GOD'S PLAN
FOR MANKIND REVEALED
BY HIS SABBATH AND
HOLY DAYS

FRED R. COULTER

York Publishing Company
Post Office Box 1038
Hollister, California 95024-1038

ISBN-13: 978-0-9675479-8-5
ISBN-10: 0-9675479-8-9
Copyright 2007 ©
York Publishing Company
Post Office Box 1038
Hollister, California 95024-1038

Table of Contents

Personal From the Desk of Fred R. Coulter... *i*

Acknowledgments.. *iii*

About the Author... *x*

Other Works by Fred R. Coulter.. *xi*

About this Book.. *xii*

Prologue... *xiv*

SECTION I — THE SABBATH

CHAPTER 1   The Background in Genesis Sermon I.................................... 1

CHAPTER 2   The Background in Genesis Sermon II.................................. 17

CHAPTER 3   The Background in Genesis Sermon III................................ 34

CHAPTER 4   The Sabbath—Sign of God... 51

CHAPTER 5   Importance of the Sabbath.. 66

SECTION II — GOD'S HOLY DAYS OVERVIEW

CHAPTER 6   Introduction—Beginning and Ending............................... 84

CHAPTER 7   Should We Keep the Holy Days?.................................... 99

SECTION III — THE PASSOVER

CHAPTER 8   Origin and Meaning of Passover.................................... 118

CHAPTER 9   The Passover—Abraham, Isaac, Israel & Christ Sermon I.......... 133

CHAPTER 10   The Passover—Abraham, Isaac, Israel & Christ Sermon II......... 148

CHAPTER 11   The Passover—Abraham, Isaac, Israel & Christ Sermon III........ 165

CHAPTER 12   The Passover Exodus and Trusting God............................ 181

SECTION IV — THE FEAST OF UNLEAVENED BREAD

CHAPTER 13   The Night to be Much Observed..................................... 198

CHAPTER 14   The Feast of Unleavened Bread Day 1—Holy Day................. 211

CHAPTER 15   The Redemption of the Firstborn.................................... 226

CHAPTER 16   The Wave Sheaf Offering Day....................................... 242

CHAPTER 17   The Special Covenant Between God the Father and Jesus Christ..... 258

CHAPTER 18   How to Count Pentecost and Count 50.............................. 271

CHAPTER 19   The Feast of Unleavened Bread Day 7—Holy Day................. 289

SECTION V — EVENTS LEADING UP TO PENTECOST

CHAPTER 20   Events Leading up to Pentecost..................................... 306

CHAPTER 21   To Walk in the Way of the Lord.................................... 321

CHAPTER 22   Day 49.. 337

SECTION VI — PENTECOST

CHAPTER 23   Pentecost—Holy Day.. 356

CHAPTER 24   Pentecost and the Sea of Glass Sermon I........................... 372

CHAPTER 25   Pentecost and the Sea of Glass Sermon II.......................... 387

CHAPTER 26   Day 50—Holy Day and the 144,000................................ 400

CHAPTER 27   More on the 144,000.. 422

CHAPTER 28   Events After Pentecost Sermon I.................................... 437

CHAPTER 29   Events After Pentecost Sermon II................................... 450

SECTION VII — THE FALL HOLY DAYS

CHAPTER 30   The Feast of Trumpets Sermon I—Holy Day.......................... 466
CHAPTER 31   The Feast of Trumpets Sermon II—Holy Day........................ 481
CHAPTER 32   The Day of Atonement Sermon I—Holy Day...................... 497
CHAPTER 33   The Day of Atonement Sermon II—Holy Day...................... 514
CHAPTER 34   The Feast of Tabernacles Day 1—Holy Day...................... 528
CHAPTER 35   The Feast of Tabernacles Day 7................................. 543
CHAPTER 36   The Last Great Day—Day 8—Holy Day............................ 557
Epilogue.. 573

God's Plan For Mankind Revealed
By His Sabbath And Holy Days
Compact Disc Directory

		Disc One
Track 1	*Chapter 1*	Background in Genesis Sermon 1
Track 2	*Chapter 2*	Background in Genesis Sermon 2
Track 3	*Chapter 3*	Background in Genesis Sermon 3
Track 4	*Chapter 4*	Sabbath - Sign of God
Track 5	*Chapter 5*	Importance of the Sabbath
Track 6	*Chapter 6*	Introduction - Beginning and Ending
Track 7	*Chapter 7*	Should We Keep the Holy Days?
Track 8	*Chapter 8*	Origin and Meaning of Passover
Track 9	*Chapter 9*	Passover-Abraham, Isaac, Israel & Christ I
Track 10	*Chapter 10*	Passover-Abraham, Isaac, Israel & Christ II
		Disc Two
Track 1	*Chapter 11*	Passover-Abraham, Isaac, Israel & Christ III
Track 2	*Chapter 12*	Passover Exodus and Trusting God
Track 3	*Chapter 13*	Night To Be Much Observed
Track 4	*Chapter 14*	Unleavened Bread Day 1 – Holy Day
Track 5	*Chapter 15*	Redemption of the Firstborn
Track 6	*Chapter 16*	Wave Sheaf Offering Day
Track 7	*Chapter 17*	The Special Covenant Between God the Father and Jesus Christ.
Track 8	*Chapter 18*	How To Count Pentecost and Count 50
Track 9	*Chapter 19*	Unleavened Bread Day 7 – Holy Day
Track 10	*Chapter 20*	Events Leading up to Pentecost
		Disc Three
Track 1	*Chapter 21*	To Walk in the Way of the Lord
Track 2	*Chapter 22*	Day 49
Track 3	*Chapter 23*	Pentecost – Holy Day
Track 4	*Chapter 24*	Pentecost and the Sea of Glass Sermon I
Track 5	*Chapter 25*	Pentecost and the Sea of Glass Sermon II
Track 6	*Chapter 26*	Day 50 – Holy Day and the 144,000
Track 7	*Chapter 27*	More on the 144,000
Track 8	*Chapter 28*	Events After Pentecost Sermon I
Track 9	*Chapter 29*	Events After Pentecost Sermon II
Track 10	*Chapter 30*	Feast of Trumpets 2004 Sermon – Holy Day
		Disc Four
Track 1	*Chapter 31*	Feast of Trumpets 2006 Sermon – Holy Day
Track 2	*Chapter 32*	Atonement 1998 Sermon – Holy Day
Track 3	*Chapter 33*	Atonement 2004 Sermon – Holy Day
Track 4	*Chapter 34*	Feast of Tabernacles Day 1 – Holy Day
Track 5	*Chapter 35*	Feast of Tabernacles Day 7 – Holy Day
Track 6	*Chapter 36*	Last Great Day – Day 8 – Holy Day

Personal

From the Desk of
Fred R. Coulter

The contemporary world in which we live encourages *individual* opinions, insisting that everyone's opinion is of *equal* validity. On the one hand, a person may consider something to be true simply because he or she *believes* it to be so—even when the facts do not support such a belief. A second person, however, may hold to an opinion exactly opposite the first—likewise accepted as fact because he or she *believes* it to be true. A dichotomy results in which truth becomes *relative.* Carrying this process one step further, when a conglomeration of divergent opinions on a subject is accepted as true, because people believe them to be true, we end up with a cacophony of opinions—which is confusion! Everyone believes and does what is right in their *own* eyes. Consequently, the majority of people today do not believe that there is *absolute truth* to the exclusion of all other opinions.

When viewing all the religions of the world—including Orthodox Christianity—we see precisely the same thing. We find a panorama of complex opinions and beliefs about God, and a confusing array of speculative schemes of men who are eager to promote their ideas about the purpose of life and the plan of God. Because learned teachers of philosophy and religion use some parts of the Word of God, their theories have a smattering of truth that sounds persuasive. Still others follow the inspiration of demons, unknowingly venerating Satan the devil himself, who appears as an "angel of light."

The result—billions of people have been deceived and wholly embrace religious falsehoods as foundational truth. Sincerely believing what they have been taught, they have dedicated their lives to false gods and false saviors through their devotion to idols, religious works, vows of poverty, life-long celibacy and virginity—all for the purpose of achieving a greater reward in heaven. Fully convinced that what they have been taught is the direct will of God—and with great sacrifice of worldly gain and even life itself—the obedient and dedicated have traveled the world over preaching their version of the Gospel, as they genuinely try to save others. Ordinary people have resolutely adhered to religious fallacies for fear of death and being forever delivered into the torments of hell. Horrifying many as well is the nightmare of being reincarnated into insects or animals because of an unworthy life. And increasingly, the world today is confronted by Islamic fanatics driven by hatred, who irrationally believe that the road to heaven is through holy jihad.

The Bible tells us: "God is not the author of confusion" (I Cor. 14:33). Therefore, we can conclude that the mainstay of all these religions, philosophies and teachings conjoined with their opinions about the purpose of life for mankind *cannot* be correct!

But where is the truth? Is it possible to find and understand it?

The answer is, *Yes!* It is found in the Bible—the true Word of God. Isaiah gives us the starting point: "And when they shall say unto you, 'Seek unto them that have familiar spirits, and unto wizards that peep, and that mutter'—but should not a people [rather] seek unto their God? Should the dead be sought on behalf of the living? To the Law [the Old Testament] and to the testimony [the New Testament]! If they do not speak according to this word, it is because there is no light in them" (Isa. 8:19-20, author's version). In other words, if we truly believe God the Father and Jesus Christ and prove that the entire Word of God is true, then we can find the truth—the absolute truth of God. We can then begin to comprehend God's plan for mankind as revealed by His Sabbath and holy days.

The Old and New Testaments combined comprise one complete book—the Word of God—the Holy Bible. To begin with, we need to understand certain fundamental truths about God as revealed in the Old Testament, which is the foundation of truth—the absolute truth of God. Here are a few scriptures that *define* the true God:

- The Lord God of the Bible is the *true* God (II Chron. 15:3; Jer. 10:10); the everlasting God (Isa. 40:28); the most high God (Gen. 14:20); the holy God (Psa. 99:9); the God of heaven (Psa. 136:26); and there is none other (Isa. 45:5).
- God is love (Deut. 4:37; 6:4-5; 7:6-9); God is merciful and gracious (Psa. 57:10; 130:8); God is forgiving (Psa. 51:1-4; 86:5; 103:3).
- The Law of God is truth (Psa. 119:142); all His commandments are truth (Psa. 119:151); His word is true from the beginning (Psa. 119:160); the Law of God is perfect (Psa. 19:7); the way of the Lord is perfect (Psa. 18:30).

From the New Testament we learn more of the truth of God:

- It is impossible for God to lie (Heb. 6:18; Titus 1:2); God is love (I John 4:8, 16). God loves the world (John 3:16); God is merciful (Luke 7:46-47; 18:13; I Pet. 1:3); God is forgiving (Luke 23:34; Eph. 1:7; 4:32; Col. 2:14; I John 1:7-10).
- Jesus Christ is God manifested in the flesh (I Tim. 3:16; John 1:1-3, 14); Jesus came to reveal God the Father (Matt. 11:27; John 14:28); Jesus is the Lamb of God, sent to take away the sin of the world (John 1:29, 36; Rev. 13:8); Jesus is Savior (Luke 1:47; 2:11; John 4:42; Eph. 5:23; Phil. 3:20; I Tim. 1:1; 2:3; I John 4:14); Jesus is full of grace and truth (John 1:14); Jesus is the First and the Last, the Beginning and the Ending (Isa. 41:4; Rev. 1:8, 11, 17; 21:6; 22:13).
- The Word of God is truth—Old and New Testaments (John 17:17; Col. 1:5; II Tim. 2:15; I Pet. 1:22); Paul and the apostles completed the Word of God—the commandments of the Lord (I Cor. 14:37; Col. 1:25; II Pet. 1:16-21; Rev. 1:11, 19; 2:1, 8, 12, 18; 3:1, 7, 14; 21:5; 22:18-19).

Once we have an overview of the entire Bible, we can see **the unity of the truth contained in both the Old and New Testaments**—how it is intricately woven together through Jesus Christ and God the Father, forming the complete Word of God, to the exclusion of all other so-called "sacred books."

In fact, the truth is personalized by Jesus Christ Himself Who said, "I am the way, and the truth, and the life; no one comes to the Father except through Me" (John 14:6). Also, Jesus emphasizes, "No one can come to Me unless the Father, Who sent Me, draws him" (John 6:44).

While some may consider this to be "spiritual snobbery," it is not. In the Bible and the Bible *alone* lies the complete revelation of God's plan.

Because God is love, He does indeed have an awesome plan and purpose for all mankind—a fantastic destiny of eternal life. Yet, **because of the sins of man**, God has concealed this vital knowledge in the writings of the Bible. But in these last days, through the inspiration of the Holy Spirit, God has unveiled the secrets of His plan as contained in His Word—by His Sabbath and holy days. This knowledge is now available to those who truly love and obey God the Father and Jesus Christ.

May God the Father and Jesus Christ bless you with the spirit of understanding, that with confidence in Christ you may comprehend and take hold of the meaning and purpose of your life—"according to *the* faith of God's elect and *the* knowledge of *the* truth that *is* according to godliness; **in *the* hope of eternal life, which God Who cannot lie promised before the ages of time**" (Titus 1:1-2).

Acknowledgments

First and foremost, all honor and glory go to God the Father and Jesus Christ for Their great and awesome "Plan for Mankind." Astonishingly, however, God has not openly revealed His plan even in the pages of the Holy Scriptures—choosing instead to deliberately *conceal* this vital knowledge. Indeed, the prophets of old—when writing the Old Testament under the inspiration of God—understood *few* aspects of His plan.

The prophet Daniel, for example, was inspired to write a major prophetic outline of events spanning from the 600s BC to the establishment of the Kingdom of God at Jesus Christ's return. Naturally, Daniel wanted to know what the prophecies meant. But God's final message to Daniel was that it was not for him to know: "And he said, 'Go your way, Daniel: **for the words are closed up and sealed till the time of the end**. Many shall be purified, and made white, and tried; but the wicked shall do wickedly: and none of the wicked shall understand; **but the wise shall understand**' " (Dan. 12:9-10).

During His ministry Jesus told the apostles that they would come to understand things that even the prophets had never understood: "**[It] has been given to you to know the mysteries of the kingdom of heaven**, but to them [the people and religions of the world] it has not been given. For whoever has *understanding*, to him more shall be given, and he shall have an abundance; but whoever does not have *understanding*, even what he has shall be taken away from him…. And in them is fulfilled the prophecy of Isaiah, which says, 'In hearing you shall hear, and in no way understand; and *in* seeing you shall see, and in no way perceive, for the heart of this people has grown fat, and their ears are dull of hearing, and their eyes they have closed….'

"But blessed *are* your eyes, because they see; and your ears, because they hear. For truly I say to you, many prophets and righteous *men* have desired to see what you see, and have not seen; and to hear what you hear, and have not heard" (Matt. 13:11-12, 14-17).

The apostle Peter reaffirms what Jesus said. "Concerning which salvation the prophets who prophesied of the grace *that would come* to you have diligently searched out and intently inquired, searching into what *way* and what manner of time the Spirit of Christ *which was* in them was indicating, testifying beforehand of the sufferings of Christ, and these glories that would follow; **to whom it was revealed that, not for themselves, but to us they were ministering these things**, which now have been announced to you by those who have preached the gospel to you by *the* Holy Spirit, sent from heaven—**into which things the angels desire to look**" (I Peter 1:10-12).

Jesus Christ provided substantially more knowledge of God's plan—the "Mystery of God"—to the apostles than any of the prophets and writers of the Old Testament. Yet, He did not reveal the *fullness* of God's plan to all of the apostles. Most of them—with the exception of John, Phillip and Andrew—died without a complete knowledge of God's plan. Jesus revealed the *final* missing pieces of the puzzle to John, who then wrote the book of Revelation and canonized the entire New Testament, with the help of Phillip and Andrew.

Indeed, the apostles received more knowledge and understanding of God's plan than any of God's servants had up to that time. It was not until the New Testament was completed and canonized, however, that God's *entire* plan for mankind was recorded. And although the complete Word of God was subsequently preserved and made widely available, the *knowledge* of God's plan remained, for the most part, *hidden*—and would continue to be a "mystery" until the time of the end, just as the Lord had told Daniel (Dan. 12:10). As we will see, the next vital step in God's plan was to raise up His true Church through Jesus Christ, His only begotten Son—God manifested in the flesh.

God Revealed His Plan to His Church—the True Church of God: Jesus Christ personally proclaimed that He would build His Church and that the gates of the grave would not prevail against it (Matt. 16:18)—and that He would always be with His Church even to the end of the age (Matt. 28:20). Jesus Christ Himself established the Church of God on the day of Pentecost in AD 30 (Acts 2). Under the inspiration and power of the Holy Spirit, Jesus Christ used the apostles to preach the true Gospel of salvation and to raise up the many congregations that would comprise the Church of God. The true Church of God is not a building, cathedral, or corporation. Rather, it consists of all the men and women whom God the Father and Jesus Christ have chosen and called out of this world. It is a "little flock" (Luke 12:32) that has been set apart and sanctified by the blood of Jesus Christ and by the Holy Spirit.

In New Testament Greek the word for "church" is *ekklesia*, which means "the assembly of called-out ones." Jesus Christ is the living Head of the Church—also called the "body of Christ" (I Cor. 12:27)—for God the Father "has given Him [Jesus Christ] *to be* head over all things to the church, which is His body" (Eph. 1:22-23). Throughout the New Testament we find that the body of Christ—which is the *true* Church of God—consists of many churches, or assemblies, of called-out believers. It was through the preaching and inspired writings of the apostles that the New Testament churches were raised up. We find the early history of the Church of God in the book of Acts, the epistles of James, Peter and John, and especially in the writings of Paul.

Jesus Christ revealed God's plan and purpose for mankind to His apostles and New Testament prophets, and they in turn taught the congregations of the Church of God. The apostle Paul, for example, wrote: "For this cause I, Paul, *am* the prisoner of Christ Jesus for you Gentiles, if indeed you have heard of the ministry of the grace of God that was given to me for you; **how He made known to me by revelation the mystery** (even as I wrote briefly before, so that when you read *this*, **you will be able to comprehend my understanding in the mystery of Christ**), which **in other generations was not made known to the sons of men, as it has now been revealed to His holy apostles and prophets by *the* Spirit**; that the Gentiles might be joint heirs, and a joint body, and joint partakers of His promise in Christ through the gospel, of which I became a servant according to the gift of the grace of God, *which was* given to me through the inner working of His power.

"To me, who am less than the least of all the saints, was this grace given, that I might preach the gospel among the Gentiles—*even* the unsearchable riches of Christ; and **that I might enlighten all *as to* what *is* the fellowship of the mystery that has been hidden from the ages in God**, Who created all things by Jesus Christ; so that the manifold wisdom of God might now be made known through the church to the principalities and the powers in the heavenly *places*, **according to *His* eternal purpose, which He has wrought in Christ Jesus our Lord**, in Whom we have boldness and *direct* access with confidence through His *very* own faith" (Eph. 3:1-12).

Paul explains that the purpose of the ministry is to teach the brethren, grounding them firmly into the perfection of Jesus Christ: "And He gave some *as* apostles, and some prophets, and some evangelists; and some, pastors and teachers for the perfecting of the saints, for *the* work of *the* ministry, for *the* edifying of the body of Christ; until we all come into the unity of the faith and of the knowledge of the Son of God, unto a perfect man, unto *the* measure of *the* stature of the fullness of Christ; so that we no longer be children, tossed and carried about with every wind of doctrine by the sleight of men in *cunning* craftiness, with a view to the systematizing of the error; but holding the truth in love, may in all things grow up into Him Who is the Head, *even* Christ from Whom all the body, fitly framed and compacted together by *that which* every joint supplies, according to *its* inner working in *the* measure of each individual part, is making the increase of the body unto *the* edifying of itself in love" (Eph. 4:11-16).

Identifying Signs of the True Church of God: There are thousands of churches claiming to be "Christian." But how does the Bible *define* and *describe* the true Church of

God? Listed below are major characteristics of the true believers who make up the body of Christ:

1. Has an unwavering belief in Jesus Christ as personal Savior—as one Who was born of the virgin Mary, was God manifested in the flesh, and was crucified for the sins of the world as the perfect sacrifice from God the Father on the Passover day in AD 30; believes that after three days and nights in the grave Jesus was raised from the dead by the power of the Father and ascended bodily into heaven to be received by God the Father as the sacrifice for the sins of the world on the first day of the fifty-day count to Pentecost; and that He returned to the earth that same day to show Himself to the apostles and give them additional instructions for 40 days—and was finally received up into heaven again to sit at the right hand of God the Father as Savior and High Priest to intercede and mediate for His people.

2. Believes that salvation is by *grace* through faith in the blood and sacrifice of Jesus Christ—on the condition of deep repentance of past sins and baptism by full immersion in water, after which God the Father gives the begettal of the Holy Spirit to the believer.

3. Has the love and faith of Jesus Christ, and keeps the commandments of God.

4. Holds to the testimony of Jesus Christ and the spirit of prophecy—meaning they will understand the prophecies contained in the Scriptures as Jesus Christ reveals them; awaits the return of Jesus Christ as King of kings and Lord of lords, at which time all who have died in Christ—with the saints who are still alive—will be raised to immortality to rule and reign with Christ on the earth.

5. Faithfully keeps the seventh-day Sabbath, the Christian Passover and the annual holy days of God according to the God-ordained calculated Hebrew Calendar. A true Christian will also reject Sunday-keeping and the religious holidays of the established Roman and Protestant "Christian" religions.

***A Brief Overview of God's True Church Through History*:** For the purposes of this book, it is not feasible to give a detailed history of the true Church of God from the first century to today. A brief overview, however, is essential if we are to understand how the knowledge of God's plan was both comprehended and disseminated by the churches of God down through the ages.

During the apostolic era, the apostles, elders and ministers of Jesus Christ spread the true Gospel into all the Roman Empire. Starting at Jerusalem, small church congregations were established over time throughout Asia Minor, as well as in Greece, Italy, North Africa, the British Isles, Ireland, Scotland and Norway. Stretching to the East, congregations were formed in Babylon, Parthia and India.

A prophetic history of the Church of God is detailed in the letters to the seven churches of Revelation 2 and 3—a period spanning from the death of the apostle John in AD 95 to the return of Jesus Christ. True to Jesus' words, there has **always** been—from the time of the original apostles to today—a small, scattered body of true, faithful believers known as the "children of God."

After the establishment of the great, state-ordained counterfeit "Christian" religion under Constantine in AD 325, the true churches of God were persecuted and thus scattered. But *true* followers of Jesus Christ—faithful, passionate and immovable—continued to keep the Sabbath, Passover and annual holy days and feasts of God in Asia Minor, Syria, Armenia and Babylon until nearly AD 1100.

Many who fled the confines of the Roman Empire in AD 325 settled in the Alps, where they were protected by God and continued to observe His Sabbath, Passover and annual festivals for 1260 years. Often referred to as Paulicans or Waldensians, they sent out teams of ministers, two by two, into all of Europe. Typically, they operated "under cover" as merchants in order to avoid persecution and arrest at the hands of Roman Catholic Church officials and clergy.

Likewise, they were able to preach the Gospel and raise up small home churches and small congregations in Switzerland, Austria, Bohemia, Germany, France, the Netherlands, Belgium, Poland and even Scandinavia. Toward the close of the 14th century, the Roman Catholic Church launched an intense campaign of persecution against the Waldensians—not only because of their adherence to the Sabbath, Passover and many of the holy days, but because they refused to acknowledge the authority of the pope and his hierarchical clergy. They were persecuted as well because they refused to accept Catholicism's anti-scriptural, "Christianized" pagan sacraments and beliefs: the Eucharist and the transubstantiation of the wine and bread, that God is a trinity, Mary worship, idol worship, prayers to the "saints," infant baptism, heaven, hell and purgatory, indulgences, Sunday-worship and the pagan holidays of the Roman Church. Thus, the Roman authorities declared them heretics and imprisoned, tortured and killed thousands of stalwart, true Christians. By 1627 the remaining Waldensians had been reduced to a pitiful few thousand who were released from prison and allowed to escape over the Alps to Geneva in the middle of winter.

Other historical records relating to the apostle Paul indicate that the gospel was preached to believers and new converts in the British Isles—as well as in Ireland and Scotland. From that time there were always small congregations of the Church of God—though called by different names. Some eventually formed what later became known as the Celtic Church in Britain. Schools were raise up in Scotland, sending evangelical teams out to preach the Gospel in Europe and Scandinavia.

After the Protestant Reformation in Europe and England, small groups of believers from the Puritans and Seventh Day Baptists fled to the American colonies, where freedom of religion and conscience allowed such groups to flourish. Continuing to call themselves Seventh Day Baptists, numerous small congregations were soon raised up throughout the northern colonies. Eventually they spread to nearly all parts of the United States, becoming collectively known as the Seventh Day Church of God or the Church of God, Seventh Day. In the 1840s, the Seventh Day Adventists church formed, splitting off from the Church of God, Seventh Day. (Detailed accounts of these events are found in two books, *A History of the True Religion* by Dugger and Dodd, and *The History of the Church of God Seventh Day* by Richard Nickels.)

While few of these small congregations of the Church of God kept the annual holy days and feasts perfectly, they did strictly observe the seventh day Sabbath and kept the Christian Passover on the 14th of Nisan—the night in which Jesus was betrayed. Though their works and knowledge were incomplete, they were nonetheless God's people.

Beginning in the early 1900s, Church of God, Seventh Day minister G. G. Rupert began a revival of the observance of the holy days and feasts of God. As he and his followers began keeping God's feasts, God began to reveal to Rupert the *meaning* of those days—and their importance in God's plan. In 1917—after studying Rupert's explanations of God's holy days—Elder Cole Sr. brought this vital information to the attention of the Church of God, Seventh Day leadership, elders Dugger and Dodd. At that time, Dugger and Dodd rejected the scriptural information concerning God's festivals. (In the 1950s, however, Dugger accepted the truth of God's holy days and relocated his organization's headquarters to Jerusalem—from which he actively preached God's Sabbath and festivals, raising up many Church of God, Seventh Day congregations on the East Coast of the United States.)

Elder Cole Sr. taught his son Otis about God's Sabbath and holy days. In 1927, Otis Cole and his family fellowshipped with a small Church of God, Seventh Day congregation near Eugene, Oregon. That same year, Herbert W. Armstrong and his wife Loma attended with Cole and began to understand God's Sabbath and holy days.

Armstrong was ordained an elder in the Church of God, Seventh Day in 1931. In 1932, Armstrong likewise presented the truth about God's holy days to Dugger and Dodd. Again, they rejected the information. Subsequently—after a split in the Church of God, Seventh Day in Eugene—Armstrong formed another congregation where he could preach the truth of God's Word, including the holy days. While still working with Church of God, Seventh Day organizations headquartered in Denver, Colorado, and Salem, West Virginia, Armstrong began intensive evangelistic campaigns. In the early 1930s, radio broadcasting was fast becoming a powerful medium for preaching the Gospel. In 1934, Armstrong began a radio ministry in Eugene, Oregon—with a program called "The World Tomorrow"—which led to the formation of what he called the "Radio Church of God." Later that same year, Armstrong began publishing *The Plain Truth* magazine, which ultimately proved to be the more effective of the two in building up church membership.

The church and radio ministry grew rapidly, prompting Armstrong to relocate to Pasadena, California, in 1947. He also founded Ambassador College that year—with a beginning class of only five students—in order to train men and women to serve the growing number of congregations God was raising up as a result of Armstrong's efforts.

In 1953, the "The World Tomorrow" program began airing on Radio Luxembourg in Europe, a major step in the growth of what Armstrong called "the Work." Indeed, "the Work" grew at an unheard-of pace throughout the 1950s and '60s. Armstrong added a second Ambassador campus in Bricketwood, England, in 1960—with a third campus established in the early 1970s in Big Sandy, Texas. Beginning in the late 1950s, the responsibility of then-worldwide radio program began to shift to Armstrong's son, Garner Ted. For the next 25 years or so, Garner Ted Armstrong would be *the* voice of "The World Tomorrow" program—which eventually grew to be heard on thousands of radio stations around the world, reaching millions of people.

But in the 1970s Armstrong's organization—which by then had been renamed the "Worldwide Church of God" (WCG)—began to experience internal strife and division. Corruption was rampant, often involving gross sexual sin; millions of dollars of income were misappropriated. Armstrong attempted to "clean house"—and was ultimately forced to remove Garner Ted in 1978 for continued and repeated sexual sin.

Ted subsequently formed the Church of God International, from which he was expelled in 1995 for similar adulterous affairs. He then founded the Intercontinental Church of God, which continued until his sudden death in September 2003.

Throughout much of the 1980s the WCG again found its stride—powerfully proclaiming the true Gospel to the world until Herbert Armstrong's death in January 1986 at age 93. By that time, worldwide attendance was around 120,000, with nearly a thousand ministers and thousands of elders. At its peak, there were nearly eight million monthly subscribers to *The Plain Truth* magazine, and "The World Tomorrow" *television* program was rated as the number two religious program in America. The WCG's annual income neared $200,000,000—more than Jerry Falwell and Billy Graham combined pulled in.

Just before his death, however, Armstrong appointed Joseph W. Tkach Sr. as his successor—a move that would prove devastating to proclaiming the *truth* of the Scriptures and would signal the impending demise of the organization. As many would ultimately come to realize, it was in fact the beginning of the *correction of God* against an apostate church and ministry.

Strongly influenced by his son, Joseph W. Tkach Jr., and other apostate ministers, Tkach set out to methodically transform the WCG, bringing it into alignment with mainstream Protestantism—primarily to attract the admiration and approval of the world's "Christian" leaders. In September 1995, Tkach died of cancer, leaving his son, Joe Tkach Jr., as successor. Almost immediately, the downward spiral accelerated: the Gospel was corrupted; the Law of God was proclaimed (as do Protestants) to be non-binding; the Sabbath and holy days were dismissed and rejected as "Jewish." Tkach Jr. began to institute the observance of Sunday and several pagan holidays. These moves caused the WCG to fragment even more—with hundreds of ministers and thousands of members leaving to form other churches of God in order to hold fast to the true teachings of the Bible and Jesus Christ.

Within the space of a few years, the glory of the WCG was gone—its ministry and membership decimated, scattered among literally hundreds of so-called "splinter" groups. Indeed—because of the widespread collective sins of the church's leadership, ministers and members—Jesus Christ, the true Head of His Church, has resoundingly brought the WCG and its colleges to "nothing." In a few short years, their memory will all but evaporate—being only a footnote recounted by history. Thus, the Armstrong era came to an ignominious end.

But Jesus Christ is true to His word—for out of the ruins of the WCG and the Armstrong era, God has raised up a remnant of numerous faithful ministers who continue today to proclaim the true Gospel—teaching the true meaning of the Sabbath and the holy days, and serving the needs of God's faithful brethren. As in ages past, they firmly stood for God the Father, Jesus Christ and the truth of the Word of God—and did not fall victim to Satan's relentless assaults against the churches of God.

Because of the widespread corruption and sins of the WCG, the author resigned on the Day of Atonement, October 1979. He and his wife Dolores made their *stand* for the truth of God—especially for the Sabbath and holy days of God (See *About the Author*). The Christian Biblical Church of God and Coulter's ministry—providing audio/video sermons, books and other literature expounding the truth of the Bible—has now grown worldwide and is serving approximately 4,500 faithful brethren. In addition, in 2006, nearly 400,000 people visited the church's Website (*cbcg.org*) to download various audio messages and written material.

According to the Bible Sabbath Association, it is estimated that the churches of God today number well over 500 worldwide—with over 340 coming from the scattering of the WCG. This includes large and small church organizations in virtually every nation, comprising thousands of ministers and hundreds of thousands of true believers who keep God's Sabbath and holy days. Of the known churches of God, the majority are located in the United States—not counting the tens of thousands of "house churches" across the nation and around the world.

In addition, there is an unknown number of small churches of God and isolated faithful believers around the world who live by the Bible, keep the Sabbath and *some* the holy days. The Seventh Day Adventist movement has grown into a vast organization with nearly three million members worldwide, including approximately 100,000 who also observe the annual holy days of God. Finally, it is estimated that there are ten million Sabbatarian Christians worldwide—including hundreds of thousands of underground Sabbath-keepers in China alone.

This short overview gives a thumbnail sketch of the history of the true Church of God from the time of Jesus Christ until today. It is quite different from the traditional "Orthodox" history presented by the counterfeit "Christianity" of this world.

Remember Jesus' instruction to His disciples: "[It] has been given to you [the true disciples and the true Church of God] to know the mysteries of the kingdom of heaven, but to them [the world with its counterfeit religions] it has not been given" (Matt. 13:11). Thus, the true scriptural knowledge and understanding of God's plan for mankind—as revealed by His Sabbath and holy days—will not be found in the churches of Orthodox Christianity. God only imparts this knowledge to those who love Him and keep His commandments—including His commanded seventh-day Sabbath and annual holy days. On the other hand, all who reject God's Sabbath and holy days—and instead observe Sunday and various pagan holidays—are excluded from this vital, *revealed* knowledge. As Jesus said, in "seeing, they see not; and hearing, they hear not; neither do they understand. And in them is fulfilled the prophecy of Isaiah, which says, 'In hearing you shall hear, and in no way understand; and *in* seeing you shall see, and in no way perceive; for the heart of this people has grown fat, and their ears are dull of hearing, and their eyes they have closed…' " (verses 13-15).

Consequently, very little of the knowledge of God's plan for mankind that you will read in this book and hear from the CD messages will be found in the Orthodox Christianity of this world. It is *only* found in the Word of God and revealed to those ministers and congregations of the *true* Church of God who observe the Sabbath and annual holy days. As Jesus said to His disciples, "**Blessed *are* your eyes, because they see; and your ears, because they hear. For truly I say to you, many prophets and righteous *men* have desired to see what you see, and have not seen; and to hear what you hear, and have not heard**" (verses 16-17).

May Jesus' blessing be upon you as you read and study this book and listen to the sermons—so that you may be able to truly understand the biblical truth about God's plan for mankind as revealed by His Sabbath and holy days.

Further Acknowledgments: Special heartfelt and loving thanks to my lovely wife, Dolores, who gave her encouragement and help in editing much of the introductory material of this book. Thanks to Jim and Betty Hyles—who first suggested that we produce this book. Jim personally assists the author in numerous aspects of serving the brethren, including writing letters and handling administrative and technical matters for the CBCG. His wife Betty reproduces and mails out our four special "Care Packages" of studies and sermons to people who request them.

A special thanks goes to those who did the wearisome work of transcribing the sermons that comprise the main text of this book: Carolyn Singer, Michael Schwartz, Bonnie Orswell, Judith Anderson and Sasha Vogele. John and Hiedi Vogele did the tedious job of compiling and laying out the pages of the book. Dick and Bette Young proofread many of the transcripts. We acknowledge our editor, Philip Neal, for his editing of the non-transcript portions of the book. Finally, special thanks go to Cindy Curley—Curley Creatives—for the beautiful art work and design of the front cover. None of this, however, could have been accomplished without the ongoing love, prayers and support of thousands of God's people.

All of us together can affirm what Jesus told His apostles: "My meat is to do the will of Him Who sent Me, and to finish His work. Do not say that there are yet four months, and *then* the harvest comes. I say to you, look around. Lift up your eyes and see the fields, for they are already white to harvest. And the one who reaps receives a reward, and gathers fruit unto eternal life; so that the one who is sowing and the one who is reaping may both rejoice together. **For in this the saying is true, that one sows and another reaps. I sent you to reap that in which you have not labored; others have labored, and you have entered into their labor**" (John 4:34-38). How true this is today! Indeed, we have entered into the sowing and reaping of nearly two thousand years of God's true ministers and servants down through history—many of whom willingly gave their lives in standing up for the truth so that we, in the end times, may reap of their labor. May God the Father and Jesus Christ count us worthy to receive and share the knowledge of this awesome plan for mankind as revealed in the Word of God.

Fred R. Coulter
Winter 2007

About the Author

Fred R. Coulter attended the University of San Francisco and graduated from San Mateo State College before graduating from Ambassador University (Ambassador College), Pasadena, California, with a BA in Theology in 1964. He was ordained a minister of Jesus Christ in 1965 and pastored churches of God in the Pacific Northwest, the Mountain States, the greater Los Angeles area and Monterey, including the central coast area of California. Coulter completed advanced biblical and ministerial studies from 1972 to 1975 under the Ambassador University Master's program. While completing these studies, Coulter was encouraged by his professor of *Koiné* Greek to consider translating the books of the New Testament.

After completing his formal instruction in *Koiné* Greek, Coulter continued to expand his knowledge of Greek for the next twenty years by undertaking a verse-by-verse study of the books of the New Testament using the Byzantine Text. In the course of his study, Coulter was ultimately moved to translate the New Testament into clear, easy-to-read English for contemporary readers. After twelve years of diligent translating, *The New Testament In Its Original Order—A Faithful Version With Commentary* was completed and published 2004.

Coulter has dedicated his life and talents to proclaiming Jesus Christ as personal Savior for all. Since 1983, he has had an active ministry as president and pastor of the Christian Biblical Church of God, Hollister, California. The CBCG has offices in the United States, Canada, Australia, New Zealand, Africa, South Africa and the United Kingdom serving thousands of people.

Each year nearly 400,000 people from around the world actively utilize the CBCG's websites—where they find timely, inspiring audio sermons and in-depth biblical study materials covering virtually every topic in Scripture.

With his ministry now spanning 42 years, Fred R. Coulter has again been inspired to undertake the publication of this book, *God's Plan for Mankind Revealed by His Sabbath and Holy Days*. This book expands upon the knowledge and information contained in another of his books, *Occult Holidays or God's Holy Days—Which?*

Other Works by Fred R. Coulter

The New Testament In Its Original Order—A Faithful Version With Commentary is a new translation and is the only English New Testament that has the books arranged in their original order. It retains the grace and grandeur of the King James Version while clarifying many of its problematic passages. Included are commentaries that answer the questions: What is the New Testament? Who wrote it? When was it written? When was it canonized? Who canonized it? Other commentaries detail the history and preservation of the Bible. Appendices contain many detailed studies of controversial New Testament teachings. This 928-page book is an absolute must for all Christians.

A Harmony of the Gospels In Modern English brings to life the message and purpose of the true Jesus, portraying His life and ministry in their true historical setting. This easy-to-understand, step-by-step account of the life of Jesus Christ is an indispensable study aid for every serious Bible student.

The Christian Passover is a book of over 500 pages that details the scriptural and historical truths of the Passover in both the Old and New Testaments, leading the reader through every aspect of one of the most vital and fundamental teachings revealed in the Bible. It fully explains the meaning of the Christian Passover—a remembrance of the sacrifice of Jesus Christ the Passover Lamb of God—in a most thorough and inspiring manner. The full meaning of the body and blood of Jesus Christ is revealed, showing the magnitude of God's love for every person.

The Day Jesus the Christ Died—the Biblical Truth About His Passion, Crucifixion and Resurrection is the ONLY BOOK to present the whole truth and nothing but the truth! It presents the "rest of the story" left out by Mel Gibson in his epic movie *The Passion of the Christ*. Without the true historical and biblical facts, no one can fully understand the meaning of Jesus Christ's horrific, humiliating and gruesome death by beating, scourging and crucifixion. The author presents the full biblical account in a most compelling way. As you will see, the truth is more astounding and profound than all of the ideas, superstitions, traditions and misbeliefs of men!

Occult Holidays or God's Holy Days—Which? For centuries the leaders of Orthodox Christiandom have sold popular holidays—Halloween, Christmas, New Years, Easter, etc.—to the masses as though they had "Christian" meaning. This book effectively demonstrates that these celebrated holidays are *not* of God—but originated from ancient, pagan religions rooted in satanic occultism, witchcraft, the feminine divine and "New Age" spirituality. Contrary to the false ideas of men, the true biblical holy days and feasts of God have deep spiritual meaning and outline God's fantastic plan of slavation for all mankind—past, present and future—as revealed in the Holy Scriptures.

The Seven General Epistles is designed for an in-depth verse-by-verse study of the epistles of James; I and II Peter; I, II and III John and Jude. As part of the living Word of God, these epistles are as meaningful today for personal Christian growth as when they were first written.

Lord, What Should I Do? is a book for Christians who are faced with a confusing world of a compromised "Christianity"—in which false doctrinal teachings undermine the true faith of the Bible. This book clarifies the problem and shows what God requires a person to do—if they are to truly find God the Father and the true faith of Jesus Christ.

On-line Studies for the serious Bible student—with written study materials and in-depth audio sermons—can be found at **cbcg.org** and **biblicaltruthministries.org**.

About This Book

God's Plan for Mankind Revealed by His Sabbath and Holy Days is unique in four major ways. First, it is intended for the advanced, serious-minded Bible student who has a sound, basic knowledge of the Bible, as well as an understanding of God's weekly Sabbath and holy days. This book contains what the apostle Paul calls "strong meat" or "solid food"—as opposed to the "milk of the Word" which is for beginners. "For everyone who is partaking of milk *is* unskilled in *the* word of righteousness because he is an infant. But solid food [strong meat] is for those who are fully grown [spiritually mature and grounded in the Word of God through years of study], who **through repeated practice have had their senses trained to discern between good and evil**" (Heb. 5:13-14).

While this book is generally not for "novices" who have newly come to the faith of Jesus Christ—or for those who are simply curious—it is possible for anyone to understand what is presented here. However, such individuals will need to apply themselves more diligently in order to fully grasp the deeper spiritual meaning of the Scriptures. Consequently, it is strongly recommend that those who are "new in the faith" first read the book *Occult Holidays or God's Holy Days—Which?* This book details the basic meaning of God's Sabbath and holy days as contrasted with the holidays of the pagan "Christianity" of the orthodox religious establishments of this world. After first reading *Occult Holidays or God's Holy Days—Which?*, the meatier material contained in *God's Plan for Mankind Revealed by His Sabbath and Holy Days* will be much easier to comprehend.

Second, this book is a compilation of sermon transcripts. As such, it is not written in customary book-style composition. Rather, the transcriptions are a literal, word-for-word rendering of some of the best in-depth sermons by the author about God's Sabbath and holy days. The sermon transcripts have a more flexible style and cadence in comparison to the more rigid style and structure of formal composition.

Third, it is not designed for passive reading. Rather, this book should be used for active, in-depth Bible study in combination with the thirty-two sermons that have been recorded on the accompanying set of four CDs (MP3 format). When you listen to the sermons and actively study along with the transcripts, you will absorb and retain the information longer because you are using *both* the sense of sight and sound in a concentrated manner at the same time.

Fourth, the bibliography for this book includes *only* the Holy Bible. No other sources have been used, with the exception of a few short quotes from historical sources that substantiate a few specific scriptures. As such, this book follows God's direct charge for ministers to preach and teach the Holy Scriptures—and not the mythological religious traditions of men. Notice Paul's charge to Timothy: "I charge you, therefore, in the sight of God, even the Lord Jesus Christ, Who is ready to judge *the* living and *the* dead at His appearing and His kingdom: **Preach the Word! Be urgent in season and out of season; convict, rebuke, encourage, with all patience and doctrine**. For there shall come a time when they will not tolerate sound doctrine; but according to their own lusts they shall accumulate to themselves *a great number of* teachers, having ears itching *to hear what satisfies their cravings*; **but they shall turn away their own ears from the truth; and they shall be turned aside unto myths** [the religious traditions of men]" (II Tim. 4:1-4).

Finally, this book lays out the critically important scriptural meaning of God's weekly Sabbath and annual holy days, which are the major keys to understanding prophecy and that reveal God's master plan for mankind. This knowledge has been concealed from the majority of people because they refuse to believe God—refuse to hear His word, to obey His laws and commandments and do not live their lives by *every* word of God. Consequently, the established Orthodox Christianity of this world disparages, rejects and refuses to keep God's Sabbath and holy days.

For those who already have a basic knowledge of the Bible, this book can systematically cement your understanding of the deeper spiritual meaning of God's Word. The reader is encouraged to start at the beginning and go step-by step through the book to the end, while simultaneously listening to the sermons. May God the Father and Jesus Christ bless you with understanding so that you may learn the inspired, deeper spiritual truths of God as you read this book and listen to the sermons.

Fred R. Coulter
Winter 2007

Prologue

As incredible as it may seem, God has deliberately hidden His plan for mankind from the wise and intelligent of this world—from the leaders in government, religion and education—as well as from philosophers, ancient and modern. In fact, God has blinded men to His true purpose throughout all ages!

Why has He done this? Surely God would want us to have an understanding of His plan, to know *why* mankind was created, *why* we are here—would He not? The answer is simple: Beginning with Adam and Eve, all humans have **sinnned and rebelled** against God (Rom. 3:9, 23). Sin is the transgression of the Law (I John 3:4). Rebellion is the refusal to walk and live God's way. Consequently, the human mind has been spiritually blinded and God has hidden His plan from mankind.

This sin and rebellion began with Adam and Eve, who had direct personal access to their Creator God in the Garden of Eden. They walked with God and talked with God. They had personal, face-to-face fellowship with Him daily—and especially on the holy Sabbath. After putting Adam in the garden to dress and keep (or guard) it, "God commanded the man saying, 'You may freely eat of every tree in the garden. But you shall not eat of the Tree of the Knowledge of Good and Evil. For in the day you eat of it, in dying you shall surely die' " (Gen. 2:16-17).

However, instead of loving and obeying their Creator, Adam and Eve chose to believe the serpent, Satan the devil. He lied to them and assured them that if they ate of the fruit of the Tree of the Knowledge of Good and Evil, that "in dying you shall not surely die." (Gen. 3:4).

As a result, true to God's word, they received in their very being a sinful nature that is enmity against God and His laws—and came under the penalty of death. Likewise, all of their descendants received by inheritance this sinful nature, which is the inner "law of sin and death" (Rom. 8:2). After Cain murdered his brother Abel, sin and rebellion against God multiplied and intensified until the whole civilization of man became so corrupt and wicked that God had to destroy all flesh with the univeral flood of Noah's time, saving only Noah and his family and the animals in the ark.

The apostle Paul describes this rebellion of men and their rejection of God—as well as God's punishment against them: "Indeed, *the* wrath of God is revealed from heaven upon all ungodliness and unrighteousness of men who suppress the truth in unrighteousness; because that which may be known of God is manifest among them, for God has manifested *it* to them; for the invisible things of Him are perceived from *the* creation of *the* world, being understood by the things that were made—both His eternal power and Godhead—so that they are without excuse; because when they knew God [before and after the flood], they glorified *Him* not as God, neither were thankful; but **they became vain in their own reasonings, and their foolish hearts were darkened. While professing themselves to be *the* wise ones, they became fools and changed the glory of the incorruptible God into *the* likeness of an image of corruptible man, and of birds, and four-footed creatures, and creeping things**.

"For this cause, God also abandoned them to uncleanness through the lusts of their hearts, to disgrace their own bodies between themselves, **who exchanged the truth of God for the lie** [Satan the devil's lie that he was god]; **and they worshiped and served the created thing more than the one Who is Creator, Who is blessed into the ages**. Amen" (Rom. 1:18-25).

As a result of mankind's sin and rebellion, both before and after the flood, God blinded their hearts and minds to His spiritual truths and abandoned them to their own devices and religions. In fact, because of their sin and worship of Satan, God deliberately hid the true knowledge of His plan and purpose for mankind.

Where then did God hide this precious knowledge? Must we go up into the heavens to find it? Or, shall we go to the bottom of the ocean to locate it? Is it written in some long lost book, or inscribed on golden tablets buried deep in the earth that are yet to be discovered? Where is the knowledge of God's plan for mankind and how do we find it?

The truth is that today, the plan of God, also called the mystery of God, is hidden in plain sight—right in front of everyone's eyes. It's in the Bible. Incredibly, however, the vast majority of the billions of people who possess Bibles do not understand God's true plan and purpose as revealed in the Scriptures. Yet, God put it there in plain sight! But people do not recognize the truth—because the truth must be revealed spiritually by God through the proper handling of the Word of God. While some people who read the Bible may know a *few* details about God's plan, the fullness of that plan has been hidden.

Why is it possible for people to have the Word of God, read it, and yet not comprehend God's plan for mankind?

First, most people do not keep the commandments of God, because they believe God's laws have been "done away": "[All] His commandments are sure. They stand fast for ever and ever, and are done in truth and uprightness…. The fear of the LORD is the beginning of wisdom: **a good understanding have all they who do his commandments**…. Blessed is the man who fears the LORD, who delights greatly in His commandments" (Psa. 111:7-8, 10; 112:1). Without *first* keeping the commandments of God, it is impossible for anyone to truly understand the Word of God and come to the knowledge of His plan.

Second, the majority of people who have the Bible have closed their eyes to God's Sabbath and holy days—which are also holy Sabbaths—and refuse to keep them. They have instead substituted their own traditions—Sunday-keeping and the holidays of this world. God's message to them is: Repent, obey My voice, and keep My laws, My commandments, My Sabbath and My holy days. As the prophet Isaiah admonished the children of Israel, and the Gentiles as well: "Thus says the LORD, 'Keep you judgment, and do justice: for My salvation is near to come, and My righteousness to be revealed [together with His purpose and plan for mankind]. Blessed is the man who does this, and the son of man who lays hold on it; that keeps the Sabbath from polluting it, and keeps his hand from doing any evil' " (Isa. 56:1-2). And again, "If you turn away your foot from the Sabbath, from doing your pleasure on **My holy day; and call the Sabbath a delight, the holy of the LORD**, honorable; and shall honor Him, not doing your own ways, nor finding your own pleasure, nor speaking your own words: then shall you delight yourself in the LORD…" (Isa. 58:13-14).

In the New Testament, in Paul's epistle to the Hebrews, he makes it abundantly clear that Sabbath-keeping is for New Testament Christians: "There remains, therefore, Sabbath-keeping for the people of God [Jews and Gentiles]" (Heb. 4:9).

Third, most do not have the Holy Spirit of God to lead them to understand the spiritual meaning of the Word of God. Jesus said, "It is the Spirit that gives life; the flesh profits nothing. The words that I speak to you, *they* are spirit and *they* are life" (John 6:63). Furthermore, God does not give His Holy Spirit unless one has repented of sin and has been baptized, and is living a life of love and obedience to God (Acts 2:38; 5:32).

Thus, we find that although people may read the Bible, they cannot understand God's plan contained in its pages. To them it is a great, unfathomable mystery!

God's Plan for Mankind is Hidden Throughout the Bible

God's plan actually begins in the book of Genesis, the first book of the Bible. That plan, however, was not fully unveiled until the apostle John wrote the Book of Revelation, the last book of the Bible, in AD 95.

Few people realize that the Lord God of the Old Testament was the One Who became Jesus Christ of the New Testament. He was the One Who created Adam and Eve and all things. He was the One Who dealt directly with the godly men of old—Abel, Enoch and Noah. He was the One Who called the patriarchs—Abraham, Isaac and Jacob—and personally dealt with them. He was the One Who called Moses to bring Israel out of their slavery in Egypt. He was the One Who gave them the Law at Mount Sinai.

He was the Word of God Who spoke to the prophets of old, such as Samuel, Isaiah, Jeremiah, Ezekiel and Daniel and all the other prophets. He inspired the Psalms of David, the Proverbs of Solomon and the other writings of the Old Testament. In every one of these inspired writings, various aspects of God's plan and purpose for mankind are concealed—they are a mystery. Though these great men of God were inspired to write the words of God, they did not fully grasp His plan or timetable for working out that plan. God intentionally did not divulge it to them. Even Daniel—to whom God revealed many prophecies that stretched from his time, in the fifth century BC, to the end of the age and the beginning of the Kingdom of God on earth—did not understand them. After receiving his final vision, he asked the Lord, "And I heard, but I understood not: then said I, 'O my Lord, what shall be the end of these things?' And he said, '**Go thy way, Daniel: for the words are closed up and sealed till the time of the end. Many shall be purified, and made white, and tried; but the wicked shall do wickedly: and none of the wicked shall understand; but the wise** [those who love and obey God] **shall understand**' " (Dan. 12:8-10).

The Teachings of Jesus Christ in the New Testament
Reveal More of God's Plan—the Mysteries of the Kingdom of God

It was more than 4,000 years after God created Adam and Eve that He began to more fully reveal His plan for mankind through Jesus Christ, the Son of God the Father. Jesus was God manifested in the flesh, born of the virgin Mary. He came to magnify the Law and make it honorable, as Isaiah prophesied: "The LORD is well pleased for His righteousness' sake; He will magnify the Law, and make it honorable" (Isa. 42:21). In magnifying the Law, Jesus brought the Law to its fullest measure, making clear its spiritual meaning and intent. The Hebrew word for "magnify" is *gadal* which means: to advance, boast, exceed; to become, do, give, make greater, increase and magnify. The Hebrew word "honorable" is *adar* which means: to expand, to be great or magnificant.

Contrary to what many religious leaders teach, Jesus did not do away with the Law. Beginning with the Sermon on the Mount (Matt. 5-7), Jesus magnified the Law by teaching the spiritual meaning of the Law and the Prophets: "**Do not think that I have come to abolish the Law or the Prophets; I did not come to abolish, but to fulfill**. For truly I say to you, until the heaven and the earth shall pass away, one jot or one tittle shall in no way pass from the Law until everything has been fulfilled" (Matt. 5:17-18). Moreover, He also said, "It is written, 'Man shall not live by bread alone, but by every word that proceeds out of *the* mouth of God' " (Matt. 4:4). (To understand how Jesus fulfilled the Law and the Prophets, see *A Harmony of the Gospels—the Life of Jesus Christ*, Coulter, pp. 73-96.)

Jesus Christ's first coming fulfilled hundreds of prophecies as recorded in the Law, the Prophets and the Psalms. In addition to magnifying the Law and the Prophets, Jesus revealed a great deal more about the meaning of God's Sabbath and holy days.

Luke writes this account of Jesus' teaching on the Sabbath day in Nazareth: "And He came to Nazareth, where He had been brought up; and according to His custom, He went into the synagogue on the Sabbath day and stood up to read. And there was given Him *the* book of the prophet Isaiah; and when He had unrolled the scroll, He found the place where it was written, '*The* Spirit of *the* Lord *is* upon Me; for this reason, He has anointed Me to preach the gospel to *the* poor; He has sent Me to heal those who are brokenhearted, to proclaim pardon to *the* captives and recovery of sight to *the* blind, to send forth in deliverance those who have been crushed, to proclaim *the* acceptable year of *the* Lord' " (Luke 4:16-19). In fact, recorded in the Gospels of Matthew, Mark, Luke and John are the direct teachings of Jesus Christ. Furthermore, the Gospel of Jesus Christ is God's message of the good news of personal salvation and the coming Kingdom of God, which is also revealed by the Sabbath and holy days.

When Jesus began His three and one-half-year ministry, He preached repentance and forgiveness of sin: "Jesus came into Galilee, proclaiming the gospel of the kingdom of God, and saying, 'The time has been fulfilled, and the kingdom of God has drawn near; repent, and believe in the gospel' " (Mark 1:14-15).

Another primary purpose of Jesus coming in the flesh was to reveal God the Father to those whom He would call: "At that time Jesus answered and said, **'I praise You, O Father, Lord of heaven and earth, that You have hidden these things from the wise and intelligent, and have revealed them to babes**. Yes, Father, for it was well pleasing in Your sight *to do* this. **All things were delivered to Me by My Father; and no one knows the Son except the Father; neither does anyone know the Father except the Son, and the one to whom the Son personally chooses to reveal *Him*'** " (Matt. 11:25-27). Jesus did not reveal God the Father to the world in general, but only to His called and chosen disciples—those truly converted believers who love Him and keep His commandments (I John 5:2-3).

For this reason Jesus spoke to the people in parables. His disciples, however, did not understand His use of parables and questioned Him: "And He answered *and* said to them, 'Because **it has been given to you to know the mysteries of the kingdom of heaven, but to them it has not been given**. For whoever has *understanding*, to him more shall be given, and he shall have an abundance; but whoever does not have *understanding*, even what he has shall be taken away from him. For this *reason* I speak to them in parables, because seeing, they see not; and hearing, they hear not; neither do they understand. And in them is fulfilled the prophecy of Isaiah, which says, 'In hearing you shall hear, and in no way understand; and *in* seeing you shall see, and in no way perceive; for the heart of this people has grown fat, and their ears are dull of hearing, and their eyes they have closed; lest they should see with their eyes, and should hear with their ears, and should understand with their hearts, and should be converted, and I should heal them.' **But blessed *are* your eyes, because they see; and your ears, because they hear. For truly I say to you, many prophets and righteous *men* have desired to see what you see, and have not seen; and to hear what you hear, and have not heard**" (Matt. 13:11-17).

The apostle Peter later confirmed Jesus' words, stating that even the prophets of old—though they had some partial knowledge and even wrote of the coming grace of God—did not understand God's plan of salvation: "Concerning which salvation the prophets who prophesied of the grace *that would come* to you have diligently searched out and intently inquired, searching into what *way* and what manner of time the Spirit of Christ *which was* in them was indicating, testifying beforehand of the sufferings of Christ, and these glories that would follow; to whom it was revealed that, not for themselves, but to us they were ministering these things, which now have been announced to you by those who have preached the gospel to you by *the* Holy Spirit, sent from heaven—into which things the angels desire to look" (I Pet. 1:10-12).

Before Jesus' death and resurrection, He revealed to His apostles and disciples additional knowledge of the mysteries of the kingdom of God—the secret plan of God. Then, on the night of Jesus' last Passover, before His arrest and subsequent crucifixion, Jesus informed them that God the Father would send the power of the Holy Spirit upon them which would give them additional insight and revelation: "But *when* the Comforter *comes, even* the Holy Spirit, which the Father will send in My name, that one **shall teach you all things, and shall bring to your remembrance everything that I have told you**…. [When] that one has come, *even* the Spirit of the truth, it will lead you into all truth because it shall not speak from itself, but whatever it shall hear, it shall speak. And it **shall disclose to you the things to come** [in prophecy and more of God's plan]. That one shall glorify Me because it shall disclose to you *the things that* it receives from Me" (John 14:26; 16:13-14). When they received the Holy Spirit, they began to comprehend the spiritual meaning of Jesus' teachings—just as He had said.

Jesus Revealed More of God's Plan to the Apostles
After He was Raised From the Dead

After God the Father raised Jesus from the dead, Jesus personally appeared to His apostles and disciples and began to explain God's plan as contained in the Old Testament. In fact, the apostles and disciples themselves did not fully fathom the meaning of the Scriptures until Jesus opened their minds: "And He said to them, 'These *are* the words that I spoke to you when I was yet with you, that all *the* things which were written concerning Me in the Law of Moses and *in the* Prophets and *in the* Psalms must be fulfilled.' **Then He opened their minds to understand the Scriptures**, and said to them, 'According as it is written, it was necessary for the Christ to suffer, and to rise from *the* dead the third day. And in His name repentance and remission of sins should be preached to all nations, beginning at Jerusalem. For you are witnesses of these things. And behold, I send the promise of My Father upon you; but remain in the city of Jerusalem until you have been clothed with power from on high' " (Luke 24:44-49).

With the exception of the apostle John, Paul wrote more about the mystery of God than any other New Testament writer. When Paul wrote to the Corinthians, he made it clear that in order to understand the mystery of God, one must have the Holy Spirit—for that mystery is spiritually revealed. All the human wisdom, philosophies and religions of the world cannot expound God's plan. Notice: "Rather, **we speak *the* wisdom of God in a mystery, *even* the hidden *wisdom* that God foreordained before the ages unto our glory** which not one of the rulers of this world has known (for if they had known, they would not have crucified the Lord of glory); but according as it is written, '***The* eye has not seen, nor *the* ear heard, neither have entered into *the* heart of man, *the* things which God has prepared for those who love Him**.'

"**But God has revealed *them* to us by His Spirit, for the Spirit searches all things— even the deep things of God**. For who among men understands the things of man except *by* the spirit of man which *is* in him? In the same way also, the things of God no one understands except *by* the Spirit of God. Now we have not received the spirit of the world, but **the Spirit that *is* of God, so that we might know the things graciously given to us by God**; which things we also speak, not in words taught by human wisdom, but in *words* taught by *the* Holy Spirit *in order to* communicate spiritual things by spiritual *means*. **But *the* natural man does not receive the things of the Spirit of God; for they are foolishness to him, and he cannot understand *them* because they are spiritually discerned**" (I Cor. 2:7-14).

When Paul wrote to the Ephesians, he again emphasized that the knowledge of the mystery of God and of Christ **must be revealed** by God Himself through His Spirit and the Word of God: "For this cause [the preaching of the Gospel] I, Paul, *am* the prisoner of Christ Jesus for you Gentiles, if indeed you have heard of the ministry of the grace of God that was given to me for you; **how He made known to me by revelation the mystery** (even as I wrote briefly before, so that when you read *this*, **you will be able to comprehend my understanding in the mystery of Christ** [God's secret plan for mankind], **which in other generations was not made known to the sons of men, as it has now been revealed to His holy apostles and prophets by *the* Spirit**; that the Gentiles might be joint heirs, and a joint body, and joint partakers of His promise in Christ through the gospel" (Eph. 3:1-6).

In writing to the Colossians, Paul revealed that part of the mystery of Christ is Christ *dwelling in* every converted believer through the power of the Holy Spirit. He also made it clear that what he was writing to them was to become part of the New Testament, thus completing the Word of God. God has perserved His Word so that those whom He would call in future generations would have the knowledge of this great mystery: "Now, I am rejoicing in my sufferings for you, and I am filling up in my flesh that which is behind of the tribulations of Christ, for the sake of His body, which is the church; of which I became a servant, according to the administration of God that *was* given *to* me for you *in order* **to complete the**

Word of God; *even* **the mystery that has been HIDDEN FROM AGES AND FROM GENERATIONS, but has now been revealed to His saints; to whom God did will to make known what** *is* **the riches of the glory of this mystery among the Gentiles; which is Christ in you, the hope of glory**; Whom we preach, admonishing every man and teaching every man in all wisdom, so that we may present every one perfect in Christ Jesus" (Col. 1:24-28).

In the early AD 60s, God revealed additional knowledge of His plan to His apostles and prophets. In some of the most eloquent and spiritually inspiring words of the Bible, Paul wrote of God's new fantastic revelation of His purpose for those whom He had called and described their personal participation in that plan: "Blessed *be* the God and Father of our Lord Jesus Christ, Who has **blessed us with every spiritual blessing in the heavenly** *things* **with Christ**; according as **He has personally chosen us for Himself** before *the* foundation of *the* world in order that we might be holy and blameless before Him in love; **having predestinated us for sonship to Himself through Jesus Christ, according to the good pleasure of His own will**, to *the* praise of *the* glory of His grace, wherein He has made us objects of *His* grace in the Beloved *Son*.

"In Whom we have redemption through His blood, *even* the remission of sins, according to the riches of His grace, which He has made to abound toward us in all wisdom and intelligence; **having made known to us THE MYSTERY OF HIS OWN WILL, according to His good pleasure, which He purposed in Himself; that in** *the divine* **plan for the fulfilling of** *the* **times**, He might bring all things together in Christ, both the things in the heavens and the things upon the earth; *yes*, in Him, in Whom we also have obtained an inheritance, **having been predestinated according to His purpose, Who is working out all things according to the counsel of His own will**; that we might be to *the* praise of His glory, who first trusted in the Christ; in Whom you also trusted after hearing the Word of the truth, the gospel of your salvation; in Whom also, after believing, you were sealed with the Holy Spirit of promise, which is *the* earnest of our inheritance until *the* redemption of the purchased possession, to *the* praise of His glory" (Eph. 1:3-14).

Paul warned the Gentile brethren in Colosse and Laodicea to hold fast to the teachings and knowledge of God's plan because there were false teachers who were trying to drag them back into the vanities of pagan religious philosophy and angel worship: "Now I want you to understand what great concern I have for you, and *for* those in Laodicea, and as many as have not seen my face in *the* flesh; **that their hearts may be encouraged, being knit together in love unto all riches of the full assurance of understanding, unto** *the* **knowledge of the mystery of God, and of** *the* **Father, and of Christ; in Whom are hid all the treasures of wisdom and knowledge**.

"Now I say this so **that no one may deceive you by persuasive speech**. For though I am indeed absent in the flesh, yet I am with you in spirit, rejoicing and beholding your order, and the steadfastness of your faith in Christ. **Therefore, as you have received Christ Jesus the Lord, be walking in Him; being rooted and built up in Him, and being confirmed in the faith, exactly as you were taught**, abounding in it with thanksgiving.

"Beware lest anyone takes you captive through **philosophy and vain deceit**, according to the **traditions of men**, according to the elements of the world, and not according to Christ. **For in Him dwells all the fullness of the Godhead bodily; and you are complete in Him**, Who is the Head of all principality and power. In Whom you have also been circumcised with *the* circumcision not made by hands, in putting off the body of the sins of the flesh by the circumcision of Christ; having been buried with Him in baptism, by which you have also been raised with *Him* through the inner working of God, Who raised Him from the dead.

"For you, who were *once* dead in *your* sins and in the uncircumcision of your flesh, He has *now* made alive with Him, having forgiven all your trespasses. He has blotted out the note of debt against us *with* the decrees *of our sins*, which was contrary to us; and He has taken it away, having nailed it to the cross. After stripping the principalities and the powers, He made a public spectacle of them, *and* has triumphed over them in it [the crucifixion and resurrection]" (Col. 2:1-15).

Paul admonished the Colossian brethren to realize that they were complete in Christ Jesus. They had true forgiveness of sin and true conversion through the baptism of Jesus Christ and the receiving of the Holy Spirit. Although as Gentiles they were not yet physically circumcised, they had spiritual circumcision of the heart in Christ Jesus (also see Rom. 2:28-29). Since they were now living a life of love and obedience to God the Father and Jesus Christ, they were keeping the Sabbath and holy days of God instead of being involved in pagan sun worship and the heathen religious holidays of the past. As a result, false teachers from outside the church at Colosse were trying to deceive them. With persuasive words they tried to convince the brethren to forsake the true way of the Lord and to once again embrace their former beliefs, which they had forsaken.

In verses 13-14,* Paul was not abrogating the laws and commandments of God or His Sabbaths and festivals. Rather, he makes it clear to these Gentile Christians that it is absolutely essential that they obey God and keep the Sabbath and holy days of God.

---

*The King James Version has a gross mistranslation of verse 14, which reads: "Blotting out *the handwriting of ordinances* that was against us, which was contrary to us, and took it out of the way, nailing it to his cross." The phrase *the handwriting of ordinances* in this verse comes from the Greek phrase το χειρογραφον τοις δογμασιν, and has been misinterpreted to mean that the laws and commandments of God as found in the Old Testament were nailed to the cross. Therefore, some wrongly conclude that Paul was doing away with the need to keep the laws and commandments of God. This phrase in the Greek does not in any way mean that the commandments of God were nailed to the cross. The phrase *the handwriting of ordinances* should be properly translated: "the note of debt with the decrees" of our sins, or "the listing of our sins" against God. The laws and commandments of God were never against anyone. God has commanded us to keep them for our good, so that it may go well with us (Deut. 4:40; 5:16, 32-33; 6:3). When we transgress the Law, we sin (I John 3:4). Our sins are against us, not the laws and commandments of God. Jesus, Who bore our sins in His body, was nailed to the cross. Therefore, the debt of our sins was nailed to the cross with Him. Hence, this verse should be properly translated "the debt against us *with* the decrees *of our sins*." Upon true repentance of sins to God the Father, He blots out the note of debt through the blood of Jesus Christ for the remission of our sins. Jesus Christ, Who knew no sin, was made sin for us. He was nailed to the cross as the sin offering for the sins of the whole world. The note of debt of our sins was symbolically nailed to the cross with Jesus Christ. The commandments of God, which stand forever, were never nailed to the cross.

The phrase *the body of Christ* in verse 17 refers to the fact that the true meaning of observing the commandments of God—including the festivals and Sabbaths—is found in Christ Himself and in the true church of God. Paul was teaching here that God's plan is understood by keeping the Sabbaths and festivals—the holy days. The phrase *new moon* is singular, and as such it is a direct reference to the use of the calculated Hebrew Calendar for determining the true dates and times to keep all of God's holy days and festivals as set by God. Detailed and technical information concerning the calculated Hebrew Calendar may be obtained by writing to the address in the front of the book, or by e-mailing your request to *www.cbcg.org.*

Colossians 2:16 does not abolish the dietary laws of clean and unclean meats, the festivals or the weekly Sabbath of God. Rather, Paul is clearly affirming that the Gentiles in Colosse were to continue to observe these commandments as they had been taught. Paul was instructing the Colossians to disregard the criticisms and harsh judgments of those outside the church—because the Sabbath and holy days continued to foreshadow things that were yet to come in God's plan (just as they still do today). By being faithful and keeping the commandments of God, the Colossians would always be worshiping the true God, be built up in Jesus Christ and never loose the understanding of God's plan. By true obedience to God the Father and Jesus Christ, they would not be deceived by vain philosophies of men, nor would they be seduced into the worship of fallen angels—Satan and his demons.

Therefore, he admonished them to not unduly worry about what other people thought, nor let anyone judge or condemn them because they were now obeying God and observing His commanded Sabbaths and festivals: "Therefore, **do not allow anyone to judge you** in eating or in drinking, or with regard to a **festival**, or new moon, or *the* Sabbaths, **which are a foreshadow of the things that are coming**, but the body of Christ. Do not allow anyone to defraud you of the prize *by* doing *his* will in self-abasement and *the* worship of angels, intruding into things that he has not seen, vainly puffed up by his own carnal mind" (verses 16-18).

Upon further examination of his epistles, it is evident that God's revelations to Paul progressively built a clearer picture of the mystery of God. Thus we understand *why* God had blinded the children of Israel—so that the Gentiles might receive salvation as well. While he did not fully understand the timing, Paul also knew that at a future time all Israel would be saved: "For I do not wish you to be ignorant of **this mystery**, brethren, in order that you may not be wise in your own conceits: that a partial hardening *of the heart* has happened to Israel until the fullness of the Gentiles be come in; and **so all Israel shall be saved**, according as it is written: 'Out of Sion shall come the Deliverer, and He shall turn away ungodliness from Jacob. For this *is* My covenant, which I will make with them when I have taken away their sins.' On the one hand, concerning the gospel, *they are* enemies for your sakes; but on the other hand, concerning the election, *they are* beloved for the fathers' sakes; because the gifts and the calling of God *are* never revoked. For just as you once did not believe God, but have now been shown mercy through their unbelief, in the same way also, **they have not believed at this time** in order that through the mercy shown to you, they also may have mercy shown *to them*. For God has given them all over to unbelief in order that He might show mercy to all" (Rom. 11:25-32).

Realizing that in the future God would most certainly save all Israel, he glorified God for the greatness of His plan: "O *the* depth of *the* riches of both *the* wisdom and *the* knowledge of God! How unfathomable *are* His judgments and unsearchable *are* His ways! For who did know *the* mind of *the* Lord, or who became His counselor? Or who first gave to Him, and it shall be recompensed to him again? For from Him, and through Him, and unto Him *are* all things; to Him *be* the glory into the ages of eternity. Amen" (verses 33-36).

At the end of his epistle to the Romans, Paul again states that in past ages the knowledge of God's mystery had been kept secret. "Now to Him who has the power to establish you, according to my gospel and the proclamation of Jesus Christ, according to *the* **revelation of *the* mystery that in past ages has been kept secret**; but now *is* made manifest, and by *the* prophetic scriptures [NT], according to *the* commandment of the eternal God, **has been made known** to all the nations unto *the* obedience of faith; to the only wise God, through Jesus Christ, *be* the glory into the ages *of eternity*. Amen" (Rom. 16:25-27). Again, we see that Paul recognized that God's revelation was not yet complete.

Later, when Paul writes to the Ephesians, he mentions that he had received additional revelations from Jesus Christ about the mystery of God—that the resurrected saints would form **a great spiritual family of God the Father**: "If indeed you have heard of the ministry of the grace of God that was given to me for you; how **He made known to me by revelation the mystery** (even as I wrote briefly before, so that when you read *this*, you will be able to comprehend **my understanding in the mystery of Christ**), which **in other generations was not made known to the sons of men, as it has now been revealed to His holy apostles and prophets by *the* Spirit**; that the Gentiles might be joint heirs, and a joint body, and joint partakers of His promise in Christ through the gospel, of which I became a servant according to the gift of the grace of God, *which was* given to me through the inner working of His power.

"To me, who am less than the least of all the saints, was this grace given, that I might preach the gospel among the Gentiles—*even* **the unsearchable riches of Christ**; and that **I might enlighten all *as to* what *is* the fellowship of the mystery that has been hidden from the ages in God**, Who created all things by Jesus Christ; so that the manifold wisdom of God might now **be made known through the church** to the principalities and the powers in the heavenly *places*, **according to *His* eternal purpose**, which He has wrought in Christ Jesus our Lord, in Whom we have boldness and *direct* access with confidence through His *very* own faith. So then, I beseech *you* not to faint at my tribulations for you, which are *working for* your glory.

"For this cause I bow my knees to the Father of our Lord Jesus Christ, of Whom **the whole family in heaven and earth is named**, that He may grant you, according to the riches of His glory, to be strengthened with power by His Spirit in the inner man; that Christ may dwell in your hearts by faith; *and* that being rooted and grounded in love, **you may be fully able to comprehend with all the saints what *is* the breadth and length and depth and height** [of God's purpose], and to know the love of Christ, which surpasses *human* knowledge; so **that you may be filled with all the fullness of God**. Now to Him Who is able to do exceeding abundantly above all that we ask or think, according to the power that is working in us, to Him *be* glory in the church by Christ Jesus throughout all generations, *even* into the ages of eternity. Amen" (Eph. 3:2-21).

The Keys to Understanding the Mysteries of God: Jesus Christ promised that His true, converted, spirit-led disciples would be given the knowledge of the mysteries of the kingdom of God. Here are the *keys* to understanding the plan of God for mankind, as revealed by His Sabbath and holy days:

- We must fully understand and absolutely believe that *all* Scripture is "God-breathed" (II Tim. 3:16) and "that no prophecy of Scripture [OT or NT] originated as anyone's own *private* interpretation; because prophecy was not brought at any time by human will, but the holy men of God spoke as they were moved by *the* Holy Spirit" (II Pet. 1:20-21).
- In order to understand the Bible and the meaning of the Sabbath and holy days, we must *rightly divide* the Word of God—which is given precept upon precept, line upon line, here a little and there a little (II Tim. 2:15; Isa. 28:9-10).
- God reveals His mysteries only to those who have the Spirit of God, truly love Him, keep His commandments and His Sabbath and holy days, and worship God the Father in spirit and truth (Mark 12:28-30; Col. 2:16; Heb. 4:9; John 4:23-24).

The Revelation of John: While the apostle Paul wrote numerous inspired passages about the mysteries of God and of Christ, God did not give him the final keys that would open the full understanding of God's plan for mankind. Rather, Jesus gave the final, pivotal revelation to the apostle John, who was the longest-lived original apostle, and the one Jesus specially loved. In approximately AD 95, Jesus gave John visions which He commanded him to record—which became the book of Revelation. This book is the most riveting book of the entire Bible because it encompasses the entire plan of God from beginning to end. In fact, Jesus revealed that *He* was the beginning and ending, the first and the last, the One Who began and would finish God's plan (Rev. 1:8, 11; 3:14; 21:6; 22:13). It is vital to note that the book of Revelation cannot be understood without being coupled with critically important passages from the rest of the Bible. A survey of Revelation demonstrates that it is structured upon the framework of God's holy days and festivals, which reveal God's plan for mankind:

- Jesus' death and resurrection (Rev. 1:18; 13:8)—pictured by the Passover.
- The mystery of the seven stars—the seven angels of the seven churches (1:20).
- The mystery of the seven lampstands—the seven churches. Chapters two and three are a prophetic overview God's church throughout history from the time of John until the return of Jesus Christ—pictured by Passover, Unleavened Bread and Pentecost.
- Chapters four and five reveal the throne of God the Father; Jesus Christ is pictured as the Lion of Judah and the Lamb of God, Who would open the seven seals and bring to pass the final, prophetic "great tribulation" of the end time as pictured by the seven seals (Rev. 6:1-17).
- Chapter seven shows the 144,000 and the great innumerable multitude—the last harvest of the saints of God, saved in the final year prior to the first resurrection, which is pictured by Pentecost.

- Chapters eight and nine show six of the seven trumpet plagues—pictured by the Feast of Trumpets.
- Chapter eleven shows the first resurrection at the seventh trumpet (Rev. 11:15-19)—pictured by Pentecost.
- Chapter fourteen shows the 144,000 who will be the bride of Jesus Christ—pictured by Pentecost.
- Chapters fourteen and fifteen show the harvest of the firstfruits—all the saints from all ages who were faithful—pictured by Pentecost.
- Chapter sixteen details the pouring out of the seven last plagues—the final wrath of God—pictured by Trumpets.
- Chapter nineteen shows the marriage supper of the bride and Christ—pictured by Pentecost—followed by the return of Jesus Christ and the saints to the earth, pictured by Trumpets.
- Chapter twenty shows when Satan will be bound—pictured by the day of Atonement (verses 1-3). Then begins the thousand-year reign of Christ and the resurrected saints—pictured by the Feast of Tabernacles (verse 4-5).
- Chapter twenty describes the final judgment of Satan and the demons—pictured by the day of Atonement (verses 7-10).
- Chapter twenty pictures the Great White Throne Judgment and the second resurrection—the first phase for all those who lived and died from the creation of Adam and Eve until the return of Jesus Christ but were never called. They will be resurrected to a second physical life to be given their first opportunity for salvation—portrayed by the feast of the Last Great Day (verses 11-13).
- Chapter twenty also depicts the final phase of the second resurrection of the incorrigibly wicked (who had committed the unpardonable sin) to a second physical life. All of the wicked will receive their final judgment of the second death as they are cast together into the lake of fire to be utterly consumed—also pictured by the feast of the Last Great Day (verse14-15).

Chapters twenty-one and twenty-two show the completion of the mystery of God—the spiritual Family of God the Father and Jesus Christ having grown great, and the coming of the New Jerusalem with God the Father to the new heaven and new earth to dwell with His family: "Then I saw a new heaven and a new earth; for the first heaven and the first earth were passed away, and there was no more sea. And I, John, saw the holy city, *the* **new Jerusalem**, coming down from God out of heaven, prepared as a bride adorned for her husband. And I heard a great voice from heaven say, 'Behold, **the tabernacle of God** *is* **with men; and He shall dwell with them, and they shall be His people; and God Himself shall be with them** *and be* **their God**.

" 'And God shall wipe away every tear from their eyes; and *there* shall be no more death, or sorrow, or crying; neither shall *there* be any more pain, because the former things have passed away.' And He Who sits on the throne said, 'Behold, I make all things new.' Then He said to me, 'Write, for **these words are true and faithful**.' And He said to me, 'It is done [the plan of God is finished]. I am Alpha and Omega, the Beginning and the End. To the one who thirsts, I will give freely of the fountain of the water of life. The one who overcomes shall inherit all things; and I will be his God, and he shall be My son.'… And **there shall be no more curse**; and the throne of God and of the Lamb shall be in it; and His servants shall serve Him, and **they shall see His face**; and His name *is* in their foreheads. And there shall be no night there; for they have no need of a lamp or *the* light of *the* sun, because *the* Lord God enlightens them; and **they shall reign into the ages of eternity**…. 'I am Alpha and Omega, *the* Beginning and *the* End, the First and the Last.' **Blessed** *are* **those who keep His commandments, that they may have the right to** *eat of* **the tree of life**, and may enter by the gates into the city" (Rev. 21:1-7; 22:3-5, 13-14).

A Prayer of Encouragement: When Paul first informed the brethren of Ephesus about the purpose of God the Father and Jesus Christ, he ended with this prayer for them. It is fitting that we also end this Prologue with his prayer. May God answer this prayer for all those who read and study about the mystery of God and of Christ in *God's Plan for Mankind Revealed by His Sabbath and Holy Days*: "I do not cease to give thanks for you, making mention of you in my prayers; **that the God of our Lord Jesus Christ, the Father of glory, may give you *the* spirit of wisdom and revelation in *the* knowledge of Him. *And* may the eyes of your mind be enlightened in order that you may comprehend what is the hope of His calling, and what *is* the riches of the glory of His inheritance in the saints, and what is the exceeding greatness of His power toward us who believe, according to the inner working of His mighty power**, which He wrought in Christ, when He raised Him from *the* dead, and set *Him* at His right hand in the heavenly *places*, far above every principality and authority and power and lordship, and every name that is named—not only in this age, but also in the *age* to come; for He has subordinated all things under His feet, and has given Him *to be* head over all things to the church, which is His body—the fullness of Him Who fills all things in all" (Eph. 1:16-23).

Thus, the prophecy of Moses is fulfilled through the New Covenant with Jesus Christ and God the Father: "**The secret things belong unto the LORD our God: but those things which are revealed** [in both the Old and New Testaments] **belong unto us and to our children for ever** [the Church of God, which is spiritual Israel, the children of God] that we may do all the words of this Law [which now includes the entire Bible]" (Deut. 29:29).

Even with all the knowledge that God the Father and Jesus Christ have revealed by the Holy Spirit through the Word of God and His Sabbath and holy days, we also realize that comprehending the absolute reality of God's spiritual plan for mankind is still like looking through a glass darkly. However, at the first resurrection we will understand the fullness of God's plan for mankind: "For we know in part, and we prophesy in part; but when that which is perfect has come, then that which is in part shall be set aside. When I was a child, I spoke as a child, I understood as a child, I reasoned as a child; but when I became a man, I set aside the things of a child. **For now we see through a glass darkly, but then *we shall see* face to face; now I know in part, but then I shall know exactly as I have been known**. And now, these three remain: faith, hope *and* love; but the greatest of these *is* love" (I Cor. 13:9-13).

"The secret of the Lord is with them who fear Him;
And He will show them His covenant."
(Psa. 25:14)

"It is the glory of God to conceal a thing;
But the honor of kings is to search out a matter."
(Prov. 25:2)

"Open my eyes to behold
Wondrous things out of your Law!"
(Psa. 119:18)

"Prove all things;
Hold fast to that which is good."
(I Thess. 5:21)

Section I

The Sabbath

CHAPTER ONE

The Background in Genesis—Sermon I

July 22, 1995

Now, let's go to the Gospel of John, please. And let's read a promise that is given to us here. And let's apply that today, because we're going to go back and look at some very basic things, beginning in the book of Genesis. And we are going to see that there is an awful lot there.

I remember making the comment sometime ago, "I wonder what it would have been like to hear a sermon by the Apostle Paul—going into the Old Testament to tell us and show this, that and the other thing that is there.

So, let's come here to John 14, and here's a promise that is given that the Holy Spirit will do for us. John 14:26 "But *when* the Comforter *comes, even* the Holy Spirit, which the Father will send in My name, that one **shall teach you all things**..." [All bold is speakers emphasis throughout.] Now, that's quite a promise, isn't it? If we have the Holy Spirit of God, which we do; and if we're yielding to God and trying to live by every word of God; will the Holy Spirit teach us all things—that is what we need to know for salvation? It's not going to teach us all information in the world, obviously. It doesn't mean that. "… and shall bring to your remembrance everything that I have told you." Now, that can't happen to us because we didn't hear the words of Jesus Christ.

Now, Chapter 16 and verse 13; here's another promise concerning the Holy Spirit: "However, when that one has come, *even* the Spirit of the truth, is come, it **will lead you into all truth**..." So there is this special blessing that comes when we really take God at His Word, study His Word, and add precept upon precept. So, here's tremendous promise given to us. So if we follow the Word of God and we do put 'line up line, here a little there a little,' and put it together **correctly,** here's a promise: "…it will lead you into all truth:…" and the Greek there means *all THE truth.* Now notice, continuing on: "…because it shall not speak from itself, but whatsoever it shall hear, it shall speak. And it shall disclose to you the things to come" (John 16:13). So this is the thing necessary for us to understand concerning how we're going to understand the truth. And I think we're going to understand this even more in relationship to the very beginning parts of the Bible.

Now, let's go to Luke 24, because here's something else that we add to the knowledge of the Scriptures. And I think this is very, very profound—if we could use the word, I know I use the word perhaps a little bit too much, but if you can help me with another word, help me with it and I could use that—but, I think it's also most comforting and understanding when Jesus gave this promise here in Luke 24:44: "And He said to them, 'These *are* the words that I spoke to you when I was yet with you…" and of course, Jesus' promise that the Holy Spirit would bring to remembrance *all things* that He said "…that all *the* things which were written concerning Me in the Law of Moses and *in the* Prophets and *in the* Psalms must be fulfilled. Then He **opened their minds to understand** the Scriptures…"

Now, we've seen and we've experienced this from time-to-time a little bit as we're going along step-by-step-by-step. And I've been working on the publication, *The Grace of God in the Bible,* and, and there's one thing I've learned with writing: you have to get in it

1

and you have to really have your mind concentrating on it and be able to know the things that are there. So, what I've been doing, I've been writing concerning the grace of God in the Old Testament. And it has brought out some very interesting things and helped me clarify and helped me understand even the first part of the Bible even more. So, I guess, when we get down to it, we will have to say that you never know anything the way that you really ought to truly know it. So, what I did, since we have—thanks to Carl Franklin making copies of it for us—we have the *Interlinear Hebrew-English Old Testament (Genesis-Exodus)* by George Ricker Berry. Now, we checked out and, unfortunately, he did not do the whole Bible. He just did Genesis and Exodus. However, I think in there is quite a bit that we can learn.

Now, this is going to help us also understand more about how important the Sabbath is right at a time when people are ***throwing away*** the Sabbath. It's almost a dichotomy that is unreal. So, let's go back. Let's take the literal translation of the Hebrew—literal translation—and let's begin in Genesis 1:1. Now, what I did, I expanded this in size so it is readable. The original text is 20 percent smaller. Now, there's something that is going to make it just a little difficult in following along, and that is that the English must be read from the right to the left, rather than from the left to the right. With the literal translation in linear form it must be done that way, because Hebrew is read from the right to the left. And we're going to see some just little different **but profound** translations of different words that really mean more to us. As you look at the interlinear translation here, you will see that there are two columns with an English translation. One is the *King James Version,* which is on the left-hand side and one is the *Revised Version,* which is on the right-hand side. Then you have the Hebrew text with the English directly below it. So let's pick it up. We're going to go into other sections of the Bible as we are going along, but let's read from the English from the *Interlinear*—and so, I'll try and get it at such a pace that you can understand it. You will also see that the verb in Hebrew is put before the subject. Just to make a clarification: *King James Version* on the left, *Revised* on the right. And then his translation—George Ricker Barry's translation—in the middle. Now, if it's a little too hard for you to follow along, then you can follow along with the *King James* or the *Revised Version,* either one. The purpose of this is because there are several sections, which are important for us to know and read and understand.

So, let's begin in verse 1: "In the beginning [when] created God the heavens and the earth…" (Gen. 1:1, *IH*)

Now, let's understand something that's important, which is this: God had to be ***before*** the beginning. Is that not correct? If God were not *before* "the beginning," then God would *be* "the beginning." As you will notice, when we're going through here, there may be some changes in your notes in your margin of your Bible—as someone just pointed out. There is only one real "**the** beginning" in relationship to us—and what the Bible reveals to us. That is "the beginning." Some people have put down there "**a** beginning" trying to indicate that there was "*a* beginning" before "*the* beginning." But you cannot have "**a** beginning before "**the** beginning," otherwise "**the** beginning" is not "*the* beginning." You have **one beginning** and you may have ***subsequent renewals***. You may have subsequent changes. You may have subsequent additions. But there is only *one* "THE beginning."

Ok—let's go on. The reason it is justified in the minds of some by saying, "**a** beginning," because some people have in mind that there was "**a** beginning" before "**the** beginning" of the heaven and earth ***as we know it***. However, in this particular case it is not talking about this, as we will see. Let's look at some other Scriptures concerning "the beginning." And John is the one who does this. Now, I'm going to go in a little more detail on this later on when I go through a very thorough word-by-word analysis of the Gospel of John, the first chapter. But, let's go to the Gospel of John, the first chapter, because there are only three places in all of the Scriptures—Old Testament and New Testament—which talks about "in **the** beginning."

Now here in the Gospel of John we find it is not "**a** beginning," but "**the** beginning." And this is very important for us to understand concerning the nature of God. I will give a little detail here and, at a later time, I will amplify it even more. "In *the* beginning was **the Word,** and the Word was **with God,** and the Word **was** God…." (John 1:1). Now the importance that we need to understand is this. "In **the** beginning"—and it can actually read here: "*before* the beginning." I don't want to get in too much detail with the Greek here "…was the Word." Now, why did He have to be in existence before the beginning? *Because He's the Creator!*

"…And the Word was with God…" Now this is very important from the point of view, as you will see in this paper concerning "the thinker" and "the thought" what they're trying to do is eliminate two beings Who are God and say there's only one Being who is God by saying that the Word was "the thought" of God. And since He was "the thought" in "the thinker" He was with God. But that's not what this means at all, because when we get to the detailed study of it, we will see it is "with"—and the Greek is "pros" which means "with or toward, face to face."

"…and the Word **was** God." So that we understand who the One it was that became Jesus Christ. And we will see later, in our in-depth study, that all of this is to counteract and go against all the philosophical doctrines of the nature of God. When we get there it is going to open your mind like you have never understood this before. But, I want to get it all prepared and laid out word for word so that you can see it clearly. I'm currently reading a book by John Goodenough, which is called *Light by Light*. And of course, it says a lot about light here, doesn't it, in the first chapter? Yes, and what he is essentially showing is the pagan's concept of the nature of God. And going through that, I can see, and with what we have in these other papers here, how that they were going *absolutely contrary* to those religions at that time, which are philosophies which are being resurrected and being dumped upon us today.

Now, let's notice something else, continuing: "He was in *the* beginning with God" (John 1:2). Which means He had to be there. Now notice what He did: "All things came into being through [**by**] **Him**…" you can also translate 'all things' as 'everything.'; "…and not even one *thing* **that was created came into being without Him**" (v 3). No such thing as creation by sub-gods. No such thing as creation by angels. No such thing as evolution. *All was made by Him*.

Now, let's go to I John 1, because we want to cover this. And since I said there were three places which talks about the beginning, we want to go ahead and have it in there. Now we're talking about something just a little bit *different* in relationship to it. We're talking about the One Who was *from* the beginning. And that is *after* everything was created, the One Who became Jesus Christ as the Lord God of the Old Testament continually existed from the time of the creation. He existed *before* the creation; He existed *after* the creation. So that is what he is saying here. And he's giving us a very, very personal account of their relationship with Jesus Christ. "That which was from *the* beginning, that which we have heard, that which we have seen with our own eyes, that which we observed for ourselves and our own hands handled, concerning the Word of life; (And the life was manifested, and we have seen, and are bearing witness, and are reporting to you the eternal life, which was with the Father, and was manifested to us;)" or that is, 'revealed' unto us "…that which we have seen and have heard we are reporting to you in order that you also may have fellowship with us; for the fellowship—indeed, our fellowship—*is* with the Father and with His own Son, Jesus Christ" (1 John 1:1-3).

Now, let's go to Hebrews 1, and we find something that adds to this concerning "the beginning," concerning God, concerning what He did, concerning what Christ was. We know that "in the beginning was God." And we know that the word for God is *Elohim*. And *Elohim* is a word which means ***"more than one."*** So, there was a time when there were the two *Elohim* and then there was a time when one of Them became the Father and the other became the Son.

So, Hebrews 1:1: "God, Who spoke to the fathers at different times in the past and in many ways by the prophets, has spoken to us in these last days by *His* Son, Whom He has appointed **heir of all things**…" So, when it says that we're going to be 'co-heirs with Christ', I don't even think that our minds can **grasp** the magnitude of what that is going to be. Because He's the heir of all things. "…by Whom..." now notice, "...also He **made the worlds**; Who being *the* brightness of *His* glory and *the* exact image of His person…" So, we're dealing with the fact that God is a person—as revealed throughout the Scriptures. That is why God wants us to have a personal relationship with Him and with Christ. Now, notice this: "…and upholding all things **by the word of His own power**," or 'by the power of His Word'—because God, we will see, when He created, when He *spoke,* it came into existence. "…when He had **by Himself**…" which we'll have to cover in more detail when we come around to the Passover time again "…**by Himself** purged our sins, sat down at *the* right hand of the Majesty on high; having been made so much greater than *any of* the angels, inasmuch as He has inherited a name exceedingly superior to them. For to which of the angels did He ever say, 'You are My Son; this day I have begotten You'?" That is when the Father ***became*** the Father. That is when the Elohim who became the Father, became the Father. That's when the Elohim who became the Son, ***became*** the Son. We'll read that again, verse 5: "…For to which of the angels did He ever say, 'You are My Son; this day I have begotten You'? And again, 'I will be a Father to Him, and He will be a Son to Me'? And again, when He brought the Firstborn into the world, He said, 'Let all *the* angels of God worship Him' " (Hebrews 1:1-6).

So this is telling us about the person and the power and the work and the activity of Jesus Christ. Now, let's go back to our *Hebrew Interlinear* in Genesis 1. And so, when we are talking about "**the** beginning" it is **the** beginning—not "**a**." Anything subsequent of "**the** beginning," is an addition or renewal or whatever, but it is not "**a** beginning. " "In the beginning [when] created God the heavens and the earth…" (Gen. 1:1, *IH*). So, as I mentioned, the verb comes before the subject. God here being *Elohim* means *more than one*. That's why, as we will see a little later, He said, "Let Us."

"(…and) the earth being a desolation and a waste…" (v 2). Now, **how** did the earth become "a desolation and a waste"? Because when He got done creating the earth it was, He said, "Behold it was ***very good***." Let's see how this came to be. Let's first understand what these two words mean, come from the Hebrew, *tohu* and *bohu*—you've probably heard that before—which means "chaos" and "confusion."

Now, is God the author of confusion? *No!* God is not the author of confusion. We find that in I Corinthians 14:33. You don't have to turn there, you might want to put it in your notes—I Corinthians 14:[33]: "For God is not the author of confusion." Now, ***how did it become this way?*** Well, the reason is there was something before human beings, which was on this earth. That's what happened. So, let's look at that. Let's look at the Scriptures, which help us with this, to give us understanding. Let's first of all go to Isaiah. Isaiah 45, and let's see what Isaiah tells us concerning God and His creation. Now, as we are turning to Isaiah 45, you will also note that the *King James* translation says, concerning in verse two that "the earth was without form and void" (Gen. 1:2).

Now, when we come to Isaiah 45, we have a very interesting, and very profound verse. Verse 18: "For thus saith the LORD that created the heavens…" now, we're talking about 'in the beginning God created the heavens and the earth'; "…God himself that formed the earth and made it; he hath established it, he created it not in vain..." *tohu*—it's not in vain. How could it become 'in vain' right at the beginning after God created it, if He didn't make it 'in vain' or in chaos and confusion? "…**he formed it to be inhabited:** I *am* the LORD; and *there is* none else" (Isa. 45:18).

All right, let's go to Jeremiah 4 and we will see another place where the expression, *tohu* and *bohu* is used. And this will give us an understanding as to how the earth **became** that way. Now, let's pick it up here in verse—it's talking about the punishment coming to Jerusalem and Judah. It's talking about the things that are happening in punishment. Verse 19, Jeremiah 4: Jeremiah says, "My bowels, my bowels! I am pained at my very heart; my heart maketh a noise in me; I cannot hold my peace, because thou hast heard, O my soul, the sound of the trumpet, the alarm of war…." Now, this is going to tell us how the earth became that way, and why the earth is so literally upside down. "…Destruction upon destruction is cried; for the whole land is spoiled: suddenly are my tents spoiled, *and* my curtains in a moment. How long shall I see the standard, *and* hear the sound of the trumpet? For my people *is* foolish, they have not known me; they *are* sottish children, and they have none understanding: they *are* wise to do evil, but to do good they have no knowledge. I beheld the earth, and, lo, *it was* **without form, and void**…" (Jer. 4:19-23). A condition subsequent to the creation. In this case, a condition subsequent to what we find of the completed creation in Genesis 1—and this is *tohu* and *bohu* or being 'a desolation and a waste.' And that's what war does.

Let's ask the question: Was there **war** in heaven **before** the creation of man? Because that becomes very important. Let's first of all, let's first of all go to Genesis 3 for just a minute, because we want to understand something here. Now, in this case, I'm just going to the *King James* because I just want to cover one thing here. In all the account that we have, concerning Adam and Eve and the garden and so forth, we have four beings who are noted in the Scriptures, correct? Besides all the animals in the creation. Who are those four beings? We have God, we have Adam, we have Eve. Now then, we also have the serpent. The serpent then, we know, is Satan the devil. He's called "the ancient serpent who is called the Devil and Satan, who is deceiving the whole world" (Rev. 12:9).

Question: Was Satan **already evil** by the time he met Adam and Eve? *Yes!* Which means then, he had to become evil and Satan, **before** Adam and Eve were created. Now, when was that, and how did that happen? Well, let's look at some Scriptures. Let's go to Ezekiel 28 and we will see. Now, Ezekiel 28 is a very interesting chapter because it talks about the "prince of Tyre"; it talks about Tyre; and it talks about the king of Tyre or Tyrus as it is listed here. But, we want to focus in on something that is very important because this tells us some very important facts.

Now, let's read it here, verse 11, Ezekiel 28. Now, this is very basic, fundamental. But, I think it's important that we go through it, because, you know, there are some people who are denying that Satan is even a being, today—even within the Church of God. Ezekiel 28:11: "Moreover the word of the LORD came unto me, saying, Son of man, take up a lamentation upon the king of Tyrus…" (vs 11-12). Now, notice over here, verse 2: "Son of man, say to the prince of Tyre, …Because thine heart *is* lifted up, and thou hast said, I *am* a God, I sit *in* the seat of God…" Well, you can't get any higher than that, can you? *No.* Why then does he address the king of Tyrus? Because, in this case, the king of Tyrus is the spirit power behind the prince, who **says** he's God. And we're going to see that this is the same spirit power that, in the book of Revelation, inspires the final beast power to say, "I am God." And all the world is going to worship him and worship the devil.

Now, let's notice what it says about this king of Tyrus which has to then be the one who became Satan the devil as we will see by what the Scriptures tell us here: "…and say unto him, Thus saith the Lord GOD; Thou sealest up the sum, full of wisdom, and perfect in beauty. Thou hast been in Eden the garden of God..." (v 12-13). Now let's ask a couple of questions here. Let's stop and we'll just ask a couple of questions, which we will confirm a little later when we go through Genesis 3.

We have the four identified who were in the garden, correct? *God, Adam, Eve and the serpent.*

- What happened after they sinned? *They were put out of the Garden of Eden.*
- And no one could enter into it, correct? *Right*

So, if he was in Eden, the garden of God, this could only be talking about the one who became Satan the devil. Because no one else came into the garden of Eden after the sin of Adam and Eve. They were cast out and cherubim were put there with flaming swords to keep the way, so they couldn't go back in there.

Now notice, we have something here that is important. "You were in Eden the garden of God" and then it talks about all of his beauty—all of the tremendous coverings and the stones, which is a sign of *regalness* and *royalty* and *exalted position.* Let's come down here to the last sentence of verse 13: "...the workmanship of thy tabrets and of thy pipes was prepared in thee in the day that **thou wast created.**"

Now, we saw that everything was created by Jesus Christ, correct? *Nothing* came into existence that He did not make. So, we have a created being. Now, let's find out a little bit more about him: "Thou *art* the anointed cherub that covereth..." Now, we know that over the ark of the covenant were two cherubs, correct—guarding it. Here we find an additional cherub which has nothing to do with the two cherubs that are over the Ark of the Covenant. Nor having anything to do with the two cherubs placed at the gate going into the garden of Eden. "Thou *art* the anointed cherub that covereth; and I have set thee *so:* thou wast upon the holy mountain of God..." Now, the garden of Eden was **not** the Holy Mount was it? *No.* This is talking about a time prior to when the earth became desolate and without form or void—or *tohu* and *bohu.* "... I have set thee *so:* thou wast upon the holy mountain of God thou hast walked up and down in the midst of the stones of fire." showing that he was right there with God in whatever this, this is talking about the way you could visualize things composed of spirit—this is what it's talking about. Verse 15: "...Thou *wast* perfect in thy ways from the day that thou wast created..." Now, it doesn't tell us how long the event was. "...till iniquity was found in thee" (vs 14-15).

We don't know how long it was, the Bible doesn't tell us. But, something happened. And it happened over a period of time.

Now, when I was back in Grand Junction I was given this little saying by Carl Quist. So I entitled it *An Old Proverb*—and this is true:

> You don't go bad in a single day,
> You just sort of shuffle along.
> Then lighten the load of your moral code
> Till you don't know right from wrong.

And I thought that was a very nice little proverb. But it's the same way with Satan the devil. Same way with the one who was the "covering cherub"—right over the throne of God.

Now, let's notice what happened: "...till iniquity was found in him" (v 15), which shows us that there had to be a period of time. There had to be an activity by the angels. Angels do not exist just to pluck on harps. Angels are greater in power and ability than human beings. So, I have to ask the question: What kind of civilization did the angels have before they fell? *We don't know.* But it had to be **greater** than ours, because they had greater abilities. But notice what it says, "by the multitude of your merchandise" (v 16). So I don't know what it was that they were doing. But what is it that Satan is inspiring the whole world to do today? *To buy and sell and trade and merchandise.* Is that what he did with the angels also, and then do it illegally, do it improperly? *It could very well be.* "… they have filled the midst of thee with violence, and thou hast sinned…" (v 16). And sin *is* the transgression of the laws and commandment of God.

- Do you not suppose that there are commandments for angels that they have to obey?
- If you have righteous angels are they not obedient angels?
- If you have disobedient angels who have become demons, then you have also to apply the principle.
- If you don't believe that there are laws and commandments for angels to follow—what is that principle?
- *Where there is no law there is no sin.*

So he could not have sinned unless there was some law that he broke or commandment that he broke. And we're going to see what that was in just a little bit here.

"…Therefore I will cast thee as profane out of the mountain of God: and I will destroy thee, O covering cherub, from the midst of the stones of fire. Thine heart was lifted up because of thy beauty, thou hast corrupted thy wisdom by reason of thy brightness:" got totally sold on himself "I will cast thee to the ground, I will lay thee before kings, that they may behold thee. Thou hast defiled thy sanctuaries…" (vs. 16-18). So there must have been some form of angelic worship with sanctuaries. With what we might call assemblies or *churches*. Now, we have to deduce that from here, because you cannot have a sanctuary unless there is some place that's set aside to be holy, can you? "Thou hast defiled thy sanctuaries by the multitude of thine iniquities, by the iniquity of thy traffic; therefore will I bring forth a fire from the midst of thee, it shall devour thee, and I will bring thee to ashes upon the earth in the sight of all them that behold thee" (v 18).

So then, it carries forth right from there to the final punishment of Satan the devil. Now, let's go to Revelation 12. And this tells us what occurred, and then we'll go from there to the book of Jude and then to the book of Isaiah. Now, let's understand something concerning fallen angels—which are called demons. Revelation 12. Because there's going to be a future war, and that future war is going to result in again, the casting down of Satan the devil to the earth—which is just somewhere in the very near future ahead of us.

Now, let's read verse 9 first, so that we can understand something with him, something about this. Verse 9: "And the great dragon was cast out, the ancient serpent…" now, what happened when he was cast out the first time? This is the second casting out, as we will see. The first one was a 'fall.' "…And the great dragon was cast out, the ancient serpent who is called the Devil and Satan, who is deceiving the whole world: he was cast down to the earth, and his angels were cast down with him" (Rev. 12:9). Those angels are called, in the Gospels, demons or unclean spirits. Now, we've seen in the past that sin causes uncleanness—spiritual and physical. Now, let's go back, let's go back to verse 1 of Chapter 12: "Then there appeared a great wonder in heaven; a woman clothed with the sun…" this is symbolic of the whole completed work of God, with the bride of Christ. This is depicting the woman, the bride of Christ. "…and *having* the moon under her feet, and on her head a crown of twelve stars: and being with child, she cried in travail, and was in pain to deliver.

And another sign was seen in heaven; and behold, a great red dragon..." which we saw was Satan the devil "...having seven heads and ten horns..." so we have the powers and principalities, "...and seven crowns on his heads; and his tail swept away a third of the stars of heaven, and cast them to the earth..." (Rev. 12:1-4).

When did that happen? That's the question now we need to ask. This first "fall," when did that happen? Let's go to Luke 10, and let's see what Jesus said. Luke 10. Let's see what Jesus said concerning Satan and the demons. Because this is also a very revealing Scripture. Luke 10:17: "Then the seventy returned with joy, saying,' Lord, even the demons [Now, the *King James* says 'devils', but that should be *demons*.] are subject to us through Your name.' And He said to them, "I beheld Satan fall as lightning from heaven" (vs 17-18). That is what we just read in Revelation 12:3-4 there, correct? "And his tail swept away a third of the stars of heaven [with him]" (Rev. 12:4).

We know that in Revelation 1, that "a star" is "an angel." So this is saying—combined together—that when Satan "fell as lightning from heaven" he "drew a third of the angels with him."

Now, let's confirm that by this Scripture in Jude—the little book of Jude, please. Let's turn there, just one little chapter—and that's why it's only the verses—and let's see what Jude wrote concerning the angels and see what he says about them. Book of Jude, last one before the book of Revelation, the book of Jude. And let's pick it up here in verse 6: "And the angels who did not keep their own original domain, but deserted their habitation..." they rebelled against God "...He is holding in eternal bonds under darkness unto the judgment of *the* great day" (Jude 6).

Now, we also know that Satan had to fall before man was created, otherwise he would not show up in the Garden of Eden as Satan. So, let's put this all together and let's see what happened. Let's go to Isaiah 14. No, before we go there, let's go to II Corinthians 4—on the way back let's stop there. Just happened to catch my eye. Let's understand that Satan is called "the god of this world." II Corinthians 4:3, and verse 4 tells us something very important: "But if our gospel is hidden, it is hidden to those who are perishing: In whom the god of this world..." Now, Jesus called him the "prince" of this world or the "ruler" of this world. He's also called, in Ephesians 2, "the prince of the power of the air. That spirit that now works within the children of disobedience." The "god of this world."

Now, let's go to Isaiah 14, and we will put this all together and we will see *when* Satan was cast down; *when* the war took place. Now, when there is war, what happens? We saw in Jeremiah 4, when there's war there's desolation and destruction—*wasting!* Now, Isaiah 14:12: "How art thou fallen from heaven..." And isn't that what Jesus said, He saw Satan fall from heaven as lightning. (Luke 10:18): "How art thou fallen from heaven, O Lucifer..." That means *light-bringer.* He was to be the "light-bringer" in God's plan, but he rebelled.

Now, let me just mention something here that's important. In all of the secret religions of the philosophies and also in masonry, they worship Lucifer as the "light-bringer." And Lucifer is declared, unequivocally, by Albert Pike, as God. And they know what they're worshipping. That's why they have to have degrees, to kind of let you in on the secret step-by-step. Because, if they told a new initiate first out, what they were doing, they would undoubtedly reject it. So, you have to be brainwashed and brought along, degree by degree by degree by degree. And when you get to be the 33rd degree, then they know that are coming to the stream of light from Lucifer. Now, you will see that in this other paper that I gave you.

8

Let's continue here in Isaiah 14: "...*how* art thou cut down to the ground, which didst weaken the nations! For thou hast said in thine heart, I will ascend into heaven..." now, this had to happen before the creation of man, correct? "I will exalt my throne above the stars of God..." stars being angels, 'above the *angels* of God'—get the advantage! "...I will sit also upon the mount of the congregation, in the sides of the north..." (vs 12-13). Which is the mountain of God, where the central government of God the Father and Jesus Christ is located. Wherever that is in the universe, and I'm convinced that it's a whole lot closer to the earth than maybe we have imagined.

"I will ascend above the heights of the clouds..." (v 14).

- Now, where are clouds? *Clouds are on the earth.*
- What do you need to make clouds? *You need water.*
- Where's the only place that they truly have found any amount of water where there can be clouds, in as far as our whole solar system is concerned? *That's the earth.*

Now, they think that on Mars they can detect some things where there used to be water. Possible. So, I just throw this into the mix, as just a thought, it makes you wonder, was there something on Mars before it was desolated in its present condition? *Could be.* So, everyone is anxious to find out what is on Mars. Some people have said that there are some temple-looking buildings or something on Mars, but the United States government is holding back the information on that. I do not know. You can read that in the *Enquire* or *Star*, which ever you prefer—ok.

The question is—"I will exalt my throne above the stars of God"—could that refer to literal stars? *Yes!* It could refer to angels. It could refer to both, and still have the same meaning. Ok, let's go on. "I will sit also upon the mount of the congregation, in the sides of the north I will ascend above the heights of the clouds; **I will be like the most High**" (vs 13-14).

Now, that is an impossibility. Why? Well, we have a lesson from Paul. He said, "Shall the thing created..." which it was "...be greater than the Creator?" *No!* Or, "Shall the thing created say to the Creator, 'What are you making?'" And that's what he's doing by this statement: "I will be like the most High."

"Yet thou shalt be brought down to hell, to the sides of the pit" (v 15). And that's what's going to happen.

Now, let's go back to Genesis 1. I can see we've made marvelous headway today—ok. So, what we are dealing with here is that after God created the heavens and the earth, in the beginning **something happened,** and the word "was" can be translated "became." Or "it's state of being *became* a desolation and a waste" (Gen. 1:2). So, then what we are dealing with here, which is true, when we are looking at the earth in this condition, what does God do from that time forward? *He renews the surface of the earth,* or recreates it, doesn't He? *Yes.*

When Christ returns, is He going to make a new heaven and a new earth? *Yes, He is!* Because all the stars are, again, out of whack, are they not? And the earth is going to be all suffering from the wars and desolation and plagues, is it not? *Yes!*

He is going to have to make a new heaven and new earth. How? *By renewing the one that is here.* It talks about that during the millennium one of the things we will be doing is helping the people rebuild the waste places, which is the result of war. Now, notice what

9

else happened here. Continuing on in verse 2, *IH*: "…(and) the earth being a desolation and waste, and **darkness** [being] upon the face of [the] abyss…" Now who is the prince of darkness? *Satan the devil.*

So, we a have dual meaning here. The light of God was not shinning, number one, because Christ is the light—and that's what John 1 tells us. Satan is the prince of darkness, so we have symbolic, the spiritual quality of the absence of light and darkness; and we have the literal darkness, that *it was dark.* Maybe a thick darkness like it was in Egypt during the plagues—I do not know. "…and darkness being upon the face of [the] **abyss**" That means just the *great deep.* "And the spirit of God was hovering upon the face of the waters…" (v 2-3, *IH*).

Now, what is one way to get rid of radiation? *You bury it in water.* And you keep it there a long time. Now, we do not know how old the earth literally is. It could be many hundreds of millions of years old, as we reckon time. Could even be billions of years old. And when you look at the geographical strata what do you see? *You see two floods.* You see the killing of the warm-blooded animals in the flood of Noah; and you see the killing of the dinosaurs in a *different* strata in a *different* time; and that is always buried way down low with the so-called "primitive rocks."

Now, I will have to say that most of the things that they test, they don't test the literal thing. I found out this concerning the testing—like they go to Africa like Professor Leeky and he's walking along the ground and sees part of a skull there. And he picks up this part of the skull and he says, "I wonder how old this is? Well, we'll take it in and do a scientific testing." So, what they do, they go and get some of the dirt and they test the dirt for the age, not the skull.

Now, if you understand the *error* in that, then you'll understand why most of these things are wrong with the carbon dating and even the argon carbon dating, though the dating [may be] correct. The age of the soil maybe totally different than the age of the bone which is found in the soil, correct? *Yes!*

Comment was made, we have, we have Betty Gramlich—she used to live back there in Utah where the dinosaur national Park (Marilyn Gramlich, Betty's her daughter, they're both here, thank you, and I'm sure you've seen it, too) the dinosaur bones right in the limestone. So, when you test the stone. Now, let's look at it this way: You could take a calf, it died, you bury it, it's left there—say, maybe 50 years. Someone comes back and does an archeological excavation. They find these bones, they want to know how old the bones are, how long has it been there? Well, if they take the bones and test the bones, they will get an accurate test. But, if they take the soil in which the calf was buried and test the soil, they're not going to get an accurate result because the soil was there long before the calf was buried in it. So, that's why you find this great divergence.

Now, how long it was that the angels were here in peace and harmony before sin, we don't know. But, God then had to renew the face of the earth—which is what He did here. So, we have the spiritual darkness and we have the physical darkness and now God is going to do something about it.

"…Then said God…" (v 3) Now, we notice, we note, that "by His Word, He commands." Now, this is going to be so *profound* when we come to the creation of Adam and Eve. Because also, this tells us our relationship and our destiny with God that God intended from the very beginning of the creation of Adam and Eve.

[So He commanded:] "…Let light be and light was. [light came into being] And saw God the light that [it was] good, and divided God between the light and (between) the darkness. And called God to the light day, [or assigned to it the name 'day'], and to the darkness he called night; and evening was and morning was, the day one" (vs 3-5, *IH*). ...in the re-creation of the earth for human existence. Because he already began with an earth that was in "chaos and confusion"—a "waste land and desolation" as a result of the war with Satan and his angels, who fell and became demons.

Now, let's also notice something here that's important: when there was night and when there was day, what do we literally have? *We have on half of the earth it is night, half of the earth it is day continuously at all times.* But, when it says "the evening and the morning were day one" the evening ended the darkness where God was when He created and called into existence the light and separated it. And the evening ended the darkness. Just like when we go through—and that follows the pattern all the way through the Bible—when you come to evening or sunset, it ends that day. So, this first evening ended the darkness because it was light just enough where God was so that it was evening; and then morning was day one.

Now, let's go on, continuing here in verse six: "And said God: Let be an expanse in the midst of the waters, and let it be dividing between waters to waters. And made God the expanse, and he divided between the waters which [were] (from) under (to) the expanse and (between) the waters which [were] (from) above [yes] (to) the expanse; [which was above] and it was so. And called God the expanse heavens; and evening was and morning was, a day second" (vs 6-8, *IH*).

Now, some people think that the waters above had to do with perhaps an envelope of water or some sort of water-covering above the earth. I do not know whether that speculation has any validity or not. Some people have said maybe there was a ring of water around the earth. And if there was a ring of water around the earth, it had to then end up being frozen, correct? Because once you get out of the temperature it's going to freeze. ***Possible!*** This doesn't tell us exactly. Let's read it in the *King James,* verse 6: "And God said, Let there be a firmament in the midst of the waters, and let it divide the waters from the waters. And God made the firmament, and divided the waters which *were* under the firmament from the waters which *were* above the firmament: and it was so" (vs 6-7).

Now, let's ask a question: Could this also refer to clouds? Are clouds full of water? *Yes!* And you know they are when it rains, right? Do they contain lots and lots and lots of water? *Yes, they do.* Especially when you get caught in some horrendous rain you wonder when it's going to stop. So, I would have to surmise from what is here that what He was doing was separating the waters from the oceans, which became the oceans, from the water which He wanted to have in the clouds. Now, whether there was a ring of water or a disc of frozen water around the earth, I do not know. It doesn't tell us. So, we have to leave that in the realm of speculation.

"...evening and the morning were the second day" (v 8).

Now, let's go to page 2 in the *Interlinear*. How are you doing reading right to left?

"And said God: Let be collected the waters (from) under the heavens unto place one, and let be seen the dry land ..." (v 9). Now, sometimes you have rearrange the words as you're reading, because it's a little awkward with the literal translation. But, it's good to have a literal translation though, really. Now, there is some evidence geologically speaking, that there was ***one major continent*** on the earth at one time and the seas all around it. Could be. This seems to lend some credence to that. And then they say that the earth was moved around and formed the continents as we have them now. How many have seen that kind of thing on television?

Well, when you look at some of these continents, you can see that it makes sense. Some of them, which are close by, you can see the difference. Like in the English Channel, you have the white cliffs of Dover on one side and then you have the white cliffs, but not as much, on the other side [in France], and you can tell that it was ripped apart and separated. However, I do not believe any of these things were gradual. I think they happened BAM! and it happened—not a gradual thing.

When you look at the mountains—especially those that go up like this—that didn't happen just a little, little, little, little—it went BAM! And it happened all at once. We can talk about that a little bit later. So there was the dry land. "…and to the collection of the waters he called [or named them] seas: and saw God that [it was] good. And said God: Let cause to spring forth the earth grass, herb seeding seed, [or grass or herbs], [and] tree of fruit making fruit **after its kind**…" (v 10-11).

Now, we're beginning to get a lesson here, as he's teaching us, that it's ***after its kind.*** And I think that if we ever do get to the point of Noah's Flood, I think it's telling us that the whole earth was corrupted. I think the animals were, the vegetables were, everything that man set his hand to do was corrupted. Just like today. Everything is becoming hybrid and cross-genetics.

Men have thought of and conceived quite a few things. If you have potatoes now that you cut open and they never turn black, you know that they have inserted a gene from a moth into that potato to keep it from turning black. They have done that, yes! They've done that with genetics. I know some may not believe it. That's what they say.

What else they can do I don't know. So, it's "after its kind." Let's continue: [and fruit] "…and tree making fruit [in] which [is] its seed (in it) after its kind; and saw God that [it was] good. and evening was and morning was, a day third" (vs 12-14. *IH*). Each one of these things in their sequence. I want you to understand that God is ***speaking*** or ***commanding*** all of these things into existence. Now, if you want to know the power of the Word of God, and if you want to know what God can do, here's part of it. He can ***command*** and it exists!

Now, let's continue on: "…And said God: Let be luminaries in the expanse of heavens, to divide between the day and (between) the night; and let them be for signs, and for seasons, and for days and years…" (v 14).

This also let's us know that since there was light and day, and we're up to the third day, the question becomes: Did God wait until the fourth day to create the moon and the sun? *No.* I think He set them back in the proper orbit that they needed to be, because I believe that they were knocked out of orbit when there was a war. The war between Satan and his demons and God and the angels.

Now, what does God use? *God uses the things that He has made.* When you look at the moon, look at it very carefully. I think you will see that the majority of those things are not really volcanoes indeed, but craters from different elements—rocks or parts of the universe—hitting it.

Now, we have an unusual thing in our solar system. We have, let's see, what is it between—I may stand corrected on this at a later date—but, I do believe, if my memory serves me correctly, there is an asteroid belt between Mars and Jupiter. Now, they know, from what they've been able to see, looking out into the heavens, that these are really just chunks of junk rock. That's all they are.

So, God, in cleaning up the universe around us, just took all of those and put them into that orbit. Now, when "stars fall from heaven" as we look at stars from heaven, is that going to be God sending a lot of those meteoroids back down to the earth and when they hit our atmosphere they're burning up. I do not know, could very well be.

But, everywhere you look in our solar system, there are signs of chaos and confusion and war. In the earth, though it's re-created for man's habitation, in Mars in particular, and with the asteroid belt that is there.

Now, some of the other planets, we would have to say we don't know if there was any habitation on them. I would have to doubt that there would be, just looking at the way that they are now.

Ok—let's go on: So then He set them for times, for seasons, for years. [And] "to give light upon the earth; and it was so. And made God the two luminaries great [lights]; the luminary greater ruling for the day [which then is the sun] and the luminary smaller for ruling the night; and the stars. And put them God in the expanse of the heaven [so this shows a re-arranging] to give light upon the earth, and to rule in the day and in the night and to divide between the light and (between) the darkness; and saw God that [it was] good" (vs 14-18, *IH*).

Now, we also know—here's another reason why the Holy Days are to be kept—they are part of the creation of God based upon seasons. Ok, let's continue on here:

[God saw that it was good] "and evening was and morning was, a day fourth. And said God: Let swarm the waters [**with**] **swarms**, soul of life…" (vs 19-20).

Let's see what it says here, verse 20 in the *King James,* yes: "… 'Let the waters bring forth abundantly the moving creature'…." "Swarming"—that's a good way—when you see some of these pictures of the schools of fish and so forth, "swarming" is a good word.

"…and fowl let fly upon the earth, upon the face of the expanse of heavens. And created God the sea-monsters great, and all the souls of [living creatures] life that creep, [with] which swarmed the waters, after their kinds, and every fowl of wing [or after every bird] after its kind; and saw God that [it was] good. And blessed them God, saying: Be fruitful, and multiply, and fill the waters in the seas, and the fowl let multiply in the earth. And evening was and morning was, a day fifth" (vs 20-23, *IH*).

So, again God is commanding this creation by the Word of His power. They're coming into existence. So therefore, let's understand something, when God told, for example: Moses or anyone who was to write the Scriptures, "Write this and put it in a book." You know, it has power to it. That's why the Word of God is, is a ***living word.***

Now let's continue on, Chapter 1 and verse 24: "And said God, let cause to go forth the earth [or from the earth or to come up out of the earth] soul of life after its kind, cattle, and creepers [the creeping things] and beast of [the] earth after its kind…' [So, you find a breakdown of the animals, as it were, as God would see it.] …and it was so. And made God the beast of the earth after its kind, and the cattle after its kind, and every creeper of the ground after its kind; and saw God that [it was] good…." (vs 24-26).

Again, God did it by speaking. Now notice, let's see what happened here. Now beginning with man. Then we'll go to Chapter 2 because there's some very interesting things concerning man: "And said God, 'Let Us…' " now this phrase "Let Us," Carl was writing in his paper *The Two Jehovahs of the Pentateuch,* he's showing that grammatically in the syntax in the Hebrew—which means *the way that it's written* and *the meaning behind the words*—this is not God talking to angels. This is not God talking to a council in heaven. This is one of Elohim saying to the other of Elohim, "...Let us make man in our image, after our likeness..." (v 26, *IH*).

Now, it's interesting, he didn't say any of the cattle or any of the birds or any other thing was after the likeness of God—they were after their **own created kind.** Now, what is true concerning an image is very important. An image is made in the likeness of something that is other than the image. In other words, in this case, being God. God is the reality from which the image was patterned. After His image, after His likeness. Supreme creation as far as the physical things are concerned. So much, so supreme that He said: "...and let them have dominion over the fish of the sea and over the fowl of the heavens, and over the cattle, and over all the earth, and over every creeper that creeps upon the earth. And created God (the) man" (vs 26-27, *IH*).

Now notice, He didn't speak, did He? **God created!** In the other cases, God created and made **by speaking.** "...created God (the) man him in his image, in the image of God he created him, male and female he created them. And blessed them God..." (v 28, *IH*).

Now, we'll finish all of Chapter 1 here, then we'll get into Chapter 2 and we will see that it was a **special** creation. And that's why it's recorded this way for us. "...and said to them God: Be fruitful, and multiply, and fill the earth, and subdue it; and have dominion over the fish of the sea, and over the fowl of the heavens, and over every beast that creeps upon the earth. And said God: Behold, I have given to you every herb seeding seed which [is] [then is translated *with the seed in itself*] upon the face of all the earth, and every tree in which [is] the fruit of a tree seeding seed, [in other words, *the seed in itself*] to you shall it be for food..." (28-29). Now, there are those who say that, at this time they did not eat any meat. We don't know whether that is exactly so. He didn't say they couldn't eat of any of the animals here at this point, but He was describing what kind of, of vegetation or fruits that they could eat—and that was with its seed within itself.

Now, today we have oranges with no seeds. They can't quite get away with it, because it pops up with a seed every once in a while. Have they come to hybridize a seedless watermelon yet? Now, I'm sure, in the scheme of things, God intended that there be certain things that man could do with plants and animals that are lawful and legal and proper. But, I'm also sure that we're entering a time where there are a lot of things that human beings are doing to plants and animals which are not lawful. And, I think we are reducing the seed reservoir, in particularly for wheat, because everyone is trying to have great abundance of wheat and rice, and they are getting into the hybridized production of those that I heard of in one show that I saw, that they are down to just maybe a dozen genesis seeds of wheat. I don't know what it is for rice, but I do remember the wheat. Now, what they're doing in the potato, they're going to South America to try and get new genetic strains from the potatoes down there—because we've pretty well destroyed the genetic strains that we have up here. They're subject to all kinds of weakness and sickness and disease.

So, you can't outdo God's way! Now, when God made this, this was tremendous, this was great! Ok, let's continue on: "...and it shall be for food; and to every beast of the earth, and to all of the fowl of the heavens, and to every creeper upon the earth, in which [is] a soul of life, [or the soul of them, which is a living soul, as it were, the soul of life] I have given..." (vs 29-30).

And, it's true. We also have something here that's important. Hold your place here and let's go to Isaiah 40 and let's understand something, which is true—absolutely, profoundly true—concerning all flesh, concerning human beings. Isaiah 40:6: "The voice said, Cry. And he said, What shall I cry? All flesh *is* grass, and all the goodliness thereof *is* as the flower of the field: The grass withereth, the flower fadeth: because the spirit of the LORD bloweth upon it: surely the people *is* grass. The grass withereth, the flower fadeth: but the word of our God shall stand for ever" (vs 6-8). And, it is actually, literally true. **We are all grass!** Even if you eat a steak, guess where that came from? *Grass.* Some kind of vegetation. You eat a chicken, where did that come from? *Grass.* And worms and a few other things.

Comment was made: "And people even smoke it." *Yes!* There are various kinds of grass: you have tobacco and then you have marijuana and you have other things. It's amazing what people do. It just, sometimes all you can do is just shake your head as how great that our creation is, of our bodies and everything. Because what mankind does to itself, and still survives is really just something else.

Now, let's finish here in verse 31 of Chapter 1, the last verse: "And saw God all which he had made, and behold, [it was] good exceedingly..." Now the Hebrew there for "good" means *gracious or beautiful.* So, in a sense, the whole creation of God was an act of **grace** by giving and providing all of these things rightly. "It was good exceedingly; and evening was and morning was, a day sixth" (v 31, *HI*).

Now, I want you to look at the Hebrew lettering for "day six." Just look at the Hebrew lettering over the English word "sixth." Now, we can't understand what they are, but we can see similarities and differences between that. I just call you attention to that.

Let's go here to the first verse of Chapter 2: "And were finished the heavens and the earth all their host. And finished God in the day seventh [or in the day seven]..." (Gen. 2:1, *IH*). Now, I want you to look at the way the Hebrew *seventh* is spelled there. Just look at the letters and compare that with *sixth.* You see the only difference between the two is a middle letter. Do you see that? Letters are the same, but there's a different letter in the middle. Now, I want you to notice at the end, on the left-hand side of the Hebrew lettering, which is seventh, there is a little "*a*". See that, see that little "*a*"—that means there's a footnote. Now, go down to the bottom and look where it says "*a*"—it says "the sixth" not "seventh." This helps us understand something. Now, it shows here, as read by the "sm" which is the *Samaritan* version, the "G" and the "S"—an intentional change. Now, this is one of these changes that were made, because God ended His work on the sixth day and rested the seventh. He didn't end His work on the seventh day. And what have we always had to say of that verse. That means He ended His work just before the seventh day began. Which may or may not be exactly true. But, if it is, God ended His work on the sixth day, what, He's following His own laws, isn't He? "Six days shall you labor and do all your work"—correct?

So, I thought this was really a very meaningful understanding of what was going on here. God finished His work in the sixth day—number six. Now notice, "...the work which He had made. And He rested in [both cases "in"] within day seventh from all His work, which He had made" (v 2). So, that helps clarify a lot, doesn't it?

Now, I know, one day I was busy doing some things and all of a sudden the fax went, because I have it going 24 hours a day now. And here was this page faxed to me from Carl, noting these things. And here I had the *Interlinear* and hadn't had a chance to get in and study it yet, and here is a very profound, meaningful understanding concerning that—that should be sixth day when God ended His work. So, in other words, God Himself also prepared for the Sabbath, correct? *Yes!* Now, let's understand something: When God created the day and night, He started the cycle. Therefore, when it came to the seventh day, He *made* that day holy versus *creating* it holy. God **created** time and the days, and then He **made** the seventh day holy. *Made* is a little less than *created.* Created is bringing it into its initial existence. Then *made* is maybe using the same thing only doing something else with the same thing, which He did here in relationship to a day. Remember, Jesus said, "The Sabbath was *made* for man." He did not say "created." He said "made." Because time had already been created, but then God made this section of time holy—the seventh day.

Well, we will get into that a little more next time, because there is an awful lot here concerning the Sabbath. And then we will get into the relationship between God and man and what God really intended is revealed, and how He created man and woman.

(End of Sermon)

Transcriber: Bonnie Orswell

The Background in Genesis—Sermon I
July 22, 1995
Scriptural References

1) John 14:26

2) John 16:13

3) Luke 24:44

4) Genesis 1:1

5) John 1:1-3

6) I John 1:1-3

7) Hebrews 1:1-6

8) Genesis 1:1-2

9) Isaiah 45:18

10) Jeremiah 4:19-23

11) Ezekiel 28:11-12, 2, 13-18

12) Revelation 12:9, 1-4

13) Luke 10:17-18

14) Jude 6

15) II Corinthians 4:3

16) Isaiah 14:12-15

17) Genesis 1:2-31

18) Isaiah 40:6-8

19) Genesis 2:1

Referenced Material:

1) *The Grace of God in the Bible* by Fred R. Coulter
2) *Interlinear Hebrew Translation of the Bible in Revise* by George Ricker Barry
3) *Light by Light* by John Goodenough
4) *The Two Jehovahs of the Pentateuch* by Carl Franklin

CHAPTER TWO

The Background in Genesis—Sermon II

July 29, 1995

Today we're going to study two very important things right in the first part of the book of Genesis. We reviewed the Creation last week. This week we're going to study more in detail the creation of man and the Sabbath.

Now, as I mentioned last week, I'm going to read some of the things from the *Interlinear* by George Ricker Berry, which is the *Hebrew Interlinear (HI)*. He only did Genesis and Exodus. And I'm very sorry that that's all that he did, because that is tremendous. He does a very good job in translating. We're going to cover some very important things and first of all I want to concentrate on creation of Adam and Eve first, because I think we're going to find this very important; because the detailed instructions of Adam and Eve and their creation have to do with the finishing of the work on the sixth day.

Let's go to Genesis 2 and let's pick it up here in verse one. I just want to cover this thing concerning the Sabbath and the seventh day and the sixth day once again. Now, remember, the very last verse in Genesis 1:31, *HI*: "And evening was and morning was a day sixth." Now, as you saw in the Hebrew last time, the difference between six and seven is one little letter inserted between two of the other letters. And that it should read this in Genesis 2:1, *HI*): "And were finished the heavens and the earth and their all their hosts. And finished God in the **day sixth** his work which he had made…" And it should be the *sixth* day, not the *seventh*. And, as you see, there's a little footnote there to verify that. Now, I'm not going to send this out on the mailing list simply because that can be checked out from some other sources. But, what I want us to do is to just review it and understand it. [Actually, God finished by *the beginning* of the seventh day].

Now, let's continue on here: "…and, he rested in the day seventh from all his work which he had made. And blessed God the day seventh and sanctified it; because in it he rested…" (Gen. 2:2, *HI*). Now, we're going to learn an awful lot concerning *rest*. Now, I want you to look at, please, I want you to look at the word "rest"—see how that is written there, those three letters, because that is the basic three letters which are used for the Hebrew word "Sabbath"—Sabbath means *rest*.

Now, we'll come back to that in just a bit. Let's come down here, let's come down here to verse seven, verse seven: "Then formed Jehovah God, (the man) [out of] dust from the ground, and breathed in his nostrils breath of life…" (Gen. 2:7, *HI*). Now, we need to understand, as I just mentioned last week, that everything else that God created, He **commanded** it and it was so. Now, let's look at some Scriptures which will verify that. Let's go to Psalm 148. And this shows that God **commanded** and everything came into existence. Psalm 148, and let's just pick it up here in verse one so we can get a flow of how everything goes—Psalm 148:1: "Praise ye the LORD. Praise ye the LORD from the heavens: praise him in the heights. Praise ye him, all his angels: praise ye him, all his hosts. Praise ye him, sun and moon: praise ye him, all ye stars of light. Praise him, ye heavens of heavens, and ye waters that *be* above the heavens. Let them praise the name of the LORD: **for he commanded, and they were created**" (vs 1-5).

He brought them into existence by the Word of His power. Now, He intended for those to tell us a story. Let's go back to Psalm 19. He intended the creation of the heavens to be a **witness** of His power and His glory, and to be perpetually that which all human beings could see so that they would understand that something greater than themselves had to create that. Psalm 19: '…The heavens declare the glory of God; and the firmament showeth his handiwork. Day unto day uttereth speech…" (vs 1-2). And there are noises that they have been able [to hear], sounds, that come out of the heavens, right? Don't they have these big gigantic tracking machines and radio, radar devices, huge great disks to try and pick up a message from outer space—maybe they're trying to communicate to us is the reasoning behind it. "…and night unto night showeth knowledge. *There is* no speech nor language, *where* their voice is not heard" (vs 2-3). In other words, the things that God has created and **commanded** into being are there in such a dynamic way that every people, every language, every generation has **learned** from it. And it's also very interesting to know that if you read the account of *Josephus* and Abraham, you find out that Abraham was a mathematician. And Abraham was the one who brought mathematics to Egyptians.

So, Abraham was no mean, grunting barbarian stumbling over the stones of the Near East. He understood these things. And, of course, this also has to do with the ultimate, concerning our salvation.

"Their line is gone out through all the earth, and their words to the end of the world. In them hath he set a tabernacle for the sun…" (v 4). Showing that the greater universe is out beyond what the tabernacle for the sun is. You could say the tabernacle for the sun is our solar system. And, it's very interesting: when you view how the different solar systems or stars in the universe are. They are shaped like discs—or, as some people would say, flying saucers. Now, I'm not going to get into a discussion of flying saucers, but I do believe there are phenomena, which are accountable for that. Verse 5: "Which *is* as a bridegroom coming out of his chamber, *and* rejoiceth as a strong man to run a race…. [In other words, always cheerful, uplifting and inexhaustible source of energy, is what it's telling us here.] … His going forth *is* from the end of the heaven, and his circuit unto the ends of it… [so they knew that things were in a circuit—wasn't flat, was in a circuit.] …and there is nothing hid from the heat thereof" (vs 5-6). And then it reflects back to the law of God beginning in verse seven.

Now, let's go to Psalm 33 and we'll understand even more concerning the creation of God and how it was that He made these things—and why then the forming of man, by God Himself, becomes a **very important** and **deep** thing for us to understand. Psalm 33:1: "Rejoice in the LORD, O ye righteous: *for* praise is comely for the upright. Praise the LORD with harp: sing unto him with the psaltery *and* an instrument of ten strings" (vs 1-2). Now, that's why on the Sabbath it is good, when we can, to sing. That's why, in the New Testament it talks about "sing with psalms in your heart." It's very important, and especially on the Sabbath, because as we will see, the Sabbath becomes a very important day and **link** to the creation of man. "Sing unto him a new song; play skilfully with a loud noise. For the word of the LORD *is* right; and all his works *are done* in truth…." Nothing wrong with what God has done and created. "…He loveth righteousness and judgment: the earth is full of the goodness of the LORD. By the word of the LORD were the heavens made; and all the host of them by the breath of his mouth" (vs 3–6). So, God **commanded**, they came into existence. That's why the Word of God is so powerful and so important. So, if God says something once, that's quite sufficient for all eternity, is it not?

Is not God eternal? *Yes!* Is not His Word forever? *Yes!*

Let's go back to Psalm 19 and see the Word of God. What that is to do for us once we understand the great and tremendous creation of God. That is to help us understand that

God is lawgiver; God does things in order; God does things in organization; and God has made everything for a purpose for its own part in God's plan that He has done. Verse 7: "The law of the LORD *is* perfect," nothing wrong with it—Psalm 19:7, now "...converting the soul..." this is the first step which leads you to conversion. Because then when you understand that the law of God is *perfect* then it becomes a standard to which you see you need to measure up to "...the testimony of the LORD *is* **sure,** making wise the simple. The statutes of the LORD *are* **right,** rejoicing the heart: the commandment of the LORD *is* **pure,** enlightening the eyes." Giving us understanding and wisdom. God made us in such a way that we are to have understanding and wisdom and judgment and righteousness and goodness. "The fear of the LORD *is* **clean,** enduring for ever: the judgments of the LORD *are* **true** *and* **righteous altogether**. More to be desired *are they* than gold, yea, than much fine gold: sweeter also than honey and the honeycomb. Moreover by them is thy servant warned..." (Psa. 19:7-11). Keeps you out of trouble—that's why the commandments are "You shall *not*."

Why did God give the commandments—now there is a positive commandment with parents: "honor your father and your mother, that the days, your days may be long on the earth." Then, the next one is: "You shall not murder." That is the extreme. You cross that line and you have sinned. Within it then there are a lot of choices that you can make: "you shall not commit adultery." They are all *negative* commands, because negative commands are the very best when you are given *a choice;* so that you determine your choices.

Now, when it says you shall not commit adultery, the positive is that you will always be faithful to your wife—that is if you're married. So they're good. They're right: "...*and* in keeping of them *there is* great reward. Who can understand *his* errors?" No one can because every way of a man is right in his own eyes, so he needs God's Word to give him the understanding of his errors. I do, you do. "...cleanse thou me from secret *faults*..." And this is really a New Testament doctrine. "Cleanse me from my secret faults"—in other words, my thoughts of sin that are in my own mind here. "...Keep back thy servant also from presumptuous *sins;* let them not have dominion over me: then shall I be upright, and I shall be innocent from the great transgression. Let the words of my mouth, and the meditation of my heart, be acceptable in thy sight, O LORD, my strength, and my redeemer" (vs 12–14). So, all of these things have to do with the tremendous creation and showing us that now *man is different.* God can command every one of these things. But, now he made man differently.

Let's go back to Genesis 2, again please. Because God did something that He did not do with any of the rest of the creation. He did several things here. Of all the rest of the creation, God commanded and it was so. And then God said to them, "Be fruitful and multiply and replenish the earth, and it was so."

Now then, with man we have something that is quite *different.* Let's go back to Chapter 1, verses 26-27 first, because none of the other creations of God were made like humankind. That's something very important for us to realize. And this is a great death-nil for evolution, because the creation of man is very special in every way—well thought out, well planned and, as we will see, formed by the hand of God. "And said God [verse 26]: Let **us** make man in **our** image, after **our** likeness..." (Gen. 1:26). God is saying here that He is giving human beings *Godlike* characteristics.

Now then, *all of the others* that God created said, "after their kind." Now, obviously, we are after the human kind and we pro-generate our own kind, but also being made in the image of God is first fundamental step of being in the God family. That's why we're made in the image of God. None of the other creatures [are]. Now you can look at apes; you can look at chimpanzees and gorillas and you can see some humanlike characteristics in them. But I'm sure God made them that way for us to realize that even though you can have humanlike characteristics—in hands and some facial features—unless you're made in the image of God you're still a beast! Rather than we evolved from this thing. We have to understand that we're made in the image and the likeness of God. And then, He gave "dominion over the fish of the sea, the fowl of the air and everything that creeps," and so forth.

Now, let's come back to the Chapter 2 again because we're going to look at the, at the continuing account of the details of the creation of man. "And created God (the) man…" (Gen. 1:27, *HI*). So, God personally formed [him]. Now this, I am sure, is telling us that God wants to have a personal relationship with this part of His creation in a way that separate and different from all the rest of His creation. That's why He made us in His image and after His likeness. And of course, the rest of the Bible then is to tell us that we're going to be after His kind. Now notice what else He did:

He did not command the man to live. He could of, because nothing's impossible with God. "… and breathed into his nostrils breath of life…" (Gen. 2:7, *HI*). Now, I think this shows that God wants us to have a close, personal, intimate relationship with Him. In other words, with this also, I believe—now, I'll just have to say, "I believe"; we'll have to draw out of this from what we see—that He breathed into man, what is called the "spirit of man" and He imparted to his mind, at the same time, a fully functioning language; because man was an intelligent, talking, responding, decision-making being from the instant of his creation. Obviously [he] had to be taught. In order to be taught he had to be teachable; in order to be teachable he had to have a language; in order to have a language, from creation it had to be put into him. So, I believe that that's what God did at this point: "…and became (the) man (for) a [living] soul" (v 7).

Now then, God began to show us a purpose in this creation. And so, I believe that the final acts of His creation on the sixth day was the creation of man—and then the final act was the creation of woman. And then the Sabbath began.

But let's carry on and see the events that happened on the sixth day. Ok, let's continue here now. "And planted Jehovah God a garden in Eden (from) east [ward] and placed there the man whom he had formed…." Now, that's interesting, He 'formed' him, He made him with His own hands and 'formed' him. "…And caused to sprout Jehovah God [or the Lord God] from the ground every tree pleasant for appearance and good for food; and the tree of life was in the midst of the garden…" (Gen. 8-9, *HI*).

Now immediately, God wanted man to know something that's symbolized by the Tree of Life. And, I am sure, there was a literal tree, number one. I am also sure that this Tree of Life symbolized the way that man would go, which then would be God's way, which would lead to eternal life—or, the other tree: And he says: "…and the tree of knowing good and evil" (v 9). So, both of them were there in the midst. Now, I don't know if they were side-by-side. It could have been that they were side-by-side. We're not told, but it says "in the midst," so I would have to take, by this account, that it was in the middle of the, the garden.

Now, the rest of it, describing where Eden was is really using the names of rivers that were known on the other side of the Flood, and so, it's very difficult to find out where Eden was, because all of that was destroyed with the Flood—and so, naming a general area where they thought it was close by *after* the Flood does not give us the direct geographical area. However, it would have to be somewhere, we would assume, in the Middle East. Some people assume that it would be somewhere in what is called "the Holy land" today or what we know as Palestine or Israel—however your division divides on that. That could be, but that's not the purpose of what we're going through here.

Let's come down to verse 15, because then God did something. And this shows, all the way through it shows *responsibility, ability* and *accountability.* Man as *ability;* he is *responsible,* and he is *accountable.* "And took Jehovah God the man and put him in the garden of Eden to till it and **to guard it"** (v 15). Very interesting translation here, isn't it. Not just to "keep" it, but to "guard" it, to protect it. To make sure that it was done the way that God would want it done. "And commanded Jehovah God (upon) the man saying…" (v 16). Now, whenever God gives a command, it is a command.

Now, hold your place here and let's go to Psalm 119—this is one of my favorite Psalms. And this is the one I always try and use to stop the mouths of the gainsayers. Now, there's not too much you can do with this—Psalm 119, and let's begin here in verse 127. Psalm 119:127, and I think this is important, verse 127: "Therefore I love thy commandments above gold; yea, above fine gold. Therefore I esteem all *thy* precepts *concerning* **all things to be right**…" (vs 127-128). Question: If God is perfect—which He is; and if God is righteous—which He is; and if God does things which are correct and beautiful and wonderful; would not all of His precepts be right concerning everything? Is any man going to go up and point out to God a sin that He has done? *No, because God does not sin!*

And so, when we come over here concerning the commandments given to Adam and Eve, I think this has a *great weight of importance;* because the whole principle of God commanding, the whole principle of God instructing then is all found right here in the first part of the book of Genesis—which tells us that man then was *responsible, accountable* and *had ability.*

So, He put them in the garden to "guard it" and "to keep it," "…And commanded Jehovah God (upon) the man, saying: From every tree of the garden eating, thou mayest eat..." In other words, anytime you want to eat, go ahead and eat. "…but, from the tree of knowing good and evil not thou shalt eat from it; for in the day of thy eating from it dying thou shalt die" (Gen. 2:16-17, *HI*). That is the literal meaning. It doesn't mean in that very instant, in that day, that you would drop dead the minute you took a bite from it. But it means that once you transgress that and do this, then you are surely going to die—just as it says in the *King James*—and that's how it's translated. Now, they had, as the sentence of their transgression, death imparted to their very being. Though they lived many hundreds of years after that, if the account of the time is correct, but they still died—yes, they did. And, I am sure that implied in that, "in dying you shall die," that also implies an aging process from which we all today suffer. So, if you want to blame anyone, you can blame Adam and Eve—ok? All right, let's go on here.

Verse 18: "And said Jehovah God: Not good [is] being (the) man's to [it says here] his separation, [and that really means *being a separate being*. It is not good for man to be alone.] I will make for him a helper as his counterpart. And formed Jehovah God from the ground [let's see] every beast of the field…and brought unto the man [all the kind]…" (vs 18-19, *HI*). Oh yeah, and every one, all of the animals that God made, God had them all pass by. So we have the animals on "review-march" with Adam, who was there. Now notice what happened here. So He "…brought unto the man to see what he would call (to) it…" (v 19). So he had a full-functioning language. Adam was able to name *all* of the animals. Now, it would be interesting to know what that was. Now, you see, he wasn't polluted with any kind of wrong thoughts. He was not polluted with wrong notions at all. He was standing right there with God and God said, "All right, now Adam, here comes this animal, what do you think you should call it?" So he gave a name to it. Now, this shows a great responsibility.

Comment was made: doesn't this indicate that the language which he had had words in it which would fit? *Yes!* So, he had a complete language. So Adam was made totally complete. There was nothing missing, except his wife. God intended that.

So, He caused all of them to pass by to see what he would name them. And the reason for this was, so that Adam would realize of everything else that God had made, there was nothing in that which was wholly compatible *for him*. So then, after that object lesson, it says here, continuing now in what he would call them: "...names to all the cattle and to the fowl of the heavens and to every beast of the field; and for a man not he did find a helper as his counterpart...." Because God wanted Adam to understand something very important, too: That only God could make for him that which would be right for him. And we find in verse 21, then: "... And caused to fall Jehovah God a heavy sleep upon the man, and he slept; and he took one from his ribs, and closed (the) flesh instead of it. And built Jehovah God the rib which He had taken from the man in to a woman, and brought her unto the man" (vs 20-22, *HI*).

Now, this also becomes very important for us to understand. As He made the woman, He also then had to breathe into her the breath of life—didn't He? *Yes!* So she could become a living soul. He also had to breath into here what would be, what we would call "the spirit of man" for human beings—and also give her a fully functioning language; because God did not want to produce an incomplete product and provide for Adam something which was not a counterpart and compatible, and somebody who knew nothing. So, she had intelligence, she had mind, she had ability and all of that sort of thing. So, the point here that is, I think the most profound thing for us to understand is this: *God made both* man and woman! And in breathing into them the breath of life. He desired with this and showing this—that's why this account is so important—that He wanted to have a personal relationship with them and be their God.

All right, let's finish the account here now: "...and brought her unto the man. And the man, this, now at last, (is) bone from my bones and flesh from my flesh;" (v 23). Which shows that God must have sat down and said, "Now, Adam, since there is nothing here for you in all of the animals and I didn't create anything for you. And I want you to see by looking and naming all the animals that there is nothing for you. So I'm going to put you asleep and I'm going to take one of your ribs and I'm going to make a woman, a help meet, a counterpart for you." That's why Adam, when he saw her, said, "This is now bone of my bone and flesh of my flesh."

Notice, in the *Interlinear* it says: "This, at last now.. " in other words after everything else had been understood "...is bones from my bones and flesh from my flesh; to this it shall be called woman, because from man this was taken. Therefore a man shall leave his father and his mother, and shall cleave unto his wife; and they shall become (for) flesh one. And were they two naked, the man and his wife, and not they were ashamed before each other" (vs 23-25, *HI*). So, this was before they had sinned. Now, we also know that there is a great lesson for us in this, concerning marriage. What we are dealing with here now is the ideal complete state of the creation of God.

Let me read to you what I have written here in *The Grace of God in the Old Testament,* so we can, this will help summarize some of these things—ok. Let's pick it up here in this paragraph:

> "In order for us to fully understand that the entire Creation was an act of love and grace, we need to examine the Scriptural account of the creation of Adam and Eve. The very words of God reveal His love and grace where He said, 'Let Us make man in Our image and after Our likeness and give them dominion' and so forth. When we consider that, of all the creation of God, only mankind was made in the image of God. Such a blessing is a profound act and expression of God's Supreme love and grace, which was created within and bestowed upon mankind.

> "To further reveal the uniqueness of the creation of mankind, when the Lord God made Adam and Eve He personally formed them with His very own hands. This act alone reveals that the Lord God intended from the very beginning to have a deep, personal and intimate relationship with them. Whereas all the other created things and beings which God created He brought into existence by the word of His command through the power of His Holy Spirit. However, in the account of the creation of Adam and Eve, notice what the Scriptures tell us. [And we just read those: formed them, breathed into them the breath of life.]

> "Apparently when God... [let's see] ...The very act of the Lord God Himself breathing the breath of life into man, reveals the intimate relationship that God desired to have with mankind."

That's why He made the garden of Eden, so He would be there with them. That's a tremendous thing. And this all relates then, when we come to it, to the very first Sabbath.

> "Apparently, when God breathed the breath of life into the man He also imparted the special spiritual essence called 'the spirit of man' which gives to mankind the special unique ability to think, to reason—hence, intelligence. Apparently, at the same time He also breathed into Adam the breath of life, God also imparted into his mind a fully functioning language. Furthermore, in order to show the close, personal relationship of love, which God intended man and woman to have as husband and wife, He personally formed Eve from one of Adam's ribs. [We just read the Scriptures on that.] And then gave her the breath of life and imparted the 'spirit of man' into her with a fully functioning language.

> "Of all the other living creatures that God created, only man and woman were created to receive and to give love in a most intimate and personal relationship [in a personal way]. None of the other created beings were made to give and receive sexual love face-to-face. That blessing was reserved for mankind alone."

Now this is also to reflect and show the personal relationship that God the Father and Christ have—that is face-to-face, though there is no sexual intimation in that because they are spirit beings. And being face-to-face, this means that God made it so that man and woman would also *grow together* and, as it were, see things God's way: eye-to-eye. So, it's really a very special thing.

> "That blessing was reserved for mankind alone. Moreover, through the process of pro-creation, all human beings were blessed with a physical, mental, emotional and spiritual ability to give and to receive love. "Greater still, only mankind was created to have a personal, spiritual, loving relationship with God, their Creator. This special blessing of love and grace was not extended to any of the other created beings which the Lord God created. "Now then, thousands of years later...[and then I put in here what David said.] (*Grace of God in the Old Testament*).

So, let's turn there. Let's go, first of all, to Psalm 8, Psalm 8—no, let's go to Psalm 139 first, then back to Psalm 8. Psalm 139. This is also one of the Psalms of David. Now, this is quite a very profound Psalm. I think we've covered this a couple of times in the past, but I think it's good for us to review and go over, because this is really very scientific and up-to-date.

Psalm 139, and let's begin in verse 13: "For thou hast possessed my reins: thou hast covered me in my mother's womb…." So, this shows that even though—in whatever the process may be—God, in creating mankind through pro-creation (legitimate or illegitimate) God is the One Who created that being.

Exactly how everything is done, I would have to surmise that each of us are able to impart *half-life*—father and the mother, the father determining the sex. I also believe that at the instant of conception that a spiritual thing takes place—whether legitimate or illegitimate—to give, because after all, the illegitimate child had no say so, did he? So God is not going to deprive him necessarily just because it was not consecrated in marriage. There are going to be enough problems beyond that. We all understand that, looking out in, in the age today. And, I know there will be some people who will say, "Well, now, legitimate or illegitimate." You might find that there are some of the people that God has used were illegitimate by birth—that is, father and mother were not married, if we can put it that way. God still, being "no respecter of persons," gives the individual the "spirit of man" or the, the beginning essence of life. So when there is that conception, God caused it to be—whether human beings by determination or by mistake caused it to be. In other words, God has a hand in every human life.

Now David continues here, he says: "…Thou hast covered me in my mother's womb. I will praise thee; for I am fearfully…" and that means **awesomely** "…*and* wonderfully made: marvellous *are* thy works; and *that* my soul knoweth right well. My substance was not hid from thee, when I was made in secret…" (vs 13-15)

Now, before an embryo becomes an embryo, which then is the stage before what they call a "fetus." It is technically called today, unless they've changed the term recently, "substance." So this is very correct in its translation.

"…when I was made in secret…" And, it's still a secret. No one really knows, do they, even with all the scientific endeavors, how human beings are created in the womb? Now, they've done a lot of scientific investigation. They're able to know and understand more than they ever have, but they still don't know! And I think it's very important for us to understand when we bring up the subject of abortion, we need to understand this: that a human being is fully formed—or nearly so—in six weeks. Every feature of a human being is there. It's just a matter of growth. Now, the only difference between a newly conceived individual and us is a matter of growth and birth and age. Because once there is the conception of a human being, it is what it is from that instant forward—have to be. You did not become yourself sometime after you were conceived. You were yourself from the instant you were conceived and it will be until the instant you die. So, when he's talking about this, I think this is very interesting here. "My substance was not hid from you…" In other words, God can know whatever He needed to. "… when I was made in secret *and* curiously wrought in the lowest parts of the earth…." Now, that's just a symbolic way of talking about 'in the womb.' Verse 16: "…Thine eyes did see my substance, yet being unperfect; and in thy book all *my members* were written, *which* in continuance were fashioned, when *as yet there was* none of them" (vs 15-16). In other words, 'until it was complete.'

Now, what they're trying to do with the genetic coding of human beings today, and they actually use this terminology: "The Book of Your Own Genetics" is what they're trying to write. And so, we find that here, this is very scientific, and this is very up-to-date in the creation of all human beings. "How precious also are thy thoughts unto me, O God! how great is the sum of them!" (v 17). So David really had an insight to the creation of human beings—his own creation—reproduction of human beings, as it were.

Now, let's go back to Psalm 8, because this tells us and gives to us an understanding concerning the reason why human beings were made in the first place—and the reason why we were made a "little lower" than God, made in His image, having abilities like He has. Psalm 8, let's pick it up here in verse 1:

Ok—Psalm 8:1, "…O LORD our Lord, how excellent *is* thy name in all the earth! who hast set thy glory above the heavens. Out of the mouth of babes and sucklings hast thou ordained strength because of thine enemies, that thou mightest still the enemy and the avenger" (vs 1-2).

And, I'm going to try and do this real soon, give a sermon concerning why God uses the least—the smallest. And here's part of it right here.This is what David was alluding to. "When I consider thy heavens, the work of thy fingers, the moon and the stars, which thou hast ordained; What is man, that thou art mindful of him? and the son of man, that thou visitest him? For thou hast made him a little lower than the angels, and hast crowned him with glory and honour" (vs 3-5).

Now, the word "angels" here in the Hebrew is *not* "angels." The word for "angels" comes from the Hebrew word *malak.* This word here, in the Hebrew, is *Elohim*—"Elohim" is translated everywhere else as God, or Gods. So, "You made him a little lower than God." Which ties right in with the creation of man and woman after the "image and likeness of God." And, "You have crowned him with honor and glory." YES! One of the most gracious acts, one of the greatest gifts that God gave mankind was the whole world. You talk about an act of grace. A tremendous gift, and God says, "Here it is. Now, all I want you to do is take care of this garden. And then from there you're to overspread the whole earth." That's tremendous, brethren. That's a wonderful, wonderful thing for us to understand.

Now, we've got greedy men in there that buy and sell and parcel it up and fight and war and shoot, and all this sort of thing and try and take the best. Well, God is going to reserve that for the saints when they're resurrected.

"Thou madest him to have dominion over the works of thy hands; thou hast put all *things* under his feet: [everything!] All sheep and oxen, yea, and the beasts of the field; The fowl of the air, and the fish of the sea, *and whatsoever* passeth through the paths of the seas. O LORD our Lord, how excellent *is* thy name in all the earth!" (vs 6-9). David understood that we were made a "little lower" than God. And this also helps reveal the purpose that we are to be eventually *in the fullness of the God family.*

Now, let's go to 1 John 3 for just a minute because we need to put this here. And this is for us to *understand* and *realize* and to *inspire us!* You know, God did not make us so that He could whip us, that He could beat us, that He could scourge us, that He could do all of those things. Now, when there is sin, sometimes some of those things are necessary. But, as we will see, even with *The Grace of God in the Old Testament,* God didn't, didn't bring those things upon people except as a very last resort.

Now, here's the whole purpose: Once we receive the Spirit of God and know the Word of God, 1 John 3:1 "Behold, what manner of love the Father hath bestowed upon us, that we should be called the sons of God…" This shows us here in the New Testament that we're going to be after the "kind"—*the God kind!* But, in order for us to be after the "God kind" we have to be made first in the image and after the likeness of God so that then we can learn of God's way and have that become a very part of our being through the power of

God's Holy Spirit. So that at the resurrection we can be born *into* the family of God. Ok—let's continue on here, 1 John 3:2: "Beloved, now are we the sons of God, and it doth not yet appear what we shall be: but we know that, when he shall appear, we shall be like him; for we shall see him as he is."

Now, remember, human beings started out face-to-face with God, correct? *Yes!* They started out in their "rest." We are to enter into the "rest" which is—now that after we have been all detoured because of the sin, have to be redeemed—but God's goal is still the same, that we are going to be in the Kingdom of God and be as God is God. And that is not a doctrine of Satan. ***That is a doctrine of God.*** However, as we are going to see, Satan counterfeited that doctrine and said, "I'm a god, you can be like god." That's is: "like me." And that is Satan's doctrine.

God's doctrine is here, that we will be "like Him.' Now, notice, this is to inspire us, verse 3: "And every man that hath this hope in him purifieth himself, even as he is pure." And that's through the sacrifice of Jesus Christ. To inspire us, to uplift us, to just thrill us to the bottom of the souls of our feet, as it were. And that's a tremendous thing, brethren. And that's what God wants for *all* human beings.

Now, let's go to Proverbs 8:36. Let's instead, go to 1 Corinthians 11. Because, even though being called and having received the Holy Spirit of God, we are Abraham's seed, where there is neither male nor female, neither Jew or Greek, neither free or bond, neither Scythian or barbarian. That still does not take away from the fact that it's our spiritual relationship with God—let's put it that way—does not take away from the fact that we are still human beings. And we still have human problems in relationship to the way that God made us and created us, and the order of things as they need to be. So, when we come here to 1 Corinthians 11, we also have some things which are very important for us to understand and realize. Let's pick it up here in verse one. "Be ye followers…" imitators, as it should read, "…of me, even as I also *am* of Christ. Now I praise you, brethren, that ye remember me in all things, and keep the ordinances, as I delivered *them* to you. But I would have you know, that the head of every man is Christ…" (1 Cor. 11:1-3). Now, when God created man and woman, He set also in order a natural order of things that God intended to be. God always intended that the man always be under God, under Christ. Meaning that everyone is under the authority of God—one way or the other. You can't get away from it even if you sin, because "the wages of sin is death" as Adam and Eve found out.

Now then, notice: "…and the head of the woman *is* the man…" (v 3). Now, in the marriage estate nothing can change that. That's just the way it is. And so, it's not a matter of going against God or trying to set down some sort of rule or something that isn't right. "…and the head of Christ *is* God" (v 3). Now, when we understand the things concerning God—let's go back here, there are a few Proverbs that we need to cover here I think are important concerning, concerning man and woman and so forth. And then we'll come back to 1 Corinthians 11 because there's a little something that we need to even cover today.

Now, let's go to Proverbs 8:35—not verse 36, I was wrong in reading it there, you know how it is, you write it down and it's not really the way it looks the first time through. I'm sure all of your handwriting is perfect, mine's not—(chuckles)—ok. Proverbs 8:35, "For whoso findeth me findeth life [that is the wisdom of God], and shall obtain favour of the LORD. But he that sinneth against me wrongeth his own soul: all they that hate me love death" (vs 35-36). So, this is just a general principle applying to all the relationships of men and women. All the relationships in our life and our relationship to God.

Proverbs 9:10, says in relationship to this then: "The fear of the LORD *is* the beginning of wisdom: and the knowledge of the holy *is* understanding." And God is the One Who gives us understanding. He's given us a mind; He's given us a language; He's given all these things so we can understand the ways of God.

Now, let's come to Proverbs 18:22, it says: *"Whoso* findeth a wife findeth a good *thing,* and obtaineth favour of the LORD." Well, God intended that to be from the very beginning. Husband and wife—man and wife—and that's the way God made it. That's the way that God intended it to be—and so should it be. Now, let's come to Chapter 19 and verse 14. It says: "House and riches *are* the inheritance of fathers: and a prudent wife *is* from the LORD" (Prov. 19:14). Because we saw in the Creation that woman was to be a counterpart to man. Now, trust me, there are a lot of instructions in here for men. And, trust me that God is going to hold men accountable as well women accountable. It is all there. And so, these things are very important for us to realize.

Let's go back to, to Proverbs 12 and verse 4: "A virtuous woman *is* a crown to her husband: but she that maketh ashamed *is* as rottenness in his bones." Well, you can turn it around the other way, too. When you have a husband who's a rotten fool and a philanderer, and goes around and does the things he shouldn't do, it's misery and wretchedness and pain and suffering and sickness and disease, too, is it not? *Yes.* And it's harder on a woman when she suffers those things because she was made to be a counterpart for man and for the man to be "the head." Now, that's why a husband and wife relations are most important in the way they need to be. Now, let's just cover one other thing while we're going back to 1 Corinthians 11. You can go through the entire Bible and you can see that God never slighted women in the least. As a matter of fact, Jesus Christ did a lot to show, and Luke did more, in showing his relationship in teaching women and things like that than any of the others.

Now, let's continue on here in 1 Corinthians 11, because there is just a slight thing that we need to cover today, which is very important, which is not a big problem but it is something that just needs to be covered. Now, we have on television—who's this woman that gets out there with all of this.....

So, today we're going to get into just a little touchy area, because I see it wherever I go and I will have to say that many women—and they have it on Star Trek, too, don't they?—bald-headed, shaved-headed women, ok. And then there's this Susan Power who encourages every woman to become whatever she can be, separate and apart from a man—whatever that may be!

Now, let's just understand something here very, very clearly. God says it's not good for a man to be alone, therefore it's not good for a woman to be alone. Whenever the circumstances are that way, and nothing can be done about it, you don't go out and create another problem by running out and marrying the first one that comes along; because now then you end up with a dual problem. Maybe you weren't made for each other—ok. And so, you get a double set of problems. So, I'm not advocating immediate running out and marriage because you happen to be alone. Ok, please understand that.

But, we're living in a time where the Babylonian woman rides supreme. And I see it everywhere I go. And sometimes it gets very obnoxious. There's also another thing about men that women also, I'm sure know; that when things get very contentious, we're cowards! We run and hide, because we don't like animosity and hatred and shouting and yelling and screaming anymore than anybody else. Even though I'm sure all of us can do a pretty good job of it if we have to.

Now, here's a principle that we need to understand, because I think this is a slight problem in the Church, which I'm sure that can be corrected very easily. Now, verse 4: "Every man praying or prophesying, having *his* head covered, dishonoureth his head...."

Now, who's the head of the man? *Christ.* And, I think it interesting that the orthodox Jews will not pray without hats. They won't go into the synagogues without them. "...But every woman that prayeth or prophesieth with *her* head uncovered dishonoureth her head:" which is the man "...for that is even all one as if she were shaven. For if the woman be not covered, let her also be shorn: but if it be a shame for a woman to be shorn or shaven, let her be covered" (1 Cor. 11:4-6). So, we're not talking about an outright sin. It is something which is a shame." It says, it says that over here in verse 14: "Doth not even nature itself teach you, that, if a man have long hair, it is a shame unto him?" (v 14). Now, we used to have that problem more than we do today. And I can never figure it out. When I watch some of these singers—like on TNT or something—they've always got to have this long hair hanging down all around, and it just makes you wonder about it. And it always looks ***bad!***—least it does to me.

It's says, "It's a shame." Now that's why, with a Nazarite vow, what happened was this: when the vow was taken, then the man shaved his head and he did not cut it—or do anything to it—until the vow was over and the hair would grow. Now, this was to show the sign of *humility* and *shamefulness.* In other words, in this vow a man was to show that he wanted to yield himself to God and so put himself in this shameful condition. When we understand that John the Baptist was a Nazarite from the beginning, from his birth, and never cut his hair, never drank wine, never took anything that was made of the grapes, nor any strong drink. He was put into that position ***physically*** because he was the one who was to announce the coming of Christ. So, we find that very important.

So, we're talking about something that is not an absolute sin, but is something which is not necessarily right—and Paul covers it here. "So let her be covered." We'll find out what the covering will be—verse 7: "For a man indeed ought not to cover *his* head, forasmuch as he is the image and glory of God: but the woman is the glory of the man." In fact, taken from his rib, made from his very inner most being. "For the man is not of the woman..." And this means, in the Greek, *for the man was not taken out from the woman*—that's why the creation was the other way around; "...but the woman of the man. Neither was the man created for the woman; but the woman for the man" (vs 7-9). So, he's saying, "Now we're going all the way back to the proper order of creation, which everything that God has done is right and everything that He's done from the beginning is true and righteous all together."

"For this cause..." because of the very creation and the fact of what God has done "...ought the woman to have power on *her* head because of the angels" (v 10). Which means here, if you have a marginal reference, ought to have a covering and sign that she is under the power of her husband because of the angels.

And so, I think the slight thing that needs to be taken care of—and I've seen this a lot wherever I go, especially in traveling—and I have not mentioned it, even though it may have been brought up to me on several occasions, but here's an appropriate time to handle it and take care of it. And I think, just as any of us who want to go ahead and do the things that are pleasing to God, that this should also be taken care of for men and women in the right way.

"Nevertheless..." he goes on to say, this doesn't take away from the fact that "...neither is the man without the woman, neither the woman without the man, in the Lord. For as the woman *is* of the man, even so *is* the man also by the woman..." and, of course, even Christ was born of the woman, right? *Yes, of Mary.* "...but all things of God. Judge in yourselves: is it comely [proper] that a woman pray unto God uncovered?" Then he says the other way around, "Doth not even nature itself teach you, that, if a man have long hair, it is a shame unto him? But if a woman have long hair, it is a glory to her: for *her* hair is given her for a covering" (vs 11–15).

And so, this is not the first age of mankind when they ran around with shorn-haired women—or shaved-headed women. Now, apparently Paul had that problem back in Corinth. So, it's not unusual that we would also have—we don't have a great raging problem concerning it—but it's something that each one should address themselves before God in their own way in their own lives. And, I'm sure that, that since these things are so, the blessings of God will come when this is taken care of in the way that's pleasing to God. So, don't ask me how long is long; don't ask me how short is short. I think it's quite evident. It's one of these things that you make a judgment. Verse 13 says you judge this yourselves. So, I'll leave the judgment to you. Now, verse 16: "But if any man seem to be contentious, we have no such custom, neither the churches of God." That is, concerning the subject that he just covered here. So, I think that since we're going back and talking about the creation of man and woman and so forth, then we need to cover this in this particular way.

Now then, so everyone will know that this is not "picking on women" time—hope you all understand that—read all the book of Proverbs, if you want to, men and women take the instruction there because there are a lot of spiritual lessons for us that we can learn.

Now, let's come back here to our translation. Now, I might mention that that's New Testament doctrine—ok. Now, let's come back and let's look at the situation concerning the Sabbath. Because this becomes very important. Let's go back to Genesis 2 and let's read that again. Then there's some things we need to learn about it. And let's understand this: the very root word for Sabbath is *rest*. The very root word for Sabbath is *rest*.

Now, it says here, *paraphrased*: Gen. 2:2: "On the sixth day God ended His work which He had made and **rested** on the seventh day from all His work which He has made and God **blessed** the seventh day." Now, when God blesses something it is for a particular purpose. "And sanctified it." Now, when God sanctifies something that means it's set aside for a Holy purpose. So this is a day which is set aside. "Because…" now the first Sabbath is very important, because "…that in it He rested from all His work which God created and made."

What was the last thing that He made? *Eve.* Now, the next morning, on the Sabbath day, what do you suppose happened on the Sabbath day? God ran off and hid some place? If God blessed it and sanctified it, He did it for a very purpose, didn't He? *Yes.*

Let's look at a couple of things showing what the Sabbath day is for, and then we'll come back and establish that the seventh day we have today is the same seventh day which they had then. Now then, let's understand just a little bit something concerning the Sabbath. All right, I'm going to read to you just a little bit out of this because I think it summarizes it quite well.

> "In addition to God's loving and gracious act of His Creation, God further expressed His love and goodness by blessing them (Genesis 1:28). To reinforce their own personal state of grace, so they would always know their Creator, so that they could be with the Lord God Himself, in His personal presence, He specifically created and made the seventh day as a perpetual day of rest and fellowship. The weekly seventh-day Sabbath was intended to be more than a memorial of God's creation. Few realize that God blessed and sanctified the Sabbath day as an act of kindness and goodness for all mankind, so that mankind could fellowship with Him, their personal Creator.

> "God specifically created and made the seventh day for mankind. Jesus Christ, Who was the Lord God of Creation, made this fact absolutely clear and declared that He and He alone was Lord of the Sabbath day—not any other day. He said, "The Sabbath was made for

man not man for the Sabbath. Therefore, the Son of man is Lord also of the Sabbath" which means that's the New Testament day of worship. We have a more profound way of understanding it today. Moreover, from the Scriptural account of this first Sabbath, combined with other Scriptural commands, we can learn a great deal about the grace of God. God personally rested and kept this very first Sabbath—obviously with Adam and Eve. Undoubtedly, He fellowshipped with them and instructed them [would he not? *Yes He would.]*

"He would have to tell them, then, about the tree of life and what it meant. He would have to tell them *why* He created them. Would not God want them to know that first? *Yes, He would.*

"From the other accounts in Genesis, Chapter 3, we know that they were personally taught by God. They saw God face-to-face. They talked with God, they walked with God before they had ever sinned. This means they kept this first Sabbath with God in a perfect state of grace in His presence.

"Therefore, there can be no doubt that God instructed them on that first Sabbath. What a marvelous day that very first Sabbath must have been. There could be no greater grace than being in the presence of, and being taught by the Lord God Himself, their very Creator" (*The Grace of God in the Old Testament*).

Now then, let's go to the book of Isaiah and let's put a couple of Scriptures together to show the whole meaning and the intent of the Sabbath. Isaiah, either 56 or 58—it's 58—Isaiah 58, very important. This is a key thing for us on how to keep the Sabbath and why we keep it the way we do.

Now here are the words of God, Isaiah 58:13. Now, do you think that God, being the "same yesterday, today and forever," would have instructed Adam and Eve any differently than this? Now, some people say because it's not told that Adam and Eve fellowshipped with Him and kept that first Sabbath, therefore there's no indication that they kept it. And I say that is reasoning from your carnal mind to destroy the Sabbath. Here is what God says concerning the Sabbath thousands of years later—so, would this not also the instruction that He would give back then?

Isaiah 58:13 "If thou turn away thy foot from the sabbath, *from* doing thy pleasure on my holy day…" When was it Holy? *When God sanctified it, when God blessed it,* that's when it was Holy, correct? It's God's Holy Day from the beginning. Now, does God run down here and destroy every person who's breaking the Sabbath? *No, He does not.* He let's them go their own way, and they are missing a tremendous blessing of God.

Now, let's notice: we're not to do "our own pleasure." That doesn't mean that we don't do things which are not pleasurable—it's a pleasure to eat; it's a pleasure to fellowship. But, why should this day be the way it is? And let's go back and think of the first Sabbath. What do you suppose that God told them? *"I'm your Creator. I'm your Maker.* This is a special day of a memorial of My Creation. This is a day in which we are going to come together *every week* and I'm going to teach you what you need to know. And we're going to have a personal relationship. I'm your Creator and you have a great and fantastic opportunity as the very first human beings."

Don't you think that God told them what was, what was going to be if they would obey Him? *Yes.*

Now notice: "…and not doing your pleasure on my holy day; and call the sabbath a delight…" And what a delight that must have been—the first one; no sin, no hostility, no animosity, no television, no radio, no driving a long way to come to Sabbath services, no worrying about anything. God provided it all—and I just wonder if God did not provide the food for the Sabbath for that very first Sabbath day. They had it all right there, didn't they? *Yes, they did.* Now, it would not be a sin on the Sabbath while you're sitting there with God and maybe God reached up and plucked some food for them to eat—I don't know. Very possible.

"…and called the sabbath a delight, the holy of the LORD…" means it belongs to Him, "…honourable; and shalt honour him, not doing thine own ways, nor finding thine own pleasure, nor speaking *thine own* words…" (v 13). Now, what does this mean? This means we're to know the words of God, speak the words of God, study the words of God. That's why today, in Sabbath services, it's important that we study the words of God—because these are not our words, are they? *No, God inspired them—this is instruction for us.* And it's the same way with our fellowship, too. It should be centered on those things in our lives which have to do with serving and loving God. And too many times, in the recent past, and I'm sure this is something that all human beings cycle through, that the Sabbath became more their own day, and their own day of doing what they were going to do for their own social things.

Now, verse 14, now when you do this, notice it is "if," verse 13; now verse 14 says: "Then…" which means that if you don't do verse 13 the "if" then you'll never understand verse 14, because 'great understanding have they *who do His commandments.*' "Then shalt thou delight thyself in the LORD…"

Now, you go back and think of all the Sabbaths that you have kept that turned out to be kind of a dud. What happened? You didn't do verse 13, did you? *No, you did your own thing.* And I found this, I'll confess, you know, it's no work to sit in front of a TV is it? So therefore, you can sit in front of a TV and kind of justify yourself, "Well, you know, this is really not working." But, is the TV from God? Did God send it into the tube for you to watch? *No!* Ok. And I found that when I have done that, when I shouldn't have done it, my Sabbath turned out to be a dud! Now, you can draw the parallel, not just TV, but whatever it may be. I've also found this: I've tried to have, or someone talked me into having a wedding on the Sabbath—it was just to be a simple affair. It became very complicated and the Sabbath was a dud. Why? *Because we were not doing what God wanted us to do.*

When we do that; when we do all of verse 13—let's read that again: "If thou turn away thy foot from the sabbath, *from* doing thy pleasure on my holy day; and call the sabbath a delight, [and] the holy of the LORD, honourable; and shalt honour him, not doing thine own ways, nor finding thine own pleasure, nor speaking *thine own* words: THEN…"

Now, they had all of that with the first Sabbath. Absolutely did! Plus being in the very presence of God. Today we have the blessing of fellowshipping with God spiritually. Then they had it face-to-face.

"Then you shall delight yourself in the Lord and I will cause thee to ride upon the high places of the earth…" (v 14). This is going clear into the spiritual salvation that God is going to give us. So, understanding God and His way, and the purpose of being created are intrinsically tied to the Sabbath. *Intrinsically tied!* The Sabbath is to be *every week* when we draw close to God to *know of His way*, to *study His Word*, to *pray to God*, to *fellowship with Him*, to *fellowship with each other*. And since this is true, going all the way back, it had to be true of that very first Sabbath.

Now, let's look at a couple of other Scriptures which will help us here—ok. Let's go back to the book of Exodus. Now, let's first of all, go to Exodus 5; and let's understand a principle that we find here which follows all the way through. Whenever you truly begin to enter into a relationship with God—or God begins dealing with you—then the Sabbath question always comes up, does it not? *Yes, it does!* Now, when Moses first went into Pharaoh—we find here in Chapter 5, verse 1: "And afterward Moses and Aaron went in, and told Pharaoh, Thus saith the LORD God of Israel, Let my people go, that they may hold a feast unto me in the wilderness. And Pharaoh said, Who *is* the LORD, that I should obey his voice to let Israel go?" After all, Pharaoh was god on earth, right? "I know not the LORD, neither will I let Israel go. And they said, The God of the Hebrews hath met with us: let us go, we pray thee, three days' journey into the desert, and sacrifice unto the LORD our God; lest he fall upon us with pestilence, or with the sword. And the king of Egypt said unto them, Wherefore do ye, Moses and Aaron, let the people from their works? get you unto your burdens. And Pharaoh said, Behold, the people of the land now *are* many, and **ye make them rest**..." (Exodus 5:1-5). Has to do with the Sabbath, the very first question was *resting*. Because you truly, truly cannot understand God, nor fellowship with Him when you're busy doing your own works and your own business.

Now, let's go to Exodus 16. A lot of people claim, "Well, there was not Sabbath-keeping from Genesis all the way here." Well, we're not going to take the time, we've proven that other places. But you know that Abraham, if he did the things that pleased God, he kept the Sabbath—so did Isaac, so did Jacob. Everyone who comes in contact with God keeps the Sabbath. If they don't, then they're not in contact with the right God or they have the wrong doctrine, one of the two. Exodus 16, we have then the renewing of the Sabbath for the children of Israel. Now, let's pick it up here in verse 23, *paraphrased*. Now, remember they started counting, didn't they? They counted day one, getting the manna, two, three, four, five, six—double manna on the sixth day. "Bake that which you have to bake today; seethe that which you have to seethe today; and keep it over for the Sabbath and it didn't breed worms, rot or stink."

Now, they were all in close quarters, weren't they? God was right there in the pillar of the cloud by day and the fire by night, wasn't He? Therefore, they were in the very presence of God.

Now, verse 23: "And he said unto them, This *is that* which the LORD hath said, To morrow *is* the rest of the holy sabbath unto the LORD..." It's to the Lord all the way through. One of the greatest arguments thrown against the Sabbath is that it was given to the Jews. Not so! Never says so in the Bible. It is the Sabbath of the Lord. "...Bake *that* which ye will..." (Exodus 16:23). I've just covered that.

Now we find out here, verse 26: "...Six days ye shall gather it; but on the seventh day, *which is* the sabbath, in it there shall be none." Now, did God cease from the work of creating the manna? *Yes!* God also rested on the Sabbath and ceased from His work, didn't He? *Yes!* What kind of work is God interested in doing on the Sabbath? *Spiritual work!* That's what He does.

Now, let's look at another one to know that they had exactly the right day. Let's go to Exodus 31:13, and then we will come back to Exodus 20 because, as I mentioned here in the article that I am writing, that the Sabbath was intended to be **more than** just a memorial of Creation. But the Creation, and the fact of it, tells us what God is, its meaning in relationship to the day. "Speak thou also unto the children of Israel, saying, Verily my Sabbaths..." now, we know this one by heart, which is plural, right? *Yes!* "...ye shall keep..." It's not an option whether we decide to or not. "...for it *is* a sign between me and you throughout your generations; that *ye* may know that I *am* the LORD that doth sanctify you" (Exodus 31:13).

Now, you cannot know the Lord unless you keep His Sabbath day. That's very simple. And with it we are sanctified. Now, continuing, verse 14: "Ye shall keep the sabbath therefore; for it *is* holy unto you: every one that defileth it shall surely be put to death: for whosoever doeth *any* work therein, that soul shall be cut off from among his people. Six days may work be done; but in the seventh *is* the sabbath of rest…" Now, here 'sabbath' and 'rest' are almost identical words, "…holy to the LORD: whosoever doeth *any* work in the sabbath day, he shall surely be put to death. Wherefore the children of Israel shall keep the sabbath, to observe the sabbath throughout their generations, *for* **a perpetual covenant**." Which, as we have covered before, is always ongoing continuously. "It *is* a sign…" that is Sabbath-keeping "…between me and the children of Israel for ever: for *in* six days the LORD made heaven and earth, and **on the seventh day he rested, and was refreshed"** (vs 14-17).

Now, this tells us that they had the same exact Sabbath seventh day as the day that God rested on. Question:

- If God tells us to keep the seventh day Sabbath, would He change the day? *No!*
- Would He hide the knowledge of it, if it's required? *No!*
- Who is the one who have put up arguments that it was changed? *Men!*

Nowhere in the Bible has the day ever, ever, ever been changed. And so, the knowledge of why we were created [and the weekly 7th day Sabbath] are *intrinsically linked* together. That's why it begins with the Sabbath day.

Now, there may be another thing or two that we can learn from this which we'll cover next time and then we'll finish this. Yes, the comment was made, is this where people take it? Well, they take it because the Jews claim that they are all of Israel and actually, when you understand how the Jews feel about the Sabbath, they don't feel anybody but Jews only should keep the Sabbath. That's why they're very anxious to get anybody who is not a Jew off from keeping the Sabbath. They *want* them keeping Sunday.

(End of Sermon)

Transcriber: Bonnie Orswell

The Background in Genesis—Sermon II
July 29, 1995
Scriptural References

1) Genesis 1:31

2) Genesis 2:2, 7

3) Psalm 148:1-5

4) Psalm 19:1-6

5) Psalm 33:1-6

6) Psalm 19:7-14

7) Genesis 1:26-27

8) Genesis 2:7-9, 15-16

9) Psalm 119:127-128

10) Genesis 2:16-25

11) Psalm 139:13-17

12) Psalm 8:1-9

13) I John 3:1-3

14) I Corinthians 11:1-3

15) Proverbs 8:35-36

16) Proverbs 9:10

17) Proverbs 18:22

18) Proverbs 19:14

19) Proverbs 12:4

20) I Corinthians 11:4-6, 14, 7-16

21) Genesis 2:2 (*paraphrased*)

22) Isaiah 58:13-14

23) Exodus 5:1-5

24) Exodus 16:23, 26; 31:13-17

CHAPTER THREE

The Background in Genesis—Sermon III

August 12, 1995

Well, today we're going to finish getting through Genesis 3. I think we learned an awful lot concerning the Sabbath; and by putting it together from the things that we've understood in other parts of the Scriptures, so that we would understand *why* God made the Sabbath. And the most important thing concerning the Sabbath being the seventh day is that God *made it for us* so that we could be in contact with Him. And of course, God wants that. God made His creation of, of man and woman so that we would be in contact with Him; so He especially created that day for the purpose of fellowshipping, of teaching and knowledge and understanding.

Now, as you know we've been going through this *Hebrew Interlinear* here. And, I'm not sending it out to the overall mailing list but just so we can have it here to go over it. Now, before we get to Genesis 3, let's understand something here. The Bible does not tell us how long it was from the Creation—and from God's initial instruction to them in the garden of Eden—how long it was from that time until the serpent was let loose.

Now, let's look at it this way: let's use a modern day example, from our own experiences within the Churches of God: How many years was it that people were in the Church of God, studied the Scriptures, got the instructions from God, knew their Bibles, and then kind of let things slack and then in came the serpent?—*almost identical!*

Coming in with another teaching by saying, "Yea! God is not two, but one or three." And what happened? People fell for it hook, line and sinker. Now, not everyone. So, I would have to conclude that since God wants—before we make a choice—He wants it to be knowledgeable for us [so] that we know what we're doing. That He certainly gave sufficient time—whatever that was—for Adam and Eve to be instructed by God, to live in the garden of Eden, to know what God wanted, to keep His commandments and so forth, before the serpent was let loose.

I do not believe that it was done the day after they were created or a week or ten days after they were created. I don't know how long, but I'm sure that it was longer than a week or ten days. So that they would know, they would have knowledgeable choices, they would understand what they were doing. And the reason I say that is because we're going to see the consequences of their sin in relationship to all human beings—and it's past on to all of us. And so, with the stakes so high and the, the situation so profound, I think God let them know in, in a pretty definitive way what His overall plan was, what they should be doing and then He let the serpent come into the garden.

Now, God *let* the serpent come into the garden. Let's pick it up here, Genesis 3:1, *IH*: "And the serpent was crafty [above] (from) every beast of the field which had made Jehovah God; and he said unto the woman: [Is it] so that has said God: Not ye shall eat from any tree of the garden?"

A direct challenge to what God had said. He said, "You could eat of every tree of the garden, you could eat, except the tree of the knowledge of good and evil." And so the

34

woman always had to correct him—isn't that so? Once you have some knowledge that is true, what is something that you do? *You try and correct the false statement.* Now, in that, you have to careful because there may be a trap set. And in this case, there was a big trap set.

So, just refuting something is not necessarily enough. Not only do you have to refute what is said in the way of a false statement, but you also then have to obey God and keep those things which are right and correct in addition to it. That's why it says that "knowledge puffs up, but love edifies"—because you can get all carried away with knowledge.

Now continuing in verse 2, *IH*: "And said the woman unto the serpent, From the fruit of the trees of the garden we may eat; but from the fruit of the tree which [is] in the midst of the garden, has said God, not ye shall eat from it, and not ye shall touch (in) it, lest ye die." Now, this shows subsequent instruction, doesn't it? Because when you read Chapter 2, He says you shall not eat of it. Now, it's "not eat" and "not touch." So, here's evidence of some subsequent instruction. I don't think, as some have concluded, that Eve added her bit to it. I think that God pretty well told them. Because you see, once you touch it then you're going to start with lust. And so, I'm sure that's why He said you should not touch it. And I think her statement was true.

"…not ye shall eat from it, and not ye shall touch (in) it, lest ye die…" and that means in dying you shall die, "And said the serpent unto the woman, not dying ye shall die. For [is] knowing God that in the day of your eating from it, then shall be opened your eyes, and ye shall become like God… (vs 3-5, *IH*).

Now, I think the *King James* says 'as God'—but it is you will be *'like'* God. You will be similar to God in a certain way. Now, you could take that statement just like we do today when you talk to the Russians about democracy. Their version of democracy is far different than ours. So, when we're communicating on a word, the understanding of that word is not the same in both minds. And so, I am sure that they had—at least Eve did—come to have the understanding that she would be *exactly* as God is.

Now, I also believe that God told them that their eventual destiny was to be in the God family. And I'm sure that He indicated to them that it would take a certain amount of time to do so. Now, here comes the serpent along and says, "Well now, you want to be like God now. Don't' wait. Now!" And that's the same philosophy that Satan has with every life. Get to it early. Get to it quick and destroy it now! And so, that's what he did with Adam and Eve here.

Here's how they would be "like God": Obviously, they wouldn't be eternal, because they didn't eat of the tree of life. Obviously, they weren't going to improve and be right-eous, because, you see, every indication is that up to this point, Adam and Eve had a neutral disposition. In order to make the choice they had to have a neutral disposition. They were neither inherently righteous nor were they inherently evil. They had to make the choice! So, here's the choice. And here's what they would be like.

Now notice, I think this is interesting in the *Interlinear* here: "…ye shall become like God, knowers of good and evil." Now, it says in the *King James*: "knowing good and evil (v 5)." "Knowers" here in this case, actually means *deciders.* "You're going *decide* what is right and what is wrong. In other words, the message is: "Who is God to tell you what is right? And Who is God to tell you what is wrong. Why don't you *decide* for yourself?"

Does that not sound like a lot of things we've heard today? *Yes!*
Is that not what is taught in the schools today? *Yes, exactly!*

You will be *deciders* of what is good and what is evil. Well, that makes you very important, doesn't it? That just lifts you up, doesn't it? You can decide. You can decide for yourself, apart from God, and this is going to make you *like* God. Now, it's also interesting, that *knowers* or *knowing*, one of the most interesting facets of all the pagan religions is this: it's **gnosticism**. It comes from the Greek word **gnosis** and that's why the English word "know" for knowledge is "kn"—it's a carry-over from the Greek with the two, two consonants there.

Now, we also find that Masonry is a Gnostic religion. And it's interesting: what is the symbol of the Masons? What is the symbol of the Masons? And of course, they have 33 degrees or steps in which they go with varying degrees of revelation of lies until they get to the top where they are told Lucifer is god. That's why they have to go through all of these degrees, step-by-step. But, the symbol of Masonry is a "G" with a square (now, what's the other part?—ok, yes) and it's in a triangle and over the triangle is the *all seeing eye!*

Now, do you have a dollar bill, or whatever. Get out a dollar bill, yes, here's an old crinkled up old dollar bill, and just to let you know that this same system is still going today, you look at the back side of the dollar bill. Now, it says, "in God we trust." However, to the left of it is a total rejection of God, which is the pyramid with the *all seeing eye*. And then it says, "the New World Order"—that's what it means. They've been trying to get the New World Order for a long time. And here the New World Order began back here with Adam and Eve—when you really understand it—with the deception that Satan brought forth. So there are still Gnostics, and that's the same thing that Satan held out to Adam and Eve, "You will be knowers and deciders of what is right and what is wrong."

And, continuing on now, verse six: "And saw the woman that good [was] the tree for food…" Now, you can't tell **by looking,** that's a very important thing to understand. That also applies to clean and unclean meats. You can't tell by looking—well, some of them you can. I mean, if you look at some of these oysters and clams, you ought to have enough sense to realize that that's not something to eat. And you can't tell. The other day I was in, what was it, Kings Table. So, we're going on down through the line, getting the things they we need and we come to this meat that looked like roast turkey. And I said, "Oh, roast turkey!" And [they] said, "No, roast pork!" And just looking at it you could not tell that is not good for you. So, God has to tell us what is right, tell us what is wrong, especially in those areas that we cannot decide.

So [by] her looking at it didn't prove a thing. Just like buying a used car. You can get one that looks good, that sounds good, because it has 90 weight oil in the crankcase; that runs quiet, because it has a little sawdust in the differential. But, you drive it home and it's a pile of junk. *So, not just how it looks, see.*

"…and the woman saw that the tree was good for food, and that a delight it [was] to the eyes, and **desirable** [was] the tree **to make wise**…" (v 6, *IH*). Now this is the proposition that Satan said, *you will be wise!* And of course, when you have intellect, when you have a mind that is designed to learn, you want to learn knowledge. You want to increase in knowledge, don't you? That's a whole life-long, driving force that God has put in us, which we need. So, here he was appealing to all of those things.

"…and she took from its fruit, and ate; and she gave also to her husband with her, and he ate. And [sure enough] were opened the eyes of those two, and they knew that naked [were] they…" (vs 6-7, *IH*). They saw something they didn't see before. Now, I'm sure they saw themselves being naked because they were brought together as husband and wife and they were naked and not ashamed.

Now, you have something that takes place here that brings about *shame*. That brings about a guilty conscience. Now continuing—now, what is not said here, and we don't want to speculate too much in what was done here. Some people say that Eve had relations with the serpent and from that comes the seed of Cain. *Not so! Not so at all!* But some people like to perpetuate their own hostilities, so they try and do it that way. Some people also try and indicate that there was perhaps a lot of sexual perversion that went on between Adam and Eve. That is possible. I do not know what it was that, that the serpent told them, or showed them, but whatever it was, it had to do with their nakedness. And they knew that they were naked. That's the first thing that they knew. They did have some understanding, didn't they?

"…and they sewed leaves of [the] fig tree, and made for themselves girdles [or coverings]" (v 7, *IH*). And it's interesting, the fig tree. Now, some say it's the fig tree from which they ate. I don't' know. It could be, it could not be. There's one reference to a fig tree back here in the book of Mark. Let's go to Mark 11. And there is a fig tree that Jesus refers to, which definitely has to do with non-productive Satan religion. Mark 11. Why did Jesus curse the fig tree? Well, let's look at the account here and maybe we can come to understand. First of all, we know that Jesus condemned the Pharisees and Sadducees for following their father, Satan the devil. So, when He's referring to the fig tree, we are going to see that He is referring to them and this may stretch all the way back to the false knowledge in the garden of Eden that never produced any spiritual fruit unto salvation.

Now, Mark 11:12: "And in the morning, after they left Bethany, He became hungry. Then, seeing a fig tree afar off that had leaves, He want *to it to see* if He might possibly find something on it. But after coming to it, He found nothing except leaves because it was not yet *the* season of figs" (vs 12-13). Well then, *why* did He go to the fig tree and try and find something on it if there were only leaves and it wasn't time for figs? Ok, the reason is, is because we're talking about here, in parable, the religion of the, of Judaism which goes right back into Satanism, which goes right back to the garden of Eden. And this tree, this fig tree, as symbolizing Judaism didn't bring forth any fruit. It didn't produce anything of any lasting spiritual value—because it was all steeped in Satanism and paganism.

Now, we have the same thing today with Catholicism. Have the same thing with Buddhism. But, since Judaism was so close and they were claiming they knew God, but they were rejecting God with all their traditions. This is why I am sure that it was a fig tree. Notice, it wasn't a peach tree or an apricot tree or an apple tree—it was a fig tree. "And Jesus responded *by* saying to it, "Let no one eat fruit from you any more forever! And His disciples heard *it*." Now, this is how we tie it in with Judaism. "Then they came into Jerusalem; and after entering the temple, Jesus began to cast out those who were buying and selling in the temple; and He overthrew the tables of the money exchangers, and the seats of those who were selling doves. Moreover, He did not allow anyone to carry a vessel through the temple. And He taught, saying to them, 'Is it not written, "My house shall be called a house of prayer for all nations"? But you have made it a den of robbers' " (vs 14-17). So, the word is *a den of iniquity*. Wherever Satan is, it is a "den of thieves." Whether it is in a church. Whether it is in a corporation. Whether it is in a government. Or whether it is in a family. It makes no difference, wherever Satan is, it's a "den of thieves." "Now the chief priests and the scribes heard *this,* and they sought how they might destroy Him; for they feared Him, because all the multitudes marveled at His teaching. And when evening came, He went out of the city. And in the morning, as they passed by, they saw the fig tree dried up from *the* roots." Right from the very ground up. "Then Peter remembered *and* said to Him, 'Look, Master! The fig tree that You cursed has dried up.' " Now, this is showing a complete repudiation of Judaism. Not the truth of God, not the laws of God, not the commandments of God, but of Judaism—and that they should have faith. "And Jesus answered and said to them, "Have faith *from* God" (vs 18-22).

Then He gave a very important lesson concerning prayer, concerning what we need to ask, how we need to ask and in what attitude: "For truly I say to you, whoever shall say to this mountain, 'Be taken away and be cast into the sea,' and shall not doubt in his heart, but shall believe that what he said will take place, he shall have whatever he shall say" (v 23). Now, we have to temper that and tie that in with other things like: "keep My command-ments" and receive the Holy Spirit, and all of those things have to be tied in with that. "For this reason I say to you, all *the* things that you ask *when* you are praying, believe that you will receive *them,* and *they* shall be *given* to you. But when you stand praying, if you have anything against anyone, forgive, so that your Father Who is in heaven may forgive you your offenses. For if you do not forgive, neither will your Father Who *is* in heaven forgive you your offenses" (vs 24-26). So, the whole lesson here is another one of these things that'll be a complete divorcement away from Judaism and into the way that Jesus Christ was teaching. And of course, one of the first things you have to have is *faith* and then you live by *prayer.* So, that's why we have that.

So, it's interesting that the fig tree was cursed and it may go right back to the garden of Eden showing that what they were doing and what they were following was harkening all the way back to some of the original teachings of Satan the devil.

Now, let's come back to Genesis 3 and continue on with the account given here. And it's interesting that God gives us all the basic knowledge we need to know:

> How did we get here.
> Who our first parents were.
> Who is God and the commandments of God
> How did we get evil.

Now, why is it that human beings are *evil?*

The question was asked: Could it be that Adam and Eve had previous encounters with Satan or the serpent was there and that maybe he "softened them up" for this point here? Now, that it's possible—it doesn't tell us, so we can't say dogmatically. But, the very fact that you mentioned that she didn't say, "who are you, what are you doing here, how did you get here?" sort of gives the credence to the question that you asked: could it be that that they knew of the serpent *before* the particular time of the eating of the tree of the knowledge of good and evil? *It's possible,* we can't rule it out, but we can't dogmatically say "yes." But at least it gives us a little more basis of understanding.

Ok—let's continue on here in Chapter 3. Ok—we just finished verse seven, let's pick it up in verse eight: "And they heard the sound of Jehovah God walking about in the garden at the breeze of the day…" so this is in the evening or the cool of the day—and it shows that they were right there with God, they had complete access to God all the time. "… and concealed themselves the man and his wife from the face of Jehovah God in the midst of the trees of the garden." [So there they were, right there] "…And called Jehovah God unto the man, and said to him: Where [art] thou?…". [Now, I don't know if there was a desig-nated place that they would meet every day at this particular time—it's very possible. So, God came down and said: 'Where are you?' "…And he said, Thy voice I heard in the gar-den, and I feared, because naked [am] I; and I concealed myself. And he said: Who made known to thee that naked [art] thou? From the tree [from] which I commanded thee to not eat (from it) hast thou eaten? And said the man…" (vs 8-12, *IH*)

Now, here's the classical case that always happens. No one likes to take blame for whatever they do. And of course, it's interesting that modern psychology is based on that. They are now understanding that people have to be responsible for what they do. But, when psychology first started this out and people get the way they were, it was blame father, blame mother, blame school, blame everybody else—you poor little thing, you can't help it—*cain't hep it!* So, that's what Adam did. He said, 'Now look…' [and the man said]: "…the woman whom thou gavest with me…" Now, it's God's fault. It's not 'my fault' it's God's fault "…she gave to me from the tree, and I ate…" So that let's 'me off the hook. Now, you know, if it wouldn't have been for the woman, Lord, I wouldn't have eaten. But there it was.' "…And said Jehovah God to the woman: What, then, hast thou done? And said the woman: The serpent seduced [or deceived] me and I ate" (vs 13).

So everyone is trying to blame everyone else. (question from audience)—answer: Ok—The reason that I'm using Jehovah is because that's the translation in the *Interlinear* and that is the really the correct pronunciation of the Hebrew word, YHVH—which is translated, *Lord*. So, to read it in the *King James* it would be "the Lord God said." (another question from audience)—answer: Well, because I'm reading, I'm reading from the English of the *Hebrew Interlinear*—that's why.

Comment was made concerning Jehovah and the Lord God. The *King James* translates YHVH as Lord, and when you first have God dealing directly with Adam and Eve it is the One Who **created** them—the Lord God, in this particular case, as we would read it in the *King James* or the One *of Elohim* Who revealed Himself as, as Jehovah—or as some people like to say Yahweh. That is not in any way indicating that we're switching over and believing in sacred names at all, we're not. And, because that is not required at all whatsoever. But, it is still; nevertheless, one of the names of God. So, in reading this, please understand that we're not trying to do that.

"And said Jehovah God unto the serpent: Because thou hast done this, cursed [be] thou from all the cattle and from all beasts of the field; upon thy belly thou shalt go and dust thou shalt eat all the days of thy life" (v 14, *IH*). And, it's interesting, when you compare our discussion that we were having before services about how human beings are made to stand upright, fully erect, and walk on two feet, made in the image of God—now here, the adversary of God now is made so he can **never** stand upright.

(Question from audience)—answer: It's possible, I do not know. The question is: Did he stand upright at one time? *It's possible, I don't know.* All we know is what we see today in the particular case. But, I think that is very profound that the one that symbolizes Satan the devil being the serpent, **cannot stand upright.** It has to go on his belly. And I think one of the most gruesome ways of eating is the way that a snake eats. It…I'm sure you've seen that on some of these Discovery programs showing how serpents eat. And so, the whole thing with the serpent is really quite a struggle. And what we're finding here is that everything that God said is true.

And, He says, verse 15: "And hostility I will put between thee and (between) the woman, and between thy seed and (between) her seed; he shall bruise thee [as to the] head and thou shalt bruise him [as to the] heel." And, of course, that did happen when Jesus was crucified. When they crucified Him and, and put the nails through His feet. It wasn't through the front part of His feet because He would have bones broken. It was prophesied "no bone would be broken." So it went through [between] the Achilles tendon and the heel, so it would go that way—and it did bruise His heel. Now, continuing on: "Unto the woman he said, Multiplying I will multiply thy trouble and thy conception…" I will greatly multiply your trouble, your sorrow—I think that's a little broader definition "…in pain thou shalt bring forth children; and unto thy husband [shall be] they longing [or your desire] and he shall rule over thee" (v 16, *IH*).

Now, God gave equal punishment to all. God is not picking on women here—please understand that. Man had his sorrow increased, and his work increased just as well. Let's see what happened here: "And to Adam he said, Because thou hast hearkened [or listened] to the voice of thy wife, and hast eaten from the tree [as to] which I commanded thee, saying: Not thou shalt eat from it; cursed [be] the ground on account of thee…" Everything that he would set his hand to do he had obstacles to overcome and problems to overcome. "…in toil thou shalt eat [of] it all the days of they life; and thorns and thistles it shall cause to sprout for thee; and thou shalt eat the herb of the field. In the sweat of thy nostrils… (vs. 17-19, *IH*).

Now, that's a literal translation. I think showing that he's going to have to not, not just the sweat of your brow, but it's going to be a breathing, difficult, very exasperating kind of existence. "…thou shalt eat bread, until thy return unto the ground; for from it thou wast taken; for dust [art] thou and unto dust thou shalt return" (v 19).

And so, that was the punishment that was given to man. Let's look at the punishments here, as it was given out to all of them. Let's first of all understand that there is a parallel for us to learn which is drawn on continually. Let's, let's see first of all, *the result* of what happened. Let's see the result as it is in relationship to Eve and then into Adam.

Let's go to II Corinthians 11, and there is a lesson for us here continually concerning the Word of God, continually concerning how Satan is going to be out there to try and turn God's way upside down and to interfere in our lives. And I think, living in the end-time we're going to experience a lot of that. We're going to see a lot of it. We're going to see a lot of obstacles brought up against us.

Now, let's pick it up here in verse two, 2 Corinthians 11: "For I am jealous over you with *the* jealousy of God because I have espoused you to one husband, so that I may present *you as* a chaste virgin to Christ. But I fear, lest by any means, [any way—"any means"] as the serpent deceived Eve by his craftiness [clever arguments, sounding good, having logic], so your minds might be corrupted from *the* simplicity that *is* in Christ" (2 Cor. 11:2-3). And that's exactly what's been happening today—coming along with philosophical and theological arguments that just *boggle* the mind. They're just so *mind-twisting* that it's difficult to even read it.

I know, I've been studying quite a bit of it now so I can *really understand* how much of the New Testament has been written to combat all of this Satanic philosophy—and it's amazing. It is *amazing* how much is there to combat everything that Satan has done. Now, notice verse 4: "For indeed, if someone comes preaching another Jesus, whom we did not preach, or you receive a different spirit, which you did not receive, or a different gospel, which you did not accept, you put up with it as *something* good". It says, "you're putting up with it, you're allowing this to happen." That's why he said that you need to be careful that you don't be deceived.

Now, let's go to 1 Timothy 2—and here's a section of Scripture which has been used against women in ways which are not exactly correct. But, as we've pointed out before, we're still male and female and God expects us to be, to live our lives in a way that He, He wants them to be lived. Verse 9: 'In like manner also, *let* the women adorn themselves with clothing that shows modesty and discretion, not with *elaborate* braidings of *the hair*, or *with* gold, or pearls, or expensive apparel;" That is, *overly done.* I don't know of any women that I've seen in church at all who was doing that—so don't take this as a personal thing "…But *with that* which *is* fitting for women who profess *to have* reverence for God—with good works. Let a woman learn in quietness and be submissive in every respect" (1 Tim. 2:9-11).

Now, "silence" can mean quietness. Let them learn in quietness. It doesn't mean you are to be still and to not ask questions or anything like that—ok.

Verse 12: "But I suffer [allow] not a woman to teach, nor to usurp [or to 'exercise,' as it should read] authority over the man, but to be in silence." That is, teaching in church. That doesn't mean that a woman cannot teach. We have the example of Aquila and Priscilla—they taught Apollos, but they were not teaching him in the church. Verse 13: "For Adam was formed first, then Eve. And Adam was not deceived; but the woman came into transgression by being deceived." Well, we're going to see that this doesn't mean that Adam didn't sin. A lot of people read this and think, well, it's just the woman, and then they get the hard-heel and put down women all the time. No, we're going to see, Adam not being deceived, KNEW what he was doing so therefore *his sin* was worse than Eve's. "But she shall be saved through the childbearing, if they continue in faith and love and sanctification with self-control" (vs 13-15).

Now, let's look at the effect concerning Adam. And what happened here to all mankind. Let's go to Romans 5—and I know Romans 5, in this particular case, is a somewhat difficult section to understand, but let's see if we can untangle it here at this particular point. Now, Adam *did sin!* And we're going to see it here, very clearly. And his sin had a great effect on all humankind.

Verse 12, Romans 5: "Therefore, as by one man sin entered into the world…" Didn't say 'woman'—'one man'. Does that mean that Adam probably could have stopped the whole thing even though Eve may have eaten of it? If he would have kept God's way and not eaten of it? *I don't know, it's possible.* I do not know—that's an open question. And that's one of those we'll have to wait for the resurrection to get the answer on, because it doesn't tell us directly.

Question from audience: The question is—we're going to deal in a little scenario now, so we'll have a little bell-ringing—what if Adam would have eaten first, instead of Eve? *I don't know, doesn't tell us.* But he ate second. But he knew better, he was not deceived. When you're deceived, you don't know better. You're deceived. He wasn't. He knew what he was doing. And, I'm sure he knew the consequences that was going to happen to the whole human race.

Now here in Romans 5, it shows us something very important that what happened. And this helps give us *an understanding* as to what happened to human nature and *why the world is so evil.* Though everyone is trying to do good in their own way, except those who are totally dedicated to evil. Verse 12: "Therefore, as by **one** man sin entered into the world…" [and the 'world' here being the human realm] "…and by means of sin *came* death; and in this way, death passed into all mankind…" so death passed on to *all* human beings, that's what it says. And so 'death' passed upon *all* men. We're as good as dead from the instant of conception—just a matter of time. Some live longer, some shorter. Now it says: "…and it is for this reason that **all have sinned…**" this means: 'for this reason **ALL** sin.' With the passing of death inherent within their genes, sin also was passed to all human beings, that we have a sinful nature. Now no longer neutral, as they were originally created. Now there was a sinful nature. And this is the reason why *all* men have sinned. Now, verse 13: "…(For before *the* law, sin was in *the* world: however, sin is not imputed when law does not exist" (Rom. 5:12-13).

So, what he's saying—in kind of double twist on the words here is—before the Covenant given to Israel, there was law in the world, that's why there was sin. Because "sin is the transgression of the law."

"Nevertheless, death reigned from Adam until Moses, upon those who had not sinned in the likeness of the transgression of Adam…" So, his sin was a *profound* sin. His sin was a *knowledgeable* sin. Now then it says: "…who was a type of the *one* Who was to come" (v 14).

41

Now, we're going to look at a couple of things in 1 Corinthians 15, concerning Adam and concerning Christ. Now, we know that Paul tells us that *all of us* have "the law of sin and death" within us. That's reflected in the carnal nature that when you want to do good you can't.

1 Corinthians 15:22—No one has been able to beat this yet. If you want to know the truth of God's Word, all have died. That verifies the truth of God's Word. No one has been able to overcome it. Everyone has tried to prolong life as long as they can. But the aging process is a very part of our being.

Verse 22, 1 Corinthians 15, *KJV*: "For as in Adam **all die,**" they all die because of the sin of Adam—death was passed on, sinful nature was passed on. "...so even **in Christ** shall all be made alive."

Now, let's turn the page, in 1 Corinthians 15 and let's get the comparison here in verse 45: "Accordingly, it is written, 'The first man, Adam, became a living soul; the last Adam *became* an everlasting Spirit" (1 Cor. 15:45). And that's what led to the question: What would the world have been like if Adam and Eve had not sinned?—and I think that video is still around some place, isn't it? So, now that I let that Adam out of the bag, if you request the tape, we'll try and find it. I did that in 1988. My, seven years ago! Yes, 1988, it was the second day of the Feast of Tabernacles.]

So, there is a comparison here. So we will just have to say, part of the tape indicates that IF Adam and Eve had not sinned, then Adam would have been the first man changed from flesh to spirit and we would all go through Adam. But now, because they sinned, we all go through Christ.

Now, it's not like the Mormons. The Mormons come along and say: "Adam and Eve had to sin so that all of these spirits up in heaven could be sent down and be put into human bodies. Because they need a human body." Well that is just demonism—that's just another version of Hinduism in the guise of a Christian-sounding religion.

So, because of that sin, we have all sinned and we come up with this human nature.

Now, let's see another verification of this. Let's go to Mark 7:21. And this is something that the world cannot figure out. **Why** is it that all human being *tend* to do evil? In varying degrees, one way or the other. Verse 21, and this shows that it's *from within, inside!* So therefore we have no one to blame but ourselves. Verse 21: "For from within, out of the hearts of men, go forth evil thoughts..." and this just almost lists out the sins as they come along in the experience of a lifetime: "...adulteries, fornications, murders..." and of course we're having in the headlines now still going on with OJ and they just finished the one with the woman who drowned her two children and people are murdered every day. "... murders, thefts, covetousness, wickedness, guile, licenciousness, an evil eye, blasphemy, pride, foolishness; all these evils go forth **from within**, and these defile a man" (Mark 7:21-23). And that kind of nature was put *into* us, *passed on* to us by inheritance from Adam and Eve down to this day. And *only God* can change it. *Only Christ* can remove it. It's the *only way*. Can't be done any other way.

Well, with a, a life like that, here let's go look at one of the most righteous kings that we have. Let's go to Psalm 51 and let's look and see what, what David said of his own conception. Now, we saw before what he said of it: how wonderfully and awesomely he was made. Now, we have the other side of it. Now we have what happens *when you are sinning* and you are confessing your sins and you really understand and realize how in-depth the sin is that human being have.

Now recently, there was a murderer down in, in San Jose`. And something worked out that they could not convict him. So he was set loose. And he says, *"You got to kill me."* "No, there's nothing we can do legally." He says, *"I'm unreformable."* At least he was honest. He said, *"I think of murder and mayhem all the time. And if you don't lock me up and do something with me and take me out of my misery, I know I'm going to do it again."* So that was really something. And you know, true confession, that a man would really admit that. And of course, these so-called "serial killers"—that they just kill one person after another, they are the same way. They get so obsessed with the evil and so compulsive with it, that every thought is to execute this evil. Every thought is to carry out this evil.

And so, when David was repenting, here's what he said: Psalm 51:1, *KJV*: "…Have mercy upon me, O God, according to thy lovingkindness: according unto the multitude of thy tender mercies blot out my transgressions." And what did he have in mind? What was it he did? *Adultery and murder*—listed in the same order right there as in Mark 7—correct? *Yes!* And he schemed and he planned and he plotted and all this sort of thing. "Wash me thoroughly from mine iniquity, and cleanse me from my sin. For I acknowledge my transgressions: and my sin *is* ever before me." When God **convicts** you of your sin it is ever before you. "…Against thee, thee only, have I sinned, and done *this* evil in thy sight: that thou mightest be justified when thou speakest, *and* be clear when thou judgest. Behold, **I was shapen in iniquity**, and **in sin** did my mother conceive me" (vs 2-5).

That doesn't mean it was a sinful, illegitimate birth, it means 'just *from the very conception* of my being *sin* was within me'—that's what it means. That's why the sweetest, nicest children—you often wonder, I wonder what Stalin was like when he was a little baby? Wonder what Hitler was like when he was a little baby? Wonder what Cleopatra was like when she was a little baby—and on and on and on and on. All little babies are sweet and lovely, but they have inherent the "law of sin and death" in them. And the more they are exposed to an evil world and Satan, the more in degree that this evil becomes more profound.

You can even take this human nature and you can raise it in a relatively good environment, with a minimal amount of influence of sin and you can come up with someone who the world would say is a "upright." That is, they are not given to too much sin. But, nevertheless, they will lie. Nevertheless, they will cheat. Nevertheless, they will covet. Nevertheless, they will still want their own way. Even in the very best. That's why "all have sinned and come short of the glory of God and none can save himself."

So, David understood that it was from right within. Now, let's look at a couple of Proverbs concerning that. There are a couple of Proverbs that we have memorized there. As a result, man's way, *man's way is the way of sin.* The way that seems right. Proverbs—you probably know where I'm going. Let's go to 16:25. There's another one which is 14:12, but let's go to 16:25. Repeats it twice, Proverbs 16:25, *KJV*: "There is a way that seemeth right unto a man, but the end thereof *are* the ways of death."

The "wages of sin is death." Man's way that seems good and right leads to death.

Now, the thing, let's come over here to Chapter 21:2—here's something else. Not only is there "a way that seems right to a man but the ends thereof are the ways of death," verse 2: **"Every way of a man *is* right in his own eyes…"** (Prov. 21:2, *KJV*). Now, that's how we have the excuse that you try and palm it off on someone else. **"Right in his own eyes."**

Now, let's look a couple of other Proverbs as we're going here. Let's come back to Proverbs 15. And because of that you can't come to God on **your terms.** Now, we're going to see that's what Cain was doing. He was going to God on *his* terms. You can never come to God on your terms. Here's why, verse 8, Proverbs 15, *KJV*:

"The sacrifice of the wicked *is* an abomination to the LORD…" If you don't repent, if you don't change, if you don't have a heart that God can work with, even whatever you do in the way of sacrifice—not only just animal sacrifice, but time, but labor, whatever it may be, is 'an abomination to the Lord.' Now, *who* is the mother of abominations? *Babylon the Great*—mother of harlots and abominations in the earth. All comes from her.

Verse 9: "The way of the wicked *is* an abomination…" And that's what, as we're going to see, happened to the world before the Flood. Verse 10: "Correction *is* grievous unto him that **forsaketh the way**…" Did that not happen to Adam and Eve? Was not their correction grievous? *Oh yes—even affects us!* "…*and* he that hateth reproof shall die. Hell and destruction *are* before the LORD: how much more then the hearts of the children of men?" (vs 10-11). So God knows the heart. That's why in Mark 7:21, it tells us what our human hearts are like.

Now, let's come down here to verse 15: "All the days of the afflicted *are* evil…" And that's what it was before the, before the Flood. It got so bad, so bad. And it's just like God has always done. When people come to a certain point that they just turn their backs on God, God says, "Okay, you can have it all. All your own way and I don't have to do anything but just let it run its course." And then history is written.

Come down here to verse 25: "The LORD will destroy the house of the proud: but he will establish the border of the widow. The thoughts of the wicked *are* an abomination to the LORD…" So, we have the "way of evil" is an abomination; and we find here—all the way through here—these things are called "abominations." That is amazing! Verse 27: "He that is greedy of gain troubleth his own house…" Didn't that happen to Adam and Eve? They were "greedy of gain." They wanted to be made "wise" in their own way? *Yes! Yes,* this is something the way that these parallels really follow along.

Now, let's come back to the book of Genesis and let's come to Chapter 4. We'll finish off Chapter 3 here and then we'll come to Chapter 4. Now, God had to do something. He withdrew the opportunity of salvation until the Messiah should come. With the exception of those few that He would call.

Genesis 3 and we finished with verse 19: "for dust you are and unto dust you shall return."

"And called the man the name of his wife Eve; for she became mother of every living [being]. And made Jehovah God for Adam and for his wife tunics [coats] of skin, and clothed them" (vs 20-21). That is to clothe their nakedness. Now, some people say that this was also an offering for a "sin sacrifice." *It's possible,* but if you read what a "sin sacrifice" how they handled it, everything had to be burned: the skin, the innards and everything had to be burned. So, it's possible that it was, but I am not going to completely say that this was an animal sacrifice for sin.

Verse 22, now, here's what God had to do: "And said Jehovah God: Behold, the man has become like one of us, to know [or that is 'to decide'] good and evil…" And now—which he can't do, he just thinks he can do—God is the One Who decides *what is good,* and God is the One Who decides *what is evil.* But, now that mankind had taken it to themselves they were "like God" in that particular sense, to decide *good* and *evil.*

"…and now, lest he put forth his hand and take also from the tree of life, and eat, and live for ever…" v 22, *IH*). So, now God closed off the way to the Tree of Life. And the reason being is, not that He wasn't going to bring salvation at a later date, which He was, without a doubt; but **you cannot live _forever_ in a state of sin.** And, I know I've said this before: How would you like to live forever the way you're living now? With the pulls of sin, with the pulls of the flesh, and all this sort of thing—forever and ever and ever? So therefore, He cut off the way of the Tree of Life.

"…(and) [so] sent him Jehovah God from the garden of Eden to till the ground [from] whence he was taken (there from). And he drove out the man, and he stationed (from) East [of] (to) the garden of Eden the Cherubim and the flame of the sword whirling itself about to guard the way of the tree of life" (vs 23-24, *IH*). Now, it's interesting, it's called *"**the way** of the Tree of Life"*—symbolizing *a way to live!* I'm sure there was a literal tree. Now, what happened to the Tree of Life? *I don't know.* I do know that after the Flood it was no longer mentioned in the sense that it was here.

Now, could it be that God took the tree back with Him, *I don't know,* at the time of the Flood? *It's possible.* Could it be that the tree was destroyed? Well, then the question comes up: if it's a Tree of Life can it be destroyed? *I can't answer that either.* So, you see we'll have to wait for God to tell us quite a bit.

Now then, we start the whole chronicle of human sin! And sin starts in the family. Let's pick it up here in Chapter 4 and verse one.

"And Adam knew Eve his wife [which means they had sexual relations] and she conceived…" (Gen. 4:1, *KJV*). **It wasn't with the serpent,** trust me! and the Word of God, that if Cain was the offspring of the serpent, God would have made it clear. But then you're also violating the laws of God, which is kind after kind. And so, you cannot have something, which then would, would be impossible to take place. So he was human as human can be and his father was Adam and not the serpent. And here's what she said: "…and bore Cain, and said: I have gotten a man from the Lord" (v 1). So right away she began to think this was the "One" that was prophesied about. That Cain was the "One" who was going to then bring the deliverance to them.

"And she again bore his brother, Abel. And Abel was keeper of sheep, but Cain was a tiller of the ground" (v 2). Now, in the account of *Josephus* it shows that the "process of time" was perhaps as much as 120 years. Now then, those of you who like to do a little mathematics—and I've seen this in some publications—you take 1500 years, which is 1550-some years from the time of Adam and Eve until the Flood. And you start out with two and then you start increasing the population. And it's estimated that there could have been as many as a billion and a half people on the earth at the time of the Flood. Now, when you consider there is a tradition—and I will have to put it that way—that Adam and Eve had 56 children. Now, that would not be hard to believe that they had 56 children. All God gives us is the *loose* linage of the line of Cain; and the *exact* linage of the line coming down to Noah. Nothing else is preserved for us. Everything else of the world before the Flood has been obliterated.

Let's continue on the account here: "And in process of time it came to pass, that Cain brought of the fruit of the ground an offering unto the LORD" (v 3). Now, we know that firstfruits are to be brought. We also know that a tithe of the ground was to be brought. So this was an **improper** offering; and I think it's probably true—the tradition that they had—that Cain was forcing the ground and doing things that he shouldn't have been doing. And Abel, he also brought of the firstlings of his flock and of the fat thereof…. [There are some people who believe that this could have been on a Holy Day—*it's possible.* It doesn't say that it was, doesn't say that it wasn't.] …And the LORD had respect unto Abel and to his offering…" (v 4). Why? *Because he did it according to the commands of God, that's why!* And whenever you do anything according to the commands of God, He will have respect unto you.

Verse 5: "But unto Cain and to his offering he had not respect. And Cain was very wroth, and his countenance fell." He got mad at God. "…And the LORD said unto Cain, Why art thou wroth? and why is thy countenance fallen? If thou doest well, shalt thou not be accepted?" (vs 5-7). All He said was, "Look, Cain, all you have to do is do what's right. Won't you be accepted?" "…and if thou doest not well, sin lieth at the door" (v 7).

Now, there's a couple of interesting things here, which may fit into this: When they brought their offering, where did they bring it? I'm sure that God was still in the garden of Eden, so when they came up to the east gate, where the Cherubim were—now remember, what is over the altar of God in the tabernacle and the temple, but the Cherubim. So, I think this: when they brought an offering, they came to the entrance—the east entrance of the garden of Eden, where the Cherubim were—and there was an altar for offerings. And that's where they offered it. And if they did well, they were accepted of God.

So, when He says, "Sin lies at the door," could it be that He is telling Cain that "Your offering here at the door is sin"? *Could be.*

"And unto thee *shall be* his desire, and thou shalt rule over [it] him…" (v 7). You have to be responsible and control your own self—so Cain didn't accept that.

So, then we have the account here concerning Cain killing his brother. And God knows. *God knows everything.* And so "Cain rose up against Abel his brother, and slew him. And the LORD said unto Cain, Where *is* Abel thy brother? And he said, I know not: *Am* I my brother's keeper?" (v 8-9).

Immediately, right in the family here is the strife going on. When you have children, do you have fights with the kids? *Yes.* Is there strife between them? *Yes.* Nothing new. Started out with the first family. That's part of the sorrows that Eve would go through. More than just the pain of bearing children, but also the turmoil and the sorrow of fighting and arguing and, you know, rearing the children. "And he said, What hast thou done? the voice of thy brother's blood crieth unto me from the ground. And now *art* thou cursed from the earth, which hath opened her mouth to receive thy brother's blood from thy hand; When thou tillest the ground, it shall not henceforth yield unto thee her strength; a fugitive and a vagabond shalt thou be in the earth…" So then, he was cast out. "…And Cain said unto the LORD, My punishment *is* greater than I can bear. Behold, thou hast driven me out this day from the face of the earth [or the face of the land]; and from thy face shall I be hidden…" (vs 10-14). No more access to God—totally cut off from God. Now, no more could he come up to the entrance of Eden and make an offering. No more, *totally cut off.*

So you have a double removable in this particular case. Adam and Eve were put out of the garden for their sin—which was the first removal. They still had access to God coming to the entrance of Eden on the east side. Now Cain, because of his sin, is removed even further—to wander, to travel, to have no roots, to have nothing permanent. And he said: "…I shall be a fugitive and a vagabond in the earth; and it shall come to pass, *that* every one that findeth me shall slay me. And the LORD said unto him, Therefore whosoever slayeth Cain, vengeance shall be taken on him sevenfold. And the LORD set a mark upon Cain, lest any finding him should kill him" (vs 14-15).

What was the mark? *I don't know.* There's been a lot of speculation, but I have not found any validation to any of the speculation. I have thought maybe it was an "X" or a mark or a cross and perhaps that was the origination of the cross—*I do not know*. But, what-ever it was, I'm sure his children, when they got up on his knees and said, "Grandpa, what is that?" I'm sure that he told the biggest fib in the world. I'm sure that he said, "God put this on me to set me apart from *and make me special* above all men." You can almost hear the story.

Now, the question is, where did Cain get his wife? Obviously, from one of the daughters of Adam and Eve. And obviously, it was at that time, because of the inheritance that they had, determined that they could marry their own sisters because they had not had—how shall we say—enough intermarriage where then it would create problems genetically. Had to be. "…and she conceived, and bare Enoch…" (v 17).

Now the reason I suspect that Cain told all of his descendants that this was a special mark from God—not a sign of a curse—is because you read the names of the linage of those of the line of Cain and they are very similar to the names that you find in the linage from Adam and Seth on down to Noah, very similar.

Well, we won't go through any more in Chapter 4 or Chapter 5. Let's come to Chapter 6 and we will end this study here, in Chapter 6, to see what the earth became like. When you have people having the "law of sin and death" in them and just give them free reign and let them do whatever they're going to do, it's going to be a mixture of good and evil.

Now Chapter 6 and verse 1: "And it came to pass, when men began to multi-ply…" (Gen. 6:1, *KJV*). Now, you reach a certain point in human reproduction that you're having a multiplying factor. Right now they say there are what, 5.5 billion people on the earth—somewhere close to that. And they say that within 20 years that it will double! Now, they're doing all they can to try and stop this with abortion and so forth, but they reached the same point here: "…began to multiply on the face of the earth, and daughters were born unto them, That the sons of God saw the daughters of men that they *were* fair…" (vs 1-2). Now, these were those who were called "sons of God." These are not some special, giant "Nephilim," as they are called. This is not some sort of "angels" intermarrying with human being to produce a super race. "…the sons of God saw the daughters of men that they *were* fair and they took them wives of all which they chose…" rather than do it the way that God said. "…And the LORD said, My spirit shall not always strive with man," so there it is: "man"—that's how we know those sons of God were men, because he says so. "…for that he also *is* flesh: [not an angelic being] yet his days shall be an hundred and twenty years" (vs. 2-3).

God pronounced sentence right then: he's only going to live 120 years longer.

[And] "There were giants in the earth in those days…" Do we have giants today? *Yes, we do! Yes, we do.* All you have to do is stack up the watusi along side of the Japanese and you'll see, there are giants. "…and also after that, when the sons of God came in unto the daughters of men, and they bare *children* to them, the same *became* mighty men which *were* of old, men of renown" (v 4). Or men renamed, renamed after the term: "sons of God." So here they were building up the master race. That's what they were doing—"mighty men." "And God saw that the wickedness of man *was* **great** [absolutely incredible] in the earth, and *that* every imagination of the thoughts of his heart *was* only evil **continually**" (v 5).

Now, we're reaching the same point again today, aren't we? How far advanced were they technologically? *We don't know.* Could they have been advanced as we are? *Could be, maybe even more.* We don't know, but the end result of man's way, under Satan's influence, is that "his heart was only evil continually." And it was so bad: "…it repented the LORD that he had made man on the earth, and it grieved him at his heart. And the LORD said, I will destroy man whom I have created from the face of the earth; both man, and beast, and the creeping thing, and the fowls of the air; for it repenteth me that I have made them" (vs 6-7).

Now, why would God destroy every living thing? *I do not know, except that you have to make a guess.* Was it that they were having genetic engineering at that time, on a grander scale than we understand today? Why does it say—let us read on here: "But Noah found grace in the eyes of the LORD. These *are* the generations of Noah: Noah was a just man *and* perfect in his generations" (vs 8-9)—or his pedigree or his progeny. Is that telling us that the rest of mankind was *so twisted and defiled?* Is that telling us that they were doing things with animals that they should not have been doing? Doing things with animals and human beings combined together that they should not have been doing? *I don't know.* I think I've mentioned this a time or two, but I'll mention it here since we're covering this very basic fundamental section of the Scriptures. There is, in mythology, the man's torso on a goat's body. And this was called one of the gods. Could it be that that actually happened? *I don't know. I do not know.* But, I'll tell you one thing, today they are looking for as many ways as they can to enhance a super race, so that they can do something with the genes to make better athletes, to make stronger men, make smarter men. They have a whole university dedicated to that, many different places, but in particularly, the Rockefeller University in their genetic section there. Very advanced into this.

Question is (from audience): Could this refer to Noah being the firstborn? *It could but it doesn't say firstborn.* It says he was "perfect in his generations." And I think that whenever we have something referring to a "first born" it lists them as firstborn. So it's possible that it could, but it's also possible that in his pedigree or his genetic makeup there was nothing foreign in it. There had to be reason why God had to kill all life. ALL LIFE! *Now that's drastic.* ALL human beings and ALL life. And we can see the evidence of the Flood everywhere.

Now notice: "And Noah begat three sons, Shem, Ham, and Japheth. The earth also was **corrupt** before God, and the earth was **filled** with violence…" Now, being corrupt, this is talking about the earth. Everything was corrupted. Now, let's continue on here: "…And God looked upon the earth, and, behold, it was **corrupt**; for **all flesh had corrupted** his way upon the earth" (vs 10-12). Now, what do you mean "all flesh had corrupted"? Does that mean it was rotting? *No!* This would have to be that all flesh was all mixed up. I would have to conclude "all mixed up" genetically. And it was so bad and the evil was so rife that "God said to Noah: [Verse 13] The end of all flesh is come before me; for the earth is **filled with violence** through them; and, behold, I will **destroy** them with the earth."

So then, He told him to make the ark. And that was some, some big vessel. And God is the One Who *sent* the animals to Noah. So apparently God picked out those animals that had a pure strain in their, in their genes, so that on this side of the Flood—which we live on now—things would not be all mixed up and twisted around. But this whole phrase here: "that ALL flesh" not just human beings. See, there's a differentiation here.

Let's go back to verse 5: "And God saw that the wickedness of **MEN** was great in the earth, and that every imagination of the thoughts of his heart was only evil **continually."** Now, we come here to verse 12: "And God looked upon the earth, and, behold, it was corrupt; for **ALL flesh** [not just human flesh—**ALL FLESH**] had corrupted his way upon the earth. And God said unto Noah, The end of **ALL flesh** is come before me; for the earth is filled with violence through them; and, behold, I will destroy them with the earth.

Now, let's come to Matthew 24, because there's also a prophecy that in our time that it's going to get very similar to it. Yet, at the same time, when all of this evil is going on, as it was back then—we saw that "all flesh had corrupted its way and **the earth was filled with**

violence." Matthew 24:37: "Now as *it was in* the days of Noah, so shall *it* also be *at* the coming of the Son of man. For as in the days that *were* before the Flood, they were eating and drinking, marrying and giving in marriage, until the day that Noah entered the ark… (vs 37-38).

So, in spite of all the violence, in spite of all the corruption, there were the normal functions going on which human beings were doing. And to them, they had been so accustomed to their way of life, *so accustomed to the evil* that was on every side about them, that they just took everything for granted. And they didn't have a clue until the Flood came.

Comment was made that the scientists are doing what they can to try and alter the genetic substance of certain of the monkey family and, in particularly, pigs, to try and have replaceable livers and hearts from pigs and other animals. That's something! That's something!

Which reminds me, the greatest blow to the abortion movement took place this week. Which was, the woman who was Jane Roe in Roe vs Wade has changed and repented and is now a pro-lifer. And the thing that did it—you know, sometimes the *overwhelmingness of evil* will get to you—and she said that the thing that got to her was when she opened up a freezer at the Planned Parenthood or the abortion clinic that she was working in, and saw a freezer full of fetuses. She said, *"that was it."* Even though she's now pro-life she says it's still all right in the first trimester. Well listen, as we have studied in the past, a baby is fully, fully formed—it's just a matter of growth—with just six weeks. So, by the time a woman has definite conformation that she is pregnant the new little person is already formed—it's only an inch long.

(Comment from audience—speaker's answer:) Yes, she was baptized by a Baptist preacher, yes that's correct. So, at least in the letter of the law she's doing something reasonable. But, it's interesting, she still hasn't come all the way to abhor all abortion. So, she's trying to, you know like you do when you repent of your sins to a certain degree, you kind of like to straddle the fence to so you can still justify what you've done in the past, but, kind of say you're getting away from it. So that's what's she's doing.

But, I thought that that was profound when she opened up the freezer and it was *full* of fetuses—so that the doctors could use them for experiments and all those things that they want to do. (Comments from audience) Yes, sure they do, yes! They sell them, make money on them. Yes, the Chinese are going to have population control by having very strict laws—execute people for the smallest little crime so they can kill them and sell their heart and sell their liver and their eyes and all that sort of thing.

So, we'll just finish this by saying: History repeats itself without a doubt. And we don't know how bad it's going to get. And we don't know what the technology is going to do. Now, there, I am sure there are lot of propagandistic statements put out which are not true. But, nevertheless, I think they are endeavoring in trying to do that.

And one of the things they want to do is come up with the "divine" man. One who's going to live forever. One who's going to be smarter than ever before. And that's Satan's whole goal. And, I think this—I'll just have to give you a little speculation here: I think that when the Beast comes on the scene it's going to be the result of a tremendous and profound Satanic religious experience. Which is, for those religions of the world in Masonry and all that sort of thing, they are going to have a "divine" man. And once they get this "divine" man then I think they are going to conclude that many more people can now follow in his footsteps *if they just make an image to the Beast.*

I'll let you think on that. Well, we'll end here. We're through with our little study there in Genesis, but I think it's been very good to go back to the very basics and understand that and come forward from there.

(End of Sermon)

Transcriber: Bonnie Orswell

The Background in Genesis—Sermon III
August 12, 1995
Scriptural References

1) Genesis 3:1-7

2) Mark 11:12-26

3) Genesis 3:8-19

4) II Corinthians 11:2-4

5) I Timothy 2:9-13

6) Romans 5:12-14

7) I Corinthians 15:22, 45

8) Mark 7:21:23

9) Psalm 51:1-5

10) Proverbs 16:25

11) Proverbs 21:2

12) Proverbs 15:8-11, 15, 25-27

13) Genesis 4:1-15, 17

14) Genesis 6:1-13, 5, 12

15) Matthew 24:37-38

CHAPTER FOUR

The Sabbath—Sign of God

May 25, 1991

What does the word *Babel* mean? Anybody remember? This is going to be kind of an open Sabbath, so we can have questions and answers and different things. [It means] confusion. Do you think this world is in confusion today? Yes, it is. Remember President Bush announced the New World Order? Well, that hasn't come together the way he thought has it? Because the other day with the assignation of Rajiv Gandhi, he said, "What kind of world is this?" And it is confusion.

Now, Evelyn gave me this: It's *Prophecy in the News* by J. R. Church and he does quite a bit keeping up on what the Jews are doing, but let us end a myth about Jews and Jewish religion today. There are as many, what we would call denominations, of Judaism as there are [of] Catholicism, and Protestantism. [That's] just the way that it is.

Now here is a headline, *Jews believe Messiah came at Passover* [1991]. How is that? Okay, and that there are going to be two Messiah's—one called Messiah Ben Joseph, and he is going to die for the sins of the people. Now you see what kind of rebellion this is toward Christ? You see they won't accept Christ, but now [they write] we are going to create our own Messiah and he is going to die for the sins of the people. Then there is the other one, and the first of the two Messiahs would come Passover 1991, we can't confirm he actually appeared. And Messiah Ben Joseph is to die for the sins of the people, then guess who is going to come as king? Who is the greatest king that the Jews look to? David. Messiah Ben David is going to come and conquer Gog and Magog.

Then it [the article] shows all the pictures here, I'll let you take a look at it here. Here are the Jews with their long beards and curly locks and everything, and you know that's supposed to get them righteousness, but it doesn't. It doesn't get them righteousness.

Then it shows the Bar Kofka coin which was a rebellion against God [131-135 AD], and let's see, there are a couple of other things in here. Meet the man who plans to rebuild the Jewish temple. So you've got all of this division here. Now he says, "Well, they don't need to offer sacrifices, but they can just make a big synagogue out of it. Then some of the Jews believe that Elijah has arrived and that's in the person of Rabbi Menachem Schnerson. It shows his picture with his long locks and his big beard and his black hat on there. Now I don't want to ridicule him from that point of view because I do believe that the two witnesses are going to be Jews, and I think it is going to be the Governor of Judea and the priest at the temple that they rebuild, because that's what Zechariah [3 and] 4 tells us.

Then he's got advertisements of all the tapes and it goes through here showing some other things. So the thing I just want to bring out is that the Jews are as much denomination-alized and confused about religion, and their own religion, and their own Bible as Protestants and Catholics are about theirs.

And then Belinda brought this in which really is something we need to pay attention to, so I'm going to go through this article, because it's very, very important for us to know. *Europeans Primed for New Age* and this is under the section of alternative religions which was found written by Don Lattin. He is the religious writer for the San Francisco Chronicle.

51

And it's written more from the point of view, as you will see when I read it, that we Californians were right in the first place, with our New Age religion and all of our freakisms here in San Francisco.

Now we know San Francisco is confused, don't we? All you have to do is drive in San Francisco, I mean you know that. Here, let's go to Revelation 17, and we have understood, and I have said for quite a while which is nothing to my credit, you know—If I believe something is in the Bible and then I say this is going to happen because it's in the Bible, now it is nothing to my credit, you understand that. So I am not going to be like some ministers and stand up and say, "See, I am great. I told you this years ago. So therefore, you better believe me because I said this years ago." No, that's not the case. God had this in the Bible before any of us were here. So if I come along after the scene and understand it, and God's Spirit leads us to understand it (that this is correct) and then I say, "Hey, according to the Bible let's look and see that this is going to happen in the future." And lo, and behold, it does happen in the future—that's because the Word of God is true and not that I as a person am anything special. Now with that caveat, Revelation 17, and you know what it is there, it is the great whore, verse 5, that is called "...MYSTERY, BABYLON THE GREAT, THE MOTHER OF THE HARLOTS AND OF THE ABOMINATIONS OF THE EARTH." As it should read.

Now, all religions, all modern day religions are resurrections of the [ancient] Babylonian worship system that has been in Babylon from time immemorial under different guises and different names and different whatever you want to call it.

Now then, Satan has never changed in his desire to corrupt the whole world, has he? No. But what he has to do, he has to make the old look new, so he has dressed up his lady with new clothing. But then some of them are really happy that it's the old lady in new clothing, because they still believe in the old lady. See, so now they are able to believe anything they want to believe, and what is it that we have said? We have said that the Catholic Church will probably umbrella all of these under their <u>hierarchy</u>.

Let me read you this: "New religious movements are finding fertile ground in Europe where low church attendance and a changing world order has led to a search for spiritual alternatives. There are several indications that California is no longer the undisputed Mecca of the new and unusual." Hooray, finally, good—the land of fruits and nuts and they tilted the whole U. S. and they all rolled out here to California. "When the Berlin Wall came down, the first encounter many East Germans had with the West was provided by the Church of Scientology." How many know what the Church of Scientology is? Yes, L. Ron Hubbard and the book *Dianetics*, and you see it advertised all the time on television. That's the book that first came out that is this: I'm OK, You're OK—which sounds <u>great,</u> but it is: I accept myself with all my perversions that I have and I accept yourself with all the perversions that you have, so then, therefore, I'm OK, and you're OK—which is the same philosophy that we are having today in acceptance of all of the evil abominations under the sun under the guise that you cannot discriminate, right? Right. [Continuing with article]: "And they posted staff members at the wall to hand out free German language copies of *Dianetics*." Well now, after being under Communism for so long, this sounds great! You see, so the way that Satan sets something up to do. What he wants is maybe [to] destroy something old, but then what he brings in as the new is really something that is older than what he destroyed that was old, so he can still get you. So that's what they are doing.

Dianetics—What does *Dianetics* mean anyway? [Continuing with article]:"In the Swiss town of Dodesville violent demonstrations broke out when a spiritualist group predicted the end of the world and nothing happened." So what's new? Look when the end of the world is going to come, all you need to do is read Revelation 16, it is not going to be some little flash in the pan; it's going to shake the whole world. (The word Dianetics is not in the little 40,000-words handbook dictionary that you can carry in your purse. We just found that out.) [Continuing with article]: "Holistic healing centers are springing up across Poland. There are about fifty New Age magazines in England, many of them targeting Neo-Pagans." There are people who say, "I want to be Pagan." Can you believe that?

The comment was made that there is a new bumper sticker out that says... *Born Again Pagan.* Now what is a born again Pagan? Let's think about this for a minute. What is a born again Pagan? It's a new philosophy. Somebody's tapped into the spirit world. Bob? [his comments are not heard] Someone's rediscovered the old teaching, right—and tapped into the spiritual power of Satan. Did they have a spiritual experience? Yes! Sure they did. The comment was made that Dianetics is trying to get a lot of the...I don't think trying to, I think they already have a lot of the actors and actresses and musicians and, you know, all that sort of thing and then they control them by fear, and that's the way Satan always does. He says, "Try a little, you'll like it." Then after you're hooked he says, "How dare you."

All right let's read on in this article because this is really very revealing. "Neo-Pagans—In Italy the motherland of Roman Catholic Church and it is abuzz with the revival of Renaissance magic and occultism with some two hundred esoteric groups operating." Now what does the word Esoteric mean? Esoteric means that it is held within a small secret group. What is Exoteric? [It is] something that everybody shares in and knows.

Now the reason the Catholics are going to take hold of this officially as a church, is because the exoteric, the outer knowledge that they give to the world appears to be biblical. The esoteric, the inner knowledge that the hierarchy knows is Satanism. That's how all of these now then can communicate.

Now what Satan is going to do, he is going to go, "Voila!" and everybody is going to believe the same thing—what a great and marvelous thing, and the Pope will have miracles, and all the New Agers will fall, bang, right in line.

So these esoteric groups have inner secret rituals that they perform, many of them being what—black magic, yes, they are all black magic one way or the other. I talked to a man the other day—he says he works with this woman who is very religious, but she says she is a witch and worships the earth. I said, "That's true." Human sacrifices—that's correct.

" 'Europe...' " quoting now, " '...has become the growth market for the new religious movement,' said Gordon Melton, Director of the Center for the Study of American Religion in Santa Barbara. Gurus who settled in America and built a movement here are now expanding into Europe at the same time,' Melton added, 'many of Europe's burgeoning occult sects and Neo-Pagan movements are not exotic American transplants, but native to Europe. Many came to believe that the new religions of Europe resulted from a migration eastward across the Atlantic to California,' said Melton, who has spent the past few years examining the development of new religions in Europe. He argued that the modern occult revival was not created by Americans, but by such spiritual leaders as the Austrian Franz Messmer 1733–1815, Emanuel Swedenborg of Sweden 1688–1772, Louie Claudeseine Martin of France 1743–1803, and Britain's Allister Crowley 1875–1947.

"Melton, who brought about sixty scholars from around the world last week to the Solvang Holiday Inn Resort near Santa Barbara..." (which is one of the nicer places of the world, you see) "...For the Fifth Annual International Conference on New Religions said, 'Europe has at least three times as many new religious groups per capita as the United States.

The Maharishi Mahash Yoga, the Indian guru who founded the Transcendental Meditation...' " Whose guru was he—the Beatles, yes, correct—where did they get the inspiration for their music then, huh?

And remember the series I did what, about four years ago, three years ago, I don't expect you to remember it, but the one we did on the Catholic Church in transition? Remember the book written by Malachi Martin, where he was lamenting the fact that the New Age religion was taking over Catholicism, still is and will continue to do so—how he pointed out that at the turn of the century that they had this international religious symposium and they brought in this Indian guru and they found so many things of Hindu religion that were so much like so-called Christianity, that they couldn't believe it, and that's when all of this really started taking hold in America. You see? Well, Satan is going to bring it all back.

"And an infamous Indian guru, the late Begawan..." I like that name "Begawan Sheri Rashi Rashni". Who is he? He is the one who had the sex cult up there in Oregon, and they finally ran him out of town, remember that? His followers were so gracious that he had thirty Rolls Royce. He died at the wonderful old age of 51 from spiritual and sexual exhaustion. That's what that religion is.

Continuing now, " 'There can be no doubt that in Europe in 1991 there is taking place a comprehensive religious change,' " and he says that 'the religious world view in Europe is subtly shifting from Christianity to a westernized version of Buddhism and Hinduism. Most Europeans are not formally converting to new religious faiths,' he stressed, 'But their New World view is shifting away from one grounded in Christian teaching (i.e. the Bible) to that of these religions.' At a three-day conference some European scholars in attendance described the view as New Age and see it as an outgrowth of the hippie culture of San Francisco's Haight-Ashbury and the human potential movement of the sixties with the Eslon Institution at Big Sur as the mother church.' " Okay, I won't read the rest of it, but it goes on saying here "We're about five to ten years behind the U.S. in the reviving of these things."

Watch, it is in every TV program you will see, either robotism or reincarnation and, by the way, Mormonism is just another version of reincarnationism. You will see things mentioned on TV programs such as Karma. Have you ever heard that mentioned? Karma or fate. What is Karma? Karma is another word for reincarnation and that the gods have control over you, and the great god of the Indians who is it, Krishna? Is that it? A substitute name for Christ. Krishna, Jesus Christ—isn't that something? He says, "It doesn't matter what god you worship because any of the gods that you are worshipping, you are really worshipping me." Now if you want to know the results of that kind of religion, just look at India.

Now that all gets down to one of the reasons why I have been translating 1 John. I won't get into it today, but because at that time there was a tremendous movement against the truth, which we have today. There is a tremendous movement against the truth in the Bible. So what did John say was the thing that was one of the ways that we know that we are doing the truth? By keeping His Commandments. Let's go to 1 John 3 for just a minute. There are two important things, two important things that we are to remember concerning our behavior. What are the two important things that we are to do, summarized in a summary? Okay, actually there are three important things that we need to do, and we find those right here in 1 John. 1 John 3:1, it says, "Behold!..." I couldn't find a more adequate word than *behold* because in the Greek it really means *See, pay attention, look*. That's what behold means. You can't translate it that way, I mean you would soon have so many words you would never get through the verse. So I just used behold, but then I was stuck on "what manner of love" manner, kind, and I really researched the word out and I translated it "Behold, what *glorious* love" and that's what it means. It's a very highly exuberant expression of this, you see, "…the Father has given to us, that we should be called the children of God:" That is a glorious love. We understand that. The children—the word there for sons is *Teknon* which means *children* and should not be translated sons, so that all you women know that God is not slighting you in a masculine put-down of the female gender, okay? God made women; God made men. Enough said on that. "…For this very reason, the world does not know us…" or is not knowing us, or does not comprehend us "…because it did not know Him."

Now let's go to 1 John 5. So the first thing is: the love of God to us and our love back to God—Number 1 absolutely, importantly Number 1. Numbers 2 and 3 we find right here, 1 John 5:2: "By this…" now that expression is used throughout here and I was really laboring over this because it is an expression in the Greek and it's pronounced *en touto* which means *by this* and then what is understood by that expression must be supplied in English. It's not supplied in the Greek but the thought is there in the Greek. But in the English, it's not there, so they translated it *herein, hereby, therein* which in this case I said, I think I had it, "In this or by this…" I think I translated it "…one standard, one method, one way…" I think it is I did it here, "by this *standard* we know that we love the children of God…" Now why does John stress this? It's in relation to the Commandments, exactly correct, but it goes one step further. Why does he stress this? Let's look at the question the other way around, because they were having trouble in the New Testament church then. What happens when there is strife in the church? There is division, and what is the first thing the division does? [It] allows Satan to come in that's correct. What is another thing that it does on a more personal level? Destroys love. Now hold your place right here.

Let's go back to John 13:34 and John reiterates this Commandment time and time and time and time again. Verse 34: "A new commandment I give to you: that you love one another…" Now this is in a command sense. This is a command! Okay, and it means be loving. (Comment was made he heard a Presbyterian minister say that there are now eleven commandments because the word commandment is there.) Well, you could probably go through on different things and actually have more than ten, you see, but you have to also keep in mind Matthew 22:37-40 which is: "the first commandment is love God with all your heart and mind and soul and being. The second one is to love your neighbor as yourself, and on these two hang all the law and prophets." [Paraphrased.] You see, all the law and the prophets, everything hangs on those two, but here is a new commandment especially given for brethren. Why is this important? Because we have all been beaten up enough by the world, God wants us to quit beating up on each other in the church, okay? It's that basic and it's that simple—to love each other.

So he says, "A new command I give to you, That you love one another;" and He gives the standard "…as I have loved you, that you also love one another. By this shall all know…" who all, the whole world? Well, if the world doesn't know us, how is it going to know? The *all know* means: all of those in the church. This is a reverifying thing with God's Spirit to us. That's why it's so difficult when you have a church that gradually becomes so unloving that every little problem or big problem that a person may have, now makes you cannon fodder and a target. That's not what God wants it to be. You see that's why it's very, very important. So what He is stressing here in 1 John 5 is this, he says, "By this shall everyone know that you are My disciples—if you love one another" (John 13:35). And it is something that you have to keep working at—something you have to really be diligent at.

Now I know from experience, and you ought to know for experience, those of you who are married, that marital love has its ups and downs. And it has its high points and it

55

has its low points, and there are times when there are more lower points than there are higher points! And that's just the way that it is. So it doesn't mean that, necessarily, that you've got to be on this super plane of high love all of the time—it doesn't mean that, because love sticks in there even in the low times and even in the down times and even in the bad times, sure. Even in marital love, even Paul said the older women teach the younger women to love their husbands. Love is not this something magical thing that happens like it is portrayed in the world and now everything is happy from there on. For example: No woman knows the pain of childbirth until she has a child, correct? So there are certain things that you never know until you experience them. Lots of times the down points we get even in the church and in married life, both, are so that we appreciate what is right when we come around to doing what is right in loving each other, and then we treasure that. But the first thing that Satan is going to do in a church is, he is going to get in there and start casting doubt, and start cutting down love.

So back to 1 John 5:2, so he is giving us our bearings—where we need to go, what we need to do, how we need to head, because one of the first things that happens after you start this kind of thing with brethren is that you start taking away from keeping the Commandments of God. Isn't that true? [It] always happens—that's a tactic. 1 John 5:2: "By this *standard* we know that we love the children of God: when we love God and keep His commandments." The two go hand-in-hand, you cannot say you love God and [yet] break His Commandments. You cannot say you keep the Commandments if you don't love God. They go hand-in-hand, it's just like water. Okay, now I've got [a bottle] here, I was thirsty—I don't know where they came up with that name, but it's an interesting name; it says Cobb Mountain. (Oh thank you, we have an expert on-hand who says this is actually a geographical place near Napa called Cobb Mountain. So it comes from the spring at Cobb Mountain. Thank you. Now we know, the mystery is removed.) I have in my hands here, some water. What does water do? [It] quenches thirst, waters, causes things to grow, like God's spirit, cleans you, you bathe in it. What else? It's so vital to life that you could say it's life itself, especially if you're an Arab and you live in the desert. You can have all that oil, but you can't drink it, you've got to have the water, right? And what is the Mohammedan's view of heaven—an oasis where there is lots of water. What is coming out of the throne of God, literally, in Revelation 22, but the pure rivers of living water, yes. But what makes up water? Hydrogen and oxygen, true? Separate hydrogen and separate oxygen are the most inflammable things in the world, right?

I saw a report, as I mentioned the other day, on blimps and Zeppelins. Remember the German Von Hindenburg Zeppelin, the last one that flew over here? Because the Nazi government took over the finalizing and building of the Von Hindenburg, and it was owned by the Nazi party at that time, there was an embargo on selling helium to Germany because of the government. Now helium is different than hydrogen, it's non- flammable, it can burn, but it's not dangerous. So they decided that since they couldn't get the helium from the U. S. which was the only place in the world to get it at that time, that they would put the hydrogen gas into the Von Hindenburg. Well, I don't have to tell you the rest. When they got here it was just after an electrical storm and guess what, boom, it caught fire and it was a miracle that 65 people survived. Today that's nothing in the way of a tragedy, but at that time they thought it was one of the greatest tragedies in the world.

The point is: when you have the right proportion of hydrogen and oxygen, you have something which will put out fires, but if you have them separately and not together in the right combination, you can blow things apart. So that's a very good analogy as to what will happen if you try loving brethren without keeping the Commandments or try keeping the Commandments and don't love the brethren and don't love God. You've got the wrong mix and it's going to blow up! And we have all experienced little and big booms haven't we, because of that very factor.

So He's stressing here something that is absolutely and vitally important. He says, in 1 John 5:3: "For this is the love of God: that we keep His commandments; and His commandments are not burdensome." They are not grievous, not burdensome. So that is an absolutely basic, fundamental thing.

Now, we have had some people who have said that… let's look at it this way: Which Commandments do people not like most of all? Let's go to Romans 8, and let's see something about the carnal mind and we all know this. (Oh, there was an article in the paper this morning, quite a long one about deception, how that it's inherent in all human beings and all human beings must be deceptive to survive.) Now does that sound a little biblical? "The heart is deceitful above all things and desperately wicked." That's the best of our hearts. Here is why. Romans 8:7: "Because the carnal mind…" that is the mind devoid of the Spirit of God "… *is* enmity against God…" that's the same word for enemy, e-n-m-i-t-y, All you have to do is just substitute the i-t and put an e in there and you have enemy, and it's the same in the Greek. "…For it is not subject to the law of God; neither indeed can it *be*." So when you have religious people in the world, I don't care what religion that they are of, but let's look at some of those who claim they are Christians. What two Commandments do they always disagree with…actually there are three, but basically two and the third one is subject to the second one. Now they may be nice people. They may be kind people. They may be what the society would say would be model citizens, but what is it that they always do not agree to? Sabbath—and what is the other one? Idols—[Commandments] Two and Four.

Now what is the third one then, subject to the second one, the Sabbath? The Holy Days. Now there are some people who say, "God, I believe I ought to keep the Sabbath, but not the holy days." And I listened to this tape, I think I mentioned it last week, from this Protestant minister who said that, "Since Jesus was resurrected on Sunday, and since Pentecost is on Sunday, therefore, I keep Sunday. Case over and done, case closed." Now does he have an open mind? No. He said also, "And I don't want to hear any more of this Sabbath bit. Because you are not to go out and just lay around and be lazy and stay in your bed all day Saturday." So guess what he knows, he knows something doesn't he? He knows which day is the seventh day, doesn't he? Yes, he does.

Now let's go to Genesis 2, because this becomes very important and I have never heard this explained this way, okay? Who was the Sabbath made for? You all said it was made for man. Where do you find that scripture? Yes, Mark 2:27 that is correct and 28. Now this minister quoted here, Genesis the second chapter and I have never heard it this way. Let me read it to you, because he forgot his New Testament, he forgot what Jesus said about the Sabbath that He was Lord of the Sabbath. Genesis 2:1: "Thus the heavens and the earth were finished, and all the host of them. And on the seventh day God ended his work which he had made; and he rested on the seventh day from all his work which he had made. And God blessed the seventh day, and sanctified it: because that in it he had rested from all his work which God created and made." Therefore the Sabbath was made for God. Now of all of the years I've been in the church and all of the Sabbath arguments I've heard, you know, not to make fun of anyone who has false teeth because you need them, but if I had false teeth they would have fallen right out of my head. That's how shocking it was to me. Can you believe that it was only made for God?

Now, then we go to Exodus 20, we don't have to go there, we ought to have all of that memorized, right? Why are we to remember the Sabbath? To keep it Holy. Why? That's right: He set it apart right here, and why? Because God is Holy. Let's go to Exodus 20. Remember what we went through here recently, Exodus 16, that God gave them the Sabbath day so therefore it is said, which we will read in a minute, that it was given to them for a sign. And the Catholics later on, as you find in this book by Samuele Bacchiocchi con-

57

cerning the enmity between Christians and Jews when Sunday worship was coming [into the early Church]. And I want you to understand that when John was writing the Epistle of 1 John, what was starting to come into vogue? <u>Sunday</u> <u>worship</u> was starting to come into vogue!

Now, Exodus 20, God gave them the Sabbath. Before we get to Exodus 20, let me finish the thought here. In the book *Anti-Semitism or Anti-Judaism and the Origin of Sunday* those who were the initiators of Sunday-keeping which later became the Catholic Church said that God cursed the Jews with the Sabbath to set them aside for punishment. Isn't that something? Now God doesn't say anything about that here in Exodus 20. He says, "Remember the Sabbath to keep it holy." And of course they just had the lesson of getting it with the manna. "Six days shall labor be done and do all your work, But the seventh day *is* the Sabbath of the LORD…" yes, it is His, but He doesn't say that I made it for myself to rest on, did He? No, He didn't.

However, this becomes very, very important, because I know for sure that it's not going to be too long before there are going to be people we know that were keeping the Sabbath who are going to be keeping Sunday. You can be almost guaranteed of it.

Now let me finish where we got interrupted when I ran to the end [of the tape], sorry about that. Exodus 20:10: "…In it you shall not do any work, you, nor your son, nor your daughter, nor your manservant, nor your cattle nor your stranger that is within your gate:" verse 11, for this reason: "For in six days the LORD made heaven and earth, the sea, and all that in them is, and rested the seventh day: wherefore God blessed the Sabbath day, and hallowed it." For whom? For all of mankind, that's correct. Did He bless it just for Himself? Did He sanctify it for just Himself? Wherever God is and whatever God does it is Holy, correct? Moses went up on the mountain, and God said, "Take off your shoes because you are standing on holy ground." So God didn't make it [the Sabbath] for Himself.

Now let's go to Mark 2:27. I know that this is very basic, but it's something that is the very key as to why there were the problems going on in the early New Testament Church. And I still like the answer that was given when asked by a Protestant when it became obvious that this particular person was keeping the Sabbath and all of the rest on this tour to the Holy Land were keeping Sunday. They came up to this man and he was a minister that I knew and they said, "By the way, what day do you keep?". And his answer was, "The same day Jesus did. What day do you keep?" Now you cannot argue with that can you? Remember that if someone ever corners you and asks you, "What day do you keep?" You just tell them, "Well, I keep the same day that Jesus kept. What day do you keep?"

Now, here is why, verse 27 of Mark 2, again, this we should memorize. " And He said to them, 'The Sabbath was made for man…" and that means *on account of the creation of man*. That's what it means. "…*and* not man for the Sabbath; ' " and what does that phrase mean? That phrase means that man has no jurisdiction over the Sabbath. That's what it means. "Therefore, the Son of man is Lord even of the Sabbath." Now what is this telling us? Very simple—Jesus is LORD of the Sabbath, so therefore which day is the LORD's Day if Jesus Christ is your LORD, which day is the LORD's day—<u>the</u> <u>Sabbath</u>. Right? It's got to be. It can't be anything else.

Now Jesus said in John 14, which we covered recently so I won't belabor the point, that "…if you are loving me, you are keeping my sayings, my words." [Paraphrased.] Did Jesus say this? Yes, He did. Now if, and let's take this a little bit further, if the Sabbath was made for a curse to put on the Jews, then why didn't Jesus when He brought the New Covenant, reveal that and relieve us from that curse? He didn't because that is not a true statement, you see? It is not a curse.

Now, let's look at a couple of other things here concerning this. There are several other places we can go to. Let's go to Ezekiel. Ezekiel 20 is a very instructive verse, set of verses. Let's ask the question: When has obedience to God ever been a curse? Nowhere. Now obedience to God may cost you your life, in some cases it's going to be martyrdom, but is that a curse, or is that a witness? It is a witness. What does the curse come from? Not keeping it—Deuteronomy 28. You read Deuteronomy 28, what does it say? It says, "If you will, indeed, listen to my voice and hearken to my commandments, and do all of that which I say, blessed shall you be in the city, in the country, in the fruit of your womb, in your basket, in your store, and fighting your enemies and all those things: But if you will not listen and will not keep my commandments, cursed shall you be [paraphrased]." So the curse comes not from obedience but from <u>disobedience</u>, correct.

Here in Ezekiel 20, it talks about what God did for the children of Israel. Verse 1. Let's get the scene before we go through some of the verses. "And it came to pass in the seventh year, in the fifth *month*, the tenth *day* of the month, *that* certain of the elders of Israel came to enquire of the LORD, and sat before me. Then came the word of the LORD unto me, saying, Son of man, speak unto the elders of Israel, and say unto them, Thus saith the Lord GOD; Are you come to enquire of me?" (Ezekiel 20:1-3). Now remember that they were in captivity. They were in this place of captivity. Why were they in captivity? Disobedience, that's correct. So now they are wanting to come to God and say to God, "Now God, <u>why</u> am I in this captivity?" So God answered and said, "…Are you come to enquire of me? *As I* live, says the Lord GOD, I will not be enquired of you." In other words, what are you going to do to come and question God? "Will you judge them, son of man, will you judge *them*? Cause them to know the abominations of their fathers; And say unto them, Thus says the Lord GOD; In the day when I chose Israel and lifted up mine hand to the seed of the house of Jacob, and made myself known to them in the land of Egypt, when I lifted up mine hand unto them, saying, I *am* the LORD your God;" (Ezekiel 20:4-6).

I want to ask you a question: If God would have promised to give the blessing that He promised to give to Abraham, if it would have been through someone other than Abraham and someone else's descendants; (Okay, this is a hypothetical question) which laws do you think that God would have given to them? <u>The</u> <u>same</u> <u>ones</u>! <u>Yes</u>! Why? Because they came from God, right? What does it say of God in the person of Jesus Christ in Hebrews 13:8. "<u>Jesus</u> <u>Christ</u> *is* <u>the</u> <u>same</u> <u>yesterday,</u> <u>and</u> <u>today,</u> <u>and</u> <u>forever.</u>" So therefore, He would have given them <u>exactly</u> <u>the</u> <u>same</u> <u>laws</u>. And what did He tell them through Jeremiah the Prophet? He said, "You go tell those sinning children of Israel that had I gone to some other nation, they would have kept my laws until now. But unfortunately I'm stuck with these rebellious children." [Paraphrased.] Because God promised, once you promise, you can't get away from it, right? Yes. He says, "But Israel has changed from Me being their God, to serving all of these idols." So God really indicted His people didn't He? Isn't that something? Look at the Indians in India, I mean we could stand up here and say, "Boy look at all these Hindus. What a mess their religion is, which is true." But God is saying, "Had I gone to those people, they wouldn't have done to Me what you have done to Me." So He made it known.

Ezekiel 20:6: "In the day *that* I lifted up mine hand unto them, to bring them forth out of the land of Egypt into a land that I had espied for them, flowing with milk and honey, which *is* the glory of all lands: Then I said to them, Cast away every man the abominations of his eyes, and defile not yourselves with the idols of Egypt: I *am* the LORD your God." So right when God was getting the Ten Commandments, guess what they did. You know what they did, they made the golden calf, worshipped it, had a great sex orgy there, the whole thing—I mean just like one of our rock concerts that we have today. All right, no different, same thing going on (Ezekiel 20:6-7).

Then we come down here to verse 10: "Wherefore I caused them to go forth out of the land of Egypt, and brought them into the wilderness. And I gave them my statutes, and shewed them my judgments, which *if* a man do, he shall even live in them. Moreover also I gave them my sabbaths…" plural, sign there are the holy days involved. Now you see there are some people who are good enough to accept Jesus, to accept the Sabbath, but not accept the holy days. So you see you are confronted with a problem in that particular case. Now they try and doctrinally somehow show that these are tied in with the sacrifices, but they had sacrifices on every day, so the argument of sacrifices being on the holy days [and] whether they ought to keep the holy days or not or the Sabbath or not is really having no bearing whatsoever to do on the Sabbath or the holy days—none whatsoever.

So He gave the "…Sabbaths as a sign between me and them, that they might know that I *am* the LORD that does sanctify them." Okay, in the next verse it says, "But the house of Israel rebelled against me in the wilderness: they walked not in my statutes, and they despised my judgments, which *if* a man do, he shall even live in them; and my sabbaths they greatly polluted:" So then He poured out His fury (Ezekiel 20:10-13).

Now if God is merciful, which He is, anybody doubt that God is merciful? And if God gave the Sabbath for a curse, which some people believe that He did, don't you think that God being merciful would remove that curse and tell them about another day? Wouldn't that make sense? For those of you who believe in logic, is that not logical? Yes, it is. So they despised God's way. Then He even said to their children after He took care of them in the wilderness, you know, and you saw all of them dying. Then He said to them <u>again</u>, verse 20: "…Hallow my sabbaths; and they shall be a sign between me and you, that you may know that I *am* the LORD your God." So <u>they</u> rebelled.

Now then, we come to Chapter 22 and we find that the priests are in on this, the prophets are in on this. You know the problem is not with ordinary people as much as it is with the leaders.

A person comes to a minister, maybe a Protestant minister, and says, "Boy, you know Pastor, I've been reading my Bible and you know, I think that we ought to keep the seventh day. And I really see there in Jeremiah 10 that it's also telling us not to have Christmas trees. And in Ezekiel 7 that we are not to have hot cross buns and all this Easter stuff, and furthermore, I went to the library and looked it up in the encyclopedia and those things are Pagan. Now what do you think?" [The minister might answer] "Well now, Jesus has delivered us from those things. We don't have to keep them and besides we have Christianized Christmas and we have Christianized Easter so now it's all okay." So the person, not wanting to offend the minister, the minister after all is what? He is the expert, right? So they take his word. But notice what God says here in Ezekiel 22:25. It's like this one minister who said, "Well about Saturday, we're not to sleep all day Saturday." Okay, well, we're not. If any of you are sleeping here, wake up. I hope you're not, no you're not. It's not too hot. There are times when you feel like you need to.

"*There is* a conspiracy…" and that's a nasty word today. Anyone who talks about a conspiracy, you're mentally off because you're imagining something. Listen, who is the greatest conspirator in history? Satan the Devil. Is he conspiring, is he working? Yes. Who does he want to get? If he gets one minister then he gets how many hundreds or thousands of people? "*There is* a conspiracy of her prophets in the midst thereof, like a roaring lion devouring the prey, they have devoured souls…" Now that's especially vivid in my mind because I just saw one of these wild, wild, documentaries, you know, and it showed the lions, and boy, I tell you those lions—they can jump on top of a zebra or a wildebeest and one big gash right on the back of the neck, you know, and that's it. And then they devour them—the whole pride of lions comes in and you talk about table manners boy, you talk about conversation around the table. They are fighting, tearing and the poor little kids [cubs] have got to get in there and try and get something. Well just picture that with these ministers. That's what they are <u>spiritually</u> <u>doing</u> <u>to</u> <u>people</u>! And they come and say, "Oh Mr. Minister I read my Bible and it looks like we ought to keep the seventh day." "Which day is the seventh day?" Conspiracy. "…They have devoured souls; they have taken the treasure and precious things; they have made many widows in the midst thereof. Her priests have violated my law, and have profaned my holy things; they have put no difference between the holy and profane…" Who made the difference between holy and profane? God did, He is the one. That's why the Sabbath is Holy, because God made it Holy. That's why the days that we keep are called *Holy Days* because they are days that God made Holy.

So they violated, "…they haven't shown any difference between the holy and profane, neither have they shewed *difference* between the unclean and the clean…" And just on the way up I was listening to the news and guess what they were saying, cholera has spread because of unclean cooks serving unclean food, namely shrimp and clams and those unclean things that should not be eaten which God said, "Don't eat them." Not because He wants to take some tidbits away from you that you may like, but because there are certain things in these animals that may make you sick, may make you prone to disease, so later you are going to have problems. So they "…have hid their eyes from my sabbaths, and I am profaned among them." So that becomes important. Now I know this is really basic, but I haven't gotten to the point that I want to get to yet.

If you find yourself in this terrible and horrible condition that you are trying to find God, now there are a lot of people out there trying to find God, right? Some people say, "Well, if God would show me a sign, I would believe Him." Isn't that what they said to Jesus, and isn't that what people say today? "If I could see God, I would believe Him." There is a man who was a minister of God. Before he was a minister he was a quadriplegic. (This is an experience within the Church of God now.) And he was paralyzed from the neck down. When he came to the knowledge of the truth and felt he had faith that God would heal him, he called for the elders of the church and was anointed. Within ten days he was walking. It was such an unusual thing that even the Veterans Administration, when he went to say, "My conscience is overloading me, I cannot bear it. God has healed me. I am walking. Please take me off of disability…" they said, "We don't believe it; we are not going to take you off disability." He said, "Okay, my conscience is clean, I can receive my check every month and it's clean. I tried." And he tried two or three times to do that. And he was a pretty powerful minister. He was always in pain even though he had this and he would get around and he would still limp and things like that, and he was a very friendly and gregarious, outgoing man and could really speak in power, and sing and lead songs—a tremendous, fantastic person! He would tell you about how God healed him. Furthermore, he married the nurse that was taking care of him. Now then, because of men within the church, and because of difficulties that he had, now he doesn't believe in keeping the Sabbath, when God led him to it, or necessarily the holy days.

So if someone asks you the question: Give me a sign O God and how can I find you? God has already given the sign and He has already given the thing that you can do. You don't have to be a cripple to find God or to see the sign. What is that sign—<u>the</u> Sabbath, <u>Yes</u>! And why is it such a fantastic sign, because in spite of all of the calendar manipulations by men, the seventh day on the calendar on your wall today, unless it's been changed by some modernists as it has in some areas of the country and Europe, what day is the seventh day of the week—Saturday, The Sabbath. You can verify that by asking any Jew who still keeps the Sabbath. You can verify that by asking any Protestant which day is the first day of the week—It's the day after the Sabbath, right? [There is] No doubt. So there is the miracle and there is the sign.

Now, what if you <u>really</u> want to get right with God? Let's go to Isaiah 56:1: "Thus says the LORD, Keep judgment, and do justice..." I talked to a man the other day and he says, "Boy, the first place to begin to solve all the political problems is to pass a law, if you could, if you think that would be possible, to outlaw all politicians from being attorneys as professionals" (Laughter). Sounds like a good thing, but you see it won't work. That's why God has to destroy the system because you can't repair it. God can repair an individual life, but He is not going to repair the system, He is going to destroy it. So there is no justice, there is no judgment. Now notice continuing, "...for my salvation *is* near to come..." When is God's salvation coming—when Christ returns, exactly right. Are we close to that? We can also say when Christ came the first time too, right? Yes. "...And my righteousness to be revealed." And this is a prophecy then for the end time. Anyone at the end time who wants to get right with God, who wants to draw close to God, who wants to serve God, here is what God says, "Blessed..." not cursed "...*is* the one..." because man there is in the general sense of a human being "...*that* does this..." Now that's a pretty specific thing isn't it, huh? "...*That* does this, and the son of man *that* lays hold on it;" that takes a hold of this thing as something to do. "...That he keeps the Sabbath from polluting it, and is keeping his hand from doing any evil" (Isaiah 56:1-2).

Now then the question comes up: What if he is not an Israelite or a Jew? Because the argument is always made, "Well, the Sabbath is for the Jews, but Sunday is for the stranger or the Gentile" and that is a name that the Jews have coined which is really a misnomer and it should be *the nations*. Let's go on, verse 3: "Neither let the son of the stranger..." gentile, someone other than an Israelite, "...that has joined himself to the LORD, speak, saying The LORD has utterly separated me from His people: Neither let the eunuch say, Behold, I *am* a dry tree." That is: "God, why can't I have any kids?" Verse 4: "...Thus says the LORD unto the eunuchs that keep my sabbaths..." Now we have the holy days involved here too, don't we, huh? "...that keep them.." Now I don't know what more you can do except look at that, "that is keeping..."

Mr. Minister, which day should we keep? I heard one minister say when it was brought up to him that we shouldn't keep Christmas. He said, "Look, I'll put on the beard, and the Santa Claus suit if it's going to bring more people into this church." I mean think about that for a minute. Got all the priorities totally backward. The Bible says what if you gain the whole world, but lose your soul? The wicked, though they walk hand-in-hand, are all going to fall. God says, "that you keep my sabbaths, ... and choose *the things* that please me, and take hold of my covenant" which is a prophecy of what—<u>the New Covenant</u>, Yes! Isn't that something? (Isaiah 56:3-4).

Now, let's go to 1 John 3. Hold your place here in Isaiah because we'll be back in that vicinity again. You know sometimes we get so bogged down in technical things and sometimes we get so bogged down in detailed, interesting doctrine in teaching which we can learn, because we've been in the church a long time and we need to learn those things, but you know it's absolutely amazing and fantastic how you can go back to a basic thing like the Sabbath which is so vitally, vitally, important and ask the question: Is that important for me to return to God? Yes. Especially in light of the situation that, you know, the sermon I gave concerning the Sardis Church and Laodicean Church and things like that, you see, because there are a lot of people out there that just feel justified, because they're hurt by a man, to give up on God. No one is justified to give up on God because they are hurt by a man. Listen, human beings are going to hurt you over and over and over and over again, why, because they are human beings—don't be surprised. Even the best intentions sometimes hurt people. Why, because they are misunderstood. And if you're wanting to be hurt, you're going to be hurt. If you are looking to be hurt, it's going to come, but don't let it take you away from God.

Now 1 John 3:22, I want you to notice the similarity between this verse and what we just read in Isaiah 56. Verse 22: "And whatever we may ask we receive from Him, be-cause…" here is the cause "…we keep his commandments, and practice…" and that means *practice* "…those things that are pleasing in His sight." Now hold your place here and go back to Isaiah 56 and look at that verse again. Isaiah 56:4: "…Thus says the LORD unto the eunuchs that keep my sabbaths, and choose *the things* that please me, and take hold of my covenant" not too much different is it? Why was Jesus always faithful? Yes, He said, "I always do those things that please God." Did Jesus keep the Sabbath? Yes, He kept the Sabbath. Did that please God? Yes, that pleased God.

Back here in Isaiah 56—that's amazing isn't it? Now let's continue on verse 4, we just read it, now verse 5: "Even unto them will I give in my house…" which is the house of God—the church. "…And within my walls a place and a name better than of sons and of daughters…" Now what did we just read concerning one of the churches of God? Behold I will give you a new name which no man knows, but he who receives it, right? So there it is right there, New Testament doctrine. "… I will give them an everlasting name, that shall not be cut off. Also the sons of the stranger, that join themselves to the LORD, to serve him, and to love the name of the LORD, to be his servants, every one that is keeping the sabbath from polluting it, and is taking hold of my covenant. Even those will I bring…" where, what was the sermon topic for Pentecost? Come to the mountain, right? "Even them will I bring to my holy mountain, and make them joyful in my house of prayer…" then it says some burnt of-ferings and so forth, that's when they had them, but now we have the offerings—what are the offerings that we have? They are offerings of praise, the offerings of thanksgiving, the offerings of glory to God through our prayers, through our life because we worship Him in spirit and in truth (Isaiah 56:4-7).

Now, let's come over to Isaiah 58:1 and God is now talking to the children of Israel. Now He's got something to say to them. He just talked to all the Gentiles, right, in Isaiah 56. Now let's go on to Isaiah 58. Now He is talking to the children of Jacob, verse 1: "Cry aloud, spare not, lift up your voice like a trumpet, and show my people their transgression, and the house of Jacob their sins." What were they? Let's go clear back to the first chapter. Hold your place here, because we'll be there. Now here is a famous Scripture that a lot of people turn to to say that we should not keep the Sabbath. Now notice Isaiah 1: 14: "Your new moons and your appointed feasts my soul hates…" that's right after He said in verse 13, "Bring no more vain oblations; incense is an abomination unto me; the new moons and sab-baths, the calling of assemblies, I cannot away with; *it is* iniquity, even the solemn meeting."

Question, very basic simple question: Whose sabbaths, whose new moons, whose feast days—God's or theirs—theirs, right? So when the Protestants say, "My sabbath is Sunday, what is he saying? His sabbath—what does God say about their sabbath? He says, "My soul hates…" I will remember this as long as I live. I had the unusual duty of being the minister in Salt Lake City which was the heart of Mormon land, and so I was driving, and this was when I first moved there, and I was driving down this road and here is the sign "Remember the Sabbath to keep it Holy—See you in church on Sunday." I almost wrecked the car (Laughter). This is the Sabbath that God hates, but that's how people…they take the name that God has and [they] put it on their days. That's what he hates. This has nothing to do with God's Sabbaths.

Now let's ask one more question, because people are very mentally astute today: Can a person keep the seventh-day of the week as we know it, the true Sabbath, and still be not a Sabbath to God, but a Sabbath to themselves even though it's on God's day? Yes, they can. How can they do that? Keep it their own way, add so many man-made traditions on it like the Jews do today, that the Sabbath is an absolute total burden. You know like they do in Israel if a car goes down the street, they stone it. Now which is more work, the person driving the car down the street, or the stoning of the car? Can you imagine that? Stoning a car, that's something.

Now let's go back here before we get to Isaiah 58, let's go to John 4, because here is what it has to be in worshipping God—the day is important, but what is secondary importance on that day, actually the primary importance, primary importance, but you've got to have the right day in order for this to work. John 4:20 the woman of Samaria said, "Our fathers worshipped in this mountain, but you say that the place where it is obligatory to worship is in Jerusalem. Jesus said to her, 'Woman, believe Me, the hour is coming when you shall neither in this mountain nor in Jerusalem worship the Father. You do not know what you worship. We know what we worship, for salvation is of the Jews. But the hour is coming, and now is, when the true worshippers shall worship the Father in spirit and in truth...' ". Now that's what makes the seventh-day the spiritual day to keep, when you worship the Father in spirit and in truth. " '...For the Father is indeed seeking those who worship Him in this manner. God *is* Spirit, and those who worship Him must...' " and the word there in the Greek is *ordained*, *obligatory*, *mandatory* " '...worship in spirit and in truth' " (John 4:20-24).

Now let's go back to Isaiah 58 and I hope we have enough time to finish it, I think we do. So He says, verse 1: "Cry aloud, spare not, lift up your voice like a trumpet, and show my people their transgressions, and the house of Jacob their sins." What do you need to do then? You need to repent and what—worship God in spirit and in truth. Because if you are keeping the Sabbath but you're not keeping it by loving the brethren and loving God, then you are not keeping it in spirit and in truth and worshipping God. Now we all have to grow with this more, I can't say that any of us are perfect in it. Verse 2: "Yet you seek me daily, and delight to know my ways..." and boy, nothing could be truer of Americans than this. Verse 2 is so true of Americans. "In God we trust". "We are a Christian nation". "Oh, we want to know God's Word and all this sort of thing". "...As a nation that did righteousness, and forsook not the ordinance of God: they ask of my ordinances of justice; they take delight in approaching to God. Wherefore have we fasted, *say they*, and you haven't seen? *Wherefore* have we afflicted our souls, and you take no knowledge? Behold in the day of your fast you find pleasure, and exact all your labours." There was just in the newspaper today about fasting for political things and it showed this Chavez, this labor union farmer union guy, fasting and they were, you know, depicting that and showing ... the whole thing. Verse 4: "Behold, you fast for strife and debate, and to smite with the fist of wickedness..." and then he goes on saying well, you're not going to have your voice heard on high and all this sort of thing" (Isaiah 58:1-4).

Now let's come down here to verse 13, we are running out of time so I need to get here to finish it. Here is one of the conditions if you are going to return to God. "If you turn away your foot from the sabbath..." that is walking on it polluting, trampling it, doing your own thing. "...*From* doing your own pleasure on my holy day" God's holy day. "...Call the sabbath a delight, the holy of the LORD," and of course this applies to the holy days—the same thing can apply. "...honorable; and shalt honor him not doing your own ways nor finding your own pleasure, nor speaking *your own* words; Then..." now notice all those conditions "...then, you shall delight yourself in the LORD..." And that way then no man is going to stand in the way and make you bitter or turn you from God. "...And I will cause you to ride upon the high places of the earth, and feed you with the heritage of Jacob thy father; for the mouth of the LORD has spoken *it*" (Isaiah 58:13-14).

So that's why it is so very, very, important, so it comes all right back to the very basic thing that the apostle John said, he said that if we love God and keep His Commandments, this is how we know that we know God. And so brethren I know that none of you are disbelieving in keeping the Sabbath because you're all here, but it's very important for us to know and understand what God thinks about it and what we need to do so that we can also do better than we have been doing and how that it is important and right. Okay, so the next time you hear anyone say, like I did, "Well, I keep Sunday because…" then you will know that they have chosen their own sabbath which God says, "I hate." But if you want to delight in God, keep His way, keep His Sabbath, keep His Words.

End of Sermon

Transcriber: Judith Anderson

The Sabbath—Sign of God
May 25, 1991
Scriptural References

1) Revelation 17:5

2) I John 3:1

3) I John 5:2

4) John 13:34

5) Matthew 22:37-40

6) I John 5:2-3

7) Romans 8:7

8) Genesis 2:2-3

9) Exodus 20:8-9

10) Exodus 20:10-11

11) Mark 2:27-28

12) John 14

13) Ezekiel 20:6-7, 10-13, 20

14) Ezekiel 22:25

15) Isaiah 56:1-4

16) I John 3:22

17) Isaiah 56:4-7

18) Isaiah 58:1

19) Isaiah 1:14

20) John 4:20-24

21) Isaiah 58: 1-4, 13-14

CHAPTER FIVE

Importance of the Sabbath

February 4, 1995

I want to start out by reading a couple of letters. These are quite illustrative of what I have been receiving lately as well as phone calls similar to this. This past week I talked to one minister in Texas and I am convinced, as we have said, that when you don't really stay close to God and so forth, when the difficulties and troubles come, you have no reserve at all, and you really don't know what to do. So I told him I would send a care package, and in the care package would be some information on grace. And he said to me, "Oh I gave a sermon on that one time…" and [he] gave the definition of the word. And I thought to myself, "You don't have a clue." So there will be six tapes there.

Then I got a call from a woman who said she wanted to know about the covenants, and I asked her, "Are you serious?" And she said, "Yes." I said, "Do you really want to study?" She said, "Yes." So I said, "Okay, we'll send it to you." There will be twelve tapes on that plus some other things. Because you see, many times people will go through and they will give a sermon topic, and they will answer part of a question, and assume that they have answered the whole question. So that's why we do things a little differently, we stick with it until we are done with it, which helps us all understand.

So anyway he says, "I believe you know my son. He gave me a copy of your book *Lord, What Should I Do?* We were members of Worldwide for twenty-five years." Now I wonder how many <u>thousands</u> are out there in addition to the ones who are beginning to understand, who have read the Bible on their own, and are keeping the Sabbath.

Let's look at something very important here in Mark 13 and Matthew 24. I know when I first thought about this, and when I first let it penetrate into my mind to get some of the thinking of God, rather than the thinking of men about what they think God says; because some people have said, "Well you know, we've published the gospel around the world already. They have already had their witness." But those people are long since gone and the magazine they claimed that did it, now has been reduced in circulation from 8 million, to a million and a half, and the world is still going on. But here is what it says right here, verse 10 Mark 13, it's talking about the end times. "And the gospel must first be published among all nations." What do you have in your hands? You <u>have</u> the gospel. The gospel being published in all nations refers to the Word of God. [It] does not refer to someone preaching <u>about</u> the gospel. The gospel <u>will</u> be preached in all the world, Matthew 24 tells us.

Now let's go to Hebrews 4, and let's understand something concerning the Old Testament. We're going to make this just a little bit different today. We're going to answer some of the questions that some of the difficulties people are bringing up are related in some of the things that we cover here. Hebrews 4:4, now we're going to come back to Hebrews 4 and look at it a little later because we are going to see that one of the major teachings of Jesus Christ did in fact, have to do <u>with</u> the <u>Sabbath</u> day and <u>with</u> your capacity to <u>work</u> and <u>with</u> your capacity to eat and drink, verse 2, Hebrews 4: "For truly, we have had the gospel preached *to us*, even as they also did;…" Who is he talking about? The children of Israel. So they had the gospel preached unto them in the form that God gave that to them. "…But the preaching of the word did not profit them because it was not mixed with faith in those who heard." So they had the gospel preached to them as well. What is this telling us? This is telling us that the gospel includes both what is known as the Old Testament and the New Testament, does it not? Yes, indeed it surely, surely does.

Remember several weeks ago we covered the scripture—let's go there for just a minute just to review—because I think a lot of times when someone comes along with dynamite and blows up your foundation, which is what has been happening, you need to go back and repeat some things. So let's go back and repeat some of these things. Let's go to Luke 24, and here's why the gospel was also in the Old Testament and as we know a covenant is God's arrangement or agreement with you. And in every covenant, there are always the laws of God that go right through all the covenants.

Now here Luke 24 is a very, very important section in the Scriptures. Let's pick it up here in verse 25: "Then He said to them, 'O foolish and slow of heart to believe all that the prophets have spoken:' " <u>Does</u> <u>Christ</u> <u>expect</u> <u>us</u> <u>to</u> <u>believe</u> <u>the</u> <u>prophets</u>? <u>Yes</u>, <u>absolutely</u>. Is that part of the gospel? Well, it surely is. It told an awful lot about Jesus Christ didn't it? And it's telling an awful lot about what's going to happen at the end of the world isn't it? And is that not part of preaching the gospel to the whole world? Sure it is.

He says, verse 26: "Was it not necessary for the Christ to suffer these things, and to enter into His glory? And beginning with Moses…" So you see, Moses is part of the living Word of God. Verse 27: "And beginning with Moses, and from all the prophets, he interpreted to them the things concerning Himself in all the Scriptures." So that was quite a Bible study. How would you like to have been at that Bible study where Christ <u>Himself</u> was <u>telling</u> you?

Verse 28: "And *as* they approached the village where they were going, He appeared to be going on farther. But they constrained Him, saying, 'Stay with us, for it is toward evening, and the day is declining.' And He entered in *as if* to stay with them. And it came to pass, as He sat *at the table* with them, He took the bread *and* blessed *it*, and after breaking *it*, He gave *it* to them. Then their <u>eyes</u> <u>were</u> <u>opened</u>…" and that's what has to happen with Christ, <u>your</u> <u>eyes</u> <u>must</u> <u>be</u> <u>opened</u>. That's why Judaism is so dead. As we covered several weeks ago, the fig tree was cursed from the roots up. You have to have your eyes opened and only Christ can open them. "… And they knew him…" and then what did He do? He immediately "…disappeared from them" (Luke 24:25-31).

Now if you are born again, that's what you should be able to do. So there are some people who say they are born again, and they make fun of those … what was the old test, the hatpin test? Stick yourself and see if you bleed. The better one is just walk through the wall. That will be far more convincing.

Verse 32: "And they said to one another, 'Did not our hearts burn within us as He was speaking to us on the road, while He was opening the Scriptures to us?' " And they rose up that very hour *and* returned to Jerusalem; and they found the eleven and those with them assembled together, saying, "In truth the Lord has risen! And He has appeared to Simon." Then they related the things that had happeded *to them* on the road, and how He was known of them in the breaking of the bread." Verse 36: "Now as they were telling these things, Jesus Himself stood in their midst and said to them, 'Peace *be* to you.' "

Now this is part of the glory that the disciples, especially John, wrote about where he says, "…and we beheld His glory as the only begotten Son of God." Now they saw Him transfigured on the mountain. They saw Him in His glorified form at that point, and now they see Him raised from the dead. Verse 37: "But they were terrified… and filled with fear, thinking *that* they beheld a spirit. Then He said to them, 'Why are you troubled? And why do doubts come up in your hearts?' " And we need to understand that also, today, in our day. Now they had to live through the time to see Christ killed and then resurrected from the dead. Now today people come along and try and put fear in your hearts and fear in your minds and try and manipulate things to their own use.

Now as Carl and I were talking yesterday. We talk quite often, and he's got some good things coming, and we have the publication on Grace back there all ready to go. I'm going to start working on the Sabbath publication some time right after the Passover. I've got a couple of other things I need to do before then. But he said and so I wrote it down—it's just like some of the things that Ed has said through the years. Ed said, which is true, "If you have a movement, which is where you are doing something in the name of Christ, but Christ is not there—If you have a movement, you must have a monument." And we'll add to that, a dead saint.

Carl said yesterday, "It's one thing to be moved by God to do His Will..." isn't that something? That is true. And that's what God wants. God wants someone to love, because He is capable of loving the whole world perfectly, correct? Yes. God wants someone who will have a relationship with Him, with His Spirit, to love Him. So, "it's one thing to be moved by God to do His Will..." And that's why there are a lot of independent Sabbath keepers out there; they are being moved to do the Will of God. And how many people are out there doing that? And God is going to bring them. God is going to call them. I don't think we can get things up and running fast enough to meet the demand as it comes, just like with the *Beliefs* booklet, we have already done seven hundred of them and I only have a hundred left at home, all the rest are gone. And I have orders for more. Then he says, **"It's one thing to be moved by God to do His Will; it is another thing to presume that you can force God to be moved to do your will."** Now that's really quite a profound thing. "It's one thing to be moved to do the Will of God; it's quite another thing for you to presume that you can move or force God to do your will." Now this is why this is so important here, when we come to Luke 24 about understanding the Will of God.

So, "...He showed them *His* hands and *His* feet" verse 40. "But while they were still disbelieving and wondering for joy, He said to them, Do you have anything here to eat? Then they Him part of a broiled fish, and a *piece* of honeycomb. And he took these *and* ate in their presence." Verse 44: "And He said to them, 'These *are* the words that I spoke to you, when I was yet with you, that all *the* things which were written concerning Me in the Law of Moses, and *in the* Prophets and *in the* Psalms must be fulfilled.' Then He opened their minds to understand the Scriptures." That's how you understand the Bible, by Christ sending His Spirit to be with you to open your mind. Can God do that anywhere, anytime with anyone? Yes, He can. And I think God is going to demonstrate it. I think God is going to purposefully do that so that if any minister, any minister at all, or any person be so presumptuous to think that they have a corner on the market with God to force Him to do their will, God is going to do just the opposite. You can be guaranteed that.

Now let's go to Matthew 6 and let's see something concerning the Will of God, concerning what is in the law of Moses, and what is in the law of Moses that is most objected to—obviously the Sabbath, that is the most objected to. And it's even to the point now where people are being taught "Well, it's okay to work on the Sabbath if your family is starving. It's okay to go out and do good humanistic works on the Sabbath, such as build houses for Habitat for Humanity. Because, after all, God doesn't want you to starve and God wants you to provide for your family because if you don't provide for your family, you're worse than an infidel." Hear those scriptures, and yes, yes, yes, and if you're sleepy and not studying the Bible and if you don't know what the Word of God is, then you're going to be in really bad shape. But you see the truth is, the Ten Commandments are a part of the gospel, are they not? If the gospel is also contained in the Old Testament, are not then the Ten Commandments part of the gospel?

Hold your place here in Matthew 6 and let's go back and let's just read this section. Let's go to Deuteronomy 5 since we go to Exodus 20 all the time, let's go to Deuteronomy 5 where the Ten Commandments are listed there and let's just read the ones concerning the Sabbath. And then we'll ask some questions concerning the Sabbath so that we will know. Now I'm covering some of this, and I know it's <u>very</u> <u>basic</u>, and I kind of feel like the apostle Paul when he wrote the Book of Hebrews. He said, "Can't we just go beyond the principles of Christ unto perfection?" [Paraphrased.] Well, I would have to say, no, because we've got to go back and pick up the basics every once-in-a-while. Too many people are not ready to go on to perfection. I'll try and start that next week, but we need to cover this so we know exactly what we are saying.

Let's pick it up here in verse 12, this is Chapter 5 of the Book of Deuteronomy, and Deuteronomy means, *The Second Giving of the Law*. And in the Book of Deuteronomy, as we will see next week, there are many things concerning the gospel of Christ and the gospel as to how we should keep it in the New Testament—many, many things. Notice verse 12: "Keep the sabbath…" Now in Exodus 20, it says "Remember the sabbath…" Here he says, "Keep the sabbath…" Now that's pretty direct isn't it? Question: Does God want us to keep the Sabbath? Yes! Yes! It says, "Keep the sabbath day to sanctify it, as the LORD your God commanded you. Six days shall you labour and do all your work:" Unless you're unemployed, unless your family is starving—no. "But the seventh day *is* the sabbath of the LORD your God…" Now if you love God and fear God and keep His Commandments, are you going to keep it? Is it not part of the gospel of Christ? Yes, it is. "But the seventh day *is* the sabbath of the LORD your God: *in it* you shall not do any work…" Unless it's time-and-a-half, or perhaps, double-time—no, it doesn't say that does it.

So, if any man comes along and says to you, "Well now, the sabbath for us today is Christ in us, and the rest of Christ, being in us, is our sabbath." Do you know what that explanation is? Any guesses? That is mental insanity! That's not true. Christ in you <u>motivates</u> you to keep the Sabbath correctly, not the opposite to give up on it. "…You shall not do any work, you, nor your son, nor your daughter, nor your manservant, nor your maidservant nor your ox, nor your ass, nor any of your cattle, nor your stranger that *is* within your gates; that your manservant and your maidservant may rest as well as you. And remember that you were a servant in the land of Egypt…" Now when we come to the days of Unleavened Bread which we will be coming to here very quickly, it will be upon us faster than we know… what does Egypt picture? Egypt is a type of sin. The Pharaoh is a type of Satan. They're the ones who have you working seven days a week because you are slaves to the system. So he is saying remember you were a slave in the land of Egypt.

Now today if Christ were here to open our minds to tell us what it would be, it would not surprise me one bit if He said, "You are a slave to this world system. Therefore, you keep the Sabbath and on the Sabbath day, you remember what it was like to live without the Sabbath." It is quite instructive you see. "…And *that* the LORD your God brought you out with a mighty hand…" Question: Who calls any individual? God does, doesn't He? Does it take a mighty hand—sometimes something even greater than a mighty hand? What is the strongest thing in the world to change? The human mind. So when God's Spirit comes to call you and bring you out of the world, that's greater than a mighty hand, because He is not just changing your position from one place to another, He is changing your mind from being hostile to God to opening your mind to love God. That's a tremendous difference. So He "… brought you out with a mighty hand and by a stretched out arm; therefore the LORD your God commanded you to keep the sabbath day." He commanded you.

Now let's go back to Matthew 6 and see that Matthew 6 is built upon the Sabbath Commandment, since we understand that the Sabbath is part of the gospel, and we will see that confirmed when we come back to Hebrews 4. And this is very basic for us to go through, because you know brethren, there are people now who have kept the Sabbath for years and are wondering, "Should we keep the Sabbath?"

What happens when someone comes along and teaches you to sin? Does anyone know what that is called in the Bible? It is the doctrine of Balaam, yes. Because Balaam was hired by Balak to come and curse the children of Israel. You can read that in Numbers 22, 23 and 24. And he went up on a mountain and he saw all the children of Israel and all he could do was bless. So Balak gave him all this money and he was coming out of his gourd. He said, "Now look, I gave you this money, and I hired you to curse them." And he said, "And you went up here on the top of the mountain and you blessed them. Now go on up there and curse them." So he goes on up again, and he blesses them. And Balak is really getting out of shape, see, he's really getting mad. He said, "Didn't I hire you to curse them!" He [Balaam] said, "Well, I can only do what the LORD will allow." Then he [Balak] said, "Now go on up there again and curse them." So he went up and blessed them with the longest best blessing that you could read. And so Balak was really angry so Jude tells us that what Balaam did was teach Balak to cast a stumbling block in front of the children of Israel to entice them to sin so that God would have to correct them. Now that's happening within any church, Sunday keepers are doing that in relationship to Sabbath, are they not? Yes, they are. Sabbath keepers who are now ready to shift over to Sunday keeping, are they not doing the same thing by saying it's okay to work on the Sabbath, when God says you shall not do any work? It's one thing if there is an "ox in the ditch," it's another thing if a car is broken down, but you don't go to the junkyard every Sabbath and resurrect all the cars. You see, in other words, you don't throw them into the ditch, and that's what they are doing.

Now we are going to see that Matthew 6 is inexorably tied to the Sabbath; it has to be. Verse 24: "No one is able to serve two masters; for either he will hate the one and love the other…" it always happens, does it not? Have you ever worked for a partnership where the bosses were equal, and then they got into a feud? Try that some time, it'll…give you fits. "…or he will hold to *the* one and despise the other." Now is that not happening with those who are rejecting and despising the Laws of God, the Commandments of God? Yes. Yes, indeed! "…You cannot serve God and mammon."

Now hold your place right here and let's go to Mark 2. Let's look at this thing concerning master. It [master in Matt. 6:24] could also be translated *lord* because it comes from the Greek word *kurios*. Now let's look at that in relationship to the Sabbath, and you're going to hear a passel of sermons that are coming out that are going to cover a lot of these same things. Now let's come to verse 23: "Now it came to pass that He went through the grain fields…" as it should read—not corn as we understand corn, but that wouldn't be too bad. If you were back in Iowa walking through a corn field and the corn was ripe and you just reach up and snap off an ear and peeled it back… have you ever eaten that fresh, sweet corn right off the cob, raw? Oh man, it's good. "…As His disciples made *their* way *through the fields*, they were picking *and eating* the grain. Then the Pharisees said to Him…" Now this is their own law, because it says that you shall not reap the corners, you shall leave it for the poor, and if anyone is passing through your field, he can pluck a little and eat, but he is not to stop there and encamp and harvest. But the Pharisees said if you pluck a head of corn on the Sabbath, you're working, you're laboring, you're harvesting. That's not a law of God. So they said, verse 24: "…Why are they doing that which is not lawful on the Sabbath?" There was no law against it, except their own tradition. So that's why they are saying this.

So Jesus answered with another one for them to figure out which was greater and harder to figure out. Mark 2:25: "And He said to them, 'Have you never read what David did when he was hungry and in need *of food*, he, and those? How in the days of Abiathar the high priest, he entered into the house of God and he ate the showbread…' " Now the showbread, if you recall from the slides or the book on the Tabernacle, there was a loaf of bread which was especially baked and was in a special container and there was one loaf for each one of the twelve tribes of Israel and these were before the LORD constantly. They had to change them every week. The priest could eat it.

Now let's ask the question concerning David, because here is the correct answer. Who was David? Not yet, he was not yet king at that point, he was the king-designate. What was David also in addition to being the king-designate and later to be king? Was he not also a prophet of God? Yes, he was. Did he not prophecy concerning Christ in the Psalms, concerning many things in the Psalms? Yes, he did. So you see the correct answer is that, even though it was unlawful for anyone else to eat it, the truth is, to give it to David and David to give it to his men, because they had need was not against the laws of God whatsoever. Let's go on. "…And He ate the showbread, which is not lawful to eat except for the priests, and he also gave *it* to those who were with him?' " So He gave them something to try to figure out. If they are so smart and condemn people for plucking a head of grain, then go figure this one out. If you want to figure out between what is lawful and what is not lawful, because the most important thing is that you worship and serve God in spirit and truth.

So He said, verse 27: "And He said to them, 'The Sabbath was made for man…' " and as we have seen in the past, for the purpose of fellowshipping with God—not just for the purpose of fellowshipping with each other. That is necessary and that is true, but if we just fellowship with ourselves and God is not there, well then there is no reason for us to come together then is there? It was made for man for that specific purpose. "… *And* not man for the Sabbath;…' " In other words, man is not going to go tell God who made and created the Sabbath, "God, I don't want to keep your Sabbath. It gets in the way. Now I can't earn a living." Well, what do you think Satan wants to get the whole world bound up into—[being] so busy, just like in Egypt that you have to work seven days to meet the bare meager things of even living. So man is not going to come along and tell God, force God … (That's why this is so significant: "It is another thing to presume that you can force, or make God to be moved to do your will.") No it's not for a man.

Verse 28: "Therefore, the Son of man (Jesus Christ) is Lord…" Now the word for Lord is *master, kurios*. "You cannot serve two masters" Matthew 6:24. And He is saying the same thing here. The Sabbath was made for man by God, and not man for the Sabbath. Because there is one Lord of the Sabbath which is Jesus Christ. And you can't serve two Sabbaths to do the activities of men. "Therefore, the Son of man is Lord even of the Sabbath." This, brethren, tells us that the Christian Sabbath is the same day that God gave to ancient Israel, the seventh day of the week, and <u>Christ</u> is Lord of it (Mark 2:23-28)!

Now let's go back to Matthew 6 and let's read what He says, and this ties directly in with the Sabbath. Now Dwight Blevins from Grand Junction called me and he'd been studying this and so he is the one who planted the seed for today's sermon. He said, "When you read Matthew 6, is this not tied directly into the Sabbath and working?" Let's read it. Verse 25. After He says, "…You cannot serve God and mammon" That's very interesting isn't it? You can't keep the Sabbath while you are working on it to earn a living. And mammon is *living, riches*, to get money. Verse 25: "Because of this I say to you…" Go work on the Sabbath, it's okay because I know you've got to live. I know you have to survive. Now that's perfectly all right with me. <u>No</u>. He <u>doesn't</u> <u>say</u> <u>that</u>. He says, "…do not be anxious about your life *as to* what you shall eat and what you shall drink;" the very basic necessities, correct? "…Nor about your body *as to* what you shall wear. Is not life more than food, and the body *more* than clothing?" Is it not? Yes. Yes, indeed.

Now He says, "Observe the birds of heaven: they do not sow, neither do they reap, nor do they gather into granaries; and your heavenly Father feeds them. Are you not much better than they?" What is He really saying here? He is saying that, if you don't trust God to provide for you, obviously in the Sabbath keeping situation here, then you are counting yourself less than the birds. You are counting yourself in a situation that you are really actually saying, "God cannot provide for me." Which then is what? That's accusing God, is it not? Yes, it is. "…But who among you, by taking careful thought, is able to add one cubit to his stature? And why are you anxious about clothing?" He says, "Now I know you need to be clothed, don't worry about it." [Paraphrased.] Continuing with verse 28: "…Observe the lilies of the field, how they grow: they do not labor, nor do they spin; But I say to you, not even Solomon in all his glory was arrayed as one of these." God is going to clothe you, if He is going to take care of the plants, if He is going to provide for the birds, if He is going to provide for His whole creation, which He does, and His whole creation is an expression of His love to all of mankind. Verse 30: "Now if God so arrays the grass of the field, which to day is and tomorrow is cast into the oven, *shall* He not much rather clothe you, O *you* of little faith?"

Now that's why we have said that the Sabbath is a test Commandment. Is it not? Yes. Well, the truth is, every Commandment is a test Commandment. Is it not? "…Will you keep My Commandments or no?" Yes, every one is. So you have to have faith. Verse 31: "Therefore, do not be anxious, saying, 'What shall we eat?' or 'What shall we drink?' or, 'With what shall we be clothed?' " [But some will say] Boy you know, this Sabbath Commandment is pretty tough. And you know my bank account's really getting low. And my wife over here is nagging at me, and my children are hungry and they have holes in their shoes, and they're just about ready to go barefoot. Therefore God, I'm going to break the Sabbath and go work because I don't have one bit of faith in you for you to provide." That's what they're saying, are they not? What should they do? They should go to God, and if they are having a difficult time on the Sabbath day, pray and draw closer to God. Ask for His Spirit in love and do the things that please God. He'll gladly provide for you.

I just talked to a man recently, whose wife was just beating him over the head, so to speak. "Well, you turned down all these jobs because of the Sabbath. And this last one was really a good one. And now the church says you can work on the Sabbath, and yet you refused." So he held to keeping the Sabbath and God blessed him with a better job than any of those that he turned down. God was able to provide. Can He not do that? Yes.

Now verse 32: "For the nations seek after all these things." And they work seven days a week don't they? And they don't keep the Sabbath do they? So this is intrinsically bound up in the Sabbath Command isn't it? "…And your heavenly Father knows that you have need of all these things." God knows. If you know, God knows, and if God knows, He'll take care of it—maybe not in the way you think or in the means or the manner in which you suspect, maybe it will not be as much because there are other lessons to learn. Maybe it will be more than you expect because God is blessing you above and beyond. And that's all in God's hands, and that's all in God's relationship with you. "…But *as for* you, seek first the kingdom of God…" That's what it needs to be. God will take care of it. Now can you truly seek the Kingdom of God if you're not keeping the Sabbath, when the Sabbath pictures the whole situation concerning the Kingdom of God? No. "…And His righteousness…" Now let's just plug in here, the imputed righteousness of God. That's what you are to seek. Would God break His own Sabbath? Did God break His own Sabbath? No! Now if you go back and read Exodus 16 and the giving of the manna, what did God do? He gave manna for six days and five of those days, he said, "Now look you just go out and you get a certain much for everyone. Now don't keep it over to the next day because it's going to breed worms and stink. But on the sixth day, you go out and you gather twice as much, and then you prepare for the Sabbath and you can keep it over and it won't breed worms and stink." Now consider the fact that this happened for forty years, every single week. That's quite a thing isn't it? Now some of them thought, "Boy, I'm going to go out and get some manna on this Sabbath day!" So they went out to look and God said, "Now look, how long refuse you to keep my commandments?" [Paraphrased.] And that was long before the giving of the Ten Commandments.

Continuing with verse Matt. 6:33: "But *as for* you, seek first the kingdom of God and his righteousness, and all these things shall be added to you" Just exactly what you need. Now some people are going to be blessed more than others. Does that mean they are more righteous? No. No. No. No, it does not. It just means that God has blessed them more than others. So therefore, if someone has more than you, you don't get mad at God and say, "Well, You didn't give it to me, You gave it to him." No, that's not it. Here is what we are to do, verse 34: "Therefore, do not be anxious about tomorrow;" that means do not be anxious, do not be worried. If you have faith in God and trust in God, He will provide. "...For tomorrow shall take care of the *things* of itself. Sufficient for the day *is* the evil of that *day*." Now isn't it true, every day has got it's own problems, right? Yes! So handle those, day by day. The question is: How do we differentiate what I said by one person receiving more of a blessing than another, as compared with what it says in the Old Testament that if you do these things, you will be blessed? I didn't say the lack of blessing, I just said that God may give someone more, bless them with more rather than you, I'm not saying that He isn't going to bless you or provide for you (Matthew 6:24-34).

Now let's just turn the page back, Matthew 6, and let's see how this all ties in together. Matthew 6:9: "Therefore you are to pray after this manner..." which is how you develop faith, "...Our Father Who *is* in heaven, hallowed be Your name; Your kingdom come; Your will be done on earth, as *it is* in heaven:" And that's what we need. We need the Will of God. And that will answer the question, how is God going to bless us? Maybe God is going to bless us with a trial because He has a greater purpose in mind. And sometimes we don't know while we are going through those trials that He has a greater purpose in mind, but nevertheless, that's how God works. Notice the next verse, verse 11: "Give us this day our daily bread;." So that ties in with the rest of Matthew 6 where He says, "Give no thought about what you will eat, what you will drink..." so forth, for God will take care of you (Matthew 6:9-11).

Now in relationship to that let me finish this letter here, "We were members of the WCG for about twenty-five years. Then things started to change. First off, they had first, second, third tithe, tithe of the tithe, excess second tithe, building fund, and special funds, work two or three jobs if you had to, etc., to keep it up, and tithe on the gross. They live like kings in mansions and pools and two or three homes, get planes—something is rotten in California. I had to get out. Now changes again! Work on the Sabbath! Work on the Holy Days! Holy Days are not commandments. Eating unclean meats is okay, etc. Anyway, your book, *Lord, What Should I Do* is refreshing. Please send me four copies." So I will.

Here is another letter from a man, and this is pretty typical as to what we are able to do to help the people, and so he says, "Although belatedly it is with much thanks and appreciation that I send this for the package and the box of tapes forwarded. I honestly can't put into words what all this means to me. So you may never know how much you have done regarding where I am at in my pilgrimage" obviously with God. "I have listened to all but a couple of tapes so far and will have them digested very soon. Yes, I most certainly will look forward to the other package you mentioned and I will be eagerly looking forward to it. When I first wrote you, I knew God was still there somewhere, but I never thought I would feel like the Prodigal Son..."

"But I never thought I would feel like the Prodigal Son coming home to a loving father as I experienced when going through your tapes and books." That's what it needs to be. That's why I just did the video *To Return to God*. It's going to help out a lot of people. [The man wrote]: "I was very inspired with your resignation tape. If my memory serves me right, I recall that (he gives the name of the minister) being sent to that area at that time to troubleshoot after a lot of questions were raised regarding various church matters. Needless to say, it would take me many pages to relate my thanks and experience since coming into contact, but time limits me. Either you are a servant of God, or the best con-artist I have come across. I can't remember when so much care was shown to me by the ministry. The only care package I received from other groups that left WCG was a co-worker letter and small bundles of tithe envelopes. I believe very strongly in God's laws on tithing and like many others, I don't need to be reminded like that. Thanks for treating me like a child of God and not another one of the dumb sheep. Best wishes to you in your service Mr. Coulter, and I am praying for you and with you in the meantime."

So that's what happens when we send out a care package. We get many, many such letters back. And we can help that way, brethren, an awful lot. When you wrap your whole life up in serving God and then someone comes along and steals it from you, and then after they steal it they begin throwing it away, it's no wonder that there are a lot of people in just such terrible, terrible, terrible shape out there.

Now let's go back and read some commands concerning the Sabbath. Because we do need to have this basic sermon concerning the Sabbath, in the light of the things that are going on, and I just want you to understand, we related here Exodus 16 already, but let's go back there for just a minute because this is important. Exodus 16:25, after the whole incident concerning the giving of the manna, "And Moses said, Eat that today; for today *is* a sabbath unto the LORD: today you shall not find it in the field. Six days you shall gather it; but on the seventh day, *which* is the sabbath, in it there shall be none." There will be no manna there. Now what is this also telling us? What was manna? [It is] food, correct. Who provided it? God did. That ties right in with Matthew 6, is that not correct? Yes. Is not God able to provide? Yes! Does He want you to work on the Sabbath? No! No, as we saw, he said no work, not any work. And don't be throwing everything into the ditch so you have an excuse to work. There won't be any out there.

Question: If God was not going to send the manna, and there wasn't going to be anything out there for them, do you think that God will bless anyone for Sabbath breaking when they know better? Do you think that God is going to bless them with their work? Now what's going to happen to these poor people who say, "Well, I believe what so-and-so said about it being okay to work on the Sabbath. I'll go ahead and work on the Sabbath." Now what happens if they lose their job? Now they are going to be in worse shape, because with the devising of men, you are not going to force God to do your will. God is not going to bless that effort. God is not going to prosper you in what you do when it is sin. We have all tried it haven't we? Haven't we all kidded ourselves and said, "Well, God understands, this sin won't hurt a little bit. After all I'm trying to do good." That's what everyone wants to do—do good in their sinning. No. No! I've done that. Did I prosper in it? Nope. Did I do well in it? Nope. Was I happy in it? Nope. Was God pleased in it? No. Did God in His mercy and graciousness and love, lead me to repentance? Yes. Which means then, He doesn't want me to do it, right? Right. So it is the same way with any of us and in anything we do.

Now verse 27: "And it came to pass, *that* there went out *some* of the people on the seventh day for to gather..." Now these are hardworking people, right? [They are] diligent, yes, "workaholics," in this case, "mannaholics." They want to go out and get more manna. "... And they found none. And the LORD said unto Moses..." Now this is really quite something, what He said here. He didn't say, "Now I understand. You know these people have been bound up in Egypt for so long, and I know that they worked every day. Now you know I understand that they had to go and look just to satisfy their own curiosity." No! He said, verse 28: "…How long refuse you to keep my commandments and my laws?" **Now I want you to make special note of that and always remember** Exodus 16:28. **That's a very important verse**. Why? Because when people get into these arguments concerning Old Testament/New Testament Laws and Commandments and the giving of [them] and so forth; please understand that the Laws and Commandments of God were in effect before they ever got to Mt. Sinai, before God ever spoke them. That's what it is saying right here. "How long refuse you to keep my commandments, and my laws? See, for that the LORD has given you the sabbath…" It is a gift! The Sabbath is a creation and a gift from God so that you can fellowship with God, so that you can love God, so that God can love you, so that God can instruct you out of His Word. God is the one who has a corner on the Sabbath. God is the one who has a corner on the truth, not us. "…The LORD has given you the Sabbath, therefore, he has given you, on the sixth day…" So here is another gift, a miraculous gift, "…the bread of two days; abide every man in his place, let no man go out of his place on the seventh day. So the people rested on the seventh day" (Exodus 16:27-30).

Now let's come to Exodus 20:8, we're just going to read some very important things here, very fundamental for us to understand. "Remember the sabbath day, to keep it holy." No other day can be holy, except the Holy Days. Sunday is not holy. God never made it holy. Verse 9: "Six days shall you labor and do all your work: But the seventh day *is* the sabbath of the LORD your God: *in it* you shall not do any work, you, nor your son, nor your daughter, your manservant, nor your maidservant, nor your cattle, nor your stranger that is within you gates: For *in* six days…" It goes back to creation. What is the authority of the Sabbath and the Ten Commandments? It's a creation, God made it. When you keep the Sabbath, you know that, "… in six days the LORD made heaven and earth, the sea, and all that in them *is*, and rested the seventh day: wherefore the LORD blessed the sabbath day, and hallowed it (Exodus 20:8-11).

Now all the way through—let's come to Chapter 23, and let's see what He says here. The Sabbath is perhaps one of the most often mentioned commands in the whole Bible. Verse: 12: "Six days shall you do your work, and on the seventh day you shall rest: that your ox and your ass may rest, and the son of your handmaid, and the stranger, may be refreshed. And in all *things* that I have said unto you be circumspect: and make no mention of the name of other gods, neither let it be heard out of your mouth (Exodus 23:12-13).

Let's come to Chapter 31—this is just in the Book of Exodus. I mean we could go through Deuteronomy and Numbers and Leviticus and all of that. Now what I want you to do with Exodus 31 which becomes a very important thing concerning the Sabbath, which is this: Let's understand something—remember what we did a couple of weeks ago, going through and showing in Numbers 11 concerning that the church was an extension of Israel, and that those Gentiles who are called, are grafted into the olive tree of Israel? Now with that in mind, let's begin reading in verse 12: "And the LORD spoke unto Moses, saying, "Thus shall you speak unto the children of Israel, Verily my sabbaths you shall keep…" It's very important. "…For it is a sign between me and you throughout your generations; that *you* may know that I *am* the LORD that does sanctify you" (Exodus 31:12-13).

Let's ask some questions here. What is the whole purpose of the New Testament for each one of those who are called saints? Why are you called saints? Because you have the Holy Spirit of God and you are sanctified. God is the one who is sanctifying us. God is the one who sanctified the Sabbath, did He not? He blessed it and He sanctified it. Okay? [It's the] same way with us—that's why we are to keep the Sabbath. Now remember the "children of Israel throughout your generations..." If we are part of Israel, now spiritual Israel, are there still generations of Israel? Yes, indeed. Can we not have spiritual meaning out of these verses as well because it's part of the gospel? Absolutely.

Exodus 31:14: "You shall keep the sabbath therefore; for it *is* holy unto you: every one that defiles it shall surely be put to death..." maybe not that day, maybe not for many years, but what is the ultimate outcome—"The wages of sin is death." When you teach people to sin, the wages of sin is death. "...Shall surely be put to death: for whosoever does *any* work therein, that soul shall be cut off from among his people." Now I tell you what's going to happen, those who begin breaking the Sabbath by working on it because now the leader says it's okay to do it and after all, you know, "He said I could, Lord." Did he not? If he says I could, Lord, I'm going to. Therefore, I'm justified."

Let's go back to Genesis 3 for just a minute. That's the same old thing of human nature going way back, Genesis 3, when they got caught in their sins. Notice whose fault it was. Hold your place here in Exodus 31, we'll be back there. Notice what happened. God came and He was calling them, "Where are you?" They were hiding. And let's pick it up here in verse 10: "And he [Adam] said, I heard your voice in the garden, and I was afraid, because I *was* naked; and I hid myself. And he said, Who told you that you *were* naked? Have you eaten of the tree where of I commanded you that you should not eat?" Now you can put any commandment in there, right? You can put anything in there. "Have you done that which I said you should not do?" Have you—be it the Sabbath, be it idols, be it taking God's name in vain, be it any of the Commandments of God, be it anything in the New Testament; you put it there.

Verse 12: "And the man said..." Yep, I sure did. God I'm terribly sorry. No, what did he do? He said, "...The woman that you gave me..." Now what is he really saying? God you're the one. You are at fault, not me, but the woman you gave me. Now he wanted her, desired her, presented to him he said, "Now this is bone of my bone and flesh of my flesh. She shall be called woman." So you see, you're not going to have a cop-out by blaming the church leader. Even if the church leader comes and says do this or that or the other thing. If it is against the Law of God or the Commandments of God, you're not to do it!

Let's go on here verse 13. So, "...the LORD God said unto the woman, What *is* this *that* you have done? And the woman said..." Well look; it really wasn't my fault. It was this serpent that snuck in here, see? "He beguiled me, and I did eat." So God took care of them all. He said, "Look, you're not going to escape the judgement or the penalty for what you have done." [Paraphrased].

So likewise today, those who go out and work because a church leader has said it's okay to work—let's understand something concerning things like childbirth, or an accident, or something like that. There are things that need to be done, and you know, babies come because babies come, and it is called child labor; it is painful and it is in travail. So God certainly expects that to be taken care of. And I am sure that if you are coming to Sabbath services and you are in an accident, that you are going to be very happy a Highway Patrolman is there to help you, or an ambulance is there to help you. Now in this world there are those things that go on. However, how many of you have had an accident coming to Sabbath services? No hands raised. How many here (well, you might remember and you might not) had your children born on the Sabbath day? If a person is a nurse and, say, works in a hospital, there are certain things that need to be done, but I was talking to a nurse last night who called and she said, "Well, there are always plenty of people who want to come and work on Saturday, so I just swap shifts with them." So you see where your desire is to please God and serve Him, there is going to be a way. God will provide a way.

I have often had people ask me this: "Well, how do you keep the Sabbath at the North Pole?" And my answer is: "When I get a letter from someone at the North Pole, I'll answer it." In the meantime, that question cannot be answered because no one is there to keep the Sabbath. What do you do when you live in a high northern latitude and you have a whole lot of dark? Then you calculate it by what you see. And that's how you calculate the Sabbath, and it will generally work out to be approximately 24 hours long. What about when the sun never sets in the summer? Well, when it dips to its lowest point, in the middle of the lowest point, that's the ending of the day so you go from there (Genesis 3:10-13).

Now let's come back to Exodus 31:15: "Six days may work be done; but in the seventh *is* the sabbath of rest, holy to the LORD: whosoever does *any* work in the sabbath day, he shall surely be put to death. Wherefore the children of Israel shall keep the Sabbath, to observe the Sabbath throughout their generations, *for*…" look at this next word, "…a perpetual covenant." This is in addition to the covenant that was given at Sinai. This is a special Sabbath keeping covenant. Why did He make it a special Sabbath keeping covenant for a perpetual covenant? I would have to say, brethren, for the New Testament church, why else? Knowing that we would not have a temple, knowing that we would not have a priesthood, but still keep it, right? Verse 17: "*It is* a sign between me and the children of Israel forever: for *in* six days the LORD made heaven and earth, and on the seventh day he rested, and was refreshed" (Exodus 31:15-17).

Now you can go through many other places. Let's go clear over to Ezekiel 20. Why did the children of Israel go into captivity? [It was] because they broke the Commandments of God and broke the Sabbath. Ezekiel, Chapter 20—this is quite a lesson. How important is it, and when we read this, let's understand that God says in the Book of Ezekiel three times, "I don't delight in the death of the wicked, but that the wicked turn from his ways." [Paraphrased.] Now, Ezekiel 20:1: "…It came to pass in the seventh year, in the fifth *month*, of the tenth *day* of the month, *that* certain of the elders of Israel came to enquire of the LORD, and sat before me. Then came the word of the LORD unto me, saying, …Speak unto the elders of Israel, and say unto them, Thus says the LORD God; are you come to enquire of me? *As* I live, says the LORD GOD, I will not be enquired of by you." In other words, just like I started out: "It is one thing to be moved by God to do His Will; it's another thing to presume that you can force or make God to do your will." That's what He just said here. "Are you going to come and question me?" That's what God said. "…As I live, says the LORD GOD, I will not be enquired of by you." Verse 4: "Will you judge them, son of man, will you judge *them*? Cause them to know the abominations of their fathers…" So now we have a history lesson.

Hold your place right here and go to 1 Corinthians 10. Paul gave a history lesson there didn't he? What was the history lesson? Let's pick it up here in 1 Corinthians 10:5: "But with many of them God was not well pleased, for their dead bodies were strewn in the wilderness." Now we are going to read about that again in Exodus 20 here in just a minute. [But] Verse 6: "Now these things were our examples, to the intent that we should not lust after evil things, as they lusted." Now what did we just read about in Exodus 16 on lusting, going out to break the Sabbath, correct? Yes. Verse 7: "Neither be you idolaters, as *were* some of them; as it is written, The people sat down to eat and drink, and rose up to play. Neither let us commit fornication, as some of them committed, and fell in one day three and twenty thousand. Neither let us tempt Christ, as some of them also tempted, and were destroyed of serpents." Do we not tempt Christ when we reject the Sabbath? Yes, we do. "Neither murmur…" and is that not what's happening, complaining murmuring, criticizing against God, see? That's what He is saying in Ezekiel 20. "Are you going to come and enquire of me? Are you going to come and complain to me?" Go read the whole Book of Jeremiah, how merciful God was where He said over, and over, and over again "You find some people who will do what is right, and I will turn back this captivity.

I'll change it, I don't want them to die." [Paraphrased.] [I Cor. 10] Verse 11: "Now all these things happened to them *as* examples, and were written for our admonition, on whom the ends of the ages are coming." Are we living in the last days? Yes! More so than Paul? Yes! "Therefore, let the one who thinks he stands take heed, lest he fall." They are not falling now, they are pushing. Yeah, they are running [Away from God] (1 Corinthians 10:5-12).

Let's go back to Ezekiel 20 again. So let's have a little history lesson here in Ezekiel 20, quite instructive. Verse 5: "And say unto them Thus says the LORD GOD; In the day when I chose Israel, and lifted up mine hand unto the seed of the house of Jacob, and made myself known unto them in the land of Egypt…" Now has God made Himself known to you? Did God send His Spirit today to make Himself known? Yes. What is the whole thing that we are to know? We are to know God—we are to know Christ, we are to know the Father. Is that not correct? "He that says I know Him and keeps not His Commandments is a liar and the truth is not in him." Didn't we study that in 1 John? Yes, indeed. And the one who is keeping the Commandments and walking the way that Jesus did, …in him is the love of God being perfected. Correct? Yes! So just as God chose them, he chose us. Continuing in verse 5: "…When I lifted up mine hand unto them, saying, I *am* the LORD your God;" Verse 6: "In the day *that* I lifted up mine hand unto them, to bring them forth out of the land of Egypt into a land that I had spied out for them, flowing with milk and honey, which *is* the glory of all the lands:" Verse 7: "Then I said to them, Cast you away every man the abominations of his eyes…" whatever it may be, an idol, fornication, adultery, stealing, idolatry, taking God's name in vain, breaking the Sabbath, whatever it may be. "…And defile not yourselves with the idols of Egypt…"

And what are we doing today? Back in Memphis Tennessee they've got a whole pyramid back there—did you know that—where they take people through and they run them through the demonic initiations into the ancient rites of Egyptian religion—right here in the United States.

He says, continuing in verse 7: "Don't defile yourself with the idols of Egypt: I *am* the LORD your God." Verse 8: "But they rebelled against me, they wouldn't listen to me: they did not every man cast away the abominations of their eyes, neither did they forsake the idols of Egypt: then I said, I will pour out my fury upon them, to accomplish my anger against them in the midst of the land of Egypt." Verse 9: "But I wrought for my name's sake, that it should not be polluted before the heathen, among whom they *were*…" In other words, He said even while they were in the land of Egypt they were so involved in idolatry that He was even going to destroy them right <u>in</u> the land of Egypt before He ever called them out. So what did they do when they got to Mt. Sinai and Moses was up on the mountain for forty days? They said, "Aaron, make us calves."

So He didn't do it. Continuing verse 9: "…In whose sight I made myself known unto them, in bringing them forth out of the land of Egypt. Wherefore I caused them to go forth out of the land of Egypt, and brought them into the wilderness. And I gave them my statutes, and shewed them my judgments, which *if* a man do, he shall even live in them." The righteousness number one of the letter of the law. Correct? Yes. "Moreover also I gave them my sabbaths, to be a sign between me and them, that they might know that I *am* the LORD that sanctify them." Verse 13: "But the house of Israel rebelled against me in the wilderness: they walked not in my statutes, and they despised my judgements…" Can you imagine what it must have been like? No wonder Moses complained all the time, "Oh Lord you got me saddled down with all these people." You know, when they were good they were the people of God; when they were bad, they were Moses' people all the way through there. Continuing with verse 13: "…And my sabbaths they greatly polluted: then I said I would pour out my fury upon them in the wilderness, to consume them. But I wrought for my name's sake, (I held back, no I didn't do it) that it should not be polluted before the heathen, in whose sight I brought them out." Even Moses said, "Now God consider what the other nations are going to say if you kill them—that you brought them out here to destroy them. Now think about that LORD." [Paraphrased.] And He did. Verse 15: "Yet also I lifted up my hand unto them in the wilderness, that I would not bring them into the land which I had given *them*, flowing with milk and honey, which *is* the glory of the lands; Because they despised my judgements, and walked not in my statutes, but polluted my sabbaths: for their heart went after their idols."

Now what is the idol today? Mammon, money, dollars, bucks, power, prestige, notoriety, clothes, car—we have so many things out there that could be abominations— it's unreal. Continuing in verse 17: "Nevertheless mine eye spared them from destroying them, neither did I make an end of them in the wilderness. But I said to their children…" now He is referring to the Book of Deuteronomy—the children, the second giving of the Law. "…I said to their children…" before they went into the land "…Walk not in the statutes of your fathers, neither observe their judgements, nor defile yourselves with their idols: I *am* the LORD your God; walk in my statutes, and keep my judgments, and do them." What did Jesus say? "If you love me, keep my commandments." "If you love me keep my words." [It is the] same thing, exactly the same thing. Verse 20: "And hallow my sabbaths; and they shall be a sign between me and you, that you may know that I *am* the LORD your God. Nevertheless, the <u>children</u> rebelled against me…" And all you have to do is read the Book of Joshua, and the Book of Judges, and as soon as Joshua and the elders died, what did they do? [They went] Right back to Sunday keeping, right back to Christmas keeping, right back to those things, and mark my words: <u>When they quit keeping the Sabbath, that's exactly what's going to happen again</u>. It will happen.

So, "…they rebelled against me: they walked not in my statutes, neither kept my judgements to do them, which *if* a man do, he shall even live in them; they polluted my sabbaths: then I said, I would pour out my fury upon them, to accomplish my anger against them... Nevertheless I withdrew my hand…" So God just finally threw His hands up and said, "All right, if you want it I'm going to let you have your own ways, and when you get so filled with your own ways and your own idolatry, and your own pollution, and your own wretchedness, and your own rottenness, then you come crying to me, then I'll hear." [Paraphrased.]

So verse 24 He said, "Because they executed not my judgments and had despised my statutes and then polluted my sabbaths, and their eyes went after their fathers' idols. Wherefore I gave them over to statutes *which were* not good…" their own ways, their own laws, their own civil governments, correct? Yes. Their own religion. He just said, "I'll just give you over to it. If you want it, have it, you got it—the whole thing." "…*Which were* not good, and judgments whereby they should not live; And I polluted them in their own gifts…" worse thing that could happen to anyone, brethren, is just be left to wallow in your own sin. Isn't it? Yes. "…In that they caused to pass through *the fire* all that opens the womb…" In other words, they just went into the whole same situation that the Mayans down in ancient Mexico went through. The reason God destroyed those civilizations is because they were doing the same thing, going through the fire, cannibalism, offering to the gods, so evil and awful that one of their special sacrifices was to cut open the sacrificial human victim and take out the heart while it was still beating and drink the blood of it. Now you see some of these things and all the archeologists say, "I wonder why these civilizations no longer exist?" Read the Bible, okay? "…That I might make them desolate, to the end that they might know that I *am* the LORD." So sometimes God just does that—just turns you over to your own devices until you learn the lesson. Some things you can learn quite quickly (Ezekiel 20:5-26).

Let's go to the Book of Hebrews now. Let's finish off there in Hebrews 4. I'm going to have to say that this is the last sermon I'm going to give any answer to things going on in the Church of God. We have too much to do, we have so much to cover and we're going to do a series on the Love of God in the Bible that is really the whole heart and core as to why the church is going through everything it is. When you really understand it, the love of God is the greatest thing, the greatest fulfillment and attainment in your life, and it does take your life. That's why as you go through life and life is empty and you get older and there is no satisfaction—that's why the whole experience of Solomon is there. He had all these physical things and all the power, and all the money and wealth and every convenience you could ever want and he said, "I am just a bag of wind. I am just an empty, hollow, frustrated old man." Why? Because he never learned the love of God. The love of God is the greatest thing. We can't be playing third grade sandbox any more, going back to these things. If someone is not convinced they ought to keep the Sabbath after being in the Church of God twenty-five years, well then I cannot be too much help to you. You should go help yourself. Isn't that what Jesus said, "You go learn what these things mean."

Now let's come back here to Hebrews 4 and this will help us understand. Remember where we just read in Ezekiel, Chapter 20 where He destroyed those in the wilderness because they didn't believe. Then He said to the children, "Now look, you're going to go into the Promised Land, now here is what God says…" [Paraphrased.] Now let's come back to, well, let's go back to Hebrews 3:15: "As it is being said, 'Today, if you will hear His voice, do not harden your hearts, as in the rebellion. For some, after hearing, did rebel, but not all who came out of Egypt by Moses. But with whom was He indignant *for* forty years?" Now notice He didn't say angered, but grieved. "…*Was it* not with those who had sinned…" Can you have the very presence of God in the cloud by day and the fire by night, every day and every night, and have the manna come six days every week, and the Sabbath every week, and still have the gall to keep your own idols? Wow! That's something, isn't it? Yes! "…Whose dead bodies were strewn in the wilderness?" Verse 18: "And to whom did He sware *that they* should not enter into His rest…" And boy, going into the Promised Land, that's a tremendous rest—you compare that with wondering in the Sinai (Hebrews 3:15-18). I remember one time we went down to Palm Springs. Boy was it hot, and I thought, "Man, how would you like to walk in that desert in all that heat?" Yet they did and still didn't believe God. So you see that they could not enter in because of unbelief. The spies came back and said, "Oh look, they're giants. Oh we can't go in." Joshua and Caleb said, "Oh yes, God will take care of it for us."

Now Chapter 4, verse 1: "Therefore we should fear, lest perhaps, a promise being open to enter into His rest…" and that is the ultimate reward of God in the Millenium. Now we are not talking about the Promised Land, we are talking about the Kingdom of God. That's the rest we are talking about. "…Any of you might seem to come short. For truly, we have had the gospel preached *to us*, even as they also *did*; but the preaching of the word did not profit them because it was not mixed with faith in those who heard. For we who have believed, we ourselves are entering into the rest, as He has said, 'So I have swore in My wrath, "If they shall enter into My rest…" ' although the works were finished from *the* foundation of *the* world. For He spoke in a certain place about the seventh *day* in this manner…" so this is showing that the Sabbath is a continuous type of the rest of God. The rest of God is not Christ in you, so therefore, you perpetually keep the Sabbath everyday. And as one man said, "When do you work then?" See, it doesn't happen that way. "…And God rested on the seventh day from all His works; And again concerning this: 'If they shall enter into My rest…' " which we just read about in Ezekiel 20. Verse 6: "Consequently, since it remains *for* some to enter into it, and those who had previously heard the gospel did not enter in because of disobedience, Again He marks out a certain day, 'Today, saying in David…' " And what was that day? That's pictured by the Sabbath Psalm which says, "…To day…" that's what he quoted over here, "…if you will hear His voice…" "…after so long a time; 'Today, if you will hear His voice, harden not your hearts' " (Hebrews 4:1-7).

Now is this not the same thing as it is with every covenant of God? Hear His voice, obey His words, thus says the Lord, thus says Jesus, thus say the prophets, "…if you will hear his words, harden not your hearts." Verse 8: "For if Joshua had given them rest…" Now this should read Joshua and most Bibles have an explanation of it there and some of the newer translations have Joshua because they understood that it was Joshua that led them into the Promised Land. And the sense of it is this way: "For if Joshua had given them rest…" in other words, and that was the fulfillment and the completion of God's plan "…He (God) would not have spoken *long* afterwards of another day." And that other day is the coming of the Kingdom of God, that other day is the millennial rest of God!

Verse 9 [of the Faithful Version], very important: [Unfortunately the King James is not clear] "There remains, therefore, Sabbath-keeping for the people of God." Now this is an entirely different word. All the way through, the word for rest in the Greek is *katapausis* which means *rest, recline, repose* from your labor and hard work. This one, verse 9, is an entirely different word for rest and it in the Greek is *sabbatismos*, which means *a keeping of the Sabbath*. New Testament command. "Therefore, there remains for the people of God…" Who are the people of God? [They are] the ones that have the Spirit of God. Correct? "…A keeping of the sabbath…" Why? Because God's plan is not complete and the Sabbath pictures the completion of that plan, doesn't it? "There remains, therefore, Sabbath keeping for the people of God. For the one who has entered into His rest, he also has ceased from his own works, just as God *did* from His own *works*."

Now then comes a statement showing that after we have the Sabbath keeping what are we to do spiritually? Verse 11: "We should be diligent therefore to enter into that rest…" the ultimate reward of God to us "…lest anyone fall after the same example of disobedience." And what is it when you tell people you can work on the Sabbath? It is unbelief, is it not? Sure it is—plain and simple (Hebrews 4:8-11).

Now let's go to Isaiah 66 for just a minute, because when Christ returns, and every Sunday keeper knows this if they have read their Bible, and a lot of Sunday keepers read their Bibles. That's why some Sunday keepers are still either closet Sabbath keepers or they keep the Sabbath. When Christ returns He is going to obviously do away with the Sabbath because it's an inconvenience to everyone, right? Of course not! Isaiah 66:23: "And it shall come to pass, *that* from one new moon to another, and from one sabbath to another, shall all flesh come to worship before me, says the LORD" Every Sabbath.

Now since we are in Isaiah and we have just a little bit of time left here, let's go to Isaiah 56:1, is this not part of what Christ opened the mind and understanding to the disciples? Yes it is. "Thus says the LORD, Keep you judgment, and do justice: for my salvation *is* near to come, and my righteousness to be revealed." This is just before the return of Christ. Verse 2: "Blessed *is* the man *that* does this, and the son of man *that* lays hold on it; that keeps the sabbath from polluting it, and keeps his hand from doing any evil." That means all the Commandments doesn't it? Sure it does. "Neither let the son of the stranger…" the Gentile now "…that has joined himself to the LORD, speak, saying, The LORD has utterly separated me from his people: neither let the eunuch say, Behold, I *am* a dry tree." Now a eunuch is, you know, that's the most shameful thing to happen to a man, right? "…Thus says the LORD unto the eunuchs that keep my sabbaths, and choose *the things* that please me, and take hold of my covenant" Did we not just go through the things that please God? Yes. And this covenant "…takes hold of my covenant…" this can be concerning the New Covenant, but did we not read of a special covenant concerning the Sabbaths of God which include the seventh day and Holy Days in Exodus 31? Yes, we did. Verse 5: "Even unto them will I give in my house and within my walls a place and a name better than sons and daughters: I will give them an everlasting name, that shall not be cut off." You go back and read the promise to the seven churches, "…And I will give him a new name…" Correct? Yes. Verse 6: "Also the sons of the stranger, that join themselves to the LORD, to serve him, and to love the name of the LORD, to be his servants, every one that keeps the sabbath from polluting it, and takes hold of my covenant;" Isn't that amazing? Yes it is (Isaiah 56:1-6).

End of Sermon

Transcriber: Judith Anderson

Importance of the Sabbath
February 4, 1995
Scriptural References

1) Mark 13:10

2) Matthew 24

3) Hebrews 4:2

4) Luke 24:25-41, 43-45

5) Matthew 6

6) Deuteronomy 5:12-15

7) Matthew 6:24

8) Mark 2:23-28

9) Matthew 6:24-34

10) Matthew 6:9-11

11) Exodus 16:25-29

12) Exodus 20:8-11

13) Exodus 23:12-13

14) Exodus 31:12-14

15) Genesis 3:10-13

16) Exodus 31:15-17

17) Ezekiel 20:1-4

18) I Corinthians 10:5-12

19) Ezekiel 20:5-26

20) Hebrews 3:15-19

21) Hebrews 4:1-11

22) Isaiah 66:23

23) Isaiah 56:1-6

Section II

God's Holy Days
Overview

CHAPTER SIX

Introduction—Beginning & Ending

November 18, 2006

This sermon is going to be the introduction [in Second Section] for the book, *God's Plan for Mankind Revealed by His Sabbath and HolyDays.*

Now, this book will have 30 [now 37] sermons and they will all be put on three CDs, MP3. And we will also entitle this, *The Beginning and the Ending.* Because what we are going to cover needs to be for an introduction, but we'll also need to understand that what this book is: This is for those who know the Sabbath, know the Holy Days; and this book is not for someone who is brand new, who has never read the Bible. However, if you're what might be called "a neophyte" and you have some understanding of the Bible, it will be difficult for you to understand most of what we're going to cover here, so I suggest that you do this: While you begin here, you go through all the rest of the sermons in the book, and when you get to the end, come back to the beginning, so that's why we're calling it *The Beginning and the Ending.*

And I also thought on this, because at the time of doing this, we're just about ready to write the introduction, preface and things like that for the book, everything else is ready to go. And, I was wondering what I would do for the introduction. And different things came to me that is what needs to be to explained about the Holy Days, the way they fall and the meaning of them. And why it is, that only those who know the Word of God will understand this; and why those who don't know the Word of God will not understand it.

Let's come to Matthew 13. Let's see what Jesus Himself said, which we have covered at different times. Now, let's begin here in verse 10, Matthew 13: "And after He had spoken some parables… [verse 10 now, Matthew 13]: …And His disciples came to Him and asked, 'Why do You speak to them in parables?' And He answered and said to them, 'Because it has been given to you to know the mysteries of the kingdom of heaven…" Now mysteries is secret—God's secret. We'll see that it is a secret being opened for the understanding of those that God calls. And is also a mystery and a secret that is closing the minds of those who will not obey. So, we'll see what He has here, what He has to say. "…but to them it has not been given' (Matt. 13:10-11).

Verse 12: "'For whoever has *understanding*, to him more shall be given, and he shall have an abundance…" and that's what this book, *The Plan of God Revealed by His Sabbath and Holy Days* does—it gives understanding to those who have understanding and more understanding as we go along, and you will see why I say that. "…but whoever [continuing now, verse 12] does not have *understanding*, even what he has shall be taken away from him. For this *reason* I speak to them in parables, because seeing, they see not; and hearing, they hear not; neither do they understand' " (vs 12-13).

They can have the Bible, they can have Sunday services, they can have Sunday, Sunday school classes, but they keep their Halloween and Christmas and Easter and all the occult holidays. And, while I'm speaking of that, let me mention this: That if you are new to the Sabbath and Holy Days as shown in the Bible, let me suggest that you get the book, *Occult Holidays or God's Holy Days, Which?* You can e-mail us, you can write us or you can call the office and we'll be happy to send you a copy of it because you need to have the knowledge that is in *that* book before you can understand what is in *this* book.

So, continuing now: "And in them is fulfilled the prophecy of Isaiah, which says, 'In hearing you shall hear, and in no way understand; and *in* seeing you shall see, and in no way perceive; For the heart of this people has grown fat [that is through sin], and their ears are dull of hearing [because they want to do their own thing], and their eyes they have closed…'" Which we know they have done with the Word of God so they can justify the way that they teach it. Now, here's what happens: they are cut off from salvation till a later date. "…lest they should see with their eyes, and should hear with their ears, and should understand with their hearts, and should be converted, and I should heal them' (vs 13-15).

Now let's see this in operation. Let's come back here to Isaiah 29. Isaiah 29:9, and here is another prophecy concerning why people don't understand the Bible. Verse 9: "Stay yourselves, and wonder; cry ye out, and cry: they are drunken…" Put in your margin, there, Rev. 17:2—'they are drunken by the wine of the fornication of Babylon the Great,' "…but not with wine…" not physical wine, but false doctrine "…they stagger, but not with strong drink. For the LORD hath poured out upon you the spirit of deep sleep, and hath closed your eyes: the prophets and your rulers, the seers hath he covered. And the vision of all is become unto you as the words of a book that is sealed, which *men* deliver to one that is learned, saying, Read this, I pray thee: and he saith, I cannot; for it *is* sealed: And the book is delivered to him that is not learned, saying, Read this, I pray thee: and he saith, I am not learned. Wherefore the Lord said…" Now here is *a key*: you *must be serious* in your commitment to God, *not curious* about what the Bible may or may not say, "…Forasmuch as this people draw near *me* with their mouth, and with their lips do honour me, but have removed their heart far from me, and their fear toward me is taught by the precept of men: Therefore, behold, I will proceed to do a marvelous work among this people, even a marvelous work and a wonder: for the wisdom of their wise *men* shall perish, and the understanding of their prudent *men* shall be hid" (Isaiah 29:9-14, *KJV*).

Now, verse 15-16: "Woe unto them that seek deep to hide their counsel from the LORD, and their works are in the dark, and they say, Who seeth us? and who knoweth us? Surely your turning of things upside down…" And that's what the pagan 'Christianity' of this world has done—and the religions of the world, they have turned God's way upside down, and they don't understand. And the very thing they ought to keep they don't keep, and the very things that God say you shall not keep, they do keep. "…shall be esteemed as the potter's clay: for shall the work say of him that made it, He made me not? or shall the thing framed say of him that framed it, He had no understanding?"

So, what happens with that? They don't understand.

Now, let's come back here to II Thessalonians 2 and let's see something else that happens, because what needs to be—if you're dealing with the, with, with the Bible you need to understand something very important: The Bible is the Truth of God. Jesus said, "Your word is the truth." In Psalm 119 it says, "All Your commandments are true. Your law is true. All your precepts are true **from the beginning**." And so, we need to understand, unless you are willing to be honest with yourself and honest with the Word of God and apply yourself to it, as we'll see the way God wants it to be done, you will never understand. You'll be just like the one to whom the book was given and you will say, "It is sealed."

Now, let's come to 2 Thessalonians 2:9, because this is talking about the coming one-world ruler, the beast of Revelation 13, and he's going to proclaim himself to be God on earth. And there's going to be a false prophet who's going to endorse him as a manifestation of God in the flesh. Verse 9: "Even the one whose coming is according to *the* inner working of Satan, with all power and signs **and lying wonders**…" So, if you don't know the truth, you'll never know what's happening. "…And with all deceivableness of unrighteousness in those who are perishing because…" now, note this very carefully "…they did not receive the love of the truth, so that they might be saved…." You must love the truth. God is true, God cannot lie, and most preachers and minister, theologian scholars immediately accuse God of lying. "…did not have the love of the truth, And for this cause, God will send upon them **a powerful deception** that will cause them to believe *the* lie, So that all may be judged who did not believe the truth, but who took pleasure in unrighteousness" (2 Thess. 2:9-12). Now then, he commends the brethren for doing what is right.

Now, let's come back to the Old Testament again, Isaiah 28, because here's the way we put the Word of God together; and here's the way that it is understood. Now, while you're turning to Isaiah 28:9, let me quote another Scripture in the New Testament: [2 Tim. 2:15]. You must [be] "rightly dividing the Word of the Truth." Let's understand something else that is, that is readily apparent. The Bible that you have has exactly the same alphabet to print the Word of God for you, so you can read it and understand that all of the evil books of witchcraft and pornography and all of those things have to explain Satan's side of it. So that's why you have to rightly divide the Word of Truth.

Now, here's the one to whom God gives understand, as Jesus said, "It's given to you to understand." Verse 9: "Whom shall he teach knowledge? and whom shall he make to understand doctrine? *them that are* weaned from the milk…" So, that's why I say, it's not for someone brand new, because those who are brand new need the 'milk' of the Word. And Paul says we need the 'meat'. What is in this book is going to be 'meat', and what is in the introduction here, *The Beginning and the Ending,* is strong 'meat' and is going to require that you apply yourself to it to understand it. "…*them that are* weaned from the milk, *and* drawn from the breasts" (Isa. 28:9, *KJV*). And then, this ties in with 2 Timothy 2:15.

"For precept *must* be upon precept, [so you have] precept upon precept precept upon precept; line upon line, line upon line; here a little, *and* there a little" (Isa. 28:10, *KJV*). And that's how you understand the Bible. You compare the Truth with the Truth.

Now, one thing that is going to be amazing with this new book. There is going to be only one bibliography. Where as if you compare the bibliography with the New Testament, it has six pages of bibliography, because of all the commentary that goes with it. And the one book that's going to be the bibliography is the *Holy Bible, Old and New Testament.* And then I'll list a couple of Old Testaments that are also conforming to that and the *New Testament in Faithful Version.*

Now, that same process by which we understand the Word of God, [let's look at it] in reverse. Because everything that God has there are two sides to the coin. By this same process, those who don't understand, if they don't take this procedure, they're never going to understand. And that's why Isaiah 29 covers that particular thing.

Now, let's come back here to Matthew 13 again. Let's make sure we finish that up. Now, back to Matthew 13. Let's come down here to verse 16 and we'll see again what Christ is laying out for us and how important what we're able to understand at the end of the age is. And what we're going to understand, brethren: it isn't because we're anything, and it isn't because we deserve it; it is that God reveals in the time He's ready to reveal. And there's also a prophecy, a proverb, that says it's God's "delight" to hide something in the kings honor to discover it. And so, everything that God wants us to know about Him is in the Bible. And the words that are here are spiritually understood. And everything you need to know about God is contained, in between 1,000-1,500 pages, depending on the size of type and pages of the Bible that you have. Now, you compare that with the Library of Congress, and I've been there once and I was overwhelmed when I saw it, that they try and get every book that is published in the world to be there and cataloged. And yet, they don't have the knowledge of God. What a fantastic thing that God does it in one book. So, this is why you have to have "precept upon precept, line upon line" and put it together. And here's what happens, verse 16, Matthew 13: "But blessed *are* your eyes, because they see; and your ears, because they hear. For truly I say to you, many prophets and righteous men have desired to see what you see, and have not seen; and to hear what you hear, and have not heard" (vs 13-14).

Now, we're going to cover quite a few things which have not been heard. Now, every one of the things that I'm going to cover in the introduction here, I have covered in a different way in the body of the book and the transcripts for this book. But, this puts it all together so we can get a good overview of everything that we are doing.

Now, let's come to John 13 [I mean John 16]. And let's see the promise here that Jesus gave, so that in the end-time we would know. John 16 and let's pick it up in verse 12. John 16:12. "I have yet many things to tell you, but you are not able to bear them now...." See, even the apostles, they didn't understand until later when Christ revealed it to them and He said: "... However, when that one has come, *even* the Spirit of the truth..." and the Spirit of God is the *power* of God, the Spirit of Truth from the God Who is true, Who cannot lie, Who will not lie and His Word is the truth. "...the Spirit of the truth it will lead you into **all** truth..." and that's what we can claim. Not because we're anything, but because there is a time when God wants it revealed—and woe to those who understand it who don't preach it, and then claim it as some great thing because of who they are. It won't work! "...because it shall not speak from itself, but whatever it shall hear, it shall speak. And it shall disclose to you the things to come" (John 16:12-13).

And so, that's what we are going to see. Now, back to the Old Testament, let's come to Psalm 119 and let's see an *astounding* verse—119:18. And here's what we're going to do, we're going to claim this promise. And I want you to understand how tremendous this is. "Open thou mine eyes, that I may behold wondrous things out of thy law" (Psa. 119:18, *KJV*). Now, if you read in the margin, it says: Hebrew for "open," it says, *reveal*. God has to *reveal* these things. And it's quite a thing!

Now, what is contained in the law? Where are the Sabbath and Holy Days listed? *In the law!* And all that we understand from it comes from the rest of God's Word as related to the Holy Days; As related to the Sabbath. Because these are days that God has made Holy where He puts His presence. And these are days, through His Word, that are vehicles that He uses to give us understanding. Now, let's see how this is brought out by the Apostle Paul in Ephesians 1: "In Whom..." That is Christ, and He is the One Who does the revealing. He is the One Who inspired the apostles. "...we have redemption through His blood..." And everything focuses in on Jesus Christ, "...*even* the remission of sins, according to the riches of His grace, Which He has made to abound toward us in all wisdom and intelligence... (Eph. 1:7-8)"

Listen, God wants us to be *wise*, to be *intelligent*, to *educate ourselves* with His Word, and the Bible is not just something written for uneducated—as the elite establishment scholars and theologians would say for those "lower" people to understand, see. No! "We great intellects understand." No, they're blinded. They are blinded. The Bible, the Word of God, coupled with the Holy Spirit is a life-time, extended education program by God to prepare you for eternal life. Very important to understand, because He wants us to have *all* wisdom—not some, not part, *but all wisdom;* and intelligence to be able to think; to be able to make wise choices; to be able to make righteous judgment, as we covered recently.

"Having made known to us the mystery…" and it is revealed through His Sabbath and Holy Days. The "mystery" is the secret of God, which the world cannot know. "…of His own will, according to His good pleasure, which He purposed in Himself; That in *the divine* plan for the fulfilling of *the* times…" which is revealed in the Sabbath and Holy Days, "…He might bring all things together in Christ, both the things in the heavens and the things upon the earth; *Yes,* in Him, in Whom we also have obtained an inheritance, having been predestinated according to His purpose…" and that's why this book. It shows plain the plan, the purpose, the intent, the love of God, the law of God, the truth of God, the prophecies of God, the meaning of the Holy Days, what God is doing and how it's laid out there. "…Who is working out all things according to the counsel of His own will" (vs 9-11).

Now, let's come down to verse 15, after Paul talks about receiving the "earnest of their salvation" and so forth. I covered that in one of the transcripts in the book.

"For this cause, I also, after hearing of the faith in the Lord Jesus that is among you, and the love toward all the saints, Do not cease to give thanks for you, making mention of you in my prayers…" Now, here's what he prayed. Now this prayer is written here so that we know what God wants us to learn. Now notice how tremendous this is: "…That the God of our Lord Jesus Christ, the Father of glory, may give you *the* spirit of wisdom and revelation in *the* knowledge of Him…" See, that's why we're to grow in grace and knowledge; grow in understanding; grow in the Word of God. "…*And* may the eyes of your mind be enlightened…" That is the spiritual understanding that comes from God because of the interaction of God's Holy Spirit in your mind. "…in order that you may comprehend…" He wants us to know "…what is **the hope of His calling,** and what is the **riches of the glory of His inheritance** in the saints, And what is the exceeding **greatness of His power** toward us who believe, according to the inner working of His mighty power, Which He wrought in Christ, **when He raised Him from the dead,** and set *Him* at His right hand in the heavenly *places,* Far above every principality and authority and power and lordship, and every name that is named—not only in this age, but also in the *age* to come; For He has subordinated all things under His feet, and has given Him *to be* head over all things to the church, Which is His body—the fullness of Him Who fills all things in all" (vs 15-23).

Now, let's understand something: *no man is the head of the Church.* Christ is! All teachers, ministers, pastors, evangelists, apostles are on the sidelines to teach the brethren—because Jesus is the great Teacher. And John 6:45 says we'll all be "taught of the Father" and that's by the power of the Holy Spirit. And Jesus is the great Teacher. So, when Jesus said, "It is sufficient for the disciple [that is the learner] …become as his Teacher" (Matt. 10:25). And so, all of this, this book and everything that we do is to help bring you and lift you through the power of God's Holy Spirit to understand the Word of God. And never in the history of the whole world have we had the opportunity to do it, especially here in, in the western world where we have peace; where we have understanding; where we have the Word of God; where we freedom of the assembly; we have freedom of thought—and all of these things. And God expects us to be zealously in there doing, and learning, and growing and overcoming for greatest goal possible: to be spirit beings in the Kingdom of God.

Now let's see another principle. Let's come to I Corinthians 2. Now let's pick it up in verse four so that we understand. Now, realize this: this church at Corinth was the most carnal of all the churches, filled with sin, filled with carnal competition. Even Paul said, "I wanted to bring you strong meat but you weren't able to take it and I had to give you milk and you were hardly able to endure that." And Paul reminded in the book of Hebrews, Chapter 5, that now's the time to have "strong meat" rather than "milk."

And so, this what this, this book is designed to do and especially the introduction. So I say again, if you find it hard to follow, go through the whole book and come back to it periodically as you're going through it.

Now notice verse 4: "And my message and my preaching *was* not in persuasive words of human wisdom; rather, *it was* in demonstration of *the* Spirit and of power; So that **your faith** might not be in the wisdom of men, but **in *the* power of God.** Now we speak wisdom among the *spiritually* mature." Now, the *King James* says "perfect," but remember, we're to become "perfect as the Father in heaven is perfect (Matt. 5:48), but this means "spiritually mature." You have to have a level of understanding. "…however, it is not *the* wisdom of this world…" That's why in the bibliography you won't find a lot of books listed—only the Bible. "… nor of the rulers of this world, who are coming to nothing. Rather, we speak *the* wisdom of God **in a mystery**…" A mystery to the world, a mystery to those who don't know, "…*even* the hidden *wisdom* that God foreordained before the ages **unto our glory**" (1 Cor. 2:4-7).

- Now, think about what God has given us.
- Think about what God has opened our minds to.
- Think about how tremendous that is, that we are being given knowledge and understanding which was before the ages ever began. ***Before*** the world was created!

So, this is amazing, amazing understanding.

Now, verse 8: "Which not one of the rulers of this world has known [secular or religious] (for if they had known, they would not have crucified the Lord of glory); But according as it is written…" Now, ***compare*** this to what we read in Matthew 13: "…*The* eye has not seen, nor *the* ear heard, neither have entered into *the* heart of man, *the* things which God has prepared for those who **love** Him" (vs 8-9). And what is the love of God? "This is the love of God that we keep His commandments and His commandments are not burdensome." Jesus said, "If you love Me you will keep My commandments." He said, "The one who loves me will be keeping My words, and the Words which I give are not Mine but the Father's Who sent them." And that's all tied up in this verse here. Verse 10: But God has revealed *them* to us…" That is, the apostles, now written in the Word of God: "…by His Spirit…" which we saw there in John 16:13—will reveal all truth to us "…for the Spirit searches all things—even the deep things of God."

And what we're going to cover today are some of the deeper things of God, deeper understanding that has actually been there all the time and we preached on them but haven't put it together in this particular manner.

Verse 11: "For who among men understands the things of man except *by* the spirit of man which *is* in him? In the same way also, the things of God no one understands **except *by* the Spirit of God.** [now notice] Now we have not received the spirit of the world…" What is the spirit of the world? Sunday keeping, Christmas, Easter, Halloween, all of the occult holidays. "…but the Spirit that *is* **of God,** so that we might know the things graciously given to us **by God**…" So any understanding we have is through the grace of God. And He wants us to have it but He's not going to give it to those who are not going to use it. That's why Jesus said, "Don't cast your pearls before swine," because they'll trample on it. Now notice: "…Which things we also speak, not in words taught by human wisdom, but in *words* taught by *the* Holy Spirit ***in order*** **to communicate spiritual things by spiritual *means*"** (vs 11-13).

Now, hold your place here and turn to John 6—we'll come right back here—John 6. Now John 6:63. Now combine this together with everything that we have done, because what we are doing here in this sermon, in this study of the Bible, is we're doing exactly what we started out as, "precept upon precept, line upon line, here a little there a little." Now notice verse 63: "It is the Spirit that gives life; the flesh profits nothing. The words that I speak to you, *they* **are spirit and** *they* **are life**" (John 6:63). That's why Paul says, we **compare** *spiritual things with spiritual things* to understand the Word of God.

Now let's come back to I Corinthians 2:14. And as we come back here to 1 Corinthians 2:14 and 15, what we need to realize is this, verse 14—and this confirms exactly what we've been covering, said in a little bit different way. Those who have knowledge, it will be given, those who don't, their eyes will be closed and they're carnal minded. Verse 14: "But *the* natural man [the one who doesn't have the Spirit of God] does not receive the things of the Spirit of God…" Because you have to have the Spirit of God in you **to receive them** and to receive the words that Jesus taught and inspired the apostles because they are spirit and they are life; "…for they are foolishness to him, and he cannot understand *them* because they are **spiritually discerned**" (1 Cor. 2:14).

Now, with all of that said, we are ready to take the two pages of the chart; [see pages 91 and 92] and for the sake of this sermon I have numbered them #1 and #2. The chart #1 is a calendar chart showing the first month of the calculated Hebrew calendar and then an abbreviated count to Pentecost, just to save space, and then the seventh month. Now the reason being is that all the Holy Days of God are confined to the first month and Pentecost and the seventh month. Now, we're going to see certain parallels as we go through. Now I want you to look at the first month. You'll see across the top I have the days numbered with the Sabbath being the seventh day. I want you to come to the first day of the month—I have the days of the month written in the middle of the square, printed in the middle of the square. And I have a little square around them. The reason I do is this: Because, now, I'm going to **assume** you know where these Scriptures are in the book of Exodus and so forth.

First day of the first month God said—in Exodus 12—to Moses: "This is the beginning of months." So the first day of the first month is the "beginning of months." Now, come down to the first day of the seventh month—which, by the way is the Feast of Trumpets—and it is the beginning of the calendar year for the calculated Hebrew calendar. So, it has to do also with the year, but in this case, for calculating the whole year.

All right, notice again, the Feast of Trumpets, the first day of the seventh month, that's when Jesus was born. Now, you can read in the *Harmony* about that and how we came to understand that. And, the first day of the seventh month pictures when Jesus returns to **literally** put His feet on the earth and the saints with Him to take over the governments of this world. So this becomes a very important thing. Now, let's come back and look at some other things here. Let's come back to the first month. And let's come to the second Sabbath, which then is the tenth day of the first month. And this is where Moses was told by God, "On the tenth day of the first month let the children of Israel select out a lamb from the flock—a kid or a goat." *Very important!*

As we will see, and you can look in the *Harmony,* in Chapter 12 of the Gospel of John, when the voice came from heaven that was when God the Father selected Jesus Christ on the tenth day of the first month to be the Lamb sacrificed to take away the sin of the world. So you have both. You've got Old Testament and New Testament.

Now remember, as we started out, God *revealed* to us, or opened to us, "marvelous things out of Your law." This is all part of it.

THREE FESTIVAL SEASONS

1st Month

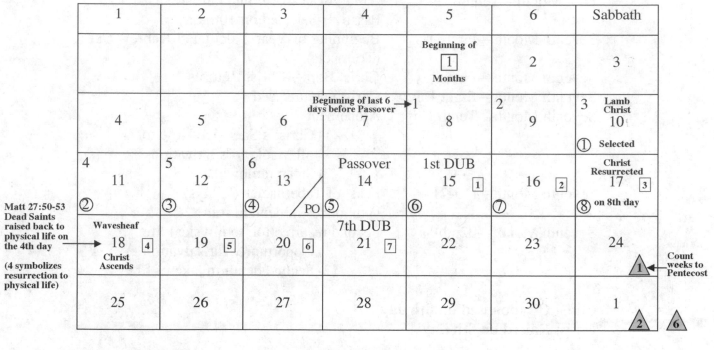

1	2	3	4	5	6	Sabbath
				Beginning of 〔1〕 Months	2	3
4	5	6	Beginning of last 6 days before Passover →1 7	8	2 9	3 Lamb Christ 10 ① Selected
4 11 ②	5 12 ③	6 13 ④	Passover 14 /PO ⑤	1st DUB 15 〔1〕 ⑥	16 〔2〕 ⑦	Christ Resurrected 17 〔3〕 ⑧ on 8th day
Matt 27:50-53 Dead Saints raised back to physical life on the 4th day → Wavesheaf 18 〔4〕 Christ Ascends	19 〔5〕	20 〔6〕	7th DUB 21 〔7〕	22	23	24 △1 Count weeks to Pentecost
(4 symbolizes resurrection to physical life) 25	26	27	28	29	30	1 △2 △6

Pentecost Count   3rd Month   7 X 7 + 1 = 50

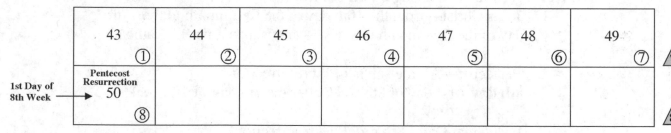

43 ①	44 ②	45 ③	46 ④	47 ⑤	48 ⑥	49 ⑦ △7
1st Day of 8th Week → Pentecost Resurrection 50 ⑧						△8

7th Month

						Trumpets 〔1〕 Beginning of Year
2	3	4	5	6	7	Christ ◄8► Circumcised
9	Atonement 10 1 Lamb for God 1 Lamb for Azazel	11	12	13	14	FOT Holyday 15 ① Millennium Begins
16 ②	17 ③	18 ④	19 ⑤	20 ⑥	Millennium Ends 21 ⑦	Last Great Day 2nd Resurrection 22 ⑧ to a Physical Life 4+4=8 ← 100 Year Period

91

First Month—First Day	Beginning of months
First Month—Tenth Day	Lamb for Passover and Christ our Passover Selected on 10th day
Seventh Month—First Day	Beginning of Year Calculated Hebrew Cal. (Trumpets)
Seventh Month—First Day	Christ Born—Christ Returns
Seventh Month—Eight Day	Christ Circumcised
Seventh Month—Tenth Day	Atonement

        (1) Christ's Sacrifice Now for
           all Mankind's Salvation
        (2) Satan removed

Seventh Month—(15-21)	Feast of Tabernacles (7 days) symbolizes millennial reign
Seventh Month—22nd Day	Second resurrection to physical life

        (1) Opportunity for salvation
        (2) Second death in lake of fire

Christ **Circumcised on 8th day**
Christ **Raised on 8th day**

All Resurrections occurring on an 8th day
    1. - Jesus Christ—from the 10th day of the first month to the 17th
      day of the first month is 8 days—and is also a weekly Sabbath

    2. - Pentecost—All the saints in 1st resurrection
      8th day - 1st day of 8th week after the 7th day of 7th week

    3. - Last Great Day - **8th day** (2nd resurrection)

	Holy Days
P.O. & DUB	2 - DUB
1+7=8	1 - Pentecost
	1 - Trumpets
	1 - Atonement
FOT & LGD	1 - Tabernacles
7+1=8	1 - LGD
	7 - Total

* All resurrections occur during the 3 festival seasons.

Now, I want you to notice something else. We have there, notice, down in the lower left-hand corner of the tenth day of the first month where "Lamb Christ" is "selected" I have a number 1 circled. Now, follow the circled count, which is the Sabbath. One, two, three, four, five. And day five is the Passover day from when Jesus was selected.

Now then, what is the number of grace? *Five*—and it's by the grace of God that we receive the blood of Jesus Christ for the remission of our sins to be under grace. Isn't that interesting.

All right, let's count six, seven, eight. Now, we're going to find that the number eight is associated with the resurrection. Jesus was resurrected *on the eighth day* after He was *selected*. And He was resurrected at the end of the Sabbath and did not ascend until the next morning. So when He was resurrected, He stood up before God, and as I've covered in some of the sermons, He thanked God for raising Him from the dead and all of the different things that we have covered there. *So remember day number eight*—very important to understand.

Now, in these verses, not verses, but in these days I also have beginning on the eighth day of the first month, which you will find detailed in the *Harmony of the Gospels,* is six days before the Passover. So, in the upper left-hand corner—not circled or boxed—I have beginning on the eighth day of the first month: one, two, three, four, five, six and after that, at sunset, that's when they kept the Passover, that's why there's that little slash line on day thirteen, showing that when the 13th day ended and the 14th day began, that's when they kept the Passover.

Now, isn't it interesting, all these things come together. Now, let's understand something else. We'll see some [other] things concerning day number eight. Write these down for day number eight. It has to do with circumcision.

Now, let's see a parallel in the seventh month, in selecting of a sacrificial lamb again, a kid of the goats—on the seventh month, on the tenth day. You can put in your notes there: Leviticus 16.

Now notice, on page two, I have "7—10": two goats selected, that's on the Day of Atonement, the tenth day. So, you have the tenth day of the first month, the lamb was selected, a type of Christ; and we have the Passover on the fourteenth. Now here, what we're dealing with in the first month is this: Number one, we're dealing with the salvation of Israel being taking out of Egypt; and then when Christ comes, we're dealing with the salvation of the individuals that God calls. Because God is not calling the world, at this time. He's not saving the world, at this time. He's only calling and saving those that He calls.

So, when Christ was selected, this is the Lamb to cover the sins of each one individually. God hasn't provided it for the world yet. But when we come to the seventh month, the tenth day—the Day of Atonement—*then God provides it.* And in order to save the world there has to be something else that takes place. That's why on the tenth day of the seventh month there were two goats selected: one for the Lord, one for Azazel because in order to get rid of sin to save the masses of the people, *you must get rid of Satan!* Because as long as he's around there's going to be sin.

That's why those that are called now for the first resurrection, given the Holy Spirit, they have to fight against Satan, they have to overcome Satan, they have to overcome the temptations of the flesh, and that's why the first resurrection is a "better" resurrection. However, before the millennium begins when the great harvest is going to take place, Satan is removed. Now, let's look again on number eight. I said, we would look to number eight, because Christ was raised on the eighth day. Let's look at some other things. What we'll do is, I'll just quote the Scriptures and we will talk about it:

Eighth day: Circumcision—that's when the young boy is accepted into the community of God. Circumcision, eighth day: that was a covenant that God made with Abraham. So put down: Genesis 17:12; Genesis 21:4; Leviticus 12:3. Now, also put down there, Luke 2:21, because Jesus was circumcised on the eighth day.

Now, before we get any further, let's look at some other things concerning the "eighth day." This has to do with uncleanness for seven days and then on the eighth day. And what we're going to see, *the eighth day represents when we stand before God.*

When Jesus was resurrected, did He stand before God? *Yes!*
When Jesus was circumcised, was that before God? *Yes!*—accepted of God.

Okay, now, when you're unclean—and we're all unclean in our sins, correct? And the ultimate uncleanness is what? *Corruption of the flesh in the grave, is it not?* And the resurrection we're going see in a little bit, will also be on an "eighth day," and we'll stand before God and be clean and pure and spiritual. Okay, cleansing: Leviticus 14:8-10, on the eighth day, after they have bathed at the end of the seventh, then they come on eighth day and bring their offering before God. Leviticus 14:23: same thing. Leviticus 15:13-15 and Leviticus 15:28-30. Let me read those again: Leviticus 14:8-10; Leviticus 14:23; Leviticus 15:13-15 and Leviticus 15:28-30.

Now, also, also, we need to look at Pentecost. The resurrection of Jesus was on the eighth day, correct? after He was selected. Now, let's come here and let's count Pentecost, let's count Pentecost. Wave Sheaf Offering Day: the eighteenth day of the first month. Now, we'll come back and look at some of these other numbers here again—okay. The first week ends on the 24th, and I number the weeks with a triangle with a number in it. So, you'll see on the twenty-fourth day of the first month there's a number one in a triangle.

On the first day of the second month there's a two with a triangle. Well, rather than just put in all the weeks, what I did: I put to the right of it a number six in a triangle. And that brings us to the seventh week. Let's count the days of the seventh week beginning with day 43: 43, 44, 45, 46, 47, 48, 49—7x7+1=50.

But, if you will notice, I also numbered them with a number in a circle, because the last week is seven days, right?: 1, 2, 3, 4, 5, 6, 7—on the seventh Sabbath. And on the morrow after the seventh Sabbath has to be the first day of the week, *can never be Monday.* And once you understand something very, very important concerning the Wave Sheaf Offering Day at the beginning up here on the day after the Sabbath. The Hebrew is *absolutely clear,* beyond any doubt, when it says, "on the next day after the Sabbath" the Hebrew for Sabbath is *ha shab-bat*—and that means "the Sabbath." All Holy Days being Sabbaths are "a" Sabbath, never "the" Sabbath. So, that should end anything concerning a Monday Pentecost. Because you cannot have a Monday Pentecost and have the day of Pentecost on the fiftieth day after the seventh Sabbath—it's an impossibility because Monday is the day after the first day which is the second day.

So, it doesn't say on the second day *after* the seventh Sabbath. It says "on the day after the seventh Sabbath."

Now, notice as you count the last week, Pentecost becomes the eighth day, doesn't it? *Yes!* And eight is associated with what? *The resurrection, a new beginning.* And the Day of Pentecost is also another thing, it's the first day of the eighth week, which is symbolic: the first day of the rest of eternity for those who are in the first resurrection. Now, go to the different sermons that we have in there concerning the resurrection.

Now, let's look at some other things here. Let's come to Matthew 27. This is *very* interesting—Matthew 27. And I think this is going to be really something. Matthew 27:50: "And after crying out again with a loud voice, Jesus yielded up *His* spirit [verse 51]. And suddenly the veil of the temple was ripped in two from top to bottom, and the earth shook, and the rocks were split. And the tombs were opened," Now follow this carefully. "…and many bodies of the saints who had died **arose."** Now, these must have been those who recently died. "…And after His resurrection…" when was He resurrected? At the end of the Sabbath, correct? When would they appear? *On the Wave Sheaf Offering Day.* So there were a lot of the things going on, on the Wave Sheaf Offering Day. "…they came out of the tombs *and* entered into the holy city, and **appeared to many**" (vs 50-53).

Now, let's look, let's look at the count here. All right, you have in another little circle, above the circle that we covered. Let's come to the fifteenth day of the first month—okay—because Jesus was put in the tomb right as the fourteenth ended and the fifteenth began. So, look at that number one in the little circle. We have one, two, three (on the Sabbath), that should read a three, and the Wave Sheaf Offering Day when they *appeared* to everyone was day four—half of a spiritual resurrection of eight, correct?

Now, question: How long was Lazarus dead before he was raised back to a physical life? *Four days!* Because Martha said, "Lord, he's been dead four days." So *four* is a resurrection number back to physical life. When God determines to bring someone back to life, in this case, it's counted as *four*. So, that's why Jesus did it. And He also brought them back to life in a physical life because you must qualify for salvation while you're in the flesh. And these were those who were called but died, never had an opportunity for salvation because the Holy Spirit was not yet given, so they came back to life and appeared to many on the Wave Sheaf Offering Day.

Can you imagine what all the Jewish leaders were going through trying to put out all these fires. Now, the reason that these saints who were resurrected had to be contemporary and were called because of the preaching of Jesus, but died before the giving of the Holy Spirit, [the] reason it had to be them, because someone who was alive could come in and say, "I'm so-and-so and I was resurrected"—and you don't know whether that's so or not. But, if you *know* that you buried Aunt Martha or your buried Uncle Charlie or you buried your mother or father and they come back and appear to you—*you know* that's who they are and that's a tremendous witness.

People who died were called, were being called and died during the, the ministry of Jesus Christ. It would have to be those.

Now, let's come to the seventh month again. Let's come to the Feast of Tabernacles, the third Sabbath, the fifteenth day of the seventh month. Oh, as you're coming down you go Trumpets. The first of the month, [then] you have the next Sabbath which is the eighth, and that's when Jesus was circumcised. He was circumcised **on the Sabbath day.** All right, now you come to the fifteenth day of the seventh month, and notice, I again have numbers in the lower left-hand corner.

How many days is the Feast of Tabernacles? *Seven days*

All right, remember how I have preached and we have learned that those who qualify for salvation during the millennium will not have to die and be buried and resurrected. There will be no resurrection of people during the millennium. They will, when they qualify for eternal life they will be in the same category as the saints who are alive when Jesus returns, who are changed in a moment, in an instant, in a "twinkling of an eye" and they will go from flesh to spirit and enter into the spiritual kingdom of God as they qualify through the sacrifice of Christ, through the grace of God, through loving God and living and proving that through God's help and Spirit that they are worthy of eternal life. Those who do not qualify do what? *They die and are buried and wait for the resurrection of the wicked.*

Now notice, there is the eighth day. And isn't it interesting, the last day—the eighth day—that's the day of what? *That's the day of the second resurrection.* See, Revelation 20 says, "...and the rest of the dead lived not again until the thousand years are finished." Eight, again, is associated with a resurrection. And in this case, back to physical life, so it's two times four, which means a second opportunity of physical life, for a first opportunity for salvation.

Now the resurrection, to have an opportunity for salvation, is the first phase of the second resurrection. (The second phase of the second resurrection is the resurrection of all of those who committed the unpardonable sin down through time.) They will all be raised together, given a physical life—those who are called to salvation and have a chance for eternal life.

[However] the second phase of the second resurrection will take place at the end of the hundred-year period. All the wicked will be raised to their second life. All of those during the Great White Throne Judgment who live a hundred years and do not accept salvation will remain alive to stand along side all the incorrigible wicked who are raised and they will all together be cast into the lake of fire. Very interesting how all of that comes together.

Now, let's look at this here. Let's come back to page two. The resurrection:

1. Jesus Christ was resurrected on the eighth day after His selection on the tenth. Ten to seventeen—now notice why it's important to count, because if you merely subtract you only have seven days. That's why you have to **count inclusively**. So that's why you have to look at the calendar to do it. So, the resurrection of Jesus occurred on the 8th day after He was selected.

2. Now come to Pentecost. All the saints in the first resurrection, which is the eighth day after the seventh Sabbath, which is the first day of the eighth week. So notice in the three seasons that, that we are to come before God, the Feast of Unleavened Bread, the Feast of Pentecost and the Feast of Tabernacles and the Last Great Day, there is a resurrection associated with each three. Christ, the saints and then:

3. The Last Great Day, when those who are raised, receive and opportunity for eternal life and the wicked are raised to die the second death. In order to die twice, you have to live twice.

Now, let's look at the symmetry of what God has done here. This is really something! We have the Passover plus the Days of Unleavened Bread is 1+7=8, correct? *Yes.*

We have Tabernacles, [it] is just the inverse: 7+1=8.

Now, let's look at the Holy Days: Though there are eight feasts, because the Passover is a feast, there are only seven Holy Days. Two during Unleavened Bread, one for Pentecost, one for Trumpets, one for Atonement, one for Tabernacles and one for the Last Great Day.

See how all of those fit together. This is really quite, quite something, when you look at how God has set this. And look at the parallels between the first month and the seventh month. The first day of the first month is the beginning of months. The first day of the seventh month is the beginning of the year—calculated Hebrew calendar. It is the day that Jesus was born. It is the day that Jesus will return.

The first day of the tenth month Christ was selected as the Lamb of God for the sins of the world. In the seventh month on the tenth day of the seventh month, you have the selection of Christ again for the world and the removal of Satan the devil. So you have a parallel. Tenth day of the first month, tenth day of the seventh month.

Isn't that interesting how that comes along. Notice, you have the fifteenth day of the first month begins the Feast of Unleavened Bread, correct? *Yes.* You have the fifteenth day of the seventh month begins the Feast of Tabernacles, correct? *Yes.*

Then of course, you have the Passover to start Unleavened Bread and then you've got the Last Great Day to end the Feast of Tabernacles. So, here we have a very interesting overview, which gives us more understanding concerning what God is doing, how God is doing it, the way that He is doing it, and what it means for us and how you can understand the Holy Days in this special book, *God's Plan for Mankind Revealed by His Sabbath and Holy Days.*

And as you view these, you're going to see why God uses the calculated Hebrew calendar. Let me just mention here: There's evidence in the beginning that it was, the year was 12 months long, 30 days in a month, 360 days in a year. That's why, have you ever wondered why in a circle they have 360 degrees? But the circle that the earth now circles the sun is not 360, and *that's because of the sins of man.* And that's because of the astronomical events that took place on the earth and also the promise that God gave to Hezekiah to move the sun back ten degrees on the sundial. Now, He didn't stop the earth and bam! everything is all destroyed 'cause you stopped the earth and you move it back. *No!*

It was calculated that the way that you get the extra 5-1/2, 5-1/4 days per years is that in order to go back ten degrees, you move the earth slightly out of its orbit by 1.4 percent. So that's why we have 365-1/4 days today. That's why the calendar must be *calculated.* And all of those who have their own visual calendar are not in sequence or in synchronization with the calculated Hebrew calendar and they're either always early or they're always late *because they don't believe God;* and they don't believe that the calculated Hebrew calendar is what God gave. They believe the propaganda and teachings of men.

So, with this overview, it shows you the comparison between the first month and the seventh month. And it shows in each one of the Feasts there is a resurrection involved. So, that's something!

All right, well I hope you're able to understand it. If not, take the chart, go back over it again and see what you can do. But this helps us understand God's plan for mankind. *And notice:* Not one book or one thing that was read from any other book than the Bible. And it all begins with the law, "reveal to me wondrous things out of Your law."

I hope that this book will illuminate you with the Word of God.

End of Sermon

Transcriber: Bonnie Orswell

Introduction—Beginning & Ending
November 18, 2006
Scriptural References

1) Matthew 13:10-15

2) Isaiah 29:9-16

3) Psalm 29:9-16

4) II Thessalonians 2:9-10

5) Isaiah 28:9-10

6) Matthew 13:16

7) John 16:12-13

8) Psalm 110:18

9) Ephesians 1:7-11, 15-23

10) I Corinthians 2:4-13

11) John 6:63

12) I Corinthians 2:14

13) Matthew 27:50-53

Referenced Scriptures not quoted:

1) Revelation 17:2

2) Psalm 119

3) Revelation 13

4) II Thess. 2:4 (Actually II Timothy 2:15)

5) Isaiah 29

6) John 6:45

7) Hebrews 5

8) Matthew 5:48

9) Exodus 12

10) John 12

11) Leviticus 16

12) Genesis 17:12, 21:4

13) Leviticus 12:3

14) Luke 2:21

15) Leviticus 14:8-10. 23

16) Leviticus 15:13-15, 28-30

17) Revelation 20

Referenced Material:

Occult Holidays or God's Holy Days, Which?
Three Festival Seasons Chart
Harmony of the Gospels

CHAPTER SEVEN

Should We Keep the Holy Days?

August 7, 1999

Should we keep the Holy Days of the Bible? Most religions that profess themselves to be Christian claim that, "No, we don't have to keep them." And many of them such as the Seventh Day Adventists, and others as well, claim that because there were sacrifices on these days; therefore, they were ritualistic and sacrificial days only and have no meaning <u>other than</u> what they meant in the Old Testament. Now is that true, and what does the Bible show, and what does the Bible teach?

Now how can people take the Bible and interpret that it's perfectly all right to keep Halloween and Christmas and New Years and Ground Hog's Day and Lent and Good Friday and Easter, and all of the Pagan holidays and say that in the Bible we can do that when it is never even listed in the Bible? How is that possible? Well, here is what happens. Let's come to 2 Corinthians 2 and the very last verse, 2 Corinthians 2:17: "For we are not like the many…" so what we are dealing with is a very, very old problem. "…Who for *their own* profit are corrupting the Word of God…" and the Word of God is corrupted by: poor translations, wrong texts, and also by corrupt interpretations, and by claiming things that are not substantiated by the Bible. So what needs to be done is this: People need to go through the Bible and they really need to put it all together as we know in Isaiah 28:13: "…Line upon Line; precept upon precept; here a little and there a little…" and also as Paul told Timothy that you have to rightly divide the Word of Truth. Now let's finish this verse: "…but we speak with sincerity as from God *and* before God, *and* in Christ."

Now we're going to look at some other Scriptures and so let's go to 2 Corinthians 4, and let's begin in verse 1.

Here, 2 Corinthians 4:1. "Therefore, having this ministry, according as we have received mercy, we are not fainthearted. For we have personally renounced the hidden things of dishonest gain,…" Now that's a very important thing to do, because the human heart is "…desperately wicked above all things, deceitful and desperately wicked; who can know it?" (Jeremiah 17:9, paraphrased). So you have to renounce that. "...Not walking in cunning craftiness,…" Now, "walking in craftiness" means walking with a hidden agenda that other people don't know, that you will craftily spring upon them at a later date. "...Nor handling the Word of God deceitfully;..." That is, by taking the Word of God and applying it to things which are not true, or to things which are not true and saying they are true. "...But by manifestation of the truth, we are commending ourselves to every man's conscience before God. But if our gospel is hidden, it is hid to those who are perishing; In whom the god of this world hath blinded the minds of those who do not believe, lest the light of the gospel of the glory of Christ, Who is *the* image of God, should shine unto them" (2 Cor. 4:1-4).

So any part of the Gospel that you have hidden from you, or blinded from you, then you need to understand that it falls into several categories here. Number one, you have misinterpreted the Word of God; number two, you have blinded your eyes to it; number three, it may be a tradition; or number four, Satan has blinded your mind to that part of it. Because Satan is trying to get all those who truly have the Spirit of God and are Christians to give up on something somewhere·along the line, because he knows that a little leaven leavens the whole lump.

Now let's also understand something here. Let's come to Matthew 7, and this is profound. Some of these Scriptures are very basic, because this is a very basic topic; as a matter of fact, so basic that I have not given a sermon on proving keeping the holy days in years and years and years and years, because I'm basically dealing with all of those who keep the holy days. But now when we come into contact with people who do not keep the holy days, nor understand the holy days, then we do need to go back and we need to reconfirm the truth as to why we do it, and so forth. But I'm going to approach this a little bit differently. Here, Matthew 7. Let's understand this. Now we have applied this to false prophets, haven't we? Because Matthew 7 talks about false prophets. And there can be a prophet who is a half false prophet by preaching half truth. So you need to understand that too. Verse 21, "Not every one who says to Me, 'Lord, Lord', shall enter into the kingdom of heaven: but the one who is doing the will of My Father, Who *is* in heaven."

That is the key. Are you doing the will of the Father? And was it the Father's will that Christ created the Sabbath? Was it the Father's will that Christ gave the holy days to the children of Israel? Was it the Father's will in these things? Now, was it the Father's will that what Christ did and what He observed part of what God wanted? Yes, absolutely. So if you are not doing the will of the Father which is in heaven, though you use the name of the Lord, though you may belong to a church, though you may have a group which really is a group that you really like, "Many will say to Me in that day, Lord, Lord, did we not prophesied through Your name?..." Now that means, "preached in Your name." And I have heard some stinging sermons against the holy days. And there are tremendous errors in their way of thinking. We'll cover that a little later. "...And *did we* not cast out demons through Your name? And *did we not* perform many works of power through Your name?" (Matt. 7:21-22).

So you see, you can have part of the fruits there. You can have some of the things that look like they come from God. You can have some of the truth of God. But unless you have the whole truth of God and you are willing to live by all the truth of God, and if when you come to understand the truth of God which you have previously not understood, you are willing to keep it. If you're not doing those things then you're going to end up in this category, verse 23: "And then I will confess to them, 'I never knew you. Depart from Me, you who work lawlessness." Now that means being against law. So since the holy days are part of the law of God, you need to make yourself very sure that you are not against the law of God as respecting the holy days. Because you see, the only thing you have different than, other than the Sabbath, you have nothing different than a Protestant. So you might as well put yourself in the same category of the Protestants if the only thing you do is keep the Sabbath. Now if that offends some people, well then, you might take your offense to God and find out from His Word what you need to do.

Now we have to keep the will of God. Now this is the attitude that we need—Psalm 143. Let's go back there. The will of God is contained in His Word. And the will of God is here for us that we're to keep. And we're going to see that it is the will of God that we keep the feasts of God. And as a matter fact, we're going to see later that the apostle Paul, with no doubt, no question whatsoever, absolutely commands the keeping of the feast. Psalm 143:10, "Teach me to do Thy will;..." So God is the one Who is going to have to teach you from His Word and with His Spirit. "...For Thou *art* my God: Thy Spirit *is* good; lead me into the land of uprightness." That is, to be righteous before God.

Now here is a New Testament expression of that very same Psalm. Let's come to Romans 12. And this is important for us to realize. Because the will of God is what we are all going to be held accountable for, right? Didn't Jesus say that? Didn't Jesus say to those who were not doing the will of the Father in heaven above that they were going to be cast into outer darkness? Yes He did. And believe me, after the experience in the lake of fire it will be outer darkness. There will be nothing left. Now here, Romans 12:1, "I exhort you therefore, brethren,..." So Paul here is sincerely asking the brethren, "...by the mercies of God, to present your bodies a living sacrifice, holy *and* well pleasing to God, which is your spiritual service. Do not conform yourselves to this world, but be transformed by the re-viewing of your mind in order that you may prove what *is* well pleasing and good, and the perfect, will of God" (Rom. 12:1-2). And so that's what we have to do. That's why the holy day issue becomes very important. So as we go through this, ask yourself, "Am I keeping all the will of God?"

Now let's notice here, very important. It says prove, renewing of your mind. So you are to use your mind. Rightly divide the Word of God, as Paul told Timothy. Rightly divide it, see, not handle it improperly. "...That you may prove..." Now how do you prove some-thing? You prove something by the facts. God is fact. His law is fact. His Word is fact, as well as truth. Now what's important here is this. You don't go on what you feel. You don't go on what you personally believe. Because a lot of personal beliefs, then, become idols be-fore God. They are idols in your mind. So you have to prove what is the good and accept-able and perfect will of God. How? As defined by His Word. That's how you do it. You don't prove it by an emotion or a feeling. See, God's Word is here. You have the whole thing, it's impartial. The problems come when people interpret things. And the problems come when they interpret them incorrectly.

So let's go here and look at some of these things and see how these are handled and what is done. Now let's go to Luke 16, and let's see one of the Scriptures which has been misinterpreted almost universally by the Catholics, by the Protestants, and by some in the churches of God; in particularly the Sabbath-keeping, non-holy day-keeping churches of God, which also includes the Seventh-Day Adventists. Let's pick it up here in verse 13. This becomes very important for us to understand. "No servant is able to serve two masters; [that's true] for either he will hate the one, and he will love the other; or else he will hold to *the* one, and will despise the other. Ye cannot serve God and mammon." Meaning, that there's only one way to serve God, and that's through His Word, and through His truth, and with His Spirit.

"Now the Pharisees who were also covetous, heard all these things; and they ridi-culed Him. And He said to them, 'You are those who justify themselves before men,...'" And that's exactly what happens with all of these false doctrines. They justify themselves before men. "...But God knows your hearts; for that which is highly esteemed among men is an abomination before God.' " Now that can apply to all the religions of men. They're very highly esteemed, aren't they? Yes. Now here's the verse that He's leading up to here. And this is something that almost everyone universally does not understand. "The law and the Prophets *were* until John:..." "Therefore, from the time of John the Baptist the laws of God have been done away." That is the conclusion. Let's read the whole thing and see what it says. "The law and the prophets were until John; from that time the kingdom of God is preached, and everyone zealously strives to enter it." Showing that to enter the kingdom of God is a difficult situation.

With the kingdom of God being preached, does that do away with the laws and com-mandments of God, including the holy days? What does it mean, "The law and the prophets were until John"? Now there's also another misconception that people are under, which is this: is that Jesus was under the Old Covenant. Not true. Jesus was under a special covenant between Him and God the Father, so He could establish the New Covenant. The New Cove-nant is the kingdom of God. The Law and the Prophets were the authority for preaching up to that time. Now then, Christ comes and the kingdom of God is preached. But notice, He wants to make it very clear concerning the laws of God. He wants you to understand that the laws and commandments of God have not been done away because there's a different emphasis in preaching. Verse 17, "But it is easier *for* heaven and earth to pass away than *for* one tittle of the law to fail" (Luke 16:13-17).

Now let's look at another scripture. Let's come to Matthew 5:17. Now especially for those who are Sabbath-keepers, you believe in the commandments of God. You believe in the Ten Commandments, and you've probably read this scripture. Well you have to apply it correctly to all the rest of the Scriptures as well. So let's read it here: "Do not think that I have come to abolish the Law, or the Prophets;..." Now that means don't let it enter into your mind. Don't even think this thought. Now, "destroy" means abolish, or do away. "...I did not come to abolish, but to fulfill." Now here's where the other miscommunication and twisting of the Scripture comes, which is this: if Christ fulfills it, then we don't have to do it. Which is where people get into the false doctrine of saying, "Well, Christ fulfilled the Sabbath for me; therefore, I don't have to keep it." Or, "Christ fulfilled the holy days; therefore, I don't have to keep them." Or, "Christ fulfilled 'You shall do no murder'; therefore, I can murder." Or, "Christ fulfilled 'Do not commit adultery'; therefore, it's all right to commit adultery." No, because then you have abolished the law. Let's find out what Jesus fulfilled, and let's find out what is yet to be fulfilled, or is still being fulfilled.

Now notice again verse 18. "For truly I say to you, until the heaven and the earth shall pass away, one jot or one tittle shall in no way pass from the Law, until everything has been fulfilled" (Matt. 5:17-18). That means everything be fulfilled. And then of course, when that is fulfilled, then if you read Revelation 21 and 22, then you have a new beginning with other things which are going to be fulfilling to a greater degree than the ones we've had in the past.

Now let's come to the book of Hebrews and see, first of all, what did Jesus fulfill? Because I know that the doctrine of not keeping the holy days, for those who keep the Sabbath, is that the holy days were part of the ritual. Well, we will see Jesus did away with the ritual. But did He do away with the days? Now let's come here to Hebrews 9, and let's see what it is that Christ did. Verse 11, "But Christ Himself has become High Priest of the coming good things, through the greater and more perfect tabernacle, not made by human hands (that is, not of this *present physical* creation)..." And Paul was referring to the physical building of the temple in Jerusalem at the time. "...Not by *the* blood of goats and calves, but by the means of His own blood, He entered once for all into the holiest, having *by* Himself secured everlasting redemption *for us*" (Heb. 9:11-12).

Now let's come all the way down here to verse 28. "...So Christ, having been offered once to bear *the* sins of many, will appear *the* second time without sin unto salvation to those who are eagerly awaiting Him." Now then, Paul goes on to explain what Christ did with His sacrifice to fulfill. And when He fulfilled it, we will see that He added to it a greater sacrifice, that is, being His sacrifice. So we're going to find that He fulfilled the animal sacrifice and the temple ritual for a special purpose.

Hebrews 10:1, "For the law, having *only* a shadow of the good things that are coming, *and* not the image of those things, with the same sacrifices which they offer continually year by year, is never able to make perfect those who come *to worship*." It is the goal of God to have everything perfected. These animal sacrifices could not do it. "Otherwise, would they not have ceased to be offered? For once those who worship had been purified, *they would* no longer be conscious of sin. On the contrary, in offering these sacrifices year by year, there is a remembrance of sins. Because *it is* impossible for *the* blood of bulls and goats to take away sins." Because it's a lesser being then a human being. How can a goat atone for human sin? How can a bull atone for human sin? No, those things were just to cover them at the temple so they could continue functioning under the Old Covenant.

"For this reason, when He comes into the world, He says, 'Sacrifice and offering You did not desire, buy You have prepared a body for Me....'' Now that's referring to Christ. "... You did not delight in burnt offerings and *sacrifices* for sin. Then said I, 'Lo, I come (*as* it is written of Me in *the* scroll of *the* book) to do Your will, O God.' " God's will and the proper worship of God, the proper forgiveness of sin before God, is what he's talking about here. It ties right in with what we talked about—the will of God. "In the saying above, *He said*, 'Sacrifice and offering and burnt offerings and *sacrifices* for sin (which are offered according to the law) You did not desire nor delight in'...." But is that the whole law? Let me ask you this question: do the animal sacrifices constitute the whole law of God, or are they part of the law of God as we find in the Old Testament? No. The animal sacrifices were a small part of the law of God. And we're going to see that when we get into it.

Verse 9, "...Then He said, 'Lo, I come to do Your will, O God.' He takes away the first *covenant* in order that He may establish the second *covenant*;..." The first covenant with the second covenant, but understand this: the covenant does not do away with law; the covenant is your relationship with God. And in every covenant there are always laws. "By Whose will we are sanctified through the offering of the body of Jesus Christ once for all. Now every high priest stands ministering day by day, offering the same sacrifices repeatedly, which are never able to remove sins; But He, after offering one sacrifice for sins for ever, sat down at *the* right hand of God...." What are we talking about here? We're not talking about doing away with law; we're talking about doing away with sin. The way to do away with sin and the way to worship God is what has been changed.

Now stop and think of this: what is sin? New Testament doctrine: Sin is the transgression of the law. So the New Covenant is how to do away with sin and your relationship with God. So Jesus' one sacrifice fulfilled all the animal sacrifices and all the temple ritual, and replaced it with His sacrifice and with the temple in heaven above. So it was done away with only in respect to that it was obsolete and not effective, and never could do away with sin. And now we have a new way of worshiping God under the New Covenant. So far having nothing to do with the Sabbath, having nothing to do with the holy days. Let's continue on.

Verse 14, "For by one offering He has obtained eternal perfection *for* those who are sanctified. And the Holy Spirit also bears witness to us; for after He had previously said, 'This *is* the covenant that I will establish with them after those days,' says *the* Lord: 'I will give My laws into their hearts, and I will inscribe them in their minds;...'" Now that is the exact opposite of doing away with anything. That is the exact opposite of fulfilling them for you as a person. "...And their sins and iniquities I will not remember ever again." Whereas the animal sacrifices were what? There was a remembrance of sin every year, correct? Yes. "Now where remission of these *is*, *it is* no longer *necessary to offer* sacrifices for sin", of animals and other rituals, because the one offering for sin was Christ.

"Therefore, brethren, having confidence to enter into the *true* holiest by the blood of Jesus, by a new and living way, which He consecrated for us through the veil, (that is, His flesh), and *having* a great High Priest over the house of God, let us approach *God* with a true heart, with full conviction of faith, our hearts having been purified from a wicked conscience, and our bodies having been washed with pure water. Let us hold fast without wavering *to* the hope *that* we profess, for He Who promised *is* faithful;..." (Heb. 10:1-12, 14-23). So what we have here is a whole new way of worship: a new temple in heaven above, a new High Priest, Who is Christ, Who is at the temple in heaven above: at the right hand of the throne of God; which is superior to the earthly temple, superior to the earthly priesthood, superior to the earthly sacrifices of the goats, and the bulls, and the turtledoves, and so forth.

So that is what has been changed. And it has been changed with the fulfillment of those things by Christ. Now Jesus said "until <u>everything</u> be fulfilled." So far the only thing that has been fulfilled is the replacing of the temporary animal sacrifices and the temporary temple tabernacle on earth with the permanent eternal one in heaven. So whenever anything has been done away [or fulfilled] it is replaced with something of a higher standard. And you can understand that when you read Matthew 5, 6, and 7, where Jesus said, "You have heard it said of old time, but I say to you..." So whenever He brought the fulfillment of the law He gave it a higher standard. He didn't do away with anything. Christ came to do away with sin.

Now let's ask another question. Let's come back to Genesis 2. And I know those of you who believe in the weekly Sabbath turn here all the time to prove that Sabbath was a day which was created. So what I want to do is ask the question: which came first—the day, by creation, or the ritual of animal sacrifice? The day came first. No doubt. The sleight of hand, the deceitful handling of the Scriptures is when you claim that the ritual sacrifices and the ritual temple things done at the temple, when those were done away with they also did away with the Sabbath and did away with the holy days. That's where the sleight of hand comes in. So therefore, we have to ask the question, which came first? Now we're not talking about evolution, the chicken or the egg. We're talking about which came first—the creation of the day, or the sacrifices? The answer obviously is the creation of the day.

Now let's pick it up here in Genesis 2:1. "Thus the heavens and the earth were finished, and all the host of them. And on the seventh day [that means, just as the sixth day ended and the seventh day was beginning] God ended His work which He had made; and He rested on the seventh day from all His work which He had made. And God blessed the seventh day, and sanctified it: because that in it He had rested from all His work which God created and made" (Gen. 2:1-3). So we know that God made the seventh day, He sanctified the seventh day. We all understand that. But is that all that God made?

Let's come over here to verse 14 of Chapter 1. The truth is, God created all days, right? But He especially made the seventh day of every week [the] Sabbath, correct? Now let's understand something else that He did here, Genesis 1:14. "And God said, Let there be lights in the firmament of the heaven to divide the day from the night; and let them be for signs, and for seasons, and for days, and years:..." Now how do we govern the weekly Sabbath? From sunset to sunset, correct? Yes. But God also created seasons, didn't He? Yes, He did.

Let's come along here, let's ask a couple of other things. Let's come to Genesis 15. Now you'll have to write for the tapes concerning the covenants of God with Abraham, and we will send them to you. Because long before the Old Covenant was ever given, Genesis 15, the covenant was given to Abraham. Now we do not have the time to go through the technical explanation of it, so I will just tell you. Let's pick it up here in verse 4. "And, behold, the word of the LORD *came* unto him, saying, This shall not be thine heir [that is, Eliezer of Damascus]; but he that shall come forth out of thine own bowels shall be thine heir. And He brought him forth abroad, and said, Look now toward heaven, and tell the stars, if thou be able to number them: and He said unto him, So shall thy seed be. And he believed in the LORD; and He counted it to him for righteousness" (Gen. 15:4-6). This was given on the fourteenth day of the first month at night, the same day in which the Passover [occurs], if you believe in the Sabbath and Passover. So we have the day first, then the significance of the day. Then the next day in which He made the covenant to take the children of Israel out of Egypt was the fifteenth, which became the first day of the Feast of Unleavened Bread.

Now let's see that by going to Exodus 12. Let's ask the question: which came first—the day or the sacrifice? We will see the day came first. The sacrifice came as later instruction. Now here's the instruction that they were to do concerning the lamb, Exodus 12:5. "Your lamb shall be without blemish, a male of the first year: ye shall take *it* out from the sheep, or from the goats: and ye shall keep it up until the fourteenth day of the same month:..." So the day came first, correct? He designated the day first. "...And the whole assembly of congregation of Israel shall kill it in the evening." Now, I'm not going to go through any technical explanation on it, except to say that this is [right] after sunset, between sunset and dark.

So God named the day, the fourteenth, verse 11, last sentence, "...it *is* the LORD'S passover." Now I assume that most of you keep the Passover. But you see, if you keep the Passover and you don't keep the Feast of Unleavened Bread, then you are cutting something off. You are not following through on the commands of God. You are throwing the commands of observation—which God has commanded to be holy days—you are throwing that into the same categories as the animal sacrifices. And they were never in the same category. Now He says in verse 13, "And the blood shall be to you for a token upon the houses where ye *are*: and when I see the blood, I will pass over you, and the plague shall not be upon you to destroy *you*, when I smite the land of Egypt. And this day shall be unto you for a memorial; and ye shall keep it a feast to the LORD throughout your generations; ye shall keep a feast by an ordinance for ever." So the day was chosen first, the sacrifice was put on the day, and God says you are to keep the day forever. Later when Christ came, when was He sacrificed? He was sacrificed on the fourteenth day [the Passover Day]. And now that becomes the sacrifice which replaces the lamb which the Israelites killed. Christ is the Lamb of God, and it's on the fourteenth day. That's why the Passover day is to be kept.

Now notice here verse 15, speaking of the Feast of Unleavened Bread. This becomes very important, because again, we're going to see that the day was there before the offering. "Seven days shall ye eat unleavened bread; even the first day ye shall [have] put away leaven out of your houses: for whosoever eateth leavened bread from the first day until the seventh day, that soul shall be cut off from Israel. And in the first day *there shall be* an holy convocation,..." Now that is the same weight and force of command as in Genesis 2 of blessing the Sabbath day—holy convocation. "...And in the seventh day there shall be an holy convocation to you; no matter of work shall be done in them, save *that* which every man must eat, that only may be done of you. And ye shall observe *the feast of* unleavened bread; for in this selfsame day have I brought your armies out of the land of Egypt: therefore shall ye observe this day in your generations by an ordinance for ever" (Ex. 12:5-6, 11, 13-17). So the day came first.

Now let's come to Exodus 20. Here is where the giving of the Ten Commandments was in Exodus 20. But in the chapter preceding it we have a special event which took place—the preparing for the giving of the Ten Commandments. Now you can write in for the tape concerning the Ten Commandments, [they] were given on the day of Pentecost. So the day came first. Now the trick is this: If you believe in the Ten Commandments, which you do, then why do you not celebrate or keep or observe, rather, the feast of Pentecost on which the Ten Commandments were given, before any animal sacrifices were offered? You need to understand that. That's the question you need to ask.

Now let's come to Leviticus 23. And Leviticus 23 is the chapter in the whole Bible where all the holy days are listed. Now again, we have established: one, the Sabbath day was before any sacrifice; two, the Passover day was established before any sacrifice. Three, the first and last day of Unleavened Bread were established before any sacrifice; four, the Day of Pentecost was established before any sacrifice, and those are holy convocations. Now let's read it here. Leviticus 23:1, "And the LORD spake unto Moses, saying, Speak unto the children of Israel, and say unto them, *Concerning* the feasts of the LORD,..." Now I want to make this very clear: they are not, never have been, never will be the feasts of the

Jews, though other people have called them the "feasts of the Jews," and though for particular reasons which John knew, he labeled the "feast of the Jews" concerning the Feast of Tabernacles, but it's the feast of the Lord. "...Which ye shall proclaim *to be* holy convocations, *even* these *are* My feasts." All of them. Then He starts off with what? "Six days shalt work be done: but the seventh day *is* the sabbath of rest, an holy convocation; ye shall do no work *therein*: it *is* the sabbath of the LORD in all your dwellings."

Now the other holy convocations are "Sabbaths of the Lord in all your dwellings" too, just as well. Now we'll see that here in just a minute. Verse 4, "These *are* the feasts of the LORD, *even* holy convocations, which ye shall proclaim in their seasons." God created the time, as we saw in Genesis 1:14 for seasons. If you believe that you are to proclaim the seventh day as a feast of God every seven days, and that you are obligated by God to keep the Sabbath and to keep it holy, then what gives you the right to go against God and proclaim that His feasts, "even holy convocations which ye shall proclaim in their seasons,"[and] you disobey that command and do not proclaim them? Now what is your reason for not proclaiming them? Well, we will look at some of them. And your reasons are going to fall apart, because it hasn't been a proper, rightful dividing of the Word of God.

"In the fourteenth *day* of the first month at even *is* the LORD'S passover." Notice, in every case He gives the day first and then the offering for that day, every one of these. "And on the fifteenth day of the same month *is* the feast of unleavened bread unto the LORD: seven days ye must eat unleavened bread. In the first day ye shall have an holy convocation: ye shall do no servile work therein. But ye shall offer an offering made by fire unto the LORD seven days:..." The sacrifices at the temple, then, were added to the days. The days came first. Likewise with Pentecost, and how to count it. If you don't know how to count Pentecost you can write in for it. We have three booklets which explain in depth the whole thing of counting Pentecost.

But verse 21, which says, "And ye shall proclaim on the selfsame day, *that* it may be an holy convocation unto you:..." Then we come down here to verse 24, "...Speak unto the children of Israel, saying, In the seventh month, in the first *day* of the month, shall ye have a Sabbath, a memorial of blowing of trumpets, an holy convocation. Ye shall do no servile work *therein*: but ye shall offer an offering made by fire unto the LORD." Again, the day is proclaimed first and then the sacrificial offering. Verse 27, "Also on the tenth *day* of this seventh month *there shall be* a day of atonement; it shall be an holy convocation unto you; and ye shall afflict your souls, and offer an offering made by fire unto the LORD. And ye shall do no work in that same day: for it *is* a day of atonement, to make an atonement for you before the LORD your God."

Now let's come down to verse 32. "It *shall be* unto you a sabbath of rest, and ye shall afflict your souls: in the ninth *day* of the month at even, from even unto even, shall ye celebrate [or observe] your sabbath." Now we've got you. Because this is the verse that all Sabbath-keepers turn to, to show that you must keep the Sabbath from sunset to sunset, but this is defining the Day of Atonement. So if this defines the Day of Atonement, and you keep the Sabbath but not the Day of Atonement, why do you take your definition from the Day of Atonement and apply it to the Sabbath, if it is not equally applicable to the Sabbath and the Day of Atonement and all the other holy days?

Then we come down here to verse 34. "...The fifteenth day of this seventh month *shall be* the feast of tabernacles *for* seven days unto the LORD. On the first day *shall be* an holy convocation: ye shall do no servile work *therein*." Same way with the eighth day, verse 36. A holy convocation; you have day one, day eight, then the sacrifices and so forth. Now notice verse 37, because it's very important. "These *are* the feasts of the LORD, which ye shall proclaim..." (Lev. 23:1-8, 21, 24-25, 27-28, 32, 34-37).

Now as you can see, I'm doing these by survey. Because in order to understand this, you must get an overview by a survey to understand. Verse 37, "These *are* the feasts of the LORD, which ye shall proclaim *to be* holy convocations,..." So if you take this statement, which is true, and it is, and you go back and you apply it in verse 1, "...the feasts of the LORD, which ye shall proclaim *to be* holy convocations, even these are My feasts," and it starts out with the Sabbath: "Six days shalt work be done: but the seventh day *is* the sabbath of rest, an holy convocation; ye shall do no work *therein*: it is the Sabbath of the LORD in all your dwellings." Now then, you're stuck, aren't you? Why do you not proclaim those other days according to God's calendar the way that they should be? Are you missing something by not doing it? Are you incorrectly dividing the Word of God because you are misapplying Scripture?

Let's go to Numbers 28, and let's go to the heart and core of the whole thing here. We'll see it. Now you're also going to be stuck with another problem if you say that, "Because they had ritual sacrifices on these days, and the sacrifices have been done away with because Christ's sacrifice superseded all the animal sacrifices..." OK, we're all together so far, right? Then what are you going to do with Numbers 28, especially the first part? Verse 1, "And the LORD spake unto Moses, saying, Command the children of Israel, and say unto them, My offering, *and* My bread for My sacrifices made by fire [because there was the tabernacle, and later the temple], *for* a sweet savor unto Me, shall ye observe to offer unto Me in their due season. And thou shalt say unto them, This *is* the offering made by fire which ye shall offer unto the LORD; two lambs of the first year without spot day by day, *for* a continual burnt offering." This is the daily burnt offering. Now, because animal sacrifices were done away, have days been done away with? No. One in the morning, one in the evening.

Now let's come down here to verse 9. "And on the Sabbath day two lambs of the first year without spot, and two tenths deals of flour *for* a meat [meal] offering, and mingled with oil, and the drink offering thereof: *this is* the burnt offering of every Sabbath, beside the continual burnt offering, and his drink offering" (Num. 28:1-3, 9-10). Now then, if you take your reasoning, which so many do to get rid of the holy days, by saying that, "The ritual sacrifices were offered on the holy days and the sacrifices were done away with; therefore we don't have to keep the holy days," now what are you going to do about the Sabbath? Because if you take the reasoning of one, you must also take the reasoning of the other, correct? Were there sacrifices on the Sabbath day? Yes. Were those sacrifices done away with and fulfilled in Christ? Yes. Then if you take the assumption that because those were true, therefore we conclude that we don't have to keep the Sabbath because the sacrifices were done away. Now you see, you're stuck in your own logic. Because if you keep the Sabbath, because God commanded it, and you don't keep the holy days because the sacrifices were done away with, then your logic traps you into your own corner, where then you must not keep the Sabbath by the same logic.

Now I've gone over—this with Church of God Seventh Day people, until I'm blue in the face. But you see, when you are dead and when your mind is set, and when you are not willing to let the truth of God enter into it, then you can come to that conclusion. But how else are you going to conclude it? If you take the reasoning that the holy days do not need to be kept because there were ritual sacrifices on those [days], and those ritual sacrifices are all done away with in Christ, so was Sabbath ritual sacrifice done away in Christ. So therefore, you're stuck in your own logic because you're not honest in handling the Word of God, and you misapply the Word of God so that you may keep the Sabbath and do away with the holy days. Now you've got to understand that. That's where you begin. Maybe other people couldn't convince you, but maybe the Word of God can convince you.

Now then, let's come to the book of Ezekiel, Ezekiel 20. Now you can go through and apply this to all the holy days here in the rest of Numbers 28 and 29. Because every one of the days had sacrifices. So you can't use that logic. That logic is a misnomer. That logic is not correct. Now if you run on to Galatians 3 [and 4] and misapply that, then you're also going to get yourself in trouble. Now if you need some understanding concerning the book of Galatians, we have at least seven or eight tapes on that which go through it and explain it. I'll see if I can cover maybe one or two of those verses a little later on.

Now then, I call your attention to, as we're here in Ezekiel 20, I call your attention to reference back to Exodus 31, where the sabbaths God said you were to keep. Now notice when we are reading here, God does not make any differentiation between which Sabbath is which. All of the holy days—please understand—are annual Sabbaths. So when we read this—let's begin here in verse 10. God says, "Wherefore I caused them to go forth out of the land of Egypt, and brought them into the wilderness. And I gave them My statutes, and shewed them My judgments, which *if* a man do, he shall even live in them. Moreover also I gave them My Sabbaths,...." Plural. That is not "the Sabbath," but "My Sabbaths," plural. Because you see, the fourth commandment in the Ten Commandments says, "Remember the <u>sabbath</u> day to keep it holy." But He gave them more than the weekly Sabbath. He gave them His annual Sabbaths, "...to be a sign between Me and them, that they might know that I *am* the LORD that sanctify them."

Now, question: If you don't keep the holy days, is there something that you don't know about the Lord? Is there something in your understanding that is missing because you're not sanctified by those days? Verse 13, "But the house of Israel rebelled against Me in the wilderness:...." Question: Are you rebelling against God if you reject His holy days? "...They walked not in My statutes, and they despised My judgments, which *if* a man do, he shall even live in them; and My sabbaths [plural] they greatly polluted:...." Verse 16, "... Because they despised My judgments, and walked not in My statutes, but polluted My sabbaths: for their heart went after their idols." Because when you take God's time and make it yours, or you declare God's holy time not holy, it becomes an idol in your mind. So then, He told them not to do it. Verse 19, He said, "I *am* the LORD your God; walk in My statutes, and keep My judgments, and do them; and hallow My sabbaths; and they shall be a sign between Me and you, that ye may know that I *am* the LORD your God. Notwithstanding the children rebelled..." (Ezek. 20:10-13, 16, 19-21).

Now I want to ask a question here. If you think that the weekly Sabbath is good and right and fine, tell me why the annual Sabbaths are not also good and right and fine. And if you don't keep them, then you are saying that God's Word is not worthy of your observance. I mean, you need to keep things on a clear, factual basis. Don't get your feelings involved in on it, because you're going to get yourself in deep trouble.

Now I'm not going to handle a technical scripture at this point. Let's come to the New Testament. Let's come to Matthew 22, and let's see what we are to do in the New Testament. And then we will see, did they in the New Testament, under the New Covenant, keep these days? Let's come to Matthew 22:37. Because you see, you're also stuck with another problem. If you say you love God, and you try and love God this way, then you have to ask yourself a question: why do I reject the holy days of God? "And Jesus said to him, 'Thou shalt love *the* Lord your God with all your heart, and with all your soul, and with all your mind. This is *the* first and greatest commandment; And *the* second *one is* like it:, "You shall love your neighbor as yourself." ' On these two commandments hang all the Law and the Prophets " (Matt. 22:37-40). And whereby Jesus said, "One jot or one tittle shall in no way pass from the Law until everything has been fulfilled." The only thing that we have seen in the Scriptures which has been fulfilled has been the animal sacrifices and the temple ritual, which have been replaced and superseded by a higher sacrifice of Jesus Christ in a greater temple in heaven above. All of the rest is still hanging on the love of God, correct? Do you love God? Do you love God in truth? Or do you want to love God your way and tell God what to do?

Let's come to John 4. Let's ask some other questions. How does God want us to worship Him today? Verse 23, "But the hour is coming, [that is, when you wouldn't worship any longer in Jerusalem, the temple would be gone, and so forth] and now is, when the true worshipers shall worship the Father in spirit and in truth;..." Now we know the commandments of God are truth; we know the laws of God are truth; we know that all of God's ways are true, and His commandments are true; so therefore, if you're going to worship God in spirit and in truth, you're going to be keeping His commandments from the heart spiritually, loving God. "...For the Father is indeed seeking those who worship Him in spirit and in truth; for the Father is indeed seeking those who worship Him in this manner. God *is* Spirit, and those who worship Him must worship in spirit and in truth" (John 4:23-24). Now the word "must" there in the Greek has the force of "obligatory." You are obligated before God to worship Him in spirit and in truth. And since all the words of God are true, and since the holy days are part of the true Word of God, you must worship Him on those days, as well as the weekly Sabbath.

Now let's come to Psalm 119. And I know here recently I brought this up concerning other topics, but it is true. Let's do a little attitude check for everybody here now, whether you agree with what I have said or not up to this point, or maybe some of the things you agree with, and some of the things you don't agree with. But you have to ask yourself the question: do I agree with God? Not whether you agree with me, or agree with another man. Because if I don't teach you the Word of God, and if I don't preach the Word of God, then it really doesn't matter what I say, even though I may misuse the Word of God and sound religious. Now here, Psalm 119:127. And this is profound. And this is the whole attitude we've got to come to concerning the will of God, concerning the commandments of God, concerning all the things of God. "Therefore I love Thy commandments above gold; yea, above fine gold."

Now hold your place here because we're going to come back, and I want you to go to 2 Thessalonians for just a minute. Because with the deception that is coming upon the whole world there is going to be a reason why it's coming. And you may be part of that deception, or caught up in that deception if you do what they do in the world. Now Satan is going to come. 2 Thessalonians 2:9, "...whose coming [this is the great beast power that is coming] is according to *the* inner working of Satan, with all power and signs and lying wonders, and with all deceivableness of unrighteousness in those who are perishing because they did not receive the love of the truth,..." Now we just read where David wrote, "I love your commandments." But if you don't love the truth, which then is all the word of God, what are you subject to? You're subject to death, because you can't be saved. And another thing takes place.

"And for this cause God will send upon them a powerful deception that will cause them to believe *the* lie, so that all may be judged who did not believe the truth, but who took pleasure in unrighteousness" (2 Thess. 2:9-12). So if you don't believe the truth of God's word, are you having pleasure and unrighteousness by rejecting them? Because if those are Sabbaths (which they are), and if they are commandments (which they are), and if they're to be kept (which they should), and if you are transgressing that, then you are sinning, and you are unrighteous, correct? And if you don't keep them then you have pleasure in unrighteousness. Is that not true? Are you not then going to blind yourself to other things further down the road? And always remember, when God gives a witness out of His Word, once is sufficient. Please understand that.

Now let's come back here to Psalm 119:127. "Therefore I love Thy commandments above gold; yea, above fine gold." And how many people do you know work on the Sabbath so they can make money because they reject the Sabbath commandment? Well, apply the same thing to the holy days. Verse 128, here's where we need to come. "Therefore I esteem all *Thy* precepts *concerning* all *things to be* right;..." Do you believe that of the will of God?

Do you believe that every precept of God is right, every command of God is right, every law of God is good and right? Notice, "...and I hate every false way." Are you willing to hate the sin that you have been committing in not keeping the holy days? Or are you going to come up with other arguments to justify your own idol? That's what it gets down to. Because those are self-justifications for your own way. There'll be no doubt about it. Do you consider <u>all</u> the precepts of God concerning <u>all</u> things to be right? If you do then you will hate every false way.

Now let's come to the New Testament, and we're going to spend the rest of the time in the New Testament, showing that, yes, the holy days were kept by those in the New Testament; and in fact, by a very command of God. Let's come to Mark 2, please. And this is one, for those of you who are Sabbath-keepers, turn to, to show that we need to keep the Sabbath in the New Testament. Well let's read it here, because this becomes very profound. Verse 27, "And He said to them, 'The sabbath was made for man,...' " No question about it. God really expects all mankind to keep the Sabbath. "...*and* not man for the Sabbath; therefore, the Son of man is Lord even of the sabbath" (Mark 2:27-28). Question: since the holy days are Sabbath, is he also Lord of those? Is He Lord of the Passover? Is He Lord of the first day of Unleavened Bread, the last day of Unleavened Bread, Pentecost, Trumpets, Atonement, Tabernacles, and the Last Great Day? The answer is yes. Now those other days and commands were made for the people of God. The Sabbath was made for mankind in general. So if you only keep the Sabbath, you're only doing what God requires of all people everywhere. The holy days have special meaning for the people of God. Now maybe you've never thought of it that way. Well, you need to think of it that way.

Let's come to Luke 2, and let's see what Jesus did. And let's understand that Jesus was not under the Old Covenant; He was under a special covenant with God the Father, which was even greater than the New Covenant, when you really come to understand it. Because with the covenant that God the Father and Jesus Christ had, Jesus could not sin once. Now I'm going to give a sermon on that here. I'm working on it: what was the covenant between God the Father and Jesus Christ? It was a greater covenant that we are under. Obviously, it had to be. Because He was God before He became a human being. But let's notice what He did here. Luke 2:40, "And the little child grew and became strong in spirit, being filled with wisdom; and *the* grace of God was upon Him. now His parents went to Jerusalem every year at the feast of the Passover. And when He was twelve years *old*, they went up to Jerusalem according to the custom of the feast." And then you know what He was doing.

Did Jesus keep the feast? Yes. Did He keep it only because His parents kept it? No. Why did His parents keep it? Because it was a law of God. But why did Jesus keep it? Because it was the law of His Father. And what was He doing there at the feast? Verse 46, "Now it came to pass, *that* after three days they found Him in the temple, sitting in *the* midst of the teachers, both hearing them and questioning them. And all those who were listening to Him were amazed at *His* understanding and His answers." Because as I point out in the series, the prophecies of Jesus, Jesus was taught every morning of God the Father. So there He was on the holy days, and afterwards, doing the Father's business. "But when they saw Him, they were astonished; and His mother said to Him, 'Son, why have you dealt with us in this manner? Look, Your father and I have been *very* distressed *while* searching for You.' And He said to them, 'Why *is it* that you were looking for Me? Don't you realize that I must be about My Father's *business*?' " (Luke 2:40-42,46-49), showing that Joseph was not His father. That's what He was clearly saying here. Was it the Father's business to send Christ? Yes. When did Christ die? On the Passover day. Was that the Father's business? Yes, it was.

Now let's see how He carried out the Father's business in His ministry. Let's come to John 2. We're going to survey some things here in the book of John for just a minute. Keep in mind this: that Jesus Christ set us an example, in Whose footsteps we should follow. Now if Jesus did no sin…now you see, some people come to the point of saying that if you keep the Sabbath and holy days you are sinning. Well, we know that if you keep the Sabbath you are not sinning. But are you sinning if you don't keep the holy days? You are. Here, if it was sin to keep them, then Jesus sinned, correct? Now let's read it. Verse 13, "Now the Passover of the Jews was near, and Jesus went up to Jerusalem…" Now the reason why John says "the Passover of the Jews" is because he is showing that Jesus was correcting them for their wrong worship of Passover, and Tabernacles, and other days. The days of the holy days are God's days.

So what did He do? He went into the temple, "…and He found in the temple those who were selling oxen and sheep and doves, and the money exchangers sitting *there*; and after making a scourge of cords, He drove them all out of the temple, *with* both the sheep and the oxen: and He poured out the coins of the money exchangers, and overturned the tables. And to those who were selling the doves, He said, 'Take these things out of here! Do not make My My Father's house a house of merchandise.' " So He got rid of them, the sin there, didn't He? Plus, He was also showing another thing, which He later on said to the Pharisee who wanted to know, which was the great commandment? He answered correctly, and Jesus said, "You are not far from the kingdom of God." Then He said, "Now go and learn what this means: I desire mercy and not sacrifice." So that's what He was teaching here. He desired mercy and not sacrifice.

Now notice verse 23, "Now when He was in Jerusalem at the Passover, during the feast, many believed on His name, as they observed the miracles that He was doing" (John 2:13-16, 23). So He was healing, and He was teaching on the feast day of Unleavened Bread, right there at the temple.

Now let's come over here to John 5:1. Now, it doesn't tell us what feast this is. But according to the chronology as we go through the book of John, we find that it is Passover, fall festival season, Passover, fall festival season, and Passover. So by chronology, this had to be one of the feast days, either Trumpets or the first day of the Feast of Tabernacles, or the last day of the Feast of Tabernacles, one of the three. It was not Atonement, because they were carrying burdens and so forth. "After these things *there* was a feast of the Jews, and Jesus went up to Jerusalem." Was He there keeping it? Yes. Did He correct them for their wrong use of the day? Yes, He did. He told the man whom He healed to pick up his bed and walk, and he walked. And so then He gave the spiritual lesson here that God is working spiritually.

Let's come over here to John 6:4. "Now the Passover, a feast of the Jews, was near." And then Jesus explained about the bread and the wine, that it symbolized His body and His blood; and made it absolutely mandatory that you keep the Passover, otherwise you don't have any life in you. Let's read that right here in John 6:53. "Therefore, Jesus said to them, 'Truly, truly I say to uo, unless you eat the flesh of the Son of man, and drink His blood, you do not have life in yourselves.' " So unless you keep the Passover properly you don't have life in you. And I just might mention here too, those who use grape juice are not keeping it properly, because it is not wine. You need to understand that.

Let's go on. John 7:1, "After these things, Jesus was sojourning in Galilee, for He did not desire to travel in Judea because the Jews were seeking to kill Him. Now the Jews' feast of tabernacles was near." His brethren—I'll just summarize it—said, "Why don't You go up and show Yourself?" And He said, "No, you go up. My time is not yet." Verse 8, so they went up to the feast. Now verse 10, "But after His brothers had gone up, then Jesus also went up to the feast, not openly, but as it were in secret." So here, in spite of the public pressure that was put against Him and all those seeking to kill Him, He still went and kept the feast, didn't He? He observed the Feast of Tabernacles, didn't He? Yes, He did.

Now notice. Here's something very important concerning the will of God and understanding. Now verse 14, "But then, about the middle of the feast, Jesus went up into the temple and was teaching. And the Jews were amazed, saying 'How does this man know letters, having never been schooled?' Jesus answered them and said, 'My doctrine is not Mine, but His Who sent Me. If anyone desires to do His will, he shall know of the doctrine, whether it is from God, or *whether* I speak from My own self.' " And Jesus was there during the Feast of Tabernacles. And there is great meaning to the Feast of Tabernacles. If you would like some tapes on those, we have almost hundreds of tapes on the Feast of Tabernacles—well over a hundred anyway—covering the feast going way back. So if you want to know about the meaning of it, you can write in for it.

Let's come over here to verse 37. "Now in the last day, the great *day* of the feast, Jesus stood and called out, saying, 'If anyone thirsts, let him come to Me and drink. The one who believes in Me, as the scripture has said, out of his belly shall flow rivers of living water.' " (John 7:1-2, 10, 14-17, 37-39). So Jesus taught on the Last Great Day, didn't He? So we find him teaching during the Feast of Unleavened Bread; we find Him teaching during the Feast of Tabernacles; we find Him teaching at the Passover time, taught His disciples during the Feast of Unleavened Bread, and so forth. Jesus did all of those things.

Now let's come to the book of Acts, and we'll do a little survey with the book of Acts. Please understand, we're into New Covenant teachings. And if the holy days were to be done away, if they were no longer to be kept, then you would hear Jesus say this statement: "You have heard it said of old time, 'You shall remember to keep the Sabbath day holy, and the holy days.' But I say unto you, you shall keep Sunday holy, and Christmas, and Easter, and New Year's." He didn't say any of that, did He? No, He did not. Now here, Acts 2 on the day of Pentecost. Acts 2:1, by the command of Christ, right? He said, "And behold, I send the promise of My Father upon you; but remain in the city of Jerusalem until you have been clothed with power from on high" (Luke 24:49). So His command was to be there and keep the day of Pentecost. If Jesus commanded His apostles to keep it, and gave the Holy Spirit on the day of Pentecost, which was the same day that the Ten Commandments were given, should you not keep the day of Pentecost?

Verse 1, "And when the day *of Pentecost,* the fiftieth day, was being fulfilled, they were all with one accord in the same place. And suddenly *there* came from heaven a sound like *the* rushing of a powerful wind, and filled the whole house where they were sitting" (Acts 2:1-2). Then you know the rest of the story, in preaching on the day of Pentecost. And that's when God started the church. So He formalized the church in the wilderness on the day of Pentecost by giving the Ten Commandments. He started the New Covenant Church on the day of Pentecost right there at the temple of God.

Let's continue on here. Let's come to Acts 12:1. "Now about that time, Herod the king stretched forth *his* hands to persecute some of those of the church: And he killed James, the brother of John, with the sword. And when he saw that it pleased the Jews, he proceeded to take Peter also. (Now those were *the* days of unleavened bread.)" Now the reason that is mentioned is because they were keeping the days of Unleavened Bread. "And after arresting him, he put *him* in prison, delivering *him* to four sets of four soldiers to guard him with the intent of brining him out to the people after the Passover *season*" (Acts 12:1-4).

Let's come to Chapter 16. Now I know all of the arguments that people will give. Acts 16:13; let's understand this. This is a time when Paul went into Macedonia and preached to them. "Then on the day of the weeks we went outside the city by a river, where it was customary *for* prayer to be *made*;..." Now the Sabbath here in the Greek actually reads "...and on the day of the weeks,..."—which is Pentecost. Hold your place here, and go back to Luke 4. And we will see that on that very day in one of the synagogues in Galilee

Jesus Christ stood up for to read, and began His ministry in Nazareth on that day. Luke 4:16, "And He came to Nazareth, where He had been brought up; and according to His custom, He went into the synagogue on the Sabbath day and stood up to read." And that is on "the day of the weeks," if you look at the Greek. So Jesus taught on Pentecost, Paul taught on Pentecost, the Holy Spirit was given on Pentecost, the day of the weeks.

Now let's come back here to the book of Acts, Chapter 18 and verse 18. "And after Paul had remained *there* many days, he took leave of the brethren *and* sailed away to Syria, and with him Priscilla and Aquila. *Now Paul* had shorn *his* head in Cenchrea because he had *made* a vow. And he came to Ephesus, and left them there; but he himself went into the synagogue, *and* reasoned with the Jews: And when they asked *him* to remain with them for a longer time, he did not consent; but took leave of them saying, 'I must by all means keep the feast that is coming at Jerusalem:…' " (Acts 18:18-21). Now the only feast, chronologically speaking, that it could be here is the Feast of Tabernacles. So he went to Jerusalem to keep it. So Paul said, "I must by all means keep the Feast.…" Now you can't say that he was keeping it under the obligation of circumcision, because he preached against circumcision.

Now let's come to Chapter 20 and verse 5. "These went on ahead *and* waited for us in Troas. But we sailed away from Philippi after the Days of Unleavened Bread;…" Now why mention going after the days of Unleavened Bread? Well, it's very simple: they kept the days of Unleavened Bread and wouldn't leave until the Feast of Unleavened Bread was over. In other words, they observed the Feast of Unleavened Bread, and then left after that. "…And in five days we came to them at Troas, where we stayed *for* seven days." So they got there on a Sunday, stayed there seven days. "Now on the first *day* of the weeks, when the disciples had assembled to break bread,…" (Acts 20:5-7). And that was then after sundown after the Sabbath ended, getting on into the first day of the week and so forth. So they kept the Feast of Unleavened Bread. That's the important thing to understand.

Now let's come here to Chapter 24 and verse 14. "But I confess to you that according to the way which they [the Jews] call heresy, so I serve the God of my fathers, believing all things that are written in the Law and the Prophets;…" And Paul himself was the one who wrote to show that the only thing that had been fulfilled and superseded by the sacrifice of Christ was the animal sacrifice and the temple ritual. And we read that earlier. He believed everything else.

Let's come here to Chapter 27 and verse 9. "And after much time had passed, and the voyage was now dangerous because the *annual* fast *day* had already passed,…" Now you may have in your reference there going back to Leviticus 23:27, referring to the Day of Atonement. So here Paul, even when he was sailing, and it was dangerous, he was still keeping the Day of Atonement on that ship. And the fast had ended. So Paul kept it.

Now let's come over here to 1 Corinthians 16:7. "For *at this time* I will not *stop* to see you, but I hope at some *future* time to stay with you, the Lord permits. But I will remain in Ephesus until Pentecost." So how were they measuring time? By Christmas? No. By Easter? No. By New Year's? No. By Sunday? No, but by Sabbath and the holy days, all the way through. Here's Pentecost.

Now let's come to 1 Corinthians 5, since we are here. And here is the command. And you need to understand this, as here is a principle: you can't have one commandment without the other. You must have all of them. And did not the apostle James say that if you keep the whole law yet offended one point, you're guilty of all the law? Correct? So if you keep the Sabbath but don't keep the holy days, then you are guilty of transgressing the holy days, and stand before God as a sinner. Especially when we have here in 1 Corinthians 5 an absolute, dogmatic command by the apostle Paul to keep the feast, and the Feast of Unleavened Bread. Now let's pick it up here in verse 7. "Therefore, purge out the old leaven,..." Because during the Days of Unleavened Bread, leaven is a type of sin. "...So that ye may become a new lump, *even* as you are unleavened." Having put it out of their houses, and they are unleavened in Christ. "For even Christ our Passover was sacrificed for us: For this reason, let us keep the feast,..." Which feast? Of Unleavened Bread, "...not with old leaven, nor with *the* leaven of malice and wickedness, but with *the* unleavened *bread* of sincerity and truth" (1 Cor. 5:7-8). So he is virtually saying here in this command to keep the feast, "If you don't keep the feast, you're not keeping the truth." There is a great command.

Now then, we need to understand another principle, which is this: People say, "Well, if it's not repeated in the New Testament, I don't have to do it." The reason a lot of these things are not repeated in the New Testament is because it would become redundant. And God didn't want to have a book of fifty volumes. He wanted one book. So that's why you have to believe the whole Word of God. Let's come to Hebrews 4. Now if you want a more in-depth study on Hebrews 4, you can write in for it, we have it. I just want to focus in on one verse, verse 9, and to summarize the part up to it, because God's plan is not yet complete. "There remains, therefore, Sabbath-keeping for the people of God." Now that becomes very important, because Sabbath-keeping, then, means more than just keeping the Sabbath. Sabbath-keeping includes all of the holy days, and the people of God include the Gentiles (1 Peter 1), not just the Hebrews.

So for people to say, "I am not convinced that we ought to keep the holy days," then what you need to do is get in and really study your Bible more, and ask yourself the question, "Do I really believe in the Word of God, and the will of God, am I willing to understand it the way God says? Or am I going to keep this in the way of personal opinion and become like all other religious people?" and end up rejecting the Word of God.

End of Sermon

Transcriber: Carolyn Singer

Should We Keep the Holy Days?
August 7, 1999
Scriptural References

1) II Corinthians 4:1-4

2) Jeremiah 17:9

3) Matthew 7:21-23

4) Psalm 143:10

5) Romans 12:1-2

6) Luke 16:13-17

7) Matthew 5:17-18

8) Hebrews 9:11-12, 28

9) Hebrews 10:1-12, 14-23

10) Genesis 2:1-3

11) Genesis 1:14

12) Genesis 15:4-6

13) Exodus 12:5-6, 11, 13-17

14) Exodus 20

15) Leviticus 23:1-8, 21, 24-25, 27-28, 32, 34-37

16) Numbers 28:1-3, 9-10

17) Ezekiel 20:10-13, 16, 19-21

18) Matthew 22:37-40

19) John 4:23-24

20) Psalm 119:127-128

21) II Thessalonians 2:9-12

22) Mark 2:27-28

23) Luke 2:40-42, 46-49

24) John 2:13-16, 23

25) John 5:1

26) John 6:4, 53

27) John 7:1-2, 10, 14-17, 37-39

28) Acts 2:1-2

29) Acts 12:1-4

30) Acts 16:13

31) Luke 4:16

32) Acts 18:18-21

33) Acts 20:5-7

34) Acts 24:14

35) Acts 27:9

36) I Corinthians 5:7-8

37) Hebrews 4:9

Section III

Passover

CHAPTER EIGHT

Origin and Meaning of Passover

April 16, 2005

What is the origin and the meaning of the Passover—especially the Christian Passover? Now let's understand something about the Bible, and this is always basic and fundamental, but it is also in depth and runs through the entire Bible on understanding. The Bible is not a book that anyone can just pick up and begin to understand like reading a novel. Now certain things that are in there which are basic; different people can understand at different times, and begin to apply them. However, to understand what we are going to cover today, we need to look at how God has designed the Bible and how it is to be understood. That's why in studying the Bible it's got to be accompanied with prayer, it's got to be accompanied with obedience, because all of those things are required. And it's got to be accompanied with an attitude of love to God and an attitude of being willing to obey what God reveals to you as you study the Word of God.

Now in I Corinthians 2, let's turn there, this tells us how we begin to understand the Bible, and this also shows us that you need spiritual help from the Spirit of God, either the Spirit of God is with you and will help lead you to understand, or if you are already baptized, the Spirit of God is in you and will lead you to understand. Nevertheless, either way the things of the Bible, as we will see, are spiritually discerned. Let's pick it up here in verse 9: "But according as it is written, '*The* eye has not seen, nor *the* ear heard, neither have entered into *the* heart of man, *the* things which God has prepared for those who love Him.'" Now if you love God, what did Jesus say? "If you love me, keep My commandments." It is not for just anybody in the world, it's not just for anybody who wants to pick up the Bible and start reading it. Oh, they can, but there are prophecies which say, even the wise men and even the priests can't understand it. Or the wise men say, "I don't know what this says, what it means." See, you have to love God. Verse 10: "But God has revealed *them*..." Now that's important. God must reveal it, and through the Spirit of God, He must open our minds to understand the Word of God. "...God has revealed *them* to us by His Spirit, for the Spirit searches all things—even the deep things of God." So God expects us to go from the beginning, from the basics and on into the deep things of God, and part of what we're going to cover today is the deep understanding of the Passover of God although it is in the simplicity of Christ. Verse 11: "For who among men understands the things of man except *by* the spirit of man which *is* in him? In the same way also, the things of God no one understands except *by* the Spirit of God" (1 Corinthians 2:9-11). Now that's important.

Therefore, when you are studying you should always ask God to help you understand. You should always ask God for His Spirit to lead you, so that you will do things according to the way that God wants them done. You will understand according to the way that God wants you to understand it, and this also tells you another reason why the world, though they call themselves Christian, cannot understand because they are not loving God the way God says, and are not keeping the commandments of God the way God says to keep them, and so therefore, when that happens they are blinded. Christ shows very clearly that if you do not believe God when you hear the Word of God, and if you're not willing to live by His Word, you automatically blind yourself and put yourself on Satan's side who is the one who blinds those from understanding the gospel.

So the way that God gives understanding to the Bible is [like] a two-edged sword. One edge for those who refuse to believe and understand—they won't. They read the words and they can't understand it. The other edge for those who want to know the Word of God, those who want to love God, then He opens their understanding to it. Now there is no other book in the world that does this, because no other book in the world is based upon the spiritual words of God, because the words Jesus spoke, they are spirit and they are life.

Now what we are going to do is we are going to look at the beginning, or the origin of the Passover. And the origin of the Passover does not begin with Exodus 12. It begins in Genesis 15. It does not begin with Israel, but it begins with Abraham, and there are more parallels. So let's go to Genesis 15. There are more parallels with the events that happen here in Genesis 15 that relate to the Passover and relate to the preaching of the gospel, as we will see, than has been understood. Now, we've gone through this quite a few times haven't we, since we first understood it—what, about five years ago, six years ago, somewhere around there? Well today we are going to learn even more. We are going to draw even more precepts out of it, we're going to have more understanding out of it, a little more here and a little more there, because it's all right there. Now there is a reason for it, and there is a reason why the Passover for the Christian Passover is not patterned after the Passover that God gave to Israel. Now that Passover, though it had types of Christ with the lamb without blemish, and the blood which would protect them from death and so forth—the timing of the Passover in Exodus 12 is different than the timing of the Passover for the New Covenant that Jesus taught the apostles on His last Passover. And what He taught His apostles on the last Passover conforms more to the flow of events here in Genesis 15 than it does to the Passover in Exodus 12, or the later slaying of the lambs at the temple by the Jews in their traditional Passover offerings that they had on the day portion of the fourteenth.

Now let's pick it up here in Genesis 15:4: "And behold, the word of the LORD *came* unto him, saying, This shall not be thine [your] heir…" That is Eliezer of Damascus would not be his heir, because here he was, what, about 85 or so, no children and God promised him a child. So here He is going to make the promise sure. "…but he that shall come forth out of thine [your] own bowels shall be thine [your] heir." So you have to be a fleshly human being first, right? And who was the one that was born to Abraham and Sarah? It was Isaac, and Isaac was the child of promise. Now we have here a physical birth, don't we? All right, keep that in mind. Verse 5: "And he brought him forth abroad, and said, Look now toward heaven, and tell the stars, if thou be [you are] able to number them…" Now the universe is quite a thing. And the heavens God designed to be glorious and awesome to lead mankind to realize that God is Creator, and to seek His purpose in creating it, because God did not do it in vain. He did it with purpose in mind.

Now hold your place here in Genesis 15, and let's come to Psalm 8, and let's see what the heavens are designed to do. Now there is a book out that is called *The Privileged Earth*—there is another one called *The Rare Earth*, and what the astronomers now have discovered is that in order for there to be physical life, in order for there to be complex life like we have on the planet, there have to be multitudinous factors that have to be there. You can't be too close to the sun or too far from the sun. The earth has to be the right size, the moon has to be the right size. The sun has to be the right size, and it must sit in the solar system [which] must be of the right composition. And you need Jupiter and Uranus to give protection from all of the asteroids that would come crashing in if they weren't there. You need to have everything in perfect balance, so it's the perfect earth, in the perfect solar system, in the perfect galaxy because the galaxy is set in such a way that from the earth you can examine the heavens like no other place in the entirety of the universe. There is no other place because there is too much gas, there are too many clouds, gaseous clouds—like if you were on Venus, you would never see the sun, and so the earth is in the perfect place because God created and put it there, and He did it for a reason—for His plan that He has for all man-

119

kind, and that's all wrapped up in Jesus Christ, and that's all wrapped up in the Passover and the holy days and so forth. Verse 1: "O LORD our LORD, how excellent *is* your name in all the earth! Who has set thy [your] glory above the heavens." Because if you can get out and see the stars and see the heavens and you know mathematically, you see this is why there are no atheist astronomers. Now you've got a lot of atheist philosophers like Carl Sagan who doesn't have a brain in his head because his mind has been closed with foolishness for rejecting God. But those who are like Carl Sagan say we are a low-class planet in a low-class galaxy, that we are nothing in the universe, and just the opposite is true. But only from the earth can you measure the sun, the moon, the stars, can you see the galaxies, and now what do we have out there? We've got the Hubble Telescope, and it looks deep into space, and the farther they go into space what do you see? More galaxies, more stars. Now there is a purpose for that; we'll see in just a minute.

Now verse 3: "When I consider thy [the] heavens, the work of thy [your] fingers, the moon and the stars, which thou hast[you have] ordained." And Isaiah 40 says that He strung out the heavens like a curtain and calls all the stars by names and has numbered them and He upholds them through Christ with the Word of His power. Then David said, verse 4: "What is man, that thou art [you are] mindful of him?" Believe it or not the creation of mankind and what God is doing here on the earth is the focal point of His plan. " ...and the son of man, that thou visitest [you visit] him? For thou hast [you have] made him a little lower than..." *Elohim*, not just the angels but *Elohim*, a little lower than God. God made us in His image for a great purpose, a great plan and that's all wrapped up in the Passover. So the first place to begin to understand God is to realize when you look out and see the heavens, that God made all of this. He keeps it in motion. He made the earth and put everything here to sustain our life. He gives us breath, He gives us food, He gives us water, He gives us air. All of that comes from God to all human beings whether they are sinners or saints. Notice, "... and hast [you have] crowned him with glory and honor. Thou madest [You made] him to have dominion over the works of thy [your] hands; thou hast [you have] put all *things* under his feet" (Psalm 8:1-6). And that's what God has done.

Now when men look out into the heavens and they reject [God and His creation], we're going to see again the same principle we covered there in 1 Corinthians 2. We are going to see exactly the same principle. Let's go to Romans 1 now, and let's see what happens when you reject this witness and testimony of God's creation. These evolutionists and scientists, they look out there and say, "Oh this just happened by accident. There was a big bang." Well, when they have a big bang with a terrorist's bomb, what do they know? They know that some human set it off, right? Well, how about the big bang that made the universe? How did it get there without someone doing it? You know, it is amazing! But you see, there is a thinking process where you cause your mind to close, and that begins with rejecting the beauty and glory and power of God as evidenced in the universe. Now let's pick it up here in Romans 1:18: "Indeed [For] *the* wrath of God is revealed from heaven upon [against] all ungodliness and unrighteousness of men, who suppress [hold back] the truth in unrighteousness..." Now any part of the truth they hold it back, they change it and what one day do they desire to get rid of more than any other day—the Passover, and under the inspiration of Satan the devil. Satan knows that if he can get people not to keep the Passover, or to keep the Passover wrongly, then he's got them on the hook, whether it's a big hook or a little hook, he's got them on the hook because sooner or later, they'll turn their backs on God, because **the Passover day is the covenant day between God the Father, Jesus Christ and those that He has called,** as we will see. And when you begin to sluff-off on that and do it in different ways, that's why there is so much confusion concerning the Passover—the 14th, the 15th, at sunset, at dark, at three in the afternoon. Is the bread leavened or unleavened? Do you have a lamb, do you not have a lamb? Should it just be the Lord's Supper and the Eucharist? Everything to move away from what the Bible says, and every step you take away from what the Bible says, you close your mind.

Now notice verse 19: "Because that which may be known of God is manifest in them; for God has shown *it* to them." Verse 20: "For the invisible things of Him from *the* creation of *the* world [are clearly seen], being understood by the things that were [are] made, both [*even*] His eternal power and Godhead—so that they are without excuse;" See, as we are going to see, the Passover is where to start and everything else flows from that, because Christ was crucified on that day, and according to the timing, as we will see, of Genesis 15. Now notice what happens, verse 21, "Because—[that] when they knew God, they glorified Him not as God, neither were thankful; but became vain in their own resonings, and their foolish hearts were darkened." Now, that's what happens when you reject the glory of God. (Romans 1:18-21.)

Now let's come back to Genesis 15, because there is another lesson for us here. Now after He told him, "Look at the stars and count them if you are able to…" and I'm sure it was a gorgeous night out there, and of course, with the Passover night it is nearly a full moon so you've got the full moon out there and you've got all the stars, you've got all this beauty and splendor that is out there, and God took Abraham out there to show him. And here is His promise, continuing in verse 5: "…and he said to him, So shall thy [your] seed be." Now there are two seeds, one is the physical seed, Isaac, and the other is the spiritual seed, those who will be born into the Kingdom of God. Now what do we have here? We have exactly what Jesus taught later. Remember when Nicodemus came to Him? And Jesus said that you cannot see the Kingdom of God unless you have been born again, and He said that which is born of the flesh is flesh, that which is born of the spirit is spirit, and this is exactly what we have here, because at the resurrection, we find in Daniel 12:3, that the righteous shall shine forth as the stars in the firmament of the heavens (Paraphrased). And in Matthew 13:49 that at the resurrection, those who enter into the Kingdom of God "shall shine like the sun." Now that shows the glory that they will have. So what do you have? You have your first birth, the physical life, and you have the second birth, projected to the resurrection, don't you—from flesh to spirit. So here, right in here you have embedded the core of what it means to be born again. Amazing! That's another precept that we can get out of here. So that's why the heavens declare the glory of God. Now let's also understand something that we will see a little bit later, that Isaac was also that type.

Now let's understand something—in this special [documentary] that was put on by the National Geographic, "In the Womb", they are able, as I mentioned, to take 3-D actual photos of the baby in the womb, much like this ad that's on television now with the baby in the womb advertising the Quiznos nacho hot sandwiches. They now know that in the womb, that the baby is nearly fully developed at 6 weeks, and that's when a woman first knows that she is pregnant. And it clearly shows that what is in her is another body and she is entrusted to bring forth that life by God—[He] created her and designed her to do so, and that the body that is in there is not hers, but another life. Now they also showed this: That the baby grows and develops. They even showed when the heart first starts beating—quite amazing, and they show how it grows.

Now the baby practices everything in the womb that it needs before it's born so when it's born it will be able to function—moves its arms, moves its legs, it turns around, it pushes, it kicks, opens its mouth, it smiles, it frowns, it sleeps, it even drinks the amniotic fluid, about a pint of it a day. It is fed by the mother through the umbilical cord. It knows the food that the mother eats because it comes to the baby. It knows the mother's voice. Babies react to music, and they have found that good symphony music relaxes the baby and guess what—rock music sends them out of their minds as it were. So even the living principles that we can see of people who have already been born and are in the world, apply to the baby in the womb. So when the baby is born, now it has to do something it has never done—it must breathe. And it will also show when it is in the womb, it's got plugs in its nostrils, and when they're born they clean out those plugs and it can breathe. Now when it is born it has practiced nursing, it knows its mother, it knows the sound of the voice, and everything like that, and the mothers are built just right so that the babies can suckle. That's the way God designed it.

Now in a parallel this way—after we're born, we grow up, we're called of God, everything that we are doing as Christians by loving God, and keeping His commandments, living by every word of God, and having the Word of God written in our hearts and our minds; we are practicing what we need for eternal life. So when we are born again into the Kingdom of God, we will be ready to start functioning, but it's going to be just like when the baby is born into the world and must begin breathing, which it's never done before. When we are born into the Kingdom of God, we are going to start functioning as spirit beings, which we have never done before. And we have all of that buried here, right in these verses.

Now notice, continuing in Genesis 15:5: "...and he said to him, So shall thy [your] seed be." Well, you can't count the stars. He didn't say, "Just a minute Lord, let me get my calculator." (Laughter) It was beyond the ability of Abraham to do. Many things are beyond our ability to do, so we [do] what? We trust God and we believe God. Now that's what Abraham did, he believed in the Lord and that's New Testament doctrine, is it not? Yes. And it was counted or imputed to him for righteousness. Now this means he was put in right standing with God because he believed God.

Now then, we know that he said, "Go ahead and you get the heifer, you get the goat, you get the ram and the turtledove and the pigeon..." (paraphrased). And he made this special sacrifice where they were cut down the middle, except for the turtledove and pigeon, and it was a real bloody sacrifice. And there was a little path between the backs of the animals that was made so God later could walk down through there, because God was going to pledge His death in order to accomplish the physical seed to come, and in order to accomplish the spiritual seed which would result from that. God had to take a maledictory oath and He had to pledge His death for the sins of mankind, and that's what He did here, and that's what the Passover is all about, and we know and we understand when we put it together, and you can read it in *The Christian Passover* book, that this occurred on the 14th day of the first month. It started at night just like our Passover does and it went on into the day portion with the sacrifices that were here, and this relates to the timing of the crucifixion and death of Jesus Christ. The Passover of Exodus 12, though it has types relating to Christ, is not of the [same] timing which relates to the crucifixion of Christ. Neither are the other sacrifices [commanded by God] at the temple related in timing to the sacrifice of Jesus Christ—this and this alone, is.

Now notice what happened, Genesis 15:12: "And when the sun was going down..." Now God has to perform this miracle in order to show Abraham that the future coming Messiah was doing to die. When did Jesus die? It says here in the gospels, at the ninth hour which is about three o'clock and that's when the sun starts going down. "...When the sun was going down, a deep sleep fell upon Abram; and lo, a horror of great darkness fell upon him." How are you going to give someone an experience of death and yet remain alive? Well, this is how you do it, and this is what God did. Then God made the promise and said that the physical seed would go into captivity and we later find out that that's into Egypt, and so He promised that He would bring them out four hundred years later in the fourth generation (verse 13). Now notice verse 17. Now we go into the next day because all days in the Bible are calculated from sunset to sunset. Verse 17: "...it came to pass, that, when the sun went down..." Now we are into the 15th day aren't we. Where was Christ on the 15th day of the first month after He was crucified on the 14th day? He was where? He was in the tomb in total darkness in total blackness. Now if you have ever gone to the Carlsbad Caverns, you get down there and they turn the lights out and they say, "Put your hand in front of your face and see if you can see it." You can't see a thing. So this is what this horror of great darkness was picturing and now with the darkness of night, then we see something else. We see God's power and pledge to fulfill what He said to Abraham. Continuing in verse 17: "…Behold a smoking furnace…" Now you might liken that to a blowtorch. "…And a burning lamp that passed between those pieces [parts]" Now that's the only way that Abraham in this horror of great darkness could comprehend that God walked down between the parts of those animals. And as He walked down between the parts of those animals, the smoking furnace just burned up those sacrifices and there was probably nothing left there but ashes. And then He made the covenant with Abraham. Verse 18: "In the same day the LORD made a covenant with Abram…" (Genesis 15:12-13, 17-18).

Now likewise with us, the covenant that Christ made with us was sealed with His death, and it was guaranteed when He was put into the tomb. Now I can't help but think of the difference between the death of John Paul II and the funeral and the accolades and all of the leaders of the world praising him there. They had five Kings, six Queens, they had seventy Presidents and Prime Ministers, and they had top officials from all governments of the world, and they had over one hundred and forty representatives of other religions of the world there. A perfect time for the spirits of Satan to massage all their self-righteousness so much so in fulfilling the will of God because Revelation 17 says what? He puts it in their minds to fulfill His will. Even the President of Israel shook hands with the President of Syria and Iran at the funeral for the Pope! Now they want him [the Pope] to be saint right now. He is a great man in this world.

Now what about Christ, I couldn't help but compare it to Christ—rejected, despised, the religious leaders hated Him. The governments of Rome did Him in and crucified Him. The people hated Him. They spit upon Him. The soldiers beat Him up and they crucified Him and He died an ignominious death that the only ones who were there to be of any help were Joseph of Arimathea and some of the women who brought spices and that was it. And where was He buried? He was buried in a grave. He was counted with robbers. And the grave was a sepulcher—no pomp, no ceremony, no circumstances, not dressed up in Santa Claus' suit, none of that, you know. What a difference, what a contrast. (The comment was made: That's why God hates religion. Yes. That's why God does hate religion).

So God promised it. Here was the [future] promise of His death—which occurred then on the Passover day in 30 A.D. Now let's come to Genesis 22 and let's see something else that is related to the Passover and has Passover significance though I cannot prove it dogmatically that this occurred on the Passover day. However, here is the lesson, you know what it was. God said take your only son—that's how He refers to Isaac as your only son—even though Ishmael was his son, he is not counted as the son of promise because it was by the conniving of Sarah that [it] occurred and so the world is paying the penalty for it ever since. And what is the greatest problem we have in the world? The fights and quarrels between the children of promise and the children of Hagar. Amazing!

So God told them go unto the mountains of Moriah and offer Isaac as a sacrifice. So he went three days' journey, and he took the wood, he took the fire, and then he loaded the wood on Isaac when they got there and he took the fire in his hand, it was probably in a pot, and he carried the coals and I'm sure they always added a little wood to it, so they could keep the fire going. So let's pick it up here in verse 7: "And Isaac spake unto [spoke to] Abraham his father, and said, My father: and he said, Here *am* I, my son. And he said, Behold the fire and the wood;" (He says, "Now I see the fire, you got it in your hand, and the wood is on my back) "…but where *is* the lamb for a burnt offering?"

OK, let's look at this for just a minute. Carrying the wood was what—like carrying a cross, and in this case Isaac was a type of Christ and Abraham was a type of God the Father and the fire was a type of fiery trial that the crucifixion would be for Jesus. Now notice the faith. And many times God doesn't do anything for us until the last second. Notice, verse 8: "...Abraham said, My son, God will provide himself [Him] a lamb for a burnt offering: so they went both of them together. And they came to the place which God had told him of; and Abraham built an altar there, and laid the wood in order, and bound Isaac his son, and laid him on the altar upon the wood. And Abraham stretched forth his hand, and took the knife to slay his son' " (verses 9 and 10).

Now why would he do that? Because he counted God powerful enough to raise Isaac from the dead in case he did go through [with] it. We find that in Hebrews 11. Now notice that a miraculous thing [happened] "And the angel of the LORD called unto him out of heaven, and said, Abraham, Abraham: and he said, Here *am* I. And he said, Lay not your hand upon the lad, neither do you anything unto him' " (verse 11).

Now let's add up the time. Abraham was called at 75. Isaac was born when he was 100. So that is 25 years. So if the lad, that would have to be between 12 and 20, were say, 18 years—so you've got 25 years and 18 years, which is 43 years. Now how long have you been in the Church? Whatever, but notice what he said, "...for now I know that thou fearest [you fear] God..." And all those trials and the things that he went through were to show whether he really loved God or not—whether he was really willing to do the things that God said or not, and to believe that God would fulfill His promise.

Now remember He said that his seed would be as the stars of heaven and as the sand on the seashore. Now if he is going to offer his son Isaac who was the only heir to carry that out. And [if] God didn't resurrect him from the dead after the sacrifice, if it would have come through, then God would have given him the greatest lie that has ever been. See we believe God because He is true and His Word is true and His Word is right, and He will do what He said, and that is what Abraham did. But notice [God's message], "...For now I know that you fear God..."

How long does it take for us to know God and love God? It takes a lifetime. Just like the baby in the womb has to be prepared for birth, we have to be prepared for the second birth of being born again at the resurrection, and that's what Abraham was doing. "...Seeing that you have not withheld your son, your only *son* from me." See, he was willing to love God and keep His commandments more than his own family. Verse 13: "And Abraham lifted up his eyes, and looked and behold behind *him* a ram caught in a thicket by his horns." Now rams normally don't get caught in thickets with their horns so as I have said, I believe God created this ram just for this particular thing—for a substitutionary sacrifice. And Christ is that substitutionary sacrifice for us. He <u>died</u> <u>for</u> <u>our</u> <u>sins</u>. So here is a type of Christ then the sacrifice was offered instead of his son.

Now notice what happened then, verse 15: "And the angel of the LORD called unto Abraham out of heaven the second time," And here is the message from God, you can't have anything greater or stronger or of a greater promise than this that God gave.

Now because of what Abraham did, God did something special. God did something He did not need to do because every word of God is true and God cannot lie and He doesn't need to swear as a man. But He said here, verse 16: "And said, By myself have I sworn, saith the LORD" Now this makes it absolutely unilateral, unequivocal, all the promises that He gave to Abraham will come true. The promises of the Messiah to come would come true, and the timing of it would come true, and it was to be exactly as God said and open the door for spiritual salvation, as we'll see here in just a minute. Continuing verse 16: " '...because thou hast done this thing, and hast not withheld thy son, thine only *son*:' " Now let's under-stand something—this is something above and beyond the commandments of God. This is something that God told him to do, and we're going to see the key important thing here in just a minute. Verse 17: "…That in blessing I will bless you, and in multiplying I will multiply thy seed as the stars of the heaven," Now in this case the spiritual is brought out first. "…And as the sand which *is* upon the seashore;" The physical seed. "…And thy seed shall possess the gate of his enemies; And in thy seed shall all the nations of the earth be blessed; **because you have obeyed my voice**. Now I gave a sermon on that, "The Simplicity in Christ—Obey My Voice."

Now also this shows in Hebrews 6, let's turn there, that God has given by these two immutable things that we just read of, in blessing I will bless. Now Hebrews 6:13. And we will see how this event that we just covered in Genesis 22 projects forward to Christ, projects forward to salvation, as we have already understood. Verse 13: "For God, after promising Abraham, swore by Himself, since He could swear by none greater, 'Saying , Surely in blessing I will bless you, and in multiplying I will multiply you.' Now after he had patiently endured, he obtained the promise. For indeed, men swear by the greater, and confirmation by an oath *puts* an end to all disputes between them. In this *way* God, desiring more abundantly…" Now who did He do this for? "…To show the heirs of the promise the unchangeable nature of His own purpose…" See, this shows the purpose of God. That's why in Genesis 15 this was done on the Passover day and then we will look at the last Passover of Jesus and we will see the importance of that day as a covenant day and the renewing of the covenant. Verse 18: "So that by two immutable things, in which *it was* impossible *for* God to lie, we who have fled for refuge might have strong encouragement to lay hold on the hope *that has been* set before us;" This was done so that we could have hope in God. So that we know that God is going to do what He has said. And this is the whole simplicity in Christ! Verse 19: "Which *hope* we have as an anchor of the soul, both secure and steadfast…" The world's going to come and go, the people are going to come and go, but God is always there, the hope of God is always there, the truth of God is always there, the love of God is always there, and then "…both secure and steadfast, and which enters into the *sanctuary* within the veil…" And what does this do? Just exactly as the voice came from heaven to speak directly to Abraham so likewise through Christ, we are able to enter into the Holy of Holies because of what Christ has done. That's why when Christ died, the veil in the temple was torn in two from the top to the bottom, to show that the way to the Holy of Holies was now open through prayer to God to Father in heaven above. Now notice, verse 20: "Where Jesus [Christ] has entered for us *as* a forerunner, having become a High Priest forever according to the order of Melchisedec" (Hebrews 6:13-20).

Now let's go back and look at one other thing concerning Abraham and then we will come to the New Testament and look at that last Passover with Jesus. Let's come to Genesis 26:4. Now He is talking to Isaac and passing the promise on to him because, you see, Jesus said of Abraham, Isaac, and Jacob to the Pharisees, "…You see Abraham and Isaac and Jacob and all the prophets in the kingdom of God, but you yourselves are cast [thrust] out" (Luke 13:28). So we know that they are going to be in glory in the Kingdom of God. So notice what He says here, verse 4: "And I will make thy seed to multiply as the stars of heaven…" There it is, the spiritual seed. Then He talks about the physical seed. "and will give unto thy seed all these countries; and in thy seed shall all the nations of the earth be blessed; (verse 5) Because…" Now this doesn't tell us whether Abraham kept the holy days or not, but this gives us an indication that he probably did. "…Because that Abraham obeyed my voice, and kept my charge, my commandments, my statutes, and my laws." Now later when God gave all these things to Israel, the holy days were called statutes. So if Abraham kept the statutes of God, and God created the sun and the moon and the stars and the earth, and gave the timing of the Passover and everything, it stands to reason that there was some kind of commemoration that Abraham had before God on this covenant day. Do we have that with the Passover today? Yes, indeed. Now, this is why in the New Testament we are called, "…if you *are* Christ's then you are Abraham's seed, and heirs according to *the* promise." (Gal. 3:29) And the promise was what? Spiritual seed, and of course, we've all been born flesh, and now we are learning how to practice, just like the babe in the womb, to learn the things we need to learn and prepare for the resurrection—tremendous!

Now let's come to the New Testament, and let's begin in John 13. Now as we're turning there to John 13 (I am going to read from the Harmony [p. 243] because I have the parallel columns here which is important for us to understand). Now I am going to go through this and I am also going to answer some questions which relate to recycling of an error concerning the Passover that the foot washing was after supper because that's what the King James says, but that's a mistranslation, because the word means: *and during supper* and the Greek verb that is used there has to do with the beginning of supper, not after supper. And so I've got a letter that I did January 19, 1975 to answer that very question. Because one man, his name is Darryl Hensen, put out a paper and said the Passover and "night to be remembered" are on the fourteenth—meaning that the feast is over on the twentieth. So look what happens when people don't do the things that God wants them to do, the way He wants them to do. But all the way through leading up to this John 13 the disciples came and said " 'Where do You desire us to prepare to keep the Passover?' and He said, 'You go into this house and you tell the master of the house that I am coming and I want to keep the Passover with my disciples at your house. You follow the man who has a pitcher of water and in that house we'll have the Passover' " (paraphrased). So when they got in there, He came at evening, sat down with the twelve, now then here, John 13, this is important for us to understand because the timing of this is very similar when you take the keeping of the Passover at night and it's the promise of eternal life, and it's the renewal of the New Covenant that's what it is, we will see. That's the same night that God gave the promises of the covenant to Abraham, isn't it. And then the sacrifices took place on the day portion and that pictured the agony and torturous crucifixion that Jesus Christ would go through to die for the sins of the world. So it goes from Abraham to Christ and to the Church. That's why it is very important for us to understand we are not to mix in the Passover of Israel with the Passover of Christ because that relates back to Abraham and not to the Passover of Exodus 12. That served a little different function, though it was the Passover, a little different function than what is served by the Passover for us today. And here again we see the same pattern, you have the physical, you have the spiritual. Well, the Passover to Israel was physical, and now Christ comes and He reveals the spiritual Passover that we are to take, and the covenant of eternal life.

Now let's begin here in John 13:2, page 274 of the Harmony: "And during supper…" That's what it means from the Greek, and I'll re-do this letter of January 19, 1975, which is more than 30 years ago, and you will see that I have always preached the same thing. "And during supper (the devil having already put into the heart of Judas Iscariot, Simon's *son*, that he should betray Him)." Why does Satan like to come—to get as close to Christ as he could. What did the apostles have to put up with—false apostles, false brethren, false practices, and that's why we have to stand for the truth. And today, for us to stand up and tell the truth, and you look at all the accolades and all the glory that was displayed with the funeral of the Pope and to stand up and say the Pope is a liar, all the doctrines are lies, everything that they are doing is a lie and that's all of Satan the devil—[people will say of us] you're an idiot, you're insane, you are rotten, you are [committing] a hate crime. Well, that's because no one is willing to prove the truth. And if you say the truth, and people don't want the truth, and hate the truth, they're going to get mad. That's why they killed Christ, wasn't it? Yes.

Now verse 3: "Jesus, knowing that the Father had given all things into *His* hands, and that He had come from God and was going [back] to God…" Where did Jesus come from? John constantly said He came from heaven. "In *the* beginning was the Word, and the Word was with God, and the Word was God" (John 1:1). Who was Christ? God manifested in the flesh. And yet, some people can go into the Bible and say, "Oh no, He was just born by the Virgin Mary. He didn't come from heaven".

So Jesus, verse 4: "Rose from supper, laid aside *His* garments; and after taking a towel, He secured it around Himself." Verse 5: "Next, He poured water into a washing basin and began to wash the disciples' feet, and to wipe *them* with the towel which He had secured." And that was the job of the lowest servant of the household to do, and that was always done at the beginning of supper, just like when Jesus went in to eat with Simon the Pharisee, and He came in and here was the woman when He sat down (or actually reclined, because they reclined on couches to eat. They didn't sit at tables like we do.) So she came and what did she do? She wiped His feet with her hair and with her tears and was repenting. And so then after Jesus asked Simon the question who is He going to forgive the most, the one that owes a lot or a little. He said, "I suppose to the one who owes a lot." And He said, "You see this woman? I came in and you didn't give me any water to wash my feet, and she has washed my feet with her tears and wiped them with the hair of her head." So that shows that foot washing should be at the beginning [of supper], not at the ending.

Verse 6: "Then He came to Simon Peter; and he (that is Simon Peter) said to Him, 'Lord, are You going to wash my feet?' " Verse 7: "Jesus answered and said to him, 'What I am doing you do not understand now, but you shall know after these things.' " Because He was going to explain it to them. Then, verse 8: "Peter said to Him, 'You shall not wash my feet, not ever.' Jesus answered (and said to him), 'If I do not wash you, you have no part with Me.' " Now let me ask you a question. Why does Satan want people to not do footwashing? Because Satan doesn't want you to have part with Jesus. Right? What is the first thing that they stop doing when they modify the Passover or what they call the Lord's Supper which is a perversion of the Passover—what do they stop first? Footwashing. "Oh well, we don't do that today. That's too humiliating to do." And see it is so simple. Jesus said to do it, and we will see He tells us to do it. Now anyone who says you don't have to do footwashing is saying, "I know more than God. I am better than Jesus Christ." They may not think those words, but that's precisely what their actions and their attitude says. So if you don't do footwashing, you have no part with Him.

Verse 9: "Simon Peter said to Him, 'Lord, not my feet only, but also *my* hands and *my* head.' Just like the way that humans do, what do they do, they want to improve on what God says. Oh, if [washing] the feet is good, how about the hands and head? You know, and if this had not occurred and been recorded, what would people be doing today—hands, head and feet wouldn't they? Now notice verse 10: "Jesus said to him, 'The one who has been washed does not need to wash *anything other* than the feet, but is completely clean; and you are clean, but not all' " (John 13:2-10).

Now there are two contradictions, not [really] contradictions but apparent contradictions if you don't understand it. "He who has been washed…" Now what does it mean to be washed? We'll see it does not mean to be bathed—that you take a bath before you come [to keep the Passover]. Obviously, the disciples did not have a chance to take a bath before they got there did they? No! What were they doing, they were walking into Jerusalem weren't they, and they were asking Jesus, "Where do you want to keep the Passover?" They were all dirty with dusty feet and sweaty from walking, and they didn't have underarm deodorant and things like this. I mean let's get down to the real nitty-gritty of life, because that's what it was. So it's not talking about being bathed in a bath.

Let's go to Act 22, and let's see what "washed" means. Now this is Paul giving an account of his calling where he was on the road to Damascus. You talk about the reach of the high priest to get people that they wanted to get! He actually had arrest warrants to go in the synagogues and get anyone who believed in Christ and haul them out and take them to prison and, yes, even have them killed. So God knocked him down, that's how He called him. Then He told Ananias, "I want you to go take care of Saul for Me." And he said, "Oh Lord, look he has come with orders to take people away." He said, "He is a chosen servant to Me" (paraphrased). So Ananias, verse 13: "Came to me; and he stood *and* said to me, 'Brother Saul, look up.' And I looked up at him at that time. And he said, 'The God of our fathers has personally chosen you to know His will, and to see the Just One, and to hear *the* voice of His mouth;' " so he was personally taught by Jesus Christ. Verse 15: " 'For you shall be a witness for Him to all men of what you have seen and heard. And now why do you delay? Arise and be baptized, **and wash away your sins**…' " (Acts 22:1-12 paraphrased, and 13-16). So the word "washed" there in John 13 is *louo* in the Greek and it's *louo* here.

Now let's come to Hebrews 10 and let's see where we have the same thing. If you are baptized, you don't need to be baptized again, you just need to have your feet washed on the Passover night. Now let's come here to Hebrews 10:22: "Let us approach *God* with a true heart…" Because we have a great High Priest over the House of God. "…with full conviction of faith, our hearts having been purified from a wicked conscience…" That's by the blood of Christ, "…and our bodies having been **washed** with pure water." That's baptism. "Let us hold fast without wavering *to* the hope *that* we profess, for He Who promised *is* faithful" (verse 23). So that's what it means there in John 13 to be **washed** and then that is accomplished through the operation of **baptism** and then you only wash the feet and therefore, as I wrote in the Passover book and in the book *The Day Jesus the Christ Died,* that foot washing <u>does</u> commemorate and renew your baptism. It also shows that you are going to walk in God's way.

Now let's come back here to John 13 again. So that's what it means to be washed. You don't have to wash anything other than the feet, verse 10: "…But is completely clean; and you are clean, but not all." And the reason He said that was because Judas was there for the foot washing and Judas went out after the foot washing.

Now the truth is, as you will see in the letter I did in 1975, is that only John mentions the exact time when Judas left, and there is no mix-up in the account in Luke 22. (John 13:11) "For He knew … who was betraying Him; this was the reason He said, 'Not all of you are clean.' " Verse 12: "Therefore, when He had washed their feet, and had taken His garments, *and* had sat down again, He said to them, 'Do you know what I have done to you? You call Me the Teacher and the Lord, and you speak rightly, because I am. Therefore, if I, the Lord and the Teacher, have washed your feet…' " And we could just add in there, the same as the lowest servant of the household. " '…you also are duty-bound to wash one another's feet.' " And that's the real meaning of the Greek, "duty-bound." So that's why Satan wants to get rid of that first. And then according to what the meaning of the Feast of Unleavened Bread [it] is what—a little leaven, leavens the whole lump, and [so] then one error after another follows each other right down the line to where even today some people say the Passover is not important.

Now notice verse 15: " '[For] I have given you an example, *to show* that you also [should] do exactly as I have done to you.' " Now, if we love God and if we keep His commandments, His love is being perfected in us (this is 1 John 2:5) and we walk in the footsteps of Jesus Christ. Now if He gave this example for us to do, what should we do. <u>What Jesus said</u>! What was the reason that the promise was given to Isaac and because of what Abraham did 'because he obeyed My voice.' Well, this is the voice of Christ speaking and if He says you are duty-bound to do it, you're what? You're duty-bound to do it! " ' For I have given you an example, *to show* that you also [should] do exactly as I have done to you. Truly, truly, I tell you, a servant is not greater than his lord: nor a messenger greater than he who sent him' " (verse 16). So those who say you don't need to do foot washing are saying what? "We are greater than the Lord. We know more than God." He says, verse 17: " 'If you know these things, blessed are you <u>if</u> <u>you</u> <u>do</u> them' " (John 13:11-17). Does that mean we should do that? Of course, of course!

Now the next part: eating the unleavened bread. Let's come here to Luke 22:19: " And He took bread; *and* after giving thanks, He broke *it* and gave *it* to them, saying, 'This is My body, which is given for you. This do in the remembrance of Me.' " Now then, He did that also with the wine. Let's continue on over here in Mark 14:23 and we'll get the wine and I'll make a very important point concerning transubstantiation—that there is no such thing as transubstantiation. It doesn't take place. Verse 23: "And He took the cup; *and* after giving thanks, He gave *it* to them; and they all drank of it. Verse 24: "And He said to them, 'This is My blood, the blood of the New Covenant, which is poured out for many' " (Mark 14:23-24). Not only the many, but each individually. Now let's understand something. When Christ did this on that night, it is not recorded that when He broke the bread, all of a sudden some of His flesh came off of His arms and leaped into the bread so His flesh would be in the bread, nor did His blood come out of His wrists and into the wine so His actual blood would be in the wine. It is symbolic. Just like your baptism is a symbolic death. Furthermore, you cannot eat the blood and flesh of Jesus Christ because after His resurrection, He had no more flesh and blood to give. And everything that is done with the Eucharist in saying that that is so, is an absolute lie, and perpetuates people in bondage, in fear, in superstition and cuts them off from Christ. When the priest stands there and holds the bread up high and everyone worships the bread, whose god is it? Who are they worshipping? You need to know where that came from. You go in [to the website] and draw down from *The Two Babylons* on the "unbloody sacrifice". Now that originally came from Egypt as an unbloody sacrifice, and that means no animal sacrifice. But in order to make it a bloody sacrifice, they've had to say it's a mystery where that even though it's apparently bread and even though it's apparently wine, it [is claimed that it] is really the flesh and blood of Jesus Christ and He is crucified again every time we say the mass. Now that is an absolute lie! That has nothing to do with the Passover. The "I.H.S." on the little wafer—now if you break the [ordinary unleavened] bread, how do you have it perfectly round? And why is it in the form of a sun disk, and why does it have "I.H.S." which is Isis, Horus and Semiramis [Seb-Nimrod]. (Comment was made: it is perforated with a cross and so they can break it into four pieces.)

Now, let's come over here to 1 Corinthians 11:25, "In like manner, *He* also *took* the cup after He had supped, saying, 'This is *the* cup *of* the New Covenant in My blood. This do, as often as you drink *it*...' " He did this with the bread, He broke the bread and said, 'Take, eat, this is My body, which *is* being broken for you. This do in the remembrance of Me' (verse 24). And likewise here '…this do as often as you drink *it*…' Now this doesn't mean as often as you would like to drink it because there is a special Greek particle that is equivalent to the English "*a*" which in the Greek is "*alpha*," and the English "*n*" which in the Greek is "*nu*" and it [the word] is pronounced "*na*." Now "*an*" is a special particle that is not translated into English, but it shows that this statement "as often as" means that there are conditions and limits to how often that you do it. And what is the condition and limit? One, the Passover is a yearly event so it is restricted to once a year. " '…As often as you do it…' " is not as often as you would like, but "until"… the other condition is: "until the Lord come." Now He hasn't come yet, so as often as we do it, year by year, "til the Lord come, we show His death." Now we'll see that here. Verse 26: "For as often as you eat this bread and drink this cup you *solemnly* proclaim the death of the Lord until He comes." When did He die—every day? No, one day, Passover day. Right? Yes. You cannot commemorate His death any other day than on the day that He died, which was what? The Passover day. "…You *solemnly* proclaim the death of the Lord until He comes. For this reason, *if* anyone shall eat this bread or shall drink the cup of the Lord unworthily, he shall be guilty of the body and *the* blood of the Lord" (1 Corinthians 11:24-29). And if you don't do it the way Jesus said, you're taking it unworthily.

Now where does that put the majority of Christendom? And yet they think they are so righteous, you see. That's why you need to prove what is the Word of God, understand what is the Word of God. Don't believe what any minister or priest or scholar or expert tells you, you read it in the Bible and prove it and you make sure that you get a good translation of the Bible so that you will have the understanding that you need. See, in the world they want to commemorate His birth and His resurrection, and forget about His death and [therefore] you have no forgiveness of sin unless you remember His death.

Now let's come to John 6 and let's see the whole meaning of this and we'll go into in a little more detail than I did last time. But you see, when we renew the New Covenant, and also John gave the words of the covenant in four chapters [we read]: John 14, 15, 16, and 17. And of course, we've gone through that with the Passover preparation.

Now let's come here to John 6:32. Let's understand the meaning of it. We have to have the foot washing, we have to have the bread, we have to have the wine, and that's the sequence in the way that we do it. Then we read the words of the New Covenant, John 14, 15, 16, and 17 and in those four chapters you'll find faith, hope, and love. You will find the whole Christian experience. You will find the promise of the Spirit given. You will find the promise of the love of Christ given. You will find the promise of the love of God the Father given, and you will find the promise that Christ would be with us even to the end of the age, and even through the preaching of those that succeeded the apostles down to the time that we have today, that these very words would be spoken and practiced and believed. Now here, John 6:32: "Then Jesus said to them, 'Truly, truly I say to you, Moses did not give you the bread from heaven;' " They were looking for the manna. " '...but My Father gives you the true bread from heaven. For the bread of God is He Who comes down from heaven and gives life to the world' " (verse 33). Now you see when I read those things, I cannot understand how [some] people believe that Jesus was not in heaven before He came to the earth! You know last time I talked about, you know, what if you had a Volkswagen Jetta and you put Rolls Royce nametags on it? Do you have a Rolls Royce, or do you have a Volkswagen Jetta? Well, you have a Volkswagen Jetta. Only the name has been changed. It is still the same thing—the Volkswagen. So, He came down from heaven " '...the bread of heaven is He Who comes down from heaven and gives life to the world.' Therefore, they said to Him, 'Lord, give this bread to us always.' " Verse 35: "Jesus said to them, 'I am the bread of life; the one who comes to Me shall never hunger; and the one who believes in Me shall never thirst at any time.' " And this is talking spiritually, not physically—spiritually. You don't have to go across the earth looking at other religions. This is what you have with God's Spirit, you'll never hunger and you'll never thirst and put in your margin there, Matthew 5 (verse 6) about if you hunger and thirst after righteousness, you shall be filled.

Now let's come to Psalm 34, because this is, as we will see, confirmed as a figure of speech. Now let's understand this—spiritually with Christ in you, that's what it results in, but you have to taste the Word of God, don't you? You have to live by every word that comes out of the mouth of God. Not by bread alone, and that's what this symbolizes as we'll see. Now let's pick it up here in Psalm 34:8. Now here is something very similar to what Jesus said. "O taste and see that the LORD *is* good..." Now you're not biting into the flesh of Christ, and you're not drinking His blood. You are, as it were, taking in the Word of God as spiritual food. "...Blessed *is* the man *that* trusteth in him." So that shows the result of it, you see.

Now let's come over here to verse 15: "The eyes of the LORD *are* upon the righteous, and his ears *are open* to their cry. The face of the LORD *is* against them that do evil, to cut off the remembrance of them from the earth. *The righteous* cry, and the LORD heareth, and delivereth them out of all their troubles." You can claim that promise. Whatever trouble you have, God promises to deliver you out of <u>all</u>, one way or the other. Now you may have to pray repeatedly, but God sooner or later will do it just like He did even at the last minute with Abraham raising the knife to offer Isaac for the sacrifice. Now notice verse 18: "The LORD *is* nigh unto them that are of a broken heart; and saveth such as be of a contrite spirit. Many *are* the afflictions of the righteous: but the LORD delivereth him <u>out</u> of <u>them all</u>." (Psalm 34:8, 15-19). Now whatever your trials and difficulties, if you're having them, you just take this Psalm, when you're praying, get on your knees open it up there, read it out loud to God, claim this promise and say, "God you have promised and I'm trusting in Your Word. God You cannot lie, God I trust in You and believe You and believe Your Word." And that's all tied here to Christ as the bread of life.

Now let's come back here to John 6. Let's come over here to verse 47: " 'Truly, truly I say to you, the one who believes in Me has eternal life.' " What was it said about Abraham? He believed in the LORD, right? Yes. It shows that Abraham is going to have eternal life. Verse 48: " 'I am the bread of life.' " Everything that Jesus was and is and stands for and gives us, through the power of the Holy Spirit, spiritual life, and at the return of Christ and at the resurrection, eternal life in the Kingdom of God forever. That's what the whole story of it is back there with Abraham. That's where it began, and it is brought to a partial completion with Christ through the Passover, and through His crucifixion and resurrection and continues on down as we will see with the church harvest leading up to Pentecost and the first resurrection. So this is really a tremendous thing when you put it all together, you see. Verse 49: " 'Your fathers ate manna in the desert, but they died.' " Isn't it true? You can eat the best food in the world—manna is the best food wouldn't you say? Even today you can eat the best food in the world, you can take care of yourself the best you can, you can exercise the best you can, you can drink your own fresh juice forever like Jack La-Lanne who is 95 and still going strong and exercising every day at 5:00 a.m. in the morning, but guess what? We are all going to die, as in Adam. So we are all looking to eternal life after death. Verse 50: " 'This is the bread which comes down from heaven so that anyone may eat of it and not die.' " Now that means, *not die forever*. " 'I am the living bread, which came down from heaven;' " How many times in this chapter did He say He came down from heaven—amazing. " '...if anyone eats of this bread, he shall live forever; and the bread that I will give is even My flesh, which I will give for the life of the world.' " This is the whole plan and purpose of God, and it goes back and the first Passover was with Abraham. Verse 52: " 'Because of this...' " Now you always have to have an argument. This is Fox News fair and balanced before it was ever on television. " 'Because of this, the Jews were arguing with one another, saying, 'How is He able to give us *His* flesh to eat?' " Well, just cut a little off His forearm and pass it around or throw a fingertip in the chili at Wendy's and sue them. "Therefore, Jesus said to them, 'Truly, truly I say to you, unless you eat the flesh of the Son of man, and drink His blood, you do not have life in yourselves' " (verse 53). That is symbolized by the bread, not His literal flesh, and by the wine, not His literal blood. Verse 54: " 'The one who eats My flesh and drinks My blood has eternal life, and I will raise him up in the last day;' " And what is the last day for us? It is not the feast of the Last Great Day. There is a feast for us which is the last day of the 50 count to Pentecost. Isn't the 50th day the last day? Isn't that [Pentecost] when we are going to be resurrected? Yes. That's what it means. " 'For My flesh is truly food, and My blood is truly drink. The one who eats My flesh and drinks My blood is dwelling in Me, and I in him.' " Wow! This was hard to take! Even these who were complaining about this were His disciples. So then He set the record straight. What does it mean? Verse 57: " 'As the living Father has sent Me, and I live by the Father; so also the one who eats Me shall live by Me' " (John 6:47-57). That's what it means. You live by Jesus Christ. You live by every word of God. That's what it means, and that goes right back to why Abraham received the blessing, because " '... Abraham obeyed My voice.' "

Now let's come to Galatians 3 (we mentioned this). Verse 26, and here is the whole meaning of the Passover and why it goes back to Abraham. "Because you are all sons of God..." Destined, what—to be as the stars in heaven, yes? The spiritual seed—yes? "...

through faith in Christ Jesus. For as many *of you* as were baptized into Christ did put on Christ." And your baptism is a conjoining to the death of Jesus. That's why we remember the death of Jesus through the Passover. We don't forget His resurrection, but His death, the death of God manifested in the flesh is the most important thing. So we're baptized into Christ, put on Christ, have the mind of Christ, the knowledge of Christ, the Word of Christ, the way that Christ lived and walked.

Verse 28: "There is neither Jew nor Greek; there is neither bond nor free; there is neither male nor female..." And that is just spiritually speaking, because I am still a man and those of you who are women are still women, and those of you who are men are still men—so in the flesh they're still a man and woman and so forth. "...for you are all one in Christ Jesus." That is for the opportunity for salvation. Verse 29: "And if you *are* Christ's, then you are Abraham's seed..." which He promised back there as the stars of heaven. "...And heirs according to *the* promise" that you will receive eternal life. And that's the origin and meaning of the Passover.

End of Sermon

Transcriber: Judith Anderson

Origin and Meaning of Passover
April 16, 2005
Scriptural References

1) 1 Corinthians 2:9-11

2) Isaiah 28:9-13

3) Genesis 15:4-5

4) Psalm 8:1-6

5) Romans 1:18-21

6) Genesis 15:5-10

7) Daniel 12:3

8) Matthew 13:43

9) Genesis 15:12-13, 17-18

10) Hebrews 6:13-20

11) Genesis 26:4

12) John 13:2-10 (Page 274 in the *Harmony of the Gospels in Modern English—The Life of Jesus Christ*)

13) Acts 22:1-12 (paraphrased) 13-14

14) Hebrews 10:22-23

15) John 13:11-17

16) Luke 22:19 (Page 276 in the Harmony)

17) Mark 14:23-24 (Page 277 in the Harmony)

18) 1 Corinthians 11:24-29

19) John 6:32, 34-35

20) Psalm 34:8, 15, 18-19

21) John 6:47-57

22) Galatians 3:26-29

CHAPTER NINE

The Passover—Abraham, Isaac, Israel & Christ–Sermon I

January 9, 2002

The title of this sermon is The Passover—Abraham, Isaac, Israel, and Christ. Most people believe that the Passover began with the children of Israel in Egypt. However, we're going to see that that is not true. It began long, long before then. And most people today believe that the Passover is only for the Jews. However, the Jews have it on the wrong day, and I've covered that very thoroughly in the book *The Christian Passover.* So let's approach this from an entirely different point of view. That's why I said, The Passover - Abraham, Isaac, Israel, and Christ.

Let's first of all go to Galatians 3. Now I'm going to read to you from my translation. Here, Galatians 3:29, and I found in translating that God inspired the Greek in such a way that if you're going to be honest in translating it, almost all the versions will be similar. And the reason being is because you can't translate it any differently.

Now, Galatians 3:29, "And if you *are* Christ's, then you are Abraham's seed, and heirs according to *the* promise." Now we'll take a look at that in detail here, in a little bit.

Let's go to the book of Hebrews, and again I'm going to read from my translation. Let's come to the sixth chapter. And I think if you go through and look at the writings of the New Testament you will be very surprised how much of the New Testament is keyed to Abraham, and then Abraham, Isaac, and Jacob, but more in particularly to Abraham.

Now let's begin here in Hebrews 6:13. "For God, after promising Abraham, swore by Himself, since He could swear by none greater, saying, 'Surely in blessing I will bless you, and in multiplying I will multiply you.' Now after he had patiently endured, he obtained the promise. For indeed, men swear by the greater, and confirmation by an oath *puts* an end to all disputes between them. In this *way* God, desiring more abundantly to show the heirs of the promise the unchangeable nature of His own purpose, confirmed *it* by an oath; …" (Heb. 6:13-17). Now I want you to understand "the unchangeable nature of His own [purpose]", because that does tie in with God's plan, and God's plan ties in with the Passover and the holy days, as well as the weekly Sabbath. So that's important to understand.

"So that by two immutable things, in which *it was* impossible *for* God to lie, we who have fled for refuge might have strong encouragement to lay hold on the hope *that has been* set before *us*; which *hope* we have as an anchor of the soul, both secure and steadfast, and which enters into the *sanctuary* within the veil; where Jesus has entered for us *as* a forerunner, having become a High Priest forever according to the order of Melchisedec" (vs. 18-20).

Now also this tells us a very important thing. That we always have to have the hope that God gave to Abraham, the hope of eternal life. We need to have that as secure and steadfast for the anchor of our soul. That way we're not going to be tossed to and fro by everything that comes along. And as we have been finding in the series in the book of Hebrews, as we're coming to now, that the thing that is important is that we have a High Priest Who is in heaven at the right hand of God, and this is the greatest most supreme thing that God could do for us while we are in the flesh.

133

Chapter Nine

Now let's come to Hebrews 13:8. And here is something that's very important that we need to understand and remember. "Jesus Christ *is* the same yesterday [that is, when He was the God of the Old Testament], and today [that is, under the New Covenant], and forever [that is in carrying out God's plan into the ages of eternity]." So these things we really need to have as a preface before getting into the Passover concerning Abraham, Isaac, Israel, and Christ.

Now let's come back to Galatians 3, and let's see something that is important, something that is profound. Now let's pick it up here in Galatians 3:6. "*It is* exactly as *it is written*: "Abraham believed God…" Now that is a profound statement. He believed God. And that's what we have to do in the New Covenant as well, see. He didn't believe in just what God had told him. Well, he did, but he believed God. And this is what it needs to be for all of us, that we believe God. When God says something, we believe it because God said it. So therefore we believe God. Now notice, "…and it was reckoned to him for righteousness." This is telling us then, when you believe God, wholly and completely, you are righteous before Him. Righteousness is imputed to you. Now we'll see how this comes when we get back to the book of Genesis in just a minute. "Because of this, *you should* understand that those who *are* of faith are the *true* sons of Abraham" (Gal. 3:6-7). That is, the spiritual sons. There were the physical sons through Isaac and Jacob, and Israel.

"Now *in* the Scriptures God, seeing in advance that He would justify the Gentiles by faith, preached the gospel beforehand to Abraham…" Now when have you heard that the gospel was preached to Abraham? There it is. And the gospel begins with what He said to Abraham, "…*saying*, 'In you shall all the nations be blessed.' *It is* for this reason [because Abraham believed] that those who are of faith are being blessed with the believing Abraham" (vs. 8-9).

So let's go back to the book of Genesis and see this. And we will see that the Passover did not begin with Israel, but rather it began with Abraham. And we'll see that it's the same day that God gave the Passover to Israel. And we will see the reason we keep the Passover today is because of Abraham. That's what it says. "If you are Christ's then you are Abraham's seed and heirs according to the promise." And so likewise, when we partake of the Passover, because we're coming up to it very shortly here, we need to understand that the words that Jesus gave, the words of the New Covenant, we need to believe.

Now let's come back to Genesis 12, KJV. Let's begin here in verse 1. "Now the LORD had said unto Abram, Get thee out of thy country, and from thy kindred, and from thy father's house, unto a land that I will shew thee:…" Now just hold your place here, and let's go to Luke 14, because I want to make something very clear. That what Abraham did fulfilled this requirement that Jesus gave in the gospel of Luke, beginning in verse 26. Let's read verse 25 and then we'll read verse 26. "And great multitudes were going with Him: and He turned, *and* said to them…" Now this is also important to understand. Multitudes of people like to use the name of Christ, like to claim that they are Christian, like to think of themselves as Christian, but they are the glad-handers just like the people who were here because they came because they were looking for the physical things. They remembered the feeding of the 4000, the feeding of the 5000, and so forth. So Jesus turned and He made a very important point here. He said, "If anyone come to Me and does not hate his father, and mother, and wife, and children, and brothers and sisters, and, in addition, his own life also, he cannot be My disciple." So it is not like the Protestants say, "All you have to do is give your heart to the Lord." No, you have to do the same thing as Abraham did. This is a requirement of Abraham, now detailed a little more closely for us. And where it says, "cannot be My disciple", it means the impossibility of being a disciple of Jesus Christ. So we can tie that together. If you do not believe God, if you do not believe Christ, if you do not keep His commandments you are not of Christ. You may claim to be, you may think you are. You may even have some important people whom you look to in this world as your spiritual leaders, but unless you do what Jesus said here, you're not His disciple.

Luke 14:27, "And whoever does not carry his cross, and come after Me,…" meaning that you have to go through whatever trials and difficulties you go through and you bear your cross. "…cannot be My disciple;" So remember what Jesus said, the broad way, the easy way. Many are going that way with the name of Christ, but it's going to end in destruction. So then He gives a little more and He says, "For which one of you, desiring to build a tower…" You can read the rest of it there. You calculate whether you have enough to finish it or not. And if you don't, people are going to mock you and say, "You began but didn't finish." Or a king, going against another, he figures out whether he can come against 20,000 with his 10,000, and if he can win or not. And if not then he goes ahead and makes peace.

Now verse 33 says, "In the same way also, each one of you who does not forsake all that he possesses cannot be My disciple." Now what is the hardest thing to give up? Many people have walked away from lands. Many people have walked away from countries. Many people have left families, but what is the hardest thing to give up? Self. You are to give up self to become a new creature in Christ.

Now let's come back to Genesis 12. Let's see how the gospel began. And what we read in Matthew, Mark, Luke, and John, and all the New Testament is a detailed fulfilling and carrying out of this promise, which was given to Abraham by God directly in Genesis 12:2. "And I will make of thee a great nation, and I will bless thee, and make thy name great; and thou shalt be a blessing: and I will bless them that bless thee, and curse him that curseth thee: and in thee shall all families of the earth be blessed." Now that is a broad, broad promise, isn't it? So therefore literally, the rest of the Bible from this point on shows how God fulfilled those promises and was carrying them out. And how that the carrying out of these promises are going to go clear on down through into the millennium, down into the Last Great Day, down into New Jerusalem coming on this earth, and on into all eternity. So that's quite a thing. "So Abram departed, as the LORD had spoken unto him;…" (Gen. 12:2-4).

Now let's come to Genesis 15. Let's see where then, God then gives a little more understanding of what He promised him. Now he believed Him. [But] He didn't give him any details. He said, "Just go, I'll bless you." So he left. Now please understand this: that's the same with us. Many times God has us do things that we don't understand right away. Later, He reveals it to us. Here's the later part that He revealed a little bit more to Abram, or Abraham. Now we're going to look and see that there are two things here. We're also going to see that this took place over a period of two days, and that these two days are the Passover, the 14th of the first month, and the first day of the Feast of Unleavened Bread, the 15th of the first month. Now, we'll prove that after we get into it.

Let's look at this now. So He gave the promise, beginning in verse 4. He said, "…Out of thine own bowels shall be thine heir." So there is a physical seed. First there is the physical, then there is the spiritual. That's what Paul said. The first man, Adam, was of the flesh. The second Adam, Christ, was from heaven. There is a natural body, which is sown in the resurrection, and raised a spiritual body. So here we have the same thing. God is giving the promise of a physical heir - a son.

Now then we have a second promise given. Verse 5, "And He brought him forth abroad, and said, Look now toward heaven, and tell the stars, if thou be able to number them: and He said unto him, So shall thy seed be." Now that's quite an awesome thing. And remember, at that time there was no smog around to obscure the vision of the stars. Now, you see the stars when? At night. What God is doing here, He is bringing the words of the covenant to Abraham. These are the words of the covenant that God gave to Abraham. Now, He expands upon that because there are two parts here: the physical seed and the spiritual seed.

Now, hold your place and let's come to Matthew 13, and we will see the promise of spiritual seed is likened unto the stars. So He is giving two promises to Abraham here. One a physical seed from his own bowels. One of spiritual seed, which would come through Christ, as we now know, Galatians 3:29, that if you be Christ's then are you Abraham's seed and heirs according to the promise.

Now let's come to Matthew 13:43. "Then shall the righteous shine forth as the sun in the kingdom of their Father. The one who has ears to hear, let him hear."

Now again let's come to 1 John 3, and let's see something very important here...how we will be when we are glorified spirit beings. 1 John 3:1, "Behold! What *glorious* love the Father has given us, that we should be called the children of God! For this reason, the world does not know us because it did not know him. Beloved, now we are the children of God, and it has not yet been revealed what we shall be; but we know that when He is manifested, we shall be like Him, because we shall see Him exactly as He is" (1 John 3:1-2).

Now let's come to Revelation 1 so we can show that when God took Abraham out there and showed him the stars, he was literally showing him the glory of his coming spiritual seed through Christ. Now, Revelation 1:13, "And in *the* midst of the seven lampstands *one* like *the* Son of man, clothed in *a garment* reaching to the feet, and girded about the chest with a golden breastplate. And His head and hair *were* like white wool, white as snow; and His eyes *were* like a flame of fire; and His feet *were* like fine brass, as if *they* glowed in a furnace; and His voice *was* like *the* sound of many waters. And in His right hand He had seven stars, and a sharp two-edged sword went out of His mouth, and His countenance [now notice] *was* as the sun shining in its *full* power" (Rev. 1:13-16). Now, what is a star? A star is a sun. We know that, don't we? Yes. So when God told Abraham they'd be like the stars, so shall your seed be, this is talking about the spiritual seed.

Now let's come to Philippians 3:20. "But for us, the commonwealth *of God* exists in *the* heavens, from where also we are waiting for *the* Savior, *the* Lord Jesus Christ: Who will transform our vile bodies..." In the Greek you can use a plural subject in a singular antecedent, but here in English it should be plural. "...Who will transform our vile bodies, that they may be conformed to His glorious body [and we just saw that in Revelation 1], according to the inner working of His own power, *whereby He is able* to subdue all things to Himself" (Phil. 3:20-21). So when God told Abraham that his seed was going to be as the stars of heaven for multitude, He's not only showing the number, He's also showing the kind of glory that they will be.

Now let's come back to Genesis 15, and let's read that again. Now some people may ask the question: "so shall your seed be," does that not just refer to physical seed? Well, what is God's plan overall for human beings? [It is] to become the sons of God.

Now let's come back here to 1 John 3 then and I'll answer the question. Because when we receive the begettal of the Holy Spirit, we receive the seed of eternal life. And in the Greek the seed is called *sperma*. Now unfortunately in 1 John 3:9 we have one of the worst translated verses in all the King James Version of the Bible, which reads, "Whosoever is born of God doth not commit sin;..." That's an entirely incorrect translation. And [it is] incorrectly interpreted by the Protestants who say that if you are born again you cannot sin. That is, if you have a conversion experience you cannot sin. Now that is not true.

Come over here to Chapter 5 and let's show the contradiction right within the translation of the King James. Verse 16, "If anyone see his brother sinning a sin *that is* not unto death,…" Does this not say that a person who is converted is capable of sin? Does it not? Is not a brother converted? Yes. And if he sins a sin not unto death, that means it's a sin he can repent of. "…He shall ask [that is, you pray for him], and He [God] will give him life for those who do not sin unto death. There is a sin unto death; concerning that *sin*, I do not say that he should make *any* supplication *to God*" (1 John 5:16). This shows two things. Converted people can sin. Converted people, according to Protestants, are born again. But that is not a correct interpretation. No one is born again until the resurrection. However, with the proper translation of verse 9, which I'll read the one that I have, which bears out in the Greek and should read this way: "Everyone who has been begotten by God [does not practice] is not practicing sin because His seed [that is from God the Father, which is the begettal, so I put in italics *of begettal*] is dwelling within him, and he is not able to *practice* sin because he has been begotten [of] by God." So when it talks about seed back here in Genesis 15, now we see that there's physical seed, and we also see that there are spiritual seed. That's why I started out that if you are Christ's then are you Abraham's seed (spiritual) and heirs according to the promise.

Ok, now let's come back to Genesis 15 because we're going to find how important this is. And I remember when we first understood this, what, about four years ago, three years ago, somewhere around there. It was really, really quite an eye-opener. So we'll go through it and we will clarify it for you. Ok, now let's come back here again to Genesis 15:5. "So shall thy seed be." Now in both instance, physical and spiritual. Verse 6, "And he believed in the LORD; and He counted it to him for righteousness." Now, let's understand something here. There was no work for Abraham to do because it's impossible to count the stars, correct? He could not have children at this point, so there was no work for him to do. He believed God. It counted to him for righteousness.

Now then, God gives him an instruction here. "And He said unto him, I *am* the LORD that brought thee out of Ur of the Chaldees, to give thee this land to inherit it. And he said, Lord GOD, whereby shall I know that I shall inherit it?" So God then, did a very profound thing. And this has to do with the very crucifixion of Christ and His death, and being put in the grave. "And He said unto him, Take Me an heifer of three years old, and a she goat of three years old, and a ram of three years old, and a turtledove, and a young pigeon" (Gen. 15:7-9). Now this means that they're all mature.

"And he took unto him all these, and divided them in the midst [meaning he cut them down the middle], and laid each piece one against another:…" Meaning the spine was close to each other and there was a path down between these animals cut and laid out. Everything was there, the blood, the guts, everything. "…But the birds divided he not." He probably put one bird on one side and one bird on the other side. Now what was the purpose of this? We'll see what the purpose of this is. This is a special maledictory sacrifice and oath, that when one takes an oath such as this they cannot break it. Now verse 11, "And when the fowls came down upon the carcases, Abram drove them away" (vs. 10-11).

"And when the sun was going down,…" That's very interesting, isn't it? First of all, back here in verse 5 we have a night, don't we? Then in the day portion of the day, which was the 14th of the first month as we will see, he did the sacrificing of the animals. Now notice there was no altar, there was no sprinkling of the blood, there was no burning of it by Abraham. Just laid out there. So much so that the fowl, which then would be the vultures and buzzards, were circling up overhead. And they came down upon the carcases, and Abram drove them away. "And when the sun was going down, a deep sleep fell upon Abram;…" Now you can read in the Passover book how this is very likened to the time when Jesus died. He died at the third hour, and the sun was going down at the third hour, is it not? Yes. Then two things happened here. "…A deep sleep fell upon Abram…" Now, a deep sleep. What is a person who dies in Christ? They are sleeping. So here's a deep sleep. This is a type of death. A type of the death of Christ, perhaps precisely at the same time that Jesus died, when He was crucified on the 14th day, the Passover, when He was crucified. "…And, lo, an horror of great darkness fell upon him. And He said unto Abram, Know of a surety that thy seed shall be a stranger in a land *that is* not theirs, and shall serve them; and they shall afflict them four hundred years; and also that nation, whom they shall serve, will I judge: and afterward shall they come out with great substance. And thou shalt go to thy fathers in peace; thou shalt be buried in a good old age. But in the fourth generation they shall come hither again: for the iniquity of the Amorites *is* not yet full" (vs. 12-16).

Now then, notice verse 17. "And it came to pass, that, when the sun went down…" Now we are into the second day, aren't we? When do the days begin and end according to scripture? At sunset. So we have the sun going down, don't we. Now remember, we started out at night in verse 4 and 5. Then we had the day portion with the sacrifice, and we'll explain the sacrifice here in just a minute. Now, we come, the sun went down and it was dark. Then God did something very profound to give to Abraham the guarantee of the promises beginning in verse 4, carried on down through verses 13, 14, and 15. Then He did something very profound. "…Behold a smoking furnace, and a burning lamp that passed between those pieces." Now what happened when God went through those parts? It doesn't tell us directly, but I would say from the context of it is here, when God walked between the parts of the sacrifice, those animals were consumed and there was nothing left but ashes.

Now verse 18. "In the same day the LORD made a covenant with Abram, saying, Unto thy seed have I given this land, from the river of Egypt unto the great river, the river Euphrates: the Kenites, and the Kenizzites,…", and so forth, all of the different tribes of Canaan. Now where else do we find a two day sequence? And how do we know this is the 14th and 15th? We can't prove it from right here, because it doesn't say 14th day of the first month, here. And it doesn't say the 15th day of the first month, here. However, if we go to Exodus 12 we do have the days numbered, and we do have it told us exactly when it took place.

Now let's come here to Exodus 12. Now again, I refer you to *The Christian Passover* book. You can go through in detail because we have great detailed explanation of everything that is here because there is great confusion over the Passover. And of course it's only logical that Satan would confuse everything concerning the Passover, because if you keep the Christian Passover today the way that Christ wants you to, at the time that He says, and the manner that He says, then you belong to Christ. So Satan's objective is to confuse it, to cause problems with it, to change the day if possible. And because the Jews today keep the Passover on the 15th, which I fully explain in the book *The Christian Passover*, they do not recognize Christ at all. Because in order to truly recognize Christ you must understand the truth of the Passover, because Christ, as we will see later, died on the Passover day, the very time that the sacrifice took place that Abraham gave and fell into the deep sleep.

Now let's read the instructions here for the children of Israel, concerning the Passover. Now we're not going to go in great detail, but what I want to point out is this, ok? Let's begin in verse 3. "Speak ye unto all the congregation of Israel, saying, In the tenth *day* of this month they shall take to them every man a lamb, according to the house of *their* fathers, a lamb for an house: and if the household be too little for the lamb, let him and his neighbour next unto his house take *it* according to the number of the souls; every man according to his eating shall make your count for the lamb. Your lamb shall be without blemish [because that's a type of Christ], a male of the first year: ye shall take *it* out from the sheep, or from the goats: and ye shall keep it up until the fourteenth day of the same month: …" Which then is the first month because he said in verse 2, "This month is the beginning of months for you." So it's the first month. "...And the whole [congregation] assembly of the congregation of Israel shall kill it in the evening" (vs. 3-6). Which means between the two evenings, between sunset and dark, which is amply proved in the book, *The Christian Passover*.

Now then, they were to eat it in that night, after taking the blood and the so forth and roasting it, and so forth. Because He says, verse 12, "For I will pass through the land of Egypt this night, and will smite all the firstborn in the land of Egypt, both man and beast; and against all the gods of Egypt I will execute judgment:..." Then He said, "And the blood shall be to you for a token upon [your] the houses where ye *are*: and when I see the blood, I will pass over you..." (vs. 12-13). Now let's understand something here very important. All of Israel was blessed because of the Passover, but the Passover spared whom? The firstborn, correct. Now there is a great parallel with that for today with God's church who are the church of the firstborn, as we will see a little later, and also the rest of the world. So how important is the church of God to the world? [It is] Far more important than we have ever calculated. As important as the firstborn of Israel in relationship to the rest of Israel, so the church of the firstborn, which we are today, is as important to God as the rest of the world. So then, they were to keep that as a memorial.

Then we have this. Let's understand something very important here, which I cover. Here is the Passover. Let's come over here verse 21. "Then Moses called for all the elders of Israel, and said unto them, Draw out and take you a lamb according to your families, and kill the passover. And ye shall take a bunch of hyssop, and dip *it* in the blood that *is* in the bason, and strike the lintel and the two side posts with the blood that *is* in the bason; and none of you shall go out at the door of his house until the morning." And that literally means sunrise. So they could not leave that night. We explain all of that in *The Christian Passover* book. "For the LORD will pass through to smite the Egyptians; and when He seeth the blood upon the lintel, and on the two side posts, the LORD will pass over the door, and will not [allow] suffer the destroyer to come in unto your houses to smite *you*. And ye shall observe this thing for an ordinance to thee and to thy sons for ever. And it shall come to pass, when ye be come to the land which the LORD will give you, according as He hath promised, that ye shall keep this service. And it shall come to pass, when your children shall say unto you, What mean ye by this service? That ye shall say, It *is* the sacrifice of the LORD'S passover, Who passed over the houses of the children of Israel in Egypt, when He smote the Egyptians, and delivered our houses. And the people bowed the head and worshipped. And the children of Israel went away, and did as the LORD had commanded Moses and Aaron, so did they" (vs. 21-28). Then at midnight He smote all the firstborn.

Now let's come here to Numbers 33:3 because we do want to get a little chronology here. Let's begin in verse 1 and not 3. "These *are* the journeys of the children of Israel, which went forth out of the land of Egypt with their armies under the hand of Moses and Aaron. And Moses wrote their goings out according to their journeys by the commandment of the LORD: and these *are* their journeys according to their goings out. And they departed from Rameses in the first month, on the fifteenth day of the first month..." (Num. 33:1-3). When does the 15th begin? Right after sunset of the 14th, correct? Yes. They went out by night, as we will see. They couldn't have gone out on the night of the 14th because they had to stay in their houses. And if they kept the Passover on the 15th then they could not have left until morning. And if they left in the morning they could not leave at night. Now that's as simple as can be. If you're going to go to work at six in the morning, you don't show up at six at night. It's that simple, see. So they left on the morrow, or that is, the day after the Passover.

Now let's come and see this. Let's see what they did when they left their homes. Now where were the homes of the children of Israel? We'll see a little later they lived in the area of Goshen. So it was in the northwest part of the delta, the very choicest part of Egypt, and they had their little villages scattered there. And so for them to leave Rameses means they had to assemble at Rameses and then leave there. So they assembled at Rameses on the day portion of the 14th. And here's what they did. Let's go back to Exodus 12:33. "And the Egyptians were urgent upon the people, that they might send them out of the land in haste; for they said, We *be* all dead *men*."

"And the people took their dough before it was leavened, their kneadingtroughs being bound up in their clothes upon their shoulders. And the children of Israel did according to the word of Moses; and they [spoiled]..." It says borrowed. They had no intention of bringing it back. "...They [spoiled] borrowed of the Egyptians jewels of silver, and jewels of gold, and raiment: and the LORD gave the people favour in the sight of the Egyptians, so that they [gave] lent unto them *such things as they required*. And they spoiled the Egyptians" (Ex. 12:33-36).

Key verse beginning in verse 37 down to verse 42. Let's read it. "And the children of Israel journeyed from Rameses to Succoth, about six hundred thousand on foot *that were* men, beside children." So this is where we get the figure of 1.8 million. If we have one woman and one child per man, then you get 1.8 million people. "And a mixed multitude went up also with them; and flocks, and herds, *even* very much cattle. And they baked unleavened cakes of the dough which they brought forth out of Egypt, for it was not leavened; because they were thrust out of Egypt, and could not tarry, neither had they prepared for themselves any victual" (vs. 37-39).

Verse 40, according to the commandment of God. Remember that we read back there in Numbers 33. "Now the sojourning of the children of Israel, who dwelt in Egypt, *was* four hundred and thirty years. And it came to pass at the end of the four hundred and thirty years, even the selfsame day it came to pass, that all the hosts of the LORD went out from the land of Egypt. It *is* a night to be much observed unto the LORD for bringing them out from the land of Egypt: this *is* that night of the LORD to be observed of all the children of Israel in their generations" (vs. 40-42). This is not the Passover because the Passover they stayed in their homes. They came out by night. Now how does this tie in with Genesis 15? It ties in this way, verse 41. "It came to pass at the end of the four hundred and thirty years, even the selfsame day it came to pass,..." Selfsame day in reference to what? In reference to Genesis 15.

Let's go back there. Let's pick it up in verse 17. "And it came to pass, that, when the sun went down [which we know begins a new day, correct?], and it was dark, behold a smoking furnace, and a burning lamp that passed between those pieces. In the same day [being nighttime] the LORD made a covenant with Abram, saying, Unto thy seed have I given this land..." Also, "this same day", what also has part of the covenant? Come back here to verse 13. "And He said unto Abram, Know of a surety that thy seed shall be a stranger in a land *that is* not theirs [that's all they were in Egypt], and shall serve them; and they shall afflict them four hundred years [it was actually 430]; and also that nation, whom they shall serve, will I judge:..." And God said He did judge them on the Passover night, correct? Yes. "...And afterward shall they come out with great substance." Did they do that? Yes. "And thou shalt go to thy fathers in peace; thou shalt be buried in a good old age. But in the fourth generation they shall come hither again: for the iniquity of the Amorites *is* not yet full" (Gen. 15:13-16). So when the sun went down, beginning the 15th, that same day God made the covenant that He would bring them out and that they would inherit the land. So that's what the "self same day" is referring to. And God did it by walking through this special sacrifice which is called a maledictory oath. Meaning that once you make this oath you cannot change. And of course then, the smoking furnace burned up all the sacrifice completely.

So then, since verse 18, "the same day" equals to the same day in Exodus 12:41, "self same day", that is the 15th day of the first month. So therefore when we come back to Genesis 15, the promises that God gave to Abraham was then on the night of the 14th, which is the same night in which we take the Passover, in which we have the promises of eternal life given to us by Jesus Christ in the words of the New Covenant, correct? Yes.

Now before we go on let's come to understand a little bit more about this maledictory oath. Let's see it here in the book of Jeremiah 34. This tells us what kind of oath this is. There is no greater, no stronger oath. And of course, in doing this not only did He make the covenant with Abraham to bring the children of Israel out, but He also foretold of His coming crucifixion. So let's see this oath, and we will see what happens when people don't keep it. This is the most solemn oath that you can have.

Verse 8, "*This is* the word that came unto Jeremiah from the LORD, after that the king Zedekiah had made a covenant with all the people which *were* at Jerusalem, to proclaim liberty unto them;" Now here's the liberty. They made a covenant. We'll see how they made the covenant. "That every man should let his manservant, and every man his maidservant, *being* an Hebrew or an Hebrewess, go free; that none should serve himself of them, *to wit*, of a Jew his brother. Now when all the princes, and all the people, which had entered into the covenant, heard that every one should let his manservant, and every one his maidservant, go free, that none should serve themselves of them any more, then they obeyed, and let *them* go" (Jer. 34:8-10).

Now notice what happened here. "But afterward they turned, and caused the servants and the handmaids, whom they had let go free, to return, and brought them into subjection for servants and for handmaids" (vs. 11). Almost like Pharaoh, right, when Moses said, "Let my people go." They couldn't get along without the servants. So the Jews, when they let them go they said, "Oh, look what we did. We've got to do the work ourselves." Too bad.

Verse 12. They went back on their word. They went back on a covenant, see. And I want you to also remember that in relationship to the coming Passover, which is a renewing of the New Covenant. "Therefore the word of the LORD came to Jeremiah from the LORD, saying, Thus saith the LORD, the God of Israel; I made a covenant with your fathers in the day that I brought them forth out of the land of Egypt, out of the house of bondmen, saying, At the end of seven years let ye go every man his brother an Hebrew, which hath been sold unto thee; and when he hath served thee six years, thou shalt let him go free from thee: but your fathers hearkened not unto Me, neither inclined their ear. And ye were now turned, and had done right in My sight, in proclaiming liberty every man to his neighbour; and ye had made a covenant before Me in the house which is called by My name: but ye turned and polluted My name, and caused every man his servant, and every man his handmaid, whom ye had set at liberty at their pleasure, to return, and brought them into subjection, to be unto you for servants and for handmaids. Therefore thus saith the LORD; Ye have not hearkened unto Me, in proclaiming liberty, every one to his brother, and every man to his neighbour: behold, I proclaim a liberty for you, saith the LORD, to the sword, to the pestilence, and to the famine; and I will make you to be removed into all the kingdoms of the earth" (vs. 12-17). Now how serious is a covenant? Mighty serious. How serious is it when you break it? And remember, they did this in the house of God. And also remember, that when we do things, we have access to God the Father in heaven above. So this is not just in a physical house upon the earth where we have a covenant, you see.

Verse 18, "And I will give the men that have transgressed My covenant, which have not performed the words of the covenant which they had made before Me, when they cut the calf in twain,…" Just like Abraham did. He cut it in two. "…And passed between the parts thereof,…" Because when anyone made that kind of covenant and passed between the parts of the animals that were sacrificed for that covenant, what they are declaring by their action is this: if I break this covenant I will be like these animals that have been sacrificed - cut down the middle.

Now continuing, verse 19. "…And [they] passed between the parts thereof, the princes of Judah, and the princes of Jerusalem, the eunuchs, and the priests, and all the people of the land, which passed between the parts of the calf; I will even give them into the hand of their enemies, and into the hand of them that seek their life: and their dead bodies shall be for meat unto the fowls of the heaven, and to the beasts of the earth" (vs. 18-20). Did not the fowls of heaven come down to try and get the sacrifices that Abraham made? Yes. So now He's going to say, "I'm going to do this to you."

"And Zedekiah king of Judah and his princes will I give into the hand of their enemies, and into the hand of them that seek their life, and into the hand of the king of Babylon's army, which are gone up from you. Behold, I will command, saith the LORD, and cause them to return to this city; and they shall fight against it, and take it, and burn it with fire: and I will make the cities of Judah a desolation without an inhabitant" (vs. 21-22). Apparently, God fought their battle for them, drove back the king of Babylon. So they said, "Thank you God for doing that. We repent. We'll let our slaves go free." And then they changed their minds. So He said, "Now I'm going to cause the king of Babylon to return, and now he's going to do in the whole city." So this tells you the seriousness of the kind of oath that there is when you make a covenant and pass between the parts. That's the oath that God made with Abraham to guarantee that he would have 1) physical seed, 2) spiritual seed, 3) that He would take them out of the land of the stranger in the same day that He made the covenant with Abraham. That very same night. So you see, the Passover, and the Feast of Unleavened Bread really began with Abraham and not with Israel.

Now let's look at the extension of this covenant, the physical seed, which would be Israel. And they would come through Isaac. Let's come to Genesis 17. And oh, the Arabs would that it would have been Ishmael. But it wasn't. So here then is a continuation of the covenant, now giving in detail the requirements for the physical seed. Let's begin in verse 1. Abraham had to wait a long time, didn't he? Now this was a year before Isaac was born. And Isaac was then the promise of the physical seed. "And when Abram was ninety years old and nine,…" Well now let's see. He left at 75, didn't he. Here we are 25 years, inclusive counting, alright? "…And [He] said unto him, I *am* the Almighty God [El Shaddai]; walk before Me, and be thou perfect." Now just put in your margin there, Matthew 5:48, because we are told to be perfect as your Father in heaven is perfect. So you see here again, it's the same requirement. It is the gospel as preached to Abraham, right? Yes. Matthew 5:48.

Now verse 2 of Genesis 17. "And I will make My covenant between Me and thee, and will multiply thee exceedingly. And Abram fell on his face: and God talked with him, saying, As for Me, behold, My covenant *is* with thee, and thou shalt be a father of many nations. Neither shall thy name any more be called Abram, but thy name shall be Abraham; for a father of many nations have I made thee." And that was before Isaac was even born. Because you see, when God says something it is as good as done. That's what's important. So when God says you will be in the kingdom of God, it is as good as done. The only condition is, you have to endure to the end and be faithful. You'll make it.

Now verse 6, "And I will make thee exceeding fruitful, and I will make nations of thee, and kings shall come out of thee. And I will establish My covenant between Me and thee and thy seed after thee in their generations…" Now this is, then, the physical seed. "…For an everlasting covenant, to be a God unto thee, and to thy seed after thee. And I will give unto thee, and to thy seed after thee, the land wherein thou art a stranger, all the land of Canaan, for an everlasting possession; and I will be their God. And God said unto Abraham,

Thou shalt keep My covenant therefore, thou, and thy seed after thee in their generations. This *is* My covenant, which ye shall keep, between Me and you and thy seed after thee; Every man child among you shall be circumcised" (vs. 6-10). So here's the covenant of circumcision. Now remember that he was blessed of God, had righteousness imputed to him, his sins forgiven him for 25 years while he was in uncircumcision so that he could be the father of the uncircumcision who receive the promise of eternal life, as well as the father of the circumcision.

Continuing verse 11, "And ye shall circumcise the flesh of your foreskin; and it shall be a token of the covenant betwixt Me and you. And he that is eight days old shall be circumcised among you, every man child in your generations, he that is born in the house, or bought with money of any stranger, which *is* not of thy seed. He that is born in thy house, and he that is bought with thy money, must needs be circumcised: and My covenant shall be in your flesh for an everlasting covenant" (vs. 11-13). And that was until it was continuous to that time. And I think for all the descendants of Israel should be, to this day. Not for salvation but for the keeping of the covenant here because we live today in the land that God gave to the descendants of Israel. Not for salvation, but for this part of the covenant because whoever are the descendants of Israel should.

Now, verse 14. "And the uncircumcised man child whose flesh of his foreskin is not circumcised, that soul shall be cut off from his people; he hath broken My covenant." Now you see, God has not required this of the Gentile and their own nations. We know that in the New Covenant circumcision is nothing, and uncircumcision is nothing, but the circumcision of the heart, and faith in Christ. But this is for the physical seed.

Now, verse 15. "And God said unto Abraham, As for Sarai thy wife, thou shalt not call her name Sarai, but Sarah *shall* her name *be*. And I will bless her, and give thee a son also of her: yea, I will bless her, and she shall be *a mother* of nations; kings of people shall be of her. Then Abraham fell upon his face, and laughed, and said in his heart, shall *a child* be born unto him that is an hundred years old? And shall Sarah, that is ninety years old, bear? And Abraham said unto God, O that Ishmael might live before Thee!" The easy way out. "And God said, Sarah thy wife shall bear thee a son indeed; and thou shalt call his name Isaac: and I will establish My covenant with him for an everlasting covenant, *and* with his seed after him. And as for Ishmael, I have heard thee: Behold, I have blessed him, and will make him fruitful, and will multiply him exceedingly; twelve princes shall he beget, and I will make him a great nation. But My covenant will I establish with Isaac, which Sarah shall bear unto thee at this set time in the next year" (vs. 15-21). It's important for us to understand that God does things at the set time. So then they had the circumcision party.

Now, Isaac was born, sure enough at the set time that God had said, and then we have something profound. Here, let's come to Genesis 21:1. "And the LORD visited Sarah as He had said, and the LORD did unto Sarah as He had spoken. For Sarah conceived, and bare Abraham a son in his old age,..." You see, God does the impossible things. That way it can never be said that it's of a man. Now you show me any 100 year old today who has a pregnant 90 year old wife, and then we will know that this was not a miraculous thing. "... At the set time of which God had spoken to him. And Abraham called the name of his son that was born unto him, whom Sarah bare to him, Isaac. And Abraham circumcised his son Isaac being eight days old, as God had commanded him. And Abraham was an hundred years old, when his son Isaac was born unto him" (Gen. 21:1-5). So that means he was pretty close to the end of his 100th year, because remember when God told him back here in Chapter 17:17, he said, "Shall a child be born of him that is a hundred years old?" So apparently he was just 100 at that point. No more than three months into his 100th year, and Isaac was born before the 100th year was out. That's how we have the chronology.

Now then, let's talk about the Passover and Isaac, because this time it talks about Isaac and Abraham. Now this we find some tremendous types coming down to the prophecy, not only the prophecy but the actual crucifixion of Jesus Christ. Here we find that in type Abraham is a type of God the Father, who has only one son. And this son is to be sacrificed. Now we do not have anything dogmatic that we could say that this took place on the Passover day. It's possible, but we don't know for sure. So we can't say that. Now here is a test that Abraham went through. Now remember what we read at the beginning in Luke 14:26. Here again he is going to be tested on this. Not only do we do that when it's called "counting the cost" where in Luke 14:26 to the end of verse 33, but we always count the cost continually as we go through our Christian life. We're confronted with many things where we must count the cost. Will we obey God or not? Will we believe God or not? Will we trust God or not? And that's on an ongoing basis. It's not just, you know, you do it once and it's over with, see. No, not at all. So here he is. We don't know how old. As we see a little later, Isaac is called a lad. So, we could say that he was probably less than 20. They even have an indication that he was say, not much more than 12. So between 12 and 20 was the age of Isaac when this event took place. Which means that from the time that God called Abraham we have 37 to 45 years when this event took place. So you see, God also tested Abraham all those years, didn't He?

Now I've got another tape that I did, you know the Abraham and his human nature, and the things that he did. Now Abraham had a little deceitful streak in him, which Isaac inherited, and also Jacob inherited. And also Jacob's mother, she had a little deceitful streak in her. So God uses some of those human weakness in His plan. But here we have between 37 and 45 years when this event took place in Genesis 22. Now let's begin in verse 1. "And it came to pass after these things, that God did tempt..." Now this means test Abraham. God does not tempt anyone with evil. Let's understand that. God puts before us choices, whether we will obey Him or not. When we are tempted with evil and drawn away of our own lusts, and then the lust conceives and brings forth sin, God did not make us sin when we do that. That's a wrong human nature. And of course that's why we have the Feast of Unleavened Bread continuously year by year, as long as we are in the church of God, so that we understand that our human nature is always here and we always have to be working on getting rid of it, just like we get rid of leaven out of our lives.

Now Genesis 22:1, "And it came to pass after these things, that God did [test, or prove] tempt Abraham, and said unto him, Abraham: and he said, Behold, *here* I *am*. And He said, Take now thy son, thine only *son*..." Now was Ishmael Abraham's son? Yes, he was. But not of Sarah. Not counted as the seed for the promise, so therefore He said, "Your son, your only son." So this is very much a type of God the Father in relationship to Christ. In this case then, Isaac being a type of Christ, Abraham being a type of the Father. "...And get thee into the land of Moriah; and offer him there for a burnt offering upon one of the mountains which I will tell thee of" (Gen. 22:1-2). Now, there were mountains in Moriah. Now the Jews claim by tradition that this was the area where the temple was built. But also one of the mountains of Moriah then would be the mount that later became to be called the Mount of Olives. So could this be, and of course you need to understand the Mount of Olives is higher than the temple mount. So could this be the mount where Christ was crucified? If the parallel follows then that could be true so I just leave that as a question.

"And Abraham rose up early in the morning, and saddled his ass, and took two of his young men with him, and Isaac his son, and [cut] clave the wood for the burnt offering, and rose up, and went unto the place of which God had told him. Then on the third day Abraham lifted up his eyes, and saw the place afar off. And Abraham said unto his young men, Abide ye here with the ass; and I and the lad will go yonder and worship, and come again to you. And Abraham took the wood of the burnt offering, and laid *it* upon Isaac his son [that's almost like a type of carrying the cross that Christ did, remember?]; and he took the fire in his hand,

…" Now that means he took a kettle of hot coals for a fire, because obviously you are not going to carry it in your hand. Because if you carry fire in your hand you're going to burn it. "…And a knife; and they went both of them together." I imagine it was kind of a silent climb up that mountain. "And [finally] Isaac spake unto Abraham his father, and said, My father: and he said, Here am I, my son. And he said, Behold the fire and the wood [I see the fire and I see the wood]: but where *is* the lamb for a burnt offering?" (vs. 3-7). Now we notice two things here. There are two acts of faith. 1) Abraham, he believed. 2) And Isaac, he also believed and did not complain. He could have said, "This is ridiculous. We're going up here and you're going to offer an offering, and I find out at the last minute it's me!" But he didn't do it.

Now verse 8. "And Abraham said, My son, God will provide Himself a lamb for a burnt offering:…" Now sometimes God waits until the very last minute for deliverance, doesn't He? Yes, He does. "…So they went both of them together. And they came to the place which God had told him of; and Abraham built an altar there,…" Now let's understand something about sin offerings and burnt offerings. On the Mount of Olives, now let's picture this in your mind. You're looking at the temple area, and you are looking north. To the right is east. To the east of the temple is the Kiddron Valley going down 600 feet. Actually 450. They built a bridge across the Kiddron Valley to go into the East gate of the temple. This bridge went to the Mount of Olives. On the Mount of Olives right near the crest of the Mount of Olives was what was called the Miphkad Altar. Now this was a special altar outside the temple area. This is where they took all the sin offerings, and they took all the skins of the sin offerings and they burnt them in the Miphkad Altar. So this was like a huge pit. And these things were constantly and continually burnt. And at the bottom of the pit there was a conduit which went down into the Kiddron Valley, at which periodically they would push the ashes out.

Now, question: could it be that where he built this altar was later where the Miphkad Altar was built? Even though this was a burnt offering, Christ was a sin offering, wasn't He? Christ was not burned, was He? No, because He had to be buried and raised so the parallel breaks down when you get out of the physical parallel and you start getting into the real sacrifice of Christ. So he "…built an altar there, and laid the wood in order, and bound Isaac his son, and laid him on the altar upon the wood" (vs. 9). Now this means that this probably tells us that he was more like 12 years old so that Abraham could pick him up and place him on the altar. If he's a full grown man, probably he couldn't do that.

Now verse 10, "And Abraham stretched forth his hand [he put down his hand], and took the knife to slay his son." Now why did he do that? His only son and the one to whom, he was told, you would have physical seed. Why was he willing to do this? Well, 1) because God commanded him to. But also what was in his mind? Was he doubting God? Was he angry at God? Here, let's come to Hebrews 11. Was he doubting God? Was he angry at God? What was it?

Now I'm going to read from my translation, Hebrews 11. Let's begin in verse 8, because this gives a real good summary of the life of Abraham. "By faith Abraham, [after] being called *of God* to go out into the place which he would later receive for an inheritance, obeyed and went, not knowing where he was going. By faith he sojourned in the land of promise, like a foreigner, dwelling in tabernacles with Isaac and Jacob, the joint heirs of the same promise; for he was waiting for the city with *the* foundations of which God *is the* Architect and Builder. By faith also Sarah herself received power to conceive seed, and gave birth *when she was well* beyond childbearing age because she esteemed Him faithful Who had personally promised *her a son*. Because of this *faith*, there came into being from one *man*—and moreover, *one* who was *reproductively* dead—*descendants* as numerous as the stars in the heavens, and as countless as the sand on the seashore" (Heb. 11:8-12).

145

Now verse 13, let's just read right on. "All these died in faith, not having received the promises, but having seen them from afar, and having been persuaded *of them*, and having embraced *them*, and having confessed that they were strangers and sojourners on the earth. For those who say such things make it manifest that they seek *their* own country, *as promised by God*. And if, on the one hand, they had let their minds dwell *fondly* on the place where they came from, they might have had opportunity to return. But now, on the other hand, they are aspiring to a more excellent *country*—that is, a heavenly *one*. Therefore, God is not ashamed to be called their God because He has prepared a city for them. By faith Abraham, when he was being tried, offered up Isaac; and he who had received the promises offered up *his* only begotten *son* of whom it was said, "In Isaac shall your Seed be called"; *because he* reckoned that God was able to raise him even from among *the* dead, from which he also received him in a figurative way" (vs. 13-19). That's why he was willing to do it. Because he knew that if it came down to the point where he did offer his son as that offering, that God would raise him from the dead.

Ok, now let's come back and we'll have just enough time to finish Genesis 22. So he took the knife, verse 10, to slay his son. And then he heard a voice from heaven. I imagine before he took out the knife that he looked around everywhere and didn't see a lamb. So then verse 11. "And the angel of the LORD called unto him out of heaven, and said, Abraham, Abraham: and he said, Here *am* I." And I imagine he said, "HERE AM I." "And he said, Lay not thine hand upon the lad, neither do thou any thing unto him: for now I know that thou fearest God,..." So how long was he tried before God really, really knew through and through that Abraham feared God? 37 to 45 years. Say, 37 years. Now is it any wonder that we still go through trials though we've been in the church for how long. See, same thing. And how many people have been in the church for so long and say, 10, 15, 20, 30 years, and then to leave? So that's why we've had the trials come upon us that have come upon us, for the same reason.

"...For now I know that thou fearest God, seeing thou hast not withheld thy son, thine only *son* from Me. And Abraham lifted up his eyes, and looked, and behold behind *him* a ram caught in a thicket by his horns: and Abraham went and took the ram, and offered him up for a burnt offering in the stead of his son." Now how did the ram get there? Well, either God drove it up there while his back was turned, or God supernaturally created a ram right there, which would be fitting, to supernaturally create one, because that would be a type of Christ who was a supernatural creation, correct? Yes. "And Abraham called the name of that place Jehova-jireh: as it is said *to* this day, In the mount of the LORD it shall be seen" (vs. 11-14). Now I wonder if that's also a prophecy of the sacrifice of Christ on the Mount of Olives? Just a question.

"And the angel of the LORD called unto Abraham out of heaven the second time, and said, By Myself have I sworn,..." Now here is where everything becomes completely irrevocable. It cannot be turned back. Nothing can stop from what God has promised. All the promises of God <u>will come</u> as He said. "...For because thou hast done this thing, and hast not withheld thy son, thine only *son*: that in blessing I will bless thee, and in multiplying I will multiply thy seed as the stars of heaven [spiritual seed], and as the sand which *is* upon the sea shore [physical seed]; and thy seed [the physical seed] shall possess the gate of his enemies; and in thy seed shall all the nations of the earth be blessed; because thou hast obeyed My voice" (vs. 15-18). Now that's the only way we're going to have the blessing of God, is if we obey the voice of God. And as we covered in our series concerning Hebrews, if you don't listen to Christ there is no eternal life.

So we'll continue on next time with Passover: Abraham, Isaac, Jacob, Israel, and Christ #2.

(End of Sermon)

Transcriber: Michael Schwartz

The Passover—Abraham, Isaac, Israel & Christ—Sermon I
January 9, 2002
Scriptural References

1) Galatians 3:29

2) Hebrews 6:13-20, 8

3) Galatians 3:6-9

4) Genesis 12:1

5) Luke 14:25-33

6) Genesis 12:2-4

7) Genesis 15:4-5

8) Matthew 13:43

9) I John 3:1-2

10) Revelation 1:13-16

11) Philippians 3:20-21

12) Genesis 15:5

13) I John 3:9, 5:16

14) Genesis 15:5-18

15) Exodus 12:3-6, 12-13, 21-28

16) Numbers 33:1-3

17) Exodus 12:33-42

18) Genesis 15:17, 13-16, 18

19) Jeremiah 34:8-22

20) Genesis 17:1-21

21) Genesis 21:1-5

22) Luke 14:26-33

23) Genesis 22:1-10

24) Hebrews 11:8-19

25) Genesis 22:10-18

CHAPTER TEN

The Passover—Abraham, Isaac, Israel & Christ–Sermon II

January 16, 2002

Now this is number two in the Passover: Abraham Isaac, Israel, and Christ. Now let's pick up where we left off last time. Let's come to Genesis 22. And I want to cover just a couple more things here concerning this type of the Passover. And as I said, there is no direct indication that you can make this happen on the Passover day. I tried hard to do so, but you can't. And so we can just take the teaching and see how it applies, not only to the Passover day, but also to the whole operation of the substitutionary sacrifice of Christ for us, just as God provided the ram instead of Isaac for the sacrifice, God has provided Christ instead of our death. And so that's important to really understand and realize.

Now let's just cover a couple things here. Let's go back to verse 15. And we can understand that when God swears something—and He doesn't need to swear—in other words, when men give an oath, that's to end a dispute between parties. But God doesn't need to swear, because He doesn't lie. So when He swears, He's giving a double emphasis that this is absolutely going to happen, with no doubt, no shadow of turning. And because He has done this, we can have absolute confidence and assurity that what God has said He will do, He will do. And now we live in the end time, when we have the benefit of seeing that, yes, He did do it. God did do it.

Now verse 15, "And the angel of the LORD called unto Abraham out of heaven the second time, and said, By Myself have I sworn, saith the LORD, for because thou hast done this thing, and hast not withheld thy son, thine only *son*: that in blessing I will bless thee, and in multiplying I will multiply thy seed as the stars of the heaven, and as the sand which *is* upon the sea shore; and thy seed shall possess the gate of his enemies; and in thy seed shall all the nations of the earth be blessed; because thou hast obeyed My voice" (vs.15-18). And this becomes a very profound and important thing. Because too much of Christianity today is based upon lawless grace. Meaning, that you don't have to obey. Oh, they claim, yes, they read the Scriptures, which say, "And if you *are* Christ's, then you are Abraham's seed and heirs according to *the* promise" (Galatians 3:29). But they don't read the thing that he obeyed.

Now, as we have seen, "the stars of heaven" apply to the spiritual seed, which then is the Church, which will then at the resurrection the saints will shine as the stars of heaven —Matthew 13:49. And "the sand which is upon the seashore," which then is the physical seed of Israel. And then He adds another promise here: "Your seed shall possess the gate of his enemies." And we'll see how that comes about a little bit more. So let's come down to Genesis 25, where then the blessing is passed on to Isaac. Actually, Genesis 26:1, "And there was a famine in the land, beside the first famine that was in the days of Abraham. And Isaac went into Abimelech king of the Philistines unto Gerar. And the LORD appeared unto him, and said, Go not down into Egypt; dwell in the land which I shall tell thee of: sojourn in this land, and I will be with thee, and will bless thee; for unto thee, and unto thy seed, I will give all these countries, and I will perform the oath which I swore unto Abraham thy father; and I will make thy seed to multiply has the stars of heaven, and I will give unto thy seed all these countries; and in thy seed shall all the nations of the earth be blessed; because that Abraham…" (vs. 1-4).

Now you see, the thing we need to understand is this: the covenant did not depend upon Isaac, it did not depend upon Jacob. It depended upon Abraham. And this has been a consternation to many, many people. Especially when they look at the nations of the ten tribes of Israel, in their modern setting, and the other nations of the world do, and they wonder, "How come we have it, and in many cases we are so bad?" Because they're looking at from the point of view, "Well, since you're so bad, you don't deserve it." See, well, God said He was going to give it because of Abraham. Now then, He also said later on that if their descendants sin, He would correct them. But He would not rescind the promise that He gave to Abraham.

And here is this famous verse we've gone over, and over, and over again, one which Protestants, I am sure, do not like to hear. Verse 5, "Because that Abraham obeyed My voice, and kept My charge, My commandments, My statutes, and My laws." Now that's also important because, as we saw, the Passover began with Abraham and not with Israel.

Now let's come to Galatians 4, and let's see the Church in relationship to Isaac. The way you counter… (*Pause–audience comment*). The comment was made that certain people will say, "Well, God had other commandments that He gave him." That's absolutely not true, because Christ is the same yesterday, today, and forever. The commandments that He gave Israel are the same commandments that Abraham obeyed. For anyone to say anything other than that, they are just Biblical illiterates. You cannot prove it from the context. The only commandments that are God's commandments, and He won't change them. Is He going to change the first one? No. Is He going to change the second one? No. Is He going to change the third one? No. Is He going to change the fourth one? No. None of them He's going to change. So he kept the commandments of God, and His statutes. Now statutes, the holy days are statutes. And He began the Passover with Abraham. So those arguments, when you really understand the Bible, do not have legs at all. They don't even have shoes. OK? They just don't stand.

Now let's come here to Galatians 4:28. Oh, by the way, in relationship to that, there are indications the way that the commandments, and the statutes, and the judgments are written out, that they are written in sections of five: 5, 5, 5, which is half of ten. So you take five and five, that equals ten. So you find "ten" all the way through the statutes and judgments there, by the way, too. A little deeper study into that. I don't have it now, but I just recall it off the top of my head. Again, verifying that these things were also things that God gave for Abraham to follow.

And we need to also understand this: Abraham had a big household. He had hundreds of people there with him. And so that means, how do you run and govern it? OK? Well, you do it by God's way. How do settle disputes among people? Well, you do it God's way. Which days do you rest and keep? God's days. So when we understand that the Sabbath was binding from creation, just like everything else God created is perpetually going on down to this day. So the Sabbath is perpetually going on down to this day. So once you know the Scriptures, and once you know the Bible, there is no question that Abraham did those things. And any of the other things that people come up with are just arguments to avoid obeying God. They don't like the word "obey." They like the word "liberty", which is another word for lawlessness.

Galatians 4:28, "Now we, brethren, like Isaac, are *the* children of promise. But as *it was* then, so also *it is* now: he who was born according to *the* flesh [that is, Ishmael] persecuted him *who was born* according to *the* Spirit. Nevertheless, what does the scripture say? Cast out the maidservant and her son; for in now way shall the son of the maidservant inherit *the promise* with the son of the free *woman*. So then, brethren, we are not children of *the* maidservant, but of the free *woman*" (v. 28-31). And we are children of promise. So here again, I'm trying to tie the things of Abraham back into the New Testament. And of course we have Abraham in Chapter 3, we have Isaac in Chapter 4.

Now let's come down to the time that the blessing is passed on to Jacob. And of course, God said before they were born about Esau and Jacob, they were two kinds of people. Esau would serve, who was the oldest, [that] he would serve the younger. And the younger would prevail. Now sometimes God does things and allows things to happen by the use of human nature. And so, we find that Jacob connived to get the blessing, or the birthright, from Esau. He didn't have to do it, because God would have given it another way. But also it was a test on Esau. Esau was willing to sell it and give it up. Then it came time for the blessing, and Mama got involved in it too. And she said, "You go in and you pretend you're Esau and get the blessing." He said, "Well how can I do that? He's a hairy man." She said, "Well, we'll put a goatskin on your neck." Now you talk about a hairy man. It must of been a real hairy man if you feel the back of the neck and it's all like the goat's hair.

So she made the stew, she put the skins on his hands and on the back of his neck because he was a smooth man. So he went in. Genesis 27:18, "And he came unto his father, and said, My father: and he said, Here *am* I; who *art* thou, [are you] my son? And Jacob said unto his father, I *am* Esau thy firstborn…" A big fat lie. Now the reason God does things like this is so that Esau would think that he just took it. But he didn't.

"…I have done according as thou badest me: arise, I pray thee, sit and eat of my venison, that thy soul may bless me. And Isaac said unto his son, How *is it* that thou hast found *it* so quickly, my son?" You know, going out and shooting venison and, you know, it takes a little while to chase it down and get it with a bow and arrow. "…And he said, because the LORD thy God brought *it* to me" (vs. 19-20). I mean, this is something.

"And Isaac said to Jacob, Come near, I pray thee, that I may feel thee, my son, whether thou *be* my very son Esau or not." So he had his doubts. "And Jacob went near unto Isaac his father; and he felt him, and said, The voice *is* Jacob's voice, but the hands *are* the hands of Esau. And he discerned him not, because his hands were hairy, as his brother Esau's hands: so he blessed him. And he said, *Art* thou my very son Esau? And he said, I *am*" (vs. 21-24). Boy, he checked him out a couple of times here, didn't he?

"And he said, Bring *it* near to me, and I will eat of my son's venison, that my soul may bless thee. And he brought *it* near to him, and he did eat: and he brought him wine, and he drank. And his father Isaac said unto him, Come near now, and kiss me, my son. And he came near, and kissed him: and he smelled the smell of his raiment, and blessed him, and said, See, the smell of my son *is* as the smell of a field which the LORD hath blessed: therefore God give thee of the dew of heaven, and the fatness of the earth, and plenty of corn and wine: let people serve thee, and nations bow down to thee: be lord over thy brethren, and let thy mother's sons bow down to thee: cursed *be* everyone that curseth thee, and blessed *be* he that blesseth thee" (vs. 25-29).

Now will see how this expanded out to the twelve tribes of Israel. "And it came to pass, as soon as Isaac had made in end of blessing Jacob, and Jacob was yet scarce gone out from the presence of Isaac his father, that Esau his brother came in from his hunting." I mean, with the movies we have now days, you can just picture this. You know- *phhft* - just got out the door. "And he also had made savoury meat, and brought it unto his father, and said unto his father, Let my father arise, and eat of his son's venison, that thy soul may bless me. And Isaac his father said unto him, Who *art* thou? And he said, I *am* thy son, thy firstborn Esau. And Isaac trembled very exceedingly, and said, Who? where *is* he that hath taken venison, and brought *it* me, and I have eaten of all before thou camest, and have blessed him? Yea, *and* he shall be blessed" (vs. 30-33). Because the blessing can only be given once. It's not like the Olympics this year, where they finally catch the French judge in cheating on the judging, and so now they give two gold medals. There's only one blessing.

"And when Esau had heard the words of his father, he cried with a great and exceeding bitter cry, and said unto his father, Bless me, *even* me also, O my father. And he said, Thy brother came with subtlety, and hath taken away thy blessing. And he said, Is he not rightly named Jacob? [which means "supplanter"], for he hath supplanted me these two times: he took away my birthright; and, behold, now he hath taken away my blessing. And he said, Hast thou not reserved a blessing for me? And Isaac answered and said unto Esau, Behold, I have made him thy lord, and all his [your] brethren have I given to him for servants; and with corn and wine have I sustained him: and what shall I do now unto thee, my son? And Esau said unto his father, Hast thou but one blessing, my father? Bless me, *even* me also, O my father. And Esau lifted up his voice, and wept" (vs. 34-38).

"And Isaac his father answered and said and to him, Behold thy dwelling shall be [far from] the fatness of the earth, [as it should read], and of [far from] the dew of heaven from above; and by thy sword shalt thou live, and shall serve thy brother; and it shall come to pass when thou shalt have the dominion, that thou shalt break his yoke from off thy neck" (vs. 39-40). That has not yet happened. Esau and Ishmael are still subject to the descendants of Jacob. Witness the latest war that we have going on right now.

"And Esau hated Jacob because of the blessing wherewith his father blessed him: and Esau said in his heart, The days of mourning for my father are at hand; then will I slay my brother Jacob" (vs. 41). Hearkens back to Cain and Abel, doesn't it?

So Jacob, he gets out of there. Rebecca says, "Look, get out of here, go hide, run away. Go to Laban, my brother. Go up there." So he left, and he went. And right before he left, here's the charge, Chapter 28:1, "And Isaac called Jacob, and blessed him, and charged him, and said unto him, Thou shalt not take a wife of the daughters of Canaan." Now remember that Esau did [that]. "Arise, go to Padan-aram, to the house of Bethuel thy mother's father; and take thee a wife from thence of the daughters of Laban thy mother's brother. And God Almighty bless thee, and make thee fruitful, and multiply thee, that thou mayest be a multitude of people; and give thee the blessing of Abraham, to thee, and to thy seed with thee; that thou mayest inherit the land where in thou art a stranger, which God gave unto Abraham" (Gen. 28:1-4). And so Isaac sent him away to Padan-aram.

And then Jacob had a dream. He saw this ladder ascending up. Verse 12, "And he dreamed, and behold a ladder set up on the earth, and the top of it reached to heaven: and behold the angels of God ascending and descending on it. And, behold, the LORD stood above it, and said, I *am* the LORD God of Abraham thy father, and the God of Isaac: the land where on thou liest, to thee will I give it, and to thy seed; and thy seed shall be as the dust of the earth, and thou shalt spread abroad to the west, and to the east, and to the north, and to the south: and in thee and in thy seed shall all the families of the earth be blessed. And, behold, I *am* with thee, and will keep thee in all places whither thou goest, and will bring thee again into this land; for I will not leave thee, until I have done *that* which I have spoken to thee of" (vs. 12-15).

And He did. Now there was still some chicanery. Now, Jacob got his punishment back, didn't he, for being deceitful and lying. What happened? Well, he came to Laban and he saw Rachel, and said, "This is it. First love. Gotta have her." Made a deal and said to Laban, "I'll work seven years for her." He says, "That's fine. You can have her." So, came the wedding night, and I guess there were all wearing burqas then, you know. So came the wedding night, and lo and behold, when he woke up in the morning, guess who it was? It was Leah. Not Rachel. So he wanted Rachel so bad, he said, "OK. I'll work another seven years for you." And Laban said, "That's fine." So he had worked 14 years. So he had a little deceit brought back upon him for his deceit. And he had to work 14 years instead of seven.

So anyway, all the children of Israel were born. You know the rest of the story. They all got jealous at Joseph. Now Joseph had quite a bit of vanity. And he came out with his coat that his father made him, and he said, "Look guys, I had a dream. And I was standing there, and I was the main sheaf. And all the other sheaves bowed down to me. That's you guys." So they got mad. Then he came out and had another dream. And so they got together and said, "Look, we gotta stop this. Let's kill him." And Judah said, "No, let's sell him. So here's what we'll do - we'll take and kill a goat, and take the coat, and spread it with the goat's blood. We'll sell Joseph for his snotty-nosed way of doing things. We'll sell him off to the Arabs when they come by."

So they came by, sold him off, and they took him down to Egypt, and you know the story that happened there. He ended up in prison, and he was able to tell the answer to the dreams that different ones had, and he was raised to be the second in charge of Egypt because he was able to tell Pharaoh the dream of the seven fat cattle and the seven skinny cattle, that a famine was coming.

So, Joseph was down in Egypt seventeen years before the famine came. Then the famine came, and God sent the sons down to get food. And he knew who they were, but they didn't know who he was. So sure enough, the prophecy came true. In order to get the corn, they had to bow down and worship him, because he was second in charge. And then remember, in order to get Benjamin, because he remembered Benjamin was his blood brother, through Rachel, he put some things in the sacks of corn. Then he told the soldiers, the Egyptian soldiers, "Now they've stolen things and hidden them in the corn. You go out and arrest them and bring them back here. "So they did. And he said, "Now look, you bring your youngest brother down here. Otherwise, I'm going to lock you all up in the dungeon." So they said, "Okay we'll bring him down." So they brought him down. And then finally he revealed himself to them that he was Joseph. And they went back and got Jacob, brought him down. Jacob came in and Pharaoh gave him all the land of Goshen.

Now we come down to the final blessings that we have that were given to the sons of Jacob, or Israel. Let's come to Genesis 48. And here's a blessing that is with us to this day, and it cannot fit the circumstances of the Jews today. What occurred here in Genesis 48 and 49 is as momentous for the physical seed as the promise given to Abraham for the spiritual seed. Now, Abraham, Isaac, and Jacob knew that they had blessings to pass on to their descendants.

Now [for] Israel, whose name was changed from Jacob to Israel, it came time for the blessing to be given. And so we find that Joseph brought his two sons, Ephraim and Manasseh. Now I might mention here that Joseph married the daughter of the High Priest of On. And a lot of people think that Joseph married a black woman. That's not the case. Egypt at that time was much like what the United States is today. It was a diverse society. So to say that you married an American today, doesn't tell you anything, does it? But in order for the blessing to be to those of the descendants of Joseph and the descendants of Jacob, he could not have intermarried with a race that was contrary to the - how should we say, the genetic inheritance which he had/ So he obviously married someone the same [ethnic stock] as he was.

Now he brought both of his - Joseph brought both of his sons to him. And Genesis 48:13 now, "And Joseph took them both, Ephraim in his right hand toward Israel's left hand, and Manasseh in his left hand toward Israel's right hand, and brought *them* near unto him." Now you would think this is just kind of all little detail, but it's very important. "And Israel stretched out his right hand, and laid *it* up on Ephraim's head, who *was* the younger…" (Gen. 48:13-14). Now, again, we have the same thing happened, right? The blessing goes to the younger first, then the older. Whereas through normal inheritance law, what do we have? The firstborn is the one who receives the inheritance.

Now I'm going through this, even though it doesn't directly relate to the Passover, because we need to understand, and I want to make the record absolutely clear that the Jews today do not represent all the twelve tribes of the children of Israel. The Jews represent one tribe, plus a substantial number of Levites. That's all of the true Jews. Now you can read the book of Josephus, and you can see where, that in the history, especially during the days of John Hyrcanus the high priest, during the days of the Maccabees, and also during the days of Herod the Great, that they forced Esauites to become circumcised Jews and follow the Jewish religion. Now they are Jews in the sense that they are proselytes. What we're talking about here are the genetic physical descendants of Jacob and his twelve sons. And we hope to have a publication here in the not too far distant future which shows how these sons came to be in their modern inheritance today. And it's very important concerning Ephraim and Manasseh. And I'll just say here for the record that Ephraim, undoubtedly, is what we call Great Britain today; and Manasseh is undoubtedly what we call the United States of America today. Now, that is before the recent years when the strangers are coming in to rise up high above us. Now we're seeing that fulfillment of prophecy because of disobedience.

But here is the prophecy of the physical seed coming down now to Ephraim and Manasseh. And when he did this, he guided "…His hands wittingly; for Manasseh *was* the firstborn." Verse 15, "And he blessed Joseph, and said, God, before Whom my fathers Abraham and Isaac did walk, the God which fed me all my life long unto this day, the Angel which redeemed me from all evil, bless the lads; and let my name be named on them, and the name of my fathers Abraham and Isaac;…" (vs. 14-15).

Now it's important to understand that he did not give that blessing to the rest of his sons. He gave different blessings to them. Though they are the descendants of Abraham, Isaac, and Jacob, the special blessing of nations and power goes primarily to Ephraim and Manasseh with this: "…And let them grow into a multitude in the midst of the earth. And when Joseph saw that his father laid his right hand upon the head of Ephraim, it displeased him: and he held up his father's hand, to remove it from Ephraim's head unto Manasseh's head. And Joseph said unto his father, Not so my father: for this *is* the firstborn; put thy right hand upon his head" (vs. 16-18). Because the primary blessing came from his right hand.

"And his father refused, and said, I know *it*, my son, I know *it*: He also shall become a people, and he shall also be great: but truly his younger brother shall be greater than he, and his seed shall become a multitude of nations." So it's no - how shall we say - incidental thing that the British Empire became to be known as the Commonwealth of nations. And it was to share the common wealth. In other words, the money. The gold. The silver. The possessions. The military. That's why it was called the Commonwealth. Now verse 20, "And he blessed them that day, saying, In thee shall Israel bless, saying, God make thee as Ephraim and as Manasseh: and he set Ephraim before Manasseh" (vs. 19-20). And so that's how it came about.

Now right before he died, Chapter 49, he gathered all the rest of his sons. "…Gather yourself together, that I may tell you *that* which shall befall you in the last days." Now the last days are now. So this gives us an identification of the nations today. "Gather yourselves together, and hear, ye sons of Jacob; and hearken unto Israel your father. Reuben, thou art my firstborn, my might, and the beginning of my strength, the excellency of dignity, and the excellency of power: unstable as water…" Now, many people believe that the descendants of Reuben are the French. Very possible. "Thou shalt not excel; because thou wentest up to thy father's bed; then defiledst thou it: He went up to my couch" (Gen. 49:2-4).

"Simeon and in Levi *are* brethren; instruments of cruelty *are* in their habitations." Now that's why the Simeonites, maybe, are more involved in Mafia within Israel, and the Levites, "instruments of cruelty," that's why they were selected for the priesthood and the slaughtering of animals. They could handle it without all the weeping and wailing and the animal rights boo-hooing, you see.

"O my soul, come not thou in to their secret; unto their assembly, mine honour, be not thou united: for in their anger they slew a man, and in their self will they digged down a wall. Cursed *be* their anger, for *it was* fierce; and their wrath, for it was cruel: I will divide them in Jacob, and scatter them in Israel" (vs. 5-7). And that's the way it is in the last days. They're scattered throughout all Israel.

Verse 8, "Judah, thou *art he* whom thy brethren shall praise: thy hand *shall be* in the neck of thine enemies; thy father's children shall bow down before thee. Judah *is* a lion's whelp: from the prey, my son, thou art gone up: he stooped down, he couched as a lion, and as an old lion; who shall rouse him up? The scepter shall not depart from Judah, nor a lawgiver from between his feet, until Shiloh come…" And that is Christ, and He came. And the disciples, then, became the lawgivers through the apostles. "…And unto Him *shall* the gathering of the people *be*. Binding his foal unto the vine, and his ass's colt unto the choice vine; he washed his garments in wine, and his clothes in the blood of grapes: his eyes *shall be* red with wine, and his teeth white with milk" (vs. 8-12). I think that describes maybe some of the things that going on in Israel today where the Jews are, doesn't it? All the bloody warring that's going on? Perhaps.

"Zebulon shall dwell at the haven of the sea;…" Now many people think that this has to do with Holland. Could very likely be. "…And he *shall be* for an haven of ships; and his border *shall be* unto Zidon. Issachar *is* a strong ass couching down between two burdens:…" Many people think this is Issachar, Issachar being Finland today. It's between the West and between the East, and they carry a great burden from Russia. "And he saw that rest *was* good, and the land that *it was* pleasant; and bowed his shoulder to bear, and became a servant unto tribute" (vs. 13-15). And of course, the Finlanders were under tribute to the Soviet Union for a long time.

"Dan shall judge his people, as one of the tribes of Israel." Now we have two aspects of Dan. We have Dan-mark, and we also have the Irish, which came from Dan. "Dan shall be a serpent by the way, an adder in the path, that biteth the horse heels, so that his rider shall fall backward. I have waited for thy salvation, O LORD. Gad, a troop shall overcome him: but he shall overcome at the last." Now a lot of people think that Gad is Switzerland. That is right there, that little small country. "Out of Asher his bread *shall be* fat, and he shall yield royal dainties." A lot of people think that this is the Netherlands. "Naphtali *is* a hind let loose: he giveth goodly words" (vs. 16-21). And a lot of people think that this is Sweden. Could very well be.

Now notice Joseph. Notice this blessing. This cannot apply to the Jews. "Joseph *is* a fruitful bough,…" (v. 22). And remember, that since before World War II, and even through the Holocaust and everything, there has never been very many more than 13 to 15 million Jews worldwide. "Joseph *is* a fruitful bough, *even* a fruitful bough by a well; *whose* branches run over the wall: the archers have sorely grieved him, and shot *at him*, and hated him:…" And we've seen this happen time and time again, haven't we? "But his bow abode in strength, and the arms of his hands were made strong by the hands of the mighty *God* of Jacob; (from thence is the shepherd, the stone of Israel:)" (vs. 22-24).

And that's where you have the great stone that is under the coronation chair which they coronate the kings and queens of England. And by the way, they coronate them as kings and queens over "Your people Israel." When you read the whole ceremony, it's not over Britain, it's not over England; it's over "Your people Israel." And she is coronated in the Jerusalem Room of the Westminster Abbey.

Now verse 25, "*Even* by the God of thy father, Who shall help thee; and by the Almighty, Who shall bless thee with blessings of heaven above, blessings of the deep that lieth under, blessings of the breasts, and of the womb: the blessings of thy father have prevailed above the blessings of my progenitors unto the utmost bound of the everlasting hills: they shall be on the head of Joseph, and on the crown of the head of him that was separate from his brethren" (vs. 25-26). So that's really quite a blessing. You cannot say that this fits the Jews as we know them today. And remember, this is a prophecy for the last days.

Now Benjamin, "Benjamin shall ravin *as* a wolf…" A lot of people think that Benjamin today is Norway, from whence we get the Vikings, who ravined as a wolf. "In the morning he shall devour the prey, and at night he shall divide the spoils" (vs. 27).

Now before we get into the Passover of Israel, let's come to Deuteronomy 33. And again, let's see some blessings which were passed on at that time. I'm just going to cover the blessing to Joseph so we can distinguish Ephraim and Manasseh, the sons of Joseph, from the Jews. Now verse 13, "And of Joseph he said, Blessed of the LORD *be* his land, for the precious things of heaven, for the dew, and for the deep that coucheth beneath, and for the precious fruits *brought forth* by the sun, and for the precious things put forth by the moon, and for the chief things of the ancient mountains, and for the precious things of the lasting hills…" (vs. 13-15). And where has most of the gold and silver and precious jewels come from? They've come from the descendants of Joseph. And in particularly, and primarily, South Africa, because South Africa was part of the Commonwealth of Britain, and part of the British Empire too.

"And for the precious things of the earth and fulness thereof, and *for* the good will of him that dwelt in the bush: let *the blessing* come upon the head of Joseph, and upon the top of the head of him *that was* separated from his brethren. His glory *is like* the firstling of his bullock, and his horns *are like* the horns of unicorns:…" And isn't it interesting that both of those things are on the seal which the British have? "…With them he shall push the people together to the ends of the earth:…" Wasn't it said of the British Empire, the sun never set on the British Empire? "…And they *are* the ten thousands of Ephraim, and they *are* the thousands of Manasseh" (vs. 16-17).

So there is the blessing given to the physical seed. Now let's come to the book of Exodus and let's look at the events leading up to the Passover with the children of Israel while they were in Egypt. But I wanted to go through and just carry those prophecies forward, showing the blessings that would come to the children of Israel, being all of the twelve tribes and of whom the ten that were carried off into captivity first were given the blessing, then the fulfillment in the last days.

Now let's come to the book of Exodus, Chapter 3. Now, we know the story. After Joseph died, then arose another Pharaoh that didn't know Joseph. And he enslaved the children of Israel. And he was bent on destroying all the male children of the children of Israel by having them drowned in the river. And you know the story of Moses. He was put in the basket, his mother watched it as it went on down. The daughter of Pharaoh found the basket and said, "This is mine. His name shall be Moses, for he came out of the water." He was raised in the court of Pharaoh. He was next in line to be Pharaoh, and then God worked it out to reveal that he was really not of the bloodline—he was not the son of Neferteri the daughter of Pharaoh, but he was the son of Levi, who was a Hebrew.

So then, in trying to rescue one of the Hebrews, because of the harsh bondage, he killed an Egyptian. And then he fled into the wilderness, straight across the Sinai desert, and he came to Midian. And then he married one of the daughters of Jethro. And then we come to the time when Moses was out there watching the sheep, and the time of the burning bush. So let's pick it up here in Exodus 3:3.

Let's go ahead, for the sake of time, and we'll summarize the burning bush thing. He went up and the thing that's important is this… let's come down here, after Moses came up to the burning bush. Exodus 3:5, "And He said, Draw not nigh hither: put off thy shoes from off thy feet, for the place where on thou standest *is* holy ground." Now this shows that wherever God is, it's holy. Now we can draw also a lesson from this concerning the Sabbath. Wherever God put His presence, that is holy time. That's why the Sabbath is holy. Now also we can project that out into what? The Passover, and all the holy days as well. That's why they are called holy days, because God put His presence in it. So wherever God is, that is holy. "Moreover He said, I *am* the God of thy fathers, the God of Abraham, the God of Isaac, and the God of Jacob" (Ex. 3:5-6). And that's the point I want to make here, is that God is following through on His promises to Abraham, Isaac, and Jacob. And remember, we started out Genesis 15, that He said that his descendants would be slaves in a land not their own and they would come out with great substance. Then He also tells them what His name is.

Now, verse 13, "And Moses said unto God…" after God said, "I will surely be with you." "And Moses said unto God, Behold, *when* I come unto the children of Israel, and shall say unto them, The God of your fathers hath sent me unto you; and they shall say unto me, What *is* His name? what shall I say unto them? And God said unto Moses, I AM THAT I AM…" Now, we find—I have a tape on that about Jesus being the "I Am." So not only does this identify the God of the Old Testament, but also it identifies that the God of the Old Testament, is the [Lord Jesus who is the] God of the New Testament [as well as God the Father].

"And He said, Thus shalt thou say unto the children of Israel, I AM hath sent me unto you. And God said moreover unto Moses, Thus shalt thou say unto the children of Israel, the LORD God of your fathers, the God of Abraham, the God of Isaac, and the God of Jacob, hath sent me unto you: this *is* My name forever, and this is My memorial unto all generations" (vs. 14-15). So He said, "You go on down there and gather all the elders. Your brother Aaron is going to meet you, and you go deliver the people." Now let's come to Chapter five. So they did that. Moses and Aaron—Chapter 4:29, let's just get this summary here.

The "I AM" verse is John 8:58. Plus there are other ones in there, which in my translation, I bring it out. He said, "If you do not believe that I AM you shall perish in your sins." So if you don't have the tape you can write for it. Write for the "I AM" tape.

Exodus 4:29, "And Moses and Aaron went and gather together all the elders of the children of Israel: and Aaron spake all the words which the LORD had spoken unto Moses, and did the signs in the sight of the people. And the people believed: and when they heard that the LORD had visited the children of Israel, and that He had looked upon their affliction, then they bowed their heads and worshiped" (Ex. 4:29-31). And went on their way.

So then, here comes the first confrontation between Moses and Aaron and Pharaoh. Now this is kind of like…how shall I put it? Beverly Hillbillies? Maybe not quite that bad, but almost. Coming in to Pharaoh. So here they come. Chapter 5:1, "And afterward Moses and Aaron went in, and told Pharaoh, Thus saith the LORD God of Israel, Let My people go, that they may hold a feast unto Me in the wilderness." Now can you imagine that? Here are two upstart people walking in to the Pharaoh of Egypt and saying, "Let the people go that we can keep a feast." Well now, he was supreme ruler. And God raised him up, as He said in the book of Romans, that He raised him up to show His power to all the earth. And the very fact that it is in the scriptures and is everywhere around the world, this story is told over, and over, and over, and over again as a witness that God is greater than Egypt. And even to this day, testifies that He is greater than Egypt.

So what was Pharaoh's response? "Why, I am so happy that you two showed up. I've been waiting for you. I had a dream from God." No. Pharaoh said, "…Who *is* the LORD, that I should obey His voice to let Israel go? I know not the LORD, neither will I let Israel go" (vs. 2). And can you imagine the effrontery which he felt with these, you know, two upstarts coming in there and telling him to let them go?

"And they said, The God of the Hebrews hath met with us: let us go, we pray thee, three days' journey into the desert, and sacrifice unto the LORD our God; lest He fall upon us with pestilence, or with the sword. And the king of Egypt said unto them, Wherefore do ye, Moses and Aaron, let the people rest from their works? Get you unto your burdens." [He's] not going hear it. "And Pharaoh said, Behold, the people of the land now *are* many, and ye make them rest from their burdens" (vs. 3-5). Now, "rest" means to sabbatize. So here we have the Sabbath in the land of Egypt long before they get to Mount Sinai. Of course they didn't understand it.

And so what did Pharaoh do? "And Pharaoh commanded the same day the taskmasters of the people, and their officers, saying, Ye shall no more give the people straw to make brick, as heretofore: let them go and gather straw for themselves. And the tale of the bricks, which they did make heretofore, ye shall lay upon them; ye shall not diminish *aught* thereof: for they *be* idle; therefore they cry, saying, Let us go *and* sacrifice to our God. Let there more work be laid upon the men, that they may labour there in; and let them not regard vain words" (vs. 6-9). So they went out and did that, and the people of Israel, they were expecting to be let go just, you know, just like that at the snap of a finger; and things didn't work out the way that they wanted, and it came down just the opposite of what they expected. Lesson: just because it doesn't work out the first time, doesn't mean that God doesn't mean what He says. He has other things in mind.

So then, what happened? They came and they told Moses, they said, "Look, this is getting worse! We're not being let go." And so, Moses and Aaron went back to Pharaoh. Verse 20—yes this is what they said here. Verse 20, here's what the people told Moses and Aaron, "…Who stood in the way as they came forth from Pharaoh: and they said unto them, The LORD look upon you, and judge; because ye have made our savour to be abhorred in the eyes of Pharaoh, and in the eyes of his servants, to put a sword in their hand to slay us. And Moses returned unto the LORD…" And see, even Moses didn't believe at this point. "…And said, LORD, wherefore hast Thou *so* evil entreated this people? And why *is* it *that* Thou hast sent me?" He was even questioning, "Well what am I doing here Lord? I went and said 'Let them go,' and he didn't let them go. Now what you want me to do?" "For since I came to Pharaoh to speak in Thy name, he hath done evil to this people; neither hast Thou delivered Thy people at all" (vs. 20-23).

So God gave him the answer. He said, "Wait, Moses. I've got a plan." "…For with a strong hand shall he let them go, and with a strong hand shall he drive them out of his land. And God spake unto Moses, and said unto him, I *am* the LORD: and I appeared Abraham, unto Isaac, and unto Jacob, by *the name of* God Almighty [which is "El Shaddai"], but by

My name JEHOVAH was I not known to them" (Ex. 6:1-3). So that's the covenant name of God for the Old Covenant: Jehovah. He says, "I'm going to release them."

Now let's come to Chapter 7. Let's see when God gets down to business what happens here. And we find this account, now we're going to find the signs, and then the plagues. Notice what God said beginning in verse 1, "And the LORD said unto Moses, See, I have made thee a god unto Pharaoh: and Aaron thy brother shall be thy prophet. Thou shalt speak all that I command thee: and Aaron thy brother shall speak unto Pharaoh, that he send the children of Israel out of his land. And I will harden Pharaoh's heart, and multiply My signs and My wonders in the land of Egypt. But Pharaoh shall not hearken unto you, that I may lay My hand upon Egypt, and bring forth Mine armies, *and* My people the children of Israel, out of the land of Egypt by great judgments. And the Egyptians shall know that I *am* the LORD, when I stretch forth Mine hand upon Egypt, and bring out the children of Israel from among them. And Moses and Aaron did as the LORD commanded them, so did they" (Ex. 7:1-6).

Now, Moses was 80 years old, and Aaron was 83. So you talk about an old church. So here's the first sign. They go in, and the Lord said, verse 9, "When Pharaoh shall speak unto you, saying, Shew a miracle for you [by me]: then thou shalt say unto Aaron, Take thy rod, and cast *it* before Pharaoh, *and* it shall become a serpent" Now this is important, because they were serpent worshipers there. "And Moses and Aaron went in unto Pharaoh, and they did so as the LORD had commanded: and Aaron cast down his rod before Pharaoh, and before his servants, and it became a serpent. Then Pharaoh also called the wise man and the sorcerers: now the magicians of Egypt, they also did in like manner with their enchantments." So you see, there are false miracles and there are things that Satan can do to make it look like it's the hand of God. "For they cast down every man his rod, and they became serpents:..." So here is a snake fight, right out in the middle of it. "...But Aaron's rod swallowed up their rods. And He hardened Pharaoh's heart, that he hearkened not unto them; as the LORD had said" (vs. 9-13).

So then we have the next sign. The second sign is blood being made from water. Now remember that the Egyptians worshipped the Nile. It was like a god. And that's why they had crocodile gods and frog gods, and so forth. So as he went out there, and stretched forth his rod, verse 20, "And Moses and Aaron did so, as the LORD commanded; and he lifted up the rod, and smote the waters that *were* in the river, in the sight of Pharaoh [right in front of him], and in the sight of his servants; and all waters that *were* in the river were turned to blood. And the fish that *was* in the river died; and the river stank, and the Egyptians could not drink of the water of the river; and there was blood throughout all the land of Egypt. And the magicians of Egypt did so with their enchantments: and Pharaoh's heart was hardened, neither did he hearken unto them; as the LORD had said" (vs. 20-22). So then after the seven days were fulfilled, then they were able to drink the water.

Now Chapter 8. They come in again. And I think that the movie, "The Ten Commandments", they did a really good job in showing this. I think they really portrayed it. That was one of the good movies that they made. Of course, it was made years ago. I know Cecil B. DeMille produced it. I think it was in the '50s, some time, it was done. And it's a classic. And every year about Passover time they always play the full version of "The Ten Commandments." So if it comes on, watch it again.

Ok, here's the third sign. Frogs. Now if you've ever seen Egyptian frogs, you will know that these are just not the little pesky little things, but these are huge—about the size of the big head. Now, I just want you to picture this: the land filled with frogs. Here's what's going to happen. God said, Chapter 8:1, "And the LORD spake unto Moses, Go unto Pharaoh, and say unto him, Thus saith the LORD, Let My people go, that they may serve Me.

And if thou refuse to let *them* go, behold, I will smite all thy borders with frogs: and the river shall bring forth frogs abundantly, which shall go up and come into thine house, and into thy bedchamber, and upon thy bed, and into the house of thy servants, and upon thy people, and into the ovens, and into thy kneadingtroughs: and the frogs shall come up both on thee, and upon thy people, and upon all thy servants" (Ex. 8:1-4). So they stretched out the rod, and guess what? All these frogs started coming out of the river. Now imagine all the sound that goes with it. All of the croaking and the urping and so forth. So the magicians did the same thing, and they brought up frogs. So three times the magicians were able to counterfeit the miracle of God.

Now this got to Pharaoh. This did get to him for a little bit. Verse 8, "Then Pharaoh called for Moses and Aaron, and said, Entreat the LORD, that He may take away the frogs from me, and from my people; and I will let the people go, that they may do sacrifice unto the LORD. And Moses said unto Pharaoh, Glory over me [you have your say]: when shall I intreat for thee, and for thy servants, and for thy people, to destroy the frogs from thee and from thy houses, *that* they may remain in the river only? And he said, Tomorrow." So Moses said, "…*Be it* according to thy word. That thou mayest know that there is none like unto the LORD our God" (vs. 8-10). So they departed. So his heart was hardened.

Now here comes the next one. God has a way of doing things that really gets your attention. Verse 16, "And the LORD said unto Moses, say unto Aaron, Stretch out thy rod, and smite the dust of the land, that it may become lice throughout all the land of Egypt." Now have you ever had lice? "And they did so; for Aaron stretched out his hand with his rod, and smote the dust of the earth, and it became lice in man, and in beast; all the dust of the land became lice throughout all the land of Egypt." And Rite Aid ran out of itching powder. (*Laughs*) "And the magicians did so with their enchantments to bring forth lice, but they could not: so there were lice upon man, and upon beast. Then the magicians said unto Pharaoh, This *is* the finger of God: and Pharaoh's heart was hardened, and he hearkened not unto them; as the LORD had said" (vs. 16-19). Now I wonder how they got rid of the lice? Who knows? It doesn't say that they removed them, does it? It doesn't say how long they endured. But I tell you what, they must of had a lice-killing program there, you know, crushing them, killing them, combing them out of the hair, cleaning out all of the beds, cleaning off all the clothes, sweeping out the house, putting them up in buckets and burning them. You know, you'd almost have to just picture how this went on. It doesn't tell us how long does what on.

But after that, now then, we have the fifth sign, which is flies. Now have you ever been bothered by a fly? Imagine swarms of them. Have you ever seen pictures of people in Africa and their cows with all of these big huge flies? Well just keep that in mind when we read this here. "And the LORD said unto Moses, Rise up early in the morning, and stand before Pharaoh; lo, he cometh forth to the water;…" See, every day it was the obligation of Pharaoh to go to the river, because he was representative of god, in their pagan religion, and he would be there at sunrise. So He says, go forth to the water, "…And say unto him, Thus saith the LORD, Let My people go, that they may serve Me" (vs. 20). And Pharaoh probably thought, "We just got rid of the lice! You're here again."

Verse 21, "Else, if thou wilt not let My people go, behold, I will send swarms *of flies* upon thee, and upon thy servants, and upon thy people, and into thy houses: and the houses of the Egyptians shall be full of swarms *of flies*, and also the ground where on they *are*. And I will sever in that day the land of Goshen, in which My people dwell, that no swarms *of flies* shall be there; to the end thou mayest know that I *am* the LORD in the midst of the earth. And I will put a division between My people and thy people: tomorrow shall this sign be." So the Lord did so. Now it says, verse 24, "…And there came a grievous swarm *of flies* into the house of Pharaoh, and *into* his servants' houses, and into all the land of Egypt:…" (vs.

21-24). And Rite Aid ran out of fly spray. (*Laughs*) No way to get rid of them. (*Pause – audience comment*) The children of Israel suffered the first four so they would understand that God is behind it, and to let them know they better listen to God and not do as Pharaoh. Let's go on here.

Now it didn't take long for Pharaoh to react this time. When you have just one fly that goes like this, you know, doing its little square flight pattern right in front of you. And you kind of sit there and wait for it to land on you, and you just wait. All you do is end up slapping your face real hard. Or there's a fly that's coming down on your food. Now imagine swarms of flies. Just crawling everywhere. Just all over your hair, all over your arm, all over the walls. You can't even walk across the room without squishing the flies that are there. And they're into the cupboards and they're eating everything, and everything is dirty. And there would have to be fly dung everywhere. I mean, let's look at this realistic as how it happens.

"And Pharaoh called for Moses and for Aaron, and said, Go ye, sacrifice to your God in the land." "Now I'm not going to let you go out. You do it in the land. I'll go halfway." So much with common ground. "And Moses said, It is not meet so to do; for we shall sacrifice the abomination of the Egyptians to the LORD our God: lo, shall we sacrifice the abomination of the Egyptians before their eyes, and will they not stone us?" (vs. 25-26). No. They were probably animal worshipers, you know, just like the Indians in India today. The Hindus, they worshiped cows. And if a miracle happens with a cow, they run and they gather the urine and they gather the dung so they can put it on themselves, and they can wipe themselves with the manure, and they can anoint themselves with the urine. Now if the children of Israel were out there sacrificing to cattle and to sheep, you know, they would really raise a big stink.

So Moses said, "We will go three days' journey into the wilderness, and sacrifice to the LORD our God, as He shall command us. And Pharaoh said, I will let you go, that ye may sacrifice to the LORD your God in the wilderness; only ye shall not go very far away: entreat for me. And Moses said, Behold, I go out from thee, and I will entreat the LORD that the swarms *of flies* may depart from Pharaoh, from his servants, and from his people, tomorrow: but let not Pharaoh deal deceitfully any more in not letting the people go to sacrifice to the LORD. And Moses went out from Pharaoh, and entreated the LORD" (vs. 27-30). So Moses went out, the flies went away, there remained not one the next day.

Now if you were the average Egyptian, and all these flies came in one day and they bothered you for however many days they had the flies, and then all of a sudden one day – *phfft* - they're gone. Now you'd begin to think that Moses and Aaron had contact with God, a greater power than, you know, the sorcerers and the magicians. But Pharaoh's heart was hardened. He didn't let them go. So again, "Then the LORD said unto Moses, Go in unto Pharaoh, and tell him, Thus saith the LORD God of the Hebrews, let My people go, that they may serve Me. For if thou refuse to let *them* go, and wilt hold them still, behold, the hand of the LORD is thy cattle which *is* in the field, upon the horses, upon the asses, upon the camels, upon the oxen, and upon the sheep: *there shall be* a very grievous murrain." Well, murrain means boils and blains. "And the LORD shall sever between the cattle of Israel and the cattle of Egypt: and there shall nothing die of all *that is* the children's of Israel" (Ex. 9:1-4). Now, you see, God was also demonstrating to the children of Israel. And the thing is, as we will see, they didn't remember these things. By time they got seven days out of Egypt to the Red Sea, they were complaining to God already. So you see, many times - and this is a lesson for us- we need to remember the things that God has done, and not be complaining to God for the things that He hasn't yet done.

Now let's continue on here, verse 5, "And the LORD appointed a set time, saying, Tomorrow the LORD shall do this thing in the land." So He did it. "…And all the cattle of

Egypt died: but of the cattle of the children of Israel died not one." So Pharaoh's getting desperate here. "And Pharaoh sent, and, behold, there was not one of the cattle of the Israelites dead. And the heart of Pharaoh was hardened, and he did not let the people go" (vs. 5-7). All right, so He put murrain, which is boils and blains, upon the cattle. And they died.

Now then, we have the seventh sign. So now it's going come on the people. Now let's pick it up here in verse 8. "And the LORD said unto Moses and unto Aaron, Take to you handfuls of ashes of the furnace, and let Moses sprinkle it toward the heaven in the sight of Pharaoh. And it shall become small dust in all the land of Egypt, and shall be a boil breaking forth *with* blains upon man, and upon beast [now that's the remainder of the beasts], throughout all the land of Egypt." So they did it. They sprinkled it to heaven. And here came the boils breaking forth. "And the magicians could not stand before Moses because of the boils; for the boil was upon the magicians, and upon all the Egyptians" (vs. 8-11). Now one boil really lays you low. How many have ever had a boil? One. The worst kind of boil is called, what? A Carbuncle? Isn't that the worst kind? And that is painful. Now I don't know if they were covered from head to toe with boils, like Job was. But what a sight that must of been.

And verse 12, "And the LORD hardened heart of Pharaoh, that he hearkened not unto them; as the LORD had spoken unto Moses. And the LORD said unto Moses, Rise up early in the morning, and stand before Pharaoh, and say unto him, Thus saith the LORD God of the Hebrews, Let My people go, that they may serve Me. For I will at this time send all My plagues upon thine heart, and upon thy servants, and upon thy people; that thou mayest know that *there is* none like Me in all the earth" (vs. 12-14). Now we get the plagues. The signs were bad enough.

So here we have the whole purpose of Pharaoh, verse 15, "For now I will stretch out My hand, that I may smite thee and thy people with pestilence; and thou shalt be cut off from the earth. And in very deed for this *cause* have I raised thee up, for to shew *in* thee My power; and that My name may be declared throughout all the earth. As yet exaltest thou thyself against My people, if that thou wilt not let them go? Behold, tomorrow about this time, I will cause it to rain a very grievous hail, such as hath not been in Egypt since the foundation thereof even until now" (vs. 15-18). So he said, "Whatever [is] left of the cattle, you get them out of there and get them under cover, because they're going to die." And that's what happened.

Verse 22, "And the LORD said unto Moses, Stretch forth thine hand toward heaven, that there may be hail in all the land of Egypt,…" Now can you imagine the weather reports today, if there were snow in Cairo? I mean, just snow. "…Upon man, and upon beast, and upon every herb of the field, throughout the land of Egypt. And Moses stretched forth his rod toward heaven: and the LORD sent thunder and hail, and the fire ran along upon the ground;…" That's probably because of the lightning. "…And the LORD rained hail upon a land of Egypt. So there was hail, and fire mingled with the hail, very grievous, such as there was none like it in all the land of Egypt since it became a nation. And the hail smote throughout all the land of Egypt all that *was* in the field, both man and beast; and the hail smote every herb of the field, and broke every tree of the field. Only in the land of Goshen with the children of Israel *were*, there was no hail" (vs. 22-26).

Now this time Pharaoh kinda, almost got the point. I mean, what does it take sometimes to get people's attention? Verse 27, "And Pharaoh sent, and called for Moses and Aaron, and said unto them, I have sinned this time: the LORD *is* righteous, and I and my people *are* wicked. Entreat the LORD (for *it is* enough) that there be no *more* mighty thunderings and hail; and I will let you go, and ye shall stay no longer" (vs. 27-28). Now I tell you what, after you hear hail and see lightning, and hear the thunder, and have that stacking up, and of course, you're used to this warm climate. Now can you imagine what all of this hail and ice is going to do? It's going to drop the temperature; you don't have any clothes for cold weather. There you are, hail all round. Man. But he still didn't quite get it.

Now verse 34, "And when Pharaoh saw that the rain and the hail and the thunders were ceased, he sinned yet more, and hardened his heart, he and his servants." And so then, God said, Chapter 10, "Now I'm going to bring another plague." Now you see, by the time all this is done, there is virtually nothing left in Egypt. Chapter 10:1, "And the LORD said unto Moses, Go in unto Pharaoh: for I have hardened his heart, and heart of his servants, that I might shew these My signs before him; and that thou mayest tell in the ears of thy son, and of thy son's son, what things I have wrought in Egypt, and My signs which I have done among them;…" (Ex. 10:1-2). So there's a time when we are to read and go through these things to know that it was the hand of God that did it.

"And Moses and Aaron came in unto Pharaoh, and said unto him, Thus saith the LORD God of the Hebrews, How long wilt thou refuse to humble thyself before Me? Let My people go that they may serve Me. Else, if thou refuse to let My people go, behold, tomorrow will I bring the locusts into thy coast: and they shall cover the face of the earth, that one cannot be able to see the earth: and they shall eat the residue of that which is escaped, which remaineth unto you from the hail, and shall eat every tree which groweth for you out of the field: and they shall fill thy houses, and the houses of all thy servants, and houses of all the Egyptians; which neither thy fathers, nor thy father's fathers have seen, since the day that they were upon the earth unto this day. And he turned himself, and went out from Pharaoh. And Pharaoh's servants said unto him, How long shall this man be a snare unto us? Let the men go, that they may serve the LORD their God: knowest thou not yet that Egypt is destroyed?" (vs. 3-7).

"And Moses and Aaron were brought again unto Pharaoh: and he said unto them, Go, serve the LORD your God: *but* who *are* they that shall go? And Moses said, We will go with our young and with our old, with our sons and with our daughters, with our flocks and with our herds we will go; for we *must hold* a feast unto the LORD. And he said unto them, Let the LORD be so with you, as I will let you go, and your little ones: look *to it*, for evil *is* before you [me]. Not so: go now ye *that are* men,…" Just the men. "I'm only going to let the men go." Verse 11, "…And serve the LORD; for that ye did desire. And they were driven out from Pharaoh's presence" (vs. 8-11).

So then what happened? Moses went out, raised his rod, and the locusts came. Covered the land. And I don't imagine they were itty-bitty things. I bet they were huge, giant devouring things. And they ate everything. Verse 15, "For they covered the face of the whole earth, so that the land was darkened; and they did eat every herb of the land, and all the fruit of the trees which the hail had left: and there remained not any green thing in the trees, or in the herbs of the field, through all the land of Egypt." Now here's worldly repentance again. "Then Pharaoh called for Moses and Aaron in haste; and he said, I have sinned against the LORD your God, and against you. Now therefore forgive, I pray thee, my sin only this once, and entreat the LORD your God, that He may take away from me this death only" (vs. 15-16). So they went out and did it. When they were gone his heart was hardened.

So then here comes another plague. Now this is quite a plague. You kind of really have to imagine this. So verse 21, "And the LORD said unto Moses, Stretch out thine hand toward heaven, but that there may be darkness over the land of Egypt, even darkness *which* may be felt. And Moses stretched forth his hand toward heaven; and there was a thick darkness in all the land of Egypt three days:" They could feel it. It would be kind of like this: have you ever been in a room with all the doors shut, and you turn out the light, and you can't see anything? Now, three days, "…They saw not one another, neither rose any from his place for three days: but all the children of Israel had light in their dwellings" (vs. 21-23).

Boy, Pharaoh, he really had it this time. "And Pharaoh called unto Moses, and said, Go ye, serve the LORD; only let your flocks and your herds be stayed:…" "All of our cattle are killed, we want yours." "…Let your little ones also go with you. And Moses said, Thou must give us also sacrifices and burnt offerings, that we may sacrifice unto the LORD our God. Our cattle also shall go with us; there shall not an hoof be left behind; for thereof must we take to serve the LORD our God; and we know not with what we must serve the LORD, until we come thither. But the LORD hardened Pharaoh's heart, and he would not let them go. And Pharaoh said to him,…" Now this kind of sounds like the last stand of Hitler, right? Very similar to it. "And Pharaoh said to him, Get thee from me, take heed to thyself, see my face no more;…" "I'm so important, you better not come in my presence and see my face any more lest you die!" Verse 29, "And Moses said, Thou hast spoken well, I will see thy face again no more" (vs. 24-29).

And so then, God said, "I have yet one more plague," the fourth plague. And this one is going to be the most devastating of all. So we'll finish verse 11 here, and the next time we'll pick it up with the Passover in Chapter 12. Let's finish Chapter 11 here. "And the LORD said unto Moses, Yet will I bring one plague *more* upon Pharaoh,…" This is the fourth plague. So you had seven signs and four plagues. "…And upon Egypt; afterwards he will let you go hence: when he shall let *you* go, he shall surely thrust you out hence all together. Speak now in the ears of the people, and let every man borrow of his neighbor,…" Now this wasn't borrow, this was spoiling. "…Of his neighbor, and every woman of her neighbor, jewels of silver, and jewels of gold" (Ex. 11:1-2). I imagine they were so frightened and fearful, that when the children of Israel went up and said, "I want your gold and I want your silver," they said, "Here!" Lest they die. Or, lest more plagues come upon them.

"And the LORD gave the people favor in the sight of the Egyptians. Moreover the man Moses *was* very great in the land of Egypt,…" Because, remember, at the beginning in Chapter 7, He says, "I have made you a god to Pharaoh." So he was very great. "…In the land of Egypt, in the sight of Pharaoh servants, and in the sight of the people. And Moses said, Thus saith the LORD, About midnight…" Now, we'll see that's the 14th day of the first month. "…Will I go out into the midst of Egypt: and all firstborn in the land of Egypt shall die, from the firstborn of Pharaoh that sitteth upon his throne, even unto the firstborn of the maidservant that *is* behind the mill; and all the firstborn of beasts." That is, which ever ones are left alive. "And there shall be a great cry throughout all the land of Egypt, such as there was none like it, nor shall be like it anymore. But against any of the children of Israel shall not a dog move his tongue, against man or beast: that ye may know how that the LORD doth put a difference between the Egyptians and Israel" (vs. 3-7).

Now let's understand something very important here concerning the Church. God has put a difference between His people and the world. A very big difference. You are the people of God. You represent God and all that He is to everyone else in the world that comes in contact with you, you see. That's very important to understand. And God has called you to be in His kingdom. Therefore, that's why He says we're not to be part of the world. We're in the world, but we're not of the world. Now, just like there could be no compromise with the children of Israel with the Egyptians in their dealings with God. So He puts a difference.

"And all these thy servants shall come down unto me, and bow down themselves unto me, saying, Get thee out, and all the people that follow thee: and after that I will go out. And he went out from Pharaoh in great anger." Boy. What a witness to Pharaoh. He says, "You get out of here and don't see my face anymore." And Moses just really said, said all

163

these words, and then left in great anger. "And the LORD said unto Moses, Pharaoh shall not hearken unto you; that My wonders may be multiplied in the land of Egypt. And Moses and Aaron did all these wonders before Pharaoh: and the LORD hardened Pharaoh's heart, so that he would not let children of Israel go out of his land" (vs. 8-10). And the reason God did that was to show the children of Israel that He was God, He alone could deliver them, He alone would fight their battles and overcome them. And if they trusted in Him, they would be released from their slavery.

Now we come to Chapter 12 and the Passover. So we'll continue next time with the Passover and the children of Israel.

(End of Sermon)

Transcriber: Michael Schwartz

The Passover—Abraham, Isaac, Israel & Christ—Sermon II
January 16, 2002
Scriptural References

1) Genesis 22:15-18

2) Galatians 3;29

3) Matthew 13:49

4) Genesis 26:1-5

5) Galatians 4:28-31

6) Genesis 27:18-41

7) Genesis 28:1-4, 12-15

8) Genesis 48:13-20

9) Genesis 49:2-27

10) Deuteronomy 33:13-17

11) Exodus 3:3-6, 13-15

12) Exodus 4:29-31

13) Exodus 5:1-5, 20-23

14) Exodus 6:1-3

15) Exodus 7:1-6, 9-13, 20-22

16) Exodus 8:1-4, 8-10, 16-30

17) Exodus 9:1-18, 22-28, 34

18) Exodus 10:1-11, 15-16, 21-29

19) Exodus 11:1-10

CHAPTER ELEVEN

The Passover—Abraham, Isaac, Israel & Christ–Sermon III

March 16, 2002

This is number three, The Passover—Abraham, Isaac, Israel and Christ. And so this time let's come to Exodus 12 and pick up where we left off last time and cover concerning the Passover with Israel—their first Passover. Now many of the details, as you know, have been written in the book *The Christian Passover*, which covers all the technicalities that we have concerning between the evenings, "between the setting times, between sunset and dark" and "sunset and morning," so I won't go into those in great detail. I will just mention them as we come to them so we have a greater understanding of it and then we will go through Exodus 16 just to really show beyond any shadow of doubt how God uses the terms *at even,* or *between the evenings,* or the Hebrew *ben ha arbaim,* meaning from sunset to dark.

First of all, let's come to Exodus 12 and let's begin here in verse 3 with the instructions that Moses gave to Israel for the Passover in Egypt. Now verse 3: "Speak you unto all the congregation of Israel, saying, In the tenth *day* of this month they shall take to them every man a lamb, according to the house of *their* fathers, a lamb for an house: And if the household be too little for the lamb, let him and his neighbor next unto his house take *it* according to the number of the souls; every man according to his eating shall make your count for the lamb. Your lamb shall be without blemish…" (verses 3-5). Of course this lamb is a type of Christ—without blemish. Continuing in verse 5: "…a male of the first year: you shall take *it* out from the sheep, or from the goats:" So it could be either one, from the sheep or from the goats. Verse 6: "And you shall keep it up until the fourteenth day of the same month…" and that means until the beginning of it which is at sunset, which is actually sunset of the thirteenth when the sun goes down after sunset of the thirteenth, then it is the fourteenth day. "…And the whole assembly of the congregation of Israel shall kill it in the evening." Now I am reading from the King James. Everett Fox translates it as *between the setting times,* and the Hebrew is *ben ha arbaim* which means between sunset and dark. So between the two evenings is another rendering of it, meaning that there is the first evening being sunset and then the second evening being dark.

And here is what they were to do and we will see the reason for it. We need to understand something very important here concerning the Passover as it was with Israel and then let's look at the Passover when we come to the one with Christ and then for us, because it has great significance and it shows God's mercy and kindness and goodness in many, many ways.

Now let's continue in verse 7: "And they shall take of the blood, and strike *it* on the two side posts and on the upper door post of the houses, wherein they shall eat it. And they shall eat the flesh in that night, roast with fire, and unleavened bread;" Now let's understanding something very simple. The entire Passover day is an unleavened bread day. That is a one-day feast, as we will see. The Feast of Unleavened Bread for seven days is a feast that follows the Passover. Now there is nowhere that you can find in the scriptures at all, anywhere, that it was allowable to eat leavened bread on the day portion of the Passover. Nowhere can you find that the Israelites did that, because at sunrise, they left their houses and assembled at Rameses. And let's understand something, there were no McDonalds' on the

165

way. So you see they didn't eat any leavened bread on the day portion of the Passover. Now we can be for sure here in verse 8 that they were to eat it with unleavened bread, that is the Passover, that they didn't have any leaven in their houses. It was to be destroyed.

Now let's continue on in verse 8: "*...and* with bitter *herbs* they shall eat it. You shall not eat of it raw or boiled at all with water..." It says, "sodden" in the King James but that means boiled. "...But roast *with* fire: his head with his legs and with the purtenance thereof." That means the heart and the liver and the kidneys were put back into the cavity from where they took out the innards. Verse 10: "And you shall leave nothing of it until the morning; and that which remains of it until the morning you shall burn with fire." Now this means this—they were to eat it that night, anything that was left they couldn't leave it until morning, but they should burn it with fire. Now God had a specific reason and purpose for doing that. Number one, it was total destruction of the Passover lamb or the Passover kid. Number two, this means that the children of Israel could not take a tooth or a bone or a hoof as a good luck charm from the Passover lamb or kid. God wanted it totally destroyed. Now you can read in the Passover book, we actually went through and found out how long it would take to burn all the skin, the intestines, and the bones and so forth in fire, and it took quite a while to burn it to ashes, and it also helped substantiate that they didn't leave their houses until morning.

Now let's continue on verse 11 here: "And thus shall you eat it; *with* your loins girded, your shoes on your feet, and your staff in your hand; and you shall eat it in haste..." Now "...eat it in haste..." is an unfortunate translation, because that gives people who believe in the fifteenth, the impression that they were to eat it in haste and hurry up and leave as soon as they ate it. Well if they did that, they had no opportunity to burn what was left, and it takes quite a few hours to burn all of those bones especially the teeth. So what we are dealing with here is this—the Hebrew means you shall eat it in <u>trepidation</u>, because of all the events which would take place, not in haste, [but] in trepidation. And of course, if you are eating it in trepidation, the chances are you are going to eat it quite quickly too, but not in haste that you can hurry and leave. Now finishing verse 11: "...it *is* the LORD'S passover." And that's what's important to understand, brethren, it's not the Jews' Passover. What we do is the Christian Passover as Jesus modified the instructions in the New Testament. Never was this the Jews' Passover. It is the LORD'S Passover, and here's why. "For I will pass through the land of Egypt this night," And we know that it was midnight. "...And will smite all the firstborn in the land of Egypt, both man and beast; and against all the gods of Egypt I will execute judgment: I *am* the LORD.

Now this becomes profound and important when we understand that God has judged all the pagan religions and gods of this world, in this Passover, and for us with the Passover of Christ. Does this not tell us that we should not go out and combine any of the things of the religions of this world—be it Judaism, be it mainstream Christianity, or whatever into any of the practices that we do because God has already judged them, hasn't He—no doubt about it, and that's why later He told the children of Israel that they were not to add anything or take away from what He gave them. They were not to go to the people of the land and say "Well how do you worship your gods, and this is a good idea and let's do so unto our God." God said, "You shall not do so unto the LORD your God."

So there is a specific reason for judging the gods of Egypt, and that is to show that they are not gods, that they are impotent, that they have no power. They are the imaginations of men and demons and are inspired by Satan the devil, and have nothing to do with the true God, nothing to do with making life right, but only having to do to keep people in the captivity, in the bondage of sin to Satan the devil and his ways. Now we need to understand that and apply that to also the Christian Passover, and the New Testament, and the New Covenant and what we are to do.

Now let's continue on in verse 13: "And the blood shall be to you for a token upon the houses where you are and when I see the blood, I will pass over you," Now this is a type of the blood of Christ. His blood causes God to pass over our sins, so we have the remission of sins that are passed. And He says, "...I will pass over you, and the plague shall not be upon you to destroy *you*, when I smite the land of Egypt" (Exodus 12:3-13).

Now let's understand something here concerning the blood and the firstborn—the firstborn of all the children of Israel, man and beast, were spared, because of the blood that they put on the doorposts and the lintels. So the firstborn became a tremendous blessing to all the children of God. Whereas the firstborn of Egypt, man and beast, became a tremendous curse because God executed His judgment not only against the gods but against the firstborn, and this literally destroyed Egypt. And by the time the children of Israel left Egypt beginning the next night, Egypt was left in destruction—there was hardly anything left. The pride and power of Egypt had been absolutely broken with the death of the firstborn of man and beast.

Now let's understand something for us. Hold your place here in Exodus 12 and let's come to Hebrews 12. There is something that we need to realize, and we need to understand in all humility, in all understanding of God's Word, with thanksgiving, but not to get us all lifted up, not to make us feel as though we are superior to other people, because we are not. But just as the sparing of the firstborn for the children of Israel in Egypt was a blessing, and of course then that blessing extended to all the rest of the children of Israel who were not the firstborn; but also we have a parallel here, because we are the firstfruits and we are the church of the firstborn. Now let's come to Hebrews 12:22: "But you have come to Mount Sion, and to *the* city of *the* living God, heavenly Jerusalem; and to an innumerable company of angels; to *the* joyous festival gathering; and to *the* church of *the* **firstborn**..." (Hebrews 12: 22-23).

So just like the firstborn being spared during the Passover that the children of Israel had in Egypt, so likewise, the firstborn who are right now begotten and those who have the Spirit of God and living today are a blessing to this entire world. Now the world doesn't know that, but we need to take that with all humility and understanding and thankfulness because of God's mercy and love. It shows His mercy, not any greatness that we could attribute to ourselves, but just in the same manner (let's come back here to Exodus 12) in the same manner that God destroyed the firstborn in Egypt and executed His judgment against **all** the gods of Egypt, so likewise in our lives in the things that we do, all the ways of the world, that's why Paul said, "The world is crucified unto me." And so brethren, when we come to the Passover we need to understand that that needs to be our attitude, in gratefulness and thanksgiving for what God has done. This ought to give us a lot of inspiration and encouragement and strength and power in the Spirit of God to do His will.

Now let's continue on back here in Exodus 12:14: "...this day shall be to you for a memorial; and you shall keep it a feast unto the LORD throughout your generations; you shall keep it a feast by an ordinance **forever**." And that's what we are to do, and it is a memorial. The Passover is a memorial, and that's why when we come to the New Testament, Jesus said, "Do this in remembrance of me."

Now then, we come to the Feast of Unleavened Bread, because the Feast of Unleavened Bread follows immediately the next day. Now verse 15, let's read it: "Seven days shall you eat unleavened bread; even the first day you shall have put away leaven" as it should read. It's past tense. Now Everett Fox in The Schocken Bible translates it: "You shall have already" or, "already on the first day..." that is as the first day comes "...you are to get rid of leaven from your houses" meaning that by time the first day comes, you shall have put away leaven from your houses. It has to be out and gone, and then of course, the Passover day being an unleavened bread day—the whole day—and that's why I have in *The*

Christian Passover book what Josephus wrote. He says that "we observe the feast for eight days of unleavened bread."

Now that does not mean that we are having a feast of unleavened bread for eight days, it means this: We have two feasts 1) a memorial feast of the Passover which is unleavened bread, 2) we have continuing seven days of the Feast of Unleavened Bread and both of these feasts have different meanings, which we will see. That's why they are both unleavened, but we will see the meaning of it in just a minute. Continuing verse 15: "Seven days you shall eat unleavened bread, even the first day you shall have put away leaven out of your houses: for whosoever eats leavened bread from the first day to the seventh day, that soul shall be cut off from Israel. And in the first day *there shall be* a holy convocation, and in the seventh day there shall be a holy convocation to you; no manner of work shall be done in them save *that* which every man must eat, that only may be done of you." So whatever is necessary on a holy day, whatever work is necessary to provide the meal because it's a feast day, you go right ahead and do it. Verse 17: "And you shall observe *the feast of* unleavened bread" Now here is the reason for the Feast of Unleavened Bread. "…For in the selfsame day have I brought your armies out of the land of Egypt: therefore you shall observe this day" That is the first day of the Feast of Unleavened Bread. "…In your generations by an ordinance <u>forever</u>" (Exodus 12:14-17).

Now the meaning of the Feast of Unleavened Bread is that that's when God brought the children of Israel out of the land of Egypt, at least it was the beginning of it, and that's why we have "the night much to be remembered". We have already covered that in the part that we did with Abraham.

Now continuing verse 18: "In the first *month*, on the fourteenth day of the month at even," Now *at even* here, comes from the Hebrew *ba erev* which means *at sunset* and sunset of the fourteenth begins the fifteenth. "…You shall eat unleavened bread, until the one and twentieth day of the month at even." Sunset then which ends the twenty-first day and begins the twenty-second day. So you have the seven complete days. Verse 19: "Seven days there shall be no leaven found in your houses for whomsoever eats that which is leavened, even that soul shall be cut off from the congregation of Israel, whether he be a stranger or born in the land. You shall eat nothing leavened; in all your habitations you shall eat unleavened bread." Now that is clear as can be. So therefore, for seven days we will do as God has said and we will eat unleavened bread.

Now during the Feast of Unleavened Bread as we know from the New Testament, leaven is a type of sin, a type of human nature—that which sours and puffs up. Now then, let's continue on a few more verses here. Verse 21: "Then Moses called for all the elders of Israel, and said unto them" Now he is giving them the detailed instructions. " 'Draw out and take you a lamb according to your families, and kill the passover. And you shall take a bunch of hysop and dip *it* in the blood that *is* in the basin, and strike the lintel and the two side posts with the blood that *is* in the basin: and none of you shall go out at the door of his house until the morning.' " Now morning here in the Hebrew means: *sunrise*. Now Everett Fox translates it: "Now you are not to go out, any man from the entrance to his house, until daybreak." That's why the blood was put on the lintels and the side posts—to show that they were not to go out of the entrance of their house, the door of his house until daybreak. Verse 23: " ' For the LORD will pass through to smite the Egyptians; and when he sees the blood upon the lintel, and on the two side posts, the LORD will pass over the door, and will not suffer the destroyer to come in unto your houses to smite *you*. And you shall observe this thing for an ordinance to you and your sons forever.

"And it shall come to pass, when you be come to the land which the LORD will give you, according as he has promised, that you shall keep this service.' " And that's in the fourteenth day of the first month. " 'And it shall come to pass, when your children shall say to you, What do you mean by this service?' " Now this means they were doing the domestic killing of the lambs otherwise the son wouldn't be able to know what was going on. You can read all about the domestic and the temple Passover in *The Christian Passover* book. Now here is what they were to answer, " 'That you shall say, It is the sacrifice of the LORD'S passover…' " Now this also verifies that it was a domestically killed lamb or kid " '…who passed over the houses of the children of Israel in Egypt, when he smote the Egyptians, and delivered our houses.' And the people bowed the head and worshiped. And the children of Israel went away, and did as the LORD had commanded Moses and Aaron, so they did" (Exodus 12:18-28).

Now you know the rest of the story. At sunrise, and by that time all the remainder that was left over would be burned the skin, the guts, the bones, and so forth of the Passover lamb or kid. There was to be nothing left of it. And at sunrise which was the signal for them to be able to go out of the door of their houses so that no one would leave early and no one would leave late. I mean you can look out and you can see when sunrise takes place. Then they were to gather at Rameses in verse 37 we find the children of Israel journeyed from Rameses. Now they had to come from their houses and their houses were in the land of Goshen. They assembled during the day portion of the fourteenth, spoiling the Egyptians along the way, and they left that night and you can go back and go over the tape that we did concerning the Passover with Abraham that God made with him—showing that this night, "night to be remembered" that He brought them out of the land.

Now let's just cover a little bit in Exodus 16 where God again, gave the Sabbath to the children of Israel. Now Exodus 16 we find that the children of Israel were there on the fifteenth day of the second month which was a weekly Sabbath, and the fifteenth day of the second month then, they had Sabbath services, and God gave them a special message. Here is what God told them. I am going to read to you from Everett Fox's Schocken Bible [Volume 1] here. And what we are going to do is see how he translates this so we can understand. Now let's pick it up here beginning in verse 4: "And the LORD said to Moses: 'Here, I will make rain down upon you bread from the heavens, the people shall go out and glean, each day's amount in its day, in order that I may test them,' " That is prove them, " '…whether they will walk in my instructions or not. But it shall be on the sixth day: when they prepare what they have brought in, it shall be a double-portion compared to what they glean day after day. Moses and Aaron said to all the children of Israel: 'At sunset' " Now since this is the Sabbath day message, what does sunset do? Sunset ends the Sabbath day, correct? Yes. " 'At sunset you shall know that it is the LORD that brought you out of the land of Egypt, at daybreak,' " which is morning. " '…You will see the Glory of the LORD when he harkens to your grumblings against the LORD—what are we, that you grumble against us? And Moses said: 'Since the LORD gives you flesh to eat at sunset,' " *ba erev*, He didn't give it between noon and sunset, now why did God not send the Quail until sunset? Well, God is Lawgiver, and God does not break His own laws—very simple. How could He teach the people to keep the Sabbath if He Himself broke it?

Now let's continue on here. " 'Since God gives you flesh to eat at sunset and at daybreak bread to satisfy (yourselves); since the LORD listens to your grumblings which you grumble against him—what are we: not against us are your grumblings, but against the LORD.' " And that certainly is true in many, many cases. You know people accuse God because things don't go the way they want. Well, God is going to make it go the way He wants. So what you need to do is yield your life and yourself to Him and understand that all things do work together for good for those who love God.

Now let's come down here to verse 11: "The LORD spoke unto Moses saying: 'I have heard the grumblings of the children of Israel—speak and say to them: Between the setting-times…' " That is *ben ha arbaim*, between sunset and dark. " '…You shall eat flesh, and at daybreak you shall be satisfied with bread, and you shall know that I am the LORD your God.' Now at sunset a horde-of-quail came up and covered the camp." Well now let's understand something. Sunset ends the day, correct? No doubt about it. So God did not send the quail until after sunset. Now verse 12 says, "Speak unto them saying, 'Between the setting-times you shall eat flesh…' " (Everett Fox's Schocken Bible Volume 1, Exodus 16:4-8 and 11-12).

Well now something is very important that we need to understand—you cannot eat the flesh until it arrives, and it didn't arrive until sunset. So therefore, here is scriptural proof that *ben ha arbaim* or *between the setting-times*, or *between the two evenings* is after sunset, *ba erev*, and there is absolutely no doubt about it, no wiggle room concerning it—no tradition can change it because these are the words of God which He spoke to Moses.

Now then, let's come to the New Testament, and if you want to just put the tape on pause and grab your Harmony, go ahead and do that because I am going to be reading mostly from the Harmony here in covering concerning the Passover—Jesus Christ and the Passover and how it relates to us. So you can go ahead and maybe put the recorder on pause and go ahead and get your Harmony.

Now there is just one thing I need to summarize concerning the Passover of the children of Israel in Egypt—The Passover pictures and commemorates as we saw there in Exodus 12, the passing over of the houses of the children of Israel in Egypt to spare the firstborn. That was the meaning of the Passover for the Old Testament. The meaning of the first day of the Feast of Unleavened Bread beginning with the "night to be remembered", is that God took them out of the land of Egypt. So we have two distinct things.

Now be sure and read in *The Christian Passover* book about how and why and when the Jews went ahead and got to taking the Passover on the fifteenth, and I think you will be surprised. What they are calling the Passover is really the beginning of the Feast of Unleavened Bread, and you need to ask the question, and I think we need to really begin to understand it which is this: When have the Jews ever had anything really right? And Jesus, soundly, roundly, absolutely condemned the traditions of the Jews in Mark 14, not in Mark 14, but in Mark 7 rather. We'll be going to Mark 14 here in just a minute.

Now we also need to understand that in the New Testament Jesus Christ changed the symbols, but He didn't change the day. He kept the literal fourteenth Passover, it was not a pre-Passover meal nor some sort of bread and wine ceremony taken from Jewish tradition. He kept the Passover.

So let's begin the New Testament here. Now if you have the Harmony of the Gospels it will be on page 241 and let's begin with the account in Mark 14:1. Now this helps establish very clearly and shows that in the New Testament they understood, New Testament time during Jesus' days, they understood that the Passover and the Feast of Unleavened Bread were two different feasts. Now let's begin in verse 1 of Mark 14: "Now after two days was the Passover and the *feast of* unleavened bread, and the chief priests and the scribes were seeking how they might stealthily lay hold of Him *and* kill *Him*. But they said, 'Not during the feast, lest there be a riot among the people.' " And then we come to where Jesus was anointed with the alabaster flask of ointment and you have all the account there concerning what happened. Now let's come to page [243 and] 274 and let's continue on with Mark 14 and verse [13]. Now remember that Jesus said that with desire, He desired to eat this Passover with them before He suffered. And He told the disciples and gave them the instructions He said, "You follow the man who has a pitcher of water and to whatsoever house he goes, you go in there and say to the master of the house, 'Where is the chamber where I will eat the Passover with my disciples?' " (Mark 14:13-14). Jesus ate the Passover. Now He had to finish the Old Testament Passover, so in the Passover that Jesus had, the last one that He had was this: they did have the lamb, but then after eating the meal He instituted the New Covenant symbols of the bread and wine. But before that took place, as we will see, there was a footwashing, and the footwashing has great and tremendous meaning. Now I've got a whole chapter devoted to that in *The Christian Passover* book.

Now let's come in the Harmony to page 274. Let's begin right at the top of the page we'll take Matthew 26:20: "And after evening had come, He sat down with the twelve." Now Mark 14:17 reads: "Now after evening had come, He came with the twelve." Now remember that *ben ha arbaim* means *between the two evenings*. The first evening is sunset and that's when they were killing the lambs and that's when the disciples said to Jesus "Where will you that we prepare the Passover for you that you may eat it?" Now the second evening is this: *at the beginning of dark*. So what we are dealing with here in Matthew 26:20 and Mark 14:17 is this very clearly: He came at the beginning of darkness, not at sunset, and the apostle Paul talks about in the night that Jesus was betrayed, so the **Passover is to be taken not right after sunset, but it's to be taken when it is getting dark**. That's when it should begin.

Now let's come down to the section here concerning footwashing, which is the first part of the New Testament Passover. Now since we will cover this in the Passover ceremony service, I'm not going to go through the whole account of it, but we'll just cover the meaning here. Let's come down here to John 13:12: "Therefore, when He had washed their feet, and had taken His garments, *and* had sat down again, He said to them, 'Do you know what I have done to you? You call Me the Teacher and the Lord, and you speak rightly, because I am. Therefore, if I, the Lord and the Teacher, have washed your feet, you also are duty-bound…' " And the Greek there means *under obligation* " '…to wash one another's feet;' " Now why are you under obligation to wash one another's feet? Because Christ said so.

Now let me tell you the first leaven that leavens getting rid of the Passover is this (based on the meaning of the Feast of Unleavened Bread "a little leaven leavens the whole lump"): the first thing they do is get rid of footwashing. And when they get rid of footwashing—if you are talked into getting rid of footwashing, then you have taken a step away from Christ and you are walking away from your part with Him, because Jesus said that if He didn't wash the feet of the disciples, they would have no part with Him. So likewise, if you do not wash one another's feet, you have no part with Christ. You need to think on that. That's profound, you need to understand it. See God does not give us complicated things to do. He doesn't give us a fancy religious ritual to do.

Now the Roman Catholic Pope has a perverted ceremony of footwashing which he does on the eve before Easter, and he has twelve seminar students sitting on chairs which are elevated and they are all dressed in their robes and white and finery, and there are prayers and incense and the mass and the whole thing and then the pope comes down and he has a special server pouring pot where he pours water over the feet of the seminar students and so then he thinks he is fulfilling what Christ has said. That is perverted nonsense. Now let's understand something important here that is true—the only time that you can wash one another's feet is when you partake of the Passover, and that is in the night of the fourteenth day of the first month, being the month Nisan according to the calculated Hebrew Calendar.

Now here is also another reason why we are duty-bound to wash one another's feet, verse 15: " 'For I have given you an example, *to show* that you also should do exactly as I have done to you. Truly, truly I tell you, a servant is not greater than his lord, nor a messenger greater than he who sent him. If you know these things, blessed are you if you do them' " (John 13:15-17).

Now let's stop and think about this for just a little bit. If you know [the commandments of Christ] and don't do them, you are not blessed. And if you are not blessed, are you then cursed? Well you need to think about that. Now let's also understand something else here, that if anyone rejects footwashing on the Passover night, they are setting themselves above Christ because He said, "The servant is not greater than his lord." If you think that you are Christ's, then you are His servant, correct? And if you say we don't have to do footwashing, you are setting yourself above Christ, are you not? So you need to think about those things. Brethren, what we do is for eternal life. These things are profound—they are important. They are absolutely necessary and required according to the commandments of Christ.

Now then the rest of that section, we have the account of Judas Iscariot taking the sop and then going on out and betraying Jesus.

Now let's come to page 276 in the Harmony, and let's pick it up here beginning in verse 19 of Luke 22: "And He took the bread; *and* after giving thanks, He broke it and gave *it* to them saying, 'This is My body, which is given for you. This do in the remembrance of Me.' " Now you see the Passover was a remembrance of the children of Israel's firstborn being spared in the land of Egypt. The Passover is a memorial of the death of Jesus Christ for us. Whose death then, gives us the forgiveness of sin or passing over of our sins and we who are the firstborn church. So we have the parallel there.

Now let's pick it up here in the section 1 Corinthians 11:23 (page 276) "For I have received of the Lord that which also I delivered unto you, that the Lord Jesus the same night in which he was betrayed…" So it shows that they took it at night. He took bread. Verse 24: "…When He had given thanks, He broke it, and said, 'Take, eat: this is my body, which is broken for you. <u>This</u> <u>do</u> in <u>the</u> <u>remembrance</u> of <u>me</u>.' " Now we are to remember everything about Christ, and Christ's entrance into our life begins with His death. And since God came in the flesh and died, that is the greatest thing that God could do and that's why we show forth and remember his death every Passover until He comes.

Now let's come to the section there 1 Corinthians 11:25 on Page 277: "In like manner He *also* took the cup after He had supped, saying, 'This is *the* cup *of* the New Covenant' " (or it should read—the new covenant and that's the way I translated it every other place. This one slipped through in this edition, but we'll get it corrected for the second edition. The new covenant the word is the same: *diatheke* which means covenant, not testament.) "This is *the* cup *of* the New Covenant in My blood. This do, as often as you drink *it*, in the remembrance of Me' " Now often means: year by year until He comes, because you can't take the Passover on any other day than the Passover day and you take it the Passover night. So this cannot be misconstrued, as the world's religions do, that they take it whenever they want on Sunday, as many times as they want, and they call it "Communion", "the Eucharist", "the Lord's Supper", and Paul made it very clear that when you come together, this is <u>not</u> to eat the Lord's Supper. Yet people insist on calling it "the Lord's Supper", and it just shows that they don't know how to understand the scriptures the way that they ought to, because if Paul says it is not to eat the Lord's Supper, it means you don't call it "the Lord's Supper", and you don't eat the Lord's Supper. The truth is the Lord ate His supper and that was on His last Passover night before instituting the symbols of the bread and wine.

Now let's continue on here 1 Corinthians 11:26: "For as often as you eat this bread and drink this cup, you *solemnly* proclaim the death of the Lord until He comes." And if it is a memorial, which it is, and if you are announcing and portraying the Lord's death until He comes, this means that the time that you eat it is on the Passover and as often as you do that, year by year on the Passover until He comes, you are announcing and portraying the Lord's death.

Now then we have something that we need to do and should all do by the time Passover comes which is this: verse 27: "For this reason, *if* anyone shall eat this bread or shall drink the cup of the LORD unworthily, he shall be guilty of the body and *the* blood of the Lord." Meaning that your sins remain on your head. Now as I covered concerning forgiveness of one another, remember that if you don't forgive from the heart each one your brother's sins, then God is going to lay back upon you your sins, and therefore you are keeping the Passover in an unworthy manner, and you are guilty of the body and blood of Christ. Now verse 28: "But let a man examine himself..." (1 Corinthians 11:26-28). Now that's what we need to do—before the Passover, examine ourselves, confess our sins to God and as I said in the message on forgiveness, you go get squared around with your brother or sister <u>before</u> Passover and then, "…and let him eat of the bread and drink of the cup accordingly because the one who eats and drinks unworthily is eating and drinking judgment to himself, discerning the body of the Lord." Which is the forgiveness of sin to put you in right standing before God. And you are under obligation then, to forgive your brothers and sisters their sins that your sins may be forgiven.

Now then, we have an argument taking place [at Jesus' last Passover]. We'll just summarize this section. I'll just say this: If they had the argument as to who was to be the greatest, don't you think they had an understanding about what they were to do? Don't you think they had an understanding about what was to come? You know after all, Christ ordained the twelve apostles didn't He? Yes. Now in this particular case, at this time Judas had already left to betray Christ. Then He gave the example that whoever is the greatest is to be your servant. We are not to be like the lords of the Gentiles and the religious leaders of the Gentiles who exalt themselves and rule over people. No brethren, anyone who is a true minister and servant of God is going to teach you to love God, to love each other, and that your relationship is directly between you and God the Father through Jesus Christ, and that you have direct access to God the Father in heaven above by just getting on your knees and saying, "Our Father." Now you see that's why it's so important. That's why it is so profound. So let's examine ourselves and make sure that we put everything under the blood of Christ and take the Passover in a worth manner, not being the worthiness which we consider worthy, but the worthiness of Christ imputed to us because of God's mercy and love and kindness and forgiveness—and that's what it needs to be.

Now since most of the rest of it here has to do with the Passover that we will take and we will cover these scriptures for the Passover ceremony, let's come ahead to the time when Jesus is betrayed by Judas. Let's come to the section now, let's begin on page 286 and let's continue here in the account of the gospel of John. Now John 18:1: "After saying these things, Jesus went out with His disciples *to a place* beyond the winter stream of Kidron, where *there* was a garden into which He and His disciples entered. And Judas who was betraying Him, also knew of the place because Jesus had often gathered there with His disciples. Then Judas, after receiving a band and officers from the chief priests and Pharisees, came there with torches and lamps and weapons. Jesus, therefore, knowing all *the* things that were coming upon Him, went forward *and* said unto them, 'Whom are you seeking?' They answered Him, 'Jesus the Nazarean.' Jesus said to them, 'I AM.' And Judas, who was betraying Him, was also standing with them. But when He said to them, 'I AM,' they went backward and fell to *the* ground." And I have often wondered—I wonder what those men who came out to arrest Christ and take Him back, I wonder what they felt when they were knocked to the ground backwards by the sound of the words "I AM"? Now you understand that that is the name of God "I AM THAT I AM" and Christ was showing His power as God in the flesh at this particular point. So I guess it didn't bother them, because they got up and so I suppose while they were lying on the ground He asked and said to them, verse 7: " 'Whom are you seeking?' And they said, 'Jesus the Nazarean.' Jesus answered, ' I told you that I AM. Therefore, if you are seeking Me, allow these to go their way'; so that the saying might be fulfilled which He had said, 'Of those whom You have given Me, not one of them have I lost' " (John 18:1-9).

173

Then we have a very interesting thing. John 18:10, page 287: "Then Simon Peter, who had a sword, drew it out and struck the servant of the high priest, and cut off his right ear. And the servant's name was Malchus." Now it is very interesting that his name was put in here by John isn't it? And it's also very interesting that John at this point, names Peter as the one who had the sword whereas Mark, who was the scribe for Peter when he wrote of the account—now let's look at the column over here Mark 14:47. He didn't name Peter. No, he said that "…a certain one of those standing near drew out a sword and struck the servant of the high priest, cutting off his ear." And I just imagine, you know, I've often wondered because Jesus then reached out and touched his ear and it was healed—I've often wondered what Malchus thought all that night. There he was standing there watching the things going on with Jesus and what the chief priests and scribes were doing, and what He was going through and I imagine he would just reach up and touch his ear just to make sure it was still there, because you know if you have your ear cut off, that's quite a thing. And so to have it instantly healed by Jesus touching it, I just wonder what he thought all that night, and what he thought after he heard that Jesus was resurrected from the dead, because surely, he heard it because he was one of the servants of the high priest.

So they took Him, bound Him, led Him away. All the disciples forsook Him and fled away. Now let's come here to Mark 14:51, page 288, "Now a certain young man was following Him, having a linen cloth wrapped around *his* naked *body*; and the young men seized him, but he *escaped*, leaving the linen cloth behind, and ran from them naked" (verse 52). Now this is Mark writing about himself, because he was probably at this time just a teenager. Later he was to serve the apostle Paul and Barnabas and Peter.

Now let's continue on in John 18, page 288, John 18:13: "And they led Him away to Annas first; for he was *the* father-in-law of Caiaphas, who was high priest that year. Now it was Caiaphas who had given counsel to the Jews that it was profitable for one man to perish for the people." Now then remember, that Jesus told Peter that he would deny Him three times, which he did. We'll see this account here. Now let's continue on in the account of John 18:15: "But Simon Peter and the other disciple followed Jesus." Now the other disciple was John—Simon Peter and John. "And that disciple was known to the high priest," in other words, he was acquainted with him, "…and entered with Jesus into the court of the high priest. But Peter stood outside at the door. Then the other disciple, who was known to the high priest, went out and spoke to the doorkeeper, and brought Peter in." Verse 18: "Now the servants and the officers had made a fire, for it was cold; and they were standing *there* warming themselves, and Peter was *also* standing and warming himself." And I just wonder what Peter was thinking because, you know, Malchus might spot him. What was he going to do, because Malchus was one of the servants of the high priest.

Let's continue on here on page 289 in the account in John 18:19: "Then the high priest questioned Jesus concerning His disciples and concerning His teachings. Jesus answered him, 'I spoke openly to the world; I always taught in the synagogue and in the temple, where the Jews always assemble, and I spoke nothing in secret. Why do you question Me? Ask those who have heard what I spoke to them; behold, them know what I said.' "

Now John 18:22 which I have here at approximately 2:00 a.m. in the morning. "But after He said these things, one of the officers who was standing by struck Jesus on the face, saying, 'Do You answer the high priest in that way?' Jesus answered him, 'If I have spoken evil, testify of the evil; but if well, why do you strike Me?' *Then* Annas sent Him bound to Caiaphas, the high priest" (John 18:13-24). So they brought Him there.

Now let's come over to continue the account in the gospel of John. Now you can follow along with the other accounts and you can read those. Just take the time to go ahead and do so. Now let's come here to the account in Luke 22 on page 291 and verse 56: "And a certain maid saw him…" (that is Peter) "… sitting by the light; and after looking at him intently, she said, 'Now this one was with Him.' But he denied Him, saying," (that is denied Christ) "saying, 'Woman, I do not know Him.' And after a little *while,* another saw him *and* said, 'You also are *one* of them.' But Peter said, 'Man, I am not.' " Verse 59: "Now after about an hour had passed, a certain other *man* strongly affirmed, saying, 'In truth, this one also was with Him, for he is indeed a Galilean.' And Peter said, "Man, I do not know what you are talking about.' And immediately, while he was yet speaking, the cock crowed. Then the Lord turned *and* looked at Peter;" Just looking right across however far it was away. "… and Peter remembered the word of the Lord, how He had said to him, 'Before *the* cock crows, you shall deny Me three times.' " And he did.

Now let's come to page 292, John 18:28: "Now then, they led Jesus from Caiaphas…" who was the high priest or the chief priest "…to the judgment hall…" Now what is the judgment hall? Well, that's the place where Pilate was, and the judgment hall was in Fort Antonia. Now Fort Antonia was Roman property and that becomes important for us to understand and to understand the next statement. "…But they did not go in…" That is, all of the scribes and Pharisees who brought Jesus there, and the priests and so forth. "… They did not go into the judgment hall, so that they might not be defiled, but that they might eat the Passover." Now this shows two things—number one: The Jews ate the Passover on the night of the fifteenth and they had a temple Passover. Now this is not all of the Jews, because perhaps the greatest number of Jews were keeping the domestic Passover, and they had already eaten it. But here we're talking about those who kept the temple Passover. Now why would they consider themselves being defiled going into the judgment hall which is in Fort Antonia being Roman property? Well it would be the same as going to another country. And Numbers 9 says that if you are in another country that you take the Passover in the second month. So they would be defiled, number one, by going into the presence of Gentiles which defiling could not be done away within a twenty-four hour period, and there was not time for a twenty-four hour period to take place, a whole day, and to bathe at evening, and so both of those have a factor as to why they didn't go in, that they might eat their Passover on the night of the fifteenth. So they sent Jesus into Pilate, they did not go into the judgment hall.

Now let's continue here on page 294, John 18:29: "Therefore, Pilate came out to them and said, ' What accusation do you bring against this man?' Verse 30: "They answered and said to him, 'If He were not an evildoer, we would not have delivered Him up to you.' " Now you see there is absolutely no proof in that statement whatsoever, but it's a claim, "If He were not, we wouldn't have done it. We are so good and have righteous judgment and can discern good from evil. Now Pilate, you know us, that we are good people. Now do you think that we would have delivered Him up if He were not an evil-doer?"

So then Pilate, let's read the account now in Luke 23:5, "But they were insistent, saying, 'He stirs up the people, teaching throughout all of Judea, beginning from Galilee even to here.' And when he heard Galilee *named,* Pilate asked whether the man were a Galilean; and after determining that He was from Herod's jurisdiction, he sent Him to Herod, *since* he also was in Jerusalem in those days. Now when Herod saw Jesus, he rejoiced greatly; for he had long been desiring to see Him because he had heard many things about Him, and he was hoping to see a miracle done by Him." Now this is Herod Antipas who was the one who killed John the Baptist. So he wanted to know. Now verse 9: "And he questioned Him with many words; but He answered him nothing." Why should He answer the one who killed John the Baptist? Verse 10: "All the while, the chief priests and the scribes stood vehemently accusing Him. Then Herod and his soldiers treated Him with contempt; and after mocking *Him*, he put a splendid robe on Him and *sent* Him back to Pilate. And on the same day, Pilate and Herod became friends with each other, because before there was enmity between them" (Luke 23:5-12). Isn't it interesting—allies in evil. And I wonder how many allies there are in evil who hate each other's guts, but they are allies and become friends for a mutual evil cause. All you have to do is read the daily paper, you'll find out who they are.

Now let's continue on in the account in John 18:31, page 295, "Then Pilate said to them, 'You take Him and judge Him according to your *own* law.' But the Jews said to him, 'It is not lawful for us to put anyone to death'; so that the saying of Jesus might be fulfilled, which He had spoken to signify by what death He was about to die." Verse 33: "Then Pilate, returned to the judgment hall and called Jesus, and said to Him, 'Are You the King of the Jews?' Jesus answered him, 'Do you ask this of yourself, or did others say *it* to you concerning Me?' " Verse 35: "Pilate answered Him, 'Am I a Jew? The chief priests and your own nation have delivered You up to me. What have You done?' Jesus answered, 'My kingdom is not of this world. If My kingdom were of this world, then would My servants fight, so that I might not be delivered up to the Jews. However, My kingdom is not of this world.' "

Now let's just stop here and understand something. This is why we are not to get involved in straightening out this world through the political process, and we are not to fight the authorities of this world because we belong to the kingdom of God and the kingdom of God is not yet here on the earth, and Christ is not yet here. It is not time for us to fight. When Christ returns, then will we fight, and we will be guaranteed that we will win! Do you think for one moment, that all of the political infighting that is done by those that are against abortion that they are going to turn back abortion? Do you think that all of the political infighting and things that are done to try and restore America to "the Constitution once delivered" is going to bring that back? And you need to stop and think and also realize and understand this: Even if those in America could get back to "the Constitution once delivered," and if there were enough time, please understand this—In two hundred years, we would again be exactly where we are today.

Now you see, who is the god of this world—Satan the devil. So if you are out there getting involved in these things, please understand very profoundly and importantly—though the United States may have the best constitution of any government on earth, it is still a kingdom of this world—and being a kingdom of this world, Satan the devil has infiltrated and taken [it] and has made it what it is today. So it is a kingdom of Satan the devil, not of God. The only reason we have the peace that we have is because the prophecies have yet to be fulfilled, and the preaching of the gospel must yet still be done, and so we have this time of peace and security and prosperity—not because of any goodness upon our part, but to give us the time to accomplish and do what God wants us to do. We need to fight the fight of faith, and we need to grow and overcome. We need not to get involved in fighting the fights of this world because the <u>Kingdom</u> of <u>God</u> is <u>not</u> of <u>this</u> world, and <u>we</u> are <u>not</u> of <u>this</u> world!

Now let's come back to the account here in John 18:37: "Pilate therefore answered Him, 'Then You are a king?' Jesus answered, '*As* you say, I am a king. For this *purpose* I was born, and for this *reason* I came into the world, that I may bear witness to the truth. Everyone who is of the truth hears My voice.' Pilate said to Him, 'What is truth?' And after saying this, he went out again to the Jews and said to them, 'I do not find any fault in Him.'

Now let's continue the account here in John 18:39, page 295: "And it is a custom with you that I release one to you at the Passover. Do you then desire that I release the King of the Jews to you?' " Verse 40: "But they all shouted again, saying, 'Not this one, but Barabbas.' Now Barabbas was a robber' " (John 18:31-40). And the other account also shows he was a murderer.

Now let's come to page 297 the account here in John 19:1: "Then Pilate therefore took Jesus and scourged *Him*." That's with a "Cat-o'-nine-tails" and it is by His stripes of scourging that we are healed.

Let's come to Isaiah 53 and let's see the prophecy of what Jesus was going to go through that was given here by Isaiah in Isaiah 53. Let's pick it up here in verse 3: "He is despised and rejected of men; a man of sorrows, and acquainted with grief: and we hid as it were (our eyes or) *our* faces from him; he was despised, and we esteemed him not. Surely he has borne our griefs, and carried our sorrows: yet we did esteem him stricken, smitten of God, and afflicted." That's what they said when they taunted Him. Verse 5: "But he *was* wounded for our transgressions, *he was* bruised for our iniquities:" And all the bruisings that He took with that "Cat-o'-nine-tails" and by His stripes we are healed. Now we need to understand that. "…The chastisement of our peace was upon him;" In other words, in order for us to have peace with God and not receive the chastisement of God upon us, that chastisement came upon Christ. "… And with his stripes we are healed" (Isaiah 53:3-5).

Verse 6: "All we like sheep have gone astray; we have turned every one to his own way…" And boy that's sure true of what it is with the church of God today. Everyone has a doctrine—doctrine, doctrine, who has a doctrine—opinion, opinion, who has an opinion—church, church, who has a church—web site, web site, who has a web site? I mean you know everyone has gone his own way. That's why unless you follow the way of the Lord, unless you follow the scriptures, then you are going your own way. You need to stop and ask the question: What are you really going to have if you insist on your own way? Have you ever thought of that?

Now what if your own way is contrary to the scriptures or your own doctrine, or your own pet theories or your own whatever? What are you going to receive? Even Jesus said that, "Many will say to Me in that day, 'Lord, Lord have we not prophesied in your name? Have we not cast out demons, and have we not done many wonderful works?' " And Jesus will profess to them, "I never knew you. Depart from Me you who work lawlessness." So you see, if you have your own way, you have the wages of sin, which is death.

So you see Jesus was beaten and scourged and crucified to cover the sins of us going our own way, but that we may repent and go God's way. And after all brethren, is that not what the Passover is all about? Is not the renewing of the New Covenant all about living the way of Christ and Christ in us in the New Covenant? Is not the footwashing also giving us a part with Christ, also renewing our baptism, also showing that we are to walk in the way of the Lord and not our own? Now you need to think about it and understand it. "We all like sheep have gone astray; we have turned every one to his own way; and the LORD has laid on him the iniquity of us all."

Verse 7: "He was oppressed, and he was afflicted, yet he opened not his mouth: he is brought as a lamb to the slaughter, and as a sheep before her shearers is dumb, so he opens not his mouth. He was taken from prison and from judgment and who shall declare his generation?" Well that's the preaching of the gospel. That's what declares it. "…For he was cut off out of the land of the living: for the transgression of my people was he stricken. And he made his grave with the wicked, and with the rich in his death; because he had done no violence, neither *was any* deceit in his mouth. Yet it please the LORD to bruise him; he put *him* to grief: when you shall make his soul an offering for sin," So that our sins could be forgiven. And God sent Christ in the likeness of sinful flesh and for sin condemned sin in the flesh and condemned human nature in the flesh and the crucifixion of Christ shows the crucifixion of human nature. And now you know why Christ said that, " If anyone comes to Me and does not hate his father, and mother, … and brothers and sisters, (lands), and, in addition, his own life also, he cannot be My disciple. And whoever does not carry his cross and come after Me cannot be My disciple" (Luke 14:26-27).

Because what God has done is so great and so fantastic and so marvelous that He would come and die for the sins of His creation. And the purpose then is that after the resurrection that there would be the children of God and that's what the next portion of this verse 10 in Isaiah 53 is about. "…He shall see *his* seed," That's us brethren—the seed of God the Father. "…He shall prolong *his* days," That is through the power of the resurrection and live forever. "… And the pleasure of the LORD shall prosper in his hand. He shall see the travail of his soul, *and* shall be satisfied:" That is God the Father will see the travail of the soul of Christ as it were and be satisfied, that is the sacrifice which brings satisfaction for the forgiveness of sins. " …And by his knowledge shall my righteous servant justify many; for he shall bear their iniquities." Verse 12: "Therefore will I divide him *a portion* with the great, and he shall divide the spoil with the strong; because he has poured out his soul unto death:" And he did and we will see that. "…And he was numbered with the transgressors; and he bare the sin of many, and made intercession for the transgressors." So quite a thing—I want you to understand about Isaiah 53 and the crucifixion of Christ and what it has to do with the Passover, what it has to do with our eternal life, and that's why brethren, that's why the Passover and renewal of the New Covenant is so profound and important.

Now let's come back to John 19, page 297 in the Harmony, and let's continue on. Verse 2: "And after platting a crown of thorns, the soldiers put *it* on His head; and they threw a purple cloak over Him, and *kept on* saying, 'Hail, King of the Jews!' And they struck Him with the palms of their hands." And it records in another place that they spit at Him. "Then Pilate went out again and said to them, 'Behold, I bring Him out to you, so that you may know that I do not find any fault in Him.' Then Jesus went out, wearing the crown of thorns and the purple cloak; and he said to them, 'Behold the man!' "

Now let's continue on page 298 here in John 19:6: "But when the chief priests and the officers saw Him, they cried aloud, saying, 'Crucify *Him*, crucify *Him*! Pilate said to them, 'You take Him and crucify *Him*, because I do not find any fault in Him.' The Jews answered, 'We have a law, and according to our law it is mandatory that He die, because He made Himself *the* Son of God.' " Verse 8: "Therefore, when Pilate heard this saying, he was even more afraid. And he went into the judgment hall again, and said to Jesus, 'Where have You come from?' But Jesus did not give him an answer. Then Pilate said to Him, "Why don't You speak to me? Don't You know that I have authority to crucify You and authority to release You?' Jesus answered, 'You would not have any authority against Me if it were not given to you from above. For this reason, the one who delivered Me to you has *the* greater sin.' " Verse 12: "Because of this *saying*, Pilate sought to release Him; but the Jews cried out, saying, 'If you release this *man*, you are not a friend of Caesar. Everyone who makes himself a king speaks against Caesar.' " Political blackmail—same old tricks that are always used in politics today, right? Yes. Verse 13: "Therefore, after hearing this saying, Pilate *had* Jesus led out, and sat down on the judgment seat at a place called *the* Pavement; but in Hebrew, Gabbatha. (Now it was *the* preparation of the Passover, and about the sixth hour.)" That's about six o'clock in the morning because John is writing here of Roman time. "…And he said to the Jews, 'Behold your King!' But they cried aloud, 'Away, away *with Him*! Crucify Him!' Pilate said to them, 'Shall I crucify your King?' The chief priests answered, 'We have no king but Caesar.' " Now you need to understand how demonic that saying was. That's the same as saying we have no king but Satan the devil. And Jesus said of those Jews that their father was the devil. (John 19:6-15).

Now let's continue on in the account in John. You can read the other accounts there in the Harmony in Matthew, Mark and Luke, page 300, verse 16: "Therefore, he then delivered Him up to them so that He might be crucified. And they took Jesus and led *Him* away. And He went out bearing His own cross to the place called *The Place* of a Skull, which in Hebrew is called Golgotha.

Now let's come here to John 19:23, page 301, "Now the soldiers, after they had crucified Jesus, took His garments and made four parts, a part for each soldier, and the coat *also*. But the coat was seamless, woven *in one piece* from the top all the way throughout. For this reason, they said to one another, 'Let us not tear it, but let us cast lots for it *to determine* whose it shall be;' that the scripture might be fulfilled which says, 'They divided My garments among them, and they cast lots for My vesture' " (John 19:23-24.) Now let's understand something here. Can God make carnal people do things to fulfill His will and His scripture and His Word and they not even know it? Those soldiers didn't know that. They didn't know that God was causing them to do that, but God did, didn't He?

Now John 19 and verse 19, page 301, "And Pilate also wrote a title and put *it* on the cross; and it was written, 'Jesus the Nazarean, the King of the Jews.' As a result, many of the Jews read this title, for the place where Jesus was crucified was near the city;" It was on the Mount of Olives just across from the temple. "… and it was written in Hebrew, in Greek *and* in Latin. Then the chief priests of the Jews said to Pilate, 'Do not write, "The King of the Jews"; but that He said, "I am King of the Jews." ' Pilate answered, 'What I have written, I have written.' " Quite a thing, quite a statement, I mean this is something brethren, you need to realize that Jesus went through all of this for us.

Now then He was mocked. Let's take the account here on page 302 in Luke 23:35: "Now the people stood *by* observing, and the rulers among them were also deriding *Him*, saying, 'He saved others; let Him save Himself, if this is the Christ, the chosen of God.' And the soldiers also mocked Him, coming near and offering Him vinegar, and saying, 'If You are the King of the Jews, save Yourself.' " Then of course, the one of the two that were crucified with Him, Jesus told him that, you know, " 'I tell you today, you shall be with Me in paradise' " (Luke 23:35-43).

Now let's come over here to the last of Jesus' life on the cross. "Now about the ninth hour, Jesus cried.' " Let's take the account here in Matthew 27:46, page 304. "…Jesus cried out with a loud voice, saying, 'Eli, Eli, lama sabachthani?' That is, My God, My God, why have you forsaken Me?' " Now that is so profound, brethren, to understand that Christ had to bear all of our sins alone, and that's why the darkness covered the earth as it were, from the sixth hour until the ninth hour, because God the Father had to leave Christ alone for that period of time and Christ, because He had such a close relationship with God the Father throughout His entire life felt as though that He were forsaken, and that fulfilled the scripture that we find in Psalm 22—"My God, My God, why have you forsaken Me?" Verse 47: "And some of those who were standing there heard and said, 'This *one* is calling for Elijah' And immediately one of them ran and, taking a sponge, filled *it* with vinegar and put *it* on a stick, *and* gave *it to* Him to drink. But the rest said, 'Let Him alone! Let us see if Elijah comes to save Him.' *Then another took a spear and thrust it into His side, and out came water and blood.* And after crying out again with a loud voice, Jesus yielded up *His* spirit." And it says there in the account in Luke that "after crying out with a loud voice, Jesus said, 'Father, into Your hands I commit My spirit.' And when He had said these things, He expired" (Luke 23:46). Or that is died.

Now then something really took place, this was something. Now back here to the account with Matthew 27:51 "And suddenly the veil of the temple was ripped in two from top to bottom, the earth shook, and the rocks were split, and the tombs were opened, and many bodies of the saints who had died arose. And after His resurrection, they came out of the tombs *and* entered into the holy city, and appeared to many." Now continuing on in Matthew, verse 54: "Then the centurion and those with him who had been keeping guard over Jesus, after seeing the earthquake" because you can see an earthquake "…and the things that took place, were filled with fear, *and* said, 'Truly this was the Son of God!' " What a testimony! The Jews rejected Him, the scribes, the Pharisees, the chief priests and the religious leaders rejected Him, but here is a Gentile, Italian centurion guard who said, "Truly, this one is the Son of God!' "

And so brethren as we go to take the Passover, let's remember what Jesus did for us. Let's remember all the things that Jesus went through, that we can come before God and have our sins forgiven, that we can be partakers of the New Covenant through His body and through His blood, and so that we may have eternal life. So let's keep the Passover with this in mind and rededicate ourselves in the New Covenant to love God with all our heart and mind and soul and being and to serve Him in those things that please Him.

End of Sermon

Transcriber: Judith Anderson

The Passover—Abraham, Isaac, Israel & Christ–Sermon III
March 16, 2002
Scriptural References

1) Exodus 12:3-13

2) Hebrews 12:22-23

3) Exodus 12:14-28, 37

4) Exodus 16:4-8, 11-13 (SB)

5) (Harmony page 241) Mark 14:1-2

6) (Harmony page 274) Matthew 26:20, Mark 14:17, John 18:13:12-17

7) (Harmony page 276) Luke 22:19, 1 Cor. 11:23

8) (Harmony page 277) I Corinthians 11:25-28

9) (Harmony page 286) John 18:1-12

10) (Harmony page 288) Mark 14:51-52, John 18:13-16

11) (Harmony page 289) John 18:18-24

12) (Harmony page 291) Luke 22:56-61

13) (Harmony page 292) John 18:28

14) (Harmony page 294) John 18:29-30, Luke 23:5-12

15) (Harmony page 295) John 18:31-40

16) (Harmony page 297) John 19:1-2

17) Isaiah 53:3-12

18) (Harmony page 297) John 19:2-5

19) (Harmony page 298) John 19:6-15

20) (Harmony page 300) John 19:16-17

21) (Harmony page 301) John 19:23-24, 19

22) (Harmony page 302) John 19:20-22, Luke 23:35

23) (Harmony page 303) Luke 23:36-43

24) (Harmony page 304) Matthew 27:46-50

25) (Harmony page 305) Matthew 27:51-54

Other References Quoted:

1) Everett Fox's Schocken Bible, Vol. 1 (SB)
2) Harmony of the Gospels (HG*)

CHAPTER TWELVE

The Passover Exodus and Trusting God

April 23, 2005

Now the apostle Paul told Timothy that he was to preach in season and out of season, be urgent in it, and so this is the season of the Passover and Unleavened Bread. So let's take a look and see some parallels of what God has done in our lives in rescuing us from the world, just how He had to intervene in the lives of the children of Israel when they were in Egypt to bring them out of slavery and out of captivity. And we will also answer a few questions as we go along as to the timing of the Passover that they had and so forth. Let's come to Exodus 10 please.

Now God performed great miracles, all the plagues and everything that God has the power to do and use, and isn't it interesting that God uses His creation to show His power. You know that is why God has created certain things so magnificently, that we can understand that only by the power of God and by His hand could things come into existence.

Exodus 10, and let's look at the last plague before the plague of the firstborn, and there are some good spiritual lessons for us here. Verse 21: "And the LORD said unto Moses, 'Stretch out your hand toward heaven, that there may be darkness over the land of Egypt, even darkness *which* may be felt.' " So this is a tremendous darkness that came upon them. It's like a dark, thick fog you could feel. Now I don't know how many have been in a mine or like in Carlsbad Caverns or whatever; I haven't been there, but I hear tell that when you get down below, you have all the lights show the way down there, and then they turn them off and they tell you put your hand in front of your face, see if you can see your hand. You can't see anything. And when I read this and the darkness that was there which could be felt, it reminds me that it had to be some kind of really powerful darkness that God brought upon them.

Now also, think of this: What is the epitome of spiritual darkness—Egypt, and what is the warning that God has always given? Don't go back to Egypt. And what is Jerusalem called in the end times? In Revelation 11, it is called Sodom and Egypt. So you see what we are seeing today is that the world is going back to Egypt in many, many ways. You see, Egypt was a land of many religions, and it was a land of ecumenism—your god is ok as long as you say my god is ok, and I accept you if you accept me. And this is exactly where the world is headed.

Now they had kind of a scare with the Pope just elected, Benedict XVI, because they thought for sure that he was going to turn the clock back. Well as it turned out, he is not going to turn it back. He is going to continue with the same things that they are doing, ecumenism with separated brethren, and dialogue with other religions, and he did not take (is what we read and it's here in the San Jose Mercury) he did not take the oath against modernism. Now that means that he is going to proceed with modernizing whatever they need to do to make Catholicism appear acceptable to people in the world. And that's all going back to Egypt. And so God wanted everyone to know that the darkness of Egypt is a spiritual lesson for us. So verse 22: "And Moses stretched forth his hand toward heaven; and there was a thick darkness in all the land of Egypt three days:" Now remember, some time previous God separated out the land of Goshen where the children of Israel were living, so none of the plagues would come upon them. So this didn't come upon them. They had light, but the Egyptians had darkness, and there is also a lesson in that. And here is how dark it was, verse

181

23: "They saw not one another, neither rose any from his place for three days: but all the children of Israel had light in their dwellings." Now there is also a lesson for us in this. Even though we live in a world of darkness, God gives us spiritual light—only in this case, not just in the land of Goshen, but wherever we are. And God also is showing, and Christ said, "I am the light." So Christ is the one Who gives us the way and shows us how to do it.

So here is what happened, just like it is in the world. How many times have good intentions come along and then people go back on them. Well, this was the story of Pharaoh. God gave him an opportunity, and then he hardened his heart, so then God hardened his heart even further. So it was kind of like a wrestling match between God, Moses, and Pharaoh. So then, verse 24: "...Pharaoh called to Moses and said, 'Go serve the LORD; only let your flocks and your herds be stayed:' " Because ours were all killed. " '...Let your little ones also go with you.' Then Moses said, 'You must give us also sacrifices and burnt offerings, that we may sacrifice unto our God. Our cattle also shall go with us; there shall not be a hoof left behind; for thereof must we take to serve the LORD our God; and we know not with what we must serve the LORD' " (or that is, how we are going to serve Him) " ' until we get there.' But the LORD hardened Pharaoh's heart, and he would not let them go. And Pharaoh said to him, 'Get you from me, take heed to yourself, see my face no more;' " That's an important one as we will see a little later. You can mark that. " '...For in the day that you see my face you shall die.' And Moses said, 'You have well spoken, I will see your face again no more' " (Exodus 10:21-29).

So then God gave him some instructions here. Now let's look at this because this becomes quite a thing here. Exodus 11:1: "And the LORD said to Moses, 'Yet will I bring one *more* plague upon Pharaoh and upon Egypt; afterwards he will let you go from there: when he shall let *you* go, he shall surely thrust you out altogether.' " Verse 2: " 'Speak now in the ears of the people, and let every man borrow of this neighbor...' " Now that should be *spoil*, not *borrow*. They weren't going to pay it back. They took it when they left Egypt. Continuing verse 2: " '...And every woman of her neighbor, jewels of silver, and jewels of gold.' " So we see here that with this they had approximately two weeks before they left in being able to get some of the riches. So they left with wages, as God says a little later on, for all their slavery that they had for all the years that they were there. Verse 3: "And the LORD gave the people favor in the sight of the Egyptians. Moreover the man Moses *was* very great in the land of Egypt, in the sight of Pharaoh's servants, and in the sight of the people." Verse 4: "And Moses said, 'Thus saith the LORD...' " Now here is the last thing that he is saying to Pharaoh. " '...About midnight...' " God says, " '...I will go out into the midst of Egypt: and all the firstborn in the land of Egypt shall die, from the firstborn of Pharaoh that sitteth upon his throne, even unto the firstborn of the maid-servant that *is* behind the mill; and all the firstborn of beasts. And there shall be a great cry throughout all the land of Egypt, such as there was none like it, nor shall be like it any more. But against the children of Israel shall not a dog move his tongue, against man or beast:' " Now this shows God's protection and God's blessing, and this is why when we have troubles and difficulties and trials, we need to trust God and trust His promises that He gives to us because He says that He will. And the reason He did was this: " '...that you may know how that the LORD does put a difference between the Egyptians and Israel.' " Now today we can take that between the church and the world. There is a difference. Then he tells Pharaoh " 'And all these your servants...' " that were standing there with him when he gave the message to him " '...shall come down unto me...' " and we will see that happen " ' ...and bow down themselves unto me, saying, Get you out, and all the people that follow you: and after that I will go out.' And he went out from Pharaoh in a great anger." And that means in the Hebrew *white hot*. He was really angry. Verse 9: "And the LORD said to Moses, 'Pharaoh will not listen to you that I may multiply all my wonders in the land of Egypt.' And Moses and Aaron did all these wonders before Pharaoh: and the LORD hardened Pharaoh's heart so that he would not let the children of Israel go out of his land" (Exodus 11:1-10).

Now then, God told them what they were to do. He told them how to prepare for the Passover, the tenth day of the first month, select a lamb. There is a parallel that happened in the time of that with Christ. Then on the tenth day, and when you have the Passover in the middle of the week, the tenth day of the month falls on a weekly Sabbath. And so they were to select a lamb on the tenth day of the first month, and they were to keep it up and they were to have it according to the number of persons in the household which if a household was too small, then they would share the lamb or the kid goat that they had with their neighbor. And He gave specific instructions for it here in verse 5, Exodus 12: " 'Your lamb shall be without blemish, a male...' " Now here we have a type of Christ that is true as I mentioned, even though the timing of the New Covenant Passover comes out of the timing of Genesis 15, we still have all the types showing that the true Messiah is going to come, and this is part of it. " '...A male without blemish of the first year: you shall take *it* from the sheep or from the goats:' " So you see, not all goats are bad. There are good goats. And the good goats are independent. So I guess we are good goats, even though we are counted as sheep.

I remember my first experience with goats that was up in Boise and I went out to visit this family and they lived up in the back hills behind Boise and to drive up there was really a trick because it was one of these roads that went up, but down the middle of it was an eroded part where when it rained, it left a trench. And so you had to be careful how you were going up. So I got up there, and they had this big tree, and I thought since it was a pretty warm day, I would park under the tree. So here I'm in, they had a house there and I'm in the house and was sitting there and talking and visiting. It was right after I had just got up to Boise and I wanted to meet everybody in the church. So all of a sudden the man got up, ran outside, and I jumped up to see what was going on and here was a goat on top of my car eating the leaves off the tree. And he knew as soon as he heard it, he knew exactly what it was because that's why he didn't park his cars under there. So I went out there and he said, "Well, you better move your car." So you see goats know how to get it when the going is tough, and they figure out what they need to do regardless of the circumstances. So here is a case of good goats. So if we're goats, let's hope we're good goats.

Verse 6: " 'And you shall keep it up until the fourteenth day of the same month:' " Now since the day begins at sundown, when does the fourteenth begin? At sundown. And if you have read the Passover book, you will know that soon as the sun goes down below the horizon, it starts the time period called *between the two evenings—ben ha arbayim* which is *between the two evenings,* or as the Schocken Bible has: *between the setting times.* So they were to " '... keep it until the fourteenth... and the whole assembly of the congregation of Israel shall kill it between the evenings (or between the two evenings)' " (Exodus 12:1-6.)

And this is where so many people just go off the deep end, because they say that it's in the evening. Well why can't it be the evening beginning of the fifteenth? Well, because then you would have kept it beyond the "until," that's why. So this was quite a spectacular thing. Now I don't know, but I have often envisioned this: Whatever their little huts were where they were living in their quarters out there and some of the slave quarters that they now have unearthed around the Sphinx and the great pyramids I can just envision their community and they had someone right up on top of one of these houses posted at different locations wherever the Israelites were, and I imagine that he was watching the sun go down, so that as soon as the sun went down, <u>bam</u>, and the fourteenth began—he gave the signal and all of the lambs were killed at the same time. So this was a spectacular event. Now when you understand that there may have been as many as 1.8 million Israelites at that time, this was no small, little task. It was a <u>big</u> task, and it was a <u>huge</u> event, and it was something that God was using to show the people His power, His forgiveness, and His mercy, as well as, since they were going to leave the land of Egypt, they needed to look to Him. So He gave them the instructions what they should do verse 7: " 'They shall take of the blood, and strike *it* on the two side posts and on the upper door post of the houses…' " which is called the lintel, " '…wherein they shall eat it. And you shall eat the flesh in that night…' " which means then if you kill it, when does it have to be? If it's on the fourteenth, then it's when the fourteenth begins. " '…eat the flesh in that night, roast with fire, and unleavened bread;' " That's why it's an unleavened bread day, and if you read the account, you can find nothing in there where they had any leavened bread at all. " ' …*And* with bitter *herbs* shall you eat it. You shall not eat it raw, or boiled at all with water, but roast *with* fire; with his legs and with the purtenance thereof' " which means that they had the heart and the liver and I don't know if the kidney was still there or not, but at least the heart and the liver. Obviously you can't roast it with all of the innards in it because if you tried to, the innards would explode and you wouldn't have anything to eat.

Now Exodus 12:10: " 'And you shall let nothing of it remain until the morning; and that which remains until the morning shall be burnt with fire.' " So anything that was left, they weren't allowed to go beyond the morning, but anything that was left, they were to burn. Verse 11: " 'And thus shall you eat it; *with* your loins girded, your shoes on your feet, and your staff in your hand; and you shall eat it…" not in haste, but "…in trepidation:' " You see a lot of people read that *in haste* in the King James and misunderstand what it means. They think it means "Well, they were eating it right then, eat it in a hurry and they left at midnight." Well, we are going to see that the instruction was, they were not to leave their houses until morning, or at sunrise. This means in trepidation. " '…It is the LORD'S passover.' " And that's where we get the name of it. The Passover—because God passed over the houses where the blood was on the doorposts and the lintel, and spared the firstborn of all the children of Israel. Verse 12: " 'For I will pass through the land of Egypt this night…' " on which day—the fourteenth. " '…And will smite all the firstborn in the land of Egypt, both man and beast:' " Now what is this telling us? And what is this important for, not only for the Israelites then, but for us today? That God gives us protection against all the satanic powers in the world, and God has the victory over them. And the satanic powers are those powers that are behind the idols and gods of Egypt.

Now I remember reading an account of a man who went to India to get enlightened, and he said he didn't think too much about idols until his third trip over there. Then he said when he was meditating on the idol, all of a sudden the power came upon him. So it was the power behind the idol or all the demonic powers that are behind all the other gods. Continuing verse 12: " '…**and against all the gods of Egypt will I execute judgement**;' " Now this is why God will never compromise and give permission to any man, any where, at any time, to go ahead and combine the true worship of God whether it was the worship of God in the Old Testament at that time; or the worship of God in the New Testament today, to combine the religions of this world with God's way. And that's why the whole thing of the ecumenical movement that is in the world is going to lead everybody back to Egypt, spiritually speaking. Now notice verse 13: " 'And the blood shall be to you for a token upon your houses where you *are*, and when I see the blood, I will pass over you, and the plague shall not be upon you to destroy *you*, when I smite the land of Egypt. This day shall be to you for a memorial; and you shall keep it a feast to the LORD throughout your generations; you shall keep it a feast by an ordinance for ever.' " Now we're going to come back to the other verses here in just a minute (Exodus 12:7-14).

Now let's come over here to verse 21: "Then Moses called for all the elders of Israel, and said to them," Now here is Moses giving God's instructions to the elders who went on back and gave the instructions to all the households, so this had to take place well before the tenth day of the first month. So everyone would know, and everyone would be ready and they would select that lamb on the tenth day of the first month. So it all had to be coordinated. So here is the coordination that went on with it. " '…And take a lamb according to your families and kill the passover. You shall take a bunch of hyssop, and dip it in the blood that is in the bason, strike the lintel and the two side posts with the blood that is in the bason; and <u>none</u> <u>of</u> <u>you</u> <u>shall</u> <u>go</u> <u>out</u> at <u>the</u> <u>door</u> of <u>his</u> <u>house</u> <u>until'</u> " —midnight: Now you see when you misread it, it makes you understand that's not what he said, but some people claim that, right? Yes. " '…shall not go out at the door of his house until the <u>morning</u>…' " And the Hebrew there is *boqer* which means sunrise. Now here is the reason. Verse 23: " 'For the LORD will pass through to smite the Egyptians; and when he sees the blood upon the lintel and the two side posts, the LORD will pass over the door, and will not allow the destroyer to come in to your houses to smite *you*.' " So God Himself, personally oversaw this, the destroyers may have been angels. It talks about an angel in another place, but God was the one Who personally did this because it was a confrontation between God and Pharaoh and the gods of Satan that were there in Egypt. So this was God's personal business. And he says, " '…Ye shall observe this thing for an ordinance to you and to your sons for ever.' "

Now here is the difference between the Passover day and the first day of the Feast of Unleavened Bread. Now we'll see what the first day of the Feast of Unleavened Bread means, though they are one day following the other, they have different meanings because they are different days and you can't combine the two together. Verse 25: " 'And it shall come to pass, when you come to the land which the LORD will give you, according as he has promised, that you shall keep this service. And it shall come to pass, when your children shall say to you, What do you mean by this service?' " Now they would obviously ask the question because this was to be a domestic sacrifice at their houses and they were to reenact it, and they were to take some of the blood and put it on the lintel and the side posts where their houses were when they got into the land. " 'And you shall say **It is the sacrifice of the LORD'S passover, who passed over the houses of the children of Israel in Egypt, when he smote the Egyptians, and delivered our houses**.' And the people bowed the head and worshipped. And the children of Israel went away, and did as the LORD had commanded Moses and Aaron, so they did."

Now if they did what was commanded, what did they do? They selected the lamb on the tenth, they killed it at the beginning of the fourteenth, they put the blood on the side posts and on the lintel, they roasted it with unleavened bread and bitter herbs, they burned the remains by morning, they didn't leave their houses until morning. Now think of this. At midnight what happened? God smote all the firstborn of the land of Egypt didn't He? Now that didn't take place all at once, I'm sure it took place as God oversaw the destroyer going in there and it was kind of like a wave that was coming along, and the screams and the cries because the firstborn were dying. Now I don't know how many of the children of Israel could hear the sound of it, but I tell you what, if you heard any sound of these people crying and screaming because of the death of the firstborn, do you think you would go out of your house before sunrise, when you were told to stay in your house until sunrise? I don't think so. Who would guarantee that you wouldn't be killed? God didn't give any guarantee unless you stayed in the house, which is a very interesting thing too, isn't it? If we stay right with God, He guarantees that He will be with us, right? Same thing today. So that's what happened (Exodus 12:21-28).

Now let's come back here for the Feast of Unleavened Bread which follows it, verse 15. Passover day is one day. The first day of the Feast of Unleavened Bread is another day. Now we'll see the meaning of the first day of the Feast of Unleavened Bread which begins on the fifteenth. " 'Seven days shall you eat unleavened bread; even the first day you shall have…" as it should read "…put leaven out of your houses: for whosoever eats leavened bread from the first day until the seventh day, that soul shall be cut off from Israel.' " In other words, you lose contact with God. " 'And in the first day *there shall be;* a holy convocation and in the seventh day there shall be a holy convocation to you; no manner of work shall be done in them, save that which every man must eat, that only may be done of you. You shall observe *the feast of* unleavened bread; **for in the selfsame day have I brought**

your armies out of the land of Egypt: therefore you shall observe this day in your generations by an ordinance forever.' "

So we have two feasts back to back, don't we? The Passover commemorating passing over—the Feast of Unleavened Bread pictures beginning to leave Egypt. Now when they left their houses, after they left them in the morning which is on the day portion of the fourteenth, where did they go? They went to Rameses. Now we figured that for some of them it was as much as 15 or 20 miles away. So it would take them all day to get there. Other ones who lived in the southern part of Goshen would be able to get to Rameses sooner, but that is where they assembled to leave. So the meaning of the Passover is passing over and the meaning of the first day of Unleavened Bread which begins at sunset and is the beginning of the fifteenth, and that's when they began to leave Egypt. Obviously, they didn't get out of Egyptian territory for some time after that, but if you are on your way with God's protection, it is as good as done.

Now then, he reiterates it here concerning the Feast of Unleavened Bread, verse 18. Now let's come over here to verse 29. Now we're going to see these two back to back. Verse 29: "And it came to pass that at midnight..." is God on time? Does He keep His word? Yes, He does. "... The LORD smote all the firstborn in the land of Egypt, from the first born of Pharaoh that sat on his throne unto the firstborn of the captive that *was* in the dungeon; and all the firstborn of cattle." Such as were still alive. Verse 30: "And Pharaoh rose up in the night, and all of his servants and all the Egyptians; and there was a great cry in Egypt; for *there was* not a house where *there was* not one dead."

Now here is a fulfilling of a prophecy two weeks before. Verse 31: "And he called for Moses..." Now let's understand that means he sent a message. Some say that Moses got up and went to Pharaoh. That's not what Moses told Pharaoh. Let's come back here to Chapter 11 and let's see it. Exodus 11:8: " 'And all these your servants shall come down to me and bow down themselves unto me saying, Get you out and all the people that follow you and after that I will go out' " That's what he told them would happen. He wasn't going to go back and see Pharaoh again because he said "You shall see my face no more again." So here they came down, he sent a message to Moses and Aaron by night. Now we know this is after midnight, how long after midnight this took place, we don't know. And he said, "Rise up, and get you forth from among my people, both you and the children of Israel; and go serve the LORD as you have said. Also take your flocks and your herds, as you have said, and be gone; and bless me also' " (Exodus 12:29-31). After all this devastation, I need a little blessing. (Laughter)

Now what was the signal for the children of Israel to leave their houses? Now just figure this: However large the community was where the children of Israel were in the land of Goshen, would they have known when the messengers came down to Moses? Would they have even known it, except those right close by? Of course not. So they would not be able to determine how soon after midnight they could leave if like some of them said, they left their houses at midnight. Well, God said don't go out 'til morning. Now what's the signal for everybody that everyone can understand? When you look out and you see the sun coming up—Sunrise. Everybody left their houses at sunrise and began to go and assemble down at Rameses.

Now let's continue on here, verse 33: "And the Egyptians were urgent upon the people that they might send them out of the land in haste; for they said, 'We *be* all dead *men.*' " That is, if we don't get them out of here, God's going to kill all of us. Verse 34: "And the people took their bread before it was leavened, their kneadingtroughs being bound up in their clothes upon their shoulders. And the children of Israel did according to the word of Moses;" Now notice, all the way through they obeyed didn't they? Yes. "...And they borrowed..." or that is spoiled "...of the Egyptians jewels of silver, and jewels of gold, and raiment:" That was just thrust upon them. The Egyptians probably figured this: God put it in their minds, "If we give them these things, we'll save our lives. Give them whatever they want." So they were loaded down. Can you imagine leaving Egypt with 200 years of wages? (The Spanish translation is: "they asked and they were given." That is probably more correct.)

Verse 36: "And the LORD gave the people favor in the sight of the Egyptians, so that they lent unto them *such things as they required*. And they spoiled the Egyptians. And the children of Israel journeyed from Rameses..." So they all had to get to Rameses. Now in the Passover book I cover all of this and I've got a map showing where Rameses is, showing where the land of Goshen is, and when you're on foot, you're walking; it's going to take some time. So they all gathered there. Now notice and they "...journeyed from Rameses to Succoth, about six hundred thousand on foot *that were* men, besides children." And that means men and women there probably together besides the children. Verse 38: "And a mixed multitude went up also with them; and flocks, and herds, *even* very much cattle. And they baked unleavened cakes of the dough which they brought forth out of Egypt, for it was not leavened; because they were thrust out of Egypt, and could not tarry, neither had they prepared for themselves any vittles." So they didn't pack up their, you know, take all their goodies.

Now let's look at this. If we are blessed, whoever those of us who are going to go to a place of safety if we live long enough to see that, God is not going to have us pack up our Petra box, so we can tell the angel, when the angel comes to take us to a place of safety, "Opp! Wait a minute. I gotta get my Petra box!" (Laughter) No, God will provide everything, whatever is necessary.

Now notice verse 40, and verse 40 and 41 is the key that unlocks the timing of Genesis 15. "Now the sojourning of the children of Israel, who dwelt in Egypt, *was* four hundred and thirty years. And it came to pass at the end of the four hundred and thirty years, even the selfsame day..." Now that's comparing something four hundred and thirty years earlier is it? Otherwise why mention the four hundred and thirty years, because that's referring to what happened in Genesis 15 and why mention the selfsame day in reference to something that occurred four hundred and thirty years before? The reason is because it's the same day of the year and of the month that occurred with the promises given to Abraham in Genesis 15. "...Even the selfsame day it came to pass, that all the hosts of the LORD went out from the land of Egypt." Now then, let's read verse 42, because some say that in observing the "Night Much to be Observed", we are adding something to the Word of God. Well, did we sneak into your house and put it in your Bible last night? (Laughter) No, of course not. "It is a night to be much observed unto the LORD for bringing them out from the land of Egypt..." when did they come out? We'll see. The night after the Passover which then was in the fifteenth day of the first month, and the Passover was the fourteenth. "...This is that night of the LORD to be observed of all the children of Israel in their generations." Because as it says, He brought them out of the land of Egypt. In other words, they started their trip out. We find that back in Chapter 12 and verse 17, we read that. Now we see where it is fulfilled that it happened that way (Exodus 12:32-42).

Now let's come down here to Chapter 13, and let's see what this day commemorates and what Moses told them to remember. And I think the movie *The Ten Commandments* with the Exodus, I think they did a very good job on the timing and showing it, and I thought it was interesting that the Jews who gave the timing in the production of it, had it right. None of them went out of the houses until morning, they assembled at Rameses, and they left Rameses just as the fourteenth was ending and the fifteenth was beginning and as you will read in the Passover book, it took quite a while for all of them to get out of Rameses, because when the children of Israel left, they couldn't all start marching at the same time and get out at the same time. That's why they came out by night. Now I'm sure that this is what Moses said as they were ready to leave and I think that the movie, *The Ten Commandments* has it right. He stood up there and they actually read the words from the Bible, verse 3: "And Moses said to the people, 'Remember this day, in which you came out from Egypt, out of the house of bondage; for by strength of hand the LORD brought you out from this *place*: there shall no leavened bread be eaten. This day came you out in the month Abib." So when you follow it through correctly, there are two days. And that follows along with what was given there in Genesis 15 (Exodus 13:3-4).

Now let's come to Numbers 33, because this gives another bit of information for us. Let's begin right here in verse 1: "These *are* the journeys of the children of Israel, which went forth out of the land of Egypt with their armies under the hand of Moses and Aaron. And Moses wrote their goings out according to their journeys by the commandment of the LORD: and these *are* their journeys according to their goings out. They departed from Rameses in the first month, on the fifteenth day of the month; on the morrow after the Passover the children of Israel went out with an high hand in the sight of all the Egyptians." Verse 4: "For the Egyptians buried all *their* firstborn" They were probably burying them as quickly as they could on the day portion of the Passover day when the Israelites were coming down to Rameses. So they buried all their firstborn "…which the LORD had smitten among them: upon their gods also the LORD executed judgments. And the children of Israel removed from Rameses, and pitched in Succoth." And then it tells the rest of the beginning of their journeys and the crossing of the Red Sea (Numbers 33:1-5).

One question—let's come to Leviticus 23 and let's ask a question here because this becomes important. Now the question is this: where did God ever say to combine the fourteenth and the fifteenth into a one-day observance? Nowhere, that's correct, nowhere. Just like, where did God ever say that He abrogated the Sabbath, the seventh day and instituted the first day? Nowhere. Now here in Leviticus 23 and then we'll look at Numbers 28 for just a minute and we'll see the difference here. Verse 4: " 'These *are* the feasts of the LORD, *even* holy convocations, which you shall proclaim in their seasons.' " God doesn't give us an option. " 'In the fourteenth *day* of the first month at even' " *ben ha arbayim*, the beginning of the day, " '…is the LORD's Passover.' " However, later you can combine them together. That's the missing verse. Don't they wish it was there? (Laughter) No it isn't there. Verse 6: "…on the fifteenth day of the same month *is* the feast of unleavened bread unto the LORD: seven days you must eat unleavened bread.' " Then the first day, the seventh day and so forth. OK, it doesn't say that (Leviticus 23:4-6).

Now let's go to Numbers 28 and here is a key, a profound key. And sometimes you get something so simple or it is so simple that you overlook what it is really telling you. Now he starts out the first part of Numbers 28, you have the morning and the evening sacrifice, and it gives everything that needed to be there. Then verse 9 he has the Sabbath day, which is a special sacrifice in addition to the daily sacrifice. Then we have verse 11, in the beginning of your months you have sacrifice there, and it lists all the things that would be there and that's in addition to the daily sacrifice.

Now come down here to verse 16. Now what He is doing, He is giving the temple sacrifice for all the days, beginning with the daily sacrifice, the evening and the morning sacrifice, the monthly sacrifice, the Sabbath sacrifice. Now verse 16 of Numbers 28: " 'And in the fourteenth day of the first month *is* the Passover of the LORD. ' " Now what does this verse tells us—by its conspicuous absence. God never required a temple sacrifice on the Passover day other than the morning and the evening sacrifice, or if it was on the Sabbath, the Sabbath sacrifice in addition. There is no God-authorized temple sacrifice of Passover lambs on the Passover day at the temple. So this simple little verse wipes out all of the traditions of the Jews—one fell swoop (Numbers 28:16-18).

Now notice verse 17: " 'And in the fifteenth day of this month *is* the feast: seven days shall unleavened bread be eaten.' " The first day holy convocation, you shall sacrifice and then on every day. Verse 24 it says, " 'After this manner you shall offer daily, throughout the seven days, the meat of the sacrifice made by fire, of a sweet savor unto the LORD: it shall be offered beside the continual burnt offering, and his drink offering. On the seventh day you shall have an holy convocation; you shall do no servile work' " verse 18. So there you have it. One simple verse tells you God never required the Passover lamb to be sacrificed at the tabernacle or the temple, which then is a later addition that the Jews added. Now that should help answer all the things concerning some of the "recycled heresies"—that's what they are.

Now there was an article in the latest journal which said that God makes no difference between the fourteenth and fifteenth. I don't know what Bible she is reading.

Now let's look at some more things. Let's come to Psalm 105 and let's see here a little summary of what we have just gone through and what we need to be doing. Now, when they left Rameses, they had to follow God and they had to trust God. And God put them through circumstances to test them. Now let's pick it up here in verse 36: "He smote also all the firstborn in their land, the chief of all their strength. He brought them forth also with silver and gold: and *there was* not one feeble *person* among their tribes." It's amazing. God prepared all of Israel though they didn't know it beforehand that there wasn't one feeble person and all those who were old had the strength and energy to walk and to go on the exodus—an amazing feat isn't it? Does God prepare ahead of time, even though we don't know that God is doing it—of course. "Egypt was glad when they departed...." I <u>guess</u>! "...For the fear of them fell upon them. He spread a cloud for a covering..." Now you're not going to go wandering out in the desert if the sun is going to be beating down on you. So not only did God prepare them so there would be no feeble ones among them when they left, but He also gave them a cloud covering. And on a real hot day, aren't you glad when a cloud comes by if you're out there working? Well, walking is work. Hiking out of Egypt and in the desert was work. So He put a cloud over them. "...And fire to give light by night." That's an amazing thing. God did this so that they would have trust in Him—that they would look to God. Verse 40: "*The people* asked, and he brought quails, and satisfied them with the bread of heaven." Even in the wilderness, God is able to provide. Nothing is impossible for God. "He opened the rock, and the waters gushed out; and they ran in the dry places *like* a river. For he remembered his promise, *and* Abraham his servant." So their exodus goes back to His promise to Abraham. The Passover that we have today, goes back to Abraham. And just like the children of Israel were brought out of the land of Egypt on the first day of the Feast of Unleavened Bread, that pictures our coming out of the world too.

Verse 43: "And he brought forth his people with joy, *and* his chosen with gladness; and gave them the lands of the heathen: and they inherited the labor of the people...." So therefore, when they harvested, the sheaf of the firstfruits, because as you know from the tapes we've sent out, the letter that I sent out concerning when we have a Passover on the Sabbath day, that the day following the Passover is the day of the Wave Sheaf offering and explained all of that through Joshua the 5th chapter because God specifically said in Leviticus 23, "You shall not eat any bread, nor grain, nor parched grain until you come into the land and when you harvest its harvest, cut the wave sheaf." Then you can eat the grain. So Joshua 5 recorded that they did and what happened on the day after they did that? The manna ceased. No more bread from heaven. Now I imagine they were happy that they had other things to eat. Nevertheless, that's all part of the covenant that God gave in the promise to Abraham.

Now notice why He did this, "...they inherited the labor of the people" verse 44, now verse 45. Why? Why has God called us out of the world? Remember in the final prayer that

Jesus gave there in John 17. He said, "They are not of the world even as I am not of the world." See He calls us out of the world. Why? "They might observe his statutes, and his laws. Praise ye the LORD." That's why. So we can love and worship God (Psalm 105:36-45).

Now let's go just a few pages over to Psalm 108. Now here is what all of this is to do for us. This shows the kind of heart and mind and attitude that we need to have. Psalm 108:1: "O GOD, my heart is fixed…." God doesn't want us changing with the vicissitudes of the world. And just like the children of Israel even though God did everything for them, led them out. What was the first thing that they did when Moses wasn't around? Well, they went and made a golden calf and worshipped it, didn't they. Their hearts weren't fixed. Their hearts were still back in Egypt. So this is something that's important for us. The only way that we come to have our hearts fixed with God is to love God and keep His commandments. And that's why in keeping the Passover and Feast of Unleavened Bread, it gives us a renewal to dedicate ourselves so that our hearts are fixed! Then we won't be changeable. Now some people might accuse us of stubbornness or hardheadedness, or whatever, but if it is stubbornness for God and hardheadedness for God, that's good! "…I will sing and give praise even with my glory." Now he talks about here, verse 4: "For your mercy is great above the heavens…." And that's what God is showing with the Passover and the sacrifice of Christ and that through His grace He gives us the opportunity to have direct access to God's mercy. "For your mercy *is* great above the heavens: and your truth *reaches* unto the clouds." And that's what we are after, brethren. And that's what God wants us to show and teach and do—the truth of God. Everything is based on the love of God and the truth of God. Verse 6: "That your beloved may be delivered:" And isn't that what the Feast of Unleavened Bread is all about—being delivered from sin, being delivered from self, being delivered from Satan? Yes, indeed. "…Save *with* your right hand, and answer me. God has spoken in his holiness; I will rejoice, I will divide Shechem, and mete out the valley of Succoth" (Psalm 108:1, 4-7).

Now drop down here to Psalm 108, verse 11: "*Will you* not, O God, who has cast us off? Will you not, O God, go forth with our hosts?" See, this pictures God being with us—God being in us. Verse 12: "Give us help from trouble: for vain is the help of man. Through God we will do valiantly:" It's by His power, His might, and His way. "…For he *it is that* shall tread down our enemies." **So remember this: whatever difficulty, whatever problem you have, as I mentioned last night during the Passover, God is there to help you. Now He may let you go a long time before He intervenes. You may have a trial and difficulty, but sooner or later if God is dealing with you, He is going to bring you to the conclusion that He wants you to come to, your trust in Him** (Psalm 108: 11-13).

Now let's come to Psalm 112 here. Verse 1: "Praise ye the LORD. Blessed is the man *that* fears the LORD." And the fear of the LORD is to lead to the love of the LORD. "…*That* delights greatly in his commandments." See because how many people are out there in the world—and what is the carnal mind—"not subject to the law of God neither, indeed, can be." So they are all out there making their excuses why they won't obey God—regardless of what they are. Now notice, here is promise. "His seed shall be mighty upon the earth: the generation of the upright shall be blessed. Wealth and riches *shall be* in his house…" (Psalm 112:1-3).

Now what I want you to think about is this—hold your place here and come to John 14. When you go through and read some of these things, let's look at the spiritual fulfillment of it. Let's look and see what Jesus said. Let's think about the house that we are going to be in, because on the Passover night Jesus talks about the Fathers house doesn't He? And what is that going to be like? And how much wealth is going to be there? I mean first of all, you start off that you're going to live forever. Now how much is that worth? I mean you can't measure that in terms of physical wealth or anything like that, can you? No. And notice this, John 14:1 " 'Let not your heart be troubled. You believe in God; believe also in Me. In My Father's house are many dwelling places;' " or that is dwelling places " '…if it were otherwise, I would have told you. I am going to prepare a place for you.' " And God is preparing that place. God is making that place. Verse 3: " 'And if I go and prepare a place for you, I will come again…' " Now this is why it is so important for us to understand that every word of God is God-breathed—meaning that it came forth out of the mouth of God and that His inspiration to those who wrote it was a special inspiration above and beyond what we get. We're to get inspiration from what God embedded in the words and the inspiration out of it, you see. But they were inspired to write it this way. And every word of God is true. So we can count on it. Christ is coming again!

Now let's come down here to verse 6, because this tells us all about Passover, the days of unleavened bread and leading up to the first resurrection. Verse 6: " Jesus said to him, 'I am the way, and the truth, and the life; no one comes to the Father, except through me' " (John 14:1-3, 6).

Now if we understand that and live God's way and realize that back here in Psalm 112, let's turn back there, that God says to those who keep His laws and commandments and fear Him, we can say, and love Him, verse 3: "Wealth and riches *shall be* in his house." What is the wealth and riches that God is going to give us? You go back to Genesis 15. What did God tell Abraham? He took him out at night and said, "You look at the stars and count them if you can. So shall your seed be." The wealth of the universe is going to be given to God's family, and those who are the firstborn. What is it that the firstborn always is given in the inheritance—a double portion. So we being in the church of the firstborn are going to have a double portion forever! So it is greater than wealth and riches here in Psalm 112. Verse 4: "Unto the upright there arises light in the darkness…" Just like the pillar of fire at night that gave light to them. "…*He is* gracious, and full of compassion, and righteous." That's how God treats us.

Now think about it this way. We know that in keeping the commandments of God, it says, there is great reward—that is true. But if we keep the commandments of God, first of all because we love Him and we know He loves us, now then, we are establishing the commandments of God through a personal relationship with God rather than just the statutes and codes that are written. So that becomes far much more meaningful does it not? Yes, indeed. So this is quite a thing.

Let's drop down here to verse 7: "He shall not be afraid of evil tidings: his heart is fixed, trusting in the LORD. His heart is established, he shall not be afraid, until he sees *his desire* upon his enemies." Now when are we going to see the desire of God and God's vengeance upon the enemies? When we are all standing on the Sea of Glass and the seven last plagues are poured out on the earth and we can see it. I tell you, that's something [when you] put all these things together (Psalm 112:7-8).

Now let's come back here to Psalm 46. Now as we are going through these things, let's also look and see how that every one of the things that we are covering as described in the Scriptures is doing what? It's putting out the leaven of human nature isn't it? And it is putting out the leaven of self.

Now notice here in Psalm 46. This is how it happens when you are trusting God, you see. Verse 1: "GOD *is* our refuge and strength, a very present help in trouble." Never forget that. Whatever the trouble is—God is there. "Therefore we will not fear, though the earth be removed and though the mountains be carried into the midst of the sea:" That's how God wants us to have trust and faith in Him, and that's why the Feast of Unleavened Bread—to get rid of trust in self. Now notice how this goes into the Kingdom of God. Verse 4: "*There is* a river, the waters thereof shall make glad the city of God, the holy *place* of the tabernacles of the most High. God *is* in the midst of her; she shall not be moved: God shall help her, *and that* right early. The heathen raged, the kingdoms were moved: he uttered his voice, the earth melted." Boy, those are powerful words! God is going to intervene and do this. This is something! "The LORD of hosts is with us; the God of Jacob is our refuge...." Now just put in your margin there, Romans 8:31, "...If God *is* for us, who *can be* against us?" Verse 8: "Come behold the works of the LORD, what desolations he has made in the earth." And that's why all of these things have happened.

Now I saw a very interesting picture. It was taken back when Napoleon Bonaparte took a small expeditionary force and went down into Egypt and conquered it (I think it was what—I forget the exact year it was—it was like 1796), and he stood there and looked at the Sphinx, and I have never seen a picture like this. You know how high the level of the ground was at the time he was there to look at the Sphinx? It was clear up to the neck of the Sphinx.

Now I believe God has done two things—He has inspired that men know more about the heavens than ever before, and more about the production of human life and how profound and precious that is. So for those who have eyes to see, and ears to hear, they will learn. He has also given us another witness. They are excavating all these places. What is the Sphinx now? Well, they got all the dirt down from it, they've got even the villages where the workers worked, they've got that all excavated out. Why? Not show how great Egypt was, but to show how absolutely sinful, and inadequate, and occult that Egypt was and why God judged it.

But you know human beings don't get the point. You can go to Las Vegas and here is the Luxor Motel in the shape of a Pyramid and those who go in there actually go through some modified religious rituals that those who went into the Egyptian religions would go through! So we have the same thing here. Don't we? Yes. God has separated us from it. And here is what He is going to do. Verse 8: "...behold the works of the LORD, what desolations he has made in the earth. He makes wars to cease unto the end of the earth...." That's the ultimate end isn't it? "...He breaketh the bow, and cutteth the spear in sunder; he burneth the chariot in the fire." You just read Revelation 16 and 19 and Revelation 8 and 9 in conjunction with that. Verse 10: "Be still, and know that I *am* God: I will be exalted among the heathen, I will be exalted in the earth. The LORD of hosts *is* with us; the God of Jacob *is* our refuge. Selah" That's why having God protect us and watch over us and that's what is pictured with the Feast of Unleavened Bread as well (Psalm 46:1-11).

Now let's come to, since we're here in the Book of Psalms, let's come to Psalm 27, and this brings this all together. Notice how this ties in with the theme of the Feast of Unleavened Bread, leaving Egypt and all of that. Verse 1: "The LORD *is* my light..." That's what God provided wasn't it. "...And my salvation..." He brought them out of Egypt didn't He. Same thing with us today—The Lord is our light, He has brought us out of Egypt, He is our salvation. "...Whom shall I fear? The LORD *is* the strength of my life; of whom shall I be afraid?" See so what God wants us to do is to take all of our sins and problems and the difficulties that we have, bring them to light before God and have them put in proper perspective that they are not as great as they appear to us when we ask God to fight our battles for us. That's why God does not want us to be held down by any of the problems of sin. That's why He has given the Feast of Unleavened Bread. That's why Jesus said on the Passover night, "Now you are clean through the words which I have spoken." So that's really profound! Don't be afraid of anything.

Now notice, verse 2: "When the wicked, *even* mine enemies and my foes, came upon me to eat up my flesh, they stumbled and fell." That will happen. I look back and see many different things how God has intervened for many, many brethren in their lives, and I see it in my life, that God has just intervened and caused people to just turn away. And He has fought the battles for us. Now notice how much confidence we are to have. So if God is our refuge and we are trusting in God notice this, "Though a host should encamp against me, my heart shall not fear: though war should rise against me, in this I *will* be confident." Verse 4: "One *thing* have I desired of the LORD, that will I seek after; that I may dwell in the house of the LORD all the days of my life..." you see how that ties in with the other Psalm and John 14? That's our desire. This is what we are to set our hearts and minds on, because this is what God is going to do to fulfill for us.

Now talk about the enemy, in the days of Hezekiah, what happened? The Asyrians came down and were mopping up everybody and even sent one of the ambassadors to go to the walls of Jerusalem and tell the people, "Don't believe anything that Hezekiah is going to tell you that God is going to fight for you, because look what we have done to all these other countries—we have wiped them out with our god." And so Hezekiah took it to God and said, "Yeah, LORD, what he says is true, that's what they have done." And God said, "I'll fight for you." And if we trust in God, He'll fight for us, and He'll bring it to pass, because this is our focus here—to be in the house of the Lord. Now continuing verse 4: "...To behold the beauty of the LORD, and to inquire in his temple. For in time of trouble he shall hide me in his pavilion:" Those are the wings of an eagle there in Psalm 91. "...In the secret of his tabernacle he shall hide me; he shall set me upon a rock" (Psalm 27:105). That's what He is going to do. That's tremendous.

Now let's come back here to the last verse, no, verse 11: "Teach me your way O LORD, and lead me in a plain path, because of mine enemies. Deliver me not over to the will of mine enemies: for false witnesses are risen up against me, and such as breathe out cruelty." Now that's a prophecy of what happened to Christ. "I had fainted, unless I had believed to see the goodness of the LORD in the land of the living." Verse 14: "Wait on the LORD..." That's the key, wait on the Lord and "...be of good courage..." not discouraged "... and he shall strengthen your heart: wait, I say, on the LORD" (Psalm 27:11-14). And that's what God wants us to do. That's how great it is.

Let's come to Psalm 62. Let's see how we are to trust in God. That's what this Feast of Unleavened Bread pictures. You know the children of Israel had to trust God for everything, didn't they? Had to trust God to take them out of Egypt, go through the Red Sea, to give them food, to give them water, all in the wilderness, to keep the cloud-cover in the daytime and the pillar of fire by night, and they had manna for 40 years. You would think that after 40 years it would be so ingrained in their brains which day was the Sabbath, right, that they would never forget it. But you see human beings are not like that. That's why we have to be renewed. That's why we have to be reinvigorated every year. That's why God has the Passover and the Feast of Unleavened Bread, so we can take all of the things and all of the mistakes and everything that has been done this past year even though we repented of them along the way, and we can know that we are starting anew. That God has called us, that God has loved us, that He is going to fight for us, see? That's what's important.

Psalm 62:1 "Truly my soul waits upon God; from him *comes* my salvation. He only *is* my rock and my salvation; *he is* my defense; I shall not be greatly moved. How long will you imagine mischief against a man? Ye shall be slain all of you: as a bowing wall *shall you be, and as* a tottering fence" because see, all of the things that are happening in the world are building to the crescendo. They are building the wall with untempered morter and when it falls it is going to be breathtaking! Verse 4: "They only consult to cast *him* down from his excellency: they delight in lies: they bless with their mouth, but they curse inwardly." That's just the way it is in the world. Verse 5: "O my soul, wait you only upon God; for my expectation *is* from him. He only *is* my rock and my salvation: *he is* my defense; I shall not be moved." See now you can come to that conviction of mind through the Spirit of God, through the Word of God, through the conviction that comes of it, you see. Verse 7: "In God *is* my salvation and my glory: the rock of my strength, and my refuge, *is* in God." Now notice verse 8, here is the key and this is one of the lessons that we need to learn continuously in life, but also to have it during the Feast of Unleavened Bread: "Trust in him at all times; you people…" trust in Him at all times. Now you can tell when you are not trusting in God at all times. That is when you try and do something and God is not behind it and it keeps failing—set it aside, take another course. Instead of seeking your way, seek God's way. Instead of seeking what you want, seek what God's wants to give you. That's what to do. "Trust in him at all times; you people, pour out your heart before him: God *is* a refuge for us" (Psalm 62:1-8).

Now just go a little diagonal across the page, Psalm 60:11 "Give us help from trouble: for vain *is* the help of man. Verse 12: "Through God we shall do valiantly: for he *it is that* shall tread down our enemies" (Psalm 60:11-12). Now you take this posture, claim these promises in your prayer and in your study, beseech God. Now you see, here is what's important. Here is how to overcome any lack of faith that you may have toward that. God cannot lie, and God will not lie! So when you go before God, you claim the promises that He has given, and remind God that He does not lie, cannot lie, and He has promised. But now then, you have to trust in Him and wait on Him, and He will provide in the time, and that time will be the time that He determines.

Now notice Psalm 62:9: "Surely men of low degree *are* vanity, *and* men of high degree *are* a lie:" I love it when you look around and see all these important men and all these important institutions and whatever and you read here what the Bible says—they are not what they appear to be. That's what God tells us. "…To be laid in the balance, they *are* altogether *lighter* than vanity." Verse 10: "Trust not in oppression, and become not vain in robbery: if riches increase, set not your heart *upon them.*" Keep your heart set upon God. Verse 11: "God has spoken once; twice have I heard this; that power *belongs* unto God. Also unto you, O LORD, *belongs* mercy: for you will render to every man according to his work" (Psalm 62:9-12). So that is really quite profound and something isn't it?

Let's end up by going to Matthew 7, since God is our rock and Christ is the rock and upon Him we are to build, notice what He says here. Matthew 7:24, now this doesn't include just what Jesus said verbally while He was in the flesh on the earth, because He was the Lord God of the Old Testament. So whenever we read anything in the Old Testament, they are the words of God and fulfills what Jesus said, "Man shall not live by bread alone, but every word that proceeds out of the mouth of God, shall man live." Now here Matthew 7:24: " 'Therefore, everyone who hears these words of Mine and practices them…' " that's what *doeth* in the King James means—*practices* them.

Like He said, "I am the way, and the truth, and the life.." (John 14:6). " '… I will liken him to a wise man, which built his house upon a rock.' " Of course, Christ is the Rock. Verse 25: " 'And the rain came down,' " Now [I] think of the weather channel and some of the movies that they show when I'm reading this. "…And the rain came down, and the floods came, and the winds blew, and beat upon that house…" So this means you are guaranteed trials, right? That's how you are going to build spiritual character, because it teaches you to trust in God. "…but it did not fall, for it was founded upon the rock." And that's what we need to do to build our lives.

Now notice those who don't do it. " 'And everyone who hears these words of Mine and does not practice them shall be compared to a foolish man, who built his house upon the sand;…" Now that's always tempting isn't it? I know down where we live we have a city called Sand City—right next to Monterey and Seaside. And all the contractors love to build there because sand is so easy to work with, because you can pour the foundation easy, it's easy to move and it compacts and everything and it looks really, really, really good. Just like this wonderful subdivision that was up in Utah, and they had a beautiful mountain scene and the river ran right in front of them and it was just gorgeous and they lived there for many years and enjoyed it, until one year when what—the rains came, the flood came, and the wind blew and washed away all those houses. And they showed it on the weather channel, and I tell you there is nothing more heart-wrenching, and that gets you in the pit of the stomach more than to see someone's house—the whole thing just go…. Well now there is a good lesson for us isn't there? Yes. We need to build upon the Rock. "…Beat upon that house; and it fell, and great was the fall of it" (Matthew 7:24-27). I mean how are you going to repair it? There is no repair; it's gone! So this is why we need to trust in God.

So tonight we are going to enjoy the "Night Much to be Observed" and it's not a concoction of a man, but it is what God says for us to do.

End of Sermon

Transcriber: Judith Anderson

The Passover Exodus and Trusting God
September 5, 2005
Scriptural References

1) Exodus 10:21-29

2) Exodus 11:1-10

3) Exodus 12:1-14, 21-28

4) Exodus 12:15-18

5) Exodus 12:29-31

6) Exodus 11:8

7) Exodus 12:32-42

8) Exodus 13:3-4

9) Numbers 33:1-5

10) Leviticus 23:4-6

11) Numbers 28:8-9, 11, 16-18, 24-25

12) Psalm 105:36-45

13) Psalm 108:1, 4-7, 11-13

14) Psalm 112:1-3

15) John 14:1-3, 6

16) Psalm 112:4, 7-8

17) Psalm 46:1-11

18) Psalm 27:1-5, 11-14

19) Psalm 62:1-8

20) Psalm 60:11-12

21) Psalm 62:9-12

22) Matthew 7:24-27

Section IV

The Feast of Unleavened Bread

CHAPTER THIRTEEN

The Night to Be Much Observed

April 12, 2006

What is the meaning of the Night to be Much Observed, and why should we keep it? Now we have already been covering on some other tapes, why the Night to be Much Observed is <u>not</u> the Passover night, so we're going to concentrate on the meaning of the Night to be Much Observed, which then begins the first day of the Feast of Unleavened Bread. Let's come to Exodus 12 and let's see where this is mentioned; let's see where it's commanded, and then we are going to see a very astounding statement which tells us something very important concerning that night and why we should observe it.

Now let's come to Exodus 12:37. All the details concerning the Passover and leading up to this we have already covered on other tapes, so I want to cover specifically, the meaning of the Night to be Much Observed. Now let's pick it up here in verse 40: "Now the sojourning of the children of Israel, who dwelt in Egypt, *was* four hundred and thirty years." Now that is a key statement to look at, because this gives a reference to something else, as we will see. Verse 41: "And it came to pass at the end of the four hundred and thirty years, even the selfsame day…" Or you could say on that very same day… "…It came to pass, that all the hosts of the LORD went out from the land of Egypt." Now this reference cannot refer to the Passover, because the Passover, the first time they took it was when—the night before. So it can't be referring to the Passover—the selfsame day—does not refer to the Passover, but it refers to something else that had occurred four hundred and thirty years earlier. Verse 42: "It *is* a night to be much observed unto the LORD for bringing them out from the land of Egypt: this *is* that night of the LORD to be observed of all the children of Israel in their generations." So here is the command—special command (Exodus 12:40-42).

Now we can understand that this is not the Passover from this point of view: that on the Passover, they were to keep the Passover and when they ate it, it was to be eaten in trepidation. That's what the Hebrew means. Now this one here, notice, the night to be much observed: one, there are no sacrifices they are to give at this point here on the first one. Later they would be giving sacrifices at the temple, but here they are leaving Egypt. So this is the first start. And so let's come over here to verse 51: "And it came to pass the selfsame day, that the LORD did bring the children of Israel out of the land of Egypt by their armies." That's talking about the day they left. Now that's where the chapter break should be. Verse 51 should actually be verse 1, Chapter 13, because verse 50 comes to a full stop, boom, and this is a whole new subject (Exodus 12:51).

Now we're going to see something about this a little bit later on, but we'll take a clue here. Verse 1 of Chapter 13: "And the LORD spoke unto Moses" the selfsame day that they were coming out of Egypt "…saying, Sanctify to me all the firstborn…" Now we'll cover that as we come to the Feast of Unleavened Bread. "…Whatsoever opens the womb among the children of Israel, *both* of man and of beast: it *is* mine. And the LORD said to the people "…Remember this day, in which you came out from Egypt, out of the house of bondage; for by strength of hand the LORD brought you out from this *place*: there shall be no leavened bread eaten" (Exodus 13:1-3). So we're going to see that this day has to do with the firstborn—has to do with the sanctifying of the firstborn, and as we will see, not in this sermon about the Night to be Much Observed, maybe, I don't know—we'll see when we get to it,

198

but we will find out when we get to Deuteronomy 16, either in this tape or another tape, that the sacrifices that they gave in Deuteronomy 16 had to do with the Night to be Much Observed.

Now let's look at something else concerning leaving Egypt. Come to Numbers 33. Let's clarify this because there is a lot of confusion concerning it, and really the main portion of the confusion concerning this stems from two sources: one, the lack of a clear translation concerning *sunset* and *between the two evenings* in the King James version of the Bible and also other translations. That's one. Number two, the tradition of the Jews of keeping a fifteenth Passover instead of a fourteenth. Now why do they keep a fifteenth Passover? Well as we saw in Numbers 9, it clearly says that in order to take the Passover, they have to be in the land—within the geographical area of the land of Israel. So if they were on a journey, they could not take a fourteenth Passover. So what happened was this: When the Jews were in exile, which they still are today, they could not, and they will tell you they cannot, keep a fourteenth Passover. So they keep the Feast of Unleavened Bread but call it—the whole thing—Passover. So when they have their meal beginning the night of the fifteenth, they are actually eating an abbreviated form of the Feast of the Night to be Much Observed, and we'll see that a little bit later.

Now here, Numbers 33. Now let's look at this because this also causes confusion, and the third reason that causes confusion is this: pre-conceived notions…you come to the Scriptures with something in mind, and you're looking to prove what you have in mind. So when you read it, you think you're proving what you have in mind because you have read it and you think that that's what it's saying. Now here, Numbers 33 is part of it, verse 1: "These *are* the journeys of the children of Israel, which went forth out of the land of Egypt with their armies under the hand of Moses and Aaron. And Moses wrote their goings out according to their journeys by the commandment of the LORD: and these *are* their journeys according to their goings out. …They departed from Rameses…" Now as we saw, the Passover was kept on the night of the fourteenth. On the day portion of the fourteenth they finished spoiling the Egyptians and assembled at Rameses, and they had to come from the land of Goshen to Rameses so they could begin their march and their journey out. So, "…they departed from Rameses in the first month, on the fifteenth day of the first month;" and we know that Leviticus 23 says "on the fourteenth day is the LORD'S Passover and on the fifteenth is the first day of the feast of unleavened bread." **So this, the fifteenth, that's when they left.** "…On the morrow after the passover the children of Israel went out with an high hand in the sight of all the Egyptians. For…" or this should read "*while* the Egyptians were still burying their firstborn, which the LORD had smitten among them: upon their gods the LORD also executed judgments" (Numbers 33:1-4).

Now what is the preconceived notion that people read into this? They read into it: This must be the morning of the fifteenth. No, it doesn't say that. It doesn't say that. They left on the fifteenth… that's when they departed. That doesn't mean the whole body of them was out, but they were departing at that point. When you have a million, eight hundred thousand people that are going to be marching out, even in a wide column, you're going to get it started. The ones who are at the end are going to come along later. And as I mentioned in the Passover book: If you observe the Rose Parade in Pasadena, California, when the parade starts, two hours later, the last crew is starting while the first crew or marching band or whatever it is or float, is finishing. So when it says departed, that doesn't mean the whole mass of them had completely gone.

Now, let's come to Deuteronomy 16, we'll just look at one verse here which is important. We will come back to Deuteronomy 16 because this will be important. Okay, verse 1: "Observe the month of Abib, and keep the passover unto the LORD…" that's one day isn't it? Yes. "…For in the month of Abib the LORD your God brought you forth out of Egypt <u>by</u>

<u>night</u>." That's why it is the night to be much observed, because they came out the next night, and as I mentioned previously, show me anywhere in the Bible where God ever combined two days together. Show me one instance… where God said, "Oops! Let's combine the two days." No, men are the ones who have combined them. So they went out by night, so you put it all together. They left with a high hand. When did they start? When does the fourteenth end—sunset on the fourteenth. Is it still light when the sun is going down? Yes. Were they leaving when the sun was going down? Yes. Did they go on into the night with their exodus? Yes, but what were the Egyptians doing when they started? Numbers 33; they were still burying their firstborn.

Now when you consider the number that were dead, if they had a population of twenty-four million—or you can pick any number you want—twenty percent are firstborn, whether it's male or female. So if you have, let's just say they only had ten million, they had 2 million dead human beings. So we'll give it the low figure, we'll low-ball it. And how about all the animals, how long do you think it's going to take to bury them? How long do you think it's going to take them to bury two million people plus all the animals? Because you know, Egypt is a hot place, and if you don't bury them right away, what happens? These gigantic flies about as big around as a half-dollar piece, come in and the buzzards and the vultures, and if you don't get them buried they get in the hot, hot sun and the bodies explode. (Comment: the question was asked: Do you think they might have burned some of them?) Who knows? It doesn't say they burned them, it says they buried them. But anyway…that's a big task, which means that you only had, counting all women and children, you only had eight million to bury two million. So if you say the adult males that were left who had to do the work and maybe some of the adult females, then you're probably down to a couple of million. (Comment: The comment was made: [Numbers 33] verse 4 in the King James says: "…The Egyptians buried all their firstborn…") And that took more than just on the day portion of the Passover to accomplish that.

See they went out with a high hand in the sight of all the Egyptians who were, what, burying their dead. Now obviously when it got dark they would quit. But obviously, if you watch anything like…Dolores watched a historical presentation of Trablinka where they started killing Jews as early as 1941, I believe, and they killed 900,000 in one place. So Trablinka was in Poland, the Nazis were killing the Polish Jews, and they would gas them and put them in this big pit, and then they would even put some lime to try and get rid of the bodies, but they couldn't do it. And they had so many dead in this big pit, and the stench was getting so bad that they had to dig them up and burn them. So when it says here "for the Egyptians buried all their firstborn…" that doesn't mean they did it on that one day.

Now they went out at night, the Night to be Much Observed, and they went out with a high hand. Now this is far different than the Passover night, which was, what, a night of fear, a night of terror, a night of trepidation.

So now, you have two operations going here: The Passover you are <u>redeemed</u>, and the Night to be Much Observed you are <u>delivered</u>. So now you're coming out.

Now let's come back here to Exodus 12 and let's read this again, and let's focus in on the time period, because the phrase "four hundred and thirty years…on the selfsame day" and we'll ask the question: What does that refer to? And what was the selfsame day? Now we know that according to the Hebrew Calendar, the selfsame day was the fifteenth. We just read it Numbers 33, right? Yes.

Now what we are going to do, we're going to find out that this actually goes back to Abraham, and God's covenant with Abraham in Genesis 15. So let's go to Genesis 15. What we're going to see in Genesis 15, is quite a tremendous thing, and then we will also go to

Genesis 22. Genesis 15 and what we are going to see is this: we are going to see a two-day sequence, which involves two nights. And the second night of which we will see is referred to in Exodus 12 as the "…selfsame day…" four hundred and thirty years later. **So in fact, we are going to see that the source and the origin of the Passover and the Night to be Much Observed began actually in Genesis 15.** Now let's come to verse 1: "After these things the word of the LORD came unto Abram in a vision, saying, Fear not, Abram: I *am* your shield, *and* your exceeding great reward. And Abram said, Lord GOD, what will you give me, seeing I go childless, and the steward of my house is this Eliezer of Damascus? And Abram said, Behold, to me you have given no seed: and, lo, one born in my house is mine heir." So he could adopt him and designate him as his heir. Verse 4: "And behold, the word of the LORD came unto him saying, This shall not be your heir; but he that shall come forth out of your own bowels shall be your heir." So this is the promise of Isaac, and also then, the promise which comes down to Jacob and to the twelve tribes of Israel.

Now notice, verse 5 is a key verse: "And he brought him forth abroad, and said, Look now toward heaven, and tell the stars, if you be able to number them:" Now when do you see the stars—at night—so we are dealing with the night. You can't see them at noon, you can't see them at sunrise, maybe you can see a few faint stars, you can't see them at sunset, except maybe a few faint stars and maybe what we call Venus and Mars today. So there must have been a lot of stars out there because He said, "…And tell…" or that is count "…the stars if you are able to number them: and he said unto him, So shall your seed be" (Genesis 15:1-5). So we have two promises here don't we, of seed: One, of Isaac the physical seed and, two, the stars of heaven which then are the spiritual seed. Because what did Jesus say? Just hold your place here and come to Matthew 13:43 and let's look at this and then Daniel 12 and we will see what the stars of heaven represent in the promise of the spiritual seed. Matthew 13:43, now this is at the return of Christ. This is talking about the resurrection. Now a little later we're going to see that we are Abraham's seed and heirs according to the promise. So the promise was given in Genesis 15: Number one of the physical seed Isaac, number two, of the spiritual seed…that would be those in the first resurrection. And notice what Jesus says of those in the first resurrection at His return, verse 43: "Then shall the righteous shine forth as the sun in the kingdom of their Father." Then He has this little cryptic statement here. "…Who has ears to hear let him hear." Now the only way you're going to understand it is if God gives you the understanding through His Word.

Now let's come back to Daniel 12 and let's look at what it says here concerning the righteous because, you see, when you understand that the sun is what; what is the sun? It's a star, right? Yes. Now let's pick it up here in verse 1 of Daniel 12: "And at that time…" that's the time of the end, the time of the resurrection, "…shall Michael stand up, the great prince which stands for the children of your people: and there shall be a time of trouble, such as never was since there was a nation *even* to that same time: and at that time your people shall be delivered, every one that shall be found written in the book." Now that's the Book of Life and this has to be the first resurrection.

Verse 2: "And many of them that sleep in the dust of the earth…" shows they were buried, "…shall awake, some to everlasting life, and some to shame *and* everlasting contempt." Now that's for those who commit the unpardonable sin and face the second death at the end of the Millennium and one hundred-year period.

Now notice verse 3: "And they that be wise shall shine as the brightness of the firmament; and they that turn many to righteousness as the stars for ever and ever" (Daniel 12:1-3). So the promise given to Abraham back here, has some big-time promises doesn't it? So that's why He said to him, as He took him out at night. Now remember [there was] no smog, no pollution, no city lights, you could see all the stars, and I'm sure that was greater… because Texas in America claims that you can see the stars clearer in Texas than any place.

201

But I just imagine that this was a whole lot better. Now notice verse 6 [Genesis 15] because you see what God asked him to do was an impossible task… So, "he believed in the LORD…" so you have to believe what God says. Now if you are dealing with God who is a God of truth, which He is, and His Word is true, which it is, and God cannot lie, which He cannot… let's come back here to Genesis 15 and let's pick it up here in verse 6. So he believed in the LORD for, what, the two promises: physical seed and the resurrected spiritual seed—very important. "…He believed in the LORD; and it was accounted to him for righteousness (or imputed to him for righteousness)." But as we know, that has nothing to do with whether he kept the Commandments of God, or not. **This was a greater righteousness—this righteousness is [being] put in right standing with God because you believe Him.**

Verse 7: "And then he said unto him, I *am* the LORD; who brought you out of Ur of the Chaldees, to give you this land to inherit it. And he said, Lord GOD, whereby shall I know that I shall inherit it?" Now as we're going to see we are on the day-portion of that day. Yes he was talking about the Promised Land, he was in the land of Canaan, but he dwelt in it never having received an inheritance in it yet. And when He says to inherit it, that includes all of his progeny as we will see. So, "… he said, Lord GOD, whereby shall I know that I shall inherit it? And he said unto him, Take me an heifer of three years old, and a she goat of three years old, and a ram of three years old, and a turtledove, and a young pigeon." Now all of these were also later used for sacrifices at the temple. But it is interesting, three years old, so you're talking about good-sized animals, right? And we are going to see that this a special sacrifice. There is no altar that is there to burn them on, there is no splashing the blood upon any altar at all, and here is what he did. Verse 10: "And he took unto him all these, and divided them in the middle…" cut them in half from head to toe.

Now when you do that, if you have watched any of the wild life documentaries on how lions get buffalo and tear them apart and eat them, so just think of this as about the size of a buffalo, African buffalo. Slit the throat and then you cut it down the middle. Now how are you going to cut it down the middle? Well, you have to virtually take a battle-ax and this is a very bloody affair, and you've got all the guts, you've got everything there and, "…he laid one piece against the other…" In other words, he put them back to back, and what he did in putting them back to back, he also created a path that went down between those sacrificial animals. Now this is a special sacrifice.

Now you can read of this in *The Christian Passover Book*. You can also read of it in the *Harmony of the Gospels*. In the *Harmony of the Gospels* I've got a chart which shows the sequence of events and how this also fits in with the death of Jesus, as we'll see a little bit later. "…But the birds he divided not." Now verse 11: "And when the fowls came down upon the carcases, Abram drove them away."

Now notice verse 12. Verse 12 is a key verse because this gives us a time-flow of the day and what we're going to see [is that] this is actually the time-flow of the Passover day and reflects directly to the crucifixion of Christ and the time of His death more than the Passover of the children of Israel in the land of Egypt. "And when the sun was going down…" it's still up, there is still a little…there is still some time…it was going down. So what happened to Abraham? "…A deep sleep fell upon Abram; and, lo, an horror of great darkness fell upon him." Now what was he experiencing in this, how shall we say, great vision that God brought upon him? He was experiencing death without dying—what it would be like to die. "The horror of great darkness fell upon him. And he said to Abram, Know of a surety that your seed shall be a stranger in a land *that is* not theirs, and shall serve them; and they shall afflict them four hundred years; And also that nation, whom they shall serve, will I judge: and afterward they shall come out with great substance" (Genesis 15:6-14). That's a prophecy of delivering the children of Israel out from captivity and taking them out of the land of Egypt. Now as it turned out it was a little more than the four hundred years, it was four hundred and thirty years. "But in the fourth generation…" so that gives us latitude here to understand it, "…the fourth generation, they shall come out from there again: for the iniquity of the Amorites *is* not yet full."

Now notice, verse 17 is another key. "And it came to pass that when the sun went down, and it was dark…" Now we're in to the next day. Let's see what happened. "…Behold a smoking furnace, and a burning lamp…" Now what was the smoking furnace doing? The burning lamp passed between those parts. What was Abraham actually seeing in this vision? Here is a burning lamp that's walking down between those parts and probably the smoking furnace came right behind it and devoured everything, just completely devoured it. So what this is, God is showing and prophesying His own death, prophesying His death and burial, which happened, when, on the Passover day and the beginning of the first day of the Feast of Unleavened Bread, He was, what, in the tomb.

So this is a special covenant oath, it's also known as a maledictory oath, meaning that in order to fulfill this, you pronounce upon yourself, you own death. And notice the promise, verse 18: "In the same day the LORD made a covenant with Abram, saying, Unto your seed have I given this land, from the river of Egypt unto the great river, the river Euphrates:" And then He lists all the land of the Canaanites that they would receive. So what God is doing with this, He is guaranteeing that on this second night, and we will see this became the night of the fifteenth; so that means the first night was the night of the fourteenth. So we have the Passover and the Night to be Much Observed right here at the, what you might say, the "prototype," the first fulfillment of it. He made a covenant. He is going to give the land to them, and He was also going to deliver them (Genesis 15:16-21).

Now when we come back to Exodus 12, what we're going to see [is] that this self-same day had to refer back to one, the delivering of the children of Israel through the Passover day, and two, the selfsame day (because the Passover day comes first then the next day is called the selfsame day) refers to this day that God made the covenant with Abraham that He would do it.

Now let's come back to Exodus 12 here for just a minute. Let's come back to verse 40 again and this will help us interpret this verse. "Now the sojourning of the children of Israel, who dwelt in Egypt…" which was prophesied, right? Yes. "…*Was* four hundred and thirty years. And it came to pass at the end of the four hundred and thirty years, even the selfsame day it came to pass, that all the hosts of the LORD went out from the land of Egypt. It is a night to be much observed unto the LORD for bringing them out from the land of Egypt: this *is* that night of the LORD to be observed of all the children of Israel in their generations" (Exodus 12:40-42). Why? Because He fulfilled His promise to deliver them. And He fulfilled His promise concerning the Passover day on the fourteenth, and His promise to deliver them that they would go out with great substance on the Night to be Much Observed and leave on the fifteenth. In both cases, what do we have? Two different days, two different meanings though connected. So this helps us understand the significance of the Night to be Much Observed.

Now then, let's come to Deuteronomy 16. As I have already previously explained with Deuteronomy 16 so we'll just review it here, but let's understand what is happening, and how that relates to the firstborn. Because the firstborn especially went out with a high hand, all the children of Israel did, but especially the firstborn because they were spared from death. So this was a significant thing. And all the firstborn belong to God. All the males and all the females, Deuteronomy 14 as we have seen, were brought to the Feast of Unleavened Bread and also to the Feast of Tabernacles and they were used as part of the offerings that they would give in peace offerings to God.

Now let's pick it up here in Deuteronomy 16:2, and we'll get a clue. And I remember the first time I understood this, because Deuteronomy 16 is difficult to understand because it seems to contradict some of the things in Exodus 12, and it seems to combine some the things in Exodus 12 and make it look like it comes on the same day, but it doesn't.

Now first of all, verse 1: "…Keep the passover…" When were they to keep the Passover? [They were to keep it on] The night of the fourteenth, right? That's one day, is it not? Yes. "…Unto the LORD your God: for in the month of Abib the LORD your God brought you out of Egypt by night…" which was what—the beginning of the night of the fifteenth. So then we have, getting in to the second day don't we? "You shall therefore sacrifice the passover unto the LORD your God, of the flock and the herd, in the place which the LORD shall choose to place his name there." Now I have a full explanation of that in the Passover book. You can go back and read that. It's very important to understand.

But here is the key that unlocks this so we have understanding. **This is not the sacrifice of the Passover lamb for the Passover, but this is in preparation for the Night to be Much Observed.** Now how do we know that? Notice the phrase "…of the flock and the herd…" As I have mentioned before: Have you ever heard of a Passover calf? No. What does it say there in Exodus 12? You are to take of <u>the</u> <u>flock</u> <u>of</u> <u>the</u> <u>sheep</u> <u>and</u> <u>of</u> <u>the</u> <u>goats</u>, but here it says herd. And the Hebrew here is *bovine*. **So this has to do with the <u>peace offerings</u>, now here called Passover offerings; not that they were for the Passover day, but for the Feast of Unleavened Bread.**

Now they probably started preparing these so they could be offered right at sunset beginning the Night to be Observed. **These had to be offered at the altar, not the Passover lamb.** Continuing in verse 2: "…In the place which the LORD shall choose to place his name there. You shall eat no leavened bread with it; seven days shall you eat unleavened bread therewith, *even* the bread of affliction; for you came forth out of the land of Egypt in haste: that you may remember the day when you came forth out of the land of Egypt all the days of your life. And there shall be no leavened bread seen with you in all your coast for seven days; neither shall there *any thing* of the flesh, which you sacrificed the first day at even, remain all night until the morning." Now then, that sounds an awful lot like the Passover doesn't it? But let's understand something, peace offerings could not be left until morning.

Okay, let's go on, "You may not sacrifice the passover within any of your gates…" and that sounds like it contradicts the commands for the Passover which they were to do at their homes, right? See, so this has to be the sacrifices for the first day of the Feast of Unleavened Bread. Now let's continue on and I will show you. Verse 6: "But at the place which the LORD your God shall choose to place his name in, there you shall sacrifice the passover at even, at the going down of the sun, at the season that you came out of Egypt." Now here is a <u>gross</u> <u>mistranslation</u> which is this, verse 7: "You shall roast and eat…" **that doesn't have to do with roasting at all!** The Hebrew here is *bashal* which is, "…you shall boil…" So we have two things that tells us the clue that these are really peace offerings which were prepared on the day portion of the Passover to be eaten after the Passover on the Night to be Much Observed. Those two key things are [number one], verse 7: "You shall boil…" Now we are going to see the Passover lamb was **never** to be boiled (I go into great detail in that in *The Christian Passover* book), and number 2, the bovine. There is no such thing as a Passover calf. Can you imagine for a family of ten trying to eat a calf? And can you imagine trying to burn the bones and the hide and everything of the calf? No (Deuteronomy 16:1-7).

Okay, let's look at the commands in Exodus 12 and then we will look at the command for a peace offering. Exodus 12, let's see what the command was. After they kill it, put the blood on the side posts and the lintels, verse 8: "And they shall eat the flesh in that night, roast in fire…" Now here it means roasted with fire. Now it didn't say with fire in Deuteronomy 16, did it, because that should not be roasted, that should be boiled. "…Roast with fire and unleavened bread *and* with bitter *herbs* shall they eat it. Eat not of it raw, nor (boiled) sodden (*bashal*) at all with water, but roast *with* fire…" (Exodus 12:8-9).

Now they even had this: the Jews' tradition was that if they had it on a spit and they were roasting it in the fire, and some of the juice from the roasting got on the staff that was through the middle of the animal, they were turning it kind of like a rotisserie and roasting it, and the juice cooked part of the meat, they had to cut that meat off and not use it because that was considered boiled in the juice. Now it says, "…not sodden with water at all, but roast with fire…" and so when you go back to Deuteronomy 16 and it says roast, it doesn't say roast with fire and that's because that's a gross mistranslation and should be boiled.

Now let's continue on and we will see the fulfillment of the Night to be Much Observed in the New Testament. Now, let me just say this: It follows along very logically according to the Word of God, not just human logic, that God commands to keep the Night to be Much Observed, doesn't He? It begins the first day of the Feast of Unleavened Bread doesn't it? So if you keep the Feast of Unleavened Bread, you should keep the Night to be Much Observed, shouldn't you? Yes, because you can't have one without the other.

Now the Passover book I'm going to mention again, because it's very important because it's over five hundred pages and there is not one page of wasted information in there: It is all vital and it covers every one of these questions concerning the Passover, the fourteenth, the fifteenth, unleavened bread, leavened bread, what time of day, covers foot washing, covers the Lord's supper, it covers all of that.

Now in the Passover book from pages 278 to 314, Chapters 22, 23, and 24, it covers the full meaning of the Night to be Much Observed beginning with the Passover and coming through the Passover night and Passover day and in to the Night Much to be Observed and showing the selfsame day.

Now one other thing that's important to understand is this: On page 307 of the Passover book there is a chart which shows the timing of Genesis 15 in the left-hand column and the death of Jesus Christ in the right-hand column, and how it parallels. Now there is one other thing that we need to understand concerning the fulfillment of this prophecy. Let's come to Joshua 5, and let's read it. Then we will get to the New Testament. Joshua 5, they entered the land and officially had ended the Exodus when they got to the land. Now remember the promises given back in Genesis 15 carried forward to the night that they were delivered out of Egypt four hundred and thirty years later, and also carried the promised of going into the land. And Joshua 5 and verse 10 says: "And the children of Israel encamped in Gilgal, and kept the passover on the fourteenth day of the month at even in the plains of Jericho. And they did eat of the old corn (and also the new corn) of the land on the morrow after the passover, (which is the fifteenth) unleavened cakes and parched *corn* in the selfsame day" (Joshua 5:10-11). That meant when they started eating the bread made from the grain of the land, the Exodus was officially over and they began the inheritance of the land on what day—the fifteenth day of the first month, the selfsame day. Amazing isn't it—how it follows all the way through.

Now let's come and see the parallels concerning the death and burial of Jesus Christ and what happened there…what occurred. Now we find we have the Passover ceremony, we have that in the Passover ceremony book, we're not going to review that, but that covers John, Chapters 13 through 17. Now we are not going to turn there, I'm just reading off of the chart. Now we have something that's important here when we come to Jesus being arrested. Let's come to the Book of John. Now to cover the Passover, go through the Passover ceremony booklet that we have for the Passover. Now let's come to John 18 first of all. After Jesus prayed, after His prayer, we come to the time of betrayal, John 18. Judas came about midnight. When did God spare the firstborn in Egypt? [He spared them] at midnight on the fourteenth. Jesus Christ was the firstborn of the Virgin Mary, right? Yes. He was also firstborn from among the dead…very important. But here in John 18 we have the betrayal of Christ which took place at midnight, and there are quite a few things that took place. And so what we really have on the Passover night is that God passed over the children of Israel, the firstborn, at midnight in Egypt. When Jesus came who was the firstborn of God; He did not pass over Him, because He <u>was</u> the Passover sacrifice.

Now what we are going to see is this: That the timing of the killing of those animals in Genesis 15 parallels, as you see in the chart here…parallels the timing the things that Jesus went through. And the bloody sacrifice of those animals parallels the beatings, the scourgings, and the crucifixion of Christ, and that when Christ died, that parallels the time when Abraham had a deep sleep fall upon him and the horrors of great darkness. And then when Christ was put into the tomb and it was sealed, it was sealed because you will see when was it sealed? When was He put in there? He was put in there just right at sunset.

So let's just do a little survey of John. Now if you have the Harmony of Gospels, go through and go back to about page 284 and go forward from there. So I am going to read here from John 18 and let's pick it up here in verse 1. I always ask the question: I wonder what those who arrested Jesus thought. And in the movie *The Passion* by Mel Gibson, it didn't show it really with all the meaning, there was too much Catholic tradition involved.

Now [reading from the Harmony of the Gospels, page 286] John 18, verse 1: "After saying these things, Jesus went out with His disciples *to a place* beyond the winter stream of Kidron, where *there* was a garden into which He and His disciples entered." And you find in the parallel accounts where He prayed, He actually prayed for three hours and then about midnight He quit praying, and verse 2: " And Judas, who was betraying Him, also knew of the place because Jesus had often gathered there with His disciples." Verse 3: "Then Judas, after receiving a band and officers from the chief priests and Pharisees, came there with torches and lamps and weapons. Jesus therefore, knowing all *the* things that were coming upon Him, went forward *and* said to them, 'Whom are you seeking?' " Now when it says "knowing all *the* things that were coming upon Him" what did He understand? He gave all the prophecies of His death didn't He? Isaiah 53, Psalm 22, Psalm 69, all of those things. Verse 5: "They answered Him, 'Jesus the Nazarene.' Jesus said to them, 'I AM.' And Judas, who was betraying Him, was also standing with them. But when He said to them, 'I AM,' they went backward and fell to *the* ground."

Now I don't know about you, but I have often wondered what those soldiers thought, and I wonder if Judas also went back. It doesn't tell us that he didn't, but they all you know, when He said I AM they went back, so that must include Judas, and fell on *the* ground." Makes you wonder why they didn't think, "Man! Do I really want to arrest this guy or not?" (laughter) Verse 8: Then "Jesus answered, 'I told you that I AM. Therefore, if you are seeking Me, allow these to go their way;' So that the saying might be fulfilled which He had said, Of those whom You have given Me, not one of them have I lost." Which we know "…not one of them have I lost…except the son of perdition." Verse 10: "Then Simon Peter, who had a sword, drew it out and struck the servant of the high priest, and cut off his right ear." Now I am sure he wasn't aiming just for the ear, and I'm sure he was aiming to lop off his head! And remember Peter was the one, Matthew 16 you go back read it, when Jesus revealed what was going to happen to Him, what did Peter say? He even took Him aside and said, "Lord, this isn't going to happen to you, I'm here, I will deliver you" And Jesus said, "Get behind me Satan, you savor the thoughts of men not the thoughts of

God" [Paraphrased]. So anyway… "And cut off his right ear. And the servant's name was Malchus. But Jesus said to Peter, "Put up your sword into the sheath; shall I not drink the cup that the Father has given Me?" And it shows in the parallel account that, what did Jesus do, He reached over and healed his ear (John 18:1-11).

Now what happens when you have a cut off something? You have blood and you kind of feeling it, right? What happens when you have a wound that is healed? Well, you feel it and see how it's going, and I imagine all the way back in, after his ear was healed, Malchus was feeling his ear. Did it really happen? So Malchus comes back in and I'm sure someone said, "Where'd you get all that blood?" "This guy over here cut my ear off." "Well, how'd it get back on?" "Now this guy over here that we arrested, touched it and it healed." A witness—do we really want to kill Him? So there are many, many things. Now remember this is the Passover night, and this is in preparation of His sacrifice on the Passover day, which parallels the animals that Abraham cut in two and God walked between.

So they took Him bound, to Annas and Caiaphas and so forth, you can read of it there in the *Harmony of the Gospels*. They beat Him, they punched Him, they had a trial, which was totally illegal, and I've got all the timeframe that is there, everything that happened. The chief priest condemns Him, Peter denies Christ three times, and then the Sanhedrin sends Him to Pilate; Pilate finds Him innocent. Now we're getting into the day portion.

But then the priests stirred up the people and they demanded Barabbas. Now it's very interesting…what does the name Barabbas mean? [It means] *son*…bar, and then abbas which is from abba, which means *son of* the *father*. So there is a total counterfeit.

So they released Barabbas and they took Jesus and they scourged Him…beat Him and scourged Him. And then after He barely was able to survive, they took the cross…now it wasn't like it was in the movie *The Passion of the Christ*; it was not a cross with two pieces. It was the crossbar that they would hang them on and what it was, they would take a tree trunk and they would put it in the ground and up at the top of it they would have a place where you could put into holders, the crossbar. So they could crucify a person on there, and then when they are dead, they'd just get them off there by lifting up the crossbar, but the tree trunk would remain in the ground. So that's what Jesus was carrying. It wasn't quite as high as what they showed in the movie there. Remember *The Passion of the Christ* is a Catholic version of the crucifixion of Christ which is made to conform to Catholic doctrine. And the reason why it says that Jesus was crucified on a tree is because the tree trunk was there…*staros*, but also for the sake of a cross, so when He carried out His cross, He was not carrying the whole thing, but He was carrying the crossbar.

Then at the very time of the sacrifices that were going on by Abraham back in Genesis 15, Christ was going through His scourging, He was being led away; at the third-hour in the morning He was crucified, and then you have the seven sayings of Jesus. Then you have darkness from the sixth hour to the ninth hour and Jesus dies at about 3:00 p.m., or the ninth hour.

Now let's come over here to John 19, and let's see something, and then this will also tell us a very important thing concerning the Night Much to be Observed by us today. Now the first night to be observed, right after the Passover and death of Jesus Christ, was not a night of rejoicing. Remember what Jesus said, He told them on the Passover night, He said, "You're going to be grieved, but afterwards you will have joy." So this one Night to be Much Observed was not a night of joy for the disciples at that time, but it was later. Because what it was, was this: Jesus performed the oath that He swore to Abraham, and He died… exactly as He said, and He was put in the grave.

Now let's follow along here and let's pick it up in verse 30 [Page 304 in the Harmony]. After Jesus received the vinegar to fulfill the prophecy, John 19:30: "And so, when Jesus had received the vinegar, He said, 'It is finished.' And bowing His head, He yielded up *His* spirit." Now the account in Mark shows that it was at the ninth hour that He died, about 3:00 p.m.. Verse [page 305 in the Harmony] 31: "The Jews therefore, so that the bodies might not remain on the cross on the Sabbath, because it was a preparation *day* (for that Sabbath was a high day, the first day of the Feast of Unleavened Bread) requested of Pilate that their legs might be broken and *the bodies* be taken away. Then the soldiers came and broke the legs of the first *one*, and *the legs* of the other who was crucified with Him. But when they came to Jesus *and* saw that He was already dead, they did not break His legs..." Why? It was prophesied He would never have a bone broken (John 19:30-33).

Now these soldiers aren't going along and saying, "Well, I read in the Bible that He was not going to have a bone broken. I'm not going to break the legs so I can fulfill the prophecy." You know... or the soldiers who were there casting lots on His vesture and on His garment, say, "Oh, let's fulfill prophecy guys." God made them do it and they had no inkling of why they were doing what they were doing.

"But one of the soldiers..." verse 34, "...had pierced His side with a spear, and immediately blood and water had come out. And he who saw *this* has testified and his testimony is true..." that's John, "...and he knows that *what* he says *is* true, so that you may believe. For these things took place so that the scripture might be fulfilled, 'Not a bone of Him shall be broken.' And again another scripture says, They shall look upon Him Whom they pierced" [Verse 38, page 307 of the Harmony]. "Now after these things, Joseph of Arimathea..." and you can read the parallel account...how he got permission from Pilate to take the body away, and then came Nicodemus, and he was bringing a mixture of myrrh and aloes, about a hundred pounds, verse 39. Verse 41, "Then they took Jesus' body and wound it in linen cloths with the aromatics..." No shroud—the Shroud of Turin is a hoax, a lie, and not true. But a church built on lies, that believes in idolatry, you know... the same rationale is used for worshiping the Shroud of Turin that is used for the false documents that they have concocted concerning President George Bush's National Guard service. They [the documents] were total forgeries, they were not true, but Dan Rather stands by it to this day, that the story is true though they are forged documents.

So the Catholic Church does the same thing with the Shroud of Turin... "Well, this may not be exactly the body of Jesus, but we have tried many, many experts, and some of them say that it is. So therefore, it's good for the faithful to worship, you know, that it's true." And the Bible that they have locked away in their little compartment on their altar says that they were <u>wound</u> much like a mummy.

Now verse 41: "Now there was a garden in the place where He was crucified, and in the garden a new tomb, in which no one had ever been laid. Because of the preparation of the Jews, they laid Jesus there; for the tomb was near" (John 19:34-42).

Now here is the point of the Night to be Much Observed for Christians today: One, God fulfilled His promise that He would die for the sins of the world as pictured by the Passover day; two, He began His three days and three nights in the tomb, beginning with the Night to be Much Observed. And think about this: the death of the one Who was God, Who became a human being—He died, and for the joy that was before Him, He endured the cross, despising the shame—so He would be able with that sacrifice to save us!

So we have joy <u>not</u> in the <u>death</u>, but in the <u>promise</u> of what He did and fulfilled, and yes, in the death from this point of view: that God applies the sacrifice of Jesus Christ to us upon repentance, for the forgiveness of our sins that we do not have the death penalty brought upon us. So that's quite a night of rejoicing. **So that if we are faithful, the Night to be Much Observed pictures this: We are redeemed by the Passover, we are delivered by the death of Jesus Christ, and now on the Night to be Much Observed, we start our walk out of spiritual Egypt—because you have to be redeemed and you have to be brought out of the world.**

Now just like the children of Israel—where were they going? They ended up at Mt. Sinai didn't they? And what was that—that was temporarily the throne of God was it not, where God gave the Ten Commandments? So likewise, our walk and our journey—(let's come to Hebrews 12 and we'll finish here) because you see, what begins with the Passover on one night, and then the Night to be Much Observed on the next night, beginning our walk then is pictured in the seven weeks of them walking to Mt. Sinai and hearing the voice of God, seeing the glory of God which then with the assembly of the people of Israel there, is a type of the resurrection and the assembly of all of the saints resurrected from the dead.

So you see, this Night to be Observed is fantastic from this point of view: That it begins our journey out of sin and from physical life to the resurrection to be resurrected and meet Christ on the Sea of Glass on Pentecost.

Now let's see what we have here. Let's come to Hebrews 12 and let's pick it up here in verse 18. We'll see the parallel; because you see, all of these are connected, Passover, Unleavened Bread and Pentecost, and those three feasts in the spring apply to the Church. Now we are going to notice something here, which I will expound more in a different sermon, concerning the firstborn. Verse 18, Hebrews 12: "For you have not come to *the* mount that could be touched…" That is the physical Mt. Sinai. They could even climb up and down on it now; God is no longer there. It's no longer a holy place. Wherever God is, it's Holy. "…And that burned with fire, nor to gloominess, and fearful darkness, and *the* whirlwind; And to *the* sound of *the* trumpet, and to *the* voice of *the* words, which those who heard *begged* that *the* word not be spoken *directly* to them. (For they could not endure what was being commanded: 'And if even an animal touches the mountain, it shall be stoned, or shot through with an arrow.': And so terrifying was the sight *that* Moses said, 'I am greatly afraid and trembling.") So that was an awesome thing!

Now we'll talk a little more about this when we come to Pentecost, but here's the parallel. In order to attain to the Kingdom of God, you: Number one, have to have your sins forgiven through the sacrifice of Jesus Christ. Number two; you have to come out of this world and walk in the ways of God, under His direction with His Spirit, with His guidance. And what did they do all the way to Mt. Sinai every Sabbath, but keep the Sabbath. Is that not correct? Yes. Verse 22: "But you have come to mount Sion, and to *the* city of *the* living God, heavenly Jerusalem; and to an innumerable company of angels; *To the* joyous festival gathering; and to *the* church of *the* firstborn…" So the death of Jesus Christ, God manifested in the flesh, the Son of The Father, was the firstborn Who was the sacrificial offering of God for the forgiveness of our sins. And the timing has nothing to do with the timing of anything at the temple, but between the timing of things in Genesis 15 with Abraham and the death of Jesus Christ (Hebrews 12:22-23).

Now then, the church of the firstborn, that's us, and so in another sermon I will bring out to you the meaning of the firstborn and why the first day of the Feast of Unleavened Bread beginning with the Night to be Much Observed is so important for us, because we are the firstborn, coming out of this world who, with Christ leading the way we are coming out with a high hand and looking forward to the resurrection, you see. "The church of *the* firstborn, registered *in the book of life* in heaven; and to God, *the* Judge of all; and to *the* spirits of the just who have been perfected; And to Jesus, *the* Mediator of *the* New Covenant;…"

which was His sacrifice "and to sprinkling of *the* blood of *ratification,* proclaiming superior things than *that of* Abel" (Hebrews 12: 23-24).

So here now we have an inkling that everything even goes back to Abel, and then that goes back to the promise that God gave there in Genesis 3:15 of His own death. So this is something, how the Bible puts it all together. So this is the meaning of the Night to be Much Observed and why we in the Church of God should keep that night beginning on the night of the fifteenth of Nisan.

Transcriber: Judith Anderson

The Night to Be Much Observed
April 12, 2006
Scriptural References

1) Exodus 12:40-42, 51

2) Exodus 13:1-3

3) Numbers 33:1-4

4) Deuteronomy 16:1

5) Genesis 15:1-5

6) Matthew 13:43

7) Daniel 12:1-3

8) Genesis 15:6-14, 16-21

9) Exodus 12:40-42

10) Deuteronomy 16:1-7

11) Exodus 12:8-9

12) Joshua 5:10-11

13) John 18:1-11

14) John 19:30-42

15) Hebrews 12:18-24

CHAPTER FOURTEEN

The Feast of Unleavened Bread

Day 1—Holy Day

April 6, 2004

And greetings brethren, this is the first day of the Feast of Unleavened Bread—2004. And you know as we have learned, as we know and have seen and understand, there is no justification at all for the religious holidays of this world to have any claim that they come from the Bible. Because as we have seen the will of man cannot be the will of God. And remember the model prayer that Jesus gave to the Father, that we are to ask that God's will be done on earth as it is in heaven. So when God spoke to the children of Israel He gave them His will. And that's what we find concerning the holy days, and the basic outline of them back in the book of Leviticus. So let's go back there right now. Let's go to Leviticus 22, and I want to read several verses at the end of Leviticus 22 before we get to Leviticus 23, so that we can emphasize and understand something very important concerning the holy days of God. And that they are just as important as the weekly Sabbath, and as a matter of fact they give the rest of the story in laying out the plan of God. Because without the holy days you cannot understand the plan of God.

So let's begin here, Leviticus 22:31. "Therefore shall ye keep My commandments, and do them: I *am* the LORD." Now whenever you see "I am the LORD" or "the LORD says," these are the words of God. And it's the recorded voice of the Word of God. And of course as we see and know and understand that we are to obey the voice of the LORD our God. Verse 32, "Neither shall ye profane My holy name; but I will be hallowed among the children of Israel: I *am* the LORD which hallow you [or, sanctifies you]…" And that ties right in with the New Testament, that we are sanctified by God the Father through Jesus Christ. Verse 33, "…That brought you out of the land of Egypt, to be your God: I *am* the LORD" (Lev. 22:31-33). And not only that, when God calls us He brings us out of the world. And Egypt symbolizes and typifies the world. So this becomes very important. And as we have seen, if you keep the holidays of this world you're going right back into Egypt. And another name that this is called by—the way—of the world is Babylon. So Babylon and Egypt, and Sodom and Gomorrah give the great definition of the end-time age that we live in.

Now let's continue right on with Leviticus 23. "And the LORD spake unto Moses, saying, Speak unto the children of Israel, and say unto them, *Concerning* the feasts of the LORD…" which we have seen and know and understand that they are His. Now you cannot take something that comes from a pagan god, as we have seen, and put the name of God on it and have some high religious figure Christianize it and sanctify it and say, "This is the will of God." No, it's very clear these are the feasts of the LORD, so if you want to keep any days to God you have to keep the ones that He says. Everything else doesn't count. "…Which ye shall proclaim *to be* holy convocations [or, appointed times], *even* these *are* My feasts." And it starts out with the weekly Sabbath because as we know and we have seen, the fourth commandment concerning the weekly Sabbath is the overarching commandment from which the holy days, which are Sabbaths, hang. "Six days shall work be done: but the seventh day *is* the sabbath of rest, an holy convocation; ye shall do no work *therein:* it *is* the sabbath of the LORD in all your dwellings" (Lev. 23:1-3).

Now we know we keep the seventh day Sabbath every week, week in and week out, and week in and week out, as we go down through the year. And when we come to the spring of the year, which this is, we have the Passover, which we have kept, and I hope that everyone had a profitable and inspiring Passover. And then we keep the Feast of Unleavened Bread. And in these things God teaches us not only His plan but His way, and how He is doing things. So that's why we have the feasts. And remember the weekly Sabbath is called a feast. So if the weekly Sabbath is called a feast, and the annual Sabbaths are called feasts, they are one in the same and belong together. So the truth is, as we already know, you can't have one without the other.

Now verse 4, "These *are* the feasts of the LORD, *even* holy convocations, which ye shall proclaim in their seasons. In the fourteenth *day* of the first month at even *is* the LORD'S passover." And we've already had that. "And on the fifteenth day of the same month [which is today] *is* the feast of unleavened bread unto the LORD: seven days ye <u>must</u> eat unleavened bread." And God says what He means and means what He says, so we eat unleavened bread. And there's a lesson in it for us, as we will see. "In the first day ye shall have an holy convocation: ye shall do no servile work therein. But ye shall offer an offering made by fire unto the LORD seven days…" So that includes that there's an offering on the seventh day, because if you start on the first day and you have an offering that you have, and of course these were also the ritual sacrifices and they did them every day. You can see them all listed out in Numbers 28. "…Ye shall do no servile work *therein*. But ye shall offer an offering made by fire unto the LORD…" (vs. 4-8). And so every one of the holy days we do take up an offering. Now today we don't offer sacrifices, but we give monetary offerings, and in a way that's likened unto a sacrifice, if you would.

Now let's come here to Deuteronomy 16 and let's see the command. Let's see what God says and let's see how that with the offerings that we take up, we are to prepare for them. We are to do the things that God wants us to do in faith and trust, and understanding that God will bless us. Verse 16, "Three times in a year shall all thy males appear before the LORD thy God in the place which He shall choose; in the feast of unleavened bread, and in the feast of weeks, and in the feast of tabernacles: and they shall not appear before the LORD empty: every man *shall give* as he is able…" Now there's a gauge. See, every time we come before God to bring an offering we have to measure it by the blessings that God has given. So if you have given and you are living by God's word and you are trusting in God, you probably have many blessings that you can count. So then God says, "…according to the blessing of the LORD thy God which He hath given thee." (Deut. 16:16-17). So that's the gauge on how we are to give our offerings.

Now we also know in the New Testament, let's come here to 2 Corinthians 9 because this is talking about the Feast of Unleavened Bread and sowing and planting, and of course it has reference then to us being the firstfruits, as we will see as we come down toward Pentecost time. Here in 2 Corinthians 9 we have an overall command with the very principles of God, and of course this is based on faith. Everything that we do then must be based on faith—to love God, to serve Him, to keep His commandments, to do the things that are right in His sight.

Now here in 2 Corinthians 9:6, "But this *I say*: the one who sows sparingly shall also reap sparingly…" And as we covered previous, long before the Feast of Unleavened Bread, that the one servant who received the one talent and didn't do anything with it, he didn't even sow it into the bank, as it were, to receive interest when Christ returns. So he didn't even do the minimum. And this is what he's talking about here. If you give sparingly then God will bless you sparingly, because the results will go hand-in-hand. "…And the one who sows bountifully shall also reap bountifully." And there are many, many blessings that come, which are more than just monetary or physical, or blessings that you can look at and see. There are the blessings of love, and joy, and peace, and longsuffering—the fruits of the Holy Spirit. There are the blessings of peace and longsuffering, there are the blessings where then you have God's Spirit, and God is giving you the strength and help to overcome. Those are all part of the blessings that God will give. "Each one as he purposes in his heart,…" So it's something that we have to do with deliberation, with thought when we come before the LORD. "…*So let him give,* but not grudgingly…" See, God wants us to keep His commandments with joy, not with grudging. Not saying, "Well, there goes that preacher again." You know, as we're going to see, we have to preach the word in season. "…or [of necessity] by compulsion [that is, because God requires it]; for God loves a cheerful giver " (2 Cor. 9:6-7).

Now here is the blessing, here is the promise. This is what we claim when we give to God our tithes and our offerings—verse 8. "For God *is* able [that means God has the power] to make all grace abound toward you so that in every *way* you may always have sufficiency in all *things, and* may abound unto every good work…" So God gives a promise that you will have sufficiency in all things. So we'll go ahead and take a pause now, and we'll take up the offering.

Now let's go to John 14, and let's look at the connection between Passover and Unleavened Bread, and a relationship with God the Father and Jesus Christ. Now remember, as we have covered, John 14, 15, 16, and 17 are the words of the New Covenant, as we covered during the Passover night. And these words also tell us exactly the way to have a relationship with Jesus Christ and God the Father. And it shows that since these words were given on the Passover night, that it is absolutely true you cannot have a connection with, or a relationship with Jesus Christ and God the Father unless you keep the Passover.

Now you know we need to be as strong as the Bible is strong and say it exactly as it is. And let's read it here. John 14:6, "Jesus said to him, 'I am the way, and the truth, and the life; no one comes to the Father except through Me.' " And Jesus Christ, as we will see, is our Passover. So unless you keep the Passover and the feasts of God you cannot get to God the Father. It is an absolute impossibility. And of course, as we have seen, everything needs to be done exactly as Jesus said it should be done.

Now let's, since we are in the Gospel of John, and I'm using the new translation from the New Testament that you have received. Let's come to John 6:53. This also shows that it has to be the way that Jesus Christ has said. Now it is an impossibility for anyone to partake of Communion anytime they want to and have a relationship with God the Father and Jesus Christ. They may think they do, but they're deceived, because no one is going to do anything contrary to the will of God, and God accept it. No one can take the Eucharist and stand before a priest, or sit before a priest who has the unmitigated gall to claim that he can command God to come and put the presence of Jesus Christ—His body and His blood—in the bread and in the wine. No, Jesus clearly showed that to eat His flesh and drink His blood is symbolized by the unleavened bread and the wine. There is nothing literal in it. It is symbolic. And it also has a meaning of what we are to do.

So let's pick it up here, John 6:53. "Therefore, Jesus said to them, 'Truly, truly I say to you, unless you eat the flesh of the Son of man, and drink His blood, you do not have life in yourselves." See, because all die. And the wages of sin is death. And there is no way out except through Christ. "The one who eats My flesh and drinks My blood has eternal life…" He's talking about the Passover, as we have seen. So if you don't take the Passover you cannot have eternal life. Now you may take a false version of it through Communion or the Eucharist, but that has no connection with God. Now it may appear to have connection with God because those who perform the service use the Scriptures, but they misuse them because they are unwilling to obey. Remember where we started—God said, "Therefore shall ye keep my commandments,…" (Lev. 22:31). And those are part of the commandments of God the Father and Jesus Christ. And He says, "...and I will raise him up in the last day; for My flesh is truly food, and My blood is truly drink. The one who eats My flesh and drinks My blood is dwelling in Me, and I in him" (John 6:53-56). So the key is again, without the Passover Christ cannot dwell in you. That's what He says.

Now here is what we are to do. This tells us exactly the meaning of it. We don't do this for some religious ritual so that somehow what we do puts us in right standing with God. We do it because God says if we do, He puts us in right standing with Him. And what are we to do after that? Verse 57, "As the living Father has sent Me, and I live by the Father; so also the one who eats Me shall live by Me.' " And it is a way of life. It is something that we do. It is something that we live by, we think by, we have our life wrapped up in. Christ is in us, God the Father is in us. It is a way to live. Christ didn't die in vain to just please men. He died to save the world His way.

Now let's see what else He says here. Let's come to verse 63. He says, " 'It is the Spirit that gives life; the flesh profits nothing." That is, our own physical flesh. And even symbolizing eating His flesh and drinking His blood, it is the spiritual meaning of it, you see. And the spiritual application of renewing the New Covenant, as we have seen on the Passover, which is kept the 14th day of the first month. "...*They* are spirit and *they* are life. But there are some of you who do not believe.' " And they didn't like the saying that Jesus said, "You have to eat My flesh and drink My blood." So what did they do? They said, "Well, it's a hard saying. I quit." See, because it went against their will. And they weren't willing to follow the will of God the Father and Jesus Christ. So that's the question. That's the whole meaning of the Feast of Unleavened Bread, as we will see. "For Jesus knew from *the* beginning who were the ones that did not believe, and who would betray Him. And He said, 'For this reason I have said to you, no one can come to Me unless it has been given to him from My Father' " (vs. 63-65). No one—it's an impossibility. Just like you cannot please God by eating leavened bread during the Feast of Unleavened Bread. It's an impossibility. So unless you come through Christ and His word, and His gospel, and His way you can't get to the Father.

Now notice, they couldn't take that. Verse 66, "From that *time* many of His disciples went back and walked no more with Him." And then, "Therefore, Jesus said to the twelve, 'Are you also desiring to go away?' Then Simon Peter answered Him, 'Lord, to whom shall we go? You have the words of eternal life; and we have believed and have known that You are the Christ, the Son of the living God.' " So Jesus wanted to set the record straight, because in Matthew 16 Jesus said to Peter when he said, "You are the Christ," He says, "Blessed are you, Simon Bar-Jona, for My Father has revealed this to you." (Matt. 16:17, paraphrased). So no one knows the true Christ unless He is revealed by God the Father. So "Jesus answered them, 'Did I not choose you twelve, and one of you is *the* devil?' " (John 6:66-70). So to believe in your own belief of what you think concerning what the Bible says, and the Word of God, will get you nowhere with God.

Now let's come to 2 Timothy 3 and let's see something very profound and important. And to show that the only way that we are going to come to God, come to Jesus Christ and God the Father, is through repentance and a broken heart, and accepting the sacrifice of Jesus Christ and living by the Words of God. Now those who then are teachers will see the command of what they are to do, and it does include the annual Sabbaths. And it does include all the commandments of God.

Now let's pick it up here in 2 Timothy 3:14. "But *as for* you [he's writing to Timothy], continue in the things that you did learn and were assured of, knowing from whom you have learned *them*..." Now let's understand something very important, verse 15. "...And that from a child you have known the holy writings..." They had, not only the scrolls of the

Old Testament in the synagogues before the time of Christ, but they also had personal scrolls. They also had the Septuagint translated from the Hebrew into Greek. "...And that from a child you have known the holy writings...", which means that he was taught in his home, if you read the first part of 2 Timothy, how that from his Grandmother and Mother, they taught him. So they had the Word of God just like we have the Word of God. Now notice, "...you have known the holy writings, which are able to make you wise unto salvation through faith, which *is* in Christ Jesus" (2 Tim. 3:14-15). So this is affirming the need to follow and obey the commandments in what is called the Old Testament.

Verse 16, "All Scripture *is* God-breathed..." It's the very Word of God. It's like when I'm speaking, breath is coming out of my mouth, isn't it? Well, God breathed. That means that God's Spirit moved these men to write the very Words of God. So it's just not the sayings or the thoughts of men. Now because of that "...[it] *is* profitable for doctrine [from which all teaching comes], for conviction..." that you have to be, not only know the truth but be convicted of the truth so you can stand for the truth, so you can love the truth, so you can live by the truth. Unless you have conviction you do not have spiritual backbone. And "...for correction..." because we all need correction—every one of us. We need to let the Word of God correct us. That's the easiest way. You read the Word of God and you change and repent when you see there's correction for you.

The next easiest way is for a minister to teach you and read the Scriptures and then you are corrected by that. Then it becomes a little more difficult. If you're not willing to listen... And many times it's not a matter of willing to listen, but because some things are hard to learn that we need the experience of trials and difficulties so that we can learn the profound importance of what God wants us to do, and how we are to live. And remember, don't complain about any trial or difficulty that you've come through. Always think on and remember the sacrifice of Jesus Christ—His beating, His scourging, and His crucifixion— that He went through, for every one of us because He loved us. So that's why Paul says all these heavy trials are just but for a light moment. And remember this: there is no trial, there is no difficulty, there is no situation that is too great for God. But in those He wants you to turn to Him. Now you see, "...for correction, for instruction in righteousness..." that we may learn how to be in right standing with God through the power of His Holy Spirit "...so that the man of God may be complete, fully equipped for every good work" (vs. 16-17). And that's not only just those who are teaching, but that's for everyone. That's why the Word of God is here. That's why we are to prove all things. That's why we are to hold fast, which is good, see.

Now then chapter 4, verse 1. "I charge you, therefore, in the sight of God, even the Lord Jesus Christ, Who is ready to judge *the* living and *the* dead at His appearing and His kingdom: Preach the Word!..." (2 Tim. 4:1-2). Now what does this tell us? How can he preach the Word if he didn't have it written down? This tells us at the time that Paul was writing to Timothy, that they had the Words of God. They had all the epistles of the apostle Paul.

Now let's come over here to 1 Timothy 6, and let's see something that's very important here. 1 Timothy 6:3. We'll come back to 2 Timothy in just a minute. 1 Timothy 6:3, "If anyone teaches any different doctrine, and does not adhere to the sound words, *even those* of our Lord Jesus Christ, and the doctrine *that is* according to godliness, he is proud and knows nothing. Rather, he has a morbid attraction to questions and disputes over words, from which come envy, arguments, blasphemy, wicked suspicions, vain reasonings of men who have been corrupted in *their* minds and *are* destitute of the truth [sounds like Biblical scholars today, to me]—*men* who believe that gain is godliness. From such withdraw *yourself* " (1 Tim. 6:3-5). Now the point is this: Timothy had to have all the gospels to know the sound words of Jesus Christ, right? Yes, indeed. So this whole thing that the Bible wasn't written until hundreds of years after the apostles, is nothing more than a Satanic lie given by atheistic scholars who don't believe the Word of God and have a secret hidden agenda that they want to destroy the Word of God and corrupt it. And in this New Testament you can read the commentary, which absolutely proves that that's so and that's their motive. There are very few honest scholars out there in the world, but just enough so that the Word of God and the history and preservation of the text will not be lost.

Now let's come back to 2 Timothy 2:4. "Preach the word!" So what is a minister supposed to do? Preach the Word. Not stories, not his ideas, not what he thinks, but the Word of God. Which means in order to preach the Word of God you have to have it. And we have the evidence right here that Timothy had the Old Testament from a child, and that he had the writings of the apostle Paul, that he had the Gospels. So by the time this second epistle is written, every book of the New Testament was available to the New Testament church except the book of Revelation. So that's amazing to understand.

Now look at the next sentence here. "Be urgent…" Not slovenly, not ho-hum. "Be urgent in season and out of season…" Now what did we read back there in Leviticus 23? That these are the feasts of the LORD which you shall proclaim in their seasons, right? Therefore all Scripture is God breathed. Therefore this is absolute proof that they were keeping the Passover and the holy days in the early New Testament church and that all of these pagan intrusions came later when the state religion was instituted by Emperor Constantine. "Be urgent in season and out of season; convict, rebuke, encourage, with all patience and doctrine. For there shall come a time when they will not tolerate sound doctrine…" Now people don't like that. "Well, that's harsh. Well, that's too rigid." You tell it to God. See if He will accept those excuses. "…But according to their own lusts…" That's where these things come from. People have lusts. They want to have it their way. They don't want to do God's way. They want their own way. They want to be satisfied in their lusts. "…According to their own lusts they shall accumulate to themselves *a great number of* teachers, having ears itching *to hear what satisfies their cravings*; and they shall turn away their own ears from the truth; and they shall be turned aside unto myths" (vs. 2-4). That's exactly what has happened.

You know, I got a letter just a couple of weeks ago. Let's go to 1 Corinthians 5 now. I got a letter just a couple weeks ago where a man wrote and said, "Well you know that in the New Testament there's no place which shows that we should keep the feasts of the Old Testament." Well, as we have already seen in the sermons leading up to the Passover and Feast of Unleavened Bread, yes. Right here in 1 Corinthians 5 you find a direct command by the apostle Paul, the apostles to the Gentiles, writing and speaking to the Gentiles commanding them to keep the Feast of Unleavened Bread because they kept the Passover.

Now let's see it here. Verse 6, "Your glorying *is* not good." And of course they were glorying about the situation with the man who had his stepmother in immoral sexual relations. But any kind of glorying is not good over things which are sin. It's a sin to say that God has delivered us to do all these abominations, meaning the pagan holidays as we already have seen and know, you see. "Don't you know that a little leaven leavens the whole lump?" (1 Cor. 5:6). A little bit of sin starts it. That's why God uses leaven as a type of sin during the Days of Unleavened Bread. And He wants us to understand, just like leaven is everywhere, leaven is in the air. And who's the prince of the power of the air that brings people to sin? Satan the devil. Leaven is so common, it's in the basic food staples that we eat. It's in bread, it's in crackers, it's in cakes, it's in all of the things that we just normally take for granted. So during the Feast of Unleavened Bread He wants us to put out the leaven and to eat unleavened bread for seven days as He has said so we learn the lesson that as God has called us out of Egypt, we have our part to do. And if we don't put the leaven out of our homes, and I've seen this time and time again down through the years for now 38 years as a minister, that when people don't put leaven out of their homes—a simple little thing—within a short period of time they no longer understand what sin is. And they redefine sin according to their own ideas, sin according to their interpretation of the Scriptures.

Now notice what He says here, verse 7. "Therefore, purge out the old leaven…" We're to go get it out of our homes, and also there's a spiritual lesson here. Purge out the old human nature, see. "…That you may become a new lump,…" that is, that you may be molded into that new person in Christ. "…*Even* as you are unleavened." Showing that they had their houses unleavened. It couldn't mean anything other than that. Now here's the reason. Some people say, "Well why do you keep the Feast of Unleavened Bread?" Turn right here, here's the answer. "For Christ our Passover was sacrificed for us" (vs. 7). Because of Christ we keep the Feast of Unleavened Bread. Now most people think because of Christ we keep Easter. God never said so. "Because of Christ we keep Lent. Because of Christ we keep Ash Wednesday." Where do you find that in the Bible? It's not there. Those are things of men who did not want to hear the truth. We read back there in 2 Timothy 4, they wanted to turn to myths and lies and have new teachings that please men, that accept all the sins of the world. That's what those are. See, we keep the Feast of Unleavened Bread and put the leaven out of our homes, and eat unleavened bread seven days because God said so. Because Christ was our Passover Who was sacrificed for us. So if you want to claim the sacrifice of Christ for the forgiveness of your sins and you do not keep the Feast of Unleavened Bread, and you do not keep the Passover, you have no part with Him. Now you see, that's very clear.

Now notice verse 8, here's the direct command. "For this reason…" Because of the fact of the sacrifice of Jesus Christ on the Passover day. That's why He's called our Passover. "For this reason, let us keep the feast…" There can be no doubt it's the Feast of Unleavened Bread. It's not Easter, it's not Lent, it's not Sunday-keeping. It is the Feast. Now notice, "…Not with old leaven, nor with *the* leaven of malice and wickedness, but with *the* unleavened *bread* of sincerity and truth" (vs. 8). And that's what God wants us to have. He wants us to have a nature that is filled with truth from the Spirit of Truth by the God of Truth and Jesus Christ, Who is the way, the truth, and the life. And the only way that that can be is if we understand that we must have our natures unleavened spiritually that we become the new creature in Christ. And that eating the unleavened bread shows us that we are to live by every Word of God and to understand that God's way is the way that it is.

Now let's come to Psalm 34. Let's see something that's very important which ties in with the Feast of Unleavened Bread, and ties in with the meaning of living by every Word of God. And this is New Testament doctrine here that we're going to read in Psalm 34. Very profound. Very important for us to understand. And this is the whole meaning of it. You see, Christ is the sinless one. Christ, Who knew no sin, became the sacrifice for us, and He is the one that we are able to continuously come to, to come to God the Father to have our sins forgiven, to grow in grace and knowledge, to understand the Word of God.

Now let's see what it says here. Psalm 34:4, "I sought the LORD, and He heard me [so you've got to come to God], and delivered me from all my fears." See, we've got to trust God. That's what the whole Feast of Unleavened Bread is picturing—you trust God. "They looked unto Him, and were lightened: and their faces were not ashamed. This poor man cried, and the LORD heard *him,* and saved him out of all his troubles. The angel of the LORD encampeth round about them that fear Him, and delivereth them." Part of the blessings of God. Part of the blessings that you hardly ever see or know or recognize. Maybe you can look back and see how angels may have delivered you from some things, but you don't know that they are there. Now notice verse 8, "O taste and see that the LORD *is* good…" That's why we keep the Feast of Unleavened Bread. We taste the Word of God, we digest it spiritually speaking, it becomes a part of us. That we think with the Word of God, we have it written in our hearts and in our minds. "…Blessed *is* the man *that* trusteth in Him" (Psa. 34:4-8). Now you see, so that's what we need to do.

Let's come down here to verse 14. This shows part of how to keep the Feast of Unleavened Bread. "Depart from evil [put the leaven out], and do good [put righteousness in]; seek peace, and pursue it. The eyes of the LORD *are* upon the righteous, and His ears *are open* unto their cry." Now verse 18, "The LORD *is* nigh unto them that are of a broken heart; and saveth such as be of a contrite spirit. Many *are* the afflictions of the righteous: but the LORD delivereth him out of them all" (vs. 14-15, 18-19). Those are the promises that God gives for keeping the Feast of Unleavened Bread.

Now let's continue on and we will follow the theme that leaven equals sin, and that we ourselves only change or become unleavened through Christ. Now here's where we begin. Let's come to Romans 3, and let's understand what we are as human beings, and where God wants us to go. The truth is that God is going to take something that is imperfect and He's going to perfect it. He's going to take us, who are sinful, and upon repentance and baptism, yielding to God and growing and overcoming, perfect us and make us righteous. It's quite a process that God is doing.

And here's where it begins, Romans 3:23. "For all have sinned, and come short of the glory of God…" So all are sinners—none are exempt, and Christ is the only way out. "…*But* are being justified freely by His grace through the redemption that *is* in Christ Jesus; Whom God has openly manifested *to be* a propitiation through faith in His blood, in order to demonstrate His righteousness, in respect to the remission of sins that are past…" (Rom. 3:23-25). So God is showing His righteousness. And that righteousness could also be called: God is showing His justification because He is taking those who are sinners (unjust) and making them in right standing with Him by justification through the sacrifice of Jesus Christ and by His blood.

Now, he says, verse 26, "…Through the forbearance of God; *yes*, to publicly declare His righteousness in the present time, that He might be just, and the one Who justifies the one who *is* of *the* faith of Jesus." Now then Paul says, "…Where *is* boasting?" It's not of self, it's not of law, it's of Christ. It's of faith. Then he also asks the question because of faith and because of grace, "Do we then make void the law?", or abolish the law? No. Let's come down here to verse 31 and see. "Are we, then, abolishing law through faith?" He says, "MAY IT NEVER BE! Rather, we are establishing law" (vs.26-27, 31), because they're written in our hearts and in our minds, you see, because we live by them. However, we still have a sinful nature. Even though we are justified, even though Christ died while we were yet sinners, even though we have the Holy Spirit shed abroad in our hearts so we can develop the patience and the love and the overcoming, we still have sin to fight.

So let's come to Romans 7 and see the predicament that all human beings are in. And one mistake that a lot of people make is that they focus on their sins because they have a sinful nature. We're going to see you have to get sin out, but not focus on sin but focus on Christ. And then we're also going to see: How does God look at us? How can God put up with us with this sinful nature, which causes us to do things that we don't want to do? And we slip and fall in sin, yet we repent and we change, we come to God. Let's see how all of this works. Let's put it all together here.

Let's begin, Romans 7:7. "What then shall we say? *Is* the law sin? MAY IT NEVER BE! But I had not known sin, except through the law [because law defines the sin]. Furthermore, I would not have been conscious of lust, except *that* the law said, 'You shall not covet.' " But something happens when God begins to call an individual. And something happens in the minds of individuals once they have the Holy Spirit. And that is they see how sinful sin is.

Now let's read it here. "But sin, having grasped an opportunity by the commandment, worked out within me every *kind of* lust because apart from law, sin *was* dead. For I was once alive without law; but after the commandment came, sin revived, and I died" (Rom. 7:7-9). Now that is obviously through the operation of baptism. He didn't die a literal death and then was resurrected, see. That's what he's talking about, and of course baptism is a death—a covenant death into the death of Jesus Christ. That's why we take the Passover.

"…Because sin, having taken opportunity by the commandment, deceived me, and by it killed *me*." Then he looked back at the law and he says, "Therefore, the law *is* indeed holy, the commandment holy and righteous and good. Now then, did that which *is* good become death to me? MAY IT NEVER BE! But sin, in order that it might truly be exposed as sin in me by that which *is* good, [that] was working out [the] death [that is, sin]; so that, by the means of the commandment, sin might become exceedingly sinful" (vs. 11-13). Now then, how is that possible?

Let's come here to John 16 for just a minute. How is it possible that we're going along and we're living our lives in the world, we have no consciousness of sin. We know some things are right, and some things are wrong, but we don't have a consciousness of sin. We don't have a conviction of sin. We don't have a need to repent of sin. Oh, when we do something wrong and we're caught doing something wrong, yeah we're sorry, but that's not repentance of sin toward God.

What changes? It is the Holy Spirit of God. Because when God begins to call someone He sends the Spirit to be with them. When they repent and are baptized the Spirit is within them. And here is what the Spirit does.

Now let's come here to John 16 and let's pick it up here in verse 7. This is talking about the activity and work of the Holy Spirit. Jesus was telling His disciples, "But I am telling you the truth. It is profitable for you that I go away because if I do not go away, the Comforter will not come to you. However, if I go, I will send it to you. And when that one has come, it will convict the world concerning sin…" (John 16:7-8). Now, what gives us the conviction of sin in our lives? What brought the apostle Paul to the point that he had this conviction of seeing how evil that human nature really was? It was by the Holy Spirit of God.

Now let's come back to Romans 7 again. So the truth is this: if you find that you're a sinner, and if you're convicted that you are a sinner, and if you find yourself doing like the apostle Paul did here, doing things he didn't want to do but still did them, what is convicting you of that? Your thoughts? No. The Holy Spirit that is with you, or in you.

Now let's notice, let's continue on in Romans 7:14. "For we know that the law is spiritual; but I am carnal, having been sold *as a slave* under sin; because what I am working out myself [that is just what I do by myself], I do not know." Isn't that true? Don't we do a lot of things that we don't know why or what we do them for? And a lot of them end up being sin. "For what I do not desire to do, this I do; moreover, what I hate, this *is what* I do. But if I am doing what I do not desire to do, I agree with the law that *it is* good" (vs. 14-16). Because you can now see that your behavior needs to be changed. That's why we need to put out the sin. And when we put the sin out, as we're going to see, we need to put righteousness in. The same Holy Spirit that convicts us of sin so we can repent and get rid of sin, it is the same Holy Spirit that gives us the power and strength to put righteousness in through Jesus Christ. And that's what we're going to see is the way that it works.

Now let's continue on here, verse 17. "So then, I am not longer working it out myself; rather, it is [the] sin *that is* dwelling within me…" All of us have sin. We'll see it's called the law of sin and death. And we have to overcome it. We can only overcome it through Christ. "…Because I fully understand that there is not dwelling within me—that is, within my fleshly being—*any* good. For the desire to do good is present within me; but how to work out that which is good, I do not find [that is, within me]. For the good that I desire to do, I am not doing; but the evil that I do not desire to do, this I am doing. But if I do what I do not desire to do, I am no longer working it out myself, but sin *that is* dwelling within me." (vs. 17-20). Now there is a solution, and the solution is Christ, and the solution is the Feast of Unleavened Bread after the Passover. Because once you have your sins forgiven, you've got to do something else. And that is: you've got to do it God's way.

Verse 21, "Consequently, I find this law *in my members*, that when I desire to do good, evil is present with me." Now you can still find that today, right? You go along, you're doing something good and then bam, all of a sudden here comes an evil thought out of the middle of nowhere. That's the law of sin and death working in you. Now we're going to see through Christ there is a way out. And what we need to focus on You see sometimes we get so "beat sin out, get sin out of your life" that all people do is just look and see, "Well, where is the sin?" Well you need to find out where the sin is. Now what do you do after that? That's the rest of the story of the Feast of Unleavened Bread. So he says concerning this, "O *what a* wretched man I am! Who shall save me from the body of this death?" Now we need to be saved from this, and only Christ can. Verse 25, "I thank God *for His salvation* through our Lord Jesus Christ. Because of this, on the one hand, I myself serve the law of God with *my* mind; but on the other hand, with the flesh, *I serve* the law of sin" (vs. 21, 24-25). In other words it is the sin within your members that causes you to do this.

Now where do we stand before God? Let's come to chapter 8, verse 1. This is what I want you to understand. This is what is so important that we need to realize what Christ does and how we stand before God and that's the whole meaning of the Feast of Unleavened Bread. Romans 8:1, "Consequently *there is* now no condemnation…" Now I want you to repeat that. "There is now no condemnation." You love God the Father, you accept Jesus Christ as your Savior, and we're going to see how there is no condemnation, in just a bit. There's no condemnation. You don't need to focus on the sin, which has brought you down, but you focus on the solution, which then is Christ in you. So when you see the sin, you put it out getting rid of the leaven. In order to replace that you have to eat unleavened bread. That's putting Christ in. That's why He has us eat unleavened bread for seven days, so that we have to understand and realize that God puts us in a very special category. There is no condemnation. The very fact that you have the law of sin and death in you and you are overcoming it, and you are looking to God to change you, there is no condemnation, because there is the forgiveness available. That's why we are in the grace of God.

Now let's read it here. Now "…*There is*…no condemnation to those who are in Christ Jesus, who are not walking according to *the* flesh…" You're not just following the dictates of the flesh. You see, before you were converted that's what you were doing. You had no consciousness of good. You had no consciousness of God. You are not convicted because of sin. You just knew somewhat of right and wrong. But now with the Holy Spirit convicting you of sin, you see sin within you. And that's the Holy Spirit revealing it to you so you can change and repent and let Christ blot that out and forgive you and give you His Spirit. Now, because you are doing that, you are walking in the Spirit and not in the flesh.

Verse 2, "Because the law of the Spirit of life in Christ Jesus has delivered me from the law of sin and death. For what *was* impossible for the law to do…" See, because the law has no power. "…In that it was weak through the flesh, God, having sent His own Son in *the* likeness of sinful flesh, and for sin, condemned sin in the flesh…" So that God could give you His righteousness, God could give you His Spirit, God could give you His mind, see. "…In order that the righteousness of the law might be fulfilled in us, who are not walking according to *the* flesh, but according to *the* Spirit:." (vs. 2-4). Now that's something.

Now let's see how this whole operation is done. Let's come to 1 John 1. Now in the New Testament, the new one, you're going to have to get used to the general epistles coming before the epistles of Paul. Let's come to 1 John 1, and here's how it is accomplished. Now let's pick it up here in verse 6. Here is the way. "If we proclaim that we have fellowship with Him..." And a lot of people do, see. "...But we are walking in the darkness..." And many are. They're not walking according to the commandments, because you see the commandment is light, and the Spirit is light, and Christ is light. He is the way, the truth, and the life. And that's the way we are to live, you see. And if we're walking in darkness, if we're keeping Sunday, and Christmas, and Easter, and all the things of the world, you're walking in darkness. You're not walking in the light. "...We are lying to ourselves..." And you see, with the Holy Spirit within you, you cannot lie to yourself very long because the Holy Spirit will convict you, and through the graciousness of God lead you to repentance. "...We are lying to ourselves, and are not practicing the Truth. However, if we walk in the light, as He is in the light, *then* we have fellowship with one another, and the blood of Jesus Christ [His sacrifice, our Passover], His own Son, cleanses us from all sin" (1 John 1:6-7). Now Jesus said on the Passover night, "You are already clean through the word that I have spoken to you." And that was after they had partaken of the very first New Covenant Christian Passover. And that's why we keep the Passover every year. That's why we keep the Feast of Unleavened Bread every year, see, it cleanses us from all sin. That's why there's no condemnation through Jesus Christ.

Now we're going to see in just a minute, how we stand before God. How does God look at you? You're going to be surprised. Now, "If we say that we do not have sin, we are deceiving ourselves, and the truth is not in us. If we confess our own sins..." We have to go to God and confess our sins. Not to a priest. It doesn't say here, "Go to a priest and confess your sins, and then you are forgiven by him." And you run out and do "Hail Mary's, and Our Father's" or whatever other kind of religious work that has been given to do. That's not of God. You confess your sins directly to God the Father through Jesus Christ. "...He is faithful and righteous, to forgive us our sins, and to cleanse us from all unrighteousness." There's no condemnation if you are cleansed from all your sins, and cleansed from all unrighteousness. How can there be condemnation? There isn't. Now notice verse 10, "If we say that we have not sinned, we make Him a liar, and His Word is not in us" (vs. 8-10).

Then he gives us encouragement here, verse 1 of chapter 2. "My little children, I am writing these things to you so that you may not sin. And *yet*, if anyone does sin..." Because as we've covered with the law of sin and death we do sin, "...we have an Advocate with the Father; Jesus Christ *the* Righteous; and He is *the* propitiation for our sins [as we read there in Romans 3]; and not for our sins only, but also for *the sins of* the whole world" (1 John 2:1-2). And in order to understand how God is going to apply it to the whole world, and when he's going to apply it to the whole world, you need to keep the feasts of God. See, here's a truth: Passover, Unleavened Bread, and Pentecost tell you what God is doing with the church. Trumpets, Atonement, Tabernacles and the Last Great Day tells you how God is going to solve the problem of the sins of the world, and when. Now keep that in mind. Very important.

Now how do you stand before God? Let's come to Ephesians 1. I want you to grasp this. I want you to understand this. I want you to fully realize how God views you through Christ. Ephesians 1:3, "Blessed *be* the God and Father of our Lord Jesus Christ, Who has blessed us with every spiritual blessing in the heavenly *things* with Christ..." The Holy Spirit, forgiveness of sin, understanding the Word of God, growing in the character of God, as we will see a little later on, how we grow and develop and build the very character and love of God within us, you see.

Now verse 4 is a very important verse. It is translated correctly here in this new translation because there is what is called, as I have mentioned before, the middle voice verb.

Showing that God has done something very special and very personal in our lives. Verse 4, "...According as He has personally chosen us for Himself..." Now that's a tremendous thing. And God did not call you to condemn you. God called you to forgive you. God called you to change you. God called you to convert you. God called you to overcome sin. God has called you to be in His kingdom, to be His very sons and daughters to share in His glory through Christ. There's no condemnation in that. That's the greatest thing that could ever be. Before the foundation of the world He had the plan already to go before He created the world. "...In order that we might be [now notice] holy and blameless before Him in love..." Now that's how you stand before God—holy and blameless because of Christ. He's got a plan for us.

Verse 5, "...Having predestinated us for sonship to Himself through Jesus Christ, according to the good pleasure of His own will..." So God is dealing in your life according to the very good pleasure of what He has determined. "...To *the* praise of *the* glory of His grace, wherein He has made us objects of *His* grace in the Beloved *Son*; in Whom we have redemption through His blood..." (vs. 5-7). And it all goes back to the blood of Jesus Christ, and it all goes back to our right standing with God through the sacrifice of Christ. See this is tremendous, brethren. That's why there's no condemnation. That's why yes, we're to put sin out. Yes, we're to overcome sin. Yes, we're to confess our sins and have forgiveness, but we need to grow, we need to change, we need to understand there is no condemnation. There's not one word of condemnation here, right? Yes, indeed.

Verse 8, "...which He has made to abound toward us in all wisdom and intelligence..." God wants you to know, God wants you to understand. He's given His Spirit, He's given His Word. That's fantastic. God wants you to have the joy of the Lord. He wants you to understand how He views you, and He does not condemn you. Now we're going to look at this just a little bit more here in just a minute. "...Having made known to us the mystery of His own will..." Do you understand the will of God? Do you understand the greatest secret that men can never grasp through everything that they do, try, work, and so forth. Now we've got the two robots up on Mars—Opportunity and Spirit. They're looking for water. They're looking for signs of life. Who knows what they'll find up there, but always remember this: even if they find water that does not mean there has been life, because there was not life in the water until God said, "Let the water bring forth the fish and all the things that are in the water." So even if they find evidence of water that doesn't mean that there was life. He's got His plan, He's got His purpose, you see. Now notice, "...having made known to us the mystery of His own will, according to His good pleasure, which He [has] purposed in Himself..." (vs. 8-9). And God is working that plan.

Let's come to Romans 5. Let's understand something very important also how God looks at us and what He does for us. And this is profound. This is something that is really absolutely marvelous. Here's what God has done for us. Ok, Romans 5:17, "For if by the offence of one man [Adam] death reigned by the one [Adam], how much more shall those who receive the abundance of grace and the gift of righteousness..." It's a fantastic gift to be put in right standing with God. Have you ever in your own mind thought that <u>you</u> can be in right standing with God through Jesus Christ? That <u>you</u> can have imparted to you, imputed to you the very righteousness of Christ? That's the only way that you can be holy and without blame, because that is imputing to you the very qualities of Jesus Christ. So that's why we are to have the joy and the understanding, and realize how great this salvation of God is and might receive "...the abundance of grace and the gift of righteousness reign in life by the one, Jesus Christ.)" So then, even as by the one transgression condemnation *came* unto all men, in the same way also, by the one act of righteousness [sacrifice and crucifixion of Christ, and His resurrection] *shall* justification of life *come* unto all men" (Rom. 5:17-18). And of course that's in God's good time.

Now, let's come down here to verse 21. "So that even as sin has reigned unto death, so also might the grace *of God* reign through righteousness unto eternal life…". God imputes the righteousness of Christ to you. That's what to understand. And that's why the lawless grace of this world and what they do with it is absolutely wrong.

Since we're here in Romans let's see what it shows we are to do. Now what are we to do with this? Wrap it up in a napkin and be all smug and say, "Oh that's good, we stand before God blameless." What are you to do? What is the obligation? Because you see, you put the sin out, you put the leaven out but you've got to put the unleaven in. And here in Romans 12:1, this shows what it is to be, that conversion is a process, and God has given this right standing before Him that we are holy and blameless before Him in love to inspire us, to want to do what Romans 12 tells us here.

Verse 1, "I exhort you therefore, brethren, by the mercies of God, to present your bodies a living sacrifice, holy, *and* well pleasing to God, which is your spiritual service." To love Him, to grow in the fruits of the Spirit, to overcome the works of the flesh—that is your spiritual service. And "Do not conform yourselves to this world [go back into the world], but be transformed by the renewing of your mind…" That's the conversion that takes place. Step by step, day by day, week by week, month by month, year by year as you grow and overcome and walk in the ways of God. "…That you may prove [so there's doing] what *is* well pleasing and good, and the perfect will of God" (Rom. 12:1-2).

Now let's come to 2 Corinthians 10, and let's see what we are to do with this carnal mind. What do you do when you're going along and all of a sudden there's an evil thought that comes along—bang. You say to yourself, "Where did that come from?" Well, it could come out of the depths of your own carnal mind. It could come because of the prince of the power of the air. It could come because there are evil spirits out there who want to bombard you with the missiles of evil that comes from Satan the devil and his demons. Now what are you to do when that thought comes along? Are you to say, "Oh, I must not be converted." No, you recognize it because of the Spirit of God. You are converted.

But now here is what you need to do, 2 Corinthians 10:4. "For the weapons of our warfare *are* not carnal…" You're not going to solve this by doing things that are motivated by the flesh. "…But mighty through God…" You are to use the weapons of God, and this is what he's talking about here. "…To *the* overthrowing of strongholds…" And of course that's referring to the carnal mind, because the carnal mind is the greatest stronghold of sin. And remember we still have the law of sin and death in us. So when these things pop up, here's what we are to do. "…Casting down *vain* imaginations…" We are to take those thoughts, literally, mentally, and grab hold of them, in the name of Jesus Christ, and cast them down. "…And every high thing that exalts itself against the knowledge of God, and bringing into captivity every thought into the obedience of Christ…" It's a process. So those things are going to happen. The Spirit of God in you is going to convict you of the sin so that you can repent and cast it down. Now notice what else it says, verse 6. "…And having a readiness to avenge all disobedience, whenever your obedience has been fulfilled" (2 Corinthians 10:4-6). Now that's the process.

Now let's see how we can put this into action even more. Let's come to Colossians 3. We put this into process even more. God expects us to do something. He will give us His Spirit to do it and accomplish it, which gives us the power to overcome. See, that's why during the Feast of Unleavened Bread we put in the Word of God. Not only do we eat unleavened bread, we put in Christ Who is unleavened, sinless. We put in the Word of God, which gives us conviction. We use the Spirit of God, which gives us power. And we realize that we have Satan to overcome, which we'll cover a little later during the feast, we have the world to overcome, we have ourselves to overcome. And the most important one to overcome is the self through the power and Spirit of God, because we overcome Satan by the blood of Christ.

So here's what He expects us to do, Colossians 3:1. "Therefore, if you have been raised together with Christ [that is, out of the watery grave of baptism], seek the things that are above, where Christ is sitting at *the* right hand of God." And when you go pray, understand that. Realize Christ is right there. Christ is our High Priest, our Savior, our Intercessor. The one Who sends the Spirit, the one Who petitions the Father. He is the propitiation for our sins, and all the things that have to do with Christ, and those are all yours because He gave Himself for you. And that ought to be a great humbling and overwhelming experience when you finally come to grasp and understand that when you're praying to God, you see.

"Set your affection on the things that are above, and not on the things that are on the earth. For you have died [again, through the watery grave of baptism], and your life has been hid together with Christ in God." Now here's a promise. Now notice how he gives this promise before he tells us what we need to do, because see, Paul wants us inspired. You can never overcome by beating the flesh. You can never overcome sin by focusing on sin. You have to focus on Christ and the solution, you see. And so that's why he shows the goal, verse 4. "When Christ, *Who is* our life, is manifested [that is, when He returns], then you also shall be manifested with Him in glory" (vs. 3-4). So he wants you to have the goal in mind before you start working on the things you need to work on to give you motivation, to give you inspiration, to help you to understand how great God is and what He's doing.

Verse 5, "Therefore, put to death your members which *are* on earth…" Grab those thoughts, cast them down. Take the lusts, get rid of them through the Spirit of Christ. These are the things: "…Sexual immorality, uncleanness, inordinate affection, evil desires, and covetousness, which is idolatry. Because of these things, the wrath of God is coming upon the sons of disobedience…" We don't want the wrath of God upon us, so put all of those things aside. This is the way, Paul says, that you used to live. He says, "…among whom you also once walked, when you were living in these things" (vs. 5-7). We're not to live in those.

Now notice, he goes through put off, put on, as we will see. Verse 8, "But now [therefore], you should also put off all *these* things…" These are the changing from carnal attitudes, carnal ways to spiritual ways, you see. "…Wrath, indignation, malice, blasphemy, *and* foul language from your mouth." Now who's he talking to? He's talking to converted Christians who have the Spirit of God but they still have the law of sin and death in them, and they have this fight that is going on. So Paul is telling them how to overcome this, and how they can build the character of God.

Verse 9, "Do not lie to one another, *seeing that* you have put off the old man together with his deeds, and have put on…" So you put off all these and now you put on the new man. Now this ties right in with Colossians 3:10-11. "…Put on the new man, who *is* being renewed…" Now notice, "is being renewed", it is a process, and it takes time. "…Being renewed in knowledge according to *the* image of Him Who created him; where there is neither Greek nor Jew, circumcision nor uncircumcision, barbarian, *nor* Scythian, slave *nor* free; but Christ *is* all things, and in all" (Colossians 3:9-11). See, God isn't going to make anyone—if you are Christ's it doesn't matter who you were before God called you. Christ is the all important thing.

Verse 12, "Put on then, as *the* elect of God, holy and beloved…" See, because you are holy and blameless before Him in love. That's why you're holy and beloved. "…Deep inner affections, kindness, humility, meekness, *and* long-suffering…" That's why God has brought together the weak of the world and all the problems that we have so that we can overcome, so that we can change. "…Forbearing one another, and forgiving one another if anyone has a complaint against another; even as Christ forgave you, so also you *should for-*

give. And above all these things *put on* love, which is *the* bond of perfection." That is the ultimate goal, as we will see. The very love of God within us to motivate us in everything that we do—that's the bond of perfection. "And let the peace of God rule in your hearts..." (vs. 12-15). Don't condemn yourself, don't have a guilty conscience, don't put yourself down. Come before God and Christ, confess your sins, let them be forgiven, walk in newness of life, pull all the vain imaginations down and cast them down and put in the Word of God, put in the love of God, put in the character of God, you see.

"Let the word of Christ dwell in you richly in all wisdom, teaching and admonishing one another in psalms and hymns and spiritual songs, singing with grace in your hearts to the Lord. And *in* everything [this is the overall thing], —whatever you do in word or in deed— *do* all in *the* name of *the* Lord Jesus, giving thanks to God and *the* Father by Him" (vs. 16-17). See, that's what God wants us to do.

Now we'll just finish with this. Let's come to Ephesians 5. This is important for us to do. How do we live our lives? "Therefore, be imitators of God, as beloved children..." That's why we study the Word of God. That's why we let God write it in our hearts, and our minds, and our inward part, that we can imitate God with His love, with His goodness, with His understanding, see. "...And walk in love [that is toward each other], even as Christ also loved us [and there's no more profound love than this], and gave Himself for us *as* an offering and a sacrifice to God for a sweet-smelling savor" (Eph. 5:1-2). Then he says all these other things are the works of the flesh—don't even let it be named among the saints. See, so the true spiritual meaning of the Feast of Unleavened Bread is this: through Jesus Christ, through renewing the New Covenant through the Passover, through keeping the commandments of God and loving God with all your heart, and mind, and soul, and being there is no condemnation. You are holy and without blame before Him in love.

End of Sermon

Transcriber: Carolyn Singer

The Feast of Unleavened Bread—Day 1—Holy Day
April 6, 2004
Scriptural References

1) Leviticus 22:31-33	13) Romans 3:23-27, 31
2) Leviticus 23:1-8	14) Romans 7:7-9, 11-21, 24-25
3) Deuteronomy 16:16-17	15) John 16:7-8
4) 2 Corinthians 9:6-8	16) Romans 8:1-4
5) John 14:6	17) 1 John 1:6-10
6) John 6:53-57, 63-70	18) 1 John 2:1-2
7) Matthew 16:17	19) Ephesians 1:3-9
8) 2 Timothy 3:14-17	20) Romans 5:17-18, 21
9) 2 Timothy 4:1-4	21) Romans 12:1-2
10) 1 Timothy 6:3-5	22) Corinthians 10:4-6
11) 1 Corinthians 5:6-8	23) Colossians 3:1-17
12) Psalm 34:4-8, 14-15, 18-19	24) Ephesians 5:1-2

CHAPTER FIFTEEN

The Redemption of the Firstborn

Unleavened Bread—Day 1

April 13, 2006

And greetings, brethren. Welcome to the first day of the Feast of Unleavened Bread—2006. And a lot of things have been going on in the world but now's the time for us to back off from all the things in prophecies and things that are happening in the world and concentrate on the feasts of God. And as we know the feasts of God give us the understanding that we need concerning His plan. Now I hope you all had a good Passover and Night to be Much Observed, and now we are going to focus on the Holy Days—the first day of Unleavened Bread, the Sabbath in-between the first and last day—the Wave Sheaf Offering Day, and then the last day of Unleavened Bread, and then soon Pentecost. Now those three feasts pertain directly to the church, and directly to each one of us so it's important that we understand and learn even more. So this year, as we have seen in understanding the little series that we did concerning the Passover and the Night Much To Be Observed, that there is a lot that we can learn from the commands concerning the firstborn.

So let's begin here in Leviticus 23 where we always begin. We've progressed all the way through verse 6. Let's begin right in verse 4: "These *are* the feasts of the LORD, *even* holy convocations, which ye shall proclaim in their seasons." Now we also find a corresponding place in the New Testament in II Timothy 4 to preach "in season and out of season" showing that the New Testament church did keep the Holy Days according to the commandments of God. Now we've already covered this, verse 5: "In the fourteenth *day* of the first month at even ["in between the evenings," or "between the two evenings" or as it is in the King James "at evening"] *is* the LORD'S passover." And as we have seen, God never at any time combined two days into one. Now notice verse 6: "And on the fifteenth day of the same month…" Now He doesn't say "combine this with the fourteenth." There are two different days. "And on the fifteenth day of the same month *is* the feast of unleavened bread unto the LORD: seven days ye must eat unleavened bread. In the first day ye shall have an holy convocation: ye shall do no servile work therein. But ye shall offer an offering made by fire unto the LORD seven days: in the seventh day *is* an holy convocation: ye shall do no servile work *therein*" (Lev. 23:4-8).

Now God expects us, when we come before Him on the Holy Days, to bring an offering as God has blessed us. So let's go to Deuteronomy 16 and see God's command here. And as we will see when we cover about the firstborn today, and the sanctifying of the firstborn and what God is doing with them, and how we fit into it, and the meaning of it for us in the church of God today, we are going to see how important it is that when we come before God we don't come before Him empty.

Now verse 16: "Three times in a year shall all thy males appear before the LORD thy God in the place which He shall choose…" And today wherever two or three are gathered together and Christ is in the midst of it, He's chosen to be there so that is the place. Now if we're able to have a fellowship group and have more than two or three, maybe have 15, 20, 30, 50, 70, whatever it may be, then that is a place where He has chosen to put His name. And also because as we have seen, we are the temple of God—individually to receive the Holy Spirit, and collectively as to what God is doing in building His church.

"…In the feast of unleavened bread, and in the feast of weeks, and in the feast of tabernacles: and they shall not appear before the LORD empty: every man *shall give* as he is able, according to the blessing of the LORD thy God which He hath given thee" (Deut. 16:16-17). And then we also know in the New Testament that the apostle Paul says that if we give, then God is able to give us sufficiency. So God challenges us, as we have seen, to prove Him for His blessing. So at this time we'll go ahead and pause and we'll take up the offering for the first day of the Feast of Unleavened Bread.

Now let's begin in an unusual place and let's see something that God has commanded concerning the firstborn. Now we've already covered much of that in Deuteronomy 16 when we covered it on the difference between the Night Much to be Observed and on the Passover, and the difference between the Passover offering there in Deuteronomy 16 that it is really peace offerings and so forth, and those are the offerings that the firstborn would bring.

Now let's come here to Numbers 3 and let's see something that's important, what God says and what He did the Passover night. And here's what He tells us, verse 11: "And the LORD spake unto Moses, saying, And I, behold, I have taken the Levites from among the children of Israel instead of all the firstborn that openeth the matrix among the children of Israel: therefore the Levites shall be Mine; because all the firstborn *are* Mine…" Now that's important for us to understand and realize. The firstborn belong to God, and we'll see how that applies to the church a little later as we go along. "…*For* on the day that I smote all the firstborn in the land of Egypt I hallowed unto Me all the firstborn in Israel, both man and beast: Mine shall they be: I *am* the LORD" (Num. 3:11-13). So this is really something. At the time that He executed His judgment against all the gods of Egypt and against all the firstborn man and beast in Egypt, then He set aside, or He sanctified, or He hallowed them. That's what it is. It means "sanctified them."

Now then there has to be a response. We can look at this as number one on the Passover, the 14th—redemption for the firstborn. Now then there has to be deliverance, and we will see that. Let's come here to Exodus 13 and we will see that all the way through. There is first redemption and then there is deliverance.

Now let's pick it up here Exodus 12:51: "And it came to pass the selfsame day [or that is "the very day"], *that* the LORD did bring the children of Israel out of the land of Egypt by their armies," which we saw and we know was the 15th day of the first month. It clearly tells us it was the 15th.

Now Exodus 13:1: "And the LORD spake unto Moses, saying, Sanctify unto Me [or that is set apart, hallow] all the firstborn, whatsoever openeth the womb among the children of Israel, *both* of man and of beast: it *is* Mine." Now I just want you to stop and think about how heinous a crime that abortion is, because most of those who are aborted are the firstborn. Now let's continue: "And Moses said unto the people, Remember this day, in which ye came out from Egypt, out of the house of bondage…" Now let's understand something: He passed over their houses on the Passover day, and on the first day of Unleavened Bread they come out of Egypt. So on the day portion of the Passover, as we saw, they assembled at Rameses so they could leave. Now notice: "…for by strength of hand the LORD brought you out from this *place:* there shall no leavened bread be eaten. This day [the 15th] came ye out in the month Abib." Then He talks about here concerning the commands for unleavened bread.

Now he says here down in verse 11: "And it shall be when the LORD shall bring thee into the land of the Canaanites, as He sware unto thee and to thy fathers, and shall give it thee, that thou shalt set apart unto the LORD all that openeth the matrix, and every firstling that cometh of a beast which thou hast; the males *shall be* the LORD'S. And every firstling of an ass thou shalt redeem with a lamb; and if thou wilt not redeem it, then thou shalt break his neck: and all the firstborn of man among thy children shalt thou redeem" (Ex. 13:1-4, 11-13). Now we're going to see about that. First we're going to concentrate a little bit on the firstborn, and let's see some things that we haven't understood before, or we haven't looked at, and we will see the theme of the firstborn coming right on down beginning with Abraham.

Now let's come to Genesis 11 and we will see Abraham was the firstborn. Now there is the right of firstborn, there is the right of the inheritance of the firstborn. And we haven't looked at it very often here, but Abraham was the firstborn of his father Terah. So let's come here to Genesis 11:26: "And Terah lived seventy years, and begat Abram, Nahor, and Haran." So Abraham was firstborn. Now we're also going to see that God redeemed Abraham. So there's a firstborn – there's a firstborn redemption. Now let's see this where He redeemed Abraham.

Let's come to Isaiah 29:22. And the deliverance, the redemption, the sanctification, and that will all tie in with what we are as those of "the church of the firstborn" as we will see later on. So this puts us in a status with God that is very important and really has profound meaning for us in our understanding and relationship with God. "Therefore thus saith the LORD, Who redeemed Abraham…" Now when did He redeem Abraham? Well we'll look at that in just a minute. "…Concerning the house of Jacob, Jacob shall not now be ashamed, neither shall his face now wax pale", etc. So He shows the redemption of Jacob along with the redemption of Abraham. But when was Abraham redeemed?

Now let's come back here to Genesis 15. I know we have been there but let's see, and we'll touch on this when we get to the New Testament to see what Paul says about this also. So Abraham was redeemed. Now remember this: beginning any relationship that anyone has with God you first have to be redeemed, which is what? The forgiveness of your sins and the application of the sacrifice of Jesus Christ to you. Isn't that correct? Yes.

Now Genesis 15:5, which we know is the Passover night: "And He brought him [Abraham] forth abroad, and said, Look now toward heaven, and tell the stars, if thou be able to number them: and He said unto him, So shall thy seed be. And he <u>believed</u> in the LORD; and He counted it to him <u>for righteousness</u>." That's when he was redeemed.

Now then what do we have? We have the sacrifice which parallels the time of the sacrifice and the crucifixion of Jesus Christ as we come down through the rest of it, and we've already covered that. But that's when Abraham was redeemed.

Now let's look at another one and see he was the firstborn, he was redeemed. Now we know that the firstborn that was counted of Sarah (because it's all that opens the womb) was Isaac. Now let's come to Genesis 22 and let's see when Isaac was redeemed. So this becomes very important for us to understand. And also we'll go to the book of Galatians here a little later on, where it says that if you are Christ's then you're Abraham's seed and heirs according to the promise, and that <u>we</u> in the church are like Isaac, the children of promise. Now let's see when Isaac was redeemed. So in every case in coming before God and God dealing with us first of all He must redeem us, and that is pictured by the Passover. Then He delivers us, which is pictured by the first day of the Feast of Unleavened Bread. And in delivering us our dedication to God begins.

Now, Genesis 22:1: "And it came to pass after these things, that God did tempt [prove] Abraham, and said unto him, Abraham: and he said, Behold, *here* I *am*. And He said, Take now thy son, thine only *son* Isaac, whom thou lovest, and get thee into the land of

Moriah; and offer him there for a burnt offering upon one of the mountains which I will tell thee of." See, because God said all the firstborn were His. And how did you redeem it? You redeemed it with a burnt offering, you redeemed it with a peace offering, as we have seen. Now then He also said that we were to redeem the firstborn, so here we find where Isaac was redeemed. And we're also going to see how he was redeemed. And we're also going to see that it is based upon faith, and based upon belief in spite of the circumstances that are involved. And we will see how God looks upon that.

Now let's continue. And of course understand Isaac was the firstborn of Sarah. Now verse 3: "And Abraham rose up early in the morning, and saddled his ass, and took two of his young men with him, and Isaac his son, and clave [split] the wood for the burnt offering, and rose up, and went unto the place of which God had told him. Then on the third day Abraham lifted up his eyes, and saw the place afar off. And Abraham said unto his young men, Abide ye here with the ass; and I and the lad will go yonder and worship, and come again to you. And Abraham took the wood of the burnt offering, and laid *it* upon Isaac his son…" Now Isaac was also a type of Christ. Isaac was the firstborn. We are going to see here in just a bit Jesus was the firstborn also. So there is a great significance in all of this and on the first day of the Feast of Unleavened Bread. Because the first day of the Feast of Unleavened Bread, as we have seen beginning with the Night Much to be Remembered, is a celebration or a great feast unto God for redeeming and delivering the firstborn who are dedicated to God. Now we need to think of that in relationship to our lives. And we need to think of that in relationship to the way that God has called us.

Now let's continue on here. He took the wood and laid it on him, you could also say it was a type of Christ carrying His cross. "…And he took the fire in his hand [he didn't have a fire in his hand but he had a little bowl where he had coals and so forth], and a knife; and they went both of them together. And Isaac spake unto Abraham his father, and said, My father: and he said, Here *am* I, my son. And he said, Behold the fire and the wood: but where *is* the lamb for a burnt offering?" (Gen. 22:1-7). Now notice Abraham's faith because he believed God.

Now hold your place here and come back to James 2 and let's understand something concerning the justification and that there are things that we need to. Once we are redeemed, once we have been set aside by God, then there are things that we need to do. And as we have seen and we know our faith, not only believing, but our faith has to have works and has to have action. Just like the children of Israel, when they left Egypt they had to believe God and His Word. Just like in keeping the Passover—they kept the Passover exactly the way that God commanded them and they obeyed Him and stayed in their houses until morning. So with belief there has got to be obedience.

Now let's pick it up here, James 2:17: "In the same way also, faith, if it does not have works, is dead, by itself." You have to do what God says. "But someone is going to say, 'You have faith, and I have works.' *My answer is:* You prove your faith to me through your works, and I will prove my faith to you through my works." In other words the works are the evidence of what you believe. So if you say you have faith and you have no works, you really have no faith. But if you truly have faith you will have the righteous works because you believe and you act upon that faith. And that's what the whole Feast of Unleavened Bread is all about—that we act upon the faith. That's why it pictures the Exodus; that's why it shows the children of Israel leaving Egypt; that's why they had to go on their journey to meet God on Pentecost at Mount Sinai. And in much the same way when we are redeemed; and we renew the covenant with the Passover; and we keep the Night Much to be Observed, and the first day of the Feast of Unleavened Bread we are taking action to walk in the way of God in obedience and <u>we</u> are on our way to the Kingdom of God. So we have the same thing.

Let's go on, verse 19: "Do you believe that God is one? You do well *to believe this*. Even the demons believe—and tremble *in fear*. But are you willing to understand, O foolish man, that faith without works is dead?" So we're going to go back and see about Abraham here because James talks about it here.

Verse 21: "Was not Abraham our father justified by works when he offered up Isaac, his own son, upon the altar?" The firstborn—Abraham was firstborn, Isaac was firstborn. "Do you not see that faith was working together with his works, and by works *his* faith was perfected?" See, because it's this way: If you believe God and do what He says and have the works of faith, you are going to have more belief because it is perfected. And the whole purpose of our calling is to be perfected, right? Yes. So there you have it. "And the scripture was fulfilled which says, 'Now Abraham believed God, and it was reckoned to him for righteousness;' and he was called a friend of God" (James 2:17-23).

Now let's come back here to Genesis 22. See, Abraham said in verse 8, let's read that again. Notice, he had to have the faith. Also Isaac had to have a certain amount of faith. He had to accept the answer that his father, Abraham, gave him. And he said: "...my son, God will provide Himself a lamb for a burnt offering: so they went both of them together. And they came to the place which God had told him of; and Abraham built an altar there, and laid the wood in order, and bound Isaac his son, and laid him on the altar upon the wood. And Abraham stretched forth his hand, and took the knife to slay his son. And the angel of the LORD called unto him out of heaven, and said, Abraham, Abraham: and he said, Here *am* I. And he said, Lay not thine hand upon the lad, neither do thou any thing unto him: for now I know that thou fearest God..." (Gen. 22:8-12). And as we mentioned before, this was over a period of years all of this occurred from its beginning of his calling.

And so likewise with us, this ties in with the scripture which Jesus said: "...the one who endures to *the* end, that one shall be saved" (Matt. 10:22). So we have to have these trials and tests upon us to see: 1) Do we love God? 2) Do we believe God? 3) Will we obey God under all circumstances? And that's what the Feast of Unleavened Bread is all about, so that every year, not only do we renew the covenant on the Passover night, not only do we keep the Night Much to Be Observed, but now on the first day of the Feast of Unleavened Bread every year we look to God in faith. We examine ourselves, we see what we need to do. We need to take the faith of Christ and overcome the sin that is within us, which is a type of leaven. But let's understand this—all of this has to be done by the power and the Spirit of God. Just like God had to lead the children of Israel out of Egypt; just like God sanctified all the firstborn unto God on the night that He killed all the firstborn of Egypt— man and beast, and therefore on the 15th is to be a celebration unto God, as we have seen, for the firstborn in bringing forth their offerings, in bringing forth offerings of thanksgiving that they are the firstborn and redeemed; also to bring forth the offering to redeem those children that were born during the year; also the offerings, as we have seen, to redeem the unclean animals; and also to bring the firstborn of oxen, and sheep, and goat, and so forth and to bring those as an offering to God. All of that together, so there's an awful lot of meaning on this day. And we find all of it jam-packed right here into Genesis 22 because this is when Isaac was redeemed—the firstborn, which belonged to God. That's why God said to Abraham, "Take your firstborn, your only son, the one whom you love and you go offer him." Because why? All the firstborn belong to God. And there's great meaning in that for us. We are the firstborn and we belong to God. So we need to understand that.

Now let's see what God provided, verse 13: "And Abraham lifted up his eyes, and looked, and behold behind *him* a ram caught in a thicket by his horns..." Now I've thought many times, as I've said before, that when they went up there if the ram would have been there they would have seen it, and they would have said, "Oh look, God has already provided a sacrifice, hasn't He." So God either caused it to go over there or God supernaturally created a ram specifically for a substitutionary sacrifice for Isaac. And this ram then became a type of Christ as a substitutionary sacrifice, which then redeems us, just like it redeemed Isaac. "…And Abraham went and took the ram, and offered him up for a burnt offering in the stead of his son." Now here's another guarantee that we have. Now notice, the guarantee that comes down through Abraham… (and this is important for us to understand) and the reason that a lot of people lose faith is: 1) Because they don't grasp the significance of their calling; 2) They don't really truly believe God in a way that they ought to. Now we'll see that in just a minute here.

Let's come down here to verse 15: "And the angel of the LORD called unto Abraham out of heaven the second time, and said, By myself have I sworn, saith the LORD, for because thou hast done this thing [faith, belief, and action], and hast not withheld thy son, thine only *son* [who was the firstborn that God already proclaimed that was His, and the firstborn were to be redeemed]: that in blessing I will bless thee, and in multiplying I will multiply thy seed as the stars of the heaven, and as the sand which *is* upon the sea shore; and thy seed shall possess the gate of his enemies; and in thy seed shall all the nations of the earth be blessed; because thou hast obeyed My voice" (Gen. 22:8-13, 15-18). Now that's something. Let's understand we are here because of Abraham and Jesus Christ.

Now let's come back to the book of Galatians and let's see the parallel between Isaac and his redemption and being the son of promise, and we become the children of promise. Come back here to Galatians 4 and let's see how important that this is. So there is a parallel for the church. And also just like the substitutionary sacrifice to redeem Isaac, Jesus Christ is the substitutionary sacrifice for us, and we become the spiritual firstborn of God.

Now Galatians 4:26: "But the Jerusalem above is free, which is *the* mother of us all; for it is written…" See, because the mother is the church of the firstborn, right? Just like Sarah was the mother of Isaac the firstborn. And that's why in Hebrews 12 it's called the "church of the firstborn." So we have been set aside and sanctified by God. "…For it is written, 'Rejoice, O barren who did not bear! Break forth and cry, *you* who were not travailing, because many more *are* the children of the desolate than of her who has the husband.' " (Gal. 4:26-27). And we, brethren, like Isaac are the children of promise. Now let's understand that. Our calling is so great and fantastic we are the children of promise just like Isaac was.

Now turn back here to Galatians 3:26: "…Because you are all sons of God…" Now let's look at this very carefully. "…Through faith in Christ Jesus. For as many *of you* as were baptized into Christ did put on Christ. There is neither Jew nor Greek; there is neither bond nor free; there is neither male nor female [that is in opportunity for salvation]; for you are all one in Christ Jesus," Who was what? The substitutionary sacrifice for us, right? Yes. "And if you *are* Christ's, then you are Abraham's seed, and heirs according to *the* promise" (Gal. 3:26-29).

Now let's come to the book of Hebrews here and let's see something very important. Let's come to Hebrews 6, and this is why we need to have the absolute faith in God and His Word, because His Word is true, God is righteous, God cannot lie, God will not lie, and He showed by that very act of redeeming Isaac, which then shows the redemption of us through Christ, which we will see in just a minute.

Now let's pick it up here in verse 13: "For God, after promising Abraham, swore by Himself…" Now let's understand how sure the promises are. God swore by His existence that there would be the spiritual seed as pictured by the stars of heaven, and we're here because of that, see. "…Saying, 'Surely in blessing I will bless you, and in multiplying I will multiply you.' Now after he [that is Abraham] had patiently endured, he obtained the promise. For indeed, men swear by the greater, and confirmation by an oath *puts* an end to all disputes between them. In this *way* God, desiring more abundantly to show the heirs of the promise the unchangeable nature of His own purpose, confirmed *it* by an oath…" Now let's look at this unchangeableness of His purpose. And His purpose then also is revealed through what? The Sabbath and Holy Days. So here is a verse which establishes them, right? Then He gives an oath and He gives this promise: "…So that by two immutable things, in which *it was* impossible *for* God to lie…" Now we need to claim that promise. You know, we have our sins and we have our problems, we have our trials and difficulties and things that we all go through. I do and you do, and we're in this together. And that's why we need the Passover, and that's why we need the Feast of Unleavened Bread, that's why we need the Spirit of God working in our lives to help us, to uplift us, to redeem us, to rescue us, you see, and so that we can produce the fruit and character that God wants us to have.

"…We who have fled for refuge might have strong encouragement to lay hold on the hope *that has been* set before *us*; which *hope* we have as an anchor of the soul, both secure and steadfast, and which enters into the *sanctuary* within the veil; where Jesus has entered for us *as* a forerunner, having become a High Priest forever according to the order of Melchisedec" (Heb. 6:13-20). So God is dealing with us that way.

Now let's come back here to Romans 3 and let's see the redemption that has been given to us through Christ just exactly as it was given to Isaac. So it's interesting to see – God redeemed Abraham, God redeemed Isaac, God redeemed Jacob, God redeemed Joseph, and God has redeemed us. And all of those follow in parallel.

Now here Roman 3:23, and this tells us how, in the same parallel as Isaac was redeemed, we are redeemed with a substitutionary sacrifice of Christ instead of the ram. Now let's pick it up here: "For all have sinned, and come short of the glory of God; *but* are being justified freely by His grace…" So what we saw back there in Genesis 22 was an act of grace, wasn't it? God provided the sacrifice, didn't He? Freely. But it also involved the belief and faith and works of Abraham and Isaac, didn't it? Yes. "…Being justified freely by His grace through <u>the redemption</u>…" See, we are redeemed, and that redemption is through Christ. And through Christ, He being the firstborn of God, because it says there in Matthew 1:18 that He was the firstborn of the virgin Mary, correct? Yes. Then it also says in Hebrews 1 that when He brought the firstborn into the world He said, " 'Let all *the* angels worship Him.' " So He's the firstborn. Now He was also the firstborn from among the dead (Revelation 1). So there we have the exact parallel that we need in our lives and will follow through as we come along here in Romans 3 and Romans 4.

Now verse 25: "…The redemption that *is* in Christ Jesus…" the substitutionary sacrifice. You go back and what did John the Baptist say? John 1:29: " 'Behold the Lamb of God, Who takes away the sin of the world.' " And it doesn't say "sins", it says "sin" because the sin of the world goes clear back to Adam, and we, with the law of sin and death, carry that in us. So he says "sin."

"…Whom God has openly manifested *to be* a propitiation through faith in His blood, in order to demonstrate His righteousness [or that is, His justification]…" Now when you have been justified then that is the first step of being sanctified, which then means you have been hallowed. When you receive the Holy Spirit you have been sanctified and hallowed. And it's up to us to keep the Holy Spirit growing through prayer and study and all the things that God has shown us here. It's justification: "…in respect to the remission of sins that are past…" Now if you have the New Testament [Faithful Version], we have in there "Justification By Faith," you can read the appendix on it. It goes through and explains everything concerning it.

Now continuing in verse 26: "...through the forbearance of God [God's mercy, God's kindness, God's loving-kindness, God's patience]; *yes*, to publicly declare His righteousness [or, justification for sin] in the present time, that He might be just, and the one Who justifies the one who *is* of *the* faith of Jesus. Therefore, where *is* boasting? It is excluded [because it's by grace and mercy]. Through what law? *The law* of works? By no means! Rather, *it is* through a law of faith." And we've seen the law of faith. You believe, you act upon it, you continue in it. That's the law of faith. And God blesses you. "Consequently, we reckon that a man is justified by faith, separate from works of law." And those works of law had to do with the rituals and the laws of Judaism, not the laws and commandments of God, as we will see here in just a minute.

"*Is He* the God of the Jews only? *Is He* not also *the God* of *the* Gentiles? YES! *He is* also God of *the* Gentiles, since *it is* indeed one God Who will justify *the* circumcision by faith, and *the* uncircumcision through faith. Are we, then, abolishing law through faith? MAY IT NEVER BE! Rather, we are establishing law" (Rom. 3:23-31). That's what's important. And that's what we need to realize.

Now let's look and see about Abraham. Here in Chapter 4, he believed God and it was counted to him for righteousness. Let's pick it up here in verse 13. The promise was given to Abraham. When was that given? On the Passover night. When was that confirmed? The Night to be Much Observed. "For the promise to Abraham, or to his seed, that he should be heir of the world, *was* not *given* through law; rather, *it was* through *the* righteousness of faith; because if those of *the* law *be the* heirs, *then* faith is made void, and the promise *is* made of no effect. For the law works out wrath; because where no law is, *there is* no transgression. For this reason *it is* of faith, in order that *it might be* by grace [God's gracious gift that we believe Him], to the end that the promise might be certain to all the seed—not to the one who is of the law only, but also to the one who is of *the* faith of Abraham, who is *the* father of us all, (Exactly as it is written: 'I have made you a father of many nations.') before God in Whom he believed, Who gives life to the dead, and calls the things that are not as though they are; *and* who against hope believed in hope..." That's why it's important to understand about the life of Abraham, Isaac, and Jacob and their faith and their works and their shortcomings and their sins that they had to repent of to give us hope, to give us understanding the way that God wants us to have. And let's understand this: Because you are having a problem, because you have circumstances that are greater than you can handle, turn them to God in faith and always have that hope. Always keep that hope going. That's what Abraham did and look how long he had to have hope. God, when He first brought him out of Haran and told him to go in Canaan, he said, "I will bless you and make your seed great." Well, it was 25 years until Isaac was born. So we have to continue with hope.

"...Who against hope believed in hope, in order that he might become a father of many nations [and he did physically, and he will spiritually], according to that which was spoken, 'So shall your seed be.' And he, not being weak in the faith, considered not his own body, already having become dead, being about one hundred years old, nor *did he consider* the deadness of Sarah's womb..." See, he had to have a child by promise, by miracle, which then was a type of the one Who became Jesus Christ. So he didn't have doubt, verse 20: "...rather, he was strengthened in the faith, giving glory to God..." (Rom. 4:13-20). Now that tells us how to have our faith strengthened by giving glory to God. And so we'll take a little break here and then we'll continue on and see how we are redeemed and how we are delivered.

Now let's continue on and see, how then, we have redemption, deliverance which then includes sanctification, justification; and also to help us as we go on our exodus leaving this world as it were and developing the righteousness of Christ.

Now let's come to I Peter 1 and let's see how he brings all of this together in this chapter. This is really quite a tremendous chapter, and we will see how it intersperses the things of the Passover—through redemption, setting aside; and also how it pictures deliverance and how it pictures our overcoming, and how it pictures how we are to grow in grace and knowledge, all in this one single chapter.

So let's begin right here in verse 1: "Peter, an apostle of Jesus Christ, to *the* elect strangers scattered in Pontus, Galatia, Cappadocia, Asia, and Bithynia [these are the Gentiles who were scattered out there]; *who have been chosen* according to *the* predetermined knowledge of God *the* Father…" So we've been chosen. So being redeemed, we've been chosen, or chosen then redeemed. "…According to *the* predetermined knowledge of God *the* Father, by sanctification through *the* Spirit…" Now this becomes very, very important: "…unto obedience and sprinkling of *the* blood of Jesus Christ: grace and peace be multiplied to you." So all of this results in grace from God, peace with God, we are delivered.

Now hold your place here and come to I John 3 and let's see how this also works together in sanctification of the Spirit, because once we have been redeemed, and delivered, and sanctified, we have been sanctified by the Spirit of God and we become part of the church of the firstborn. We belong to God. Like God said, "All the firstborn are Mine." Now you think on that a little bit more and that helps you understand the severity of the unpardonable sin.

Now, I John 3:1: "Behold! What *glorious* love the Father has given to us, that we should be called the children of God!" Not yet born—we are begotten, but we are the children of God, selected by Him, chosen by Him, redeemed by Him, delivered by Him, you see. "For this very reason, the world does not know us because it did not know Him. Beloved, now we are the children of God [just like a child in the womb is growing and developing], and it has not yet been revealed what we shall be [because we haven't been born again yet—that takes place at the resurrection]; but we know that when He is manifested, we shall be like Him, because we shall see Him exactly as He is." And that's born again at the resurrection.

Now verse 3, a very key thing concerning the hope we talked about with Abraham and the hope that we are going to talk about here in I Peter 1: "And everyone who has this hope in him purifies himself, even as He is pure." And that's what the Feast of Unleavened Bread is all about—to overcome sin, to get rid of sin, to have our minds cleansed, to have our hearts purified. You see, it is a process because God is creating in us His Holy and His perfect character through His Spirit. And this requires then our love and obedience and dedication because we've been sanctified by God.

Now here is the contrast. We are going to see this. And this is why God constantly instructed the children of Israel to not go back into Egypt, because that personifies the way of the world, the way of Satan the devil. We are not to be living in sin. Now verse 4: "Everyone who practices sin is also practicing lawlessness, for sin is lawlessness." [And the KJV says "Sin is the transgression of the law."] "And you know that He appeared in order that He might take away our sins; and in Him is no sin." There is the substitutionary sacrifice, correct? Yes. "Everyone who dwells in Him [which we are by the power of God's Holy Spirit] does not *practice* sin…" And that's the whole purpose of the Feast of Unleavened Bread that leaven is a type of sin. We are to put the leaven out of our homes, we are to put sin out of our lives, and all that ties in together. It doesn't say we don't sin, because as long as we have the law of sin and death in us, as we have seen as the apostle Paul wrote there in Romans 7, we are going to be sinning, but as long as we do not sin a sin unto death, it is a forgivable sin and upon repentance we are forgiven and the grace of God applies to us here. "…Anyone who *practices* sin has not seen Him [now he's talking about those false anti-Christ prophets that were coming around and saying it's ok to sin], nor has known Him. Little children, do not allow anyone to deceive you…" And that's another thing concerning the Feast of Unleavened Bread, because unleavened bread strips bare human nature before God and shows how then in spirit and in truth we will not then be deceived. "…Do not allow anyone to deceive you; the one who practices righteousness is righteous, even as He is righteous. The one who practices sin is of the devil because the devil has been sinning from *the* beginning." So you see, that's why Paul said, "Do we abolish law because of grace? God forbid. We establish law." See, because it's to be written in our hearts and our minds and that's the whole purpose of the Feast of Unleavened Bread because the more of the Word of God we get in, the more sin we put out; the more of the power of God's Holy Spirit we have, the more that He exposes in us the sin that is within, so we can repent. And all of those things work together, and that's what the spiritual purpose of the Feast of Unleavened Bread is for.

"For this purpose the Son of God appeared that He might destroy the works of the devil." And the first place to begin destroying it is within our lives. Now, stop and think about this in relationship to the Passover: Did He not destroy all the works of the devil in Egypt in judging Egypt with all the plagues and all the things that were there and on the Passover night judging all the gods and religious practices of Egypt? Yes, indeed. And He's going to destroy every one of the works of the devil when He returns.

Now verse 9 is a key thing: "Everyone who has been begotten by God does not practice sin because His seed *of begettal* is dwelling within him, and he is not able to *practice* sin because he has been begotten by God" (I John 3:1-9). Now let me explain this verse thoroughly to you, which is this: You have the Holy Spirit of God which is the begettal. You come along and as exposed by the Feast of Unleavened Bread and God's Spirit in you, you see sin in your life. You are convicted of what sin is and you repent of it. That is God working in your life so you don't practice sin. Now notice it doesn't say: You do not sin. It says you do not <u>practice</u> sin.

Now come over here to I John 5, and this is very important for us to understand concerning sin. Verse 16: "If anyone sees his brother sinning a sin *that is* not unto death…" In other words it is a forgivable sin as Jesus said, " 'Because of this, I say to you, every sin and blasphemy shall be forgiven to men except the blasphemy against the *Holy* Spirit; *that* shall not be forgiven to men. And whoever speaks a word against the Son of man, it shall be forgiven him; but whoever speaks against the Holy Spirit, it shall not be forgiven him, neither in this age nor in the coming *age*' " (Matt. 12:31-32). So Jesus there in Matthew 12 showed there are forgivable and unforgivable sins. So a sin that is not unto death is a forgivable sin. So if you are convicted in conscience of sin within and you repent of it, it is forgiven. It is a forgivable sin.

Now if you want to know about the unpardonable sin, go to our series in the book of Hebrews, or get the tapes on that, or in our new book that we're publishing here pretty soon we are going to have in there about what the unpardonable sin is. (*Occult Holidays or God's Holy Days—Which?*).

Now: "…he shall ask [now if you see a brother sinning, pray for him], and He [that is God] will give him life for those who do not sin unto death." In other words He'll lead them to repentance. That's all of God's purpose—to lead us to repentance. "There is a sin unto death; concerning that *sin*, I do not say that he should make *any* supplication *to God*" (I John 5:16).

So, back here to Chapter 3. We don't practice sin. Now let's read verse 10 because it becomes very important in understanding this: "By this *standard* are manifest the children of God [who are the church of the firstborn—chosen, set aside by God, redeemed, delivered by God] and the children of the devil. Everyone who does not practice righteousness is not of God, and neither is the one who does not love his brother." So there we go. Now come over here just a few more verses toward Chapter 3 and let's read this here, verse 18, here's the whole sum of it. This is where we are headed. This is the goal of our behavior: "My little children, we should not love in word, nor with *our* tongues; rather, *we should love* in deed and in truth. And in this *way* we know that we are of the truth, and shall assure our hearts before Him…" So God wants us to have the confidence. Now we go back and we can apply this to the children of Israel leaving the land of Egypt. They left with a high hand. In other words they had confidence—confidence in God, trust in God, although it didn't last very long, as we will see, because they didn't have the Holy Spirit of God. But here we have the Spirit of God and we are to assure our hearts before God and to know that we are right with God. That's what everything that God wants us to do is all about.

Verse 20: "…That if our hearts condemn us [because we've sinned—it's a forgivable sin], God is greater than our hearts, and knows all things. Beloved, if our hearts do not condemn us, *then* we have confidence toward God. And whatever we may ask we receive from Him because we keep His commandments and practice those things that are pleasing in His sight" (I John 3:10, 18-22). And that's what God wants us to do.

Now let's come back to I Peter 1, and we are going to see all of these elements here again in the first chapter concerning what God has done. Now let's begin here in verse 3. That's where we left off before with verse 2: "Blessed *be* the God and Father of our Lord Jesus Christ, Who, according to His abundant mercy, has begotten us again unto a <u>living hope</u>…" And that living hope is through the resurrection of Jesus Christ from the dead because He is the firstborn from among many brethren, and we <u>are</u> the church of the firstborn, and what we are going to look at here is the process of perfection.

Now hold your place here and come back to Hebrews 12 because I refer to this, but let's see what it is that God is doing with us, and let's see how He is doing it, and let's see the purpose in it. Sometimes we expect things to go totally perfect in our lives every day in every way and we end up with many difficulties and challenges and problems and maybe even get depressed over sinning and all of these things. Well look, that's all a part of God dealing with you so you're going to trust in Him, as we will see, and trust in Him for your deliverance because that's what the Feast of Unleavened Bread is all about.

Now here is the goal. Let's come here to Hebrews 12:22: "But you have come to Mount Sion, and to *the* city of *the* living God, heavenly Jerusalem; and to an innumerable company of angels; *to the* joyous festival gathering; and to *the* church of *the* firstborn…" That is us, and all of the saints down through time beginning with Abel and until the return of Jesus Christ. Now at the resurrection when we are born again and become the literal family of the firstborn of God, redeemed, delivered, resurrected, given eternal life—that's the goal. "…*To the* joyous festival gathering [so you see, that's why I said this also ties into Pentecost, as we will see]; and to *the* church of *the* firstborn, registered *in the book of life* in heaven; and to God, *the* Judge of all; and to *the* spirits of the just who have been perfected…" (Heb. 12:22-23). Now that's what God is doing in our lives. That's why we go through the things that we go through—to be perfected.

Now come back here to I Peter 1 and let's see how this is. You see, we have the living hope. We don't trust into the flesh. We don't trust in the physical things around us. We need them to exist as long as we are physical human beings, that is true, but we don't look at that as a great thing. We're thankful and grateful for all that God gives us and does for us and provides for us because we need it, that is true. But here is what we are looking to because our hope goes beyond this life.

Verse 4: "...Unto an inheritance <u>incorruptible</u> and <u>undefiled</u> and <u>unfading</u>, reserved in heaven for us..." See, because on the Passover night Jesus told His apostles what? "I go to prepare a place for you. And if I go, I will come again and receive you to Myself, so that where I am you may be also." That is our hope—reserved, unfading, undefiled. Now notice verse 5: "...Who *are* being safeguarded by *the* power of God through faith, for salvation *that is* ready to be revealed in *the* last time." That's the way that God does. He sets the goal, He sets the perspective whereas you could say "the vision," because without vision the people perish, and God has given this vision of the hope of our calling and where we are going and what we are doing, and that's what the Feast of Unleavened Bread is all about—that we desire to get rid of sin, that we desire to overcome human nature, that we desire to be delivered out of the difficulties and problems that we are in, and all of those work for the character of building love and hope and faith and grace and temperance and longsuffering and mercy and understanding—all the fruits of the Holy Spirit, all of the character that comes from God.

Now verse 6: "In this you yourselves greatly rejoice [which we ought to]; though for the present, if it is necessary, you are in distress for a little while by various trials; in order that the proving of your faith..." Just like God proved Abraham's faith, correct? Yes. "...Which is much more precious than gold that perishes, though it is being tested by fire, may be found unto praise and honor and glory at *the* revelation of Jesus Christ..." (I Peter 1:4-7).

Now let's look how we trust in God to redeem us and to deliver us. Hold your place here because we'll come back to I Peter 1. Let's come to Titus 2. First we must be redeemed. That's what God did with the children of Israel, right? He redeemed them. Next then we have to be delivered, and we will see that. Let's go up here to verse 11 and follow through with how Paul wrote. You know many of the things that are written in Greek, they have long run-on sentences which are unacceptable in English, but they work just fine in Greek.

Verse 11: "For the grace of God, which brings salvation for all men, has appeared..." That's Christ, His sacrifice, His resurrection. All of that is the grace of God and salvation. "...Teaching us that, having denied ungodliness and worldly lusts, we should live moderately and righteously and godly in this present world..." That's how we are to be. That's what unleavened bread is all about. "...Looking for the blessed hope and *the* appearing of the glory of our Savior and great God, Jesus Christ; Who gave Himself for us, so that <u>He might redeem us from all lawlessness</u>..." There you have it. Just like when God redeemed Israel when He slew all the first born in Egypt, He redeemed Abraham, He redeemed Isaac, and here's the purpose: "...and might purify for Himself [that's the whole process of growing, changing, and overcoming, and the purpose of Unleavened Bread] a unique people, zealous of good works." That's what we should be. "Speak these things, and exhort, and rebuke with all authority. Do not let anyone despise you" (Titus 2:11-15). So there is redemption.

Now let's look at some deliverance. When we get into the trials and difficulties that Peter spoke, of let's see how we are to look to God to deliver us. Let's come to Psalm 7. And we all need deliverance. Sometimes there are times when we go before God... I know I do. I know you do. And sometimes there are so many things pressing in upon you that the only thing you can do is like one of the psalms there where he starts out, he says, "Help." And another one says, "Hear me." And another one is, "O God, I'm so overwhelmed I can hardly lift up my head." And sometimes you get into those things. Alright, let's pick it up here in Psalm 7. Here is how we are to approach God, because first there is redemption and then there is deliverance. And deliverance is based upon hope and trust and so forth.

Verse 1: "O Lord my God, in Thee do I put my trust: save me from all them that persecute me, and <u>deliver</u> me..." And so you go before God and say, "Oh God I'm overwhelmed with this. Please just intervene, deliver me, help me, open the way, open the door, give me understanding, help me to realize why I'm going through what I'm going through. Give me of Your Spirit, give me of Your truth, deliver me from this situation." "...Lest he tear my soul like a lion, rending *it* in pieces, while *there is* none to deliver" (Psa. 7:1-2).

Now come over here to Psalm 25. This is quite a psalm of deliverance, and one that we can also apply to our prayers and our thoughts and yieldedness to God asking God to deliver us, you see. Now in deliverance there is trust. You must trust in God, which is active faith, active belief, knowing that what God has said that He's a God that cannot and will not lie, His Word is true. You know, sometimes, just like the man who wanted to have the demon cast out of his son and Jesus said, "If you believe, all things are possible." He said, "Lord, I believe. Help my unbelief." So lots of times we need to go to God in that way and we need to look to Him and just ask Him, "Help us." But that trust and faith go hand in hand with redemption.

Psalm 25:1: "Unto Thee, O LORD, do I lift up my soul. O my God, I trust in Thee..." That's what we are to do—trust in God. What is the scripture which says, "Trust no man." Every time you trust some man you get in trouble, right? Yes, we've got a long history of that, don't we? Yes.

"...Let me not be ashamed, let not mine enemies triumph over me. Yea, let none that wait on Thee be ashamed: let them be ashamed which transgress without cause." Now notice what happens then when we have that kind of attitude, and when we are trusting in God and looking to Him: "Shew me Thy ways, O LORD; teach me Thy paths. Lead me in Thy truth, and teach me..." See, this is what we need to be—teachable by God with His Spirit and in truth. "...For Thou *art* the God of my salvation; on Thee do I wait all the day." Now notice how he reminded God. When you get down and desperate and in the fiery trial that Peter was talking about here in I Peter 1, remember this, verse 6: "Remember, O LORD, Thy tender mercies and Thy lovingkindnesses; for they *have been* ever of old. Remember not the sins of my youth, nor my transgressions: according to Thy mercy remember Thou me for Thy goodness' sake, O LORD. Good and upright *is* the LORD: therefore will He teach sinners in the way. The meek will He guide in judgment: and the meek will He teach His way." And that's what the Exodus is all about—it is "the way" of God. "All the paths of the LORD *are* mercy and truth unto such as keep His covenant and His testimonies." Then he says: "For Thy name's sake, O LORD, pardon mine iniquity; for it *is* great" (Psa. 25:1-11).

Come over here to [Psalms] Chapter 27 now and let's see how this is also amplified here, and how we have trust, we have deliverance, we have yieldedness to God. Verse 11: "Teach me Thy way, O LORD, and lead me in a plain path..." And that's what we need God to do—God, with His Spirit to teach us. Then in every situation that we learn. Now many times we get frustrated in some of the things we are going through, and in overcoming there are very difficult challenges for us, but let's have Him teach us, see.

"...Lead me in a plain path, because of mine enemies. Deliver me not over unto the will of mine enemies..." Now notice, for here is a prophecy of Christ: "...for false witnesses are risen up against me, and such as breathe out cruelty. *I had fainted,* unless I had believed to see the goodness of the LORD in the land of the living [projecting forward to the resurrection]. Wait on the LORD: be of good courage, and He shall strengthen thine heart: wait, I say, on the LORD" (Psa. 27:11-14) and He will deliver us. There is no question about it.

Now let's come back to I Peter 1 here again and let's see how Peter continues going on showing all of these elements that we have concerning the Feast of Unleavened Bread and growing and changing and overcoming in faith, in truth, and love, and all of those things are all combined together here in the first chapter of I Peter. So it's really very interesting when you get in and you study the Bible and you see how God inspired them to write, you see how that all the elements of the truth of God are brought in different ways and in different manners. And so here we have this concerning many of the aspects of the Feast of Unleavened Bread and the redemption of the firstborn being sanctified and set aside by God for a special and a holy use.

Let's go over verse 7 again: "…In order that the proving of your faith…" And that's what it's all about—He's going to prove our faith. "…Which is much more precious than gold that perishes, though it is being tested by fire, may be found unto praise and honor and glory at *the* revelation of Jesus Christ; Whom, not having seen, you love; in Whom, *though* at the present time you do not see Him, you believe…" So here we have hope, we have belief, we have faith, we have love. And also: "…rejoice with unspeakable joy, and filled with glory; *and are* receiving the end of your faith—*even the* salvation of *your* souls…" Well, it's the salvation that we have been given here.

Now notice: "…concerning which salvation…" See, we've been redeemed, we have been delivered. And of course we ask God every day, "Deliver us from our sins, deliver us from the evil one." And God has intervened to do that, you see. "…The prophets who prophesied of the grace *that would come* to you have diligently searched out and intently inquired, searching into what *way* and what manner of time the Spirit of Christ *which was* in them was indicating, testifying beforehand of the sufferings of Christ, and these glories that would follow…" (I Peter 1:7-11). So it's quite a thing, isn't it?

Now let's see how that's accomplished. Come here to Colossians 1 and let's see again of the deliverance. And here in this case rescuing. God has to intervene and rescue us from Satan the devil, just exactly in the same way that He had to intervene and rescue the firstborn and the children of Israel in Egypt and deliver them.

Now let's come over here to Colossians 1:10: "…That you may walk worthily of the Lord, unto all pleasing, being fruitful in every good work and growing in the knowledge of God…" And that's what it needs to be. Every year we keep the Passover, keep the Feast of Unleavened Bread, and all the holy days of God; that we are growing in the knowledge of God so every year we learn more; we are preparing for the resurrection; we are growing in grace and knowledge; we are growing in love and faith and hope and trust and all of those things, you see.

Now notice what that does, verse 11: "…being strengthened with all power according to the might of His glory, unto all endurance [because we must endure to the end] and long-suffering with joy…" Now let's understand something: every year there are going to be saints who are going to come to the end of their lives and die. God said there is a time to die. And when you die you're going to die of something, aren't you? Yes, because your body being physical, and your body being corruptible and being weak is going to die of something. So we need to realize that. But let's look at it the way that God looks at it. He says, "Blessed in the eyes of the Lord is the death of His saints." Why? Because death is actually a graduation. You graduate from this physical life and are put in the grave and you wait the resurrection. And when you die there is no more sin, there is no more pain, there is no more wretchedness. But the next thought that you will have will be the resurrection and the angels carrying you up to meet Christ on the sea of glass in the air with all the other saints. So let's keep focused on that, that we are enduring to the end and looking to the long-suffering of God to help us to do that.

Verse 12: "…giving thanks to the Father, Who has made us qualified for the share of the inheritance of the saints in the light…" Now notice verse 13. Very important thing: "…Who has personally rescued us from the power of darkness…" Now you go back and you can see that situation with the children of Israel when they were in Egypt. Was there not the plague of darkness? Does that not signify the darkness of Satan the devil? And did He not give light to the children of Israel who were living in Goshen at that time? Yes. "…personally rescued us from the power of darkness…" Who controls the power of darkness? Satan the devil. We are rescued and delivered from the evil one. Just like God rescued the children of Israel and brought them out of Egypt and rescued them from the evil of that terrible and wretched society and the slavery in which they were held captive. "…And has transferred *us* unto the kingdom of the Son of His love…" We are under the authority of God the Father and Jesus Christ. That's what's important to understand. "…In Whom we have redemption…" So here we go right back to the redeeming of the firstborn, the delivery of the firstborn, the walking in the way of God, the exodus out of sin. "…*Even* the remission of sins…" (Col. 1:10-14).

Now let's come back and we'll finish I Peter 1 here. So you see how all of these things work, how all of these things come together, and how He saves us. Now come back here to I Peter 1 and let's pick it up here in verse 11: "…searching into what *way* and what manner of time the Spirit of Christ *which was* in them was indicating, testifying beforehand of the sufferings of Christ, and these glories that would follow; to whom it was revealed that, not for themselves, but to us they were ministering these things, which now have been announced to you by those who have preached the gospel to you by *the* Holy Spirit, sent from heaven—into which things the angels desire to look."

Now here is the lesson we need to do. Here is the lesson for the Feast of Unleavened Bread. Because of all of this… Now see you start out with Chapter 1, verse 1 and you come down here to verse 13 and he gives the summary. Now he says: "For this reason, be prepared in your minds [that's what the Feast of Unleavened Bread is all about], be self-controlled [with the Spirit of God], *and* be fully hoping in the grace that will be brought to you at *the* revelation of Jesus Christ." And the greatest grace we have to receive yet is what? The resurrection, right? Yes. Which will be when? When Christ returns.

Now: "As obedient children [this is what God wants us to be], do not conform yourselves to the former lusts, *as you did* in *your* ignorance." Don't go back and live the way that you lived. If it comes back, starts to creep back, that's just like leaven growing in your life—get rid of it. Put in the unleavenedness of Christ. And that unleavenedness comes through the Spirit of God, as obedient children, see. Don't go back [to] the way that you did in your former lust as in your ignorance. Now you are educated with the Word of God and the Spirit of God. "But according as He Who has called you *is* holy, you yourselves also be holy in all *your* conduct; for it is written, 'You be holy because I am holy.' " A perfect summation of the Feast of Unleavened Bread. We are to come from something which is leavened and unholy to something which is unleavened and holy. See, because leaven during the Feast of Unleavened Bread pictures a type of sin. And as we know that Paul said, "Let us keep the feast. Not with the old leaven, nor with the leaven of malice and wickedness." Notice how Paul and Peter agree. If you put I Corinthians 5 together with I Peter 1 they agree, don't they?

Now notice: "And if you call upon the Father, Who judges according to each man's work without respect of persons, pass the time of your *life's* journey in *the* fear *of God*; knowing that you were not redeemed by corruptible things, by silver or gold, from your futile way of living, inherited *by tradition* from *your* forefathers; but by *the* precious blood of Christ, as of a lamb without blemish and without spot…" Now that's why we need to do the things that we do. So we have that we have been redeemed, we have been set aside, that we go forward in the way that God wants us to do.

Now let's just finish a few verse here in closing. Verse 20: "…Who truly was foreknown before *the* foundation of *the* world, but was manifested in *these* last times for your sakes; *even for you* who through Him do believe in God, Who raised Him from *the* dead and gave Him glory, so that your faith and hope might be in God. Having purified your lives by obedience to the Truth unto unfeigned brotherly love through *the* Spirit, love one another fervently with a pure heart. *For* you have been begotten again, not from corruptible seed, but from incorruptible *seed*, by *the* living Word of God, *which* remains forever" (I Peter 1:11-23).

And that's the meaning of the Feast of Unleavened Bread. We are the church of the firstborn. We have been called and set aside and purified, delivered, to have faith and hope and trust and love with God. Have a good Feast of Unleavened Bread, brethren. And take these things and every day during the Feast do some extra Bible study and ask God to help you with His Spirit to grow, to change, to overcome, and to have your life transformed through this Feast of Unleavened Bread that you become more Christ-like.

(End of Sermon)

Transcribed: Carolyn Singer

The Redemption of the Firstborn
April 13, 2006
Scriptural References

1) Leviticus 23:4-8	17) Hebrews 1:6
2) Deuteronomy 16:16-17	18) John 1:29
3) Numbers 3:11-13	19) Romans 4:13-20
4) Exodus 12:51	20) 1 Peter 1:1-2
5) Exodus 13:1-4, 11-13	21) 1 John 3:1-10, 18-22
6) Genesis 11:26	22) 1 John 5:16
7) Isaiah 29:22	23) Matthew 12:31-32
8) Genesis 15:5	24) 1 Peter 1:3-7
9) Genesis 22:1-13, 15-18	25) Hebrew 12:22-23
10) James 2:17-23	26) Titus 2:11-15
11) Matthew 10:22	27) Psalms 7:1-2
12) Galatians 4:26-27	28) Psalms 25:1-11
13) Galatians 3:26-29	29) Psalms 27:11-14
14) Hebrews 6:13-20	30) 1 Peter 1:7-11
15) Romans 3:23-31	31) Colossians 1:10-14
16) Matthew 1:18	32) 1 Peter 1:11-23

CHAPTER SIXTEEN

The Wave Sheaf Offering Day

Unleavened Bread—Sabbath 2006

April 15, 2006

And greetings brethren. Welcome to the Sabbath during the Feast of Unleavened Bread, and we're going to talk about the resurrection of Christ very briefly, but we're going to focus in on the Wave Sheaf Offering Day and the meaning of the Wave Sheaf Offering Day. Not only is this going to be for the Feast of Unleavened Bread, but this is also going to be in the coming new holy day book, which is going to be a compilation of transcripts of the best sermons given through the years of all the holy days of God. So as we do with all the holy days, since this is during the Feast of Unleavened Bread, let's come to Leviticus 23 and let's begin in verse 9 where it starts talking about the Wave Sheaf Offering Day and the significance of this day as it is fulfilled through Jesus Christ. And we are going to see that this is a tremendous and absolutely wonderful day – the Wave Sheaf Offering Day – that it is a celebration for God the Father and Jesus Christ. And that's why it's not a holy day for us. But it's an important part of the fulfillment of the plan of God.

Now let's begin in verse 9: "And the LORD spake unto Moses, saying, Speak unto the children of Israel, and say unto them, When ye be come into the land which I give unto you, and shall reap the harvest thereof, then ye shall bring a sheaf of the firstfruits of your harvest unto the priest…" Now this sheaf of the firstfruits was called "the premiere sheaf." It was a special barley sheaf that was cut, and it was cut at the end of the Sabbath during the Feast of Unleavened Bread to be waved on the first day of the week during the Feast of Unleavened Bread.

Now let me just say something here very important that we need to understand and grasp. The Jews do not count (and this is the first day—the Wave Sheaf Offering Day) Pentecost correctly. They calculate it, not from the Sabbath and then the first day of the week during Unleavened Bread. They calculate it from the [first] holy day. And what this significantly does, it rejects the resurrection and ascension of Jesus Christ as the Savior of mankind. So all of those who follow what the Jews are doing are following a pattern that rejects Jesus Christ, as they have not only in the Passover but also the Wave Sheaf Offering and Pentecost. Subsequently because they reject Jesus Christ and do not accept the New Testament, they are cut off and do not have any understanding. Now you just need to realize that, that is a very important thing. That's why we have to do it the way that God says, calculate it the way that God says, count it the way that God says, and then put the scriptures together to get the full meaning of what these days mean.

Now let's see what the Priest was to do with the sheaf: "…and he shall wave [elevate] the sheaf before the LORD, to be accepted for you…" Now this shows, as we will see, the acceptance of the resurrected Jesus Christ as the perfect sacrifice for the sins of all the world, more importantly beginning with those who are the firstfruits of God, because then it goes on and connects directly to the day of Pentecost, which then is the first resurrection.

Now notice when it should be done: "…on the morrow after the sabbath…" Now notice he does not say "on the morrow after the holy convocation," being the holy day the first day of the Feast of Unleavened Bread. This is the weekly Sabbath. Then on the morrow, which means in the morning afterward: "…the priest shall wave it" (Lev. 23:9-11). Then he gives the instruction of what to do.

Now what we are to do is look at the fulfillment of this in the New Testament. And this is what becomes so important and profound in understanding the things of God, the way of God, the Word of God, and so forth.

Now let's come to I Corinthians 15 because the apostle Paul tells us the meaning of this day, and it also labels Christ as the firstfruits. And this tells us a part of the fulfillment of this day on the morrow after the Sabbath during the Feast of Unleavened Bread. And it's appropriate that it happens at that particular time because it falls right in line with the resurrection of Jesus Christ. You see this is why Jesus was crucified on the Passover day. And God uses all the holy days to fulfill major, epical, historical fulfillments of prophecy that He has given. And this is why unless you understand the holy days you cannot understand the plan of God. Now I want you to think for a minute: Do the Protestants accept the holy days? No. Do they understand the plan of God? No. Do the Catholics accept the holy days? No. Do they understand the plan of God? No. Do the Jews accept the holy days? Yes, with a caveat that they changed the Passover and they changed the Wave Sheaf Offering Day and hence they have changed Pentecost. And rejecting Jesus, do they understand prophecy? No. So you have to have both. You must have the Old Testament writings and the prophecies contained therein; you must have the New Testament writings and the interpretation and the prophecies there.

Now we are going to see a little later that Jesus opened the minds of the apostles to understand the prophecies concerning Him that are found in the Law and the Prophets and the Psalms. And that becomes profoundly important, because what Jesus is telling us is this: The New Testament interprets the Old Testament, not the other way around. So we need to remember that and grasp that.

Now let's come here, I Corinthians 15:20: "But now Christ has been raised from *the* dead; He has become the firstfruit…" Now this interprets Leviticus 23, "the premiere sheaf." "…Has become the first-fruit of those who have fallen asleep [resurrection from the dead]." That's why that wave sheaf was a special one that was bound with a special ceremonial ribbon and then was cut. It was cut right as the Sabbath ends during the Feast of Unleavened Bread, and then it was lifted up and carried to the altar of burnt offerings and laid alongside the altar of burnt offerings. Now having the firstfruit sheaf cut at that particular time signifies Christ being resurrected while He was in the tomb. But He did not ascend to the Father until the morning of the first day of the week at the time that they had the Wave Sheaf Offering, so He is the first of the firstfruits. Now verse 21: "For since by man *came* death, by man also *came the* resurrection of *the* dead. For as in Adam all die, so also in Christ shall all be made alive. But each in his own order: Christ *the* firstfruit; then, those who are Christ's at His coming" (I Cor. 15:20-23). Very important. And that has to fill in with all the holy days. So He's the firstfruit.

Let's look at a couple of other scriptures concerning this. Let's come to Colossians 1, and again we have a very misunderstood verse for those who do not accept Jesus, that He was God before He became human. And you know [what] the biggest problem with that is? You can answer the question very simply: Read the Gospel of John. That's all you have to do. Christ tells you where He came from. Christ tells you that He was in heaven before. Christ tells us that He prayed to the Father to give Him the glory that He had with the Father before the world existed. Now the only way that those who believe that Jesus was only a man can believe that is if they ignore all of this. Well, we'll see. Jesus said, "Heaven and earth will pass away, but My words shall not pass away" (Matt. 24:35, paraphrased). That's why when Jesus said... And He told the Jews that He wasn't going to give them a sign. They wanted a sign. Oh yes, they like miracles and magical things, and they can all gather around and revel in it just like people do when there is an apparition of Mary. Oh they come weeping and kneeling and rosarying and crying, and thousands coming. See, Christ would not, to those Jews, give them a sign. So He said, "The only sign I'm going to give you is the sign of Jonah the prophet. As Jonah was in the belly of the great fish for three days and three nights, so shall the Son of man be in the heart of the earth three days and three nights" (Matt. 12:40, paraphrased), and He turned and walked away.

Now since Jesus said that His words are truth, that He preached the words of the Father, He spoke nothing that the Father had not commanded Him to speak. And if the Word of God is true, it will not, cannot, ever fail, and that heaven and earth can pass away before the Words of Christ can pass away, how long was He in the tomb? Three days and three nights. And you can look in the New Testament—we have a chart there. And you can look in the *Harmony of the Gospels*—we have a full explanation of it there and a chart there showing the three days and three nights. And this year with the Passover in the middle of the week we have the same sequence of days that we had in the week when Jesus was crucified and resurrected. So that's why this is very important for us to understand.

Now come here to Colossians 1:14: "...in Whom [that is in Christ] we have redemption through His own blood..." But remember this: If Christ is not raised then you are still in your sins. If Christ did not ascend to heaven to be accepted of God the Father on the Wave Sheaf Offering Day, you have no justification. So it's very important to realize. "... In Whom we have redemption through His own blood, *even* the remission of sins; Who is *the* image of the invisible God, *the* firstborn of all creation..." Now this is where they get hung up. Now "the firstborn of all creation" does not have to do with the physical creation of things that God has made in the universe. This has to do with all of those who are created (which salvation is creation) in the image of Jesus Christ and are resurrected as Jesus was resurrected from the dead. Now we'll see this in just a minute because it interprets itself.

"...Because by Him were all things created..." So if He was the firstborn of creation, how could He create all things? So you see, you only can have the explanation that I gave. "...The things in heaven and the things on earth, the visible and the invisible, whether *they be* thrones, or lordships, or principalities, or powers: all things were created by Him and for Him. And He is before all, and by Him all things subsist." And that's what it says in the second verse of Hebrews 1—that He upholds the world by the Word of His power; and that He is the express image and the brightness of the glory of the Father.

Now verse 18: "And He is before all [things], and by Him all things subsist. And He is the Head of the body, the church; And He is the Head of the body, the church; Who is *the* beginning, *the* firstborn from among the dead..." So that's what it means. That interprets verse 14. He is the firstborn of all of those created through the resurrection of the dead. "... So that in all things He Himself might hold the preeminence. For it pleased *the Father* that in Him all the fullness should dwell..." (Colossians 1:14-19). So that's quite a wonderful thing talking about Jesus.

Now let's come to Revelation 1 and let's see what Jesus looks like and let's see what Jesus said of Himself. Let's see what the message was to John. And in the series of Revelation this becomes very important so we'll just review a few verses here. Now let's come to verse 4: "John to the seven churches that *are* in Asia..." And of course this is prophetic. It was at that time. It's prophetic and it has a fulfillment at the end-time. All three interpretations of Revelation 2 and 3 as we cover in the series on Revelation are true. "...Grace and peace *be* to you from Him Who is, and Who was, and Who *is* to come; and from the seven spirits that are before His throne; and from Jesus Christ, the faithful Witness, the Firstborn from the dead, and the Ruler of the kings of the earth. To Him Who loved us and washed us from our sins in His own blood, and has made us kings and priests to God and His Father; to Him *be* the glory and the sovereignty into the ages of eternity. Amen" (Rev. 1:4-6). Now, that is quite an introduction and is a summary of what all you're going to find in the book of Revelation.

Now let's come over here and see what John saw. Let's come first to verse 17: "And when I saw Him [now we'll read what Jesus is like in His glorified form here in just a minute], I fell at His feet as if dead; but He laid His right hand upon me, saying to me, 'Do not be afraid; I am the First and the Last, even the one Who is living; for I was dead, and behold, I am alive into the ages of eternity. Amen. And I have the keys of *the* grave and of death' " (Verses 17-18). Without Christ there is no resurrection. Without the resurrection of Christ there is no resurrection of anyone else. That's what Paul said.

Now let's see what He looks like in His glorified form. And let's understand what a profound thing this is. And I want to cover this and then we are going to look at the several men in the Bible who were able to see the glory of God. Now John was able see the glory of Jesus Christ, and as we'll see a little later when we get to Revelation 4 and 5, he also saw the glory of the Father.

Now let's pick it up here in verse 12: "And I turned to see the voice that spoke with me; and when I turned, I saw seven golden lampstands; and in *the* midst of the seven Lampstands..." Now let's understand these lampstands are in a circle, and Christ being the head of the church is in the middle. Very important to understand. This is not like the lampstand that was in the temple, otherwise Christ could not be in the middle of them.

"...Clothed in *a garment* reaching to the feet, and girded about the chest with a golden breastplate. And His head and hair *were* like white wool, white as snow; and His eyes *were* like a flame of fire; and His feet *were* like fine brass, as if *they* glowed in a furnace; and His voice *was* like *the* sound of many waters. And in His right hand He had seven stars, and a sharp two-edged sword went out of His mouth, and His countenance *was* as the sun shining in its *full* power." Now that's why it said that John wrote: "...when I saw Him, I fell at His feet as if dead..." (Verses 12-17). This is what Christ looks like in His full power and glory.

Now let's look at those who were able to see the glory of God. Now we find three distinct instances recorded in the Bible. Now let's come back to Exodus 33 and here we find that Moses... And this is why Moses was called the preeminent or the premiere prophet and law-giver of God, because he saw God in His glorified form. Not face to face, but he saw Him.

Let's come here to Exodus 33, and this is after the destroying of the golden calf and so forth, and Moses is pleading with God. He was able to intervene and persuade God not to destroy all the children of Israel for their sins. And so Moses asked God that "If I could see Your glory..." So because of the intercession of Moses the children of Israel were spared. Verse 17: "And the LORD said unto Moses, I will do this thing also that thou hast spoken: for thou hast found grace in My sight, and I know thee by name. And he said, I beseech Thee, shew me Thy glory. And He said, I will make all My goodness pass before thee, and I will proclaim the name of the LORD before thee; and will be gracious to whom I will be gracious, and will shew mercy on whom I will shew mercy. And He said [to Moses], thou canst not see My face: for there shall no man see Me, and live." And the reason being is that flesh cannot exist in the presence of the glory of God. So therefore he was only able to see a similitude of Him. "And the LORD said, Behold, *there is* a place by Me, and thou shalt stand upon a rock: and it shall come to pass, while My glory passeth by, that I will put thee in a clift of the rock, and will cover thee with My hand while I pass by: and I will take away Mine hand, and thou shalt see My back parts: but My face shall not be seen" (Ex. 33:17-23). So that happened.

So Moses hewed two more tables of stone for God to write the Ten Commandments on. Remember, the first ones that were written on were stones that God had hewed. Then He wrote the Ten Commandments on [them]. And then when Moses came down from the mount and saw all the worshipping of the golden calf and all the rebellion and everything that was going on with the children of Israel, he threw them down and broke them. So God made Moses make new ones. But also this signifies that there is a step removed from God that was caused by the people's sin because now the two tables of stone were hewn by Moses, and he took them up and gave them to God.

Now verse 5 of Exodus 34: "And the LORD descended in the cloud, and stood with him there [so there was a cloud so he couldn't see Him directly], and proclaimed the name of the LORD. And the LORD passed by before him, and proclaimed, The LORD, The LORD God, merciful and gracious, longsuffering, and abundant in goodness and truth, keeping mercy for thousands, forgiving iniquity and transgression and sin, and that will by no means clear *the guilty* [that is, without repentance]; visiting the iniquity of the fathers upon the children, and upon the children's children, unto the third and to the fourth *generation.*" (Ex. 34:5-7). And that is referring to the second commandment of those who worship idols. And if you worship idols you hate God and so therefore you bring upon your progeny to the third and fourth generation the curse of your idol worship and breaking the commandments of God. Now just an aside, stop and think here: What one physical thing can a man make or use (be it an idol, be it beads, be it a temple) that is greater than a broken heart and a contrite spirit, and seeking to worship God in spirit and in truth, and direct access to God the Father and Jesus Christ? There's nothing—nothing greater than that. And brethren, we need to understand that is a tremendous and wonderful blessing that God has opened up because of the death and resurrection and acceptance of Jesus Christ.

So, let's look at another instance. Let's come here to Isaiah 6. Now Isaiah in vision was able to see this. And we're going to see a little later the similarity between what takes place here and what is shown in the vision in Isaiah 6 that we find in Revelation 4 and 5. So we come all the way from Moses all the way up to Isaiah. Now David did see a simile of God in the holy place when he had the Ark of the Covenant in a special tent that was in his house before the temple was built. But he didn't see God as Moses did, and he did not see God as Isaiah did.

So let's pick it up here in Isaiah 6:1: "In the year that king Uzziah died I saw also the LORD sitting upon a throne, high and lifted up, and His train filled the temple. Above it stood the seraphims [now we're going to see how that connects with Revelation 4 a little later]: each one had six wings; with twain he covered his face, and with twain he covered his feet, and with twain he did fly. And one cried unto another, and said, Holy, holy, holy, *is* the LORD of hosts: the whole earth *is* full of His glory. And the posts of the door moved at the voice of him [now we will see "the post of the door" a little later on in relationship to Christ coming to be accepted of God the Father on the Wave Sheaf Offering Day] that cried, and the house was filled with smoke. Then said I, Woe *is* me! for I am undone; because I *am* a man of unclean lips, and I dwell in the midst of a people of unclean lips: for mine eyes have seen the King, the LORD of hosts." Quite a fantastic thing that Isaiah experienced. And when God does so, He does so to give inspiration to those who are going to speak, to those who are going to write that they will do exactly as God wants done. Do you think that Moses would have done anything differently than God commanded Him after talking to God on the mount after seeing His glory? Do you think that Isaiah would have written lies and prophesied lies after he had seen God in vision on His throne? I dare say, absolutely not! Would you? Of course not.

"Then flew one of the seraphims unto me, having a live coal in his hand, *which* he had taken with the tongs from off the altar: and he laid *it* upon my mouth, and said, Lo, this hath touched thy lips; and thine iniquity is taken away, and thy sin purged. Also I heard the voice of the LORD, saying, Whom shall I send, and who will go for us?" Very interesting, isn't it? Where God the Father, Jesus Christ and also the angels [are], and then Isaiah said, "…Here *am* I; send me. And He said, Go, and tell this people, Hear ye indeed, but understand not; and see ye indeed, but perceive not." And this is what happens to the average person concerning the Word of God because they don't want to obey it. They want to retain their sinful nature and their myths and their lies that they get from the religious teachers, which make them feel good and it appeals to their carnality, and it appeals to their deceitful nature. "Make the heart of this people fat, and make their ears heavy, and shut their eyes; lest they see with their eyes, and hear with their ears, and understand with their heart, and convert, and be healed" (Isa. 6:1-10). And Jesus quoted that in Matthew 13 and in the parallel accounts in Mark and Luke, that God blinds people who do not believe.

And isn't that exactly what happens in the religious world? First thing they want to do is say, "Well, God didn't mean this," and "God didn't mean that," and "We can't trust the Word of God. It was compiled by men hundreds of years later." Absolute lie. But they have that because their minds are closed, their eyes are shut and they can't understand, and they have no door to salvation unless they repent. That's why this day is so important.

Now let's come one step further. Let's come here to Matthew 17 and let's see where the disciples were given a vision of what Jesus would look like in His glorified form. And this becomes very important because what does this do? This gives equal or greater status to the apostles. And in this case it was James, Peter, and John. Not all the apostles saw this—just James, Peter, and John. So God does not show Himself to people just because they desire it. And He doesn't show Himself to anyone at anytime, and so this thing about like Pat Robertson said, "God spoke to me." No, God didn't speak to him.

Now let's come here to Matthew 17:1. Now Christ did this to give them equal and greater authority than Moses, because if God showed His glory to Moses, and if God showed His glory to Isaiah this also shows that the authority that they had came directly from God—not by any man, not by boards of men, not by rabbis, not by priests, not by Levites, but by Jesus Christ Who was God manifest in the flesh. So He wanted to encourage them. He wanted them to know exactly what it was going to be like at the resurrection.

Let's begin right here in Matthew 17:1: "And after six days, Jesus took with *Him* Peter and James and his brother John, and brought them up into a high mountain by themselves. And He was transfigured before them; and His face shined as the sun [now remember what we read in Revelation 1], and His garments became white as the light [just like we saw in Revelation 1]. Then behold, there appeared to them Moses and Elijah talking with Him." It doesn't say they were actually there because we will see this is a vision. And in vision you can see many different things, right? So here, this shows the authority that He gave to Moses, the authority that He gave to Elijah, that He is going to confer to the apostles. In this case the leading apostles—Peter, James, and John.

"And Peter answered *and* said to Jesus, 'Lord, it is good for us to be here. If You desire, let us make three tabernacles here: one for You, and one for Moses, and one for Elijah.' While he was speaking, a bright cloud suddenly overshadowed them; and behold, a voice out of the cloud said, 'This is My Son, the Beloved, in Whom I delight. Listen to

247

Him!' " Now a very important thing for us: If you want to understand about God the Father and Jesus Christ you have to listen to the words that they have spoken, which have been recorded here in the Bible. Not some man, not some priest, not some pope, not some evangelist, but Christ. Listen to Him.

"And when the disciples heard it, they fell on their faces in extreme terror. But Jesus came *and* touched them, and said, 'Arise, and do not be terrified.' And when they looked up, they saw no one except Jesus alone." Now verse 9 is the key. What happened here was not literal but a vision: "Now as they were descending from the mountain, Jesus commanded them, saying, 'Tell the vision to no one until the Son of man has risen from *the* dead' " (Matt. 17:1-9). Now these are the only occasions in the Bible where we find that men were able to see the glory of God. In the case of Moses, he saw it directly. In the case of Isaiah, he saw it in vision. In the case of the apostles, Peter, James, and John, they saw it in vision. And this is what motivated them to make sure that in the writing and canonization of the New Testament that it would be the Words of God as Christ had defined it and as Christ had taught.

Now just to emphasize that point let's come here to II Peter 1 and let's understand exactly the motivation behind writing the New Testament and why we can trust in the Words of God, and why this becomes so important, and why as we will see, this Wave Sheaf Offering Day becomes so profound in the meaning of the plan of God with the acceptance of Jesus Christ by God the Father on the Wave Sheaf Offering Day. Let's come here to verse 14: "...knowing that shortly the putting off of my tabernacle [that means he's saying he's going to die] *will come*, even as our Lord Jesus Christ has signified to me. But I will make every effort *that,* after my departure, you may always have a *written* remembrance of these things *in order* to practice *them* for yourselves..." This thing of oral tradition is just a myth and a lie by men so they can put in their own way. God has it written down. He told Moses—write; He told the prophets—write; He told Samuel—write; Hezekiah—to write; and He told His apostles to write. That way, with the inspired Word of God there isn't going to be any dispute. And it's important to understand that because what's in the Bible is how God is going to judge each one of us. Think on that for a minute. Think of the lies that come from the pulpit of men who presume to say Jesus lied, the Word of God lies. They are the liars. They are the ones who are blinded.

Now notice what Peter says here: "...for we did not follow cleverly concocted myths *as our authority*..." And what does Christendom follow today? Nothing but myths, lies, fables through the occult holidays while they reject the holy days and feasts of God. "...When we made known to you the power and coming of our Lord Jesus Christ, but we were eyewitnesses of His magnificent glory; because He received glory and honor from God *the* Father when *the* voice came to Him from the Majestic Glory, 'This is My Son, the Beloved, in Whom I am well pleased.' And this *is the* voice from heaven that we heard when we were with Him on the holy mountain [which we just read of there in Matthew 17, right? Yes, indeed]. We also possess the confirmed prophetic Word..." Now this "prophetic word" means the inspired word confirmed by Christ. Now you can't have anything greater than that, can you? "...To which you do well to pay attention [not argue with], as to a light shining in a dark place..." This is the Light of God to bring you out of spiritual darkness. "...Until the day dawns [that's the return of Christ] and *the* morning star arises in your hearts [that is when you are resurrected]..."

Now notice verse 20, and this is going to be very important when we go through the account of the resurrection and ascension of Christ: "...knowing this first [this is a primary thing to understand], that no prophecy of Scripture..." Now that does not restrict it to just prophetic things, because the "prophecy of Scripture" means anything that was spoken under the inspiration of God or written under the inspiration of God is a prophecy. "...Knowing this first, that no prophecy of Scripture originated as anyone's own *private* interpretation; because prophecy was not brought at any time by human will, but the holy men of God spoke as they were moved by *the* Holy Spirit" (II Peter 1:14-21). And the Holy Spirit is directed by Jesus Christ. And the Holy Spirit is called the Spirit of Truth. So we can have full confidence in the Word of God and the Truth of God and the things that we need to understand. And as it relates to this most important day, the Sabbath during the Feast of Unleavened Bread when the resurrection occurred and the next day, the Wave Sheaf Offering Day when Jesus was accepted as the first of the firstfruits. So this is why it's so absolutely marvelous that we trust the Word of God.

Now, one other caveat here before we go on, which is this: Carnal men like to take apparent contradictions to fight Scripture against Scripture so they can cast them aside. The way God wants us to do it is to take line upon line, precept upon precept, a little here, a little there, and add it together. And lo, guess what's going to happen? The contradictions will disappear. They will be gone, because we're dealing with the Word of Truth, which is the Word of God, and the God of truth, and the Holy Spirit of Truth, and the truth written by the apostles who were holy men, as well as the other writings contained in the Bible from the beginning to the end—all of God.

Now we're going to go ahead and we're going to look at the events that took place on the resurrection day, and then the ascension on the Wave Sheaf Offering Day.

Now let's continue on. Let's come to John 20. Now we're going to look at John and then Luke and then Mark when the women came to the tomb early the first day of the week, and we're going to understand some things concerning the resurrection of Jesus Christ. And as Jesus promised He would be in the tomb exactly three days and three nights. So He was put in the tomb just as the Passover day was ending at sunset, and that was on a Wednesday. Then you come forward three days and three nights and it puts you on the regular weekly Sabbath. Does that sound familiar where we started out? Yes, indeed. And He had to be resurrected at exactly that same time. But in order to understand what happened we need to come to the first day of the week and then put the events together that happened on the first day of the week so we can go back and see what happened when Jesus was resurrected and then we will come forward to when He ascended into heaven to the Father.

Now let's come here, John 20: "Now on the first *day* of the weeks…" Now that is the first day counting to Pentecost. That is on a Sunday, the first day of the week, and it was the Wave Sheaf Offering Day. "…While it was still dark, Mary Magdalene came early to the tomb…" Now she came alone. The other women came and joined her. They probably had already decided that in the morning they were going to go and take the spices and to do more wrapping [of] Jesus body in spices in the morning. So she started while it was still dark. But understand as she was walking the sun was rising so it was getting lighter and lighter and lighter. "…Mary Magdalene came early to the tomb; and she saw *that* the stone had been taken away from the tomb." So immediately she didn't know what to do. She didn't understand what was happening. "Then she ran and came to Simon Peter and to the other disciple whom Jesus loved, and said to them, 'They have taken away the Lord from the tomb, and we do not know where they have laid Him.' " (John 20: 1-2).

Now let's come over here in Luke 24:1: "Now on the first *day* of the weeks, they came to the tomb at early dawn, bringing *the* spices that they had prepared; and certain *others came* with them. But they found the stone rolled away from the tomb; and when they entered *it*, they did not find the body of the Lord Jesus." So here the other women came. Mary came first and ran to tell Peter and John. The other women came and found exactly the same thing. How much later it was we don't know, but they didn't know that Mary had already been there.

Now verse 4: "And it came to pass that while they were puzzling over this, suddenly two men [who were angels] in shining garments stood by them. And *as* they bowed their faces to the ground, being filled with fear, they said to them, 'Why are you seeking the living among the dead?' " So the key thing is this—let's understand a very important and profound point which is this: No one witnessed the resurrection of Jesus Christ. The women who came to the tomb didn't see it. The soldiers who were guarding the tomb didn't see it. When they came early in the morning on the first day of the week, the Wave Sheaf Offering Day, He wasn't there. There's no such thing as an Easter Sunday resurrection. That is a lie, a fiction. Jesus was gone.

They said: " 'He is not here, but has risen: remember when He spoke to you *while He* was yet in Galilee, saying, ' "It is necessary for the Son of man to be delivered into *the* hands of sinful men, and to be crucified, and to arise the third day"?' Then they remembered His words; and after returning from the tomb, they related these things to the eleven and to all the rest." So they got there while Mary Magdalene was apparently telling them, because it says in verse 10: "...Mary Magdalene and Joanna and Mary, *the mother* of James, and the others with them, who told these things to the apostles" (Luke 24:1-10), but of course they didn't believe it.

Now let's come here to Mark 16:2 and let's see the account here: "And very early on the first *day* of the weeks, at the rising of the sun..." So Mary started out when it was still dark. Now we have the sun is rising. They were coming to the tomb. This is the parallel account of Luke 24. Verse 3: "...and they were asking themselves, 'Who will roll away the stone for us from the entrance to the tomb?' For it was a massive *stone*. But when they looked up, they saw that the stone had been rolled away. And after entering the tomb, they saw a young man sitting on the right, clothed in a white robe; and they were very frightened." Now that was an angel. See there were two angels. In this case they're emphasizing seeing one. "But he said to them, 'Do not be afraid. You are seeking Jesus the Nazarene, Who was crucified. He has risen; He is not here. Look, *there is* the place where they laid Him. But go, tell His disciples and Peter that He goes before you into Galilee; there you shall see Him, as He said to you' " (Mark 16:2-7). Quite an interesting thing, isn't it?

Now let's see what happened next, and then this will help us understand about the resurrection of Jesus, because He had to be raised from the dead exactly three days and three nights from the time He was put in the tomb. So He had to be raised at the end of the Sabbath. Remember, just like as we started out when they cut that premier sheaf for the Wave Sheaf Offering, it was cut right as the weekly Sabbath had ended, or was ending. That signified Christ being raised from the dead, no longer connected to the earth, as it were. No longer earthy, if we could put it that way.

Now let's come back here to John 20 again and let's see what else occurred. Let's pick it up here in verse 3. After Mary Magdalene came, then the other women came: "As a result, Peter and the other disciple [that is John] went out and came to the tomb. Now the two ran together, but the other disciple ran faster than Peter and came to the tomb first; and he stooped down *and* saw the linen cloths lying *there*, but he did not enter. Then Simon Peter came following him, and he went into the tomb and saw the linen cloths lying, and the napkin that had been on His head, not lying with the linen cloths but folded up in a place by itself." Quite an amazing thing, isn't it? Now let's read verse 8: "Then the other disciple, who had come to the tomb first, also went in and saw *these things*; and he believed. For they did not yet understand the scripture *which decreed* that He must rise from *the* dead." (John 20:3-9). Christ had to give them that understanding later.

Now let's look at this and let's analyze this for just a minute and let's see what this is telling us. We know that when Joseph of Arimathaea and Nicodemus took Jesus' body off the cross that they had a hundred pounds of spices and aloe, and they wrapped His body. Now it was not like a shroud. The Shroud of Turin is a lying fiction. It has nothing to do with Christ. They didn't lay a shroud over Him. He was wrapped with the linen. They probably had strips of linen about like this—about six to nine inches wide. Probably more like about six inches. And they would wrap His body, beginning with His feet, and add in the spices as they were wrapping, go right on up on up His torso, all the way up and then do His body and then do His arms. And then cover His head with a special covering that was called a napkin.

Now they saw the linen cloths lying. What did they see? What would be a profound witness of the resurrection of Christ but to see the wrappings of these linen cloths still in their wrapped form but no body in it and perhaps with a little sag in the middle of the wrapped cloth showing that He wasn't there? Now what would this demonstrate? This would demonstrate that 1) No one took the body. 2) If they would have taken the body they would have taken the burial wrappings with them. Wouldn't you think? Now if they didn't want to, if they stole the body and didn't want to take the wrappings with them then they would have to unwrap it or cut it off. So they saw the linen cloths laying there to demonstrate that as a Spirit Being, Christ, as we will see a little later, did not need to have the cloth removed to be resurrected. He just simply rose through it. Now to demonstrate that He was alive we have this: The linen napkin, which was on His head, was folded and put in another place. Now do you think if anyone was going to steal His body, would they not have taken the napkin too? Do you think that they would have…whoever the group claiming that the disciples stole the body away—and of course the Jews still believe that lying fable to this day because they won't take the New Testament and read what it says and look at the evidence. Now if you were a forensic expert today what would you have to conclude? That the napkin was folded up and put in another place and no one had gone into the tomb, except Jesus was put in there when He was dead. You'd have to conclude that He was resurrected from the dead. And you would have to conclude that He deliberately folded the napkin and put it in another place to demonstrate that He was alive. That's quite an important thing to understand.

Now let's look at some psalms which bear on the resurrection of Christ. Now in Psalm 16 we find something very interesting. Let's ask the question: What do you suppose that may have been the first thoughts of Jesus when He was resurrected and He's in the tomb, and He realizes that He is alive. Because His last thought was what? On the cross saying, "Father into Your hands I commend My Spirit," and He died. So what would He think right after He's resurrected? Now if you've ever been unconscious or if you've ever had an operation where you've gone under a sedation and you wake up, your thoughts are entirely different, right? Well we have it right here, maybe these are the words of Christ. A prophecy of the words of Christ, the very first ones that He spoke when He was raised from the dead. Psalm 16:8: "I have set the LORD always before me: because *He is* at my right hand, I shall not be moved. Therefore my heart is glad, and my glory rejoiceth: my flesh also shall rest in hope. For Thou wilt not leave my soul in hell [You will not leave me in the grave]; neither wilt Thou suffer [allow] thine Holy One to see corruption." And that happened to Jesus. And probably His first thought was to praise God, to praise God for the tremendous and wonderful blessing of the resurrection, that He did not see corruption, that He didn't leave Him in the grave, that the Word of God was true and the covenant that Jesus Christ and God the Father made before Jesus came to the earth in the flesh that He would raise Him back to life when He died, was fulfilled.

Let's finish verse 11: "Thou wilt shew me the path of life: in Thy presence *is* fulness of joy…" Now we're going to see that on the Wave Sheaf Offering Day Jesus came again into the presence of God the Father. "…At Thy right hand *there are* pleasures for evermore" (Psa. 16:8-11).

Now let's come to Psalm 23. Here is another one which I think are the very words of Christ after He was resurrected in thanking and praising God. Now let's begin right here. We've covered this before. We've gone through some things concerning Psalm 23. There are many, many, many lessons we can learn out of this. But let's think of it in the praising of God the Father by Jesus Christ after He was resurrected from the dead.

Now, Jesus did not stay in the tomb very long. Where did Jesus go? Now let's understand something: He was raised from the dead; the burial clothes were there; the napkin was folded up; His first conscious thoughts were probably thanking God of the fulfillment of Psalm 16; and then since He was a Spirit Being He merely walked through the stone which covered the tomb, and the soldiers didn't see Him when He came out the other side because He would be in the heart of the earth three days and three nights. So He could not have stayed there very long at all—get right out. Where would He have gone, because He didn't ascend until the next morning as we are going to see? Well, right near there is the garden of Gethsemane, right? And in the garden of Gethsemane was the place where Jesus always prayed. And as a matter of fact, the night of the Passover, after He had the Passover with the apostles, they went there and He prayed for three hours and then was arrested. So Jesus probably went out to His, as it were, familiar or favorite praying place in the garden of Gethsemane, and perhaps this was His prayer.

Let's read it, Psalm 23: "The LORD *is* my shepherd; I shall not want [anything]. He maketh me to lie down in green pastures: He leadeth me beside the still waters. He restoreth my soul [His soul and His body would not see corruption—yes, restored it through the power of the resurrection, right?]: He leadeth me in the paths of righteousness for His name's sake [to do the will of God]. And isn't that what Jesus said? "Lo, I come to do the will of the Father Who sent Me"? Yes. "Yea, though I walk through the valley of the shadow of death [He just experienced it, right?], I will fear no evil…" Did He have any fear when He went through the scourging and crucifixion? No. "…For Thou *art* with me; Thy rod and Thy staff they comfort me. Thou preparest a table before me in the presence of mine enemies…" Quite a fantastic thing, isn't it? You talk about preparing right in the presence of the enemies. The soldiers were guarding the tomb—He walked right out. The civil government of the Romans was against Him; the religious government of the Jews was against Him; His own apostles didn't believe Him until later [when] He opened their minds. You talk about "preparing a table in the presence of my enemies." "…Thou anointest my head with oil; my cup runneth over." Remember He was anointed with oil twice before the crucifixion. "Surely goodness and mercy shall follow me all the days of my life: and I will dwell in the house of the LORD for ever" (Psa. 23:1-6).

Now let's come to Psalm 108 and let's see another prophecy about Jesus. And let's look at this as having to do with also His prayer of the resurrection: "O God, my heart is fixed; I will sing and give praise, even with my glory. Awake, psaltery and harp: I *myself* will awake early [a type of the resurrection]. I will praise Thee, O LORD, among the people: and I will sing praises unto Thee among the nations [yet to happen, isn't it?]. For Thy mercy *is* great above the heavens: and Thy truth *reacheth* unto the clouds. Be Thou exalted, O God, above the heavens: and Thy glory above all the earth; that Thy beloved may be delivered [which He was]: save *with* Thy right hand, and answer me. God hath spoken in His holiness; I will rejoice…" (Psa. 108:1-7). Quite a wonderful thing that Christ experienced.

Now one other psalm here. Let's come to Psalm 63. Although David wrote this and he did see a similitude of God in the small little tabernacle where he had the Ark of the Covenant that was in his house after it was retrieved from Kirjath-Jearim. Now here, let's look at it from the point of view of the resurrected Christ and what He was thinking: "O God, Thou *art* my God…" Think of Him now praying in the garden of Gethsemane, praying all that night thanking God for resurrecting Him from the dead and waiting for the time when it was time for the fulfillment of the Wave Sheaf Offering. "...My soul thirsteth for Thee, my flesh longeth for Thee [which it did when He was in the flesh] in a dry and thirsty land, where no water is; to see Thy power..." Because now He knew that He was going back to God the Father; now He knew that He was going to ascend into heaven; now He knew that He was going to see the sanctuary of God again. "...To see Thy power and Thy glory, so *as* I have seen Thee in the sanctuary. Because thy lovingkindness *is* better than life, my lips shall praise Thee" (Psa. 63:1-3). Quite a wonderful thing.

Now, let's talk about, a little more, the Wave Sheaf Offering Day and the ascension of Jesus Christ. Let's come to John 20:10 and let's get the story flow from here: "Then the disciples went away again to their *home*. But Mary stood outside the tomb weeping; and as she wept, she stooped down *and looked* into the tomb. And she saw two angels in white who were sitting, one at the head and the other at the feet, where the body of Jesus had been laid." Because she could see also the burial cloths. "And they said to her, 'Woman, why are you weeping?' She said to them, 'Because they have taken away my Lord, and I do not know where they have laid Him.' And after saying these things, she turned around and saw Jesus standing, but did not know that it was Jesus." Because He was able to manifest Himself in a form that she couldn't see Him as He was. And there was a specific purpose for that.

Verse 16: "Jesus said to her, 'Woman, why are you weeping? Whom are you seeking?' Thinking that He was the gardener, she said to Him, 'Sir, if you have carried Him off, tell me where you have laid Him, and I will take Him away.' Jesus said to her, 'Mary.' Turning around..." She apparently turned and was crying and wasn't looking at the man and just saying "Oh, if you'd just tell me where He is." "...Turning around, she said to Him, 'Rabboni'; that is to say, 'Teacher.' Jesus said to her, 'Do not touch Me, because I have not yet ascended to My Father. But go to My brethren and tell them that I am ascending to My Father and your Father, and My God and your God.' " (John 20:10-17). Now, this was still in the morning. When was the Wave Sheaf Offering to be elevated for the first of the firstfruits? In the morning, somewhere right around nine o'clock in the morning. So this fits the time frame. So, Mary Magdalene went and told them. [Then] Jesus ascended into heaven; He was accepted of God the Father.

Now let's see another vision, another psalm in Psalm 24 which talks about the acceptance of Christ. Then we will go to Revelation 4 and Revelation 5 and we will see the fulfillment of that. Let's come to Psalm 24. Now there's quite an interesting sequence of things here with the psalms. First of all Psalm 22 is about the crucifixion of Christ. Psalm 23 is about the resurrection. Psalm 24, which follows, is about Jesus ascension into heaven and being accepted.

Now let's pick it up here in Psalm 24, and let's think of it this way: These are some of the thoughts of Jesus as He is ascending to the Father, and He's looking down on the earth, verse 1: "The earth *is* the LORD'S, and the fullness thereof; the world, and they that dwell therein." As He's ascending He sees the earth, He sees the land, He sees the oceans. "For He hath founded it upon the seas, and established it upon the floods. Who shall ascend into the hill of the LORD? or who shall stand in His holy place? He that hath clean hands, and a pure heart..." Now this may be the angels singing as Christ is ascending, "Who shall ascend into the hill of God? or who shall stand in His holy place? He that hath clean hands, and a pure heart?" That was Christ. "...[He] who hath not lifted up his soul unto vanity, nor sworn deceitfully. He shall receive the blessing from the LORD, and righteousness from the God of his salvation." Quite a wonderful thing. Just imagine how Christ is ascending.

Now verse 7: "Lift up your heads, O ye gates..." The gates where He would walk through to go to the throne of God the Father and be accepted by God the Father as the perfect sacrifice for the sins of all the world—all mankind. "...And be ye lift up, ye everlasting doors; and the King of glory shall come in." That is Christ, the King of glory. The one Who conquered death; the one Who overcame sin; the one Who overcome the pulls of the flesh; the one Who was crucified and yet in His days of His flesh He cried out in fear and trembling to the one Who was able to save Him from death (that is God the Father), and now He's ascending; now He's at the gate; now He's walking into in just a little bit, right into the presence of God the Father. And we'll go to Revelation 4 in a minute and see what He saw.

"...Be ye lift up, ye everlasting doors; and the King of glory shall come in. Who *is* this King of glory? The LORD strong and mighty, the LORD mighty in battle." And hadn't He overcome everything? Yes. He had just overcome Satan the devil; He had just overcome all the demons; He had just overcome death; He was now resurrected, strong and mighty in battle, and that was in the battle for us. And by the grace of God He tasted death for every one of us that He could be resurrected and ascend to God the Father to be that perfect sacrifice and our High Priest at the right hand of God the Father.

"Lift up your heads, O ye gates; even lift *them* up, ye everlasting doors; and the King of glory shall come in. Who is this King of glory? The LORD of hosts, He *is* the King of glory. Selah" (Psa. 24:1-5, 7-10).

Now let's come to Revelation 4 and let's see what Jesus saw when He was resurrected to come in the presence of God the Father. Now we know this by vision that was given to John, so let's look at it this way: This is also what Jesus saw. And I want you to picture the angels singing in glory and power that Christ had overcome; that He now is going to walk down to the presence of God the Father, see God the Father, and they are going to embrace each other for the very first time since Jesus left to become a human being.

Now here's the setting that He saw. And we're blessed to have this given to the apostle John. Now let's begin in Revelation 4:1: "After these things I looked, and behold, a door opened in heaven..." Didn't we just talk about the door? Didn't we just talk about the everlasting gates? Yes. "...And the first voice that I heard *was* as if a trumpet were speaking with me, saying, 'Come up here, and I will show you *the* things that must take place after these things.' And immediately I was in *the* Spirit; and behold, a throne was set in heaven, and *one was* sitting on the throne." And this is what God the Father looks like in appearance—great, glorious and marvelous. "And He Who *was* sitting was in appearance like a jasper stone and a sardius stone; and a rainbow *was* around the throne, like an emerald in its appearance." So here is the throne of God with the Father sitting in it and a great rainbow all around the throne and the sea of glass that it sits on.

"And around the throne *were* twenty-four thrones; and on the thrones I saw twenty-four elders sitting, clothed in white garments; and they had on their heads golden crowns. And proceeding from the throne were lightnings and thunders and voices; and seven lamps of fire, which are the seven Spirits of God, *were* burning before the throne." So here is Jesus coming closer and closer. "And before the throne *was* a sea of glass, like crystal. And around the throne and over the throne *were* four living creatures, full of eyes before and behind..." And this is what Isaiah saw with the Seraphim. "...And the first living creature *was* like a lion, and the second living creature *was* like a calf, and the third living creature had the face of a man, and the fourth living creature *was* like a flying eagle. And each of *the* four living creatures had six wings respectively [and that's what Isaiah saw—six wings]; *and* around and within *they were* full of eyes; and day and night they cease not saying, 'Holy, holy, holy, Lord God Almighty...'" Now it doesn't mean that they did this repeatedly without stopping. There were certain times when this occurred, because as we will see when it occurred the twenty-four elders bowed down and worshipped. So this was at certain set times that this was done.

" '...Lord God Almighty, Who was [now referring to Christ], and Who is, and Who *is* to come.' And when the living creatures give glory and honor [so it wasn't continuously] and thanksgiving to Him Who sits on the throne, Who lives into the ages of eternity, the twenty-four elders fall down before Him Who sits on the throne; and they worship Him Who lives into the ages of eternity, and cast their crowns before the throne, saying, 'Worthy are You, O Lord, to receive glory and honor and power because You did create all things, and for Your will they were created and exist' " (Rev. 4:1-11). Everything that there is, is by the will of God for His great plan for all of humanity. And Christ is going to be the one Who is going to execute this plan all into the future. And so this Wave Sheaf Offering Day, when Christ ascended into heaven, this is what He saw. This is Whom He met, and He came to God the Father and presented Himself.

Now there must have been some portion of blood yet left in Christ that He took with Him when He ascended into heaven so that the holy place could be sanctified with His blood in heaven above so that He would be the propitiation for our sins. And that the blood of Jesus Christ can cover the sins of all mankind, that is for those who repent.

Now let's see Chapter 5 because this also tells us something else. Not only is He there with God the Father, but Christ is there to carry out the will of the Father from heaven, to complete the plan of God. Now let's read here Revelation 5:1: "And in the right hand of Him Who sits on the throne I saw a book [this is the rest of the book of Revelation], written within and on *the* back, which had been sealed with seven seals." Now a key important thing: Nothing is going to be understood without Christ revealing it. Remember that. Whatever we understand in the Bible it's because of what God has written in the Spirit of God. Whatever understanding that we have of the prophecies it's because God reveals it, therefore we must be very careful in interpreting prophecies, that we interpret them correctly according to the will of God.

"And I saw a strong angel proclaiming with a loud voice, 'Who is worthy to open the book and to loose its seals?' But no one in heaven, or on the earth, or under the earth was able to open the book, or to look inside it." And so John said: "And I was weeping greatly because no one was found worthy to open and to read the book, or to look into it. Then one of the elders said to me, 'Do not weep. Behold, the Lion Who is of the tribe of Judah [that's Christ], the Root of David, has overcome to open the book, and to loose its seven seals.' Then I saw, and behold, before the throne and the four living creatures, and before the elders, *was* standing a Lamb..." So we have the two aspects of Christ—the Lamb as Savior, and the warrior of Judah. And David was a man of war—the two aspects of Christ. That's why He's coming as conquering King. Here it is the Lamb: "...as having been slain, having seven horns and seven eyes, which are the seven Spirits of God that are sent into all the earth..." Now if you don't have the tape on the "Spirit of God—The Seven Spirits of God," write in for it.

"...And He came and took the book out of the right hand of Him Who sits on the throne [that's of the Father]. And when He took the book, the four living creatures and the twenty-four elders fell down before the Lamb, each having harps and golden bowls full of incense, which are the prayers of the saints." So our prayers come right up before God the Father. "And they sang a new song, saying..." And this is a new song for the saints that they are going to sing this song when they are resurrected. And this is what we will sing when we come before God the Father: " '...Worthy are You to take the book, and to open its seals because You were slain, and did redeem us to God by Your own blood [not the elders—the saints], out of every tribe and language and people and nation, and did make us unto our God kings and priests; and we shall reign on the earth.' " So the first thing we are going to know when we are resurrected is what God has in store for us to be ruling and reigning with Christ as kings and priests.

And now then he saw a great and spectacular thing. Remember, the angels were rejoicing in the gates opening and Christ walking in to come down to God the Father. "And I saw and I heard *the* voices of many angels around the throne…" So just picture this: here's the throne of God; twenty-four elders; Christ standing right there at the right hand of God; the rainbow around the throne and a vast sea of glass. And all on the sides of that a tremendous chorus of angels going all around behind the throne, and on this side of the throne. All around the throne were the voices of many angels around the throne. "…And *the voices* of the living creatures and the elders, and thousands of thousands…" Great and marvelous was this Wave Sheaf Offering Day and the ascension of Jesus Christ. "…Saying with a loud voice, 'Worthy is the Lamb Who was slain to receive power, and riches, and wisdom, and strength, and honor, and glory and blessing.' " And if you don't have the "Messiah", you get the "Messiah" and you listen to this song. Great and fantastic is this song. This finishes off the whole "Messiah"—the reception of Jesus Christ at the throne of God.

" '…Worthy is the Lamb Who is slain to receive power, and riches, and wisdom, and strength, and honor, and glory and blessing.' " And the whole creation is going to rejoice. And we are going to join Christ there at the first resurrection and we are going to be given the things that God wants to give us to rule and reign with Christ. And just as Christ came and received this great blessing, we will be resurrected and the angels will rejoice. The angels will carry us up to the throne of God to the sea of glass and we will sing praises to God. We will see Jesus Christ. We will see the twenty-four elders. We will see the four living creatures. We will see the thousands and thousands and thousands of angels, and we will look back on the earth just like it was here.

"And every creature that is in heaven, and on the earth, and under the earth, and those that are on the sea, and all the things in them, I heard saying, 'To Him Who sits on the throne, and to the Lamb, *be* blessing, and honor, and glory, and sovereignty into the ages of eternity.' " Fantastic thing. This is what happened on the Wave Sheaf Offering Day—the reception of Jesus Christ by God the Father as the perfect sacrifice for the sins of all mankind. The Creator had died, but was resurrected back to save His creation. Later in that day He came back to the earth and appeared to the apostles and so forth. You can read of that in the *Harmony* or in Matthew, Mark, Luke, and John.

Now let's finish it off here, verse 14: "And the four living creatures said, 'Amen.' " That part of the plan of God with the ascension of Jesus Christ to the throne of God to carry on the work of the church from then on was finished—Amen. "And the twenty-four elders fell down and worshiped *Him Who* lives into the ages of eternity" (Rev. 5:1-14). This is the fulfillment of the Wave Sheaf Offering Day. And this is the meaning of Revelation 4 and 5.

End of Sermon

Transcriber: Sasha Vogele

The Wave Sheaf Offering Day
Unleavened Bread—Sabbath—April 15, 2006
Scriptural References

1) Leviticus 23:9-11

2) I Corinthians 15:20-23

3) Matthew 24:35

4) Matthew 12:40

5) Colossians 1:14-19

6) Revelation 1:4-6, 17-18, 12-17

7) Exodus 33:17-23

8) Exodus 34:5-7

9) Isaiah 6:1-10

10) Matthew 17:1-9

11) II Peter 1:14-21

12) John 20:1-2

13) Luke 24:1-10

14) Mark 16:2-7

15) John 20:3-9

16) Psalm 16:8-10

17) Psalm 23:1-6

18) Psalm 108:1-7

19) Psalm 63:1-3

20) John 20:10-17

21) Psalm 24:1-5, 7-10

22) Revelation 4:1-11

23) Revelation 5:1-14

CHAPTER SEVENTEEN

The Special Covenant Between God the Father and Jesus Christ

January 10, 2004

This will be number 27 in the series of Hebrews that we've been going through. And this is going to be a different kind of sermon from the point of view of trying to uncover and understand even more the Word of God. See now we're told in Isaiah 28 that the Word of God is understood "line upon line, precept upon precept, a little here and a little there." And that it has to be put together rightly, as Paul told Timothy, "Rightly divide the Word of God." And also there are degrees of understanding.

Let's take one verse in particular—John 3:16, and let's look at this for just a minute. There are degrees of understanding that people have concerning this verse depending upon their involvement with God; depending upon what they've been taught in whatever church that they go to; and depending upon their personal relationship with God; depending upon the experiences that they have gone through.

Now John 3:16 says: "For God so loved the world, that He gave His only begotten Son, that whosoever believeth [believes] in Him should not perish, but have everlasting life." Now some people read that and they think, "Well, we're going to heaven." Some people read that and say, "All you've got to do is believe" and they don't understand much more beyond that. But how is it that God loved the world; and how is it that He gave His only begotten Son; and how did it come about the way that it came about? Well, the only way we're going to understand this is to realize that in the Word of God, since it's inspired by the mind of God, that there are certain things that come along that God reveals to give us a deeper understanding of it.

Now Paul wrote of that. Let's come to I Corinthians 2. It's not something that anybody can pick up like a book and just read it. It isn't understood that way. Yes, it can be read that way, but whether it is understood that way or not is another whole question. And it's interesting with the commentary that we have with the coming New Testament where we show, not only from the Scriptures themselves but also from history and from the textural criticism, that all the words in the Bible are God-breathed. Now this comes out at a time when the world is saying, and even those who are supposed to be ministers—or I should put it this way: Who are what the world calls "men of the cloth." And if you want some real shocking things and you are on-line, go to Dr. Spong [John S. Spong] and look at some of the things that he has written, because there is a vast movement, not only out in the world to get rid of God and have a Christianity without God, but there is also a vast movement of lying men of the cloth within what is called the church establishment of the world, if I could use that, and they are preaching directly against God; directly against the inspiration of the Word of God. And when you read some of the things that they have it's almost like reading the myth of the story of evolution. They have a story that they tell, and the substance of it is this: That those who said in the New Testament or the Old Testament who wrote it, [that] they didn't write it. But their disciples, they told the story verbally and it was gradually formed together, and then they lay it all at the footsteps of the Roman Catholic Church that they created the New Testament. And so this is the commonly perceived thing that's in the world.

What we show is the exact opposite: God intended the New Testament to be written; and it was written by the ones who said they wrote it; and it is the inspired Word of God; and it is the Word of God that is only understood by the Spirit of God.

Now here in I Corinthians 2:6: "Now we speak wisdom among the *spiritually* mature; however, *it is* not *the* wisdom of this world, nor of the rulers of this world, who are coming to nothing." And I think Saddam Hussein is a good example of that, right? Did he not come to nothing?

"Rather, we speak *the* wisdom of God...", which is different. That has to be with the Word of God. "...We speak *the* wisdom of God in a mystery..." That is a mystery to the world. And even a mystery to religionists who do not read the Word of God as it is the Word of God. "...*Even* the hidden *wisdom* that God foreordained before the ages unto our glory..." Now what Paul is saying here is that the understanding of the plan of God and the Word of God was foreordained before the ages for the very purpose that we be born into the Kingdom of God. Now that's quite a statement, isn't it? Now this means that God calling the weak of the world, which we all are, and as he says over here in Chapter 1 that we are nothing to bring to nothing the things that are. You see, God has given us a high calling and a great mission according to His plan and His purpose and His will in His timing. Not that we go out and we take over the reins of government now, but when we do all those things that have infuriated you when you watch the news and watch the government speakers speak their doublespeak and all this sort of thing, and the things that are going on—guess what? Christ is going to give us the authority to straighten it all out. So you see, salvation is more than just people living a good life; people have some understanding of the Word of God. It is a fantastic and a tremendous calling which was set forth before the foundation of the world, and today we're going to see some of the deep things that Paul talks about here of the things between God the Father and Jesus Christ.

So let's continue here now. Verse 8: "...Which not one of the rulers of this world has known (for if they had known [it]..." So you know, it's no surprise that when you hear the rulers of the world speak they don't know anything. See, the Bible tells us they don't. "...(For if they had known, they would not have crucified the Lord of glory); but according as it is written, '*The* eye has not seen, nor *the* ear heard, neither have entered into *the* heart of man, *the* things which God has prepared for those who love Him.' " See, now that's a key thing that's important. And you can put in your margin there Romans 8:28 that <u>all</u> things work together for good to those who love God and who are called according to His purpose. <u>All things</u>. Not one thing excluded. Even the difficult things. Even the problematic things. Even the disappointments. And yes, even death. That's the whole point and the purpose of Jesus' coming.

Verse 10: "But God has revealed *them* to us [first to the apostles and then to the brethren] by His Spirit..." And that's the whole important thing concerning the calling of the apostle Paul who was what? A very high mucky-muck in Judaism, right? And what did he know about God? Very little. What did he understand though he was one of the most righteous of Pharisees that could have been, and the son of a Pharisee? What did he say of all of that? "I count it by dung, to win Christ." So God had to reveal it to him. God had to reveal it to the apostles. God has to reveal it to us by His Spirit, as we study His Word, as we hunger and thirst after righteousness, as we yield to God to understand. "...God has revealed *them* to us by His Spirit, for the Spirit searches all things—even the deep things of God." Now today we are going to understand, hopefully, a little bit more about one of the deep things of God.

Verse 11: "For who among men understands the things of man except *by* the spirit of man which *is* in him? In the same way also, the things of God no one understands except *by* the Spirit of God." And to whom does God give His Spirit? To those who obey Him.

Verse 12: "Now we have not received the spirit of the world…" And I know Robert Martin gave me a tape from the Jesus Seminar concerning the Nag Hammadi Gnostic gospel of Mary Magdalene. And I tell you it was so evident—that made this verse just stand out. Here they are intelligent, studied for years and years—you know, Dr., Dr., Dr., Ph.D., Ph.D., Ph.D.; study all these languages, know all of them, be able to read the fragments of the Nag Hammadi Library and all of that and they don't have a clue. They're all wandering out here in the mist of their super-intellectual thoughts and emotions. And it was awfully hard getting through that tape, but I got through that tape. But nevertheless that's the spirit of the world.

"…But the Spirit that *is* of God [is what we have received], so that we might know…" Now God wants us to know but He wants us to search for it. And He wants us to search for it in the right way: "…that we might know the things graciously given to us by God; which things we also speak, not in words taught by human wisdom, but in *words* taught by *the* Holy Spirit *in order to* communicate spiritual things by spiritual *means*. But *the* natural man does not receive the things of the Spirit of God; for they are foolishness to him, and he cannot understand *them* because they are spiritually discerned" (I Cor. 2:6-14). And some of what we're going to cover today falls exactly in that category, and falls in that category because you go along and you study and you grow in knowledge and understanding and all of these things come together bit by bit, step by step, week by week, month by month, year by year, decade by decade. Now if we look around and see all of our gray heads, and yet there is still more to learn. And the way that we learn these things is because we still ask questions. So let's come to Hebrews 10 and let's pick it up where we left off and let's see what we can learn here.

Now I preached on this once some years ago, but what we're going to do is examine the covenant between God the Father and Jesus Christ. A lot of people claim that Jesus was under the Old Covenant. No, He was not under the Old Covenant. If He were under the Old Covenant then He would have offered sacrifices, correct? Jesus was not under the New Covenant because the New Covenant hadn't been given. But what we are going to see is that Jesus was under a special covenant between Him and God the Father.

Where do we find this? Well, Paul leads up to it. Let's begin here Hebrews 10:1: "For the Law, having *only* a shadow of the good things that are coming, *and* not the image of those things, with the same sacrifices which they offer continually year by year, is never able to make perfect those who come *to worship*. Otherwise, would they not have ceased to be offered? For once those who worship had been purified, *they would* no longer be conscious of sin." See, so that's part of our repentance and coming to God and asking God to cleanse our heart and mind and conscience, and to get rid of the sin within. That's the whole goal of overcoming, you see.

I'm reading from the new translation. Verse 3: "On the contrary, in *offering* these *sacrifices* year by year, *there is* a remembrance of sins because *it is* impossible *for the* blood of bulls and goats to take away sins." Now why is that even though it was, as we saw, for the removal of sin to justify them to the temple? Because it requires something greater than a human being to forgive human sin. And it's also true that no animal is even equal to a human being let alone greater. So that's why this was given to show that there has to be something greater than that.

Now verse 5: "For this reason, when He comes into the world, He says, 'Sacrifice and offering You did not desire, but You have prepared a body for Me.' " Now this is talking about Christ. And we'll got back and we'll look at the psalm concerning this and where it came from and we will see that this is accurately quoted from the Septuagint. We'll see in the King James it's just a little bit different. And by the way, I might mention, someone sent me a study using the latest Tanakh, and the Tanakh is the Hebrew publication of the Old Testament. Well, what do you suppose they've done in the latest ones? They've gone through and sanitized all of the prophecies concerning Christ to make them read slightly different. So if you want to study the English translation by the Jews of the Hebrew Old Testament, what you do is this: You go back and you get a 1908 or 1905, something like that (I have one of those) and you compare that with the newest Tanakh.

So anyway, here's quite a thing: " '…You have prepared a body for Me.' " A physical body for Christ. And we will see there were certain things that God promised in doing that. And also this has to do with the church, because the church is the body of Christ of which He is the Head, correct? So we can get many things out of this.

Now then again he repeats it: " 'You did not delight in burnt offerings and *sacrifices* for sin.' " Now here's a key verse, verse 7. Verse 7 becomes the important verse: " 'Then said I, "Lo, I come (*as* it is written of Me in *the* scroll of *the* book) to do Your will, O God" ' " (Heb. 10:1-7). Ok, now we'll examine this in just a little bit here.

Where is "the scroll of the book"? Where in the Old Testament is this scroll? Well let's look where it's quoted from in Psalm 40 and we will see that this is just a quote. And then we'll ask some questions concerning "the scroll of the book" and so forth, and see what we can come up with. Let's pick it up here in verse 6: "Sacrifice and offering Thou didst not desire…" Now instead of saying "You prepared a body for Me," it says: "…Mine ears hast Thou opened: burnt offering and sin offering hast Thou not required. Then said I, Lo, I come: in the volume of the book *it is* written of Me…" Now where can you find that? What book? What scroll? "…I delight to do Thy will, O My God: yea, Thy law *is* within My heart" (Psalm 40:6-8). Now let's ask another question: Are there books in heaven? Yes, there are. What do we have? We have the book of life, don't we? And all those who have the Spirit of God, their name is written there. We also have to have a book… And the book of life by the way includes first and second resurrection, would it not? It would have to. And consider this: God says that a sparrow doesn't fall that the Father's not aware of it. So God is in close communication with the earth through the things that He has created. A lot of people think that God is way off someplace, but He's not way off someplace.

Ok, now then there are also because the wicked have to be resurrected and judged, don't they? Then there has to be a book of those whose names are written in there for the resurrection of the incorrigible wicked.

Now then there are other books aren't there? Let's come to Revelation 10. Now here was a special book. Let's pick it up right here in verse 1: "Then I saw another strong angel coming down out of heaven, clothed with a cloud: and *with* a rainbow on his head; and his face *was* like the sun, and his feet *were* like pillars of fire; and he had in his hand a little book *that was* open…" So there's another book in heaven. "…And he placed his right foot on the sea, and *his* left *foot* on the earth, and cried with a loud voice, as a lion roars. And when he cried, seven thunders uttered their voices. And when the seven thunders spoke *with* their voices, I was about to write. But I heard a voice from heaven say unto me, Seal what the seven thunders spoke, and do not write them." Apparently it's going to be so devastating that it would be such a horrible thing to write it.

So then: "Then the angel whom I had seen standing on the sea and on the earth lifted up his hand to heaven, and swore by Him Who lives into the ages of eternity, Who created the heaven, and the things in it, and the earth and the things in it, and the sea, and the things in it, '*There* shall be no more delay.' " And then it says: "…but in the days of the voice of the seventh angel, when he is about to sound *the* trumpet, the mystery of God shall also be completed, according to the gospel *that* He declared to His servants the

261

prophets. Then the voice that I heard from heaven spoke to me again, and said, Go take the little book that is open in the hand of *the* angel who is standing on the sea and upon the earth. And I went to the angel, *and* said to him, 'Give me the little book.' And he said to me, Take *it,* and eat it, and it shall make your belly bitter, but in your mouth is shall be as sweet as honey" (Rev. 10:1-9). So he took the book, he did so, and what he was to do then was to prophecy.

Let's come back here to Revelation 5 and let's see that there is what we call the "book of prophecy." See, the first three chapters are the letters to the seven churches. The fourth chapter is showing the throne of God and where everything is taking place. The fifth chapter, let's begin here in verse 1 to show that there is a book there. "And in the right hand of Him Who sits sat on the throne I saw a book written within and on *the* back, which had been sealed with seven seals. And I saw a strong angel proclaiming with a loud voice,"Who is worthy to open the book and to loose its seals?" And no one in heaven, or on the earth, or under the earth was able to open the book, or to look into it" (Rev. 5:1-3). So here what do we have? What does this book contain? All the rest of the book of Revelation.

Now there were certain things that were done before the foundation of the world. Let's come to Revelation 13. You see, God had this all planned out before He even began the process. And part of the scroll that it was written in, we are going to see, was a special scroll. Now verse 8, it talks about the coming beast and how the world's going to worship him and so forth. The only ones who are not going to worship him are those whose names are in the book of life. The ones: "…whose names have not been written in the book of life [so there again we have the book of life here, right?] of the Lamb slain from *the* foundation of *the* world." So this was planned before the foundation of the world.

Now how did they plan it? How did they work it out? Well, let's see if we can pick up some clues. Let's look at one of them: "You have prepared Me a body and it's written in a scroll of a book" (Heb. 10:5, 7, paraphrased, *KJV*). Now since God is a covenant God… and what do we have here contained in the Bible? We have the Old Covenant, we have the New Covenant, we have lesser covenants and promises and things given, don't we? And it's written. Do you suppose that there was a special book written that contained the agreement of God the Father and Jesus Christ? Now between themselves alone they wouldn't need it written down, but why would they write it down? So that when all of those who are resurrected enter into the Kingdom of God they can see the record of how it was planned.

Now, let's look at the body. Let's come to Psalm 16. Could this have been written in the scroll of the book, because "in the scroll of a book it's written of Me"? So everything to do with the ministry of Christ was written there.

Now before we get into Psalm 16 let's just review something we already know. What do we know concerning God in the Old Testament? "In the beginning God…", and what is the Hebrew word? Elohim. And in studying the Bible and searching it out the Bible reveals that there were two that were Elohim. One became the Father, one became the Son. They had an agreement. We'll get to Psalm 16 in a minute, come over to Psalm 2 first. Let's pick it up before the body is formed and we will see what God had to do, what the one Who became the Son, had to do. And there had to be absolute trust and absolute belief and absolute faith in each other—God the Father and Jesus Christ—in order to do what God did. You know today in this world they break every agreement that they have. And if God the Father were not righteous and God Who loves, and if Jesus Christ were not righteous and God Who loves, then the one Who became a human being could have been snuffed out by the one Who didn't, right? There was a time when the one Who became the Son gave up His power and glory as God to be begotten in the virgin Mary.

Now let's come here to Psalm 2:7: "I will declare the decree: [that] the LORD hath said unto Me…" Now this is probably written in that scroll because everything about Christ was going to be written in that scroll. "…Thou *art* My Son; this day have I begotten Thee." Now there was a day when that happened. We have that recorded in Luke 1, don't we? Yes. What did God have to do to do that? What did Jesus have to do, the one who became Jesus Christ? Let's add a little bit more before we go to Psalm 16. Let's come back here to Philippians 2, and let's see what Jesus had to do in order to become a human being. And this is what is so confounding to people in the world, religious people whatever their theology is. And that's why it's almost—I don't know. Some of these religionists, you wonder if you can do anything to get the truth into their heads.

Now the one who became the Son had a body prepared for Him. What does this mean "prepared?" The first thing that had to happen before the body could be prepared—and of course in preparing the body, however Christ reduced Himself down in power and glory, it had to be made compatible with genes and chromosomes, correct, in order for that begettal in Mary to produce a human being. Now with the knowledge we have of science today we can understand that a little bit more.

Ok, Philippians 2:5: "Let this mind be in you, which *was* also in Christ Jesus [setting the example of humility and giving up]; Who, although He existed in *the* form of God [and that is the correct translation], did not consider it robbery to be equal with God, but emptied Himself…" It means He gave up His power, His glory, His splendor, His rule, His authority and handed it all over to God the Father. It's going to be interesting…I'm anxious to see if there is that book, which I'm convinced that there is, and to understand what's in it because this was a tremendous thing for God to do. "…*And* was made in *the* likeness of men, *and* took the form of a servant; and being found in *the* manner of man, He humbled Himself, *and* became obedient unto death, even *the* death of *the* cross" (Phil. 2:5-8). And we're going to see there are some other things that were promised.

Now let's come to Hebrews 1 and then we'll go to Psalm 16. When He was born God commanded that the angels worship Him. Now that's something. And they did. Remember the account in the book of Luke? The shepherds were out there and all of a sudden the heavens lighted up and here were a host of angels singing "Glory to God in the Highest." So when Paul writes here beginning right here in verse 1, this is profound: "God, Who spoke to the fathers at different times in the past and in many ways by the prophets, has spoken to us in these last days by *His* Son…" Now how profound is that when compared to a human being even though He became a human like we are human. "…Whom He has appointed heir of all things, by Whom also He made the worlds…" So the very Creator Who made the heavens and the earth under the authority of God the Father was the one Who divested Himself and became a human being. You can't have any greater authority and power than that to forgive your sins, can you? No.

Verse 3: "…Who, being *the* brightness of *His* glory and *the* exact image of His person, and upholding all things by the word of His own power…" Now you think about that for a minute. The very one Who upholds the universe by the word of His power says that "If you confess your sins, I will forgive your sins." That's why you need to believe that that is so. And that's why we need to have faith and love and all the attributes that God can give us, you see.

"…When He had by Himself…", since He was the Creator of human beings; since He gave the judgment of the law of sin and death to Adam and Eve and that passed on to all human beings, He alone… And this is why it cannot be that the one who was Jesus Christ was just another man, because this has to save all humanity, see. "…When He had by Himself purged our sins, sat down at *the* right hand of the Majesty on high; having been made so

263

much greater than *any of* the angels, inasmuch as He has inherited a name exceedingly superior to them. For to which of the angels did He ever say, 'You are My Son; this day I have begotten You'?" That's a one-time occurrence. "And again, 'I will be a Father to Him, and He will be a Son to Me'?" And that was part of their agreement.

"And again, when He brought the Firstborn into the world…" Now the King James says "begotten," but that's incorrect—it's "firstborn." It means when He was born of the virgin Mary. And remember what he was commanded to call Him? Jesus. What's another name? Emmanuel. And what does that mean? God with us. "…When He brought the Firstborn into the world, He said, 'Let all *the* angels of God worship Him' " (Heb. 1:1-6).

Now then we are ready for Psalm 16. Let's go there. Here's part of the promise. Now we can pick up a few clues from some of the psalms and some of the other scriptures. Verse 10, this is a promise of the resurrection. Since He was going to become a human being and suffer death He had to have the promise that God would fulfill, right? Here's part of the promise: "For Thou wilt not leave My soul in hell [that means the grave]; neither wilt Thou suffer Thine Holy One to see corruption." You can go back to Psalm 2 and see where Peter preached that on the Day of Pentecost concerning Christ. "Thou wilt shew Me the path of life: in Thy presence *is* fulness of joy; at Thy right hand *there are* pleasures for evermore" (Psa. 16:10-11). So He promised that He would not let His body corrupt.

Let's come to Isaiah 9. Now Isaiah 9 is a very profound section of scripture. Verse 6: "For unto us a child is born, unto us a son is given: and the government shall be upon His shoulder: and His name shall be called Wonderful…" Now look, all of these are names and attributes of God. So here it's said of this little child that would be born: "…Wonderful, Counsellor, The mighty God…" As much of God as could be in the flesh, that's what Jesus had. We've also seen that it's impossible for God in His glorified form to fill a human body. Why? Because it would disintegrate it. That's what God told Moses. He said, "You cannot see My face and live." So therefore God had to divest Himself of His glory and power and honor and become a human being to become a child to be born.

Now let's continue on here in Isaiah 9: "…and His name shall be called Wonderful, Counsellor, The mighty God, The everlasting Father…" And I've had a lot of people ask me the question: "Well, when is Jesus going to be the everlasting Father? And what about God the Father? Does this not present a conflict?" Well, no. God the Father is the Father of all of those who are going to be in the first resurrection. He will not be the Father of all those who come into the Kingdom of God during the Millennium. Jesus Christ will be the Father of all of those, and the church ruling with Christ will be the Mother of them. So henceforth then at that time the one that we know as the Father is our Father but will be their Grandfather, if we could put it into human terms. So that's when Jesus will be the everlasting Father, The Prince of Peace.

"Of the increase of *His* government and peace *there shall be* no end [just like there's no end to the universe], upon the throne of David, and upon His kingdom, to order it, and to establish it with judgment and with justice from henceforth even for ever. The zeal of the LORD of hosts will perform this" (Isa. 9:6-7).

Now when Jesus came in the flesh now you will understand even more Isaiah 50. And understand this: The current thing that is going around about Jesus is this, and if you got tired of watching all the Christmas shows over the Christmas holidays and so forth and you turned on History Channel, you saw a lot of stories out of the Bible. And one of the stories that keeps coming out over and over and over again is Jesus was a Jew born into a Jewish family and He was taught by the Rabbi's, and Jesus Himself was a Rabbi. Well (and I believe that this is part of the covenant that was written in that scroll), since Jesus gave up everything to become a human being… And you know when a baby is born, outside of just certain functions that God has programmed into the mind of a baby such as responding to love, being able to nurture, being able to have some few rudimentary movements and things like that, the brain is virtually empty of any knowledge. There is no programmed knowledge in there. They don't come out speaking a language: "Oh, Hi Mom. Boy, I'm sure glad to be here. It was kind of dark and wet in there for all these nine months."

God could not leave the mind of Jesus Christ to be taught and programmed by liars, because what the Rabbi's follow is based upon their traditions, which are lies against the Word of God. So He was taught by the Father directly, and I think beginning at a very early age, probably almost immediately. Question: Do newborn babies begin responding to mother and father and the environment around them? Yes, immediately, don't they? Yes. Well, we've covered this before but we will cover it again.

Isaiah 50:4, and this is a prophecy, as we have noted in the *Harmony* and also in the coming New Testament, of Jesus education. We'll go there in just a minute (in John 7). Isaiah 50:4: "The Lord GOD hath given Me the tongue of the learned…" And isn't that what they wanted even at age twelve when He was there at the temple and He was talking to all the teachers and priests. They were [saying], "My, where did he get all this understanding?" See, at age twelve where did He get it? Did Mary teach it to Him? Did Joseph teach it to Him? No. "The Lord GOD hath given Me the tongue…" It came from God, see. The one Who became God the Father taught His Son: "…that I should know how to speak a word in season to *him that is* weary [which is a prophecy of the Gospel of the good news]: He wakeneth morning by morning [every morning God the Father woke up Jesus], He wakeneth Mine ear to hear as the learned." That's how He was taught. God didn't leave it to sinful men to teach Jesus. He taught Him directly. And we would have to conclude that that is absolutely necessary, otherwise what? Jesus would, as a young child, be led into sin, correct? Yes, indeed. So it couldn't have happened except this way. "…He wakeneth mine ear to hear as the learned. The Lord GOD hath opened mine ear, and I was not rebellious, neither turned away back" (Isa. 50:4-5). Then it jumps forward into the things that would happen at the crucifixion.

And you find this in the Old Testament. That's why the Old Testament is a precept here, a line here, a bit here, and you put it together. Because now here we have verses 4 and 5 are about His first coming and His education. Then immediately it jumps forward to His scourging. And you find that in the Old Testament. When you understand that that's how the Old Testament is written then you'll be able to understand it. But what is the key for understanding the Old Testament? The New Testament. That's what Jesus said: He opened their minds to the things concerning Him out of the Law, the Prophets, and the Psalms. So the New Testament interprets the Old.

Ok, let's go forward here. Now with this in mind let's come to John 5. Let's see what was part of the covenant that Jesus had to respond to, because He had His part. His part was that when He was here as a human being He had an obligation of what He was going to say and what He was going to do. And God the Father taught Him that, didn't He? Yes. Ok, John 5 and let's pick it up here in verse 17 when they came to Him because He healed a man on the Sabbath: "But Jesus answered them, 'My Father is working until now, and I work.' " See, they did not understand that there is a spiritual work always going on. And the greatest work that is accomplished on the Sabbath is the spiritual work, which comes through study, prayer, God's Spirit, fellowshipping with God the Father and Jesus Christ—all come together on the Sabbath day. And it has to be a participation spiritually with those who are teaching and those who are learning that altogether with God's Spirit, you see, that we all learn. So that's a spiritual work. And of course on the Sabbath the Jews couldn't understand that.

"So then, on account of this *saying*, the Jews sought all the more to kill Him, not only because He had loosed the Sabbath…" Now the King James says "broke the Sabbath," and as we went through the series on Refuting Sunday-keeping, those who do not understand the Greek nor understand what the New Testament is teaching say, "He broke the Sabbath to set the example that we can keep Sunday." That's a carnal mind trying to understand something spiritual. No, He loosed that law which said you can't carry, as we would say today, a sleeping bag on the Sabbath. He loosed the Sabbath. "…But also *because* He had called God His own Father, making Himself equal with God."

Now verse 19. Here's part of what was Jesus' responsibility. "Therefore, Jesus answered and said to them…" What I want you to do is also keep in mind what the scriptures tell us of Lucifer and Satan, who rebelled and went against God and said, "I will be like God," and "I will exalt my throne above the stars of heaven," and all of that. Now compare that with the attitude of what Christ had here. And of course this had to be because also Christ has to judge Satan the devil. And in order to judge Satan the devil, that's part of the reason He came in the flesh so that He could overcome him as a human being, which is a lesser existence than God, a lesser existence than an angel. God can overcome Satan any time, can't He? Angels fight back and forth—the good angels and the evil angels, don't they? You can read that in Daniel 9 and 10. But to overcome Satan as a human being (Which, who did not do [it]? Adam and Eve.), He had to do it.

So He had an obligation. Now keep that in mind when we read verse 19: "Therefore, Jesus answered and said to them, 'Truly, truly I say to you, the Son has no power [*dunamis*] to do anything of Himself…' " That was His agreement. He would take no power to Himself to do anything of His own. " '…But only what He sees the Father do.' " Does that not verify Isaiah 50, that He saw the Father? Yes, indeed. " 'For whatever He does, these things the Son also does in the same manner. For the Father loves the Son, and shows Him everything that He Himself is doing' " (John 5:17-20). So what I want you to do is think of the tremendous spiritual relationship that Jesus Christ had with God the Father all during His life while this was going on, you see. [That's] something, I mean really something. So then that's why He was given authority as the Son of man and so forth.

Now let's come back here to John 3:31. This was also part of it and this also verifies it: " 'He Who comes from above is above all. The one who is of the earth is earthy, and speaks of the earth. He Who comes from heaven is above all;…' " Isn't it interesting—people wonder where Jesus came from. And here it is—He comes from heaven. Verse 32: " '…And what He has seen and heard,…' " Now that's what the Father taught Him, right? Had to be. " '…This *is what* He testifies; but no one receives His testimony. The one who has received His testimony has set his seal that God is true; for He Whom God has sent speaks the words of God;…' " That was Jesus' obligation under this covenant.

You see, just like when we are baptized and put into the watery grave and we enter into that covenant relationship with God, it is a covenant relationship unto death (that's why it is a burial) and we are co-joined to the death of Christ Who paid for our sins. Now then, when we come out of that watery grave we have an obligation to do, based upon the terms of the covenant, don't we? Yes, indeed. We are to obey God, we are to love God, we are to believe God, we are to trust in Him. All of those things are our obligation. Just like with the covenant that Christ had between Him and God the Father, He had an obligation, didn't He. His obligation was to speak what God told Him to speak. Whatever the commandment was He told Him to speak, He spoke. And so that we understand, and then this becomes much more profound, you see, that these words are the words which God the Father has given. So when anyone rejects Christ they reject the Father. That's why John said, "He who has not the Son has not the Father."

Verse 34: " 'For He Whom God has sent [now that's referring to Christ] speaks the words of God; and God gives not the Spirit by measure *unto Him*. The Father loves the Son and has given all things into His hand. The one who believes in the Son has everlasting life; but the one who does not obey the Son shall not see life, for the wrath of God remains on him' " (John 3:31-36).

Now let's come to John 7. Isn't it interesting that a lot of these things that we're picking up, which had to be part of that covenant that was written in the scroll of the book, we find in the Gospel of John. John 7. Now we've covered this before but let's look at just a couple of things that are important here. Let's just talk about the Feast of Tabernacles for a minute because this is what John 7 is talking about. Let's ask a question: Would Jesus command His brothers and mother to sin? No. Did He tell them to go up to the Feast? Yes, He did. So therefore anybody who says that keeping the Feast of Tabernacles is a sin is accusing Jesus of commanding sin. They don't think of it that way, but that's what they're doing.

Now His brothers said, "Go up and show yourself to the world." Let's come here to verse 6: "Therefore, Jesus said to them, 'My time has not yet come, but your time is always ready. The world cannot hate you; but it hates Me because I testify concerning it, that its works are evil. You go up to this feast.' " There it is, He said go to the Feast, the Feast of Tabernacles. " 'I am not going up to this feast <u>now</u>…' " What He wanted to happen was for them to leave and be on their way then He would come up privately, because He was going to the Feast but He had a plan in mind that He was going to do when He got there, and He couldn't do it if He went with them. Because what would happen? Now I'm sure they didn't have binoculars in those days, but I'm sure they had everybody up there looking: "Well, there's Mary and James and Joseph, and so forth. There they are. Where's Jesus? We don't see Him." See, so that's why He said (He had a plan in mind, we'll see what it is). He says: " 'You go up to this feast. I am not going up to this feast now [that means at this present minute], for My time has not yet been fulfilled.' And after saying these things to them, He remained in Galilee. But after His brothers had gone up, then Jesus also went up to the feast, not openly, but as it were in secret. As a result, the Jews were seeking Him at the feast, and said, 'Where is He?' Now there was much debating about Him among the people. Some said, 'He is a good man.' But others said, 'No, but He is deceiving the people.' However, no one spoke publicly about Him for fear of the Jews."

"But then, about the middle of the feast, Jesus went up into the temple and was teaching." So He was there keeping the feast all the time but didn't show Himself till the middle of the feast. Now notice the reaction here, verse 15: "And the Jews were amazed, saying, 'How does this man knows letters [that means how does He understand the scriptures], having never been schooled?' " Now let's stop here and think for a minute. We have the Sadducees, we have the Pharisees, we have the Essenes, we have all of the Rabbi's. We have the school of Hillel, we have the school of Gamaliel—those were the two main schools in Jerusalem. So if you wanted to become some mucky-muck in Judaism you had to go to one of these two schools. Don't you think, since this is the Feast of Tabernacles just before His crucifixion, don't you think that all of the leading Jewish Rabbi's checked out with one another from the very beginning and said, "Did he go to your school?" "Did he go to your school? Who taught this guy?" Now what do you think they would have done to the Rabbi who had taught Him? Sayonara (good old Japanese phrase). He would have been tried and convicted. "How dare you teach someone to usurp our authority." You know, whatever you want to add to it.

Now then, verse 16: "Jesus answered them and said, 'My doctrine is not Mine, but His Who sent Me. If anyone desires to do His will, he shall know of the doctrine, whether it is from God, or *whether* I speak from My own self' " (John 7:6-17). There it is—His obligation. This was part of His covenant with God the Father. So the one Who became the Father said, "Alright, I'll watch over You, I'll teach You while you grow up, and when the times comes for the beginning of Your ministry," which we find there in Mark 1, the beginning of the Gospel of Jesus Christ and so forth, "then You are to teach and say only My words." Which is what He did all the way through.

Now let's come over here to Chapter 8, verse 28: "Then Jesus said to them, 'When you have lifted up the Son of man, then you yourselves shall know that I AM, and *that* I do nothing of Myself. But as the Father taught Me, these things I speak.' " How many times did He say that over and over and over again, you see. " 'And He Who sent Me is with Me. The Father has not left Me alone because I always do the things that please Him' " (John 8:28-29).

Now then, was keeping the Feast of Tabernacles in the manner that He kept it pleasing to God? It had to be. That was part of His obligation: Always speak the words that God the Father taught Him; always do the things that please Him. So you see this is the separate covenant that Jesus was under, and the covenant between Him and God the Father. Now it's going to be very interesting when we're resurrected and we meet the Father and we see where these books are written. And I'm sure that they're going to open them up and say (how ever they keep time in heaven in relationship to the earth), "This was our agreement."

Ok, now let's look at another one. Let's come to John 10:14: " 'I am the good Shepherd, and I know those who *are* Mine, and am known of those who *are* Mine. Just as the Father knows Me, I also know the Father; and I lay down My life for the sheep.' " That was part of His agreement—to lay down His life. He had to do the hardest thing , [more] than any human being could do—lay down His life into the manner that it was taken. We'll have more to talk about that when we come down toward Passover time. " 'And I have other sheep that are not of this fold. I must bring those also, and they shall hear My voice; and there shall be one flock *and* one Shepherd. On account of this, the Father loves Me: because I lay down My life, that I may receive it back again.' " Now that's the proper translation. He didn't take it back. This is passive—receive. Because God the Father had to give it back to Him, didn't He? Remember what happened when Jesus was on the cross, one of the very last things He said? "Father, into Your hands I commend My Spirit," and He gave up the ghost—the Spirit. That's when He died, because He had to be dead. And it's not docetism where a spirit being called Christ imposed itself into the body of a man called Jesus. And so therefore [they claim] Jesus Christ did not die. The Spirit Christ went back to the Father, and the man Jesus died. That's not what it was. " '...I may receive it back again.' "

Verse 18: " 'No one takes it from Me, but I lay it down of Myself.' " Of His own accord He did it. " 'I have authority to lay it down [that's part of the covenant agreement that they had] and authority to receive it back again. This commandment I received from My Father' " (John 10:14-18). So that's quite a thing. That helps you understand the voluntary choice and will of God to do this. Now think back and go back to the verse we started with, John 3:16, where it says that "God so loved the world"—think what the Father and the Son worked out. Think of what they did. This is a tremendous thing. This is a tremendous covenant that they had.

Now let's look at some other things concerning this. Let's look and see and understand when He says "I lay My life down," let's see what He knew was going to happen. Let's come to Isaiah 53. He knew this was going to happen. He gave this prophecy Himself. Did Jesus understand exactly what was going to happen to Him? Yes, He did. Isaiah 53 is a very profound chapter. This is why the sacrifice of Jesus Christ saves all who repent. This is why God alone can help people in these situations because He went through it all.

Isaiah 53:1: "Who hath believed our report?" How many people really believe God? "And to whom is the arm of the LORD revealed? For He shall grow up before Him as a tender plant [that's Christ's childhood], and as a root out of a dry ground: He hath no form nor comeliness; and when we shall see Him, *there is* no beauty that we should desire Him." So He's just an ordinary looking man. Notice what kind of life He lived. You think you've got troubles, this is what God had to suffer in the flesh among His own. It says there in John 1 He created the world and the world didn't know Him and He came to His own and His own didn't receive Him. So if you're down and out, if you're alone, if you think nobody likes you, no one loves you, no one cares for you—look up, pray to God. Look to Jesus Christ, He'll help you. "He is despised and rejected of men; a man of sorrows, and acquainted with grief…" And this has to do when they saw Him on the cross: "…And we hid as it were *our* faces from Him; He was despised, and we esteemed Him not."

"Surely He hath borne our griefs, and carried our sorrows…" That's why it says in Matthew 11, "All you who are heavy burdened, come unto Me for My yoke is easy and My burden is light" (Matt 11:28-30, paraphrased), because you can put all of those on Christ. "…Yet we did esteem Him stricken, smitten of God, and afflicted." Yeah, they came by and said, "Well…" And even one of the two robbers said, "Well, if You're the Christ save Yourself and save us." The other one said, "You don't even know what you're talking about. We're here because we did it. We're here justly, but He not justly." Then he said, "Lord, remember me when You come into Your kingdom."

"But He *was* wounded for our transgressions [not for anything He did], *He was* bruised for our iniquities: the chastisement of our peace *was* upon Him…" In other words in order for us to have peace with God, the penalty of our sins had to be slashed upon His back with the scourging of crucifixion to bring peace. "…And with His stripes we are healed. All we like sheep have gone astray; we have turned every one to his own way; and the LORD hath laid on Him the iniquity of us all [because He was responsible]. He was oppressed, and He was afflicted, yet He opened not his mouth: He is brought as a lamb to the slaughter, and as a sheep before her shearers is dumb, so He openeth not His mouth. He was taken from prison and from judgment: and who shall declare His generation? for He was cut off out of the land of the living: for the transgression of My people was He stricken. And He made His grave with the wicked…" See, all of this was there. All of this had to be written in the scroll that is all about Christ and the covenant that God the Father and Jesus Christ had, and then we are given some of it here and some of it there and put all together. And the key thing that really got me started on this was there was no place where that part which says "it's written of Me in a scroll of a book," there's no place in the Bible where you can find what was written, except you get a bit here and a bit there.

"And He made His grave with the wicked, and with the rich in His death; because He had done no violence, neither *was any* deceit in His mouth. Yet it pleased the LORD to bruise Him…", even though He did. And that goes back to Genesis 3:15, doesn't it? Yes. Even though it pleased God to do it to solve the problem of sin and His creation of human beings, it still was so gruesome that when it came down to the final three hours of Christ on the cross, it became dark and Jesus had to do it alone. So that was something. That's why they had this covenant. That's why this agreement was there.

"…He hath put *Him* to grief: when Thou shalt make His soul an offering for sin…" Now then out of that: "…He shall see *His* seed…", because as it is in the great congregation (as it says back there in Hebrews 2, "I will declare Your name unto My brethren in the great congregation.") That, brethren, has got to be at the resurrection. Here is Christ, all of us are resurrected and we meet Him in the air, and He turns to God the Father and says, "Here are the children that You have given Me." And He's going to go right down the line and give everyone a new name. We'll have to save that for Pentecost. We'll go on.

269

"…He shall prolong *His* days, and the pleasure of the LORD shall prosper in His hand. He shall see of the travail of His soul, *and* shall be satisfied [takes care of all sin]: by His knowledge shall My righteous servant justify many; for He shall bear their iniquities." Only God can do that. No human being, no animal. This had to be carefully prepared and worked out well ahead of time. "Therefore will I divide Him *a portion* with the great, and He shall divide the spoil with the strong [that's giving a reward to all of us]; because He hath poured out His soul unto death: and He was numbered with the transgressors; and He bare the sin of many, and made intercession for the transgressors" (Isa. 53:1-12).

Now let's come back to Hebrews 10 and let's read that again. Maybe this will give us more understanding. And is one of these things that we come to realize after we've been converted a long time and have really studied the Word of God. Let's come back here and read it, verse 5: "For this reason, when He comes into the world, He says, 'Sacrifice and offering You did not desire, but You have prepared a body for Me. You did not delight in burnt offerings and *sacrifices* for sin. Then said I, "Lo, I come (*as* it is written of Me in *the* scroll of *the* book [the covenant between God the Father and Jesus Christ]) to do Your will, O God" ' " (Heb. 10:5-7).

So that's something brethren, and we're part of it, and here we're living right at the end of the age and it's going to be really profound to see what God is going to do. So that is a covenant (since God is a covenant God) that God the Father and Jesus Christ made when He came to the earth.

End of Sermon

Transcriber Carolyn Singer

The Special Covenant Between God the Father and Jesus Christ
January 10, 2004
Scriptural References

1) John 3:16	13) Isaiah 9:6-7
2) I Corinthians 2:6-14	14) Isaiah 50:4-5
3) Hebrews 10:1-7	15) John 5:17-20
4) Psalm 40:6-8	16) John 3:31-36
5) Revelation 10:1-9	17) John 7:6-17
6) Revelation 5: 1-3	18) John 8:28-29
7) Revelation 13:8	19) John 10:14-18
8) Hebrews 10:5,7	20) Isaiah 53:1-12
9) Psalm 2:7	21) Matthew 11:28-30
10) Philippians 2:5-8	22) Genesis 3:15
11) Hebrews 1:1-6	23) Hebrews 10:5-7
12) Psalm 16:10-11	

CHAPTER EIGHTEEN

How to Count Pentecost and Count 50

October 2006

And greetings brethren this is a special video which will also be part of the coming new book, and we want to go through how to count Pentecost and the meaning of counting to fifty. And what we need to understand is this, as we've mentioned before, everything concerning the Holy Days is keyed to the Passover. And the Passover is most important because it is the crucifixion of Jesus Christ. Now, that starts out in Genesis 3, as we have already understood. And goes through to Genesis 15, Genesis 22, Exodus 12, and then on down to the time of Christ when on the Passover night He instituted the New Covenant symbols, and then on the day portion of the Passover He was crucified. Then we immediately go into the Feast of Unleavened Bread which is connected with it, then on to the Wave Sheaf Offering Day, on to Pentecost, down to Trumpets, down to Atonement, down to Tabernacles and the Last Great Day.

Now, if we count the Passover as one of the Feasts of God, which it is, and then we have seven Holy Days; we have a total of eight [feasts]. And Pentecost is the fourth Feast of the eight, or the middle Feast. As you will see when you get into the transcripts concerning events to take place before Pentecost, and then events to take place after Pentecost, you will see that Pentecost is the tipping point in history. Now we've also understood that Satan likes to confuse everything. Satan likes to destroy the knowledge of the true Christian Passover. So we have all of the counterfeits concerning that. We've covered a lot of that. Then [that] does away with Unleavened Bread, substituting it with Lent and with Easter. And the Wave Sheaf Offering Day is then made to be the resurrection day, which is not the resurrection day. And Pentecost also is confused. Not only by those who profess Christianity, but also by those who profess to know the truth, that is being the Jews. And we will see how Judaism also affects the things concerning the understanding of the Holy Days of God. And because the Jews are not in the land of Palestine, they do not keep a fourteenth Passover, but they keep a fifteenth Passover. And if you read the Passover book, I have a chapter in there, "The Passover of the Rejected" and why they do it on the fifteenth. So likewise, as we'll see a little later, they always have their Pentecost on a fixed day of the calendar because they begin counting in the wrong place with the exception of one of the five variations of when Passover occurs.

Now, let's come to Acts the 2nd chapter, and let's see how that Pentecost pictures, as we know, the receiving of the Holy Spirit. And this becomes important for us to understand and how it's all tied together with Unleavened Bread, Wave Sheaf Offering Day, and all of these things. But let's begin right here, in verse 36 of Acts the 2nd chapter. Now, let's come back to the first verse because we'll refer to this later. Acts 2:1, "And when the day *of Pentecost*, the fiftieth day, was being fulfilled, they were all with one accord in the same place" (Acts 2:1). So it's not the day before, it's not the day after; it's during the fiftieth day that it is being fulfilled. Now then, the apostles preached, God gave them the ability to preach supernaturally in all the languages of those who were gathered there at the temple. And God began it at the temple to show the sign of His authority, and that it was directly from Him. Now, let's come over here to verse 36, because what I want to do is show you this, is that in order to receive the Holy Spirit, it has got to go back to the Passover and the sacrifice of Jesus Christ, and then the Wave Sheaf Offering, and Jesus' acceptance for our sins as the perfect sacrifice of God in the throne of God in heaven above. So right here, verse 36, "Therefore, let all *the* house of Israel know with full assurance that God has made this *same* Jesus, Whom you crucified, both Lord and Christ." So here we are in Pentecost going back to Passover because see they fit together as a unit. And as you study the things concerning the seven churches, and all of those things which in this transcription book of study of the Holy Days, you will have all of those things combined to show the various meanings of the seventh week and the fiftieth day. But today we're going to look at it from another different point of view. Verse 37, "Now after hearing *this*, they were cut to the heart; and they said to Peter and the other apostles, 'Men *and* brethren, what shall we do?' Then Peter said to them, 'Repent and be baptized each one of you in the name of Jesus Christ, for *the* remission of sins, and you yourselves shall receive the gift of the Holy Spirit.' " And so the day of Pentecost pictures the day in which the Holy Spirit was given in power. And it pictures the day which also commemorates us receiving the Holy Spirit. And we will see that this fiftieth day, though we receive it at other times whenever we are baptized, but the meaning is with the Feast of Pentecost, that it has to do with our receiving of the Holy Spirit. And it's connected back to the Passover, and the Feast of Unleavened Bread. Verse 39, "For the promises is to you and your children, and to all those who are afar off, as many as *the* Lord our God may call" (Acts 2:36-39).

Now, let's look a just a couple of other things here, that's important for us to understand and realize. Let's come here to Romans the 5th chapter, Romans 5:6. And then we are going to see with this how important that it is everything ties back to the Passover and the crucifixion of Jesus Christ. Romans 5, and let's begin here in verse 6. "For even when we where without strength, at the appointed time..." See even Paul in writing and preaching it goes back to the crucifixion of Christ on the Passover Day. At the appointed time, and it was not at any other time. "... [Christ] died for *the* ungodly. For rarely will anyone die for a righteous man, although perhaps someone might have the courage even to die for a good man. But God commends His own love to us because, when we were still sinners, Christ died for us. Much more, therefore, having been justified now by His blood..." Now justification is a two-step operation. It is the sacrifice of Jesus Christ and His acceptance of the Wave Sheaf Offering Day, which begins the first day of the Count to Pentecost. "...Justified now by His blood, we shall be saved from wrath through Him. For if, when we were enemies, we were reconciled to God through the death of His own Son, much more *then*, having been reconciled, we shall be saved by His life" (Rom. 5:6-10).

Now, come back over here to Romans 4, and let's pick it up here concerning faith and imputation of righteousness through having your sins forgiven. And using the example of Abraham here in Romans the 4th chapter, let's to verse 23, in Romans 4. "But it was not written for his sake alone, that it was imputed to him: Rather, *it was* also *written* for our sakes, to whom it shall be imputed—to those who believe in Him Who raised Jesus our Lord from *the* dead." Now it's very important to understand, as we'll see on some charts later on that the year in which Jesus was crucified, the Passover fell in the middle of the week, on a Wednesday. With the Passover services taking place on Tuesday night before the day portion of the Passover. And the appointed time that we read of over here in Romans the 5th chapter is that very day. And it is also backed up by what Jesus said, that He would be in the tomb three days and three nights. So, we'll have to come through to the Wave Sheaf Offering Day, and then we will look at how to count Pentecost. But notice, "Who raised Jesus our Lord from *the* dead: Who was delivered for our offenses..." delivered to the crucifixion and death, "...And was raised for our justification" (Rom. 4:23-25). And as Paul said, "If Christ was not raised; you're still in your sins." And if you're still in your sins you have no justification, do you? No.

Now let's see how this applies here concerning the blood of Christ, and concerning these things that we're covering here. Let's come back to Hebrews the 10th chapter, and we'll see about the sacrifice of Christ. And again, as you go through and study the Bible, and the New Testament in particular, I want you to understand that everything is keyed on the Passover; the death of Jesus Christ. The next event then, His resurrection at the end of the weekly Sabbath during the Feast of Unleavened Bread. [Calendar month charts can be found in pages 280–287 that show this in detail.] If you want a full explanation of when Jesus was resurrected you can read *The Harmony of the Gospels* which shows the three days and three nights of Jesus in the tomb, or the appendix in the New Testament. And we also have it in the book *The Day Jesus the Christ Died*. So there are plenty references to it, so you go ahead and read and study those.

Now let's come here to Hebrews 10, and let's read what he said here concerning Hebrew 10:12. Now what you might do is key this in your margin going back to Genesis 3:15. Where it talks about [it], that's the first prophecy of the death of Jesus Christ after the sin of Adam and Eve showing that there had to be a penalty paid for their sins. Now, when Jesus was crucified, here is the meaning of it. Verse 12, "But He…" now this is contrasted to the priest who offered sacrifices daily, "…After offering one sacrifice for sins forever…" because Jesus was God manifested in the flesh He alone can take away the sins of the world because He is the creator of all mankind, and don't be fooled by any false doctrine that He was not God before He became God manifested in the flesh. "…One sacrifice for sins forever, sat down at *the* right hand of God." Now that took place on the Wave Sheaf Offering Day for His presentation, He came back to the earth for forty days and forty nights, and He showed Himself to His apostles. Then ascended on the fortieth day for the final time, and has been sitting at the right hand of God, as it says here "…Waiting until His enemies are placed *as* a footstool for His feet." So that is the tipping point of history, the beginning of the return of Christ and the resurrection of the Saints, as we will see. Verse 14, "For by one offering He has obtained eternal perfection *for* those who are sanctified" (Heb. 10:12-14). So this is, again, relating back to the crucifixion.

Come over here to [Hebrews] Chapter 9, and let's pick it up here in verse 11; showing about Christ's activity as our High Priest in heaven right now. And also it goes back to His crucifixion. See, every thing keys back to the Passover, and ties together. All the Holy Days of God are connected in a plan and [in] a revealed step-by-step sequence of what God is doing. Now let's pick it up here in verse 11 of Hebrews 9. "But Christ Himself has become a High Priest of the coming good things, through the greater and more perfect tabernacle, not made by *human* hands (that is, not of this *present physical* creation). Not by *the* blood of goats and calves, but by the means of His own blood, He entered once for all into the holiest…" that's in the heavens above, "…Having *by* Himself secured everlasting redemption *for us*. For if the blood of goats and bulls, and *the* ashes of a heifer sprinkled *on* those who are defiled, sanctifies to the purifying of the flesh. To a far greater degree, the blood of Christ, Who through *the* eternal Spirit offered Himself without spot to God, shall purify your conscience from dead works to serve *the* living God" (Heb. 9:11-14). Now that's why He is mediator of the New Covenant; so that through death, He provided the release of our transgressions for us.

Now's let's come here to I John the 1st chapter; and let's see again the blood of Jesus Christ. And as you study through the Bible I want you to continuously keep that in mind. All of what God is doing is keyed to the Passover. And that's why it's so important. Now if you don't have the Passover book, write in for it, we'll send it to you. Five hundred pages explaining the truth about the Passover; exposing all the errors; going through step-by-step-by-step-by-step to show the magnitude of the Passover and why it is profoundly important and related to salvation, that unless you keep the Passover the way that God has said, you do not have salvation. Now let's come here, I John the 1st chapter, and let's pick it up here in verse 7. It says, "However, if we walk in the light, as He is in the light…" Now notice the "IF." The "if" is always on us. The "if" is never on God. "…We walk in the light, as He is in the light, *then* we have fellowship with one another, and the blood of Jesus Christ, His own Son, cleanses us from all sin" (I John 1:7). Now that's what we need to really understand and realize. See again here, John is writing this and he starts out—read how he starts out—and it comes down then to the sacrifice of Christ, and the forgiveness of our sins. And that's why the Passover is so important. We take the Passover to commemorate—and the sacrifice of Jesus Christ—to renew the New Covenant. And then that keeps us established under the grace of God, so that through the grace of God and the confession of sins we can continually have our sins washed away even on a daily bases, through the blood of Jesus Christ.

Alright now let's carry this a little bit further here, let's go to Acts 20:28. And let's see how this reflects to the church. Because here again, we see Paul in preaching to the elders at Ephesus who came down to meet him in Miletus. He refers back again to the sacrifice of Christ and His blood. And let's read it here, Acts 20:28, he's talking to the elders. So this is a good verse for all the elders, ministers, and teachers to understand, you see. Because no man is to put himself forward. God has to lead and guide him, you see. Verse 28, "Take heed therefore to yourselves and to all the flock, among which the Holy Spirit has made you overseers, to feed the church of God, which He purchased with His own blood." So again, our sins are forgiven through the blood of Christ; the blood of Christ covers everything that we do on a continuous basis in establishing our relationship with God; the blood of Christ; the body of Christ that has to do with the New Covenant and renewing it. And here he purchased the church with His own blood. Then He gives a warning, "For I know this: that after my departure grievous wolves will come in among you, not sparing the flock." And that's what's happened to the church of God; and that's what's happened to worldly Christianity. They've given themselves over to Satan the Devil and his ways, and all the counterfeit things that are there. "And from among your own selves men will rise up speaking perverse things to draw away disciples after themselves" (Acts 20:28-30). And so that's why we find there's so much confusion today in the things that are done, and in relationship to the Passover, Unleavened Bread, and the resurrection of Jesus Christ.

Now, let's come here and see about the assention of Christ; the receiving of the Holy Spirit, because the Holy Spirit was not given until Christ sent it on the day of Pentecost, and what that has meaning for us. Let's come back here to Ephesians the 1st chapter, and let's see where again Paul in starting out he connects this, now notice the connection from Passover, Unleavened Bread, [and] Pentecost. And that's the pattern. Come here to Ephesians the 1st chapter. Now let's pick it up in verse 7, and we'll see the progression of it. "In Whom we have redemption through His blood, *even* the remission of sins, according to the riches of His grace, Which He has made to abound toward us in all wisdom and intelligence; having made known to us the mystery of His own will..." See, God has brought you into His confidence to understand His will. This is just not a matter of comparative religions that you go out and say "Well, I wonder what religion I could be comfortable with? I wonder how I feel in this church." See that has nothing to do with truth. You've got to have the true Jesus; the true Word of God; understand the truth of the Passover and Holy Days; and you've got keep the commandments of God; love Him. It's not a matter of a place where you have a psychological rearranging of your brains to be a good person in the world. See, you're qualifying for eternal life. "Having made known to us the mystery of His own will, according to His good pleasure, which He purposed in Himself; that in *the divine* plan..." And that's what this book is all about; the divine plan of God, step-by-step-by-step, and as you will see when you go through the transcriptions, you listen to the sermons in this book about Gods' revealed will and His plan for mankind, that Pentecost has indeed the greatest number of sermons in there because it is the tipping point in history. Because not only does it commemorate our receiving the Holy Spirit, we will also see as you get into the meaning of Pentecost, that it commemorates and looks forward to the resurrection when Jesus returns. Now we will see that right here in Ephesians the 1st chapter. "...He might bring all things together in Christ, both the things in heavens and the things upon the earth, *yes*, in Him, in Whom we also have obtained an inheritance, having been predestinated according to His purpose…" Now think about that for a minute. God Himself has personally called you; God Himself has personally given you the begettal of the Holy Spirit; God Himself wants to give you eternal life if you remain faithful. So notice all the responsibility that has been given to us, and the way that God has given us the understanding of these things. This is a magnificent thing indeed. "That we might be to *the* praise of His glory…" Now I want you to just think about that for a minute; that God has called you; given you His Spirit and is creating in you the very mind of Christ; and is going to resurrect you, as we'll see as the Feast of Pentecost pictures, the first resurrection, so that all those in the first resurrection will be to the praise of His glory. "…Who first trusted in the Christ; in Whom you also trusted after hearing the Word of the truth…" And the Word of truth involves: repentance, baptism, and so forth as we've already seen. "…The gospel of your salvation; in Whom also, after believing, you were sealed with the Holy Spirit of promise." And that's the first meaning of The Feast of Pentecost. "Which is *the* earnest of our inheritance until *the* redemption of the posession, to *the* praise of His glory" (Eph. 1:7-14). See, so it is the down payment. And Pentecost pictures the down payment of the Holy Spirit; and Pentecost pictures the fulfillment of the redemption on Pentecost. So this is really quite a thing, really something for us to understand.

Now let's look at something else that's important concerning counting, concerning Pentecost, and why God did it this way. Let's come here to Luke the 4th chapter, and then we will go back to the Old Testament, and we will read how to count Pentecost, we will read about the number 50 and what it means. Now, let's come over here to Luke the 4th chapter, because this becomes a very important section for us to understand, and again, Jesus is showing and preaching on a day that's important to show what the gospel is all about, and what it means. Now let's pick it up here in Luke 4:14. "Then Jesus returned in the power in the Spirit to Galilee…" Now that was after He was baptized. "…And the word about Him went out into the entire country around. And He taught in their synagogues, *and* was glorified by all. And He came to Nazareth, where He had been brought up; and according to His custom, He went into the synagogues on the Sabbath day…" Now in the New Testament you'll find the foot note there which means, this Sabbath was a unique Sabbath; because it is called in the Greek *te hemera toon sabbatoon*, and it means, on the day of the weeks; which has reference to Pentecost. Now I want you to focus in on the message that he gave from Isaiah, which is from Isaiah 61, you can go back and read it there. "…And he stood up to read. And there was given Him *the* book of the prophet Isaiah; and when He had unrolled the scroll, He found the place where it was written." Now you see, we're told to preach in season and out of season, correct? Jesus taught in season and out of season as well, because that's the method of how God wants us to understand things. So He taught in season. Here it is on the Feast of Weeks or the Feast of Pentecost, He reads, "*The* Spirit of *the* Lord *is* upon Me; for this reason, He has anointed Me to preach the gospel to *the* poor…" And that relates to fifty days as we will see. " '…He has sent me to heal those who are broken-hearted, to proclaim pardon to *the* captives and recovery of sight to *the* blind, to send forth in deliverance those who have been crushed, to proclaim *the* acceptable year of *the* Lord' " (Luke 4:14-19).

Now what is the acceptable year of the Lord? What is it talking about? Now let's come back to Leviticus 25, before we go to Leviticus 23 for the count on Pentecost. Let's see the only other holy year, if we can put it that way, where there is a count to fifty; and it ties right in with the message that was given here by Jesus on Pentecost. Leviticus 25—and it has to do with the Jubilee. So what Jesus was doing here on Pentecost was preaching the Jubilee. Now let's read it, let's come back here to Leviticus 25:8. Now I'm reading from the new translation which you'll receive sometime in the fall of 2007. "And you shall number seven Sabbaths of years to you, seven times seven years." That's forty-nine; we'll see forty-nine when we get to counting Pentecost for the Holy Day. "And the time of the seven Sabbaths of years shall be forty-nine years to you. Then you shall cause the trumpet of the jubilee to sound on the tenth *day* of the seventh month; in the Day of Atonement, the trumpet shall sound throughout all your land." Now notice what this is physically. Now we know that every seven years there's to be a release of debt. Now here is seven times seven years—forty-nine—then we come to the fiftieth year. Verse 10, "And you shall make the fiftieth year holy..." So here is a parallel counting one through fifty. And seven complete cycles of seven years for forty-nine years. Now that will tie in when we count the weeks. "...And proclaim liberty throughout the land to all its inhabitants." All debts forgiven; everything set aside. "It shall be a jubilee to you, and you shall return each man to his possession, and you shall return every man to his family." Now when you read what's going to happen during the millennium, everyone is what? Going to sit under his own fig tree, and he's going take care of his own food, his own garden, right? Yes. "That fiftieth year shall be a jubilee to you. You shall not sow, neither reap that which grows of itself in it, nor gather in it of your undressed vine." See because God said He would give you three years worth of food in the last year. That is the year forty-eight. So you go forty-nine and fifty, and then the third year you have the food, see. "For it *is* the jubilee. It shall be holy to you. You shall eat the increase of it out of the field." You're not to gather; you're not to reap it; but you can go out and eat whatever there is. "In the year of this jubilee you shall return each man to his possession. And if you sell anything to your neighbor, or buy from your neighbor's hand, you shall not oppress one another. According to the number of years after the jubilee" (Lev. 25:8-15). Then it's the instructions on how to handle the land. But the point is this, number fifty pictures the jubilee. So when we come to Pentecost and counting fifty, what we are actually doing is counting a mini jubilee; and that ties in with God's plan for the resurrection. When we first receive the earnest of the Holy Spirit, let's see what we receive. We'll talk about that a little bit later.

Let's come back here and see how to count Pentecost, because this becomes important for us, and to have it the right way. Now again, in the new translation, what we're going to find is this, that we have it explained in the translation so there doesn't have to be any misinterpretation on how to count Pentecost. So let's come to Leviticus 23 and let's pick it up here in verse 9. And this gives us some very important information and understanding too; when we understand the Hebrew; and when we have the right translation; and when we understand what God is saying; and how to count Pentecost; and how it's going to come about. Now verse 9, "And the LORD spoke to Moses, saying, 'Speak to the children of Israel and say to them, "When you have come into the land which I give to you, and shall reap the harvest of it..." and of course we're the firstfruits harvest, you see, "...Then you shall bring *the premier* sheaf of the firstfruits of your harvest to the priest." And that first of the firstfruits pictured Christ. You're to bring it. And you can read in the Passover book all the details concerning that. "And he shall wave the sheaf before the LORD to be accepted for you." And that's what we read that Christ did when He ascended to heaven, correct? To be accepted for us, as the one sacrifice once for all. And His blood covered it. But you see now with the Wave Sheaf and the Wave Sheaf Offering Day we're going to see must take place on the first day of the week which is called Sunday today. Now just remember, though the names of the weeks have pagan names on them today that does not detour from the fact that seven days of the week are still the seven days of the week as God gave it in the creation. Now here's what he says, verse 11, "And he..." that is the priest, "...shall wave the sheaf before the LORD to be accepted for you. On the next day after the Sabbath the priest shall wave it." Now this becomes important because the Hebrew here is *ha shabbat*, which means the weekly Sabbath. And yet Judaism today follows the pharisaical count of counting from the first Holy Day. And that's how they end up with their Pentecost on *Sivan* 6. Now we're going to go through, and we're going to look at some charts here in just a minute and see how to count Pentecost and how this mini jubilee fits in for Christians. Now let's continue on. Now here's something he says—verse 12—what they were to do with the offering and so forth, the grain offering, the meal offering and so forth. Now, it says—and this was to be when they came into the land—see because it says here in verse 14, "And you shall eat neither bread, nor parched corn, nor green ears, until the same day, until you have brought an offering to your God. *It shall be* a statue forever throughout your generations in all your dwellings." So all during the time they were wandering in the wilderness they ate no bread from grain; they ate manna, bread from heaven. Now we'll take a little pause and we'll come back and see how to count Pentecost.

Now let's come to Leviticus 23 where we left off and let's begin to count. Let's begin to see how Pentecost is counted. It's very important; this is a special day; this is a special thing; and there's special meaning to Christians today concerning counting Pentecost and coming to the fiftieth day Pentecost. Then what it pictures is a mini jubilee within a Christian's life. Now let's read it, verse 15 Leviticus 23. "And you shall count to you beginning with the next day after the Sabbath..." *ha shabbat*, "...Beginning with the day that you brought the sheaf of the wave offering; seven Sabbaths shall be complete." Now when we read it there in Leviticus 25 it was seven Sabbaths of years. So we have the same thing. "Seven Sabbaths shall be complete." Now this means this, a complete week, beginning with day one through day seven. You cannot have partial weeks because then you get into completely discombobulating the instructions here, and miscounting. Now notice verse 16, "Even unto the day after the seventh Sabbath you shall number fifty days" (Lev. 23:9-11, 14-16). Now the fiftieth day then is always the first day of the week after the weekly Sabbath, the seventh Sabbath. And it's also the first day of the eighth week, which then we will see has meaning for us as Christians in relating to the mini jubilee. Now, we have other sermons that go through and explain all about the grain offerings, and the two wave loaves, and everything like that.

So what we're going to do now, I'm going to show you some charts of the calculated Hebrew calendar and show you the [four] different ways, or the [four] different days at which Passover can occur during the year as you go through time. We'll see there is a Passover on Monday, and on Wednesday, and on a Friday, and on Sabbath; and we'll see all of those and see how to count with those circumstances and how the variation of Pentecost will occur on a monthly bases from the fifth of *Sivan* to the tenth of *Sivan*. So having it fixed on the sixth on *Sivan* violates the way to properly count because there would be no use in counting if it where a fixed day of the month. So we'll take a look at these charts here and go through them one-by-one, (pages 280-287). Let's take a look at this chart. This is count to Pentecost with a Monday Passover because everything's keyed to the Passover. Now let's understand something with this. On a Monday Passover it is observed Sunday night. Then we have the Feast of Unleavened Bread through here, and this is the weekly Sabbath during Unleavened Bread. Then this is the Wave Sheaf Offering Day. And we're to count beginning with this day which is inclusive counting, and we number the days. And you also have this chart in the book; and when we send this sermon out we'll send all of these charts with it as well. Okay, Wave Sheaf Offering Day is one. And it goes down, you have seven, here's the first week. Now, we have each day counted, and each day of the count toward Pentecost is in a circle. Now let's come down to the next month here, *Iyor*, you have *Nisan* then *Iyor*, so here is week two; and you come down, week three; week four; week five, and each day is listed; week six, forty-two days, week seven, forty-nine days. And then Pentecost over here which when the Passover is on a Monday, observed Sunday night, Pentecost comes out to be on the 10th of *Sivan*. Quite interesting isn't it? So this is a sequence of how you count when you have a Monday Passover.

Now we're going to look at another chart. Now let's look at when Passover is on a Wednesday, again remember, everything is keyed to the Passover. So Wednesday Passover, middle of the week, you observe it the night before. And this is the same sequence as it was in the year that Jesus was crucified. So you come down here to the 17th, then which is the weekly Sabbath during the days of Unleavened Bread; and toward the end of the Sabbath Jesus was resurrected; and then ascended to the Father on the 18th, the Wave Sheaf Offering Day. So that's why you count this as day one, always Wave Sheaf Offering Day. Now let's count through the days here and then the weeks. One, two, three, four, five, six, seven and again we have the days in the circle, and then the weeks in the square. Week one, week two, week three, week four, five, six, seven which is forty-nine days then, to the morrow after the seventh Sabbath; Pentecost, the fiftieth day, which then is on the eighth of *Sivan*. So that's how you count it when you have a Wednesday Passover.

Now let's look at it when we have a Friday Passover. Now here is the sequence of months beginning with *Nisan*, when you have the Passover on a Friday, and it's observed Thursday night. The Holy Day, which then is the fifteenth, is also the weekly Sabbath; but remember it's on the day after the weekly Sabbath, which then always puts the Wave Sheaf Offering Day on the first day of the week; now that's important when we get to the next one with a Sabbath Passover day. So the Wave Sheaf Offering Day is on the first day of the week, and it is day one. Always, must be counted. So then we have the seven days to the first week, which ends in the Sabbath; second week, which end with the Sabbath; third week ending in the Sabbath, same way with the fourth week, fifth week, sixth week, seventh week. Then we have Pentecost here on the fiftieth day on the day after the seventh Sabbath, fifty days. And that is on sixth of *Sivan*. So you see the difference. You have the tenth of *Sivan*, and the eighth of Sivan, now here you have the sixth of *Sivan*.

Now when we look at the next sequence of when the Passover is observed, which is on the weekly Sabbath, then we have some special circumstances to look at, so we'll look at that chart next. Now this is the last one, when the Passover day falls on the Sabbath, and presents some special difficulties which always have caused people some problems. Now the reason that it has caused problems is because the Passover day is on the Sabbath and you then observe it Friday night. Now, in this case, you do not have a Sabbath during the days of Unleavened Bread, except [after] the last Holy Day; but then if you start counting the Wave Sheaf Offering Day after the last Holy Day then you loose the whole sequence of things and [because] the Wave Sheaf Offering Day cannot be outside the Day's of Unleavened Bread. So what is the solution? The solution is very simple. Since Passover is also an Unleavened Bread Day, therefore this becomes **the** Sabbath. And the next day after the Sabbath then is a Holy Day, the fifteenth day of the first month. So you have a combination here of the Holy Day and the Wave Sheaf Offering Day on the rare occurrence when you have a Sabbath Passover. Now for years, and years, and years we did not have a Sabbath Passover, and we made the mistake of saying that it's day after the weekly Sabbath during the Feast of Unleavened Bread, which was incorrect. It should be the first day of the week during Unleavened Bread is the day that you begin counting on, then which is this day right here. So let's see how this counts. One, two, three, four, five, six, seven complete weeks ending with the Sabbath, which is also a Holy Day. Now, we come down: week two, week three, four, five, six, seven and that's forty-nine days, seven weeks. On the day after the Sabbath you have Pentecost, right here. And in this case it occurs then on the fifth of *Sivan*. Now you see this is why we are to count Pentecost because there will a variation all based upon when the Passover occurs.

Now I'm sure that those charts will help you understand how to count to Pentecost. And how to get the correct way to do it; and I want to emphasize this, that for years—I'll just repeat what I said—for years it was said that it has to be the Sabbath during the Feast of Unleavened Bread. That is true in three out of four cases when you count Pentecost because there's the regular Sabbath during the Feast of Unleavened Bread. However when you have it when the Passover is on Sabbath, then the first Holy Day is on the Wave Sheaf Offering Day because the only Sabbath during Unleavened Bread has got to include the Passover in that, because the Passover is an Unleavened Bread day. Now there are still a lot of people who say "Well you only have to eat unleavened bread for the Passover, and then you can have leavened bread until sundown the next day." Well that's not true. Passover was an Unleavened Bread day. And just keep this in mind, very simple thing to remember, the children of Israel ate unleavened bread for the Passover, which we do too. We eat unleavened bread, correct? When they left their homes at sunrise there was no place for leaven to be around, right? They had unleavened bread; they ate it on the Passover; the Passover day, and Passover ceremony is a day of Unleavened Bread. Now keep this in mind, it's easy to understand, as they were making their way to Ramses to assemble for the beginning of the exodus, there were no McDonald's to stop at to get a egg McMuffin's, or toast, or biscuits. It was by practice an Unleavened Bread Day. So therefore when you come to the Passover being on Sabbath, then the first Holy Day, being the first day of the week, becomes the Wave Sheaf Offering Day because it is the only first day of the week during the Feast of Unleavened Bread. Now I hope that makes things a whole lot more clear for you.

Alright, now, let's come to Romans 8 and let's see the beginning of the mini jubilee for Christians. And this is when you receive the Holy Spirit. Romans 8:1, "Consequently, *there is* now no condemnation to those who are in Christ Jesus, who are not walking according to *the* flesh, but according to *the* Spirit; because the law of the Spirit of life in Christ Jesus has delivered me from the law of sin and death." Now that takes place when you receive the Holy Spirit, after you have repented and have been baptized. And that's where we started. Repent and be baptized and receive the Holy Spirit. You have a mini—beginning of a mini jubilee at that particular time—and then regardless of what it was during the year when you where baptized and receive the Holy Spirit, you come full circle around the Passover and then Unleavened Bread and Wave Sheaf Offering Day, and so forth. And all of that has to do with receiving the Spirit, it is the earnest of the inheritance. So you have been delivered from the law of sin and death. That's the beginning of the mini jubilee for all Christians, if we could put it that way, in their lives. Now let's continue on here in Romans 8 because this is important. "For what *was* impossible for the law to do" (Rom. 8:1-3). The law could not overcome the law of sin and death that is within us, you see. And the only way we can be delivered by it is with God's Spirit. So when you receive God's Spirit that's when you're able to overcome.

Now, let's come to I John the 3rd chapter, and let's see that the beginning of the mini jubilee for every Christian is when they receive the Holy Spirit. Now the mini jubilee, just the rest of your life from the time that you're baptized until the time of your resurrection, that is the jubilee. So you begin the jubilee by receiving the Holy Spirit. That's why Christ came; that why He preached that message in Luke the 4th chapter. Now, here in I John the 3rd chapter let's see what it talks about with receiving God's Spirit which it the begettal, the seed of the Holy Spirit. Now let's pick it up here in verse 9. I John 3:9, "Everyone who has been begotten by God does not practice sin..." You don't live your life in sin because you have been delivered from the law of sin and death inasmuch as that with the Holy Spirit and growing and overcoming, and yielding to God, you're then able to be delivered in a progressive way from the law of sin and death. Now the full deliverance from death does not come until later at the resurrection. But let's finish this here. So you don't practice sin, "... Because His seed *of begettal* is dwelling within him..." That's the beginning; the earnest; the down payment as we saw in the beginning of the Holy Spirit. "...And he is not able to practice sin because he has been begotten by God" (I John 3:9). Now let's see the end of the jubilee, or the symbolism for Christians concerning the fiftieth day, because the fiftieth day—just like the fiftieth year in the jubilee year—is a complete deliverance from everything. So if you grow, change, and overcome, and die in the faith; then the final jubilee is going to be for everyone who dies in the faith; for everyone who is still alive when the resurrection occurs is going to be that day of the resurrection which is pictured by Pentecost; the full deliverance; the full jubilee for Christians.

Now what we need to do is come back to Ephesians the 1st chapter. And let's read verse 13 and 14 again though we've already covered it as we need to remember that number fifty is a complete jubilee. And Pentecost is the fiftieth day; a mini jubilee as I have said for all Christians. So it's fitting that this mini jubilee which will be the great first resurrection is going to be the total redemption that we have so that we are no longer flesh but spirit. Totally redeemed of Christ, and now ready as spirit being in the kingdom of God to do the work of God. So let's go back to Ephesians 1:13. Speaking of Christ, "In Whom you also trusted after hearing the Word of the truth, the gospel of your salvation; in Whom also, after believing, you were sealed with the Holy Spirit of promise." Which is the beginning as he says here, "Which is *the* earnest of our inheritance..." This is the guarantee, the down payment, and we're trusting in God because God cannot lie, will not lie, His Word is truth, the resurrection is going to occur. Now notice the rest of this, "...Until *the* redemption of the purchased, possession..." and that redemption comes for all Christians at the same time on the fiftieth day being the day of Pentecost. "...To the praise of His glory" (I John 3:13-14).

Now let's come to II Timothy the 4th chapter. And we will see what Paul said. Come to II Timothy the 4th chapter and let's see how Paul kind of gives us a little summary of this. Now he's says here, verse 6 of II Timothy the 4th chapter. "For I am now ready to be offered..." He knew that he was going to be martyred. "...And the time of my departure is at hand." So you can say well this is day forty-nine for Paul. For whatever [day] it is for when we die that's day forty-nine for us. "I fought a good fight, I have finished the course; I have kept the faith. From this time forward..." That is when he's dead and in the grave, "...A crown of righteousness is laid up for me, which the Lord, the righteous Judge, shall give me in that day..." The jubilee day for all Christians. "...And not to me only, but also to all who love His appearing" (II Tim. 4:6-8). Now this is why when we come to the book of Hebrews that it shows the jubilee day.

Now let's come here to Hebrews the 12th chapter. Now we've covered this in other sermons that we have in the transcripts in the book concerning the day of Pentecost but let's just input it right here. Hebrews 12 and let's pick it up here in verse 22. This ends the mini jubilee for all Christians and it all occurs at the same time on the fiftieth day, which then is the day of the resurrection. So you can take all of the other things that we have studied leading up to Pentecost, the meaning of Pentecost, you put it all together and it shows the great meaning of the day of Pentecost and the resurrection. Verse 22, Hebrews 12, "But you have come to Mount Sion, and to *the* city of *the* living God, heavenly Jerusalem; and to an innumerable company of angels." And that's what it's going to be, and as we have seen when the saints are resurrected they're brought to the sea of glass, as we find, you can study that in the other transcripts that we have in the book; and everyone is on the sea of glass and it's going to be called, as he says here in Hebrews 12:23, "*To the* joyous festival gathering." Because it is the total deliverance from the flesh; it is the total deliverance from death; it is the total deliverance from sin; because as resurrected human beings, now spirit beings, you no longer have the ability to sin. So it is the complete jubilee that happens for all of those in the first resurrection on the day of Pentecost, which then brings the final jubilee for every one of us. "*To the* joyous festival gathering; and to *the* church of *the* firstborn, registered *in the book of life* in heaven; and to God, *the* Judge of all; and to *the* spirits of the just who have been perfected" (Heb. 12:22-23). And so that's really quite a thing, isn't it? The harvest of the firstfruits; and that's why it is counted. And that's why it must be on the fiftieth day, and the fiftieth day then is the first day of the eighth week.

Now let's understand something else. There is also symbolic significance for us in the fiftieth day, which then is the beginning of the eighth week. Eight is the number of a new beginning. And the resurrection day of Pentecost, being the fiftieth day, and the first day of the eighth week is a new beginning for all eternity; for all the resurrected saints, is it not? Yes. So that's important to understand the mini jubilee as it applies to Christians. And why it has to be fifty days; and why it has to be seven complete weeks unto the day after the seventh Sabbath. So that's why Pentecost is fifty days, and that's the meaning of the counting of fifty days; so all Christians at the resurrection on Pentecost are going to share in eternal life; the fiftieth day beginning the first day of eternity, of a new beginning.

(End of Sermon)

Transcriber: Sasha Vogele

How to Count Pentecost and Count 50
October 2006
Scriptural References

1) Acts 2:1, 36:39

2) Romans 5:6-10

3) Romans 4:23-25

4) Hebrews 10:12-14

5) Hebrews 9:11-14

6) 1 John 1:7

7) Acts 20:28-30

8) Ephesians 1:7-14

9) Luke 4:14-19

10) Leviticus 25:8-15

11) Leviticus 23:9-11, 14-16

12) Romans 8:1-3

13) 1 John 3:9, 13-14

14) II Timothy 4:6-8

15) Hebrews 12:22-23

Count to Pentecost—Monday Passover

NISAN

Sunday	Monday	Tuesday	Wednesday	Thursday	Friday	Sabbath
		1	2	3	4	5
6	7	8	9	10	11	12
13	14 **Passover** Observed Sunday Night	15 **Holy Day**	16	17	18	19
20 **Wave Sheaf Offering Day** ①	21 **Holy Day** ②	22 ③	23 ④	24 ⑤	25 ⑥	26 ⑦ Week 1
27 ⑧	28 ⑨	29 ⑩	30 ⑪			

281

Count to Pentecost—Monday Passover

IYAR

Sunday	Monday	Tuesday	Wednesday	Thursday	Friday	Sabbath
				1 ⑫	2 ⑬	3 ⑭ **Week 2**
4 ⑮	5 ⑯	6 ⑰	7 ⑱	8 ⑲	9 ⑳	10 ㉑ **Week 3**
11 ㉒	12 ㉓	13 ㉔	14 ㉕	15 ㉖	16 ㉗	17 ㉘ **Week 4**
18 ㉙	19 ㉚	20 ㉛	21 ㉜	22 ㉝	23 ㉞	24 ㉟ **Week 5**
25 ㊱	26 ㊲	27 ㊳	28 ㊴	29 ㊵		

SIVAN

Sunday	Monday	Tuesday	Wednesday	Thursday	Friday	Sabbath
					1 ㊶	2 ㊷ **Week 6**
3 ㊸	4 ㊹	5 ㊺	6 ㊻	7 ㊼	8 ㊽	9 ㊾ **Week 7**
10 **Pentecost** ㊿	11	12	13	14	15	16
17	18	19	20	21	22	23
24	25	26	27	28	29	30

Count to Pentecost—Wednesday Passover

NISAN

Sunday	Monday	Tuesday	Wednesday	Thursday	Friday	Sabbath
				1	2	3
4	5	6	7	8	9	10
11	12	13	14 **Passover** *Observed Tuesday night*	15 **Holy Day**	16	17
18 **Wave Sheaf Offering Day** ①	19 ②	20 ③	21 **Holy Day** ④	22 ⑤	23 ⑥	24 ⑦ **Week 1**
25 ⑧	26 ⑨	27 ⑩	28 ⑪	29 ⑫	30 ⑬	

IYAR

Sunday	Monday	Tuesday	Wednesday	Thursday	Friday	Sabbath
					1 ⑭	**Week 2**
2 ⑮	3 ⑯	4 ⑰	5 ⑱	6 ⑲	7 ⑳	8 ㉑ **Week 3**
9 ㉒	10 ㉓	11 ㉔	12 ㉕	13 ㉖	14 ㉗	15 ㉘ **Week 4**
16 ㉙	17 ㉚	18 ㉛	19 ㉜	20 ㉝	21 ㉞	22 ㉟ **Week 5**
23 ㊱	24 ㊲	25 ㊳	26 ㊴	27 ㊵	28 ㊶	29 ㊷ **Week 6**

Count to Pentecost—Wednesday Passover

SIVAN

Sunday	Monday	Tuesday	Wednesday	Thursday	Friday	Sabbath
1 ㊸	2 ㊹	3 ㊺	4 ㊻	5 ㊼	6 ㊽	7 ㊾ **Week 7**
8 **Pentecost** ㊿	9	10	11	12	13	14
15	16	17	18	19	20	21
18	19	20	25	26	27	28
29	30					

Count to Pentecost—Friday Passover

NISAN

Sunday	Monday	Tuesday	Wednesday	Thursday	Friday	Sabbath
						1
2	3	4	5	6	7	8
9	10	11	12 **Passover** *Observed Tuesday night*	13	14 **Passover** *Observed Thursday night*	15 **Holy Day**
16 **Wave Sheaf Offering Day** ①	17 ②	18 ③	19 ④	20 ⑤	21 **Holy Day** ⑥	22 ⑦ Week 1
23 ⑧	24 ⑨	25 ⑩	26 ⑪	27 ⑫	28 ⑬	29 ⑭ Week 2

IYAR

Sunday	Monday	Tuesday	Wednesday	Thursday	Friday	Sabbath
30 ⑮	1 ⑯	2 ⑰	3 ⑱	4 ⑲	5 ⑳	6 ㉑ Week 3
7 ㉒	8 ㉓	9 ㉔	10 ㉕	11 ㉖	12 ㉗	13 ㉘ Week 4
14 ㉙	15 ㉚	16 ㉛	17 ㉜	18 ㉝	19 ㉞	20 ㉟ Week 5
21 ㊱	22 ㊲	23 ㊳	24 ㊴	25 ㊵	26 ㊶	27 ㊷ Week 6
28 ㊸	29 ㊹					

Count to Pentecost—Friday Passover
SIVAN

Sunday	Monday	Tuesday	Wednesday	Thursday	Friday	Sabbath
		1 ㊺	2 ㊻	3 ㊼	4 ㊽	5 ㊾ Week 7
6 **Pentecost** ㊿	7	8	9	10	11	12
13	14	15	16	17	18	19
20	21	22	23	24	25	26
27	28	29	30			

How to Count Pentecost and Count 50

Count to Pentecost—Sabbath Passover

NISAN

Sunday	Monday	Tuesday	Wednesday	Thursday	Friday	Sabbath
1	2	3	4	5	6	7
8	9	10	11	12	13	14 **Passover** Observed Friday night
15 **Holy Day Wave Sheaf Offering Day** ①	16 ②	17 ③	18 ④	19 ⑤	20 ⑥	21 **Holy Day** ⑦ **Week 1**
22 ⑧	23 ⑨	24 ⑩	25 ⑪	26 ⑫	27 ⑬	28 ⑭ **Week 2**
29 ⑮	30 ⑯					

IYAR

Sunday	Monday	Tuesday	Wednesday	Thursday	Friday	Sabbath
		1 ⑰	2 ⑱	3 ⑲	4 ⑳	5 ㉑ **Week 3**
6 ㉒	7 ㉓	8 ㉔	9 ㉕	10 ㉖	11 ㉗	12 ㉘ **Week 4**
13 ㉙	14 ㉚	15 ㉛	16 ㉜	17 ㉝	18 ㉞	19 ㉟ **Week 5**
20 ㊱	21 ㊲	22 ㊳	23 ㊴	24 ㊵	25 ㊶	26 ㊷ **Week 6**
27 ㊸	28 ㊹	29 ㊺				

Count to Pentecost—Sabbath Passover

SIVAN

Sunday	Monday	Tuesday	Wednesday	Thursday	Friday	Sabbath
			1	2	3	4
			㊻	㊼	㊽	㊾ **Week 7**
5 **Pentecost** ㊿	6	7	8	9	10	11
12	13	14	15	16	17	18
19	20	21	22	23	24	25
26	27	28	29	30		

CHAPTER NINETEEN

The Feast of Unleavened Bread

Day 7—Holy Day

April 12, 2004

And greetings brethren. This is the last day of the Feast of Unleavened Bread – 2004. And we look back at all the feasts that we've kept down through the years. And we've never realized that the time would go this long. But it's going this long and the days around us are more evil than we have ever expected. And so we just need to, through this Feast of Unleavened Bread, as we have been doing, draw close to God. Now with the last day of the Feast of Unleavened Bread we're going to go ahead and take up an offering as we've already seen on the first day of Unleavened Bread that there is an offering on the last day. We're going to go ahead and take up that offering with the same understanding that we've had before. Remember the blessings of God, remember how God has promised to give you all sufficiency in all things. And giving the offerings and tithes are all a part of living by every Word of God. And so I hope that you really appreciate the things that we've been able to do, and I hope that you're enjoying the New Testament. So we'll just go ahead and take a break, and we will pick up after the offering is taken up.

And on this last day of the Feast of Unleavened Bread, the very theme of this feast is—The Lord Shall Fight For You. And God is the one Who is going to give salvation. So we are to see the salvation of the Lord. Now let's understand what happened with the children of Israel before they were released on the first day of the Feast of Unleavened Bread. Let's start back and look at everything that took place just in a summary—what God did to save the children of Israel, or rescue them from Egypt. And also let's understand something very important concerning this, is that God raised up Pharaoh and all of the evil apparatus with it to show His power, to declare His salvation, to rescue Israel, and so that His name would be glorified in all the earth. And it certainly has because we have it recorded for us, and we preach it every year.

Now remember the thing that was important. Let's come back here to Exodus 6 and let's see something that is very important so we understand… Actually it's Exodus 7, so that we understand the office of Moses, and how God was using Moses and Aaron to defeat all the God's of Egypt. And as we have seen on the Passover night when God struck all the firstborn of the Egyptians, all their animals and all the firstborn of men and beasts, that He judged all the god's of Israel. And of course the children of Israel didn't understand that the judgment against all those gods meant that why should they be so foolish as to go to these other gods who were not gods.

Now here, Exodus 7:1, "And the LORD said unto Moses, See, I have made thee a god to Pharaoh…" Now that's how Pharaoh would look upon him because Pharaoh could not see the true God. That was reserved for Moses. So since Pharaoh was called a god, since Pharaoh was worshipped as god, since they worshipped all the animals and things that they did in Egypt, and worshipped the river Nile all of these plagues came upon them because of that. So there are six signs and there are four plagues that took place. So let's look at the six signs.

First of all was the rod of Aaron that turned into a serpent. Well, the magicians were able to go ahead and counterfeit that, but the rod of Aaron was able, as a serpent, to eat up the serpents of the magicians.

The second sign was, which was pretty powerful. Now remember the Nile was considered the river of the gods, or a god, and they worshipped the water and they worshipped the river. It gave life and all of this sort of thing. So the first thing God did was cause, in the next sign, because Pharaoh hardened his heart, and it was a joint venture. Pharaoh hardened his heart, and God hardened his heart. And God was raising him up for the purpose of the destruction of Egypt. Now God is the one Who can do that because He's God. So what did He do? For seven days He turned the river into blood.

Then the third sign was frogs. Now these were the gigantic frogs that come out of the Nile river, and they just filled the whole land. And when that sign was over they just put them in heaps and it stank.

Fourth sign—dust turns into fleas and lice and just covered all the animals, covered all the human beings, you see. And the whole lesson in all of this is: no one has the power to fight against God. And if God be for us, as we're going to see, who can be against us? Now let's think on that as we're going through this.

So after that, still Pharaoh hardened his heart so then we have the swarms of flies. Nice big flies going everywhere. However, number five is the sign of grace, and in the land of Goshen where the children of Israel were there were no swarms of flies. So God separated it.

The sixth sign was murrain caused by the ash. Moses took some ash and threw it in the air. God caused it to go everywhere throughout all the land of Egypt and they had boils from the top of their head to the foot of their soul. All the animals, all the horses, camels, oxen, all human beings. Well, Pharaoh called "uncle" on this and so he recanted a little bit. And so he asked Moses if he would cause it to go away. So he said, ok, he would. And then Pharaoh hardened his heart again all the way through. Now here come the four plagues.

The first plague was hail. Now for it to hail in Egypt is an unreal thing because that's right in the desert. And it had never done this from the creation of the world, or since Egypt was a nation. And there was thunder and lightening and all of this going on at the same time they had the plague of hail.

Well then after that came the plague of locusts. Locusts everywhere and ate everything that was not in a container. And that wasn't good enough, they still didn't repent, so there was the plague of darkness. Darkness so thick that they could feel it. And it was so oppressive that the only thing that they could do was stay in bed. Now all the Israelites had light but the darkness covered Egypt.

Now the fourth one, as we have seen, is the important one. This is where then God passed over the houses of the children of Israel and spared their firstborn, executed judgment against all the gods of Egypt, and killed all the firstborn of the Egyptian children. After that they let them go. So the children of Israel went out with a high hand. And of course, God did not take them the easy way. And here's a lesson that's important for us: God doesn't take us the easy way. There are some hard things for us to do. And so if you are a good-time Christian and you're just a glad-hander, and you are a social creature, and you attend church because it's just nice and wonderful and comfy and all your friends are there, know for sure you're going to have a trial that's going to come to test you, to see whether you love

God with all your heart, and mind, and soul, and being, and whether you really trust Him. That's the whole lesson of the last day of the Feast of Unleavened Bread.

Now let's come to Exodus 14 because we see the whole lesson here. And this is the way God led them, instead of by the way of the Philistines going on over to the holy land, which would have been easy because that just follows right along the coast of the Mediterranean Sea and they would be there in a few days. Well God had other plans in mind. So He took them down by the way of the Red Sea and they were encamped along the Red Sea—big long line of the children of Israel. And the Egyptians then had second thoughts about letting them go. So they said, "Well, look we don't have any slaves. We can't do these things." So Pharaoh said, "I know what I'll do. I'll get all my armies, I'll get all my chariots and we'll go get them and we'll bring them back. And so when the children of Israel saw that they became afraid. Well God intervened and He put a cloud wall between the Egyptians and the children of Israel. To the Egyptians it was dark, to the children of Israel it was light. And so let's pick it up here in Exodus 14. Let's see the reaction of the children of Israel, because herein is a great lesson for us, see. You have to trust God in the tough times as well as the good times.

Verse 10, "And when Pharaoh drew nigh…." Now we can also draw the analogy of Pharaoh and his armies as Satan and the demons. That's true. We can also look at it as the world coming after us. That is true. But what we're interested in is the reaction of the children of Israel. "And when Pharaoh drew nigh, the children of Israel lifted up their eyes, and, behold, the Egyptians marched after them; and they were sore afraid: and the children of Israel cried out unto the LORD. And they said unto Moses…" (Ex. 14:10-11). Immediately begin complaining. Immediately begin accusing. Immediately displaying absolutely no faith. Now the reason I went over the six signs and the four plagues was to show what God had done and the power that God had used to cause the children of Israel to be extracted from the land of Egypt. Now you would think that they would have said, "Oh look at all that God has done for us. Now these Egyptians, God took care of them in Egypt so let's just trust Him to do it now." That's not what they did. Let's notice it.

"And they said unto Moses, Because *there were* no graves in Egypt [in other words there was plenty of room for graves there], hast thou taken us away to die in the wilderness? Wherefore hast thou dealt thus with us, to carry us forth out of Egypt? *Is* not this the word that we did tell thee in Egypt, saying, Let us alone, that we may serve the Egyptians? For *it had been* better for us to serve the Egyptians, than that we should die in the wilderness" (vs. 11-12). Well that's not what they said. They cried to God and said, "Oh God, get us out of this slavery." Now what were they doing? They were looking back and comparing what they thought was how good they had—everything in Egypt. It's just like people when they first come into the church and the first trial comes along, they say they've never experienced anything like this before they were converted. There must be something wrong. No, there is nothing wrong. That's the way it is. And here's the reason for it, and here's why we go through these things.

Now verse 13, "And Moses said unto the people, Fear ye not, stand still, and see the salvation of the LORD…" And that's what we need to do. We need to stand. Stand for the Word of God, stand for God, stand against evil, stand against human nature, stand against all the forces that are against us and to realize that with the power of the Holy Spirit we can do it, with the conviction of God, God will fight for us. Now then he says, "…see the salvation of the LORD, which He will shew to you to day: for the Egyptians whom ye have seen to day, ye shall see them again no more for ever. The LORD shall fight for you…" (vs. 13-14). Now I want you to mark that. I want you to understand this: the Lord shall fight for you and you shall hold your peace. In other words don't complain to God. Ask God to intervene and help you. Ask God to intervene and change the circumstances. Ask God to intervene and fight your battles for you because He has more power than you do. So you've got to trust God. Now God will do many great and fantastic things to fight your battles for you, but you have to place it all in God's hands, just like it is here: stand still and see the salvation of the Lord, and don't complain, and don't gripe, and don't whine. Let the peace of God rule in your heart, as we covered on the first day of the Feast of Unleavened Bread, you see.

So the Lord said, "...Wherefore criest thou unto me? speak unto the children of Israel, that they go forward..." (vs. 15). And that's the whole key for the Feast of Unleavened Bread—that we go forward in spite of everything and anything that comes along. That we know God, we love God, we understand His Word, we live by it and we go forward. So you know the rest of the story of what happened there. God told Moses, "Take your rod, hold it over the sea. And that night He caused a tremendous east wind to blow, and He also parted the waters a great distance, probably a place as much as ten miles wide, and then all of the children of Israel, in the morning watch just before the sun came up, they all crossed the Red Sea at the same time. A divine miracle. God intervening and showing them His power. And of course you know what happened to the Egyptians. They came up there and they looked to the right, and they looked to the left, and they said, "Go." And right when he got in the middle of where the sea was going to be God had the angels start taking the wheels off their chariots and they drug heavy, the ground then became mud, and then all of a sudden the waters came crashing back, and that was the end of the Egyptians. Just like God had said. Well now the children of Israel were very happy, but you see, let's look at what they said. This is really a tremendous lesson for us.

So here's what they did, Exodus 15:1. "Then sang Moses and the children of Israel this song unto the LORD, and spake, saying, I will sing unto the LORD, for He hath triumphed gloriously: the horse and his rider hath He thrown into the sea." Now notice verse 2, "The LORD *is* my strength and song, and He is become my salvation: He *is* my God, and I will prepare Him an habitation; my father's God, and I will exalt Him. The LORD *is* a man of war: the LORD *is* His name" (Ex. 15:1-3). So you see, that's what we need to look at. If you have a problem that needs to be overcome, take it to God. If you have a complaint against God, go repent and ask Him to intervene and help you. If you have a situation that is greater than you can handle, ask God to handle it for you. Let Him fight your battles, but you put it all in His hands and realize that that's the way that it has to be.

Now all the way down through history, as we find in the Bible, we see the salvation of God, the power of God, the intervention of God. Some in great and fantastic things. Some in small and little things. Now the first great thing that happened was the flood, and God saved all mankind through Noah because Noah walked with God and kept His commandments and he found grace. So God had to destroy the whole world—everything there.

Now then after that, during the days of Abraham we have the story of Lot. Now Lot was actually what you would call, though he was righteous, he was weak in the faith. And he was confronted with many situations that we are being confronted with now, the onslaught of the homosexuals. Who knows, they probably had homosexual marriages in Sodom and Gomorrah, and all the people thought that that was a great thing. But if it weren't for Abraham, Lot would not have survived. But Abraham intervened and Lot survived. And you know what happened to Sodom and Gomorrah. And of course then, the one who had the lack of faith and didn't follow was his wife. And the angel said, "Don't look back." That's an important lesson because Jesus said later, "Remember Lot's wife." So we're not to look back. But nevertheless Lot was saved.

Then we have with the children of Israel all the miracles that took place while they were going through the wilderness, and everything that God did. The miracle of the manna every morning. God took care of them, blessed them, watched over them. The water out of the rock. Oh but they didn't want to follow God so they rebelled. They didn't believe God after all that so then God had to punish them for their rebellion and it took another 38 ½ years of wandering in the wilderness, so everyone over 20 died, except for Caleb and Joshua. Then they went into the Promised Land and God fought their battles for them when they did what God said. When they didn't do what God said, He didn't fight for them. They moaned and groaned and complained to God. "Oh why can't we overcome our enemies?" Well, it was because some were stealing the gold which belonged to God. So the whole history of going through the Bible shows how God will fight for you if you believe Him. God will fight for you if you trust in Him.

Now let's come to Psalm 18 and let's see a Psalm dedicated to that. David's Psalm. Quite a Psalm. We're going to look at several Psalms in here because this shows how God intervenes to help, to fight, to save on behalf of those that He loves. Here let's notice, Psalm 18. Now this was after one of the great deliverances of God. Psalm 18:1, "I will love Thee, O LORD, my strength." See, our whole relationship with God is based on the love of God, as we saw on the Sabbath during this feast. So he says, "I will love Thee, O LORD, my strength." Are you weak? That's where you get strength from. "The LORD *is* my rock, and my fortress…" Now we can think what Jesus said there in Matthew 7. We are to build our house upon a Rock (Matt. 7:24), aren't we? And 1 Corinthians 10 says that Rock is Christ (1 Cor. 10:4). He's our Rock. "…My fortress, and my deliverer; my God, my strength, in whom I will trust; my buckler, and the horn of my salvation, *and* my high tower" (Psalm 18:1-2). And if you're in a high tower no one can get at you, can they? No. So that's why he said that.

Now notice verse 3, "I will call upon the LORD…" That's how God will intervene for you. You have to love Him, praise Him, worship Him, call upon Him, you have to trust in Him, you have to look to Him to be your salvation, your savior, the warrior, the fighter. He's going to fight your battles for you. Now we're going to see some more of these things as we go along.

Verse 3, "I will call upon the LORD, *Who is worthy* to be praised: so shall I be saved from mine enemies. The sorrows of death compassed me…" Now how close was he to tragedy in the end? Right at the brink. "…And the floods of ungodly men made me afraid. The sorrows of hell compassed me about: the snares of death prevented me. In my distress I called upon the LORD…" So we're going to have times when we have distress. Now remember, David was a man after God's heart. "In my distress I called upon the LORD, and cried unto my God: He heard my voice out of His temple, and my cry came before Him, *even* into His ears" (vs. 3-6).

Now let's go back and let's see another Psalm here. Let's come to Psalm 12:1. This is pretty much the situation that we find ourselves in, in the world today. Verse 1, "**Help**…" That's how this one starts out. You know—"Help, LORD; for the godly man ceaseth…" Where's someone who's godly? There aren't any. "…For the faithful fail from among the children of men. They speak vanity every one with his neighbour: *with* flattering lips *and* with a double heart do they speak." And that's just the way this world is. It's just nothing but lies and double-speak. "The LORD shall cut off all flattering lips, *and* the tongue that speaketh proud things: who have said, With our tongue will we prevail; our lips *are* our own: who *is* lord over us?" (Psa. 12:1-4). Perfect description of this society, isn't it? Anything goes. If we don't like a law, we'll change it. Just like up in San Francisco, they've been marrying thousands of same sex, so called couples, in defiance against the law. But they don't think they are breaking the law. But when Judge Roy Moore defied a federal judge and his ungodly illegal order to get rid of the Ten Commandments monument, they said he ought to obey the law of the land. See, and that's just the way that it is in the world.

Verse 5, "For the oppression of the poor, for the sighing of the needy, now will I arise, saith the LORD [God is going to take action sooner or later]; I will set *him* in safety *from him that* puffeth at him." Let's come down here to verse 8, "The wicked walk on every side, when the vilest men are exalted" (vs. 5, 8). And that is a perfect description of our political system.

Now, let's again see how we are to pray when we are in trouble. See, instead of complaining to other people, accusing the ministers, accusing other brethren—go repent. Ask God to help you, ask God to fight your battles. Psalm 4:1, "Hear me when I call [He will], O God of my righteousness: Thou hast enlarged me *when I was* in distress; have mercy upon me, and hear my prayer. O ye sons of men, how long *will ye turn* My glory into shame? *how long* will ye love vanity…" That's just the way it is in the world. Love the vanity, love the lies. Verse 3, "But know that the LORD hath set apart him that is godly for Himself: the LORD will hear when I call unto Him." God will hear. We can be guaranteed of that. Now verse 4, Now you see, when people get discouraged and get distressed and get down and begin to give up, they give in to their weaknesses and sin. That's why it says, "Stand in awe, and sin not…" (Psa. 4:1-4). So God will hear our prayers.

Let's come to Psalm 37. This is one to keep in mind. This is really a good Psalm. Ok now here, Psalm 37. This is good counsel and advice for us, that's why it's here. You look out and you see the world and all the things that are wrong, all the sin that is going wrong, and somehow they seem to be getting along better—but they're really not.

Now then, Psalm 37:1, good advice. "Fret not thyself [in other words don't be frustrated] because of evildoers, neither be thou envious against the workers of iniquity. For they shall soon be cut down like the grass, and wither as the green herb. Trust in the LORD…" Now that's where we need to put our trust. Not in other human beings, not in circumstances, not in physical things, but trust in the Lord. "…And do good; *so* shalt thou dwell in the land, and verily thou shalt be fed. Delight thyself also in the LORD…" So this shows that you're happy, that you're joyful, that you understand that Christ has saved you, that you understand that you have the Holy Spirit of God in you, you understand that God the Father has begotten you so that you, at the resurrection, can become a son or daughter of God. Look, you have eternal life ahead of you. That's what's important, you see. So, "Delight thyself also in the LORD…" Now notice, "…and He shall give thee the desires of thine heart" (Psa. 37:1-4). Of course according to His will. And the greatest desire of our heart needs to be that we are going to be in the kingdom of God. The greatest desire that we ought to have is to, as the Psalm said, to see God; and as Revelation says, face to face, and to be there in that resurrection.

Now here's how you do it, verse 5. Of course you do this through prayer, you do this through study, you do this through everything that you do. Everything that you do, see. Not just when, as some people would look at it, not just when you get religious and pray—but your whole life and everything you do. See verse 5 says, "Commit thy way unto the LORD [everything you do]; trust also in Him; and He shall bring *it* to pass." Now this means concerning health, concerning healing. Of course we have our parts to do. Concerning employment, concerning marriage, concerning whatever your life is involved in. Commit yourself unto the Lord, trust in Him, and He shall give you the desires of your heart. He shall bring it to pass.

Verse 6, "And He shall bring forth thy righteousness as the light, and thy judgment as the noonday. Rest in the LORD, and wait patiently for Him…" See, because God's timetable is always different than our timetable, so we have to wait patiently for Him. "…Fret not thyself [that is, don't become frustrated, worried, or concerned] because of him who prospereth in his way, because of the man who bringeth wicked devices to pass. Cease from anger, and forsake wrath: fret not thyself in any wise to do evil" (vs. 6-8). Because you see, that's what people do. They're not trusting in God in the way they ought to be. They're not patient waiting for the Lord, so something happens and they get all angry. Well you see, that's why you had the trial, so that you can get rid of your anger and see and know and understand that you have it.

Verse 27, "Depart from evil, and do good; and dwell for evermore." And that's what the whole Feast of Unleavened Bread is all about, isn't it? Put out the leaven, which is sin. Put in the unleaven, which is righteousness. Put out the way of man and put in the way of Christ. That's why Christ said, "You have to eat My flesh and drink My blood" showing that you will live by Him, which means by every Word of God. So, "Depart from evil, and do good; and dwell for evermore. For the LORD loveth judgment, and forsaketh not His saints…" So if you ever think you've been forsaken—you haven't, and you need to go repent of that and ask God to help you to trust in Him. "…They are preserved for ever: but the seed of the wicked shall be cut off. The righteous shall inherit the land, and dwell therein for ever" (vs. 27-29). That means the kingdom of God and all the earth and everything that is there.

Verse 34, "Wait on the LORD, and keep His way…" Now isn't that the message of the last day of the Feast of Unleavened Bread, that we first went through in Exodus 14? Stand still and see the salvation of the Lord. "Wait on the LORD, and keep His way [never give up on doing it], and He shall exalt thee to inherit the land: when…" So there is a timing in all of this. There is a time. Now the kingdom of God is not here, therefore we don't fight. But when we come back with Christ we are going to fight, and we are going to be in charge of putting away all evil. Now they will either repent or they will be "*histoi.*" "…When the wicked are cut off, thou shalt see *it.* I have seen the wicked in great power, and spreading himself like a green bay tree. Yet he passed away, and, lo, he *was* not: yea, I sought him, but he could not be found." Very important—verse 37, "Mark the perfect *man…*" Now as we have seen, if you are in Christ, which you are, and God has imputed the righteousness of Christ to you and you stand before Him holy and blameless, before God you are perfect. Now you have to then be perfected in attitude, be perfected in character, and it's an ongoing project as we have seen. "…And behold the upright: for the end of *that* man *is* peace. But the transgressors shall be destroyed together: the end of the wicked shall be cut off" (vs. 34-38). And the finality of that is going to be with the last part of the Last Great Day when all the wicked are cast into the lake of fire and there are no more wicked around.

Verse 39, "But the salvation of the righteous *is* of the LORD: *He is* their strength in the time of trouble." That's why we need to trust God. Now we're going to see some other things how God intervenes, because He's really performed some great and tremendous things. "And the LORD shall help them and deliver them: he shall deliver them from the wicked, and save them, because they trust in him" (vs. 39-40). Do you trust in God? That's all a part of the Feast of Unleavened Bread—that you get rid of the sin of doubt, you get rid of the sin of lack of trust. But you trust God, you believe God, you walk in His way in everything that you do.

Now let's come to 2 Chronicles 20 and let's see how God intervened in great and fantastic ways to save those who feared God and trusted Him, and looked to Him to fight their battles. Now this is the case of King Jehoshaphat. He had a great army. The children of Moab and Ammon, and the Assyrians were all coming against him to destroy him, and destroy Judah. Now notice what he did. 2 Chronicles 20:3, "And Jehoshaphat feared, and set himself to seek the LORD, and proclaimed a fast throughout all Judah." So you see, when you have trouble and difficulty you need to fast and draw close to God, ask for His help, ask for His intervention. So he called them all together for a prayer. And then he got the answer from one of the prophets of God. A Levite came who was one of the sons of Asaph.

Now verse 15, and here's the message, "And he said, Hearken ye, all Judah, and ye inhabitants of Jerusalem, and thou king Jehoshaphat, Thus saith the LORD unto you, Be not afraid nor dismayed by reason of this great multitude; for the battle *is* not yours, but God's." Now that's what we need to understand—the battle is not ours but it is God's, so we trust in Him in faith.

So verse 17, "Ye shall not *need* to fight in this *battle:* set yourselves, stand ye *still,* and see the salvation of the LORD…" Now that sounds just like Exodus 14, doesn't it? Yes. "…O Judah and Jerusalem: fear not, nor be dismayed; to morrow go out against them: for the LORD *will be* with you."

Now verse 20, so here's what they did on the morrow. "And they rose early in the morning, and went forth into the wilderness of Tekoa: and as they went forth, Jehoshaphat stood and said, Hear me, O Judah, and ye inhabitants of Jerusalem; Believe in the LORD your God, so shall ye be established; believe His prophets, so shall ye prosper." Profound and important message. We are to believe and trust, and have faith and confidence, and lay it all before God just like Jehoshaphat did here. "And when he had consulted with the people, he appointed singers unto the LORD, and that should praise the beauty of holiness, as they went out before the army, and to say, Praise the LORD; for his mercy *endureth* for ever." So here the priests went out first before the army, and that's the way God said they should fight their battles—and God was with them.

"And when they began to sing and to praise, the LORD set ambushments against the children of Ammon, Moab, and mount Seir, which were come against Judah; and they were smitten" (vs. 22). So what God did, He just turned them all against each other and they killed each other, and what did they do? They went out there and they found that they were all dead. So what did they do? Verse 25, "And when Jehoshaphat and his people came to take away the spoil of them, they found among them in abundance both riches with the dead bodies, and precious jewels, which they stripped off for themselves, more than they could carry away: and they were three days in gathering of the spoil, it was so much." Now that was a tremendous battle, wasn't it? God intervened, gave them the blessing. God fought for them. Now if God could do it for them we know God can do it for us. So regardless of what the situation is, regardless of what the trouble may be, God is there, He will help just like this. Now we're going to look at another example here in a minute and see how God intervened to fight and to save His people.

Now let's see another example of how God intervened for king Hezekiah. And what he did when he got the notice from the Assyrians that they were coming and conquering, and that they had destroyed all the nations coming right on down the line. And they sent a letter to Hezekiah, "Now you surrender or we're going to do to you like we did to all these other nations and their gods." So here, 2 Kings 19:1, "And it came to pass, when king Hezekiah heard *it* [that is, heard the letter read], that he rent his clothes [that means he ripped his clothes], and covered himself with sackcloth, and went into the house of the LORD." And he said in verse 3, "And they said unto him, Thus saith Hezekiah, This day *is* a day of trouble, and of rebuke, and blasphemy: for the children are come to the birth, and *there is* not strength to bring forth." Now sometimes you feel like that. So that's what Hezekiah did. He took it before God.

Let's come over here to verse 14. "And Hezekiah received the letter of the hand of the messengers, and read it: and Hezekiah went up into the house of the LORD, and spread it before the LORD." Took his troubles right to God—very first thing. He didn't stop and ask anyone else's advice. He went right to the Lord. "And Hezekiah prayed before the LORD, and said, O LORD God of Israel, which dwellest *between* the cherubims, Thou art the God, *even* thou alone, of all the kingdoms of the earth: Thou hast made heaven and earth. LORD, bow down Thine ear, and hear: open, LORD, Thine eyes, and see: and hear the words of Sennacherib, which hath sent him to reproach the living God" (vs. 14-16). Then he said, "Of a truth, LORD, he did conquer all of them."

He says here, verse 19, "Now therefore, O LORD our God, I beseech Thee, save Thou us out of his hand, that all the kingdoms of the earth may know that Thou *art* the LORD God, *even* Thou only." This is a perfect example of how we need to go to God with our problems. You go to God and you state the problems. You don't accuse Him, but you glorify Him. You don't complain to Him, but you show what the problem is, and you ask God to fight because you are His. You belong to Him. You are His property. He's promised to take care of you.

So that's exactly what happened. He got the message, "I will defend this city for David, My servants sake" (vs. 34, paraphrased). Now verse 35. Here's what God did. Even greater miracle than what happened there with Jehoshaphat. "And it came to pass that night, that the angel of the LORD went out, and smote in the camp of the Assyrians an hundred fourscore and five thousand [185,000 were slain by the angel]: and when they arose early in the morning, behold, they *were* all dead corpses." In other words He spared the king and probably a few of his advisors, but all of his army was dead. "So Sennacherib king of Assyria departed, and went and returned, and dwelt at Nineveh" (vs. 34-36). And of course as he was worshipping in the house of his god, someone came in and assassinated him. Well now, question: did this take care of the enemy? It sure did. Did they have to lift the sword to fight? No, they didn't, but they trusted in God. Perfect example of what we need to do.

Now let's come to the New Testament and let's see some things here that are important for us to understand so that we can realize how then we need to look to God. Now we have to overcome self, we have to overcome the sins in us. And let's understand what kind of determination that we need to have, and what kind of faith that we need to have. Now let's come to Hebrews 12 and let's see what the apostle Paul wrote to the Hebrews telling them what they need to do to overcome and change, and what kind of resolve that they need to have in serving God.

Now after the apostle Paul had listed out many of the things that where God fought for the children of Israel, coming on down through the faith chapter and Chapter 11, we come to Chapter 12 and Paul writes: "Therefore, *since* we are surrounded by such a great throng of witnesses…" That's what the Old Testament is there for. These are examples that we can look to, to see the examples of right and wrong, and good and evil. The examples of God intervening and fighting our battles for us. These are the examples that we need to look to. So here's what Paul writes, "…let us lay aside every weight…" Every problem, every difficulty—set it aside. You see, God does not want us to dwell on the problem. He wants us to dwell on Him and the solution. So you set it aside. "…And the sin that so easily entraps *us*…" You repent of that. We've already covered how you do that. Confess your sins to God. "…*And* let us run the race set before us with endurance…" (Heb. 12:1). That's what we need to do. We have got to finish the course.

Here's how to do it, verse 2, "Having *our minds* fixed on Jesus, the Beginner and Finisher of *our* faith; Who for the joy that lay ahead of Him endured *the* cross, *although* He despised *the* shame, and has sat down at *the* right hand of the throne of God." That's what we need to do. Always have our mind on Christ. Always have our minds on what He did, how He did it, why He did it. And He did it because He loved us. God the Father sent Jesus Christ because He loves the world and loves us, and we are part of the eternal plan of God. So Paul writes, "Now meditate deeply on Him Who endured such great hostility of sinners against Himself…" That's why we need to study the Gospels. That's why we need to understand what Jesus did and what He went through. Here's the reason, "…so that you do not become weary and faint in your minds" (vs. 2-3).

Chapter Nineteen

Now there is a proverb which says that if you faint in the day of your adversity, you have very little strength. See, so who is our strength? Christ. Who is our Savior? Christ. Who is our redeemer? Christ. Who is there to fight our battles for us? Christ is. And as we have seen He also has the angels to do His work for him too, doesn't He? Yes, indeed. See, now this is why.

Now verse 4 becomes very important. And in all the struggles and difficulties that we have gone through, verse 4 is very profound. "You have not yet resisted to the point of *losing* blood in your struggle against sin." I've never anointed anyone for bleeding because they've been fighting against sin. What does this show? This shows the effort and determination and steadfastness that we need to have in serving and loving God and in overcoming. And we do it by fixing our mind on Christ. And don't get discouraged and don't get down because God is doing this for a tremendous and wonderful purpose.

Verse 5, "And you have already forgotten the admonition that He addresses to you as to sons: "My son, do not despise *the* chastening of *the* Lord, nor grow weary of being reproved by Him; For whom *the* Lord loves He chastens, and He severely disciplines every son whom He receives" (vs. 5-6). That's why, see. God didn't call us to have good perfect lives in the flesh. If you want to join a social club, go to a social club. If you want to go to where everything is smooth and nice, I don't really think you can find any place on the face of the earth today that's like that, can you? No, and times are getting difficult and harder, and harder to come by aren't they? So we need to realize that. And God is helping us to develop the character, as we saw just last Sabbath, to have the faith and virtue and character, and eventually come to the point of having the very love of God perfected in us. That's what God is doing. So yes, there is going to be some correction. Yes, there are going to be some things that change and come along here. Yes indeed, because that's just the way it's going to be.

Now let's look at some other things here—the reason for all the trials. Let's come here to 1 Peter 5 and let's see what Peter says about this, and why we go through these things. And he also shows that a great deal of it, yes a great deal of what we go through is because we're fighting Satan the devil, as well as self, as well as sin, as well as the world. So we've got a big battle out there and the way we do it is keep our minds fixed and focused on Jesus Christ, that we know what's in the Gospels, we know what's in the Epistles of Paul, we know what's in the General Epistles, that we live by every Word of God—that's what's the important thing for us to realize and understand.

Now let's come here to 1 Peter 5. Now let's pick it up here in verse 5. "In the same manner, *you* younger men be subject to *the* older men; and all *of you* be subject to one another, being clothed with humility…" That's the whole purpose of it. "…Because God sets Himself against *the* proud, but He gives grace to *the* humble. Be humbled therefore under the mighty hand of God so that He may exalt you in *due* time; casting all your cares upon Him, because He cares for you" (1 Peter 5:5-7). Now here's a great mistake a lot of people do. They get worried, they get frustrated, they get upset, and they pace back and forth and they wonder what they're going to do. But they haven't cast all their cares upon God, see. So rather than worry and fret and stew and wonder—go pray. Lay it all before God. Cast all your cares upon Him because He cares for you. He has called you. He loves you. He wants you in His kingdom. He wants you to succeed and grow and overcome, and He will give you the strength and the power and perform the work for you if you trust in Him and rely upon Him. It's like it said where we started, "Stand still and see the salvation of the Lord, and go forward." Don't be discouraged, don't be down, don't let anything, anything take you away from Christ.

Now here's the reason for it. Verse 8, "Be sober!" Now that means don't get involved with the spiritual drunkenness of this world. "Be vigilant!" That's why we have the

Feast of Unleavened Bread come along so that it reminds us every year we need to be vigilant. That means on watch, on guard. "For your adversary *the* devil is prowling about as a roaring lion, seeking anyone he may devour." Yes, we're going to have battles against Satan, and he's going to come after the people of God. That's just all part of the situation the way that the reality of it truly is. Now here's how we fight him, verse 9, "Whom resist, steadfast in the faith…" Not wavering back and forth, as James said, and be double-minded man and unstable as water. Steadfast in the faith. "…Knowing *that* the same afflictions are being fulfilled among your brethren who *are* in *the* world" (vs. 8-9). And don't think that any trial you're going through is some sort of strange thing that has come upon you. Everyone has them. And you have them, so you take them to God.

Now here's a promise. And you claim this promise. When you're going through a trial, ask God to help you understand it, ask God to help you learn the lesson, ask God to help you fully comprehend what is going on so that you can take that and make it part of your life and character of the very lesson that you're going to learn. And then claim this promise, verse 10, "Now may the God of all grace, Who has called us unto His eternal glory in Christ Jesus, after *you* have suffered a little while, Himself perfect you [so God is perfecting you —individually], establish, strengthen, *and* settle *you*." That's the purpose of the trials and the difficulties that we go through, so that we can let God fight our battles for us. Then he says, "To Him *be* the glory and the power into the ages of eternity. Amen" (vs. 10-11). So that's the way we unleaven our lives in Christ, by Christ in us, by growing, by overcoming, by looking to God to fight our battles for us so that we can realize that we are called unto eternal glory. And keeping our minds fixed and focused on Jesus Christ.

Now let's look at some other things here which are important for us to realize. Let's come here to Ephesians 6. Since this talks about fighting against Satan the devil let's come to Ephesians 6 and let's see what we need to do—the very spiritual preparation. Let me tell you this. If you're not praying, if you're not studying, if you're not living by every Word of God when a trial comes upon you it's going to hit you like a blockbuster. And you are not going to know what to do because you're weak spiritually, you're weak mentally, you're weak physically. All of those things go hand in hand. And so when they come, you're overwhelmed and you get discouraged. Now here's what we need to do. We need to be strong in the power God.

Ephesians 6:10. Satan is out there after us like a roaring lion, as we saw. And he is clever and slick and has all kinds of devices to try and entrap and even deceive the very elect. So when we have problems and difficulties to come by, do exactly like Moses told the children of Israel—"Hold your peace, stand still, see the salvation of the LORD and go forward." And the obvious implication is: not backward into Egypt.

Now Ephesians 6:10, "Finally, my brethren, be strong in *the* Lord…" And that comes with patient study, prayer, walking in every way of God, living your life the way that God wants you to do it. That's how you're strong in the Lord "…and in the might of His strength" because He is going to fight for us. "Put on the whole armor of God…" So not only is God going to fight for us but we have our part. "Put on the whole armor of God so that you may be able to stand against the wiles of the devil because we are not wrestling against flesh and blood, but against principalities *and* against powers, against the world rulers of the darkness of this age, against the spiritual *power* of wickedness in high *places*" (Eph. 6:10-12). And we see that more so in this age now. There's just an acceleration of evil everywhere. And that is deliberate, and let's understand something. Let's just be frank—we ain't seen nothing yet because Satan and his forces and troops are out there to destroy every vestige of Christianity that they can through any means that they can. And those are all part of the wiles of the devil, and we're fighting against those wicked spirits in high places.

Chapter Nineteen

Verse 13, "Therefore, take up the whole armor of God so that you may be able to resist in the evil day, and having worked out all things, to stand." Just like Moses said, "Stand still and see the salvation of God." Verse 14, "Stand therefore, having your loins girded about with truth…" And that is the Word of God, which is true. "…And wearing the breastplate of righteousness, and having your feet shod with *the* preparation of the gospel of peace. Besides all *these*, take up the shield of the faith, with which you will have the power to quench all the fiery darts of the wicked one…" (vs. 13-16). Because he's there just trying to lob them in. Missiles of lust, if we could put it that way. Because, as it says there in Chapter 2, he is the prince of the power of the air, he is the one who comes along to tempt and to induce into sin. He is there. If there's any one thing Satan would like you to do is get discouraged and down and come to the point that you're going to give up on God because you have a trial that you're going through. Well now, you can't let that happen.

Verse 17, "And put on the helmet of salvation, and the sword of the Spirit, which is the Word of God…" See, so it shows an active, growing, overcoming, praying, trusting in God, focusing on Christ. Verse 18, "…Praying at all times…" That you pray every day, that you pray many times during the day, just like Paul wrote in 1 Thessalonians 5:17, cease not praying. Not only do you pray and put your life in God's hands every day when the day begins, but during the day you pray and ask God for help, for wisdom, for truth, for understanding, for bringing into captivity every thought unto Christ and casting down vain imaginations that rise up in your mind against God. And that's how sin so easily besets us. So it is a continuous daily thing that we do—praying at all times. "…With all prayer and supplication in *the* Spirit, and in this very thing being watchful with all perseverance and supplication for all the saints…" (vs. 17-18). Because brethren, we all need the prayers of everyone. And I know my prayer every day is for all the brethren. For those that need to be healed, those that need to fight their battles, those that need to be raised up, those who are distressed and brokenhearted. Christ came to heal the brokenhearted. Christ came to relieve the distressed. So you turn all of that to Him, you see. He is there. He will help. He will fight. He has promised. It doesn't depend on your goodness, it doesn't depend on your righteousness. Oh, you have your part to do, but it depends on Christ because He has promised. And those promises are sure, and those promises are true and good like we've already seen and Jesus Christ has promised that He will not <u>ever</u>, <u>never</u> leave us and forsake us. Now that's something. So we can have the total faith and confidence in what God wants us to do in trusting Him to fight our battles.

Now let's come over here to Ephesians 2 again and let's see this. Let's again see what we are operating against. Christ has saved us, reached down and saved us, saved us from our sins in this world. Now Ephesians 2:1, "Now you were dead in trespasses and sins…" That's how we were before God. And God reached down and had mercy on every one of us individually. "…In which you walked in times past according to the course of this world, according to the prince of the power of the air, the spirit that is now working within the children of disobedience…" This is what God has saved us from, that's why we are not to go back into it. "…Among whom also we all once had our conduct in the lusts of our flesh, doing the things willed by the flesh and by the mind, and were by nature *the* children of wrath, even as the rest *of the world*. But God, Who is rich in mercy, because of His great love with which He loved us, even when we were dead in *our* trespasses, has made *us* alive together with Christ (*For* you have been saved by grace.)" (Eph. 2:1-5). And that's through the sacrifice of Jesus Christ, through the power of the Holy Spirit, through the Word of God.

Now notice what we are to do here. Verse 8, "For by grace you have been saved through faith, and this *especially* is not of your own selves; *it is* the gift of God…" And always remember this: you have nothing you didn't receive. Everything we have is of God. "Not of works, so that no one may boast. For we are His workmanship…" God is creating Himself in you. We are His workmanship, "…created in Christ Jesus…" Because you see, salvation is creation—creating in us the mind of Christ, the love of God, the character of God, all the fruits of the Holy Spirit of love, and joy, and peace, and longsuffering, and faith, and gentleness, and kindness, and goodness, and meekness, and temperance, against such there is no law. That's what He is creating in us. And we are "...created in Christ Jesus unto *the* good works that God ordained beforehand in order that we might walk in them" (vs. 8-10). That is the way of the Lord. That is what He has done for us.

Now let's come to Romans 8 and let's understand how we are to look at these things, how we are to look at the world, how we are to look at ourselves, how we are to view the circumstances in which we find ourselves and what God is going to do for us. Now let's pick it up here in verse 9. We'll cover a good deal of Romans 8 because this is a profound chapter. Romans 8:9, "However, you are not in *the* flesh, but in *the* Spirit, if *the* Spirit of God is indeed dwelling within you. But if anyone does not have *the* Spirit of Christ, he does not belong to Him." And that's the important thing. The Spirit of God. Now as we have seen, if you let that lax and you're not exercising, then you have to do as Paul said—stir up the Spirit of God that is in you. And that's what the Feast of Unleavened Bread is all about, as we have seen, to stir up the Spirit of God which is in us, you see.

Now verse 10, "But if Christ *be* within you, the body *is* indeed dead because of sin..." Because you are baptized. All your sins died with Christ and He died for you. And whenever you confess your sins, you put them in the hands of God. They are covered with the blood of Jesus Christ and His sacrifice, you see. So you're not living in sin. "... However, the Spirit *is* life because of righteousness." Now here is a great and tremendous promise. "Now if the Spirit of Him Who raised Jesus from *the* dead is dwelling within you, He Who raised Christ from *the* dead will also quicken your mortal bodies because of His Spirit that dwells within you. So then, brethren, we are not debtors to the flesh, to live according to the flesh..." We're not to live in the carnal way of this world, "...because if you're living according to the flesh, you shall die; but if by *the* Spirit you are putting to death the deeds of the body, you shall live" (vs. 10-13). Just like we saw on the first holy day. We are to put to death the deeds of the flesh. We are to put all of that out, and we are to put in Christ. That's what he's talking about here. Now if you do that you shall live, and that means to eternal life.

Here's the key, verse 14. Never forget this, "For as many as are led by *the* Spirit of God, these are *the* sons of God." Now let's understand something very important here. The Spirit of God is not going to force you. The Spirit of God will lead you, but you have to choose to yield to God, and you have to choose to ask God to help you be led of the Spirit of God. "As many as are led of the Spirit of God, they are the sons of God." Now this is also important for us to understand because Satan, as we have seen, wants to come in and give us a spirit of fear, give us a spirit of doubt, give us a spirit of contention, give us a spirit of argument with God. "Now you have not received a spirit of bondage again unto fear, but you have received *the* Spirit of sonship, whereby we call out, 'Abba, Father.' The Spirit itself bears witness conjointly with our own spirit, *testifying* that we are *the* children of God" (vs. 14-16). That's what it is brethren, see.

Now notice, these next few verses are profound. "Now if *we are* children, *we are* also heirs—truly, heirs of God and joint heirs with Christ..." Now stop and think for a minute. What did Christ inherit? All things. That means the universe. We are joint heirs with Christ. That means we will own part of whatever God gives us of the universe, and He says, "Here, this is yours, but with Christ." That is a fantastic and tremendous thing that God has called us to. And I think that we can understand more, and more, and more about God; and more, and more about how we need to grow and change and overcome, if we keep that right in the forefront of our minds and be led of the Holy Spirit of God.

Chapter Nineteen

Now notice, here's a promise—a promise of suffering. "...If indeed we suffer together with Him, so that we may also be glorified together <u>with</u> Him." Now the apostle Paul was called to suffer more than any other man except Jesus Christ. And he did suffer. And how did he look upon those sufferings? Well, he came to rejoice in them because he understood the end result. And so likewise with us, you see, we need to rejoice in them because we understand the end result. Not be like the children of Israel at the Red Sea who complained against God and the circumstances they were in because they couldn't see the outcome. They didn't have faith in God, though He did a miraculous intervention to extract them from the land of Egypt. No, see, we're going to be glorified together but we have to suffer, see. "For I reckon that the sufferings of the present time *are* not worthy *to be compared* with the glory that shall be revealed in us." Now I want you to understand these next verses here to give us some perspective. "For the earnest expectation of the creation itself is awaiting the manifestation of the sons of God..." How important are the sons of God? How important is God to you? So important that Jesus Christ gave His life for you and for everyone individually because you see the sacrifice of Christ is applied to each of us individually, continually, standing in the grace of God. And the whole creation is waiting. The world is waiting. Have you ever thought of it this way: the world is waiting for you, and you, and you, and me, and all the sons of God down through history. It's waiting. It's needing us because we are the solution in God's set time, of course. "...Because the creation was subjected to vanity, not willingly, but by reason of Him who subjected *it* in hope..." And we are part of that hope through Jesus Christ. "...In order that the creation itself might be delivered from the bondage of corruption into the freedom of the glory of the children of God. For we know that all the creation is groaning together and travailing together until now" (vs. 17-22). You see, waiting for us.

Now let's come down here to verse 28. Let's understand something that's important. Let's realize this, regardless of your circumstances, regardless of the difficulties, regardless of your physical condition, regardless of whether you are young or whether you are old, whether you are rich or whether you are poor, God loves you and has a purpose for you. And everything in your life is going to work out for good. Now let's read it, verse 28, "And we know that all things work together for good to those who love God..." That's why we've covered how important the love of God is. "...To those who are called according to *His* purpose [and you have been] because those whom He did foreknow [and if you have God's Spirit in you He has foreknown you], He also predestinated *to be* conformed to the image of His own Son, that He might be *the* firstborn among many brethren." So that's what our destination is, our predestination. "Now whom He predestinated, these He also called; and whom He called, these He also justified; and whom He justified, these He also glorified" (vs. 28-30). Because you see, God is looking at the finished product in you. He's not looking at you the way that you are. He's imputed the righteousness of Christ to you so that you stand before Him blameless and holy, in love. He is looking to you as if you are now glorified. In other words He sees and knows what you will be at the resurrection. Now we've received a bit of the glory of God by receiving the Holy Spirit of God. We've received a bit of the glory of God by having His Word, which we can know and understand and live by. Absolutely true.

Now verse 31, "What then shall we say to these things? If God *is* for us, who *can be* against us?" There is no trouble, there's no difficulty, there is no battle, there is nothing that can be against us. Now claim that promise through the blood and sacrifice of Jesus Christ. "He Who did not spare even His own Son, but gave Him up for us all, how shall He not also grant us all things together with Him?" Say, "Come, inherit the kingdom prepared for you by My Father." "Who shall bring an accusation against *the* elect of God?" Well, people can. But that has no standing before God. "God *is the one* Who justifies. Who *is* the one that condemns?" See, Satan comes and accuses us day and night before God, but we overcome Him with the blood of Christ, right? Yes, indeed. "*It is* Christ Who died, but rather, Who is raised again, Who is even *now* at *the* right hand of God…" to fight our battles for us, to give us of His Spirit, to strengthen us, to help us overcome. "…*And* Who is also making intercession for us. What shall separate us from the love of Christ?" Now think on this. Is there anything that's going to separate you from the love of God, the love of Christ? See, the reason that we keep the commandments of God and the holy days of God, and the feasts of God is so that we understand this: nothing can separate us from God. "*Shall* tribulation, or distress, or persecution, or famine, or nakedness, or danger, or sword?" (vs. 31-35). None of those things and we're probably going to face every one of these things in the coming years.

"Accordingly, it is written, "For Your sake we are killed all the day long; we are reckoned as sheep for *the* slaughter. But in all these things [even if that happens] we are more than conquerors through Him Who loved us." And this is the persuasion we need to come to. This is the attitude that we need. And this is the whole finality of the Feast of Unleavened Bread. "For I am persuaded…" Are you? Are you fully persuaded "…that neither death, nor life, nor angels, nor principalities, nor powers, nor things present, nor things to come, nor height, nor depth, nor any other created thing, shall be able to separate us from the love of God, which *is* in Christ Jesus our Lord" (vs. 36-39). That's the meaning of today. Stand still and see the salvation of the Lord, and go forward with the power and the might and strength of God.

End of Sermon

Transcriber: Carolyn Singer

Unleavened Bread—Day 7
April 12, 2004
Scriptural References

1) Exodus 7:1

2) Exodus 14:10-15

3) Exodus 15:1-3

4) Psalm 18:1-6

5) Matthew 7:24

6) I Corinthians 10:4

7) Psalm 12:1-5, 8

8) Psalm 4:1-4

9) Psalm 37:1-8, 27-29, 34-40

10) II Chronicles 20:3, 15, 17, 20-22, 25

11) II Kings 19:1,3, 14-16, 19, 34-36

12) Hebrews 12:1-6

13) I Peter 5:5-11

14) Ephesians 6:10-18

15) I Thessalonians 5:17

16) Ephesians 2:1-5, 8-10

17) Romans 8:9-22, 28-39

Section V

Events Leading up to Pentecost

CHAPTER TWENTY

Events Leading Up to Pentecost

May 14, 1994

In the past I have always run out of time preaching on Pentecost, and I have run right up to the end and the tape goes off and I have to put it on a C100 and squeeze it down. So what I have decided to do is what I have done with the Feast of Tabernacles which I started what, ten years ago? Remember there is so much to preach on the eighth day that what I did, I went ahead and said, OK, let's preach the things about the seventh day and the end of it on the last day of the Feast of Tabernacles and then the things for the eighth day we will preach on the eighth day. So I have decided that I am going to do the same thing with Pentecost, which is the events leading up <u>to</u> Pentecost, I will now do on the Sabbath <u>before</u> Pentecost, and then the events <u>of</u> Pentecost itself, I will do on Pentecost. So what we are going to do—you could also entitle this *When You Forget Pentecost*, because it could be exactly the same thing.

Let's begin in a rather unusual place because I will refer you to Exodus 19 and 20 which we will cover partly tomorrow concerning the first Pentecost and the giving of the Ten Commandments at Mount Sinai, and let's go all the way to Exodus 33, and let's begin there because this I think points out the situation—what happens when you forget Pentecost or you forget God.

Now I think God will tolerate some people being confused on how to count Pentecost—at least they are attempting to keep it. And I can understand the various reasons for people doing it the various ways they have done it, however, in each case in thoroughly examining it, I have found that they are missing vital elements of scriptural understanding to handle it in the proper way. So what we are going to do is concentrate on the events that happened after Moses went up on the mountain, and I think we are going to see some very important things. Let's pick it up here in Exodus 33:1: "And the LORD said unto Moses, Depart, get you down from here and unto the people which you have brought up out of the land of Egypt..." Now, here is where they start this exchange—your people, Moses, and Moses says to God, "Your people, God." So they are kind of pushing the people back and forth as to who is responsible. You know, it's just like when mother and father have a child that disobeys. The one who finds out that they've done wrong runs to the father and says, "Your son..." and then it's the other way around, "Your, son..." So here Moses is being told, "Now look, these are your people..." Continuing verse 1: "...unto the land which I swore unto Abraham, to Isaac, and to Jacob, saying, Unto your seed will I give it: And I will send an angel before you; and I will drive out the Canaanite, the Amorite, and the Hittite, and the Perizzite, the Hivite, and the Jebusite: Unto a land flowing with milk and honey: for I will not go up in the midst of you;" that's a very interesting statement. Hold your place right here and let's go back to Exodus 25 for just a minute. Exodus 25:8. The instructions that God was giving Moses says, "...let them build me a sanctuary; that I may dwell among them." Now He says, "I will not go up in the midst of you." Exodus 33:3. So what are we dealing with here? A lot of people are wondering: Where is God? Same experience, and when we go through this, I want us to relate it to the experience we are going through today, and later when we get into another section here in Jeremiah, I want you to relate it to the world and the parallel course within the Church. And I think we are going to see some astounding parallels. So He says, "...I will not go up in the midst of you; for you *are* a stiffnecked people: lest I consume you in the way. And when the people heard these evil tidings, they mourned: And no man did put on his ornaments." Now remember the ornaments they received—the ornaments of gold and silver. What do you suppose these ornaments really were? They were the idols of the gods of Egypt. That's what they were—or the crosses, or the crucifixes or, what is that cross they have—the Ankh cross that has the eggshape on top? So they took off their ornaments. What did they do with these ornaments in Chapter 32? They made a golden calf—right? Yes. Continuing in verse 4: "...no man did put on his ornaments. For the LORD had said unto Moses, 'say unto the children of Israel, You *are* a stiffnecked people: I will come up into the midst of you in a moment, and consume you: Therefore now put off your ornaments from you, that I may know what to do with you.' And the children of Israel stripped themselves of their ornaments by mount Horeb" (Exodus 33:1-6).

Now can we think of a New Testament lesson concerning idolatry? What did the apostle Paul say concerning an idol? To whom an idol is nothing, it is nothing. These people were going back to idolatry—so strip them away. "You can't be trusted. You see this thing and it becomes a god to you. I am God in your presence," God was virtually saying "in the pillar of cloud and fire, and yet you won't honor Me." I'm just sort of summarizing some of the things that we are going to come across here.

Now notice what Moses did. He "...took the tabernacle..." So they had a little tabernacle there, before they built the big one, which is called the Tent of the Meeting, where God would meet with Moses. "...And pitched it outside the camp"—that's what *without* means. "...Afar off from the camp, and called it the tabernacle of the congregation. And it came to pass, *that* every one which sought the LORD went out unto the tabernacle of the congregation, which *was* without the camp" (verse 7).

Now let's think about this: In a church and in our lives can we do actions which will cause God to exit? Yes. Maybe some people asking what's going on in church today ought to ask the question: Did God leave because they forced Him out because of believing things which were idolatrous against God? [It is] very possible—probably absolutely true. Verse 8: "And it came to pass, when Moses went out unto the tabernacle, *that* all the people rose up, and stood every man *at* the door of his tent..." Now we're getting a little bit of discipline here aren't we. Now when Moses went out the whole camp—this is on a formal occasion, obviously—the whole camp had to stand up and watch Moses walk out of the camp and go to the tabernacle of the congregation. Then when he got there, then it says, verse 9: "And it came to pass, as Moses entered into the tabernacle, the pillar of cloud descended and stood *at* the door of the tabernacle, and *the* LORD talked with Moses. And all the people saw the cloudy pillar stand at the tabernacle door: And all the people rose up and worshiped, every man *in* this tent." Put off on the side. Verse 11: "And the LORD spoke to Moses face to face, as a man speaks to his friend. And he turned again into the camp: But his servant Joshua, the son of Nun, a young man, departed not out of the tabernacle." So he had Joshua out there guarding it. Verse 12: "And Moses said to the LORD, See, you say unto me..." Now here is this argument going back and forth, "...Bring up this people: and you have not let me know whom you will send with me." So he said, "Now if you are going to leave us, now how are we going to do this?" Continuing verse 12: "...Yet you said, I know you by name and you have found grace in my sight. Now therefore, I pray you, if I have found grace in your sight, show me now your way that I may know you, that I may find grace in your sight: and consider that this nation *is* your people" (Exodus 33:7-13).

So you know, some church leaders may be right when they say that certain members in their congregation are their people, because they're taking a possession that belongs to God. Because no one having the Spirit of God belongs to a minister—just a little insight as we are going along here.

307

Verse 14: "And he said, 'My presence will go *with you*, and I will give you rest.' And he said unto him, 'If your presence go not *with me*, carry us not up from here. For wherein shall it be known here that I and your people have found grace in your sight? *Is it* not in that you go with us? So shall we be separated, I and your people, from all the people that *are* upon the face of the earth.' And the LORD said to Moses, 'I will do this thing that you have spoken for you have found grace in my sight, and I know you by name' " (Exodus 33:14-17). So God said, "All right, now I'm going to go ahead and go back there"

Let's continue on now in Exodus 33:18 "And he said, 'I beseech you, show me your glory.' And he said, 'I will make all my goodness pass before you, and I will proclaim the name of the LORD before you; and will be gracious to whom I will be gracious, and will show mercy to whom I will show mercy.' And he said, 'You cannot see my face: for there shall no man see me, and live.' And the LORD said, 'Behold *there is* a place by me…' " So forth, " …when I pass I will cover you and you will see my glory " (Exodus 33:18-22).

Chapter 34 and verse 1, "…The LORD said to Moses, 'Hew out two stones like the first and I will write on them ' " So he did that and so verse 4: "Moses took the stones like the first, rose up early in the morning, and he went up on Mount Sinai as the LORD commanded him, and he took in his hands the two tables of stone. The LORD descended and passed by proclaimed all of his glory saying, …'The LORD, The LORD God, merciful and gracious, longsuffering, and abundant in goodness and truth, Keeping mercy for thousands, forgiving iniquity and transgression and sin, and that will by no means clear *the guilty*; visiting the iniquity of the fathers upon the children, and upon the children's children, unto the third and to the fourth *generation*' " (verse 7). Verse 8: "And Moses made haste, and bowed his head toward the earth and worshiped. And he said, 'If now I have found grace in you sight, O Lord, let my Lord, I pray you, go among us; for it *is* a stiffnecked people; and pardon our iniquity and our sin, and take us for your inheritance.' And he said, 'Behold, I make a covenant:' " So He had to re-do the whole old covenant again because they broke it with their idolatry. Continuing, verse 10: " Behold I make a covenant: before all your people I will do marvels, such as have not been done in all the earth, nor in any nation: and all the people among which you *are*…" that is going to go, "…shall see the work of the LORD: for it *is* a terrible thing that I will do with you. Observe all that which I command you this day…" (Exodus 34:1, 4-11). Then He goes and He reiterates the things that He did with the first giving of the Ten Commandments.

Let's come all the way down here to verse 21. It says, "Six days shall you work, but the seventh day shall be rest: in earing time and in harvest shall you rest. And you shall observe the feast of weeks, of the firstfruits of your wheat harvest and the feast of ingathering at the year's end" (verse 22). And then He reiterates everything that He shows all the way down, let's come on down here to verse 28: "And he was there with the LORD forty days and forty nights; he did neither eat bread, nor drink water. And he wrote upon the tables the words of the covenant, the Ten Commandments." So He re-did the whole thing again.

Verse 29: "And it came to pass, when Moses came down from mount Sinai with the two tables of testimony in Moses' hand, when he came down from the mount, that Moses didn't know that the skin of his face shone while he talked with him. And when Aaron and all the children of Israel saw Moses, behold, the skin of his face shone; and they were afraid…" Verse 31: "And Moses called unto them; and Aaron and all the rulers of the congregation returned unto him: and Moses talked with them. And afterward all the children of Israel came near: and he gave them in commandment all that the LORD had spoken with him in mount Sinai. And *till* Moses had done speaking with them, he put a veil on his face" (Exodus 34:21-22, 28-33).

Now then we come down here to Exodus 35. The question was asked: He didn't eat or drink for forty days. Does that mean that when Christ was fasting that He didn't eat or drink for forty days? It is very possible. I've said before maybe Christ even drank water while He was fasting, but this may be a good indication that He didn't need to—absolutely, yes. Thank you for bringing that up.

I missed an important part back in Exodus 32, where that when Moses came down the first time and saw all the people were naked and verse 26 of Chapter 32, "Then Moses stood in the gate of the camp, and said, 'Who *is* on the LORD'S side? Let him come to me.' And all the sons of Levi gathered themselves together unto him. And he said unto them, 'Thus says the LORD God of Israel, Put every man his sword by his side, and go in and out from gate to gate throughout the camp, and slay every man his brother, and every man his companion, and every man his neighbor.' " That is all of those who were involved in the nakedness of the orgy that they were involved in and worshiping the golden calf. Verse 28: "And the children of Levi did according to the word of Moses: and there fell of the people that day about three thousand men" (Exodus 32:26-28). Then he went back up on the mountain. A very interesting parallel could also be happening with the Church too.

Now let's go to Jeremiah 5, and let's see something that is so very important for us to realize and that is: Very seldom have the people of God stayed really faithful and true to God—the Israelites didn't, the Judahites didn't, and look what happened to Solomon. I mean Solomon is really a great case to study of what happens when you have everything given to you and laid out on a platter for you. And even God spoke to Solomon twice, but what did he do? He made Jerusalem the center of Baal worship! That's what he did—built temples to every god under the sun. So here is where it degenerated to in Jeremiah 5, just before God was ready to destroy Jerusalem. And so let's draw the parallel in the nation with what's happening today. It's almost incredible. Hardly anybody in the government today can tell the truth. It is unreal. When you watch the news shows on Sunday morning, if you watch them—I've given up watching them because they just become nothing but political propaganda gristmill anymore—what they tell you, virtually take the opposite and know that that's the truth. So it is the same thing here. It's throughout the whole society, and I think we're also dealing with a situation that when the society, which applies to a church as well, comes to a certain point then God just gives it over to its own devices and He leaves. That doesn't mean that God has given up, it just means that He has excused Himself from their presence because their behavior and their attitude is so idolatrous that God will not stay there. So that's why Moses had to plead with God, "Please come back into the camp and take these, your people." And so God did.

Here He wants to give mercy so He says, Jeremiah 5:1: "Run you to and fro through the streets of Jerusalem, and see now, and know, and seek in the broad places thereof, if you can find a man…" A man, one single person, and that's almost the way it is in society to-day. Can you find one person who will do this: "…if there be *any* that seeks judgment, that seeks the truth…" That's the hardest thing in the world for people to really seek—the truth, "…and I will pardon it." God says He was willing if they found a man, to say: "OK, I'll pardon all the inequity of it, and I will spare the people for one man." Verse 3: "O LORD, *are* not your eyes upon the truth? Have you not stricken them, but they have not grieved; you have consumed them, *but* they have refused to receive correction: they have made their faces harder than a rock; they have refused to return. Now we can say that in relationship with the society. We can say that in relationship with the church. Verse 4: "Therefore I said, Surely these *are* poor; they are foolish: for they know not the way of the LORD, *nor* the judgment of their God. I will get me to the great men, and will speak unto them; for they have known the way of the LORD, and the judgment of their God…" But he says after going to them, "…but these have altogether broken the yoke, *and* burst the bonds" (Jeremiah 5:1, 3-5).

I have a chart showing that every one of the leading persons in the current United States Government to all of the appointee offices: Secretary of State, Secretary of Treasury, Secretary of Transportation, and so forth—every single one down through three layers all belong to the Council on Foreign Relations—every single one. And if you know anything about them and the world conspiracy, guess what? And so this is what Jeremiah experienced, he went to the wise men, he went to the leaders saying, "Boy, surely they ought to have God's judgment, surely they ought to know. " …But these have altogether broken the yoke, *and* burst the bonds." Verse 6: "Wherefore a lion shall come out of the forest and slay them, *and* a wolf of the evenings shall spoil them, a leopard shall watch over their cities: every one that goes out of there shall be torn in pieces…" Now again, let's apply this spiritually and physically. Didn't we just have a cougar attack on a woman out jogging? Ok, now I'm not saying that's a great fulfillment of this, but I'm saying: Are we entering times when those things are going to be that way—certainly.

Now let's apply this people-wise. Are there people who are called wolves? Yes, they are—false prophets, right? What do they come to do—seek to kill, and destroy, and take, right? Yes—the same thing. So we can have these parallels going all the way down. Here is the reason (continuing in verse 6): "…because their transgressions are many, *and* their backslidings are increased" (Jeremiah 5:6). This is so true.

When I go down to the area of Southern California and have a Bible study down there, believe me: They are all so backslidden that so many of them can hardly stand to take the truth. It is incredible, but that's what has happened.

Verse 7: "How long shall I pardon this? Your children have forsaken me and have sworn by *them that are* no gods" changing the truth of God into that which is a lie. And one of the leading evangelists in Worldwide just what, two months ago in Modesto, preached and said that the Worldwide Church of God never taught that there were two Elohims, never taught that Christ was the Logos, never taught any of these things. Continuing in verse 7: "…and have sworn by *them that are* no gods…" Is that in the society? Yes. Is it in the church? Yes. Continuing verse 7: "…and when I fed them to the full, they committed adultery, and assembled themselves by troops in the harlots' houses." And we have the leading trooper as President.

Verse 8: "They were *as* fed horses in the morning: every one neighed after his neighbor's wife. 'Shall I not visit for these *things*?' says the LORD: And shall not my soul be avenged on such a nation as this?", or church such as this? Verse 10: "Go you up on her walls, and destroy; but make not a full end: take away her battlements; for they *are* not the LORD'S. For the house of Israel and the house of Judah have dealt very treacherously against me, says the LORD. They have belied the LORD, and said, It is not he; neither shall evil come upon us; neither shall we see sword nor famine…" (Jeremiah 5:8-12). And that's exactly what people are saying in the world today, people are saying in the church today.

Verse 13: "And the prophets shall become wind, and the word *is* not in them: thus shall it be done unto them." That's why we have to check out every doctrine. What does it say? "Don't be carried about with every sleight of the wind of doctrine by cunning of men." "Their prophets shall become wind." There it is right there—a foretelling of it in the Old Testament which Paul said was fulfilled in the New Testament.

Verse 14: "Wherefore thus says the LORD God of hosts, Because you speak this word, behold, I will make my words in your mouth fire, and this people wood, and it shall devour them." And of course, they don't like it. You don't have to get all vain, and you don't have to get all uppity…, you just have to speak the truth.

Verse 15: "Lo I will bring a nation upon you from far, O house of Israel, says the LORD; It *is* a mighty nation, it *is* an ancient nation, a nation whose language you know not, neither understand what they say." And isn't it interesting what religious doctrines are being brought into the Church of God—the same religious doctrines that are coming from this nation, mainly Chaldeanism.

By the way, Carl Franklin's got a book where he finds the exact sayings of Stavrinides which come right out of ancient Chaldean philosophy—word for word quotes which are now becoming doctrines of the church. And God says He is going to visit for this. And He goes on and shows what He is going to do. Let's pick it up here in verse 17. After He says He is going to cause all these things to take place, that "...they are going to eat up your harvest, and your bread *which* your sons and daughters should eat: take your flocks and your herds, eat up your vines... they shall impoverish your fenced cities, wherein you trusted with the sword" (Jeremiah 5:3-17). All of the defenses that are put up are not going to work. And it is the same way in the church. What was the defense of the church? Don't read anybody else's literature—that defense is gone. Don't talk to anyone who is not in this church—that defense is gone. I know in talking to a man who called me the other day, I said, "Well, we take the opposite philosophy. We figure that you can read anything and if you can't understand the truth, then you better get grounded in it because denying people to read something is not going to keep them from the difficulty." Now it is don't study the Bible unless a minister is there.

Now verse 19: "And it shall come to pass when you say..." so they come back and they talk back to God. " ...Wherefore does the LORD our God do all these *things* unto us?" Now we will see when we get to Revelation here, because I am tying this into the events that lead up to the things happening in the church in the Book of Revelation: Do we have a church that talks back to God? Yes. Same thing here, right? Yes. Continuing in verse 19: "...then you shall answer them, Like as you have forsaken me and served strange gods in your land, so shall you serve strangers in a land *that* is not yours." But today we are seeing strangers are coming in. And you go to your local supermarket, and it's like going to a different nation.

Verse 20: "Declare this in the house of Jacob, and publish it in Judah, saying, Hear now this, O foolish people, and without understanding; which have eyes, and see not; which have ears, and hear not:" (Jeremiah 5:20-21). Is that not also in the church as well as in the world? Yes. You tell people the real old plain truths—"Well, we never said that."

Verse 22: "Won't you fear me?" says the LORD: will you not tremble at my presence, which have placed the sand *for* the bound of the sea by a perpetual decree, that it cannot pass it: and though the waves thereof toss themselves, yet can they not prevail; though they roar, yet they cannot pass over it? But this people has a revolting and a rebellious heart; they have revolted and are gone. Neither say they in their heart, Let us now fear the LORD our God, that gives rain, both the former and the latter, in his season: he reserves unto us the appointed weeks of the harvest" (Jeremiah 5:22-24). So that's why the second title I had was, *When You Forget the Feast of Pentecost.*

So He says, verse 25: "Your iniquities have turned away these *things*, and your sins have withholden good *things* from you. For among my people are found wicked *men*: they lay wait, as he that sets a snare; they set a trap, they catch men. As a cage is full of birds, so are their houses full of deceit:" so true.

When I was reading and preparing for this sermon, I just could not get over the parallels that are in the society and in the church. It is unreal. Continuing now in verse 27: "... Therefore they are become great and waxed rich." They have grown rich and yet there are people today who say that the gauge of a church's spirituality is how much money they have. Be careful. "They are waxen fat, they shine; yea, they overpass the deeds of the wicked: they judge not the cause, the cause of the fatherless, yet they prosper; and the right of the needy they judge not. Shall I not visit for these *things*? says the LORD: shall not my soul be avenged on such a nation as this? An awesome…" that's what it means, "…wonderful and horrible thing is committed in the land; The prophets prophesy falsely, and the priests bear rule by their means; and my people love *to have it* so: and what will you do in the end thereof?" (Jeremiah 5:19-31). When God calls it to account. I was just stunned when I read that with just all the things that have been happening.

Now let's go back to Daniel 9, and let's see what Daniel did. Daniel was one of the ones who really repented. Daniel was one of the ones who really turned back to God. Daniel 9:1 "In the first year of Darius the son of Ahasuerus, of the seed of the Medes, which was made king over the realm of the Chaldeans; In the first year of his reign I Daniel understood by books the number of the years, whereof the word of the LORD came to Jeremiah the prophet, that he would accomplish seventy years in the desolations of Jerusalem." So he didn't understand what Jeremiah wrote until way toward the end of the seventy years. So then he repented. He said, verse 3: "I set my face unto the Lord God, to seek by prayer and supplications, with fasting, and sackcloth, and ashes:" and frankly brethren, that's what the Church of God needs to do. Verse 4: "And I prayed unto the LORD my God, and made my confession, and said, O LORD, the great and dreadful God, keeping the covenant and mercy to them that love him, and to them that keep his commandments; We have sinned, and have committed iniquity, and have done wickedly, and have rebelled even by departing from your precepts and your judgments: Neither have we listened to your servants the prophets, which spoke in your name to our kings, our princes, and our fathers, and to all the people of the land. O LORD, righteousness *belongs* to you, but unto us confusion of faces…" and doesn't that tell you what's going on in the country and in the church—confusion, everybody is confused. Why, because they have left God. "…As it is this day; to the men of Judah, and to the inhabitants of Jerusalem, and to all Israel, *that are* near, and *that are* far off, through all the countries whither you have driven them…" and isn't the church being scattered today? Yes it is—it parallels, it's amazing, stunning. "…Because of their trespass that they have trespassed against you. O LORD, to us *belongs* confusion of face, to our kings, to our princes, and to our fathers, because we have sinned against you." And I tell what, there isn't going to be any straightening out of doctrine or knowledge of truth and doctrine until this kind of repentance and admission is made before God. It won't happen. Verse 10: "Neither have we obeyed the voice of the LORD our God, to walk in his laws, which he set before us by his servants the prophets." And then he goes through and says, "Oh God, all these things have happened" (Daniel 9:1-8, 10).

Now let's come down here to verse 18: "O my God, incline your ear, and hear…" and that's what we need to do for this Pentecost, brethren—have an ear to hear. Isn't that something when you run the parallel there? God will hear us when? When we hear Him. So he says, "…incline your ear and hear; open your eyes, and behold our desolations, and the city which is called by your name: for we do not present our supplications before you for our righteousnesses, but for your great mercies." And that's what needs to happen with the whole church—all the brethren everywhere.

Daniel 9:19 "O LORD, hear; O LORD, forgive; O LORD, listen and do; defer not, for your own sake, O my God: for your city, for your people which are called by your name." And then he was given what? He was given the prophecy of the seventy weeks of the coming of the Messiah. (Daniel 9:18-19).

Now let's go back to Revelation 2 and 3, and we are going to see some tremendous parallels, because part of the thing we are dealing with, with the events leading up to Pentecost, are the things that are happening within the Churches of God. Let's pick it up here in Chapter 1 and verse 18. After seeing the vision of Christ, He says to John, "Even the one Who is living; for I was dead, and behold, I am alive into the ages of eternity. Amen. And I have the keys of *the* grave and of death." In other words: God is going to judge whom He is going to resurrect, when He is going to resurrect, and what resurrection it will be. "…And of death." He is the only one Who can give us life. Verse 19: "Write the things that you saw, …" Up to this point, "…and the things that are, and the things that shall take place. The mystery of the seven stars that you saw in My right hand, and the seven golden lampstands, *is this*: the seven stars are *the* angels of the seven churches: and the seven lampstands that you saw are *the* seven churches" (Revelation 1:18-20). And Christ said He would walk in the midst of them.

Now let's go to Revelation 5, and let's understand something as we put this together, because Revelation 2 and 3 is everything that we have pretty well understood that it is. Yes, it is the seven churches which were literally then. Yes, it is a prophecy of God's church down through time. We have defined it in the past as eras. That's not necessarily wrong, but it was not as clear-cut as people like to make it be understood that they thought it was—because we see that these are also the seven attitudes that you find at any one time within the church. These are all the major problems that will confront the church, etc. Now Chapter 5 and verse 5: "Then one of the elders said to me, "Do not weep. Behold, the Lion Who is of the tribe of Judah, the Root of David, has overcome to open the book, and to loose its seven seals." Then I saw, and behold, before the throne and the four living creatures, and before the elders, *was* standing a Lamb as having been slain,…" that is Christ alone "…having seven horns and seven eyes, which are the seven Spirits of God that are sent into all the earth" (Revelation 5:5-6).

Now let's back up and we want to focus in on the seven horns. Why would the symbol of Christ, being a lamb, have seven horns? Well, we can answer the question this way. What do horns in the Book of Daniel represent? Each horn we know, we won't go back there and turn there, each horn represents a king or a kingdom, correct? Yes. So if you have a horn in the head of Christ—seven of them—let's ask some other questions. Who is the head of the Church? Christ. Can we conclude properly then that these seven horns represent the Churches of God through history that Christ is the head of? Yes, I think that would be a fair statement. We can also conclude that it refers to the seven churches as we found in Revelation 2 and 3. That would also be another conclusion we can come to without stretching the Scriptures at all—because we know Christ is the Head of the Church. He dwells in the midst of the Church, He is the Lamb which takes away the sins of the world, He was the Lamb Who was slain, and now He is the Lamb with the seven horns. (Answer to comment from congregation): I am sure the seven Spirits of God also apply to the seven churches, I am sure that applies to the seven angels of the seven churches, because it is both. Yes, good comment.

Now let's just review parts on Revelation 2 and 3, I am not going to concentrate on it. So we have we know definitely—not definitely, but we can conclude from the things we have seen that there is every reason to believe that this has to do with the history of the churches. It has to do with the seven churches, has to do with the attitudes of the churches, has to do with the practices of the churches, and it has to do with the major confrontation of the churches and Satan the Devil. All of those you can put all together.

Now the first church—it is interesting as you look back in your Christian life, I think you are going to see that many of these things you have gone through and you have experienced. Now the first church: **Ephesus**. He said, "I know your works, and your labor, and your endurance, and that you cannot bear those who are evil; and *that* you did test those who proclaim *themselves* to be apostles, but are not, and did find them liars;" (Revelation 2:2).

313

What is one of the biggest problems we have to do today? Is that not it? Have we not found, now I'm not talking about in someone's personal life that they may tell a lie because they are weak, or they feel as though the truth would be too damaging in some little low-level thing here. That could be repented of, and Christians tell lies, they shouldn't, but Paul said, "Lie not one to another" didn't he? Yes, he did. But what have we found? When you really get to the truth of examining the doctrines which we have learned, and some of the doctrines, which were mistakes—some of them which were not true; what have we found? Everyone we held in high esteem, we found to be a liar—right? Now I could name names, but no use naming names. Any name you can think of would be it. Are we to find them liars? Yes we are, especially concerning doctrine. So we have to do that.

Now then, they had their problem—they did a lot of work, they had a lot of patience, but they lost the first love, verse 4. So they had to repent. And then He says in Revelation 2, verse 7: "The one who has an ear, let him hear what the Spirit says to the churches. To the one who overcomes I will give *the right* to eat of the tree of life that is in *the* midst of the paradise of God" (Revelation 2:4,7).

Then He says unto the angel of **Smyrna**. Now here is the one you wouldn't think would be a Church of God because they are thrown in jail, they are ridiculed, they are put down, they are killed, they are slaughtered, they are poor—despised by everyone. And I tell you what: The world loves a winner.

Here in this area we have a sports phenomena—it is the San Jose Sharks. And everyone will know what I mean. No one was interested in hockey. No one could care about hockey, and the first two years, they were the dregs and the pits of the National Hockey League. All of a sudden, they made it to the play-offs, and then they beat the number one team, and everyone now is jumping on the bandwagon, right? Yes, because people love a winner. Remember when the Oakland Athletics were doing great and winning pennants? Everyone loves a winner, but when you are down and out, no one wants you. Now it was the same with Christ. Remember when He fed the five thousand? Boy, we got a winner! We're going to make Him king, John the sixth chapter. They were going to come by force and make Him king, because we love a winner. So He escaped. When He was on the cross, they said, "We'll give you one last chance to be a winner." I am sort of paraphrasing here. "You come down off that cross and we will believe that you're the Son of God." So when everything is going good, every one wants to jump on the bandwagon, but what does God have to do when you've got a bandwagon full of bandwagoners, and not the "real McCoy"? He's got to shake the bandwagon, right? Because the ones who jump on the bandwagon because they love a winner, are not really "true blue". That's why the church at Smyrna is such a powerful church. That's why Christ said, "You are rich, even though you are poor." He said, "Don't fear death. I have died." And He says, verse 11: "The one who has an ear, let him hear what the Spirit says to the churches…" and all the way through, it's all the churches. Ok, the reason I'm going through this is because the seven weeks to the harvest is the time of the harvest of the seven churches, and that pictures everything that the church is going to do. So He says to the churches, "…The one who overcomes shall not be hurt of the second death" (Revelation 2:8-11).

Then we come to two of the most problematic churches there are. The church of **Pergamos**, right there, right in Satan's capitol—Do the ways of the world affect the Church? Yes, they do. What's one of the biggest problems that has happened to the Church of God today—the same thing here, two of their great sins: Organized according to a corporate structure, hierarchical authority from the top down. If the minister says it, I'm off the hook, because the Bible has assured me that he is going to stand before God and my judgment. Now people don't phrase it that way, but that's how they look at it. And you still hear today, "Oh brethren, come and attend this church. If you are here you are going to receive salvation." Not so. They had the doctrines of Balaam, ate things sacrificed to idols, committed fornication, spiritual and everything there. You can read it in the book *Lord, What Shall I Do?* So He says, You have to overcome this, verse 17.

Then you have the next church, **Thyatira**. And here we have all the women's libbers. We have a woman prophetess, Jezebel. That tells what kind of doctrines they were getting—calls herself a prophetess. They went clear into the depths of Satan, but God wanted to make everyone know something clear and sure, verse 23: "…I will kill her children with death; and all the churches shall know that I am He Who searches *the* reins and hearts; and I will give to each of you according to your works." So God made sure that everyone knew that everyone was responsible for taking care of it. So He tells them to overcome, keep the first works, "…keeps My works … I will give authority over the nations;" (verse 26).

Then in history, we come to the church which is called **Sardis** and after all the things that you go through with these other churches, you come up to Sardis—they're dead, they have a little life and they are just about ready to collapse and have only a couple of things left, and God says, "I'll be merciful to you. You keep those few things that you have and I will not deny you before My Father." Now isn't that something? You think about that. For Christ says, "You do those few things and I won't deny you…" which tells us what? That if you don't do those things, you're denying Christ and He'll have to deny you, right? Didn't Jesus say, "The one who denies me, I shall also deny" (Revelation 3:1-6 paraphrased)?

Then you come to the church of **Philadelphia**. And I think there is something most interesting about the Philadelphians—a true Philadelphian does not know who he really is because you read the parable of the goats, and the sheep, and you remember what He said to the sheep? He said, "Enter into the Kingdom." He said because when I was hungry, when I was down and out, when I was in prison, and so forth, you came and visited me." And they said, "Lord, when did we do that?" They didn't know they had done it, did they? And He said, "…because you have done it to the least of these, my brethren, you have also done it unto me." So we won't belabor the point with the Philadelphians, we've had plenty enough sermons going over that, pro and con. But He says, verse 13: "The one who has an ear, let him hear what the Spirit says to the churches" (Revelation 3:7, 13).

Laodicea— "And to the angel of the church of *the* Laodiceans, write: These things says the Amen, the faithful and true Witness, the Beginner of the creation of God" verse 14. Now we come to a contemporary time which is, talking back to God, not believing God, being rich and increased with goods, but spiritually taking off their cloths because they are naked. They are literally taking off their spiritual cloths and telling God "I'm in good shape." Because we know, let's go back to Revelation 19, we know that the white clothing or the white raiment is the righteousness of the saints. Let's come back here to Revelation 19:8: "And it was granted to her that she should be clothed in fine linen, pure and bright; for the fine linen is the righteousness of the saints." So they are not doing the righteousness of God. So here we have all of these churches and let's just throw into the mix of it all the problems of the churches at Corinth—divisions, following men because they are a man, not building on the foundation of Christ, thinking they have already got it made, all kinds of prophecies, all kinds of Psalms, talking in tongues, bowing down before idols, all of those problems.

Now then, let's come to Revelation 5, because there is going to come a time when all of this is going to come to a screeching halt, and we are all going to be brought to the reality of things that are going to happen. And it is going to come as a shock, much as the shock that has come to Rwanda where they have killed about 150,000 people by slaughtering and hacking and killing and shooting. I heard a news clip just yesterday over the radio, where there is now a special organization where they go around the world and they are getting rid of mine fields. Did you know that 1,200 people a month are killed from mine fields that have been laid in 60 different countries that have been in various forms of fighting and guerilla warfare since World War II? Twelve hundred people are killed! They said mines can go off after twenty or thirty years. You just walk across a field and "boom!" you are either gone, lost a leg, lost an arm, blow out your eyes, or whatever. And that is how it is going to happen, brethren. It's going to come in a day and Bam! And it's going to be something!

Then we are going to come to the time that we have right here when God says, "That's it! Now is the time!" And this is when Christ is given the scroll. Revelation 5:1: "And in the right hand of Him Who sits on the throne…" that is God the Father "…I saw a book, written within and on *the* back, which had been sealed with seven seals. And I saw a strong angel proclaiming with a loud voice, 'Who is worthy to open the book, and to loose its seals? But no one in heaven, or on the earth, or under the earth was able to open the book, or to look inside it." So this is telling us that there are some things in there that no one understands yet. We have a bare little glimpse of it don't we. Verse 4: "And I was weeping greatly because no one was found worthy to open and to read the book, or to look into it. Then one of the elders said to me, 'Do not weep. Behold, the Lion Who is of the tribe of Judah, the Root of David, has overcome to open the book, and to loose its seven seals" (Revelation 5:1-6). And then he saw the Lamb with seven horns.

Then we come all the way down here to verse 11: "And I beheld, and I heard the voice of many angels round about the throne and the living creatures and the elders: and the number of them was ten thousand times ten thousand, and thousands of thousands; Saying with a loud voice, Worthy is the Lamb that was slain to receive power, and riches, and wisdom, and strength, and honor, and glory, and blessing." Now every man that wants to set himself up as a prophet, and one of them is ready to proclaim himself one of the two witnesses any time someone comes up with enough evidence—read this! OK? Christ is going to do it! He alone is going to open it. Verse 13: "And every creature which is in heaven, and on the earth and under the earth, and such as are in the sea, and all that are in them, heard I saying, Blessing, and honor, and glory, and power, *be* unto him that sits upon the throne, and to the Lamb forever and ever. And the four living creatures said, Amen. And the twenty-four elders fell down and worshiped him that lives forever and ever" (Revelation 5:11-14).

Then the seals are opened. The first seal is the white horse. A lot of these things we know, we've gone over many times. So let me just review them. I've said in the past, verse 2, "…I saw, and behold a white horse: and he that sat on him had a bow; and crown was given unto him: and he went forth conquering, and to conquer" (Revelation 6:2). And we have always looked at that and said, "Well, that's got to be the Catholic Church." Well, it fits the Catholic Church up to a certain point. Let's think of it beyond just the Catholic Church and let's understand that the reason a horse is used is because things happen suddenly. And I think the world is ready for a great common religious, spiritual, revival to bring together all religions, and I think we've given enough sermons in the past to show that that's the way it's going—which will include the Catholic Church and all of those, so called Christians, and also all the other religions of the world.

I still remember the ad that Belinda brought from IBM which showed the Tower of Babel which was crumbled down and they boasted, "We are now able to finish what they started." Wasn't that it? Something like that.

So this is going to come suddenly. This is part of the events leading up to the fulfilling of Pentecost—and they are going to do miracles! Right now there are a lot of people talking about aliens come to help us! What if they bring a new religion? And everyone says this is wonderful. We can now have peace, we can now get along, and there are miracles that are performed, because everyone likes a winner—remember that. And when there comes along this great religious movement, everyone's going to be considered a winner. It's going to be a wonderful event for them. So I would have to say we need to think in that term, along those lines.

Then verse 3, the second seal: "...I heard a voice say, Come and see. And there went out another horse *that was* red: and *power* was given to him that sat thereon to take peace from the earth, and that they should kill one another: and there was given to him a great sword" (Revelation 6:2-4). And I think that's going to happen, brethren, which we'll see where that fits in.

Let's go to Revelation 13, because when the great religious leader comes on, there is also going to be the great military leader and it's going to come on. He is going to come and it will come to this point—All the world is going to worship him. He is going to receive the deadly wound that will be healed. Now verse 4: "And they worshiped the dragon which gave power to the beast: and they worshiped the beast, saying Who *is* like unto the beast? Who is able to make war with him?" In other words, you can't resist his war-making powers. That is what it is saying.

Now I want you to just think on this, (cowbell rings indicating an opinion) there is my cowbell. I want you to think of the UN. How many members vote? You have ten, plus five who are the permanent members. What if they add two more permanent members—Japan and Germany? Now how many do you have—seven and ten. Is that not correct? Yes. Think on it—very possible. What if, and I have heard this suggested: The way we can have world peace is to turn over all nuclear weapons under UN control. Think on that for a minute. Who is able to make war with the beast? Now then, think what is going to happen when whoever the leader of the UN is, is killed and comes back to life or one of the seven heads. That disturbs the peace. Then he is going to go make war and here is what's going to happen, verse 5. I think the second seal and verse 5 fit exactly together. Revelation 6 verses 3 and 4 tie in together with Revelation 13, verses 4 down through 8. Who is able to make war with him? Now verse 5 of Revelation 13: "And there was given him a mouth speaking great things and blasphemies; and power was given unto him to continue forty *and* two months." That is after the deadly wound was healed. Verse 6: "...He opened his mouth in blasphemy against God, to blaspheme his name, and his tabernacle and them that dwell in heaven. And it was given unto him to make war with the saints, to overcome them: and power was given him over all kindreds, and tongues, and nations. And all that dwell upon the earth shall worship him, whose names are not written in the book of life of the Lamb slain from the foundation of the world. If any man have an ear, let him hear" (Revelation 13:3-9). So that means we need to really pay attention.

Now then, of the events leading up to Pentecost, let's continue back in Revelation 6. We have the third seal a black horse, famine, shortage of food. That can come on us quickly. How long could you last in the event you couldn't buy any food at the grocery store or there was war or [it was] cut off. Let's reverse the question. How many times a month do you go to the store? Or if that is too many? How many times a week do you go to the store? Now you might be able to calculate that, but I know there are times when I go to the store three or four times, because it's close, right? Any of you experience that? How long could you exist—not very long. So you see you don't have to wait for any great monstrous event to take place, it's just going to happen once and that's going to be it.

Then we come to the fourth seal which then is death as a result of that. And I tell you, we have these super viruses, super bacteria, super this and that and everything else, it's going to come and when there is starvation, lack of food, lack of water, guess what happens—wham! Throw in the mix all kinds of rats. Throw in the mix all kinds of insects.

Throw in the mix all kinds of insane people running around killing, taking, looting, and stealing. Throw in the mix, cannibalism. All that will be part of it.

Then they are going to come after us, Revelation 6:9. The fifth seal is the martyrdom of the saints. That's going to be something! And then there is going to be an event that leads up to the fulfilling of the next to the last and the last Pentecost which is going to startle this whole earth. Verse 12: "And I beheld when he had opened the sixth seal, and, lo, there was a great earthquake; and the sun became black as sackcloth of hair, and the moon became as blood; And the stars of heaven fell unto the earth, even as a fig tree casts her untimely figs, when she is shaken of a mighty wind. And the heaven departed as a scroll when it is rolled together; and every mountain and island were moved out of their places." Now you're not going to watch this on NBC, CBS, ABC, or CNN, or CBNC newscasts. This is going to happen suddenly—so much so that, "...the kings of the earth and the great men, and the rich men, and the chief captains, and the mighty men, and every bondman, and every free man, hid themselves in the dens and in the rocks of the mountains;" Why—because everything is going to be in an upheaval. Verse 16: "And said to the mountains and rocks, Fall on us, and hide us from the face of him that sits on the throne, and from the wrath of the Lamb: For the great day of his wrath is come; and who shall be able to stand?" (Revelation 6:12-17). So this is going to be something! What's going to happen when that scroll of heaven rolls back? What is going to be seen? They are going to see something. They're going to know it is something coming from outer space. They may not call Him Christ. The False Prophet is going to call Him Antichrist.

Let's go back to Matthew 24, because this is the event leading up to the fulfilling of the next to the last Pentecost and the last Pentecost, and I will just say right here—I believe that the sixth seal happens on the next to the last Pentecost. I won't ring the bell with that because I think that is based on fairly sound Scriptures, as we will see. Matthew 24, and let's pick it up here in verse 21: "For then shall be great tribulation, such as was not since the beginning of the world to this time, no, nor ever shall be. And except those days should be shortened, there should no flesh be saved:" or that is living, "...but for the elect's sake those days shall be shortened. Then if any man shall say to you, Lo, here is Christ, or there; believe *it* not. For there shall arise false Christs, and false prophets..." Now let's do this, let's figure that they don't all have to be religious. Do we not have saviors for the economy? Yes. Do we not have saviors for increasing the human race genetically? Yes. Do we not have prophets telling us how good things are going to be? Yes. Do we not have religious people doing that? Yes. So let's put it all in the whole mix. Someone mentioned to me that he thought this might be a possibility, I don't know so I will ring the bell (Bell rung). That's an opinion. His opinion was that he felt that Rush Limbaugh was a secular prophet telling them the truth and telling the truth to people that you can't get to listen to from a spiritual prophet, but God is going to make sure that they hear it! I would say, that's a reasonable opinion. So we need to realize that there are going to be those, there are also going to be false prophets.

Now notice what they are going to do. So mark it, brethren, watch, there are going to be more miracles done. (Comment was made that they are going to allow religious programming, and I think that means within programs, religious scenes of prayers and things like that on prime time.) But I tell you what: What's going to happen when there are five hundred television channels? I mean if you are fed up with the garbage with just twenty-plus [channels], times that by five and by five. Five times twenty is one hundred; times five is five hundred. But that is going to give opportunities isn't it? Yes. So watch, there are going to be miracles that are going to be done, great signs and wonders. Some of them can be medical signs and wonders—not only just healings, but they can be all kinds of things going on. "...and shall show great signs and wonders; insomuch that, if *it were* possible, they shall deceive the very elect" (Matthew 24:24). Now I want us to grasp this. We've got to really be on the ball constantly or the deception will be so great, we could be deceived. It's going to be hard to say that these bona fide, absolutely provable, documented miracles are of Satan. The world won't believe it. Why? Because they love a winner, and this is going to be a winner.

Verse 25: "Behold, I have told you before. Wherefore if they say unto you, Behold, he is in the desert; go not forth: behold, he is in the secret chambers; believe *it* not. For as the lightning..." Now let's focus in on verse 27 because this ties in with Revelation 6 and verse 12. "For as lightning coming out of the east, and shining unto the west;" that is only the sun, that cannot be a bolt of lightning—because lightning goes up, lightning comes down, lightning goes north and south and east and west and at all angles. "...So shall the coming of the Son of man be. For wheresoever the carcass is, there will the eagles be gathered together" (Matthew 24:25-28). And He gives us this statement which really it's hard to understand. The carcass, the body, the eagles are gathered that must have some reference to the church, some reference to protection.

Let's go on verse 29: "Immediately after the tribulation of those days..." This is the sixth seal. This happens on next to the last Pentecost, which I will prove. "Immediately after the tribulation of those days shall the sun be darkened, and the moon shall not give her light and the stars shall fall from heaven, and the powers of heaven shall be shaken: And then shall appear the sign of the Son of man in heaven:" What is the sign of the Son of man in heaven? When does it all of a sudden appear? Bam! When the heavens are rolled back like a scroll, and they see Christ as a sun, s-u-n. When they first see Him, notice it says shining from east to west. Which means that it's going to be far enough out in space that the gravitational pull of the earth is not going to affect it—because the earth will continue on its orbit and every eye is going to see it. And I believe, brethren, that from the next to the last Pentecost to the last Pentecost that that is going to get closer, and closer, and closer, and closer to the earth. And then on the last Pentecost, which we will cover tomorrow, when the first resurrection takes place it's going to come down into the clouds over Jerusalem. Now that's going to make a lot of excited people on earth, right? Militarists and otherwise. So the sign of the Son of man shall appear in heaven, "...then shall all the tribes of the earth mourn, and they shall see the Son of man <u>coming</u> in the clouds of heaven with power and great glory. And he shall send his angels with the sound of a great trumpet..." Did you realize the trumpet was blown on Pentecost? We'll cover that tomorrow. "...And they shall gather together his elect from the four winds, from one end of heaven to the other" (Matthew 24:29-31). So let's do it this way: verse 30 is the next to the last Pentecost, verse 31 is the last one. And we will cover that a little bit more tomorrow.

Let's see, I'm just about done here. Let's go to Luke 17, and let's cover the same thing there concerning His return. Luke 17:22: "And he said to the disciples, The days will come, when you shall desire to see one of the days of the Son of man, and you shall not see *it*." Longing for the good ol' days. Verse 23: "And they shall say to you See here; or, See there: go not after *them*, nor follow *them*. For as lightning that lights out of one *part* under heaven, shines unto the other *part* under heaven; so shall also the Son of man be in his day" (Luke 17:22-24).

We know that a day fulfilled in prophecy is one year. And what we're going to do is look at His day, from the next to the last Pentecost, to the last Pentecost and we will do that tomorrow on Pentecost, and put all of these events together.

End of Sermon

Transcriber: Judith Anderson

Events Leading Up to Pentecost
May 14, 1994
Scriptural References

1) Exodus 33:1-22

2) Exodus 25:8

3) Exodus 34:1, 4-11, 21-22, 28-33

4) Exodus 32:26-28

5) Jeremiah 5:1, 3-17, 19-31

6) Daniel 9:1-8, 10, 18-19

7) Revelation 1:18-20

8) Revelation 5:5-6

9) Revelation 2:2, 4, 7-11, 17, 23, 26

10) Revelation 3:1-7, 13-14

11) Revelation 19:8

12) Revelation 5:1-6, 11-14

13) Revelation 6:2-4

14) Revelation 13:3-9

15) Revelation 6:5-9, 12-17

16) Matthew 24:21-31

17) Luke 17:22-24

CHAPTER TWENTY-ONE

"To Walk in the Way of the Lord"

Pentecost—Day 49

June 3, 2006

And greetings, brethren. This is the Sabbath before Pentecost. Now let's come back here to Leviticus 23 and let's see something about counting Pentecost. We're going to rehearse it just a bit, and then we will see the message that is for us out of the word of God which culminates in this last day of the seven weeks. Now let's come here to Leviticus 23:9, "And the LORD spake unto Moses, saying, Speak into the children of Israel, and say unto them, When ye be come into the land..." So this ceremony could not take place until they came into the land. And as we know, that happened, as we find, in Joshua 5. "...Which I give unto you, and shall reap the harvest thereof..." So it was the harvest of the land. They didn't plant it, it wasn't their harvest; it was theirs inasmuch as that when God gave them the land they owned it. "...Then ye shall bring a sheaf of the firstfruits of your harvest unto the priest..." Now the thing that's important to understand is this: "...And he shall wave sheaf before the LORD, to be accepted for you: on the morrow after the Sabbath..." Now the term "Sabbath" here is *ha shabbat*, and it always means the weekly Sabbath. Then you were to count seven sabbaths.

Now let's come down here and see the count in verse 15: "And ye shall count unto you from the morrow after the Sabbath..." So that is the Sabbath which falls during the days of Unleavened Bread, and then the next day puts it on the first day of the week. "...From the day that ye brought the sheaf of the wave offering; seven sabbaths shall be complete..." Now this is seven sabbaths, and "shall be complete," meaning each week ends in a Sabbath. Now when you tie that together with Deuteronomy 16 where it says that you are to count seven weeks, so you put it together. These are whole weeks ending in a Sabbath. Now here is a thing that is important, verse 16: "Even unto the morrow after the seventh Sabbath [so that's today, the seventh Sabbath] shall ye number fifty days..." (Lev. 23:9-11, 15-16). And so if you take that and line that all up, it always comes out on a Sunday.

Now let's come to Deuteronomy 2. Because—let's liken the seven weeks that it took the children of Israel to come out of Egypt in order to receive the Ten Commandments from God at Mount Sinai, let's liken that to an extended travel that they had all through the wilderness. And remember, God provided for them. He led them by the pillar of cloud by day and the fire by night; He gave them manna; and as we will see, their clothes didn't even grow old, and so forth. Now let's come here to Deuteronomy 2:7: "For the LORD thy God hath blessed thee in all the works of thy hand..." Now this is what we want God to do for us in our personal lives, and our family lives, and in our church lives. "...He knoweth thy walking through this great wilderness…"

Now today we live in a different kind of wilderness, a spiritual wilderness filled with all kinds of physical things. "…These forty years the LORD thy God *hath been* with thee; thou hast lacked nothing." Now we find in Exodus 16 when God first began to give the manna to the children of Israel, He said that He was going to do this to prove them, to test them whether they would walk in His law or not. Now that's the same thing for us. Are we going to walk in God's way, even in spite of the world in which we are living?

Now let's come to Leviticus 26:2, and let's see what God says about walking in His way. And if you want a title for this sermon, it will be, "To Walk In the Way of the LORD." Now, "Ye shall keep My sabbaths…" Now there again, we have plural, referring to the weekly Sabbath and holy days, "…And reverence My sanctuary: I am the LORD. If ye walk in My statutes, and keep My commandments, and do them..." all the way through. Then He says He will bless them, give them peace, and things like this. So today we are living in a world where there is very little peace, there is nothing but trouble and difficulties. All of us in our lives, we have things that we are confronted with all the time. But let's understand that God has given us the way. He has given us the truth. He has given us the life through Jesus Christ.

Now come over here to verse 11: "And I will set My tabernacle among you…" Now today it's quite different because each one of us are a temple of God. "…And My soul shall not abhor you. And I will walk among you…" Now we're going to see how this applies to the church a little later; "…and will be your God, and ye shall be My people. I *am* the LORD your God, which brought you forth out of the land of Egypt, that ye should not be their bondmen; and I have broken the bands of your yoke, and made you go upright" (Leviticus 26:2,11-13). Now that's what God has done with us spiritually. Just like the children of Israel, as we saw during the days of Unleavened Bread, were rescued from Egypt; Pharaoh was a type of Satan, and that his armies were a type of the demons, and how God rescued them, and so forth; did all the things that He did to bring them out of the land of Egypt and bring them into the promised land. And when we come here to the book of Deuteronomy— let's come back here to Chapter 8, and let's see the things that God warned them of. And then let's see how this applies to the church today and how it applies to our lives, and how not only do we need to do the things that please God, but we also need to beware of the difficulties and problems that we're confronted with in the world today.

Now let's begin right here in Deuteronomy 8:1: "All the commandments which I command thee this day shall ye observe to do…" Now I'm going to give a sermon here sometime soon which will be, "Which commandments should we keep?" And we'll understand the error of where most of the professing Christianity of this world falls into and the difficulties that they have in rejecting the commandments of God. "…That ye may live…" And God wants us to live. God wants us to grow spiritually. God wants us to live in His way. "…And multiply, and go in and possess the land which the LORD sware unto your fathers. And thou shalt remember all the way which the LORD thy God led thee these forty years in the wilderness…" Just like we are to remember that God has called us out of the world. We are to remember that we are not to go back to spiritual Egypt. Now here is what God is doing in our lives. And here is why we go through the things that we do, the same exact process that they went through, only for our spiritual good and our spiritual benefit. Now He did this forty years in the wilderness, "…to humble thee, *and* to prove thee…"

Now let's just look at our lives. How many have been in the church of God, how long? Some have just been baptized, and some have been in the church of God 40 or 50 years. So we have the same thing. How are we walking in the world? And is God testing us and proving us? Yes, all the time, "…to know what *was* in thine heart..." And this is what God wants to know. And when we see about the seven churches a little bit later, it all has to do with the heart and how they stand before God, and what the problems of the world pressing in on the church caused them. "…To know what *was* in thine heart, whether thou wouldest keep His commandments, or no [and also whether we would love God or not]. And He humbled thee, and suffered thee to hunger, and fed thee with manna, which thou knewest not, neither did thy fathers know; that He might make thee know that man doth not live by bread only, but by every *word* that proceedeth out of the mouth of the LORD doth man live" (Deuteronomy 8:1-3). And then he gave them some other instructions in showing that even their clothes didn't wax old and their shoes didn't wear out. And then he warns them beware lest they forget.

Now let's come back to the New Testament. Let's come to II John, and let's see how this applies to us. Now let's look and see how we are to walk in God's way. II John 4. There are no chapters there, so it's just II John 4. "I rejoiced exceedingly that I have found among your children those who are walking in [the] truth..." So that's what God wants us to walk in—walk in the truth. We are sanctified by the truth, which is the word of God. "...Exactly as we received commandment from the Father." Now notice how this parallels with what we read back there in the Old Testament. Now verse 5, "And now I beseech you, lady [which then is the type of the church], not as though I am writing a new commandment to you, but that which we have *observed* from *the* beginning, that we love one another. And this is the love *of God*: that we walk according to His commandments. This is the commandment, exactly as you heard from *the* beginning, that you might walk in it" (II John 4-6,).

Now we also know this, that God gives us some warnings about how we are walking and how we're living in the world. Let's come to II Corinthians 6, and let's see why God does this. If you think that the children of Israel had all of their problems because they didn't follow in the way that God wanted them to do, well just think about the church of God today. We're going to talk about that a little later, so I just want you to get this in your mind. Let's come here to II Corinthians 6:14: "Do not be unequally yoked with unbelievers..." Now that's especially true in the sense of what the world would call Christianity. And one of the biggest errors that the church of God has done in recent time has gone to the Christianity of this world and say, "What do you know about God?" Well you've seen the results of that because they don't really know the way of God very well.

Now here is what we need to watch: "...For what do righteousness and lawlessness *have* in common? And what fellowship *does* light *have* with darkness? And what union *does* Christ *have* with Belial?" Now Belial means "the son of foolishness." "...Or what part *does* a believer *have* with an unbeliever? And what agreement *is there between* a temple of God and idols?" Now here's the whole key, which is important: "...For you are a temple of *the* living God..." That's why our calling is special. That's why it is important. That's why we need to always follow the way of God. You are a temple of the living God, "...exactly as God said: 'I will dwell in them and walk in *them*...' " Now if Christ is in you, how should you walk? We'll see about this a little bit later on here. "'...And I will be their God, and they shall be My people. Therefore, come out from the midst of them and be separate,' says *the* Lord, 'and touch not *the* unclean, and I will receive you; and I shall be a Father to you, and you shall be My sons and daughters, says *the* Lord Almighty' " (II Corinthians 6:14-18).

And this is what we want to attain to, because, as we'll see, tomorrow pictures the Resurrection. Tomorrow pictures the completion of this journey and the walk that we are walking in. Now let's come back here to Psalm 86, and let's see some other things which tie into this and help us understand how we need to walk, and help us understand how God is dealing with us. Now we all know we have things we need to change and overcome, and righteousness that we need to grow in, and that's all a part of the meaning of the Feast of Unleavened Bread. But in order to fulfill the completeness of the Feast of Unleavened Bread we've got to get to the final goal, which is the Resurrection.

Now let's come here to Psalm 86:11: "Teach me Thy way, O LORD..." Now if we're going to walk in the way of the Lord we have to examine the word of God and know what it is and He has to teach us. "...And I will walk in Thy truth..." Now see how that combines with what we have already talked about here, walking in the truth. "...Unite my heart to fear

Thy name. I will praise Thee, O LORD my God, with all my heart…" And this is what God wants from all of us—that we love God with all our heart; that we walk in God's way with all our heart; that we believe God with all of our heart; that we trust in God with all of our heart. "…And I will glorify Thy name for evermore. For great *is* Thy mercy toward me: and Thou hast delivered my soul from the lowest hell."

Now down here to verse 14: "O God, the proud are risen up against Me…" And there are a lot of things that are coming against a lot of brethren today. "…And the assemblies of violent *men* have sought after my soul; and have not set Thee before them. But Thou, O LORD, *art* a God full of compassion, and gracious, longsuffering, and plenteous in mercy and truth." Now here's the whole key in verse 16: "O turn unto me…" Now if we return to God, God promises He will return to us. Remember, God has called us and chosen us, and given us His Spirit, and He is walking in us. This is why we need to let the Spirit lead us— lead us in the way that we think, in the way that we live, on a daily basis. Not just on the Sabbath, not just when we feel "religious." "O turn unto me, and have mercy upon me; give Thy strength unto Thy servant, and save the son of thine handmaid" (Psalm 86:11-17). God has helped us and comforted us.

Let's come to another couple of Psalms here. Let's come to Psalm 119:1. Now let's see what happens when we're walking in the way of the LORD; our journey, as it were, to spiritual Mount Sinai. "Blessed [so this results in blessings, as we will see] *are* the undefiled in the way, who walk in the law of the LORD." So we have the way the Lord equals the way of truth, the way of His commandments, the way of His laws; the way of statutes and judgments; the way of keeping His Sabbath; the way of keeping His holy days; the way of taking care of our bodies and minds; even the way of eating, that we eat the things are right, and so forth. All of those are part of the way of the Lord. Now notice, "Blessed *are* they that keep His testimonies, *and that* seek Him with the whole heart." We're going to find all the way through here that it has to do with the heart. "They also do no iniquity: they walk in His ways" (Psalm 119:1-3). Now let's understand this: when you have this kind of attitude toward God and you're walking in His ways, you have no sin imputed to you. But you have the righteousness of Christ imputed to you. And that's what is important.

Let's come to Psalm 138:1. Let's see some other things about walking in the way of the Lord, walking in the way of God. And here's what it needs to do for us: "I will praise Thee with my whole heart: before the gods will I sing praise unto Thee. I will worship toward Thy holy temple, and praise Thy name for Thy lovingkindness and for Thy truth: for Thou hast magnified Thy word above all Thy name" (Psalm 138:1-2). Very important to understand. Now let's translate this into things that we have for the New Testament. When we pray, when we study, when we come before God we are coming right into the holy of holies in heaven above through the very sacrifice of Jesus Christ so that we can do these things.

Now let's come down to verse 6: "Though the LORD *be* high, yet hath He respect to the lowly: but the proud He knoweth afar off. Though I walk in the midst of trouble…" And we're going to see that the church is always confronted with difficulties and problems and troubles because we're living in this world, even though we know we're not part of this world. "…Thou wilt revive me: Thou shalt stretch forth Thine hand against the wrath of mine enemies, and Thy right hand shall save me. The LORD will perfect that which concerneth me…" And that's the whole goal. That is the whole goal that God wants us to understand—He is perfecting us. Now continuing, "…Thy mercy, O LORD, *endureth* for ever: forsake not the works of Thine own hands" (Psalm 138:1-2, 6-8).

Now let's apply that to us. We are the workmanship of God created in Christ Jesus, correct? And let's always understand this: the way that we always keep the perspective we need to have is to realize how great and marvelous our calling is, and what God is doing for us, and to us, and through us, and in us, and where He wants us to go. And He wants us to be faithful to the end and attain to the Resurrection. So this is a great and marvelous thing that we always need to keep in mind, and to realize this above all things.

Now let's come to the book of Revelation. Here in Revelation 1, let's see what it says about Christ, and let's see that Christ is intimately involved in His church. And it is the focus of His whole attention at the present time. Now there are things that are going on in the world which He is also directing, but the central focus is His church. Now let's pick it up here in Revelation 1:8. Now this helps us understand how important it is that Christ is dealing with each one of us, and how important the plan of God is. And as we have seen, it's all on the framework of the holy days of God. And as we have seen, every one of the holy days are all connected together and have meaning.

" 'I am the Alpha and the Omega, *the* Beginning and *the* Ending,' says the Lord, 'Who is, and Who was, and Who is to come—the Almighty.' " Christ is going to return, and His return is going to be so powerful and so glorious—we're going to see about that tomorrow. And it's going to be so spectacular that our thoughts and imaginations of it are just very minuscule compared to what it is really actually going to be. Then John, who was given this vision by Jesus Christ [wrote], "I, John, who *am* also your brother and joint partaker in the tribulation and in the kingdom and endurance of Jesus Christ, was on the island that *is* called Patmos because of the Word of God and the testimony of Jesus Christ. I was in *the* Spirit on the day of the Lord; and I heard a loud voice like a trumpet behind me, saying, 'I am the Alpha and the Omega, the First and the Last'; and, 'What you see, write in a book, and send it to the churches that are in Asia…' "

So this is a written message. And as we know, John canonized the whole New Testament. So this can also refer to that as well, the whole inclusive thing. But what he writes in the book here, the letters to the seven churches, have to do with how God deals with His church; how Christ, Who is the head of the church, is working with His church and how the church, with God's Spirit living in the world, has the difficulties and trials that they need to overcome, and how God is dealing with us. And this is why we need to go back and over this, especially at this time of year. Because this shows that the seven churches picture the seven weeks leading up to Pentecost. And it is just like the harvest of the seven weeks of the wheat harvest that takes place, the seven churches are the spiritual harvest of God.

Now He names them here: Ephesus, Smyrna, Pergamos, Thyatira, Sardis, Philadelphia, and Laodicea. Now as we're going to see, these seven churches picture the churches that were then, number one. Number two, it is also a prophecy of all the churches of God down through history from the time that it was formed in 30 A.D. with the coming of the Holy Spirit until the return of Jesus Christ and the Resurrection at Pentecost. Number three, it pictures the spiritual condition and attitude of the churches in general and individuals in particular. So it includes all of that. Now it includes one more thing, which is this: the churches at the end. So what we really have is this: [1] the seven churches that were there, [2] the seven—and people like to call them the seven church eras, or stages of the church down through history, and [3] the seven churches at the end.

Now I think if we view things from the point of view like the Bible Sabbath Association, and look at the different publications that come out; and for us, when we look at what is called *The Journal*, we can see in *The Journal* different parts of messages which go to the churches of God. And it's quite an interesting thing that that is what it is. And what you see when you read *The Journal*, you see how that there are various different doctrines and teachings which also are reflected here in Revelation 2 and 3, as we will see in just a minute, and what we need to do about those. Because some of these teachings are not in accord with the word of God.

Now notice verse 12, "And I turned to see the voice that spoke with me; and when I turned, I saw seven golden lampstands…" Now this is just like in a circle. This is not a replica of the candle, or the lamp-holder that is found in the Temple. Because as we will see, the seven golden lampstands—now notice verse 13, "And in *the* [middle] midst of the seven lampstands *one* like *the* Son of man…" Christ is in His church. Now if Christ is in you, and in me, and in all the brethren, all the brethren consist of the church. And the church is a spiritual organization. It is not a corporate organization. Any corporate organization only has to do with conducting business in this world. And so He is in the midst of His church. Then it shows His great glorified—how Christ is, with the countenance shining as the sun in full strength.

And when John saw this, he says here in verse 17: "And when I saw Him, I fell at His feet as if dead; but He laid His right hand upon me, saying to me, 'Do not be afraid…',", And this is what we need to also understand: do not be afraid. If there are things we need to change, we'll change. If there are things we need to repent of, we can repent of those, because that's the whole story of the seven churches as recorded in Chapter 2 and 3. " '…Do not be afraid; I am the First and the Last, even the one Who is living; for I was dead, and behold, I am alive into the ages of eternity. Amen. And I have the keys of *the* grave and of death.' " Now let's understand one thing. Like the apostle Paul said very clearly, if Christ is not raised, then there is no resurrection of the dead; and if there is no resurrection of the dead, we have no hope. But here is the message from Christ. These of the words of God: He has the keys of the grave and death.

Now notice verse 19. God wants us to know. This is why it was written: " 'Write the things that you saw [everything up through verse 18 to this point], and the things that are [that's the seven churches which exist, the state of the church at that particular time], and the things that shall take place hereafter.' " Because this comes from the time of John—yes, even reaching back to the beginning of the church in 30 A.D. on Pentecost, and goes clear to the return of Christ on into the millennium, and on into New Jerusalem, and on into the first stages of the ages of eternity. So this is a fantastic book. And it starts with churches. Now let's ask the question—we all get interested in news, don't we? And we all like to see what's going on in the world, right? We like to see, are the prophecies being fulfilled? Well the answer is yes, they're all being fulfilled exactly the way that God wants them fulfilled. Now stop and think for a minute. Since God gave prophecies concerning all the major events in the world, do you not think that He would also give a prophecy of His church? Yes. That's what He's done in Revelation 2 and 3.

Now verse 20, " 'The mystery of the seven stars that you saw in My right hand, and the seven golden lampstands, is *this*: the seven stars are *the* angels of the seven churches; and the seven lampstands that you saw are *the* seven churches' " (Revelation 1:8-12, 17-20). Now let's see the message to them. This is written to us. These are the sayings of Christ so that we might know what to do in any circumstances that we are confronted with in our Christian life, as individuals, in our community, as it were, in our congregations and fellowship when we get together. And what we will see is this: is that God through Christ lays out all the things that we need to be aware of and what's going to happen with His church.

Now just like—and we will see there's a parallel here; we will see many, many, many of the things that happened to the church as it goes down in time in history, were also the same things that happened to Israel as they walked in the wilderness for the 40 years. Now let's begin in Revelation 2:1, " 'To the angel of the Ephesian church, write…' " Now let's understand something. When God has it written, and God has it preserved, and He has it for us today, then we better pay very deep, serious concern about it, and understand that these are the living words of God given to us. So when we ask the question, "What would Jesus say to His church today?" Right here we have it. This is the message for us.

" '…These things says He Who holds the seven stars in His right hand [and to do His work; that's why it's in the right hand], Who walks in *the* midst of the seven golden lamp-stands.' " Christ is right there, just like we read, He is walking in us, and we are walking in His way. And we are to let the light of Christ lead us. Now notice, He knows everything about us, doesn't He? He says, " 'I know your works, and your labor, and your endurance, and that you cannot bear those who are evil; and *that* you did test those who proclaim *them-selves* to be apostles, but are not, and did find them liars…' " Now this is why there are so many warnings in there: "Beware of false prophets; beware that you're not deceived. Test those. Prove all things." This is what they were doing. And this is what we have to do in everything that we do. And this is how, then, we let ourselves be led by the Spirit of God; and how also that the Word of God and the Spirit of God then corrects us, encourages us, uplifts us, leads us in the things that we need to do; convicts us of the shortcomings and problems that we encounter, and also encourages us. As it says in verse 3, " '…And *that* you have borne *much* and have endured, and for My name's sake have labored and have not grown weary…' " So that's the important thing to do—never grow weary.

" 'Nevertheless…' " So here comes a little correction. As we will see, God has correction for His church in every sense. " 'Nevertheless I have *this* against you, that you have left your first love' " (Revelation 2:1-4). And this is what happens in any organization. They start out with zeal. They start out with love. They start out with dedication, and then everything gets kind of "socialized" as with people. And when you leave the first love, what is happening you're letting the world come in. You're letting others come in. And even though you may be fighting off false doctrine, as it says here, that they "tried them who were apostles and were not, and tested them," that means you test the message. You listen to what they have to say.

And I'll just mention this now, but I also am going to mention it again, but one of the doctrines that is coming to test the church today, which a lot of people are failing, is this: the false doctrine that Jesus did not exist as God before He came in the flesh; and that He did not exist until He was begotten in the womb of the virgin Mary. Now you already have the letter that I wrote on it. You already have the series that we have done on it. But how does that come about? Right here. Let's come back here to Mark 12 and let's see what it was where it says they lost their first love. Now a lot of people refer to this as the first love that people have when they're first called and understand the truth and understand the way of God. That is true to a certain extent. But that's not what it's talking about, because the Greek back there for "first" comes from the word *protos*, which also means "primary."

Now let's come here to Mark 12:28. And this is what we need to keep always right in the forefront of our minds. "And one of the scribes who had come up *to Him*, after hearing them reasoning together *and* perceiving that He answered them well, asked Him [that is, asked Jesus], 'Which is *the* first commandment of all?' " The primary commandment. What's the most important thing? And once you understand this and realize this, it will bring everything else together. " '…"Hear, O Israel: *the* Lord our God is one Lord. And you shall love the Lord your God with all your heart…" ' " Now I want you to notice the effort that is put into it, the effort that is required.

Now the reason that this is important is this: is because eternal life, to live forever is a tremendous and wonderful thing. And view it this way: everything that we're doing right now is preparing and getting ready for the event that tomorrow pictures, the Resurrection; and getting ready to live eternally, and getting ready to know how to rule and reign with Christ, and preparing us to complete what God has given us to do. So, "Love the Lord your God with all your heart," not part-time. Don't let your heart be divided, your mind be divided. Because it says there in James 1 that if you are divided in heart and mind, then you are double-minded and you are unstable. Maybe that will explain a lot of difficulties that people have. You judge yourself in that yourself. " ' "...And with all your soul, and with all your mind, and with all your strength." ' " So our calling is an all-out effort on our part. nd then God gives His all-out effort to us.

Let me ask you a question: did not Jesus Christ give an all out effort when He was here in the flesh? Did He not give His all to save His creation, and to save you individually? Yes He did. That's why we need to understand what it's talking about there in losing the first love. " '...This is the first commandment.' " So the primary love is loving God. And the primary commandment is to love God. " '...And *the* second *is* like this: "You shall love your neighbor as yourself." There is no other commandment greater than these' " (Mark 12:28-31). And then Jesus also said of us that we are to love one another as Jesus loved us.

Now if you are loving God with all your heart and mind and soul and being—let's just answer some other questions here as we are going along—would you get wrapped up in doctrines and teachings of men? No. If you are proving everything like they did back here in the church at Ephesus, are you really seeking the truth? There's a difference between seeking the truth of God, walking in the truth, being sanctified of the truth, living by the truth, and seeking a position. Not a position of power, but a religious position which is not connected with God. So that's why we have to prove all these things.

Now let's come back here to Revelation 2 again, and let's continue in verse 5. Now this is what we are to do. And this is what God wants us to do as we are walking the walk. We'll also need to be "talking the talk" if we could put it that way, that which is right. " 'Therefore, remember from where you have fallen, and repent, and do the first works...' " That's what we need to do.

I was talking to a man here the other day and we were talking about the condition of the church and how many people have fallen into this position, which is similar to Laodiceanism, but not exactly the same thing. And how many people are out there kind of treading water. Now have you have ever tread water out in the ocean? You can tread water and you think you're keeping yourself afloat, and granted you're not sinking; but you can tread water, but there is one thing with treading water—you don't have your feet on the ground. And when you're treading water and the currents are coming, it's moving you along and it's moving you maybe in a direction that you really don't want to go, and you're not aware of it. And then all the sudden, just like a wave comes upon the land—if you're treading water, just like this, it's going to catch up with you. So we have this. He says repent and to the first works. Go back and do the things that you know that you need to do and recapture that first love.

Now let's continue on and learn some more things that we need to understand out of this. He calls them to repent. And He says, "Unless you repent I'm going to remove your lamp stand." Now let's look at this in several different ways. Number one, God corrects His own church. Number two, God corrects each one of us individually, and He expects us to repent. Now if there is not repentance then He says he's going to remove you. Let's look at Number one. Did God remove a church before our very eyes? Yes He did. Has God removed false brethren, false ministers, false teachers? Yes, because they did not repent. They lost their first love. They quit loving God with all their heart and mind and soul and being, and got wrapped up in themselves, and their own doctrines, and their own positions, and their own religiosity. And that's cause for removal. But they did have one thing, that they hated the works of the Nicolaitans. And the Nicolaitans are those who have a rigid hierarchy and lorded over the brethren. And the Nicolaitans are also those who have a false grace, as we'll see here in just a little bit.

Now here in verse 7, " 'The one who has an ear, let him hear with the Spirit says to the churches...' " (Revelation 2:7). Very important. God's Spirit is in you. Christ directs the Spirit. It is to lead you and it is to bring you to repentance. And that's all a part of our Christian walk. Because we are in the process of being perfected, step by step, day by day, week by week, month by month, year by year. That's why we are always to walk in faith, believe in hope, and live in love. And that's how we are to conduct our lives.

Now let's go on. Because even in the world today we have those who are dying for Christ. Even within the churches of God there are those in very treacherous and evil places in the world that have suffered death because of those who follow Satan the devil. Now let's read it here, the church of the Smyrnans: " '…These things says the First and the Last, Who was dead but is alive. I know your works and tribulation and poverty (but you are rich)…' " And when you come to the Laodiceans, because they have an abundance of physical things, that they think they are rich, that they are spiritually right before God. But God looks at it the other way. Remember this: God looks at it with other eyes. So they are rich even though they're suffering tribulation,

" '…And the blasphemy of those who declare themselves to be Jews and are not, but *are* [of] a synagogue of Satan.' " A very interesting way to put it, isn't it? A synagogue of Satan. Let's talk about another synagogue of Satan—radical Muslimism. And they are the ones who are killing brethren. There have been some who have been associated with the churches of God in Africa who have been killed by Muslims. So this is a living part of the church today. And yes, these brethren may not have the understanding of doctrine, may not realize all the things that we do or understand the depths of the plan of God, but they believe Christ. They are willing to die for His name. They are willing to stand up and be counted. And so God says to them, don't fear any of the things that you're about to suffer: " '…Behold the devil is about to cast *some* of you to prison that you may be tried, and you shall have tribulation ten days. But be faithful unto death and I will give you a crown of life' " (Revelation 2:8-9).

Now let's look at the other situation too. What did Jesus say at the end? "He who endures to the end, the same shall be saved." And what we see all the way through here with the churches of God is the lack of true spiritual endurance and consistency. So those who die, they are going to receive a crown of life. And God looks at them with far greater love and favor than those who may have more truth, those who may understand more doctrine but treat it with disdain and contempt, familiarity, and [end] up treading water in their spiritual lives, and that God has to correct them. Here with the church at Smyrna, those who go through and suffer these things, they don't have any correction Christ has to give them because their hearts are right with Him.

Now let's come to the next two churches, or perhaps the most infiltrated with satanic doctrine. Because Satan wants to bring in satanic doctrine into the church. Because he knows if he can get you to move away from the truth just a little bit, just like a ship that is off one degree, it's going to miss the port at the other end. Or if you're sending a satellite up into orbit, if you are off just a little bit it's not going into orbit. Now let's read here in Revelation 2:12, " 'And to the angel of the church in Pergamos write: These things says He who has the sharp two-edged sword…' " Which we find in the book of Hebrews, that's the word of God—sharper than any two-edged sword, and cuts asunder to the dividing of the soul and spirit and joints and marrow, and is a discerner of the thoughts and the intents of the heart (Hebrews 4:12, *paraphrased*), the word of God. Christ, Who is called the Word of God and the Spirit of God. So He wants them to understand, there is correction coming.

He says, " 'I know your works and where you dwell, where the throne of Satan *is*; but you are holding fast My name, and did not deny My faith, even in the days in which Antipas *was* My faithful witness, who was killed among you, where Satan dwells.' " Now let me tell you something, when you get in the middle of where Satan is, and Satan is deceiving this whole world, and he's got his ways of doing things. He has a counterfeit Christianity. He has his counterfeit way of doing things. And with all the pressures coming upon people and these things, it's awfully hard to resist those things. " 'But I have a few things against you because you have there *those* who hold the teachings of Balaam...' " (Revelation 2:12-14).

Now what is the teaching of Balaam? The teaching of Balaam is this: "Let's amalgamate the religions together." Let's take the best of this, and the best of that, and the best of the other thing. And isn't that what the Catholic Church did, and is this not really the brethren who repented in Pergamos, then they left what later became the Catholic Church because the doctrine of Balaam is that. " '...Who taught Balak to cast a stumbling block before the children of Israel, to eat things sacrificed to idols and to commit fornication.' " Both physically and spiritually, and to sacrifice unto idols. Now if you want to know any one thing that the Bible teaches, which is this: "Thou shalt have no other gods before Me. Thou shalt not make unto thee any graven image, or any likeness of any thing that is in heaven above, or that is in the earth beneath, or that is in the water under the earth. Thou shalt not bow down thyself to them, nor serve them: for I the Lord thy God am a jealous God, visiting the iniquity of the fathers upon the children unto the third and fourth generation of them that hate me;" (Exodus 20:3-5). And if there's any one thing that is pounded through the whole Bible, that is it. But today people have different idols. They have idols of their minds. They have idols of their doctrines. They have idols of their way of life. They have idols of the things about them that their hands have made. And so that's all part of it.

" '...Moreover, you also have *those* who hold the doctrine of the Nicolaitanes, which thing I hate.' " Now when it comes to doing things which God hates—and the church is guilty of it—know that correction is going to come. Just like when the children of Israel were on their way in coming to Mount Sinai to meet God. Did He not have to correct them? Did He not have to teach them? Did He not have to, in a sense, punish them? Yes indeed. Notice what He says here in verse 16: "Repent!..." And that's what God wants us to do all the time. Repentance doesn't happen just at the time before you're baptized, but repentance happens daily. Because as we're overcoming sin, as we're overcoming carnal nature, as we overcome the things of this world we need to repent. We need to have our minds cleansed. We need to have our hearts purified. " '...For if *you* do not *repent*, I will come to you quickly and will make war against them with the sword of My mouth' " (Revelation 2:14-16).

Now just stop and think for a minute. Is it not a sad situation indeed that Jesus has to fight against His own church? Think on that for a minute. Look back at what happened to ancient Israel. Did not God have to fight against His own people because of what they did? Yes indeed. So there needs to be some repentance among the churches of God. There are too many people out there with their own ideas. And one of the big idols that is out there today is various calendars schemes. Because they do not count God worthy of understanding the universe. And they have to have their own calendar schemes.

Now if you are caught up in some of that, I suggest to you do exactly like [it says] here, repent. And we've got a stack of material that shows without a doubt that God gave the calculated Hebrew calendar so that we would all be able to keep the feasts on the right day that He has appointed. Because when we have our own calendar schemes, what do we end up doing? We appoint days that God didn't appoint. And yet many of those who do that are staunchly for the Sabbath and the holy days and against Sunday. But if you establish your own holy days contrary to the way that God has given it, what are you doing? It's the same thing as establishing Sunday, right? Yes indeed. But God says, "Repent!"

Now let's come down here to Thyatira. Thyatira really got carried away. And as you look at the state of some of the churches of God today you understand how that can happen. Because as we learned with the Feast of Unleavened Bread, a little leaven leavens whole lump; and if you let it grow, and grow, and grow, and grow, and grow, and grow, and you don't understand the magnitude of the problems and difficulties until it gets out of hand. Just look at the immigration problem in all the nations of the ten tribes of Israel today. It is out of hand.

And that's what happened to the church at Thyatira, though they started out well. Let's read it: " 'And to the angel of the church in Thyatira, write: These things says the Son of God, He Who has eyes like a flame of fire, and His feet *are* like a fine brass. I know your works, and love, and service, and faith, and your endurance [so they were doing well], and your works; and the last *are* more than the first [so some of them repent]. But I have a few things against you, because you allow that woman Jezebel, who calls herself a prophetess, to teach and seduce My servants into committing fornication and eating thing sacrificed to idols' " (Revelation 2:18-20). And that's exactly what happens when you have your own Passover, you have your own Unleavened Bread—just one step away from this kind of idolatry.

But look what happened here. Jezebel was the daughter of the high priest of Baal. And Jezebel married Ahab, and Ahab lead the children of Israel into sin. And it even caused problems for Elijah. So God means what He says. Now if you are out there with the world, living like the world, being like the world, acting like the world, then you are spiritually fornicating with the world. Now juxtaposition that with this: how much do you study? How much do you pray? How much do you really believe God?

Now verse 21, " 'And I gave her time to repent of her fornication...' " God gives us all space and time to repent. That's why He doesn't come down upon us until He sees what we're going to choose and do. He sends little warnings. He sends thoughts in our minds. He sends situations to bring us up short, to alert us as to what is taking place. And sometimes we react to them right away, other times we kind of let them linger. And then the problem gets more, and more, and more, and then finally Christ has to do what He does here, in a way, He brings us up short and helps us to understand where we have been going wrong. That's why He said here, " 'And I gave her time to repent of her fornication, but she did not repent.' " So if there's not repentance, what comes next? " 'Behold, I will cast her into a bed, and those who commit adultery with her into great tribulation, unless they repent of their works' " (Revelation 2:21-22).

Now let's understand this. Let's come back here to Psalm 86 again. Let's understand something about God that we really need to realize. And if you have things in your life that you know you need to repent of, then remember this: God is waiting for you to repent. And God will receive you when you repent. Now Psalm 86:1, "Bow down Thine ear, O LORD, hear me: for I *am* poor and needy [now that's repentance]. Preserve my soul; for I *am* holy..." And every one that God calls and every one that has the Holy Spirit is holy. "... O Thou my God, save Thy servant that trusteth in Thee." So now you've got to reestablish that trust with God, and here's how you do it. "Be merciful unto me, O LORD: for I cry unto thee daily." Get right back with God. "Rejoice the soul of thy servant: for unto thee, O LORD, do I lift up my soul. For Thou, LORD, *art* good, and ready to forgive..."

So the problem is never with God. That's why there are no conditions on God. Where there are conditions it is, "if you—" then "God will—." So if you repent, then God will forgive. But that repentance has to be from the heart, and it has to be, as we covered at the first, reestablishing the true love. "For Thou, LORD, *art* good, and ready to forgive, plenteous in mercy unto all them that call upon Thee. Give ear, O LORD, unto my prayer; and attend to the voice of my supplications. In the day of my trouble I will call upon Thee: for Thou wilt answer me" (Psalm 86:1-7). And so that's the appeal that was made here by Christ to the church at Thyatira: "Don't be taken down by any of these things."

331

Let's think about it for a minute too. Let's equate all of these things together that we see happening in the churches of God concerning their attitude toward God, concerning their attitude toward doctrine, concerning their health—spiritually and physically—concerning the world that we are living in, and all of that, God weighs all of those factors together and we need to really draw close to God and realize that He is there to help us if we repent.

Now let's come back here to Revelation 2:22,..."unless they repent of their works." And if they don't, He says, " 'And I will kill her children…' " In other words, whatever you are going to do, if you don't repent and are not right with God, it is going to come to nothing. " 'And I will kill her children with death; and all the churches shall know that I am He Who searches *the* reins and [the] hearts [because Christ is in us all the time]; and I will give to each of you according to your works.' " Now how far can a person go and still recover themselves? God alone makes that decision. But look at the next verse here: " 'But to you I say, and to *the* rest who *are* in Thyatira, as many as do not have this doctrine, and who have not known the depths of Satan, as they speak; I will not cast upon you any other burden. But hold fast what you have until I come.' " And then all the way through to every one of the churches—let's read it right here in verse 29: " 'The one who has an ear, let him hear what the Spirit says to the churches' " (Revelation 2:23-25, 29).

Do you have an ear to hear? How is your walk with God? How are you steadfast with God? Because God is going to bring you to Mount Zion in heaven above, as we will see, and the day of the Resurrection is going to happen. And Christ wants you ready. Christ wants you prepared. That's what this is all about.

Then we have the ones who are the absolute—how shall we say—perhaps even the worst church of all, the church at Sardis, that they have a name that they live, but they are dead. Now notice the warning that He gives them here. He says in Revelation 3:2, " 'Be watchful, and strengthen the things that remain [whatever little bit is remaining, strengthen it], which are about to die. For I have not found your works complete before God.' " Now there are spiritual works we are to do, and God wants us to do them, and they need to be complete. " 'Therefore, remember what you have received and heard, and hold on *to this*, and repent [again, repentance]. Now then, if you will not watch…' " And Jesus tells us to watch: watch ourselves, watch the world, " '…I will come upon you as a thief…' " Because God will always visit for the sins. This is not talking about His second return here. This is talking about Jesus dealing with each one of us. " '…And you shall by no means know what hour I will come upon you.' "

And isn't that the way it always is? When you least expect it and are least prepared, because you have come into a state of near deadness, then Christ is going to come upon you. Now, a little encouragement here, " 'You have a few names even in Sardis who have not defiled their garments, and they shall walk with Me in white because they are worthy. The one who overcomes shall be clothed in white garments; and I will not blot out his name from the book of life, but I will confess his name before My Father and before His angels.' "

Now let's understand something here, very important to realize: our names written in the book of life [and] are there and will remain there so that at the resurrection we will be raised from the dead. But let's also understand this, if we allow ourselves to get into these kinds of spiritual conditions, it [our names] can be erased. And as God told Moses, "I will blot out whom I will blot out" (Exodus 32:33 *paraphrased*). So that's quite a warning isn't it? Notice verse 6, " 'The one who has an ear, let him hear with the Spirit says to the churches' " (Revelation 3:2-6). Then it talks about the Philadelphians. We'll be there in a little bit. We'll end up with that one. But let's come over here to the Laodiceans. Now you've heard this many, many times over. So let's go to the message to the Laodiceans that we find in the book of Colossians, Colossians 2. Because this is important for us to understand and realize. Not only was this written to the Colossians, but he also gave instructions then when it was done being read to the Colossians that it was to also be read in the church of Laodicea.

Now let's notice the focus here, especially in Colossians 2. Because this also has to do with what we are confronted with today, with all of the Satanic spiritism that is out there. And what we need to understand is this: this world is absolutely going to go after Satan the devil and all of these teachings. Now just the other night I was channel surfing, because there's hardly anything to watch; and I got on the National Geographic channel. And guess what they were showing? Witchcraft, séances, appealing to demons and devils, and even using the name of Jesus with it. Now that's one of the great problems with the Laodiceans. They get involved in philosophy. And philosophy then changes the nature of God, which then is why there are people who are involved in this "one God only in number" false doctrine, and saying that Jesus was not God before He became a human being. And Paul is dealing with that here in Colossians 2.

Now let's begin right here in Colossians 2: 1, "Now I want you to understand what great concern I have for you, and *for* those in Laodicea…" Now remember, these are the inspired words of God. God has concern for all of His brethren, "…as many as have not seen my face in *the* flesh; that their hearts may be encouraged, being knit together in love…" Now notice how this ties in with the message to all the churches: "…knit together in love unto all riches of the full assurance of understanding…" Not physical goods and physical riches. To the riches of the full assurance of understanding that you know God, that you know Jesus Christ, that you know the word of God, that you know how to live your life before God the way He wants you to. "…Unto *the* knowledge of the mystery of God, and of *the* Father, and of Christ…" He wants us to know the great, fantastic things that He has for us. "In Whom are hid all the treasures of wisdom and knowledge." You're not going to gain any knowledge from the philosophies of this world. They come from men who profess themselves to be wise, but have become fools. And they believe when you believe in "only one God in number," you're talking about a god who is the transcendent god, who has no form, no shape, no being. And that's the philosophical god of all the pagans. In Christ are hidden all the treasures of wisdom and knowledge.

"Now this I say so that no one may deceive you by persuasive speech." Just because a person presents an argument, remember this: not all logic is truth. But all truth is logical. "For though I am indeed absent in the flesh, yet I am with you in spirit, rejoicing and beholding your order, and the steadfastness of your faith in Christ. Therefore [here comes the warning], as you have received Christ Jesus the Lord [as you find in the Scriptures], be walking in Him…" Now put together all these other scriptures that we have seen here [up to this point], "…being rooted and built up in Him, and being confirmed in the faith, exactly as you were taught, abounding in it with thanksgiving" (Colossians 2:1-7).

Now let's come to I John 2 and let's see "be walking in Him." How does it tell us we're to be walking in Him? Let's see it. Very basic, in verse 3, "And by this *standard* we know that we know Him: if we keep His commandments. The one who says, 'I know Him,' and does not keep His commandments, is a liar, and the truth is not in Him." Now stop and think about this for a minute. Is it not then foolish for the people and ministers in the churches of God to go to Sunday-keeping churches, whose ministers are liars, and ask, "How do you understand the Scriptures?" Just think on that for a minute. "On the other hand, *if* anyone is keeping His word, truly in this one the love of God is being perfected…" And that's what God wants in our lives, that the love of God be perfected. That's why we're here. That's why we're doing what we're doing, so that we can do—as we go back to the very first message that was given to the church at Ephesus—that we don't lose our first love, that it is being perfected. And if it is, he says, "By this *means* we know we are in Him." And also that means we know that He is in us.

Now verse 6 is the key: "Anyone who claims to dwell in Him is obligating himself also to walk even as He Himself walked" (I John 2:3-6). Isn't that something. That's how we're to do it. That's how we're to live God's ways. And that's why where we started out that John was pleased when he heard that they were walking in the truth.

So what Paul is writing about here back in Colossians 2:6—now let's go back there—"Therefore, as you have received Christ Jesus the Lord [and that means the whole Bible together], be walking in Him; [now notice] being rooted and built up..." So you have roots that go down for stability, and you are being built up—your faith and love is being perfected. "...Built up in Him, and being confirmed in the faith, exactly as you were taught, abounding in it with thanksgiving." Verse 8, a very key one, "Be on guard so that no one takes you captive through philosophy and vain deceit, according to the traditions of men, according to the elements of the world, and not according to Christ" (Colossians 2:6-8).

Very important. Look at all of these different doctrinal proposals that come along, and what do you see? They are all designed and presented with persuasive speech. They're all designed to lead you just a little away from Christ, and a little more, and a little more, and a little more. Satan knows that he can't get those who have the Holy Spirit of God to reject it instantly. So he comes along with a program, a step by step, by step, by step, by step to get rid of it. And that's how he does it. That's how he accomplishes it.

Now let's come back here to Revelation 3 and let's talk a little bit more about Laodiceanism. So if that's the problem—which it is; and was it not philosophy brought by a Greek native professor, doctor of philosophy, which set the stage to take down one of the largest churches of God in the history of the churches of God? Yes indeed. Because philosophy changes the nature of God. And if you believe that Jesus did not exist until He was conceived, you are changing the nature of God. Now what happens when you get into that state? Let's pick it up here. It says they're neither hot or cold, lukewarm, %be spewed out of His mouth. Now verse 17, " 'For you say, "I am rich, and have become wealthy"...' " Now notice this. This is the only church that talks back to God. None of the others do that. "God, how can You accuse me of this? Look all these blessings that we have." No, " ' "... And have become wealthy, and have need of nothing;" and you do not understand that you are wretched, and miserable, and poor, and blind, and naked.' " How are you clothed spiritually? So He says He doesn't want you to be naked. So He gives us counsel. And this is what we need to do, brethren, " '...to buy from Me gold purified by fire so that you may be rich [the true riches, like those in Smyrna had], and white garments so that you may be clothed, and the shame of your nakedness may not be revealed; and to anoint your eyes with eye salve so that you may see.' "

Now let's understand this. In all of this, though it is pointing out the errors and the problems and the difficulties, this is not a matter of condemnation to put people down. This is a matter of an urgent message to wake people up, from the point of view that God is dealing with us. He says, " 'As many as I love, I rebuke and chasten. Therefore, be zealous and repent' " (Revelation 3:17-19). And when we have that repentance, how are we to implement it? Let's come over here and look at the church at Philadelphia, which then is the key model. Everyone wants to be a Philadelphian. Not everyone can. But nevertheless, when we repent of these things, whether Laodiceans, or Sardisites, or Thyatira, or Pergamos, or Ephesus, whichever attitude we are in, which ever church in the world that there is today that we are in, we can look at this as the model on how we need to behave ourselves and how we need to react to God.

He says here in Revelation 3:8, " 'I know your works. Behold, I have set before you an open door, and no one has the power to shut it because you have a little strength [God is holding it open], and have kept My word…' " There it is, as we read back there in the beginning, Deuteronomy 8, which is also in Matthew 4 and Luke 4, "Man shall not live by bread alone but by every word that proceeds out of the mouth of God." " '…You have kept My word, and have not denied My name.'" When you bring in all of these false doctrines and things that we have covered, you're denying the name of Christ. "'Behold, I will make those of the synagogue of Satan…' " Which He's telling us here, do not worry about the world. Do not worry about the conspiracies that are out there, which are out there, which are all of Satan who is deceiving the world. God is going to turn the tables on them. " '…Who proclaim themselves to be Jews and are not, but do lie—behold, I will cause them to come and worship before your feet, and to know that I have loved you.' "

Now think about that for a minute. That's what God is going to do to the rich and the great of this world. They're going to come and humble themselves before the feet of the resurrected children of God and acknowledge that we are of God, and that they were of Satan. Now notice, here is a blessing and a promise which Christ has given: " 'Because you have kept the word of My patience [so God recognizes and understands what you do], I will also keep you from the time of temptation which is about to come upon the whole world to try those who dwell on the earth.' " A great worldwide event which is coming, which is the antichrist, and the false prophet, and the mark of the beast, and all of these things at the end time are coming. He is going to keep us and protect us. Exactly how He will do that, God knows. So what we do is leave it in His hands to show us what to do. Trust in Him to watch over us.

He says, " 'Behold, I am coming quickly; hold fast that which you have so that no one may take away your crown.'" Don't lose what you have had. Heed the warnings here. Repent of the things that are wrong. Hear, give ear to the Spirit. "'The one who has an ear, let him hear with the Spirit says to the churches. The one who overcomes [which we can, and we're victorious in Christ] will I make a pillar in the temple of My God, and he shall not go out anymore; and I will write upon him the name of My God, and the name of the city of My God, the new Jerusalem, which will come down out of heaven from My God; and *I will write upon him* My new name. The one who has an ear, let him hear with the Spirit says to the churches' " (Revelation 3:8-13).

So brethren, in our walk with God as we are coming closer, and closer, and closer to the end, as we are reaching that time when the kingdom of God is going to come on this earth, when we're reaching the time when we're going to graduate from this physical life and enter into the grave, and await the Resurrection, we need to heed the warnings and teachings of God and just ask God to be with His people, to forgive them, to heal them, to raise them up, and to help us all love God with all our hearts, and minds, and soul, and being.

End of Sermon

Transcriber: Michael Schwartz

Chapter Twenty-one

"To Walk in the Way of the Lord"
Pentecost—Day 49 – June 3, 2006
Scriptural References

1) Leviticus 23:9-11, 15-16
2) Deuteronomy 2:7
3) Leviticus 26:2,11-13
4) Deuteronomy 8:1-3
5) II John 4-6
6) II Corinthians 6:14-18
7) Psalm 86:11-17
8) Psalm 119:1-3
9) Psalm 138:1-2, 6-8
10) Revelation 1:8-12, 17-20
11) Revelation 2:1-4
12) Mark 12:28-31
13) Revelation 2:5
14) Revelation 2:7
15) Revelation 2:8-9

16) Revelation 2:12-14
17) Hebrews 4:12
18) Revelation 2:14-16
19) Revelation 2:18-20
20) Revelation 2:21-22
21) Psalm 86:1-7
22) Revelation 2:23-25, 29
23) Revelation 3:2-6
24) Exodus 32:33
25) Colossians 2:1-7
26) I John 2:3-6
27) Colossians 2:6-8
28) Revelation 3:17-19
29) Revelation 3:8-13

CHAPTER TWENTY-TWO

Day 49

June 10, 2000

Greetings brethren. This is day 49 the day before Pentecost, the year 2000. And as you know every year we go through the holy days. And every year we learn a little bit more, and every year we try and understand some other aspects of the holy days, other aspects of God's word in relationship to it so that we can grow in grace and knowledge and understand. And so likewise with Pentecost we're going to do the same thing today, and then tomorrow.

And it seems like the time has really flown since the Passover and Feast of Unleavened Bread. As with us here, we've really been busy just trying to get everything done and get all the mailings and everything out so we can get them out to you to cover everything in a timely manner. And I hope that you've gone over the tapes that we sent out for the Seven Church Harvest, because that goes through all of the churches and shows the spiritual harvest of God, which we'll cover a little bit more tomorrow. But all of that is in preparation so that when we are preaching in season and out of season we're always relating everything to the way of God pointing to the holy days. And I'm going to have some very good information for you concerning the holy days in the near future, which is really going to be I think very, very helpful in understanding so that we will be able to have greater confidence in the holy days of God, greater confidence in God's way, greater confidence in what God is doing. And that all adds to faith. That adds to love. That adds to hope, and then gives us a greater understanding, and that's what God wants us to have.

So as we always do for the holy days, let's begin in Leviticus 23 and continue the story and the flow of the holy days through the year as we are coming up to Pentecost. Now we know that this began with the wave sheaf offering day, and I hope you went over that tape that we did for the wave sheaf offering day because that is very significant. As a matter of fact that is the whole key for everything coming down to Pentecost.

Now let's begin here in Leviticus 23:9. "And the LORD spake unto Moses, saying, Speak unto the children of Israel, and say unto them, When ye be come into the land…" So now Pentecost with the grain harvest and everything, was not to happen until they came into the land because as long as they were in the wilderness they didn't have any grain, they had manna, and that was their food. And I'm sure that Pentecost was kept because as we'll see, the Ten Commandments were given on Pentecost, and so Pentecost was kept even though they did not have the grain. But when they got into the land we'll see what happened, what they did according to God's instruction here. "…When ye be come into the land which I give unto you, and shall reap the harvest thereof, then ye shall bring a sheaf of the firstfruits of your harvest unto the priest: And he shall wave the sheaf before the LORD, to be accepted for you: on the morrow after the sabbath the priest shall wave it" (Lev. 23:9-11). Now this was the very first of the firstfruits, and that's what Christ is called. He is called the first of the firstfruits.

Now let me read to you out of the Schocken Bible because he gives a little bit different description of it, which I think points more toward the resurrection than just the wave sheaf offering as we have it translated in the King James Version.

337

Verse 10, "Speak to the Children of Israel and say to them: When you enter the land that I am giving you, and you harvest its harvest, you are to bring the premier sheaf…" Now the premier means the most important. "…The premier sheaf of your harvest to the priest. He is to elevate the sheaf before the presence of [The LORD] YHWH, for acceptance for you" (Lev. 23:10-11, Schocken).

Now since Christ was the firstfruit, Christ was the firstborn, the premier one is this. Hold your place there in Leviticus 23 and let's go to Romans 8 and let's see where we have a fulfillment of this in describing Christ. And also it includes us because you see, Christ had to be first because as Paul said if Christ be not raised then you are dead in your sins, and your faith is empty and vain. So here in Romans 8 we have the fulfillment now of the firstfruits and also the firstborn. So remember the firstfruits and the firstborn are very connected in the plan of God.

Now we have it right here. Let's pick it up in Romans 8:28. "And we know that all things work together for good to those who love God, to those who are the called according to *His* purpose." And brethren I've seen that through the years over and over and over again. Everything works to good but we have to let it exercise us so we can understand how it is good for us, and the trials and difficulties that we go through. But when you take a long perspective of it and you take and look back through the years you see how that everything works for good. God designed it that way. God is involved in our lives. God has called us. God has given us of His Spirit. God is leading us and guiding us and bringing us to His Kingdom. So when we understand that everything Christ went through, and that all worked for good.

Now let's come here to Romans 8:29. "Because those whom He did foreknow, [and He's foreknown us] He also predestinated, *to be* conformed to the image of His own Son, that He [that is His Son] might be *the* firstborn among many brethren."

So what we have in the harvest of the firstfruits, let's go back to Leviticus 23 now, you have this: you have the premier sheaf, which is cut first. No other grain was to be harvested. No other things were to be eaten until that was cut. Now when that was cut, that is signifying being cut from the earth, meaning that it is no longer earthly bound, if we could put it that way. And let's transfer that to Christ in a figure. Then the priest elevates it. And elevating is just like a resurrection. And remember there in John 20:17 when Jesus spoke to Mary Magdalene. She came to hug Him, to hold Him, and He said, "Do not touch Me, because I have not yet ascended to My Father. But go to My brethren and tell them that I am ascending to My Father and your Father, and My God and your God." And so she did. So Jesus immediately, right after that, ascended into heaven, was accepted of God the Father as the sacrifice, as the first of the firstborn, the first of the firstfruit, and that perfect sacrifice to redeem all mankind. So that was the start. So the wave sheaf offering day is a very important and key thing.

Now let's continue on here. "He is to elevate…" Now Leviticus 23:11, I'm still reading from the Schocken Bible. "He is to elevate the sheaf before the presence of [the LORD] YHWH, for acceptance for you; on the morrow of the Sabbath…" Now that means on the morrow after the Sabbath. "…The priest is to elevate it." This is the regular weekly Sabbath during the Feast of Unleavened Bread.

Now when Passover falls on a Friday night and then Sabbath day is the Passover day, then that day becomes the Sabbath of the Unleavened Bread because the Passover is also an unleavened bread day. So therefore the first day right after that becomes the wave sheaf offering day. Now this year we didn't have that. This year we had the Passover in the middle of the week. We had the three days and three nights in the tomb, we had the resurrection at the end of the Sabbath. Then we have Christ ascending on the wave sheaf offering day on the morrow after the Sabbath to be accepted for us, when He was accepted.

Now then, let's continue on, I'll read out of the King James. And it says, "And ye shall offer that day when ye wave the sheaf an he lamb without blemish of the first year for a burnt offering unto the LORD (Lev. 23:12)." This was also a type of Christ. "And the [meal] meat offering thereof *shall be* two tenth deals of fine flour mingled with oil, an offering made by fire unto the LORD *for* a sweet savour: and the drink offering thereof *shall be* of wine, the fourth *part* of an hin. And ye shall eat neither bread, nor parched corn, nor green ears, until the selfsame day that ye have brought an offering unto your God..." (Lev. 23:13-14). So here's what we have. After they entered into the land, and after they had the very first wave sheaf offering, from that time on then they could eat the old corn and the new corn. Of course then every year coming up to that time then they could always eat the old corn coming up to the time of the wave sheaf offering day but they couldn't eat any of the new corn, or that is the new grain. They couldn't take it and dry it and parch it like it says here. "And ye shall eat neither bread, nor parched corn, nor green ears, until the selfsame day that ye have brought an offering unto your God: *it shall be* a statute forever throughout your generations in all your dwellings" (Lev. 23:14).

Now hold your place here and let's go to Joshua 5, and let's see how it was fulfilled when they came into the land. Now this becomes very important and this is one of those weeks where the weekly Sabbath was the Passover day. So therefore the first day of the Feast of Unleavened Bread being the first day of the week after the Passover Sabbath, became the wave sheaf offering day. Now let's read it here.

Joshua 5:10, "And the children of Israel encamped in Gilgal, and kept the Passover on the fourteenth day of the month at even in the plains of Jericho. And they did eat of the old corn of the land on the morrow after the passover, unleavened cakes, and parched *corn* in the selfsame day" (Josh. 5:10-11). So the morrow after the Passover was the 15th. And that was the wave sheaf offering in that day, that year rather, when they entered into the promised land, so therefore they could eat of the old corn, which was the harvest that they got from conquering on the east side of the Jordan. So they had stores of grain, they had the new harvest already planted and grown ready to harvest. So what they did, they took a premier sheaf right from the harvest that had been planted. The priest waved it before God, elevated it, and it was accepted on the morrow after the Sabbath, and the Sabbath being the Passover day, and that's why this took place. Now notice they also ate unleavened bread with it.

Now let's read verse 12. "And the manna ceased on the morrow after they had eaten of the old corn of the land; neither had the children of Israel manna any more; but they did eat of the fruit of the land of Canaan that year." So there it was fulfilled. There was the command that God gave, and we saw it fulfilled.

Now let's come back to Leviticus 23 and again I'm going to read from the Schocken version of the Bible. And this tells us then how we are to count because counting is very important and there's still some people who believe in a Monday Pentecost. Well, unfortunately there's no such thing as a Monday Pentecost. Has never been and can't be, especially when you understand the counting.

Now let me read from the Schocken Bible beginning in verse 15. "Now you are to number for yourselves, from the morrow [and that means beginning with the morrow] of the Sabbath..." Now the reason that is is because you have to count that first day because Christ was accepted on that day. He ascended to the Father, and His ascension made Him accepted as the sacrifice for our sins. So that day must be counted. "...From the morrow of the Sabbath, from the day that you bring the elevated sheaf, seven Sabbaths-of-days, whole (weeks) are they to be; until the morrow of the seventh Sabbath you are to number—fifty days, then you are to bring-near a grain-gift of new-crops to [the LORD] YHWH. From your settlements you are to bring bread as an elevation-offering, two (loaves of) two tenth-measures of flour are they to be, leavened you are to bake them, as firstfruits to [the LORD] YHWH" (Lev. 23:15-17, Schocken).

Now let's go back and analyze these two verses just a little bit more. First thing, number 1. You are to number beginning with the morrow after the Sabbath. From the day, that means including the day, that you bring the wave sheaf offering day. So that's number 2. Number 3, you are to have seven Sabbaths of days. That means seven Sabbaths. Number 4, whole weeks are they to be. Now this is very easy to figure out once you understand. You start day one, which is the wave sheaf offering day, which is on a Sunday. Seven days you come to Sabbath. So then you count seven Sabbaths, 1, 2, 3, 4, 5, 6, 7. That gives you 49 days. Then until the morrow of the seventh Sabbath you are to number 50 days. Now if you went to Monday you would actually be numbering 51 days. So this is 50 days.

Now, on the morrow of the seventh Sabbath you are to number 50 days, ok so that's number 5 to the morrow of the seventh Sabbath, number 50 days, number 6. Number 7 then you are to bring a grain offering of the new crop to the LORD, that's number 7. So you've got those seven steps that you are to do.

Now then this offering which was to come, was the only meal offering, or bread offering where God required that leaven be put in it. Leaven was never in any of the other offerings except peace offerings. They were always unleavened. Now there's a reason for them being leavened and I'll let you come back tomorrow and find out what that reason is. I'll sort of leave you in suspended animation here. However, there's a distinct purpose in it. Now, just understand this: during the Feast of Unleavened Bread leaven is a picture of sin. On Pentecost leaven here pictures something entirely different. Now I used to say that it was that God accepted us even though we have the law of sin and death in us, which is a true statement. But I'll cover a little bit more of that tomorrow so we'll understand more about that.

Now, let's come on here and read some more, verse 18. "And you are to bring-near along with the bread seven sheep, wholly-sound, a year old…" Isn't that interesting? What is the Church called? The Church is called the flock of God. Sheep are of the flock. Is it interesting that we have seven sheep. Are those a type of the seven churches in Revelation that we've covered already? Could very well be. "…And one bull, a young of the herd, and rams, two, they shall be an offering-up for [the LORD] YHWH…" And so exactly what all of these picture other than whole burnt offerings, complete dedication to God, that's what that shows. "…With their grain-gift and their poured-offerings, a fire-offering of soothing savor to [the LORD] YHWH. And you are to perform-as-sacrifice: one hairy goat for a [atonement] *hattat*, and two sheep, a year old, for a slaughter-offering of [a peace offering] *shalom* [and that is so you can have peace with God, sit down and eat with Him, as it were]. The priest is to elevate them, together with the bread of the firstfruits as an elevation-offering before the presence of [the LORD] YHWH, together with the two sheep; they shall be a holy-portion for [the LORD] YHWH, for the priest. And you are to make-proclamation on that same day…" (Lev. 23:18-20). Now you see you have the 50 days, you have the same day. We don't go to the 51st day.

Now tomorrow we will see, when we come to Acts 2, what it's talking about there, the very first verse talking about Pentecost means from the Greek, and I have written a booklet on it and we also have two other booklets on counting Pentecost, so if you don't have those be sure and write for them. But the one is "The True Meaning of Acts 2:1". And the Greek there has a very special construction which is called an articular present tense infinitive, meaning that when the day of Pentecost was being fulfilled, or when the 50th day was being fulfilled, or accomplished, or being completed, not yet finished. So that shows that you cannot move over to the 51st day. They didn't wait until the day there…till the day after the 50th day, they did it on that day.

Now then let's look at some other things concerning Pentecost and how those fit in to the meaning of it. Now let's come back here to Exodus 19:1. Now we also have a tape that we put out with a chart, and it's called "From Egypt to Sinai". And it took the children of Israel seven weeks to get from Egypt to Sinai. Not quite. Seven weeks less three days.

Let's pick it up here in verse 1, "In the third month, when the children of Israel were gone forth out of the land of Egypt, the same day…" Now this particular phrase means the same day of the week. Now the Passover that Israel had in Egypt was in the middle of the week, on a Wednesday. So Tuesday night is when they ate the passover. Tuesday night is when the firstborn were killed, the death of the firstborn. And then Wednesday morning, our time, then they got up and they gathered all the spoil of the Egyptians and assembled at Rameses and then that Wednesday night beginning the first day of the Feast of Unleavened Bread, the night much to be observed, 430 years after the promise given to Abraham, they departed from Rameses. That is the same day of the week that they came into the wilderness of Sinai.

Now let's notice what happened, verse 3. "And Moses went up unto God, and the LORD called unto him out of the mountain, saying, Thus shalt thou say to the house of Jacob, and tell the children of Israel; Ye have seen what I did unto the Egyptians, and *how* I bare you on eagles' wings, and brought you unto Myself. Now therefore, if ye will obey My voice indeed…" And brethren I want to emphasize this again over and over and over again. The whole key is to obey the voice of God. Now remember in Deuteronomy 8:3 it says, "…Man doth not live by bread only but by every *word* that proceedeth out of the mouth of the LORD doth man live." And here we have all the words that God has for us that He spoke or inspired, one of the two, and it's out of the mouth of the LORD. It's the key thing. Same thing you find with Abraham. Same thing you find with all of those who were the prophets of God. They obeyed the voice of God.

Now notice, "…and keep My covenant…" So not only do you have to obey the voice but you have to keep the covenant. That's for us today too in the same way. "…Then ye shall be a peculiar treasure unto Me above all people: for all the earth *is* mine: And ye shall be unto Me a kingdom of priests, and an holy nation. These *are* the words which thou shalt speak unto the children of Israel" (Ex. 19:3-6).

"And Moses came and called for the elders of the people, and laid before their faces all these words which the LORD commanded him. And all the people answered together, and said, All that the LORD hath spoken we will do." So they came and told the elders, the elders went and told the people. The people said yes, we'll do it. The elders came back and told Moses, yes we'll do it. "And Moses returned the words of the people unto the LORD" (Ex. 19:7-8).

Now how was Israel going to be a peculiar nation, a kingdom of priests? Let's go to Deuteronomy 4. We'll come right back here again and we'll finish this. Let's go to Deuteronomy 4 and see what they were supposed to do. Let's pick it up here in verse 1. Again we have the same thing all the way through the Bible, obeying the voice of God.

"Now therefore hearken, O Israel, unto the statutes and unto the judgments, which I teach you, for to do *them*, that ye may live, and go in and possess the land which the LORD God of your fathers giveth you. Ye shall not add unto the word which I command you, neither shall ye diminish *ought* from it, that ye may keep the commandments of the LORD your God which I command you." Now just to make a point, and we covered this on the "Seven Church Harvest" tape #3, concerning Baalim. "Your eyes have seen what the LORD did because of Baal-peor…" That's what the Moabites came in and enticed the Israelites to come and do sacrifice to their gods. And that was under the instruction of Baalim to Balak to do so. "…For all the men that followed Baal-peor, the LORD thy God hath destroyed them from among you." So He wants you to learn. Don't go do what the others did. Don't go out and bring something from the world and bring it in and try and make it a part of God's way. The same thing applies today. We're not to do that. "But ye that did cleave unto the LORD your God *are* alive every one of you this day. Behold I have taught you statutes and judgments, even as the LORD my God commanded me, that ye should do so in the land whither ye go to possess it" (Deut. 4:1-5).

Now here's how they were to be a kingdom of priests and a holy nation. "Keep therefore and do *them*; [that is all the commandments, statutes, and judgments of God] for this *is* your wisdom and your understanding in the sight of the nations, which shall hear all theses statutes, and say, Surely this great nation *is* a wise and understanding people. For what nation *is there so* great, who *hath* God *so* nigh unto them, as the LORD our God *is* in all *things that* we call upon Him *for*? And what nation *is there so* great, that hath statutes and judgments *so* righteous as all this law, which I set before you this day?" (vs. 6-8). Now brethren that's why no one can improve upon God's way.

Now if the word of God needs to be changed God will change it. And He did so in the New Covenant when Christ made all the laws more spiritually binding, raised them to a higher level of obedience than we've had in the past. And we need to understand this concerning law-keeping and grace. Under the New Covenant, because we have the laws of God written in our heart and in our mind through the power of God's Holy Spirit, and we stand in the grace of God when we keep the commandments today, we are doing so as an operation of grace because we do it from the heart filled with the Holy Spirit. Now that's something you need to understand because a lot of Protestants will tell you that what you do is to keep the law and the law is against grace. No such thing. The law is there to show us, to teach us, to lead us, to guide us. And if we sin the law is there to convict us of sin. And when we repent through the operation of grace then we're restored to God.

Now for the children of Israel, they were to do this for the whole world, and needless to say, they failed. But God said never the less, that's what He wanted. Now let's come back here to Exodus 19 and continue on with the rest of the account leading up to the day of Pentecost when the Ten Commandments were given. And that's something very important to really understand.

Now verse 10, "And the LORD said unto Moses, Go unto the people, and sanctify them to day and to morrow, and let them wash their clothes, and be ready against the third day…" (vs. 10-11). So you have Friday, Sabbath, and Sunday. Sunday is the third day. So what did they do? They washed their clothes on Friday and got all prepared. They kept the Sabbath because that sanctified them. And then God came down the third day and brought the Ten Commandments.

Now let's see how that went, ok. Verse 14, "And Moses went down from the mount unto the people, and sanctified the people; and they washed their clothes. And he said unto the people Be ready against the third day: come not at *your* wives. And it came to pass on the third day in the morning…" (vs. 15-16). Now we're going to see there are parallels between this and Acts 2 when we come to Acts 2 tomorrow, because it was in the morning that the events took place in Acts 2. Same way here.

Now how's this to wake up? How'd you like to wake up to this? "…There were thunders and lighnings, and a thick cloud upon the mount, and the voice of the trumpet…" Now there's something to understand. The trumpet is always blown on every holy day. The Feast of Trumpets is a memorial of blowing of trumpets all day long. That's why it's called the Feast of Trumpets. "…Exceeding loud [here it is the trumpet]; so that all the people that *was* in the camp trembled. And Moses brought forth the people out of the camp to meet with God [what an absolutely awesome thing that must have been]; and they stood at the nether part of the mount [that is beneath the mountain]. And mount Sinai was altogether on a smoke, because the LORD descended upon it in fire: and the smoke thereof ascended as the smoke of a furnace, and the whole mount quaked greatly" (vs. 16-18).

So here imagine this whole thing just all of the sound of the thunder and the lightning, and it's recorded back in Hebrews 12, and the wind that was with it, and the earth quaking. And if there's one thing that really puts fear into people, that's to have the ground beneath them shaking. And that's exactly what was happening here. Now we live in California, we know what that's like. Those of you back in the midwest and east you have tornadoes. You know what that's like, you can get afraid of that. So it's the same thing.

"And when the voice of the trumpet sounded long, and waxed louder and louder, Moses spake, and God answered him by a voice. And the LORD came down upon mount Sinai, and on the top of the mount: and the LORD called Moses *up* to the top of the mount; and Moses went up. And the LORD said unto Moses, Go down, charge the people, lest they break through unto the LORD to gaze, and many of them perish" (vs. 19-21). Because you see you can't look upon the glorified form of God as a physical human being and live. That's what God told Moses when he said, "I beseech thee, shew me thy glory" (Ex. 34:20). He said, "Thou canst not see my face: for there shall no man see me, and live" (Ex. 34:20). Because God in His glory living eternally in spiritually, you see, has that power just radiating from His very body. And so this is what happened here. So He says, "...to gaze, and many of them perish" (vs. 21).

"And let the priests also, which come near to the LORD, sanctify themselves, lest the LORD break forth upon them. And Moses said unto the LORD, the people cannot come up to mount Sinai: for Thou chargedst us, saying, Set bounds about the mount, and sanctify it. And the LORD said unto him, Away, get thee down, and thou shalt come up, thou, and Aaron with thee: but let not the priests and the people break through to come up unto the LORD, lest He break forth upon them. So Moses went down unto the people, and spake unto them" (vs. 22-25).

Now then God gave the Ten Commandments. You know what they are, we've gone over these many, many, many times. But let's understand something very important here in relationship to Pentecost and the Sabbath. God gave the Ten Commandments on the day of Pentecost, which is a holy day. God pronounced that the Sabbath was to be remembered and to be kept so there is no excuse by any Sunday-keeper to claim because the New Testament church began on Pentecost that therefore the first day of the week is the day that God wanted to keep instead of the seventh day. Not so. If you accept Pentecost, you accept the commandments of God, you accept the Sabbath of God, you accept the words of God. Now God spoke all those words.

Now it was too much for the people to bear. Exodus 20:18, "And all the people saw the thunderings, and the lightnings, and the noise of the trumpet, and the mountain smoking: and when the people saw *it*, they removed, and stood afar off. And they said unto Moses, Speak thou with us, and we will hear: but let not God speak with us, lest we die: (Ex. 20:18-19). And of course then what did that do? That gave them one person removed from God, and so then they could say, "Well Moses said" instead of "God said". So remember this, everything Moses said was what God said he was to say. So this was a carnal excuse showing that the carnal mind is not subject to the law of God neither indeed can be and that it cannot hear the laws of God. That's the whole lesson here with this. And that's why when you go to Deuteronomy 18, that's why God said he would send Jesus Christ to come in the flesh, to speak to them as a man rather than speak to them as God. To speak to them with words that they could hear and understand rather than speaking with such great power and force that you are so afraid that there was hardly anything you could remember. And yet they rejected Christ. That's the way that the carnal mind is.

Now let's continue on here. Let's see some things which are important concerning this. Now then, Moses went back up on the mount. God gave him all the statutes and judgments. Let's come over here to Exodus 23. Let's understand something that's very important. On the very day that God gave the Ten Commandments He also gave the holy days. Do you realize that? Let's read it.

Exodus 23:12, He reiterates the Sabbath. "Six days thou shalt do thy work, and on the seventh day thou shalt rest: that thine ox and thine ass may rest, and the son of thy handmaid, and the stranger, may be refreshed. And in all *things* that I have said unto you be circumspect: and make no mention of the name of other gods, neither let it be heard out of thy mouth" (Ex. 23:12-17).

This precludes anything concerning Christmas and Easter and New Years, and any of the pagan holidays that any of the nations had, and they go right back to the very same thing that we see in the world today. God said don't even mention it. That is in the way that that is something that you would do. And yet look what happened to the Worldwide Church of God—totally taken down, totally subverted, totally back into the world, have forgotten the words of God, have forgotten the commandments of God, have had every lying excuse under the sun to get rid of the Sabbath, to get rid of the holy days, and to embrace Sunday, and Christmas, and Easter, and all of that. So you see, now you understand why God puts these warnings in here, over and over, and over, and over, and over again. Perhaps taking up as much as one third of the whole Bible to tell you to beware to don't do the things that the pagans do. And yet some people never get it. They never get it.

Now notice, verse 14. "Three times thou shalt keep a feast unto me in the year. Thou shalt keep the feast of unleavened bread: (thou shalt eat unleavened bread seven days, as I commanded thee, in the time appointed of the month Abib; for in it thou camest out from Egypt: and none shall appear before me empty:) And the feast of harvest, the firstfruits [which is Pentecost, which we will keep tomorrow] of thy labours, which thou hast sown in the field: and the feast of ingathering, *which is* in the end of the year [now that means the end of the harvest season], when thou hast gathered in thy labours out of the field. Three times in the year all thy males shall appear before the Lord GOD" (vs. 14-17). So there it is right there. On the same day that God gave the Ten Commandments with the Sabbath; He also gave the holy days.

Now then let's understand something important. If you accept one then you have to accept all because if you do not accept all, what are you doing? You are diminishing from it. And when you diminish from it what is the natural proclivity to do but to add to it. And that's what the children of Israel did. That's their whole history.

Now let's come back here, continue on. Chapter 24 is where the covenant was made. Here is where the marriage covenant between the Lord GOD Who became Jesus Christ for the New Testament is to be found. This is the marriage covenant between the Lord GOD and Israel that took place. The Old Covenant was a marriage covenant. Now let's see that beginning here in verse 1.

"And he said unto Moses, Come up unto the LORD, thou, and Aaron, Nadab, and Abihu, and seventy of the elders of Israel; and worship ye afar off." And we will see why all of them came up. "And Moses alone shall come near the LORD: but they shall not come nigh; neither shall the people go up with him. And Moses came and told the people all the words of the LORD, and all the judgments: and all the people answered with one voice, and said, All the words which the LORD hath said will we do" (Ex. 24:1-3).

Now when there is a marriage you ask, "According to the covenant do you accept? Do you promise to love and obey [for the wife] to submit to your husband in all things as unto the LORD, whether in sickness or in health, whether in want or in wealth?" Now it's the same way with the man. "Do you promise and covenant with God to faithfully love your wife, to cleave to her, to cherish her, to honor her, to provide for her?" And he says, "Yes I do." That then is a marriage covenant. That's what this is. These words are the words which God said, "that ye should be mine" (Lev. 20:26).

Now verse 4, "And Moses wrote all the words of the LORD…" God always has His covenants written down. That is the record (That's why we have the new Covenant written down. That is the record.). "…And rose up early in the morning, and builded an altar under the hill, and twelve pillars, according to the twelve tribes of Israel. And he sent young men of the children of Israel, which offered burnt offerings, and sacrificed peace offerings of oxen unto the LORD" (Ex. 20: 4-5). Now the reason he took young men, now these may have been Levites, but the Levitical priesthood was not yet consecrated. So therefore he took the young men, and I'm sure they were Levites.

Next notice what happens because there is no covenant that is made without blood. And without the shedding of blood there is no covenant. "And Moses took half of the blood, and put *it* in basins; and half of the blood he sprinkled on the altar." So he put it in basins. He put two basins, half in one basin, half in another basin. He sprinkled half of it on the altar. "And he took the book of the covenant, and read in the audience of the people: and they said, All that the LORD hath said will we do, and be obedient. And Moses took the blood, and sprinkled *it* on the people, and said, Behold the blood of the covenant, which the LORD hath made with you concerning all these words" (Ex. 20:4-18).

Now I want you to notice that this covenant was made on the day after Pentecost. And we will see tomorrow that, that is significant in relationship to the eternal covenant that God is going to make with the Church when the Church is resurrected.

Now let's continue on here in verse 9. "Then went up Moses, and Aaron, Nadab, and Abihu and seventy of the elders of Israel: and they saw the God of Israel: and *there was* under His feet as it were a paved work of a sapphire stone, and as it were the body of heaven in *his* clearness" (vs. 9-10). This is called in the New Testament the sea of glass. And so whenever God comes down and is in a particular place, if He's there for any length of time then there is the sea of glass. Now this sea of glass was also so that the people could not see up in toward God. But the elders who were right up close could see up into it, but the people couldn't. Now this was to establish the fact for all the people who the seventy elders represented that they saw God and that this covenant was sure and that it was true.

Now let's also notice something else that took place. Verse 11, "And upon the nobles of the children of Israel he laid not his hand: also they saw God, and did eat and drink." Now what did they have? They had a wedding feast. And in this particular case, since God was dealing with carnal human beings He could not come down and eat with them directly. This wedding feast then had the representatives of Israel being the seventy elders, and the representatives of the priesthood being Aaron, Nadab, and Abihu, and the representative of the high priest being Moses, who was a type of Christ. He was the One Who went to the Father. He was the One now in this case, Who became Jesus Christ.

Now verse 12, "And the LORD said unto Moses, Come up to me into the mount, and be there: and I will give thee tables of stone, and a law, and commandments which I have written; that thou mayest teach them. And Moses rose up, and his minister Joshua: and Moses went up into the mount of God. And he said unto the elders, Tarry ye here for us, until we come again unto you: and, behold, Aaron and Hur *are* with you: if any man have any matters to do, let him come unto them. And Moses went up into the mount, and a cloud covered the mount. And the glory of the LORD abode upon mount Sinai, and the cloud covered it six days: and the seventh day he called unto Moses out of the midst of the cloud" (vs. 12-16). So Moses had to wait seven days. I'm sure after Nadab, Abihu, and Aaron and the seventy of elders had finished eating, they went back down to be with the rest of the children of Israel. Moses went up into the mount.

"And the sight of the glory of the LORD *was* like devouring fire on the top of the mount in the eyes of the children of Israel. And Moses went into the midst of the cloud, and gat him up into the mount: and Moses was in the mount forty days and forty nights" (vs. 17-18). Well we won't get into much of the rest of the story that took place there lest we get away from understanding about the day of Pentecost. And I'm covering it in the Old Testament today on day 49 so that will lead us up to the New Testament tomorrow.

Now let's look and see that this was a marriage. Let's come to Isaiah 54. And this tells us very clearly that what happened there with the covenant that was made. It was a marriage covenant on the day after Pentecost with the blood of the covenant that was sprinkled on the people, that was sprinkled on the altar. And Moses read all the words that God commanded them to do. And they said, "Yes we will do that."

Now here Isaiah 54 we find where it talks about Israel being the wife of the LORD. Let's pick it up here Isaiah 54:5. "For thy Maker *is* thine husband…" Now this not only is talking about Israel, because Israel was married to God, but in this particular case this is also a prophecy of the New Testament Church. "…The LORD of hosts *is* His name; and thy Redeemer the Holy One of Israel; The God of the whole earth shall he be called. For the LORD hath called thee as a woman forsaken and grieved in spirit [that is while they were down in Egypt], and a wife of youth, when thou wast refused, saith thy God" (Isa. 54:5-6). So Israel refused even though they said yes, their whole action said we refuse. That's why God had to divorce them. That's why God had to put them away. That's why God had to leave them and forsake them because they left God and forsook God for other gods and broke the covenant. Now brethren we need to understand that concerning the covenant with Jesus Christ because it is His body which is broken for us. And it is His blood which is shed for us, and that is the blood of the New Covenant.

Now let's understand the children of Israel, they broke the covenant. They were punished for it. But if we break the covenant, the covenant with Christ, the covenant unto eternal life then we have nothing to look forward to but eternal death. Because you either will love God and keep His commandments, accept Jesus Christ, or you will be in the lake of fire. Now some people may even get mad at me for saying that. But let's understand something. When I bring the series in Hebrews you're going to understand that's exactly what Hebrews says. You either follow Christ, obey Him, love God the Father, keep all of His commandments, or you have the lake of fire to look forward to. Under Moses they were stoned. But when you do despite to the Spirit of grace you are cast into the lake of fire and you are eternally dead. There's no resurrection from that.

Now let's come to the New Testament. Let's come here to Matthew 13. Now Matthew is a very important chapter because this shows that what Christ was working out from the time He came until the end of the age is likened unto a harvest. That's why Pentecost is the harvest of the firstfruits beginning with the first one, the wave sheaf offering or the premier sheaf was accepted of God. Christ was the first. The rest of it is what He is doing. It is a harvest. It is a planting. And that's what God is doing.

Now we need to understand these parables here. Let's just begin in verse 18. Don't have enough time to read through it all. Let's begin in verse 18 showing the harvest. "Hear ye therefore the parable of the sower:" Now the sower was Christ. "When any one hears the word of the kingdom, and does not understand *it*, the wicked *one* comes and snatches away that which was sown in his heart." Now that is something we need to understand. Brethren, don't let Satan come and take that away which was sown in your heart. Now we have seen some where that has happened to, and I'm afraid that there are going to be great problems. "This is the one who was sown by the way. Now the one who was sown upon the rocky places is the one who hears the word and immediately receives it with joy; but because he has no root in himself, he does not endure; for when tribulation or persecution arises because of the word, he is quickly offended" (Matt. 13:18-21). Now we can't let that happen to us either. And we've also seen that take place haven't we? That's why all things work together for good for those who love God and are called according to His purpose. [But not for those who reject God's Way and Will.]

Verse 22, "And the one who was sown…" So this is a planting. We'll see when the harvest takes place, because there's another aspect of it that we have to understand here. "… Among the thorns is the one who hears the word, but the cares of this life, and the deceitful-ness of riches, choke the word, and it becomes unfruitful."

Now then, remember the parable of the rich man who came to Christ and said "Good Master, what good *thing* shall I do, that I may have eternal life?" And He said, "…Keep the commandments." And he said, "Which?" So He listed off all the commandments having to do with loving your neighbor. Of course they were living in a land where they were keeping the Sabbath. That was not the issue. They were keeping the holy days. That was not the issue. They had the right God. That was not the issue. They had no idols there. That was not the issue. So that's why Jesus didn't mention the first four commandments in that account in Matthew 19:16-23.

Now let's come back here to Matthew 13. "But the one who was sown on good ground…" as compared to the others and the rich man, you know, he went away very sorrowful because he had many riches. Typical example of the one where the seed is sown among the thorns and the weeds, the cares of the world, the deceitfulness of riches. "But the one who was sown on good ground, this is the one who hears the word and understands, who indeed brings forth fruit and produces—one an hundredfold, another sixtyfold *and* another thirtyfold" (Matt. 13:22-27).

So then He gave another parable and saying, "…The kingdom of heaven is compared to a man who was sowing good seed in his field; But while men were sleeping, his enemy came and sowed tares among the wheat, and went away." Then the tares and the wheat grew up together. "And the servants came to the master of the house *and* said to him, 'Sir, did you not sow good seed in your field? Then where did these tares come from?' " (Matt. 13:27).

Well you see, we've seen the same thing too. We've lived through that haven't we? The enemy, Satan the devil, infiltrates the Church and what do we have? We have tares. We have false doctrine. Right alongside those who are producing the good.

So Christ said, "No, don't tear them up. But you wait until the harvest." And Pente-cost is the harvest. Let's see that. Let's pick it up in verse 37. "He answered and said unto them, He that soweth the good seed is the Son of man; and the field is the world; and the good seed, these are the children of the kingdom; but the tares are the children of the wicked *one*" (vs. 37-38). And as we find in 1 John, they are the ones who are practicing lawless-ness. And I'm going to have a lot to say about the mystery of lawlessness as we go down here in the next few weeks, or maybe even before Pentecost. I'll just see how it works out. But I tell you that is something, the mystery of lawlessness, or the mystery of iniquity is really an awesome thing indeed.

"Now the enemy who sowed them is the devil; and the harvest is *the* end of the age, and the reapers are the angels." Now we'll see this takes place concerning the resurrection. "Therefore, as the tares are gathered and consumed in the fire, so shall it be in the end of this age" (vs. 39-40). Now we're going to see when this age ends.

Ok, let's continue on here in Matthew 13. Now verse 41, "The Son of man shall send forth His angels, and they shall gather out of His kingdom all the offenders, and those who are practicing lawlessness; And they shall cast them into the furnace of fire; there shall be weeping and gnashing of teeth. Then shall the righteous shine forth as the sun in the kingdom of their Father. The one who hath ears to hear, let him hear" (vs. 41-43). And we'll see that's very important when we come to the harvest that God has.

Now then there are seven weeks to the harvest. This Sabbath ended the seventh week to the harvest. Then there was the 50th day offering that took place. Now let's come here to Revelation 2 and 3, which we've already covered, but I just want to cover it very quickly. Well, we won't go to Revelation 2 and 3, you've already had that. We have seven churches and I think that the seven churches represent, not necessarily just in time sequence, but represent in type the seven weeks to the harvest. And that is the Church age, and that is the Church harvest. And they will be in the first resurrection. Now there will be more in the first resurrection, which we will see, and we will cover that tomorrow because there is also the 50th day harvest which then is the harvest of God. So the seven churches represent the 49 day harvest.

Now let's come back to Matthew 22 because we're going to ask the question, and we will try and answer it tomorrow, but we will ask the question: Will everyone in the first resurrection be the bride of Christ? Now we've thought in the past, yes that is so. Let's read the parable here in Matthew 22. Let's pick it up here right in verse 1. There's a lot for us to learn right here. "And again Jesus answered and spoke to them in parables, saying, The kingdom of heaven is compared to a man *who was* a king, who made a wedding feast for his son [now the king is God the Father, the son is Christ], and sent his servants [which then began with the apostles and whoever the true servants of God are] to call those who had been invited to the wedding feast; but they refused to come." Now these are the guests. "Afterwards he sent out other servants, saying, 'Say to those who have been invited, "Behold, I have prepared my dinner; my oxen and the fatted beasts are killed, and all things *are* ready. Come to the wedding feast" ' " (Matt. 22: 1-4). Of course there was going to be a marriage supper.

Now we saw there was a marriage supper with the first covenant with Moses, and Aaron, and Nadab, and Abihu, and the 70 elders of Israel. They did eat and drink. That was the marriage supper. So here's the supper all ready to go.

Verse 5, "But they they paid no attention and went away, one to his farm, and another to his buisiness. And the rest, after seizing his servants, insulted and killed *them*. Now when the king heard *it*, he became angry; and he sent his armies *and* destroyed those murderers, and burned up their city." Now this is exactly what Christ did to Jerusalem. "Then he said to his servants, 'The wedding feast is indeed ready, [so there's going to be a time when the wedding is going to be ready], but those who were invited were not worthy; Therefore, go into the well-traveled highways, and invite all that you find to the wedding feast.' And after going out into the highways, those servants brought together everyone that they found, both good and evil; and the wedding feast was filled with guests" (vs. 5-10). So there is going to be God the Father, Who is the King, going to perform the ceremony. There's going to be Christ. There is going to be the bride. There are going to be guests. And all of them will be there for this event. Now is this telling us that not everyone in the first resurrection will be part of the bride of Christ? Perhaps it is.

Now notice in this parable. "And when the king came in to see the guests, *he* noticed a man there who was not dressed in *proper* attire for *the* wedding feast; . And he said to him, 'Friend, how did you enter here without a garment *fit* for *the* wedding feast?' But he had no answer. Then the king said to the servants,'Bind his hands and feet, *and* take him away, and cast *him* into the outer darkness.' There shall be weeping and gnashing of teeth". Well in this parable it can't be shown about the resurrection because this is showing about the wedding. In other words, no one is going to get there unless they have the wedding garments. Now they won't get there because they'll have to be in the first resurrection. And if they're not in the first resurrection then they rejected the call, and they didn't do what God wanted to do, then sure enough they will be cast out into outer darkness and there will be weeping and gnashing of teeth. "For many are called, but few *are* chosen" (vs. 14).

Now let's look at the parallel account back here in Luke 14, and I think this is quite profound when we put the whole chapter of Luke 14 together and see the things as they took place. Let's begin here in verse 15. " Then one of those who sat *at the table* with *Him*, after hearing these things, said to Him, 'Blessed *is* the one who shall eat bread in the kingdom of God.' But He said to him, 'A certain man made a great supper, and invited many. And he sent his servants at supper time to say to those who had been invited, "Come, for everything is now ready." But everyone with one *consent* began to excuse himself. The first said to him, "I have bought a field, and I need to go out to see it; I beg you to have me excused." And another said, 'I have bought five pairs of oxen, and I am going to try them out; I beg you to have me excused.' And another said, 'I have married a wife, and because of this I am unable to come' " (Luke 14:15-20). Now all of these are good and valid excuses, aren't they? I mean in the modern work-a-day place that we live in today. But that has nothing to do with valid excuses for obeying God. Now you've been given the invitation. Are you going to come? Well, we'll see.

"And that servant came and reported these things to his lord. Then the master of the house was angry; *and* he said to his servant, 'Go out quickly into the streets and lanes of the city, and bring in here the poor, *the* crippled, *the* lame and *the* blind.' " And of course that's all of us because we are spiritually poor and maimed, and halt and blind. "And the servant said, 'Sir, it has been done as you commanded, and there is still room.' Then the lord said to the servant, 'Go out into the highways and hedges, and compel *them* to come in, so that my house may be filled.' " So God is going to accomplish His work. It's going to be filled. There is going to be the wedding. There will be Christ, there will be the bride, there will be the guests. "For I tell you, not one of those men who were invited shall taste of my supper" (vs. 21-24).

Now then notice, this ties in with the other parable where many are called but few are chosen, and here is why only few are chosen—because few repent. And few repent with this kind of attitude. So what you need to do when we read these scriptures, you apply them to yourself. I'll apply them to myself, because this is the qualification for the wedding invitation, right here.

Notice what Jesus said, " And great multitudes were going with Him; and He turned *and* said to them, If anyone comes to Me and does not hate his father, and mother, and wife, and children, and brothers and sisters, and, in addition, his own life also, he cannot be My disciple " (vs. 25-26). And you cannot be in the first resurrection, whether you're called to be part of the bride or whether you're called to be a guest. Have we done that? Do we continue to do that? Have we set our minds that we are going to always do that? That we will be faithful. That we will be loving. That we will be obedient to God in all circumstances, and that we have this set before us. That's all a part of counting the cost. That's what we did when we were baptized, and that's what we continually do as we go down through the walk that we have with God in walking in the truth, and walking in the light, and serving God in the way that we do.

Now notice, "And whosoever does not carry his cross [whatever the difficulty may be], and come after Me, cannot be My disciple" (vs. 27). And the Greek there is the very strongest. It means ο δυναται. That's what the Greek is, and that translated means "it is impossible to be His disciple". And if you're not His disciple, you won't be in the first resurrection and you won't be in the resurrection for guests, or as the bride either one.

Now let's carry this a little bit further. Let's come here to Hebrews 12, we'll see a parallel between Mt. Sinai and Mt. Zion in heaven above, showing what is going to happen to those who will be, in what is called the Church of the Firstborn. That is us. We are the firstfruits. Christ is the first of the firstfruits. Christ is the firstborn of the firstborn. We are going to be part of the Church of the Firstborn. Now let's read that here in Hebrews 12. And notice how it starts out here in Hebrews 12. How that it is Christ that we need to look to. And brethren we need to really understand that. We don't know what the days are going to be. We don't know what the times are going to be. We don't know exactly when these things are going to come, but I'll guarantee you according to the word of God that we are a whole lot closer to the end than when we first believed. You can guarantee that.

Now here's a whole example. Let's begin right here in Hebrews 12:1. " Therefore, *since* we are surrounded by such a great throng of witnesses, let us lay aside every weight, …" And that's what we need to do brethren. Every care, every problem, every weight, everything that is dragging us down. "…and the sin that so easily entraps *us*;…" Yes we're weak in the flesh, yes we have the law of sin and death in us, yes these things come upon us. But they can be set aside through Christ. "…*and* let us run the race set before us with endurance, …" And today too many people have slowed down to a walk. They aren't even trotting. And many of them are just sitting along the sidelines. They aren't even participating in anything. They've just given up (Heb. 12:1-6, 14-29).

Now the way that you continue in this way is this, verse 2. "Having *our minds* fixed on Jesus, the Beginner and Finisher [or the beginner and finisher] of *our* faith…" We always need to look to Christ because He's the head of the Church. He's the One Who set us an example. He is the One Who is our Savior. He is the One Who is our sacrifice. It is His blood that pays for our sins. It is His sitting at the right hand of God so that we are justified, that we have the grace of God given to us.

Now notice, "…Who for the joy that lay ahead of Him [look how He counted the trial that He went through] endured *the* cross, *although* He despised *the* shame, and has sat down at *the* right hand of the throne of God. Now meditate deeply on Him Who endured such great hostility of sinners against Himself, so that you do not become weary and faint in your minds." And I put a little note to myself in my Bible, "…and give up". Brethren we are not to give up. We are not to let these things slip away from us. We are not to let these things fall into disrepair because of neglect and disuse. No, we have to do as it says here, verse 4. "You have not yet resisted to the point of *losing* blood in your struggle against sin" No, you haven't. Yes we're going to have correction. Verse 6 says "For whom *the* Lord loves He chastens, and He severely disciplines every son whom He receives". He chastens so that we can be better, so that we can grow, so that we can bring forth more fruit.

Now let's come over here and see what all of this is going to do. Let's come over here. Let's pick it up here in verse 14. "Pursue peace with everyone, and sanctification, without which no one will see the Lord; Looking diligently, lest anyone fall from the grace of God; lest any root of bitterness springing up trouble *you*, and through this many be defiled;" People can fall from the grace of God. It is an absolute lie to say, "Once saved – always saved", that once you have been saved you have eternal security and regardless of what you do you cannot fall away. That is a blatant lie because it says right here, "...lest anyone fall from the grace of God; lest any root of bitterness springing up trouble *you*, and through this [and when that happens] many be defiled; lest *there* be any fornicator or godless person, as Esau, who for one meal sold his birthright; Because you also know how that afterwards, when he wished to inherit the blessing, he was rejected; *and* he found no room for repentance, though he sought it earnestly with tears" (vs. 14-17).

Now verse 18, now notice what Paul does here. He immediately shifts this right over into the spiritual reality of our existence in standing before Christ. "For you have not come to *the* mount that could be touched and that burned with fire, nor to gloominess, and fearful darkness, and *the* whirlwind; And to *the* sound of *the* trumpet, and to *the* voice of *the* words, which those who heard, *begged* that *the* word not be spoken *directly* to them." which we read back there in Exodus 19 and 20. Now we haven't come to that mount, no. "...which those who heard, begged that *the* word not be spoken *directly* to them. (For they could not endure what was being commanded; 'And if even an animal touches the mountain, it shall be stoned, or shot through with an arrow;' And so terrifying was the sight, *that* Moses said, 'I am greatly afraid and trembling.)" (vs. 18-21).

Now with this setting the tone, now then notice what Paul says. Heb. 12:22-23, "But you have come to Mount Sion, and to *the* city of *the* living God, heavenly Jerusalem; and to an innumerable company of angels; *To the* joyous festival gathering; and to *the* church of *the* firstborn,..." That's where we have come to. You are part of the Church of the Firstborn. You are part of that general assembly, notice, "registered *in the book of life* in heaven;..." Your name is in the book of life, and only you can take it out. "...and to God, *the* Judge of all; and to *the* spirits of the just who have been perfected..." So this is quite a thing brethren, to be counted in this group, to be of this part. To be of this harvest, to be there and be able to be on Mt. Zion with Christ. "And to Jesus *the* Mediator of *the* New Covenant; and to sprinkling of *the* blood of *ratification*, proclaiming superior things than *that* of Abel" (vs. 22-24). So I tell you it's really quite a thing.

Then he gives a warning. "Beware that you do not refuse to *hear* Him Who is speaking! For if they did not escape *judgment*, who refused *to hear* the one Who was on the earth divinely instructing *them*, how much more *severely will we be judged*, if we ourselves apostatize from Him Who speaks from heaven;" (vs. 25). I tell you that's something. The resurrection is going to be something. It is going to be a powerful thing that is going to take place.

Notice. "Whose voice then shook the earth; but now He hath promised, saying, 'Yet onc.0e more I will shake not only the earth, but heaven also." And we find back in Hagai 3, and the sea and the dry land, and all of it. So the return of Jesus Christ is going to be absolutely tremendous. "Now the *words* "once more" signify the removing of the *things* being shaken, as of things that were made, so that those *things* which cannot be shaken may remain." And that's us. "Therefore, since we are receiving a kingdom that cannot be shaken, let us have grace, through which we may serve God in a pleasing *manner* with reverence and awe; For our God *is* indeed a consuming fire." (vs. 26-29). And we are going to meet Him at the resurrection.

Now let's answer the question here concerning the guests. Let's come to Revelation 19. Now we'll sort of get over into tomorrow by going to Revelation 19 but that's ok, we'll come back for tomorrow. Now let's read it here beginning in verse 1. "And after these things [now this is after the resurrection and we'll see this is after being on the sea of glass and so forth] I heard *the* loud voice of a great multitude in heaven…" Now they're in heaven – that is the first heaven where the sea of glass is, because we meet Christ in the air. That's not in the heaven of heavens where God's throne is. That is in the heavens where those who are resurrected meet Christ in the air on the sea of glass. "…great multitude … saying, Hallelujah! The Salvation and the glory and the honour and the power *belong* to the Lord our God. For true and righteous *are* His judgments; for He has judged the great whore, who corrupted the earth with her fornication, and He has avenged the blood of His servants at her hand. And they said a second time, Hellelujah! And her smoke shall ascend upward into the ages of eternity. And the twenty-four elders and the four living creatures fell down and worshipped God, Who sits on the throne, saying, "Amen. Hallelujah!" (Rev. 19:1-4).

"For her sins have reached as far as heaven, and God has remembered her iniquities. Render to her as she has rendered to you; and give to her double, even according to her works. In the cup that she mixed, give her back double. To the degree that she glorified her-self and lived luxuriously, give to her as much torment and sorrow. For she says in her heart, 'I sit a queen enthroned, and am not a widow; and in no way shall I experience sorrow.' For this very reason, her plagues shall come in one day—death and sorrow and famine; and she shall be burned with fire; for *the* Lord God, Who executes judgment upon her, *is* powerful. Then the kings of the earth who have committed fornication with her and have lived luxuriously, will weep and lament for her, when they see the smoke of her burning." (Rev. 18:5-9). So all of those who are called to the marriage supper, all of those who are called to the wedding have a great and a fantastic blessing from God. The bride and Christ, when they are married, they will be in a special relationship forever. And we will see that tomorrow. So as Paul Harvey says, tune in for the rest of the story.

End of Sermon

Transcriber: Carolyn Singer

Day 49
June 10, 2000
Scriptural References

1) Leviticus 23:9-11

2) Romans 8:28-29

3) John 20:17

4) Leviticus 23:12-14

5) Joshua 5:10-11

6) Leviticus 23:15-20

7) Exodus 19:1, 3-8

8) Deuteronomy 4:1-8

9) Exodus 19:10-21

10) Exodus 34:20-25

11) Exodus 20:18

12) Exodus 23:12-17

13) Exodus 24:1-3

14) Leviticus 20:26

15) Exodus 20:4-8, 9-18

16) Isaiah 54:5-6

17) Matthew 13:18-22

18) Matthew 19:16-23

19) Matthew 13:22-27, 37-43

20) Matthew 22:1-14

21) Luke 14:15-27

22) Hebrews 12:1-6, 14-29

23) Revelation 19:1-4

Section VI

Pentecost

CHAPTER TWENTY-THREE

Pentecost—Holy Day

June 4, 2006

And greetings brethren, welcome to the Feast of Pentecost–2006. And this is really quite a tremendous and wonderful day when we understand the full significance of it and what it means to us, because this is the day that all true Christians are looking for, as we will see. This day is the harvest of the firstfruits. And the firstfruits then are those in the first resurrection.

Now let's come back to Leviticus 23 and we're going to see that on the fiftieth day it tells us what they were to bring. So there were special offerings that they were to bring. One has significance for the prophetic meaning of Pentecost, and the other has to do with the offerings that we are to take, because in Deuteronomy 16 it says that when we have Pentecost, also called the Feast of Weeks after you count out seven weeks and you're to have the Feast of Weeks, which then is the fiftieth day as Leviticus 23 points out. And it says here verse 17: "Ye shall bring out of your habitations two wave loaves of two tenth deals: they shall be of fine flour; they shall be baken with leaven…" And it is the only offering other than a peace offering where they could bring leavened bread with the offering. But the leavened bread was not ever to be burned. Only unleavened bread was to be burned. The other was to be eaten. "…*They are* the firstfruits unto the LORD." So there's a significance in relating to those who are going to be in the resurrection and the church. And then it gives the offering that they were to offer—all of the rams and the lambs and so forth: "…an offering made by fire, of sweet savour unto the LORD." Then it talks about the sacrifice of the peace offering and sin offering, verse 19.

Verse 20: "And the priest shall wave them with the bread of the firstfruits…" So waving is the same thing when you come back to the first day. What do you have on the first day of the count? You are to have the premiere sheaf that was specially cut, that is waved before the Lord. And we know this symbolizes the ascension of Jesus into heaven on the first day of the count toward Pentecost to be accepted of God the Father as the sacrifice for the sins of the whole world. So now we have the same thing here with: "…the priest shall wave them with the bread of the firstfruits *for* a wave offering before the LORD…" And so if it applies to Jesus ascending and being accepted of God the Father on the first day, then this also has to apply to those who are in the church to be waved and accepted by God on the day of Pentecost.

Now let's continue on here. It says: "…with the two lambs: they shall be holy to the LORD for the priest. And ye shall proclaim on the selfsame day [that very day—the fiftieth day], *that* it may be an holy convocation unto you: ye shall do no servile work *therein: it shall be* a statute for ever in all your dwellings throughout your generations" (Lev. 23:17-21).

Now since this is a holy day and we do take up an offering and it is the firstfruits. Now we need to understand, God said you shall not fail to bring your firstfruits to Him. It's very, very important. And also the offering that we bring we need to understand that we need to apply ourselves in the offering; we need to plan for the offerings; we need to realize that just as we are part of the firstfruits, which are going to be harvested when the resurrection occurs, so likewise as we are planning to grow in grace and knowledge in character to be able to be raised from the dead when that time comes, then likewise when we bring an offering to God we need to plan it. We need to prepare for it. And that's why Paul gives it here in II Corinthians 9. So let's come to II Corinthians 9:6 and here is a living principle. And I've seen this over and over and over again in the lives of people, not only in the world but especially in the church.

"But this *I say*: the one who sows sparingly shall also reap sparingly; and the one who sows bountifully shall also reap bountifully." Now this is a living principle. And it's just the way that it is. If you're a curmudgeon with God, He's going to be a curmudgeon with you. It's just that simple. Whether it be in our character, our prayers, our growing, our overcoming, our studying, our thinking, our giving of tithes and offerings. It's all the same thing.

Now verse 7 is the key: "Each one as he purposes in his heart..." because we are to give according to the blessings that God gives us. Not only just the physical blessings but also the spiritual blessings. "...*So let him give,* but not grudgingly or by compulsion; for God loves a cheerful giver." In other words this: instead of saying, "Oh. It's a holy day and I know the minister is going to ask for an offering. Well, alright I'll give it." No, it's just like everything else—you need to look forward to it and you need to perform it from the heart with a willing attitude. And here is what God is able to do, see. Because those who are curmudgeons do not believe verse 8: "For God *is* able to make all grace abound toward you so that in every *way* you may always have sufficiency in all *things*, *and* may abound unto every good work..." (II Cor. 9:6-8). And so that's what we need to look at with the offerings that God wants us to bring.

So keep that in mind because you see, when it comes down to tithes and offerings we're not dealing in our own property, we're dealing as custodians or stewards of the property of God. And He wants us to have it with a right heart, and a right mind, and a right attitude. So you need to trust God. He's able to make all grace abound toward you. And let me just say this: as we have seen and as we know, that if you do not do from the heart what God wants you to do in everything that you do, not only in giving, but since we're talking about offerings and giving, as one man wrote, he didn't tithe and he didn't give offerings but you know what he did? He spent all of that money on things in his life which amounted to penalties against him because he wasn't right with God in his heart and his mind and his attitude. And he wrote and said, "I spent the tithe all the way to bankruptcy court." Then he learned the lesson: if you can't get along on the 90% that God gives you, then you're surely not going to get along on the 100% which you're claiming. So we just need to keep that in mind because today on the Feast of Pentecost we're going to see the great blessing that God has in store for us as pictured by this holy day. So we'll pause and take up the offering at this time.

(Pause)

There are many things we could cover on Pentecost. Some of these things we are going to review rather than get in great detail in it because we cover different aspects of it every year when we do. But God gave the Ten Commandments on the day of Pentecost. And the day of Pentecost did not picture the firstfruits until after they got into the land, as far as the harvest was concerned. But it did picture the firstfruits of God in calling Israel as the first nation. And it also pictures those people that God has called beginning with Seth and all through the righteous line that we find before the flood, and then with Abraham after the flood and so forth, who we know that Jesus said will be in the first resurrection. So when we come to Leviticus 23 let's go back and review verse 17 just a minute: "Ye shall bring out of your habitations two wave loaves of two tenth deals: they shall be of fine flour; they shall be baken with leaven; *they are* the firstfruits unto the LORD." Now this was a special firstfruit offering. Now why would God have the Feast of Unleavened Bread where leaven at that time is pictured to be sin, and now He says put leaven into this offering? Well you see, because there is also a good application of leaven. Because see, when you put leaven into your dough and it rises and then you bake it, now what you do, you permanently set that dough in the baked condition. It can never go back, you can never beat it down to where it would be flat again. Once it's baked it is set.

Now let's look at a good application of leaven as it is pictured the type of the Kingdom of God. Let's come to Matthew 13 because you see we know that the Kingdom of God is going to be righteousness, don't we? It's not going to be sin, so leaven here in this particular case referring to the Kingdom of God has got to refer to the leaven that is there in the wave loaves.

Now here in Matthew 13, we find something very interesting too, don't we? We find that the whole work of God in calling people and growing and producing has to do with a harvest, has to do with planting. And He talks about the seed that fell in the different places where that they didn't produce, and then the ones who do produce. Now then the harvest, He says, is at the end of the age. And we'll talk about that a little bit later, but let's look at it here. Let's come to the one where the Kingdom of God is likened unto leaven.

Let's pick it up in verse 33: "Another parable He spoke to them: " 'The kingdom of heaven is compared to leaven which a woman took and hid in three measures of flour until all was leavened' " (Matt. 13:33). Then when you bake it, like with the two wave loaves which were offered, then you have something that is permanent; you have a finished product. Because what you do, you start out, just like it is here with the seeds that are planted. Then what has to happen is this: it has to grow; it has to be harvested; it has to be milled; you have to add to it the salt and the sweetening; you have to mix it and you have to add the leavening, and then you have to wait for it to rise. And generally you have to beat it down several times so you can get a nice real firm good kind of loaf of bread. And then you let it rise for the last time, and then you stick it into the oven and roast it or bake it. So when it's baked it is finished. It is a complete product. And that's what the wave loaves back there in Leviticus 23 pictured. One has got to be for those who enter into the Kingdom of God from the time of Adam down to the time of the beginning of the Church. And then from the Church forward to the return of Christ. And this happens on Pentecost. It doesn't happen on Trumpets. Trumpets is entirely different. And Trumpets cannot be the day of the resurrection simply because a trumpet is blown, but from a concordant type study; [we learn that it is different] because the trumpet is blown on every holy day. And remember what happened at Mount Sinai when the Ten Commandments were given. What was it? The trumpet blew long and loud and louder and louder and louder and then God spoke the Ten Commandments. So we'll look at some of that here in just a little bit later.

Let's come to Acts 2 because here we have several things going on the day of Pentecost. And the day of Pentecost was when the Church began with the power of the Holy Spirit being given to it. And there are, as we have covered, several reasons why God did it here on the day of Pentecost at the Temple: (1) Because now the Holy Spirit was given to empower the people to keep the commandments of God; (2) it was given at the Temple so there is a consistency of the place where God chose to put His name, and it was at the Temple; (3) and also since it was the power of God's Holy Spirit to do it, and that it was going to be the Gospel that was to be preached in all the world then He caused the miracle of the speaking of the apostles so when they spoke in their own language it came out in the language of wherever they were of the Jews who came there to keep the Feast of Pentecost. And so this was a tremendous thing that God was showing. This was also a prophecy that now then, men are going to have access to God the Father through the Spirit into the Temple in heaven above. So this was also a prophecy of the coming demise of the whole temple system and the sacrificial system. And we know what happened.

Let's read verse 1: "And when the day *of Pentecost*, the fiftieth day, was being ful-filled…" And that's the accurate translation from the Greek, and we have a booklet on that. If you don't have it write in for it. "…They were all with one accord in the same place. And suddenly *there* came from heaven a sound like *the* rushing of a powerful wind, and filled the whole house where they were sitting. And there appeared to them divided tongues as of fire, and sat upon each one of them. And they were all filled with *the* Holy Spirit; and they began to speak with other languages, as the Spirit gave them *the words* to proclaim." And so what did they do? They preached the crucifixion and resurrection of Jesus Christ, and the receiv-ing of the Holy Spirit through repentance and baptism. A brand new thing. It had not been done before. And God was signaling the way of how now He was going to deal with His Church and His people. And a very important thing that took place here is this: When Peter preached and they were convicted in their hearts and minds about what had happened with the crucifixion of Jesus Christ, he was actually preaching to those of whom some of them may have even been in the mob demanding that Jesus be crucified. So when it really got to them and they repented and were baptized, that was a tremendous event. Because you see, on that day the words that Jesus said, "Father, forgive them for they know not what they are doing," was applied to them. Quite a wonderful thing that happened.

Now let's pick it up in verse 37 and we'll see how this follows along with what we read back there in Leviticus 23. Verse 37: "Now after hearing *this*, they were cut to the heart; and they said to Peter and the other apostles, 'Men *and* brethren, what shall we do [because there's always something we need to do]?' Then Peter said to them, 'Repent and be baptized each one of you in the name of Jesus Christ for *the* remission of sins, and you yourselves [meaning personally, coming from God] shall receive the gift of the Holy Spirit. For the promise is to you and to your children, and to all those who are afar off, as many as *the* Lord our God may call.' " So he made it clear right from the beginning, it is a calling that comes from God and fulfills what Jesus said, "None can come to the Father except they come through Me, and none can come to Me except the Father draw them." And here it is fulfilled right here.

Now verse 40: "And with many other words he earnestly testified and exhorted, say-ing, 'Be saved from this perverse generation.' " Now if there's any perverse generation, it is today. And it's going to get much more perverse—so perverse that just like God had to de-stroy the temple system, destroy Jerusalem, that He's going to have to nearly destroy this world in order to cleanse it and purify it from all of the sins and corruption and Satanism and perversity that's in the world today.

Verse 41: "Then those who joyfully received his message were baptized; and about three thousand souls were added that day" (Acts 2:1-4, 37-41, *FV*) —the day of Pentecost. So this day has a great meaning for us. And this is why God gave the Holy Spirit on that day. So it starts on this day and it ends on this day. Think about that for a minute. And we'll look at all the different things now.

Let's look at some of the things concerning the resurrection. Let's come back here to I Corinthians 15. And we need to understand this. We need to realize it to the depths of our being. As I covered yesterday, there are people out there even within the ranks of the Church of God that want to come in with their own doctrines. And just like it says here, if you don't believe that Jesus is raised from the dead then your faith is in vain. And if you don't believe that Jesus Christ was God before He became a human being; that He was God manifested in the flesh, you don't understand the sacrifice of Jesus Christ, and you cannot comprehend the deep love that God the Father and Jesus Christ have for not only the church and the people that He calls, but also for all humanity. Because in God's great plan through the things that we know from the holy days, He is going to save the vast majority of man-kind. And God is going to offer them the kind of repentance and forgiveness that we have.

But God has called us as the firstfruits. And as the firstfruits we have a great and a tremendous promise—greater than anyone else who comes into the Kingdom of God after that. And so we need to really... Let's understand this: The Bible also says, "Without vision the people perish." And that's why a lot of people fall out of the church. They just don't have the vision. So you've got to understand the greatness of the plan of God, and you've got to keep that in the forefront of your mind, that it will lead you, that it will inspire you, that it will give you hope, that it will give you the strength, that it will give you the endurance.

Now let's come down here to I Corinthians 15:12. Now we need to understand this because there were those, even in the Church of God back there... He says here in verse 34: "Awake to righteousness, and do not sin, for some *of you* do not have the knowledge of God. I say *this* to your shame." See. And there are a lot of people who do not have the knowledge of God as they ought to.

Now let's come back here to verse 12: "But if Christ is being preached, that He rose from *the* dead, how *is it that* some among you are saying that there is no resurrection of *the* dead? For if there is no resurrection from *the* dead, neither has Christ been raised. And if Christ has not been raised, then our preaching *is* in vain, and your faith *is* also in vain." Now let's understand this: Any minister, any man, any church that preaches that you go to heaven is preaching in vain because they are not preaching the resurrection of Christ. Now think about that.

"And we are also found *to be* false witnesses of God..." And God isn't going to back up any liars, is He? No, they are excluded from the Kingdom of God. "...Because we have testified of God that He raised Christ, Whom He did not raise, if indeed *the* dead are not raised. For if *the* dead are not raised, neither has Christ been raised. But if Christ has not been raised, your faith *is* vain; you are still in your sins, and those who have fallen asleep in Christ have then perished. If in this life only we have hope in Christ, we are of all people most miserable." Because you suffer in vain; you go through trials in vain; you're not developing the character of God; you have a false belief in Christ, and all of that sort of thing.

Now verse 20: "But now Christ has been raised from *the* dead..." And they haven't ever produced the body; they haven't ever produced the witnesses who carried Him away; they have never produced the bones, because He was raised from the dead. "...He has become the first-fruit of those who have fallen asleep." That goes back to the wave sheaf offering day—the first of the firstfruits—the premiere sheaf that was accepted of God the Father. "For since by man *came* death, by man also *came the* resurrection of *the* dead. For as in Adam all die, so also in Christ shall all be made alive." Notice: "But each [one] in his own order: Christ *the* firstfruit; then, those who are Christ's at His coming" (I Cor. 15:34, 12-23). Now we're going to see about His coming—that it is going to be quite a fantastic event. And it's not going to be something that happens [*slaps hands*] just in one day. We'll see that. We'll understand that.

Now let's apply this to ourselves. Let's come to James 1 and let's see what it says here concerning the Church. And this is important for us to understand. And let's pick it up here in verse 17. And here it shows that we are firstfruits: "Every good act of giving and every perfect gift is from above, coming down from the Father of lights, with Whom there is no variation, nor shadow of turning. According to His own will..." Now you see how important it is to remain faithful, because God of His own will and desire "...begat us by *the* Word of truth [His Holy Spirit], that we might be a kind of firstfruits of all His created beings" (James 1:17-18).

Now let's look at it here. Let's come to the book of Hebrews again. We're going to see "firstfruits" and "firstborn," and we are called the Church of the Firstborn. And here's where we get the parallel between the giving of the law at Mount Sinai and all the things that took place after that, and our coming to the resurrection, and our being part of coming to Mount Zion, which is the city of the living God.

Now let's come down here to Hebrews 12:18: "For you have not come to *the* mount that could be touched and that burned with fire, nor to gloominess, and fearful darkness, and *the* whirlwind; and to *the* sound of *the* trumpet, and to *the* voice of *the* words..." See, they heard God speak. Now none of us have heard that, but we have greater than that. We have the begettal of God the Father in us—the firstfruits of the Holy Spirit. "...Which those who heard, *begged* that *the* word not be spoken *directly* to them. (For they could not endure what was being commanded: 'And if even an animal touches the mountain, it shall be stoned, or shot through with an arrow'; and so terrifying was the sight *that* Moses said, 'I am greatly afraid and trembling'.)" Now we're going to see what they all experienced there is nothing compared to what it's going to be like when Christ returns, because it's going to be an awesome, fantastic event. And if we could say, "Let's get the big picture," of what's going to take place worldwide at that time.

"But you have come to Mount Sion [Not Mt. Zion on the earth, but Mount Sion], and to *the* city of *the* living God, heavenly Jerusalem; and to an innumerable company of angels; *to the* joyous festival gathering..." Now that's what it means in the Greek. So this has got to be the day of Pentecost, which <u>is</u> a festival gathering—the greatest gathering and the great congregation that we have talked about concerning the resurrection and how that's going to take place. "...And to *the* church of *the* firstborn..." And then we read in Romans 8:29 that Christ is the firstborn among many brethren. So we have the first of the firstfruits, we have the first of the firstborn, and then we have the firstfruits and then we have the church of the firstborn. That's what we are called. "...Registered *in the book of life* in heaven; and to God, *the* Judge of all; and to *the* spirits of the just who have been perfected; and to Jesus, *the* Mediator of *the* New Covenant; and to sprinkling of *the* blood of *ratification*, proclaiming superior things than *that of* Abel" (Heb. 12:18-24). So this sets the stage.

Now let's look at how this is going to take place. Let's see how these events are going to transpire. Now let's come here to Revelation 11. Now we know (if you don't have the series on Revelation and Daniel, be sure and write for it, and the chart and everything that goes with it.) there's going to come a time when the beast and the false prophet will come on the earth. They will precede the two witnesses. And there will be a time of peace, as Paul writes in I Thessalonians 5, for when they say peace and prosperity then sudden destruction is going to come upon them. Now there's going to come a time when Satan is going to be cast down and he's going to persecute the church, as we find in Revelation 12. Then there will be some few who will be taken to a place of safety. Those who remain behind, Satan is going to make war against them. And as we are going to see that is the martyrdom of the saints. But before that begins to take place (and as you will see on the chart that we have laying out the number of days, and so forth, of the two witnesses—when they end, when they begin, and so forth) that the two witnesses begin just before winter. And here is what they are going to do. This is going to be a key event. And it's going to precipitate all of the events that are going to take place leading to the return of Christ and the resurrection.

So he says here, verse 1: "Then *the angel* gave me a measuring rod like a staff, saying, 'Arise and measure the temple of God, and the altar, and those who worship in it. But leave out the court that *is* within the temple *area*, and do not measure it because it has been given *up* to the Gentiles; and they shall trample upon the holy city *for* forty-two months. And I will give *power* to My two witnesses, and they shall prophesy a thousand two hundred *and* sixty days, clothed in sackcloth. These are the two olive trees, and *the* two lampstands that stand before the God of the earth.' " Now these are special two witnesses that God is going to raise up and empower in a way of a direct giving of the Holy Spirit to give to them. These will be the two most powerful men of God that the world has ever seen. Greater than Moses, greater than Aaron. Of course not greater than Christ, but just as human beings representing God. That's why they are called the two olive trees, and the two lampstands that stand before the God of the earth. Now if you don't have the tape "Who Are The Two Witnesses and Elijah" write in for it.

" 'And if anyone attempts to harm them, fire will go out of their mouths and devour their enemies.' " So this is going to be a fantastic thing. So here [is] the confrontation of the two that represent Satan the devil and the two that represent God right at Jerusalem. And it's going to take place in a powerful way because the beast is going to enter into the Temple and proclaim himself that he is God, as we have already seen. And that is the abomination of desolation that is spoken of by Daniel the prophet. We'll go there in just a minute in Matthew 24.

Now here's what's going to happen. It says: " 'For if anyone attempts to harm them, he must be killed in this manner. These have authority to shut heaven so that no rain may fall in *the* days of their prophecy; and they have authority over the waters, to turn them into blood, and to smite the earth with every plague, <u>as often as they will</u>.' " That's going to be an awesome thing. Then it says: " 'And when they have completed their testimony, the beast who ascends out of the abyss will make war against them, and will overcome them, and will kill them' " (Rev. 11:1-7). But God has a surprise for them, as we will see a little bit later on.

Let's come here to Matthew 24 and let's see something very important concerning Matthew 24 and when the tribulation begins, and then we will go to Revelation 6 and we will see the parallel events and how these come down to Pentecost and the resurrection.

Now let's pick it up here in verse 15: " 'Therefore, when you see the abomination of desolation, which was spoken of by Daniel the prophet, standing in the holy place (the one who reads, let him understand) [that's John's note that we have to be watching and looking], then let those who are in Judea flee into the mountains. Let the one *who is* on the housetop not come down to take anything out of his house; and let the one *who is* in the field not go back to take his garments. But woe to those *women* who are expecting a child, and to those who are nursing infants in those days! And pray that your flight be not in *the* winter, nor on *the* Sabbath; for <u>then</u>...' " Now this is the key to understanding when the great tribulation starts. And this is the key that locks in the beginning of all the events in Daniel and Revelation that lead up to the return of Jesus Christ and the establishing of the Kingdom of God on earth. " '...For <u>then</u> shall there be great tribulation, such as has not been from *the* beginning of *the* world until this time, nor ever shall be *again*.' " Now what we need to understand is this brethren: We are facing humungous worldwide problems. And what we are going to see is that what God did to Egypt back in the book of Exodus with Pharaoh and Jannes and Jambres, God is going to do to the whole world, and to the beast and the false prophet, and their armies and all of those with him. It is going to be a time that has never been from the beginning of the world. So we've got to really understand that. " 'And if those days were not limited...' " Now it says "cut short" in the King James, but it means "limited." God is not going to cut short the three and a half years (three and a half days in prophecy). And the reason being is this: He has limited it to three and a half years. And we'll see the events that take place there. " '...But for the elect's sake those days shall be limited' " (Matt. 24:15-22).

Now we'll come back here to Matthew 24 again a little later, but let's come to Revelation 6 and let's see how these events are going to unfold on the earth. And this is then going to lead us up to how Christ is going to return, and lead us up to the time of the resurrection. Now let's pick it up here in verse 1. Christ is the one who opens the seals: "And I looked when the Lamb opened one of the seals; and I heard one of the four living creatures say, like the sound of thunder, 'Come and see.' And I looked, and behold, *there was* a white horse…" Now this is not Christ, because Christ opened the seal and out of the seal that Christ opened here comes a white horse. This is the false Christ. This is the false religion. This then has to be first the anti-Christ, the false prophet who is coming. Now let's understand this: both the beast and the false prophet are anti-Christs.

"…And the one who was sitting on it had a bow, and a crown was given to him; and he went out conquering, and to conquer." This tells us, as the other prophecies (this is a summary of how many of the other prophecies), that there is coming a great one world religion. And it is going to come. Now then, when it comes time for the beast power to go into the Temple and sit down and proclaim himself God as II Thessalonians tells us, then we come to verse 3. So this is the timing: "And when He opened the second seal, I heard the second living creature say, 'Come and see.' And another horse went out *that was* red [symbolic of war]; and *power* was given to the one sitting on it to take peace from the earth…" When does the tribulation begin? <u>When</u> you see the abomination spoken of by Daniel the prophet standing in the Holy place. So what is going to happen? We've put all of the scriptures together—the king of the north is going to come down; he is going to enter into to the Temple of God, proclaim himself God; the false prophet is going to say, "Yes, he is God." The two witnesses are going to say, "No, he is not God." And then the great tribulation begins on the whole world. And that's what this second seal pictures.

And immediately what happens with that? "And when He opened the third seal, I heard the third living creature say, 'Come and see.' And I looked, and behold, *there was* a black horse; and the one sitting on it had a balance in his hand. And I heard a voice in *the* midst of the four living creatures say, 'A measure of wheat for a silver coin, and three measures of barley for a silver coin: and *see that* you do not damage the oil and the wine.' " So immediately whenever there's war, food supplies are cut short. And don't we have that today? Just think about how quickly death, destruction, and famine is going to take place when people do not have access to their markets; people do not have access to their shopping mall. And that's what's going to happen.

So then what happens after that? Immediately follows the fourth seal. So these come one-two-three, quite quickly. "And when He opened the fourth seal, I heard *the* voice of the fourth living creature say, 'Come and see.' And I looked, and behold, *there was* a pale horse; and the name of the one sitting on it *was* Death, and the grave followed him; and authority was given to them over *one* fourth of the earth…" Now exactly where that is going to be we don't know. But when the tribulation begins it's going to affect one fourth of the earth. Now three fourths of the earth will not be affected by it. But when they see this take place they are going to start building their armies and getting them up to speed, because later, as we will see, there's an army of two hundred million that is going to come, and come toward the Holy Land. So we're looking at big-time global events that are going to take place.

Now then, they are going to a fourth part of the earth: "…to kill with *the* sword and with famine and with death, and by the beasts of the earth" (Rev. 6:1-8). So this is going to be one of the most gruesome times on earth. That's why Jesus said that if the time weren't limited there would be no flesh saved alive because of all of the weapons we know that men have, because of all of the things that are going to take place. And unless God intervened, and we're going to see how He's going to intervene, and get their attention and let them know what's going to happen, we'll see that in just a little bit.

Now let's continue right on here in Revelation 6. Now let's coordinate this with Revelation 12. So hold your place here in Revelation 6 and let's come back to Revelation 12 and let's see what's going to happen. Satan is going to be cast down. He's going to persecute the Church. After those who go to a place of safety have gone, then we pick it up here in the very last verse of Revelation 12, verse 17. This is when the martyrdom of the saints begins to take place. And let's understand something here, there is a great principle, which is this: The one who seeks to save his life shall lose it, and the one who loses his life in Christ shall save it. Now that is accomplished in two ways: (1) if you think you're going to go to a place of safety, be guaranteed you aren't; (2) and if you think you're going to avoid martyrdom, be guaranteed, unless you die before these events take place, you're not. So we might as well face the reality of the truth of the things at the end-time as Jesus said—the worse things that have ever happened on the face of the earth since the beginning of the creation are going to take place. So we might as well gear ourselves up for that thinking and ask God for the help, the strength, the character that we need, because this is not going to be "good-time Charlie" and "wonderful Sally time" when these things and events take place. That's why Jesus said, "Woe." And then we're going to see what God is going to do about it.

Last verse: "Then the dragon was furious with the woman and went to make war with the rest of her seed, who keep the commandments of God and have the testimony of Jesus Christ" (Rev. 12:17). Now when war comes against the saints they are going to know wherever true Christians are, because all of those who are true Christians will not have the mark of the beast and they will know where you are. Now granted, some can flee from city to city but they're going to track you down, because there are going to be traitors. There will be people who are looking to kill Christians because, combined with the two witnesses, they are the ones who are causing all the problems on the earth.

Now let's pick it up here in Revelation 6:9. Brethren, I want you to understand the magnitude of these things. I want you to understand how awesome these events are going to be where we are not talking about little events at the end-time that are going to take place and all of a sudden, like the Protestants believe, there's going to be a rapture. There isn't going to be any rapture. Only the few that go to the place of safety—and they are only there to fulfill what Jesus said, that the mouth of the grave would not prevail against the Church. So there's going to come a time when all of the rest—just the few that are in the place of safety—and I don't think many of us are going to make that, because we have to be a witness for Christ. And just like Christ was a witness to the world and gave His life that we may live, we have to give our lives for Christ. And we need to understand that. And if you have not counted yourself already dead to sin, and dead because you have been buried in the watery grave, then you are not mentally prepared for the things that are coming. And so part of what I'm trying to do is to help us have a big picture of what's going to take place, and to give us strength and courage by the power of God's Spirit to stand for what is right; to know what we need to do; to realize that God is there, Christ is there, they will help us, they will strengthen us; but we have to be a witness against all of the bloody wretchedness of this world, even in giving our lives. And you look back at the prophecy that we are going to read here, and many others have done so down through history. And what makes us think that we are so all-fired good that we are going to avoid it. A little colloquialism: It ain't a gonna happen.

Now verse 9: "And when He opened the fifth seal, I saw under the altar the souls of those who had been slain for the Word of God [because they believed God], and for the testimony that they held…" to tell them that just like the two witnesses are saying to the beast and the false prophet, "You are of Satan the devil. You are not of God. These plagues are coming down and we call them as a demonstration against your evil and your wickedness."

"…And they cried out with a loud voice, saying, 'How long, O Lord, holy and true, do You not judge and avenge our blood on those who dwell on the earth?' And white robes were given to each of them; and they were told that they should rest a short time yet…" In other words they are still dead. But this is just a vision to give you an understanding what's going to happen at the end-time in comparison to those who had been martyred before us, you see.

"...Until *it* be fulfilled *that* both their fellow servants and their brethren also would be killed, just as they had been." Now when it comes time that all of those that Satan makes war against—he finally gets them—that ends the "church age." Then something new is going to begin, and as we know from past sermons and so forth, the next event that's going to take place is going to be approximately eighteen months before Christ and the saints put their feet on the earth. Now I want you to begin to think what's going to happen here.

Verse 12: "And when He opened the sixth seal, I looked, and behold, there was a great earthquake; and the sun became black as *the* hair *of* sackcloth, and the moon became as blood..." Because if there's a great earthquake and it's anywhere near volcanoes you're going to have all of this exploding at the same time. "...And the stars of heaven fell to the earth, as a fig tree casts its untimely figs when it is shaken by a mighty wind. Then *the* heaven departed like a scroll..." There is going to be a new thing that's going to take place. God is going to reveal in a great and a powerful way, just like He said back there in the book of Haggai, "I'm going to shake the heavens. I'm going to shake the earth. I'm going to shake the sea." And that's what this is right here. And then the heavens are going to depart as a scroll and a new thing is going to be revealed.

Let's see what it is: "...and every mountain and island was moved out of its place. And the kings of the earth..." Now God is going to get the attention of the whole world. This is going to be an awesome and fantastic thing. "...And the great men, and the rich men, and the chief captains, and the powerful men, and every bondman, and every free *man* hid themselves in the caves and in the rocks of the mountains; and they said to the mountains and to the rocks, 'Fall on us, and hide us from *the* face of Him Who sits on the throne, and from the wrath of the Lamb because the great day of His wrath has come, and who has the power to stand?' " (Rev. 6:9-17).

Now what is this going to be like when this takes place. How is this going to take place? Look, I want you to understand this is the beginning of the return of Christ to the earth. But He has to come from the third heaven, however far away that that is. So the heavens roll back as a scroll and then they see something that they have never seen before. Let's come to Matthew 24. And this is what they are going to see. The whole world is going to see this. It's not going to be that every eye is going to see Him just kind of a flick of a second and every eye sees Him. No, we are going to see that this is going to be something that they are going to be aware of for approximately a year and a half. And it's going to be a new thing. And it's going to frighten the whole world.

Now let's pick it up here, Matthew 24:27: " 'For as the light of day, which comes forth from *the* east and shines as far as *the* west, so also shall the coming of the Son of man be.' " That's how it's going to start. Now the light of day is what? The sun. When the heavens roll back as a scroll then, as we're going to see, this is called the "sign of the Son of man." And it's going to be like a new sun that is going to suddenly appear. And what are the men on earth going to say? Why are they going to be willing to fight? The whole world has been programmed with UFO's and aliens, right? It's going to be declared as the alien invasion of the world and we must save ourselves from them. And in a sense they will be right because Jesus Christ and God the Father and the angels of God are indeed alien to the inhabitants of the earth. But it's going to be greater than that, as we will see.

Now verse 29: " 'But immediately after the tribulation of <u>those</u> days...' " That's the tribulation against Israel. We'll see that when we come to Revelation 7. There's a great tribulation which compasses the whole world. There is the tribulation that is against Israel for God's punishment which lasts two full years, as we find in Hosea 5 and 6. " 'But immediately after the tribulation of those days, the sun shall be darkened, and the moon shall not give her light, and the stars shall fall from heaven, and the powers of the heavens shall be shaken.' " I mean the whole universe. The return of Christ, when it begins, is going to affect the whole universe. " 'And then shall appear the sign of the Son of man in heaven...' ", which in verse 27 says is like the light of day which shines forth from the east unto the west. So here's a new sun. The earth is down here turning on it's axis and it looks like it's a new sun that goes around, that is like a second light. That's why it shines from the east to the west because the earth is on it's axis turning. So that's going to be quite a thing, isn't it? " '...And then shall all the tribes of the earth mourn, and they shall see the Son of man coming...' " And He's going to come: " '...upon the clouds of heaven with power and great glory.' " And it's going to arrive at, verse 31: " 'And He shall send His angels with a great sound of a trumpet; and they shall gather together His elect from the four winds, from one end of heaven to *the* other' " (Matt. 24:27, 29-31).

Let's go back to the book of Revelation and see how this thing is going to be. Because when this comes down it's going to be something. God is going to shake the heavens, God is going to shake the earth, God is going to reveal Himself. Let's come back to Revelation 1. Why will all the tribes of the earth mourn? Why will all people be willing to fight against Christ? Because they're following the anti-Christ and the false prophet. And they are going to declare that this is an alien invasion from outer space. That's why all the armies are going to be gathered together.

Now let's read this here, Revelation 1:7: "Behold, He is coming with the clouds..." So as it appears in heaven, then it's going to come closer, and closer, and closer, and closer to the earth until it reaches a point in the clouds above the earth. And that's going to give plenty of time for all the armies of the earth to gather together. "Behold, He is coming with the clouds, and <u>every eye shall see Him</u>, and those who pierced Him [that's a direct reference to those who crucified Him; and of course our sins killed Christ, so every eye is going to see Him]; and all the tribes of the earth shall wail because of Him. Even so, Amen." (Rev. 1:7).

Now let's come back to Revelation 7. Let's see what's going to happen. So the sign of the Son of man is there. Time is going on. The earth is still turning on it's axis. Now then, God stops the tribulation against Israel and He begins His final harvest. And there's every reason to believe that Revelation 7 is going to take place on the next to the last Pentecost as Christ is returning, because He's going to be coming, coming, coming, coming, coming, coming, coming to the earth. It's not going to be all of a sudden—*whoop*, one day here's Jesus; *whoop*, one day here's the resurrection; and *whoop*, we all return to the earth on the same day. It isn't going to happen that way because you have to ask the question: Why are all of those on the earth going to be fighting against each other and fighting against Christ. Why are all the armies of the earth gathered at Armageddon? Because they're going to fight this alien invasion, and we are going to see that it's going to get worse for them.

Now God intervenes. Remember this: Before any event takes place God gives space of repentance. So here's a space of repentance that God gives to Israel: "And after these things I saw four angels standing on the four corners of the earth..." Now look, this is big time stuff. "...So that the wind might not blow on the earth, or on the sea, or on any tree. Then I saw another angel ascending from *the* rising of *the* sun, having *the* seal of *the* living God; and he cried out with a loud voice to the four angels, to whom it was given to damage the earth and the sea, saying, 'Do not damage the earth, or the sea, or the trees until we have sealed the servants of our God in their foreheads.' And I heard the number of those who were sealed: one hundred forty-four thousand, sealed out of every tribe of *the* children of Israel."

Now if you don't have our study paper on who the hundred and forty-four thousand are, write in for it. Because if you have the Spirit of God today you cannot be one of the hundred forty-four thousand who are saved in the next to the last Pentecost before Christ and the saints return to the earth. These are of all the tribes of Israel. It is a special harvest of God, and they receive the Holy Spirit of God in a special and particular way, because there are no ministers there to baptize them; there is no one to counsel them; their repentance is because they [have gone] through the tribulation and fulfills the promise of Deuteronomy 28 and Leviticus 26 that if while in captivity you seek the Lord your God with all your heart, then He will save you. And this is what happens. And it starts out with the tribe of Judah first to fulfill the prophecy that God is going to save the tents of Judah first. And then it lists the twelve tribes. Then after that there is a great innumerable multitude because the hundred and forty-four thousand are not the only ones who are going to repent. This is the result of the harvest of the preaching of the two witnesses to Israel and Judah [and] all the tribes of the earth. And now we have a great innumerable multitude, see. So if anyone says that there are only going to be a hundred forty-four thousand in the first resurrection, know that they are lame-brained idiots, because the Bible says, verse 9: "…a great [innumerable] multitude… out of every nation [that takes care of sacred-namers doesn't it?] and tribe and people and language…" And what are they going to be? They're going to be in the resurrection. So here's the vision that portrays them "…standing before the throne and before the Lamb, clothed with white robes and *holding* palms in their hands;…" So they're going to be in the first resurrection.

Verse 14 says: " '…They are the ones who have come out of the great tribulation; and they have washed their robes, and have made their robes white in the blood of the Lamb' " (Rev. 7:1-4, 9, 14,). Quite a thing, isn't it? And by their repentance, that's what's going to happen. Then we come to all the events that take place then in Revelation 8 and Revelation 9 and Revelation 10 and all those events that take place.

Now let's come back here to Revelation 11 and let's see what's going to happen because we come to the last Pentecost. That's when the harvest is going to take place. So here, all this time during this whole year the wars have been going on, on the earth (Revelation 8, 9, and 10); the hundred forty-four thousand and the great innumerable multitude have been spared and they have been saved, waiting the resurrection because we're all going to be resurrected at the same time.

Now then we are going to see when the resurrection is going to take place, because this is important for us to understand because it does not take place on the Feast of Trumpets. It takes place on Pentecost because from the time of the resurrection of Christ and His ascension to heaven we have seven continuous weeks of the harvest, and God is harvesting, God is harvesting all the way down through it. And then the resurrection is going to take place on the fiftieth day. That's when the two wave loaves are brought, when there will be permanent change from flesh to spirit.

Now let's come back here to the two witnesses. Revelation 11:7: " 'And when they have completed their testimony, the beast who ascends out of the abyss will make war against them, and will overcome them, and will kill them.' " See, because what Satan is always allowed to do is to believe that he's going to win. See, that's what happened with Pharaoh when he went and chased the children of Israel to the Red Sea and thought, "Man, they got across there—I'm going across." So they're going to think that they're going to win. So God is going to let them finally kill the two witnesses. And everyone with their cell phones everywhere will be able to see this. They'll see it on television, they'll hear it on radio, they'll have the broadcast. This is going to be a worldwide event. They're going to say, "Let's have a feast." Yes.

" 'And their bodies *will lie* in the street of the great city, which spiritually is called Sodom and Egypt [that's Jerusalem], where also our Lord was crucified. Then those of the peoples and tribes and languages and nations shall see their bodies three and a half days, for they will not allow their bodies to be put into tombs. And those who dwell on the earth will rejoice over them, and will make merry, and will send gifts to one another, because these two prophets had tormented those who dwell on the earth.' "

Now notice—surprise, surprise, God has a big one in store for them: "Then after the three and a half days, *the* spirit of life from God entered into them and they stood on their feet; and great fear fell upon those who were watching them. And they heard a great voice from heaven, say, 'Come up here!' And they ascended into heaven in a cloud; and their enemies saw them *rise*." So what do we have here? Another fulfillment of the Word of God. The last two martyred are the first two raised to life.

"And in that hour there was a great earthquake, and a tenth of the city fell; and seven thousand men were killed in the earthquake. And the rest were filled with fear, and gave glory to the God of heaven. The second woe is past. Behold, the third woe is coming immediately. Then the seventh angel sounded *his* trumpet [right as soon as they got out of their sight the trumpet sounds, and this is the resurrection of the rest of the saints, the rest of the firstfruits]; and *there* were great voices in heaven, saying, 'The kingdoms of this world have become *the kingdoms* of our Lord and His Christ, and He shall reign into the ages of eternity' " (Rev. 11:7-15). Now this is going to be something. This is a fantastic thing that is going to take place. So when that trumpet sounds let's look at two places where it talks about the trumpets, and the resurrection, and let's think and talk about the resurrection here for just a minute in relationship to the rest of the world.

Let's first of all come to I Corinthians 15, and let's pick it up here in verse 49: "And as we have borne the image of the *one* made of dust, we shall also bear the image of the heavenly *one*. Now this I say, brethren, that flesh and blood cannot inherit *the* kingdom of God, nor does corruption inherit incorruption. Behold, I show you a mystery: we shall not all fall asleep..." Because there will still be some [in the place of safety] who will be alive when Christ returns—plus the hundred forty-four thousand, the great innumerable multitude—they are waiting the resurrection. They will be changed from flesh to spirit in an instant, in the twinkling of an eye. "...But we shall all be changed, in an instant, in *the* twinkling of an eye, at the last trumpet; for *the* trumpet shall sound..." Now notice these are not trumpet<u>s</u>, but trumpet. "...And the dead shall be raised incorruptible, and we shall be changed. For this corruptible must put on incorruptibility, and this mortal must put on immortality. Now when this corruptible shall have put on incorruptibility, and this mortal shall have put on immortality, then shall come to pass the saying that is written: 'Death is swallowed up in victory' " (I Cor. 15:49-54). And it's going to be.

Now let's come over here to I Thessalonians 4 and let's see what's going to happen. Let's see how this is going to take place, then we'll go back to Revelation 14 and see what's going to transpire because this is going to be an awesome event indeed. Now let's pick it up here in verse 13: "But I do not wish you to be ignorant, brethren, concerning those who have fallen asleep, that you be not grieved, even as others, who have no hope. For if we believe that Jesus died and rose again, in exactly the same way also, those who have fallen asleep in Jesus will God bring with Him." Now how's He going to bring them with Him because they're dead in the grave? We're going to see that in just a minute.

"For this we say to you by *the* Word of *the* Lord, that we who are alive and remain unto the coming of the Lord shall in no wise precede those who have fallen asleep..." So the dead will be raised first. Those who are living will follow. "...Because the Lord Himself shall descend from heaven with *a* shout of command, with *the* voice of an archangel and with *the* trumpet of God; and the dead in Christ shall rise first..." (I Thes. 4:13-16).

Now what's that going to look like? Now let's picture this for just a minute here. Let's put all of this together. We'll see it in Revelation 15 here in just a minute. The sign of the Son of man appears in heaven. It's coming closer and closer and closer and closer and closer to the earth over the space of a year. And then it comes right down into the clouds. Now the clouds are restricted up to about 50,000 to 60,000 feet down to almost ground level. Now then the sign of the Son of man when it comes into the clouds is going to be transformed into a great sea of glass. We'll see that in Revelation 15. But the resurrection takes place, and the angels are going to, as we saw, carry them up to, as we will see, the sea of glass.

Now I believe the whole world is going to see this. And what are they going to say? "The aliens have come and they've got this huge space craft right there hovering over Jerusalem, and they are snatching bodies." Has the world been prepared mentally for that through movies and things? Yes. So here they'll see all of the saints being resurrected who are in the graves. The graves opening up and here they come—thousands and thousands and thousands of them. And then those who are alive, the hundred forty-four thousand and great innumerable multitude and those who are in the place of safety, they will be resurrected and they will come to the sea of glass. Now this is going to make the world even more angry at this alien invasion. And they are going to feel that unless we can get rid of this, unless we can marshal all the armies of the world against this mighty invasion from outer space, that we are going to be taken over by the aliens.

Now let's come back here to Revelation 14 and Revelation 15. Let's see how the harvest is like. Let's pick it up here in Revelation 14, verse 14: "And I looked, and behold, a white cloud, and *one* like *the* Son of man sitting on the cloud, having a golden crown on His head; and in His hand *was* a sharp sickle." The harvest of the firstfruits. Tie that in with Matthew 13—the harvest is at the end of the age, and the reapers are the angels carrying all of the saints up to the sea of glass. And this is going to bring the greatest confrontation that the world has ever, ever seen. "And another angel came out of the temple, crying with a loud voice to Him Who was sitting on the cloud, 'Thrust in your sickle and reap, because the time has come for You to reap; for the harvest of the earth is ripe.' " And that's the harvest of the firstfruits. Now the harvest of the wicked comes after that. "And He Who was sitting on the cloud thrust forth His sickle upon the earth, and the earth was reaped" (Rev. 14:14-16).

Now let's come to Revelation 15 and let's see something. Alright, verse 1: "Then I saw another sign in heaven, great and awesome: seven angels having the seven last plagues, for in them the wrath of God is filled up. And I saw a sea of glass mingled with fire, and those who had gotten the victory over the beast..." That means over Satan the devil, so that goes all the way back to Abel. "...And over his image..." That includes all of the idolatry beginning with Cain and all the way down through history to our time. "...And over his mark...", which is at the end-time with the mark of the beast that's going to be enforced upon all human beings. "...*And* over the number of his name, standing on the sea of glass, having *the* harps of God." Now, when you're resurrected, where are you going to be taken? If the angels take you, where are they going to take you? They are going to take you to the sea of glass. See, now that's not a doctrine of Fred Coulter. That's what I read out of the scriptures.

Now if you don't have the tape, "What's Going To Happen On The Sea Of Glass" I'll just review it for you. (1) We're all going to receive our garments—the righteousness of the saints. (2) We're going to receive our new name. (3) We're going to meet Jesus Christ.

(4) The marriage of the Lamb is going to take place. (5) We will see the declaration of Jesus Christ to God the Father. When all the saints are resurrected and on the sea of glass, He is going to turn to the Father (and we'll probably all see this at the same time) and say to the Father, "Behold all the brethren that you have given Me." And all of our rewards are then going to be given. We're going to have to know what to do; which cities we're going to rule over; who are we going to work with; how's it going to be done? We're going to also have to understand how to ride those white horses that we're going to be given. Because now we are going to be the army of God coming back to the earth, you see. And we don't come back to the earth until it's pictured by Trumpets. So we are on the sea of glass all during the time from the resurrection of Pentecost until we come back with Christ on Trumpets. And we're going to see all the events that take place, standing on the sea of glass having the harps of God.

"And they were singing the song of Moses…" proclaiming how great and powerful God is—a man of war. "…*The* servant of God, and the song of the Lamb, saying, 'Great and awesome *are* Your works…' " This is going to be the greatest and biggest thing that has ever happened or has occurred in the history of the whole world from the beginning of the creation of man until the resurrection of His Church. And it's going to be this great world-wide thing.

" '…Righteous and true *are* Your ways, King of the saints. Who shall not fear You, O Lord, and glorify Your name? For *You* only *are* holy; and all the nations shall come and worship before You, for Your judgments have been revealed' " (Rev. 15:1-4). Well, they're not going to come and worship before God until the government of God is set up on the earth and they begin to beat their spears into pruninghooks and their implements of war into plows and come and learn the way of God. And if they don't come and keep the Feast of God, as we know, there are going to be plagues, there are going to be things that will come upon them because God is not going to establish the Kingdom of God and have men continuously rebel. It's going to come in power, it's going to come in awesome destruction, as we will see here, Revelation 16 leading up to returning to the earth with Christ. This is going to be big time—absolutely the biggest thing that has ever been in the history of the world.

So what I want you to understand brethren, is this: God has called us with the greatest calling possible. We are in training for eternal life. God has given us of His Spirit. He is going to resurrect us from the dead. He is going to give us power and authority to rule under Christ. He is going to bless us with joy and greatness for all eternity and we will forever be the Church of the Firstborn—the harvest of the firstfruits of God, resurrected on Pentecost in great joy and power and wonder and magnificence. And now we are going to be ready for the biggest fight that the world has ever seen. But you have to come back for Trumpets in order to see that.

End of Sermon

Transcriber Carolyn Singer

Pentecost—Holy Day
June 4, 2006
Scriptural References

1) Leviticus 23:17-21

2) II Corinthians 9:6-8

3) Matthew 13:33

4) Acts 2:1-4, 37-41

5) I Corinthians 15:34, 12-23

6) James 1:17-18

7) Hebrews 12:18-24

8) Romans 8:29

9) Revelation 11:1-7

10) Matthew 24:15-22

11) Revelation 6:1-8

12) Revelation 12:17

13) Revelation 6:9-17

14) Matthew 24:27, 29-31

15) Revelation 1:7

16) Revelation 7:1-4, 9, 14

17) Revelation 11:7-15

18) I Corinthians 15:49-54

19) I Thessalonians 4:13-16

20) Revelation 14:14-16

21) Revelation 15:1-4

CHAPTER TWENTY-FOUR

Pentecost and the Sea of Glass—Sermon I

Pentecost—1999

April 17, 1999

Now on my trip I had several people ask me about the Sea of Glass. And there have been…other letters that have been written about the Sea of Glass in relationship to Pentecost. And Pentecost being the first resurrection…since those who have been in the Church of God for years and years, especially Worldwide Church of God, have thought that because of the teachings of the Church, that the resurrection would be on the Feast of Trumpets. And, just to give you a little background on that so you kind of know what happened in Worldwide and how they came to a Monday Pentecost. And many people don't know this. I came across this when I was up in Eugene, Oregon.

In 1952 in Eugene, Oregon when the Church was still very, very small, Eugene, Oregon being the mother Church and they had the College down in Pasadena just starting and so forth, they had a big *difficulty* over how to count Pentecost. And I think at that time they had just less than a dozen members up in Eugene, and all but one of them went with a Sunday count of Pentecost. So Herbert Armstrong sent Raymond Cole up there to solve the problem and to try and save the Church. And then he had Hermon Hoeh go ahead and do a study on it to find out from the scriptures. Well, they concluded that it ought to be on a Monday.

So what happened was that this came up again and again during the years from then until 1974. And in 1974 it came up again and there was really a big difficulty about it and there was more knowledge concerning the Hebrew and concerning the Greek and so forth. So again they had another study on it and there was a ministerial conference over it and I was there at the conference and I heard Hermon Hoeh give his confession as to how he came up with a Monday Pentecost, which was this. In Leviticus 23 he went ahead and said that the word Sabbath *ha shabbath* meant "weeks." *Ha shabbath* never means "weeks" but he concluded in his mind that since Herbert Armstrong was the apostle of God that the apostle of God could not be wrong with a Monday Pentecost, so he sought a way to justify it and that's how he justified it. So he had to admit at this conference that *ha shabbath* meant "Sabbath" and "Sabbath" only, and *shabua* meant "weeks." "Week or weeks," the *shabua* is the week.

So that's how we came to have a Monday Pentecost in the Worldwide Church of God. And all of those years and all of those problems could have been solved going clear back to 1952 if it would have been handled rightly. And since that time there are many, many people who have tried to justify a Monday Pentecost and we'll see how they do it, one of them, because before we begin Pentecost we need to go through and review how to count it. First of all I'm going to show you how to count it correctly, and I'm going to use the Schocken Bible, Volume 1, The Five Books of Moses. Now when I was on my trip back east I mentioned the phone number for Christian Book Distributors. And I gave you the wrong number so I'm going to give you the right number: Christian Book Distributors— 978-977-5000. And I called the number to verify that it was correct, and it is correct. Now then, you cannot get it by asking for the Schocken Bible because it is under the *First Five Books of Moses*. So here is the order number at CBD: Stock Number — 40616 .

Now the Schocken Bible has the first five books of Moses and it is a translation, which is based upon the more literal reading of the Hebrew and it is really excellent. And when I first got it I was shocked at how that he was able to get it published at Schocken Publishing Company, because that is the largest Jewish publication company in the world. And I've since figured out how he was able to get the clarity of scripture but get it past the Rabbi's, because the Rabbi's are not interested in scripture, they're interested in commentary. So he gave many of the traditional Rabbinical commentaries in the commentary section and so it got through and got published. Because here he says…let's go to Leviticus 23, but let me just tell you very clearly concerning another dispute that centers around Passover…that is when "between the two evenings" or *ben ha arbaim* is. And he translates it correctly "between the setting times," which I think is a good, very good translation. But he makes this definition of it and he proves it in Exodus 16. Now I'm not going to go back and do that, we've already done that. But he says concerning "between the setting times" is between the time that the sun is below the horizon, no longer visible, and total darkness. An idiomatic rendition would be "at twilight." There, from one of the foremost experts in the world on Hebrew.

Now he also translated this from the Ben Asher-Ben Napthalai text, which is the Levitical Masoretic text. Most people don't realize that there is also a Rabbinic Masoretic text, which comes from the Ashkenazi manuscripts, which come out of Poland and East Germany. And those are not the texts that Luther and Tyndale used to translate the Old Testament. That's another story I won't get into it, but suffice to say we have here a proper Levitical Hebrew text underlying the Schocken translation.

Now let's come to Leviticus 23 and let's pick it up here in verse 10, and we will go through on how to count it and I'm going to show you five checkpoints that gives us absolute certainty that it is the 50th day and it is on a Sunday. Now, many people are familiar with double entry bookkeeping. Double entry bookkeeping gives you two reference points so that you can balance the books. Now if you want to balance the books without balancing the books you do like this little joke. There's a little cartoon came out, the auditor came in and was auditing this business and he said, "Well I see your books are in perfect shape they all balance, but I have just one question." And the bookkeeper looked up and said, "Well, what's that?" He said, "What is this ESP account? That seems be a very large account and I don't know what it is?" And she said, "Oh, that means "error some place". (Laughter) Whenever there's an error I just put it in the ESP account and the books balance."

Well a lot of people do that with the Bible. They don't properly put it together, but double entry bookkeeping rightly handled gives you the correct perspective and it gives you a double check that all your figures are right. Now then if you are on the ocean or on the land and you want to figure a precise place where you are then you do a three point not a two point. You do what is called a triangulation, and you can pick the exact spot as to where you are or the exact spot as to where you want to go. So here with Pentecost we don't have double entry bookkeeping, we don't have triangulation, we have five points which prove and give us a definition on how to come to the 50 days.

Now, you can't have any one of these five points wrong and you cannot have a Monday Pentecost or a 6th of Sivan Pentecost, except in rare occasions where you have all five of these correct. You must break some of them in order to do that. So let's read it here beginning here in verse 10, and this picks up right after what I gave on the Sabbath during Unleavened Bread.

"Speak to the Children of Israel and say to them: When you enter the land that I am giving you, and you harvest its harvest…" Now you see all during the wilderness all they had was manna. Manna, manna, manna, manna, manna, manna. (Laughter) They could boil it, they could bake it, they could deep fry it, they could eat it raw, they could mix it in with other vegetables if they had it, but all they had was manna. And they could not eat bread nor eat grain until they got in to make the first harvest of the land. Now continuing, "...and you harvest its harvest, you are to bring the premier sheaf..." Now the King James says "the sheaf of the firstfruits." ok. The premiere sheaf because that means "the first of the first" in the Hebrew. That's why he translates it "premiere sheaf," it is the first and most important, and that's why this pictures the resurrection of Christ, the ascension of Christ, not his resurrection—I beg your pardon. He was already resurrected at the end of the Sabbath, but His ascension.

And another thing that is important to remember is this: the premiere sheaf had a special time of harvest. And the special time of harvest was right after the regular Sabbath, during the Feast of Unleavened Bread; was ending. Now in Temple times they would do this: they would send out the Priests and they would send out the watchers, and they had a special barley plot right on the Mount of Olives. So they would come across the bridge Kidron, go over to this special ceremonial barley plot and they would then be ready to harvest the sheaf because they had put a scarlet thread around it to mark it off. They marked it off before the Sabbath. Then the men who were the watchers would be up on top of the hill, and they would be watching for sundown. So they would go out there right at the end of the Sabbath, that was less then a Sabbath day's journey because it was only from the Temple over to the Mount of Olives, which was just across the bridge Kidron. And the watchers would look out west and those who were with the group would ask them three times, "Is the sun set?" "No." "Is the sun set?" "No." Finally the third time, "Is the sun set?" "Yes." And they would harvest the sheaf. Now that's a type of when Christ was lifted from the earth, as it were, right at the end of the Sabbath. Just as the first day of the week was beginning. He already had spiritual life given back to Him. So He was the first harvest, the premier sheaf. This was the one then that was to be taken to the Priest.

Now notice verse 11. It says in the King James, "...he shall wave" it. But in the Schocken it says, "He is to elevate the sheaf..." Now, elevate means to "lift up" and that's more like an ascension into heaven than it is just waving back and forth. "He is to elevate the sheaf before the presence of [the LORD], for acceptance for you..." And that's exactly what happened on the day that Jesus ascended into heaven to be accepted of the Father as a sacrifice on our behalf for us. And the "us" means we're the rest of the firstfruits.

Now let's notice, "...on the morrow of the Sabbath..." That means "on the day after the Sabbath." Question: when does the day after the Sabbath begin? At sunset. It's the whole day. You count the whole day. See, because as the day the Sabbath was ending they cut the sheaf, so they had it cut at the beginning of the day. Then in the morning at 9 o'clock they would take it to the Priest and "...on the morrow of the Sabbath [shall] the priest... elevate it."

Now let's come down to verse 14, it gives all the things that they were to do on that day when they waved the wave sheaf offering there. "Now bread or parched-grain or groats, you're not to eat, until that same day..." Now that, you go to Joshua 5 and that tells you when that same day occurred when they entered into the land and harvested it's harvest. Now you go back up here to verse 10 and it says, "...and you harvest its harvest...," see. Some people made the argument that they had to wait until they planted their own grain and harvested their own harvest, which then would put it a year later. But no, you harvest its harvest because when they came in and took over those areas that were already planted, whose grain did it become? It became theirs. So they couldn't eat any "...bread or parched-grain or goats, you are not to eat, until [that] same day..." So if you think eating unleavened bread for seven days is difficult, try 40 years with no bread. That would be, when you really get bread, then that would be kind of like a strange new food, especially all this manna, ok.

Now, you're not to eat it "...until you have brought the near-offering of your God—(it is) a law for the ages, into your generations, throughout all your settlements."

Now verse 15 is the key. "Now you are to number..." That is to count. Counting is different from adding and subtracting. I use this example many times and I'll use it again because we're familiar with it, ok. When you went to high school you went four years, didn't you? If you count the years, they're 9, 10, 11, and 12, correct? Inclusive counting. Now if you take 9 and subtract it from 12, you don't get 4 but you get 3. And that's where people make a lot of mistakes. Another example: you work from Monday to Friday. That includes Monday, does it not? Now just to give you an example, if your boss would do subtracting instead of counting, you would come and get your paycheck and say you were to make $100 a day. And you come in to get your paycheck and you expect the gross amount to be $500, and you look on it and it's $400. So you ask your boss, "Well, I'm short $100 here." Well he says, "No, you agreed to work from Monday to Friday, see, so since it's from Monday I'm not counting Monday because it's from Monday." Well how long would you work for him? (Laughter) You would tell him, "Look, you either pay it..." (Laughter) And then what would you do? If you belonged to a union you'd get a grievance, right? If you didn't belong to the union you'd go to the Fair Employment Practices, right? And you would get your day's pay of $100. Well, this is what people have done concerning Pentecost. They're not doing it correctly, ok.

Now, verse 15, "Now you are to number for yourselves, from the morrow of the Sabbath..." Which means "including that day" because the Hebrew is *m moh-'ghorahth*, which means "including that day." Cause you're counting <u>from</u> the Sabbath. You are not counting <u>from</u> Sunday. You are including Sunday. Let's put it this way. The first day of the week, because that follows the seventh day of the week, correct? Yes. So you have to count from that Sabbath. That's #1, see. You are including the morrow from the Sabbath. You're counting the first day of the week.

Now, to reemphasize it. From the day that you bring the wave sheaf. That's all part of number 1, cause that's included on that day. Now there's only one day to bring the wave sheaf. Every one agrees on the wave sheaf with the exception of the Jews who say it's on the holy day rather than Sabbath, and that's a Pharisaical way of reckoning it, and that's how they come up with the 6th of Sivan.

Now then it says what you're to do here, "...seven Sabbaths-of-days..." (vs. 15), that's #2, seven Sabbaths. Now you're going to miss out on the Sabbath, one Sabbath if you go a 6th of Sivan, so that can't be right. And you're going to miss out on a Sabbath if you're counting to a Monday Pentecost. We'll see there's another checkpoint. So there have to be seven Sabbaths, ok. That's #2, seven Sabbaths of days.

#3, "...whole (weeks) are they to be..." (vs. 15). Now it says, in the King James, "complete weeks" doesn't it? Now what is a whole week? A whole week is seven consecutive days. That is a whole week. That is a complete week. What is a deficient week? A deficient week is when you start, say like on Monday, and if you count from Monday to Monday you're dealing with deficient weeks. All seven weeks are deficient, are they not? You don't have whole weeks. A whole week is day one through day seven including one and including seven. That is a whole week. If you go from day two to day two you have deficient weeks and they are not whole weeks, and they're not complete weeks, see. "Whole weeks are they to be."

Ok, now #4, verse 16. "Unto the morrow of the seventh Sabbath..." So you're to go unto the morrow of the seventh Sabbath, so there again it's not the day after, the day after the Sabbath, see. When you have a Monday Pentecost you're coming to the day after the day after, the Sabbath, correct? "Unto the morrow of the seventh Sabbath you are to number fifty days," which then is #5 [number fifty days].

Now in order to come to the right counting of it you must have all five of these conditions met. Let's go back and review it again so we get it clear here. You are to number unto yourselves:

#1–from the morrow of the Sabbath from the day you bring the wave sheaf.
#2–seven Sabbaths of days
#3–whole weeks are they to be
#4–until the morrow of the seventh Sabbath
#5–you are to number fifty days

You can take any calendar and you can start out on any Sunday and you can count seven full weeks and come to the day after the seventh full week and you will be on a Sunday. There is no way that can be missed.

Now then what they were to do, they were to bring the offering we find here, verse 17. And what they did after that, they brought two loaves of two tenths meal, flour they are to be, firstfruits unto the LORD. Now these firstfruits are different than the others, ok. Notice verse 17, "…leavened you are to bake them…" This is the only offering that God required to be leavened [except peace offerings]. All other meal or bread offerings were to be unleavened. The leavening of these then symbolizes the two covenants, or the two ages of when people would be brought into the Kingdom of God. One being the Covenant with Israel, and of course that goes on back including the other patriarchs going back to that. And two, would be the New Testament Church. That's why there are only two. That's why there are not three, there are not six, there are not ten, there are only two.

Now notice, let's come down here to verse 21. "And you are to make-proclamation on that same day…" Now I want you to really emphasize this, fifty days—that same day. "…a proclamation of holiness shall there be for you, any-kind of servile work you are not to do—a law for the ages, throughout your settlements, into your generations." Ok.

Now we're going to look at a very clever slight of hand which is done by some people where they use the word in verse 16 where it says "…fifty days, then you are to bring the grain [offering] of new-crops to [the LORD]." Now in the King James it says, "and" instead of "then," "and." But this "then" does not mean an afterward "then," but it means inclusive.

Let's come here to Leviticus 15, let's show where they go to try and prove their point. Because they use that as a device to say that we should go to the 51st day by saying that after you have counted the 50 days then you are to go to the 51st day by using the word "then" or "and" as it were. Now let's come here to Leviticus 15:13, this time I'll read in the King James. "And when he that hath an issue is cleansed of his issue [that could be of any wound, sore, infection, anything that was draining or issuing]; then he shall number to himself seven days for his cleansing, and wash his clothes, and bathe his flesh in running water, and shall be clean."

Now verse 14, "And on the eighth day he shall take to him two turtledoves…" and he shall go and that will be his offering. That will be an atonement, see. So what they say is this: that the seven days in counting here is likened unto numbering the 50 days in Leviticus 23. So when you get done numbering the 50 days then you must go to the 51st day. But you see it doesn't say number eight days here. It says count and number to himself seven days. Then on the eighth day he is to go do his offering. It doesn't say count the eighth day. You count seven days and then that eighth day you go do it. Whereas back here it says, number to yourself 50 days and on that same 50th day you are to bring the offering. It does not say, and on the 51st day then you are to bring your offerings.

So what is missing is this, here in Leviticus 15:14, it specifically mentions the eighth day, correct? Yes. In Leviticus 23 it does not mention specifically a 51st day. So if there was to be a parallel in thought then it would have to say, then on the 51st day you are to bring a near grain offering or meal offering. So this is the cleverest slight of hand that I have heard. Because people get tripped up over reading this and there are some people who fervently, adamantly believe in a 51st day Pentecost, a Monday Pentecost based upon what I just said.

See, what happens if you did that, you would go on to the morrow after the morrow, see. So what happens is this, you violate the very last point, see. Or the fourth point rather, under the morrow of the seventh Sabbath. And if you have a Monday Pentecost you are not on the morrow after the seventh Sabbath. You're on the morrow after the morrow of the seventh Sabbath and then you can't avoid the situation down here in verse 21. "And you are to make-proclamation on that <u>same</u> day…" (Lev. 23:21, Schocken). Now if this were referring to the 51st day that's where it would say it. "That same day".

Now let's go to the New Testament here for just a minute. And that's all of Schocken for this situation here, and I'm glad I have the phone number correct for you. Ok, let's go to John 20:1 and we will see that there is a sequence of days, a sequence of counting that lead up to the 50 days. And on "The first *day* of the weeks [or the first of the weeks]…" Now the Greek there is plural *ton sabbaton*, which means "on the first of the weeks". Now which day is the first day of the weeks? The morrow after the Sabbath, correct? And this is counting toward Pentecost. "…Mary Magdalene came early…" and so forth. That is the day that Jesus ascended.

Let's come here to verse 16, we'll just summarize this. "Jesus said to her, 'Mary'. Turning around, she said to Him, 'Rabboni', that is to say, 'Teacher'. . Jesus said to her, 'Do not touch Me; because I have not yet ascended to My Father. But go to My brethren and tell them that I am ascending to My Father and your Father and My God and your God'." So she came and told them. "…bring word that she had seen the Lord, and that He had said these things to her. Afterwards, as evening was drawing near that day, the first *day* of the weeks,…". Apparently just right before the sun was setting, still on that day, the first day of the week. "…And the doors were shut where the disciples had assembled for fear of the Jews, Jesus came and stood in the midst, and saith unto them, 'Peace *be* to you'." (vs. 16-19). And then you know the rest of the story.

Let's come over here, verse 26. "Now after eight days…" So now we've got eight days. We have day one. We have day eight. "…His disciples again were within, and Thomas with them. Jesus came after the doors were shut,…" Jesus appeared to them. All right, now let's come over here to Acts 1. So we have a numbering of the days. Now let's come over here to Acts 1. Let's pick it up right here in verse 1. "The first account I indeed have written, O Theophilus, concerning all things that Jesus began both to do and to teach, Until the day in which He was taken up, after giving command by *the* Holy Spirit to the apostles whom He had chosen; To whom also, by many infallible proofs, He presented Himself alive after He had suffered, being seen by them for forty days, and speaking the things concerning the kingdom of God" (Acts 1:1-3). Now there were a great many brethren that saw Him. Hold your place here and go to 1 Corinthians 15. God did not want this to be some little thing done in a corner. The whole ministry of Christ was public, absolutely if we could put it this way, of great notoriety. And of course to the Scribes and Pharisees—notorious. But they were the notorious ones.

Now let's pick it up here in 1 Corinthians 15, and let's begin in verse 3. "For in the first place, I delivered to you what I also had received: that Christ died for our sins, according to the Scripturres: And that He appeared to Cephas, *and* then to the twelve. Then He appeared to over five hundred brethren at one time, of whom the greater part are alive until now, but some have fallen asleep" (1 Cor. 15:3-6). So He was seen by many, many, many. Many infallible proofs. I don't know all the infallible proofs that it says there. It would be interesting to know what they were, but it doesn't tell us. So when we're resurrected and we meet the apostles and those who saw it, we can ask them what they were. We'll find out at that time.

Now let's come back to the book of Acts, Chapter 1. "And while *they* were assembled with *Him*, He commanded them not to depart from Jerusalem but to 'await the promise of the Father, which' *He said*, 'you have heard of Me. For John indeed baptized with water, but you shall be baptized with *the* Holy Spirit after not many days.' " (Acts 1:4-5). How many days was it from that? Well, we had 40 days. On the 40th day He ascended. The disciples really didn't quite understand it.

Verse 6, "So then, when they were assembled together, they asked Him, saying, 'Lord, will You restore the kingdom to Israel at this time?' " You see because they were promised to sit on thrones weren't they, so they wanted to know, "Lord is the throne coming?" See. "And He said unto them, 'It is not for you to know *the* times or *the* seasons, which the Father has placed in His own authority;." That's what it should read, not power—authority, cause the Greek here is *exousiaz* not *dunamis*. "But you yourselves shall receive power when the Holy Spirit has come upon you, and you shall be My witnesses, both in Jerusalem, and in all Judaea and Samaria, and unto *the* ends of the earth" (vs. 6-8), then which is a continuing ongoing prophecy of the gospel going out to the world. "And after saying these things, *as* they were looking at *Him*, He was taken up, and a cloud received Him out of their sight." Now that would be an experience, wouldn't it? Today we have television or movies and we can see things simulated like that, but to actually see the real thing…and of course this was a one time thing for them.

"Now while they were gazing intently up into heaven…" I wonder what they were thinking when He was going up. I wonder what they were thinking in their minds. "Look, He's going higher and higher, higher and higher. Wow, I can't see Him. There He goes right into a cloud. Look at that." "...as He was going up, two men in white apparel (these were angels) suddenly stood by them, Who also said, '…You men of Galilee, why do you stand *here* looking up into heaven?' " Once the event is finished God wants you to get on with the business, you see. "…This *same* Jesus, Who was taken up from you into heaven, shall come in exactly the same manner as you have seen Him go into heaven" (vs. 10-11). So they returned. Now then, that was the 40th day.

Now let's come to Acts 2. And I'm not going to go through this in great detail, but you can…we have three booklets in Care Package #2. Many, many people have received Care Packages, but you haven't received Care Package #2. And there are a lot of things in Care Package #2 that you need, three of which are: how to count Pentecost, when is Pentecost, and all the peculiar details of it that I've just covered here. So you need to write in for Care Package #2 if you don't have it. And in it, I have the booklet where I go into quite technical detail concerning verse 1, Acts 2. Now let's read it here in the King James.

"And when the day of Pentecost was fully come, they were all with one accord in one place." Now those who believe in a Monday Pentecost and will not refuse to let go of it say that this means "when the Day of Pentecost had ended." But unfortunately that is not what it means. "When the Day of Pentecost was fully come" that doesn't mean the day after, it doesn't mean the day before. Now in the Greek it means this: "and when the day, namely the 50th day was being fulfilled." That's what it means in the Greek. Now if you want to prove that then you have to write in for Care Package #2 and get the Pentecost articles because the "being fulfilled" is a peculiar thing to Greek which is not in any other language, maybe in some other languages, but at least it is not in English. It is in Greek and that is what is called an articular infinitive. That means this: that you put the definite article "the" in front of an "ing" verb. "The coming," "the going," "the keeping," "the fulfilling." And that's what it means—during the fulfilling of the day, namely the 50th day. So it wasn't the day before and it wasn't the day after.

Now let's look at some of the same language here that we find in Leviticus 23. You know what happened there on the Day of Pentecost, I'll cover it for Pentecost. Now let's look at the same…you know what happened, I'll cover this when the day of Pentecost comes but this, look at the fulfilling of not only the wave sheaf offering on the Wave Sheaf Offering Day, the first day, but also the fulfilling of the bringing the loaves of leaven for the 50th day.

Now let's read it right here, Faithful Version, verse 37, "Now after hearing *this*, they were cut to the heart; and they said to Peter and the other, 'Men *and* brethren, what shall we do?' Then Peter said to them, 'Repent, and be baptized each one of you in the name of Jesus Christ for *the* remission of sins, and you yourselves shall receive the gift of the Holy Spirit. For the promise is to you and to your children, and to all who are afar off, as many as *the* Lord our God may call.' And with many other words he earnestly testified and exhorted, saying, 'Be saved from this perverse generation'. Then those who joyfully received his message were baptized; and about three thousand souls were added that day [notice the same wording as back in Leviticus 23, 'the same day'] " (Acts 2:37-41). So there is a fulfilling of the wave offering loaves on the 50th day.

So you have the same exact thing as we find in Leviticus 23 and that's what those loaves were picturing because this was a great and a momentous event, wasn't it? Yes, great momentous event. It just occurred to me that these loaves could also signify more than just what I said, Old Testament, New Testament. It could also signify Jew and Gentile as relating to receiving the Holy Spirit after baptism, because the Gentiles were given the Holy Spirit in the same way that the Jews were, and in the same manner, by the way, Acts 10.

Ok, now that we have that taken care of that, and therefore I won't have to repeat it on Pentecost. I'll do it ahead of time. There are too many things to bring out on Pentecost so I'm doing some of this ahead of time. Let's go to Hebrews 12 and let's see the comparison between Hebrews 12 and Exodus 19 and 20. Hebrews 12, let's go there first. And this is also a very important chapter which also shows us why the first resurrection is on Pentecost and not on the Feast of Trumpets. There will be other things, which I will show to prove that. But I never will forget the first Pentecost that we kept on the first day of the week in 1974. At that time, we were still living in Pasadena and I was pastoring Torrance and Santa Monica and we had combined Torrance and Santa Monica services down at the Los Angeles Convention Center, and Gerald Waterhouse was the speaker. Well, I led the songs and everything. I think someone else brought the Sermonette, but I led the songs and took the announcements and I had to announce to everyone, "Well brethren, here we are the first time keeping Pentecost on the right day." And trying to help them understand a little bit about it, you know, not getting into scripture or anything. But I mentioned just off-handedly, and I said, "Who knows? Maybe we will find out that the first resurrection is really on Pentecost." And Gerald Waterhouse is sitting out there, and I'm thankful that it just sailed over his head, because I'm sure I would have been lambasted up one side and down the other for having said such a presumptuous thing. But later it's turned out to be true. Let's see some of the reasons for it today. Not all of them, we'll cover some of those on Pentecost, but we need to get some of this out before Pentecost.

So let's pick it up here in verse 18. Hebrews 12:18, "For you have not come unto *the* mount [now that's referring to the one back in Exodus 19, Mt. Sinai] that could be touched, and that burned with fire, nor to gloominess, and fearful darkness, and the whirlwind:, and to *the* sound of *the* trumpet…" I want to emphasize "a trumpet." We're going to see that's important. Now the reason I'm emphasizing it is because "trumpets" is plural, "trumpet" is singular. We also need to understand this: on every holy day, you'll read this in Numbers 10, the trumpet was to be blown. So a trumpet was blown on the first day of Unleavened Bread, the seventh day of Unleavened Bread, the day of Pentecost. And then on the Feast of Trumpets, now they had a different day, it was a memorial or a blowing of trumpets all the day long. Of which I think the Buddhists perversion is where they have these big long horns you know. And they all get up there on whatever day they have, they go whhhhh, these big old horns going. And they're all decked up and all these demonic costumes and running around firing off firecrackers and jumping in the air and doing all sorts of silly things to drive the demons away.

Question? Is God going to stop blowing trumpets on the Feast of Trumpets because the pagans do this? Because they have a counterfeit of it? No. Just because pagans have a counterfeit of anything that we do does not mean that we stop doing it because they have something that they have done.

Now, let's continue here. "And to *the* sound of *the* trumpet, and to *the* voice of the words, which those who heard, *begged* that *the* word not be spoken *directly* to them: (For they could not endure what was being commanded: 'And if even an animal touches the mountain, it shall be stoned, or shot through with an arrow [now a dart means an arrow]:' And so terrifying was the sight, *that* Moses said, 'I am greatly afraid and trembling'.)" Now we're going to see so did all the people. Now he's making a comparison here. And the comparison has to do with the Feast of Pentecost, because that's when the Ten Commandments were given. "But you have come to Mount Sion, and to *the* city of *the* living God, heavenly Jerusalem; and to an innumerable company of angels; *To the* joyous festival gathering, and to *the* church of *the* firstborn…and to God *the* Judge of all, and to *the* spirits of the just who have been perfected;." (vs. 19-23). Now the Greek has it here "to the general assembly." The general assembly here means "to the festal gathering of the church of the firstborn." Now when is the festal gathering of the church of the firstborn going to take place? Well, let's see. "…which are written in heaven…" and so forth.

Now, let's come back here to Exodus 19, let's look at some parallels. Let's pick it up here in verse 16, which then is the day of Pentecost and I've got a chart, the Count Pentecost Chart,. showing that, and that's in the Care Package #2. All right. "And it came to pass on the third day in the morning, that there were thunders and lightnings, and a thick cloud upon the mount, and the voice of the trumpet…" Now we have "a trumpet," now we have "the trumpet". It wasn't many trumpets. "…exceeding loud; so that all the people that *was* in the camp trembled. And Moses brought forth the people out of the camp to meet with God; and they stood at the nether part of the mount [that is up close to the base of the mountain]. And mount Sinai was altogether on a smoke because the LORD descended upon it in fire: and the smoke thereof ascended as the smoke of a furnace, and the whole mount quaked greatly. And when the voice of the trumpet sounded long, and waxed louder and louder, Moses spake, and God answered him by a voice. And the LORD came down upon mount Sinai, on the top of the mount: and the LORD called Moses *up* to the top of the mount; and Moses went up" (Ex. 19:16-20). And I imagine all the people…[sound of sucking breath in]. Boy, that must have been a sight with him going up.

"And the LORD said unto Moses, 'Go down,'…" So he climbed and down this mountain. Boy, Moses really was a mountain climber here. "Go down, charge the people, lest they break through unto the LORD to gaze, and many of them perish. And let the priests also, which come near to the LORD, sanctify themselves, lest the LORD break forth upon them.' And Moses said unto the LORD, 'The people cannot come up to mount Sinai: for Thou chargedst us, saying, 'Set bounds about the mount, and sanctify it.' And the LORD said unto him, 'Away, get thee down, and thou shalt come up, thou, and Aaron with thee: but let not the priests and the people break through to come up unto the LORD, lest He break forth upon them.' So Moses went down unto the people, and spake unto them" (vs. 21-24). And then God gave the Ten Commandments.

And of course the people couldn't stand it. Now this must have been some awesome display. Here Exodus 20:18, "And all the people saw the thunderings, and the lightnings, and the noise of the trumpet, and the mountain smoking: and when the people saw *it*, they removed, and stood afar off." No chance of them running up the hill. "And they said unto Moses, [You] speak with us, and we will hear: but let not God speak with us, lest we die" (vs. 19). So this must have been such a loud noise and so much happening that the vibrations of the noise and the thunder and the lightning was just going through their system so much that it affected them to the point that they felt they were going to die. Have you ever had any loud noise affect you that way? Well that's how it affected them. Ok.

Now, let's look at a scripture here which is important for us to understand. Hold your place cause we're coming right back here. Let's go to Jeremiah 2, because we're going to see that with the giving of the Ten Commandments and the events that took place right after that, the day after Pentecost, that ties right in with the Church and the marriage of the Lamb and so forth. Let's come in here with Jeremiah 2. Let's pick it up in verse 1.

"Moreover the word of the LORD came to me, saying, 'Go and cry in the ears of Jerusalem, saying, 'Thus saith the LORD; I remember thee, the kindness of thy youth, the love of thine espousals, when thou wentest after Me in the wilderness, in a land *that was* not sown. Israel *was* holiness unto the LORD'…" Now, when did they become holiness unto the LORD? We'll see. "…*and* the firstfruits of His increase:…" When did they become the firstfruits? See because they were literally harvested out of Egypt, were they not? And had a seven week journey coming up to Mt. Sinai. So they became firstfruits and became holiness to the LORD on Pentecost and then the sealing of it on the day after Pentecost when the covenant was sealed and the marriage took place. "…firstfruits of His increase: all that devour Him shall offend; evil shall come upon them, saith the LORD. Hear ye the word of the LORD, O house of Jacob, and all the families of the house of Israel…" (Jeremiah 2:1-4). And then He asked, "What happened to you? I brought you out of Egypt, why did you reject Me? If I were sent even unto other nations, why they would have rejected their gods and accepted Me and would have kept Me, but you've forsaken Me."

Now let's come to Isaiah 54 just a few pages back. Isaiah 54:5, "For thy Maker *is* thine husband; the LORD of hosts *is* His name; and thy Redeemer the Holy One of Israel…" Now when did the LORD become the husband to Israel? Now you see there are going to be parallels with Christ and the Church with this. Parallels with Mt. Sinai and Mt. Sion. Parallels with the festal gathering at the foot of Mt. Sinai to receive the Ten Commandments and the festal gathering which will take place at the resurrection, which we will see, and the marriage of the Church and the Lamb.

Now let's come back to Exodus 20 again. Let's continue on. The rest of Exodus 20, 21, 22, and 23 are all the basic statutes and judgments based upon the Ten Commandments. Now we come to Chapter 24. This becomes important because this finishes off the day of Pentecost. And the day after Pentecost then is when the marriage took place. And the marriage took place when they accepted the covenant because this was a covenant ceremony.

Chapter Twenty-four

Exodus 24:1, "And He said unto Moses, 'Come up unto the LORD, thou, and Aaron, Nadab, and Abihu, and seventy of the elders of Israel; and worship ye afar off. And Moses alone shall come near the LORD: but they shall not come nigh; neither shall the people go up with him'" (vs. 1-2). So Moses came, then he came down. So he went up, came down… Moses doing a lot of walking here. "…And told the people all the words of the LORD, and all the judgments: and all the people answered with one voice, and said, 'All the words which the LORD hath said will we do.'" Now what do we have in a marriage ceremony? Do you accept this woman as your lawful wedded wife? I do. Do you accept this man as your lawful wedded husband? I do. This is what Israel and the LORD did here. And it's always a written contract. God never enters into a covenant without some kind of written contract. God is the author of law, so God is legal. So He makes sure that it's done legally and technically correct.

Verse 4, "And Moses wrote all the words of the LORD, and rose up early in the morning [so then this is after Pentecost], and builded an altar under the hill, and twelve pillars. according to the twelve tribes of Israel. And he sent young men of the children of Israel, which offered burnt offering, and sacrificed peace offerings of oxen unto the LORD. And Moses took half of the blood, and put *it* in basons; and half of the blood he sprinkled on the altar. And he took the book of the covenant, and read in the audience of the people…" These are the words of the marriage covenant between Israel and God, which took place the day after Pentecost. Years ago I thought it was done on Pentecost but it's obvious, "and in the morning," so that's the next day. "…Read it in the audience of the people: and they said, 'All that the LORD hath said will we do, and be obedient.' And Moses took the blood and sprinkled *it* on the people, and said, 'Behold the blood of the covenant…" Now when you understand covenant relationships and you understand that a covenant is cut. It is binding until death. That's why when Christ came to be human, one of the functions He served in dying, was the husband to physical Israel died to loose that marriage. Now either He had to die or all of Israel had to die. So God died. That loosed the Old Covenant. No longer binding (Rom. 7:1-4). That has nothing to do with the laws and commandments because all covenants have laws and commandments and if you don't understand that write for the series on "The Covenants of God." We have 15 tapes which go through all the covenants, ok. "…Blood of the covenant [this is serious business], which the LORD hath made with you concerning all these words." (Exodus 24:1-8). So we have the marriage of Israel to God.

When the Church is resurrected there will be the marriage of Christ and the Church and there will be a new covenant at that time. It will be a marriage covenant for all eternity. I don't think many people really understand that. The covenant we are under now is renewed every year by us with the bread and wine and foot-washing. Christ doesn't have to renew it because He gave His life. That's why He said He would not eat of the bread or drink of the wine, especially of the wine. Of course He's not going to eat of bread because there's no…well He ate bread later but that wasn't in the covenant ceremony of the Passover. He ate bread and fish there we find in John 21. But He's not going to drink of the fruit of the vine until it's in the Kingdom. And when its going to be when He drinks it, It will be the wine of the marriage ceremony when the Church is married to Christ.

Now let's look at where and when and how this is going to happen. But first of all let's answer a question here and let's get into the situation concerning what is called the sea of glass, which we pick up right here beginning in verse 9. "Then went up Moses, and Aaron, Nadab, and Abihu, and seventy of the elders of Israel: And they saw the God of Israel: and *there was* under His feet as it were a paved work of a sapphire stone, and as it were the body of heaven in *his* clearness" (vs. 9-10). There is a sea of glass, or a pavement of what you would call glass. Now why did He come down to there? So that they could see Him but not look upon Him. They saw the outline of Him but they couldn't see it clearly. So Moses had to go up and to be up there on this pavement with God.

Now notice what they did. "And upon the nobles of the children of Israel He laid not His hand: also they saw God, and did eat and drink." So they had a special ceremony there, didn't they, commemorating the marriage of Israel and God. "And the LORD said unto Moses, 'Come up to Me into the mount, and be there: and I will give thee tables of stone, and a law, and commandments which I have written; and thou mayest teach them.' And Moses rose up, and his minister Joshua: and Moses went up into the mount of God. And he said unto the elders, 'Tarry ye here for us, until we come again unto you: and behold, Aaron and Hur *are* with you: if any man have any matters to do, let him come unto them. And Moses went up into the mount, and a cloud covered the mount. And the glory of the LORD abode upon mount Sinai, and the cloud covered it six days: and the seventh day He called unto Moses out of the midst of the cloud. And the sight of the glory of the LORD *was* like devouring fire on the top of the mount in the eyes of the children of Israel. And Moses went into the midst of the cloud, and gat him up into the mount: and Moses was in the mount forty days and forty nights" (vs. 11-18).

Well, you know what happened there. The children of Israel couldn't stand it. They thought, "I wonder what's happening. I wonder what happened to that Moses, he's still up there. You know, this has been like unto three weeks and where is this guy? I bet he's fallen into the volcanic explosions up there and he's been all devoured. Yeah, well we better go to Aaron here. He said go to Aaron, so let's go to Aaron." And they came to Aaron and said, "You know Aaron, look we don't know where he is, we don't have a God, now what you should do, you just make us gods." And Aaron said, "Ok, bring all your gold and all of this…" And I love the excuse when Moses came down and said, "Aaron why did you do this?" He said, "We just threw the gold in the fire and out jumped these calves." You know. But just as an aside, what happened? The children of Israel didn't want God's pure way, they wanted a religion. Remember that, I'll talk about that later on.

Ok, let's go on. Let's look at the presence of God and the sea of glass. Here we find the sea of glass. Now there's some people very angry at me because I say that when we're resurrected we're going to be on the sea of glass. Well, we'll get to that verse in a minute. Then what you need to do is also be very angry at God because God only talks of the prophet twice by name. And is the false prophet going to do a lot of damage? Yes indeed. So please understand something about scripture, which is this: once is sufficient.

Now let's come to Psalm 11. Let's talk about God's throne because that also has to do with the sea of glass. Psalm 11:4, "The LORD *is* in His holy temple, the LORD'S throne *is* in heaven: His eyes behold, His eyelids try, the children of men." So God is in heaven. How close is the heaven of God's throne to the earth? I can't tell you but I don't think it's in the far, far, far north, because we're going to see that it's probably a whole lot closer to the earth but men cannot see it at the present time.

Ok, let's come to Psalm 45, it talks about the throne of God. Psalm 45:6, "Thy throne, O God, *is* forever and ever: the sceptre of Thy kingdom *is* a right sceptre. Thou lovest righteousness, and hatest wickedness: therefore God, Thy God, hath anointed Thee with the oil of gladness above Thy fellows" (Psalm 45:6-7). That's a direct prophecy that Christ would be, or was, and is God. Right there. His throne is forever and ever.

Psalm 47:8, "God reigneth over the heathen: God sitteth upon the throne of His holiness. The princes of the people are gathered together, *even* the people of the God of Abraham [now that could have an allusion to the resurrection]: for the shields of the earth *belong* unto God: He is greatly exalted" (Psalm 47:8-9).

Now, let's come to Ezekiel 1. We have something here in Ezekiel 1 that is very unusual, and I don't think that anyone can properly explain about the Cherubim, exactly how they look like. I know people have tried to draw pictures of them. When I read it I think of something of a jet plane and the things that look…the way that they look, I don't know how to explain it other than just it's in there. What he wrote he wrote and for us to try and decide what it is, is very difficult for us to do indeed. But let's just clarify something here that is important. Everything in this room is made of the dust of the earth, including us. Even though we are composed of the dust of the earth and are flesh we have life, whereas this microphone doesn't, nor the stand doesn't, nor the rug, and so forth. We have things which bring us light which are called lights and have electricity in them, but those are still made of physical fleshly things. There are things in heaven which are made of spiritual things which are not living beings. For example, New Jerusalem is going to be made out of spiritual material but it is not a living being. So likewise here with this, whatever these Cherubim are, it is God's chariot.

So let's pick it up here in verse 20. "Whithersoever the spirit was to go, they went, thither *was their* spirit to go; and the wheels were lifted up over against them: for the spirit of the living creature *was* in the wheels. When those went, *these* went; and when those stood, *these* stood; and when those were lifted up from the earth, the wheels were lifted up over against them [Now that seems to me kind of like the wheels were folded up in just like an airplane today. That's what it seems like to me. I don't know]: for the spirit of the living creature *was* in the wheels." Now the "spirit", that could be just the power of the living creatures. "And the likeness [now here's what I want to get to] of the firmament upon the heads of the living creature *was* as the colour of the terrible [or that is awesome] crystal…," so beautiful to behold. So there we have something now in kind of like a rainbow over them like crystal. Not a sea of glass, but just to show you that there are things composed of spirit.

And verse 23, "And under the firmament *were* their wings straight, the one toward the other: everyone had two, which covered on this side, and every one had two, which covered on that side, their bodies. And when they went, I heard the noise of their wings, like the noise of great waters, as the voice of the Almighty, the voice of speech, as the noise of an host: when they stood, they let down their wings." So it's just like, you know, the closest I can come to that is like propellers. And when the plane lands you turn off the propellers they stop. The propellers are kind of like wings. That's the best I can do.

Verse 25, "And there was a voice from the firmament that *was* over their heads, when they stood, *and* had let down their wings. And above the firmament that *was* over their heads *was* the likeness of a throne [So this was to carry a portable throne of God], as the appearance of a sapphire stone: and upon the likeness of the throne *was* the likeness as the appearance of a man above upon it. And I saw as the colour of amber, as the appearance of fire round about within it, from the appearance of His loins even upward, and from the appearance of His loins even downward, I saw as it were the appearance of fire, and it had brightness round about." So here he's seeing just a glorified spirit being who's obviously God. "As the appearance of the bow that is in the cloud in the day of rain [so there was a rainbow round about this whole Cherubim], so *was* the appearance of the brightness round about. This *was* the appearance of the likeness of the glory of the LORD. And when I saw *it*, I fell upon my face, and I heard a voice of one that spake" (Ezek. 1:20-28). "And He said unto me (Ezek. 2:1), 'Son of man, stand upon thy feet, and I will speak unto thee.'" So here God came right down to Ezekiel. Boy, that's quite a thing, you see. Stood him on his feet, gave him His message and everything. "And the spirit entered into me when He spake unto me, and set me upon my feet, that I heard Him that spake unto me" (vs. 1-3). And then He gives him his commission that he is to do. So that's quite a thing.

Now let's come to Ezekiel 3:12. "Then the spirit took me up, and I heard behind me a voice of a great rushing, *saying*, 'Blessed *be* the glory of the LORD from His place.' *I heard* also the noise of the wings of the living creatures [so apparently he got a ride on this

Cherubim] that touched one another, and the noise of the wheels over against them, and a noise of a great rushing. So the spirit lifted me up, and took me away, and I went in bitterness, in the heat of my spirit; but the hand of the LORD was strong upon me. Then I came to them of the captivity at Telabib, that dwelt by the river of Chebar…" (vs. 12-15). So apparently Ezekiel had a ride on a Cherubim.

Now this is probably very similar as to what happened to Enoch when he was carried away, and Elisha when he was carried away. They were carried away to a separate place and the chariot of the LORD took them away, ok. The reason I'm bringing that out is because I want you to see that there are things made of spirit which must then be manifested to the human eyes that you can't see otherwise and God uses those things. Ok.

Let's come to Isaiah 6 and let's see where Isaiah was also before the throne of God. As we're turning to Isaiah 6 let's understand something. Maybe this will convince some people who want to profess themselves to be prophets, to maybe not be prophets any longer because maybe the Cherubim is going to come and correct you rather than give you a ride. God may come and correct you with some pretty severe things. That's why no one should set himself up as a prophet. Look at how Ezekiel was set up. Look at how Jeremiah was set up. Look how Isaiah was set up here. God did it directly. Let's read it here beginning in verse 1.

"In the year that king Uzziah died I saw also the LORD sitting upon a throne, high and lifted up, and His train filled the temple." So he saw the throne and the temple. "Above it stood the seraphims: each one had six wings; with twain he covered his face, and with twain he covered his feet, and with twain he did fly. And one cried unto another, and said, 'Holy, holy, holy, *is* the LORD of hosts [Now we'll see in Revelation 4 this is pretty similar to what we have back there]: the whole earth *is* full of His glory.' And the posts of the door moved at the voice of him that cried, and the house was filled with smoke. Then said I, 'Woe *is* me! for I am undone; because I *am* a man of unclean lips, and I dwell in the midst of a people of unclean lips: for mine eyes have seen the King, the LORD of hosts.'" Actually saw God in vision. "Then flew one of the seraphims unto me, having a live coal in his hand, *which* he had taken with the tongs from off the altar: and he laid *it* upon my mouth, and said, 'Lo, this hath touched thy lips; and thine iniquity is taken away, and thy sin purged.'" So God has more than one way of forgiving sin doesn't He? This was to show Isaiah that God was going to use him. "Also I heard the voice of the LORD, saying, 'Whom shall I send, and who will go for us?' Then said I, 'Here *am* I; send me.' And He said, 'Go, and tell this people, Hear ye indeed, but understand not; and see ye indeed, but perceive not. Make the heart of this people fat, and make their ears heavy, and shut their eyes; lest they see with their eyes, and hear with their ears, and understand with their heart, and convert, and be healed'" (Isa. 6:1-10). Now how many times was that quoted in Matthew and by the apostles in the New Testament, yes, and even by Christ Himself.

Ok, let's continue on this with the throne of God. Let's come to Acts 7. Now this is when Stephen was martyred. Let's just pick it up here in verse 51. You talk about a witness. And this was one of the last profound witnesses to the leaders of Judaism. And with this, with this, this sealed the doom of Jerusalem and the temple and everything. "O stiffnecked and uncircumcised in heart and ears! You do always resist the Holy Spirit; as your fathers *did*, so also *do* you. Which of the prophets did your fathers not persecute? And they killed those who foretold the coming of the Righteous One, of Whom you have become the betrayers and murderers; Who received the law by *the* disposition of angels, but have not kept *it*." And here they thought they were the most righteous people in the world. "And when they heard these things, they were cut to their hearts [not unto repentance], and they gnashed their teeth at him…" Not on him but against him. They were sitting there gnashing their teeth. "But he, being filled with *the* Holy Spirit, looked intently into heaven, *and* saw *the* glory of God, and Jesus standing at the right hand of God…" (vs. 51-56). So again, how close is the throne of God to the earth? We don't know. But Stephen looked up and saw it, and Christ standing at the right hand.

Now let's understand something about being at the right hand. When someone is at the right hand that is a sign of equality. That is a sign of equality, standing at the right hand of God. Notice He wasn't sitting there. You come to Revelation the last verse and it says "To the one who overcomes will I give *authority* to sit with Me in My throne even as I also overcame, and sat down with My Father in His throne." (Rev. 3:21). So this time He was standing. He was standing there looking on to what was going on, not just sitting viewing. So He wasn't a passive participant in this, but active—standing.

And Stephen said, "…Behold, I see the heavens opened, and the Son of man standing at the right *hand* of God.' Then they cried out with a loud voice [They couldn't stand this, couldn't stand this. The one whom they killed and crucified, rejected], *and* stopped their ears, and rushed upon him with one accord, and cast *him* out of the city, *and* stoned *him*…" (Acts 7:56-58). There comes a point some people just won't listen to the truth at all and there's no repentance available.

Now let's continue on with this concerning the throne of God. Let's come to Revelation 4. Let's begin in verse 1. I'm so out of time I don't have time to finish this. There's too many important things that I need to cover about the sea of glass.

End of Sermon

Transcriber: Carolyn Singer

Pentecost and the Sea of Glass—Sermon I
April 17, 1999
Scriptural References

1) Leviticus 23:10-11, 14-17, 21, (SB)

2) Leviticus 15:13-14

3) John 20:1, 16-19, 26

4) Acts 1:1-11

5) Acts 2:1, 37-41

6) Hebrews 12:18-23

7) Exodus 19:16-24

8) Exodus 20:18-19

9) Jeremiah 2:1-4

10) Isaiah 54:5

11) Exodus 24:1-18

12) Psalm 11:4

13) Psalm 45:6-7

14) Psalm 47:8-9

15) Ezekiel 1:20-28

16) Ezekiel 2:1-3

17) Ezekiel 3:12-15

18) Isaiah 6:1-10

19) Acts 7:51-58

20) Revelation 3:21

CHAPTER TWENTY-FIVE

Pentecost and the Sea of Glass—Sermon II

Pentecost—1999

May 1, 1999

This is tape 2 on the sea of glass leading up to Pentecost. And I've done it this way so that when you come to day 49 and day 50 for Pentecost then you can put the whole picture together. And I have tried in the past to get it all together on day 49 and day 50 but everywhere I went on my trips I always had questions, "Can you tell us more about the sea of glass?" And so in giving this I ran out of space last time to get it all on one tape so I said, "Ok we will do it on two tapes." And then you can put this together with day 49 and day 50 when they come. So let's back up and just talk a little bit now about the throne of God and how the throne of God and the sea of glass are combined together, as we will see. But let's go back and look at some of the scriptures that we ended up, just in review.

Let's go to Psalm 11. And I think the thing that is most interesting is this in viewing the things concerning William Tyndale, which I've discussed a little bit, but that those who really have the Spirit of God and want to teach the word of God, as William Tyndale did, and as anyone that God will use, they will preach the words of Christ. They will use the scriptures. And when you stop and think about it, there is nothing greater that you can use. There is nothing greater that you can preach on than the word of God. Because the word of God is true. The word of God has been sent to us so that we may understand. The word of God is given to us to bring us eternal salvation through Christ and the Holy Spirit of God. So we have here in our hands sitting in front of us the greatest possession that you could have. That's why David said, "Therefore I love thy commandments above gold; yea, above fine gold." (Psa. 119:127). Because there is no wealth in the world that can buy this. There is no wealth in the world that can buy what William Tyndale did over 460 years ago. And he did it so that it is a blessing for us today.

And part of understanding the word of God is to go through it and put it together and let God lead us in it, you see. Christ gave the promise that the Spirit will lead us into all truth, and will lead us into understanding the things which are to come. But it's also based upon, do we love God? Because if we don't love God then that's not going to happen. God will leave us to our own devices. If we love power and prestige and money and things of this world, then God will leave us to our own devices. Before then He will correct us, He will work with us to bring us to repentance that we may change and grow.

And I think when we're looking at this thing concerning Pentecost and when we are looking at the old teachings that we had in Worldwide, I think that part of the problem was this, is that in keeping a Monday Pentecost we never understood the truth of the resurrection being pictured by the day of Pentecost. That was part of the penalty that we had. And yet down through the years it was always bragged upon that, "Well, God blessed us though we kept a Monday Pentecost and what was bound on earth was bound in heaven." Well if it was, why did God change it? Why did God bring it to their attention to do it correctly? Well that's so those of us who remain can understand the truth. So when we get into the sea of glass we need to understand about the throne of God. And so we're going to cover some scriptures about the throne of God and then we will go on through and into the book of

Revelation and then we will see why Pentecost has to be on and pictured by the first resurrection rather than Trumpets.

Here, Psalm 11:4, "The LORD *is* in His holy temple, the LORD'S throne *is* in heaven: His eyes behold, His eyelids try, the children of men." So God knows. Now remember the account when Stephen was martyred in Acts 7? He said he saw heaven opened and the Son of man standing at the right hand of the throne of God looking down and seeing what was going to happen. "The LORD trieth the righteous: but the wicked and him that loveth violence His soul hateth. Upon the wicked He shall rain snares, fire and brimstone, and an horrible tempest: *this shall be* the portion of their cup." And we see in the book of Revelation, does God do that? No doubt about it. "For the righteous LORD loveth righteousness; his countenance doth behold the upright " (Psa. 11:4-7). So God is on His throne.

Let's come here to Psalm 45 and let's see what kind of throne this is. This is really… this is a prophecy of Christ Himself. Psalm 45:6, "Thy throne, O God, *is* for ever and ever: the sceptre of Thy kingdom *is* a right sceptre [or a righteous sceptre]." "Thou lovest righteousness, and hatest wickedness: therefore God, Thy God, hath anointed Thee with the oil of gladness above Thy fellows" (Psa.45:6-7). That's a direct prophecy of Christ. And of course Christ is right at the very throne of God.

Now let's come over here to Psalm 47 and let's pick it up here in verse 7. "For God *is* the King of all the earth: sing ye praises with understanding. God reigneth over the heathen: God sitteth upon the throne of His holiness" (Psa. 47:7-8).

Now let's see what happened to the throne of God during the days of Ezekiel. Let's go back and review that, because part of understanding about the sea of glass is this: that wherever God goes when He's not on His throne He has a portable throne that's in the Cherubim. And that's what Ezekiel saw. Now I'm not going to go back and try and understand all of that, and try and tell you what it was that Ezekiel saw. I don't think any man can really figure out exactly what he said. I know I've seen people draw pictures of it and it kind of looks like a combination of a jet plane and a flying saucer and all of that sort of thing, so I don't know what it looks like. But it's very possible.

But nevertheless let me just review and say this as we discussed last time. Everything that we see in this room and see around us in the world is made of the dust of the earth. Now, we're made of the dust of the earth but that, in the flesh of human beings, is formed into a different kind than the soil out here, or the grass, or the trees, or the carpet that we have on the floor here, or the lights that we have overhead. Likewise with God. God makes things out of spirit which are not necessarily living creatures. Now, that's the best I can explain about the Cherubim. The Cherubim may in fact be living creatures but you look at it in another way and they may in fact not be living creatures as they're attached to this thing called the Cherubim and it is a chariot of God.

So let's pick it up here in Ezekiel 1:21, and here's how it went. "When those went, *these* went; and when those stood, *these* stood; and when those were lifted up from the earth, the wheels were lifted up over against them…" Kind of sounds like collapsing wheels, doesn't it? Almost like wheels of an airplane that they land on the wheels and when they take off the wheels close up. That's what it sounds like to me. "…For the spirit [that is the power] of the living creature *was* in the wheels. And the likeness of the firmament upon the heads of the living creature *was* as the colour of the terrible crystal…" (Ezek. 1:21-22). So notice we're going to see that the sea of glass, and around God's throne, crystal is referred to as crystal. But I'm sure that it is something that is made out of spirit that is spirit substance that is created into the thing that God moves around in. Just like your car. Your car is made out of the dust of the earth. But you stop and think about how the dust of the earth has to be refined to make the car, to make the plastic, to make the metal, to make the tires, to give you all the things that you have with heating, with air conditioning, with the radio, with…you know, if you have a record player or a cd player…all of those things.

Now if we can do this as human beings, cannot God do more and greater with spirit? I mean after all, consider New Jerusalem that's coming down out of heaven. That's wholly made out of spirit, ok. So here's "…terrible crystal, stretched forth over their heads above." So it's kind of like an arch. "And under the firmament *were* their wings straight, the one toward the other: every one had two, which covered on this side, and every one had two, which covered on that side, their bodies. And when they went, I heard the noise of their wings, like the noise of great waters…" Kind of like a big power thrust taking off. And that's what the shuttle launch sounds like when you listen to it, see. And it's got the fire breathing out the back, ok. "…As the voice of the Almighty, the voice of speech, as the noise of an host: when they stood, they let down their wings" (vs. 22-24). So in other words, when it came to a stand still they let down their wings. Reminds me more of a helicopter, doesn't it, with the wings?

"And there was a voice from the firmament that *was* over their heads, when they stood, *and* had let down their wings. And above the firmament that *was* over their heads *was* the likeness of a throne [now we're talking about the throne of God], as the appearance of a sapphire stone: and upon the likeness of the throne *was* the likeness as the appearance of a man above upon it. And I saw as the colour of amber, as the appearance of fire round about within it, from the appearance of His loins even upward, and from the appearance of His loins even downward, I saw as it were the appearance of fire, and it had brightness round about. As the appearance of the bow that is in the cloud in the day of rain…" Now we're going to see when we come back to Revelation 4 that the rainbow surrounds God's throne. So this goes wherever He goes. "…so *was* the appearance of the brightness round about. This *was* the appearance of the likeness of the glory of the LORD. And when I saw *it*, I fell upon my face and I heard a voice of one that spoke" (vs. 25-28).

Now Chapter 2:1, "And He said unto me, 'Son of man, stand upon thy feet, and I will speak unto thee.' And the spirit entered into me when He spake unto me, and set me upon my feet, that I heard Him that spake unto me. And He said unto me, 'Son of man, I send thee to the children of Israel, to a rebellious nation that hath rebelled against Me; they and their fathers have transgressed against me, *even* unto this very day'" (Ezek. 2:1-3).

Ok, let's come to Chapter 3:10, "Moreover He said unto me, 'Son of man, all My words that I shall speak unto thee receive in thine heart, and hear with thine ears." Boy what a lesson for us today. Absolutely, what a lesson. Do we receive all the words of God and put them in our heart and hear with our ears, let it lead us and guide us as God's Spirit leads us? Verse 11, "'And go, get thee to them of the captivity, unto the children of thy people, and speak unto them, and tell them, Thus saith the Lord GOD; whether they will hear, or whether they will forbear.'" So there comes a time when you have to give a witness whether they will hear or whether they won't hear. And that's one of the reasons why we do the things that we do. Now we don't hear from everyone who we send a care package to, but at least it is a witness to them. And if they don't act upon it, it is a witness against them.

And as I mentioned the last time, sometimes a witness is just what people would consider a very small thing. Like God told Jeremiah, "You write this witness against Babylon. You give it to one of the captives and when they get to Babylon have them throw it in the river for a witness against them." Well, how many people saw that? I'm sure the king of Babylon was not on the bridge when he threw it in the river, but it was still a witness against him. So what I want us to do in some of these things as we're going along, let us really think, let us really think on the word of God and think of what God has for us. And to understand the words of God like this here. "Then the spirit took me up, and I heard behind me a voice of a great rushing, *saying*, 'Blessed *be* the glory of the LORD from His place.' *I heard* also the noise of the wings of the living creatures that touched one another, and the noise of the wheels over against them, and a noise of a great rushing" (vs. 12-13).

So Ezekiel got a ride in the Cherubim (laughter), that's what he did. "So the spirit lifted me up, and took me away, and I went in bitterness, in the heat of my spirit; but the hand of the LORD was strong upon me. Then I came to them of the captivity at Telabib, that dwelt by the river of Chebar..." So he was actually just brought right into the captives internment center there. "...and I sat where they sat, and remained there astonished among them seven days" (vs. 14-15). So God just took him down and put him right there and he just sat there astonied for seven days, and I imagine everybody came by, "Who is this? Did you see how he got here? He was just kind of dropped right here."

"And it came to pass at the end of seven days, that the word of the LORD came unto me, saying, 'Son of man, I have made thee a watchman unto the house of Israel: therefore hear the word of My mouth and give them warning from Me. When I say unto the wicked, 'Thou shalt surely die'; and thou givest him no warning, nor speakest to warn the wicked from his wicked way, to save his life; the same wicked *man* shall die in his iniquity; but his blood will I require at thine hand" (vs. 16-18). Now you talk about a responsibility, huh, God laid it upon him. Now we need to think about that in relationship to what we are doing. Not that I want to, by any way intimate that we are going to be Ezekiel's watchman on the wall (chuckle). As I've mentioned, I know of at least 8 or 10 ministers who claim that. And I think the wall is getting a little crowded you see (laughter).

Nevertheless this is why I keep encouraging the brethren, if you know other brethren, reach out to them. Send them a tape. Ask God to give you understanding which would be the best tape for you to send to them. Just this week I got...just yesterday rather, I got three letters from people who had tapes sent to them and they wrote in saying please send us care package #1. And so it is working, and we need to reach out to them, and that's the best way we can. I don't know who they are. I don't know where they are. But many brethren in many places know some where they are, and others know some where they are, and we can help them in that manner.

It was recommended that one tape you could give them is called "The Living Dead." Ok, yeah that's when I took a Passover book up to a man who was still in Worldwide and he just looked like he was dead spiritually. But nevertheless it helped revive him. So you see, and we hope to get the Passover book out...I don't think we're going to make it [complete it] until sometime after Tabernacles, but we're going to get it out and it's going to be some book. And that we're going to give out free. All of our things we give out free. God will provide enough so we can do that. We'll keep the overhead down, we'll run it lean, and clean, and slim so we can send out things for the brethren.

Now continue here. Here's the warning, "Yet if thou warn the wicked, and he turn not from his wickedness, nor from his wicked way, he shall die in his iniquity; but thou hast delivered thy soul. Again, When a righteous *man* doth turn from his righteousness, and commit iniquity, and I lay a stumblingblock before him, he shall die: because thou hast not given him warning, he shall die in his sin, and his righteousness which he hath done shall not be remembered; but his blood will I require at thine hand." Well boy, God really requires a lot, doesn't He? We really need to think on these things, and we all need to take it personally. Not that we all become an Ezekiel, but the word of God is for us, and we need to heed it and use it. "Nevertheless if thou warn the righteous *man*, that the righteous sin not, and he doth not sin, he shall surely live, because he is warned; also thou hast delivered thy soul" (vs. 19-21). So that was quite a message after riding on the chariot, you know, after being taken in God's chariot over to the slave camp there where the Israelites were. Then God laid it out to be absolutely clear for them. And then you read the book of Ezekiel and you will see that he had one of the toughest, most difficult ministries to do. And the book of Ezekiel is really a very heavy book of death and destruction, and slaughter, because the people rejected God and had forgotten God. And I think we can look at what's happening in our day and realize the same thing is going to happen again.

Now, let's come over here to Isaiah 6, and again we have a situation where Isaiah was brought before the throne of God, as it were. Let's pick it up in verse 1, "In the year that king Uzziah died I saw also the LORD sitting upon a throne, high and lifted up, and His train filled the temple." Now I'm convinced after reading these scriptures, the ones that I've read in preparation for this sermon, that we'll see in Revelation 4 and 5, that God's throne is much closer to the earth than we have realized. But God has not given us the ability to see how close it is. He has to open up our eyes, or as we will see in Revelation 6, roll back the heavens and then the whole world will see. So there are going to be some things that are going to happen. God is not going to let this world come to an end without great and awesome things taking place.

Verse 2 now, "Above it stood the seraphims: each one had six wings; with twain he covered his face, and with twain he covered his feet, and with twain he did fly. And one cried unto another, and said, 'Holy, holy, holy, *is* the LORD of hosts: the whole earth *is* full of His glory. And the posts of the door moved at the voice of him that cried, and the house was filled with smoke" (vs. 2-4). Here hold your place here and go back to Psalm 24, it talks about the posts and I think that has to do with Psalm 24. It just dawned on me as we're going through here. Psalm 24:7, "Lift up your head, O ye gates; and be ye lift up, ye everlasting doors; and the King of glory shall come in." Now I think that's what it's talking about here in the posts. When Christ was accepted of God the Father the posts said this, the gates opened....

Now, back here to Isaiah 6. "...and the house was filled with smoke." Then verse 5, "Then said I, 'Woe *is* me! for I *am* undone..." Boy if you would be right up before God's throne and see that you'd feel the same thing too, wouldn't you? Because human beings when they see awesomeness of the spiritual things of God, are just like that. You realize that you are absolutely nothing. So Isaiah said, "...I *am* undone; because I *am* a man of unclean lips, and I dwell in the midst of a people of unclean lips: for mine eyes have seen the King, the LORD of hosts. Then flew one of the seraphims unto me, having a live coal in his hand, *which* he had taken with the tongs from off the altar:" So he's right there before the temple of God in the spirit. "And he laid *it* upon my mouth, and said, 'Lo, this hath touched thy lips; and thine iniquity is taken away, and thy sin purged.' Also I heard the voice of the LORD, saying, 'Whom shall I send, and who will go for us?' Then said I, 'Here *am* I; send me.' And He said, Go, and tell this people, Hear ye indeed, but understand not; and see ye indeed, but perceive not. Make the heart of this people fat, and make their ears heavy, and shut their eyes; lest they see with their eyes, and hear with their ears, and understand with their heart, and convert, and be healed'" (vs. 5-10). So God has deliberately closed the eyes of many in the world.

Let's go right on into Revelation 4. Now as I will mention on Pentecost, go into some detail, the seven churches in Revelation 2 and 3 picture the harvest of seven weeks, beginning with the first day, the day after the Sabbath, including that and seven whole complete weeks coming down to seven whole weeks. Then the 50th day is Pentecost. And you will see that the 50th day is God's special day of salvation for the 144,000 and the great innumerable multitude. Well what I want to do here in the book of Revelation is to look at the whole situation concerning the throne of God and the sea of glass and why at the resurrection we will be taken to the sea of glass. So let's begin right here Chapter 4 and verse 1.

Now the church age ends with the Laodicean epic. And so that's why it is cut off right here. Then when the martyrdom of the saints occurs, the only Christians in the flesh alive will be in wherever the place of safety is. They're the only ones left alive in the flesh. So that's then why God raises up the 144,000, and He does His work, and He does His ministry, ok.

So after the church age, right when it is coming to a close, Revelation 4:1. "After this I looked, and, behold, a door opened in heaven; and the first voice that I heard *was* as if a trumpet were speaking with me, saying, 'Come up here, and I will show you *the* things that must take palce after these things.' And immediately I was in *the* Spirit; and, behold, a throne was set in heaven, and *one was* sitting on the throne. And He Who *was sitting* was in appearance like a jasper stone and a sardius stone: and a rainbow *was* around the throne..." So again we have the rainbow. Remember we had the rainbow back in Exodus 24, where there was the sea of glass or the paving where they saw God standing. "...And a rainbow *was* around the throne, like an emerald in its appearance. And round about the throne *were* twenty-four thrones [They are actually lesser thrones.]: and on the thrones I saw twenty-four elders sitting, clothed in white garments; and they had on their heads golden crowns. And proceeding from the throne were lightnings and thunders and voices; and seven lamps of fire, which are the seven Spirits of God, *were* burning before the throne" (Rev. 4:1-5).

Now what I want you to do, I want you to think how similar this is compared to when God came down on Mt. Sinai in Exodus 19 and 20 and brought the Ten Commandments, when there were thunderings, there were lightnings, there was the voice of the trumpet sounding exceeding loud. And remember that was done on the day of Pentecost. Now the seven Spirits, we'll see a little later that their job is to go to and fro in the midst of the earth and see who's seeking God. How does God call someone? Because He does it personally. Well I think first of all one of the seven Spirits has to find out and spy out who is seeking God and let God know. Then God decides whether this individual is seeking Him in truth or not and begins to call them, begins to deal with them. How did you first begin to understand the truth? What happened? What turned the switch in your mind, because it had to happen, and it was a spiritual miracle to occur. So the seven Spirits do that.

Now verse 6, "And before the throne *was* a sea of glass, like crystal..." So here's the sea of glass. Wherever the throne of God is there is a sea of glass. There is a rainbow, or in the case of the Cherubim it is a temporary throne and goes where God goes. "...And around the throne and over the throne, *were* four living creatures, full of eyes before and behind; And the first living creature *was* like a lion, and the second living creature *was* like a calf, and the living creature had the face of a man, and the fourth living creature *was* like a flying eagle" (vs. 6-7). And that ties right in with the appearance of the Cherubim. So wherever God goes on the Cherubim He has his portable throne and He has His small replica of it just like His main throne that we're seeing right here in Revelation 4.

"And each of *the* four living creatures had six wings respectively [now that ties in with what we read in Isaiah 6]; *and* around and within *they were* full of eyes; and day and night they cease not saying, 'Holy, holy, holy, LORD God Almighty, Who was, and Who is, and Who *is* to come. And when the living creatures give glory and honor and thanksgiving to Him Who sits on the throne, Who lives into the ages of eternity, The twenty-four elders fall down before Him Who sits on the throne; and they worship Him Who lives into the ages of eternity, and cast their crowns before the throne, saying, 'Worthy, are You, O Lord, to receive glory and honor and power because You did create all things, and for Your will they were created and exist" (vs. 7-11). Now you think about that brethren. For God's pleasure you were and are created, and understand that salvation is creation right now in you. A spiritual creation that is taking place. And that you were created for His pleasure.

Now come back to Ephesians 1. Hold it here for just a minute and we'll be back there to Revelation…let's come here to Ephesians 1 and let's pick it up here in verse 3. "Blessed *be* the God and Father of our Lord Jesus Christ, Who has blessed us with every spiritual blessing in the heavenly *things* with Christ;" because one day we're going to be there with Christ. One day we're going to be on the sea of glass before the throne of God. "According as He has personally chosen us for Himself before *the* foundation of *the* world in order that we might be holy and blameless before Him in love; having predestinated us for sonship to Himself through Jesus Christ, according to the good pleasure of His own will…" (Eph. 1:3-5). So let God do His good pleasure in you. Let Him create in you Christ. Let Him create in you the spiritual character and strength, which comes from God, because that's the whole purpose of your life. Ephesians 2:10, "For we are His workmanship, created in Christ Jesus unto *the* good works that God ordained beforehand in order that we might walk in them." And if we do that then there's going to be the day we will come before the throne of God.

Now then let's come back to Revelation 5 again here. So just remember that, all things were created by God and for His pleasure. In other words God has a great and a marvelous thing that He is going to do for all of His creation and we are the firstfruits. Now Chapter 5, it talks more about the throne of God and how that Christ then was counted worthy to open the seals. Now we've gone through this several times here in recent past so I'm not going to go through the whole thing in great detail but let's pick it up here in verse 5 in Revelation 5.

"Then one of the elders said to me, 'Do not weep. Behold, the Lion Who is of the tribe of Judah, the Root of David, hath overcome to open the book, and to loose its seven seals.' Then I saw, and, behold, before the throne and the four living creatures, and before the elders, *was* standing a Lamb as having been slain, having seven horns and seven eyes, which are the seven Spirits of God that are sent into all the earth;" (vs. 5-6). Now the seven horns pictures that Christ is the head of the seven churches of Revelation 2 and 3. And Christ is the head of the Church. That's why the seven horns are in the head of the Lamb.

Now notice, "And He came and took the book out of the right hand of Him Who sits on the throne [which is God the Father]. And when He had took the book, the four living creatures and the twenty-four elders fell down before the Lamb, each having harps and golden bowls full of incense, which are the prayers of the saints" (vs. 7-8). So somehow when our prayers go to God they help bring them to God. Just how that works I don't know but we're told in Romans 8 that the spirit makes intercession for us with sounds or groanings which we cannot utter. And the best way I can explain that is this. The spirit eliminates out of our prayers all the stupidity that enters in because of the weakness of our minds. Have you ever been praying and all of a sudden the thought of something having nothing to do with prayer came in? Like maybe you left the oven on, or you left the keys in your car, or you didn't lock the door, or whatever. Or the one that bothers me is when I'm praying and then all of a sudden a stupid commercial comes clattering through my mind, you know, that I've heard on television or radio. Well that doesn't go to God. I think the Spirit filters that out. The Spirit conveys your true heart to God. And then it comes before God, and it comes before His very throne, and it comes before the golden altar. So that's something. One of these days we're going to see that whole thing, ok.

Now, let's come over to Chapter 6, and as I explain on Pentecost, this is somewhere down into two years of the 3 ½ years of the tribulation. Revelation 6:12, let's notice what happens here. "And when He opened the sixth seal, I looked, and behold, there was a great earthquake; and the sun became black as *the* hair of sackcloth, and the moon became as blood; and the stars of heaven fell to the earth, as a fig tree casts its untimely figs, when it is shaken by a mighty wind. Then *the* heaven departed like a scroll that is being rolled up, and every mountain and island was moved out of its place. And the kings of the earth, and the great men, and the rich men, and the chief captains, and the powerful men, and every bond-man, and every free *man* hid themselves in the caves and in the rocks of the mountains; and they said to the mountains and to the rocks, 'Fall on us, and hide us from *the* face of Him ? Who sits on the throne, and from the wrath of the Lamb:'" (vs. 12-16). So the world gets a glimpse of God's throne. Not like we will, but they get a glimpse of it, ok.

Come over here to Chapter 7. The 144,000 and the great innumerable multitude. Now let's pick it up in verse 10. I cover that on Pentecost so I'm not going to repeat it here. This is God's 50th day harvest, ok. Verse 10, "And they were calling out with a loud voice to Him Who sits on the throne and to the Lamb, saying..." No go back to verse 9. "After these things I looked, and behold, a great multitude, which no one was able to number, out of every nation and tribe and people and language, was standing before the throne and before the Lamb, clothed with white robes and *holding* palms in their hands; And they were calling out with a loud voice to Him Who sits on the throne and to the Lamb, saying, 'The salvation of our God *has come* ' " (vs. 9-10). So they're standing right before the throne of God. When you're resurrected you're going to come before the throne of God. That's what this is telling us. When the 144,000 and the great innumerable multitude are resurrected they come before the throne of God. What is underlying the throne of God? The sea of glass.

Verse 11, "Then all the angels stood around the throne, and the elders and the four living creatures, and fell on their faces before the throne and worshipped God, saying, 'Amen: Blessing, and glory, and wisdom, and thanksgiving, and honor, and power and strength *be* to our God into the ages of eternity. Amen.' And one of the elders answered *and* said to me, 'These who are clothed with white robes, who are they, and where did they come from?' Then I said to him, 'Sir, you know.' And he said to me, 'They are the ones who have come out of the great tribulation; and they have washed their robes, and have made their robes white in the blood of the Lamb' " (vs. 11-14).

So there they are before the throne of God. "For this reason, they are before the throne of God and serve Him day and night in His temple; and the one Who sits on the throne shall dwell among them. They shall not hunger any more, nor shall they thirst any more; neither shall the sun nor the heat fall upon them," So this is a projection clear into New Jerusalem, Revelation 22. "Because the Lamb Who *is* in *the* midst of the throne will shepard them, and will lead them to fountains of living waters; and God will wipe away every tear from their eyes" (vs. 15-17). So there is the throne, the sea of glass, and every-thing that takes place there.

Now let's come to Chapter 11. Let's see what happens at the last trump. Now I want you to understand that whenever it talks about the resurrection it talks about "the trump" or "a trump" as we'll see in just a minute, never "trumpets." And the Feast of Trumpets is plu-ral, trumpets, a memorial of blowing trumpets all day long. So let's read it here beginning in verse 15. "Then the seventh angel sounded *his* trumpet; and *there* were great voices in heaven, saying, 'The kingdoms of this world have become *the kingdoms* of our Lord and His Christ, and He shall reign into the ages of eternity.' And the twenty-four elders, who sit before God on their thrones, fell on their faces and worshipped God..." So he's looking again at the throne of God. And the throne of God has the sea of glass. All those who are going to be resurrected will come before the throne of God won't they? And there has to be the sea of glass. We'll see that in a little bit when we get to Chapter 14. "...Saying, 'We give You thanks, O Lord God Almighty, who is, and Who was, and Who *is* to come; for You have taken *to Yourself* Your great power, and have reigned'" (Rev. 11:15-17).

"For the nations were angry, and Your wrath has come,...." Cause see the resurrec-tion takes place before the wrath of God, not after. The wrath of God comes between Pentecost and Trumpets. Now notice continuing verse 18, "…and the time for the dead to be judged, and to give reward to Your servants the prophets, and to the saints, and to *all* those who fear Your name, the small and the great; and to destroy those who destroy the earth'" So all of the saints have to be individually given their reward. We also know from Revelation 2 and 3 they have to be given a new name, they have to be given the name of the Father, the name of the new city Jerusalem, they have to be given Christ's new name. All of that has to take place after they are resurrected.

Now notice verse 19, "And the temple of God in heaven was opened, and the ark of His covenant was seen in His temple; and there were lightnings, and voices, and thunders, and an earthquake and great hail." Again I call your attention to Exodus 19 and 20, which was on Pentecost.

Now let's ask the question concerning the resurrection before we get to Revelation 14. Let's go back to Matthew 24. When we are resurrected we don't remain on the earth. Now if we don't remain on the earth where do we go? And yet we see in Zechariah 14 that we come back to the earth, don't we? "The Lord comes and all the saints with Him." Well, when they're resurrected they're taken up from the earth. Let's read it, verse 30, "And then shall appear the sign of the Son of man in heaven…" That's after the…let's go to verse 29 so we get the story flow here. "But immediately after the tribulation of those days, the sun shall be darkened, and the moon shall not give her light [that goes right back to Revelation 6, goes right back to Revelation 11], and the stars shall fall from heaven, and the powers of the heavens shall be shaken. And then shall appear the sign of the Son of man in heaven; and then shall all the tribes of the earth mourn, and they shall see the Son of man coming upon the clouds of heaven with power and great glory." But the saints are not with Him yet. We're going to see it says we're going to meet Christ in the air.

Verse 31, "And He shall send His angels with a great sound of a trumpet…" So there is a trumpet, not trumpets plural. We'll see later it's called "the trumpet." "…And they shall gather together His elect from the four winds, from one end of heaven to *the* other." Why do they have to be gathered? Because they're not left on the earth. They meet Christ in the air. Where in the air will Christ be? We'll see in just a little bit, ok.

Let's come to 1 Thessalonians 4, and this gives us a little more understanding concerning it. 1 Thessalonians 4:14, "For if we believe that Jesus died and rose again, in exactly the same way also, those who have fallen asleep in Jesus will God bring with Him." But in order to be brought with Him you've got to come out of the grave to meet Him. Because Christ is not coming down to the earth to go into the grave to get you. He's going to send the angels to catch you up after you've been resurrected out of the earth.

Verse 15, "For this we say to you by *the* Word of *the* Lord, that we who are alive and remain unto the coming of the Lord shall in no wise precede those who have fallen asleep." So all the dead are going to rise first. "Because the Lord Himself shall descend from heaven with *a* shout of command, with *the* voice of an archangel and with '*the* trumpet' of God, and the dead in Christ shall rise first;…" and be carried by the angels, as we will see, to the sea of glass before the throne of God. After all if you're resurrected why can't you come up to God's throne? God is on His throne isn't He? Should we not go there to worship Him the very first thing we do? No doubt about it.

Ok, hold your place here and come back to 1 Corinthians 15 and then we'll finish it off here in 1 Thessalonians 4. Now here's what's going to happen to us when the trumpet sounds. Dolores and I always used to joke whenever we go past a cemetery, especially when it's filled with all kinds of headstones and everything. We said the first thing that's going to happen, they're going to be resurrected and knocked cold. (Laughter) No that won't happen. Physical things won't bother you.

Ok, now verses 51-52, "Behold, I show you a mystery: we shall not all sleep, but we shall all be changed, in an instant, in *the* twinkling of an eye (snapped fingers)[just like that], at the last trumpet [which is the seventh trump-not the Feast of Trumpets]; for *the* trumpet shall sound, and the dead shall be raised incorruptible, and we shall be changed." Now when we are changed the angels gather us and take us up to meet the Lord in the air.

Now let's come back to 1 Thessalonians 4:17, let's see that. "Then we who are alive and and remain shall be caught up together with them in *the* clouds..." Now when Christ comes He's going to come first, then the sign of the Son of man will be seen and will be coming closer and closer and closer to the earth perhaps during the space of about a year and a half, not quite a year and a half, a little over a year. And then it's going to come right into the clouds, and then it's going to stop in the clouds. Then I believe those clouds where it stops are going to be right over Jerusalem so that when we are raised we are going to be raised and be brought to the sea of glass. We are caught up in the air to meet him "...in *the* clouds for *the* meeting with the Lord in *the* air [and that is for the meeting with the Lord in the air]; and so shall we always be with *the* Lord." Now Zechariah 14 shows we're going to come to the earth with Christ, but that won't happen until the Feast of Trumpets. "Therefore, encourage one another with these words" (vs. 17-18).

Now, let's come to Revelation 14. Now I will cover this in detail on Pentecost but let's just come here in Revelation 14:14. This is talking about the first resurrection. Now the first resurrection is typified by the grain harvest, as we will see in Matthew 13 when we come to the day of Pentecost. Verse 14, "And I looked, and behold a white cloud, and *one* like *the* Son of man..." So here's Christ. Christ comes down to the clouds, correct? We are going to meet Him in the clouds, correct? Yes. "...having a golden crown on His head; and in His hand *was* a sharp sickle. And another angel came out of the temple, crying with a loud voice to Him Who was sitting on the cloud, 'Thrust in your sickle, and reap...'" Now that's what you do with grain. You take a sickle and you cut it, and then you gather it. And who gathers it? The angels. And where do they take it? They take the firstfruits to the sea of glass before God. "...Because the time has come for You to reap; for the harvest of the earth is ripe" (Rev. 14:14-15). Then it talks about the harvest of the wicked, the rest of the chapter which I explain on Pentecost.

Now, Chapter 15:1, "Then I saw another sign in heaven, great and awesome: seven angels having the seven last plagues; for in them the wrath of God is filled up." So the resurrection occurs before the seven last plagues, doesn't it? Now you read Chapter 16, especially come over here Chapter 16:12 to show you that there is a space of time between the resurrection and coming back to the earth. "And the sixth angel poured out his vial into the great river Euphrates; and its waters were dried up, so that the way of the kings from the rising of *the* sun might be prepared. Then I saw three unclean spirits like frogs *come* out of the mouth of the dragon, and out of the mouth of the beast, and out of the mouth of the false prophet. For they are the spirits of demons working miracles, going forth to the kings of the earth, even of the whole world, to gather them together to *the* battle of that great day of the Almighty God" (Rev. 16:12-14). Now then, how long does it take to move an army even with trucks, even with planes? How long did it take us to prepare for Desert Storm? Four months. So there's got to be a four month period which is just about the length of time between Pentecost and Trumpets, ok.

So let's come back here to Revelation 15:2, "And I saw a sea of glass mingled with fire..." That is to look at it. In other words, created out of spirit and just shone brightly. "...And those who had gotten the victory over the beast..." We know that Satan is the beast. Satan has been around here since whenever, Adam and Eve, correct? So you get victory over the beast. Do all Christians through all time have to get victory over the beast? Yes. Did Abel get victory over the beast? Yes. And Satan, who is the beast, used Cain to kill him. Yes, he got victory over him. "…And over his image…" And we know that there was an image of the beast going clear back into Babylon, right? Where Shadrach, Meshach, and Abednego got the victory over the beast idol that Nebuchadnezzar had made, correct? Yes. "…And over his mark [which is coming], *and* over the number of his name [which is coming], standing on the sea of glass, having *the* harps of God." Now question: How many times in scripture does a thing have to be said in order for it to be true? Once is sufficient. Where does it say we will stand? It says we will stand on the sea of glass. What is also on the sea of glass? The throne of God. The temple of God. Didn't say right here in…yes, we'll see it in just a minute…talks about the temple of God.

Ok, verse 3, "And they were singing the song of Moses, *the* servant of God, and the song of the Lamb, saying, 'Great and awesome *are* Your works, Lord God Almighty; righteous and true *are* Your ways, King of the saints. Who shall not fear You, O Lord, and glorify Your name? For *You* only *are* holy; and all the nations shall come and worship before You, for Your judgments have been revealed. And after these things I looked, and behold, the temple of the tabernacle of the testimony in heaven was opened. And the seven angels who had the seven *last* plagues came out of the temple…"(vs. 3-6). So there we are on the sea of glass. The throne of God is there. The temple of God is there, and we see the seven angels come out and get the seven vials for the seven last plagues. And then as I point out on Pentecost, God gives us the blessing of His promise that He said that His vengeance we would all see. And the only way that can happen is if we are on the sea of glass with the throne of God and all these things happen according to the way that Revelation shows us.

Now then, let me tell you why that Pentecost pictures the first resurrection and not Trumpets:
1) Firstfruits is a harvest of grain, which we are.
2) The Holy Spirit was given on Pentecost, which is the earnest. So why not on Pentecost receive the fullness?
3) It is a continuous harvest from the time of Christ until His return. Just like seven weeks is a continual count from the beginning of the ascension of Christ to be accepted of the Father, until the day of Pentecost 50 days later.
4) Seven churches equal the seven weeks of harvest.
5) 144,000 and great innumerable multitude equal the 50th day harvest of God.
6) We are raised at the seventh trumpet, the last trump. The trump, not trumpets.
7) We have the meeting with Christ in the air.
8) We are on the sea of glass.
9) We have to receive our reward.
10) We have to be given our new name.
11) We have to be given our assignments.
12) The marriage of the Lamb takes place, and according to Revelation 19 is the last thing to occur.

Now then, let me just say this. Here's why it is not on Trumpets:
1) Trumpets is not a harvest feast. It is a feast picturing war, death, destruction, which is going to happen with the seven last plagues, ending in the return of Christ and the saints on the earth.
2) It is never "trumpets," but it is the "seventh trump", or the "last trump." .
3) We return to the earth after the seven last plagues and judgment of great Babylon, not before.
4) The marriage of the Lamb and the Bride must take place, and that is not pictured by Trumpets but is pictured by Pentecost and the Book of Ruth is a type of that, where Ruth marries Boaz. And that was during the barley harvest.

Yes, and I mentioned that Trumpets is not a grain harvest. Let's go ahead and finish by…I know this will be a little short but we don't have much time here in our meeting hall today, we have to get right out. But nevertheless I've covered everything that I need to cover.

Let's go to Hebrews 12 and let's finish right here, because this is also a prophecy of our being resurrected to be on Mt. Zion. Zion in heaven above as it were. Hebrews 12, and let's pick it up in verse 18. I know we've covered this a little before but it's good to end it right here. "For you have not come to *the* mount that could be touched and that burned with fire, nor to gloominess, and fearful darkness, and *the* whirlwind; and to *the* sound of *the* trumpet, and to *the* voice of *the* words; which those who heard *begged* that *the* word not be spoken *directly* to them. (For they could not endure what was being commanded: 'And if even an animal touches the mountain, it shall be stoned, or shot through with an arrow'; And so terrifying was the sight, *that* Moses said, 'I am greatly afraid and trembling.') But you have come to Mount Sion, and to *the* city of *the* living God, heavenly Jerusalem; and to an innumerable company of angels; *To the* joyous festival gathering; and to *the* church of *the* firstborn, registered *in the book of life* in heaven; and to God, *the* Judge of all; and to *the* spirits of the just who have been perfected; and to Jesus, *the* mediator of *the* New Covenant; and to sprinkling of *the* blood of *ratification*, proclaiming superior things than *that of* Abel" (Heb. 12:18-24).

And so that's why Pentecost pictures the first resurrection and not Trumpets. And why when we are resurrected we will be on the sea of glass, we'll be brought up there by the angels. And boy, what a time that's going to be. We're going to be able to…you talk about fellowship.

Oh, there's one other thing, one other thing we'll add here. Christ is going to do a solo song. Did you know that? Christ is going to bring us special music. Hebrews 2, and let's pick it up here in verse 9. "But we see Jesus, Who *was* made a little lower than *the* angels; crowned with glory and honor on account of suffering the death, in order that by *the* grace of God He Himself might taste death for everyone;" And then we'll see all of those resurrected and on the sea of glass with Him and know that He died for each one individually and personally. "Because it was fitting for Him, for Whom all things *were created*, and by Whom all things *exist*, in bringing many sons unto glory, to make the Author of their salvation perfect through sufferings. For both He Who is sanctifying and those who are sanctified *are* all of one…" Just like Christ prayed in John 17: "That they may be one as You Father…You and I are One. I in them, You in Me, that they may become one in Us" [that's what will take place right there]. " …For which cause He is not ashamed to call them brethren, saying, 'I will declare Your name to My brethren, in *the* midst of *the* church I will sing praise to You" (Heb. 2:9-12). And that will be in the midst of the Church because the Church will all be resurrected and on the sea of glass. He's going to sing praise to God the Father. We are going to sing the song of Moses. We're going to sing the song of the Lamb. We are going to learn how to play those harps, and I don't have a clue today, see. And we're going to be able to meet all those you've wanted to meet, all the apostles. And I especially want to meet, after I'm able to meet Christ and see Him face to face, I'm going to especially want to meet the apostle Paul, and I'm sure there will be a long line for that. And I will especially want to meet William Tyndale, because he gave his life for the Word of God and the testimony thereof. And so brethren, that's why Pentecost pictures the first resurrection and not Trumpets.

End of Sermon

Transcriber: Carolyn Singer

"Sea of Glass—Sermon II"
Pentecost—1999
Scriptural References

1) Psalm 11:4-7

2) Psalm 45:6-7

3) Psalm 47:7-8

4) Ezekiel 1:21-28

5) Ezekiel 2:1-3

6) Ezekiel 3:10-21

7) Isaiah 6:1-4

8) Psalm 24:7

9) Isaiah 6:5-10

10) Revelation 4:1-11

11) Ephesians 1:3-5

12) Revelation 5:5-8

13) Revelation 6:12-16

14) Revelation 7:9-17

15) Revelation 11:15-19

16) Matthew 24:29-31

17) I Thessalonians 4:14-15, 17-18

18) I Corinthians 15:51

19) Revelation 14:14-15

20) Revelation 15:1-6

21) Revelation 16:12-14

22) Hebrews 12:18-24

23) Hebrews 2:9-12

CHAPTER TWENTY-SIX

Day 50—Holy Day—and the 144,000

Pentecost—June 11, 2000

(Part I)

Now for the Feast of Pentecost, the year 2000, there's a tremendous meaning for this feast, and there are a lot of things that God wants us to know and to understand as we go forward and in keeping the holy days. And all of the holy days really show us and teach us the ways of God. Now it's very interesting but in the Septuagint version of the Bible, when you go through Exodus 31, all the way through there with the exception of the seventh day Sabbath, it says, "My Sabbaths", plural. So you see you can't have one without the other. If you have the seventh day Sabbath, which you keep, then you must also keep the annual Sabbaths.

Now this day of the Feast of Pentecost pictures the finality of the harvest of the firstfruits. And it all begins with Christ on the wave sheaf offering day, as we saw yesterday. Let's go back to Exodus 34 and let's pick it up here in verse 26 because as we have seen Christ is the first of the firstfruits. And so for ancient Israel God wanted the children of Israel to always remember that the first of the firstfruits belonged to God.

Verse 26 says, "The first of the firstfruits of thy land thou shalt bring unto the house of the LORD thy God." Christ was the first of the firstfruits as we saw in John 20. That He ascended to the Father on the morrow after the Sabbath. He was the premier sheaf that was elevated by the priest to be accepted on our behalf. In other words as the very sacrifice of Jesus Christ for the forgiveness of our sins plus the resurrected Christ for the justification to put us in right standing with God, and for Christ to be at the right hand of God the Father, to carry out His plan and carry it forward.

Now let's come to 1 Corinthians 15 and let's see some very important things concerning the resurrection, and of course everything starts with the resurrection of Christ. And as we saw yesterday that the firstfruits is a firstfruit harvest. It is harvest holy day to celebrate the completing, the accomplishing of the firstfruits of the grain. Now that's not all the firstfruits which follow after that. There are the firstfruits of the fruit of the tree, there are firstfruits of other products, other vegetables, other things that come along. Those all belong to God. But this is a special one. And the harvest that God has with the Feast of Pentecost relates to and begins with Christ Who is the first of the firstfruits.

Now let's come to 1 Corinthians 15 and let's understand something very important concerning the resurrection of Christ. And especially in this day. Now we need to understand too, and I'm going to emphasize again that you must have the right Bible. And the right Bible is the one that is based upon the right Greek text and Hebrew text. And so the King James Version has been based upon the proper texts. Now I've been doing a translation, and it is all complete. I used the same Greek text that was used that the translators of the King James Version used, which is the Byzantine text, also known as the authorized text, or the received text, or the text of 1550 by Stephens. And so that's the one that I have used. Now let's read here in the *New Testament in Its Original Order—A Faithful Version With Commentary.*

Let's begin here in verse 12, because this is important. "But if Christ is being preached that He rose from *the* dead, how is it that some among you are saying that there is no resurrection of *the* dead?" So immediately Satan is there. As soon as the seeds have been sown Satan is there bringing his tares and infiltrating into the Church, bringing false doctrine and saying, "Why there's no resurrection. We're all going to heaven." No.

Notice Paul's argument here. "For if there is no resurrection from *the* dead, neither has Christ been raised. And if Christ has not been raised,…" Now I want you to notice the strength of his argument. And I want you to know how dogmatically he brings it because this is important. "For if there is no resurrection from *the* dead, neither has Christ been raised. And if Christ has been raised, our preaching is in vain…" In other words they're preaching a myth. You're preaching something that is empty, that is hollow, that has no meaning. "…And your faith *is* also in vain. And we are found to be false witnesses of God; …" Now this is an important statement. Anytime someone makes a statement that is not in conformity with the word of God, is a false witness for God. Meaning that he is testifying of something which is not true, and claiming that God has sanctioned it. Which then is false witnessing for God. Taking the name of God in vain, using the name of God in futility and vanity. "…Because we have testified of God that He raised Christ, Whom He did not raise, if indeed *the* dead are not raised. For if *the* dead are not raised, neither has Christ been raised. And if Christ has not been raised, your faith *is* vain; you are still in your sins," (vs. 13-17).

In other words there is no forgiveness of sin unless Christ, Who is the first of the firstfruits, ascended unto the Father to be accepted on the morrow after the Sabbath during the Feast of Unleavened Bread, which then is the first day beginning the 50 day count. Unless that occurred there is no forgiveness of sin. And you can also trust and be reassured that any other scheme of the forgiveness of sin will not bring the forgiveness of sin because Christ is the way and the truth and the life. And there is no other way that it can be done than except through Jesus Christ.

Now continuing verse 18, "And those who have fallen asleep in Christ have then perished." Cause there's no hope. "If in this life only we have hope in Christ we are of all people most miserable." Why? Because you're believing in something that is false, if the dead are not raised. But notice how Paul concludes his argument. "But now Christ has been raised from *the* dead; He has become the firstfruits of those who have fallen asleep. For since by man *came* death, by man also *came* the resurrection of *the* dead. For as in Adam all die,…" Because we all have inherited the law of sin and death within us, and so as in Adam we die. Just like God told Adam. "Dust you are and unto dust you shall return" (Gen. 3:19). "So also in Christ shall all be made alive" (vs. 18-22). That is all the resurrections. The three resurrections in the Bible. The first resurrection, the second resurrection of those who have not committed the unpardonable sin, and the other part of the second resurrection, which is the resurrection of those who have committed the unpardonable sin. All will be made alive in Christ. Whether for eternal life, or whether for eternal death.

Now notice verse 23, very important. "But each in his own order: Christ *the* firstfruit;…" And as we saw yesterday, we are the Church of the Firstborn. We are the firstfruit of the harvest but Christ is the first of the firstfruits. "…then those who are Christ's at His coming." And so that's when the first resurrection is going to be, at His coming.

Now we're going to see then "at His coming", how this pictures the day of Pentecost as the day of the resurrection. And let's understand that that is the only day that it can signify. Well then someone will surely say, "Well then you're saying you know when the return of Christ is." No we're saying we know when the resurrection will be. And the reason is we can go back this way. Let's look at it from what we already know. Is Christ our Passover, Who was crucified for us? Answer: yes. When was He crucified? On the Passover day. Did God do it on the time and in the day that He prophesied, and in the way and the manner that He said that He would do it? Yes.

Now it's exactly the same thing concerning the resurrection of Christ. When was He raised? Right at the end of the Sabbath after being in the grave three days and three nights. When did He ascend to the Father? On the wave sheaf offering day. And then we saw how there are seven churches. And those seven churches represent the harvest of the church age. And the harvest of the church age then is part of the main harvest of God. And that's from the time that Christ ascended to heaven until the time of the first resurrection, which we will see. Then every man in his own order. We know that at the end of the thousand years there will be the second resurrection of those who have not committed the unpardonable sin. And then the other half of the second resurrection, for those who committed the unpardonable sin, that all the wicked may be thrown in the lake of fire at once.

So the holy days picturing God's plan, these things happen on the holy days. So let's keep that in mind. And let's understand something that of the day of Christ's coming no one really knows because I'll show you why. I'll show you why a little bit later. So let's continue on here, and let's pick up the story now in Acts 1 and let's see what Luke wrote concerning the things, the events that took place after Christ was raised from the dead.

Now let's begin here in Acts 1:3, concerning Christ, "To whom also, by many infallible proofs, He presented Himself alive after He had suffered, being seen by them for forty days,…" Now isn't it interesting that Christ was seen of the apostles from the time of His ascension until the time of His second ascension into heaven. His first one to be accepted, and then His second one to remain in heaven. He was seen of the apostles 40 days. But also isn't it interesting that after Pentecost, and the covenant that was made with Israel and the wedding supper of Israel with the 70 elders, as I explained yesterday, that Moses was on the mount with God 40 days. So in either case we have 40 days. In Christ's case it's 40 days before Pentecost. And in Moses case it's 40 days from the day after Pentecost. So it's 40 days.

"…And speaking the things concerning the kingdom of God. And while they were assembled with Him, He commanded them not to not depart from Jerusalem but to 'await the promise of the Father, which,' *He said*, 'you have heard of Me.' For John indeed baptized with water, but you shall be baptized with *the* Holy Spirit after not many days." Which was just 10 days away. "So then, when they were assembled together, they asked Him, saying, 'Lord, will you restore the kingdom to Israel at this time?' And He said to them, 'It is not for you to know *the* times or *the* seasons, which the Father has placed in His own authority' " (Act. 1:3-7). Remember this was before any of the New Testament was written. And this was written before the book of Revelation was written by John. And the book of Revelation is to reveal. And all of the New Testament is to reveal the will of God and His word and His truth.

Verse 8 now, "But you yourselves shall receive power when the Holy Spirit has come upon you, and you shall be My witnesses, both in Jerusalme and in all Judea and Samaria, and unto *the* ends of the earth." And so that is a continuous thing that is going on today. And God has made it known. And God has sent it out. And there are Bibles in over 250 languages. The New Testament in over 1,200 languages, and the book of Mark in over 2,000 languages, and all of that is preaching the gospel. And so it is going out. We all have our part to do our preaching. We all have our part to do our witnessing. And brethren, pray that God will open whatever doors are necessary for us to reach out and to reach new people.

Now with our new web-site we're able to reach out into all the world, 24-hours a day, seven days a week, and to anyone who has a computer can get on there and find out information concerning many things. Now if you haven't gotten on there yet go ahead and try it. I'll give you the .com address right here. It is www.cbcg.org . Now we have a lot of information and literature on there. We have tapes on there. We have sermons on there. And we have some things especially concerning the beliefs booklet, which none of those who fellowship with the Christian Biblical Church of God have ever heard because we haven't mailed them out. We've done them especially for the web-site. And we're going to have some other things put on there, and hopefully this will also, what you're seeing today will be on the web-site in the audio form.

Now let's continue on here, verse 9. "And after saying these things, as they were looking at Him, He was taken up; and a cloud received Him out of their sight." Just disappeared to go sit at the right hand of God the Father. "Now while they were gazing intently up into heaven as He was going up, behold, two men in white apparel suddenly stood by them," That's two angels. Angels look like men. "Who also said, You men of Galilee, why do you stand *here* looking up into heaven? this *same* Jesus, Who was taken up from you into heaven, shall come in exactly the same manner as you have seen Him go into heaven" (vs. 9-11).

Now let's go ahead and come here to Acts 2 and let's see how tremendous and momentous this event was, and how important it is to understand the real meaning of verse 1. And as I mentioned yesterday, we have the booklet, which is "The True Meaning of Acts 2:1", because everyone has misconstrued this, twisted the scriptures to their own destruction to make it say something that it really doesn't say. So let's read it in the King James version.

"And when the day *of Pentecost,* was fully come…" And some people say, "The 50th day was over. They were all assembled with one accord in one place. So see, that means they were there on the 51st day." That doesn't relate to what the Greek really means. The Greek here has a special articular infinitive, the present tense. And this should be translated: "and during the fulfilling", or "the accomplishing of the 50th day", not the 51st. If it were the 51st day then it would clearly say the 50th and first day. But it doesn't say that in the Greek.

And now let's read Acts 2:1 in the Faithful Version. "And when the day of *Pentecost*, the fiftieth day, was being fulfilled, they were all with one accord in the same place." Why? They were assembled for the holy day, which is a holy convocation. That's why they were there.

"And suddenly *there* came a sound from heaven…" Now you see here is the re-enactment of what we saw yesterday at Mt. Sinai. Only instead of at Mt. Sinai it's at the temple of God because that's where God placed His name. So anything that God was going to do, any authorization and change in the way that things were done would come from God. And in this case by the power of His Holy Spirit, and right at the temple, so that it would be fully established that this was by the authority and the power of God, undeniable. "…a sound like the rushing of a powerful wind, and filled the whole house where they were sitting. And there appeared *to* them divided tongues as of fire…" Remember the fire on top of Mt. Sinai. So this is showing the same fulfillment now only spiritually, of the day of Pentecost, as when the law was given on the day of Pentecost. "…and sat upon each one of them. And they were all filled with *the* Holy Spirit; and they began to speak with other languages, as the Spirit gave them the words to proclaim." (vs. 2-4). Now let's understand something very important here. God is not the author of confusion, so whatever the Holy Spirit did was something that was sound, it was intelligible, it was understandable, and it was for a specific purpose. And that's what happened on this day of Pentecost.

And here's the reason. "Now *there* were *many* Jews who were sojournaing in Jerusalem, devout men from every nation under heaven. Now when word of this went out, the multitude came together, and were confounded, because each one heard them speaking in his own language" (vs. 5-6). So there was a double miracle. There was a miracle in the preaching. Because in the minds of the apostles they were thinking and speaking with their own language, but in everyone who was listening it came to them in their own language. Now this is a profound thing to understand. Not only just for Jews because remember the New Testament says, to the Jew first and then to the Greek. So we have here to the Jew first, but also to those who were assembled there in Jerusalem who came from every nation on earth. And please understand that the stories that went back from those who were up at Jerusalem during the Passover and the Feast of Unleavened Bread, and all the events that took place that we have already covered. How that Christ was crucified and raised from the dead, and all the stories that were told by the scribes and Pharisees to tell the lies that the disciples stole the body away. And so now they knew that something big was going to happen on Pentecost, because it was a holy day of God. And this was big. This was great. This was fulfilling the prophecy of God giving His Spirit to men. And He began with the apostles.

And it says here, verse 7, " And they were all amazed, and marvelled, saying to one another, 'Behold are not all these who are speaking Galilaeans? Then how is it *that* we hear each one in our own language in which we were born?" (vs. 7-8). They were hearing, they were understanding, and then it lists all of the nations that they were from. And the last part of verse 10 says Jews and proselytes. Now proselytes were circumcised Gentiles who would embrace the religion of Judaism.

Now the last part of verse 11, "…we hear them speaking in our own languages the great things of God." So this day was tremendous. "And they were all amazed, and greatly perplexed, saying to one another, 'What does this mean?' But others were mocking *and* saying, 'They are full of new wine.' Then Peter, standing up with the eleven, lifted up his voice and spoke out to them; 'Men, Jews, and all those of you who inhabit Jerusalem, let this be known to you, and pay attention to my words. For these are not drunken as you suppose, for it is *only the* third hour of the day" (vs. 11-15). Now that is in the morning. The third hour of the day. When did God appear on Mt. Sinai? In the morning. When did He give the law? On the day of Pentecost. When did He give the Holy Spirit, in other words to give them the heart now to keep God's laws? Because remember, when He gave the Ten Commandments He said there in Deuteronomy 5:29, He said, "Oh that there were such a heart in them that they would fear Me and keep My commandments always." Now God is supernaturally giving the heart, by the circumcision of the heart through the power of the Holy Spirit so that they would have, that they would have the ability now to keep the laws of God. Greater than that. God's Spirit and power would write them in their hearts and in their minds so they could keep them with a willing heart, with a willing attitude. And in service to God. But first there has to be repentance as we will see in just a minute.

Then Peter went on and gave this tremendous and powerful sermon. Now notice verse 16. "But this is that which was spoken by the prophet Joel: " Now we'll see how this ties in with Revelation 7 in just a little bit. ""And it shall come to pass in the last days," says God, "*that* I will pour out My Spirit upon all flesh, and your sons and your daughters shall prophesy, and your young men shall see visions, and your old men shall dream dreams; And even upon My servants and upon My handmaids will I pour out My Spirit in those days, and they shall prophesy; And I will show wonders in the heaven above and signs on the earth below, blood and fire and vapors of smoke. The sun shall be turned into darkness and the moon into blood, before *the* coming of the great and awesome day of *the* Lord." (vs. 17-20). Well now He gave this prophecy. It's recorded here in Acts 2, but this has not yet occurred. The only thing that has occurred of this is that the Holy Spirit was given. The rest of it has not occurred. That is for a future day of Pentecost, as we will see. And so we need to keep that in mind. We'll see that when we get to the book of Revelation.

" And it shall come to pass *that* everyone who calls upon the name of *the* Lord shall be saved. Men, Israelites, listen to these words: Jesus the Nazarean, a man sent forth to you by God, as demonstrated by works of power and wonders and signs, which God performed by Him in your midst, as you yourselves also know; Him, having been delivered up by the predetermined plan and foreknowledge of God, you have seized by lawless hands *and* have crucified and killed. *But* God has raised Him up, having loosed the throes of death, because it was not possible *for* Him to be held by it;"(vs. 21-24). Now then he finished giving the sermon saying that David was not resurrected from the grave but it was Jesus, even though He gave the promise to David.

Now let's pick it up here in verse 34, "For David has not ascended into the heavens, but he himself said, 'The LORD said to my Lord, "Sit at My right hand ..." So they understood those Psalms. Remember the very first time that they saw Jesus in the evening on the day that He ascended to the Father, back there in Luke 24, what did He do? He opened their understanding concerning Him and the law, and the prophets, and the Psalms. So here he's quoting the Psalm here. Psalm 110. "...Until I have made Your enemies a footstool for Your feet." (vs. 34-35).

Verse 36, "Therefore, let all *the* house of Israel know with full assurance that God has made this *same* Jesus, Whom you crucified, both Lord and Christ." That was a powerful sermon, and notice what happened. "Now after hearing *this*, they were cut to the heart; and they said to Peter and the other apostles, "Men *and* brethren, what shall we do?"(vs. 37) Now this is what has to happen to every one of us. This is what has to happen to everyone who God calls. They are pricked in their heart so they will understand what Christ went through to die for their sins and become the sacrifice for all of mankind. And God leads you to repentance to understand that.

And let's understand something very important too. Repentance is a continuous, ongoing thing in our lives. By the operation of the grace of God, and He is the One Who leads us to it. You know, just like the parable of the prodigal son, remember what happened to him? He got his inheritance and went out and spent it, squandered it in a strange land and was out feeding the hogs good food. He couldn't even eat it. And it says there, "...and when he came to himself..." Now this is what you need to do concerning repentance. You need to come to yourself. That is understand where you are. Understand your nature, understand your sins, and repent to God. Now that's what they did here. "...They were pricked in their heart, and said unto Peter, and to the rest of the apostles, Men *and* brethren, what shall we do?" (vs. 37). Because there are things that God wants us to do.

"Then Peter said unto them, Repent...", and repentance means to turn from your sin, turn from the way you're going. Turn back and come to God. Just like God said through Ezekiel, "Turn you, turn you, for why will you die O house of Israel." So it's the same way with us. And I hope there are brethren out there who are turning back to God. Why will you die O Church of God, you that have gone astray? Turn you, turn you, come back to God. Let your hearts be pricked.

"...Then Peter said to them, "Repent and be baptized each one of you in the name of Jesus Christ for *the* remission of sins, and you yourselves shall receive the gift of the Holy Spirit. . For the promise is to you and to your children, and to all those who are afar off, as many as *the* Lord our God may call." And with many other words he earnestly testified and exhorted, saying, "Be saved from this perverse generation." (vs. 38-40).

Now verse 41 is a very key important verse. "Then those who joyfully received his message were baptized; and about three thousand souls were added that day." Which day? During the fulfilling of the 50th day. So that is a tremendous thing that happened. So imagine the account that every one went back and told the story of being there at the temple, and this tremendous event took place. And that one that was called Jesus Christ was raised from the dead, and how the power of the Holy Spirit came on them. This was a tremendous event. And so we'll project forward to the last Pentecost here in just a minute.

But now I want to go back and pick up something that's very important. Let's go back and let's pick up concerning in Leviticus 23 the two loaves that were baked with leaven. And let's ask ourselves a couple of questions concerning this and let's see if we can determine the true scriptural use of leaven here in Leviticus 23, and what that pictures in it's fulfillment. Now remember, all during the Feast of Unleavened Bread leaven represents sin. Outside the Feast of Unleavened Bread leaven does not represent sin. Now what we are looking at here is a good use of leaven, is it not? Let's read it.

Now in Leviticus 23:17, and this is to be done on the 50th day. "Ye shall bring out of your habitations…" Now this is all who assembled up at the temple area, that they were to bring out of their habitations. "…Two wave loaves of two tenth deals: they shall be of fine flour; they shall be baken with leaven…" Why would God have them put leaven in these? Now this has to be a good use of leaven because it's waved before God. Now I think we were right in our past understanding that one loaf equals those were qualified for the first resurrection under the Old Covenant, and the other loaf represents those who qualify for the resurrection under the New Covenant. Now then, why leaven? Now what does it say these are? "…*they are* the firstfruits unto the LORD." Baked.

Now let's go to Matthew 13 and let's see something important here, where there is defining the kingdom of God with the parable of the leaven, which is a good use of the leaven. Matthew 13:33, "Another parable He spoke to them: "The kingdom of heaven is compared to leaven …" Now you can't say that this is a bad use of leaven. You cannot say that leaven here is picturing sin because then you would have to say that the kingdom is likened unto sin. And the kingdom is likened unto righteousness, not sin, correct? Yes. So it's likened unto leaven "…which a woman took and hid in three measures of flour until all was leavened."

Now what happens to bread… Now all dough when you first make it is unleavened. When it's baked in unleaven then it's permanently in that form. That is permanently until it's eaten. Now, when you put the leaven in it, it rises. It completely changes the form of the bread. And when you bake it, it is permanently in that changed form. It can't be…well, I suppose it could but it's dough. It can't be beaten back as though to make it flat again like you do when it rises and then you beat it back, let it rise a couple more times so that you really get everything leavened. So here is a good use of leaven.

Now what does this picture? This pictures the new spirit body, which we will receive. All of those from the Old Covenant that qualified, and going all the way back to Abel. And those who under the New Covenant, beginning with the day of Pentecost as we saw who received the Holy Spirit at the resurrection, they will be changed. Now let's see that in 1 Corinthians 15.

Now this becomes very important, very profound. You are not going to be raised with the same body that you have in the flesh today. Now let's notice how the apostle Paul describes this. Let's begin here in verse 34. Now remember he also condemned them already as we saw earlier, that there were some who did not believe in the resurrection. "Awake to righteousness, and do not sin, for some *of you* do not have the knowledge of God.

I say *this* to your shame." Can you imagine that? Sitting in the Church of God and not having the knowledge of God? Well we see the same thing being repeated today. How can people sit there in the Church of God and have not the knowledge of God? Well number one, they have not been taught; and number two, some of them may be tares; and number three, some of them may be Laodiceans or whatever attitude of the seven churches that be there.

Now continuing on in verse 35. "Nevertheless, someone will say, "How are the dead raised? And with what body do they come? " Now hold your place here and let's come to John 12 and let's see how Jesus explained it concerning Himself, likening it also unto grain. And remember that Jesus was the first of the firstfruits, right? He was the premiere sheaf of the harvest of the grain, correct? Yes. Now let's begin here in John 12:24. "Truly, truly I say to you, unless a grain of wheat falls into the ground and dies, it remains alone;" Now this is a sowing, isn't it? And we covered part of that yesterday, didn't we in Matthew 13? Yes. "... but if it dies, it bears much fruit. The one who loves his life shall lose it, and the one who hates his life in this world shall keep it unto eternal life" (John 12-24-25). So Christ is likening even His own death as a grain being planted that dies.

So let's come back here to 1 Corinthians 15. It's the same thing here. "...Fool! What you sow does not come to life unless it dies. And what you sow *is* not the body that shall be; rather, *it is* bare grain—it may be of wheat, or one of the other *grains*; And God gives it a body according to His will, and to each of the seeds its own body. *Likewise*, not all flesh *is* the same flesh. ..." So he goes on to explain it in quite detail here. "...Rather, *there is* one flesh of men, and another flesh of beasts, and another of fish, and another of birds. And *there are* heavenly bodies, and earthly bodies; but the glory of the heavenly *is* different, and the *glory* of the earthly *is* different. *There is* one glory of *the* sun, and another glory of *the* moon, and another glory of *the* stars; for *one* star differs from *another* star in glory. So also *is* the resurrection of the dead. It is sown in corruption; it is raised in incorruption. It is sown in dishonor; it is raised in glory. It is sown in weakness; it is raised in power. It is sown a natural body; it is raised a spiritual body. There is a natural body, and there is a spiritual body; " (vs. 36-44). Now notice how it's talking about the harvest continually. It is sown, it is sown. That's why the day of Pentecost pictures the resurrection because that's a finality of the firstfruits harvest for the grain.

Now let's pick it up here in verse 45. "Accordingly, it is written, "The first man, Adam, became a living soul; the last Adam *became* an ever-living Spirit." That is Christ through the power of the resurrection. "However, the spiritual *was* not first, but the natural— then the spiritual. The first man *is* of the earth—made of dust. The second man *is* the Lord from heaven. As *is* the one made of dust, so also *are all* those who are made of dust; and as *is* the heavenly *one*, so also *are all* those who are heavenly. And as we have borne the image of the *one* made of dust, we shall also bear the image of the heavenly *one*. " (vs. 45-49). And when we bear the image of the heavenly we're going to see here that we will be changed, just like a lump of dough is changed when leaven is put in it, and then when it's baked in it's final form, it is permanently in a changed form. So that's exactly what it will be with us for the resurrection.

Now let's continue on, verse 50. "Now this I say, brethren, that flesh and blood cannot inherit *the* kingdom of God, nor does corruption inherit incorruption. Behold, I show you a mystery: we shall not all fall asleep, but we shall all be changed, In an instant, in *the* twinkling of an eye, at the last trumpet; for *the* trumpet shall sound, and the dead shall be raised incorruptible, and we shall be changed. " (vs. 50-52). Now we will see in a little bit that in Revelation 11 the last trump is defined as the seventh trump. And that is the resurrection.

Now notice, "For this corruptible must put on incorruptibility, and this mortal must put on immortality. Now when this corruptible shall have put on incorruptibility, and this mortal shall have put on immortality, then shall come to pass the saying that is written: "Death is swallowed up in victory. " (vs.53-54). Now notice here. We will be changed. Permanent change. Now that is what the leaven of the two loaves picture on the day of Pentecost. And of course when all the thousands of them came there were thousands and thousands of those loaves. And they waved them before the Lord and then that became part of their keeping of the Feast of Pentecost.

Now let's continue on brethren because this really gets exciting. Now let's go back and we'll just review. We won't turn there but turn to the book of Revelation and let's come to Chapter 6 here for just a minute. But we'll review Chapters 2 and 3. And Chapter 2 and 3 we have the seven churches. And that pictures the seven churches that were then. That pictures the seven churches down through history. That pictures perhaps even the seven churches at the end time. If we have seven from which comes seven, out of which comes seven, which is the pattern of the book of Revelation then we probably have seven churches in the end-time which will match up to the seven churches in Revelation 2 and 3. These seven churches represent the seven weeks harvest. Now let's see when the seven week harvest comes to an end and then we are left once again with the 50th day harvest, which will be God's harvest.

Now, right after Revelation 2 and 3 we have Revelation 4 and 5 showing the events that are going on there, and how that Christ is the only One to open the seals. And then He was given power to open the seals, and that is after the time that God the Father gave Christ the authority to do so. Now let's begin in Chapter 6 because here we will see where we have the end of the Church age.

Let's begin, " And I looked when the Lamb opened one of the seals;..." Now I'm reading out of my translation here. "...and I heard one of the four living creatures say, like the sound of thunder, "Come and see." And I looked, and behold, *there was* a white horse; and the one who was sitting on it had a bow, and a crown was given to him; and he went out conquering, and to conquer. And when He opened the second seal, I heard the second living creature say, "Come and see. " (Rev. 6:1-2). Now this is a picture of the false religion going out in conquering and to conquer. We see that happening right now bringing all coalesced into the coming one world government.

"And another horse went out *that was* red; and *power* was given to the one sitting on it to take peace from the earth, ..." (vs. 3-4). This is the time of Revelation 13 after the beast receives the deadly wound and that is healed and he comes back, and authority is given him over all kindreds and tongues and nations, and it was given him authority to make war against the saints. Now we will see that will happen here in the 5th seal in just a minute.

Verse 5, "And when He opened the third seal, I heard the third living creature say, "Come and see." And I looked, and behold, *there was* a black horse; and the one sitting on it had a balance in his hand. And I heard a voice in *the* midst of the four living creatures say, "A measure of wheat for a silver coin, and three measures of barley for a silver coin: and *see that* you do not damage the oil and the wine." And when He opened the fourth seal, I heard *the* voice of the fourth living creature say, "Come and see." And I looked, and behold, *there was* a pale horse; and the name of the one sitting on it *was* Death, and the grave followed him; and authority was given to them over *one* fourth of the earth, to kill with *the* sword and with famine and with death, and by the beasts of the earth." (vs. 5-8).

Now then, here's what we have, verse 9. This is when the Church age ends. "And when He opened the fifth seal, I saw under the altar the souls of those who had been slain for the Word of God, and for the testimony that they held;" Now this was in vision. This is not saying that they are immortal souls. But this is a way of God conveying to John, and to us, the events that are going to take place. "And they cried out with a loud voice, saying, "How long, O Lord, holy and true, do You not judge and avenge our blood on those who dwell on the earth?" And white robes were given to each of them; and they were told that they should rest a short time yet, until *it* be fulfilled *that* both their fellow servants and their brethren also would be killed, just as they had been" (vs. 9-11).

So we have two categories of Christians at this particular point. We have those who have gone to a place of safety, as we find in Revelation 12. But also in Revelation 12 we find that Satan goes after to make war of the remnant of her seed, which have the testimony of Jesus Christ and keep the commandments of God. This is the war pictured right here by the 5th seal. Now there will come a time when all of those who are not in a place of safety will be martyred. And that will end the Church harvest. That will finish the harvest of the seven churches. That will finish the seven-week harvest. But there is still one more day, and one more day of the harvest which God Himself is going to do in a way different than dealing with us.

Now let's see how that begins. Verse 12, " And when He opened the sixth seal, I looked, and behold, there was a great earthquake; and the sun became black as *the* hair *of* sackcloth, and the moon became as blood; And the stars of heaven fell to the earth, as a fig tree casts its untimely figs when it is shaken by a mighty wind. Then *the* heaven departed like a scroll that is being rolled up, and every mountain and island was moved out of its place. " (vs. 12-14). This is a tremendous event. This is the event which is spoken of there in Haggai 2 where the Lord says, "And yet one more time I will shake the earth and the heavens and the dry land, and the sea." And then Christ will appear. This is it, right here. Now we'll see another of this in Matthew 24 in just a minute.

Notice what happens then. " And the kings of the earth, and the great men, and the rich men, and the chief captains, and the powerful men, and every bondman, and every free *man* hid themselves in the caves and in the rocks of the mountains; And they said to the mountains and to the rocks, "Fall on us, and hide us from *the* face of Him Who sits on the throne, and from the wrath of the Lamb. Because the great day of His wrath has come, and who has the power to stand? " (vs. 15-17).

Now let's see in Matthew 24 where this occurs. Jesus talked about this. Matthew 24:21 is talking about the tribulation because see, the tribulation begins with the second seal. Then we have the third seal, the fourth seal, and then the fifth seal is the martyrdom of the saints. They are blamed by the beast as causing all of these problems on the earth. And as soon as we get rid of them then we're going to solve all the problems on the earth and we'll have one government, we'll one religion, we'll have one mind, and all of these nasty Christians will be exterminated. So when they come to the point of killing every Christian they can find, because they'll be able to find them. Because even without the mark of the beast, which none of the true Christians will have, they have the global positioning system, and they can track down any human being on earth within 100 square feet. So there is no mountain you can go to, no cave you can go to, no cellar that you can go to, because when God has determined it is His will that those who are to be martyred will be martyred, they will be martyred. And at that time God will give great strength to be able to give a witness, and to prophesy against the evil powers of Satan and the world.

Matthew 24:21 "For then shall there be great tribulation, such as has not been from *the* beginning of *the* world until this time, nor ever shall be *again*. And if those days were not limited,..." Now the Greek here doesn't mean, "cut short", shortening up less than 3 ½ years. It means, "limited", those days are limited. God has in advance set a limit of the days of the tribulation. "…there would no flesh be saved; but for the elect's sake those days shall be limited. Then if anyone says to you, 'Behold, here *is* the Christ,' or, '*He is* there,' do not believe *it*. For there shall arise false Christs and false prophets, and they shall present great signs and wonders, in order to deceive, if possible, even the elect. Behold, I have foretold *it* to you. Therefore, if they say to you, '*Come and* see! He is in the wilderness'; do not go forth. '*Come and* see! *He is* in the secret chambers'; do not believe *it*." (Matt. 24:21-26).

Now here, this ties in with the beginning of the sixth seal with the rolling back of the heavens as a scroll rolled up together. Matt 24:27 King James Version, "For as the lightening cometh out of the east, and shineth even unto the west…" Now this is not talking about a bolt of lightning. Unfortunately this is not a good translation. This should read, "and as the light of day." Because lightning does not just proceed from the east. It proceeds from the east, from the west, from the north, from the south. From the clouds down to the ground. From the ground back up to the clouds. It goes sideways, it goes at every angle. So this cannot be talking about lightning as a bolt of lightning, but the light of day, which comes out of the east because that's where the sun rises, and shines even unto the west because that's where the sun sets. "…So shall the coming of the Son of man be." This is called the sign of the Son of man. So what is going to happen? When the heavens roll back as a scroll there is going to appear this brightness as if it's another sun, and of that day, and of that hour knows no man.

Now let's see it here in the Faithful Version, Matthew 24, verse 29. But immediately after the tribulation of those days, the sun shall be darkened, and the moon shall not give her light, and the stars shall fall from heaven, and the powers of the heavens shall be shaken. Because we saw the tribulation come up to a certain point. And when we come to the book of Revelation we are going to see that it shifts from the tribulation of man against man to the more dastardly part of it of demons and men against the angels of God with the seven trumpet plagues. So this becomes important to understand.

"And then shall appear the sign of the Son of man in heaven [as a sun just being exposed – never there before]; and then shall all the tribes of the earth mourn, and they shall see the Son of man coming upon the clouds of heaven with power and great glory" (vs. 30). And so because of the time that is left, as we will see, that sign of the Son of man must be like a sun coming closer and closer, and closer, and closer, and closer, and closer to the earth. And then when it comes time for the resurrection then it will, I believe, lock into orbit right over Jerusalem. And that's where the sea of glass will be. How high it will be, I don't know. It says it's going to be in the clouds. How high are the clouds? Clouds can be as high as 50,000 feet. They can be as low as 2000 or 3000 feet. So we don't know but we are going to meet Christ in the air in the clouds. So Christ is coming with the clouds. Now notice, when the resurrection occurs this is what is going to happen. "And He shall send His angels with a great sound of a trumpet; and they shall gather together His elect from the four winds, from one end of heaven to *the* other. " (vs. 31).

Now we got ahead of the story a little bit, but let's go back to Revelation 7 because we need to look at the 50th day harvest of God. And this is a special harvest of God. Now let's pick it up here beginning in verse 1. Now remember how we ended with Revelation 6. They saw the sign of the Son of man in heaven. "Because the great day of His wrath has come, and who has the power to stand?" Now then God does something very important. He intervenes to fulfill a prophecy. He intervenes to show His mercy. He intervenes because He does not want, with the end of the Church age, that there lack human beings who are converted and qualify for the kingdom of God.

Now let's pick it up here in verse 1. "And after these things I saw four angels standing on the four corners of the earth, holding back the four winds of the earth, so that the wind might not blow on the earth, or on the sea, or on any tree. Then I saw another angel ascending from *the* rising of *the* sun, having *the* seal of *the* living God; and he cried out with a loud voice to the four angels, to whom it was given to damage the earth and the sea, Saying, "Do not damage the earth, or the sea, or the trees until we have sealed the servants of our God in their foreheads" (Rev. 7:1-3).

(Part II)

Now then, let's understand something very important and very profound here. Of the 144,000 in Revelation 7, that cannot be anyone who is in the Church today. And that's why the Jehovah Witnesses are completely wrong on their 144,000 and their interpretation and understanding of it. Why is it that I say that the 144,000 of Revelation 7 cannot be any of us? Well let's answer the question by scripture. Let's first of all go to 2 Corinthians 1 and let's see that we are now sealed with the Holy Spirit of God. Whenever you receive the Holy Spirit you have been sealed. Now let's see that and let's understand that. So we will see that the 144,000 were not sealed with the Holy Spirit until this particular time down into the tribulation. So we'll see that very clearly.

Now let's pick it up here, 2 Corinthians 1:20. "For whatever promises of God *there are*, in Him *is* the yes, and in Him the Amen, with glory to God by us ." And that's one thing we can do brethren. We can claim the promises of God. Not because we're anything. Not because we're something that we have done on ourselves and we now deserve it. No, we claim the promises of God for the sake of Christ. For the sake of His word. For the sake of His truth. For His righteousness. And it's always yes, because He won't deny the promise. He will fulfill it.

Now notice, "But He Who establishes us with you in Christ, and Who has anointed us, *is* God, Who has also sealed us and has given the earnest of the Spirit in our hearts (vs. 21-22). Now the earnest of the Spirit is the down payment. See, we are just like the unleavened bread now. When we are leavened in our spiritual form then we will have the fullness of the Spirit, and that's why leaven is pictured in good cause at that particular time. We only have the earnest of it now.

Let's go to Ephesians 1 and let's see how he explained it to those at Ephesus, concerning the Holy Spirit. Now notice how this begins here. Now let's pick it up in verse 12. "That we might be to *the* praise of His glory, who first trusted in the Christ; In Whom you also trusted after hearing the Word of the truth, the gospel of your salvation; in Whom also, after believing, you were sealed with the Holy Spirit of promise, Which is *the* earnest of our inheritance until *the* redemption of the purchased possession, to *the* praise of His glory. " (Eph. 1:12-14). So if you have the Holy Spirit of God now, you have been sealed. So you cannot be any of the 144,000 of Revelation 7.

Now let's go back to Revelation 7 and let's see who the 144,000 there are. And this will show how true God's word is. Now let's pick it up here in verse 3. "Saying, 'Do not damage the earth, or the sea, or the trees until we have sealed the servants of our God in their foreheads' " We've already been sealed so these are those who are now at that time called and converted by God's supernatural act.

Now notice… Let's go back and just review the things in Revelation 6 for just a minute. How that all of those things that the prophet Joel said concerning the heavens, the sun, the moon, the stars, and the earthquake, and the pouring out of the Spirit of God, how even Peter prophesied that that would be before the great and notable day of the Lord. And so this is showing it right here. That's what happened. Now here is the fulfillment of the Pentecost harvest, or the 50th day harvest by God. This is a separate harvest. Separate from the

Church. This is God's divine intervention to fulfill and complete His word and call those especially that He is determined to call.

Now let's see who the 144,000 are, beginning verse 4. "And I heard the number of those who were sealed: one hundred forty-four thousand, sealed out of every tribe of *the* children of Israel. From *the* tribe of Judah, ..." Now isn't it interesting that in the book of Zechariah, God says that the tents of Judah will be saved first. So here is Judah first. "... twelve thousand *were* sealed; from *the* tribe of Reuben, twelve thousand *were* sealed;...". Now Dan is left out. The reason Dan is left out is because the book of Genesis says of the prophecy of Dan that he would wait for his salvation. And of course Dan is the tribe of Israel that is so involved in idol worship and Catholicism. So God is going to save them later. They're not included in this 144,000. So this is a special category that God has saved for Himself.

Now let's understand when in time frame does this take place in the tribulation. We know that the overall tribulation is 3 ½ years. So this is an event which takes place before the 3 ½ years has expired. So let's go back to the book of Hosea, Chapter 5, the very last verse there, and we will see that this gives us a prophetic time frame as to when this took place. Hosea 5:15 God says concerning Israel, "I will to *and* return to My place, till they acknowledge their offence, and seek My face: in their affliction they will seek Me early."

Now the prophecies are true. Israel is going into captivity. Now there are some people out there who say, "Israel is not going into captivity today." That is a lie and that is a false prophet. And he is teaching things that are not according to the scriptures. Oh, that it would be, that Israel could be in such a condition before God that they wouldn't have to go into tribulation. But you read all of the prophecies concerning where Israel is when Christ returns and all of them show that they are in captivity. So here are the children of Israel in captivity and out of those who are in captivity 144,000 are brought to repentance and are sealed. Now when during the [tribulation] Millenium does this take place?

Let's go to Hosea 6:1. Here it is speaking of Israel during this time of repentance. "Come, and let us return unto the LORD: for He hath torn, and He will heal us; He hath smitten, and He will bind us up. After two days will He revive us..." Now in prophecy how long is a day? In prophecy a day is a year. So this is after two full years. That's when the sign of the Son of man is going to appear in heaven and God will then begin to raise them up. Now notice, "...He will revive us: in the third day..." That is, beginning in the third year of the tribulation, which means there's a whole year to the third year left and there is another six months making a total of a year and a half. So the whole tribulation is 3 ½ years altogether, broken down into the first two years, coming down through the opening of the seals until the sign of the Son of man appears in heaven. And then we come down to the time now of Revelation 7 where that we have what? We have then the 144,000 of Israel sealed just like it says right here in Hosea 6. "...In the third day He will raise us up, and we shall live in His sight" (Hosea 6:1-2).

Now notice also the prophecy. "Then shall we know, *if* we follow on to know the LORD: His going forth is prepared as the morning; and He shall come unto us as the rain, as the latter *and* former rain unto the earth" (vs. 3). So this is what we have back in Revelation 7. God intervening to save them.

Now then, what does it say concerning the preaching of the gospel? It says to the Jews first, which includes Israel as we've seen here. All Israel. Then who does it go to after that? To the Greek or the Gentile. Now God is also going to reach down and supernaturally seal, and supernaturally by the power of God's Holy Spirit through this angel who is commissioned to do so. Now let's understand something. All of these will receive the Holy

Spirit first, then they will be baptized just like it was with Cornelius' household. They received the Holy Spirit first, then they were baptized. Now can God do that? Yes, He can. God chooses to do that whenever it is His choice to do so, like He did with Cornelius. But do they still have to be baptized? Yes they do. So then what will happen then? There will be great baptismal ceremonies taking place with the 144,000.

Now then, since it goes to the Gentile also, the same thing is going to occur. But notice this, Revelation 7:9 "After these things I looked, and behold, a great multitude, which no one was able to number…" So this shows contrary to the preaching of some, that God is not just restricting those that He is calling from the time of Christ until His return, to 144,000. Such a thing could never be. Because if even on the very first day, as we saw of Pentecost, 3000 were converted and thousands were added. Another place it says, "…and 5000 souls were added." Great multitudes in Jerusalem believed. And we saw where James told Paul when Paul came up to visit James there in Acts 22. What did James say? He said "Behold the thousands that believe in Christ and are zealous for the law." So anybody who says that God is only calling 144,000 in this age just doesn't know what he's talking about and he's twisting and turning the scripture to his own destruction.

Now here it says, "…a great multitude, which no one was able to number…" Where did they come from? "…out of every nation and tribe and people and language, was standing before the throne and before the Lamb, clothed with white robes and *holding* palms in their hands; " You know just like we saw yesterday. White robes, they're called to the wedding. These are some of the guests who are called at the very last minute out of the highways and out of the byways, and out of the places that God is doing it at the last minute. So this undoubtedly, let's just say this, since this is prophesied in Acts 2 to happen with all the signs preceding it, and it happened on the day of Pentecost there in Acts 2, therefore this has to happen on the next to the last Pentecost before Christ puts His feet on the earth. Or the Pentecost before the resurrection. So we have these people here now who in these circumstances will be converted for one year. These people, the 144,000 and the great innumerable multitude then are reckoned as the laborers who are put into work and hire at the eleventh hour. So there's only one hour left. And in this case that pictures one year left. So is God able to do that? Yes He is. No doubt about it. So they're going to receive salvation.

Now notice, let's just finish here Chapter 7. "And they were calling out with a loud voice to Him Who sits on the throne and to the Lamb, saying, 'The salvation of our God *has come*.', because that's what they're going to receive. "Then all the angels stood around the throne, and the elders and the four living creatures, and fell on their faces before the throne and worshiped God, 'Saying, "Amen. Blessing, and glory, and wisdom, and thanksgiving, and honor, and power and strength *be* to our God into the ages of eternity. Amen" ' ". "And one of the elders answered *and* said to me, 'These who are clothed with white robes, who are they, and where did they come from?' Then I said to him," 'Sir, you know.' "And he said to me, 'They are the ones who have come out of the great tribulation; and they have washed their robes, and have made their robes white in the blood of the Lamb. For this reason, they are before the throne of God and serve Him day and night in His temple; and the one Who sits on the throne shall dwell among them. They shall not hunger any more, nor shall they thirst any more; neither shall the sun nor the heat fall upon them, Because the Lamb Who *is* in *the* midst of the throne will shepherd them, and will lead them to fountains of living waters; and God will wipe away every tear from their eyes.' "

So this projects forward to the time that we know in Revelation 21 showing the finality of God's plan. So what this is doing it's showing, now what is God going to do with the 144,000 and great innumerable multitude? First of all He's showing that they're going to be resurrected. Of course they're not going to be resurrected until the first resurrection takes place. But it also shows that they are not going to enter into the Millenium as physical human beings. They're going to be spirit beings. So now we have a good setting to go on and understand what we're talking about with some of the other scriptures concerning the day of Pentecost and the resurrection.

Ok, let's go ahead now. Now I'm just going to summarize Chapter 8, and Chapter 9, but each of them are the seven trumpet plagues. The seventh seal is opened and then the first angel goes out. Now isn't it interesting it talks about the first angel going out and blows his trumpet. Then the second angel, then the third angel, then the fourth angel, then the fifth angel, then the sixth angel. Now let's come over here to Revelation 11 and we will see when the seventh angel sounds, and the seventh angel is the last trump. That's what we need to understand. And the saints are resurrected at the last trump, not trumpets. As I mentioned yesterday, the Feast of Trumpets is a day of war, memorial of blowing of trumpets. So here we have a sequence of seven trumpets. Now if you don't have the "Outline of Revelation" #1 and #2, and the chart that goes with it, be sure and write for it. Cause it will show that the first trumpet is blown shortly after the Pentecost where the 144,000 are sealed and the great innumerable multitude. And that comes down through the time sequence to when we come to the seventh trump, which then has to be on the day of Pentecost, or right there abouts.

Now let's pick it up here concerning the two witnesses, because then this leads on up until up to the resurrection. Now, God allowed the two witnesses to be killed. Revelation 11:8, "And their bodies *will lie* in the street of the great city, which spiritually is called Sodom and Egypt, where also our Lord was crucified." Now Sodom tells us the morals of the peoples. Egypt tells us the religion of the people because the coming one world religion is going back to the whole thing of Egyptian religious worship. That's why it's defined here.

Now notice, it also says, "…where also our Lord was crucified." And that is typified by Jerusalem because Jerusalem, even though it was city that God chose to place His name there when the temple was built there. It has never been faithful, with the exception of a few of the kings, as we find recorded in a history recorded in the books of Kings and Chronicles. Now then, when they die, "Then those of the peoples and tribes and languages and nations shall see their bodies three and a half days, for they will not allow their bodies to be put into tombs. And those who dwell on the earth will rejoice over them, and will make merry, and will send gifts to one another, because these two prophets had tormented those who dwell upon the earth." The last two enemies now to be killed. So the world thinks. "Then after the three and a half days, *the* spirit of life from God entered into them and they stood on their feet…" Now can you imagine how everyone is going to view that and take that. And it says, "… and great fear fell upon those who were watching them" (vs. 9-11).

Then here is an example, a perfect example in the scripture concerning the first shall be last and the last shall be first. The two witnesses were the very last two who were martyred for Christ's sake. And they are the very first two who are resurrected. Notice after they stood on their feet, verse 12, "And they heard a great voice from heaven, say. 'Come up here!' And they ascended into heaven in a cloud; and their enemies saw them *rise*. And in that hour there was a great earthquake, and a tenth of the city fell, and seven thousand men were killed in the earthquake. And the rest were filled with fear, and gave glory to the God of heaven." The second woe is past:…" And the second woe was introduced with the sixth trumpet. "…Behold the third woe is coming immediately" (vs. 12-14).

Now verse 15, "Then the seventh angel sounded *his* trumpet; and *there* were great voices in heaven, saying, "The kingdoms of this world have become *the kingdoms* of our Lord and His Christ, and He shall reign into the ages of eternity." And the twenty-four elders, who sit before God on their thrones, fell upon their faces and worshipped God, saying, "We give You thanks, O Lord God almighty, Who is, and Who was, and Who *is* coming, that You have taken *to Yourself* Your great power and have reigned." For the nations were angry, and Your wrath has come, and the time for the dead to be judged, and to give reward to your servants the prophets, and to the saints, and to *all* those who fear Your name, the small and the great; and to destroy those who destroy the earth" (vs. 15-18). Now then, that is the resurrection, is it not? The resurrection occurs at the seventh trump. The last trump, just as Paul said.

Now let's go back here to 1 Thessalonians 4 and let's see where then, as we saw in Matthew 24, the angels will pick us up as we are resurrected and will bring us up to the sea of glass, because there is going to be the meeting with the saints. And then we will see what has to happen here. 1 Thessalonians 4:14, "For if we believe that Jesus died and rose again, in exactly the same way also, those who have fallen asleep in Jesus will God bring with Him. For this we say unto you by *the* word of *the* Lord, that we who are alive and remain unto the coming of the Lord shall in no wise precede those who have fallen asleep because the Lord Himself shall descend from heaven with *a* shout of command, with *the* voice of an archangel and with *the* trumpet of God; and the dead in Christ shall rise first: then we who are alive..." Now who are those who are alive? One, those who are of the Church in the place of safety. Two, the 144,000 of Revelation 7 and the great innumerable multitude. So after all the dead in Christ have been raised, "Then we who are alive and remain shall be caught up together with them in *the* clouds for *the* meeting with the Lord in *the* air; and so shall we always be with *the* Lord" (1 Thes. 4:14-17).

Now then, let's come to Revelation 14 and let's see when that will take place. Notice, I want you to understand. There are a lot of things that have to take place after the resurrection before we come back to the earth. Now it is true that the Feast of Trumpets pictures the day when Christ and the saints put their feet on the earth on the Mount of Olives. But the coming of Christ began with the sign of the Son of man in heaven, and He kept coming closer and closer, and closer, and closer to the earth.

Now let's come there to Revelation 14 and let's see the harvest of the firstfruits. Let's see what it says there. Then when we're done with this we'll go back and we'll examine the 144,000 again of Revelation 7 and the 144,000 of Revelation 14. But first let's get us all resurrected first. Let's have that all taken care of.

Let's begin here in verse12. "Here is *the* patience of the saints, here *are* the ones who keep the commandments of God and the faith of Jesus." And that means having Jesus very own faith. "And I heard a voice from heaven, say to me, "Write: Blessed *are* the dead who die in *the* Lord from this time forward. Yes, says the Spirit, so that they may rest from their labors; and their works follow them." And I looked, and behold, a white cloud, and *one* like the Son of man sitting on the cloud, having a golden crown on His head; and in His hand *was* a sharp sickle." Now what do you cut grain with? A sickle. "And another angel came out of the temple, crying with a loud voice to Him Who was sitting on the cloud, "Thrust in your sickle and reap, because the time has come for You to reap; for the harvest of the earth is ripe" (Rev. 14:12-15). Which Jesus said the harvest is the end of the age. The age ended with the seventh trump. And this then is the resurrection of the seventh trump. So as the age is ending the sickle is put to the grain and all then are resurrected.

Now verse 16, "And He Who was sitting on the cloud thrust forth His sickle upon the earth, and the earth was reaped." There is the first resurrection. That occurs on Pentecost. Then it jumps forward to another harvest. And this is the harvest of the destruction of the wicked through the seven last plagues. So let's see this now.

"And out from the altar came another angel, who had authority over fire; and he called with a loud cry to the one having the sharp sickle, saying, "Thrust in your sharp sickle, and gather the clusters of the earth, because her grapes are fully ripe." These are the true grapes of wrath. "Then the angel…" Now notice, the one who did the first harvesting was like unto the Son of man, that's Christ. Here now we have an angel with a sickle. "Then the angel thrust his sickle into the earth, and gathered the vine of the earth, and cast *its fruit* into the great winepress of the wrath of God. And the winepress was trodden outside the city, and blood spewed out from the winepress as high as the horses' bridle, to the distance of a thousand six hundred furlongs" (vs. 18-20). This is the judgment and the valley of judgment.

Now let's come right on to Revelation 15 here, verse 1. "Then I saw another sign in heaven, great and awesome: seven angels having the seven last plagues, for in them the wrath of God is filled up. And I saw a sea of glass mingled with fire…" Now remember yesterday how we saw the sea of glass was there when Christ came down on the mountain. And then He had Moses and the seventy elders and Aaron, Nadab, and Abihu come up. And they all saw Him because it was pavement under His feet. So here we have, if we're going to meet Christ in the air, what are we going to do? How are we going to be suspended? Well, there is a sea of glass which we can walk on. That's where the angels take us. "…A sea of glass mingled with fire…" That is because of it's brilliance there.

"…And those who had gotten the victory over the beast…" Question? When did the beast first appear? Well in the person of Satan the devil in the Garden of Eden. Have all of those who enter in to the first resurrection, have they had to get victory over the beast? Yes. Then He continues here, "…over his image…" Has there not been a female goddess worship in the image to the beast from going clear back when? Yes, at least we know that it came after the flood. So we know that they just reconstructed what they had after the flood from what they did before the flood. So there's the image of the beast. "…And over his mark…" Now at the end time we're going to have the mark of the beast. It's called the Digital Angel, which is inserted in the right hand or in the forehead either one. "…*And* over the number of his name, standing on the sea of glass, having *the* harps of God" (vs. 2)

Now notice this includes the Old Testament, those who have been resurrected and qualified from the time of Abel on down to the time of Christ. And notice what they do, verse 3. "And they were singing the song of Moses, *the* servant of God…" So this is those of the Old Testament. The loaf of the Old Testament. "…And the song of the Lamb…", which then is the loaf of the New Testament. "…Saying, "Great and awesome *are* Your works, Lord God Almighty; righteous and true *are* Your ways, King of the saints. Who shall not fear you, O Lord, and glorify Your name? For *You* only *are* holy; for all the nations shall come and worship before You; for Your judgments have been revealed." Now there's a prophecy of what's going to happen on down into the Millenium.

Now before we get into the seven last plagues let's go back and let's look at the 144,000 of Revelation 7, then we'll come back and look at the 144,000 of Revelation 14. Now in Revelation 7 we find this, verse 4. "And I heard the number of those who were sealed: one hundred forty-four thousand, sealed out of every tribe of *the* children of Israel;" So these are from the children of Israel only. Twelve thousand from each tribe. Why are they sealed at this particular time? Number one because they are in captivity because they were unfaithful to God even in the letter of the law. But, here they repent. We'll see that's very important. Now we also find the great innumerable multitude. Now there are no other distinguishing characteristics of these other than the fact that they are sealed at the beginning of the third year during the tribulation of 3 ½ years. And they then qualify for the first resurrection. These are the laborers of the 11th hour, as we find in the Gospel of Luke 11.

Now let's come here to Revelation 14:1 and let's look at the 144,000 of Revelation 14, and we are going to see that these 144,000 are a different group. And we are going to see the distinguishing and qualifying things for this 144,000. Now let's begin, verse 1.

"And I looked, and beheld *the* Lamb standing upon Mount Sion..." Now we read that yesterday, didn't we, in Hebrews 12? That we have come unto Mt. Zion, the Church of the Firstborn. "...And with Him one hundred *and* forty four thousand, having His Father's name written on their foreheads. Then I heard a voice from heaven, as *the* sound of many waters, and like *the* sound of great thunder: and I heard *the* sound of harpers, playing their harps. And they were singing a new song before the throne, and before the four living creatures and the elders. And no one was able to learn the song except the hundred *and* forty four thousand, who were redeemed from the earth" (Rev. 14:1-3). Now this is a separate song from the song of Moses, and the song of the Lamb. This is a third song that only this 144,000 could sing. No one else could sing it. All the rest were able to sing, the one concerning Moses for the Old Covenant, the one concerning the Lamb for the New Covenant, and now we have a third category here of the 144,000 with their song.

Now notice carefully, vers 4. "These are the ones who were not defiled with women..." Now what does it mean to be defiled with women? You go right back to Revelation 17, that we have mystery Babylon the Great, the mother of harlots and abominations of the earth, and she is called the great whore. So this means that once they were converted they did not defile themselves with any of the religions or the religious practices of this world. Now we're going to see that's very important when we go back and look at the seven churches in Revelation 2 and 3. "...They are virgins..." And of course Christ would only marry a virgin, correct? "...These are the ones who follow the Lamb wheresoever He may go. These were purchased from among men *as* firstfruits..." Now that's the correct translation. Not "these were purchased from among men, the firstfruits", because in the Greek there is no definite article. You can even drop off the "as". "These were purchased from among men - - firstfruits unto God and to the Lamb." (vs. 4). This then, we have Christ Who was the first of the firstfruits, and then we have these who are apparently the first group of the firstfruits. All the rest being the firstfruits in general. Now notice verse 5. "And no guile was found in their mouths; for they are blameless before the throne of God."

Now let's go back and let's analyze all of this and let's see what separates these even further from the 144,000 in Revelation 7. All right, let's list them out.
#1. They have the name of the Father written in their foreheads.
- That doesn't say that about the 144,000 in Revelation 7. All of these are distinguished from the 144,000 in Revelation 7. Plus the first thing that we need to understand is as we go along here because it says that they were not of the children of Israel, but they were redeemed from the earth.
#2. No one was able to learn the song except the 144,000.
#3. These 144,000 were redeemed from the earth probably over a period of time.
#4. These are they which are not defiled with women.
- That is they remained virgins, or they remained totally faithful to God in everything that they did in their conversion and were never defiled by women.
#5. They are virgins.
- Now remember that the warning that the apostle Paul gave to the Corinthians in 2 Corinthians 11, where he said, "For I am jealous over you with *the* jealousy of God because I have espoused you to one husband, so that I may present *you as* a chaste virgin to Christ" (2 Cor. 11:2). But they became non-virgins because they committed spiritual fornication. Now maybe they were able to repent of it, just like any woman who looses her virginity through sin, she can repent of it but she's no longer a virgin. So likewise, if it is those who have received the Holy Spirit, if they give up their virginity by being enticed by Satan the devil and getting involved in other religious practices, or other religious doctrines within the Church then they lose their virginity.

#6. These follow the Lamb wherever He goes.
- Meaning, that they're always following Him regardless of where they're spiritual life takes them.

#7. These were redeemed from the earth, from among men..

#8. Firstfruits unto God, and to the Lamb.

#9. In their mouth was no guile.

#10. For they are without fault before the throne of God.

Now let's go back and just quickly review the seven churches, and we will see that out of the seven churches only two of the seven remained virgins. Let's read it. Ephesus, remember we already covered that. They lost their first love and Christ told them, "Except you repent, I'm going to remove your candlestick." Loosing your first love, that is loosing your virginity.

Now then we come to the one at Pergamos where we saw that they ate things sacrificed to idols and committed fornication. And had the doctrine of Balaam, and the doctrine of the Nicolaitans, which thing God says He hates and He would fight against them with the sword of His mouth. So those at Pergamos, even though they repented because they were told to repent, even those at Pergamos who repented they lost their virginity. They can be put back in right standing with God but once you lose your virginity you have lost it. That doesn't mean you can't recoup it. You can, to be in the first resurrection. But the question is: will you still be part of the bride of Christ? Because the question is when describing the 144,000 here in Revelation 14, are they not the ones who are the bride of Christ because they remain virgins?

Ok, let's continue on with the church at Thyatira. They had the woman Jezebel, they committed fornication, they ate things sacrificed to idols, and they also had those who knew the deep things of Satan. In other words those who infiltrated into that church were bringing in the doctrines of Satan worship under the guise that you're worshiping Christ. Obviously they lost their virginity.

Then you have Sardis. Now what do you have in Sardis? Sardis was dead. They had a name that they lived but they are dead. With having dead practices they surely were not virgins before God. Because they somehow defiled themselves, and remember what Christ said to them. "Repent."

Same way with the Laodiceans. The Laodiceans became lukewarm, had need of nothing, and God was spewing them out of His mouth. And God told them to repent. So we have Ephesus, Pergamos, Thyatira, Sardis, and Laodicea. Five of the seven churches were commanded to repent of their sins. So they lost their virginity.

Now of the two churches left were Smyrna and Philadelphia. Smyrna: no command to repent. Now the Smyrnaites were the ones who were then martyred, and they were faithful unto death, which they were. And they held their virginity unto death. We have the Philadelphians who resisted everything concerning the synagogue of Satan, and they patiently kept the word of God. They were the ones who were faithful, the most faithful of all. The true Philadelphians, and there is no call to repentance there. And to the church at Philadelphia Christ said, "To him that overcomes will I write upon him the name of My Father, and the name of the city, New Jerusalem, and I will write upon him My new name." So to the Philadelphians, if you have the name of the Father, and if you have the name of Jerusalem, and you have the name of Christ upon you, you belong to part of the bride of Christ.

Now just like we learned yesterday, not all of those in the first resurrection are going to be part of the bride of Christ. So does this tell us here in Revelation 14, because of all of these conditions that this 144,000 represents those who have been called down through time, who have been faithful unto God, who were virgins, never deviated from it. Once they were baptized and received the Holy Spirit they never got involved in any of the religions of this world, or any of the doctrines of this world. And brethren now I hope you understand why it is so important that we remain faithful.

Now those who have not remained faithful, we pray that they will repent and not lose their reward. So this is really important for us to understand. Let's go back to 1 Corinthians 3 and let's see. They can repent, but they have been building wooden shacks and straw huts and their works are burned up because they were not virgins. The only ones who are virgins in this case, in 1 Corinthians 3 as we will see, are those who build on the virginity, keep it, and build the gold, silver, precious stone, and not the wood, hay, and stubble.

Now let's read it here in 1 Corinthians 3:11. "For no one is able to lay any other foundation besides that which has been laid, which is Jesus Christ. Now if anyone builds upon this foundation gold, silver, precious stones, wood, hay *or* stubble, The work of each one shall be manifested; for the day *of trial* will declare *it*, because it shall be revealed by fire; and the fire shall prove what kind of work each one's is. If the work that anyone has built endures, he shall receive a reward. If the work of anyone is burned up, he shall suffer loss; but *he* himself shall be saved, yet as through fire. " (1 Cor. 3:11-15). Now is this describing the difference between the 144,000 of Revelation 14 who become part of the bride of Christ because they remain faithful, as differentiated from those who started out but ended up sinning, ended up repenting and coming back much like the prodigal son, and they lost their virginity. So they lost some of the inheritance that they would have had otherwise. So this is really a tremendous thing for us to understand brethren.

Now let's come back to Revelation 15 again. Now I don't have time to go through the seven last plagues except that the seven last plagues represent the harvest of the wicked, as depicted in the last part of Revelation 14. And all of these plagues will be poured out in the presence of the saints. And these are righteous judgments. And these are true judgments. And for any who say that the God of the Old Testament was an angry and a harsh God, but the one of the New Testament is loving and kind and sweet, please understand that this is the wrath of the Lamb which is being poured out on all those sinners.

Now let's end up where we ended up last time. Let's come to Revelation 19:1 again. Before we begin let's also understand this too. God knows for the resurrection, based upon the works and the faithfulness of the individuals that He is going to select those who will be in the 144,000 of Revelation 14. And if those are the ones who consist of the bride of Christ, God the Father is the One Who chooses them. So we don't have to worry about it. We don't have to look around and accuse people, or suspect them, because it says, ..."Blessed are those who are called to the wedding supper of the Lamb..."(Rev. 19:9). Those who are called to the supper will participate in the first resurrection in power, and in glory just like the rest. But only the bride of Christ will be with Christ in where He is.

Now let's pick it up in verse 1. "And after these things I heard *the* loud voice of a great multitude in heaven, saying,...", because that's all of those who were resurrected standing on the sea of glass. And it's in the first heaven where the clouds are. "...'Hallelujah! The salvation and the glory and the honor and the power *belong* to the Lord our God. For true and righteous *are* His judgments; for He has judged the great whore, who corrupted the earth with her fornication, and He has avenged the blood of His servants at her hand.' And they said a second time, 'Hallelujah!' And her smoke shall ascend upward into the ages of eternity. And the twenty- four elders and the four living creatures fell down and worshipped God, Who sits on the throne, saying, 'Amen, Hallelujah!' And a voice came forth from the throne, saying, 'Praise our God, all His servants, and all who fear Him, both small and great.' " (Rev. 19:1-5).

"And a voice came forth from the throne, saying, 'Praise our God, all His servants, and all who fear Him, both small and great.' And I heard a voice like that of a great multitude, and like *the* sound of many waters, and *the* sound of mighty thunderings, saying, 'Hallelujah! For *the* Lord God Almighty has reigned. Let us be glad and shout with joy; and let us give glory to Him; for the marriage of the Lamb has come, and His wife has made herself ready.' And it was granted to her that she should be clothed in fine linen, pure and bright; for the fine linen is the righteousness of the saints. And he said to me, 'Write!" Blessed *are* those who are called to the marriage supper of the Lamb'. And he said to me, 'These are the true words of God.' " (vs. 6-9).

So we have a tremendous blessing brethren, whether we have been called to be part of the bride of Christ, which I hope whoever you are that that is true. We can't judge for ourselves how it's going to be. God is going to make that judgment. But also realize this. There is a great and a fantastic and eternal blessing to be called to the first resurrection and to be one of the guests at the wedding of the Lamb and His bride. So that is the full meaning of the day of Pentecost. Brethren, I hope it's been a wonderful day for you.

End of Sermon

Transcriber: Caroline Singer

Day 50—Holy Day and the 144,000
Part I and Part II
Pentecost—June 11, 2000
Scriptural References

1) Exodus 31

2) Exodus 34:26

3) John 20:17

4) I Corinthians 15:12-23

5) Genesis 3:19

6) Acts 1:3-11

7) Acts 2:1-20

8) Deteronomy 5:29

9) Acts 2:21-24, 34-35

10) Psalm 110:1

11) Acts 2:36-37

12) Ezekiel 33:11

13) Acts 2:2-15

14) Deteronomy 5:29

15) Acts 2:16-24, 34-40

16) Leviticus 23:17

17) Matthew 13:33

18) I Corinthians 15:34-35

19) John 12:24-25

20) I Corinthians 15:36-54

21) Revelation 6:1-17

22) Matthew 24:21-31

23) Revelation 7:1-3

24) II Corinthians 1:20-22

25) Ephesians 1:12-14

26) Revelation 7:3

27) Revelation 6:4-8

28) Hosea 5:15

29) Hosea 6:1-3

30) Revelation 7:9-17

31) Revelation 21

32) Revelation 11:8-18

33) I Thessalonians 4:14-17

34) Revelation 14:12-20

35) Revelation 15:1-3

36) Revelation 7:4

37) Revelation 14:1-5

38) II Corinthians 11:2

39) I Corinthians 3:11-15

40) Revelation 19:1-9

CHAPTER TWENTY-SEVEN

More on the 144,000

Pentecost—2000

June 17, 2000

Now I want to answer some questions concerning the bride and the guests and maybe a little bit concerning the 144,000. I might mention that I'm working on a booklet on the 144,000 and so we'll be able to cover that. I also have a booklet that I've been wanting to do for a long time. I've a lot of it done which centers on the series I did on Sabbath-keeping, on "The Holy Sabbath". But now with some of the information that we have, especially concerning Hebrews 4 and *sabbatismos* and the various verb forms of it and the Septuagint Greek version of the Old Testament, we are going to make that Sabbath booklet a whole lot stronger. And it's not going to be based upon Old Testament doctrine. It's going to be based on New Testament doctrine, and it's going to be put in such a way that there will be no doubt whatsoever that Sunday-keeping never came from God.

Let's come to Matthew 20, and what I want to do is cover a little part concerning the 50th day harvest of the 144,000 and great innumerable multitude. And we might add a little bit more to it. Now let's pick it up here in verse 1. "The kingdom of heaven shall be compared to a man, a master of a house, who which went out early in *the* morning to hire workman for his vineyard. And after agreeing with the workmen on a silver coin *for* the day's *wage*, he sent them into his vineyard. And when he went out about the third hour, he saw others standing idle in the marketplace; and he said to them; 'Go also into the vineyard, and whatsoever is right I will give you.' And they went" (Matt. 20:1-4). Now this is interesting isn't it? Because one thing that we have to get rid of is the Gerald Waterhouse mentality that it's all stacked up according to his four-hour sermon. See, it's not that way because God is going to determine who will be where and what position. And that's all a part of this, as we will see. So he didn't tell them very much, or he said, "Whatever is right I will give you." So they went their way.

"Again, after going out about *the* sixth hour and *the* ninth hour, he did likewise." So he went out there at 6 a.m., 9 a.m., noon, 3 p.m. "And about the eleventh hour [which then is 5 o'clock cause the 12th hour then is 6] he went out *and* found others standing idle, and said to them, 'Why have you been standing here idle all the day?' They said to him, 'Because no one has hired us.' He said to them, 'Go also into my vineyard, and whatever is right you shall receive.' And when evening came, the lord of the vineyard said to his steward, 'Call the workman and pay them *their* hire, beginning from the last unto the first' " (vs. 5-8). Now this tells us an awful lot, doesn't it? And as we will see the whole parable tells us that God does not think like we think. Now especially if you ever belonged to a union. I mean this would be called the greatest scab operation that they had ever come across.

"And when those who *were hired* about the eleventh hour came, they each received a silver coin. But when the first ones came, they thought that they would receive more;..." Now this is judging by human standard, correct? Yes. "...but each of them also received a silver coin. And after had receiving *it*, they complained against the master of the house, saying, 'These *who came* last have worked one hour, and you have made them equal to us, who have carried the burden and the heat of the day.' But he answered *and* said to them, 'Friend,

I am not doing you wrong. Did you not agree with me on a silver coin *for the day*?" (vs. 9-13). So this tells us what? That God is going to do what He is going to do. He is going to reward whom He is going to reward in the way He is going to reward them. And that all of our complaining or comparing isn't going to change it. And that also means that…and I know there are to be some people who say, "Well, who are you to say that we're not going to be part of the bride?" Well, the truth is, Christ is going to determine who it is, and I'm sure God the Father is going to select the bride. Don't you think so? Ok.

Now just recently I had a wedding, and I love weddings. Weddings are my favorite thing. And it was really a wonderful outdoor wedding. Andy Davis and Jennifer, his wife. And it was beautiful. Only thing is it was at noon and 95 degrees, so it was a little warm. But just as we started there was a breeze that came up and made it livable. So I finished the ceremony in 10 seconds. [Laughter] No, I didn't. Went through the ceremony fully, all the way. And then we went on over where they were going to have the wedding supper. And they had a wedding supper. And as I was sitting there, and my wife was sitting there, and we were enjoying everything. And here the bride and groom came in and they took the first dance, ok. And I thought this is just exactly what the Bible is talking about. Now we're here and we're enjoying it, and I was happy to have a part in doing the ceremony, but there is the husband and there is the bride and all the rest of us are guests. And I though, you know, that's just the way it's going to be in the resurrection. And God is the One Who's going to have to decide.

Now let's continue on here verse 14, "Take *what* is yours and go, for I also desire to give to the last *ones* exactly as I gave to you. And is it not lawful for me to do what I will with that which *is* my own? Is your eye evil because I am good? So the last shall be first, and the first *shall be* last; for many are called, but few *are* chosen" (vs. 14-16). Now this almost sounds like what we read about in Job here just a little earlier, wasn't it? "Will you disannul My judgment that you may be righteous?" That's what they're trying to do here, see.

Now, hold your place here and let's look at the literal last, because we'll come back. Let's go to Revelation 7 and then Revelation 11. Now are not these in Revelation 7 the 144,000 from Israel. And I think that's very clear that they are different from the 144,000 in Revelation 14. Now, as we covered on Pentecost Revelation 7 is approximately at the end of two full years of the 3 ½ year tribulation. Meaning that there's one year and six months left. This, I believe, is the 50th day harvest that belongs to God. Now here it gives no inclination of any reward at all does it? Except that it says, after you get through the 144,000 then you come down here the great innumerable multitude, which no man can number. And then it says here in verse 14, "Then I said to him, 'Sir, you know.' And he said to me, 'They are the ones who have come out of the great tribulation; and they have washed their robes, and have made their robes white in the blood of the Lamb." So these here may very well be a good portion of the number of guests, because if they're in white then those are the wedding garments of the guests. We'll go back to Matthew 22 here in just a little bit. These are part of the last, which will probably be some of the first who are resurrected. But that doesn't mean that they're going to necessarily be first in reward.

Now let's come to Revelation 11 and let's look at the very two last, the two witnesses. Let's pick it up here in verse 3. "And I will give *power* to My two witnesses, and they shall prophesy a thousand two hundred *and* sixty days, clothed in sackcloth. These are the two olive trees, and *the* two lampstands that stand before the God of the earth. And if anyone attemps to harm them, fire will go out of their mouths and devour their enemies. For if anyone attempts to harm them, he must be killed in this manner" (Rev. 11:3-5). So this is going to be quit a thing. And I can just see it now, CNN News there which Christiane Amanpour, whatever her name is, you know. And Peter Arnett out there, you know, giving the news. "Boy did you see that? Fire came out of their mouth and look, here are the ashes…" You know talking to different ones. "…And what are we going to do to stop them? They're upsetting this thing of the One World Government."

Verse 6, "These have authority to shut heaven so that no rain may fall in *the* days of their prophecy; and they have authority over the waters, to turn them to blood, and to smite the earth every plague, as often as they will. And when they shall have completed their testimony, the beast who ascends out of the abyss [who then is talking about Satan and the man that he possesses] will make war against them, and will overcome them, and kill them." Well this is just like with Christ. Satan thought he had it made when Christ was killed. But He was resurrected and totally defeated him. So here the beast will think boy, we finally have it made. And we'll teach them a lesson. "And their bodies *will lie* in the street of the great city, which spiritually is called Sodom and Egypt, where also our Lord was crucified" (vs. 6-8). And of course the coming one world religion is going to be nothing more than a re-warmed Egyptian version of the New Age religion.

Did you know that Mormonism, when you read this book, "Primitive Christianity In Crisis", Mormonism is nothing more than modern Gnosticism. When you read this it will blow you away. Cause the Gnostics believe that we were spirits up here in heaven and that we had to come down and possess a human body. That's a basic tenant of Mormonism. Very basic tenant of Mormonism. Ok, let's not get too detracted here.

Verse 9, "Then those of the peoples and tribes and languages and nations shall see their bodies three and a half days, for they will not allow their bodies to be put into tombs." Now when it talks about "all the world shall see it", it means they will see it. And today we understand that statement. I think it will be with television. No question about it. "And those who dwell on the earth will rejoice over them, and will make merry, and will send gifts to one another,…" I can just hear the beast. "Brethren of the world. We have finally conquered these two men who were disturbing and upsetting our wonderful one world government. They have caused plagues, and killed people, and drought, and now they are dead. Let us celebrate. I proclaim a feast." [Laughter] That's what's going to happen. And my wife thinks it's going to be Wilhelm Clinton. Could be. The longer he sticks around the more I think: Hey, there could be something to it. "…And will send gifts to one another, because these two prophets had tormented those who dwell on the earth" (vs. 9-10).

"Then after the three and a half days, *the* spirit of life from God entered into them and they stood on their feet;…" Can you imagine that? Can you imagine the breathlessness of all of the television reporters? You can just see them, you know. Peter Jennings, Tom Brokaw, and Dan Rather, all breathlessly reporting this. And Christian Amamadpur, you know, and all the cameras are there. And then we have our discussion, you know. Larry King live. They'll have a Rabbi, and they'll have you know, "What do you think of this." They won't quite have time for that but you can almost just see the whole thing going on here see. And right when they're talking about how good it is that they're dead, all of a sudden the cameras pointing on their bodies see them rise up on their feet. "…And they stood on their feet; and great fear fell upon those who were watching them. And they heard a great voice from heaven, say, 'Come up here!' And they ascended into heaven in a cloud; and their enemies saw them *rise*" (vs. 11-12). These are the last two who are killed, who are what? The first resurrected. Perfect example of the last shall be first.

"And in that hour there was a great earthquake, and a tenth of the city fell; and seven thousand men were killed in the earthquake. And the rest were filled with fear, and gave glory to the God of heaven. The second woe is past. Behold, the third woe is coming immediately." That's what it means. Not just quickly, immediately. "And the seventh angel sounded *his* trumpet; and there were great voices in heaven, saying, 'The kingdoms of this world have become *the kingdoms* of our Lord and His Christ, and He shall reign into the ages of eternity" (vs. 13-15). Here then is the resurrection. But just prior to the resurrection, the two witnesses, the last two are raised first.

Now let's come back to Matthew 20:16. "So the last shall be first, the first *shall be* last; for many are called, but few *are* chosen." Then we have this, the next section. And Jesus went up. He told them He was going to be betrayed and so forth. Now let's come down to verse 20 because this ties right in with it, see.

"Then the mother of the sons of Zebedee came to Him with her sons, worshipping Him and asking a certain thing from Him. And He said to her, 'What do you desire?' She said to Him, 'Grant that these my two sons may sit one at Your right hand and one at *Your* left *hand* in Your kingdom" (vs. 20-21). Boy, now you talk about a political move to make it good for my two boys. But this has the same thing to do with the first and the last. Only from a little different perspective. Only this time instead of the first and last being the general laborers that were out in the vineyard, now we here have it with the 12 apostles. And He gives the lesson here.

"But Jesus answered *and* said, 'You do not know what you are asking. Are you able to…' ", you see because her two sons were right there. You know they wouldn't want to march up and say, "Lord, give it to us. Look how good we are." "But Mom, you are so persuasive. Why don't you do it for us?" You know. "…Are you able to drink the cup that I am about to drink, and to be baptized *with*?" And He just told them that He was going to be crucified. "They said to Him, 'We are able' " (vs. 22). And of course they didn't know what that was. You know it's kind of like a Marine recruit. "Are you able to go up and capture that enemy machine gun nest?" "Yea, I can." Don't even know what you're saying. Never been under fire. "We are able."

"And He said to them, 'You shall indeed drink of My cup, and shall be baptized *with* the baptism that I am baptized *with;* but to sit at My right hand and at My left *hand* is not Mine to give, but *shall be given to those* for whom it has been prepared by My Father." So the Father is in charge of all of this, right? Yes He is. Not just us as human beings, or just Christ alone. "And after hearing *this*, the ten were indignant against the two brothers" (vs. 23-24). Because they got there first. The other 10 would have liked to have gotten there first to ask. That's what they were mad at. Cause, you know, just carnal human, wanting to be the best, the greatest, and all this sort of thing.

"But Jesus called them to *Him and* said, [He's giving the lesson here] 'You know that the rulers of the nations exercise lordship over them, and the great ones exercise authority over them.' " And of course the exercised dominion is *katakurieuo*, which is "downward". And the other one is *kataexousio*, which is "authority downward". "However, it shall not be this way among you; but whoever would become great among you, let him be your servant; and whoever would be first among you, let him be your slave; just as the Son of man did not come to be served, but to serve, and to give His life *as* a ransom for many " (vs. 25-28). Now that all ties in with those who are going to be in the resurrection.

Now, let's come over here to Matthew 22 and let's look at the guests. Matthew 22:1. "And again Jesus answered and spoke to them in parables, saying, 'The kingdom of heaven is compared to a man *who was* a king, who made a wedding feast for his son,' " Now the king there is God the Father, and the son obviously has to be Jesus Christ, Who is giving a parable. "And sent his servants to call those who had been invited to the wedding feast; but they refused to come" (Matt. 22:1-3). Let's stop right here. The king who is God the Father is going to have the marriage and He is going to select the bride. Have to be.

He "...sent his servants to call those who had been invited to the wedding feast; but they refused to come. Afterwards he sent out other servants, saying, 'Say to those who have been invited, "Behold, I have prepared my dinner; my oxen and the fatted beasts are killed, and all things are ready. Come to the wedding feast." ' But they paid no attention and went away, one to his farm, and another to his business. And the rest, after seizing his servants, insulted and killed *them*." Just a summary of the life of the apostles. "Now when the king heard *it*, he became angry; and he sent his armies *and* destroyed those murderers, and burned up their city." Now that is Jerusalem, and the fall of it in 70 A.D. "Then he said to his servants, 'The wedding feast indeed is ready, but those who were invited were not worthy; Therefore, go into the well-traveled highways, and invite all that you find to the wedding feast.' And after going out into the highways, those servants brought together everyone that they found, both good and evil;..." Now this is talking about people who are bad people and good people, not in a sense of spiritually speaking but just in their lives. And of course both the bad and the good have to repent. It's harder for the good to repent because they don't see the sins that they have done. "...And the wedding was filled with guests" (vs. 3-10).

Now here the parable breaks down a little bit because obviously this is referring to the first resurrection, but there is not going to be anybody in the first resurrection who's going to be there without the proper wedding garment. But in order to show that you have to apply yourself and have to have the proper wedding garment, this is here in the parable. So when will those who do not prepare to be guests, when will they be cast into outer darkness? Well that will be the lake of fire, which will be at the end of the Millenium and the Great White Throne Judgment. So in order for the sake of the parable to show it, it has to be combined here. Let's read it.

"And when the king came in to see the guests..." Now the king being God the Father, maybe this helps answer the question: when we are resurrected will we see God the Father? Why not? Will we be spirit beings? Yes. Are we not His children? Yes. Would He not want to see His children just resurrected, born from the dead? Yes. Would we not want to see Him? Absolutely. As well as Christ? No doubt. So this says He came to see them. "...*He* noticed a man there who was not dressed in *proper* attire for *the* wedding feast; And he said to him, 'Friend, how did you enter here without a garment *fit* for *the* wedding feast?' But he had no answer. Then the king said to the servants, 'Bind him hands and feet, *and* take him away, and cast *him* into the outer darkness.' There shall be weeping and gnashing of teeth. For many are called, but few *are* chosen" (vs. 11-14).

Let's go to Matthew 25. Now let's hope we can understand this a little bit more. Verse 1, "Then shall the kingdom of heaven be compared *to* ten virgins, who took their lamps *and* went out to meet the bridegroom." Now here we have the virgins and the bridegroom. Before we had the guests coming to the wedding. This is obviously a different category of people. "...Went out to meet the bridegroom. And five of them were wise, and five *were* foolish. The ones who were foolish took their lamps, *but* they did not take oil with them" (Matt. 25:1-3).

Now you need to understand about the lamps. The lamps that they had were probably as you see the top of this little teapot here. A little bigger than this and maybe just a little deeper as it sits over on it's side. And there was a little wick that came out on the side. Olive oil was put into the middle of it and the wick would hang over the edge of it and give light. Well obviously if you only have oil in your little lamp here you don't have very much. So that's why they should have had some with them to carry an extra amount to pour in there when they needed it.

"But the wise took oil in their vessels *along* with their lamps. Now when the bridegroom was gone a long time, they all became drowsy and slept." Showing that they will all have their own individual problems. "But in *the* middle of *the* night there was a cry: 'Look, the bridegroom is coming! Go out to meet him.' Then all those virgins arose and trimmed their lamps. And the foolish said to the wise, 'Give us *some* of your oil, because our lamps are going out.' But the wise answered, saying, '*No,* lest *there* not *be* enough for us and *for* you. But instead, go to those who sell, and buy for yourselves' " (vs.4-9). Now this obviously showing that they did not have enough spiritual character in order to qualify as part of the bride.

"And while they went to buy, the bridegroom came…" Now again in a parable it can't fit everything to the exact facts. "…The bridegroom came; and those who were ready went in with him to the wedding feast, and the door was shut. And afterwards the other virgins also came, saying, 'Lord, Lord, open to us.' But he answered *and* said, 'Truly I say to you, I do not know you.' " Now in this case he doesn't say, "Depart into outer darkness and there shall be weeping and gnashing of teeth." So this does not necessarily show a loss of salvation. But this shows a loss of being part of the bride. The door to being the bride is shut. It doesn't say they won't be in the kingdom of God, but it does tell us they won't be part of the bride. "Watch therefore, for you do not know the day nor the hour in which the Son of man is coming" (vs. 10-13).

Now then, I think that that's the best understanding I've been able to derive from this. In other words these virgins by the virtue of the fact, now it says they were virgins, but by virtue of the fact that they didn't exercise the spiritual character they should have had they, in a sense, disqualified themselves from the marriage. Now it doesn't necessarily say that they sinned and lost the, what we would call the spiritual virginity, but it does show that they were very negligent.

Now let's answer the question concerning the firstfruits. Let's go to 1 Corinthians 15:20. "But now Christ has been raised from *the* dead; He has become the first–fruit of those who have fallen asleep." Now we know that this is the first of the firstfruits by several things. Number 1, God says in Exodus 34 that you are to bring the first of the firstfruits unto the Lord. We also know by the wave sheaf offering that was elevated on the wave sheaf offering day, that that signified Christ ascending to the Father to be accepted as the firstborn from the dead. So we have Christ Who is the first of the firstfruits.

Now let's notice. "For since by man *came* death, by man also *came the* resurrection of *the* dead. For as in Adam all die, so also in Christ shall all be made alive. But each in his own order:…" (vs. 21-23). Notice, every man in his own order. So there is an order to the resurrection. Part of what we have of the order that we saw was what? The last shall be first and the first shall be last. Now if Adam repented and made it, is he going to be the last one resurrected? I don't know. But the ones who are going to be the very last, who are going to be resurrected, are those who are alive when Christ returns. I Thessalonians 4 says that they which are dead in Christ shall rise first, then we which are alive will be caught up in the air together with them and meet the Lord in the air. Now meeting the Lord in the air can also have the meaning "for the meeting with the Lord in the air". So there's an order. Ok, the bride is the firstfruits.

Let's go to James 1:18. Here in James 1:18 we are called firstfruits. All those in the first resurrection are called firstfruits. Christ is called firstfruits. So Christ is the first of the firstfruits, now let's look at the rest. "According to His own will, [that's speaking of the Father] He begat us by *the* Word of truth, that we might be a kind of firstfruits of all His created beings." Now that means of His creation, meaning those of us who are created in Christ Jesus. That's what it's referring to. So we are called firstfruits. Christ is also called the firstborn, isn't he? Romans 8:29, "…that He might be *the* firstborn among many brethren." We're also called "*the* church of *the* firstborn", Hebrews 12:23.

Now then let's go back to Revelation 14 and let's see concerning the 144,000 here. And the distinction between this and the 144,000 in Revelation 17 becomes very clear when we analyze all the differences. What is said of the 144,000 in Revelation 7 is that they are 12,000 from the 12 tribes of the children of Israel. It lists Joseph, and it lists Manasseh, and it does not include Dan. Now that's because of the prophecy that Dan will wait for his salvation.

Now here in verse 1, "And I beheld *the* Lamb standing on Mount Sion,…" Now that's what we are to come to, correct, the Church of the Firstborn, Hebrews 12? "…And with Him one hundred *and* forty-four thousand…" Now when you look at Revelation 7 with the innumerable multitude and 144,000…let's go back there.

Revelation 7:9, "After these things I looked, and behold, a great multitude, which no one was able to number, out of every nation and tribe and people and language, was standing before the throne and before the Lamb, clothed with white robes and *holding* palms in their hands;" Now you have to have the white robes in order to be a guest, correct? Yes. This is probably indicating that these are all guests. They stood before the throne. That is out around before the throne. "And they were calling out with a loud voice to Him Who sits on the throne and to the Lamb, saying, 'The salvation of our God *has come.*' Then all the angels stood around the throne, and the elders and the four living creatures, and fell on their faces before the throne and worshipped God, saying, 'Amen. Blessing, and glory, and wisdom, and thanksgiving, and honour, and power and strength *be* to our God into the ages of eternity. Amen'" (Rev. 7:9-12).

"And one of the elders answered and *said* to me, 'These who are clothed with white robes, who are they, and where did they come from?' Then I said to him, 'Sir, you know.' And he said to me, 'They are the ones who have come out of the great tribulation; and they have washed their robes, and have made their robes white in the blood of the Lamb. For this reason, they are before the throne of God and serve Him day and night in His temple; and the one Who sits on the throne shall dwell among them. They shall not hunger any more, nor shall they thirst any more; neither shall the sun nor the heat fall upon them, Because the Lamb Who is in *the* midst of the throne shall shepherd them, and will lead them to fountains of living waters; and God will wipe away every tear from their eyes'" (vs. 13-17).

Now let's come back and compare that with the 144,000 in Revelation 14. 144,000 at mount Sion "…having His Father's name written on their foreheads. Then I heard a voice from heaven, like *the* sound of many waters, and like *the* sound of great thunder; and I heard *the* sound of harpers playing their harps. And they were singing a new song before the throne, and before the four living creatures and the elders. And no one was able to learn the song except the hundred *and* forty-four thousand, who were redeemed from the earth. These are the ones who were not defiled with women, for they are virgins; they are the ones who follow the Lamb wherever He goes. These were purchased from among men as first fruits to God and to the Lamb;…" Now since we are all called firstfruits what category are these? Verse 5, "And no guile was found in their mouths; for they are blameless before the throne of God" (Rev. 14:1-5).

Now let's go back and just analyze this just a little bit more. Let's begin with firstfruits. These were redeemed from among men, not the children of Israel. Can be from any race or people or whatever. Firstfruits unto God and the Lamb. Now Christ is called firstfruits so we know He is the first of the firstfruits. Could we say then if this 144,000 represents the bride, are these the next category of firstfruits because it says everyone in his own order. And then all of the rest in the first resurrection will be called firstfruits. So we have three categories of firstfruit. Christ the first, the bride next, all the rest of us after that. And I think if we put the scriptures together properly we can see how that will be.

Let's go back and look at this a little bit more. Last part of verse 3, "who were redeemed from the earth". It says "redeemed from the earth". Again showing that it's from all nations. But this is differentiating it from the children of Israel. "These are the ones who were not defiled with women,..." Now what does it mean to be defiled with women?

All right, let's look at it. Let's go to Revelation 17. What does it mean to not be defiled with women? Who are the women that defile the saints of God? That's another way of answering the question, see. Revelation 17:1, "And one of the seven angels who had the seven vials came and spoke with me, saying to me, 'Come here; I will show you the judgment of the great whore who sits upon many waters; With whom the kings of the earth have committed fornication, and those who dwell on the earth were made drunk with the wine of her fornication.' Then he carried me away in *the* spirit to a wilderness; and I saw a woman sitting upon a scarlet beast that had seven heads and ten horns, full of names of blasphemy. And the woman *was* clothed in purple and scarlet, and was adorned with gold and pearls and precious stones; *and* she had a golden cup in her hand, filled with abominations and *the* filthiness of her fornication; And across her forehead a name *was* written, **MYSTERY, BABYLON THE GREAT, THE MOTHER OF THE HARLOTS AND OF THE ABOMINATIONS OF THE EARTH**" (Rev. 17:1-5). So it could be mother Babylon or any one of her daughters that can defile the saints. So these 144,000 of Revelation 14 were never defiled by false doctrines. The false doctrines of the churches of this world.

"They are the ones who follow the Lamb wherever He goes" (Rev. 14:4) because it says then Christ and the bride say…let's go back here to Revelation 22. And this a summary of what goes on during the Millennium. Revelation 22:17, "And the Spirit [Who is Christ] and the bride say, 'Come.' And let the one who hears say, 'Come.' And let the one who thirsts come; And let the one who desires partake of the water of life freely." So this is Christ and the bride. Everything in the Millennium will flow from Christ and the bride. Who will it flow to? Well let's go to Revelation 20:6. "Blessed and holy is the one who has part in the first resurrection;…" Now that's a blessing upon all. "…over these the second death has no power. But they shall be priests of God and of Christ, and shall reign with Him a thousand years." Now we also know from Matthew 25 that there will be those who are reigning over cities. We know also from Jesus explaining about who's going to sit on the 12 thrones of the children of Israel, that it's going to be each one of the apostles. So they will be kings. Here we have priests. We will reign as kings and priests with Christ. But the 144,000 are with Christ wherever He goes. Whereas those who are priests will be where ever Christ sends them to be priests. So it's a little bit different situation.

Now let's go back and look at this right here. Revelation 14, Verse 1. "Having His Father's name written on their foreheads. …"

Now let me clarify something here. Let's come to Revelation 14:4. "These are the ones who were not defiled with women, for they are virgins;" Now that means from the time of baptism. See, that has to mean from the time of baptism. Now hold your place here and let's go to 2 Corinthians 11 and let's see that. Verse 1, Paul writes, "I would *that* you might bear with me in a little nonsense; but indeed, do bear with me. For I am jealous over you with *the* jealousy of God because I have espoused you to one husband, so that I may present *you as* a chaste virgin to Christ. But I fear, lest by any means, as the serpent deceived Eve by his craftiness, so your minds might be corrupted from *the* simplicity that *is* in Christ. For indeed, if someone comes preaching another Jesus,…" Now that's when after you have been baptized and you believe in a different form of Christ, then you are not really believing in the true Christ. So these were the false apostles coming and teaching false doctrines. And so in believing these false doctrines and following these false doctrines then those who were once virgins lose their virginity spiritually. But they can repent and still be in the kingdom of God.

Ok, let's go back here to Revelation again. The question was asked: is the 144,000 a literal number or a symbolic number? Well if you have a symbolic number then what does that mean as a literal number because we have 144,000 literally of the children of Israel, those who were sealed. And then we have the great innumerable multitude, which then no one can number, so how could you say there could be a symbolic number with the great innumerable multitude because there's no number. So I would be more inclined to think that the 144,000 is perhaps a literal number. Now how is God going to choose that? Well, He alone knows. Will there be other virgins who were just slovenly, who are still going to be in the kingdom of God. Yes we had the parable of the 10 virgins. But the door to the wedding to be part of the bride was closed. But it doesn't say they were excluded from the kingdom of God, they just couldn't be part of the bride.

Now let's clarify something else. During the break it was brought up that there were these classes of the firstfruits. Christ the first of the firstfruits. Then the seven church harvest represented by the seven churches, Revelation 2 and 3. That's a second category. They are firstfruits. The third category is the 144,000 of Israel. The fourth category is the great innumerable multitude. And the fifth category would be the 144,000 of Revelation 14. So you have five categories all together, and five is the number of grace. So there may be something to that, but that helps substantiate what we covered in 1 Corinthians 15, Christ the firstfruits, and after that those that are His at His coming, but every man in his own order. So how Christ is going to order that out we don't know.

Now let's look at Revelation 2 and 3 and we will see that out of the seven churches... Now as I mentioned in the "Seven Church Harvest", these seven churches represent:

#1 The seven churches that were then.
#2 The projection of the history of the Church down through history.
#3 Represents the attitudes of Christians at anytime during any period.

And some of us can identify with several of the churches with our various attitudes as we have gone through our Christian life. So it's awfully hard to say exactly where each person belongs. And in that sense it is good from the point of view that God is the One Who is going to make the decision, and salvation is by faith. Salvation is not knowing which category you are in. Salvation is by faith. And I think we can trust God to know what He's doing, and we can trust God that to be in the first resurrection in any category is a blessing. Because it says in Revelation 19:9, "Blessed *are* those who are called to the marriage supper of the Lamb." So it's all a blessing. But what it does do, it shatters some of our carnal approaches to who we may think we are. [Laughter] Lest we pull a Job and tell God who we are and God tells us we're not who we say we are. But you are who I say you are. See.

Now let's look at the seven churches here. First one is Ephesus. Now they're commended for their works. They have good works, they have patience, they labor. You can't stand them which are evil. I'm just sort of summarizing here. And you've tried them which say they are apostles and are not and have found them liars. Now some people get mad when you do that. Well we still do that today, don't we? Yes. And someone said, "Well take me off your mailing list because of what you say about Herbert Armstrong and that if anyone doesn't agree with you well then you'll have nothing to do with them." No that's not the case brethren.

I wish there were 10,000 faithful ministers. Just think what could be done. I have tried working with other ministers, to get beat up, knocked down, mailing list stolen, and the whole works. Now I'd be happy to work with any minister. But I'll tell you one thing I will not do. I will not compromise or play politics to please anybody, because if we do not please Christ then it doesn't matter who else you please. All bets are off. Paul said, "...For if I am yet pleasing men, I would not be a servant of Christ." (Gal. 1:10) And he wouldn't even give one minute to any man to come against what Christ had revealed to him. And he should not. And so likewise I'll just take the same attitude that Paul had. You know. Be glad to work with any man but don't come and steal from us. Don't come and take brethren. Don't come and have your own personal thing. I don't set myself up as some big thing. I just want to teach the word of God and serve and love the brethren. I don't want people to look up to me as some big mucky-muck because I'm not. But in handling the word of God I won't countenance one minute people twisting and turning the word of God.

Now what we're doing here for the Bible Study tonight, we're trying to understand some difficult to understand scriptures, wouldn't you say? Yes. Maybe not everything we have here is exactly correct yet. But what we're doing, we're thinking it through, comparing the scriptures, looking at the scriptures to try and have it so we can understand the word of God even more. And there is nothing wrong with that at all. And that's something that we should do. If we find ourselves wrong in anything we'll change. We'll change. If someone finds something that I'm doing wrong that I shouldn't do, or say something I shouldn't say let me know, and I'll correct it. No problem with that. But I don't want the brethren to be beat up, and I don't want to be beat up. And I've been beaten up enough. I fought the hierarchy within Worldwide from 1972 on and it was really a tough situation. And I've seen what they did to each other and to the brethren. And that should never be. And yet we called ourselves the church of brotherly love, right? Everyone wants to be a Philadelphian, we'll look at that one in just a minute, but it's very obvious that not everyone can be.

Now those at Ephesus, he says here in verse 4. "Nevertheless I have *this* against you, that you have left your first love." Now what is losing your first love? That's not just being excited and knowing the truth when you first come to it. The first love is loving God with all your heart, and mind, and soul, and being. That's what they lost. Now how could they lose it? Could it be from negligence? Could it be letting in some idolatry? I don't know but they lost it. So He says, "Therefore, remember from where you have fallen…" So He considers this a great sin. "…And repent, and do the first works…"(Rev.2:4-5). So we can conclude from what we have here that those who did this and lost their first love probably have defiled their garments. Probably have lost their spiritual virginity from baptism, but then if they repent and do the first works they can be restored. Now the question is will they be part of the bride of Christ? That is God's judgment. But if we look at it from Revelation 14 we can say that these have defiled themselves with women.

Now then we come down here to the church of Smyrna. Now this one there is no correction at all, no calling to repentance. He says, verse 9, "I know your works and tribulation and poverty (but you are rich), and the blasphemy of those who declare themselves to be Jews and are not, but *are* a synagogue of Satan. Do not fear any of the things that you are about to suffer. Behold, the devil is about to cast *some* of you into prison, that you may be tried; and you shall have tribulation ten days. Be faithful unto death, and I will give you a crown of life" (vs. 9-10). No correction. They didn't submit to any of the false things that came along. Whether it was persecution by the Jews. Whether it was persecution by the pagans. Whether it was inquisition of the Roman Catholic Church. They didn't give in to any of it so they kept their spiritual virginity.

Now Pergamos really got themselves in trouble. Pergamos and Thyatira, wow. It's self-explanatory here. They had the doctrine of Balaam, which I will talk about here in the very near future. They also had the doctrine of Nicolaitanes. They ate things sacrificed unto idols. So He says verse 16, "Repent! For if *you* do not *repent*, I will come to you quickly, and will make war against them with the sword of My mouth." So here Christ has to fight against His own Church here. But notice Pergamos is right where Satan's capitol is. And when you are so close to the things of Satan it's awfully hard to not inculcate some of those

431

practices into your daily way of doing things. But that's what happened. We've had some of that today in this form. Not exactly, well we've had some of this very same thing recently with the demise of Worldwide Church of God going clear into Sunday-keeping. But we have had some of it even within the ministry and teaching that they bring out a lot things of psychology instead of preaching the word of God. And so that's getting so close to the world that you look at the things that the world has which is good and you bring in that and equate that with righteousness of God. The goodness of this world comes from which tree? The tree of the knowledge of good and evil. It is good. It can do good things. But it doesn't equal the righteousness of Christ. Now we've seen that.

Then we come to Thyatira. Boy Thyatira is perhaps the best and the worst all combined together here. It talks about their... It says, "I know your works, and love, and service, and faith, and your endurance, and your works; and the last *are* more than the first. But I have a few things against you, because you allow the woman Jezebel, who calls herself a prophetess, to teach and to seduce My servants into committing fornication and eating things sacrificed to idols" (vs. 19-20). Well there it is right there. Most of those in Thyatira, even in repenting, could not be considered virgins after they were baptized, because talking about their condition after they were in the Church because the message was to the church at Thyatira. So it's not before they were in the Church but after they were in the Church.

Then we come to Sardis and when you get the "Seven Church Harvest" with Sardis in there I did an in-depth study on that and it was really quite a revealing thing here. Chapter 3:1, "And to the angel of the church in Sardis, write: These things says He Who has the seven Spirits of God and the seven stars. I know your works, *and* that you have a name as if you are alive, but are dead." I tell you this is perhaps the worst spiritual condition. This is worse than lukewarm. At least lukewarm you're still alive. But here you're a corpse with just a pulse. "Be watchful, and strengthen the things that remain, which are about to die. For I have not found your works complete God. Therefore, remember what you have received and heard, and hold on *to this*, and repent. Now then, if you will not watch, I will come upon you as a thief, and you shall by no means know what hour I will come upon you. You have a few names even in Sardis who have not defiled their garments, and they shall walk with Me in white because they are worthy. The one who overcomes shall be clothed in white garments; and I will not blot out his name from the book of life, but I will confess his name before My Father, and before His angels" (Rev. 3:1-5). So here they just make it by the skin of the teeth. I don't even say skin of the teeth. Boy. But only a few are going to make it. I mean when you go through and you look at these things and you ask the question: how much does our choice count in all of this? Everything, as far as our responsibility is concerned.

Now over here to the Laodiceans. We beat up on the Laodiceans long and often and hard and difficult so we won't get in here and beat up on them too bad. But being lukewarm, talking back to God saying, "For you say, 'I am rich, and have become wealthy,...'" (vs. 17). Sounds a little bit like Job doesn't it, talking back to God? "...And have need of nothing'; ..." Well now as I wrote in a letter recently it's all taken away. It is all gone. Ok, now He commands them to... They are so bad they are vomited out of the mouth of Christ. Christ is outside knocking on the door to get in. They can repent. They can receive salvation. They can sit in the throne of judgment as Christ sits in the throne of judgment, but they have to become zealous.

Now let's look at Philadelphia and let's compare that to the 144,000 of Revelation 14. And the church at Philadelphia comes the closest to describing Revelation 14 and the 144,000 there, with the exception that we have to also do as Christ did in commending Smyrna. That they had no faults before God. Now let's read it here, verse Revelation 3:7. "And to the angel of the church in Philadelphia, write: These things says the Holy One, the one Who *is* true; the one Who has the key of David, Who opens and no one shuts, and Who shuts and no one opens." We always like to look to the open door but there's a time when God shuts it. And I think we've lived in the time where God has shut the door of radio and television as an effective way of reaching people. Now He's going to open another door, and when He does we have to be prepared and be ready. Whatever it may be Christ will have to open the door for any one of the seven churches here, but in particularly for those who really love God, He's got to open the door. Why? We'll see.

Verse 8, "I know your works. Behold, I have set before you an open door, and no one has the power to shut it because you have a little strength, and have kept My word, and have not denied My name." So here is a small church. Little strength. "...And have kept My word..." Now no other church is commended of really keeping the word. Now if you're going to keep the word that means you have to number one, you have to have it. Number two, you have to know it, because how can you keep something that you don't know? You can't. "...And have not denied My name."

Now that's a little different than over here with Pergamos. It says Revelation Chapter 2 verse 13, "I know your works and where you dwell, where the throne of Satan *is;* but you are holding fast My name, and did not deny My faith, even in the days in which Antipas *was* My faithful witness, who was killed among you, where Satan dwells." So they only held on as long as they had Antipas for their leader. After that everything went to hell in a handbasket to Balaam, and to the doctrine of the Nicolaitanes, which this book "Primitive Christianity..." does an excellent job of bringing out what that really means.

"Behold, I will make those of the synagogue of Satan..." (Rev. 3:9). Now who's the synagogue of Satan? The synagogue of Satan combines the economics, the religious, and the political affairs of this world, who control the world. And we are living in a time when that synagogue of Satan is coming to the fore again like it never has. Now I'm going to give a sermon here in the very near future on the beast that was and is not and yet is. And I think we will understand it even more clearly. And that we are living in those times.

Now these we can just say, those of the synagogue of Satan are rewarded by Satan. How does he reward them? What did he promise Christ if He would worship him once? The whole world. So those who control the world and the world establishment in banking, in religion, and in politics are all part of the synagogue of Satan with all of their followers and all of their subordinates with them, and those who truly are part of the synagogue of Satan worship Satan directly and get their orders directly from him. And we are in a struggle brethren. We are in a fight, and I'm going to bring out, well I won't bring it out tomorrow but I'll bring out a little bit about it. But we are in a fight for the word of God. We are in such a position today that no longer can we say, "Look it up in your Bible. Read it in your Bible." Now we've got to tell them, "Look, before you can even look it up in the Bible, you better make sure you have the right Bible." Cause you may not find it in the one Satan has perverted through Westcott and Hort, and through the New International Version, and the New American Standard Bible, and some of the others. I mean it's a horrendous thing that they have done to it. And that's all part of the synagogue of Satan, "...who proclaim themselves to be Jews and are not, but do lie—behold, I will cause them to come and worship before your feet, and to know that I have loved you."

Now Christ loves His whole Church but there is a special love that God has for the Philadelphians, why? Because they love Him. That's why. And you can't love the brethren truly unless you love God first. Now you can have a social club. You can get along with each other, you can like each other, you can be desirous to be in each other's company, but to truly love the brethren with the love of God, that's got to come from God. It has to come from God.

Now notice verse 10, "Because you have kept the word of My patience..." Now notice. Twice He says, "...and have kept My word, and have not denied My name", verse 8. Then He says, "Because you have kept the word of My patience [or patiently kept My word]", which means what? In spite of the synagogue of Satan, in spite of anybody else around, in spite of the consequences that comes to you, in spite of what you go through, you stay faithful and keep the word of God. He says, "...I also will keep you from the time of temptation which *is* about to come upon the whole world to try those who dwell on the earth. Behold, I am coming quickly; hold fast that which you have so that no one may take away your crown" (vs. 10-11). Showing that there is a battle, there's a fight. That you're having to fight against all of the odds that are coming. Someone trying to take your reward, take your crown.

Now notice verse 12. Notice how closely this ties in with Revelation 14 more than any other. "The one who overcomes will I make a pillar in the temple of My God, and he shall not go out any more [follow Christ wherever He goes]; and I will write upon him the name of My God [which Revelation 14 says], and the name of the city of My God [which is not back there in Revelation 14], the new Jerusalem, which will come down out of heaven from My God; and *I will write upon him* My new name."

Now the bride always what? Takes the name of Her husband, which is a new name. Now, since there have always been Philadelphians down through time, is this out of these kinds of Christians, are these the ones who are going to be part of the bride of Christ? Of all that we have examined of all the firstfruits, being the seven churches, being the 144,000 of Israel, the great innumerable multitude, and the 144,000 of Revelation 14, this attitude here ties in more closely with Revelation 14. So the only thing we can say is the parallel is very close. But, lest we get carried away with categorizing things ourselves and saying, "He is, he isn't. She is, she isn't. We are, they aren't." We'll just say it is all in God's hands and let Him take care of it. And when it comes time for the resurrection we'll all find out then won't we? And regardless of what it is, we're all going to be happy about it. The whole goal is to be in the kingdom of God and receive eternal life. God is the One Who is going to give the rewards. God is the One Who is going to pick the bride. Christ is the One Who is going to marry the bride. And if we can be there as guests, why hey: I'm all for that, because it says, "Blessed and holy is he that is called to the marriage supper of the Lamb."

So at least this will give us something to think on. Give us something to study more into, and we don't want to get carried away with anything and treat what we've had with... now we have something new and we can beat everybody over the head with, because that's not correct, you know. Because whatever we understand comes from God. Now when we try and understand these things and the understanding that comes from God will then lead us to change any of our understanding in the future, then by all means we'll change. No question about it. I don't want to be in a category of holding on to any teaching or doctrine which isn't correct.

But let's understand this, the knowledge of this does not change your salvation. Does it? No. In other words it gets right back to the same thing that we covered in Matthew 20 when we started. When Christ told the mother of John and James the sons of Zebedee, "You don't know what you're asking for and it's not Mine to give, but the Father's." So here the Father has to make the decision doesn't He? All we can do is look at it and say, the most we can come to is that these scriptures give us a little better understanding and some indications of what God is going to do. That's the most that it can do for us. If we try and make any more out of it, then we will get carried away with our own self-importance. We don't want to do that at all. And we certainly don't want to pull a Job and walk up and tell God what to do. You know, that didn't work then, and it won't work now. And I'll just close with this. The longer that I have been in the Church, the more that I understand that there is really literally nothing that we haven't received. Everything comes from God. And the most important thing we need to concentrate on…[God and His Way].

Let's finish with this by going to 2 Corinthians 10. Here's the most important thing, and this is the greatest tool for overcoming. Begin in verse 1. "Now I Paul am personally exhorting you by the meekness and gentleness of Christ, On the one hand, when present with you I *am* base; but on the other hand, when absent I am bold toward you. But I am beseeching *you* so that, when I am present, I may not have to be bold with the confidence with which I intend to show boldness toward some, who think that we are walking according to *the* flesh" (I Cor. 10:1-2). And walking according to the flesh is as according to human reason, human rational, human ideas and things like this. Or as Paul was fighting it, philosophy, as he brought out in the first part of 1 Corinthians 1.

"For although we walk in *the* flesh [which we do], we do not war according to *the* flesh…" And as I mentioned concerning psychology and psychological methods of overcoming. No, you don't do that. Here's the way we overcome. "For the weapons of our warfare *are* not carnal, but mighty through God to *the* overthrowing of strong holds,…" And this is the battle we have to keep at. "Casting down *vain* imaginations, and every high thing that exalts itself against the knowledge of God, and bringing into captivity every thought into the obedience of Christ," (vs. 3-5). Now that's what we have to work on. That's what's the most important thing. Why? Because in your mind is where sin begins. And your mind and your thoughts of self and importance, and all of the things of the world to puff up the self then are idols before God. Meaning that anything that you think that you understand or know, or can do, earns you salvation or earns you something or makes you more special than someone else, becomes an idol.

For us to proclaim, "We are Philadelphians and anyone who is not with us is not a Philadelphian" [is not right]. Look, we don't know. That would be an imagination. A thought exalting itself against God. So when thoughts like that of self-exaltation or thoughts that come along of sin, or whatever it may be, you are to grab that thought, bring it into captivity and cast it down and bring your mind into obedience to Christ. And this is what we need to do. Now, I don't know about you but I have a struggle with my own mind. Just like Paul did, see. So that's why it's so important we keep our perspective in this.

And verse 6, "And having a readiness to avenge all disobedience, whenever your obedience has been fulfilled." Wow, that's quite a statement, isn't it? How do you fulfill your obedience? Ok, everything that you do and it starts in your mind, see. "Do you look on things after the outward appearance? If any man trust to himself that he is Christ's, let him of himself think this again, that, as he *is* Christ's even so *are* we Christ's." And that's what we really need to keep in mind.

So anyway, it's late so we'll have to quit here. It's after 10 o'clock. Let's see, shall we be back at seven? [Laughter]

End of Sermon

Transcriber: Carolyn Singer

435

Chapter Twenty-seven

More on the 144,000—Pentecost 2000
June 17, 2000
Scriptural References

1) Matthew 20: 1-4, 9-16

2) Revelation 7:14

3) Revelation 11:3-15

4) Matthew 20:16, 20-28

5) Matthew 22:1-14

6) Matthew 25:1-13

7) I Corinthians 15:20-13

8) Exodus 34:26

9) James 1:18

10) Romans 8:29

11) Hebrews 12:23

12) Revelation 14:1-5

13) Revelation 7:9-17

14) Revelation 17:1

15) Revelation 22:17

16) Revelation 20:6

17) Matthew Chapter 25

18) Revelation 14:1,4

19) II Corinthians 11:1

20) Revelation Chapters 2-3

21) Revelation 19:9

22) Revelation 2:4-5, 9-10, 16, 19-20

23) Revelation 3:1-5, 7, 17

24) Revelation 2:13

25) Revelation 3:9-12

26) I Corinthians 10:1-2

27) II Corinthians 10:4-6

CHAPTER TWENTY-EIGHT

Events After Pentecost—Sermon I

June 21, 2003

Now let's look at some other things which cover the Pentecost story, but in some of those things which take place <u>after</u> Pentecost. So it's proper to go ahead and cover it here. Let's understand something very important. Come to 1 Corinthians the first chapter please. God is doing a phenomenal thing with His people and His Church. And God never works like men work. He works entirely differently, and He has called us, those that the world does not even consider worthy of counting as existing. And it is like I told one Protestant, I said, "You know, that's always the way it's been with the Church of God. Every Sabbath there are millions of Christians who believe in Jesus Christ and His grace and salvation by <u>faith</u>, who keep the Sabbath, and you don't even have a clue as to where they are. You don't even recognize who they are." So callous are they in their beliefs that they are right, the Protestants even in the face of reading *Rome's Challenge to the Protestants*, insist on keeping Sunday.

Now that's an aside, but it does prove a point. And the point is that God has called us because to the world we are insignificant and foolish. Now let's read it here, 1 Corinthians 1:25 "Because the foolishness of God is wiser than men, and the weakness of God is stronger than men." Of course God doesn't have any foolishness, He has — well, let's put it this way: even if God had foolishness and even if God had weakness then it would be greater than men or the best efforts of men. Verse 26: "For you see your calling, brethren, that *there are* not many who are wise according to the flesh, not many who are powerful, not many who are highborn *among you*. Rather, God has chosen the foolish things of the world so that He might put to shame those who are wise…" and the confounding of the wise will not be completed until after the resurrection. "…And God has chosen the weak things of the world so that He might put to shame the strong things." And so you think about that. That's why we have so many problems and difficulties that we go through, but God is with us. God is with us in all of it.

Verse 28: "And the low born of the world, and the despised has God chosen — even the things that are counted as nothing…" you know today, how many people in the world know that we are keeping the Sabbath here, or that we even exist — hardly any. He has done this to bring to nothing the things that are. So all of the rich, all of the powerful, all of the governments, all the great things of the world are going to be coming to nothing through us. So that's why I said on Pentecost, we've been called to the greatest thing that there is! That's why God does not want you to look at what you <u>are</u>, but God wants you to <u>focus</u> <u>on</u> <u>what</u> <u>will</u> <u>be</u>! Because that is the spiritual reality that is going to take place. Now here is the reason. Verse 29: "So that no flesh might boast in His presence." No flesh should glory in His presence (1 Corinthians 1:25 –29).

Now God told the children of Israel the same thing. Let's come to Deuteronomy 5 — because it shows that God works His mysterious way opposite according to the way that men think. Because He is doing something greater because it is His work that He is working in us. Not what we can do for God, but what we can do for God we need to do. Whatever He says that we need to do, or sets before us to do, we need to do it. But the question is what can God do for us? Or, let's put it another way. What can you do without God? Nothing. Not even any man in the world can do anything without God—though he rejects Him because God created him and gave him everything that he has anyway. And in His mercy God sends the rain on the just and on the unjust, and the sunshine, and the food, and everything like this God gives to all human beings, and they only exist because of the will of God. Which means then, whatever they do, even though they sin contrary to the will of God, the only reason that they are not snuffed out instantly is because of God. So hence, they can do nothing without God.

I think it is interesting, but I heard a man talking about the solar system and the universe and the videos that they put out on that, who is an astronomer, and he said he didn't know a single astronomer who did not believe in God. It is amazing isn't it? It doesn't mean that they obey Him, but they can understand this didn't all spontaneously happen from nothing. You know like God told the environmentalist. He said, "Go create your own dirt before you start. Don't use mine." (Laughter).

Now here is what God said to the children of Israel. Let's pick it up here in verse 22, and then we'll go back and look at something there in Exodus in just a minute. Deuteronomy 5:22: "These words the LORD spake unto all your assembly in the mount out of the midst of the fire, of the cloud, and of the thick darkness, with a great voice:" *and he ceased to talk*…now that's what it means. It doesn't mean *he added no more*. A lot of people say, "Well God didn't add any more." He ceased to talk at that point, but as we will see He added a considerably lot more didn't He? But the Ten Commandments, which He spoke, were the basis of everything that He gave them later on. "And he wrote them in two tables of stone, and delivered them unto me. And it came to pass, when you heard the voice out of the midst of the darkness, (for the mountain did burn with fire,) that you came near unto me, *even*, all the heads of your tribes, and your elders; And ye said, Behold, the LORD our God has showed us his glory and his greatness, and we have heard his voice out of the midst of the fire: we have seen this day that God does talk with man, and he lives. Now therefore why should we die?" Now they didn't want to hear the voice of God anymore. "…For this great fire will consume us: if we hear the voice of the LORD our God anymore, then we shall die." (Deuteronomy 5:22-25).

You know that's the way people are today. This same kind of spirit is what is behind removing God from government, from public education, from media, and yes, from the new versions of the Bible also by perverting and twisting and destroying it.

Verse 26: "For who *is there of* all flesh, that has heard the voice of the living God speaking out of the midst of the fire, as we *have*, and lived? You go near, and hear all that the LORD our God shall say: and speak thou unto us all that the LORD our God shall speak unto thee; and we will hear *it*, and do *it*." Verse 28: "And the LORD heard the voice of your words, when ye spoke unto me; and the LORD said unto me, I have heard the voice of the words of this people, which they have spoken unto thee: they have well said." They mean well. "…They have well said all that they have spoken."

Here is the key. Verse 29: "O that there were such an heart in them, that they would fear me, and keep all my commandments always, that it might be well with them, and with their children forever!" (Deuteronomy 5:26-29).

Now God also said something over here in Chapter 7, just turn the page there. And why did God do this? Just like with us—why did God call us? Well, we have already seen it, so He explained it to them there. Deuteronomy 7:6: "For thou *art* an holy people unto the LORD thy God: the LORD your God hath chosen thee to be a special people unto himself, above all people that *are* upon the face of the earth." Now you need to realize this: God the Father, Himself, has personally chosen you, and personally selected everyone one that He gives the Holy Spirit to. So we are special. Verse 7: "The LORD did not set his love upon you, nor choose you, because ye were more in number than any people; for you *were* the fewest of all people:" Verse 8: "But because the LORD loved you, and because he would keep the oath which he had sworn unto your fathers…" that is Abraham, Isaac, and Jacob "…hath the LORD brought you out with a mighty hand, and redeemed you out of the house of bondmen, from the hand of Pharaoh king of Egypt. Know therefore that the LORD thy God, he *is* God, the faithful God, which keepeth covenant and mercy with them that love him and keep his commandments to a thousand generations…" then repays to the face those who hate Him—destroys them. So he says, "Thou shalt therefore…" verse 11, "keep the commandments, and the statutes, and the judgments, which I command thee this day, to do them." Then He shows the blessings and cursings that would follow. (Deuteronomy 7:6-11).

Now let's tie this in with Pentecost, and let's go forward from here. Let's come to Exodus—we have already had a review of it there in Deuteronomy the fifth chapter. So let's see what happened after God called Moses up on the mountain again.

Now when we understand—which I have done on other sermons, what was it, *From the Red Sea to Sinai*—coming up showing that it was when the law was given on the Day of Pentecost. Then these events took place after Pentecost—part of them, from the last part of Chapters 20, 21, 22 [and] 23, God gave all this information to Moses, and then he came back down. Since they assembled before the mount in the morning, they heard the voice of God through the cloud, through the trumpet, through the whirlwind, through all of the things that were going on and the mountain was literally burning and smoking. That's why they were afraid. So then Moses went back up and he got this information.

Now beginning in Chapter 24 we see that another day takes place <u>after</u> Pentecost where then He <u>seals</u> the covenant. So let's read this. Exodus 24:1: "And he said unto Moses, Come up unto the LORD, thou, and Aaron, Nadab, and Abihu, and seventy of the elders of Israel; and worship ye afar off. And Moses alone shall come near the LORD: but they shall not come nigh; neither shall the people go up with him." So Moses came. Now verse 3, Moses comes down, "…Moses came and told the people all the words of the LORD…" now I want you to pay attention to what happened on this part of Pentecost, and then let's see what happened the next day because that will be significant when we come to the New Testament. "…Told the people all the words of the LORD, and all the judgements: and all the people answered with one voice, and said, All the words which the LORD hath said will we do. And Moses wrote all the words of the LORD, and rose up early in the morning…" now we are in the next day aren't we—the day after Pentecost. "… and builded an altar under the hill…" that means right at the base of the hill not under the literal hill. "…And twelve pillars, according to the twelve tribes of Israel. And he sent young men of the children of Israel, which offered burnt offerings, and sacrificed peace offerings of oxen unto the LORD." Verse 6: "And Moses took half of the blood, and put *it* in basins; and half of the blood he sprinkled on the altar. And he took the book of the covenant, and read in the audience of the people: and they said, All that the LORD has said we will do, and be obedient." (Exodus 24:1-7).

See now when God makes a covenant there are *words of the covenant*. That's why when we take the Passover we entitle the words: *The Words of the New Covenant*, because the covenant is an irrevocable contract that God makes, and when there is a contract it is to be <u>written</u> so that there should not be any dispute. That's what he did. And they said again, "All that the LORD hath said will we do, and be obedient. And Moses took the blood, and sprinkled *it* on the people, and said, Behold the blood of the covenant…" Now that ties right in with the new covenant Passover doesn't it? Yes it does. See, when they had the Passover sacrifice in Egypt, that was the setting aside of them at the beginning of their calling to be set-aside for God. God did not enter into covenant with them on Passover. God entered into covenant with them <u>after</u> Pentecost. And we'll see there is a parallel between this and what will happen with us.

I'll just telegraph a little bit of it here. Before we go about the business of running the world under Christ, we are going to enter into a special covenant with Christ. Because the New Covenant that we renew every Passover is for what—forgiveness of sin, and the promise of eternal life. Now when you are resurrected and you receive eternal life, then there has to be a New Covenant made, because now you are in a different category, and this is a fore-type of it here in Exodus 24. We'll see that's one of the things that have to take place.

OK let's go on. Now then, verse 9: "Then went up Moses, and Aaron, Nadab, and Abihu, and seventy of the elders of Israel: And they saw the God of Israel…" not talked to face to face, but they saw Him. The reason God did this was so that they would know that it was God. They would come down and they would be witnesses to the people that—yes, it <u>was</u> God. Because remember, a little later on they forgot that it was God didn't they—when they made the golden calf. So they had no excuse.

Now notice the next sentence here. "…and *there was* under his feet as it were a paved work of a sapphire stone, and as it were the body of heaven in his clearness." Now what is this? This is the thing that separated God and Aaron and Nadab and Abihu and the seventy elders that went up to see God. So they could look up through this and they could see God. Now what is this describing, other than a sea of glass?

Verse 11: "And upon the nobles of the children of Israel he laid not his hand: also they saw God, and did eat and drink." Now when they said, "I do" at this particular point, what kind of covenant was this? It was a marriage covenant. "…And they did eat and drink" now it doesn't say what kind of food they had. It doesn't say how they got it. It doesn't tell us that they brought it up there. It doesn't say they didn't bring it up there. It doesn't say that God provided it, and it doesn't say that He didn't provide it. So I'll let you figure out what it is. Now it is very possible they took it up there. Verse 12: "And the LORD said to Moses, Come up to me into the mount, and be there: and I will give thee tables of stone, and a law, and commandments which I have written; that thou mayest teach them. And Moses rose up, and his minister Joshua: and Moses went up into the mount of God. And he said unto the elders, Tarry ye here for us, until we come once again…" so apparently Joshua went up so far, and then Moses went up beyond that. That's the only thing we could figure out, because Joshua did not talk to God face to face. "…And, behold, Aaron and Hur *are* with you: if any man have any matters to do, let him come unto them. Moses went up into the mount, and a cloud covered the mount. And the glory of the LORD abode upon mount Sinai, and the cloud covered it six days: and the seventh day he called unto Moses out of the midst of the cloud." So after they had eaten, apparently, they went on down—that is the elders and so forth. Verse 17: "And the sight of the glory of the LORD *was* like a devouring fire on the top of the mount in the eyes of the children of Israel. And Moses went into the midst of the cloud, and gat him up into the mount: and Moses was in the mount forty days and forty nights." Now there are a lot of things that went on those forty days and forty nights. We are not going to go through that. (Exodus 24:1-18).

Let's come and see the parallel that the apostle Paul writes about in Hebrews 12. There is a New Testament fulfillment of this. Hebrews 12, and let's pick it up here in verse 18: "For ye are not come unto the mount that might be touched, and that burned with fire, nor unto blackness, and darkness, and tempest, And the sound of a trumpet, and the voice of words; which *voice* they that heard intreated that the word should not be spoken to them any more: (For they could not endure that which was commanded, And if so much as a beast touch the mountain, it shall be stoned, or thrust through with a dart…" and that's probably an arrow. And so terrible was the sight, *that* Moses said, I exceedingly fear and quake:).

Now here is what you need to understand how great that God is dealing with us, verse 22: "But ye are come unto mount Sion, and unto the city of the living God, the heavenly Jerusalem, and to an innumerable company of angels, To the general assembly and church of the firstborn, which are written in heaven, and to God the Judge of all, and to the spirits of just men made perfect, And to Jesus the mediator of the New Covenant, and to the blood of sprinkling, that speaks better things than *that of* Abel." (Hebrews 12:18-24). So there is a spiritual parallel. That is quite a thing!

Now let's talk about some things concerning this mount Sion, and we'll talk about some things concerning the sea of glass. We'll get to it in just a little bit, but first of all let's cover something that's very important.

The Bible shows there are three heavens: 1) the atmosphere around the earth, 2) the universe that you can look out and see, and 3) the third heaven where God's throne is. Now no one can see the third heaven unless God makes it possible. Paul said that he was taken up into the third heaven whether in body or whether in spirit he didn't know, and he heard things that it is not lawful for a man to speak. And we are going to see that John also had that privilege.

Now when I fly and go some place as I have said, I come from heaven. The plane I fly on goes either in the clouds or above the clouds, and when it lands I have just descended from heaven. Matter of fact when they fly at 33,000 to 37,000 feet, I think the highest I have flown on a plane was a cross-continental flight, non-stop, and they went at 37,000 feet. Now that is higher than the birds fly, but it is still part of the first heaven, which is part of the earth. Question: Do people today travel in heaven? Yes—on airplanes and some few in rockets. Because we're going to see a place here a little bit later on, that talks about the sound of much people in heaven—which one, where? How did they get there? Because as Peter said on Pentecost, "David has not ascended into heaven." John wrote, as we covered last time, that only Jesus has ascended into heaven. No man has ascended into heaven, but Jesus. So we need to get some of these things a little clearer and defined, don't we?

Now then, you can go back and you can do this, I'm not going to do it now, but you can go back and study about the cherubim in Ezekiel the first chapter and Ezekiel the tenth chapter. You can talk about the vision of Isaiah and seeing the throne of God in heaven above and so forth—so it is there. Now let's see if we can put this all together.

Now let's come to Revelation 12:9. So we'll go here and then we will work backwards. And part of this dawned on me yesterday, as a matter of fact, last night. Let's pick it up here in verse 9 so we come to the point where we see that these events begin. Now this is going to take place. Let's pick it up here in verse 7: "And there was war in heaven…" now that's going to happen again. "…Michael and his angels warred against the dragon, and the dragon and his angels warred," so the angels of Satan are fallen angels who are called demons. Verse 9: "And the great dragon was cast out, the ancient serpent who is called the Devil, and Satan, who is deceiving the whole world…" he is actively doing it "…he was cast down to the earth, and his angels were cast down with him." (Revelation 12: 7-9).

Now we don't know how much time there is left, so we don't know how big the space station is going to get, do we? But they want to build a pretty enormous space station up there. And now apparently the Chinese are going to start getting into the act because they're going to, some time this year, send their first man into space—thanks to the guidance system that so-and-so sold under Bill Clinton to the Chinese, so it would go.

Could it be that in this space station that Satan possesses the beast? He gets in a rocket and he goes up there and all the demons of Satan are there, and there is war right around that space station? And the beast possessed of Satan escapes and comes back to the earth? Now just consider I rang my cowbell—that is a little speculation. But nevertheless, one way or the other, Satan is going to be cast to the earth.

Now notice verse 10: "And I heard a great voice in heaven say, 'Now has come salvation, and the power, and the kingdom of our God, and the authority of his Christ: because the accuser of our brethren has been cast down, who accused them day and night before our God. But they overcame him through the blood of the Lamb, and through the word of their testimony; and they loved not their lives unto death." See because they knew, and we need to know and understand that God has called us to become part of the greatest thing that is ever going to happen to this earth since it was created! God hasn't called you to save your neck from burning in ever-burning hell. God has called you for a great and fantastic purpose, as His sons and His daughters! And the first resurrection is going to be the greatest thing that will happen, and you and I and all those who have the Spirit of God, will be part of that! It is not going to be some secret rapture! When Christ returns, the world is going to know, and all of these people that think they are going to escape in a secret rapture before the tribulation, are deceived, and they are going to pay the price by going through it! (Revelation 12:10-11).

Now let's read on, Revelation 12:12: "Therefore, rejoice you heavens, and those who dwell in them. Woe to those who inhabit the earth and the sea! For the Devil has come down to you, having great wrath, *because* he knows that he has *only* a short time. And when the dragon saw that he was cast down to the earth, he persecuted the woman who had brought forth the man *child*. And two wings of a great eagle were given to the woman, so that she might fly to her place in the wilderness, where she is nourished *for* a time, and times, and half a time, from the face of *the* serpent." Now there are going to be some who are going to be taken to a place of safety. But I do believe that many of those who thought they would save their necks because they read the article, *There is a Way of Escape* years ago, probably are no longer in fellowship with the Church of God. (Revelation 12:13-14).

Now why are there going to be some in a place of safety? Now just put in your notes there, Luke 17. Those who go to a place of safety, will be taken there by the angels. It is not a rapture because you're not going to heaven. You may fly through the first heaven as the angels take whoever is going to go to a place of safety and will be there, but God is going to choose and select the ones to go. No man or woman is going to appoint himself [or herself, saying,] "I deserve to go." The minute you say that, you are unworthy, because you are judging yourself rather than God. God is going to see who is going to be worthy or not. He is going to make the decision, and so that's another reason why the church had to be destroyed, because there were too many people there with their Petra boxes thinking that they were going to save their physical necks. Now the ultimate reason why there are some who go to the place of safety, comes down to a very simple thing. Now we will cover that in just a minute.

Now from here, we are going to back up, after we finish this chapter. Let's go through it. So "...the serpent cast water out of his mouth as a river, so that he might cause her *to be* carried away by the flood. The earth helped the woman, and the earth opened its mouth and swallowed up the river that the dragon cast out of his mouth." Now look, can God protect you if He wants to? Yes, indeed! What can He even do? Well, He'll even open up the earth and consume all the water! Now verse 17: "And the dragon was furious with the woman and went to make war with the rest of her seed..." and these are the ones who do not go to a place of safety. Now the remnant here should rightly be translated *the others* not meaning just a small few left behind—*the others*. Now notice, "...which keep the commandments of God, and have the testimony of Jesus Christ." These people have been chosen to be martyrs. God is the one who makes the decision, but He will strengthen you with whatever strength you need if you are chosen to be a martyr! Because if you love God with all of your heart, mind and soul and being, and you have already forsaken your own life and your own way and buried it in Christ, then when it comes time that you—whoever you may be—that you must be a martyr; then God will give you the strength. He will give you a mouth to speak. You will say the Words of God, and you will not be afraid of anything that anyone can do to you because they can't take away eternal life. Even killing the body is not going to stop the plan of God.

Now let's come back here to Revelation 6 just a few pages back. I am not going to repeat what I already covered on Pentecost. Revelation 6 and let's come here to verse 9, which is the fifth seal. And I am going to give here very soon a sermon on the mark of the beast. Like I said when I gave the sermon, *The Mark of the Beast—It is Here Already* and I said it's going to become so natural and such a regular thing that when it comes time to receive it, people are going to say, " Yea, give it to me." except those who have the Spirit of God, and those who don't will be martyred. You can tie that in with Revelation 13. If you don't bow down to the image of the beast and you don't receive the mark of the beast, you're history as far as the world is concerned, but you are preserved in Christ. Remember He said if you lose your life, you are going to preserve it.

Now Revelation 6:9: "And when He had opened the fifth seal, I saw under the altar the souls of those who had been slain for the Word of God, and for the testimony that they held:" you tie that in with Revelation 12:11 how they got there—they didn't love their lives unto death. "And they cried out with a loud voice, saying, 'How long, O Lord, holy and true, do You not judge and avenge our blood on those who dwell on the earth?' And white robes were given to them; and it was said unto them, that they should rest a short time yet..." showing that they are in the grave actually though this is symbolically speaking here "...until *it* be fulfilled *that* both their fellow servants and their brethren also would be killed, just as they had been." Now when this takes place, remember, Satan makes war against the remnant of her seed, so this takes place just right after the second seal, the third seal, the fourth seal, the fifth seal comes real quickly—bam, bam, bam, bam, bam! So the martyrdom goes on for just a little less than two years. And I am sure; I'm convinced that God will allow Satan to think that he has destroyed the Church by killing all of those who are the saints of God. So there will come a time, as I said on Pentecost, this ends the Church harvest—martyrdom of the saints.

Now how does that tie in with the place of safety? That's so Jesus can keep His Word. Now let's come to Matthew 16. We'll come back to Revelation here in just a minute. What is another reason why they go to a place of safety? Because Jesus made a promise—not just a place of safety—He made another promise that also applies to those who go to a place of safety. Let's pick it up here in verse 16, after He asked them, "Whom do men say I am?" "Then Simon Peter answered *and* said, You are the Christ, the Son of the living God." Verse 17: "And Jesus answered *and* said to him, 'Blessed are you Simon, Bar-jona:' " that is the son of Jona "...for flesh and blood did not reveal *it* to you, but My Father which *is* in heaven." A very key, important thing, anything you understand out of the Bible, God reveals it to you, right? Yes. "...I say also to you that you are Peter..." you know the whole thing—Petros, "...but upon this Rock" Petra "I will build My church," Now here is the promise "...and *the* gates of hell" or that is the mouth of the grave "...shall not prevail against it." (Matthew 16:16-18). Now to fulfill that promise, there are those who go to a place of safety, because all of the rest that Satan makes war against are going to be killed. And if He didn't put some in a place of safety to preserve their physical life, the church would have died out, would it not? So that's another reason why there is a place of safety.

There have to be some remnant alive in the flesh, not counting the 144,000, great innumerable multitude, you see, but Christ made the promise here that the gates of hell would never prevail against it, therefore, it would never die out! And that is the whole premise of the Mormon Church—it died out, therefore it had to be revealed to Joseph Smith.

Now let's come back here to the Book of Revelation, Chapter 6. Now I'm not going to repeat everything that I did on Pentecost, I'll just refer you to the tape. Now then, let's pick it up here in verse 12, and let's understand that if we put the Scriptures properly together concerning the time frame, we know that in Revelation 12 we have "time, times, and a half a time" which we understand to be three and a half years. So we know that the time at the end is three and a half years. That's referred to as <u>the</u> <u>great</u> <u>tribulation</u>. It is referred to as <u>the</u> <u>day</u> of the Lord—the whole period. We also know that if we have put Hosea 5:21 and 6:1-3 together, that out of the great tribulation there is the tribulation against Israel, which ends in two years. It says that He'll raise them up in the third year. So this means that as we are looking at the three and a half year period if there are two years that are gone, there is roughly a year and a half left, correct?

Now then let's begin in verse 12, and I believe that this takes place right at the end of two years into the tribulation, and this is going to be the great event that is going to take place. It is going to be an awesome thing indeed! The whole world is going to know it! The return of Jesus Christ is going to be a spectacular event, which will be witnessed, the coming of it, for a year and a half! Every eye is going to see Him. Everyone is going to know that something spectacular is happening. So let's begin right here in verse 12 of Revelation 6:12 " And when He opened the sixth seal, I looked, and behold, there was a great earthquake; and the sun became black as *the* hair *of* sackcloth, and the moon became as blood; And the stars of heaven fell to the earth, as a fig tree casts its untimely figs when it is shaken by a mighty wind."

Now here is the event that is going to <u>startle</u> the world! Verse 14: "Then the heaven departed like a scroll that is being rolled up;" that is going to absolutely <u>shock</u> the world! And we just might understand what a fantastic thing this is—it <u>affects</u> the <u>whole</u> <u>earth</u>! "… And every mountain and island was moved out of its place. And the kings of the earth, and the great men, and the rich men, and the chief captains, and the powerful men, and every bondman, and every free *man*, hid themselves in the caves and in the rocks of the mountains; And they said to the mountains and to the rocks, Fall on us, and hide us from *the* face of Him Who sits on the throne…" that's God the Father "… and from the wrath of the Lamb: Because the great day of his wrath is come; and who has the power to stand?" (Revelation 6:12-17). Now that's the ultimate end result of it.

But what's going to happen when the heavens depart as a scroll? Wouldn't you say that the heavens departing as a scroll is a new thing in the heavens as people observe it? Have to be—yes, a brand new thing.

Now let's come back to Matthew 24. Now remember there in the Book of Haggai—while we're turning to Matthew 24—God says He is going to shake the heavens. He is going to shake the earth. He is going to shake the sea. We find in the Book of Isaiah that the earth is going to reel like a drunken man. Now here is what is going to be, when they say, "Here is Christ, there is Christ, don't believe it." Here is how He is going to come. Verse 27: "For as the light of day…" as I have said many times, is the light of day "…which comes forth from *the* east and shines as far as *the* west, so also shall the coming of the Son of man be." So when the heavens depart as a scroll, something brand new is going to happen, bam! The whole sky, the whole universe, and everything is going to be instantly changed, and once they recover from the shock of it, they're going to look up there and they are going to see, here is a brand new sun we never knew existed out there. And the reason that it looks like it shines from east to west is because the earth is still turning on its axis and however far out this sign is, the sign of the Son of man like a new sun, it's going to be out there. Now remember, this takes place at the end of two years in the tribulation. Now what is the world going to be convinced that this is? They won't know at first. They'll look at it, they'll watch it, they'll observe it, but what will they conclude? This is the invasion from outer space that we have been expecting. That's what they will conclude. And the aliens are coming to invade the earth. That will be their ultimate conclusion of it. So that's going to be a spectacular event.

Now let's come back to Revelation 7 and then we'll also do a little more overview. Revelation 7, we already covered about the 144,000 and great innumerable multitude. So you see what happens when that sign of the Son of man appears—the heavens depart as a scroll, then God intervenes to do His fiftieth-day work, as we have seen in the 144,000 of the children of Israel; which we have already seen are different than the 144,000 of Revelation 14, and the great innumerable multitude. Which means then, not everyone is going to start fighting Christ or think that it is an invasion from outer space; they are going to repent! Because you see, no one receives salvation without repentance, so 144,000 repent, God sends the Holy Spirit to them, the great innumerable multitude repent, God sends the Holy Spirit to them, because it is His independent work in saving all of these people. These will be the harvest of Pentecost, from one Pentecost to the next Pentecost within that eighteen-month period. This fulfills the prophecy of the laborers that went to work in the vineyard—some started at the first hour in the morning and some came the eleventh hour of the day and worked just a little bit and when they got paid, they all received the same amount which is symbolic of eternal life. The first shall be last and the last shall be first.

Now also we need to plug in here, that also during this timeframe there are two witnesses in Jerusalem aren't there—having a very powerful witness, and just before the resurrection, they are martyred. So God is going to give Himself a fantastic witness! God is not going to have anyone say, "Oh! You came to the earth? When did You come to the earth?" (Laughter). The whole world is going to know it!

Now then, let's show that they meet Christ on the sea of glass. Now we need to talk about the sea of glass, so we need to go to Revelation 14 and 15, and then we need to work our way back and we'll see some very important things. Remember what we covered there in Exodus 24, that <u>after</u> Pentecost they went up and they had that meal in the presence of God. They saw God standing on a little portable sea of glass so they could look up and see God. Now some people think the sea of glass is just kind of a symbolic thing! Well that shows that they neither understand what God is doing, nor do they understand the magnitude of what God is going to perform!

Now let's ask the questions: Today, why do we come to Sabbath services? Why do we study the Bible? Because we are preparing for eternal life, correct? God has His Work in it; Christ has His Work in it; we have our work in it, but it is something for a preparation correct? Yes! What we will do, we will show the silliness, what we used to believe, that the resurrection would be on the Feast of Trumpets—we'd all be resurrected, meet Christ in the air and come right back to the earth. Well since, if you are resurrected, we're going to see that a lot of things need to happen before you're ready to come back to the earth. And that's why the resurrection is on Pentecost, because it pictures the first fruits, and it's called the church of the firstborn, and there are a lot of things that have to be done before we come back with Christ to the earth! Now since you have never experienced being a spirit being, you're going to have to learn how you operate, right? Of course!

Now let's look at the resurrection. Hold your place here, we got ahead of ourselves. Let's go back to Matthew 24, and let's look at the resurrection. If we did not go to the sea of glass, why then take us up into the air at the resurrection? What would be the purpose of that? Why not just stay on earth and let Christ come all the way to the earth? No one has ever asked that question before. Verse 29: "But immediately after the tribulation of those days, the sun shall be darkened, and the moon shall not give her light, and the stars shall fall from heaven, and the powers of the heavens shall be shaken. And then shall appear the sign of the Son of man in heaven:" and He gets closer, and closer, and closer to the earth, as we will see. "...Then shall all the tribes of the earth mourn, and they shall see the Son of man coming upon the clouds of heaven with power and great glory." They are going to see this. Now notice first of all verse 27, it starts out like a new sun appearing in the heavens, by the time it comes time for the resurrection, where does this sign come to—the clouds. Where are the clouds? Well, the clouds are not in the second heaven, because there aren't any out in the universe are there? No. The clouds are not in the third heaven, necessarily, but where are the clouds—the first heaven. So it comes down into the clouds.

Now what happens when you have something coming from outer space that comes to the earth? What does the magnetic force do? When it comes just so far to the earth—it locks it into a stationary orbit. We have many satellites, don't we, that they lock into stationary orbit—it's going around the earth this way while the earth is turning this way. They have satellites that are designed to go the exact speed of the rotation of the earth so it sits in the same spot all the time, don't they?

Now then, I believe that when it comes down into the clouds, and it doesn't tell us how high that is—clouds range anywhere from earth level as fog up to 50,000 feet, so you pick your altitude if you want to put it that way. But they are going to see this, so it comes down and stations itself right over Jerusalem. Now what's the first thing to happen when it stations itself right over Jerusalem—Revelation 11, the two witnesses are the first resurrected. The last shall be first. Where did they die? They died in Jerusalem. You read Revelation 11, and a voice came and said, "Come here" and they stood on their feet and lived, and so apparently some angels, which they didn't see, got them and carried them up to the sea of glass. Let's ask the question: If you ascend into the clouds to meet Christ—you've got to meet Him some place don't you? Yes.

Now after the two witnesses are raised, verses 31 of Matthew 24, "And He shall send his angels with a great sound of a trumpet..." because isn't it interesting when you read Revelation 11, the two witnesses are raised first, and then the trumpet sounds, the seventh trump sounds. So they are the first two raised. " ... And they..." that is the angels, as we will see, "... shall gather together His elect from the four winds, from one end of heaven to *the* other." Now what is this telling us? This is telling us the prospective of looking down on the earth—that the angels are going around the whole earth and gathering up those that are resurrected from the dead. Where are they going to take them? How many are going to be there? Let's answer that question, because this is going to be a great thing!

Now let's ask another question: Will the people of the earth see the resurrection take place and these people being raised out of the grave and the angels taking them up to meet Christ? That's possible. Did they see the two witnesses go up? Yes! Revelation 11, they stood and watched them go up! Now wouldn't that be a phenomenal thing—see all the saints resurrected, what a witness to this whole world, huh? You know this is not going to be some secret rapture done in a corner someplace, this is an earthshaking event!

Will they know that this is God doing it? Well, Satan is still on the earth and he is going to say, "It's the antichrist who is doing it, and what is happening, what you are seeing is the aliens from outer space have come and they are taking all of the aliens that were living among us." Have you seen a movie to that effect? It's like my wife has said many times— Satan telegraphs what he is going to do in the movies that he produces for people to watch today. Since this is an invasion from outer space, now then, look at how many aliens were among us. And of course, what are we called, but strangers and sojourners in the earth. Amazing stuff isn't, huh? We can use our imagination this way and ask God to lead us with His Spirit. If this isn't correct, we'll change. But it's got to happen some way. It's got to happen somehow, and if we can discern from the Scriptures from what we are told how it's going to happen, then that's fine.

Now let's understand something concerning this. This information is interesting. Hopefully, it's inspiring. Hopefully, it is true to the Word of God. However, understand this, it is not salvational. In other words, if we understand this today because we live in the time we live in, and know that these things can happen, and we have all of the Word of God and we can put it together—does that mean that those who came before us who knew nothing of it will not be saved? No. That's why it's not salvational. You understand the difference there? OK.

Now let's come to 1 Thessalonians 4 and here it talks about the resurrection again. Now if I have to finish it next time, I'll finish it next time, but I think if we can put it together and really understand it, brethren, this will inspire us so much more, and give us strength of faith, conviction of heart, and trust in God to know that what He is going to do with us is going to be a great and a marvelous, and a fantastic thing, you see. And when we are resurrected and our bodies are changed in a moment in the twinkling of an eye, all the things and aches and pains and sickness and disease and death and all of the wretchedness of human life is over.

Now let's pick it up here in 1 Thessalonians 4:13: "But I do not wish you to be ignorant, brethren, concerning those who have fallen asleep…" that is; they died in Christ, "…that you be not grieved, even as others, who have no hope. For if we believe that Jesus died and rose again, in exactly the same way also, those who have fallen asleep in Jesus will God bring with Him." Since they are buried and in the ground and must be resurrected, how is He going to bring them with Him unless they go to meet Him? It won't happen, will it? Because no man has ascended to heaven, correct? Yes. So let's go on. Verse 15: "For this we say to you by *the* Word of *the* Lord, that we who are alive and remain unto the coming of the Lord …" which now we understand are going to be those in the place of safety, and we also understand it will be the 144,000, great innumerable multitude, "…shall in no wise precede those who have fallen asleep. Because the Lord Himself shall descend from heaven with *a* shout of command, with *the* voice of an archangel and with *the* trumpet of God; and the dead in Christ shall rise first;" of course, the two witnesses will be the first of the first. Verse 17: "Then we who are alive and remain shall be caught up together with them in *the* clouds…" where is Christ coming to—to the clouds. "…for *the* meeting with the Lord in *the* air;…" Now I translated it this way: for *the* meeting with the Lord in *the* air. "…So shall we always be with *the* Lord. Therefore, encourage one another with these words." (1 Thessalonians 4:13-18).

Now let's look and see how this is going to happen. Let's first of all look at the sea of glass in Revelation 4 and 5. Now, let's understand something—just because there is the first heaven, which is the atmosphere around the earth; and the second heaven, which includes all of the universe, all the stars and galaxies and everything out there; and we know about the third heaven—does not mean that the third heaven is further removed than the second heaven. Just in a numerical way of doing things, we would think that. So Christ does not have to come from the outer reaches of the universe, does He? How close is the throne of God, which sits on the sea of glass, to the earth? Can anybody tell us? No, we don't know.

Hold your place here in Revelation 4, and let's come to Acts 7, because we have an indication that it may be a whole lot closer than we have imagined, but we just can't see it yet! Acts 7, this is with the stoning of Stephen, right toward the end of the chapter there. Let's pick it up here in verse 54: "And when they heard these things…" that is the Sanhedrin, all the Jewish leaders, "…they were cut to their hearts, and they gnashed their teeth at him…" I thought at one time that they went out and bit him, but it doesn't mean that. It means they gnashed their teeth at him—sat there and ground their teeth at him, they were so angry. Have you ever seen someone so angry that their jaws were biting. That's what it means. Verse 55: "But he, being filled with *the* Holy Spirit, looked intently into heaven, *and* saw *the* glory of God, and Jesus standing at the right hand of God. And he said, 'Behold, I see the heavens opened, and the Son of man standing on the right *hand* of God.' " That did it! Now, does this tell us that the throne of God is closer to the earth than we have imagined? Let's look at it this way: Jesus sits in the throne of God doesn't He? He said that in Revelation 3:21 "…set down with my Father in His throne." Hebrews 4, He is at the right hand of God, isn't He? He is our High Priest to make intercession for us. (Acts 7:54-56).

Here we have… He is not sitting; He is standing. So what is Jesus doing? He is looking down to see what's going on. Now how far away do you suppose that is? Close enough that He can stand and look down and see what's going on. He wanted to see what the Jews would do. He wanted to see what Stephen was going to do. And notice he had the same attitude that Christ had. Verse 59: "And they stoned Stephen, who called upon *God*, saying, Lord Jesus, receive my spirit. And he knelt down, and cried with a loud voice, Lord, do not lay this sin to their charge. And after he had said this, he died." Showing he died. So just by the way that this is written and what was seen and how it was done, does this tell us that the throne of God is closer to the earth than we have imagined? I do not know. He did not see God; he saw the glory of God. He didn't see God, but he saw the Son of man standing at His right hand.

Now let's come to Revelation 4 and let's begin right here in verse 1, and let's see some things concerning the sea of glass. Revelation 4:1: "After these things I looked, and behold, a door opened in heaven, and the first voice that I heard *was* as if a trumpet were speaking with me, saying, 'Come up here, and I will show you *the* things that must take place after these things. And immediately I was in *the* spirit: and, behold, a throne was set in heaven, and *one* was sitting on the throne. And He Who *was* sitting was in appearance like a jasper stone and a sardius stone; and a rainbow *was* around the throne, like an emerald in its appearance. And round about the throne *were* twenty-four…" as it should read "… thrones…" smaller thrones "… twenty-four elders sitting, clothed in white garments;…" Now the question has been asked: Who are the twenty-four elders? We don't know. We do know that God has twenty-four elders, because He tells us that. Apparently they are special created beings that help assist God in running the universe. I said, apparently, that's the best we can do with that. Other than that we don't know, but one of these day we are going to find out, and we'll know of sure. And they were, "…clothed in white garments; and they had on their heads golden crowns. And proceeding from the throne were lightnings and thunders and voices…" this is the center of the power of the universe, if we can put it this way—amazing thing isn't it? "…And seven lamps of fire, which are the seven Spirits of God, were burning before the throne." Now we will see what the seven Spirits of God do a little bit later here. Verse 6: "And before the throne *was* a sea of glass, like crystal. And around the throne and over the throne *were* four living creatures, full of eyes before and behind. And the first living creature *was* like a lion, and the second living creature was like a calf, and the third living creature had the face of a man, and the fourth living creature *was* like a flying eagle. And each of *the* four living creatures had six wings respectively; *and* around and within *they were* full of eyes; and day and night they cease not saying, Holy, holy, holy, Lord God Almighty, which was, and is, and is to come." Now this is quite a scene.

Now so far, who have we identified on the sea of glass: God the Father, Jesus Christ, twenty-four elders, and the four living creatures. That's it. When John saw this, no one was resurrected, correct? We haven't come to the time of the resurrection. So here we have the sea of glass with the throne of God, and we'll see a little later there are a great innumerable multitude of angels that are with it, but no saints yet. Why? Well, the resurrection of the dead hasn't taken place. So this is going to be a phenomenal thing.

Now let's finish off Chapter 4, and this will end it for us today, because this is a natural place to break here. Verse 9: "And when the living creatures give glory and honor and thanksgiving to Him Who sits on the throne, Who lives into the ages of eternity, The twenty-four elders fall down before Him Who sits on the throne; and they worship Him Who lives into the ages of eternity, and cast their crowns before the throne, saying, 'Worthy are You, O Lord, to receive glory and honor and power because You did create all things, and for Your will they were created and exist (Revelation 4: 1-11). So God is going to fulfill His purpose.

So the only thing we can conclude is that the throne of God and the sea of glass are probably closer to the earth than we have imagined, and if it's out there a little further at the present time; it's going to come closer. We'll see that next time, and maybe we can answer the question of the mystery of the sea of glass.

End of Sermon

Transcriber: Judith Anderson

Events After Pentecost—Sermon I
June 21, 2003
Scriptural References

1) 1 Corinthians 1:25-29	8) Matthew 16:16-18
2) Deuteronomy 5:22-29	9) Revelation 6:12-17
3) Deuteronomy 7:6-11	10) Matthew 24:27
4) Exodus 24:1-18	11) Matthew 24:29-31
5) Hebrews 12:18-24	12) I Thessalonians 4:13-18
6) Revelation 12:7-17	13) Acts 7:54-56, 59-60
7) Revelation 6:9-11	14) Revelation 4:1-11

CHAPTER TWENTY-NINE

Events After Pentecost—Sermon II

July 5, 2003

Let's go ahead—*The Events After Pentecost #2*, or re-titled, *What Are We Going To Do on The Sea of Glass*? Very intriguing question isn't it? Now let's ask a couple of questions to go into this. Does God plan things? Yes, He does, and He says that He has made known to us the mystery of His plan. Does He prepare for things? Yes, He does. Did He not prepare Abraham? Yes, He did. Did He not prepare Moses in the wilderness before leading the children of Israel out? Yes, He did. Did He not prepare the way for the coming of Christ with John the Baptist? Yes, He did. Did He not send Jeremiah—let's back up a little bit—was not Jeremiah prepared and sent to the people of Judah to warn them before the captivity took place? Yes, He did.

Now the greatest event that's going to take place since the creation of the world is going to occur at the first resurrection! Now don't you think that it is rather, silly, dumb and ignorant if the resurrection took place on Trumpets—we all meet Christ in the air and hurry up and come back down to the earth. Or must there be some kind of preparation before we come back to the earth? But of course there has to be—there is preparation right now isn't there? We are preparing right now for the first resurrection, are we not? Yes, indeed. Now with all that preparation do you think it is going to be a hurry-scurry thing and that God is going to say ... "Let's go! Get on your horse." I never rode one of these in my life! Are you not going to have to understand how this new body works? This is going to be the greatest invasion in the history of the world! So, therefore, we've got to be prepared and ready. We have to have instructions and understanding.

So, let's see what's going to take place on the Sea of Glass. Let's come to 1 John 3. So let's back up here just a little bit. The first thing that's going to happen when we are resurrected and see the angels and they take us up to meet Christ on the Sea of Glass, 1 John 3:1: "Behold, what manner of love the Father has bestowed upon us, that we should be called the sons of God: therefore the world knows us not..." and they don't know us. Like I told one man, the man that I bought the 1550 Stephens Text from—he is a dyed-in-the-wool Protestant, and I let him know that we keep the Sabbath and holy days and I said, "Look you need to understand this." I said, "Every Sabbath there are millions of Christians who believe in Jesus Christ, who keep the Commandments of God, who keep the Sabbath, and a good number of them the holy days, and they are not looking for salvation by works." I said, "You need to understand that. But you never hear about us do you? You don't even know that we exist, do you?" And he was dumbfounded. No, the world doesn't know us. How many people out there driving by, drive by and say, "Well, yes, we know there are Christians, true Christians that have the Spirit of God, meeting in that building." Of course not. We walk down the street, we go in the supermarket, we don't carry a placard, you know, "I'm a true Christian, and all the rest of you are damned." (Laughter) Try that in San Francisco today. Now we should be called the sons or the children of God—the world doesn't know us, "... because it knew Him not." See God knows what He is doing in selecting those that He is preparing for the first resurrection. "Beloved, now are we the children of God, and it does not yet appear what we shall be but we know that when he shall appear..." we already covered that how He is going to come back to the earth and where the Sea of Glass will be and so forth. "...We shall be like him; for we shall see him as he is" (1 John 3:1-2). That's one of the first things that are going to take place. We are going to see Christ!

Now let's go to Revelation 15. Let's look at the Sea of Glass here just a little bit, where it talks about the Sea of Glass, and we'll read through some Scriptures, and then we'll go back and analyze them; then we'll ask some questions, and we'll see if we can fill in the blanks. Revelation 15:1: "And I saw another sign... great and awesome:...." Okay now he sees the seven angels, but he also sees the Sea of Glass too. So this is an awesome thing. "...Seven angels having the seven last plagues, for in them the wrath of God is filled up. And I saw a sea of glass mingled with fire, and those who had gotten the victory over the beast, and over his image, and over his mark, *and* over the number of his name, standing on the sea of glass, having *the* harps of God."

Now what's one of the very first things that is going to happen—let's read all the way through here down to verse 5 and then we'll go back and see what's going to happen here. Verse 3: "And they were singing the song of Moses, *the* servant of God, and the song of the Lamb..." we'll cover that in a little bit, both of them. "...Saying, Great and awesome *are* Your works, Lord God Almighty; righteous and true *are* Your ways, King of the saints. Who shall not fear You, O Lord, and glorify Your name? For *You* only *are* holy; and all the nations shall come and worship before You; for Your judgments have been revealed. And after these things I looked, and behold, the temple of the tabernacle of the testimony in heaven was opened." Now that's got to be right close to where—that's got to be right close to the Sea of Glass, does it not? And who is in the tabernacle but God the Father and His throne, right? Yes, indeed (Revelation 15:1-5).

Now then, the first thing that is going to happen is that Christ is going to receive us. Now let's go back to Psalm 24 and let's see how Jesus was received when He ascended to heaven to be received of God the Father after He was resurrected. Psalm 24—and do you not think that there is going to be a reception for us? Yes, indeed, and Christ is going to do the welcoming, and we will see what He will do. Psalm 24, and let's pick it up here in verse 7. Now I want you to picture this: Just as Christ is coming to the Sea of Glass, as we covered last time (Revelation 4 and 5) to be received of the Father, and remember when we saw that Sea of Glass there were no saints there, just the Father, and Christ, and the angels. But picture this: Christ coming to walk down whatever aisle between the angels to be received of God the Father and here is what they sing. Verse 7: "Lift up your heads, O you gates; be lifted up you everlasting doors; and the King of glory shall come in. Who *is* the King of glory? The LORD strong and mighty, the LORD mighty in battle." Because yes, He is going to come back in battle isn't He? And we are going to be with Him. Remember what He said, "If my kingdom were of this world, then would my servants fight." And if you have been waiting for a good fight, you are going to get it. And you'll have the tools and power to carry it out. Verse 9: "Lift up you heads, O you gates; even lift *them* up, you everlasting doors; and the King of glory shall come in. Who *is* the King of glory? The LORD of hosts, he is the King of glory." So when He was received, that's what the angels sang.

Now Christ is going to receive us isn't He? Now what is He going to do? Let's go back to Hebrews 2; let's see what He is going to do. See there has to be a reason for the sea of glass, because there are a lot to things that have to take place, and a lot of things have to occur for us, and these things are in the Word of God which shows that they must take place. Now let's pick it up here beginning in verse 5, Hebrews 2: "For *it* is not to *the* angels *that* He has placed in subjection the world to come, of which we are speaking." No He has put it in subjection under us. "But in a certain place one fully testified, saying, 'What is man, that You are mindful of him, or *the* son of man, that You visit him? You did crown him with glory and honor, and You did set him over the works of Your hands;' " That's our ultimate destiny. Verse 8: "You did put all things in subjection under his feet. For in subjecting all things to him, He left nothing *that was* not subjected to him. But now we do not yet see all things subjected to him." But the day is coming when it will be. "But we see Jesus, Who *was* made a little lower than *the* angels, crowned with glory and honor on account of suffer-

451

ing the death, in order that by *the* grace of God He Himself might taste death for everyone;" So Christ has a tremendous stake in this doesn't He? All those who are resurrected are those who have had the character of God, Christ in them developed. Correct? Yes, indeed. Verse 10: "Because it was fitting for Him, for Whom all things *were created*, and by Whom all things *exist*, in bringing many sons unto glory…" And that takes place at the resurrection. "…To make the Author of their salvation perfect through sufferings. For both He Who is sanctifying and those who are sanctified *are* all of one;" and the only time that is going to be with everyone, everywhere from the beginning of creation to the return of Christ [is] when they are all resurrected and meet Christ in the air on the Sea of Glass—all of one. See at this present time, we're a few here and few there, there are some in this country, there are some in that country. When are they going to be all one? Now notice what happens when they are all one. "…For which cause He is not ashamed to call them brethren, Saying…" Now here is what Christ is going to do when we're resurrected and we're on the Sea of Glass. What is the first thing that He is going to do? <u>Christ</u> <u>is</u> <u>going</u> <u>to</u> <u>declare</u> <u>us</u> <u>to</u> <u>the</u> <u>Father</u>, and say, "Behold, the work of your hands." Continuing in verse 12: "…'I will declare Your name to My brethren; in *the* midst of *the* church I will sing praise to You.' And again, 'I will be trusting in Him.' And again, 'Behold I and the children whom God has given Me.' " And I believe that's the first thing that Christ is going to say—all resurrected spirit beings (Hebrews 2:5-13).

Now let's come to Psalm 22 and let's see a prophecy of this. I mean, brethren, we're talking about the greatest thing since the creation of the world is going to happen. And we, you know—let's get out of our minds a crippled concept of salvation because we have so been tainted by Protestantism and Catholicism and the insipidness of this stupid world, that we haven't yet gotten in our minds that we are called to the greatest, greatest thing that has been! God is just not going to save you so you can be saved. Salvation is not escaping ever-burning hell! Salvation is being called to serve God through all eternity at the first level under Jesus Christ! And the church of the firstborn will be at that level for all eternity! I don't know if there is any way we can shake up some these sleeping Laodiceans and Sardisites that are almost dead, you know—I don't know. You see, the reason people give up on things so easily is because they were never convinced in the first place, and they were never taught in the second place, and they never studied their Bibles to really know, in the third place! So I don't know what can be done to wake up these people—especially those that have forsaken the Sabbath and the holy days and have gone back into the vomit and swill of the order of the Roman Catholic Church to keep Sunday! Who they [the Roman Catholic Church] arrogantly say that those Protestants and those other people who keep Sunday, "You are just following us. You are hypocrites. We determined Sunday, not the Scriptures. You are following us, not God. You don't believe your Bible, you believe us!" All you have to do is just read *Rome's Challenge to the Protestants*—there it is. That is a <u>profound</u> piece of work, and when your enemy is so confident that he will come out and deride you like that, and then people give up on God.

Now let me tell you one very profound, important lesson: Because of a man who is supposed to be a servant of God, [but who] turns out to be evil and corrupt because he was gotten to by Satan the Devil; <u>do</u> <u>not</u> <u>ever</u> <u>give</u> <u>up</u> <u>on</u> <u>God</u>. I don't care who you are, where you are, where you have been, what you experienced, salvation will overcome every bit of whatever you may have gone through. You need to understand that.

Psalm 22:22. Here is what Christ is going to do—we come up on the Sea of Glass, the angels bring us up there, and we get our sea legs as it were, and stand on the Sea of Glass, "I will declare your name unto my brethren:" He is going to say, "My brethren whom God has given me—Here is the Father!" Now we'll be able to see the Father, won't we, as spirit beings if we see Christ as He is? Will we not see God the Father as He is? Yes, indeed. "…In the midst of the congregation…" as we saw back there in Hebrews 2, the great congregation, and the great congregation is all the resurrected saints, you see. "…In the midst of the congregation I will praise you. You that fear the LORD, praise him;" Now I just imagine after Jesus says, "Behold the children you have given me" and the children behold the Father—I imagine the angels ten thousands times ten thousands are going sing praises to God the Father. I mean this is going to be absolutely the most electrifying and penetrating event that we will ever experience, and then we'll praise God. Verse 23: "You that fear the LORD, praise him; all you seed of Jacob, glorify him; and fear him, all you the seed of Israel." And who is the true seed of Israel? The Church [is]. That is going to be a magnificent thing to take place (Psalm 22:22-23)!

Let's come to Isaiah 8:16. We are going to read of the work of the apostles. He says here, verse 16: "Bind up the testimony, seal the law among my disciples. And I will wait upon the LORD, that does hide his face from the house of Jacob, and I will look for him. Behold, I and the children the LORD has given me…" again that refers to Hebrews the second chapter doesn't it? "…*Are* for signs and for wonders…" and we will be to the world, won't we? Yes, we will be. "… From the LORD of hosts, which dwells in mount Zion." Now what are we coming to? Mount Sion in heaven above, correct? Yes. Okay, put it all together (Isaiah 8:16-18).

The next thing we are going to do, **Number Two**—Okay **Number One**, you can put down there: Christ proclaims us to the Father. **Number Two**: We sing the victory song. Now we're going to do a lot of singing. Remember it says there we have harps, right? Now, I have never played a harp. So whatever it is that God does when we are resurrected, to give us the ability to do so, He will. So all the harps have to be passed out don't they? Now in this remember, the angels are going to be busy assisting in all of this. Okay, since we're here in Isaiah, let's come to Isaiah 40. No, let's go to Psalm 35. Beg your pardon, instead of Isaiah let's go to Psalms, and that's not the airlines. Psalm 35:18. Now this also has to do with Christ. "I will give you thanks in the great congregation…" now the great congregation then is the resurrected saints. "…I will praise you among much people."

Now since we are right here just go across the page to Psalm 33. Let's begin in verse 1. We are going to sing some songs. We are going to sing more than just the song of Moses and the song of the Lamb. We'll get to that in just a bit. Verse 1: "Rejoice in the LORD, O you righteous: *for* praise is comely for the upright. Praise the LORD with the harp:" That's what we're going to do. We have the harps of God don't we? Yes. "…Sing unto him with the psaltery *and* an instrument of ten strings. Sing unto him a new song;" it's going to be one we have never sung. "…And play skillfully with a loud noise. For the word of the LORD *is* right; and all of his works *are done* in truth." Is that part of the song we are going to sing? What is the greatest work of His hands—those who have been resurrected. Yes, indeed (Psalm 33:1-4).

Now let's come to Psalm 149:9—No, Psalm 144:9, I'm getting you all messed up here today, aren't I? Psalm 144:9: "I will sing a new song unto you O God: upon a psaltery *and* an instrument of ten strings I will sing praises unto you. *It is he* that gives salvation unto kings:" Are we going to be kings and priests? Have we not received salvation? Yes, indeed. He "…delivers David his servant from the hurtful sword." Then it blends on back to a contemporary time (Psalm 144:9-10).

Now let's go to Isaiah 40:8. Okay, now that you're there, we will save this until we come to the rewards because this is talking about the rewards.

Now, song of victory—let's see the song of Moses because it says we are going to sing the song of Moses the servant of God. So let's go back to Exodus 15 and we will pick up part of it here, but remember now, we will expand this beyond just destroying the Egyptians at the Red sea.   Verse 1: "Then sang Moses and the children of Israel this song unto the LORD, and spoke, saying, I will sing unto the LORD, for he has triumphed gloriously: the horse and his rider he has thrown into the sea.   The LORD *is* my strength and song, he is become my salvation: he *is* my God, and I will prepare a habitation; my father's God, and I will exalt him.   The LORD *is* a man of war: the LORD *is* his name."   And we are going to see a little later that Jesus returns to the earth and He makes war in righteousness doesn't He? He is a man of war.   And it talks about Pharaoh being cast down, and this is all likened then unto the judgment that will come against Babylon.   And then we also have over here, verse 20: "And Miriam the prophetess, the sister of Aaron, took a timbrel in her hand; and all the women went out after her with timbrels and with dances.   And Miriam answered them, 'Sing unto the LORD, for he has triumphed gloriously;...' "   Now think what is going to be the triumph with all the resurrection of the saints.   "...The horse and his rider has he thrown into the sea.   So Moses brought Israel from the Red Sea, and they went into the wilderness..." and so forth, the rest of the story goes back from there (Exodus 15:1-3, 20-22).

Now let's come to Revelation the fifth chapter and see some of the songs we are going to sing.   This is part of the song of the Lamb.   You know we have often wondered—what was the song of the Lamb?   Well, I think we can answer it here.   And this is when the Lamb came, verse 8: "...When he took the book, the four living creatures and the twenty-four elders fell down before the Lamb, each having harps and golden bowls full of incense, which are the prayers of the saints.   And they sang a new song, saying,...." and this is the song that we are going to sing.   "...Worthy are You to take the book, and to open its seals because You were slain, and did redeem us to God by Your own blood, out of every tribe and language and people and nation, And did make us unto our God kings and priests; and we shall reign on the earth."   That is part of the song of the Lamb, I believe.   And I believe another part of the song of the Lamb is that we will sing unto Him because He was the Lamb slain from the foundation of the world.   So all of that will be part of the song of the Lamb. (Revelation 5:8-10).

Now let's look in the Book of Psalms and see if we can see some other things which may be connected with the song of the Lamb.   You know, you've heard it said that the saints are going to shout for joy.   Well, we are!   I mean this is going to be a tremendous thing, brethren.   Let's come to Psalm 18:46.   This is extolling God as a fighter, as a warrior, and is Christ going to be fighting and warring this time when He comes back to the earth?   Without a doubt.   Psalm 18:46.   Could this also be part of the song of the Lamb?   "The LORD lives; and blessed *be* my rock; and let the God of my salvation be exalted.   *It is* God that avenges me, and subdues the people under me."   And isn't that what's going to happen when we come back to the earth?   Isn't the earth going to be subdued under all the saints?   Yes, indeed.   "He delivered me from my enemies: yea, he has lifted me up above those that rise up against me: and he has delivered me from the violent man.   Therefore I will give thanks unto you, O LORD, among the heathen, and sing praises unto your name.   For Great deliverance gives he to his king;" liken that unto the resurrection, that's the greatest deliverance of all isn't it—being delivered from death.   "...And showed mercy to his anointed, to David, and to his seed forevermore."   We are going to be doing a lot of singing, I believe.   So that will be good (Psalm 18:46-50).

Let's come to Psalm 47.   Maybe this is going to be one of the songs that we'll sing. Maybe this is part of the song to the Lamb.   Verse 1, Psalm 47: "...Clap you hands, all you people; shout unto God with the voice of triumph."   It's going to be something isn't it!   Yes, we have been overcomers.   Yes, we triumph over death through Jesus Christ.   Yes, we're going to triumph over all the forces of evil in this world.   "...The LORD most high is awesome," that's what terrible means.   Psalm 47, verse 2: "...*he is* a great King over all the earth.   He shall subdue the people under us, and the nations under our feet."   That's why we come back to the earth to fight.   I don't know about you, but this makes a lot of sense to me and you know, I have never put it together this way before, but when asked the question: what's going to happen on the Sea of Glass—I guess one thing leads to another. Verse 4: "He shall choose our inheritance for us, the excellency of Jacob whom he loved. God is gone up with a shout, the LORD with the sound of a trumpet." Of course that will occur on the Feast of Trumpets, right? "Sing praises to God, sing praises: sing praises to our King, sing praises. For God *is* the King of all the earth: sing you praises with understanding. God reigns over the heathen: God sits upon the throne of his holiness. The princes of the people are gathered together, *even* the people of the God of Abraham:" and that's us, "...for the shields of the earth *belong* unto God: he is greatly exalted." All of this is going to help prepare us for the coming battle. So that is the victory song (Psalm 47:1-9).

Now let's come to the third thing that is going to take place on the Sea of Glass. **Number Three**: We are going to receive a new name. Now each one is going to receive a new name. Now how many people are there that are going to be resurrected? Well, millions and millions—don't you think it is going to take some time for us to receive our new names? Okay, let's see that. Let's come to—first of all let's see that Jesus is going to have a new name. Let's come to Ephesians 1. And He is going to have the greatest of the new names, but you see just like God has done before the resurrection, He names things for what they will be. He changed Abram's name to Abraham because he was going to be a father of many nations—and *is* he going to be surprised at the resurrection (Laughter). Ephesians 1, verse 20 talking about the greatness of God's power, verse 20: "Which He wrought in Christ, when He raised Him from *the* dead, and set *Him* at His right hand in the heavenly *places*," verse 21: "Far above every principality and authority and power and lordship, and every name that is named—not only in this age, but also in the *age* to come; For He has subordinated all things under His feet, and has given Him *to be* head over all things to the church, Which is His body—the fullness of Him Who fills all things in all." We'll accomplish the will of God (Ephesians 1:20-23).

Now we see that name back here in Revelation 19. We see two things about the name of Christ. Let's begin here in verse 11: "And I saw heaven open; and behold, a white horse; and He Who sat on it *is* called Faithful and True, and in righteousness He does judge and make war." Now we are getting into the events coming to the Feast of Trumpets now here. "And His eyes *were* like a flame of fire, and on His head *were* many crowns; *and* He had a name written, that no one knows except Him." So He is going to have one name that is above all names, but also we are going to see He has other names. Let's come over here to verse 16: "And *His* garment and on His thigh He has a name written: King of kings, and Lord of lords" (Revelation 19:11-12, 16).

Now we have to have a new name. Let's come over here to Revelation 2. Let's see where that promise is given, and we won't know what it is until we are given it. So I imagine that Christ is already working on the names—He and God the Father are putting together the names that He has for us—getting all prepared. You see God is getting prepared. Jesus Christ is getting prepared, and all the preparation it is going to take for the first resurrection. Revelation 2:17: "The one who has an ear, let him hear what the Spirit says to the churches. To the one who overcomes I will give *the right* to eat of the hidden manna;..." So we are going to eat when we are spirit beings. Now what is the hidden manna? I can't tell you, it's hidden, but we'll know at that time. "...And I will give him a white stone, and on the stone a new name written,..." And I wonder if this stone is going to be something that we will hold in our hands, you know a symbol of authority. "...And in the stone a new name written, which no man knows except the one who receives *it*." So, no one will know it until you receive it, then you will know it (Revelation 2:17).

Now let's come to Chapter 3 and let's see that there is also another name. Not all are going to receive the same name. Each one is going to be different. And, after all, each one of us at the resurrection is going to be a special creation of God the Father and Jesus Christ. We are going to have a new body, have a new mind, we're going to have a new name. We're going to have a new job, we're going to eat new food, and we're going to do new things. Now verse 12, Revelation 3: "The one who overcomes will I make a pillar in the temple of my God,..." Now that doesn't mean, you know, that you're going to be made into a pillar; because the temple of God is going to consist of the people of God—because ultimately, as we will see for the Last Great Day, in New Jerusalem there is no temple. All temple builders will be unemployed (Laughter). "...And he shall not out any more; and I will write upon him the name of My God, and the name of the city of my God,..." Now this is in addition to your individual name. So these are names then, which distinguish work and authority—it would have to be. "...The New Jerusalem, which will come down out of heaven from my God; and *I will write upon him* My new name." Now exactly how all that is going to work, I can tell you exactly how you're going to find out—you make it to the resurrection, and when you see it done, you'll understand it, and until then, I'll ring my bell (the cowbell sounds). We don't know, except that it says it (Revelation 3:12). The question was asked: Could not these names also signify titles? Very well—could very well be. We'll find out.

Okay now let's come to Isaiah—I mean this new name is going to be something. Let's come to Isaiah 56. I imagine God the Father and Jesus Christ are having a great time selecting the names. Isaiah 56 and let's see the promise given here. Verse 1: "Thus says the LORD, Keep you judgment, and do justice: for my salvation *is* near to come, and my righteousness to be revealed. Blessed *is* the man *that* does this..." Now the Protestants think you are cursed. "...And the son of man *that* lays hold on it: that keeps the sabbath from polluting it, and keeps his hand from doing any evil. Neither let the son of the stranger, that has joined himself to the LORD, speak, saying, The LORD has utterly separated me from his people: neither let the eunuch say, Behold I *am* a dry tree. For thus says the LORD unto the eunuchs that keep my sabbaths..." <u>plural,</u> holy days, "...and choose *the things* that please me, and take hold of my covenant; Even unto them will I give in my house and within my walls a place and a name..." Now this is talking about at the time of the resurrection. "...Better than of sons and of daughters: and I will give them an everlasting name, that shall not be cut off." So it's going to go for all eternity. Tremendous promise isn't it (Isaiah 56:1-5)?

Now since we're in Isaiah, let's turn a few pages over to Isaiah 62. You know, and some names really need to be changed—God is going to change them. Isaiah 62 and let's pick it up here in verse 1: "For Zion's sake I will not hold my peace, and for Jerusalem's sake I will not rest, until the righteousness thereof goes forth as brightness, and the salvation thereof as a lamp *that* burns." Now that is bringing salvation to the whole world during the Millennium. Verse 2: "And the Gentiles shall see your righteousness, and all kings your glory:" And we will be the kings won't we? Yes. "...And you shall be called by a new name which the mouth of the LORD shall name." It's going to come directly from God. Now that's going to be an exciting thing isn't it? So you might ask the question: What is in the name of a son or daughter of God? His eternal standing and position. Verse 3: "You shall also be a crown of glory in the hand of the LORD and a royal diadem in the hand of your God." We've got lots of work to do (Isaiah 62:1-3).

Now finally let's go to Ephesians the third chapter and see that there is going to be the whole Family name. So not only are we going to have a new first name, we're going to have a new last name. Now let's pick it up here in verse 11, showing that God has purpose and part of what we are reading is the purpose of God for us, you see. Ephesians 3 and verse 11, God is busy doing and preparing for this, and I am sure the angels as well. Now notice, "According to *His* eternal purpose, which He has wrought in Christ Jesus our Lord, In Whom we have boldness and direct access with confidence through His *very* own faith. So then,..." Paul writes, "...I beseech *you* not to faint at my tribulations for you, which are *working for* your glory." Now I can understand why Paul was very positive about the things that he went through. I imagine when he saw the third heavens in vision, that he was given an inkling of some of these things. Verse 14: "For this cause I bow my knees to the Father of our Lord Jesus Christ, Of Whom the whole family in heaven and earth is named,..." Now we are going to be the family of God (Ephesians 3:11-15).

Now there was a man who, another Protestant, who when he found out that we believe that God is a Family, said that this is heterodoxy, if not heresy. Well, what does it say? Yes, Hillary reads this: "...In whom the whole village is named." No, it doesn't say that—it says family. Who made and created the family? God did. Who said be fruitful and multiple to create a physical family? God did. God is creating His family isn't He? Yes, indeed, there it is. So we're going to have a family name as well.

Now let's come to **Number Four**: We will receive our reward. Now what is our reward going to be? The New Testament talks quite a bit about rewards. So let's look at some of these and let's see them. Now we have some rewards here, we have other rewards in heaven to be brought with us. "His reward is with Him."

Let's go to Isaiah. Now we'll go to Isaiah 40. Now we've got it in the right place—sorry about that. He is going to bring it with Him. Isaiah 40:9: "O Zion..." now that's talking about the Church "...that brings good tidings..." which we will bring to the world, "...get you up into the high mountain; O Jerusalem, that brings good tidings, lift up thy voice with strength; lift *it* up, be not afraid; say unto the cities of Judah, Behold your God! Behold, the Lord God will come with strong *hand*, and his arm shall rule for him: behold, his reward *is* with him, and his work before him. He shall feed his flock like a shepherd: he shall gather the lambs with his arm, and carry *them* in his bosom, *and* shall gently lead those that are with young" (Isaiah 40:9-11).

Now let's see some more about rewards. Let's look at some of the rewards that we are looking forward [to] today. Now, God is the one who knows all things, He is the one who is working up the rewards, He is the one who is preparing them for us, isn't He? Let's come to Matthew 5:12. Here is an inkling of the reward. Now it talks here in verse 11: "Blessed are you, when they shall reproach you, and shall persecute you, and shall falsely say every wicked thing against you, for My sake. Rejoice, and be filled with joy, for great *is* your reward in heaven;..." which He is going to bring with Him. Now what is a great reward? We're not told, but it says it's great, and if it's going to be great—guess what—it is going to be great (Matthew 5:11-12)!

Let's come over here to Chapter 6. You can look up the different ones, the different rewards, but here Chapter 6 and verse 1. Now you can lose your reward, we'll see that in a little bit. Matthew 6:1: "Beware *that* you do not bestow your alms in the sight of men in order to be seen by them; otherwise you have no reward with your Father Who *is* in heaven." So your reward depends upon your conduct. In other words, don't do it for glory of men. Whatever you do don't do to be seen of men. Whatever you do, don't do it for politics. You know, He talks about those who blow the trumpets when they give their alms—they've had their reward, they were seen of men. Likewise, you can go and read the whole chapter there it talks about the reward, but it talks about the treasures that we lay up for heaven, verses 19 and 20.

Now let's come to 2 John 1 verse 8 and here it says something very unusual. 2 John 1 verse 8: "Watch out for yourselves in order that we may not lose the things we have accomplished, but *that* we may receive a full reward." Rather than just partial [reward]—a full reward. Or you might say the fullness of your reward, either one would be okay. That would be all right.

Let's come to 1 Peter 1:3: "Blessed *be* the God and Father of our Lord Jesus Christ, Who, according to His abundant mercy, has begotten us again unto a living hope through *the* resurrection of Jesus Christ from *the* dead; Unto an inheritance incorruptible and undefiled and unfading, reserved in heaven for us," Which He is going to bring with Him. He comes with His reward (1 Peter 1:3-4).

Now part of that reward, as we are going to see, is going to be our assignments! We are going to have to receive our assignments as well. So let's come to Matthew 25, and let's see what some of those assignments are going to be. Now with these assignments, we're going to have to know where to go, aren't we? So that's going to be all laid out in the plan, isn't it? Have to be. Here it talks about the reward and the assignment. Let's pick it up here in verse 14. This is the parable of the talents. The parable of the pounds is Luke 19. You can just put that in your notes, we won't turn there. Matthew 25:14: "For *the kingdom of heaven is* like a man leaving the country, who called his own servants and delivered to them his property." Now God has given you the Spiritual goods of His Holy Spirit and His Word is delivered to you. Now it depends on what you do with it. Verse 15: " Now to one he gave five talents, and to another two, and to another one; he *gave* to each one according to his own ability, and immediately left the country. Then the one who had received five talents went and traded with them, and made an additional five talents." See God expects us to take the initiative. The way God does things, He doesn't do it like in a corporation where some-one is there supervising you and looking after every little detail. He says, "Here is the job, here is the goal, here is the mission; go do it." [One might ask,] "Well, how do I do it Lord?" [And the Lord might answer,] "Well, you study My Word and all this sort of thing, but you do it!" You have to use your initiative. You have to use your choice and so forth.

So, "In the same way also, the one who had *received* two *talents* also gained two oth-ers." He that received the one, we won't dwell on that one. He went and digged in the earth and hid his Lord's money. Verse 19: "Now after a long time, the lord of those servants came to take account with them. Then the one who had received five talents came to *him and* brought an additional five talents, saying, 'Lord, you delivered five talents to me; see, I have gained five other talents besides them.' And his lord said to him, 'Well *done*, good and faithful servant! *Because* you were faithful over a few things, I will set you over many things. Enter into the joy of your Lord.' " Likewise the one, [with] the two, "…good and faithful servant… enter into the joy of the Lord" (Matthew 25:14-21).

Now let's go to Luke 19. It's necessary that we go there because this is the other half of the story. What is the reward? Everybody is going to get a reward, and that's going to take some time isn't it? It's going to take some time for everybody to get their rewards, just think how many are going to be resurrected—you know—all at once. See we look around us, and we are few today. Just think what it is going to be like in the resurrection with millions, and millions, and millions and we say, "O God what have you been doing down though the ages?" And He is going to say, "Look—all of this, how is that?" And Abraham, Isaac and Jacob are going to say, "Praise God, look at what He did." Especially Abraham because all he had was Isaac. And now look at all the physical nations on the earth and look at all now the spiritual nations that God is resurrecting. The first resurrection—that's going to be awesome.

Okay, let's pick it up here in verse 15, Luke 19:15: "And it came to pass that when he returned after receiving the kingdom, he directed that those servants to whom he had given the money be called to him, in order that he might know what each one had gained by trading." See, God doesn't want you to stay the same. Never be happy and satisfied with what you are today. Thank God that you are able to do what you do, that you can grow and overcome, but there is <u>more</u> that you can do, there is <u>more</u> that you can learn, there is <u>more</u> that you can grow into—you've got to apply yourself. It isn't going to come by osmosis. It is not going to come by a funnel in the top of the head.

Verse 16: "And the one came up, saying, 'Lord, your pound has gained ten pounds.' Then he said to him, 'Well *done*, good servant; because you were faithful in a very little, you shall have authority over ten cities.' " Now when is he going to know which cities those are? It's got to be at the resurrection on the Sea of Glass before we come back to the earth—how are you going to know where to go? "Which city, Lord? I've never been up here in the atmosphere, and looking down I can't tell."

Verse 18: "And the second one came, saying, 'Lord, your pound has made five pounds.' Then he also said to this one, 'And you be over five cities.' " And then the one who didn't do anything with it, you see, the one who didn't do anything with it was the Sardisite who is dead and who had defiled his garments and didn't receive the reward because he was lazy. Now if you're dead, you've got to be lazy, right? How much can a corpse do (Laughter)? Not very much, right? Okay, so we receive our rewards.

Number Five: There is going to be a New Covenant. Now as compared to the old covenant, we are in the New Covenant today. But just like the covenant that God made with Abraham, when He expanded the covenant, what did He do, He changed his name from Abram to Abraham, didn't He. So likewise, when we are spirit beings, I believe there is going to be a New Covenant. Now the covenant first of all has got to start out with the marriage of the Lamb and the bride. Is not the marriage ceremony a covenant? Yes. Are not our new assignments and the new work and our new existence, is that not going to require a New Covenant—a new agreement? But of course (Luke 19:15-20).

Let's come to Revelation 19. Now you might want to go ahead and expand the thing on rewards and look up in a concordance and add a little more study to it and so forth—and expand on it because it talks about the reward of a prophet, the reward of a righteous man if you give a cup of water to one of the disciples, etc., etc. And some of those rewards, I believe will take place in the second resurrection—not necessarily the first.

Now, Number Five: The New Covenant. Let's pick it up here in verse 1: "And after these things I heard *the* loud voice of a great multitude in heaven..." Now that's not the third heaven. That is on the Sea of Glass, which is in the atmosphere where the clouds are, which is the first heaven. "...A great multitude in heaven, saying,".... Now we're getting ready to come back to the earth—this is the finale. "...'Hallelujah! The salvation and the glory and the honor and the power *belong* to the Lord our God. For true and righteous *are* His judgements; for He has judged the great whore...' " Now we'll see that a little later. "...'Who corrupted the earth with her fornication, and He has avenged the blood of His servants at her hand.' And they said a second time, 'Hallelujah!'. And her smoke shall ascend upward into the ages of eternity. And the twenty-four elders and the four living creatures fell down and worshiped God, Who sits on the throne, saying, 'Amen; Hallelujah!' " Now this is the finale before we come back to the earth. So this is really a tremendous send-off isn't it? And the thing that is going to take place, I believe, the last part of it that will take place will be the marriage of the Lamb. Then we come down to the earth just like it lays out here. Verse 5: "And a voice came forth from the throne, saying, 'Praise our God, all His servants, and all who fear Him, both small and great.' " There we will be on the Sea of Glass, and we'll praise God. Verse 6: "And I heard a voice like that of a great multitude, and like *the* sound of many waters, and *the* sound of mighty thunderings, saying, 'Hallelujah! For *the* Lord God Almighty has reigned' " (Revelation 19:1-6).

Now then, here comes the marriage of the Lamb. Verse 7: "Let us be glad and shout with joy, and let us give glory to Him, for the marriage of the Lamb has come, and His wife has made herself ready". Now I believe that God the Father will perform the ceremony, who else? "And it was granted to her that she should be clothed in fine linen, pure and bright, for the fine linen is the righteousness of the saints. And he said to me, 'Write, Blessed *are* those who are called to the marriage supper of the Lamb.' " So these are the guests. Now we don't know exactly how all of that is going to work, but we know that it says there are going to be guests at the wedding. So not everyone who is resurrected in the first resurrection will be part of the bride, but there will be guests, and they eat at the marriage supper. So the last thing we're going to do is have a great big feast! Marriage of the Lamb is going to take place, we'll have the great feast of the marriage supper of the Lamb, and then get ready for Trumpets—the angels are going to bring all the horses for us (Revelation 19:7-9).

Now let's look and see if we can get some hints of this covenant here—will be an extension of a covenant already of the new covenant. Let's come to Hebrews 13:20. Just like the covenant that God made with Abraham in Genesis 17 was an extension of the covenant He made with him in Genesis 15. So likewise, with us, we will be part of the everlasting covenant. Hebrews 13:20: "And *may* the God of peace, Who raised our Lord Jesus from among the dead—that great Shepherd of the sheep—through *the* blood of *the* everlasting covenant..." So when we receive our new name, we receive our rewards, we receive our assignments, we will have a New Covenant—part of the everlasting covenant that started out when you were baptized. This will be a new phase of it, an extension of it because we will live forever (Hebrews 13:20).

Let's come to Psalm 110. Let's see part of the covenant that God made with Melchizedek—the Lord who was Melchizedek. And being priests and kings under Christ, we then will become part of the Melchizedek priesthood directly. So not only does this apply to Christ, Psalm 110, let's begin here in verse 1—not only does it apply to Christ, but it will also have to extend to those who are going to be kings and priests under Christ. Wouldn't you believe that would be so? Have to be. "The LORD said to my Lord, 'Sit you at my right hand, until I make your enemies your footstool.' " That's the whole prophecy of what God is doing. Verse 2: " The LORD shall send the rod of your strength out of Zion: rule in the midst of your enemies. Your people *shall be* willing in the day of your power, in the beauties of holiness from the womb of the morning: you have the dew of your youth." Verse 4: "The LORD has sworn, and will not repent, You *are* a priest forever after the order of Melchizedek." Now that is a covenant. So likewise, there is going to be a marriage covenant; there will be the covenant for the new priests and the new kings (Psalm 110:1-4).

Okay, now Number Six. **Number Six**: <u>will</u> <u>be</u> <u>the</u> <u>pouring</u> <u>out</u> <u>of</u> <u>the</u> <u>seven</u> <u>last</u> <u>plagues</u>. Let's come back to Revelation 15 and we'll see that. All of this takes place while we are on the Sea of Glass before we return to the earth, and then we'll finish here. And then you have to come back for Trumpets so we can continue the story. See because all of the holy days are connected together and have meaning.

Revelation 15 and then on into Revelation 16, the pouring out of the seven last plagues, and let's pick it up here in verse 5: "And after these things I looked, and behold, the temple of the tabernacle of the testimony in heaven was opened. And the seven angels who had the seven *last* plagues came out of the temple; they were clothed in linen, pure and bright, and girded about the chest with golden breastplates. And one of the four living creatures gave to the seven angels seven golden vials, full of the wrath of God, Who lives into the ages of eternity. And the temple was filled with smoke from the glory of God, and from His power; and no one was able to enter inside the temple, until the seven plagues of the seven angels were fulfilled" (Revelation 15:5-8).

Now then, God's vengeance is given. Remember God said to all of us, "Vengeance is mine, says the Lord." Now God is going to do a unique thing. He is going to show all the saints, all at the same time, the vengeance of God on this whole ungodly world system, and fulfill His promise, that if you wait for the vengeance of God, you <u>will</u> see it.

Revelation 16:1: "Then I heard a loud voice from the temple say to the seven angels, 'Go and pour out the vials of the wrath of God upon the earth.' " Men are going to learn that they are feeble, indeed, fighting against God. God doesn't use guns and cannons, and bombs. God uses things that affect the human body in a way to debilitate it. And He uses the same plagues that He used when He destroyed Egypt. And this is to show that God is the same yesterday, today, and forever, and these weapons—these are the greatest weapons of mass destruction that have ever been.

Now verse 2: "...And the first *angel* went and poured out his vial onto the earth; and an evil and grievous sore fell upon the men who had the mark of the beast, and upon those who were worshiping his image." They are probably going to break out with boils and blains and carbuncles, from head to toe. Remember what happened to Job? He was so covered with boils that he just sat there in the dust and took a broken potsherd and just scraped the puss-caps off—those boils that he had, and then threw ashes on it. And he was sitting there and you know the flies just came all around him, that's why he said, "The worms eat this body." There were probably some maggots crawling around in some of these sores that he opened up. So just picture the same thing here. That's why don't receive the mark of the beast. It may be convenient for a while, but you're going to pay the penalty, friend.

Verse 3: "And the second angel *went and* poured out his vial into the sea; and it became blood, like *that* of a dead *man;* and every living soul died in the sea died." So when Christ comes to this earth when we come with Him to this earth, the earth is going to be nearly dead, lifeless, plagued, sick, destroyed, dead bodies everywhere. Yeah, there will be some people still alive—how many we don't know. So you talk about shell shock, you talk about plague shock, yes.

Verse 4: "And the third angel poured out his vial upon the rivers, and into the fountains of waters; and they became blood. Then I heard the angel of the waters say..." Now there is an angel in charge of the waters of the earth. So he said, "...You are righteous, O Lord, Who are, and Who was, even the Holy One, in that You have executed this judgment. For they have poured out *the* blood of saints and of prophets..." Now you need to understand the blood of the saints and the prophets is worthy that they receive this. "...And You have given them blood to drink; for they are worthy. And I heard another *voice* from the altar say, Yes, Lord God Almighty, true and righteous *are* Your judgments." Now men look at this and say God is evil and mean and nasty and hateful and terrible. Well, what have men done to God? All those who are against God, remember, there is a day called payback time, and here it is.

Verse 8: "And the fourth angel poured out his vial upon the sun; and *power* was given to it to scorch men with fire." You think 130 degrees in Iraq is pretty tough? It doesn't say how hot this is, but it scorches them like with fire. "Then men were scorched with great heat..." now apparently just a big blast for a certain period of time—did they repent? No. How hard is the heart once it is given over to Satan the Devil? Pretty hard isn't it? "... And they blasphemed the name of God, Who has authority over these plagues, and did not repent to give Him glory." We're going to make it to the end. We're going to fight these invaders from outer space.

Verse 10: "And the fifth angel poured out his vial upon the throne of the beast; and his kingdom became full of darkness; and they gnawed their tongues because of the pain,..." it's much like the darkness that they had in Egypt. It was so thick they could feel it. Can you imagine having such a darkness that is so totally black and so absolutely oppressive that you can reach out and feel it and there is nothing you can do? "...And they gnawed their tongues because of the pain, And blasphemed the God of heaven because of their pains and their sores; yet they did not repent of their works." Now there is going to be a little respite after that. Now here comes the last desperate hoorah of mankind against God.

Verse 12: "And the sixth angel poured out his vial into the great river Euphrates;..." because after Revelation 9, it began to flow again. "...And its waters were dried up, so that the way of the kings from the rising of *the* sun might be prepared." So that the rest of the army of 200 million could come. And they thought, "Oh! This is fantastic! The river is dried up, now we can get to our enemies over there to Jerusalem and we can fight this invasion from outer space! Now is our opportunity. We can still do it in spite of everything that has gone on."

Verse 13, So they are going to get spiritual communication, "Then I saw three unclean spirits like frogs *come* out of the mouth of the dragon, and out of the mouth of the beast, and out of the mouth of the false prophet;" Now these are going to convince them that if we all gather together, if we just come together—you talk about Pharaoh being convinced that he could run down into the Red sea which was opened and he could see the dry ground and he looked to his right, and the water was way down at the other end, and he looked to his left and the water was way down at that end. So likewise, they are going to be deceived into thinking, "Boy, if we gather together, we're going to make it. This is our last chance!"

Verse 14: "For they are spirits of demons working miracles, going forth to the kings of the earth, even of the whole world, to gather them together to *the* battle of that great day of the Almighty God." This is going to be an awesome battle—all the armies gathered around. They are going to be able to see the Sea of Glass. They are going to be able to get their armies there and they are going to say, "Okay, let's all get here—all of our rockets, all of our tanks, all of our bombs, everything we can shoot up there. And we are going to blast this thing out of the air and they'll come tumbling down, and we'll kill them all!" Well, the Sea of Glass is going to be perfectly protected. All those missiles and everything are just going to bounce off. They are going to know they are in <u>deep</u> trouble then.

So here is a little warning to all the saints. Verse 15: "Behold, I come as a thief. Blessed *is* the one who is watching and is keeping his garments, so that he may not walk naked and they *may not* see his shame." In other words: Lest you who know the truth, don't watch and keep your garments clean by loving and obeying God and by repentance through the blood of Christ, you're going to be ashamed and you're going to end up the same way. Now verse 16: "...He gathered them together the place that in Hebrew is called Armageddon."

Verse 17: "Then the seventh angel poured out his vial into the air; and a loud voice came out of the temple of heaven, from the throne, saying, 'IT IS FINISHED.' And there were voices and thunders and lightnings; and there was a great earthquake, such as was not since men were upon the earth, so mighty an earthquake, *and* so great." This is the finale. You know, like a great and tremendous symphony that just builds, and builds, and builds, and builds, and builds, and finally it comes to the end. Oh, instead of kettledrums going and trumpets blowing it's going to be the angels who are shouting and here it's building right to the end and the seventh angel poured out his vial. It's going to be something so great, verse 19: "And the great city was divided into three parts; and the cities of the nations fell..." I just imagine every skyscraper that man has ever built is going to come crumbling to the ground. "...And Babylon the Great..." now we'll talk about the judgment of Babylon leading up to Trumpets here. "...Was remembered before God to give her the cup of the wine of His wrath. And every island disappeared, and no mountains were found; And great hail, *each stone* the weight of a talent, fell down from heaven upon men; and men blasphemed God because of the plague of the hail, for the plague was exceeding great." Now we'll see this doesn't kill all the men. This doesn't kill all the armies yet. They recover after this—the hail comes down, and what happens after hail is down on the ground for a while? Well, sooner or later, it melts away (Revelation 16:1-21).

Then, now if you want to know the rest of the story, come for Trumpets.

End of Sermon

Transcriber: Judith Anderson

Events After Pentecost—Sermon II
July 5, 2003
Scriptural References

1) I John 3:1-2

2) Revelation 15:1-5

3) Psalm 24:7-10

4) Hebrews 2:5-13

5) Psalm 22:22-23

6) Isaiah 8:16-18

7) Psalm 35:18

8) Psalm 33:1-4

9) Psalm 144:9-10

10) Isaiah 40

11) Exodus 15:1-3, 20-22

12) Revelation 5:8-10

13) Psalm 18:46-50

14) Psalm 47:1-9

15) Ephesians 1:20-23

16) Revelation 19:11-12, 16

17) Revelation 2:17

18) Revelation 3:12

19) Isaiah 56:1-5

20) Isaiah 62:1-3

21) Ephesians 3:11-15

22) Isaiah 40:9-11

23) Matthew 5:11-12

24) Matthew 6:1

25) II John verse 8

26) I Peter 1:3-4

27) Matthew 25:14-21

28) Luke 19:15-20

29) Revelation 19:1-9

30) Hebrews 13:20

31) Psalm 110:1-4

32) Revelation 15:5-8

33) Revelation 16:1-21

Section VII

The Fall Holy Days

CHAPTER THIRTY

The Feast of Trumpets—Sermon I—Holy Day

September 16, 2004

Greetings, brethren, to the Feast of Trumpets, 2004. And here we are with the time going by. We're at the fourth holy day of the year. The first holy days of the year apply directly to the Church. The last four: Trumpets, Atonement, Tabernacles, and the Last Great Day apply to the world, and also to the Church. And in this, this Feast of Trumpets, as we come down through Leviticus 23, it lists all the holy days. All the holy days are important to God, and they tell the plan and the story that God wants us to know so we can understand why we're here, where we're going, what God is doing, how He's doing it, approximately when He is going to do it so we can have understanding, faith, and hope. That's why we have the holy days.

Now the Feast of Trumpets is an unusual feast inasmuch as that it pictures being a war-feast from this point of view. Let's go to Leviticus 23, which we always do, and here we have the Feast of Trumpets. It says in verse 23, "And the LORD spake unto Moses, saying, Speak unto the children of Israel, saying, In the seventh month, in the first *day* of the month, shall ye have a sabbath, a memorial of blowing of trumpets, an holy convocation" (Lev. 23:23-24). Now the "memorial of blowing of trumpets" means that the trumpets were to be blown all day long. So this is a feast where then it incorporates everything that it talks about what the trumpets are used for in Numbers 10. We're going to see this as we go through the explanation of the day.

Let's come over here to Numbers 10 and let's go back and review the use of the trumpet. There were two special trumpets that were made. One, Numbers 10:2 - the calling of assembly. Verse 5. And this is calling of assembly, as we will see. God is going to gather all nations there at Armageddon. And then it's blown for an alarm or a warning, which this day is. And then it's also, verse 9, if you go to war. So this is a war feast. But also, after the war is over you have the recovery of it, so you also have the trumpet here. "… In the day of your gladness, and in your solemn days, and in the beginnings of your months, ye shall blow with the trumpets over your burnt offerings, and over the sacrifices of your peace offerings;…" (Num. 10:2, 5, 9-10). So the trumpet had a lot to do with the ceremony at the temple. And of course, as we will see as we already have leading up to Pentecost, that the trumpet plagues in Revelation 8 and 9 have an awful lot to do with the fulfilling of God's plan and the carrying out of what He's doing leading up to the return of Jesus Christ.

Now in Leviticus 23 it says that on this day we are to offer an offering made by fire unto the LORD. And of course we always take up an offering on the holy days. An offering is something that you need to determine, something that you need to plan for, something that reflects your thankfulness to God for the blessings that He has given you, and it has to be from your heart.

And so God expects us to do that and then we in turn use this money to help the brethren. Everything that you send in is used to produce books, booklets, tapes, CD's, pay for mail, pay for office help, and all of these things. So if you appreciate receiving the tapes, if you appreciate receiving the things then you can express it back in an offering, which will then be honored by God because you give from a willing heart and attitude. So at this time we'll pause and take up the offering.

(Pause)

Now as we saw leading up to Pentecost and including Pentecost, that the return of Jesus Christ is a spectacular event. And it's something that is not just done in an instant, and it's something the whole world will understand when the time comes. And it will be something that no one is going to be able to avoid. It's not going to be a secret rapture. It's not going to be a secret coming. It is going to be known in power and strength and glory, and especially as we will see for the Feast of Trumpets, because the Feast of Trumpets caps off the return of Jesus Christ to this earth.

Now when Jesus was talking to His disciples on the Passover night, He said, "If I go I will come again and receive you to Myself, so that where I am you may be also." So Christ is going to receive us to Himself. But many people don't believe in the return of Jesus Christ anymore. We're going to find that that is going to be more and more of a problem. And also that people are so deceived with the Rapture, even to the point that some of them say, "Well, you can receive the Mark of the beast and still go to heaven." Well I don't read that in the Bible. The Bible says you have to have victory over the beast and over his mark, and over his number, and over his name. But nevertheless they are not going to believe it, because there is going to be, as we'll see a little later, a false messiah, a false prophet and they are going to deceive the whole world under the spiritual power of Satan and the demons.

Now the apostle Peter wrote of this in II Peter 3, so let's turn there. And while you're turning there remember this: That Jesus even said when He comes will He find faith in the earth? Of course there will be some with His church. But even then, the quality of faith is in question. Now here in II Peter 3 is what Peter wrote. He said, "Now, beloved, I am writing this second epistle to you; in *both*, I am stirring up your pure minds by causing *you* to remember *in order* for you to be mindful of the words that were spoken before by the holy prophets, and of the commandment of the Lord and Savior, *spoken* by us, the apostles; knowing this first, that in the last days *there* will come mockers, walking according to their own personal lusts, and asking, 'Where is the promise of His coming? For ever since the forefathers died, everything has remained the same as from *the* beginning of creation' " (II Peter 3:1-4). And so they have ignored the facts of history, as he says there in verse 5. They have ignored the facts in the geological table of the earth. They have believed in evolution. They don't believe in God. They don't believe in the second return of Jesus Christ. And so when Jesus Christ comes, you wait and see, He is going to be counted as an alien. He and His angels and all the saints with Him. We're going to see this.

Let's look at some of the prophecies which tell us about the setting up of the kingdom of God on earth at the return of Jesus Christ in power and in glory, and in a scope that is going to be awesome indeed. Far greater than even most of us in the church have ever assumed or ever thought of. It is going to be something else.

Now here, let's go back to the book of Daniel. And of course the whole book of Daniel tells us some of the things here about the return of Christ and when these things will be, and how they are going to happen, and what it is going to be like. Let's come to Daniel 2 because here is a promise that was given to Nebuchadnezzar in the interpretation of the dream that he had, which Daniel interpreted for him. Now I'm not going to go through the whole thing, but we'll just come here to Daniel 2:44. We're going to see how this fills in, in the book of Revelation a little later.

"And in the days of these kings…" So there's coming a time when all of these things will be. And they're going to be done on time according to God's schedule, according to His plan as outlined by the holy days, and God has predetermined all of this. You know, the apostles wanted to know, "Are You at this time going to restore the kingdom to Israel?" And He said, "No, you go your way and you preach. That's given into the hands of the Father and that's under His authority."

It talks about it. "And in the days of these kings shall the God of heaven set up a kingdom, which shall never be destroyed:…" Notice how it's going to come. "…And the kingdom shall not be left to other people,…" It's going to be given to the saints and we're going to rule, and we're going to reign. And we're going to help straighten out this whole earth. You see, the Protestants focus in on having sin forgiven so they can be right with God, and they can be saved, and they can go to heaven. And they never get past the beginning. God wants us to grow in character, grow in knowledge, grow in understanding. He wants us to develop the character so that we can rule and reign with Jesus Christ, because it's not going to be left to other people, it's going to be for the saints. And this whole civilization of this world is going to come to a destructive end. And that's what this feast pictures—the destruction of the civilizations of this world. And it's pictured right here.

"…It shall break in pieces and consume all these kingdoms, and it shall stand for ever. Forasmuch as thou sawest that the stone was cut out of the mountain without hands, and that it brake in pieces the iron, the brass, the clay, the silver, and the gold; the great God hath made known to the king what shall come to pass hereafter: and the dream is certain, and the interpretation thereof sure" (Dan. 2:44-45). Now all of the details are not given here.

Some of the details are given a little later in Chapter 7. Let's come over here and see this. This is quite a thing. Brethren, God has called us to the greatest calling, to the greatest event, to be able to be partakers of it, to be able to be part of it, to be able to help solve all the problems of this world. And know for sure they're going to get worse.

Daniel 7:13, "I saw in the night visions, and, behold, *one* like the Son of man came with the clouds of heaven,…" That's how He's coming. That's how He left. That's how He's returning. And the book of Revelation says every eye shall see Him. "…And came to the Ancient of days, and they brought Him near before Him. And there was given Him dominion, and glory, and a kingdom, that all people, nations, and languages, should serve Him: His dominion *is* an everlasting dominion, which shall not pass away, and His kingdom *that* which shall not be destroyed." Now you see, this is going to bring the beast, the false prophets, the nations of the world into a head-on confrontation with the return of Jesus Christ and the saints of God. But as we are going to see, they are going to lose. And they are going to lose big time.

Now when we come to verse 27, again we'll see that dominion was given to Christ, and then He gives some of that dominion to us to rule and reign with Him. "And the kingdom and dominion, and the greatness of the kingdom under the whole heaven, shall be given to the people of the saints of the most High, whose kingdom *is* an everlasting kingdom, and all dominions shall serve and obey Him" (Dan. 7:13-14, 27). But the thing that is profound and important is the way this is going to happen and how big an event this is going to be. It is going to be almost beyond the scope of our imagination. So maybe we can help expand that a little more today, to understand that we are called to the greatest most significant and most profound event to ever occur since the creation of the world. And that's what this Feast of Trumpets is all about.

Now let's look and see a little bit more here. We'll come back to Chapter 8 when we get to the feast a little bit later on. But let's come over here to Daniel 12:1. "And at that time shall Michael stand up, the great prince which standeth for the children of thy people [so this is going to rescue the physical tribes of Israel]: and there shall be a time of trouble, such as never was since there was a nation *even* to that same time: and at that time Thy people shall be delivered, every one that shall be found written in the book." Now we saw that. We saw how the first resurrection takes place on Pentecost. And we're going to look at the events that take place after we are on the sea of glass leading up to the literal return of Christ and the saints on the earth.

Now let's come to Jeremiah 25 and let's see what a tremendous event this is going to be. This is going to be something just affecting the whole world. Jeremiah 25:12, "And it shall come to pass, when seventy years are accomplished,…" Now, it finishes off with the seventy year captivity of the Jews in Babylon, but then it extends out way beyond to the end. So this prophecy begins here and then projects to the return of Jesus Christ. "…I will punish the king of Babylon, and that nation, saith the LORD, for their iniquity, and the land of the Chaldeans, and will make it perpetual desolations. And I will bring upon that land all My words which I have pronounced against it, *even* all that is written in this book, which Jeremiah hath prophesied against all the nations." Now you go back and you read Jeremiah 50, 51, and 52 and you see how profound this is going to be. He's going to bring to pass all His words. Continuing in Jeremiah 25:14-16, "For many nations and great kings shall serve themselves of them also: and I will recompense them according to their deeds, and according to the works of their own hands. For thus saith the LORD God of Israel unto me; Take the wine cup of this fury at My hand, and cause all the nations, to whom I send thee, to drink it. And they shall drink, and be moved, and be mad, because of the sword that I will send among them." So then Jeremiah said, verse 17, "Then took I the cup at the LORD'S hand, and made all the nations to drink, unto whom the LORD had sent me:…" And He starts right at Jerusalem. Then it lists all the nation.

Now come over here to verse 26 and let's see how far this goes. "And all the kings of the north, far and near, one with another, and all the kingdoms of the world,…" So when we come to the end-time and we're talking about the return of Jesus Christ, we are talking about world-wide events. And we are living in a time when all of these things are possible. They weren't possible 25 years ago, 30 years ago, 100 years ago, 500 years ago, 1000 years ago. But now they are possible. "…All the kingdoms of the world, which *are* upon the face of the earth:…" Now that's very inclusive, isn't it? That's quite a thing to understand.

Now notice what it's going to be. Verse 29, "For, lo, I begin to bring evil on the city which is called by My name,…" Now God is saying, "I want you to understand something very important. If I start correcting and bringing evil upon the city that is called by My name, the rest of you are not going to escape." And we're going to see the things at Jerusalem is going to key these end-time events as never before. And we can see how that is coming more, and more, and more, and more, can't we? Now notice, He says, "…Which is called by My name, and should ye be utterly unpunished? Ye shall not be unpunished: for I will call for a sword upon all the inhabitants of the earth, saith the LORD of hosts." Now how all encompassing is that? That's profound. Remember Jesus said, "It is a time of trouble that has not been since there was a nation on earth, nor no ever shall be." And unless God had not limited that time all flesh should be destroyed. So we need to get our thinking caps on and we need to think big. We need to think huge. We need to use the Spirit of God to understand as greatly as possible, as much as we can, what God is going to do.

Now what you need to do is understand this: because these events are coming this way—do not be fearful! Do not be cowardly. Do not run and try and hide in a corner. God wants us to be courageous. God wants us to stand for the truth. God wants us to understand one thing very important—we are on God's side and there is nothing that anyone can do to us to turn back what God has promised for us and to turn back the hand of God.

Just like He told Jeremiah when He said, "I want you to go." He said, "I'm going to give you a forehead of flint so you will speak the words that I want you to speak, and don't be afraid of them, don't be afraid of their faces, don't be afraid of their threats. So likewise with the events that are coming here at the end-time, don't be afraid. But you know, as Luke wrote, "Look up and rejoice for your salvation is near."

Jeremiah 25 verse 30, "Therefore prophesy thou against them all these words, and say unto them, The LORD shall roar from on high, and utter His voice from His holy habitation; He shall mightily roar upon His habitation; He shall give a shout, as they that tread *the grapes,* against all the inhabitants of the earth." That's why the book of Revelation is so profound because it shows how this is going to happen worldwide. "A noise shall come *even* to the ends of the earth; for the LORD hath a controversy with the nations, He will plead with all flesh; He will give them *that are* wicked to the sword,..." When we read the book of Revelation, the deaths are going to be astounding. It's going to be something. "Thus saith the LORD of hosts, Behold, evil shall go forth from nation to nation, and a great whirlwind shall be raised up from the coasts of the earth. And the slain of the LORD [as we're going to see this in Revelation 16 a little later] shall be at that day from *one* end of the earth even unto the *other* end of the earth: they shall not be lamented, neither gathered, nor buried; they shall be dung upon the ground" (Jer. 25:12-17, 26, 29-33). Then He lays it all at the feet of the pastors and the shepherds. So there we have quite a situation with this as it is coming.

Let's come back here to Revelation 13. Let's see how all of this is going to develop. Now after seeing the events that have been taking place in Iraq, seeing the events that are transpiring with the United Nations, I'm more convinced in my own mind—so this is my own opinion—but I'm more convinced in my own mind than ever before that the United Nations is going to have to be reformed and reconstituted. And I think that it will probably take place in Europe. Now there are a lot of scandals coming out concerning how the U.N. has been run. There are some books coming out which are going to expose it, so that means that it's going to have to be reformed. Which means that we have more time than the end coming just next year or the year after, or however long it will be. But you see, there is one thing we need to do: we need to always be ready. And as it says in the King James - we need to occupy. That means we need to be doing. And as we see the day coming closer we need to put forth the effort, we need to draw close to God, we need to be filled with His Spirit.

Now, Revelation 13 tells us how this whole world–wide system is going to develop. And it's going to be awesome indeed. And there is going to come out of it the false Christ, the false messiah who is called the beast. And the world is being set-up for it. Part of it has to do with the movie "The Passion," part of it has to do with *The Da Vinci Code* and the holy grail, and the movie that is coming out. Part of it has to do with how everything is being organized worldwide. Part of it has to do with the mark of the beast. Part of it has to do with the other events that are taking place, but they are all focusing together on fulfilling Revelation 13 to an absolute "T."

Now let's begin in Revelation 13:1. John saw this prophecy taking place. "And I stood on the sand of the sea; and I saw a beast rising up out of the sea, having seven heads and ten horns,..." - the signs of Satan the devil. This is his system. And it's going to be his grandest most glorious system. "...And on his horns ten crowns, and upon his heads *the* name of blasphemy." Now this is going to be an unusual political set-up because it's going to amalgamate and bring in the best of all the civilizations in the past, so that it is going to look like this is a wonderful and a magnificent thing.

"And the beast that I saw was like a leopard [so it's going to have swift military], and his feet like *the feet* of a bear [it's going to have power], and his mouth like *the* mouth of a lion; and the dragon gave him his power, and his throne and great authority." So all of this comes from Satan the devil. God is going to let Satan the devil rise to where he's going to be convinced in his own mind that he's going to fulfill Isaiah 14 and finally have the forces, and finally have the ability, and finally have the capacity to rise and usurp the throne of God. And we will see how he's going to try and convince the nations to do that. And it's going to be quite a deception indeed.

Now let's continue on. Verse 3, "And I saw one of his heads as *if it were* slain to death, but his deadly wound was healed; and the whole earth was amazed *and* followed the beast." And you can see how quickly this will take place. You can see what a fantastic thing this is going to be. So here we have, if the prophecies are correct back there in Daniel 9, which they are. All the prophecies are correct. It's just a matter of our interpretation. So when we come to a final seven year period we're going to have the first three and a half years be some of the most astounding things with false prophets, with miracles, with calling fire down from heaven, with nations giving their power and authority to the beast, with peace coming on the earth. And yet the prophets of God and the ministers of God are going to be saying, "Don't be deceived. This is a deception and it's not going to work because this is not of God—this is of Satan the devil." And there are going to be some fanatics. Now we don't know who they are but maybe they're going to be fanatical Jews who will come and try and assassinate the beast so he receives a deadly wound, but his deadly wound is healed.

Now notice what happens after the deadly wound is healed. We'll see this here. "And they worshiped the dragon,…" That's why every vestige of Christianity must be destroyed in this plan that they're bringing about, so that Satan–worship, and witchcraft, and all of these things will be the predominant form of worship. And that's the only way that they are going to bring in a whole one-world religion, which will be an amalgamation. It will have parts of all the religions of the world just like the civil authority here has parts of all the great kingdoms of the world. But just like all the kingdoms of the world are going to give their power to the beast, all the religions of the world are going to give their power and authority to the second beast.

Now here's what they're going to do. "And they worshiped the dragon, who gave *his* authority to the beast. And they worshiped the beast, saying, 'Who *is* like the beast? Who has the power to make war against him?' And a mouth speaking great things and blasphemies was given to him; and authority was given to him to continue *for* forty-two months." So after the deadly wound is healed he continues for forty and two months. The same exact time that it talks about in Revelation 11 that Jerusalem is trodden down of the Gentiles. So one of the first moves that he makes, as we find in Daniel 11, is he's going to come against the king of the south, and he's going to go into the holy land and stand in the temple and he is going to say that he is God. Now won't that be interesting and profound if the beast power claims that he is of the Monrovian king line of Europe. And then everybody's going to be convinced (because of the movie "The Da Vinci Code", and other movies, and the book and so forth, that's coming out) that he actually has the genes of the physical Christ through Mary Magdalene. Isn't that something?

Now here's what's going to happen when he's possessed of Satan the devil, when he is raised up from that. "And he opened his mouth in blasphemy against God, to blaspheme His name, and His tabernacle, and those who dwell in heaven." You can put in your notes there II Thessalonians 2, that he goes into the temple of God and says that he himself is God. Well you know that's not going to stand. Now notice, "And he was given *power* to make war against the saints,…" So here is something that God always allows the wicked to do: to think that they are winning. And that's what happens—"…given *power* to make war against the saints, and to overcome them; and he was given authority over every tribe and language and nation." So here's the great counterfeit kingdom. Now notice, "And all who dwell on the earth will worship him, whose names have not been written in the book of life of the

Lamb slain from *the* foundation of *the* world. If anyone has an ear, let him hear." So there we have it. That's how it's going to be.

Now he's going to have a partner and that partner is going to be another beast. And that partner is going to be the false prophet. And he is going to do great signs and great wonders. Let's read it here, verse 11. "And I saw another beast rising out of the earth; and he had two horns like a lamb, but spoke like a dragon; and he exercises all the authority of the first beast before him; and he causes the earth and those who dwell therein to worship the first beast, whose deadly wound was healed. And he performs great wonders, so that he even causes fire to come down to the earth from heaven in the sight of men." Now you know the old saying: seeing is believing. And if he says "I am from God" and people see this they're going to say he's from God. But the question needs to be: which God? The God of heaven, or the god of this world? Because Satan is called the god of this world.

"And he deceives those who dwell on the earth by means of the wonders that were given to him to perform in the sight of the beast, saying to those who dwell on the earth that they should make an image for the beast, which had the wound by the sword, yet was alive. And he was given *power* to give life to the image of the beast, so that the image of the beast also could speak; and he causes everyone who will not worship the image of the beast to be killed." And that's when (how shall we say, the qualifying exam to receive the mark of the beast), to show that you are loyal to this new world government is going to be whether you will make the image, and fall down and worship the image. That's why it's absolutely profound that in every Catholic catechism the second commandment concerning idolatry is removed from the Ten Commandments. Yet, in their own Bibles, to show the gall, the hypocrisy, and to show how confident they are in their lying ability to change the Word of God, right in their own Bible they leave in the second commandment. So we're going to make that one of the first things on Biblical Truth Ministries: "Lies From the Pulpit", which by the time you view this video it will be up and going for quite a while, and I think you're really going to like it.

Now let's continue on here. "And he…" Now this "he" refers back to the first beast. And the second beast, undoubtedly the false prophet, is undoubtedly going to be the pope. It can't be anyone else. And all the religions of the world will acknowledge him just like they do the first beast. And they say, "Ah, now we have a wonderful system. We have cultural diversity. We have all of the good things that we have here: multi-culturalism and every one loves each other and accepts each other, except for those people who won't go along with this system and receive the mark of the beast, so they're going to be killed."

"And he causes all, the small and the great, and the rich and the poor,…" See, because it has to be a government edict to do it, to make it a requirement. "And he causes all, the small and the great, and the rich and the poor, and the free and the bond, to receive a mark in their right hands, or in their foreheads; so that no one may have the ability to buy and sell unless he has the mark, or the name of the beast, or the number of his name" (Rev. 13:1-9, 11-17). You can see how that is coming. I'm going to bring some sermons on the mark of the beast, which I hope to have out before the Feast of Trumpets. But it's going to be something. It's going to be everywhere, and in everything—this whole system, until the final thing is the mark of the beast in the right hand or in the forehead. Now it's going to be quite a thing that's going to take place.

Now let's come over here to Revelation 15 and 16, and let's see what's going to happen because this fills in the gap from Pentecost up to Trumpets. And it's going to be quite a thing. Let's ask the question: as we saw on Pentecost first there's the sign of the Son of man in heaven that shines like the light of day. And apparently it comes closer and closer, and closer, and closer, and closer to the earth. Everyone is going to see that. Everyone is going to know that something profound has happened, because as we saw on Pentecost the heavens are rolled back as a scroll. And God shakes the heaven and shakes the earth and shakes the sea and the dry land and everything that there is. It's going to be an awesome time indeed. Then the resurrection takes place and every one meets Christ in the air on the sea of glass. Now how big will the sea of glass be when it finally comes down to the earth close enough in the clouds? And I think it's going to be plenty close enough so that the people of the world are going to be able to see it, and that they are going to figure that this is an alien invasion, which is actually true from this point of view: We, and Christ, and the angels are the aliens. Not these silly looking things they depict in the movies, those are not aliens. Those are silly things for people to be deceived.

Now how big will the sea of glass be? How high will it be? It's going to be in the clouds. Now the highest clouds are 60,000 feet. So maybe it's going to be like 10,000 or 15,000 feet, but every eye is going to be able to see it. Now when the saints are resurrected on Pentecost does the sea of glass move around the earth in accordance with the sun, and the dead are raised and brought up to the sea of glass all during the time that it makes it's trip around the earth? And then does it stop and hover over Jerusalem? Now that's a very distinct possibility. How big will this be? Well it's going to be enough to accommodate all the saints, right? Yes, it will be. So let's read that again.

Let's review here in Revelation 15. "Then I saw another sign in heaven, great and awesome: seven angels having the seven last plagues,…" And this is going to lead up to the finality of Trumpets which will cap it off. "…For in them the wrath of God is filled up. And I saw a sea of glass mingled with fire, and those who had gotten the victory over the beast, and over his image, and over his mark, *and* over the number of his name, standing on the sea of glass, having *the* harps of God." So how big is this sea of glass going to be? We'll just review it here. They sing the song of Moses, they sing the song of the Lamb and then it says, verse 4, " 'Who shall not fear You, O Lord, and glorify Your name? For *You* only *are* holy; and all the nations shall come and worship before You,…' " Now that won't take place right away. That's a prophecy—shall. " '…For Your judgments have been revealed' " (Rev. 15:1-4). And then right after that we'll take a look at what happens.

Let's set the stage and see what the world is going to be like, and then bring it altogether in Revelation 16. First of all let's go to Isaiah 13:6. Let's see where it talks about the day of the Lord, and this is the day of the Lord, which He is going to execute upon the earth. Now it talks about the burden of Babylon in verse 1. So this is Babylon the great, as it's called there in Revelation 18. Babylon the great.

Verse 6, "Howl ye; for the day of the LORD *is* at hand; it shall come as a destruction from the Almighty. Therefore shall all hands be faint, and every man's heart shall melt: and they shall be afraid: pangs and sorrows shall take hold of them; they shall be in pain as a woman that travaileth: they shall be amazed one at another; their faces *shall be as* flames. Behold, the day of the LORD cometh, cruel both with wrath and fierce anger, to lay the land desolate: and He shall destroy the sinners thereof out of it." As we have seen before this is going to be so fantastic that, like it confirms here in verse 10, "For the stars of heaven and the constellations thereof shall not give their light: the sun shall be darkened in his going forth, and the moon shall not cause her light to shine. And I will punish the world…" Now I want you to understand and grasp that all of this is a world-wide setting. "…I will punish the world for *their* evil, and the wicked for their iniquity; and I will cause the arrogancy of the proud to cease [and that is personified in the beast and the false prophet], and will lay low the haughtiness of [men] the terrible. I will make a man more precious than fine gold; even a man than the golden wedge of Ophir. Therefore I will shake the heavens, and the earth shall remove out of her place, in the wrath of the LORD of hosts [the wrath of God is contained in the seven last plagues], and in the day of His fierce anger" (Isa. 13:6-13). And so God is going to execute His wrath.

Now as we've talked about, let's come here to Joel 2 and let's see where it describes the armies of Revelation 8 and 9, and then that leads up to where we will be in Revelation 15 and 16 again. So we need to set the stage so we know what is going on here. But notice the warning that is given. Joel 1 talks about the Day of the Lord. And the Feast of Trumpets is the Day of the Lord to execute His vengeance.

Joel 1:15, "Alas for the day! for the day of the LORD *is* at hand, and as a destruction from the Almighty shall it come." This is from God. This is not from man. But this is from God. We saw how men have their armies, how the things take place in Revelation 6. Then Revelation 8, it's the angels of God against Satan and the demons. And now here, God set's His hand. That's what it's going to culminate in. Now then, it talks about this army that comes from the east - the army of 200 million.

Now it talks about the Day of the Lord. Joel 2:1, "Blow ye the trumpet in Zion, and sound an alarm in My holy mountain: let all the inhabitants of the land tremble: for the day of the LORD cometh, for *it is* nigh at hand;…" And that's why we have to have the Feast of Trumpets so that we know, we understand that Christ is going to return. The Day of the Lord is coming, and it needs to be a warning for us that we get our lives right. And a warning for the world that they are going to know that it is God Who's intervening. The very God they rejected, the very one that they have despised, the very one that they figure is going to be a nice meek little lamb is coming and returning in power and glory and authority such as the world has never, never seen in the most awesome and profound way that will ever be. There will never be another day like this. We need to understand it, brethren. God has called us to participate in some awesome things.

Now let's continue here in Joel 2. "…A day of darkness and of gloominess, a day of clouds and of thick darkness, as the morning spread upon the mountains: a great people and a strong; there hath not been ever the like, neither shall be any more after it, *even* to the years of many generations" (Joel 2:1-2). That means all the way down through the Millennium. Of course when Christ is here ruling during the Millennium nothing like this is going to happen. This is the culmination and the end of the rule of man and Satan the devil, and it is coming in such a way that it is literally going to destroy almost everything on the earth. You see, the great cities of the nations need to be destroyed. All their temples, all their idols, everything that men have made is going to be destroyed. And so we're going to have quite a job rebuilding this earth. It is going to be something. I want us to have a little broader scope and understanding of what's going to take place. This is going to be God directly intervening and doing it.

Now then it talks about the army. And it's very interesting, the army comes and runs upon the walls and climbs in the houses. You know they have uniforms right now that they are developing for soldiers that will actually give medication to their bodies instantly when they are wounded so they can keep on going and fighting. And it sounds much like what they have here. And who knows what will happen. Will they develop an army where they implant chips? Will they put it into them and program them to go fight a battle and the generals are back there and the commanders are back there running all of these by remote controls? You know, all of these things are possible. We need to think about these things. This is going to be something.

Now let's ask the question: Where will the sea of glass finally come and be stationary? That's going to be over the area of Palestine. How big will it be? I've asked the question before, and I've asked it to myself many times because I've been thinking on this. Now Ben Ambrose wrote a very wonderful paper. He got together with a mathematics instructor and figured out the math of what it would take for every eye to see the return of Jesus Christ; how far out it would have to be when the sign of the Son of man is first seen; and how close it comes to the earth, and so forth. And he has the question: how big will the sea of glass be? Well it's going to have to be big enough to accommodate all the saints down through all the history of the world. So who knows how big that is going to be. Is it going to be fifty by fifty miles? Now that's pretty big. And what is the world going to think when they look up there and see this? And how do we know that it's going to be over Palestine? Right over Jerusalem? Well Joel 3 tells us.

Joel 3:2, "…I will also gather all nations, and will bring them down into the valley of Jehoshaphat, and will plead with them there for My people and *for* My heritage Israel, whom they have scattered among the nations,…" He's going to bring them down to the valley of Jehoshaphat. That is in the land of Palestine. We also will see a little later that that is called Armageddon. And it shows in other prophecies that the blood is going to run up to the horses bridle. You can figure blood being six to eight feet deep in the valley of Jehoshaphat. God is going to bring about a slaughter that is going to be just almost unreal. But that's the only way that God is going to be able to conquer this earth, get rid of Satan the devil, get rid of the demons, get rid of the armies, get rid of all of the things that man has done against God.

Now let's come here to Revelation 15. Now when they see the sea of glass up there and they begin to experience some of the things that God is doing to them, we're going to see what they're going to do. Now if you haven't seen the movie "Independence Day" you be sure and see that, because that shows how that in the midst of aliens from outer space coming to this earth, that all the nations get together and rescue the earth.

Let's come back to Revelation 15 and see how this is going to happen. Now we're going to change views. Now we're going to be looking at it from God's point of view down on the earth, rather than on the earth just seeing what is here. We're going to see it all and we're going to see how God is going to do it. This is going to be something. And this is going to fulfill another promise that God has given to all the saints where God has said, "Vengeance is Mine, says the Lord." And He's going to execute it.

Before we get into Revelation 15 let's come back to Psalm 149. This is quite a verse when you understand what it's saying here. And I believe this is talking about the time being on the sea of glass. Psalm 149:1, "Praise ye the LORD. Sing unto the LORD a new song, *and* His praise in the congregation of saints." Well, when is the congregation of the saints going to be all congregated together? At the resurrection. And where is that? On the sea of glass. "Let Israel rejoice in Him that made him: let the children of Zion be joyful in their King. Let them praise His name…" And isn't that what it says we do back in Revelation 15? We sing the song of Moses, the song of the Lamb, and here's another one we're going to sing. "Let them praise His name in the dance: let them sing praises unto Him with the timbrel and harp. For the LORD taketh pleasure in His people: He will beautify the meek with salvation." And that salvation is to be in glorified form, isn't it? And we receive that and we're on the sea of glass. "Let the saints be joyful in glory:…" You're going to look at your new body, you're going to look at your new self and we're going to be joyful in that. God is going to give us something marvelous. "…Let them sing aloud upon their beds. *Let* the high *praises* of God *be* in their mouth, and a two-edged sword in their hand; to execute vengeance upon the heathen, *and* punishments upon the people; to bind their kings with chains, and their nobles with fetters of iron; to execute upon them the judgment written: this honour have all His saints. Praise ye the LORD" (Psa. 149:1-9). So we're going to do it.

Now let's go to Psalm 2 and let's look down on the earth and God's perspective and see what's happening. "Why do the heathen rage, and the people imagine a vain thing?" To even imagine that they can fight against God and win - is anything more vain than that? "The kings of the earth set themselves, and the rulers take counsel together, against the

LORD, and against His anointed,…" So they're going to say, "Look, if we can turn back these aliens, which are up here on whatever kind of apparatus this is,…" And I imagine that they're trying to shoot rockets up there, they're trying to shoot off other things to try and destroy it and it just bounces off as if it's nothing. They are really going to be really raging. This is going to be something indeed.

"…*Saying,* Let us break their bands asunder, and cast away their cords from us. He that sitteth in the heavens shall laugh: the Lord shall have them in derision. Then shall He speak unto them in His wrath, and vex them in His sore displeasure. Yet have I set My king upon My holy hill of Zion. I will declare the decree: the LORD hath said unto Me, Thou *art* My Son; this day have I begotten Thee. Ask of Me, and I shall give *thee* the heathen *for* thine inheritance, and the uttermost parts of the earth *for* thy possession. Thou shalt break them with a rod of iron; thou shalt dash them in pieces like a potter's vessel" (Psa. 2:1-9).

Now let's come back to Revelation 15 and see how that's going to be, because that's exactly what we're looking at here. Viewing now from the sea of glass, here's what's going to take place. Verse 5, "And after these things I looked, and behold, the temple of the tabernacle of the testimony in heaven was opened." So here the saints are going to see all of that. "And the seven angels who had the seven *last* plagues came out of the temple; they were clothed in linen, pure and bright, and girded about the chest with golden breastplates." Quite a thing, isn't it? Here are these angels to do the will of God. This is how God is going to fight against them - directly from Him. Right out of His temple. "And one of the four living creatures gave to the seven angels seven golden vials, full of the wrath of God, Who lives into the ages of eternity. And the temple was filled with smoke from the glory of God, and from His power; and no one was able to enter inside the temple until the seven plagues of the seven angels were fulfilled" (Rev. 15:5-8,).

Then Revelation 16:1, "Then I heard a loud voice from the temple say to the seven angels, 'Go and pour out the vials of the wrath of God onto the earth.' And the first *angel* went and poured out his vial onto the earth; and an evil and grievous sore fell upon the men who had the mark of the beast, and upon those who were worshiping his image." Now, it's going to be something because the Mark of the Beast is not just an accounting system, and buying and selling system. It is for total control. And so when these people give up their free moral agency to Satan the devil they are going to pay the price. And so this grievous sore, whatever it's going to be … I don't know if it's going to start where the Mark of the Beast is and spread to the whole body—on their hand or on their forehead - it doesn't tell us. But that is their just punishment. Probably most of them will die.

Verse 3, "And the second angel *went and* poured out his vial into the sea; and it became blood, like *that* of a dead *man*; and every living soul in the sea died." The whole ocean is going to become a putrefying stench of dead fish, and dead whales, and dead men, and sunken ships. It's going to be awesome. See, when Satan and men get together and defy God, and think that they can turn back the hand of God then God has to intervene and let them know Who is in charge. And notice all of these weapons God can use at any time. These are the same weapons that He used back when He fought against Pharaoh, right? Remember in the book of Exodus? Yes, indeed.

Verse 4, "And the third angel poured out his vial upon the rivers, and into the fountains of waters; and they became blood." Now what's this going to do to all the eco-freaks out there? Environmental Nazis. You see, God is going to destroy it. We need to understand that. We need to understand this: The only thing worth saving on this earth will be Israel, and the people that repent. Otherwise God would utterly destroy it all. But because He says He won't, He's not going to.

Now, how did the angels view this? How should we view this kind of destruction? There are going to be some people who say, "Well, that's not the Jesus that I worship." Well let me tell you something. If the Jesus you worship is not Almighty and can't do these things, he is not the true Jesus Christ of the Bible.

Here's how the angels view it. "Then I heard the angel of the waters say, 'You are righteous, O Lord, Who are, and Who was, even the Holy One, in that You have executed this judgment. For they have poured out *the* blood of saints and of prophets, and You have given them blood to drink; for they are worthy.' " So there is the complete vengeance of God. "And I heard another *voice* from the altar say, 'Yes, Lord God Almighty, true and righteous *are* Your judgments.' " True and righteous—that God says, "Yes, the men on this earth deserve this." This is His judgment. Well, that's why Jeremiah said that the dead are going to be strewn from one end of the earth to the other end of the earth, as far as the eye can see.

"And the fourth angel poured out his vial upon the sun; and *power* was given to it to scorch men with fire." And notice the attitude [of men] of all these things coming. You would think that they would repent. You would think that they would have some fear of God, wouldn't you? No, they don't. What happens? "...They blasphemed the name of God, Who has authority over these plagues, and did not repent to give Him glory." That's quite a thing.

Now then, to show how profound and evil that the beast, and the false prophet, and Satan are, "...the fifth angel poured out his vial upon the throne of the beast; and his kingdom became full of darkness; and they gnawed their tongues because of the pain,..." So can you imagine having the Mark of the Beast, the grievous sore, having blood to drink instead of water, having been scorched by the sun, and now it's so dark, probably just like it was back there in Egypt, that they felt the darkness. Back then they stayed in bed for three days. Couldn't go out. And yet, it says, "...they did not repent of their works."

Now here's the last ditch effort that's going to take place. You talk about Satan deceiving to the very end, and men being gullible to believe it. Let's read it here. "And the sixth angel poured out his vial into the great river Euphrates; and its waters were dried up, so that the way of the kings from the rising of *the* sun might be prepared." So the armies are still there. You see, God hasn't done this to everybody, everywhere. The armies are still going to come. "Then I saw three unclean spirits like frogs *come* out of the mouth of the dragon, and out of the mouth of the beast, and out of the mouth of the false prophet; for they are spirits of demons working miracles, going forth to the kings of the earth, even of the whole world, to gather them together to *the* battle of that great day of the Almighty God." So they're all being gathered for this battle. And this is the final climactic battle of all the disasters and wars and holocausts that have taken place in the great tribulation. This is the finality, and that's what this day of Trumpets pictures—the final battle, the final war, the final end of these things.

And then He gives a little warning here. "Behold, I come as a thief. Blessed *is* the one who is watching [now this is a warning for us] and is keeping his garments, so that he may not walk naked and they *may not* see his shame." In other words, here's a warning to the Laodiceans when they're reading these things that they better get their lives squared around. Instead of being lukewarm and ho-hum, and all glad-handing and all socializing and all of these things, brethren, we have got a tremendous mission ahead of us. We've got the greatest thing to look forward to that has ever been since the creation of the world, and we are going to be a part of all of these events that are going to culminate in the end of the rule of man and Satan the devil. Now that's something. And when you read back there in Romans 8, the world is waiting for the manifestation of the sons of God. That's us. The first thing they're going to do though, is fight against God.

Now verse 16, "And he gathered them together to the place that in Hebrew is called Armageddon [valley of Jehoshaphat]." Now they're all there. They're all ready to fight, and God ends it quickly. "Then the seventh angel poured out his vial into the air; and a loud voice came out of the temple of heaven, from the throne, saying, 'IT IS FINISHED.' And there were voices and thunders and lightnings; and there was a great earthquake, such as was not since men were on the earth, so mighty an earthquake, *and* so great." That's something. You read through the book of Revelation—this earth is going to be shaken, and shaken, and shaken, and shaken, and shaken, over and over again all during that last three and a half year period. And here's the greatest earthquake that has been.

"And the great city was divided into three parts; and the cities of the nations fell;..." All their buildings are going to collapse. Everything in these big cities is going to be utterly ruined and destroyed. "...And Babylon the Great was remembered before God to give her the cup of the wine of the fury of His wrath. And every island disappeared, and no mountains were found;..." So there's no place to go hide. God is going to make it: you either repent and get right with Him or the end is here. "...And great hail, *each stone* the weight of a talent [180 pounds], fell down from heaven upon men; and men blasphemed God because of the plague of the hail, for the plague was exceedingly great" (Rev. 16:1-21). What an awesome thing that this is. That's how Christ is going to return. It is going to be something. It is going to be absolutely just the most fantastic thing that we could ever imagine.

Now let's come to Revelation 19 and we'll see the finale. Verse 1, "And after these things I heard *the* loud voice of a great multitude in heaven,..." That is on the sea of glass, up in the clouds, in the first heaven—not the third heaven. But Christ is coming down. God the Father will come down, perform the marriage and the time of giving rewards to the saints and all of this sort of thing, so we understand what we're going to do and how we're going to do it and so forth. And after the seventh last plague is poured out the great multitude in heaven saying, " '...Hallelujah! The salvation and the glory and the honor and the power *belong* to the Lord our God [now this is the hymn we're going to sing]. For true and righteous *are* His judgments; for He has judged the great whore, who corrupted the earth with her fornication, and He has avenged the blood of His servants at her hand.' And they said a second time, 'Hallelujah! And her smoke shall ascend upward into the ages of eternity.' " In other words that smoke is going to go up and go out into the vastness of the universe and there will be specks of it just going on clear out through the whole galaxy and the universe.

"And the twenty-four elders and the four living creatures fell down and worshiped God, Who sits on the throne, saying, 'Amen. Hallelujah!' And a voice came forth from the throne, saying, 'Praise our God, all His servants, and all who fear Him, both small and great.' And I heard a voice like that of a great multitude, and like *the* sound of many waters, and *the* sound of mighty thunderings, saying, 'Hallelujah! For *the* Lord God Almighty has reigned. Let us be glad and shout with joy; and let us give glory to Him; for the marriage of the Lamb has come, and His wife has made herself ready.' " Now this is the beginning of the salvation of the world. So know and understand this: when God sets His hand to save the world He's going to save it. But in order to save it, it's going to have to be nearly destroyed.

"And it was granted to her that she should be clothed in fine linen, pure and bright; for the fine linen is the righteousness of the saints. And he said to me, 'Write: Blessed *are* those who are called to the marriage supper of the Lamb.' And he said to me, 'These are the true words of God.' " So they are going to take place. They are going to come to pass. And see, the world won't know this because they don't keep the feasts of God. They don't keep the Sabbath, the Passover, Unleavened Bread, Pentecost, Trumpets, Atonement, Tabernacles, or the Last Great Day. They don't know what God is doing. But God has revealed that to us—His mystery and His secret plan that He has proposed in Himself. And we are an intricate part of this. So brethren, see, these words are the true Words of God.

"Then I fell at his feet to worship him. And he said to me, 'See *that you do* not *do this*! I am a fellow servant of yours, and of your brethren, who have the testimony of Jesus. Worship God. For the testimony of Jesus is the spirit of prophecy.' And I saw heaven open; and behold, a white horse; and He Who sat on it *is* called Faithful and True, and in righteousness He does judge and make war." Now the final battle comes. This is going to be awesome indeed.

"And He eyes *were* like a flame of fire, and on His head *were* many crowns; *and* He had a name written that no one knows except Him. And *He was* clothed with a garment dipped in blood; and His name is The Word of God." Now that goes right back to the beginning of the Gospel of John. "And the armies in heaven were following Him on white horses; …" That's going to be us. So we're going to be given a spiritual horse. We're going to get on it and we're going to go. "…*And* they were clothed in fine linen, white and pure." Now Christ is going to do the fighting. "And out of His mouth goes a sharp sword, that with it He might smite that nations; and He shall shepherd them with an iron rod; and He treads the winepress of the fury and the wrath of the Almighty God." See, God is saving up all of this for one last final battle. And it's going to be something.

"And on *His* garment and on His thigh He has a name written: King of kings and Lord of lords. Then I saw an angel standing in the sun; and he cried out with a loud voice, saying to all the birds that fly in *the* midst of heaven, 'Come and gather yourselves together to the supper of the great God so that you may eat *the* flesh of kings, and *the* flesh of chief captains, and *the* flesh of mighty *men*, and *the* flesh of horses, and of those who sit on them, and *the* flesh of all, free and bond, and small and great.' And I saw the beast and the kings of the earth and their armies, gathered together to make war with Him Who sits on the horse, and with His army." So here John was looking down and seeing that. That's what we're going to see when we start coming down off the sea of glass, and we're on those white horses and we're coming down with Christ and here are the birds flying, circling, coming for all this flesh that is going to be. And here we're coming down out of the clouds with Christ on our horses. And so that's going to be quite a thing.

Let's go back to the book of Zechariah now and let's pick up some more, as Paul Harvey would say "the rest of the story." Now let's see what's going to happen to those that fight against Christ. This is going to be quite a thing. There's no defense for this. It doesn't matter what kind of army that you think you have. It doesn't matter what weapons you think you may have. No one's going to be able to fight against this. Zechariah 14:12 (hold your place there when we're done with it because we'll come back there again in a minute), "And this shall be the plague wherewith the LORD will smite all the people that have fought against Jerusalem;…" That's where He's gathered them, right? Yes. "…Their flesh shall consume away while they stand upon their feet, and their eyes shall consume away in their holes, and their tongue shall consume away in their mouth." In other words the flesh is just going to fall off their bodies, and the flesh is just going to collapse and the skeletons fall over, and that's the end of the enemy. Now you tell me what man has any power against God to stop that? No man has.

Now let's come back to Revelation 19. The first thing that needs to be done is you need to get rid of the leaders. Verse 20, "And the beast was taken, and with him the false prophet who worked miracles in his presence, by which he had deceived those who received the Mark of the Beast and those who worshiped his image. Those two were cast alive into the lake of fire, which burns with brimstone;…" So God preserves them alive. Their flesh doesn't fall off them like the others. But they just look at their armies and see all of this going on and all of their soldiers just becoming like crumpled heaps of rotten flesh and bones, and blood spewing everywhere, and guts spewing everywhere. You know, this is going to be an awesome sight. "And the rest were killed by the sword of Him Who sits on the horse, *even the sword* that goes out of His mouth; and all the birds were filled with their flesh" (Rev. 19:1-21).

Now back to Zechariah 14. Here's what's going to happen, because we are coming back to this earth. Christ is going to stand on the Mount of Olives. Now remember, when Christ ascended into heaven, from where did He ascend? From the Mount of Olives. So He's coming right back to the Mount of Olives. And what did the angels say when the apostles were looking up and wondering what was happening to Him? He said, "Why are you gazing up into the heavens? This same Christ is going to return in the same way" (Acts 1:11, paraphrased). Yes, and to the same place. Amazing, isn't it?

Now let's pick it up in verse 3. "Then shall the LORD go forth, and fight against those nations, as when He fought in the day of battle. And His feet shall stand in that day upon the mount of Olives, which *is* before Jerusalem on the east, and the mount of Olives shall cleave in the midst thereof toward the east and toward the west, *and there shall be* a very great valley;…" So the whole geography is going to change, isn't it? Yes indeed. So much for the Temple Mount. That's going to be utterly destroyed, isn't it? Yes indeed. "And ye shall flee *to* the valley of the mountains; for the valley of the mountains shall reach unto Azal: yea, ye shall flee, like as ye fled from before the earthquake in the days of Uzziah king of Judah: and the LORD my God shall come, *and* all the saints with Thee." We're going to put our feet on the mount of Olives with Him. Now notice verse 9, "And the LORD shall be King over all the earth:…" (Zech. 14:3-5, 9). That's what it's going to be.

Now the rest of the story is continued with the next holy day—the Day of Atonement, because there is yet one more judgment that needs to be taken place, and that is to get rid of Satan the devil.

End of Sermon

Transcriber: Carolyn Singer

The Feast of Trumpets—Sermon I—Holy Day
September 16, 2004
Scriptural References

1) Leviticus 23:23-24

2) Numbers 10:2, 5, 9-10

3) II Peter 3:1-4

4) Daniel 2:44-45

5) Daniel 7:13-14, 27

6) Daniel 12:1

7) Jeremiah 25:12-17, 26, 29-33

8) Revelation 13:1-9, 11-17

9) Revelation 15:1-4

10) Isaiah 13:6-13

11) Joel 1:15

12) Joel 2:1-2

13) Joel 3:2

14) Psalm 149:1-9

15) Psalm 2:1-9

16) Revelation 15:5-8

17) Revelation 16:1-21

18) Revelation 19:1-21

19) Acts 1:11

20) Zechariah 14:12, 3-5, 9

CHAPTER THIRTY-ONE

The Feast of Trumpets—Sermon II—Holy Day

September 23, 2006

Greetings brethren, welcome to the Feast of Trumpet's 2006. And we've certainly seen a lot of things transpire this past year. And every year we get closer and closer to the fulfillment of the events that are prophesied in the Bible, and of course the Feast of Trumpet's is one of the key important—as you might say—fulcrum points in history because this day pictures the establishing of the Kingdom of God on earth by Jesus Christ and the saints.

Now let's come to Leviticus 23. Let's also understand all of the holy days are connected, the Sabbath puts us in contact with God, the holy days tell us what he's doing—and let's understand something about the holy days—though they seem unimportant to the world, they are absolutely important to God. Because what people don't understand about the holy days is this: Every one of the holy days pictures an epical historical event that God fulfills. For example, the Sabbath, right after the creation of man: It was given as a day of rest, sanctified to be holy. It was an epical beginning of man and his relationship with God. And then we come down to the Passover, epical historical event with Abraham, with the children of Israel, an epical historical event with the killing of the firstborn, the destruction of Egypt, and then the first day of the Feast of Unleavened Bread, the exodus to leave. Pentecost, the giving of the 10 Commandments, an epical historical event.

And then we come right down through the New Testament with all of these. Passover, the greatest event to take place from the beginning of the history of the world, the prophecy of the death of the Son of God. Who would save the world from sin, happened on the Passover day. And the first day of the Feast of Unleavened Bread, He was, right as it began, He was put into the tomb. Three days and three nights later, He was resurrected, toward the end of the Sabbath. And then on the wave sheaf offering day, He ascended to heaven, an epical historical event. And then Pentecost, the beginning of the church, an epical historical event, and the resurrection from the dead for the first resurrection on Pentecost. An epical historical earthshaking event as we saw on the day of Pentecost. And now we come down to the Feast of Trumpets, and again, it is going to be an epical and historical event, and profound, telling the plan of God, lying out step-by-step how He's going to fulfill it. And it's not generally revealed to the world because the world doesn't know, the world doesn't understand. And especially today, as Satan is deceiving the whole world with all of these false gospels, and Gnostic gospels, and things like this, and people just going after it head over heels.

So we come to the Feast of Trumpets, and the Feast of Trumpets is an epical event that is going to take place. Now let's come to Leviticus 23, and pick up here in verse 23, "Then the LORD spoke to Moses, saying, 'Speak to the children of Israel, saying: "In the seventh month, on the first *day* of the month, you shall have a Sabbath…" so all the holy days are a Sabbath, " '…a memorial of blowing of trumpets, a holy convocation. No servile work is to be done, and to make an offering made by fire unto the LORD' " (Lev. 23:23). And so with all the holy days because these picture major events that God is going to do, these are special, and we should bring an offering that is special to God. And we should always realize that we are to seek first the kingdom of God in His righteousness.

481

And then the blessings that God gives us then, are to be reflected in the offerings that we give to God. So you know all about that, and brethren, just realize that we try and use everything that God sends us to preach the word of God, to publish the gospel, to send out books to people, to help them in their circumstances. And we are not here to build an organization; we are not here to build up the name of any man. We are here to preach the truth of God, to help and serve the brethren, and to make known the word of God as much as possible, as God will open the doors for us to reach out to the world, which we're doing in a very dramatic way with the book now that was published this last summer, "Occult Holidays or God's Holy Days—Which?" And in there, it contains the entire plan of God, and it is going to be a fantastic book, having an impact on people such as never has been in recent years. So keep all of that in mind when you send in your tithes or offerings for the holy days, and remember that God is able to give back to you in blessing [so] that all of us will have sufficiency in all things. So at this time we'll take a pause, and we'll take up the offering.

And now brethren, let's continue on and see the meaning of the day of the Feast of Trumpets, which is going to be one of the most, as we can say earthshaking events to hit the world since its creation. Now, let's come to Matthew the 6th chapter, Matthew the 6th chapter because this is part of our prayer, when we pray, according to the model prayer. So let's pick it up here, Matthew 6:9, "Therefore, you are to pray after this manner: 'Our Father Who *is* in heaven, hallowed be Your name.' " Now, when you are praying that way, just remember, you're coming before God the Father on His throne, Jesus Christ at His right hand, the 24 elders out in front before the throne, and around the throne is a rainbow and it sits on the sea of glass. There are thousands, and thousands, and 10,000 times 10,000 angels there praising God, and the message is "Holy, Holy, Holy, Lord God Almighty, which was, and is to come, for all these things have been created for your will, and your pleasure." So when we say "Your will be done, on earth as *it is* in heaven" (Matt. 6:9-10), now it's always going to be done that way. But the reason that we pray for it this way, is because there is always a space of repentance that God gives. And whenever there's something that comes along that is going to be a disaster that's going to happen, that there is going to be a judgment by God, He always gives a time and space of repentance. Now we'll see that in several instances here, as we go through. That's why in Ezekiel 33, God says, you know, "O Israel, turn you, turn you, for I have no pleasure in the death of the wicked but that the wicked would turn from his way" (Ezek. 33:11, *KJV paraphrased*) And so, in everything that God does, there is that measure of repentance because God has given free moral agency and choice, and who knows what people will do. And so, that's why there is given that space. So, we need to realize that that's part of the will of God. And the reason that we do this, is this: So when we come to God, we don't come to God and pray to Him and pray for our will to be endorsed by God. Now it is true, as Jesus said that when we ask He will answer, and whatever we desire, He will give. Now that's according, if it is according to, the will of God.

Now, "Your Kingdom come," comes in two different ways. Number one, it comes to us upon conversion. Let's come back to Colossians the 1st chapter, and see that. Colossians 1, it comes to us when we are converted, not that the Kingdom of God becomes within, as some people say. That's not true. But we come under the jurisdiction of the kingdom of God and Jesus Christ, as our Lord, and Master, and High Priest in heaven right now, and soon coming King, when Jesus returns. Now let's pick up here in Colossians the 1st chapter, and let's see how the Kingdom of God comes to us, and in our Christian lives, in the way that we live, and walk, and so forth. Now He says in verse 10, Colossians 1, "That you may walk worthily of the Lord…" and this is our goal, this is what we need to do in everything we do. And we're going to talk about how we need to have the right kind of attitude and mind set in the end-time, so that we can do the will of God in our lives; that God will be with us; that God will help us; that God will bless us and strengthen us. "…unto all pleasing, being fruitful in every good work and growing in the knowledge of God." And all of this has to do with preparing for eternal life. See, because we are in training for eternal life; we're in training to be kings and priests; we're in training to rule this world. And the first place that begins is to let Christ rule in us. Now, verse 11, "Being strengthened with all power according to the might of His glory, unto all endurance and longsuffering with joy." So, regardless of our circumstances, we're always looking to God the Father; we're always looking to Jesus Christ. We are developing, and growing in heart, in mind, and spirit, in knowledge of God. And this gives us the strength, and this gives us the conviction, and this gives us the endurance of the longsuffering, "Giving thanks to the Father, Who has made us qualified for the share of the inheritance of the saints in the light." Now that's what God is doing and we have a literal, absolute, inheritance. Now we talked about that in the past. Now, verse 13, "Who has personally rescued us from the power of darkness and has transferred *us* unto the kingdom of the Son of His love" (Col. 1:10-13). Now that means this, that once we have been called, and have repented, and have been baptized, and received the spirit of God, then we are brought under the jurisdiction of Jesus Christ. We are under the jurisdiction of the Kingdom of God. So when we pray, "Your Kingdom come", we're praying, that in the first instance, that we are always subjected to the Kingdom of God, that is to God the Father and Jesus Christ.

Now when we understand that, we realize that there is no room for a hierarchical authoritarian government in the ministry of God, or as the Catholics have with their hierarchy. They say, outside of the hierarchical Catholic Church there is no salvation. Well that's a bunch of humbug. There is no salvation *in it* because salvation comes from God. So that's how we are there.

Now let's notice how it is to work in our lives, and in our hearts, and in our minds. Let's come over here to Chapter 3, and verse 14. And the reason I'm going through things is so that we can see, how do we have the attitude to face all the horrendous things that are going to take place as pictured by the Feast of Trumpets? Now last year, we saw all those hurricanes hit America, we had the tsunami, we've had earthquakes, we've had wars. And as we're going to see, that's just a start. Because what the Feast of Trumpets pictures—in the intervention of God, and the kingdom of God, coming on this earth, and God's judgment on the world. Because just as the Passover pictured the judgment of God against all the gods of Egypt, and against the firstborn in Egypt, so likewise from the time of Pentecost down through Trumpets it pictures the judgment of God on this world, and it is going to make what happened in Egypt look like child's play.

Now Chapter 3, verse 14, "Above all these things..." and He list all the character things as we covered during the Feast of Unleavened Bread, "*put on* love…" and that is the key. You must be fortified with the love of God, by loving Him with all your heart, all your mind, all your soul, all your being, and you're going to hear me say that over, and over, and over again because that is where our strength comes from. Because that is where we're going to receive the resolve that is going to guarantee that we will be faithful unto the end. That will give us the mind set, as we're going to see here, in a little bit, that we need to have to be able to be faithful to Christ in the face of the worst disasters that are going to come upon the face of the earth.

Now granted, many of us who are older, God is going to spare us, He is going to take us to the grave in peace and that will be our place of safety. That's fine, that's all part of God's purpose. But there are those of us who are going to have to live through it, and we're going to have to be strengthened with the Spirit of God. And you're not going to be strengthened when you see these things happening and all of the sudden, you start praying, and all of the sudden, you start studying—too late! You have to build and develop the character now. Verse 15, "Let the peace of God rule in your hearts, to which you were called into one body, and be thankful. Let the word of Christ dwell in you richly…" Now that's the whole key, we're to live by every word of God; we're to live by the words of Christ. And we're to have His words dwelling in us richly. Now let's look at it this way, if Christ is going to dwell in us, which He is, and God the Father is going to dwell in us, which He is, then the words of Christ ought to richly dwell in us too. Because that establishes our minds, establishes our hearts, establishes our thoughts, and gives us the defense against all the events that are going to take place in the world because you need to be defended here, mentally and spiritually first. Now notice, "…rule in your heart…" So let Christ rule in you. You stop and think about this for a minute—we have to just do a little sidebar here, as they call in legalese—Christ is to rule you, not the ministry. The Holy Spirit of God is to lead you, not the ministry. Yes, the ministry is here to teach, and to help, and give counsel, and advice. But the greatest advice is: Look to God the Father and Jesus Christ, not what we would do of ourselves, or the ministry would do for you. "To which you are called into one body and be thankful…" Yes, "Christ dwell in you richly in all wisdom, teaching and admonishing one another in psalms and hymns and spiritual songs, singing with grace in your hearts to the Lord" (Col. 3:14-16).

Now stop and think a minute, when Paul and Silas were cast into prison, what did they do? They prayed to God, and they sang, and God intervened and helped them, see. So in all circumstances, Paul was one who really set the standard here. Now, let's realize this, the kind of attitude we need to have is this: We need to be tenderhearted to God, and Jesus Christ, and the brethren. Now then, we need to have a mind and a forehead of flint, toward all the evils, and troubles that are coming in the world.

Now let's see that, let's come to Jeremiah the 1st chapter. Jeremiah the 1st chapter, and let's see what God told Jeremiah. Now Jeremiah had a really lonely ministry. He had no friends, he had no brethren, the only one he had was his secretary Baruch. And you read through the book of Jeremiah, and see the things that Jeremiah went through. God knew it was going to be difficult, so here's what He told him. He says here, Jeremiah the 1st chapter and let's pick it up in verse 15, Jeremiah 1:15, " 'For, lo, I will call all the families of the kingdoms of the north," now on the end-time God is going to call all the nations, He's going to gather all the nations, "saith the LORD; and they shall come, and they shall set every one his throne at the entering of the gates of Jerusalem, and against all the walls thereof round about, and against all the cities of Judah." That is all the armies of Nebuchadnezzar. "And I will utter my judgments…" Now, we're going to see that ties in with also with the Feast of Trumpets. "Against them touching all their wickedness, who have forsaken me, and have burned incense unto other gods, and worshipped the works of their own hands," And those two things apply to us today as never before. "Thou therefore gird thy loins, and arise, and speak to them all that I command thee: Be not dismayed", or that is discouraged, "at their faces, lest I confound thee before them." In other words, don't look to the circumstances and how other people react because that really doesn't make any difference. You have to be looking to God. " 'For, behold, I have made thee this day a fortified city, and an iron pillar, and brasen walls against the whole land, against the kings of Judah, against the princes thereof, against the priests thereof, and against the people of the land. And they shall fight against thee; but they shall not prevail against thee; for I *am* with thee,' saith the LORD, 'to deliver thee' " (Jer. 1:15-19).

Now let's understand, at the end-time, it's going to be very similar to the same thing. Did we not see on Pentecost how there's coming the martyrdom of the saints, and how are we going to endure that? We are going to be offered many different ways out aren't we, [we will be] given a chance to recant, given a chance to accept the beast, and the mark, and all the things that are there. Because remember, Revelation 13 says, what? That into the hands of the beast are given all nations and languages and kingdoms, and he goes to make war against those who have the spirit of Christ. And there's going to be that martyrdom.

Now let's come to, Isaiah 50, let's see how Jesus was strengthened, in a very similar way. How did Jesus endure everything that he had to do, through the crucifixion, the scourging, and the beating? Or, remember when he finished that prayer, and angels strengthened Him. And so, likewise, we need the power of God to strengthen us, and let's see what kind of mind that God gave him. Now tender toward God the Father inside, but there had to be the strength and the power on the outside, to not be overwhelmed with all the things that He was going to experience. Isaiah 50:5, "The LORD God hath opened mine ear, and I was not rebellious, neither turned away back." When we get into those situations, understand this, if you have opened the door for Christ in your mind, and Christ rules in your heart and mind, you have closed the door to turn back. It's exactly what happened with Christ. Now notice, so He could do this, "I gave my back to the smiters, and my cheeks to them that plucked off the hair:" Where they beat him and pulled his beard and smashed him in the face. "I hid not my face from shame and spitting. For the LORD God will help me; therefore shall I not be confounded; therefore have I set my face like a flint, and I know that I shall not be ashamed" (Is. 50:5-7). So this is the only way we're going to be able to face these things in the future.

Let's come to Ezekiel the 3rd chapter, and let's see what God told Ezekiel. Now of all the prophets, the two that had the most difficult ministry to do, were Jeremiah, but Ezekiel had the worst one of all. And if you read the book of the Ezekiel, just take it and read a couple chapters every day, and think about what he had to go through, think about what he had to endure.

Now let's pick up here in verse 4, Ezekiel 3, "And he said unto me, Son of Man, go, get thee unto the house of Israel, and speak with my words unto them. For thou *art* not sent to a people of a strange speech and of an hard language, *but* to the house of Israel; not to many people of a strange speech and of an hard language, whose words thou canst not understand. Surely, had I sent thee to them, they would have hearkened unto thee. But the house of Israel will not hearken unto thee; for they will not hearken unto me:" Now, the reason is this: When, as Jesus said, that lawlessness shall be multiplied, and the love of many shall grow cold, there's going to come a time of great evil, and people are not going to want to listen to the truth of God. That's why God has to intervene with the events that we see here. That's why God sends the two witnesses and their ministry. So we're talking about big earthshaking events that are going to take place. "For all the house of Israel *are* impudent and hardhearted. Behold, I have made thy face strong against their faces, and thy forehead strong against their foreheads. As an adamant harder than flint have I made thy forehand: fear them not, neither be dismayed at their looks, though they *be* a rebellious house. Moreover, he said unto me, Son of Man, all my words that I shall speak unto thee receive in thine heart, and hear with thine ears" (Ezek. 3:4-11). Then he was to preach that.

So this tells us, that when we come down to these times, we are not to back off from the message of God. We're not to make it softer and easier so that we don't offend people. Because Jesus said, "many are going to be offended", and it's going to be a time of great trouble and great difficulty.

Now let's come to Matthew the 24th chapter, and let's see something here. Let's see what it is going to be like. Great historical events of a magnitude that is unimaginable to the human mind—if you think the destruction of the tsunami was great, or if you think that some of the volcanic actions that we have had are great, or the earthquakes, or the floods, or the storms, hang on because they now know the global warming is a general warming of the whole solar system. Even Mars is having a global warming experience, and of course there's not one single gas driven car up there, is there, nor factories with huge smokestacks belching out carbon dioxide, right? Yes. Now there are two electrical satellite vehicles up there, and surely they are not causing Mars to have a global warming experience. And all of this is part of the things leading up to the time of the end, and all of this is going to upset the weather even more.

Now let's come here to Matthew 24. Now let's see something that's important concerning the day of the Lord. Matthew 24, and he says here, verse 15, "Therefore, when you see the abomination of desolation, which was spoken of by Daniel the prophet, standing in the holy place (the one who reads, let him understand), Then let those who are in Judea flee into the mountains. Let the one *who is* on the housetop not come down to take anything out of his house; And let the one *who is* in the field not go back to take his garments. But woe to those *women* who are expecting a child, and to those who are nursing infants in those days! And pray that your flight be not in *the* winter, nor on *the* Sabbath;" So here again, even in the midst of great trouble and difficulty what does God say, "remember the Sabbath day and to keep it holy." "For then shall there be great tribulation..." Now, how great? "...Such as has not been from *the* beginning of *the* world until this time, nor shall ever be *again*" (Matt. 24:15-21). Now we need to let those words sink in.

Now let's come back here to the book of Amos, and let's ask the question—so many ministers have used, "Oh, the events are speeding up! Oh, we really need you to send in more money so we can preach the gospel! Oh, we've got to hurry and get this done, and hurry and get that done!" Because what they do is that they want to speed up the day of the Lord, so they can kind of glory in their own self predictions of it. And those are the prophecies that Paul said would fail, and they've all failed, haven't they? Why? Because they're not relying on God, and they're not looking to the outline of God, as God has said. Now it hasn't happened yet because we have not comprehended how great God is going to let the kingdom of Satan become before He intervenes directly. And we don't know how many people God is going to call, and lead to repentance between now and that point. See, because God is interested in mercy, and not sacrifice. But when the time comes that God says it's going to happen, because it's under the authority of God the Father and Jesus Christ, it is going to happen. So preachers and men are not to get out there and say, "Oh hurry, the day of the Lord is coming!" And you look back at all the events. "Jesus is going to set his foot on the earth" in all these different years, it never happened, did it? Why, because they're not willing to put it in God's hands to let it happen. So here's God's answer to them, Amos 5:18, "Woe unto you that desire the day of the LORD! to what end *is* it for you? the day of the LORD *is* darkness, and not light. As if a man did flee from a lion, and a bear met him; or went into the house, and leaned his hand upon the wall, and a serpent bit him." So He's telling us very clearly, there is not going to be any relief once this starts. Yes, we'll see, Psalm 91, that God will protect you, but also up to a certain point, because there's going to be a martyrdom of the saints. And this is why we have to have the mind and attitude that Jesus Christ has. So we ask for a tender heart before God the Father and Jesus Christ, and loving the brethren in each other, but we ask for a forehead of flint against all the evil, and against all the things that are coming. Because if you get emotionally involved in all these events, as we're going to read about from here on, that's going to literally turn this world upside down, you will not be able to handle it. So we need to ask God for the strength so we can handle it. Now verse 20, "Shall not the day of the LORD *be* darkness, and not light? even very dark, and no brightness in it?" (Amos. 5:18-20)

Yes, now let's come to Zephaniah the 1st chapter, Zephaniah, since we're right close here, just over a couple of pages, and we'll get to the book of Zephaniah, and that's right before Haggai, so just a few pages over. Sometimes I try and have the scriptures so they're convenient to go to, other times I can't do that. Now let's pick it up here, in Chapter 1, verse 13, "Therefore their goods shall become a booty, and their houses a desolation: they shall also build houses, but not inhabit *them*; and they shall plant vineyards, but not drink the wine thereof. The great day of the LORD *is* near, *it is* near..." That's the message for our time.

Notice: He doesn't say exactly how far, or how close, but it's near. And even though we've had all these false alarms down through time, guess what, it is nearer than when we first believed. "…and hasteth greatly, *even* the voice of the day of the LORD: the mighty men shall cry there bitterly. That day *is* a day of wrath, a day of trouble and distress, a day of wasteness and desolation, a day of darkness and gloominess, a day of clouds and thick darkness, A day of the trumpet…" Because it is a memorial of the blowing of trumpets, and actually the fulfillment of the Feast of Trumpets is reserved for the end-time, and the very day of the Lord. There's only one fulfillment of the Feast of Trumpets that we find in the Old Testament, and that is in I Chronicles, the 5th chapter, when the temple was dedicated, and on the Feast of Trumpets. God put his presence in the temple. The only other fulfillment is the return of Christ. "…against the fenced cities…" No defense is going to help. "…against the high towers." Doesn't matter what weapons you have. "And I will bring distress upon men, that they shall walk like blind men, because they have sinned against the LORD: and their blood shall be poured out as dust, and their flesh as the dung" (Zeph. 1:13-17). And as Jeremiah said, in Jeremiah 25, "…the LORD has a controversy with the nations…" (Jer. 25:31). He's going to bring them all to Jerusalem, and in that day, the dead will be from one end of the horizon to the other end of the horizon.

Now let's see if we can at least begin to grasp this, perhaps no more than 1/10th of all the population of the earth is going to survive through the tribulation, and enter as physical human beings into the kingdom of God. So it's going to be a horrendous time. There will never ever, ever, ever, ever again be a day like this. Verse 18, "Neither their silver nor their gold shall be able to deliver them in the day of the LORD'S wrath; but the whole land shall be devoured by the fire of his jealousy: for he shall make even a speedy riddance of all them that dwell in the land" (Zeph. 1:18). Now God is going to spare some. There will be some who will escape, that is true.

Now since we're here, let's come back just a few pages, to the book of Joel. Let's come to Joel the 1st chapter, and let's see again the warning concerning the day of the Lord, and all the way through here, it is a day that has never ever had a historical parallel, not even in the destruction of Jerusalem. This is going to be a worldwide event, not like it was in Egypt, where He dealt with just one nation, but this is all nations, all peoples. And so, when we understand the plan of God, we need to realize, it covers the great and the major events in the Bible, and God has given us the knowledge and the understanding of it. Now here, Joel 1:15. "Alas for the day! for the day of the LORD *is* at hand, and as a destruction from the Almighty shall it come." And it's going to come. Chapter 2, verse 1, "Blow ye the trumpet in Zion…" Now I don't know what's going to happen when that Feast of Trumpets is fulfilled, and we'll get to the book of Revelation here in a minute, and see how it unfolds step-by-step-by-step. "Blow ye the trumpet in Zion, and sound an alarm…" So that means continuously blowing. "…in my holy mountain:" Where's it going to start. It's going to start from Mt. Zion in heaven above, and the sound, and the trumpets, and the blasting is going to come from God. And we'll see how that's going to be here in just a bit. "For the day of the LORD cometh, for *it is* nigh at hand; A day of darkness and of gloominess, a day of clouds and of thick darkness, as the morning spread upon the mountains: a great people and a strong; there hath not been ever the like…" We're going to see in Revelation 9, [there will be] huge armies, and one of them 200 million. And God is going to judge the world, and God is going to judge the nations, and they're all going to fight against Christ. "There hath not been ever the like, neither shall be any more after it, *even* to the years of many generations. A fire devoureth before them…" Great modern weapons that we have today, "And behind them a flame burneth: the land *is* as the garden of Eden before them, and behind them a desolate wilderness; yea, and nothing shall escape them. The appearance of them *is* as the appearance of horses;" and we'll read the fulfillment of that in Revelation, in just a bit. "So shall they run. Like the noise of chariots on the tops of mountains shall they leap, like the noise of a flame of fire that devoureth the stubble, as a strong people set in battle array. Before their face the people shall be much pained: all faces shall gather blackness." Because of all the events that are going to take place, "They shall run like mighty men…"

Now, I've read articles recently, where they're trying to improve the battle worthiness of troops on the ground. Where they have armor that cannot be penetrated with weapons, where they have medication put right into the garments themselves, so if any wound happens it immediately starts working to heal it, and keep them from getting any infection. They are working on putting chips in the minds of the soldiers to be able to give them instant recall to make them better in battle. So what it's talking about here, we could not picture this in the past until now, [but] we know what it's going to be like. "They shall climb the wall like men of war; and they shall march every one on his ways, and they shall not break their ranks: Neither shall one thrust another; they shall walk every one in his path: and *when* they fall upon the sword, they shall not be wounded." Isn't it amazing that today that's exactly what they're working on? "They shall run to and fro in the city; they shall run upon the wall, they shall climb up upon the houses; they shall enter in at the windows like a thief. The earth shall quake before them…" Now I want you to kind of, if you can, turn on the vision of your mind, to see, what an awesome event this is going to be. "The heavens shall tremble: the sun and moon shall be dark, and the stars shall withdraw their shining: And the LORD shall utter his voice before his army: for his camp *is* very great: for *he is* strong that executeth his word: for the day of the LORD *is* great and very terrible…" That is awesome for all the power and destructions that's going to take place. "Who can abide in it?" That is, live in it?

Now notice, whenever it comes to that point, there's a space of repentance. "Therefore also now, saith the LORD, turn ye *even* to me with all your heart, and with fasting, and with weeping, and with mourning: And rend your heart, and not your garments, and turn unto the LORD your God: for he *is* gracious and merciful, slow to anger, and of great kindness, and repenteth him of the evil" (Joel 1:15, 2:1-13).

Now this is a message directly to the children of Israel, of the hundred and forty-four thousand who repent, and are saved on that next to the last Pentecost.

Now let's continue on brethren. Let's come to Isaiah 13, and again, it's talking about the day of the Lord. Now let's understand something. It is a day of judgment, of death, of destruction; such as never has been since the creation of the world. And this day is going to be talked about all the way through the Millennium. And everybody is going to remember *this* day as we now remember what happened to Egypt, because what happened to Egypt, on the Passover, and the events leading up to the Passover, is going to happen to the whole world—the events leading up to Trumpets and the return of Christ. Now Isaiah 13:6, "Howl ye; for the day of the LORD *is* at hand; it shall come as a destruction from the Almighty. Therefore shall all hands be faint, and every man's heart shall melt: And they shall be afraid: pangs and sorrows shall take hold of them; they shall be in pain as a woman that travaileth: they shall be amazed at one another; their faces *shall be as* flames. Behold, the day of the LORD cometh, cruel both with wrath and fierce anger, to lay the land desolate:" And we will see, that goes out to the whole world. "And he shall destroy the sinners thereof out of it. For the stars of heaven and the constellations thereof shall not give their light: the sun shall be darkened in his going forth, and the moon shall not cause her light to shine. And I will punish the world for *their* evil…" So that's why God is letting all the evil increase, giving everyone a chance to have their fill of evil, whatever it may be, but also giving an opportunity of repentance, if they would. "…And the wicked for their iniquity; and I will cause the arrogancy of the proud to cease, and I will lay low the haughtiness of the terrible." Now that's the beast, and false prophet, and Satan the devil. "I will make a man more precious than fine gold;" Because 9/10th of the population is going to die in these events that are going to take place. "Even a man than the golden wedge of Ophir. Therefore I will shake the heavens, and the earth shall remove out of her place, in the wrath of the LORD of hosts, in the day of his fierce anger" (Is. 13:6-13).

Now let's come to Isaiah 24. Here's what God is going to do, He's going to literally shake this earth in a way that has never been. Let's pick it up here, in verse 18, Isaiah 24:18, "And it shall come to pass, *that* he who fleeth from the noise of the fear shall fall into the pit; and he that cometh up out of the midst of the pit shall be taken in the snare: for the windows from on high are open, and the foundations of the earth do shake."

Now going to Revelation here in just a minute and see that taking place. "The earth is utterly broken down, the earth is clean dissolved…" or that is, torn asunder; great earthquakes are born "the earth is moved exceedingly." It's going to affect the orbit of the earth. It says, "And the earth shall reel to and fro like a drunkard, and shall be removed like a cottage; and the transgression thereof shall be heavy upon it; and it shall fall, and not rise again. And it shall come to pass in that day, *that* the LORD shall punish the host of the high ones that *are on* high…" (All the leaders of the world all of the powers and principalities of Satan the devil) "And the kings of the earth upon the earth. And they shall be gathered together, *as* prisoners are gathered in the pit, and shall be shut up in the prison…" And we're going to see, God is going to entrap them in that war. "And after many days shall they shall be visited. Then the moon shall be compounded, and the sun ashamed, when the LORD of hosts shall reign in Mount Zion, and in Jerusalem, and before his ancients gloriously" (Is. 24:18-23). And of course the ancient ones are going to be all of those who've been raised from the dead.

Now let's come back to the book Revelation. Now let's come to Revelation the 6th chapter, and let's pick it up where we left off in Pentecost. Because remember all the holy days are connected one with another, and here in Revelation 6, we see, between Revelation 6 and Revelation 7, that after the heavens roll back as a scroll, and this is what we just read about here in the Old Testament that is going to take place. And after the martyrdom has taken place, then there comes a space of time of repentance in Chapter 7 with 144,000 and the great innumerable multitude, are then sealed, waiting for the next Pentecost. So from Pentecost, when they are converted, to the last Pentecost, a space of one year, these are the laborers who were hired at the eleventh hour. Now they're going to be saved, they're going to enter into the Kingdom of God. Then, we come to Chapter 8. Now, let's picture this: It is running from Trumpets to Trumpets, from the next to the last Trumpets to [the last] Trumpets. And as we come down in time, when the resurrection takes place, there is still four months left until the Feast of Trumpets and its fulfillment. So we have here a whole year, and if our estimation of time is correct, it is a 13 month year. So that gives a little more space of time. But here's what happens, here is how it's fulfilled, we read a lot of it, but here is how it's going to be fulfilled beginning with next to the last of the Feast of Trumpets down to the last of the Feast of Trumpets, before Christ and the saints put their feet on the earth. Now let's begin, Revelation 8, "Now when He opened the seventh seal, *there* was silence in heaven *for* about a half hour." So there again, a time, a respite, and we read of that back in Joel the 2nd chapter, a time of repentance, that God always gives, before He starts pouring out his wrath. Now we'll talk about the wrath of God here, a little bit later. "Then I saw the seven angels who stand before God, and seven trumpets were given to them. And another angel, who had a golden censer, came and stood at the altar; and much incense given to him, so that he might offer *it* with the prayers of all the saints on the golden altar that *was* before the throne." Now this is a time, all the brethren, all the saints, are going to be calling out to God day and night. There isn't going to be any laxness in prayer in these days. It's going to be almost constant prayer. "O, Lord help me, O, Lord watch over me, O, Lord spare me, O, give me strength. Let my mind be fixed. Let me have the same attitude as Jesus Christ and Jeremiah and Ezekiel, to withstand all the events that we're going through." So they're coming up before God, "And the smoke of the incense went up before God from *the* hand of the angel, ascending with the prayers of the saints." So we're all directly involved in this. Now here's what's going to happen. God begins fighting against men, who are led by Satan and his demons. He's going to fight against them with His angels. Now here is direct intervention from heaven above. Everything else that took place in Revelation the 6th chapter, where all of those things that took place because of the efforts of men, and their armies, and so forth. And those seals that were opened, ended then, with the sixth seal, in their Revelation of the sign of the Son of Man in heaven above.

Now God begins to deal in a different way because this is the day of the Lord, from Trumpets to Trumpets, the year of the Lord. "And the angel took the censer, and filled it with fire from the altar, and cast *it* into the earth; and there were voices, and thunderings, and lightnings, and an earthquake" (Rev. 8:1-5). We're going to see they're going to be a lot of earthquakes. It says, back there in Isaiah 40, "Every valley shall be exalted, and every mountain and hill shall be made low:" (Is. 40:4). So when it says they're turning the earth upside down, what it is, it's turning of the surface of the earth upside down. That's going to result in earthquakes, and volcanoes, and it's going to be a horrendous thing. That's why I want us to grasp, and to understand how important the holy days really are: that they picture the major mammoth events, orchestrated and carried out, and fulfilled by God the Father, and Jesus Christ, and the angels. And here's the angelic intervention, verse 6, "Then the seven angels who had the seven trumpets prepared themselves to sound *their* trumpets. And the first angel sounded *his* trumpet; and there was hail and fire mingled with blood, and it was cast upon the earth; and a third of the trees were burnet up, and all green grass was burnt up." Now what's going to happen with all the hail, and darkness, and everything? Well, there's going to be a lot of rain storms that will come right after that, just like we see every year, right? We see fires out here in California, and fires burn up grass. See fires in forest and the mountain areas; we see fires in Florida, and all of that. And then what happens after that? The rain comes, and the floods and destruction.

Now verse 8, "Then the second angel sounded *his* trumpet; and *there* was cast into the sea as *it were* a great mountain burning with fire, and a third of the sea became blood." Now with all of these things taking place and all of those who are dying on the earth because of it, those who survive are going to be firmly convinced that this must be war from heaven—which it is. There's no convincing about it, you see. And that the aliens are preparing to invade the world, which they are, Jesus Christ and the saints. And, as I mentioned on Pentecost, when they see the resurrection take place, and I think they're going to see the resurrection take place, all these people being taken up to the sea of glass—well I'm getting a little ahead of myself here in the flow of the events, but nevertheless, they are going to be absolutely convinced of this alien invasion, and an asteroid hitting the earth, because that's what is being described here, "a great mountain burning with fire." An asteroid hits the earth, think of the tsunamis, think of the earthquakes, think of what's going to happen then. And when that happens then, "a third part of the sea became blood," So it doesn't affect the whole earth yet. It's in different areas of the earth. So if we can look at the orb of the earth, and kind of picture—well it happens here, say, in the Atlantic Ocean, or in the Indian Ocean, and it happens later over in the Pacific Ocean, and so forth. Here's what's going to happen, "And a third of the living creatures that *were* in the sea died, and a third of the ships were destroyed." You think about the giant mammoth ships they're building now, being destroyed. Think about all of these tankers carrying the oil, being destroyed and split open. Verse 10, "And the third angel sounded *his* trumpet; and *there* fell out of heaven a great star, burning like a lamp; and it fell upon the third part of the rivers, and on the fountains of waters. Now the name of the star is called Wormwood." So because they wouldn't obey God, and they martyred the saints, God is going to give them the bitterness of their way back to them. "And a third of the waters became wormwood; and many men died from *drinking* the waters because they were made bitter." They are going to be so thirsty, they're going to say, "Oh let us drink of it, if we live, we live. If we die, we die." "Then the fourth angel sounded *his* trumpet; and a third part of the sun was smitten, and the third part of the moon, and the third of the stars; so that a third of them was darkened; and a third part of the day did not shine, and likewise *a third part of* the night." This is why God has to intervene. He is showing exactly what He is going to do. Now all of this that I read up to this point, through verse 12, are just softening up the world for what is coming. Because as God says, He is going to judge the world, He's going to judge the inhabitants thereof; He's going to judge the nations thereof. And in a final analysis, we're going to see He gathers all nations together. And they are going to fight against Jesus Christ, and fight against the saints. So these are huge worldwide events that are taking place. Now verse 13, "And I looked; and I heard an angel flying in the midst of heaven, saying with a loud voice, 'Woe, woe, woe to those who are dwelling on the earth, because of the voices of the remaining trumpets of the three angels who *are* about to sound *their* trumpets" (Rev. 8:6-13). So you see, it intensifies, and gets greater, and men are going to be mad in their thoughts, desperate in what they are going to do, motivated. Now you see because the angels of God have done this, now Satan gets permission for the legions of his demons who are bound in the abyss to be released, to strengthen men so that they will fight even more, to give them strength, and power, and energy, and to release—as we will see—a secret weapon.

And this is what's going to happen as we read back there in Daniel the 12th chapter, the King of the North is going to come against the King of the South, and then when he's there for awhile, he is going to hear of trouble from the north, and from the east, and he is going to go and make waste against them. So Revelation 9 is a fulfillment of this. And he's going to have an awesome secret weapon.

Now let's begin, Chapter 9 and verse 1, "And the fifth angel sounded *his* trumpet;" This is the first woe. "And I saw a star that had fallen from heaven to the earth, and there was given to him the key to the bottomless abyss." That's where the demons are in prison, "And he opened the bottomless abyss; and there went up smoke from the pit, like *the* smoke of a great furnace; and the sun and the air were darkened by the smoke from the pit." So here come out all these millions, and millions of demons, bound in there, now ready to fight against God, ready to fight against whomever that they're directed against. This is going to be a mad frenzy. "Then locusts came onto the earth from the smoke; and power was given to them, as the scorpions of the earth have power." So they are going to go out, and it's going to be a secret occult major weapon against all the forces of the north and the east, and temporarily they're going to have a victory. "And it was said to them that they should not damage the grass of the earth…" Because all the grass burned up, but now because of the rain and things that comes along in spite of all the destruction, the grass still grows. So here months later, the grass has come back, and now it said, "…do not damage the grass of the earth, or any green thing…" Because the trees come back. "Or any tree, but only the men who did not have the seal of God in their foreheads." So over here, wherever they are, are the hundred and forty-four thousand. Then scattered through the earth, are the great innumerable multitude, wherever they are gathered. And God gives them special protection. Just like at the same time, in the plagues that came against Egypt, God brought the first number of plagues against the Egyptians, and they also came against the Israelites. Then with the one plague concerning the Moraine, God severed the children of Israel from the rest of Egypt. So likewise here, He severs those who have the Holy Spirit of God, who were sealed by the angel, as we see there in Revelation 7.

Now the reason they received the Holy Spirit that way is very simple. There's nobody out there, no ministers out there to baptize them. So they repent and God gives the Holy Spirit to them directly that way, sealed by a hand of an angel. Verse 5, "And it was given to them…" that is these satanic powers "that they should not kill them, but that they…" that is the enemy "…that they should be tormented five months; and their torment *was* like *the* torment of a scorpion when it stings a man." So they are going to be virtually paralyzed, hardly able to move, and it will take them five months to recover.

When they recover, we're going to see what happens. Just picture this, this is sent to Russia, and China, and India, and Southeast Asia, and Japan, and Mongolia, and Kazakhstan, and in Uzbekistan, and all the stans that go to the east, and against all the Moslem countries there involved. So they're going to have this come upon them. They are going to think, "Boy, this is fantastic. We have stopped them in their tracks." But it's only going to last for five months. And during that time, verse 6, "And in those days men will seek death but will not find it; and they will desire to die, but death will flee from them. And the appearance of the locusts *was* like horses prepared for war; and on their heads *were* crowns like those of gold; and their faces *were* like *the* faces of men; And they had hair like women's hair, and their teeth were like *those* of lions. And they had breastplates like iron breastplates; and the sound of their wings *was* like the sound of chariots drawn by many horses running to war; And they had tails like scorpions, and stinger; and they were *given* power to injure men with their tails *for* five months."

Demonic weapons used by men, possessed by demons, going out to battle. Now notice, verse 11, "And they have over them a king, the angel of the abyss, his name in Hebrew *is* Abaddon, but *the* name he has in Greek tongue *is* Apollyon." So this is Satan the devil. "The first woe is past." So there comes a respite, "Behold, after these things two woes are still to come. And the sixth angel sounded *his* trumpet;" which is the second woe. Now then, they recover from their five months of this super secret weapon inspired by demons that have them paralyzed for five months. They're able to recover. They're able to gather their armies. Now they begin to launch their super secret demonic weapons. So now we have demons against demons, angels of God against men and demons, men against men, demons against demon, all carrying out the will of God. "And I heard a voice from the four horns of the golden altar that *is* before God; and it said to the sixth angel, who had the trumpet, 'Loose the four angels who are bound in the great river Euphrates." So God has demons buried in the earth, imprisoned there for a certain time, for a certain thing to be done. Now it's going to be a mammoth thing to dry up the river Euphrates.

Now someone sent me an article that different countries are seeking to build dams on the river Euphrates, and so that's how it's going to dry up. It isn't going to happen that way. It's going to happen the way it says here. So they were loosed. "Then the four angels. Who had been prepared for the hour and day and month and year, were loosed..." a specific time determined by God, "So they might kill a third of men;" And remember, back in Revelation 6, a fourth of mankind was already killed, so a third of them is another fourth. So here we have fifty percent of mankind killed already, to say nothing of the other events that are going to take place. Verse 16, "And the number of *the* armies of the horsemen..." Now you think back there in Joel the 2nd chapter, was 200,000,000, army of 200 million. So it's going to come, as we will see, from what we might say, the middle of Iraq. All the way, the army is strung all the way back to the Far East. And I think it's very profound, very interesting, that in order to get the oil from Kazakhstan to China, which they have been doing by rail tanker cars. Now they are building huge pipelines to go to the east to China. But also along with that, they are building a huge highway, so they can service all of that. And that's going to come into China, and that's going to go right by the world's biggest dam, which is going to be opened about 2010, and is going to become a world tourist event. And the Chinese are going to have Olympic Games in 2012, and they're the rising power of the world. So just think, these armies stringing from the middle of Iraq all the way back—two hundred million. You can't have them all in one place, so they're all strung out back there, and they come in waves, and they come in waves, you see, two hundred million. "And I heard the number of them." So here's how they're going to come. All their demonic secret weapons, "And so I saw the horses in the vision, and those sitting on them, who had fiery breastplates, even jacinth and brimstone. And the heads of the horses *were* like heads of lions, and fire and smoke and brimstone shoot out of their mouths. By these three, a third of men were killed: by the fire and the smoke and the brimstone that shoot out of their mouths. For their power is in their mouths; for their tails are like serpents, and have heads, and with them they inflict wounds."

Now this must be some kind of weapon protruding out of it. However that is, that you know, they are developing weapons now that are going to be awesome. And I think we're going to see how it's going to be fulfilled to the very nth degree of what it's talking about, here in Revelation 9. "...And with them they inflict wounds. But the rest of the men who were not killed by these plagues..." Now this is to show you the hardness of heart that men have, and how absolutely self-centered on their power, and worshiping Satan the devil, who gives them that power, that they want to hold on to it. And yes, this is Satan in his desperate battle, in fighting against God, as we will see that he wants to hold onto the power of this earth, for all the earth has been given over to him. Remember the temptation with Jesus, when Satan said, "If you worship me I'll give you all the kingdoms of the world, for they are given to me. And I give them to whomsoever I will." Now Satan and men are going to be losing this power, losing these things. Satan is going to be desperate, he is going to be absolutely furious, he's going to be doing everything that he can. He is going to be given the power to cut loose everything, in the demonic world to fight against God, and use men in that way. So we need to understand how fantastic these events are going to be. Now notice, even at that, the whole point of the thing, is so that God will give them a space to repent. Now you talk about being hardhearted, and you talk about having your minds set to serve evil. Listen to it here, "But the rest of the men which were not killed by these plagues still did not repent of the works of their hands, that they might not worship demons, and idols of gold and silver and brass and stone and wood, which do not have the power to see, nor to hear, nor to walk:" So this is a repeat of God's judgment of the gods of Egypt, correct? Now only the gods of all the world. But will they repent and turn to God? No. Now, verse 21, "And they did not repent of their murders, nor of their sorceries, nor of their fornications, nor of their thievery" (Rev. 9:1-21). Quite an army, quite a thing that takes place.

Now then, Chapter 10 talks about the seven thunders, and what's going to take place there. No one knows what they're going to be because God instructed John, "Don't write it." So whatever the seven thunders do—and please understand—the seven thunders were never the seven churches of Revelation 2 and 3. We're way down in to the last year before Christ sets his feet on the earth, and it has nothing to do with the churches. These have to do with the angelic powers of God.

Then we come to Chapter 11, which we've already covered. The sea of glass is there, the armies have been all fighting, the resurrection takes place, they see all the saints up there, and they get together and they say, "Oh, we're being invaded by invaders from outer space. Let's gather together, let's quit fighting each other." We're going to see that in just a minute. "We have got to gather to fight this! Look at this [the Sea of Glass] sitting there [in the clouds]." And it's got to be over Jerusalem doesn't it? Because He gathers all the armies to where? To the valley of Meggedo, doesn't He? "And he treads out the wine press and the fierceness of his wrath and the blood is going to rise to the horses bridles." Just think, 5-6 feet of blood of the carnage of human rebellion against God. So that Sea of Glass has got to be up there.

Now let's come to Revelation 15, and let's bring us up to date here. After we're all resurrected on the Sea of Glass, all the saints are then going to see the final judgment against God, and against the wickedness of man, against the nations of the world, and against Satan and his demons. After all that we have been through, after all that the saints have gone through, beginning from Abel clear down to the two witnesses who were the last two resurrected; everything that the saints have suffered through, all of those who've been martyred, lost their heads for the word of Christ, burned at the stake because of the evil of the beast and the false prophet, and the evil of Satan's religions, and armies—down through the history of the world. They are going to be resurrected as spirit beings. And we are all, from the Sea of Glass, going to view the seven last plagues of God, which is His final judgment for the nations of the earth, before the Kingdom of God begins.

Now let's pick it up here, in verse 5, of Revelation 15, "And after these things I looked, and behold, the temple of the tabernacle of the testimony in heaven was opened." The direct intervention of God with His angels. This is the final sequence of battle that's going to take place. "And the seven angels who had the seven *last* plagues came out of the temple; they were clothed in linen, pure and bright, and girded about the chest with golden breastplates." Now remember, this is going to come upon the armies that are right there. The other armies are spread all the way to the east. So they are going to come, as we will see, in Revelation 19 [Back to Revelation 15]: "And one of the four living creatures gave to the seven angels seven golden vials, full of the wrath of God, Who lives into the ages of eternity. And the temple was filled with smoke from the glory of God, and from His power; and no one was able to enter inside the temple until the seven plagues of the seven angels were fulfilled" (Rev. 15:5-8). "Then I heard a great voice..." Chapter 17 and verse 1 [16:1], "from the temple say to the seven angels, 'Go and pour out the vials of the wrath of God onto the earth. And the first *angel* went and poured out his vial upon the earth; and an evil and grievous sore fell upon the men who had the mark of the beast, and upon those who were worshipping his image."

Now we've had many, many sermons on the Mark of the Beast. We'll have more before it's finally instituted. But the first judgment is given against them, why? Because they gave up their freewill to the beast with the mark, and to Satan the devil. So they're the first one's going to be hit. "And the second angel *went and* poured out his vial into the sea; and it became blood..." All the oceans of the world, "like *that* of a dead *man*; and every living soul in the sea died." So you see, when God begins to repair the earth, there's going to have to begin the healing water that flows from Jerusalem to the east and to the west, and is going to heal the whole ocean. An amazing thing. Verse 4, "And the third angel poured out his vial upon the rivers, and into the fountains of waters; and they became blood." Now, as we're all watching this, and seeing this going on—and they're going to be some people say, "Oh how can a God who is a God of love, do this?" Let's reverse it, how could men and demons do this to a God of love, and not expect judgment back upon themselves?

Let's go on. Here's how the angels view this, here's how we're going to view this, "Then I heard the angel of the waters say, 'You are righteous, O Lord, Who are, and Who was, even the Holy One, in that You executed this judgment. For they have poured out *the* blood of the saints and of prophets..." Now God honors that, and His judgment is given all at once. He has stored up this last generation for this judgment. Just like Jesus said, "This generation, shall not pass away until all these things be fulfilled." This is the generation, this is the one that we are looking at today, and it's going to come. "...and You have given them blood to drink; for they are worthy.' And I heard another *voice* from the altar say, 'Yes, Lord God Almighty, true and righteous *are* Your judgments.' And the fourth angel poured out his vial upon the sun; and *power* was given to it to scorch men with fire." So there's going to be a big burst from the sun, and this heat is going to come like a great flash upon the earth, where it talks about, back in one of the prophecies, seven times hotter than normal. So this great flash is going to come, and scorch men. Now there are going to be some who will survive, who will not be out in the open, but whoever is in the open, it's going to burn them. "These men were scorched with great heat; and they blasphemed the name of God, Who has authority over these plagues, and did not repent to give Him glory." You talk about hardhearted, you see.

Now think about this, if these evil men, inspired of Satan the devil and demons, can set their will to not repent, don't you think that we ought to go to God, and ask Him to give us the tenderheartedness toward Him, and Jesus Christ, and the saints, but have minds of pillars of brass, and iron, and flint, to withstand all these things that are coming, and to be able to stand firm for God. You know, too many people give up easily on God because it's not comfortable, and it's not the kind of nicey-nicey thing that I've always wanted. Well listen, it isn't going to be nicey-nicey. You need to understand that. Now notice, "…And they blasphemed the name of God, Who has authority over these plagues, and did not repent to give Him glory. And the fifth angel poured out his vial upon the throne of the beast; and his kingdom became full of darkness; and they gnawed their tongues because of the pain, And blasphemed the God of heaven because of their pains and their sores; yet they did not repent of their works." See, in every case, God gave them a chance to repent, but didn't do it. "And the sixth angel poured out his vial into the great river Euphrates;" Because after it was dried up once, then it came back flowing again. So now it's got to be dried up again. "…So that the way of the kings from the rising of *the* sun might be prepared. Then I saw three unclean spirits like frogs *come* out of the mouth of the dragon, and out of the mouth of the beast, and out of the mouth of the false prophet;" After all the things that happened, they've got to be convinced by supernatural spiritual demonic power, that they ought to go fight this alien invasion. This is their last hope. Verse 14, "For they are the spirits of demons working miracles, going forth to the kings of the earth, even of the whole world, to gather them together to *the* battle of that great day of God Almighty." And they are going to come. And now He gives a warning again. Now notice how this is a pattern in the Bible, "Behold, I come as a thief. Blessed *is* the one who is watching and is keeping his garments, so that he may not walk naked and they *may not* see his shame." Direct reference to the Laodiceans, and the five foolish virgins of Matthew 25. "And He gathered them together to the place that in Hebrew is called Armageddon." See, Armageddon is the battle of God against the armies of this world. "Then the seventh angel poured out his vial into the air; and a loud voice came out of the temple of heaven, from the throne, saying, 'IT IS FINISHED.'" Now we're going to hear that because we are on the Sea of Glass. We'll hear that. "And there were voices and thunders and lightnings; and there was a great earthquake, such as was not since men were on the earth, so mighty an earthquake, *and* so great. And the great city was divided into three parts; and the cities of the nations fell;" And all of their super high building "And Babylon the great was remembered before God to give her the cup of the wine of the fury of His wrath. And every island disappeared, and no mountains were found;" Because they were lowered, and the valleys were raised. "And great hail, *each stone* the weight of a talent, fell down from heaven; and men blasphemed God because of the plague of hail, for the plague was exceedingly great" (Rev.16:1-21).

Now see, maybe some had protection, maybe they were in their tanks and the hail didn't smash out their tanks, or whatever it may be. Because you see, now they're going to come and gather to the final battle. It is here, in Revelation 19. And all the saints are going to come, and all of us are going to descend with Christ to the earth. And verse 14, "And the armies in heaven were following Him on white horses; *and* clothed in fine linen, white and pure. And out of His mouth goes a sharp sword, that with it He might smite the nations;" All God has to do is command, and it's done. "That with it He might smite the nations; and He shall shepard them with a iron rod;" That's what it's going to take to bring these unrepentant people of the ten percent that are left, after all of this, that are going to enter into the millennium, and be the first living, human beings in the kingdom of God, administered by Christ and the saints. "And on *His* garment and on His thigh He has a name written: King of kings and Lord of lords. Then I saw an angel standing in the sun; and he cried out with a loud voice, saying to all the birds that fly in *the* midst of heaven," See God's going to clean up the mess. "Come and gather yourselves together to the supper of the great God so that you may eat *the* flesh of kings, and the flesh of chief captains, and *the* flesh of mighty *men*, and *the* flesh of horses, and of these who sit on them, and *the* flesh of all, free and bond, and small and great. And I saw the beast and the kings of the earth and their armies, gathered together..." So all the remnant that are left, they gathered together. "...To make war against Him Who sits on the horse, and with His army."

And so, God is going to send an angel. The first thing is going to be done: The beast is going to be taken. Verse 20, "And the beast was taken, and with him the false prophet who worked miracles in his presence, by which he deceived those who received the mark of the beast and those who worshiped his image. These two were cast alive into the lake of fire, which burns with brimstone; And the rest were killed by the sword of Him Who sits on the horse, *even the sword* that goes out of His mouth; and all the birds were filled with their flesh" (Rev. 19:14-21).

And then we come down to Zechariah 14:4, "And his feet shall stand in that day upon the mount of Olives..." (Zech. 14:4). And all the saints with him. And then, the next major most important event, from the time of the Garden of Eden, is going to take place as pictured by the Day of Atonement.

End of Sermon

Transcriber: Carolyn Singer

The Feast of Trumpets—Sermon II—Holy Day
September 23, 2006
Scriptural References

1)	Leviticus 23:23	13)	Zephaniah 1:18
2)	Matthew 6:9-10	14)	Joel 1:15, 2:1-13
3)	Ezekiel 33:11 (paraphrased)	15)	Isaiah 13:6-13
4)	Colossians 1:10-13	16)	Isaiah 24:18-23
5)	Colossians 3:14-16	17)	Revelation 8:1-5
6)	Jeremiah 1:15-19	18)	Isaiah 40:4
7)	Isaiah 50:5-7	19)	Revelation 8:6-13
8)	Ezekiel 3:4-11	20)	Revelation 9:1-21
9)	Matthew 24:15-21	21)	Revelation 15:5-8
10)	Amos 5:18-20	22)	Revelation 16:1-21
11)	Zephaniah 1:13-17	23)	Revelation 19:14-21
12)	Jeremiah 25:31	24)	Zechariah 14:4

CHAPTER THIRTY-TWO

The Day of Atonement—Sermon I—Holy Day

September 30, 1998

Brethren, this is the Day of Atonement, 1998. One of the most important holy days of God. A day where we fast, where we don't eat, we don't drink any liquids, and we come to God realizing how very important that He is and that He is our whole life totally. Now let's go to Leviticus 23:26, and let's see the command here. "And the LORD spake unto Moses, saying..." And of course everything that Moses taught was what God told him to say. Everything is... "The LORD said tell the children of Israel." "...Saying, also on the tenth *day* of this seventh month [which is today] *there shall be* a day of atonement: it shall be an holy convocation unto you; and ye shall afflict your souls, and offer an offering made by fire unto the LORD" (Lev. 23:26-27). Now, in afflicting your souls, we know that that means with no food and no water. And when you do that you really realize how weak that you are.

Now also it says you shall offer an offering made by fire. And we always take up a holy day offering on each one of the holy days every year as they come to us. When we come to God we are to not appear before Him empty. And when we come we are to be prepared. And when we come, especially on this Day of Atonement, it should be a special offering to God because this shows when we will really be at one with God. And this shows that when all of our battles with Satan the devil will be over. So this should be a wonderful opportunity to present an offering to God, and we know that God desires that from the heart.

Now let's come down here to verse 38. And it says, "Besides the sabbaths of the LORD..." So all the holy days are Sabbaths. "...And beside your gifts,..." So there are gifts that we give during the year. "... And beside all your vows,..." That is what you determine to give God in your heart. "...And beside all your freewill offerings,..." And all the offerings are to be freewill offerings. We don't want to take any money under any false pretenses or to leverage the brethren or to merchandise the brethren, or any of those physical carnal things which have been done by so many people for so long. So it should be a freewill offering from the heart which you give unto the Lord. So at this time we'll go ahead and take a small break and take up the offering for the Day of Atonement.

Now let's continue on in Leviticus 23. And we know that as the apostle Paul said, we are to be instant in season and out of season, and to preach the word. You see, the word of God is what we are to preach, just exactly like the Lord told Moses, whatever is in the Scriptures. And that is what we are to teach. And that is what we are to cover for the whole meaning of the Day of Atonement, and it's importance in the plan of God. And we will see that this is one of these days in which it's very important to complete the plan of God. All of them are, beginning with the Passover and Unleavened Bread, and Pentecost and Trumpets, and so is Atonement as we come to it, and so will the Feast of Tabernacles and the Last Great Day when <u>we</u> come to it. All of that portrays all the various aspects of God's plan.

So let's continue on right here in Leviticus 23, continuing now in verse 28. "And ye shall do no work in that same day:..." None at all. Now we'll see a little later He double affirms it by saying, "You shall not do <u>any</u> work." "...For it *is* a day of atonement, to make an atonement for you before the LORD your God." Now we're going to see that the Day of Atonement also is an application of forgiveness. Now we have our forgiveness with Passover, but the world is going to have their forgiveness beginning with the Day of Atonement. So you see the Passover is for us. Day of Atonement has a direct meaning for us also, but it also is going to have a tremendous meaning for the people in the world.

"For whatsoever soul *it be* that shall not be afflicted in that same day, he shall be cut off from among his people" (vs. 29). Now, one of the worst things to do is to be cut off from God. And the people who do not keep the Sabbaths of God, and don't keep the holy days of God, don't realize they're cut off from God. They're just out there doing their own thing. And so it's a terrible thing to be cut off from God. So that's why the Day of Atonement is so important. We want to be at one with God. The opposite of being cut off from God is to be at one with God, because the Day of Atonement, "at-one-ment," gives us the meaning of the word, that we are at-one with God. And we can't be at one with God unless we do what He says.

"And whatsoever soul *it be* that doeth any work in that same day, the same soul will I destroy from among his people." And we've also seen that happen. We've seen people who've come along, been in the Church for years, and years, and years, who've given up on the Day of Atonement, and they have been destroyed. Not dead, but just their lives have been destroyed. "Ye shall do no manner of work: *it shall be* a statute for ever throughout your generations in all your dwellings. It *shall be* unto you a sabbath of rest [and it is a real resting Sabbath], and ye shall afflict your souls:..." And here, He gives a precise time. You see, God does not want any misunderstanding as to when the Day of Atonement begins, because you can't have people starting it at three in the afternoon, and others starting it when it gets dark at seven or eight at night. That way then you would have a five to six hour difference in the beginning and ending of the Day of Atonement. And you can't possibly all be at-one with God if you're all beginning and ending at different times. So God makes it very clear. And this tells us precisely how every Sabbath is to be calculated. He says, "...in the ninth *day* of the month at even, from even unto even, shall ye celebrate your sabbath" (vs. 30-32). So from sunset, *Ba erev*, to sunset, *Ba erev*, shall you keep your sabbath. And so when the sun dips below the horizon, the Day of Atonement begins. It ends the ninth day, begins the tenth day. Then when the whole day comes around and the sun dips below the horizon again, then it ends the tenth day. That is the Day of Atonement.

Now, let's look and see all the meaning that we are going to have for the Day of Atonement, because it's really something. So we're fasting. Now this day of fasting is very important for us to realize because it shows that we're just made of flesh, and the flesh does not last long. And it means that we can't trust in the flesh because when you realize how weak you are, and how helpless you are, what good is that going to do against Satan the devil? What power are you going to exercise out of your own self? Can you save yourself? Can you make yourself right? No, you can't. Only God can.

Now it also then teaches us total reliance on God. Because everything we have comes from God. And it means, as I already mentioned, "at-one-ment." And we're going to see that you cannot overcome Satan the devil with physical means. If you try and overcome Satan with physical means, that's exactly what Satan wants you to do because he's got you. You can only overcome Satan the devil with spiritual means, by the Spirit of God, by the power of God.

And also it shows that sin can never be totally removed while Satan is around. Now we're going to see all the aspects of this Day of Atonement and we're going to see why God has to put him away, and how that fits into God's overall plan. <u>First of all, let's see how Satan began.</u>

Let's go to Ezekiel 28, because there is a Satan the devil, and Revelation 13 shows that the whole world is going to worship Satan the devil, worship the dragon, and worship the beast, who gave him his power. Satan has always wanted to be God, as we're going to see. Now, Satan was originally Lucifer, as we will see, and he was a created being. Let's read it right here beginning in Ezekiel 28:11. "Moreover the word of the LORD came unto me, saying, Son of man, take up a lamentation upon the king of Tyrus [a type of the final beast]…" Now the power behind the king of Tyrus was Satan the devil, as we will see, because everything he has to say here has nothing to do with the king of Tyrus, but it has to do with the one who became Satan the devil. "…And say unto him, thus saith the Lord GOD; Thou sealest up the sum, full of wisdom, and perfect in beauty." That can't be said of any man. "Thou hast been in Eden, the garden of God;…" Now we're going to see a little bit later that the only other one who was in the Garden of Eden besides God and Adam and Eve, was Satan the devil. So this statement means it's talking about Satan the devil. The king of Tyrus could not possibly have been in the Garden of Eden, because the Garden of Eden was long destroyed through the flood before the king of Tyrus was ever a being, a person. Then it says, "…every precious stone *was* thy covering,…", and it lists all of them. And it says, "…the workmanship of thy tabrets and of thy pipes was prepared in thee in the day that thou wast created" (Ezek. 28:11-13). Now this is a created being.

"Thou *art* the anointed cherub that covereth…" Now that's what Lucifer originally was. "…And I have set thee *so*: thou wast upon the holy mountain of God [right there where God's throne is]; thou hast walked up and down in the midst of the stones of fire." That means what you could liken unto, as we've discussed before, the sea of glass, the stones of fire. "Thou *wast* perfect in thy ways…" That's why we know that this has to be referring to Lucifer before he fell. "Thou *wast* perfect in thy ways from the day that thou wast created, till iniquity was found in thee" (vs. 14-15). So he sinned.

Now here's how he sinned. "By the multitude of thy merchandise…" Now whatever Satan did to merchandise, he merchandised the angels. Whatever he did in not doing what God wanted him to do. And of course then merchandising has to do with lust, and covetousness, and greed. "…They have filled the midst of thee with violence…" See, because evil goes into deeper depths. And we'll cover that a little bit later on. And that's why we learned the lesson with the Feast of Unleavened Bread, that a little leaven leavens the whole lump. And now here God is showing how the leaven of sin leavened Lucifer so that he would fall. "…They [the sinful merchandising] have filled the midst of thee with violence, and thou hast sinned: therefore I will cast thee as profane out of the mountain of God: and I will destroy thee, O covering cherub, from the midst of the stones of fire" (vs. 16).

Now let's hold your place right here in Ezekiel 28, and let's go to Luke 10, and let's see what Jesus said. This also tells us something very important that we need to understand. This also confirms that Jesus was God before He became a human being. That's why the two most fundamental verses you need to know and know that you know, and have memorized are the verses of John. "In the beginning was the Word, and the Word was with God, and the Word was God." And then it says in John 1:14, "And the Word was made flesh." See, you really need to understand that, and have that sunk deep into your heart and mind.

Now here's a verification of that. And after the seventy came back they were all joyful because they were able to heal the sick and raise the dead and cast out the demons, "And [Jesus] said to them, 'I beheld Satan fall as lighting from heaven" (Luke 10:18). As a lightning streak, just fall from heaven because he was cast down. It says he fell. So there's the fall of Satan. And the greatest sin is not the sin of Adam and Eve when they fell. The greatest fall is the fall of Satan the devil.

Now He says, continuing with His disciples here, "Behold, I give you authorit to tread upon serpents and scorpions, and upon all the power of the enemy..." And we'll see how that power is, brethren, because Christ has given that to us. "...And nothing shall injure you in any way. Yet do not rejoice in this, that the spirits are subject to you; but rejoice that your names are written in heaven" (vs. 19-20). And brethren, with this Day of Atonement we need to understand that our names are written in heaven and we are to be at-one with God. This is a tremendous day for us. Absolutely marvelous day.

Now let's come back to Ezekiel 28:17. "Thine heart was lifted up..." Now what did Jesus say? "He who exalts himself shall be abased." Satan exalted himself, didn't he? Was he abased? Yes, he was. "Thine heart was lifted up because of thy beauty, thou hast corrupted thy wisdom by reason of thy brightness: I will cast thee to the ground,..." That's why he fell, he fell as lightning. He was cast back to the earth. "...I will lay thee before kings, that they may behold thee. Thou hast defiled thy sanctuaries by the multitude of thine iniquities,..." So whatever kind of worship service the angels had in their sanctuaries in worshipping God, this is what it's referring to. And one third of the angels, Revelation 12, fell with him. "...By the iniquity of thy traffic; therefore will I bring forth a fire from the midst of thee, it shall devour thee, and I will bring thee to ashes upon the earth in the sight of all them that behold thee" (vs. 17-18). Now it blends back into the king of Tyrus [A type of the final beast who shall be destroyed in the lake of fire.].

Now let's go to Isaiah 14, very basic scriptures. These are scriptures we should know and understand, but this is the time and season when we are to go back and see them, and we are to understand that there is a Satan the devil, that he is the enemy of God, that he is the adversary, that he is against us, that he wants to destroy us and wants to destroy what God is doing in us. And we need to understand and realize that, because one of the first things that Satan wants you to do is discount Satan. And then say that, "Well, he's just a myth." And then he's got you.

Now here, Isaiah 14:12. "How art thou fallen from heaven, O Lucifer,..." Now there's only one being that that happened to. Lucifer means, light-bringer. And now the light that he brings is darkness indeed. "...O Lucifer, son of the morning [or, the day star]! *How* art thou cut down to the ground, which didst weaken the nations! For thou hast said in thine heart..." And you see, that's where sin begins - in the heart. And that's why Satan wants to inspire sins in people. That's why he wants them, through lust and covetousness, to get them with their heart to sin. So we have it right here. "For thou has said in thine heart, I will ascend into heaven, I will exalt my throne..." You see, exaltation doesn't come from the north or the south, or the east or west. It comes from God. And Satan says, "I'm going to do it, and I'm going to exalt my throne", "...above the stars of God [above all the angels of God]: I will sit also upon the mount of the congregation, in the sides of the north: I will ascend above the heights of the clouds; I will be like the most High" (Isa. 14:12-14). And you can't do that because there's only one Most High. And this is what Satan has wanted to do all the time. He's wanted to be God. That's why, we'll see a little later, he's called the god of this world, because the world is now once again, in all the occult that is coming back on this whole world, as inspired by Satan the devil, they're going to worship him as God.

"Yet thou shalt be brought down to hell, to the sides of the pit." And we're going to see that Satan is going to be cast into a pit, a bottomless pit. "They that see thee shall narrowly look upon thee, *and* consider thee, *saying, Is* this the man that made the earth to tremble, that did shake [the] kingdoms" (vs. 15-16). Is he the one that caused all of this destruction? Yes, indeed, he certainly was.

Now let's go to Genesis 3, and let's see how Satan is subtle. He is subtle. And I think we can see the subtleties of this with the episodes that we've had with Bill Clinton as

President. He twists and turns the truth just like Satan. There is a good example of someone who is a son of Satan. And we'll talk about that a little bit later on. There's a difference between being a son of God and a son of Satan. Now you see, the first proposition that Satan gave to Eve was that you will become like God, but that's not to become like God as God, because that's the whole plan of God. But to become as a god like Satan considers himself. That's what he was really talking about. And he always comes with an accusation. Let's read it here.

Genesis 3:1, "Now the serpent was more subtil than any beast of the field which the LORD God had made. And he said unto the woman, Yea, hath God said, Ye shall not eat of every tree of the garden?" Well, that's not what God said. God said, "You may eat of every tree of the garden freely, except the tree of the knowledge of good and evil. For in the day that you eat thereof you shall surely die." "And the woman said unto the serpent, We may eat of the fruit of the trees of the garden: but of the fruit of the tree which *is* in the midst of the garden, God hath said,…" So she knew what God had said. God talked to her. There are some people who think, "Well, God only talked to Adam, and then Adam talked to his wife." No, she knew what God said. "…Ye shall not eat of it, neither shall ye touch it, lest ye die. And the serpent said unto the woman, Ye shall not surely die" (Gen. 3:1-4). In other words, one of the tactics of Satan the devil is to come along and take the words of God and say, "Well, God didn't mean what He said." Now you think about that in relationship to all the doctrinal problems that have come about. One of the first things that is said is that God didn't mean what He said. That brethren, is a Satanic message. Now it may sound spiritual, it may sound religious, but it is not of God. It is of Satan the devil from one of the most basic elements that we need to understand back here in Genesis 3.

Now then, furthermore he goes on and accuses God. "For God doth know that in the day ye eat thereof, then your eyes shall be opened, and ye shall be as gods, knowing good and evil" (vs. 5). Now the word here is *elohim*, and that refers also to pagan gods. So he's saying you will become as a god the way I, Satan the devil, am a god knowing good and evil. Does Satan know good? Yes. Does he know evil? Yes. No question about it.

"And when the woman saw that the tree *was* good for food [lust of the eyes], and that it *was* pleasant to the eyes, and a tree to be desired to make *one* wise [vanity, to be exalted up in your own self], she took of the fruit thereof, and did eat, and gave also unto her husband with her, and he did eat. And the eyes of them both were opened…" Yes, opened to see and understand evil, but closed their eyes to understand the life and truth of God. Now that's what's happened, because we will see that it says that Satan the devil has blinded the eyes of those who follow him. So this opening of the eyes was a closing of the eyes. "…And they knew that they *were* naked…" (vs. 6-7), and so forth. Well, you know the rest of the story there.

Now let's continue on. Let's come to Leviticus 16. Now Leviticus 16 tells us one of the most important things that's going to happen on the Day of Atonement. And this is the removal of Satan the devil. There is no other being in the whole Bible that is called, or referred to as a God, except God the Father and Jesus Christ. And Satan the devil is not a God. Satan the devil is a fallen archangel who now is Lucifer, Satan the devil. But to people in the world, they cannot distinguish between Lucifer and the true God. And this is the whole story, and the whole meaning of Leviticus 16. Now, if you are having problems thinking that both of the goats mean that they both belong to God, well then you write in for our 1994 Day of Atonement, which I did showing that it cannot possibly be both goats referring to Jesus Christ. Absolutely an impossibility.

Now, let's see what was to be done on this Day of Atonement. A very important ceremony was to take place. First of all the Priest was allowed to go into the Holy of Holies once a year, and this was the day. No other day. They could only come into the first part of the temple to take care of the altar of incense, the showbread, and to light the lamps. (Now, we'll see that on the first day of the Feast of Tabernacles when you are there to see the first holy day.) Then he was to have a special atonement for himself, an atonement for his family, and only after he was atoned for himself with very specific offerings, was he then to come back and to take of the two goats.

Now, let's pick that up here in Leviticus 16:5. "And he shall take of the congregation of the children of Israel, two kids of the goats for a sin offering, and one ram for a burnt offering. And Aaron shall offer his bullock of the sin offering, which *is* for himself, and make an atonement for himself, and for his house [household]. And he shall take the two goats,..." See, he had to have the atonement for himself first. "And he shall take the two goats, and present them before the LORD *at* the door of the tabernacle of the congregation [right in front of God]. And Aaron shall cast lots upon the two goats; one lot for the LORD, and the other lot for the [Azazel] scapegoat." And Azazel means the one to be removed. And of course, Christ was never removed. "And Aaron shall bring the goat upon which the LORD'S lot fell, and offer him *for* a sin offering" (Lev. 16:5-9). Now that's very important to understand. This is Christ as our sin offering. This is Christ as the offering for the sins of the whole world.

Here, hold your place and let's go back to 1 John 2 now, because this is important and it will show us that our sins come through Passover. The sins of the world come through Atonement. And John makes that distinction very clear, what he's saying here. 1 John 2:1, "My little children, I am writing these things to you so that you may not sin. And *yet*, if anyone does sin, we have an Advocate with the Father; Jesus Christ *the* Rghteous; and He is *the* propitiation for our sins..." And we know that through the covenant renewal of the Passover, don't we? Yes. Now notice, "...And not for our sins only, but also for *the sins of* the whole world" (1 John 2:1-2). And so the Day of Atonement is when God is going to be dealing with the sins of the whole world, because the world today cannot distinguish between the god of this world [Satan the Devil] and the true Jesus Christ. That's why this ceremony back in Leviticus 16...let's go back there now.

So the lot for the Lord was to be offered for a sin offering. Now we will see what happens with that sin offering. "But the goat, on which the lot fell to be the scapegoat, shall be presented alive before the LORD, to make an atonement [upon] with him..." Not with him, upon him. "...*And* to let him go [for the one to be let go, Azazel] for a scapegoat into the wilderness" (Lev. 16:10). And we are going to see that in the wilderness is one of Satan's abodes.

And so Aaron, then he will bring all of the things for his offering, and he shall present that. Now let's come down to verse 15. "Then shall he kill the goat of the sin offering, that *is* for the people, and bring his blood within the veil..." Now if you bring in the blood, and you have the sin offering, and you have an atonement and you have forgiveness of sins, the sins are forgiven, are they not? No question about it. Otherwise why do it if they were not forgiven? "...And bring his blood within the veil, and do with that blood as he did with the blood of the bullock, and sprinkle it upon the mercy seat, and before the mercy seat: and he shall make an atonement..." Now notice, "...for the holy *place*, because of all the uncleanness of the children of Israel, and because of their transgressions In All Their Sins:..." Now it doesn't say some of them, does it? No. It says all their sins. "...And so shall he do for the tabernacle of the congregation, that remaineth among them in the midst of their uncleanness" (vs. 15-16). And so this is forgiving all of their sins.

So then he says, verse 17, "And there shall be no man in the tabernacle of the congregation when he goeth in to make an atonement in the holy *place*, until he come out, and have made an atonement for himself, and for his household, and for all the congregation of Israel." Now if the atonement through the propitiation of the sacrifice has already been effective in forgiving the sins of the people, then when he comes to the one upon which the lot fell for Azazel, now we have a totally different application. And let's read that.

Let's come down here to verse 20. "And when he hath made an end of reconciling the holy *place*, and the tabernacle of the congregation, and the altar, he shall bring the live goat:" Now this is symbolic that it cannot die. A live goat. "And Aaron shall lay both his hands upon the head of the live goat, and confess over him all the iniquities of the children of Israel, and all their transgressions in all their sins, putting them upon the head of the goat, and shall send *him* away by the hand of a fit man into the wilderness:" (vs. 20-21). Now that's a very unusual thing to do. Now if you have all the sins forgiven already by a sin offering, why this confession of sins again over the goat for Azazel? Well there's a very profound reason for it, which is this: as long as Satan the devil is around, who's the author of sin, he is always going to inspire people to sin. And he is the one who has caused it. And so God is making allowance for it here and showing what He's going to do. That He is going to remove the one who causes sin.

"And the goat shall bear upon him all their iniquities unto a land not inhabited: and he shall let go the goat in the wilderness. And Aaron shall come into the tabernacle of the congregation, and shall put off the linen garments, which he put on when he went into the holy *place*, and shall leave them there: and he shall wash his flesh with water in the holy place, and put on his garments, and come forth...", because you see, that represents an unclean spirit. So then he had to wash himself. Same way with the fit man who took him out into the wilderness. He had to wash himself and bathe himself because he was dealing with all the uncleanness, an unclean spirit who caused the sins of all the children of Israel. "...And offer his burnt offering, and the burnt offering of the people, and make an atonement for himself, and for the people. And the fat of the sin offering shall he burn upon the altar. And he that let go the goat for the [Azazel] scapegoat shall wash his clothes, and bathe his flesh in water, and afterward come into the camp" (vs. 22-26). And then it talks about the sin offering.

Now here's something very important to understand. This is why this goat cannot represent Christ. The goat for Azazel cannot represent Christ. Verse 27, "And the bullock *for* the sin offering, and the goat *for* the sin offering, whose blood was brought in to make atonement in the holy *place*, shall *one* carry forth without the camp;..." That is, over to the altar where they burned all the sin offerings to ashes at the Miphkad Altar. And that represents Christ. Now that's something really important to understand. Now notice what else happens. "...And they shall burn in the fire their skins, and their flesh, and their dung. And he that burneth them shall wash his clothes, and bathe his flesh in water, and afterward he shall come into the camp" (vs. 27-28).

"And *this* shall be a statute for ever unto you: *that* in the seventh month, on the tenth *day* of the month [that's this day], ye shall afflict your souls, and do no work at all, *whether it be* one of your own country, or a stranger that sojourneth among you: For on that day shall *the priest* make an atonement for you, to cleanse you, *that* ye may be clean from all your sins before the LORD. It *shall be* a sabbath of rest unto you, and ye shall afflict your souls, by a statute for ever. And the priest, whom he shall anoint, and whom he shall consecrate to minister in the priest's office in his father's stead, shall make the atonement, and shall put on the linen clothes, *even* the holy garments: and he shall make an atonement for the holy sanctuary, and he shall make an atonement for the tabernacle of the congregation, and for the altar, and he shall make an atonement for the priests, and for all the people of the congregation. And this shall be an everlasting statute unto you, to make an atonement for the children of Israel for all their sins once a year. And he did as the LORD commanded Moses" (vs. 29-34). So there we have the fullness of the meaning of the Day of Atonement here in Leviticus 16.

Now later on…well, let's just do it right now. Let's go to Revelation 20, and we're going to see the fulfillment of this, and then we'll come back and we'll see some other things as it relates to Satan the devil, and our calling, and the things that we need to do, and how we need to overcome him, and a more complete meaning of this day.

Now after Christ returns, sets His feet on the earth on the day of Trumpets, Satan then, on the Day of Atonement, Revelation 20:1, "Then I saw an angel descending from heaven [this is what the type of the fit man was], having the key of the abyss…" Didn't we read that he was going to be put into the pit? Yes. "…And a great chain in his hand. And he took hold of the dragon, the ancient serpent, who is *the* Devil and Satan, and bound him *for* a thousand years" (Rev. 20:1-2). So Satan is not going to be around all during the Millennium. It's going to be a completely different world. A completely different administration. A completely different set of circumstances. And we will be there with Jesus Christ to serve and to help the people, and to rule them, and to train them, to teach them, to qualify them to come into the Kingdom of God. And what a glorious reign that is going to be as we will see when we keep the Feast of Tabernacles.

"Then he cast him into the abyss, and looked him *up*, and sealed *the abyss* over him, so that he would not deceive the nations any longer until the thousand years were fulfilled…" (vs. 3). And we're going to find out on the Last Great Day why he is let out for that very short period of time. The seventh and eighth day of the Feast of Tabernacles. The last day of the Feast of Tabernacles, day seven, and the Last Great Day, the eighth day. We'll see why.

Now today we're still confronted with Satan the devil, aren't we. And we're still confronted with what we need to do, so let's understand something concerning the things that we need to do. Let's come to Ephesians 2. Let's see how Satan the devil works. And he is working grandly today. And he's got all the powers and tools and people in his hands, using them, manipulating them, preparing the way, making his coming, great one world to be an awesome and a mighty thing indeed.

And here, Ephesians 2:1, "And you were dead in trespasses and sins…" Because if you're living in sin, you're dead. You have no spiritual life. You may be alive physically, but you are dead spiritually. And there was a time when we are living in our sins and transgressions that we are dead. And when God in His mercy has called us and raised us up out of that, granting us forgiveness and giving us the gift of repentance, and the gift of eternal life, and the gift of the Holy Spirit, and the gift of imputed righteousness of Christ. That is what it is to be made alive in Christ, see. But we were once dead in our sins and trespasses.

"In which you walked in times past according to the course of this world [that is the way that this world is], according to the prince of the power of the air, [and he is] the spirit that is now working within the children of disobedience." So Satan has a power, and Satan has his spirit that can go out and have power and cause people to do things that he wants them to do. Now, people can resist it. There's a way to resist. But you can only resist so much in the flesh. You have to resist in the spirit and have the spiritual armament. Now notice how he works here. "Among whom also we all once had our conduct in in the lusts of our flesh, doing the things willed by the flesh and by the mind…" And of course, all of those things seems so good. "…And were by nature *the* children of wrath, even as the rest *of the world*" (vs. 2-3).

Now let's go to 1 John 2, because it tells us here also about how Satan appeals to the flesh, to the lust of the eyes, the pride of life, and the love of the world. And all of that is part of Satan's world. Now here, 1 John 2:15, "Do not love the world, nor the things *that are* in the world." Because that's how Satan gets you, because then you become carnal minded. You become material minded. So you're not minding the things of God, of the Spirit. You're minding the things of the flesh. "If anyone loves the world, the love of the Father is not in him. Because everything that *is* in the world..." I want you to think about this statement, brethren. "...Everything that *is* in the world—the lust of the flesh, and the lust of the eyes, and the pretentious pride of physical life—is not from the Father, but is from the world. And the world and its lust is passing away, but the one who does the will of God abides forever" (1 John 2:15-17). Brethren, that's important to understand. But notice how Satan uses all the physical things of the world. The lust of the flesh. The lust of the eyes and the pride of life. Those are his tools, and he is the god of this world.

Now let's go to 2 Corinthians 4, and here we're going to see that Satan the devil is called the god of this world. Now, verse 1, "Therefore, having this ministry [Paul is talking about his ministry], according as we have received mercy, we are not fainthearted. For we have personally renounced the hidden things of dishonest gain..." Now these are the things that the false prophets and teachers use. Dishonesty, walking in craftiness, handling the word of God deceitfully. Anyone who is a true minister of God will have renounced all those carnal things. "...But by manifestation of the truth..." (2 Cor. 4:1-2), which is the word of God, in teaching the word of God, and speaking the word of God, in helping people understand the word of God. Not using and abusing and manipulating, deceitfully handling it, you see. Now that's how you can tell who is a false teacher and who is not.

"But if our gospel is hidden, it is hidden to those who are perishing; in whom the god of this world has blinded the minds..." Now that's what happened with Adam and Eve. He blinded their minds. And yet they thought their minds were opened. Quite a different thing indeed. "...Of those who do not believe..." And that's what happens when Satan the devil blinds your mind. You believe not. "...Lest the light of the gospel of the glory of Christ, Who is *the* image of God, should shine unto them." So He cuts them off so that they won't understand it. And God turns them over to it because this is not the age of Christ [and His kingdom]. This is the age of man and Satan. "For we do not preach our *own* selves, but Christ Jesus *the* Lord, and ourselves your servants for Jesus' sake" (vs. 3-5). And so that's the way that the apostle Paul did.

Now, let's come over here to 2 Corinthians 11:13, and let's see how the false preachers and teachers and apostles behaved themselves. It says here, "For such *are* false apostles..." And part of it was here, he's talking about the things that were done, is that they were turning them from the simplicity of Christ. They were merchandising them. They were feeding them with philosophy, which are the doctrines of the religion of Satan the devil. For he says, "For such *are* false apostles—deceitful workers, who are transforming themselves into apostles of Christ. And *it is* no marvel, for Satan himself transforms himself into an angel of light." And yet his light is darkness. "Therefore *it is* no great thing if his servants also transform themselves as ministers of righteousness—whose end shall be according to their works" (2 Cor. 11:13-15). Now we have to fight against this, don't we? That's how Satan works.

Let's see also how he works as the prince of the power of the air. Remember what he did with Job. One day the sons of God appeared before the Lord, and Satan was among them, going up and down, to and fro in the earth. And then you know all the rest of the story of Satan the devil. We come here to 1 Peter 5:8, Satan as a roaring lion, is going about seeking whom he may devour. And how will he devour. Well, let's see how he does. He sends out his impulses, his airwaves as it were, because he's the prince of the power of the air, and inspires people to sin. He even got to King David.

Now let's go back here to 1 Chronicles 21:1, and let's see one of the great sins that David committed. It says right here that he was inspired of Satan the devil. "And Satan stood up against Israel, and provoked David to number Israel." So Satan is the one who did it. Provoked him. Caused him to do it. "And David said to Joab and to the rulers of the people…" See now, God said, "Don't number them. Don't look to them for a number." [But David said] "…Go, number Israel from Beer-sheba even to Dan; and bring the number of them to me, that I may know *it*. And Joab answered, The LORD make His people an hundred times so many more as they *be*: but, my lord the king, *are* they not all my lord's servants? Why then doth my lord require this thing? why will he be a cause of trespass to Israel?" (1 Chron. 21:1-3). And so then, you know what happened there. Seventy thousand in Israel died because David sinned. Satan does things like that.

Let's come here to Matthew 16. Let's see what Satan also appeals to. Right here, Matthew 16:21, "From that time Jesus began to explain to His disciples that it was necessary for Him to go to Jerusalem, and to suffer many things from the elders and chief priests and scribes, and to be killed, and to be raised the third day. But after taking *Him* aside, Peter personally began to rebuke Him, saying, '*God will be* favorable to you, Lord. In no way shall this *happen* to You.' " Now Peter thought he was doing something good and fine. He's going to save the Savior. I mean, think of that. Those are kind of conflicting words, aren't they? Now notice what Jesus did. "Then He turned and said to Peter, 'Get behind Me, Satan! You are an offence to Me: because your thoughts are not *in accord* with the things of God, but the things of men" (Matt. 16:21-23). And so Satan appeals to those things that be of men.

Now let's come here to Luke 22:31, and let's see that Satan really desired to have Peter. And if he really could have had Peter, the true apostle, instead of Peter, a false apostle, perhaps he thought he could have had a greater false church. "Then the Lord said, Simon, Simon, listen *well*, Satan has demanded to have you…" And the Greek there means demanded to have you. "..To sift *you* as wheat. But I have prayed for you, that your faith may not fail; and when you are converted, strengthen your brethren" (Luke 22:31-32). So Satan really wanted Peter. And Satan did get to Peter, we find there in Galatians 2 when he fell hook, line, and sinker back into Judaism. And so Peter was spared that, but he had to be saved from that, see.

Now let's understand something else here too. When Satan really has you… Let's come to John 13:27, Satan entered into Judas. "And after the sop [that is after Judas took the sop] Satan entered into him." Totally possessed of Satan the devil. Now that's going to happen again with the Beast and the False Prophet, that the Beast is going to be totally possessed of Satan and he is going to go into the Temple of God, and he is going to say that he is God, and be worshipped as God. Those are all the means and devices of Satan the devil.

Now, let's understand something. Something very important for us to realize. There are the children of the devil. And there are the children of God. And we're going to look at the difference between them. Now John Morgan made a very interesting comment… Let's go to Matthew 13 while we're commenting on this. He said that there are two ways, and there's a great in-between between the two ways, and that's the vastness of the deceived world. But you have the children of Satan on one hand, and the children of God on the other hand. And the children of Satan the devil are indoctrinated in a course, or a process called perversion. And the children of God are, through a process, converted. So that each has a process. One to perversion. One to conversion. One leads to eternal death. The other leads to eternal life. And we are going to see, that yes the children of the devil do come in amongst our midst and they are called tares. And they are the ones who cause us problems. And Satan loves a hierarchy, so he can get someone in authority to sit there and wait. These are called, as Peter said, false teachers who stealthily snuck in and began to teach against the truth. We'll see that in just a minute.

Now let's pick it up here in Matthew 13:37. This is the parable of the sower. "And He answered *and* said to them, 'The one Who sows the good seed is the Son of man; and the field is the world; and the good seed, these are the children of the kingdom [that's us]; but the tares are the children of the wicked *one* [so we have the two here, don't we?]; Now the enemy who sowed them is the devil; and the harvest is *the* end of the age [and we're living in the end of the world right now]; and the reapers are the angels." And eventually the finality of this is going go take place at the resurrection. "Therefore, as the tares are gathered and consumed in the fire..." And I think right now God is gathering the tares together in their own little groups. And God is gathering the children of the Kingdom in their groups. "...So shall it be in the end of this age. The Son of man shall send forth His angels, and they shall gather out of His kingdom all the offenders and those who are practicing lawlessness; and they shall cast them into the furnace of fire; there shall be weeping and gnashing of teeth. Then shall the righteous shine forth as the sun..." So then we have the two rewards. We have the two things. We have the children of the wicked one, we have the children of the Kingdom. We have the process, the ending up of being burned in the fire of the wicked ones, and the children of the Kingdom entering into the Kingdom to shine in the glorious being as the sun shines, "...in the kingdom of their Father. The one who has ears to hear, let him hear" (Matt. 13:37-43).

Now let's look at, that there is a difference between the children of the Kingdom, who are the children of God, and the children of the devil. Now let's go to 1 John 3:4, and here is where it shows very clearly. Now I'm going to read to you from my translation of it, because I've translated it correctly. "Everyone who practicing sin is also practicing lawlessness, for sin is lawlessness." Now the King James says, "Whosoever committeth sin transgresseth also the law: for sin is the transgression of the law." That is an accurate translation too, but this is even stronger because lawlessness means *anomia*, which means against law. And Satan is against all the laws of God. He has his own. But he's against God.

Now, verse 5, "And you know that He appeared in order that He might take away our sins [that is Christ]; And in Him is no sin. Everyone who dwells in Him does not *practice* sin..." Now that's what it means, because we're talking about practicing sin up in verse 4, and the thought in the Greek is carried on down here to verse 6, "...does not practice sin." "Anyone who *practices* sin has not seen Him, nor has known Him. Little children, do not allow anyone to deceive you; the one who practices righteousness is righteous, even as He is righteous." Because we have the imputed righteousness of Christ. "The one who practices sin is of the devil because the devil has been sinning from *the* beginning. For this purpose the Son of God appeared that He might destroy the works of the devil. Everyone who has been begotten by God does not practice sin..." that's what it should read, "...because His seed *of begettal* [from the Father] is dwelling within him, and he is not able to *practice sin* because he has been begotten by God" (1 John 3:5-9).

Now let's understand why it means practice sin, because here in 1 John 5:16, let's turn there for just a minute because it tells us something that's important we need to understand. There is a sin which is not a sin unto death. Let's read it here. "If anyone sees his brother sinning a sin *that is* not unto death..." That means any sin that it can be repented of. That's why when we go pray, we say "Forgive us our sins." But we are not practicing sin. Those who are practicing sin have no consciousness of sin. It is their way of life. "...he shall ask, and He will give him life for those who do not sin unto death. There is a sin unto death [now that is the unpardonable sin]: concerning that *sin*, I do not say that he should make *any* supplication *to God*." So here in 1 John 3 we have the same thing, don't we? Practicing sin.

Now let's read verse 9 again. "Everyone who has been begotten of God does not practice sin because His seed *of begettal* is dwelling within him, and he is not able to *prac-*

tice sin because he has been begotten from God." And God the Father will reveal to him that he is sinning so he can repent. Verse 10, "By this *standard* are manifest…" That is the one who is practicing righteousness, the ones who are practicing lawlessness. "By this *standard* are manifest the children of God and the children of the devil…" Satan has his children. Satan has those who do his bidding. And there is a process of perversion that they go through. "…Everyone who does not practice righteousness is not of God, and neither is the one who does not love his brother" (vs. 9-10). Now you think how importantly brotherly love then is.

Now let's first of all, we'll take a look at the process of perversion. Then we will look at the process of conversion. And then we will see how we need to overcome Satan the devil. Now let's come to Romans 1. Again I'm going to read my own translation taken from the series that we did in the book of Romans. And we did finally finish that and it took us a little over two years and about almost two months to get it all done. But we have it done, 21 tapes now altogether.

So let's come back here to Romans 1:19. "Because that which may be known of God is manifest among them…" God always reveals Himself in the physical things to them. We'll see that. "…For the invisible things of Him are perceived from *the* creation of *the* world, being understood by the things that were made—both His eternal power and God-head—so that they are without excuse" (Rom. 1:19-20). Now, when they come to that point of rejecting God, knowing and having everything there to show that there is a God, they are, number one, without excuse.

"Because when they knew God, they glorified *Him* not as God, neither were thankful, but they became vain in their own reasonings…", number two. When you reject God then you become number two, vain in your own reasonings, your own imaginations. "…and their foolish hearts were darkened" (vs. 21) Again, the light of Satan the devil is darkness.

Number three happens then. When they become vain in their own imaginations, "While professing themselves to be *the* wise ones, they became fools…" So that's the third step. And of course they think they are wise. Now the fourth step. "…And changed the glory of the incorruptible God into *the* likeness of an image of corruptible man, and of birds, and four-footed creatures, and creeping things" (vs. 22-23). So now then you go back into idol worship, or the green movement, if you want it that way. That's all part of it. And where is all of this eco stuff coming from today, but straight out of the cauldron of the goddess Gaia. So number five, "For this cause, God also abandoned them to uncleanness through the lusts of their hearts…" That's number five. Then God does something. He turns them over and lets Satan have them even more. That's why all of these, you'll understand this even more, all of the secret societies have degrees of initiation. And each degree goes further and further, and further, and further into the depths of Satan the devil.

Now, number six. "…To disgrace their own bodies between themselves." Number seven, "Who exchanged the truth of God for the lie…" Now they believe the lies. "…And they worshiped and served the created thing more than the one Who is Creator, Who is into the ages. Amen" (vs. 24-25). So then they get into the full worship of man and how great he is, and of Satan the devil, the created thing. That's number seven.

Number eight, "For this cause, God abandoned them…" So then God then gives them over some more. That's number eight. "…God abandoned them to disgraceful passions; for even their women exchanged the natural use *of sex* into that which is contrary to nature. And in the same manner also the men, having left the natural use *of sex* with the women, were inflamed in their lustful passions toward one another—men with men shamefully committing lewd *acts*, and receiving back within themselves a fitting penalty for their error." Number nine, "And in exact proportion as they did not consent to have God in *their* knowledge, God abandoned them to a reprobate mind, to practice *those* things that are immoral" (vs. 26-28). So there are the nine steps of the process of perversion into the depths of Satanism.

Let's read the rest of it. "Being filled with all unrighteousness, sexual immorality [now this is the whole summary of it], wickedness, covetousness, malice, full of envy, murder, strife, guile, evil dispositions, whisperers, slanderers, God-haters, insolent, proud, boasters, inventors of evil things *and practices;* disobedient to parents, void of understanding, covenant-breakers, without natural affection, implacable *and* unmerciful; who, knowing the righteous judgment of God, that those who commit such things are worthy of death, not only practice these things themselves, but also approve of those who commit *them*" (vs. 29-32). And so they arrive at the depths of Satan the devil.

Let's go to Revelation 2, and let's see where God talks about how that even one of the Churches of God, got involved in it. And you will see this at the Feast of Tabernacles, the story of the Waldensians, or the Church at Thyatira. And because they listened to that woman the prophetess Jezebel, who is the Catholic church… Let's pick it up here in verse 19. Then God had to punish them, and He did it in [a] very, very profound way. "I know your works, and love, and service, and faith, and your endurance, and your works; and the last *are* more than the first. But I have a few things against you, because you allow the woman Jezebel, who calls herself a prophetess, to teach and to seduce My servants into committing fornication and eating things sacrificed to idols" (Rev. 2:19-20). So you see, that going down into Satanism, can even happen to people who are converted if you give yourself over to it. Because you have to fight against Satan the devil. And we will see how we need to do that after we get done here.

"And I gave her time to repent of her fornication, but she did not repent. Behold, I will cast her into a bed, and those who commit adultery with her into great tribulation, unless they repent of their works." And there was great tribulation during the time of the Waldensians. And when you see "The Israel of the Alps" video you're going to be shocked as to what happened to them. And they finally were fully compromised. Now notice what God says He's going to do. "And I will kill her children with death; and all the churches shall know that I am He Who searches *the* reins and hearts [God knows]; and I will give to each of you according to your works. But to you I say, and to *the* rest who *are* in Thyatira, as many as do not have this doctrine, and who have not known the depths of Satan, as they speak; I will not cast upon you any other burden" (vs. 21-24). So there is the depths of Satan to which people go. And it can happen, and we just read the process here in Romans 1.

Now let's look at the process of conversion. And there is a process to that which Peter describes in 2 Peter 1, the process of conversion. And it is step by step. And it is degree by degree. And it's something that we have to work at. Just like the children of the devil have to work at what they do and are dedicated into what they are doing, and that's how they are raised in elevation to great offices of responsibility and authority in this world, because they've proved that they can serve Satan and lie, so he raises and elevates them and rewards them. So likewise brethren, we need to realize that we have a reward coming too. But our reward comes the other way. Our reward comes this way, we have to understand the promises that God has given us, and that's what this Day of Atonement is all about, that we can have the same nature of God. That we can be as God is. That we can live in all eternity as the sons and daughters of God.

Now notice, 2 Peter 1:2. "Grace and peace be multiplied to you in *the* knowledge of God and of Jesus our Lord, according as His divine power has given to us all things that *pertain* to life and godliness…" And it's all right here in the word of God, brethren. Everything that we have, plus His Spirit, plus the gift of righteousness, plus access to Him. Brethren, it's a wonderful thing that God has called us to. "…All things that *pertain* to life and godliness, through the knowledge of Him Who called us by *His own* glory and virtue: through which He has given to us the greatest and *most* precious promises, that through these you may become partakers of *the* divine nature…" (2 Pet. 1:2-4). Think of that. That is tremendous brethren. That's what God wants to give us, the divine nature. Not human nature. Not Satan's nature. The children of the devil have Satan's nature. The children of God have God's nature of love, and joy, and peace, and longsuffering, and all the things of God.

So then he goes on to give the process here. He says, "…partakers of *the* divine nature, having escaped the corruption *that is* in *the* world through lust. And for this very reason also, having applied all diligence besides, add to your faith, virtue…" So here are the steps: faith, then virtue. "…And to virtue, knowledge; and to knowledge, self-control; and to self-control, endurance; and to endurance, godliness [having godly character]; and to godliness, brotherly love; and to brotherly love, the love *of God*" (vs. 4-7). That's the whole process of conversion. So you see the two. One goes into the depths of depravity, and one goes to the height of being exalted in the Kingdom of God at the resurrection.

Now we also understand, we have to fight Satan the devil. Let's go to Matthew 4 and see Jesus Christ fought Satan the devil, and what He did, and how He did it. And this gives us understanding on what we need to do to fight Satan the devil, because we still live in this world. And we still have to overcome Satan the devil. And we have to overcome the Beast, and we have to overcome the number. We have to overcome the mark, and the name. So we have a lot of Satanic things that we need to overcome in this world. And we cannot do it on our own. We cannot do it with our own strength. We cannot do it with fleshly means. That's why here in Matthew 4 we have it that Jesus fasted 40 days and 40 nights. And this shows that our weapons are not carnal, but spiritual to the pulling down of strong holds, as the apostle Paul said. We follow the example of Christ and how He fought Satan the devil.

Let's look at it here. Matthew 4:1, "Then Jesus was led up into the wilderness by the Spirit…" That's where Satan was. That's why the goat of Azazel was taken out to the wilderness, because that's Satan's abode. There is nothing there but death and wilderness, and desolation. That's the legacy of the children of Satan. "…In order to be tempted of the devil. And when He had fasted *for* forty days and forty nights, afterwards He was famished. And when the tempter came to Him, he said, 'If You are the Son of God…' " Always challenging God. Always questioning what you believe. That's why we have to be alert doctrinally, because Satan comes along and he's always testing. Is there a weakness in this doctrine? Is there a weakness in your understanding? Is there a weakness in what you believe? If this is true? If the Sabbath is the day of God, why do so many Christians go on Sunday? Gotcha! So he said to Christ, " 'If You are the Son of God, command that these stones become bread.' But He answered *and* said, 'It is written…' " Here is the key. You overcome Satan the devil with the word of God, properly applied. "…Man shall not live by bread alone…" Not just by the physical means. And that's why He was fasting the 40 days and 40 nights. And that's why we are fasting today, brethren, so we understand exactly the same lesson, that we don't "…live by bread alone, but by every word that proceeds out of *the* mouth of God" (Matt. 4:1-4). That's how we are to live. That's why Satan the devil comes along and he said to Eve, "Well, did God say this?"

Now continuing, verse 5, "Then the devil took Him to the holy city and set Him upon the edge of the temple, and said to Him, 'If You are the Son of God, cast Yourself down; for it is written…" Satan and his ministers will quote scripture. They will even quote it correctly, but they will misapply it. No question about it. They will always misapply it. But they will use it and they will quote it. And like the apostle Paul said, handle the word of

God deceitfully. "…It is written, 'He shall give His angels charge concerning You, and they shall bear You up in *their* hands, lest You strike Your foot against a stone.' " Jesus said to him, 'Again, it is written, "You shall not tempt *the* Lord your God." ' After that, the devil took Him to an exceeding high mountain, and showed Him all the kingdoms of the world, and their glory…" (vs. 5-8). And Luke says, in the moment of time. This is why Satan is called the god of this world. This is why the goat for Azazel. Right here is the confrontation that we see between Christ and Satan. Between the goat for the LORD, and the goat for Azazel in the wilderness. Here is the confrontation right here, you see.

"And said to Him, 'All these things will I give You, if You will fall down and worship me [—as God].' " That's the whole goal of Satan the devil. "Then Jesus said to him, 'Begone, Satan! For it is written, "You shall worship the Lord your God, and Him alone shall you serve." ' " Not that He's telling that Satan would, because won't. But He's saying that's what man should do, what Christ should do, what we should do. "Worship the Lord your God, and Him alone shall you serve. Then the devil left Him; and behold, angels came and ministered to Him" (vs. 9-11). So you see, it's quite a thing that we have here. It's quite a process that we are going through. And this day of Atonement shows us how we can escape the things of Satan the devil, and how we need to do it, and why we need to do it. And what we need to do to overcome it.

Now, let's go to Ephesians 6, and let's understand something. Something that's very clear as we are going to Ephesians 6. Those who are the children of Satan the devil come to think like the devil. Those who are of the children of God are to come to have the mind of Christ and think like Christ. Very important. That's the whole goal of being at-one with God. To be as Christ is. To think as Christ. Now brethren, if we can understand that, that's why you never hear me say, "Follow me as I follow Christ." No, I don't have to say that because now we have the whole scriptures here. I want you to follow Christ. I want to follow Christ. I don't want you to think as me. I don't want you to think as any other human being. I want you to think as Christ thinks. To have the mind of Christ. That then becomes the full total conversion. Because you see, we are told that we are going to have our confrontation with the synagogue of Satan. We know that and we are told right here in Ephesians 6 that the wiles of the devil are there. And we are battling, and fighting, and warring against great powers. And this struggle that we are in is a great struggle.

So let's read it. Ephesians 6:10, "Finally, my brethren, be strong in *the* Lord…" And that's what we need brethren. Please be strong in the Lord. "…And in the might of His strength." See that you are armed with the word of God. You are armed with the Spirit of God. You are armed with all the defenses of God. "Put on the whole armor of God…" See, it's something you have to do. Something we have to do. And if we don't put it on then we will be victimized by Satan the devil. "…So that you may be able to stand against the wiles of the devil" (Eph. 6:10-11). And he's got plenty. And he has many. And he has been at it for over 6000 years, and he is the slickest thing around. And if you think slick Willy is slick, you ain't seen nothing compared to Satan the devil.

"Because we are not wrestling against flesh and blood…" No, it's not just a physical power. "…But against principalities *and* against powers, against the world rulers of the darkness of this age…", who are the children of Satan the devil, who have gone through the depths of perversion to come to the depths of power that they have. "…Against the spiritual *power* of wickedness in high *places*." And yes, they've even gotten into the Church and have torn the Church asunder. "Therefore, take up the whole armor of God…" And brethren we are going to need it the closer and closer we come to the year 2000, the more we are going to need the whole armor of God. We don't know exactly what's going to happen, but it's going to be significant. "…So that you may be able to resist in the evil day…" Whatever that evil day is, whether it is a day of trial for you, a day of trouble for you, a day of temptation for you, a day of weakness for you. Whatever it may be "…so that you may be able to resist in the evil day, and having worked out all things, to stand" (vs. 12-13).

"Stand therefore, having your loins girded about with truth [just a part of your being], and wearing the breastplate of righteousness, and having your feet shod with *the* preparation of the gospel of peace, besides all *these*, take up the shield of the faith, with which you will have the power to quench all the fiery darts of the wicked one." To put them out, to extinguish them, that the burning passions of lust do not get to you. When it comes you say, "Get you hence, Satan." "And put on the helmet of salvation, and the sword of the Spirit, which is the Word of God; praying at all times with all prayer and supplication…" (vs. 14-18). Yes, brethren, we always need to pray. That is our spiritual life. Every single day. And these are the things we need to do.

Now let's see what else we do to overcome Satan the devil. Let's come here to Revelation 12:9, and this is important too. And we may be called upon to do this. "And the great dragon was cast out [he's going to be cast out again], the ancient serpent who is called the Devil, and Satan, who is deceiving the whole world [and the whole world is under his sway]: he was cast down to the earth, and his angels were cast down with him. And I heard a great voice in heaven say, 'Now has come the salvation and the power and the kingdom of our God, and the authority of His Christ because the accuser of our brethren has been cast down, who accuses them day and night before our God. But they overcame him…" And we <u>will</u> overcome him, brethren. We can overcome him through the very power of the Holy Spirit of God and all the things that God has, and all the armor of God. We can overcome him. "…Through the blood of the Lamb…" That is by having our sins forgiven and cleansed and washed. "…And through the word of their testimony…" That we have the word of God and the testimony which comes from Christ. "…And they loved not their lives unto death" (Rev. 12:9-11). No, we consider God's way above everything that we do. So this is what God wants us to do.

And we're going to have that confrontation with Satan the devil. Let's come back here to Revelation 3:9 and see that, and see why this Day of Atonement is so important for us. And we'll finish right here in Revelation 3, speaking to the Church at Philadelphia. He says, "Behold, I will make those of the synagogue of Satan…" So all of the great ones in the world, all of those who have gone through the depths of the perversion that you have seen, that we have read about here. "…Who proclaim themselves to be Jews, and are not, but do lie—behold, I will cause them to come and worship before your feet, and to know that <u>I</u> have loved you." Understand, God the Father loves you, Jesus Christ loves you. "Because you have kept the word of My patience, I also will keep you from the time of temptation which *is* about to come upon the whole world to try those who dwell on the earth. Behold, I am coming quickly; hold fast that which you have so that no one may take away your crown." And don't let anyone take your crown. Don't let Satan get it. Don't let any man get it, who is inspired of Satan the devil, take it from you. "The one who overcomes will I make a pillar in the temple of My God, and he shall not go out any more; and I will write upon him the name of My God, and the name of the city of My God, the new Jerusalem, which will come down out of heaven from My God: and *I will write upon him* My new name" (Rev. 3:9-12). Because you are at-one with God the Father and Jesus Christ.

End of Sermon

Transcriber: Carolyn Singer

The Day of Atonement—Sermon I—Holy Day
September 30, 1998
Scriptural References

1) Leviticus 23:26-27, 38, 28-32

2) Ezekiel 28:11-16

3) Luke 10

4) John 1:14

5) Luke 10:18-20

6) Ezekiel 28:17-18

7) Isaiah 14:12-16

8) Genesis 3:1-7

9) Leviticus 16:5-9

10) I John 2:1-2

11) Leviticus 16:10, 15-17, 20-32

12) Revelation 20:1-3

13) Ephesians 2:1-3

14) I John 2:15-17

15) II Corinthians 4:1-5

16) II Corinthians 11:13-15

17) I Chronicles 21:1-3

18) Matthew 16:21-23

19) Luke 22:31-32

20) John 13:27

21) Matthew 13:37-43

22) 1 John 3:4-9

23) I John 5:16

24) 1 John 3:9-10

25) Romans 1:19-32

26) Revelation 2:19-24

27) II Peter 1:1-7

28) Matthew 4:1-11

29) Ephesians 6:10-18

30) Revelation 12:9-11

31) Revelation 3:9-12

CHAPTER THIRTY-THREE

The Day of Atonement—Sermon II—Holy Day

September 25, 2004

And greetings brethren. Welcome to the Day of Atonement, 2004. And of course this is a very important holy day, and also we're going to see that just as the Passover prepares those who are in the church for Unleavened Bread and Pentecost, so likewise Trumpets and Atonement prepares the world for what God is going to do as pictured by the Feast of Tabernacles and later the Last Great Day. So there's quite a connection between the two of them. So we're making our way through the holy days of God, the annual feasts of God. And of course as we have been learning all of the Bible is structured around the Sabbath, Passover and the holy days. And without those it's impossible to understand the plan of God. And without that knowledge men go ahead and do their best in creating what they think is a plan of God, and the will of God. And in the various religions and denominations that are in the world, unfortunately their best intentions can never match the will of God.

Now let's come to Leviticus 23, and we'll pick it up here in the flow of the holy days. Verse 26 "And the LORD spake unto Moses, saying,…" Now you see, as we have learned these are the days of God. So God spoke to Moses, Moses then told the children of Israel. "…On the tenth *day* of this seventh month [which is today] *there shall be* a day of atonement: it shall be an holy convocation unto you; and ye shall afflict your souls,…" And of course we know from Psalm 35:13 that that is without food. And in the case of Moses up on the mountain, it was without food and water for forty days. Now God doesn't require that of us, but we are to fast this one day as a commanded feast in addition to other times during the year whenever it is necessary. "…And offer an offering made by fire unto the LORD."

Now let's come to Numbers 28 and 29 because this depicts all of the official offerings that were to be given throughout the whole year. And it starts out in Numbers 28 with the daily offering and then the Sabbath offering, and then the monthly offerings, and then the Feast of Unleavened Bread. And of course as we have noted concerning the Passover, at the temple or tabernacle there were no sacrifices required for that day. You can read that in Numbers 28:16.

But let's come over here to Numbers 29. It comes from Unleavened Bread down to Pentecost and then there's a break because it goes to Numbers 29. Now I don't think in the Hebrew there is a break there. There very well may be, but it groups all of the commanded offerings at the temple; This was in addition to the individual offerings of burnt offerings and peace offerings and meal offerings that people would give.

Now here are the commandments for the Day of Atonement found in Numbers 29:7. "And ye shall have on the tenth *day* of this seventh month an holy convocation; and ye shall afflict your souls: ye shall not do any work *therein*: but ye shall offer a burnt offering unto the LORD *for* a sweet savour; one young bullock, one ram, *and* seven lambs of the first year; they shall be unto you without blemish: and their meat [meal] offering *shall be of* flour…" (Num. 29:7-9). And it gives a description there. And then it explains concerning the goats for the sin offering, and so forth. And so whenever we come to the holy days, when we come before God on these special occasions, we do take up an offering. And an offering that we give to God is not measured in terms of dollars, though in a sense it is, in a

514

physical way. But our offerings to God should be a measure of our love to God, our attitude toward God, and our willingness to serve Him and obey Him. And also our willingness to prove Him, as He says there in Malachi 3 that He says, "Now prove Me herewith, that you shall not have sufficiency in all things, whether you will or not" (Mal. 3:10, paraphrased). Because we will. And God also promises that. Many of the blessings of God that come from God are not counted in terms of monetary equivalency, or remuneration. The blessings of God include many, many, many different things: Our life, our health, our protection, our family, our employment, the things that we are doing. And as we will see today, keeping us from the evil one. All of those are blessings that God gives. So in taking up the offering, we'll pause in just a minute and take up the offering, but you do it according to the blessings that God has given you, and realize that on this Day of Atonement we are to be at-one with God.

Isn't it a marvelous thing indeed, that that which men count the least or the most unimportant, are the very things that God uses to teach and reveal His will and purpose? Such is the case of the holy days being all listed together. And this is the only chapter in the whole Bible that has all the holy days listed together—and it's in the Old Testament. A lot of people say, "Well, you know, we don't need to keep this. It's nailed to the cross", and so forth. And all they are doing with that is cheating themselves out of the true knowledge of the plan of God. See, because it is true, anytime anyone thinks that they know better than God they're going to get themselves in trouble. They're going to cut themselves off from God. Now the Day of Atonement is a particular holy day, which emphasizes that.

Now let's continue reading here in Leviticus 23:28, "And ye shall do no work in that same day:…" Now you see when we read this it makes it very clear. These are not hard to understand words. This is not some secret allegorical meaning that is contained in here. It's very simple. "…For it *is* a day of atonement, to make an atonement for you before the LORD your God. For whatsoever soul *it be* that shall not be afflicted in that same day, he shall be cut off from among his people." He's still among them, but he's cut off from them. Isn't that interesting? Think about how many people today who used to be in the church of God. Whether they were converted or not, that's in God's hands. Only God knows. But how many people have been cut off from God and from among the people and from the church because they no longer keep the Day of Atonement? It's an amazing thing when you think about it.

Look at it on the other hand this way: It is an amazing thing how much God reveals to us when we do keep these days year after year, after year, after year. And every year we learn more. And every year we understand more because that's the way God has inspired and caused the Bible to be written. We're reading the things which are inspired by the mind of God, though a man wrote it. Though Moses originally wrote these words down, and though they have been translated, the meaning of it is very clear.

Now let's continue on, verse 30. "For whatsoever soul *it be* that shall not be afflicted [that is fast without food and water in that day, with the exception of some who are pregnant or childbirth, or medical situations like that] in that same day, he shall be cut off from among his people. And whatsoever soul *it be* that doeth any work in that same day, the same soul will I destroy from among his people." Now how God is going to do that, you can just look out and see how God has intervened in different ones lives.

Now to emphasize it again He says in verse 31, "Ye shall do no manner of work: *it shall be* a statute for ever throughout your generations in all your dwellings." Now then, how long does that mean? Well, if we are the descendants of the children of Israel physically, it's binding upon us. And if we are the children of Israel spiritually because we, as Gentiles have been grafted into that tree, and then the branches drink of the sap that comes

515

from the roots and is fed by the roots, then it means for us—in your generations, in your dwellings.

"It *shall be* unto you a sabbath of rest,…" Now all the holy days are called Sabbaths. And it's strange that the Seventh Day Adventists really don't understand that. Now they can keep the seventh day but how much do they lose because they don't keep the holy days of God? So you see, there are the contradictions that come along here [in their thinking]. "…And ye shall afflict your souls:…" Again He mentions it, so that's three times.

Now also it gives us a definitive time of when the day begins and ends. "…In the ninth *day* of the month at even [Hebrew *ba erev*, meaning the sun has just dropped below the horizon. That beings the new day. *Ba erev* of the ninth ends the ninth day, so when the sun drops below the horizon you're beginning the tenth day. "…From even unto even [from the even of the ninth to the even of the tenth], shall ye celebrate [observe] your sabbath" (Lev. 23:26-32). And it's very interesting because in the Septuagint the Greek means, you shall sabbathize your Sabbath. Quite important, isn't it? So there we have it.

Now let's go to Exodus 31 and let's see again how these things are binding upon us. Now every time God asks us to do something, why does He ask us to do it? Why does He command us to do it? 1) Because God is love; 2) God loves us; 3) God has called us; 4) God wants us to be in right standing with Him through Jesus Christ and the sacrifice for our sins, and having been justified from them. And He wants to bless us so that in doing the things that He commands us, He will bless us because He loves us, because He's called us, because we are those that He has called to be in His family. So in order to prepare for that we need to have the education and understanding which comes from God through His word and through His Spirit, so we can learn to have the mind of Christ, and so when the resurrection takes place we will be able to work with Christ and do the things that He wants and help usher in the kingdom of God on the earth. So you see that's why God commands these things.

Now here again in Exodus 31:12, "And the LORD spake unto Moses, saying, Speak thou also unto the children of Israel [and we are the spiritual Israel of God], saying, Verily my sabbaths ye shall keep: for it is a sign between Me and you throughout your generations; that ye may know that I *am* the LORD that doth sanctify you." And then you combine that with the New Testament where Jesus said, "Your Word is truth, sanctify them with Your Truth." Now this is part of where it's God's Word, isn't it? Yes, it is. So keeping the Sabbaths, and it's plural therefore it includes all of them.

Now it mentions the seventh day Sabbath as the main one on which all of these are sanctified and it says you will keep it. It says, verse 15, work six days. Now verse 16 says, "Wherefore the children of Israel shall keep the sabbath, to observe the sabbath throughout their generations, *for* a perpetual covenant. It [that is the keeping of the sabbaths] *is* a sign between Me and the children of Israel for ever: [and to always remember that God is Creator] for *in* six days the LORD made heaven and earth, and on the seventh day He rested, and was refreshed." So that's a tremendous thing that God has given here.

Now after He gave that commandment, verse 18, "And He gave unto Moses, when He had made an end of communing with him upon mount Sinai, two tables of testimony, tables of stone, written with the finger of God" (Ex. 32:12-18). You think about it for a just a minute. How dare a man take upon himself the prerogative to change the Word of God and to change what God has spoken, and to alter or reject what God had written with His own finger on those two tables of stone.

Now let's continue on with the Day of Atonement. Let's see when sin entered into the world, because sin and the removal of sin has everything to do with the Day of Atonement. And we're going to see that just the removal of sin alone without the removal of Satan the devil is not sufficient. By the time we get all the way through the holy days, we're going to understand that Satan, the author of sin, must be removed and dealt with forever. That's all in God's plan.

Now we know the account here in Genesis 3, of how God told them "You shall not eat of the tree of the knowledge of good and evil, for in the day that you eat thereof you shall surely die." And of course Satan came in, and God wanted to test them. Would they obey His voice or not? Would they keep His commandments or not? Would they eat of the tree of life, and would they not eat of the tree of the knowledge of good and evil? See, God had to do that because in giving free moral agency, God did not make us robots. And if you give free moral agency you have to give free moral agency so that a person can choose one way or the other. Now just like He told the children of Israel in Deuteronomy 30, "I command you to choose life that you may live." So likewise He commanded Adam and Eve not to eat of the tree of the knowledge of good and evil because He loved them, He created them, and His plan was to come forth from them. But He had to know—did they really love Him; did they really believe Him; were they willing to do what God had said?

So, you know the story. The serpent came and said to the woman, "Is it really true that God said you can't eat of any of the fruit of the trees in the garden?" Bringing up a preposterous proposition because he knew that was not so. And so Eve had to correct him and say, "No, we can eat of the fruit of all the trees except the one that's in the midst of the garden. God said, 'You shall not eat of it neither shall you touch it lest you die.' " And of course Satan always wants to get you on his side. And he makes sin appear as if it's not sin. So he said, "You shall not surely die." And isn't that the way it is in the world today? Don't people want to live in their sins and yet receive the blessings for obedience? But it doesn't mix. It's not that way. And then he accuses God. Anyone who accuses God, especially of what God has done, then you'll never, never, never understand the Word of God. What you need to do is admit that you don't understand and ask God for understanding, and He will give it as you study His Word, and as you pray, and as you live according to God's will. But Satan lied. He's the father of lies, he did not stand in the truth and there's no truth in him. So when he speaks a lie, he speaks of his own because he's the father of it.

So Satan said, "You shall not surely die, for God knows in the day that you eat thereof your eyes will be opened [the exact opposite happened—their eyes were closed], and you shall be as gods." No, they weren't as gods. Isn't it interesting here—"be as gods"? Does Satan consider himself to be a god? But of course. So he's saying, "You'll be like me." Not the true God. But the only way that they would become "as god" is if some of the qualities of God would be: 1) they took upon themselves to judge God instead of accepting and believing in faith what God had told them and commanded them; 2) to judge for themselves (by exercising their free moral agency incorrectly) what they would determine to be right and wrong. And that's the whole story of the tree of the knowledge of good and evil. So you know they took it. It appealed to the senses. Why didn't Eve say, "Well, God told us no. We're not going to. We believe God, we love Him, we're not going to do it." End of the story. They didn't do that. I did a tape years ago called "What would the world have been like if Adam and Eve had not sinned?" Well, it would have been a different world indeed. So if you want that tape you can write for it. However, please understand this: They did sin, and we are the end result of the progeny of mankind from Adam and Eve, and we still sin.

So it appealed to her senses, it was good for food, pleasant to the eyes, a tree to be desired to make one wise, and she took of the fruit, she ate of it, she gave it to her husband and he ate it. The eyes of both of them were opened—not to spiritual reality, but to sin and evil. Whenever Satan says, "Your eyes shall be opened," they will be—to evil and wretchedness, and sin. Not opened to understand the plan of God. Only God can do that, only through Christ.

So, their eyes were opened, they were both naked, and you know what happened. God came and judged them, and in sentencing and judging them He started right out with the serpent. Let's come back up to verse 11 after Adam and Eve hid themselves. Of course God knew where they were all the time. Someone wrote and said, "Well, it's kind of dumb of God to walk through the garden and say "Adam, where are you?" You see, that kind of attitude is never going to understand the Bible. He knew where he was, but He wanted Adam to respond to Him. So Adam said, "I hid myself when I heard Your voice because I was naked."

Now verse 11, "And he said, Who told thee that thou *wast* naked? Hast thou eaten of the tree, whereof I commanded thee that thou shouldest not eat? And the man said, The woman…", of course he didn't want to say, "Yeah, I did it." He pointed immediately to the woman and said, "The woman You gave me. God, it's Your fault, You gave me this woman." "Well boy, when I gave her to you, hey, that was the greatest thing there ever was, wasn't it? And now you're accusing her."

"…She gave me of the tree, and I did eat. And the LORD God said unto the woman, What *is* this *that* thou hast done? And the woman said, The serpent beguiled me, and I did eat [I was tricked into it]. And the LORD God said unto the serpent,…" So He began to meet out the punishment. Even if you are tricked into it, even if you are deceived into it, you still have a penalty to pay because sin is sin and the wages of sin is death. And that's what God told them about the tree of the knowledge of good and evil.

So He said to the serpent, "Because thou hast done this, thou *art* cursed above all cattle, and above every beast of the field; upon thy belly shalt thou go, and dust shalt thou eat all the days of thy life: and I will put enmity between thee [the serpent] and the woman, and between thy seed [that is all the physical serpents and the demons] and her seed [Who was to be the Christ];…" So right at the first sin God revealed there had to be a redeemer who had to overcome the power of sin and Satan. And that's what this day pictures. "…It [that is the seed] shall bruise thy [the serpent's] head, and thou shalt bruise his heel [a prophecy of the crucifixion that it would take the death of God to pay for the sins of mankind]."

And then the woman—she had her punishment. "…He said, I will greatly multiply thy sorrow and thy conception; in sorrow thou shalt bring forth children;…" And because the women bring forth the children and when the children do wrong as they're growing up and the different things that happen, they have sorrow and grief and look at how it is in the world today, and look at how women suffer because of the very nature that their offspring have. And just imagine the sorrow that was there when Cain killed Abel. So it's not just the pain of the child labor alone.

And He says, "…And thy desire *shall be* to thy husband, and he shall rule over thee. And unto Adam he said, Because thou hast hearkened [listened] unto the voice of thy wife, and hast eaten of the tree, of which I commanded thee, saying, Thou shalt not eat of it: cursed *is* the ground for thy sake; in sorrow shalt thou eat *of* it all the days of thy life; thorns also and thistles shall it bring forth to thee; and thou shalt eat the herb of the field; In the sweat of thy face shalt thou eat bread, till thou return unto the ground; for out of it wast thou taken: for dust thou *art,* and unto dust shalt thou return" (Gen. 3:1-19). And that's the fate of all human beings. No one has escaped death except Jesus Christ. No means that man or Satan have devised to try and trick man into thinking that he has an immortal soul and he's going to live forever, causes any life to be at all is because life comes from God, life comes from love, life does not come from sin, life does not come from death. Now let's see how it affected the whole world. So you see, it says that Eve was deceived, but Adam sinned.

Now let's come to the New Testament, Romans 5, and see what happened to the world when Adam and Eve sinned. Because it was quite a thing. The sentence that God gave them was the sentence of death within their members. And also as Paul wrote of later, to have along with that the law of sin—the corrupted human nature which naturally sins.

Now here in Romans 5 Paul explains it very clearly. Let's begin in verse 12 because here's where it brings us to Christ and His sacrifice for us on the Passover day, and then likewise when we come to the Day of Atonement then we will see this is when God is going to make that sacrifice of Christ available on a universal basis to everyone in the world—but not until the meaning of the Day of Atonement has been fulfilled, which we can summarize in this way: You can never be at-one with God as long as you have a sinful nature, and as long as you are in the flesh you can never be totally at-one with God. That cannot happen until there is first the process of conversion, and then enduring to the end, and then the resurrection, and then being born into the family of God. Then and only then can we be at-one with God. But it is sin that separated all mankind. And we know that Satan is the author of sin.

Now Romans 5:12, "Therefore, as by one man sin entered into the world, and by means of sin *came* death;…" The sentence of death was passed on and we all inherit it. The scientists know that there is a death gene in us, and it activates upon certain things that happen. But even if we have a good long physical life and live a long time, the death gene still activates and we die. "…And by means of sin *came* death; and in this way, death passed into all mankind; *and it is* for this reason that all have sinned." Because you see, with a nature of death there is no way that human beings can avoid sin, because it is a more imperfect product because of that (the nature of death) than what God originally created Adam and Eve to be, which is another whole different story. So the Day of Atonement pictures when God is going to open the way for all.

Now let's come here to II Corinthians 4, and we're going to see that Satan the devil is called the god of this world. And of course as we have seen, Satan likes to come in and twist and turn the Word of God, and he has many willing agents to do it. He has many willing people who desire to do this—and they think they are doing the will of God, but they're not. So he says here, II Corinthians 4:1, "Therefore, having this ministry, according as we have received mercy, we are not fainthearted. For we have personally renounced the hidden things of dishonest gain [now, that has to be], not walking in *cunning* craftiness [not having another agenda secretly below doing the will of God], nor handling the Word of God deceitfully;…" And that's what all the false apostles have done. And as we have been seeing in "Lies From The Pulpit" they handle the Word of God deceitfully. "…But by manifestation of the truth, we are commending ourselves to every man's conscience before God. But if our gospel is hidden, it is hidden to those who are perishing; in whom the god of this world has blinded the minds of those who do not believe,…" Because Satan the devil is deceiving the whole world (Revelation 12:9), and he has all of his agents out there doing it. The powers, the principalities, the demons, those in government, education, and everything. This whole world is in the grips of a diabolical deception that comes from Satan the devil. Yes, there is a little good here, and a little good there, but we're going to see that the evil is going to triumph temporarily. But the Day of Atonement pictures when God is fully triumphant. Because not only must you get rid of sin on an individual basis, which God does through the sacrifice of Jesus Christ and His mercy, forgiveness, and justification, but you also must get rid of the author of sin who is called the god of this world.

And here is what he does: "…Blinded the minds of those who do not believe, lest the light of the gospel of the glory of Christ, Who is *the* image of God, should shine unto them" (II Corinthians 4:1-4), to have the knowledge of God in truth and understanding. See, any time anyone rejects any part of the Word of God, they are rejecting God in degree. And as we have learned from the Days of Unleavened Bread, a little leaven leavens the whole lump. So a little sin breeds more sin.

Now let's come back to Leviticus 16 and let's see in the ceremony on the Day of Atonement that God commanded the children of Israel to do, that here He pictures one of the strangest offerings that we find in the entire Bible. And it's only on this one day—on the Day of Atonement.

This was to be done at the tabernacle or the temple. The priest was to go through his ritual—bathe himself and dress himself with the holy garments. And the thing concerning the Day of Atonement is this: This is the only day in the entire year that the high priest could go into the holy of holies. Once a year. And he had to give the offerings for himself, and so forth, as Paul said not without blood. Now I want you to compare that to the blessing that God has given to those who He has called, and who have the Holy Spirit now, that we have the ability through prayer to come in to the very presence of God anytime we desire. Quite a different thing, isn't it? Yes, indeed.

And so through this there is the offering of the two rams. Leviticus 16:7, "And he shall take the two goats, and present them before the LORD *at* the door of the tabernacle of the congregation." Now that's not even before the altar, nor the tabernacle of the congregation. That's right up past the altar of burnt offerings, right up where you go into the temple itself. And there he was to perform a special ceremony. This is not done on any, underline any other sacrifice that is done, because these two goats were to be as identical as possible. And there was a special ritual that was done by the priest to show which of these two goats was the true sin sacrifice of God.

And so he cast lots. "…One lot for the LORD, and the other lot for the scapegoat." And the Hebrew there is *Azazel*, which is another name for Satan the devil. Before Satan fell he was the cherub that covered, and he comes to this world saying, "I am God." And the world can't distinguish the difference between the true Christ and the false christ; between the true God and the false god. So this is symbolized by these two goats, where then God would have to select the one which was the true sin offering. Then the one that was the true sin offering, he was told after he went in and cleansed the ark and everything, verse 15, "Then shall he kill the goat of the sin offering, that *is* for the people, and bring it's blood within the vail, and do with that blood as he did with the blood of the bullock, and sprinkle it upon the mercy seat, and before the mercy seat: and he shall make **an atonement for the holy *place*,** because of the uncleanness of the children of Israel, and because of their transgressions in **All THEIR SINS:**…" Now here was one sacrifice that was given to represent the forgiveness, or the atonement of all the sins of the children of Israel. And once they have been atoned for they have been atoned, so the live goat is another proposition. And it's interesting that the ceremony took place at the temple, but the live goat was never sacrificed. Because the live goat is symbolic of Satan the devil, who's the god of this world, who is the author of sin. Because as soon as Satan was let into the Garden of Eden, Adam and Eve sinned. And as we are going to see when we come to the final conclusion of the Feast of Tabernacles where God yet has another mission for Satan to do, that unless the author of sin is removed, sin will occur again. And that's the whole lesson we have within our bodies with the law of sin and death, and overcoming, and things like this.

Now then when he has done that, then we come down here to verse 20. "And when he hath made an end of reconciling the holy *place,* and the tabernacle of the congregation, and the altar, he shall bring the live goat: and Aaron shall lay both his hands upon the head of the live goat, and confess over him all the iniquities of the children of Israel,…" Because you see, all of the sins that people do as instigated by Satan the devil, and of course since he's the author of sin, all sin comes back to him. So therefore, having their sins forgiven, now God goes to the one who has caused them, Satan the devil, and puts it upon his head that he bears his own sin. There is no atonement for Satan the devil.

"...Putting them upon the head of the goat, and shall send *him* away by the hand of a fit man into the wilderness: and the goat shall bear upon him all their iniquities unto a land not inhabited: and he shall let go the goat in the wilderness." Now the wilderness is a very important part of this whole thing, as we will see. And very important in relationship to Satan the devil.

Then the fit man, as we will see a little later, is a type of an angel who binds Satan the devil. He would come back and wash himself. The priest would wash and cleanse himself. Now notice verse 29. "And *this* shall be a statute for ever unto you: *that* in the seventh month, on the tenth *day* of the month, ye shall afflict your souls, and do no work at all, *whether it be* one of your own country, or a stranger that sojourneth among you: for on that day shall *the priest* make an atonement for you, to cleanse you, *that* ye may be clean from all your sins before the LORD. It *shall be* a sabbath of rest unto you, and ye shall afflict your souls, by a statute for ever." And then it says here, verse 34, "And this shall be an everlasting statute unto you, to make an atonement for the children of Israel for all their sins once a year. And he did as the LORD commanded Moses" (Lev. 16:7, 15-16, 20-22, 29-31, 34). Now we're going to see in just a little bit, the significance of the wilderness and what that has to do with removing Satan the devil that Jesus Christ will do, and to atone for our sins.

Now let's see the connection between the wilderness and Satan. Let's come in the New Testament now to Matthew 4, and here we have one of the most important battles of the entire ministry of Jesus Christ. Now it's important from this point of view: Jesus could not begin His ministry until He had conquered Satan the devil. Now let's think about this. If Jesus manifested Himself as God is God, to fight a battle with Satan, obviously He would win because He won the battle when Satan rebelled and a third of the angels went with him and they were cast back down to the earth, weren't they? So there's no question that He would win. Now when you come to this: If Jesus were an angelic being (we see in the book of Daniel that the angels of God fight against the angels of Satan, and there is war that goes on), He probably could have beaten him, and overcome him if He would have been manifested in angelic form. But now, here Christ was manifested, God in the flesh, as a human being. Now in order to overcome Satan the devil it was necessary that He do so in the flesh. Because Satan is the one who has caused all human beings to sin. So before He began His ministry He had to overcome Satan the devil, and to defeat him, which He did.

Now after He was baptized, Matthew 4:1, "Then Jesus was led up into the wilderness by the Spirit in order to be tempted by the devil. And when He had fasted *for* forty days and forty nights, afterwards He was famished. And when the tempter came to Him, he said, 'If You are the Son of God, command that these stones become bread.' " Now we'll notice in all the answers that Jesus gave, He gave the answers that God gave to man in order to serve God.

"But He answered *and* said, 'It is written,...' " Good example. How do you overcome demonic and satanic problems but by the Word and the Spirit of God. There it is right there. " 'It is written, "Man shall not live by bread alone, but by every word that proceeds out of *the* mouth of God [Deuteronomy 8:3]." ' " Then the devil took Him to the holy city and set Him upon the edge of the temple,..." From the highest pinnacle of the temple to the floor of the Kidron Valley is 650 feet. So this was like being on a 65 story building. "And [Satan] said to Him, 'If You are the Son of God, cast Yourself down; for it is written, "He shall give His angels charge concerning You, and they shall bear You up in *their* hands, lest You strike Your foot against a stone." ' " Jesus said to him, 'Again, it is written, "You shall not tempt *the* Lord your God." ' " And that's quite a statement isn't it? No human being is to tempt God.

Now that's another whole sermon in itself. You tempt God by not believing; you tempt God by accusing Him; you tempt God by imputing to Him things that are not His - such as imputing to Him the things that Satan the devil does. That is how you tempt God. And you shall not tempt Him to make a spectacle of yourself so that **you, by your actions, are commanding God to do something which God will not do**. And so the whole bottom line of this is that **no one is going to command God**. That's what this is all about.

Now verse 8, "After that, the devil took Him to an exceedingly high mountain, and showed Him all the kingdoms of the world and their glory,...", and Luke adds "in a moment of time." Now notice what he said to Him. " 'All these things will I give You, if You will fall down and worship me.' " Well, the meaning of that is, "You worship me as God. Instead of God, You worship me." That's exactly the same test that Adam and Eve failed by eating of the tree of the knowledge of good and evil. They didn't believe God. They didn't listen to His voice, and that is the most important thing. And the Word of God that we have here today is the voice of God. That's what's important. That's why it's so absolutely important that whoever does any preaching and teaching, and this applies to everyone of us, that we better teach the Word of God as Paul said, in season and out of season, because these are the Words of God. And we better handle it with love, and respect, and obedience, and fear, and awe because this is God's Word.

So what did Jesus say to him? " 'Begone, Satan! For it is written, "You shall worship the Lord your God, and Him alone shall you serve." ' " And of course that's to human beings—not to Satan. Satan would never worship God. But that's quite a statement, isn't it? You take this to yourself. You shall worship the Lord your God, and Him alone shall you serve. Even Job had to learn that lesson, didn't he? Without a doubt. So "Then the devil left Him..." (Matt. 4:1-11), and as it says in Luke "for a short season."

Now let's see how we are to look at these things. Let's see what God tells us to do in praying every day. Let's come over here to Matthew 6:13. This is what we need to pray: "And lead us not into temptation (or that we don't have to be led into trials), but rescue us." Now that's from the Greek—deliver, save, rescue us all applies here, from the evil one, who is Satan the devil. Now we are rescued from Satan the devil by the power of God through Jesus Christ with the Holy Spirit of God. And by yielding to Him, and obeying Him, and not living in sin and doing the will of Satan the devil. So we have to be rescued from it.

Now let's see how great this rescue was. I don't think many of us realize it. You know, many people have come out of this so-called Christian church or that so-called Christian church and all you're doing in many cases is changing Saturday for Sunday and the holidays for the holy days, which you need to do. There's nothing wrong with that. That needs to be. But the question comes down to this point: Are we really converted? Do we really believe? And do we really understand that even in that religious setting, which was a Satanic deception cleverly interwoven with the Word of God to make it look really good and Christian, because you see that's the whole lesson of the two goats of Leviticus 16. You cannot of your own self discern the true God from the false god. And unless you have the Word of God and the Spirit of God, you can't discern between Satan as god and God. You cannot discern between false prophets and false apostles and false brethren, and all of these things, and you're going to fall as a dupe again for Satan the devil. How else can you explain: Where have all the brethren gone? Well many of them were false brethren. And many of them came not for the reasons of loving God and obeying His voice, and believing Him and having faith in Christ. Many of them came because they saw the institution, and they saw the elegance of it and the desire of it. So they didn't come to serve God. You might say they were fair weather Christians, as it were. Just like it says in the parable: When persecution and trouble comes, they give up and flee.

Now here in Colossians 1:9, Paul is also setting the stage (as we have seen in Colossians 2) to avoid the subtlest most powerful deceptions of Satan the devil through philosophy and angel worship. So in what he's writing, he's trying to establish them firmly in the truth of God and for them to know and understand what God has done for each one of them, and hence for each one of us.

Verse 9, "For this cause we also, from the day that we heard *of it*, do not cease to pray for you and to ask that you may be filled with the knowledge of His will in all wisdom and spiritual understanding; that you may walk worthily of the Lord,..." Remember what we've said: **You walk in faith**, **believe in hope**, **and live in love**. And that is the core of your relationship with God. And that's what he's talking about here. "...Unto all pleasing, being fruitful in every good work and growing in the knowledge of God;..." And that is continuous "...Being strengthened with all power..." That's what God wants to be in us. To be strengthened with the power of God's Holy Spirit, "... according to the might of His glory,..." Since we live in the world "...unto all endurance and long-suffering with joy; giving thanks to the Father, Who has made us qualified for the share of the inheritance of the saints in the light;..."

Now notice verse 13. This is one of those middle voice Greek verbs. "...Who has personally rescued us from the power of darkness..." Now, you think about that for a minute. Why are you here in the church of God, with the knowledge of God, and the Word of God, and the Spirit of God, and the understanding of God, and you are not out there—that is, in the world? Because God has called you, and God is the one Who qualifies you. Not because we are greater than anybody else because we're not. We're the least. That's just the way it is. And that's why the Day of Atonement is a tremendous holy day, brethren, because it is to be a spiritual feast that we feast on the Word of God and on the Spirit of God and not the flesh. So it's tremendous.

"...Personally rescued us from the power of darkness and has transferred *us* unto the kingdom of the Son of His love..." (Col. 1:9-13). Now we're not in the kingdom of God yet. That won't come till the resurrection because flesh and blood cannot inherit the kingdom of God. But we are under the jurisdiction of the kingdom of God through the Holy Spirit of God, through Jesus Christ, through the Word of God. And then all of our allegiance, and all of our politics, as it were, are in heaven and not on earth. We await the kingdom to come and we will enter into it. So, isn't that something? "...**Who has personally rescued us from the power of darkness**." Quite a fantastic thing.

Now let's come to I John 5 and let's compare that with what the world is. I John 5:19), "We know that we are of God,..." We have to know that. If you have any doubts whatsoever, you take it to God in prayer through Jesus Christ, and study the Word of God and know that you have the Spirit of God, and know that you understand and do these things because God has given you the desire to do it, and that you are of God.

"We know that we are of God, and *that* the whole world lies in *the power of* the wicked one." Or, lies in the wicked one, but it means the power of the wicked one. Isn't that something? It reminds me of the song... "He's got the whole world in his hands, he's got the whole wide world in his hands..." And the Day of Atonement pictures when it's going to be taken out of his hands. Quite an important thing, and profound for us to realize and know and understand.

Now let's see what God is going to do. Let's see what the Day of Atonement pictures in dealing with Satan the devil. Let's come to the book of Revelation and see this, then we will see how God will begin to deal with Israel and grant to them repentance. But first, this must be done: The author of sin must be removed. Now notice as we saw on the Feast of Trumpets, how Christ and all of us, the saints, are going to return to the earth. There's going to be this great battle on the earth and the first thing that happens is that Jesus sends an angel to take the beast and the false prophets and cast them into the lake of fire where they are burned to a crisp. So in order to stop that kind of human activity you have to get the two top leaders—the beast and the false prophet. Then you have to go one step further: You have to get rid of Satan the devil who set up the beast and the false prophet and brought sin to the whole world. So here we see the fulfilling of Leviticus 16 where the goat is taken to the wilderness and let go. Taken away, gotten rid of. Now then we have an add-on at this point as revealed in the book of Revelation. Something has to happen in order for Satan to be removed and for the Millennium to start.

Let's begin. Revelation 20:1, "Then I saw an angel descending from heaven, having the key of the abyss, and a great chain in his hand." Now that is the prison of the demons and Satan—the abyss. "And he took hold of the dragon, the ancient serpent, who is *the* Devil and Satan, and bound him *for* a thousand years." Now He doesn't get rid of him entirely. He binds him. "Then he cast him into the abyss, and locked him *up*, and sealed *the abyss* over him, so that he would not deceive the nations any longer until the thousand years were fulfilled; and after that it is ordained that he be loosed *for* a short time" (Rev. 20:1-3). And when we come to that last part of the Feast of Tabernacles we'll see what happens. Namely this: As soon as he is let loose sin reigns again. So the Day of Atonement pictures that you must get rid of the author of sin. You cannot bring in everlasting righteousness with him around. It is an impossibility.

Now let's see what God is going to do with Israel. Let's come to Ezekiel 36. Quite an amazing thing. See, once you get rid of the author of sin, and you get rid of the blindness, and you get rid of all of those wrong influences—and remember what they all went through, it's really quite a thing that is done here.

Ezekiel 36:16, "Moreover the word of the LORD came unto me, saying, Son of man, when the house of Israel dwelt in their own land, they defiled it by their own way…" Now isn't that interesting? "There is a way that seems right to a man, the ends thereof are the ways of death" (Prov. 16:25, paraphrased). And it seems right. "…By their own way and by their doings: their way was before Me as the uncleanness of a removed woman. Wherefore I poured My fury upon them for the blood that they had shed upon the land, and for their idols *wherewith* they had polluted it: and I scattered them among the heathen, and they were dispersed through the countries: according to their way and according to their doings I judged them. And when they entered unto the heathen, whither they went, they profaned My holy name, when they said to them, These *are* the people of the LORD, and are gone forth out of His land." Isn't that true? Even today there are people who say, "We're the people of God", but they're not.

Now then He says, "But I had pity for Mine holy name, which the house of Israel had profaned among the heathen, whither they went. Therefore say unto the house of Israel, Thus saith the Lord GOD; I do not *this* for your sakes, O house of Israel, but for Mine holy name's sake…" God is going to save the world and Israel, and all nations because of His plan and His holiness, and as we know, because of His covenant with Abraham.

He says, "I'm going to do this for My holy name's sake…which ye have profaned among the heathen, whither ye went. And I will sanctify My great name, which was profaned among the heathen, which ye have profaned in the midst of them; and the heathen shall know that I *am* the LORD…" Though Israel didn't know God, now God is going to reveal Himself not only to Israel but to the heathen. He says they, "…shall know that I *am* the LORD, saith the Lord GOD, when I shall be sanctified in you before their eyes." In other words, what God is going to do when He brings Israel out of captivity, and grants them repentance, which this Day of Atonement pictures, and restores them back to Him, all the heathen are going to know that it is God. "For I will take you from among the heathen, and gather you out of all countries,…" And that's what this Day of Atonement pictures the regathering of the children of Israel back to the land. "…And will bring you into your own land. Then will I sprinkle clean water upon you [get rid of all the filthiness and so forth], and ye shall be clean: from all your filthiness, and from all your idols, will I cleanse you. A new heart also will I give you, and a new spirit will I put within you:…" So not only is it going to be a recreation of the earth because of the desolation of all the things that take place on the earth, as we saw from Pentecost and Trumpets, but also now that Satan is removed He's going to take away the penalty that He gave to Adam and Eve when they first sinned in giving them a sinful nature.

So now He says, "A new heart also will I give you, and a new spirit will I put within you: and I will take away the stony heart out of your flesh, and I will give you an heart of flesh." That means a normal human mind and heart and capacity without all of the pulls of human nature. Now that's going to change the world, see. But in order to change the world you've got to change the people. This is what God is doing. That's why we're called first. That's why we live in this world though we're not of the world, because in order for God to do this and bring it to the whole world we have to be changed, we have to be converted; and just count that all the saints from Abel on down to the last two witnesses. We all have to be changed first before we can do what God wants us to do. So before He puts them back in the land, He's going to take away this hard-heartedness and blindness that they have. Verse 27, "And I will put My spirit within you [they're going to be converted], and cause you to walk in my statutes, and ye shall keep my judgments, and do *them*" (Ezek. 36:16-27). **Hello! What does it take to keep the commandments and judgments of God? His Spirit. That doesn't do away with them, does it? No, it gives you the means and the ability to keep them. But you see, since the carnal mind that they had before, the heart of stone, they had a religion where they did not want to do the will of God**. They wanted the part of it that they agreed with, but the other part they wanted to remake in their own image, and polluted it and caused all the deception and lies, and Satan the devil was right there saying, "Yeah, do it." Now it's going to be changed. **You can't change the world unless you change the people. And you can't change the world unless you get rid of Satan the devil. And you can't change the people unless you have the proper leadership through Christ and the saints.**

Now let's go to Ezekiel 37:15 and let's see another way of explaining it here. "The word of the LORD came again unto me, saying, Moreover, thou son of man, take thee one stick, and write upon it, For Judah, and for the children of Israel his companions: then take another stick, and write upon it, For Joseph, the stick of Ephraim, and *for* all the house of Israel his companions: And join them one to another into one stick; and they shall become one in thine hand." That is part of the meaning of the Day of Atonement bringing back the children of Israel—all twelve tribes, all together, all serving God.

Now, verse 18, "And when the children of thy people shall speak unto thee, saying, Wilt thou not shew us what thou *meanest* by these? Say unto them, Thus saith the Lord GOD; Behold, I will take the stick of Joseph, which *is* in the hand of Ephraim, and the tribes of Israel his fellows, and will put them with him, *even* with the stick of Judah, and make them one stick, and they shall be one in Mine hand. And the sticks whereon thou writest shall be in thine hand before their eyes. And say unto them, Thus saith the Lord GOD; Behold, I will take the children of Israel from among the heathen, whither they be gone, and will gather them on every side, and bring them into their own land [bring them back as one]: and I will make them one nation in the land upon the mountains of Israel; and one king shall be king to them all: and they shall be no more two nations, neither shall they be divided into two kingdoms any more at all: neither shall they defile themselves any more with their idols, nor with their detestable things, nor with any of their transgressions: but I will save them out of all their dwellingplaces, wherein they have sinned, and will cleanse them: so shall they be My people, and I will be their God." There is the meaning of the Day of Atonement for the future repentance, conversion, and bringing at-one-ment the whole nation of Israel. Just as Paul wrote, so all Israel shall be saved. And here it is. This is for the Day of Atonement. And we know, as He says in Zechariah 12, He starts out with the tribe of Judah first. He's going to save the tents of Judah first. And we found that confirmed in Revelation 7 when we saw the sealing of the 140,000 of the children of Israel [Judah is first].

Now let's see what also God is going to do, verse 24. "And David My servant *shall be* king over them [Christ will be King over all the earth, and David will be king over Israel]; and they all shall have one shepherd: they shall also walk in My judgments, and observe My statutes, and do them." You see, it's amazing isn't it, how that in the Old Testament it shows that you need the Spirit of God to keep the commandments of God. And that's what God was saying all along. Clear back when He first dealt with Israel and gave the Ten Commandments, He said, "O that there were such a heart in them that they would fear Me, and keep My commandments always,…" (Deut. 5:29). Here we see, they have a new heart. Here we see the Day of Atonement then paves the way for the beginning of the Millennium.

"And they shall dwell in the land that I have given unto Jacob My servant, wherein your fathers have dwelt; and they shall dwell therein, *even* they, and their children, and their children's children for ever: and My servant David *shall be* their prince for ever. Moreover I will make a covenant of peace with them; it shall be an everlasting covenant with them: and I will place them, and multiply them, and will set My sanctuary in the midst of them for evermore. My tabernacle also shall be with them:…" So now we're getting in to the meaning of the Feast of Tabernacles. "…Yea, I will be their God, and they shall be My people. And the heathen shall know that I the LORD do sanctify Israel, when My sanctuary shall be in the midst of them for evermore" (Ezek. 37:15-28).

Now then, that takes care of the children of Israel. Now let's come back to us, and see the prayer that Jesus gave to us so that we can understand that in order to be in the kingdom of God the Day of Atonement pictures for us being at-one with God. And this was the prayer that Jesus gave at His last prayer there in John 17. So let's turn there and let's see the prayer that Jesus gave.

Let's pick it up here in verse 13, " 'But now I am coming to You [that is, to the Father]; and these things I am speaking *while yet* in the world, that they may have My joy fulfilled in them.' " Now that's after the resurrection and we're in the kingdom of God. For the fullness of that, see. We are to have joy now, but just think what it's going to be after the resurrection and we're one with God.

" 'I have given them Your words, and the world has hated them because they are not of the world, just as I am not of the world.' " So in order for us to be at-one with God we have to have the Spirit of God, we have to be sanctified by God. Even though we're not of the world, now notice what He says here. " 'I do not pray that You would take them out of the world, but that You would keep them from the evil one.' " When we stay at-one with God knowing His plan and purpose, and having His Spirit and His grace and His love, God will keep us from the evil one. We will not be deceived. We will not go astray. " 'They are not of the world, just as I am not of the world. **Sanctify them in Your truth; Your Word is the truth** [that's how it's accomplished]. Even as You did send Me into the world, I also have sent them into the world [referring to the apostles]. And for their sakes I sanctify Myself, so that they also may be sanctified in *Your* truth. I do not pray for these only, but also for those who shall believe in Me through their word;…' " And this prayer of Jesus is being fulfilled right to this very day, and will continue to be down through until He returns and beyond.

Now notice, here is the prayer, here is the ultimate goal—that is, spiritual Israel, " '...That they all may be one, even as You, Father, *are* in Me, and I in You; that they also may be one in Us, in order that the world may believe that You did send Me. And I have given them the glory that You gave *to* Me, in order that they be may one, in the same way *that* We are one: I in them [Christ in you], and You in Me [Christ and the Father working together], that they may be perfected into one...' " (John 17:13-23).

So this Day of Atonement pictures that perfection, and pictures when we will no longer have any sin at all but be totally at-one with God. This is the meaning of the Day of Atonement.

End of Sermon

Transcriber: Carolyn Singer

The Day of Atonement—Sermon II—Holy Day
September 25, 2004
Scriptural References

1) Leviticus 23:26-32

2) Psalm 35:13

3) Numbers 28:16

4) Numbers 29:7-9

5) Malachi 4:10

6) Exodus 31:12-18

7) Genesis 3:1-19

8) Romans 5:12

9) II Corinthians 4:1-4

10) Revelation 12:9

11) Leviticus 16:7, 15-16, 20-22, 29-31,34

12) Matthew 4:1-11

13) Deuteronomy 8:3

14) Matthew 6:13

15) Colossians 1:9-13

16) I John 5:19

17) Revelation 20:1-3

18) Ezekiel 36:16-27

19) Proverbs 16:25

20) Ezekiel 37:15-28

21) Deuteronomy 5:29

22) John 17:13-23

CHAPTER THIRTY-FOUR

The Feast of Tabernacles—Day 1—Holy Day

September 30, 2004

And welcome brethren, to the first day of the Feast of Tabernacles, 2004. Now we're going to start a little differently here. Let's come to I Corinthians 1, because you see, more and more the holy days are coming under attack, especially by the Protestants. And they have been by Seventh Day Adventists, and they have been by the Church of God Seventh Day. And we're going to understand something here very important concerning the holy days from the point of view of how we understand.

Now here, I Corinthians 1:17. The apostle Paul writes: "For Christ did not send me to baptize, but to preach the gospel—not with *the* wisdom of words [that is, the words and philosophies of men], lest the cross of Christ be made void. For to those who are perishing, the preaching of the cross [and of course that includes the whole plan of God] is foolishness; but to us who are being saved, it is the power of God. For it is written, 'I will destroy the wisdom of the wise, and I will nullify the understanding of those who understand.' Where *is the* wise? Where *is the* scribe? Where *is the* disputer of this age? Did not God make foolish the wisdom of this world?" And you compare the holy days of God and the whole plan of God to everything that the world has and their religions and their holidays—it is foolishness and yet they think it is wisdom. And they look at what we do and think we are foolish, and think that we are going back under the law. That's not the case because you see, keeping the commandments of God and having the faith of Jesus Christ (Rev. 14:12) go hand in hand. [They think that] He's destroyed them. Verse 21: "For since in the wisdom of God the world through *its own* wisdom did not know God, it pleased God to save those who believe through the foolishness of preaching" (I Cor. 1:17-21). Now how are we going to understand not only the preaching, but the writings, the Word of God, what the apostles have written and preserved for us, what God inspired and had written and preserved for us in the Old Testament?

Now let's come here to I Corinthians 2:9. "But according as it is written, '*The* eye has not seen...' " So people are not going to understand these things by just sitting down and reading alone. " '...Nor *the* ear heard, neither have entered into *the* heart of man, *the* things which God has prepared for those who love Him.' " And God is preparing for us. And God is preparing for this world. "But God has revealed *them* to us by His Spirit..." So there is an absolute dividing line, and that dividing line is determined by the Spirit of God. You understand the things in the Scriptures by the Spirit of God. And as we have seen: Line upon line, precept upon precept, here a little and there a little, and rightly dividing the Word of God to put it together. And also to have the understanding and the attitude that the Word of God teaches us His plan. Now that has to be revealed. "...For the Spirit searches all things..." Not just the New Testament, but all things: the Old Testament; each individual that comes into being in the world; all of those that God calls—searches all things. "...Even the deep things of God" (I Cor. 2:9-10). And the holy days, and the understanding of the holy days are part of the deep things of God.

"For who among men understands the things of man except *by* the spirit of man which *is* in him? In the same way also, the things of God [now the holy days are part of the things of God] no one understands except *by* the Spirit of God." And we've seen the problem that has happened in the church here in recent years. They begin bringing in the spirit of the world. And as they brought in the spirit of the world they brought in the world and their beliefs and pushed out the Spirit of God and the truth of God. That's why Paul says here, verse 12: "Now we have not received the spirit of the world, but the Spirit that *is* of God, so that we might know the things graciously given to us by God; which things we also speak, not in words taught by human wisdom, but in *words* taught by *the* Holy Spirit *in order to* communicate spiritual things by spiritual *means*" (verses 11-13). And that's why the holy days are important because these are the appointed times of God, the appointed seasons of God. And these are commanded convocations.

Now let's come to Psalm 119 and let's see another thing that God wants us to know to understand. And this is important because you see, the Word of God is inspired by God. And as Jesus said: " 'The words that I speak to you, *they* are spirit and *they* are life' " (John 6:63). And so when we come here to Psalm 119 we also see where David was inspired to write something very profound. He says: "Open Thou mine eyes, that I may behold wondrous things out of Thy law" (Psa. 119:18). And that's what we are going to do with the holy days. We are going to see the wondrous things out of God's law, out of God's Word—Old Testament, New Testament, put it all together and see and understand the plan of God and the meaning of the Feast of Tabernacles.

So let's first of all go, as we always do, to Leviticus 23, because one of the secret things of God that He has hidden, where He says that it is God's honor to hide something, or prerogative to hide it. But it is the honor of the king to dig it out. So that's what we have with all the holy days in Leviticus 23. Because it's awfully easy bringing in the spirit of the world, bringing in the spirit of the worlds religions to say: "Well, look at that, that's in the Old Testament." See, well they take that attitude because they do not understand and realize that Jesus Christ (Who they say they love, Who they say they follow, which they do not); that "The God of the Old Testament was harsh and mean. And these laws and these things we no longer have to do." And by that very thing they cut themselves off from God.

So let's begin here, Leviticus 23:33. Now you see we started out: Passover, Unleavened Bread, Pentecost, Trumpets, Atonement, and now here we are at the Feast of Tabernacles. And all of these things we have seen portrays a step-by-step revelation of the plan of God. And this is what we are to know, what we are to understand, and how we are to live our lives. And in these days, if we love God, if we serve God, if we are faithful to God and have God's Spirit in us, He will reveal more and more of His will out of His Word just like David said: "Open my eyes that I may behold wondrous things out of Your Word." And as Paul wrote, they are revealed by God's Spirit.

So let's begin here, verse 33: "And the LORD spake unto Moses, saying, Speak unto the children of Israel, saying, The fifteenth day of this seventh month *shall be* the feast of tabernacles *for* seven days unto the LORD. On the first day *shall be* an holy convocation [which is today]: ye shall do no servile work *therein*. Seven days ye shall offer an offering made by fire unto the LORD [now we're going to look at that in Numbers 29 in just a minute]: on the eighth day shall be an holy convocation unto you; and ye shall offer an offering made by fire unto the LORD: it *is* a solemn assembly; *and* ye shall do no servile work *therein*" (Lev. 23:33-36).

Now verse 37. Let's pay clear attention to this because one of the ways that people attack the Word of God and attack what we do, try to discredit what we do is because they say that we are keeping the feasts of the Jews. And that is an abominable lie. Notice what God says here: "These *are* the feasts of the LORD, which ye shall proclaim *to be* holy convocations…" This is a summary of the whole chapter up to here. The Sabbath commandment sanctifies the Passover and all the holy days. That's why it's given in the first part of the chapter. Now notice: "…to offer an offering made by fire unto the LORD, a burnt offering, and a meat [meal] offering, a sacrifice, and drink offerings, every thing upon his day: beside the sabbaths of the LORD, and beside your gifts, and beside all your vows, and beside all your freewill offerings, which ye give unto the LORD" (verses 37-38).

Now let's come to Numbers 29 and let's see the commanded offerings that they were to give. These were the official offerings to God for the whole nation of Israel. Now the Feast of Tabernacles is different in relationship to the offerings that are given on the other days. First of all He showed in Numbers 29 that there was to be the morning and the evening sacrifice. And of course then they had the meal offering and the wine offering and the incense that would go with it. Then on the Sabbath they had special Sabbath offerings in addition to the continual burnt offering. And then He goes right through all of the holy days (the new moons, the holy days) and it is very interesting that there is no commanded sacrifice at the tabernacle or temple for the Passover day because it was (as we have written extensively in *The Christian Passover* book) a domestic home kept feast.

Now let's come to Numbers 29:12. Let's see the tremendous offerings that were given. Now we also know this: that during the days of Solomon they had, beginning with the Feast of Trumpets, then they had (including the Feast of Trumpets) seven days dedication of the temple. Then they took a break so they could have Atonement and so forth, and then they come to the Feast of Tabernacles. And they had so many thousands of people there, and so many thousands of sacrifices that were offered that they had to make smaller altars in different locations on the temple grounds. And it was literally a fantastic and mammoth feast.

But here were the required offerings. Let's begin in Numbers 29:12: "And on the fifteenth day of the seventh month ye shall have an holy convocation; ye shall do no servile work, and ye shall keep a feast unto the LORD seven days: and ye shall offer a burnt offering, a sacrifice made by fire, of a sweet savour unto the LORD; thirteen young bullocks [one for every tribe], two rams, *and* fourteen lambs of the first year; they shall be without blemish..." (Num. 29:12-13). And then their meal offering and the wine offering and so forth and a kid goat for a sin offering. That's besides the continual morning and evening sacrifice and their meal and drink offerings.

Now each day of the feast the number of bullocks (while all the rest would remain the same) was decreased by one. And each one of these things shows a type of fulfillment and a progression in the plan of God. Now let's come over here to verse 32: "And on the seventh day seven bullocks, two rams, *and* fourteen lambs of the first year without blemish [their meal offering, their drink offering and so forth, and a goat for a sin offering]..." (verses 32-36). Now it says then on the eight day it reverts back to one bullock.

Now let's come down here to verse 39 and let's read this again. "These *things* ye shall do unto the LORD in your set feasts, beside your vows, and your freewill offerings, for your burnt offerings, and for your meat [meal] offerings, and for your drink offerings, and for your peace offerings." So there are the free-will offerings, there are the vows, and there are many things to consider.

That's why God says when they would come to a feast they were not to appear before the Lord empty. Now let's see here (Deuteronomy 16) the command for an offering. And we'll take up the offering here in just a bit. "Three times in a year shall all thy males appear before the LORD thy God in the place which He shall choose; in the feast of unleavened bread, and in the feast of weeks [which is Pentecost], and in the feast of tabernacles: and they shall not appear before the LORD empty: every man *shall give* as he is able..." (Deut 16:16-17). Now this is in addition to the burnt offerings, the peace offerings, the meal offerings and so forth that they were to give. Just like we find in Deuteronomy 14, that if the way was too far they were to go ahead and sell the bullocks, and sell the lambs, and the rams and so forth, and take the money and come to Jerusalem and then use that money on whatever their soul desires. And of course, as we see in Luke 21, which was the time leading up to the Passover when Jesus was crucified, there were many coming and giving gifts into the treasury. And so it wasn't just animal sacrifices and meal offerings and incense and wine offerings. They also had monetary offerings. And so since Christ, in fulfilling the Law and the Prophets, the part that He fulfilled in the law was all the rituals and all the sacrifices that were given under the Old Covenant. But the whole thing of free-will offerings and giving to the Lord, especially on the holy days, continues through till today.

Now you see, the daily offerings given, that was at the temple for the priests to do. That didn't mean that everyone was to come in and give an offering: part of an offering on one day, part of an offering on another day, part of an offering on another day all through the eight days. That had to do with the commanded sacrifices for the whole nation of Israel. So when we come to the New Testament it carries over because there is no temple, there is not a priesthood—Christ is our High Priest. And when we come together we are still to honor God by bringing an offering to Him. And so I just bring this out in a way so that you understand how then we can go into the Old Testament, how with the Spirit of God we can understand what needs to be done.

So at this time we'll take a pause and take up the offering. And be sure and put your full name and address on the envelope please.

The Feast of Tabernacles is what the whole world is waiting for. That is, the rule of God on earth. The kingdom of God governing the whole world. Now in the world today we are seeing that God is letting man, under the guidance of Satan the devil and also by His plan and purpose, just exactly like He told the Jews before they went into captivity that He raised up Nebuchadnezzar for the very purpose of taking them into captivity. And that if they fought against him, God would fight against them. And at the time that Jesus came the Jews were actually looking for the Messiah. They knew He was the Messiah. But you see, they didn't want to accept Him because He did not align Himself with them. See, they were expecting the Messiah to come to align with all of their institutions—the temple, the sacrifices, the government, throw out the Romans, and fight for them. Well, when Jesus came the first time that's not what it was.

Now let's come here to John 18 and let's see what Jesus told Pilate when he was questioning Him before He was scourged and sent out to be crucified. Let's pick it up here beginning in verse 33: "Then Pilate returned to the judgment hall and called Jesus, and said to Him, 'Are You the King of the Jews?' Jesus answered him, 'Do you ask this of yourself, or did others say *it* to you concerning Me?' Pilate answered Him, 'Am I a Jew? The chief priests and your own nation have delivered You up to me. What have You done?' Jesus answered, 'My kingdom is not of this world.' " (John 18:33-36). See, because God had a greater plan. God has a greater purpose. God knows that the world cannot be run in the kingdom of God unless there is planning, unless there is preparation, and unless the fullness of the plan of God comes to fruition.

And He said: " 'If My kingdom were of this world, then would My servants fight, so that I might not be delivered up to the Jews. However, My kingdom is not of this world.' " So Pilate couldn't understand that. Because you see, one of the reasons that they delivered Him to Pilate was because He said He was king. And so then the Jews falsely accused Him of wanting to usurp authority over Caesar. And so, it put all the pressure on Pilate as to what to do. So therefore verse 37: "Pilate therefore answered Him, 'Then You are a king?' Jesus answered, '*As* you say, I am a king. For this *purpose* I was born, and for this *reason* I came into the world, that I may bear witness to the truth. Everyone who is of the truth hears My voice.' Pilate said to Him, 'What is truth?' " (verses 36-38). That's exactly where we are today with the death of truth in this world. So then he said he found no fault in Him.

Now let's look at another thing concerning the kingdom of God because the scribes and Pharisees were expecting it to appear immediately. And they didn't understand that this was going to be a spiritual kingdom run by spiritual sons and daughters of God <u>over</u> the human beings on the earth. They wanted their own human power to be right under the Messiah so they could exercise the authority. Well you see, God is not going to leave the kingdom to people—only the sons and daughters of God, and they didn't understand that.

Let's pick it up here in Luke 19:11. "Now as they were listening to these things, He went on to speak a parable, because He was near Jerusalem, and they thought that the kingdom of God was going to appear immediately." They thought He was going to Jerusalem to take over; announce that He was the Messiah; rally all the armies of the Jews around; supernaturally with their armies and the power that He had, to destroy the Romans and get them out, and set up the kingdom of God on earth. So He wanted them to know it wasn't going to be that way.

"Therefore, He said, 'A certain nobleman set out to a distant country to receive a kingdom for himself, and to return' " (verse 12). Now they understood this because Herod went to Rome to be coroneted (this is Herod the Great), and then when he came back, it took him three years to come back and conquer the Jews to be the king over Judea, as the Romans had sent him. So they understood what He was talking about here.

Now verse 13: " 'And after calling ten of his servants, he gave to them ten pounds, and said to them, ' "Trade until I come *back*." ' " Now this tells us a little bit about what we are going to do that I'm going to talk about tomorrow—how do we prepare to rule and reign with Christ. He said: " ' "Trade until I come *back*." But his citizens hated him and sent an ambassador after him, saying, ' "We are not willing to have this man reign over us." ' " (verses 13-14). One of the very first things that has to be is Christ has to rule over you. But they didn't want Him to rule over them.

" 'And it came to pass that when he returned after receiving the kingdom, he directed that those servants to whom he had given the money be called to him…' " (verse 15). Then it went through one gained ten pounds, one gained five pounds, and the other one gained two pounds and so forth. Then we have someone who didn't do what they were supposed to do. And he said, verse 21: " ' "For I was afraid of you, because you are a harsh man." ' " Isn't that interesting? Isn't that what the Protestants accuse the God of the Old Testament of being? And is that not one of the reasons that they don't do the things that Jesus has said? Is that not one of the reasons why the Catholic Church exists? Yes, they don't want Christ to rule over them in their lives. They want a pope to worship and to rule over their lives. Absolutely amazing, isn't it? " ' "You take up what you did not lay down, and you reap what you did not sow [see, because it's spiritually built]." ' Then he said to him, ' "Out of your *own* mouth I will judge you, *you* wicked servant!" ' " (verses 21-22). Now that's something you need to understand. Every single one of us are going to be judged according to our works, and what we say, and what we do. And there are times when we say things that you better be very, very careful what you say because God may take you up on what you say as your judgment, just like here.

" ' "You knew that I am a harsh man, taking up what I did not lay down and reaping what I did not sow. Then why didn't you deposit my money in the bank, so that at my coming I might have received it with interest?" ' And he said to those who were standing by, ' "Take the pound from him, and give *it* to the one who has ten pounds." ' (And they said to him, ' "Lord, he has ten pounds." ')" And Jesus said, verse 26: " ' "For I tell you that to everyone who has, *more* shall be given; but the one who does not have, even what he has shall be taken from him." ' " Now verse 27: " ' "Moreover, bring my enemies, those who were not willing *for* me to reign over them, and slay *them* here before me" ' " (verses 22-27). Now that's just a very good short summary of the return of Christ—slay them.

Now we also know that the apostles, the very last thing just before Jesus ascended into heaven for the final time, they said, "Lord, will You restore the kingdom to Israel at this time?" And He says, "It's not given to you to know the times and seasons which the Father has put under His authority. But you go…" (Acts 1:6-7, paraphrased). In that case, go to Jerusalem and wait for the Holy Spirit. But for all of us we are to do that. We are not only to learn and know and understand the Word of God, but we are to go and we are to do, and we are to preach, and we are to teach, and we are to do these things, and we are to occupy by doing these things until Christ returns.

We are also going to see something very important here. Because when Jesus told Pilate that "to this end was He born," He was making very clear that He fulfilled this prophecy. Now He didn't make it clear to Pilate because Pilate didn't understand it. But as we go back and as we know and understand the prophecies and read them and put all the Scriptures together, then we understand that's precisely what Jesus was talking about because He was born to be a king. We're going to see you have been born, and I have been born, and all of those that God has called have been born, and having been converted, we are called to be kings and priests. And that's a tremendous thing as we will see.

Isaiah 9:6: "For unto us a child is born, unto us a son is given: and the government shall be upon His shoulder [He is going to reign, He is going to rule into the ages of eternity as it says in the book of Revelation]: and His name shall be called Wonderful, Counsellor, The mighty God, The everlasting Father, The Prince of Peace." Because only Christ can bring peace. And when Christ returns He is going to become a father by those who are converted (as we will see as we go down through the Feast of Tabernacles) by those who were converted during the Millennium as we rule and reign on this earth.

Now notice verse 7: "Of the increase of *His* government and peace *there shall be* no end…" So God's plan is going to go on into the ages of eternity. Quite a tremendous and magnificent thing that God is going to do. "…Upon the throne of David, and upon his kingdom, to order it, and to establish it … from henceforth even for ever. The zeal of the LORD of hosts will perform this" (Isa. 9:6-7). There's no getting around it. This is going to be done. It doesn't matter whether people believe or not, whether they understand or not—it is going to happen.

Now as we saw, the resurrection is on Pentecost, and we are there to receive our rewards and to receive our new name, the marriage of the Lamb and all those things that take place. Then the seven last plagues are poured out. Then Christ and all of the saints on the sea of glass return to the earth. And He's going to be King over all the earth. And that's going to be a tremendous day indeed.

Now let's see something else here—we share in that. Now let's look at this. Let's come to Revelation 20. Let's follow that progression down. After Satan has been put away, and during the Millennium Satan won't be around. Now on the seventh day of the feast we'll talk about why Satan is loosed for a short season. There's a purpose in that. So Satan is taken, he is bound, cast into the abyss. The next thing to take place is this, verse 4: "And I saw thrones; and they that sat upon them, and judgment was given to them; and *I saw* the souls of those who had been beheaded for the testimony of Jesus, and for the Word of God, and those who did not worship the beast, or his image, and did not receive the mark in their foreheads or in their hands; and they lived and reigned with Christ a thousand years" (Rev.

20:4). Now that's quite a thing. This is the whole purpose and goal as to why we are called—so that we can be with Christ, so that we can rule and reign with Him. That's the most important thing for us to understand. And tomorrow we'll cover what is the most important thing we need to have and develop now so we <u>can</u> rule and reign with Christ.

Then it says: "(But the rest of the dead did not live again until the thousand years were completed.)" Then referring back to verse 5 it says: "This *is* the first resurrection. Blessed and holy…" Now that's quite a thing, isn't it? Who is also called blessed and holy? God is. And as we know, we are to share the very glory of Christ. So it says: "Blessed and holy is the one who has part in the first resurrection; over these the second death has no power. But they shall be priests of God and of Christ, and shall reign with Him a thousand years" (verses 5-6). So that's going to be a tremendous thing. Absolutely marvelous.

Now let's come back here to Revelation 2 and let's see that's one of the promises. When we come to Revelation 2 and 3 even though there's a message to each one of the churches it always ends with "he that has an ear, let him hear what the Spirit says to the churches." So let's read it here. Revelation 2:25: "But hold fast what you have until I come. And to the one who overcomes, and keeps My works unto *the* end [so there are works to be kept], I will give [power] authority over the nations; and he shall shepherd [rule] them with an iron rod, as vessels of pottery are broken in pieces; as I have also received from My Father…" (Rev. 2:25-27). Now you see, we are going to have full authority and control. Christ is going to be King. The twelve apostles will be sitting on twelve thrones judging the twelve tribes of Israel. And beyond that of Elijah and Moses, we don't have too much of an inkling of who's going to be doing what. But don't fear, God has it all planned out and it's going to be all according to His will.

Now here just recently we have seen the transfer of sovereignty to the Iraqi's. And we also have seen, leading up to it and afterward, the terrorists attacks and so forth. And we've had all the bleeding hearts in the press say, "Oh, things went terribly wrong. Oh, there have been great mistakes that were made," and so forth. I think we need to understand: you cannot—it will be impossible to have a one-world government unless the Islamic nations are tamed and brought into the modern world. That's what all of this is going to lead to. But yes, there are those things that took place in killing, and bombing, and kidnapping, and beheading and things like this.

Now I saw a very interesting documentary when it was leading up to the memorial of D-Day, and there were more mistakes and more casualties made on that first day on D-Day when the troops landed there. They had 5000 casualties just the first day alone. And some of them landed at the wrong place. And some of the supplies didn't get to them the way that they should have. But never the less they overcame all those mistakes and they went in and the invasion was a success. And they said as it got to the end of the war, "Now how are they going to democratize Germany and Japan?" Well, it hasn't been reported very much but right after the Germans surrendered, do you know what the German renegades (or what we would call today, insurgents) were doing? They were blowing up railroad tracks, blowing up trucks, they were cutting telephone lines. And it took a total of three more years before the occupational forces got it underhand to where they could work with the Germans to bring about peace. And that finally wasn't resolved until the Cold War ended and the wall was torn down.

Now from that we're going to learn a lesson. And that lesson is: What is it going to be like when the Millennium begins? Because we're going to rule and reign with Christ a thousand years, are we not? And we are going to enforce and bring the government of God, are we not? And are we not going to have authority over the nations to rule them, or shepherd them with a rod of iron? Yes, we are.

So let's come back here to Isaiah 2 and let's see what it tells us about this. And let us see something very important and then we will look at the Scriptures which show how then it will be done. Now many times we read these things and go over them and we don't really fully expound them, or go through them in detail. But we're going to today.

Now let's pick it up here, Isaiah 2:1: "The word that Isaiah the son of Amoz saw concerning Judah and Jerusalem. And it shall come to pass in the last days, *that* the mountain of the LORD'S house..." Now as we know, it's a type of God's government. And we read in Isaiah 9 that the government is going to be on His shoulders and He's going to delegate to all the saints who are in the first resurrection so that they can rule and reign with Him. That's what it says—will reign a thousand years with Him. "...Shall be established in the top of the mountains...", because there will be other nations, but this is going to be the leading one. The sons and daughters of God in the kingdom of God ruling on earth will be with Christ ruling over the whole world. "...And shall be exalted above the hills; and all nations shall flow unto it" (Isa. 2:1-2).

And also as we have seen in Zechariah 14, one of the first things they are going to do is keep the Feast of Tabernacles. And if they don't keep it, what's going to happen? For those nations who don't keep it, then they aren't going to get any rain. And the Egyptians who don't come up, if they don't come up they're going to get the plague. Now that's what it means to shepherd with a rod of iron. And God has weapons far better than any army. God has power to execute these things far better than bombs, and tanks, and planes, and all of the specialty things that men have developed for war.

Now notice, continuing: "...and all nations shall flow unto it." Jerusalem! And it says here Judah. Isn't it interesting? Because it will be filled with resurrected sons of God who are considered spiritual Jews. Isn't that correct? Yes, indeed. Very interesting how these Scriptures come together.

Now let's continue on. Isaiah 2:3: "And many people shall go and say..." Now notice it doesn't say all people. Now that's important. So there will be those who will want to yield to God, the kingdom of God, and as we will see, it will start with Israel first. "...And say, Come ye, and let us go up to the mountain of the LORD, to the house of the God of Jacob; and He will teach us of His ways, and we will walk in His paths: for out of Zion shall go forth the law..." The very law that the Protestants hate. And the law of God has never changed. You need to understand that. Only the rituals and sacrifices have been superceded by greater [By the sacrifice of Jesus Christ and His priesthood]. Now notice: "...and the word of the LORD from Jerusalem. And He shall judge among the nations, and shall rebuke many people..." Why? "...And they shall beat their swords into plowshares..." See, so there's still going to be these insurgents, and terrorists, and remnants fighting against the implementation of the kingdom of God on earth. And just like everything else that God does: He gives man choice and He gives man leeway to see whether they will obey or not. And if they will not, after a given period of time, then He's going to exercise His power and His authority over them so they are going to learn, because God is not going to be mocked. "...And they shall beat their swords into plowshares, and their spears into pruninghooks: nation shall not lift up sword against nation, neither shall they learn war any more" (Isa. 2:1-4). See, so He's going to judge the nations afar off. That's exactly what He's going to do.

Now let's see, since we have seen the kind of attitude and the kind of things that we have in the Middle East, and with the Muslim religion and so forth, let's come to Ezekiel 38 and see one of the most profound things that's going to take place after the return of Christ, after Israel is brought back from captivity and in the land. And it's going to take a number of years. How long that will be we do not know. But all of those nations to the north and to the east, out of which came the army of 200 million that fought against Christ, as we saw there in Revelation 16 with the seven last plagues. Just remember there are billions, and billions, and billions of people over there and they're not all going to die. God has a plan. He knows that just like a lot of these insurgents that were after WWII in Germany, and that are in Iraq now after the transfer of sovereignty and all the things that have been going on there, they have to be ferreted out and they have to be put down, and they either have to repent or be exterminated. That's how God is going to handle it. That's what He means "rebuke them afar off."

Now let's see what happens here, and what it's going to do for the Millennium. The beginning of the Millennium is going to be a very difficult time indeed. Some people will come and say, "Oh, let's go up and learn God's way." A lot of other people are going to say, "Well, we don't know about this. This looks like these are the aliens from outer space. We better go up and we better fight against them. We better take back the world to ourselves." And that's exactly what they're going to try and do.

Now Ezekiel 38:1: "And the word of the LORD came unto me, saying, Son of man, set thy face against Gog, the land of Magog, the chief prince of Meshech and Tubal, and prophesy against him…" (Ezek. 38:1-2). Now we're going to see… Come over here to verse 11 so that we understand the time setting. "And thou shalt say, I will go up to the land of unwalled villages…" Now you can't call Jerusalem unwalled villages. As a matter of fact they're building walls, aren't they? Yes. "…I will go to them that are at <u>rest</u>…" Because you see God deals with Israel first, then the rest of the world. So God is going to deal with Israel first, and those nations who volunteer to come under the sovereignty of the kingdom of God and the rule of Jesus Christ and the saints. There will be some who won't want to. And as it says, great nations afar off He's going to rebuke. Well all these nations we're talking about here are afar off from Jerusalem.

Now back here to verse 3 and let's follow the story flow. "And say, Thus saith the Lord GOD; Behold I *am* against thee, O Gog, the chief prince of Meshech and Tubal: And I will turn thee back, and put hooks into thy jaws, and I will bring thee forth, and all thine army, horses and horsemen, all of them clothed with all sorts *of armour, even* a great company *with* bucklers and shields, all of them handling swords: Persia, Ethiopia, and Libya [which actually means Kush and Phut from India] with them; all of them with shield and helmet: Gomer, and all his bands; the house of Togarmah of the north quarters, and all his bands: *and* many people with thee. Be thou prepared, and prepare for thyself, thou, and all thy company that are assembled unto thee, and be thou a guard unto them. After many days thou shalt be visited…" (verses 3-8). So God is going to rule on earth beginning in Jerusalem; bring back the captivity of the children of Israel out of their captivity; establish them in their land. They will be building. They will be planting. God will be blessing them. And then these nations out there who don't want to submit, they're going to know what's going on.

"After many days thou shalt be visited: in the latter years thou shalt come into the land *that is* brought back from the sword, *and is* gathered out of many people, against the mountains of Israel, which have been always waste [that is, since the fall of Jerusalem in 70 AD]: but it is brought forth out of the nations, and they shall dwell safely all of them. Thou shalt ascend and come like a storm, thou shalt be like a cloud to cover the land, thou, and all thy bands, and many people with thee. Thus saith the Lord GOD; It shall also come to pass, *that* at the same time shall things come into thy mind, and thou shalt think an evil thought: and thou shalt say, I will go up to the land of unwalled villages; I will go to them that are at rest, that dwell safely, all of them dwelling without walls, and having neither bars nor gates, to take a spoil…" Because you see, they are going to be prosperous, they are going to have plenty, God is going to be blessing Israel, and they are going to want to take it. "…And to take a prey; to turn thine hand upon the desolate places *that are now* inhabited, and upon the people *that are* gathered out of the nations [so Israel is back in the land], which have gotten cattle and goods, that dwell in the midst of the land. Sheba, and Dedan, and the merchants of Tarshish, with all the young lions thereof, shall say unto thee, Art thou come to take a spoil? hast thou gathered thy company to take a prey? to carry away silver and gold, to take away cattle and goods, to take a great spoil?" (verses 8-13). "Are you going to come and take away the blessings that I God have given to the children of Israel who are at rest? Are you going to resist the kingdom of God? Are you going to resist the rule of Christ and the saints? Are you going to come with your power and your armies and think that you are going to conquer and take back and take away?"

God has something special for them. Verse 14: "Therefore, son of man, prophesy and say unto Gog, Thus saith the Lord GOD; In that day when My people of Israel dwelleth safely, shalt thou not know *it?* And thou shalt come from thy place out of the north parts, thou, and many people with thee, all of them riding upon horses, a great company, and a mighty army [a reoccurrence of Genghis Khan, if we could put it that way]: and thou shalt come up against My people of Israel, as a cloud to cover the land; it shall be in the latter days, and I will bring thee against My land…" Here's the purpose. Why does God do all of this? Because you see, He wants everyone to submit through repentance and choice voluntarily. Those who won't He's going to make an example that there will never ever, ever again during the Millennium (except at the end as we will see) will war, rebellion, and anarchy, and killing rule again. He's going to make this an example. "I will bring thee against My land, that the heathen may know Me…" They don't know God. They know Buddha, they know Confucius, they know Mohammad, they know Islam. They know whatever kind or form of religion that they have, but not the true God. And in India they've got so many gods that there is hardly any naming of them all. They don't know God. "…That the heathen may know Me…" God is going to do this for a perpetual and everlasting lesson that is going to carry right through the Millennium. "…When I shall be sanctified in thee, O Gog, before their eyes" (verses 14-16).

"Thus saith the Lord GOD; *Art* thou he of whom I have spoken in old time by My servants the prophets of Israel, which prophesied in those days *many* years that I would bring thee against them? And it shall come to pass at the same time when Gog shall come against the land of Israel, saith the Lord GOD, *that* My fury shall come up in My face. For in My jealousy *and* in the fire of My wrath have I spoken, Surely in that day there shall be a great shaking in the land of Israel; so that the fishes of the sea, and the fowls of the heaven, and the beasts of the field, and all creeping things that creep upon the earth, and all the men that *are* upon the face of the earth, shall shake at My presence, and the mountains shall be thrown down, and the steep places shall fall, and every wall shall fall to the ground. And I will call for a sword against him throughout all My mountains, saith the Lord GOD: every man's sword shall be against his brother" (verses 17-21). So they're going to get all there and then God is going to set them in confusion. They're going to start fighting among each other and killing each other. You know, God has done that before. That's one of the weapons that God does. He puts it in their minds to fight against each other. Now that won't be too terribly hard to do. I mean, all you have to do is just look at the radicalism of the different groups that are out there today. They fight against each other. So it's going to be something.

"And I will plead against him with pestilence and with blood; and I will rain upon him, and upon his bands, and upon the many people that *are* with him, an overflowing rain, and great hailstones, fire, and brimstone." So when they come up and they're going to go and try and attack and take over the land of Israel with Israel back in the land living in peace and prosperity, and worshipping God and keeping the Sabbath and the holy days, and all the things that God wants them to do, and they're going to come up and want to take over. So God is going to fight with the same weapons He's always fought with. You can read this in the book of Exodus when He freed the children of Israel from Egypt. You can read of this in the book of Revelation with the seven last plagues and so forth. These are the weapons of God that He uses against men. Now notice what this is going to do: "Thus will I magnify Myself, and sanctify Myself; and I will be known in the eyes of many nations, and they shall know that I *am* the LORD" (verses 22-23). Well, that's going to be pretty powerful, isn't it? And if there are any left back in the homeland, they're going to go back and say, "It is God! Forget everything you've ever thought that you're going to do. Repent and submit." So that will be something, won't it? I mean you think about it.

Now let's look at the first few verses in Chapter 39. "Therefore, thou son of man, prophesy against Gog, and say, Thus saith the Lord GOD; Behold, I *am* against thee, O Gog, the chief prince of Meshech and Tubal: and I will turn thee back, and leave but the sixth part of thee…" (Ezek. 39:1-2). So out of all of those that are left, even subtracting out all of those that were killed in the seven last plagues and the battles leading up to it, then He's only going to leave one sixth left. See, God is not going to put up with rebellion and anarchy. When the kingdom of God, with Christ ruling, comes to this earth it is going to rule in love, in peace, in understanding. But for those who rebel it's going to be power, and force, and pestilence, and fire, and brimstone, and hailstones. So that's going to be what they're going to be faced with. I couldn't help but think of that when I saw the documentary about what happened in Germany after WWII, and then seeing what is happening after the conflict here in Iraq and the supposed war on terror. And it's also another lesson: a few sinful men can do a great deal of damage. And God is not going to allow that. That's why He says in Revelation 2 that we are going to rule them (that is shepherd them, but rule them) with a rod of iron. And if they don't do the will of God, they're going to be broken in pieces just like you take a pot and just bust it into shards. Because Jesus Christ is going to show that no one can come against Him. No one can come against the spiritual saints of God that are ruling this world. Look at the weapons. That's going to be something. A sixth part of you.

"…And will cause thee to come up from the north parts…" Just like everything else, God raises up the evil ones by letting them do their own thing. And they think that they have power and success because they are accomplishing these things and they don't know that they are on their way to meet their Maker. And He says: "…[I] will bring thee upon the mountains of Israel: and I will smite thy bow out of thy left hand, and will cause thine arrows to fall out of thy right hand. Thou shalt fall upon the mountains of Israel, thou, and all thy bands, and the people that *is* with thee: I will give thee unto the ravenous birds of every sort, and *to* the beasts of the field to be devoured." So immediately God sends in the animals and birds, which are His servants to clean up all the flesh. "Thou shalt fall upon the open field: for I have spoken *it,* saith the Lord GOD. And I will send a fire on Magog, and among them that dwell carelessly in the isles: and they shall know that I *am* the LORD." So when the last rebellion is put down then there will be universal peace. But God is going to let them go their own way. God is going to rebuke them. God is going to set them up for the fall. Because the word will go out. They will know. They will have been told that Christ is here ruling from Jerusalem. They will have had an opportunity to go up like the other nations, but refuse to do so. They will have an opportunity to repent so that they can receive the Spirit of God, and that they can stop all of their hateful warmongering and just bloodthirsty and barbarous ways. But they refuse to take it. Now we'll finish here with verse 7. "So will I make My holy name known in the midst of My people Israel; and I will not *let them* pollute My holy name any more: and the heathen shall know that I *am* the LORD, the Holy One in Israel" (verses 2-7).

Now let's go on. Let's see what happens. There has to be a tremendous clean up program after all the birds and animals clean up all the rotten flesh and so forth. And as we read these prophecies and God has given us understanding on how these things unfold through His word, and I just imagine that down through time, from the time of the death of the apostles on down until the beginning of what we would call the modern age, it was really difficult for them to understand these Scriptures. So brethren, we need to be thankful that we can understand it. But also know and realize that with this understanding also comes a responsibility. Because no man is given the truth of the knowledge of the Word of God so that it can be taken lightly, or that it can be looked upon as a thing of human discovery, rather than as we started out as God's revelation through His Spirit.

Now verse 8: "Behold, it is come, and it is done, saith the Lord GOD; this *is* the day whereof I have spoken. And they that dwell in the cities of Israel shall go forth, and shall set on fire and burn the weapons…" You know, just like they are doing in Iraq today. There are great truck convoys going out of Iraq into Turkey carrying weapons; rifles, cannons, bombs, to be all melted down. And so: "…both the shields and the bucklers, the bows and the arrows, and the handstaves, and the spears, and they shall burn them with fire seven years…" Now you stop and think about that. How huge is this army going to be? And I'm sure that not only on the mountains of Israel but as these armies spread back toward the homelands in the north and the east there's going to be those things there too. "So that they shall take no wood out of the field, neither cut down *any* out of the forests; for they shall burn the weapons with fire: and they shall spoil those that spoiled them, and rob those that robbed them, saith the Lord GOD" (verses 8-10). Now that's something.

"And it shall come to pass in that day, *that* I will give unto Gog a place there of graves in Israel, the valley of the passengers on the east of the sea: and it shall stop the *noses* of the passengers [because right at first, because of the stink of it]: and there shall they bury Gog and all his multitude: and they shall call *it* The valley of Hamon-gog. And seven months shall the house of Israel be burying of them, that they may cleanse the land." Just like we're seeing in Iraq today. How long is it going to take to search out and get all these weapons? Because they now know that what was said of the representatives of Iraq trying to get uranium from the country of Niger was true! And they are finding weapons of mass destruction here and there. Amazing, isn't it? Well, it's going to be the same way here. They are going to have to go out and cleanse all of that. "Yea, all the people of the land shall bury *them;* and it shall be to them a renown the day that I shall be glorified, saith the Lord GOD" (verses 11-13). And so here it is, they're going to have continual employment, verse 14 and so forth. And so that's what's going to happen.

So it's going to be when we're dealing with human beings, and the problems of war, and the destruction of the earth (which we are going to be confronted with when we come back to this earth with Jesus Christ and set up the kingdom of God), we're going to be confronted with massive real human problems. And we're going to have to correct all of them. Christ is going to have to give us guidance and understanding so we know what to do. But God is going to really make a name for Himself with this. You stop and think about the mammoth proportions of what's going to happen with Gog and Magog, and it's really a fantastic thing. There won't be a rebel left. That's how God is going to solve the problem.

Now let's come to Psalm 47. Let's look at some of the psalms here and see how these things fit in with what we found there in Ezekiel 38 and 39. And I tell you—it's going to be something. God isn't going to allow or tolerate rebellion. But what He's going to do is gather up all the rebels together and let them come, and take care of them all at once.

Now Psalm 47:1: "O clap your hands, all ye people; shout unto God with the voice of triumph." That's what Israel is going to do when they see how God has fought against Gog and Magog, and Meshech and Tubal, and all of the countries of the north and the east and everything. They're going to shout with joy. "For the LORD most high *is* terrible [awesome—look what He did]; *He is* a great King over all the earth." Literal fulfillment. "He shall subdue the people under us, and the nations under our feet." And that refers to us who are going to rule and reign over the heathen. Amazing thing, isn't it? There it is right in the Word of God. "He shall choose our inheritance for us, the excellency of Jacob whom He loved." And of course Jacobs name was changed to Israel, and we are spiritual Israel. "God is gone up with a shout, the LORD with the sound of a trumpet. Sing praises to God, sing praises: sing praises unto our King, sing praises. For God *is* the King of all the earth: sing ye praises with understanding" (Psa. 47:1-7). Now you know how He's going to be King over all the earth, and the great power He's going to exercise, and our part in it. And the part of the children of Israel, the physical children of Israel brought back out of captivity.

Now notice verse 8: "God reigneth over the heathen: God sitteth upon the throne of His holiness [ruling out of Jerusalem]." Now remember what we read in Isaiah 2: The throne of God is going to be there and many people are going to come and say, "Let us learn of His ways." The law is going to go forth out of Zion. Here it's explaining it right here. "The princes of the people are gathered together, *even* the people of the God of Abraham…", which then are what? The spiritual children of God ruling with Jesus Christ. Now you put that together with the understanding of the covenant that God gave Abraham back in Genesis 15. So you see, the plan of God goes way back before the creation of the earth. But it is solidified through Abraham and comes down through the children of Israel, and then down to the church—the spiritual children of Abraham. And that's what it's talking about here. "…*Even* the people of the God of Abraham: for the shields of the earth *belong* unto God: He is greatly exalted" (verses 8-9). Now then there will be the peace which will come.

Psalm 50:1: "The mighty God, *even* the LORD, hath spoken, and called the earth from the rising of the sun unto the going down thereof." In other words around the whole earth. That's what it's talking about. "Out of Zion, the perfection of beauty, God hath shined. Our God shall come, and shall not keep silence: a fire shall devour before Him, and it shall be very tempestuous round about Him. He shall call to the heavens from above, and to the earth, that He may judge His people [and judge the world]. Gather My saints together unto Me; those that have made a covenant with Me by sacrifice." Now we'll expand on that tomorrow because that has to do with our relationship with God and how we prepare to be kings and priests. "Hear, O My people, and I will speak; O Israel, and I will testify against thee: I *am* God, *even* thy God." (Psa. 50:1-5, 7). So we need to listen to what God has to tell us.

Now let's come over here to Psalm 98. So this is what it means—the Millennium. This is the fulfilling of the Millennium. And day one pictures the institution of the Millennium. Christ is on the earth, Satan is put away, and now the kingdom of God begins. The government of God begins.

"O sing unto the LORD a new song; for He hath done marvellous things: His right hand, and His holy arm, hath gotten Him the victory." We just went through and described it, didn't we? Yes, indeed. "The LORD hath made known His salvation…", and the heathen know Him. And now has been sanctified in Gog and Magog, and all the earth will be under the control and power of Jesus Christ and the saints of God. Marvelous thing. "…His righteousness hath He openly shewed in the sight of the heathen. He hath remembered His mercy and His truth toward the house of Israel: all the ends of the earth have seen the salvation of our God" (Psa. 98:1-3). And that's what this day is going to picture when Gog and Magog have been put down and destroyed, and the last human enemies against the imposition of the kingdom of God on earth.

"Make a joyful noise unto the LORD, all the earth: make a loud noise, and rejoice, and sing praise. Sing unto the LORD with the harp; with the harp, and the voice of a psalm. With trumpets and sound of cornet make a joyful noise before the LORD, the King. Let the sea roar, and the fulness thereof; the world, and they that dwell therein. Let the floods clap *their* hands: let the hills be joyful together before the LORD; for He cometh to judge the earth: with righteousness shall He judge the world, and the people with equity" (verses 4-9). Amazing thing, isn't it?

Brethren, let's understand we have been called to the greatest calling possible. We have understanding that as Jesus said that other people do not have. And with that comes a great responsibility that we serve God with love, with joy, with zeal, with loyalty, with determination, with understanding, with faith, with hope, with all the attributes of the Holy Spirit because this is the greatest thing that we could possibly be involved in, in ushering in the rule of Jesus Christ and the kingdom of God on earth.

Now notice Psalm 99: "The LORD reigneth…" Now there are several psalms that say "the LORD reigns." "…Let the people tremble: He sitteth *between* the cherubims; let the earth be moved. The LORD *is* great in Zion; and He *is* high above all the people. Let them praise Thy great and terrible name; *for* it *is* holy" (Psa. 99:1-3). That goes right back to Psalm 2, doesn't it? Yes, it does. It's going to be an amazing thing.

Now let's see, after we get all of this done, what is going to be the outcome of it? Let's come to Isaiah 11. We're going to see what happens. See, God has the power. God is going to change and recreate and reform the earth, and with His Spirit with Israel, with bringing conversion to the heathen, bringing His way to the whole earth, then we are going to see what will happen here.

"And there shall come forth a rod out of the stem of Jesse, and a Branch shall grow out of his roots: and the spirit of the LORD shall rest upon him, the spirit of wisdom and understanding…" This is going to be the rule that we are also going to bring in, and it has a lot to do with how we prepare to be kings and priests, which we'll cover tomorrow. "…The spirit of counsel and might, the spirit of knowledge and of the fear of the LORD; and shall make him of quick understanding in the fear of the LORD: and he shall not judge after the sight of his eyes, neither reprove after the hearing of his ears: but with righteousness shall he judge the poor, and reprove with equity for the meek of the earth: and he shall smite the earth with the rod of his mouth [just like it says back there in Revelation 2—"smite them with a rod of iron"], and with the breath of his lips shall he slay the wicked. And righteousness shall be the girdle of his loins, and faithfulness the girdle of his reins" (Isa. 11:1-5). And then everything is going to be changed—human nature, animal nature. The way that the earth is, is going to be beautiful, and marvelous, and harmonious.

And not only are they not going to learn war anymore, there's also going to be a change in the nature of the animals. Verse 6: "The wolf also shall dwell with the lamb, and the leopard shall lie down with the kid; and the calf and the young lion and the fatling together; and a little child shall lead them." Boy, entirely different, isn't it. I look at that and every time I read that I think, "Hey, there are not going to be very many plastic toys for the children to play with, right?" Yes, sure there will be some toys. But not like it is today. They're going to have the real thing. They're going to have lions and tigers and all of these things. "And the sucking child shall play on the hole of the asp, and the weaned child shall put his hand on the cockatrice' den." Now that's to show the contrast of the world today with the kingdom of God tomorrow. "They shall not hurt nor destroy in all My holy mountain [which ties right in with Isaiah 2, that the mountain of the house of the LORD shall be exalted]: for the earth shall be full of the knowledge of the LORD, as the waters cover the sea" (verses 6, 8-9). That's something, isn't it? Yes. So that's how the Millennium will start.

End of Sermon

Transcriber: Carolyn Singer

Chapter Thirty-four

The Feast of Tabernacles—Day 1—Holy Day
September 30, 2004
Scriptural References

1) I Corinthians 1:17-21

2) Revelation 14:12

3) I Corinthians 1:9-13

4) John 6:63

5) Psalm 119:18

6) Leviticus 23:33-38

7) Numbers 29:12-13, 32-36, 39

8) Deuteronomy 16:16-17

9) John 18:33-38

10) Luke 19:11-15, 21-27

11) Acts 1:6-7

12) Isaiah 9:6-7

13) Revelation 20:4-6

14) Revelation 2:25-27

15) Isaiah 2:1-4

16) Ezekiel 38:1-23

17) Ezekiel 39:1-13

18) Psalm 47:1-9

19) Psalm 50:1-5, 7

20) Psalm 98:1-9

21) Psalm 99:1-3

22) Isaiah 11:1-6, 8-9

CHAPTER THIRTY-FIVE

The Feast of Tabernacles—Day 7

October 6, 2004

And greetings, brethren. Welcome to the seventh day of the Feast of Tabernacles, which is technically the last day of the feast because the Feast of Tabernacles is seven days long. However it is eight days because of the Last Great Day. And so there is still a whole lot more that we can learn. But let's understand something as Christ has said, there's a beginning, there's an ending. So just as we started the feast and we went down through every day, now there is the ending of the feast, and then we have the finale with the Last Great Day.

So let's continue on and let's see how important that this is and what this day represents. And we're going to ask some questions as we go along. We're going to answer those questions and find out a little bit more about what the Millennium is going to be like as it's revealed in the Word of God, and what we need to be doing, and how we need to be doing it. But brethren, you know, we all need to be thankful because of the Word of God that gives us the understanding. Now in order to understand these things it's not that we're anything great, it's not that we are more intellectual than other people or whatever it may be. No, it's because the calling of God, the Spirit of God, and the Word of God. So let's continue on with it. We're going to also understand and realize that not only is this so, but also that when we come to the end of the Millennium there are going to be a couple of things that it's very difficult for some people to grasp and understand, so we'll see if we can do it this time.

But in the mean time let's pick up where we left off on day six and let's come to Isaiah 32. And we are going to see how the Millennium is going to be. Now we know the Spirit of God is going to be available. We know that salvation is going to be given to everyone at that time all during the Millennium. And we know that it is going to be absolutely (in human existence) nearly the greatest time that has ever been. And I say "nearly" because we don't know what it's going to be like for the one hundred year period that follows the Millennium, which is interesting—the one hundred year period is actually a tithe of the thousand years, is it not?

Alright, let's come back here, Isaiah 32:15. It says: "Until the spirit be poured [out] upon us from on high…" Now doesn't that sound a little bit like what happened in Acts 2 on the Day of Pentecost when the Holy Spirit came? Yes. Well the Holy Spirit's going to be available to all people. "…And the wilderness be a fruitful field, and the fruitful field be counted for a forest. Then judgment shall dwell in the wilderness, and righteousness remain in the fruitful field. And the work of righteousness shall be peace…" (Isa. 32:15-17). So here again we're not talking about just the physical place, but we are talking about the work of conversion all during the Millennium. Just like we have the parables of the sower in Matthew 13 and the parallel columns that we have in Mark and in Luke. Very important to understand. This is talking about that spiritual harvest that is going to take place. So it's really saying that it's a universal salvation that is going out to all people.

Now notice: "…And the effect of righteousness quietness and assurance for ever." See, no more fear. No more crime. No more—none of this. "And My people shall dwell in a peaceable habitation, and in sure dwellings, and in quiet resting places…" Now those resting places are typical of living during the Millennium. And it says: "When it shall hail, coming down on the forest; and the city shall be low in a low place. Blessed *are* ye that sow beside all waters, that send forth *thither* the feet of the ox and the ass" (verses 17-20). In other words, so that there will be plenty of that. But it's very interesting here. We can tie in … just put in your margin there Psalm 1, concerning: "Blessed *is* the man that walketh not in the counsel of the ungodly, nor standeth in the way of sinners … But his delight *is* in the law of the LORD; and in His law doth he meditate day and night. And he shall be like a tree planted by the rivers of water, that bringeth forth his fruit in his season…" (Psa. 1:1-3). And that's what's going to happen. All during the Millennium every one is going to bring forth fruit (spiritually speaking) in season. And God is going to harvest it. It's going to be the greatest harvest. The greatest thing that has happened since the creation of the world. Just think how many billions will be converted and added to the kingdom of God.

Now, we need to also understand that God did not create the universe in vain. He created that on purpose, for a purpose. And the more that they get out and study into the universe, the more they are awed by the very power of it. So in the final analysis God is going to need billions, and billions, and billions to help to produce what God wants to produce with the vastness of the universe that He has created. So as I said before, we need to not only think big, we need to think gigantic.

Ok, let's come back here to Isaiah 25:6. This is going to be really quite a wonderful time for everything here. And here's what God is going to do for all people. He says so right here. "And in this mountain shall the LORD of hosts…" Now "the mountain of the LORD" is where? In Jerusalem on Mount Zion. "…The LORD of hosts [shall] make unto all people a feast of fat things [that's all the good things that you'd ever want], a feast of wines on the lees, of fat things full of marrow, of wines on the lees well refined." I mean that is a time that we could say the greatest and the best will be produced. There will be no more Thunderbird wine. There will be no more Andre Champaign. There will be no more hard, tough steaks. There will be none of this. Plus, everyone is going to be converted. It's going to be quite a time. A sinner, as we're going to see a little bit later on, they're not going to be allowed to be around. They're either going to repent, or they're going to have to face the consequences.

Now notice verse 7: "And He will destroy in this mountain the face of the covering cast over all people, and the vail that is spread over all nations." See, so they're going to have their blindness removed. See, God has got to do this at the beginning of the Millennium. And we'll see that when the beginning of the Last Great Day starts, He also has to do that with those people. "He will swallow up death in victory; and the LORD GOD will wipe away tears from off all faces [He's going to]; and the rebuke of His people shall He take away from off all the earth: for the LORD hath spoken *it*" (verses 7-8). Now this is really quite a thing, isn't it? That's what's going to happen all during the Millennium.

Now verse 9: "And it shall be said in that day, Lo, this *is* our God; we have waited for Him, and He will save us: this *is* the LORD; we have waited for Him, we will be glad and rejoice in His salvation." So that's a tremendous thing, brethren. Just think of this attitude all through the Millennium, all people. Just think of the things that are going to be taught. How right, how good, how pure, how lovely. Every kind of description that you would like to give. It will apply. And so God is going to have an increase. God is going to produce. The whole world is going to learn. And we are going to be the ones who will be teaching them.

Since we are here in Isaiah let's come over to Chapter 30 and let's see. Here, this describes part of our job. And you know, God is going to have us active and busy all during the Millennium, all during the one hundred year period, and all during the rest of the ages of eternity. So God has called us to a tremendous and absolutely mind-boggling calling. Whereas most religions in the world, what do they do? They have things set up so that you can get along a little better in this life. But you ask them, "Why were you born? What is God doing? When is Christ returning? What are these things that are going to happen?" They don't know. They don't even believe in the resurrection in most cases, though they mouth the words. All of their so-called immortal souls go to heaven. And if you don't have the book *Primitive Christianity in Crisis* by Alan Knight, well you make sure you get a copy of it. We do have a few copies here in the office. But let me tell you something: you cannot understand how those false doctrines came into the church unless you have read his book. How did it happen? Well you see, during the Millennium none of this is going to happen. Everyone is going to know God. Everyone is going to know who their teachers are. Everyone is going to know who their rulers are. Everyone is going to keep the Sabbath, keep the holy days. And they are going to work and produce, and life is going to be the way that God wants it to be. And let me tell you something, it's going to make this modern world look like an absolute conglomeration of insane idiots.

Now here, Isaiah 30:18: "And therefore will the LORD wait, that He may be gracious unto you…" That is, that's why He's not bringing the Millennium now. In His set time it will come, you see. "…Be gracious unto you, and therefore will He be exalted, that He may have mercy upon you: for the LORD *is* a God of judgment: blessed *are* all they that wait for Him." Now that includes us who are now waiting. But let me tell you something else: everyone during the Millennium is going to be doing the work and the will of God the way God wants it done. So they'll be waiting on God, as it were. "For the people shall dwell in Zion at Jerusalem: thou shalt weep no more: He will be very gracious unto thee at the voice of thy cry; when He shall hear it, He will answer thee" (Isa. 30:18-19). Now it says in another place that He is going to really do some fantastic things. He's even going to answer right while you're asking. And that ought to help us to be able to have more faith in prayers that we have to God. I'll tell you one way to never have a prayer answered. That is go pray your heart out, be as fervent as you can, get all done and say "Amen," and then stand up on your feet and say, "I wonder if God will answer this prayer?" You've just undone everything that you've asked for.

"And *though* the LORD give you the bread of adversity, and the water of affliction, [that is in the past to bring them to the point of conversion], yet shall not thy teachers be removed into a corner any more…" No, it's not going to be like it was in the past. There are not going to be those trials and tribulations. "…But thine eyes shall see thy teachers…" That will be our jobs. Isn't that going to be fantastic? Verse 21: "And thine ears shall hear a word behind thee, saying, This *is* the way, walk ye in it, when ye turn to the right hand, and when ye turn to the left" (verses 20-21).

Now, let's stop and think on this for a minute. Let's look at the three existences of converted people who are resurrected. The first existence is in the womb right after conception. And now they've been able to take 3-D pictures, which show babies as young as 12 weeks old who are able … and they see them doing things in practice so when they are born they will have all of these things down pat. They practice walking. Their legs are going like this. That's to build and strengthen the muscles. Their arms are going like this. They suck their thumbs. They open their eyes, but they can't see because it's totally dark in the womb. They smile. They're disturbed at outside noises coming in to them. And remember, water is a great conductor of sound. So it's very incumbent upon mothers to be careful what kind of sounds that they have coming upon them. And it just makes me wonder, all these people who are involved in some of these awful things called music today, and all that sound coming into their ears, to the body, into the unborn. But never the less they also yawn, they smile, and they are getting ready to be born.

Now there's a set time for them to be born. And when they have been born they come into this world, and they do something for the very first time—they breathe and they are no longer dependent upon the umbilical cord to be fed. But in the process of growing, right after being born and so forth, they have mother's milk, which is the best thing, and should be. All mothers should nurse their children. God designed it many ways which are totally beneficial to the mother and to the child. This is not the place to get into it. But anyway if someone is not cut off because of an untimely or early death, they live in this physical life.

Now if God calls them then God's plan is still working, isn't it? He's given us minds. He's given us understanding. He's called. He's given us His Spirit. And now He is teaching us. And what are we doing in this life but in loving God and keeping His commandments, and learning of His Word, walking in His way, repenting and changing and growing—what are we doing? Well, we are practicing for being born again, are we not? Yes, indeed.

So when we die and are put into the grave, or we're still alive and changed when Christ returns, we are born into the kingdom of God. Then all of a sudden we are spirit beings, correct? Now we have another form of existence, don't we? Yes. So we're going to be doing things for the first time that we have never ever done in our whole lives. Just like when a newborn is born and starts breathing, then it's doing that for the very first time. And isn't it interesting because "breath" is likened unto "spirit." So just as the newborn takes a first breath, so when we are born into the kingdom of God we are going to be spirit beings. So as it were, our breath will be the fullness of the Spirit of God. Now likewise with all of those that we are teaching in the Millennium, they will know this. They will know who God is. They will know who we are. We are going to be teaching and training them. It's going to be an amazing thing indeed.

Now let's come over here to Micah 4. (Hosea, and hold it at Amos because we'll go back to Amos here in just a minute. Amos, Jonah, and then Micah.) Now let's pick it up here in verse 4. I just want to cover this. After not learning war anymore … and just stop and think about it: God is not going to have any more exploiting corporations to exploit people and control them, and destroy their lives. No. Verse 4: "But they shall sit every man under his vine and under his fig tree; and none shall make *them* afraid…", all during the Millennium. It says: "Of the increase of *His* government and peace *there shall be* no end…" (Isa. 9:7). "…For the mouth of the LORD of hosts hath spoken *it*" (Micah 4:4).

Now back here to Amos 9. Let's see what kind of thing that they will have, what kind of agriculture it is going to be. It's going to be something. Just like we read earlier. God is going to make them a feast of all the fat things. Well it's going to come, and come, and come. The produce, the food, the things that are produced, as well as then you can also understand all the things that will be produced in making clothes, making shoes, making things, making whatever machines that we will need at that time. It's going to be an amazing thing. But here it starts with the agricultural base.

Amos 9:13: "Behold, the days come, saith the LORD, that the plowman shall overtake the reaper, and the treader of grapes him that soweth seed; and the mountains shall drop sweet wine, and all the hills shall melt." It's just going to be an overflowing abundance. Now you compare that with what is in the world today with the war and the famine and starvation and so forth. Verse 14: "And I will bring again the captivity of My people of Israel [and this means bring them out of their captivity], and they shall build the waste cities, and inhabit *them;* and they shall plant vineyards, and drink the wine thereof…" Now all you teatotelers listen up. Now sure, there's not going to be alcoholism. You can be guaranteed that. But it's going to be used in the right way, and the best of it "…They shall also make gardens, and eat the fruit of them. And I will plant them upon their land, and they shall no more be pulled up out of their land which I have given them, saith the LORD thy God" (Amos 9:13-15). Now think of this starting out the beginning of the Millennium where there's still some wars going on as we saw, and then coming all the way down through the Millennium.

Now let's come to Isaiah 60 and let's see something here, how it's going to be. Economically we've seen how it is for agriculture. Now let's see how it's going to be for commerce and industry. Verse 16: "Thou shalt also suck the milk of the Gentiles, and shalt suck the breast of kings..." That is symbolic language that you're going to receive the best of everything. So will all of them during the Millennium. "...And thou shalt know that I the LORD *am* thy Saviour and thy Redeemer, the mighty One of Jacob." So you see, as great as the coming new world order is going to appear in the eyes of men, what God is going to do during the Millennium is going to pale into absolute insignificance this coming great new world order of Satan the devil.

Let's see what He's going to do here, verse 17. Here's how rich they are going to be: "For brass I will bring gold, and for iron I will bring silver, and for wood brass, and for stones iron..." Now there's going to be a lot of industry going on using all of these things. And we're no longer going to have these counterfeit notes, which most currencies are today. They are counterfeit notes put out by fake banks which say they are central banks. No more. God is a god of real wealth. God is a god of real power. God is a god of real righteousness. And that's how it's going to be. Now notice: "...I will also make thy officers peace, and thine exactors righteousness." So that's going to be us. They are going to be able to give their tithes and offerings and so forth. God is going to bless them because of obedience. God is going to bless them with His Spirit. God is going to bless them with conversion. Amazing.

"Violence shall no more be heard in thy land, wasting nor destruction within thy borders; but thou shalt call thy walls Salvation, and thy gates Praise" (verse 18). This is an amazing thing, brethren, what God is going to do. And when we leave this Feast of Tabernacles, which we will do after the Last Great Day, I want you to keep these things in mind. Because this is the vision that God has given us so that in the times of trouble and difficulty that we are going to face after the feast (which all of us are going to face one way or the other because we're still living in the world) keep your mind focused on these things.

Now let's come back to Isaiah 33 please. And this will be really quite a wonderful thing when we see right here in the Word of God it talks about it. Let's begin here in verse 20: "Look upon Zion, the city of our solemnities: thine eyes shall see Jerusalem a quiet habitation, a tabernacle *that* shall not be taken down; not one of the stakes thereof shall ever be removed, neither shall any of the cords thereof be broken. But there the glorious LORD *will be* unto us a place of broad rivers..." That's just likened unto God's Spirit. Remember, as we will see tomorrow, that the crystal clear waters will flow out of the throne of God (Revelation 22). So this is likened unto it. "...Wherein shall go no galley with oars, neither shall gallant ship pass thereby. For the LORD *is* our judge, the LORD *is* our lawgiver, the LORD *is* our king; He will save us" (Isa. 33:20-22). So that's really quite a description, isn't it? So just like the world today is all focused in and is going to come to the point of worshiping Satan the devil, so likewise in the Millennium all are going to be focused in on worshiping God and His way and His truth and His righteousness.

Now come over here to Isaiah 35:1. "The wilderness and the solitary place shall be glad for them; and the desert shall rejoice, and blossom as the rose." Now you tie that in with Amos 9 there again. "It shall blossom abundantly, and rejoice even with joy and singing: the glory of Lebanon shall be given unto it, the excellency of Carmel and Sharon, they shall see the glory of the LORD, *and* the excellency of our God" (Isaiah 35:1-2). So it's going to really be a tremendous thing that's going to happen.

547

"Strengthen ye the weak hands, and confirm the feeble knees [that's what we're going to do]. Say to them *that are* of a fearful heart, Be strong, fear not: behold, your God will come *with* vengeance [He already has. This is coming into the Millennium], ... and save you. Then the eyes of the blind shall be opened, and the ears of the deaf shall be unstopped. Then shall the lame *man* leap as an hart, and the tongue of the dumb sing..." (verses 3-6). That's going to be our job. Can you imagine what it's going to be like to heal blind people? To heal those who cannot speak? To heal those who have had limbs destroyed? It's going to be an amazing thing because if the lame is going to leap as the hart, that's what it's talking about.

Now notice verse 7: "And the parched ground shall become a pool, and the thirsty land springs of water: in the habitation of dragons, where each lay, *shall be* grass with reeds and rushes." Then it talks about: "...[the] highway shall be there, and a way, and it shall be called The way of holiness; the unclean [person] shall not pass over it..." (verses 7-8). No, we're going to see in just a little bit that during the Millennium there's going to be a division between the righteous and the sinners. And God is going to make that division and they're going to have to choose. God is not going to let the wicked prosper. Now we'll talk about how God will deal with them in just a little bit.

Let's continue on here just a minute. "No lion shall be there, nor *any* ravenous beast shall go up thereon [no, the lions are going to be the pets back at home as we saw there in Isaiah 11], ... but the redeemed shall walk *there:* And the ransomed of the LORD shall return, and come to Zion with songs and everlasting joy upon their heads: they shall obtain joy and gladness, and sorrow and sighing shall flee away" (verses 9-10). So there's the whole mission statement for the thousand years.

Now let's look at Psalm 145. See, it is amazing, isn't it? Let's think about it for a minute. The key to understanding the Bible is what the religionists in the world do not want to do. And that is: obey God and love Him. For example: as I tell people who want to know about the Sabbath and what it's for, and so forth (and they are really serious), I say, "Ok, you do this: you go ahead and keep the Sabbath. And on the Sabbath day study about the Sabbath. And you do this for several months, you will understand the Sabbath. But if you don't obey, you're not going to understand." So likewise with the holy days. We don't understand them unless we obey and keep them. And then with God's Spirit and God's Word, He opens up our understanding so we can realize what it really is.

Now here, Psalm 145, listen to this. This is a fantastic description of what it's going to be like all during the Millennium. Verse 1: "I will extol Thee, my God, O king; and I will bless Thy name for ever and ever. Every day will I bless Thee; and I will praise Thy name for ever and ever" (Psa. 145:1-2). Just think of this: every day people are going to be praying to God. Every day they're going to be thanking and blessing God. It's going to be an amazing place. It's going to be an amazing thing. And we, brethren, are the ones who are going to administer this with Christ. That's what's so fantastic about it.

"Great *is* the LORD, and greatly to be praised; and His greatness *is* unsearchable. One generation shall praise Thy works to another, and shall declare Thy mighty acts." So all during the Millennium this is what is going to happen, isn't it? "I will speak of the glorious honour of Thy majesty, and of Thy wondrous works. And *men* shall speak of the might of Thy terrible [awesome] acts: and I will declare Thy greatness. They shall abundantly utter the memory of Thy great goodness, and shall sing of Thy righteousness." And here's what they're going to be singing: "The LORD *is* gracious, and full of compassion; slow to anger, and of great mercy" (verses 3-8). And you wonder in the midst of all of this, why would people choose to sing? We'll talk about that in just a little bit.

"The LORD *is* good to all: and His tender mercies *are* over all His works. All Thy works shall praise Thee, O LORD; and Thy saints shall bless Thee. They shall speak of the glory of Thy kingdom, and talk of Thy power; to make known to the sons of men His mighty acts, and the glorious majesty of His kingdom. Thy kingdom *is* an everlasting kingdom, and Thy dominion *endureth* throughout all generations" (verses 9-13). In other words not only during the time of the Millennium, but down through all eternity because there are ages of eternity.

Now let's look at a couple things here and begin to ask some questions and see what's going to happen. Now human nature is this way: once you get used to something because you're born into a certain set of circumstances in society... And for example: I doubt if there are any children today who even have a thought that there was never a time when we were using electricity, and had lights and cars and all the things we have today. Now, they get used to it. And what happens when children have everything? They get spoiled. Now just think what's going to happen to human nature as we progress down through the Millennium. They're going to be taking these things for granted. They are going to be able to see their teachers and they're going to take it for granted. And also, there's going to be enough human nature around that there are going to be some who are going to want to sin. So let's look and see two things. Number one: How long are people going to live during the Millennium. Number two: What happens to the righteous? Number three: What happens to the sinner?

Now let's come here to Isaiah 65. Now I know that we apply this to the one hundred year period, that's true. And it's probably going to be exactly the same for the Millennium and for the one hundred years of the Great White Throne Judgment period.

Now let's pick it up here, Isaiah 65:17: "For, behold, I create new heavens and a new earth: and the former shall not be remembered, nor come into mind. But be ye glad and rejoice for ever *in that* which I create: for, behold, I create Jerusalem a rejoicing, and her people a joy. And I will rejoice in Jerusalem, and joy in My people: and the voice of weeping shall be no more heard in her, nor the voice of crying" (Isa. 65:17-19). So that applies all during the Millennium, doesn't it? That also will apply during the Great White Throne Judgment too, without a doubt.

"There shall be no more thence an infant of days [that is an infant of days who does not fulfill his life], nor an old man that hath not filled his days: for the child shall die an hundred years old..." That means live to be a hundred years old. And we're all destined to die, with the exception where God makes the exception, and we will see it. "...But the sinner *being* an hundred years old shall be accursed" (verse 20). Now, let's look at it this way. You can read the rest of it and it shows, again, the Millennium setting.

Let's come to an unusual circumstance that we find in the New Testament and let's apply that to us. Let's come here to I Thessalonians 4. Because there is a time when those who are truly converted at the return of Christ and are still living—now it says they don't die. Now, I've gone back and forth in trying to understand this, which is this: Hebrews 9:27 (paraphrased): "It's given to man once to die. After that the judgment." Now it says here in I Thessalonians 4 concerning those which are alive when Christ returns. So let's read that and let's think about this for a minute. Is their change kind of... I don't know how to phrase it. Let's read it first and then we'll think about it here.

I Thessalonians 4:14: "For if we believe that Jesus died and rose again, in exactly the same way also, those who have fallen asleep in Jesus will God bring with Him. For this we say to you by *the* Word of *the* Lord, that we which are alive and remain unto the coming of the Lord shall in no wise precede those who have fallen asleep. Because the Lord Himself shall descend from heaven with *a* shout of command, with *the* voice of an archangel and with *the* trumpet of God; and the dead in Christ shall rise first; Then we who are alive and remain shall be caught up together with them in *the* clouds for *the* meeting with the Lord in *the* air; and so shall we always be with *the* Lord" (I Thess. 4:14-17).

Now, they are changed instantaneously, aren't they? Now how this works, I don't know. Is this change considered an instantaneous death and transformation to spirit. Death of the human body. I mean it's going to be transformed because it says there in Philippians 3:21 (let's go back there)... In talking about when Christ returns: "Who will transform our vile bodies, that they may be conformed to His glorious body, according to the inner of His own power, *whereby He is able* to subdue all things Himself." So we don't know the exact process. But it does say in Isaiah 65 that "the infant shall die a hundred, and the sinner dying at a hundred shall be accursed."

Now then, what would it serve for those who are righteous, for those who have (as we shall say) through the process of God's salvation been qualified for salvation, what would be the purpose for them to die and be buried? Well, they'd have to be resurrected. Well then let's tie that in to what we have at the end. What purpose would it be for those who are righteous at the end, to die and be buried, but rather, shall be changed and transformed as Paul said: "In an instant, in *the* twinkling of an eye, at the last trumpet;...we shall all be changed" (I Cor. 15:52). Just like those being resurrected out of the graves will be changed. So is it that at that point of a hundred years, that the righteous when they are changed, there is a death of the physical body and they have it converted into a spiritual body.

Now, I suggest this: that we all wait until we see how it happens when we are ruling and reigning with Christ. Then we will know for sure. Otherwise these are just some thoughts to help give us some understanding.

Now let's continue on brethren. Let's ask the question: What does the Bible teach us, and how does God show us that He deals with people who have sinned, and sinned greatly enough that they should die, but God allows them to live? See, because that's going to be the quandary during the Millennium. What are you going to do with people who die?

Now, during the first part of the Millennium they can die, be put in the grave, and every time there is a funeral that takes place everyone is going to know that that person has committed the unpardonable sin. Because they die as sinners and are accursed. That's their first death. So keep that in mind also for tomorrow.

Now when we come down to the last generation there's not going to be time for them to live a hundred years. There's not going to be time to be able to have them die the death at a hundred, being accursed [Because there is less than 100 years left in this Millennium]. Now let's ask the question. Let's come back here to Genesis 2 and let's look at something here for just a minute. And also, I think this will help us understand how God is going to do it.

Now, was the Garden of Eden the ideal setting that God wanted? Yes. And didn't we cover the restitution of all things? Yes. Now what happened with Adam and Eve? Obviously they sinned enough to die. He gave them the death sentence. He put within them the law of sin and death because of their transgressions, but He let them live, didn't He? So what did He do? Now this has also been brought up (I brought it up before) as referring to the last generation. But could it also happen to those during the Millennium who sin grievously and have to be removed? Will there be a place of exile of all sinners, gross sinners, which would be a minority of people by the way. But still there will be, because God is not going to take away free choice from anybody. It's still going to be there. It's still going to be whether you're going to choose to love God and serve Him, or go your own way. It's like with Adam and Eve. So what did He do?

Now, here's what He did. He cut them off from the tree of life, didn't He? And He sent them out of the Garden of Eden, didn't He? Genesis 3:24: "So He drove out the man [and obviously his wife]; and He placed at the east of the garden of Eden Cherubims, and a flaming sword which turned every way, to keep the way of the tree of life." Now then, are we going to have something similar during the Millennium? Now I know I've applied it to the last generation of the Millennium, but could it be that there is going to be a place of exile that those who just say, "Well look, I just want to choose which ever way I want to go." And God is going to say, "Ok. If you do that, you're going to go over here to this place of exile. And if you repent you can come back. But if you don't repent you're going to live out your life a hundred years and you're going to die accursed and you're going to be buried." Now, I don't know. But it's very likely, based upon what we have here in Genesis 3. So if we're going to have the restitution of all things, as we saw there at the beginning of the feast, are we not also going to have a means of handling those who have committed grievous sins? Now obviously if someone commits something like murder, then the sentence is death right there. And of course the one who has been murdered can be resurrected. But however, during the Millennium it says very clearly that "no one is going to hurt or destroy in all My holy mountain." So I highly doubt whether we are going to have murderers around. I'm sure that there are going to be those who are going to try and steal (that's only part of human nature), and lie, and things like that. That's all part of human nature. And people can repent of those things. Those are sins which are sins not unto death.

But what happens when you have someone who comes to the point that they are just incorrigible and you cannot have them around? Well we also have the principle too, don't we, of this way: that we are not to become part of the world. We are separate. We are told that "be separate from the way of the world and sinners" right? Yes. So it's very possible that God will have this.

Now why is this necessary? Because God has decreed that all sinners will die twice. All unrepentant sinners will suffer the second death, which we will get into tomorrow. So here they are exiled. Now where do you suppose would be the best place to exile them. Ok, let's see, maybe we have an answer in the New Testament. And then we're going to see something that has been very hard for people to understand. So let's see if we can put it together. Now I realize that we are into areas that are not absolutely totally dogmatic in the things that I have just said here. I understand that. So in thinking the process through, which God wants us to do, we understand that the ultimate reality of it is going to be when we see how God truly does it. But in the mean time it's certainly not wrong for us to try and get some understanding of the Scriptures based upon what we know. So let's come to Revelation 20 and let's see part of the enigma in trying to understand these Scriptures, and how God is going to handle it.

Now let's come to Revelation 20. Now we saw that the angel came down (verses 1 and 2) and put the devil into the abyss. It says, verse 2: "And he took hold of the dragon, the ancient serpent, who is *the* Devil and Satan, and bound him *for* a thousand years." So all during the Millennium Satan is not going to be around to tempt them. Which also tells us one thing very important, because that also goes back to the time of when Adam and Eve sinned. The beginning was when they let Satan persuade them to go against God. And as soon as Satan enters the scene, sin prospers. When Satan is removed then not all sin, but the sins that Satan inspires, will be gone. So: "Then he cast him into the abyss, and locked him *up*, and sealed *the abyss* over him, so that he would not deceive the nations any longer until the thousand years were fulfilled; and after that it is ordained that he be loosed *for* a short time" (Rev. 20:2-3). Now why would God do that? Because He needs Satan for one more mission. And let's see what that is. He let's them out. He lets Satan, and of course then the demons too, He let's them out with a purpose that's necessary to be fulfilled.

All during the Millennium sinners who die are accursed. That's their first death. When we come down to the last generation you are going to have righteous people who are living who will probably live over into the Great White Throne Judgment period so they can live to be a hundred and then be transformed. Then you are also going to have the sinners who are exiled. They're still going to be alive. They're going to have to die their first death. Because you cannot have the Great White Throne Judgment one hundred year period begin until certain things are done.

So let's see it here. Let's come down to verse 7: "Now when the thousand years have been completed, Satan shall be loosed out of his prison…" Why does God let him out of his prison? You see, the prison that he is put into in, the abyss, is a temporary punishment. Because as we will see the fulfillment of the seventh day of the Feast of Tabernacles also gives the final judgment on Satan the devil as well. That has to be reserved until the end of the Millennium, as we will see.

"And he shall go out to deceive the nations that *are* in the four corners of the earth, Gog and Magog…" Now this brings us right back to the very first day of the Feast of Tabernacles, about how Gog and Magog came down and wanted to attack and take away the kingdom from beginning when Christ returns at the beginning of the Millennium. But they are destroyed. Their names are (as we will say) the total epitome of evil to come down and fight Christ at the beginning of the Millennium. Now Gog and Magog in this particular case then has to be a geographical area in Gog and Magog. Now why do I say that? I say that because of this: that if God is going to give free moral agency and free choice to everyone to choose, do you not think that at the beginning of the Millennium when all of those armies of Gog and Magog have been destroyed, that they're going to be the physical descendents of Gog and Magog who are going to be converted? Yes. Because God says that with that event of destroying the armies of Gog and Magog at the beginning of the Millennium, all the heathen (which includes the rest of those of Gog and Magog who are still alive) are going to know that Christ is the Lord, and that God is ruling on this earth so this is not the people of Gog and Magog, but part of the territory of Gog and Magog. And [the ones at the end in exile are like] those who have the rebellious attitude that Gog and Magog had at the beginning of the Millennium. And so it says "to deceive the nations." Not deceive Gog and Magog alone. So "that *are* in the four quarters of the earth" Gog and Magog describes that part of the earth where they have been exiled to.

Now notice, here's his mission: "…of whom the number *is* as the sand of the sea…" Now God uses that to show it's a great number but it's not determinable (the exact number) and why. Why? Because there is choice. And if they choose to sin, God has not predetermined who is going to choose to sin and who is going to choose not to sin. God reserves that for every individual that He calls, or exposes them to the truth. And God is not going to take away that from anybody. He didn't take it from Adam and Eve. He hasn't taken it away from us. He's not going to take it away from the people who live during the Millennium. He's not going to take it away from the people in the last generation of the Millennium.

But you see, those who are incorrigible sinners at that time will not have one hundred years to live, to die, and be buried accursed. So God has to execute His plan so that they will die their first death in a very unusual manner. And He uses Satan to do it. He releases Satan. And he goes over to where they are in the area of Gog and Magog, and you can almost hear it. "Boy, I've been fighting this for a thousand years, and I really am the true God. You were right in rejecting God. You were right in coming over here. You were right in exercising your free moral agency to do what you want to, and now I am here as God to rescue you. Worship me." And you know they will. What else do you think that Satan is going to do? What did he do with Adam and Eve? What did he do when Christ had His confrontation with Satan the devil to be tempted of him? Did he not say, "Worship me"? Yes, indeed. So no doubt, he's going to do it again. However it's going to be a deception because he set out to deceive **these people who have already rejected salvation. They're not deceived out of salvation. By choice they have rejected it. Just like every one who commits the unpardonable sin, by choice they reject God.** So there we have it.

Now what does he do? "...To gather them together for war" (verse 8). And every time Satan is around there is war. Without a doubt. Look what happened with Cain and Abel. The first murder, right? Yes. War, death and destruction.

Now then, in preparing for war they're probably going to make various weapons. We don't know how much technology they are going to be able to develop in a short time. It says he must be loosed for a short time or a short season. We don't know how long that is. Is that three and a half years as some of the other areas where it is for a "short season" referred to, or a short time? It's possible. It's going to be long enough for them to prepare for war. It's going to be long enough for them to make enough armaments that they think that they are going to be able to conquer the saints down in Jerusalem. And you see, if you go conquer Jerusalem and you take the capital, and you take over God's throne... Oh boy, doesn't that sound like a repeat of Isaiah 14? Yes, indeed. If you do that then you can finally be god. You can finally rule over the world. And then you see, "You can be rewarded," Satan is going to tell them. "You can be rewarded. And you can take over and rule and you can dispose of all of these people." It will be a very convincing thing. I mean all we have to do is just piece together what Satan has said down through the years and put it together again. See, Satan can't do anything new. Whatever he does is just a repeat.

Ok, so here's what happens, verse 9: "Then *I saw* them go up upon the breadth of the earth and encircle the camp of the saints..." Now the camp: could this be something that is going to happen during the Feast of Tabernacles? I do not know. "...And the beloved city..." Now they are going to think that they are going to have success. But God has His execution in mind for them. "...And fire came down from God out of heaven and consumed them..." Now when all of those who are sinners and chosen to sin, who have been exiled to Gog and Magog, are worked up into their armies and brought down to Jerusalem, they will have finished completing the unpardonable sin. The wages of sin is death as it always has been. So here, for them, is their first death. They're yet going to suffer the second death, as we will see tomorrow. But all sinners who are incorrigible sinners; those who won't repent or never repent, God has decreed that they will die twice. So what we are reading of here in Revelation 20 then, is the first death of those wicked in the last generation of the Millennium who have not had enough time to die a natural death, and die a sinner accursed and be buried. Now I think we can understand it that way, is about the best way we can understand it.

Now here's something else that has to take place. Because (just as we saw during the Millennium) the only way that righteousness is brought in, is not only by having the government of God here; not only by having the resurrected saints rule and reign and teach and so forth, but Satan must be removed. Now then, Satan's work is done at this point. There is no other purpose for Satan the devil. Now's the time for judgment against Satan. So let's see what this is. Let's see how it's going to be accomplished. And we will see that Satan's judgment must be done before the beginning of the Last Great Day, and the meaning and fulfillment of the Last Great Day. So he is sentenced and he is judged.

Now let's read it here, verse 10: "And the Devil, who deceived them..." And of course the devil—what [else] do you have with the devil? All of his demons because he's king over the abyss. So when Satan is cast into the abyss, all the demons are cast into the abyss. So when Satan is let out, all the demons are let out. So when this judgment comes upon Satan, it's going to come upon all the demons. "And the Devil, who deceived them, was cast into the lake of fire and brimstone [now this is a proper translation with a correct interpretation of Revelation 19, which we will look at in just a minute], where the beast and the false prophet *had been cast...*" Now when were the beast and the false prophet cast into the lake of fire? So this also tells us that there is going to be a lake of fire active during the Millennium, both. So you're going to have two things. You're going to have the totally incorrigible who may commit a crime that demands instant death. They'll probably, during the Millennium, be cast into the lake of fire. Those who sin and never repent but haven't done the incorrigible sin until the very end of their lives by not accepting the salvation of God, and they die as sinners being a hundred years old. So we probably have two things going here.

But let's go back to Revelation 19:20 and let's see what happens to the beast and the false prophet. Now this is important to understand. Verse 20: "And the beast was taken, and with him the false prophet who worked miracles in his presence [two human beings—flesh and blood], by which he had deceived those who received the mark of the beast and those who worshiped his image. Those two were cast alive into the lake of fire, which burns with brimstone..." Now when people are cast into the lake of fire, what happens? They burn up. Now just think of it this way. Think of it as a lake of molten lava. Now any human being, being flesh and blood, cast into that is burned up and they are no more. So that's why I translated it this way so it clears up the mistranslation that most people believe that the beast and the false prophet were there being tormented all during the Millennium. It cannot be because human beings are not tormented in fire. See, that's a misinterpretation and not a clear translation, because people believe in an ever-burning hell. So I translated it properly.

Now back to Revelation 20:10: "...where the beast and the false prophet *had been cast...*" Now understand this: the beast was possessed of Satan the devil, correct? Yes. And the false prophet by probably the next highest demon under Satan the devil. Those demons then, along with Satan, were cast into the abyss and the seal shut up over them all during the Millennium. Then they were let out as we saw and so forth. Now, here's the final judgment of Satan the devil. "...And they..." Because it is in the Greek "they shall be tormented." But that cannot refer to the beast and the false prophet because they are burned up. So the "they" has to refer to Satan and the demons. "...And they, *Satan and the demons,* shall be tormented day and night into the ages of eternity." So God is going to have Satan the devil and the demons being tormented day and night forever into the ages of eternity. Now that's what the Greek says. Now a lot of people can argue back and forth and say, "Well, couldn't God convert them into a human being and then destroy him and he's burned up?" Well anything is possible with God, but is that what God is going to do? You read in Hebrews 1 where it says that never did He say to any of the angels at any time, " 'You are My Son; this day I have begotten You' " (Heb. 1:5). So I see no reason why He would convert them into being human beings. But it does say that they are going to be tormented day and night forever. So that's quite a thing.

Let's come back here to Isaiah 14. Let's see where it talks about the punishment of Satan the devil. And of course if that's the case then, which it undoubtedly is because that's what the Scriptures tell us, then there will always be a constant reminder for all eternity to all of the rest who enter into the kingdom of God that sin and rebellion and going against God will never succeed.

Now here, Isaiah 14:12: "How art thou fallen from heaven, O Lucifer, son of the morning! *how* art thou cut down to the ground, which didst weaken the nations!" And he did. So what we have here right now is this: we have an amalgamation of everything that Satan stands for, a reference back to his first rebellion, a reference to his continuous rebellion, and a reference to the last rebellion that we just read of in Revelation 20.

"For thou hast said in thine heart [and he has never changed], I will ascend into heaven, I will exalt my throne above the stars of God [stars being the angels of God, but also the creation of the universe of God out there as well]: I will sit also upon the mount of the congregation, in the sides of the north…" [He thinks] going to be God. That's what he has always wanted to do—to replace God. "I will ascend above the heights of the clouds; I will be like the most High. Yet thou shalt be brought down to hell, to the sides of the pit [which is the abyss]. They that see thee shall narrowly look upon thee, *and* consider thee, *saying, Is* this the man [this could also be "is this the one"] that made the earth to tremble, that did shake kingdoms…" (verses 13-16). And of course all down through history Satan has possessed various men: the king of Babylon, other kings through time. And as we can see in our day, obviously had great influence with those dictators of World War II that we knew like Hitler, and Mussolini, and Tojo. Probably a combination of Satan and the high principalities and powers that serve under Satan the devil. And so people are going to look at him and they're going to say, "Is this the one?" It's going to be an object lesson, isn't it?

And you stop and think, if this happens all during the Millennium that people can come to the sealed abyss, will they be able to look down into the abyss and see Satan and the demons down there, and yet turn around and go sin? Will not that unpardonable sin be even more determined and premeditated than what we do today? Amazing, isn't it? So that's going to be Satan's judgment. That's the last thing that's going to take place during the Millennium.

So now what do we have? We have undoubtedly those human beings who were righteous, who are converted, who have the Spirit of God. They will live on over. And I've been torn between this too at different times, and different sermons. So if you go back and hear some other sermons where it's not exactly the same as this, just understand that. I've said in the past there are no more human beings alive. Well why not have those who have not reached a hundred years live on over into the hundred year period to help set the example for all those who will be resurrected in the second resurrection? So then you will have those human beings who will live over into the Great White Throne Judgment period. You'll have all the sons of God, all of those of us who are in the first resurrection. You'll have all of those who came into the kingdom of God all during the Millennium. And then we are ready for the finality of God's plan, which you'll have to come back tomorrow to get the rest of the story. Because that will be the finishing and completing of the plan of God.

End of Sermon

Transcriber: Carolyn Singer

Chapter Thirty-five

The Feast of Tabernacles–Day 7
October 6, 2004
Scriptural References

1) Isaiah 32:15-20

2) Psalm 1:1-3

3) Isaiah 25:6-9

4) Isaiah 30:18-21

5) Micah 4:4

6) Isaiah 9:7

7) Amos 9:13-15

8) Isaiah 60:16-18

9) Isaiah 33:20-22

10) Isaiah 35:1-10

11) Psalm 145:1-13

12) Isaiah 65:17-20

13) Hebrews 9:27

14) I Thessalonians 4:14-17

15) Philippians 3:21

16) I Corinthians 15:52

17) Genesis 3:24

18) Revelation 20:2-3, 7-10

19) Revelation 19:20

20) Hebrews 1:5

21) Isaiah 14:12-16

CHAPTER THIRTY-SIX

The Last Great Day—Day 8—Holy Day

October 7, 2004

And greetings brethren. Welcome to the Last Great Day. The eighth day of the feast. We've had seven days of the Feast of Tabernacles. And you know, it's very interesting how God starts out the feasts season. He starts out with the Passover, which is one day, plus seven days, equals eight. So we have one plus seven equals eight. And then we count seven weeks to Pentecost. And then on that eighth day we have Pentecost, don't we? We have the first resurrection. And then we come down to Trumpets and Atonement and then the Feast of Tabernacles. And now the Last Great Day. So He ends it with seven plus one equals eight. He starts it out with one plus seven equals eight. And those juxtaposition, or are like bookends for the plan of God.

Now let's go to Leviticus 23, because this is where it tells us about the eighth day and that it's a holy convocation. Verse 34: "Speak unto the children of Israel, saying, The fifteenth day of this seventh month *shall be* the feast of tabernacles [we've already done that] *for* seven days…" First day is a holy convocation. They were to make their offerings, which we covered on the first day in Numbers 29.

Now verse 36 in the middle of the verse: "…on the eighth day shall be an holy convocation…" So this is an appointed feast of God. And it is probably the most insignificant feast that is in the Bible. It's mentioned once in the book of John, which we will see a little bit later. You hear of the Jews keeping the Feast of Tabernacles, but hardly do you hear them keeping the Last Great Day. And of course the Protestants and Catholics know nothing of it.

But here's what He says: "…on the eighth day shall be an holy convocation unto you; and ye shall offer an offering made by fire unto the LORD: it *is* a solemn assembly; *and* ye shall do no servile work *therein*." Now verse 37 reads: "These *are* the feasts of the LORD, which ye shall proclaim *to be* holy convocations…" And these are the feasts. Notice how He ends it.

Let's come back here to verse 4. So this again ties it in. Verse 4, and verse 37. "These *are* the feasts of the LORD, *even* holy convocations, which ye shall proclaim in their seasons." Now we do take up an offering on the holy days. We know that we are not to come before God empty. And knowing and understanding the plan of God, you think about how much God has blessed you and the knowledge that He has in your consideration of the offering. So at this time we'll take a pause and take up the offering.

(Pause)

Now let's begin by going to the Gospel of John 7. And here it talks about the feast of the Last Great Day. And here again is showing that Jesus kept the feast, but He also prophesied of it's meaning and gave a fulfillment of it, as we find here in John 7. We know that in verse 2 it says that it was the time of the Feast of Tabernacles. And of course Jesus went up and kept the Feast of Tabernacles. Now let's come down here to verse 37. And this was a special ceremony called the Ceremony of Water, which took place as the sun was going down to end the seventh day, and the beginning of the Last Great Day.

Now let's pick it up here John 7:37: " 'Now in the last day, the great *day* of the feast, Jesus stood and called out, saying, "If anyone thirsts, let him come to Me and drink [prophecy of universal salvation]. The one who believes in Me, as the scripture has said, out of his belly shall flow rivers of living water' " (John 7:37-38). Again, a type of spiritual life, spiritual truth, spiritual cleansing. And all of these things are all a part of what we have here in what Jesus is explaining. And there has to come a time when God undoes all evil. And this is the day that pictures when God does that—when He gets rid of all evil in the whole human family.

Now verse 39: "But this He spoke concerning the Spirit, which those who believed in Him would soon receive; for *the* Holy Spirit was not yet *given* because Jesus was not yet glorified." So it had it's fulfillment beginning when they received the Holy Spirit when the church began. And it's going to have it's fulfillment in the end. But what is the meaning of the Last Great Day? And why do we call it the Last Great Day? Well first of all we're going to see that just like God has always done, that which is considered least among men produces the most for God.

Now let's come to Isaiah 14 and let's see what God has declared. And the first thing we need to understand and <u>always</u> remember is that God has a purpose and He is going to carry it out. He is God and He looks down on the nations and as far as compared to Him what are they but a drop in the bucket. They aren't even weighty enough to be counted as dust in a scale of balances, is it? No.

Now here Isaiah 14:24. Let's read this: "The LORD of hosts hath sworn, saying, Surely as I have thought, so shall it come to pass; and as I have purposed, *so* shall it stand..." Whatever God's purpose is, it's going to stand. That's why God has given His word, has given His Spirit, and also has given choice—whether we believe in God, whether we love God, whether will keep His commandments, whether we will do the things that are pleasing in His sight. And as I mentioned yesterday: the way that you understand God's plan is by keeping His commandments. That's what it says in Psalm 111: "A good understanding have all they who do *His commandments*..." (Psa. 111:10).

Now verse 26: "This *is* the purpose that is purposed upon the whole earth..." Yes, it talks about breaking the Syrian, which is a type of the beast as fulfilled in Revelation 19, as we saw yesterday. So He has a purpose that is proposed upon the whole earth. "...And this *is* the hand that is stretched out upon all the nations." God's hand. He's going to do it. You know, and I just imagine that the throne of God is a whole lot closer to the earth than we think. But you see, being spiritual we don't see it. "For the LORD of hosts hath purposed, and who shall disannul *it?* and His hand *is* stretched out, and who shall turn it back?" (verses 26-27). So God is going to do His purpose. He is going to accomplish His purpose. No man, no angel, not even any of the demons are going to turn back the hand of God. It is just not going to happen.

Now let's come to the New Testament to the book of Ephesians here and let's understand something that is very profound. And God has called us to reveal His secret to us. And the understanding of this Last Great Day is the greatest fulfillment of the plan of God and it is a secret that God reveals to us. It's a mystery to the world because they cannot understand it because they will not obey Him.

Now let's come here and begin in Ephesians 1:3. Now see, the whole first chapter of Ephesians is in English the worst sentence in the world. But in the Greek it is one long sentence. Two at the most. So let's get the thoughts together here.

Verse 3: "Blessed *be* the God and Father of our Lord Jesus Christ, Who has blessed us with every spiritual blessing in the heavenly *things* with Christ..." And those spiritual blessings are going to be fulfilled when we enter into the kingdom of God and are the spirit glorified sons and daughters of God. But He has given us the earnest, the down payment of it now.

Verse 4. I want you to mark verse 4 because this is the correct translation here. "According as He has <u>personally</u> chosen us…" Now that's what it means in the Greek with the special middle voice verb as I have covered before. And I want you to understand: think about you. And if you're sitting there and you're thinking, "Well, little old me—what do I have to offer God?" You have love, obedience, and God's calling and God's education for you. But God personally has: "…chosen us for Himself before *the* foundation of *the* world…" And that means in His plans He said, "Ok, I'm going to call the firstfruits. They will be in the first resurrection." This is not fatalism, by the way, where most of the churches in the world believe in fatalism. And that is, if you're called you're going to make it and go to heaven. If you're not called you are going to go to hell and be tormented for ever and ever. And this day shows that that lie cannot possibly be true. So the predestination of this whole thing is that He had the plan before the foundation of the world.

"…In order that we might be holy and blameless before Him in love; having predestinated us for sonship…" That is, all of those who are in the first resurrection have been predestinated for a special sonship, by a special personal calling of God the Father and Jesus Christ. "…For sonship to Himself through Jesus Christ, according to the good pleasure of His own will, to *the* praise of *the* glory of His grace, wherein He has made us objects of *His* grace in the Beloved *Son*; in Whom we have redemption through His blood, *even* the remission of sins, according to the riches of His grace, which He has made to abound toward us in all wisdom and intelligence; having made known to us the mystery of His own will…" (verses 4-9). When you understand the plan of the holy days of God you are being invited by God Himself to understand His will. And the mystery is that if you don't keep the holy days, and if you don't keep them the way that God has said and Jesus Christ has shown, you'll never understand it. See, because the Jews have rejected Christ, they don't understand anything. And they believe just as much as the immortality of the soul as any of the religions in the world. Because even though they have the form of the law, they don't keep it; even though they have all of the prophecies, they don't keep it; even though they have all of the prophecies of Jesus Christ, they don't recognize Him. And so you see, God has called you, God has called me, God has called all the brethren. And down through time, as much as they are able to learn and know and understand. And here we are at the end of the age and what can we do? God has given us His will, His truth, His Word, time to study, to know, to grow, to change, to overcome, and all of these things. And to realize that the very purpose and plan that God thought of at the beginning before the foundation of the world, He has made known to us. Now that ought to be very humbling indeed.

God has made known to us, see. "…Having made known to us the mystery of His own will, according to His good pleasure, which He purposed in Himself; that in *the divine* plan for the fulfilling of *the* times…" And that's what this is. The Last Great Day is the fulfilling of the last of the times of salvation. "…He might bring all things together in Christ, both the things in the heavens and the things upon the earth…" (verses 9-10). Yes, God has a plan. God has the purpose. He has called it. We are part of it. It is fantastic and tremendous for us to realize and understand.

However, now let's look at the world. Let's understand something very profound. God has chosen the few. Many are called but few are chosen because few repent. Now let's understand something else here. That God has done something that He alone is responsible for. Number one: He's given all human beings the law of sin and death within them (a miniature part of the nature of Satan the devil). He's allowed them to go their own ways. He has let them be ruled by Satan the devil. And God is responsible for that. As a result—

as a result how many people have been killed and died in wars and all of the things that have gone on down through time because men just reject God and cannot stand Him? But God is responsible.

Now we're going to see, yes, there is the unpardonable sin as we have covered in the book of Hebrews in going through that series. Which by the way I hope to finish after the feast. But never the less, here's what God has done. Let's come to Isaiah 29:13. People love to have their religions. Oh they love to take the name of God in a religious sense; condemn all of those who swear and curse; but those who take the name of God in vain in a religious sense are <u>worse</u> than the people who swear and curse and are just totally blinded. And those who are the religious ones don't realize that they are blinded because they don't want to do everything that God has said. An amazing thing, isn't it? Now you stop and think about that—what a fantastic miracle that it is that you understand, that God has opened your mind; that God has called you.

Now notice, Isaiah 29:13: "Wherefore the LORD said, Forasmuch as this people draw near *Me* with their mouth [Oh yes, got to have religion], and with their lips do honour Me [God bless America], but have removed their heart far from Me, and their fear toward Me is taught by the precept of men [not by the Word of God]: therefore, behold, I will proceed to do a marvellous work among this people, *even* a marvellous work and a wonder: for the wisdom of their wise *men* shall perish, and the understanding of their prudent *men* shall be hid. Woe unto them that seek deep to hide their counsel from the LORD, and their works are in the dark, and they say, Who seeth us? and who knoweth us? Surely your turning of things upside down shall be esteemed as the potter's clay: for shall the work say of him that made it, He made me not? or shall the thing framed say of him that framed it, He had no understanding? *Is* it not yet a very little while, and Lebanon shall be turned into a fruitful field…" (Isa. 29:13-17), and so forth. And He's showing the solution to the problem.

Let's look at some things here which are important for us to realize and carry through on this. Let's come to Matthew 13 now, and let's see where this is fulfilled. And this will help us to answer a couple of very difficult Scriptures in the New Testament to understand. And here we have Christ's explanation of this even a little bit more. Matthew 13:13: " 'For this *reason* [He said to them explaining why He spoke in parables] I speak to them in parables, because seeing, they see not; and hearing, they hear not; neither do they understand.' " Now isn't it amazing that people can have a Bible and not understand it? They can read the words and not comprehend them. They can hear the things said but it's meaningless to them.

Now notice verse 14: " 'And in them is fulfilled the prophecy of Isaiah, which says, "In hearing you shall hear, and in no way understand; and *in* seeing you shall see, and in no way perceive [and that is true concerning the meaning of the Last Great Day]; for the heart of this people has grown fat, and their ears are dull of hearing, and their eyes <u>they have closed</u>…" They have chosen to do this. So God has selected their delusion, but also to serve His purpose and have mercy on them at a later time. "…Lest they should see with their eyes, and should hear with their ears, and should understand with their hearts, and should be converted, and I should heal them." ' " Well now doesn't this go against mainstream Protestantism, which says, "We have to save everybody. And if you're not saved in our church you're going to go to hell and burn in everlasting fire for ever and ever." How's God going to do that? Who is responsible for all of this? God is.

Verse 16, He says to the apostles, which means to us: " 'But blessed *are* your eyes, because they see; and your ears, because they hear. For truly I say to you, many prophets and righteous *men* have desired to see what you see, and have not seen…' " Even Daniel didn't understand. Moses didn't understand. Isaiah, Jeremiah, Ezekiel—none of them understood. And even the apostles themselves did not fully understand. We have been blessed at the end of the age to understand this far more fully than they did. " '…and to hear what you hear, and have not heard' " (Matt. 13:13-17).

Now let's look at a couple more Scriptures so we can understand what God has said. Let's come to I Timothy 2. Now here is an enigma. And this is a hard one to answer. And really the answer is found in the meaning of the Last Great Day. This is important. Let's come to I Timothy 2:3, and here is God's desire. But remember God's desire is always modified by the choice of the individual. Let's read it: "For this *is* good and acceptable before God our Savior [that is to pray for quietness and so forth], Who desires all men to be saved [now that's what He desires] and to come to *the* knowledge of *the* truth" (I Tim. 2:3-4). Now question: If He blinds them, how can they come to the knowledge of the truth? Now what if they lived a full life and died without having the knowledge of the truth, how can they be saved? Because they must be called. And if God has blinded them then obviously God is not going to call them, right? So how's God going to solve this problem?

Let's come here to II Peter 3. Let's see what is said here in II Peter where Peter was writing about the very same thing. And he says in verse 9: "The Lord is not delaying the promise *of His coming*, as some in their own minds reckon delay; rather, He is longsuffering toward us, not desiring that any should perish, but that all should come to repentance." So He wants them all to come to repentance. And He wants them all to be saved. Now how is He going to do this? If He cuts them off so they don't understand it, how's that going to happen? Now we also have this: that He has used Satan the devil to blind their minds, hasn't He (II Corinthians 4:4), that they cannot understand? Yet it says He wants them all to be saved. So how's God going to do this?

Well, let's come over here to Romans 9. Let's take a little look into that. Let's see what the apostle Paul wrote. Now we're going to see in these Scriptures that we're going to cover here in Romans 9 (and also Romans 11 in just a minute), that the understanding that we have today Paul didn't quite have it. He knew that it was going to happen. But you see, God had not given the revelation to the apostle John yet, so those Scriptures were not available for him to understand it.

Now let's come to Romans 9:14: "What then shall we say? *Is there* unrighteousness with God?" That is, because He loved Jacob and hated Esau. Or we could say, because He called some and didn't call others, is God unrighteous? No, because God has to lead a person to repentance. He wants them all to come to repentance. He wants them to all be saved. But He has closed their minds. He has blinded their eyes, and shut their ears, and put them in this predicament. Is God unrighteous in it? Or is not God righteous in doing so? Because you see, the Last Great Day is the rest of the story.

Let's go on. "What then shall we say? *Is there* unrighteousness with God? MAY IT NEVER BE! For He said to Moses, 'I will show mercy to whomever I show mercy, and I will have compassion on whomever I have compassion.' So then, *it is* not of the one who wills, nor of the one who runs; rather, *it is* of God, Who shows mercy" (Rom. 9:14-16). So if God has called us and shown us mercy, then we ought to be thankful and happy and grateful that God has done it.

And then he goes on to show that yes, He raised up Pharaoh for the very purpose, you see. Verse 17, quite a verse here: "For the Scripture said to Pharaoh, 'For this very purpose I raised you up in order that I might show in you My power, so that My name may be declared in all the earth.' " And it is. In the Bible, His name and what He did to Egypt is there for anyone to read from that time forward to glorify the name of God. "So then, He shows mercy to whom He will, and He hardens whom He will. Will you then reply to me,

'Why does He yet find fault?' " In other words, why does He still punish people for sin if He blinds their eyes? Because sin has penalties, that's why. So He's not going to take that away. Otherwise how are you ever, ever, ever going to know what's right and wrong? " 'For who has opposed His purpose?' Yes, indeed, O man, who are you to answer against God? Shall the thing that is formed say to the one who formed *it*, 'Why did you make me this way?' " (verses 17-20).

Then he goes on to explain here a little bit about a potter and all the things that are done there. He says: "Or doesn't the potter have authority over the clay to make from the same lump of clay one vessel unto honor, and another vessel unto dishonor? And *who dares to question His purpose* if God, willing to show *His* wrath and to make known His power, chose in much long-suffering to put up with *the* vessels of wrath which were created for destruction…" Now if God created them for that, how is He going to save them? How is He going to solve the problem? That's the answer of this day. "In order that He might make known the riches of His glory unto *the* vessels of mercy, which He prepared before for glory…" (verses 21-23).

Now let's come here to Romans 11. Now he's talking to the Gentiles and he's saying the Gentiles were seeking God, but not the way that they should have. So they were broken off. Even God cut off His own people that He says He loves. Now he's talking to the Gentiles and he says, verse 18: "Do not boast against the branches; but if you are boasting against *them, remember that* you do not bear the root; rather, the root bears you." Isn't that interesting? It shows that it comes all from the Word of God.

Verse 19: "Will you then say, 'The branches were broken off in order that I might be grafted in'? *That is* true! Because of unbelief they were broken off, and you stand by faith. Do not be high-minded, but fear…" (verses 19-20). A good lesson for us. Because God has given us the understanding of His plan and has called us, let's not be high-minded and hooty-snooty and self-righteous and look down on the world.

Verse 21: "For if God spared not the natural branches, take heed lest He not spare you either. Therefore, behold *the* graciousness and *the* severity of God: upon those who fell, severity; and upon you, graciousness, if you continue in *His* graciousness; otherwise you also will be cut off. And they also, if they do not continue in unbelief, shall be grafted in because God is able to graft them in again. For if you were cut off from an olive tree which by nature is wild, and contrary to nature were grafted into a good olive tree, how much more shall those who according to nature *were from the good olive tree* be grafted back into their own olive tree?" (verses 21-24).

Verse 25: "For I do not wish you to be ignorant of this mystery, brethren, in order that you may not be wise in your own conceits: that a partial hardening *of the heart* has happened to Israel until the fullness of the Gentiles be come in…" God is going to resolve the problem. Verse 26: "And so all Israel shall be saved…" He doesn't know when. But at this time, verse 32: "For God has given them all over to unbelief in order that He might show mercy to all." When? Verse 33: "O *the* depth of *the* riches of both *the* wisdom and *the* knowledge of God! How unfathomable *are* His judgments and unsearchable *are* His ways! For who did know *the* mind of *the* Lord, or who became His counselor?" See, so here we have it. "Or who first gave to Him, and it shall be recompensed to him again? For from Him, and through Him, and unto Him *are* all things; to Him *be* the glory into the ages of eternity. Amen" (verses 25-26, 32-36).

So now let's look and see how God is going to begin to solve the problem. Let's come here to Revelation 20. And again, it deals with the Millennium. And again, it tells us something that is very important. And it tells us something which shows the mind of God.

And it tells us something about the plan of God. So let's come here, Revelation 20:5. Now verse 4 talks about the resurrection of the saints. They will live and reign with Christ a thousand years.

Verse 5: "(But the rest of the dead did not live again until the thousand years were completed.)" So at the end of the Millennium there's going to be a resurrection. Because it says "the rest of the dead shall not live again until the thousand years were completed." Quite an amazing and a profound thing, isn't it? Yes, it is.

Let's look at some other Scriptures which help us understand this a little bit here. Who are the rest of the dead? Well we know (I Corinthians 15) as we learned on the Day of Pentecost tells us that Christ is the firstfruit, and then all of those who are Christ's at His coming—that's the first resurrection. Well what about all the other people? What about all of those that God blinded? What about those people who were sincere but never knew, never understood, never had the Spirit of God? Are they lost? Are they cut off? Are they destined to have no opportunity for salvation at all? And if the rest of the dead, all of those who were not in the first resurrection, why are they to be resurrected? What is the purpose in doing so? Well, we get a clue.

Let's come back here to John 11 for just a minute, and let's ask the question. We may not read some verses there for the sake of time, but you know that talks about the resurrection of Lazarus. Now why was Lazarus resurrected? Remember, he died and was in the grave for four days. But why did Jesus resurrect him? Even in coming to the tomb Jesus said, "If you believe that I am the resurrection." And his sister said, "Yes, I believe that he'll be raised up at the last day" (John 11:23-27, paraphrased). But she wasn't thinking that he would be raised right then. But, Jesus loved Lazarus, didn't He? Jesus had called Lazarus, didn't He? But he died before a very important thing could take place in his life. He had not received the Holy Spirit. And if he had not been raised from the dead he would not have been in the first resurrection, because you have to receive the Holy Spirit of God and to grow in grace and knowledge and to be resurrected when Christ returns. So therefore he was brought back to life. Same way with the saints who were resurrected, came back to a second physical life in the flesh as we find there in Matthew 27, so that they could receive the Holy Spirit and be saved.

Now this tells us how God operates. Let's come to Romans 2 because this tells us something very important. Because let's talk about the so-called "good sincere people" out there in the world, because there are many of them out there. Many of them. God hasn't called them. They're blinded. Have they sinned a sin unto death? Have they committed the unpardonable sin? No. As a matter of fact, a lot of them are trying to live fairly decent lives, aren't they? Yes.

Now God talks about this. Romans 2:14: "For when *the* Gentiles, which do not have *the* law [and we could say today - do not understand the law], practice by nature the things contained in the law..." They don't believe in stealing, they don't believe in committing adultery, they don't believe in lying and all of those things. They try and live good decent lives. They try and be honest. But their minds are not open to the Sabbath, not open to the holy days, not open to the Scriptures. But maybe they're even trying in some way to be (as some of the Sunday professing Christians are) trying to lead a decent life. But God hasn't opened their minds to understanding. And the reason that God does this is so that everyone is going to know that no one is going to receive salvation because of the works that he or she is doing. God has to give it. But in cutting people off from having the understanding of the Word of God, then we have a vast area of decent people out there down through all time who have not committed the unpardonable sin. And it talks about here in verse 14, that we've been reading.

"…Practice by nature the things contained in the law, these who do not have *the* law are a law unto themselves; who show the work of the law written in their own hearts, their consciences bearing witness, and their reasonings also, as they accuse or defend one another;) …" Now notice verse 16: "In a day when God shall judge the secrets of men by Jesus Christ, according to my gospel" (Rom. 2:14-16). Now we know this: our names are written in the Book of Life. But what about all of those people out there who have died in wars, and famine, and pestilence, and starvation. What about all of those who died in accidents and floods? What about all of those who were under the influence of Satan the devil before the flood of Noah? What about all of those that have been deceived, that don't know, that never heard the name of Jesus Christ? And long before there were any Protestant missionaries, hundreds of millions of people down through history have died having not known the way of God. And even a lot of the children of Israel and Judah have not known God because He's blinded them. Yes, they've had the Scriptures. Yes, they've had the Word of God, but they don't know God.

Here, let's go to John 5 now and let's see what Jesus said so that we understand all of those who are to be resurrected… Now we'll cover this in just a minute. We're not going to delve deeply into the unpardonable sin. But here in John 5:25 where Jesus tells us this: " 'Truly, truly I say to you, *the* hour is coming, and now is, when the dead shall hear the voice of the Son of God; and those who hear shall live.' " They'll be raised. That's what happened to Lazarus. That's what happened to the others that He raised. " 'For even as the Father has life in Himself, so also has He given to the Son to have life in Himself; and has also given Him authority to execute judgment because He is *the* Son of man. Do not wonder at this, for *the* hour is coming in which all who are in the graves [that means all who have died] shall hear His voice and shall come forth: those who have practiced good unto a resurrection of life, and those who have practiced evil unto a resurrection of judgment' " (John 5:25-29).

And there are two kinds of judgments, as we will see. The judgment of the unpardonable sin, and the judgment of the person who has not committed the unpardonable sin. So we can extrapolate from what we know from the Scriptures. One: there is a Book of Life, and our names are written in it right now. Could we also say that in order for all of those who have not committed the unpardonable sin, that their names are also written in a separate book of life to be raised in a resurrection. Have to be, otherwise how can they be resurrected. And we can also extrapolate that there has to be a book of the dead for those who have committed the unpardonable sin to die the second death. Now as we continue we'll go ahead and take a look at those scriptures which show this.

…and see where it talks about "the rest of the dead who live not again till the thousand years were finished" (Rev. 20:5). Now remember, they cannot come out of the graves. They cannot be resurrected from the dead unless Jesus resurrects them. Now these are all the people who never had an opportunity for salvation. And I know there are a lot of hard shelled Baptists out there in the world who don't want to give people a second opportunity. Well, what if they never had a first opportunity? What if they need a second life in the flesh (as we will see, this is in the flesh) for a first opportunity for salvation? If God is going to do as He wants to have them come to repentance and be saved, He's got to do it someway, somehow, doesn't He? This is how He's going to do it.

Now, Revelation 20:11: "Then I saw a great white throne [that's why this is called the Great White Throne Judgment Day] and the one Who was sitting on it, from Whose face the earth and the heaven fled away; and no place was found for them." Billions, and billions, and billions, and billions of people. "And I saw the dead [Which dead? The rest of the dead who lived not again until the thousand years were finished.], small and great, standing before God; and *the* books were opened; and another book was opened, which is *the book* of life…" (Rev. 20:11-12). Now they're going to have an opportunity for eternal life. Amazing, isn't it? "And the dead were judged out of the things written in the books, according to their works." Now their first life surely couldn't qualify them for salvation. And you can't say because they are good sincere people, therefore they earned salvation a little differently than the rest. Because Jesus said that He is the door, and if they come in any other way they are thieves and robbers. So it's not going to be another way. It's going to be according to God's way, see. So here is how God is going to do it.

Now let's see in the book of Ezekiel where it does talk about this. And then we'll come back to the New Testament again. Let's come to Ezekiel 37, and let's see where there is a resurrection to a second physical life of those who were never called to receive salvation in their first physical life.

This is quite a long one here so we need to read all of this section in Ezekiel 37 because this is the meaning of this day—when the rest of the dead live again. And we're going to see that it is a second life in the flesh. And as we will see, for a first opportunity for salvation, which they never had before, because number one: God didn't call them. Number two: God blinded their eyes. Number three: they lived before Christ came. They were in other nations other then Israel. And of course this helps answer the question too. Look at all of the things that Israel went through. And this proves a point, which is this: There was not universal salvation granted to those under the Old Covenant. They were required to obey in the letter of the law. But there was no salvation granted to them. Only to the prophets and certain of the kings, and that was it.

Now Ezekiel 37:1: "The hand of the LORD was upon me, and carried me out in the spirit of the LORD, and set me down in the midst of the valley which *was* full of bones, and caused me to pass by them round about: and, behold, *there were* very many in the open valley; and, lo, *they were* very dry." It was like looking out in a valley and all you see are bones. All human bones. "And He [that is the LORD] said unto me, Son of man, can these bones live? And I answered, O Lord GOD, thou knowest" (Ezek. 37:1-3). He couldn't tell Him whether they could live or not.

"Again He said unto me, Prophesy upon these bones, and say unto them, O ye dry bones, hear the word of the LORD. Thus saith the Lord GOD unto these bones; Behold, I will cause breath to enter into you, and ye shall live…" Now what kind of life? The answer's right here. Verse 6: "And I will lay sinews upon you, and will bring up flesh upon you…" Let's stop here for a minute before we go on and analyze this any further. First of all, if you see all these dry bones out there, what does it tell us? It tells us these were people who were alive once, correct? Otherwise how are you going to get the bones? It also tells us that it's people who have died. So now here we have the details on how the rest of the dead are going to live after the Millennium is finished. He says: "And I will lay sinews upon you, and will bring up flesh upon you, and cover you with skin, and put breath in you, and ye shall live; and ye shall know that I *am* the LORD" (verses 4-6). So here's a group of people that didn't know the Lord. Now then, if their eyes are blinded and if their ears are stopped, there is no way they could know the Lord, right? They lived and died without knowing God. Now then He's going to give them a second physical life to what? To know God.

"So I prophesied as I was commanded: and as I prophesied, there was a noise, and behold a shaking, and the bones came together, bone to his bone. And when I beheld, lo, the sinews and the flesh came up upon them, and the skin covered them above: but *there was* no breath in them" (verses 7-8). So here they were. They look like human beings again, recreated in the flesh according to the genetics that God gave them when they were first conceived. Amazing, isn't it? No breath in them.

"Then said He unto me, Prophesy unto the wind, prophesy, son of man, and say to the wind, Thus saith the Lord GOD; Come from the four winds, O breath, and breathe upon these slain, that they may live. So I prophesied as he commanded me, and the breath came into them, and they lived, and stood up upon their feet, an exceeding great army." Well the next question is: Who are they? Well it's answered the next verse. "Then He said unto me, Son of man, these bones are the whole house of Israel…" (verses 9-11). And this tells the rest of the story that Paul was writing about there in Romans 11, that they were cut off—the whole house of Israel, all twelve tribes.

"Behold, they say, Our bones are dried, and our hope is lost: we are cut off for our parts." They lived lives that were "the wages of sin is death and all have sinned and come short of the glory of God" even though they may have tried to do the best that they could. "Therefore prophesy and say unto them, Thus saith the Lord GOD…" Now listen carefully to these next verses: "Behold, O My people, I will open your graves, and cause you to come up out of your graves, and bring you into the land of Israel. And ye shall know that I *am* the LORD, when I have opened your graves, O My people, and brought you up out of your graves…" Now it says graves four times, right? Yes. They were dead. They were in their graves. This is picturing the resurrection from the dead to a second life in the flesh. It has to be. But notice verse 14: "And shall put My spirit in you…" An opportunity for salvation. There you go. "…And ye shall live, and I shall place you in your own land: then shall ye know that I the LORD have spoken *it,* and performed *it,* saith the LORD" (verses 11-14).

Now we come to the book of Matthew. We find something very interesting. Because this happens to Israel. Well, what happens to all the rest of the nations then? There's a principle in the New Testament, as we are turning to Matthew 12 to understand this, which is this: to the Jew first and then to the Gentile. Or, to the Israelites first and then the Gentiles. What happens to Israel also happens to the Gentiles. Very important principle to remember.

Now here we have in Matthew 12:32. Here's something to understand. This gives us a little definition of the unpardonable sin. Since we have covered that in the book of Hebrews, I'm not necessarily going to cover it here. But the unpardonable sin is the total rejection of God, total rejection of being led to repentance, a total rejection of the Spirit of God, total rejection of God's way completely. Now that is the unpardonable sin against the Holy Spirit of God.

Now verse 32: " 'And whoever speaks a word against the Son of man, it shall be forgiven him; but whoever speaks against the Holy Spirit, it shall not be forgiven him, neither in this age nor in the coming *age.*' " Now we're talking about the coming age—the Last Great Day. " 'Either make the tree good and the fruit good, or make the tree corrupt and its fruit corrupt; for a tree is known by its fruit. Offspring of vipers, how are you able to speak good things, being evil? For out of the abundance of the heart the mouth speaks. The good man out of the good treasure of his heart brings out good things; and the wicked man out of the wicked treasure brings out wicked things. But I say to you, for every idle word that men may speak, they shall be held accountable in *the* day of judgment.' " God is going to judge us by our words. That's talking about the unpardonable sin here. " 'For by your words you shall be justified, and by your words you shall be condemned' " (Matt. 13:32-37). And then the Pharisees, they wanted to have a sign. And He said it would be the sign of Jonah three days and three nights and so forth.

Let's come to verse 41: " '*The* men of Nineveh shall stand up in the judgment…' " Now isn't that what we read in John 5? Some to a resurrection of life and some to a resurrection of judgment. The Last Great Day is called the Great White Throne Judgment, to be given an opportunity for salvation for those who have never had an opportunity, and they are given a second life in the flesh.

Now notice: " '*The* men of Nineveh shall stand up [that means be resurrected] in the judgment <u>with</u> this generation [which shows that this is going to take place at the same time that Ezekiel 37 is fulfilled when all Israel is resurrected] and shall condemn it, because they repented at the proclamation of Jonah; and behold, a greater than Jonah *is* here. *The* queen of *the* south [now removed by well over a thousand years from the men of Nineveh] shall rise up in the judgment [that is be resurrected] with this generation [that's at the same time] and shall condemn it, because she came from the ends of the earth to hear the wisdom of Solomon; and behold, a greater than Solomon *is* here' " (verses 41-42). So here we have right from the Scriptures a resurrection to life of Israel (all twelve tribes) and Gentile nations at the same time. Be resurrected and given an opportunity for salvation. Be brought back to life in the flesh, just like Lazarus and the saints were brought back to physical life so they could have an opportunity for salvation.

Now let's see what kind of world that they are going to come back to. So what is the sum of this, brethren? Well, the sum of it is this: All those who have lived and died and have not committed the unpardonable sin are going to be raised to have an opportunity for salvation. And I think we can just refer to what we covered yesterday. They are going to live a hundred years. Now there are going to be some people who were righteous at the end of the Millennium who are going to also live on through into that time.

Let's come here to Revelation 20 and let's see something that's important for us to understand. Many people have misunderstood this, which is this: remember Revelation 10, it talks about that Satan the devil is cast into the lake of fire and brimstone. He is put away. When these people are resurrected and stand in the judgment, and God is going to be fair in the judgment that He is giving them. That He is giving them an opportunity for salvation. And they are going to be judged just like we are today. What does it say of the church? "For judgment is upon the house of God. And if it begin with us, where will the sinner and the ungodly be?" (I Peter 4:17, paraphrased). So likewise they are going to be judged and have an opportunity to live. And in this second life Satan is not going to be anywhere around. Now let's just stop and ask the question: Don't you think that living one life under Satan the devil is quite sufficient? So, Satan is not going to be around. They're going to have the opportunity for salvation. And this is when God is going to fulfill that He wants all men to come to repentance and be saved. And as Peter said, He wants all men to be saved. And this is how He's going to do it.

And you see then we have the situation which comes with the unpardonable sin. Now then we have what is called the second death. Since all men who reject the salvation of God must die twice regardless of when they lived. Therefore there has to be another phase of this second resurrection, which is the resurrection of the wicked. Now it says here...

Let's just continue the story before we get to that. Revelation 20:13: "And the sea gave up the dead *that were* in it, and death and *the* grave [hell] gave up the dead *that were* in them; and they were judged individually, according to their works." Now that's a very interesting situation here. Each one is judged individually. Now then, when they qualify for life what's going to happen? They are going to enter into life just like those during the Millennium. When it came the end of the hundred years they would enter into life. All of those who do not qualify for salvation, or at this time reject the salvation of God (which they have the choice to do), then there's going to be something else that's going to happen. All those who qualify will enter into the kingdom of God. All of those who do not qualify will be left standing waiting their fate. Because it is judgment. Judgment unto life or judgment unto the second death. So what's going to happen is this: all of those who committed the unpardonable sin all the way down through history are all going to be resurrected and they are going to stand waiting their judgment to the lake of fire.

Verse 14: "And death and *the* grave were cast into the lake of fire. This is the second death. And if anyone was not found written in the book of life, he was cast into the lake of fire" (verses 14-15). And if they are cast into the lake of fire they are burned up, they are ashes, there is no more torment. And as it says concerning the wicked, that the righteous are going to walk on the ashes of the wicked in Malachi 4.

Now let's look at a very interesting parable that Jesus gave in Luke 16 concerning Lazarus and the rich man. When you read this it looks like that people are tormented in hell forever. You see, and that's part of the problem with the translation in the King James Version, because it says, "and in hell." That's not correct. The Greek word *hades* is "the grave."

So let's pick it up here Luke 16:19: " 'Now there was a certain rich man, and he was clothed in purple and fine linen, and daily indulged himself in luxury. And there was a certain poor man named Lazarus, who was laid at his porch, full of sores. And he longed to be nourished with the crumbs that fell from the rich man's table; and the dogs even came and licked his sores.' " No one to comfort him but a dog. That's why God gave dogs—to comfort people when no one else will. " 'Now it came to pass *that* the poor man died, and he was carried away by the angels into Abraham's bosom' " (Luke 16:19-22). Now, when is he carried away? He dies. When is he carried by the angels? At the resurrection—Matthew 24. Into Abraham's bosom because Abraham, Isaac, and Jacob are going to be in the kingdom of God. So this is the first resurrection.

" 'And the rich man also died and was buried. And in the grave he lifted up his eyes and was in torment...' " (verses 22-23). Now when, because obviously this man had committed the unpardonable sin. Not just because he was rich. When is he going to lift up his eyes in the grave? See, that's why it's misleading where the King James says "and in hell." And I just imagine there have been thousands and thousands of fire and brimstone preachers preaching this about being tormented in hell. Not so. "In the grave he lifted up his eyes." When would that be? We just read it back there in Revelation 20. After the Great White Throne period of one hundred years. The second phase of the second resurrection takes place and the incorrigible wicked are raised to face their judgment of the second death. So this is what happened with the rich man. "And was in torment." Why was he in torment? Because he could look out and see the lake of fire out there.

" '...*For* he saw Abraham afar off, and Lazarus in his bosom. And he cried out *and* said, "Father Abraham, have compassion on me and send Lazarus, so that he may dip the tip of his finger in water and cool my tongue; for I am suffering because of this flame" ' " (verses 23-24), that is by seeing it. You'd be tormented too. How much fear would you have if you were standing on the edge of a volcano and you thought you were going in there? I mean you think about that the next time you watch Kilauea volcano in Hawaii blow up and all that lava is flowing down. "<u>Because</u> of this flame," not <u>in</u> the flame. It's a wrong translation.

" 'Then Abraham said, "Child, remember that in your lifetime you received good things to the full, and likewise Lazarus evil things. But now he is comforted, and you are suffering. And besides all these things, between us and you a great chasm has been fixed [The difference between physical life and spiritual life. That's fixed]; so that those who desire to pass from here [facing the second death] to you are not able, nor can those from there pass to us [To go back and become a human being again. It's not possible.]." And he said, "I beseech you then, father, that you would send him to my father's house, for I have five brothers; so that he may earnestly testify to them, in order that they also may not come to this place of torment." Abraham said to him, "They have Moses and the prophets. Let them hear them" ' " (verses 25-29). Very important thing. Now are we talking about the difference between eternal life and eternal death? Yes, indeed. What is the difference? You must hear Moses. And as II Corinthians 3 has said, that in Christ the veil of the eyes is taken away at the reading of Moses when you have the Holy Spirit of God. So isn't it interesting. Moses and the Prophets are necessary for salvation, are they not? Have to be.

"But he said, "No, Father Abraham, but if one from *the* dead would go to them, they would repent." ' " No, you see, because people will not be convinced unless they choose to repent. Unless they are convicted in heart of their sins there is no way that they will repent. And besides you're also dealing here with the unpardonable sin with the rich man. So notice verse 31: " 'And he said to him, "If they will not hear Moses and the prophets, they would not be persuaded even if one rose from *the* dead" ' " (verses 30-31). So this parable of the rich man takes place when the dead, the incorrigible wicked who have committed the unpardonable sin, are raised from the dead to stand alongside the lake of fire with all of those who have committed the unpardonable sin, and they are all going to be cast alive into the lake of fire as God's final judgment. See, God has told all the righteous down through time, "You will see the final judgment of God. You will see the vengeance of God." And it's necessary for a demonstration of the righteousness of God that all of the wicked die together just as all who are saved will live together.

And with this lake of fire God is going to do something. He is going to prepare the whole earth for the new heavens and the new earth. Let's come to II Peter 3 again, and let's see where it talks about the destruction of this earth in preparation for the new heaven and the new earth. Now the destruction of the earth is going to be that the lake of fire is going to envelop everything on the earth. And it will be a great renewing of the surface of the earth. Now as spirit beings, that will not affect us.

We'll pick up where we left off with the verse about repentance there. II Peter 3:10: "However, the day of *the* Lord shall come as a thief in *the* night in which the heaven itself shall disappear..." Now Peter didn't have all the knowledge and understanding that John did in Revelation. So his account here is a little deficient. But we put it together a line here, a line there, a little here, and a little there, precept upon precept and that gives us understanding. But notice: "...in which the heaven itself shall disappear [now that's the heaven around the earth] with a mighty roar, and *the* elements shall pass away, burning with intense heat [and they will], and *the* earth and the works in it shall be burned up." So when the wicked are cast into the lake of fire, like it says there in Revelation 12 "death and hell are cast into the lake of fire," it envelops the whole earth. And when it does it destroys all the oceans. We'll see that in just a minute.

Now verse 11: "Since all these things are going to be destroyed, what kind of *persons* ought you to be in holy conduct and godliness, looking forward to and striving for the coming of the day of God, during which *the* heavens, being on fire, shall be destroyed, and *the* elements, burning with intense heat, shall melt? But according to His promise, we look forward to a new heaven and a new earth, in which righteousness dwells" (verses 11-13).

Now let's come back to Revelation 21 and let's see the fulfillment of this that was given to John approximately thirty years after Peter wrote this, thereabouts. And here then it gives us a glimpse into the final fulfillment of the kingdom of God. Revelation 21:1: "Then I saw a new heaven and a new earth; for the first heaven and the first earth were passed away, and there was no more sea." Now you see at that time, as spirit beings, we will no longer need oceans. We need them today as physical human beings to keep the temperature on the earth suitable for human life. So there's no more sea.

Here's the new earth. Now God is going to begin to replenish the new earth. Let's see what He does. Verse 2: "And I, John, saw the holy city, *the* new Jerusalem, coming down from God out of heaven, prepared as a bride adorned for her husband. And I heard a great voice from heaven say, 'Behold, the tabernacle of God *is* with men [that is, all men now made perfect being born again into the kingdom of God]; and He shall dwell with them, and they shall be His people; and God Himself shall be with them *and be* their God. And God shall wipe away every tear from their eyes; and *there* shall not be any more death, or sorrow, or crying; neither shall *there* be any more pain, because the former things have passed away' " (verses 2-4). Now we enter into the glorious kingdom of God. We look forward to the new Jerusalem made by the very hands of God the Father and Jesus Christ and the angels prepared for His church.

Verse 5: "And He Who sits on the throne said, 'Behold, I make all things new.' Then He said to me, 'Write, for these words are true and faithful [It's going to happen. It's going to come to pass.].' And He said to me, 'It is done. I am Alpha and Omega, the Beginning and the End.' " From the very beginning of the creation of Adam and Eve, clear down to the very end Christ is going to carry out and fulfill His plan as He has told us. Now then: " 'To the one who thirsts, I will give freely of the fountain of the water of life. The one who overcomes shall inherit all things; and I will be his God, and he shall be My son' " (verses 5-7).

Now then He gives a warning here which is very important for us to understand. " 'But *the* cowardly...' " Someone said, "Well the King James says "fearful." Now aren't we to fear God?" Well this is not the same kind of fear. This is that you don't have enough courage to be a Christian the way you ought to be, and you give up on God. The cowardly. " 'But *the* cowardly, and unbelieving, and abominable, and murderers, and fornicators, and sorcerers, and idolaters, and all liars, shall have their part in the lake that burns with fire and brimstone; which is *the* second death' " (verse 8).

Then there is this great vision that he sees of new Jerusalem coming down out of heaven. Fifteen hundred miles cubed. New Jerusalem: streets paved with gold, made with all of the most fine and precious stones. And I am sure that all of these, as it lists all of the stones, the wall, the gates, the pearls, and everything like that, I'm sure that he is seeing not just the physical thing of it but he is seeing that which is composed out of spirit but looks like these things. Because you see in verse 21 it says: "...and the street of the city *was* pure gold, as transparent *as* glass." Well see, that has to be spiritual. We're going to be spirit beings. Everything that we have will be made out of spirit, whether it be the clothes that we have, new Jerusalem that we dwell in, or whatever our place is. Remember Christ said in John 14 that He went away to prepare a place for us. So right now Jesus Christ is active, busy, preparing that place in new Jerusalem for us, looking forward to this day.

Now verse 22. Something very profound and important. "And I saw no temple in it; for the Lord God Almighty and the Lamb are the temple of it." Amazing thing to be in the family of God. We're going to see God. We are going to see Jesus Christ. We're going to live with Them, we're going to dwell with Them. No need of a temple. "And the city has no need of the sun, or of the moon, that they should shine in it..." It doesn't say that they aren't there. It just says they have no need that they shine on it. "...Because the glory of God enlightens it, and the light of it *is* the Lamb" (verses 22-23).

"And the nations that are saved..." So here, all the nations from the Millennium, all of those through the Great White Throne Judgment, all of those of the saints down through time. But here all the nations that are saved shall walk in the light of it. See, those who are in the first resurrection are going to live and dwell in new Jerusalem. All of the rest who are saved are going to live outside of Jerusalem and they are going to come to new Jerusalem. These are the nations that are saved. "...Shall walk in its light; and the kings of the earth shall bring their glory and honor into it." Yes, there's going to be ruler ship. There are going to be kings. "And its gates shall never be shut by day; for there shall be no night there. And they shall bring the glory and the honor of the nations into it" (verses 24-26). So God is going to have us busy, producing, making, creating, doing. If God by Himself (with the help of the angels and the twenty-four elders and Jesus Christ) created all the heavens and the earth, I wonder what sort of thing He's got planned for us. See, because this indicates there's going to be a fantastic amount of things going on. We're not going to be there humdy-dumdy strumming on harps, or as the beatific vision is: look at the face of God like you're staring at some thing you never understand. No, this is real spiritual life, greater, better than the best of human life.

Now then he gives another warning: "And nothing that defiles shall ever enter into it, nor shall *anyone* who practices *an* abomination or *devises* a lie; but *only* those who are written in the Lamb's book of life" (verse 27).

Now then it concludes with one of the most tremendous chapters in the whole Bible—Revelation 22. Now let's think on this for just a minute. You have seven plus one, don't you, making eight? How many chapters do we have? We have three sections of seven in the book of Revelation. That makes twenty-one. Plus one is twenty-two. And moreover twenty-two is also the number of letters in the Hebrew alphabet. So here we have the eighth one again, don't we? Showing the newness of God's way and everything.

"Then he showed me a pure river of *the* water of life, clear as crystal, flowing out from the throne of God and of the Lamb." So through all eternity the righteousness and power of God's Spirit is always going to be flowing. "*And* in the middle of *the* street, and on this side and that side of the river, *was the* tree of life…" Now I don't quite understand all of this completely, but it says: "…*the* tree of life, producing twelve *manner of* fruits, each month yielding its fruit; and the leaves of the tree *are* for *the* healing of the nations" (Rev. 22:1-2). Now the Greek there is *therapeian*, which could also mean "for the maintenance of the nations." I don't know exactly how this will fit in, but I'll tell you how we will understand it. Be there in new Jerusalem and you will know.

And now this here's a great thing, verse 3: "And there shall be no more curse; and the throne of God and of the Lamb shall be in it; and His servants shall serve Him, and they shall see His face; and His name *is* in their foreheads" (verses 3-4). Complete oneness with God. Here, everything that God has done in His plan has now all come together and we are ready in the family of God to begin to do the work of God which He has for us for the rest of eternity down through the ages of that eternity.

Now notice it says: "And there shall be no night there; for they have no need of a lamp or *the* light of *the* sun, because *the* Lord God enlightens them; and they shall reign into the ages of eternity" (verse 5). For ever and ever and ever. And that's the kind of life that God wants us to have. That's how it's going to be. That's why it says that: "The eye has not seen and the ears have not heard, neither has it entered into the heart of man the things that God has prepared for those who love Him" (I Cor. 2:9, paraphrased). That's why we need to love God with all our heart, and all our mind, and all our soul and being.

Now we come back to the closing part here, verse 6: "And he said to me, 'These words *are* faithful and true [see, they're going to happen]; and *the* Lord God of the holy prophets sent His angel to show His servants the things that must shortly come to pass.' " And that's really true right now. It's going to come to pass shortly. " 'Behold, I am coming quickly. Blessed *is* the one who keeps the words of the prophecy of this book [meaning the whole Bible].' Now I, John, *was* the one who saw and heard these things. And when I heard and saw, I fell down to worship before the feet of the angel who *was* showing me these things. But he said to me, 'See *that you do* not *do this*! For I am a fellow servant of yours, and of your brethren the prophets, and of those who keep the words of this book. Worship

God.' And he said to me, 'Do not seal the words of the prophecy of this book because the time is near' " (verses 6-10). In other words, when we come close to the time of the end we're going to understand it. And I think today we understand the book of Revelation more than any other time in the history of the whole world. Because we are living in the times when we see these things coming to pass.

And then he says: " 'Let the one who is unrighteous be unrighteous still; and let the one who is filthy be filthy still; and let the one who *is* righteous be righteous still; and let the one who *is* holy be holy still. And behold, I am coming quickly; and My reward is with Me, to render to each one according as his work shall be. I am Alpha and Omega, *the* Beginning and *the* End, the First and the Last.' " God's plan has now been completed and then He's going to open up the rest of it to our understanding. And he finalizes by this: " 'Blessed *are* those who keep His commandments, that they may have the right to *eat of* the tree of life, and may enter by the gates into the city' " (verses 11-14). Now that's the full meaning of this day, the holy day the Last Great Day. And you know why it is The Great Day.

End of Sermon

Transcriber: Carolyn Singer

The Last Great Day—Day 8—Holy Day
October 7, 2004
Scriptural References

1) Leviticus 23:34, 36-37, 4

2) John 7:37-39

3) Isaiah 14:24, 26-27

4) Psalm 111:10

5) Ephesians 1:3-10

6) Isaiah 29:13-17

7) Matthew 13:13-17

8) I Timothy 2:3-4

9) II Peter 3:9

10) II Corinthians 4:4

11) Romans 9:14-23

12) Romans 11:18-26, 32-36

13) Revelation 20:5

14) John 11:23-27

15) Romans 2:14-16

16) John 5:25-29

17) Revelation 20:11-12

18) Ezekiel 37:1-14

19) Matthew 12:32-37, 41-42

20) I Peter 4:17

21) Revelation 20:13-15

22) Luke 16:19-31

23) II Peter 3:10-13

24) Revelation 21:1-8, 21-17

25) Revelation 22:1-14

26) I Corinthians 2:9

Epilogue

In reviewing the contents of this book and its accompanying CDs, we humbly stand before God the Father and Jesus Christ, praising Them with thanksgiving for Their love, mercy and grace—and for Their awesome plan for mankind as revealed by the Sabbath and annual holy days. It is certainly true that we are the recipients of Their loving kindness and grace in these last days. They have opened up to our understanding this profound knowledge, which has long been hidden from the world. As promised in the book of Daniel—and as later reaffirmed by Jesus Christ—God has granted more understanding to His Church at this time than He previously granted to all the prophets, apostles, ministers and brethren of past ages. On the other hand, the Word of God is not *bound*, because God Himself has inspired all the knowledge contained in the Bible. As Jesus said, "It is the Spirit that gives life; the flesh profits nothing. **The words that I speak to you,** *they* **are spirit and** *they* **are life**" (John 6:63).

Apart from the Word and Spirit of God, even the greatest minds throughout history have failed to understand God's plan for mankind. It was simply not possible—for God's truth is spiritually discerned and God Himself must choose to *reveal* His plan. As Paul wrote: "But according as it is written, '*The* eye has not seen, nor *the* ear heard, neither have entered into *the* heart of man, *the* things which God has prepared for those who love Him.' **But God has revealed** *them* **to us by His Spirit, for the Spirit searches all things—even the deep things of God**. For who among men understands the things of man except *by* the spirit of man which *is* in him? In the same way also, **the things of God no one understands except** *by* **the Spirit of God**. Now we have not received the spirit of the world, but **the Spirit that** *is* **of God, so that we might know the things graciously given to us by God**; which things we also speak, not in words taught by human wisdom, but in *words* taught by *the* Holy Spirit *in order to* communicate spiritual things by spiritual *means*" (I Cor. 2:9-13).

Even with the understanding God has granted, we still do not comprehend as we ought to. Indeed, we are still "looking through a glass darkly." There are many things, however, that God will no doubt yet reveal to His church and ministers as we come closer to the return of Jesus Christ. And while we may see many aspects of God's plan more clearly than those of past church ages, we need to continue to grow in the grace and knowledge of the Lord Jesus Christ—so that we may be counted worthy to receive eternal life and share in the glorious inheritance of Jesus Christ as spirit-born sons and daughters of God the Father, thus fulfilling God's plan and purpose.

We will conclude with Paul's inspired prayer of thanksgiving for the knowledge of God's plan and purpose given to him through Jesus Christ for us: "For this cause I, Paul, *am* the prisoner of Christ Jesus for you Gentiles, if indeed you have heard of the ministry of the grace of God that was given to me for you; how **He made known to me by revelation the mystery** (even as I wrote briefly before, so that when you read *this*, you will be able to comprehend my understanding in **the mystery of Christ**), **which in other generations was not made known to the sons of men, as it has now been revealed to His holy apostles and prophets by** *the* **Spirit**; that the Gentiles might be joint heirs, and a joint body, and joint partakers of His promise in Christ through the gospel, of which I became a servant according to the gift of the grace of God, *which was* given to me through the inner working of His power.

"To me, who am less than the least of all the saints, was this grace given, that I might preach the gospel among the Gentiles—*even* the unsearchable riches of Christ; and **that I might enlighten all** *as to* **what** *is* **the fellowship of the mystery that has been hidden from the ages in God, Who created all things by Jesus Christ**; so that the manifold wisdom of God might now be made known through the church to the principalities and the powers in the heavenly *places*, **according to** *His* **eternal purpose, which He has wrought in Christ Jesus**

our Lord, in Whom we have boldness and *direct* access with confidence through His *very* own faith.

"So then, I beseech *you* not to faint at my tribulations for you, which are *working for* your glory. For this cause I bow my knees to the Father of our Lord Jesus Christ, of Whom the whole family in heaven and earth is named, **that He may grant you, according to the riches of His glory, to be strengthened with power by His Spirit in the inner man**; that Christ may dwell in your hearts by faith; *and* **that being rooted and grounded in love, you may be fully able to comprehend with all the saints what** *is* **the breadth and length and depth and height, and to know the love of Christ, which surpasses** *human* **knowledge; so that you may be filled with all the fullness of God**.

"Now to Him Who is able to do exceeding abundantly above all that we ask or think, according to the power that is working in us, to Him *be* glory in the church by Christ Jesus throughout all generations, *even* into the ages of eternity. Amen" (Eph. 3:1-21).

Additional Audio Messages and Transcripts Available:

From our Website ***www.cbcg.org*** we have additional audio messages and transcripts that are available for further study. You may download them to your computer and print out the transcripts and listen to the audio messages. For the Spring Holy Days—Passover through Pentecost, we have over 60 additional messages and transcripts. For the Fall Holy Days—Trumpets through the Last Great Day, we have over 70 other messages and transcripts. These will help give you a greater biblical insight into the meaning of God's ordained feasts and holy days that reveal God's plan for mankind.

Notes

576